MANAGEMENT of WILDERNESS and ENVIRONMENTAL EMERGENCIES

MANAGEMENT of WILDERNESS and ENVIRONMENTAL EMERGENCIES

Edited by

Paul S. Auerbach, M.D.

Assistant Clinical Professor of Medicine
University of California, San Francisco
Attending Physician, Emergency Services
San Francisco General Hospital
San Francisco, California

Edward C. Geehr, M.D.

Assistant Clinical Professor of Medicine
University of California, San Francisco
Medical Director of Emergency Medical Services
City and County of San Francisco
San Francisco, California

Macmillan Publishing Company
NEW YORK

Collier Macmillan Canada, Inc.
TORONTO

Collier Macmillan Publishers
LONDON

Macmillan Publishing Company
866 Third Avenue, New York, New York 10022

Collier Macmillan Canada, Inc.
Collier Macmillan Publishers · London

Library of Congress Cataloging in Publication Data
Main entry under title:

Management of wilderness and environmental emergencies.

  Bibliography: p.
  Includes index.
  1. Outdoor life—Accidents and injuries.   2. Medical
emergencies.   3. Environmentally induced diseases.
I. Auerbach, Paul S.   II. Geehr, Edward C.
RC88.9.O95M36   1983   616.9'8   83–9807
ISBN 0–02–304630–9

Printing 1 2 3 4 5 6 7 8   Year: 3 4 5 6 7 8 9 0

Retinal photographs (Color Plate 1, opposite p. 18) taken by Dr. Murray McFadden, University of British Columbia, Vancouver, B.C., in association with Dr. Charles Houston, Burlington, Vermont; Dr. Gary Gray, Defense and Civil Institute of Environmental Medicine, Toronto, Ontario; and Drs. John Sutton and Peter Powles, McMaster University, Hamilton, Ontario.
The study wherein the photographs were taken was supported by National Institutes of Health grant no. HL 14102 and in part by the Canadian Armed Forces and the U.S. Army Medical Research and Development Command (No. DAM D7-77-C-7029). It was part of the High Altitude Physiology Study (HAPS) of the Arctic Institute of North America.
The above authors do not necessarily endorse any conclusions drawn from the above photographs.

This book is dedicated to my parents; to my wonderful wife, Sherry; and to my good friends, Bert Cashman, Phil Asack, Chip Potter, John Mustalish, York Miller, Ralph Bundy, Stan Steindorf, and Cayce Hafe.

A special thanks goes to Ed Geehr. Without his collaboration this book wouldn't have been half the fun.

P.S.A.

This book is dedicated to my mother and father.

I gratefully acknowledge the patience and support of my wife, J. T., and the contribution and friendship of my energetic co-editor, Paul Auerbach.

E.C.G.

PREFACE

Emergency and primary care physicians, unpredictably confronted with disorders of every variety, need access to descriptions of and therapeutic guidelines for common and uncommon diseases. Our purpose is to provide the clinician with a body of knowledge concerned with the interactions between people and the natural environment.

What some may consider peripheral, we see as mainstream and vital for spiritual and recreational health. Environmental encounters, however, are not without risk, even for the prepared. As increased wilderness activity leads to a rising incidence of misfortune, medical personnel must sharpen their awareness of environmental hazards. Competitive athletics, and underwater and aerospace exploration have engendered medical subspecialties. Because wilderness and environmental medicine are poorly organized in the medical literature, we direct this book toward defining the field and gathering the best available information. We have solicited contributions from experts in diverse specialties who have a common bond of recreational and wilderness pursuits.

Their vast experience and irrepressible enthusiasm are evident in this work.

The chapters that discuss wilderness rescue, forest fires, aerospace medicine, and disaster planning are designed as a primer to introduce the reader to unfamiliar terminology and equipment, define resources, and explore emergency management strategies. More detailed clinical information is included in the chapters that address the commonly encountered physical forces such as sun, heat, cold, lightning, altitude, and barotrauma and the biologic toxins such as plant poisons, animal bites, insect stings, and marine envenomations. In addition, because industry and nuclear technology threaten the environment in ever-increasing fashion, we have added a chapter on inhalation injuries and an appendix on the management of radiation incidents. The true focus of our work and space limitations prevent us from fully exploring the environmental and health impact of modern technology.

The text is intended to serve emergency and primary care physicians as a definitive therapeutic guide, to provide residents in training and medical students with an authoritative reference source, and to offer nurses and paramedic personnel a background in the health consequences of environmental stress.

The need for medical education is self-evident. A larger issue is that of conservation and the environment. Sadly, much of our land and resources have been exploited, polluted, and consumed. This book is a plea for thoughtful management and preservation of the wildernesses of the world. The harvesting of wildlife and elimination of ecosystems for economic gain threaten to be the undoing of the wilderness as we know it. What we do not actively protect will be endangered by those unconcerned with or unaware of the history, fragility, and natural order of things. It is our wish to make the wildlands safer through greater awareness and to foster the spirit of conservation. We encourage our colleagues to encounter the wildlands, and wish them safe expeditions.

P. S. A.
E. C. G.

CONTRIBUTORS

Paul S. Auerbach, M.D., Assistant Clinical Professor of Medicine, University of California, San Francisco; Attending Physician, Emergency Services, San Francisco General Hospital; Base Station Medical Director, City and County of San Francisco.

Cameron Bangs, M.D., Clinical Instructor in Medicine, University of Oregon Health Sciences Center, Portland, Oregon.

Charles A. Berry, M.D., M.P.H., President, National Foundation for the Prevention of Disease, Houston, Texas; Professor of Aerospace Medicine, Wright State University School of Medicine, Dayton, Ohio; Former Director of Life Sciences, Hq. National Aeronautics and Space Administration, Washington, D.C.; Former Director, Medical Research and Operations, Lyndon B. Johnson Space Center, Houston, Texas.

Michael A. Berry, M.D., Vice President, National Foundation for the Prevention of Disease; Adjunct Assistant Professor of Aerospace Medicine, University of Texas School of Public Health, Houston, Texas; Former Chief, Flight Medicine Clinic, NASA/Johnson Space Center, Houston, Texas.

Warren D. Bowman, Jr., M.D., F.A.C.P., Clinical Assistant Professor of Medicine, University of Washington School of Medicine; Internist and Hematologist, Billings Clinic, Billings, Montana; Medical Advisor, National Ski Patrol System, Inc.

Michael L. Callaham, M.D., Associate Clinical Professor of Medicine and Director, Emergency Medicine, University of California, San Francisco.

Mary Ann Cooper, M.D., Associate, Professor Department of Emergency Medicine, University of Louisville, Louisville, Kentucky.

P. William Curreri, M.D., Professor and Chairman, Department of Surgery, University of South Alabama, Mobile, Alabama.

Jefferson C. Davis, M.D., Director, Hyperbaric Medicine, Southwest Texas Methodist Hospital, San Antonio, Texas; Founder and First Chief, Hyperbaric Medicine, U.S. Air Force School of Aerospace Medicine; Past President, Undersea Medical Society.

Kathleen M. Davis, Plant and Fire Ecologist, Western Region, National Park Service, U.S. Department of the Interior, San Francisco, California.

Gail E. Drayton, M.D., Assistant Clinical Professor of Medicine and Dermatologist, University of California, Los Angeles.

Wade R. Eckert, M.D., Senior Orthopedist, Alpine Medical Clinic, Mammoth Mountain, California.

Charles Farabee, Jr., Assistant Chief Ranger, Grand Canyon National Park, U.S. Department of the Interior.

Jacques Foray, M.D., Chief of Staff, Hospital de Chamonix-Mont-Blanc, Chamonix, France.

Edward C. Geehr, M.D., Assistant Clinical Professor of Medicine, University of California, San Francisco; Medical Director, Emergency Medical Services, City and County of San Francisco; Attending Physician, Emergency Services, San Francisco General Hospital.

Joel Geiderman, M.D., Attending Physician and Research Coordinator, Department of Emergency Medicine, Cedars-Sinai Medical Center; Clinical Assistant Professor of Medicine, University of California, Los Angeles.

Bruce W. Halstead, M.D., Director, International Biotoxicological Centre, World Life Research Institute; Medical Director, Halstead Preventive Medical Clinic, Loma Linda, California; Consultant on Toxicology, World Health Organization; Editorial Board Member, *Clinical Toxicology.*

Murray P. Hamlet, D.V.M., Director, Cold Research Division, U.S. Army Research Institute of Environmental Medicine, Natick, Massachusetts.

Herbert N. Hultgren, M.D., Professor of Medicine, Stanford University; Chief, Cardiology Service, Palo Alto Veterans Administration Medical Center; Medical Committee Member, American Alpine Club.

Brian D. Johnston, M.D., Vice President, Janzen, Johnston and Rockwell, Santa Monica, California; Clinical Instructor in Medicine, University of California, Los Angeles; Emergency Physician, White Memorial Medical Center, Los Angeles, California.

Richard P. Kaplan, M.D., Adjunct Assistant Professor, Division of Dermatology, University of California, Los Angeles.

Donald Friday King, M.D., Division of Dermatology, University of California, Los Angeles.

Eric Lewis, M.D., Dermatologist and Dermatosurgeon, Beverly Hills, California; Associate, Department of Medicine, University of California, Los Angeles.

Arnold Luterman, M.D., F.R.C.S., F.A.C.S., Associate Professor of Surgery, University of South Alabama; Director of Trauma Services, University of South Alabama; Trauma Project Director, Southwest Alabama Emergency Services, Mobile, Alabama.

Charles McElroy, M.D., Clinical Associate Professor of Medicine, University of California, Los Angeles; Internist, Pacific Palisades, California.

Frederick A. Mettler, M.D., M.P.H., Associate Professor of Radiology and Chief, Diagnostic Imaging, University of New Mexico School of Medicine, Albuquerque, New Mexico.

Sherman A. Minton, M.D., Professor of Microbiology and Immunology, Indiana University School of Medicine, Indianapolis, Indiana.

Robert W. Mutch, Fire Staff Officer, USDA Forest Service, Missoula, Montana; Faculty Affiliate, University of Montana.

Paul M. Paris, M.D., Program Director, University of Pittsburgh Affiliated Residency in Emergency Medicine; Associate Medical Director, Emergency Medical Services, City of Pittsburgh, Pennsylvania.

Sydney W. Porter, Jr., C.H.P., President, Porter Consultants, Inc. (Radiological Protection and Environmental Services), Ardmore, Pennsylvania.

Jan Stehlick, M.D., Associate Orthopedist, Alpine Medical Clinic, Mammoth Mountain, California.

Ronald D. Stewart, M.D., Assistant Professor of Medicine, University of Pittsburgh; Director, Center for Emergency Medicine; Medical Director, Emergency Medical Services, Pittsburgh, Pennsylvania.

Willis A. Wingert, M.D., Professor of Pediatrics, Community Medicine, Public Health and Emergency Medicine, University of Southern California; Director, Pediatric Ambulatory Service, Los Angeles County—University of Southern California Medical Center, Los Angeles, California.

CONTENTS

Preface   vii

Contributors   ix

Color Plates 1 and 2   After page 18

Color Plates 3 and 4   Facing page 19

1. High-Altitude Illness
   Herbert N. Hultgren, M.D.   1

2. Hypothermia and Cold Injuries
   Cameron Bangs, M.D., and *Murray P. Hamlet, D.V.M.*   27

3. Heat Illness: Current Perspectives
   Charles McElroy, M.D., and *Paul S. Auerbach, M.D.*   64

4. Wilderness Rescue and Preparation
   Warren D. Bowman, M.D., F.A.C.P., Charles Farabee, Jr., and *Jacques Foray, M.D.*   82

5. Alpine and Nordic Ski Injuries
   Wade R. Eckert, M.D., and *Jan Stehlik, M.D.*   134

6. Diving and Barotrauma
   Jefferson C. Davis, M.D.   164

7. Submersion Incidents: Drowning and Near-Drowning
Ronald D. Stewart, M.D. — 189

8. Hazardous Marine Life
Paul S. Auerbach, M.D., and Bruce W. Halstead, M.D. — 213

9. Aquatic Skin Disorders
Gail E. Drayton, M.D. — 260

10. Arthropod Envenomation
Sherman A. Minton, M.D. — 270

Protection from Blood-Feeding Arthropods
Richard P. Kaplan, M.D. — 304

Mites and Lice
Richard P. Kaplan, M.D. — 307

11. Domestic and Feral Mammalian Bites
Michael L. Callaham, M.D. — 310

12. Venomous Snake Bites
Willis A. Wingert, M.D. — 352

13. Toxic Plant Ingestions
Edward C. Geehr, M.D. — 379

14. Plant Dermatitis
Don Friday King, M.D. — 426

15. The Sun and the Skin
Eric Lewis, M.D. — 432

16. Wildland Fires: Dangers and Survival
Kathleen M. Davis and Robert W. Mutch — 451

17. Burn Wounds
Arnold Luterman, M.D., F.R.C.S., F.A.C.S., and P. William Curreri, M.D., F.A.C.S. — 481

18. Lightning Injuries
Mary Ann Cooper, M.D. — 500

19. Aerospace Medicine: The Vertical Frontier
Charles A. Berry, M.D., M.P.H., and Michael A. Berry, M.D. — 522

20. Disaster Planning
Joel Geiderman, M.D., and Paul M. Paris, M.D. — 556

21. Inhalation Injuries
Brian D. Johnston, M.D. — 585

Appendix: The Emergency Response to Radiation Accidents
Frederick A. Mettler, M.D., M.P.H., and Sydney W. Porter, Jr., C.H.P. — 606

Index — 647

MANAGEMENT of WILDERNESS and ENVIRONMENTAL EMERGENCIES

1 | # HIGH-ALTITUDE ILLNESS

Herbert N. Hultgren, M.D.[*]

The exposure of climbers, trekkers, and tourists to high altitude has increased remarkably over the past few years. Mountain tours and safaris provide access to high mountain regions previously explored by only the hardiest climbers. Each year more than 5000 people climb Mount Rainier (14,408 feet), and on an average summer day about 3600 people drive to the summit of Pike's Peak (14,110 feet). Many ski resorts in the Rocky Mountains are located at 8000 feet or higher, with lifts carrying zealous flatlanders to 11,000 and 12,000 feet. Air travel provides easy access to these resorts from any part of the United States within 1 day.

High-altitude illness has become a unique problem among travelers; deaths due to high-altitude pulmonary edema and high-altitude encephalopathy continue to occur despite our knowledge of appropriate preventive measures. For these reasons, physicians, paramedical personnel, trip leaders, and mountain travelers should be acquainted with the physiologic and medical consequences of high-altitude exposure in order to prevent illness, disability, and death.

Definitions

It is useful to consider three levels of altitude at which medical problems occur.

HIGH ALTITUDE—8000–14,000 FEET

It is rare for significant altitude illness to occur below 8000 feet. Altitudes exceeding 14,000 feet are rarely attained in the continental United States or in those foreign high-altitude areas that are readily accessible to tourists.

VERY HIGH ALTITUDE—14,000–18,000 FEET

These altitudes are frequently encountered by climbers in many parts of the world and

---

[*] The assistance of Peter Hackett, M.D., in the preparation of this chapter is gratefully acknowledged.

are the usual location of base camps for higher climbing. It is very dangerous to ascend to this altitude range without acclimatization.

EXTREME ALTITUDE—18,000–29,028 FEET (MOUNT EVEREST)

These elevations are reached only by expert expeditionary climbers, and then only for a relatively short period of time. Medical problems at such altitudes are more frequently related to terrain and weather (avalanches, frostbite, hypothermia) then to high-altitude illness, since at such elevations climbers are usually acclimatized and those who are susceptible to high-altitude illness have returned to lower elevations.

At these elevations, a prolonged stay is commonly associated with progressive high-altitude deterioration. For example, the mining community of Amincha is located in the Chilean Andes at 13,100 feet, with the local mines at 19,600 feet. The miners who live in the community refuse to live at the elevation of the mines because of the difficulty in sleeping and the progressive altitude deterioration. Each day, they travel by truck and on foot from the village to work and return at night.

Members of the 1960 Himalayan Scientific and Mountaineering Expedition spent more than 6 weeks at 19,000 feet at Mingbo La near Mount Makalu. While the group appeared to acclimatize well, all members of the party lost weight. Newcomers to the mountain, after 4–6 weeks of acclimatization, were, if anything, fitter and more active than the men who had wintered at 19,000 feet (37).

Major Physiologic Consequences of High-Altitude Exposure

It is convenient to refer to physiologic changes as acclimatization or adaptation to altitude, but it should be realized that not all physiologic processes are necessarily beneficial; indeed, some physiologic changes may be exaggerated and thus lead to unfavorable consequences. Physiologic responses to high-altitude exposure have been reviewed by Tenney (49) and Lenfant (31) and are outlined below.

HYPOXIA

Hypoxia is probably the single most important factor in causing high-altitude illness.

Barometric pressure decreases with increasing altitude, so that at 18,000 feet the atmospheric pressure is one-half that at sea level. Since the percentage of oxygen in the atmosphere is the same at sea level as at high altitude, the partial pressure of oxygen (PIo_2) is halved at 18,000 feet. Increased ventilation will partially, but not completely, compensate for this decrease. Thus, a decrease in arterial oxygen pressure (Po_2) will occur at high altitude in proportion to the altitude, as shown in Table 1 (values are derived from normal, resting, awake subjects).

Two other important factors that result in a further decrease in arterial Po_2 at high altitude are exercise and sleep.

At sea level, heavy physical exercise is accompanied either by no change or by a slight

TABLE 1
Gas Tensions at Various Altitudes

Altitude (feet)	Barometric pressure (mmHg)	Inspired Oxygen Tension (mmHg)	Arterial Oxygen Tension (mmHg)	Arterial CO_2 Tension (mmHg)	Arterial Oxygen Saturation (mmHg)
24,000	280	52	34	16	50
18,000	379	69	40	29	71
12,000	483	91	52	35	83
8000	564	108	60	37	89
5000	630	122	66	39	92
Sea level	760	149	94	41	97

Source: Data from Reference 16.

rise in arterial P_{O_2}, due to more complete pulmonary perfusion. At high altitude, exercise is accompanied by a fall in arterial P_{O_2}. The decrease is proportional to the level of exercise and the altitude, as demonstrated in Figure 1. This is due to the limitation of the pulmonary diffusing capacity, which cannot fully equilibrate capillary blood with alveolar oxygen because of the increased velocity of the blood flow (51). This may be an important factor in limiting heavy physical work at high altitude. Frequent rest stops are required to allow the decreased arterial P_{O_2} to return to the resting level. Thus, at sea level, it appears that the circulatory system (cardiac output) is the factor that limits heavy exercise, while at high altitude, it is the lungs (diffusing capacity) that limit heavy exercise. This appears to be part of the explanation for the observation that maximal heart rate and maximal work capacity are progressively decreased at higher altitudes.

During sleep at sea level, normal subjects exhibit a decrease in ventilatory drive that results in a small drop in arterial P_{O_2} and a slight rise in carbon dioxide pressure (P_{CO_2}). In patients with sleep apnea or the obesity-hypoventilation syndrome, periods of hypoventilation or apnea may be associated with marked falls in arterial P_{O_2}. At high altitude,

sleep hypoventilation is more intense, and even in normal subjects with no history of sea-level sleep disorders, profound decreases in arterial P_{O_2} may occur (48). Arterial oxygen saturation may decrease from levels of 70 to 60% at 17,300 feet; saturations as low as 50% may occur in some subjects, as shown in Figure 2.

It has long been known that acetazolamide (Diamox) will ameliorate the symptoms of acute mountain sickness (11). An important aspect of this beneficial effect may be the amelioration of hypoventilation and hypoxia during sleep, as shown in Figure 2. Acetazolamide will also reduce the frequency and incidence of periodic breathing (Cheyne-Stokes respirations). In studies on Mount Logan at 17,300 feet, acetazolamide reduced the incidence of periodic breathing in normal sleeping subjects from 80 to 35%. The average oxygen saturation during sleep was increased from 72 to 79%, and the lowest arterial saturation was increased from 61 to 72% (48).

The roles of low P_{CO_2} and alkalosis in the generation of mountain illness are under investigation.

RESPIRATORY

An increase in the depth of respiration with a minimal increase in rate occurs, which is mediated by the carotid bodies that sense a decrease in arterial P_{O_2}. During an ascent, the resting minute volume increases from 4.8 liters/minute at sea level to 6.6 liters/minute at 14,000 feet. Ventilation does not increase significantly until an altitude of greater than 10,000 feet is reached. This is accompanied by an increase in the work of breathing, which is greatly increased at extreme altitudes, particularly during heavy physical work when the accessory muscles of respiration are employed. On the summit of Mount Everest, the oxygen cost of the work of breathing may be so great that there is little reserve left over for climbing or other physical activity. Abnormalities of ventilation may occur during sleep, which consist of periods of hypoventilation with periodic decreases in arterial P_{O_2} and Cheyne-Stokes breathing, with alternating cycles of hyperpnea and apnea. Pronounced sinus arrhythmia and sinus bradycardia have been de-

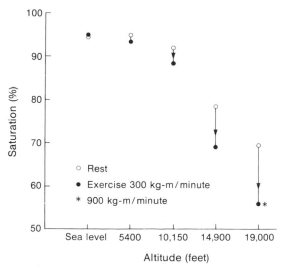

FIGURE 1 Resting arterial oxygen saturation (open circles) and saturation during exercise (closed circles) at various altitudes.

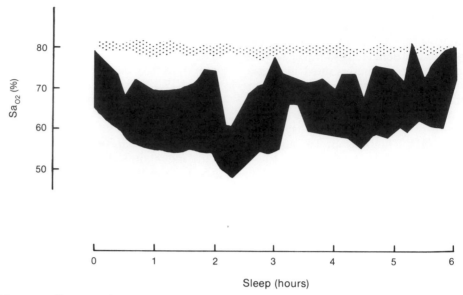

FIGURE 2 Ranges of arterial oxygen saturation (Sa_{O_2}%) in one subject during sleep at 17,500 feet with acetazolamide (Diamox) (upper stippled area) and without acetazolamide (lower black area). (Reprinted with permission of the *New England Journal of Medicine*, **301**:1329, 1979.)

scribed at high altitude during sleep, probably in relation to periodic breathing. During sleep at sea level, a slight decrease in ventilation and arterial P_{O_2} occurs in most individuals. This may be considerably more severe at high altitude and may be one of the causative factors of high-altitude illness, such as acute mountain sickness (AMS) (41). In persons with decreased sensitivity to hypoxemia, such as patients with chronic obstructive pulmonary disease, the hypoxic stimulus to breathing may be further blunted, resulting in more profound hypoxemia. Commonly used sedative-hypnotics may dangerously reduce the hypoxic drive to breathe when used at high altitude.

A slight decrease in vital capacity occurs in most subjects during the first hours of high-altitude exposure (50). The decrease is small (3–4%) and is of no consequence. It is probably due to an increase in pulmonary blood volume. The pulmonary diffusing capacity is not increased in lowlanders who ascend to high altitude, but it is increased in high-altitude residents by 20–30% (52).

Chronic habitation at high altitude leads to a reduction in the hypoxic ventilatory drive. Native highlanders have one-half the ventila-tory drive of acclimatized lowlanders. Highland residents also have a much lower ventilatory response to exercise, experiencing less dyspnea on exertion.

BLOOD GAS CHANGES

Despite the increase in minute ventilation, a decrease in arterial P_{O_2} occurs. Not only is P_{O_2} decreased at rest, but further decreases occur during exercise and sleep. The mean resting arterial oxygen saturation in acclimatized residents at 12,000 feet is approximately 83%, and the P_{O_2} is 52 mmHg (Figure 3; Table 1).

As a consequence of hyperventilation, arterial P_{CO_2} decreases and a respiratory alkalosis occurs. Arterial P_{CO_2} at 12,000 feet is approximately 35 mmHg. The respiratory alkalosis is compensated for by the renal excretion of bicarbonate, which restores the pH to normal. This is a slow process that requires 10–14 days to complete.

CHANGES IN BLOOD

Within a few hours of ascent to high altitude, there is a rapid decrease in plasma vol-

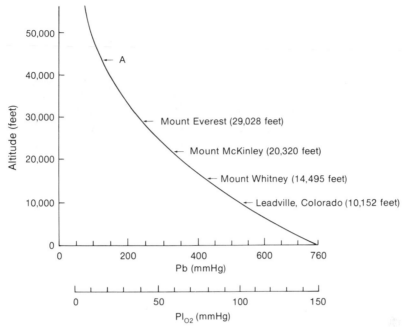

FIGURE 3 Relationship of altitude and barometric pressure (Pb) and partial pressure of oxygen (PIo_2) at representative elevations. *A* represents the upper limit of altitude where 100% oxygen at ambient pressure fails to maintain consciousness.

ume of 10–20%. This is easily detected by a rise in hematocrit (46). The decrease in plasma volume is due to the movement of water from the vascular bed both into cells and into the interstitial space. Hypoxic cells tend to increase their water content due to disruption of normal ion transport complexes. Erythropoietin activity increases within a few hours after ascent and is responsible for the gradual increase in red cells, which may require 2–4 months to become complete.

The partial pressure of oxygen at which hemoglobin attains 50% saturation (P_{50}) and the oxygen-hemoglobin dissociation curve are shifted to the right. This was thought to facilitate oxygen delivery at the capillary level, but recent studies have refuted this concept. Oxygen delivery to the tissues is facilitated by a rise in 2,3-diphosphoglycerate (2,3-DPG). This elevation is noted within 24 hours after ascent and disappears rapidly upon descent (32). High-altitude residents have higher levels of 2,3-DPG than do sea-level dwellers. The clinical importance of increased 2,3-DPG is controversial. Improvement in oxygen-hemoglobin unloading at the tissue level may be offset by hemoglobin's decreased affinity for oxygen in the lung capillary bed.

Hemoglobinopathies that lead to poor hemoglobin-oxygen binding, along with the sickle cell disorders, render certain persons especially susceptible to the consequences of high-altitude hypoxemia. Persons with the sickling hemoglobinopathies S-S hemoglobin, S-C hemoglobin, and S-β thalassemia appear to be most vulnerable to hypoxia-induced sickling crises, leading to pulmonary and splenic infarction. Any black person at high altitude with complaints of chest, back, or abdominal pain, shortness of breath, or arthralgias should have sickling crisis included in the differential diagnosis. Four case reports described the splenic syndrome (left upper quadrant abdominal pain, anorexia, vomiting) in whites who engaged in recreational mountain travel (7a).

CIRCULATORY CHANGES

Acute exposure to high altitude produces a tachycardia which is probably due to increased activity of the sympathetic nervous system. In response to hypoxia, venous tone is increased, as is the urinary excretion of nor-epinephrine. Cardiac output is increased during the first few days, but after 10 days, the cardiac output for a measured exercise is decreased as a consequence of a significant reduction in stroke volume. This compromise of stroke volume is present with both submaximal and maximal exercise. The heart rate during maximal exercise at high altitude is decreased compared to that at sea level. This decrease is proportional to the altitude. Coronary blood flow is decreased at high altitude, but the decrease is proportional to the decrease in stroke volume and cardiac work (13,21).

Ascent to high altitude results in a prompt, modest increase in pulmonary arteriolar resistance due to hypoxic vasoconstriction (21). Left ventricular filling pressures are normal or decreased. The rise in pulmonary artery pressure may show individual variation, since individuals who have had prior episodes of high-altitude pulmonary edema have a greater rise in pulmonary artery pressure.

CENTRAL NERVOUS SYSTEM

Hypoxia results in cerebral vasodilatation and increased cerebral blood flow. This may be accompanied by a slight increase in cerebrospinal fluid pressure. Conversely, hypocapnia and respiratory alkalosis cause cerebral vasoconstriction and a decrease in cerebral blood flow. Retinal blood flow is increased at high altitude.

TISSUE CHANGES

In acclimatized natives and animals, there is evidence of an increased number of capillaries per unit of tissue in brain, skeletal muscle, and myocardium.

Increased amounts of myoglobin are present in the tissue of humans and animals at high altitude. While myoglobin may act as a store for oxygen, its major function may be to facilitate the diffusion of oxygen.

It has been shown that the number of mitochondria is increased in the myocardium of cattle living at 13,000 feet. The size of the mitochondria is not increased (35). Succinic dehydrogenase activity may be increased independently of the increase in mitochondrial mass.

PLASMA VOLUME

Recent reports of the possible beneficial effect of hemodilution upon high-altitude performance have focused attention upon the significance of changes in plasma volume at high altitude. During rapid ascent to high altitude, a prompt decrease in plasma volume occurs due to diuresis. Thereafter, diurnal variation in plasma volume can be detected during the first few days at high altitude. Plasma volume is lower in the morning than in the evening, probably due to sleep hypoxia. Short periods of heavy exercise will usually cause a prompt decrease in plasma volume, which is reversed within a few minutes after the cessation of exercise (20). This is probably related to the movement of fluid out of the vascular bed as pressure and flow increase in exercising muscles, as well as to fluid loss from the lungs. Prolonged exercise for several hours at sea level and high altitude is accompanied by a slight rise in plasma volume (3,36). This may be an adaptive phenomenon designed to maintain cardiac output and tissue perfusion. The magnitude of all these changes in plasma volume is small, involving only 10–20% of the total plasma volume, or the equivalent of 300–500 ml of plasma. In climbers at extreme altitudes, greater decreases in plasma volume may occur, with resultant hematocrits as high as 65% (38,55). For example, after a 6 week sojourn at 19,000 feet at Mingbo La, the mean hematocrit in climbers was 56%. This was accompanied by an 18% decrease in plasma volume, although total blood volume was increased by 21% due to the great increase in the red cell mass.

On Mount Everest, no correlation was found between the hemoglobin level and the climbing performance. The range of hemoglobin values was 17.6–23.0 g per 100 ml (49). It has been proposed that hemodilution at extreme altitudes may improve climbing performance and prevent deterioration during exhausting alpine-style ascents. Field studies have shown an increase in hematocrit from 50% at the start of an alpine-style ascent to 54% at the end of the climb (55). In some climbers, more marked increases in hematocrit have occurred. Hemodilution is performed at base camp before ascent by the administration of either stabilized human serum, plasma, or blood substitutes after withdrawal of an equivalent quantity of blood. The infusion of 500–750 ml will decrease the hematocrit and allegedly decrease blood viscosity, improve the microcirculation, and counteract the effects of a decrease in plasma volume due to dehydration (53). However, controlled studies to establish that hemodilution will improve the physical work capacity at extreme altitudes are lacking. While hemodilution may minimize the effect of dehydration, an appropriate intake of salt and water during a climb should accomplish the same objective. It is unlikely that blood viscosity will be significantly altered by a 20% increase in plasma volume. Infusion of human serum preparations in the field is hazardous and involves the risk of hepatitis transmission, and can induce a life-threatening allergic reaction. A rapid increase in plasma volume could precipitate pulmonary edema; this may well have occurred in one subject who was hemodiluted on a 1978 Everest expedition.

It is quite likely that severe decreases in plasma volume may occur during prolonged climbs at extreme altitudes and may contribute to impaired physical performance and collapse. Severe hypoxia, dehydration due to fluid loss via the lungs, inadequate intake of fluid and food, and hypothermia will all act to decrease plasma volume. Further studies are clearly needed to elucidate this problem.

Renal Changes

A spontaneous bicarbonate diuresis by the kidneys usually occurs after 24–36 hours, serving to compensate for the respiratory alkalosis. This diuresis usually coincides with an improvement in oxygenation and an amelioration of symptoms. The loss of bicarbonate necessitates a certain amount of free water loss, contributing to the dehydration experienced at high altitude.

Acclimatization

The multiple processes of acclimatization permit a sea-level dweller to carry out graded heavy physical activity at high altitude without the risk of developing altitude illness. The time required for acclimatization is variable, depending upon the adaptive processes involved. An increase in 2,3-DPG occurs within

hours, while an appropriate degree of polycythemia may require months.

For practical purposes, partial acclimatization for a sojourn at high altitude (8000–14,000 feet) can be achieved by a 2–4 day stay at an altitude of 5000–7000 feet (9). For climbs to very high altitude (14,000–22,000 feet), an additional 2–4 day stay at 10,000–12,000 feet is useful. The first day at a higher altitude should be a rest day with minimal physical exertion. At altitudes above 14,000 feet, even acclimatized individuals may develop altitude illness if climbing is too fast or continuous. Climbing at a rate of 1000 feet/day, with a rest day every other day or every third day, is a useful precaution.

The sleeping altitude is critical in the development of mountain illness, proving the truth of the climbers' rule to "climb high and sleep low." One should not fly or drive to altitudes above 8000 feet unless one is acclimatized. It is far better to start at an intermediate altitude and walk up. If one is transported to an altitude greater than 8000 feet, the first day should be spent at rest. Discontinuous exposure to high altitude does not provide optimum acclimatization. Heavy physical training at sea level does not protect one from altitude illness. An acclimatized individual who returns to sea level or an altitude below 8000 feet will lose acclimatization in 7–14 days. There are no pharmacologic agents that will hasten true physiologic acclimatization. While acetazolamide may minimize altitude illness and ameliorate sleep hypoxia, it should not be used as a substitute for acclimatization. It is a helpful adjunctive measure if used when previous altitude illness has occurred despite acclimatization, or if one is forced to ascend rapidly, as in a rescue situation.

HIGH-ALTITUDE ILLNESSES

High-altitude medical problems may be classified according to severity as follows:

1. Serious; may be fatal; prompt recognition and management essential
   a. High-altitude pulmonary edema (HAPE)
   b. High-altitude encephalopathy (HAE)
   c. Venous thrombosis and pulmonary embolism
2. Disabling but nonfatal
   a. Acute mountain sickness (AMS)

b. Chronic or subacute mountain sickness (SAMS)
c. High-altitude deterioration (HAD)
3. Minor, rarely disabling, nonfatal
a. Systemic edema at high altitudes (HASE)
b. High-altitude retinal hemorrhages (HARH)
c. High-altitude flatus expulsion (HAFE)
d. Ultraviolet keratitis (snow blindness)
e. Altitude throat
f. Chronic mountain polycythemia
g. Pulmonary hypertension at high altitudes

High-Altitude Pulmonary Edema (HAPE)

Of the various forms of high-altitude illness, HAPE is the most serious. It continues to result in many deaths annually worldwide despite current knowledge of prevention and treatment. HAPE occurs not only in mountaineers but also in tourists, trekkers, skiers, and hikers. In earlier years, deaths in climbers attributed to "pneumonia" were probably instances of HAPE. Ravenhill (39) described instances of HAPE in the Bolivian Andes in 1913, but little attention was paid to this syndrome until Hurtado's case report appeared in 1937. In this work, he described a native of Casapalca (altitude 13,665 feet) who traveled frequently to sea level. On one occasion, upon returning to the mountains, he developed acute pulmonary edema which rapidly improved upon descent to Lima. Hurtado correctly diagnosed pulmonary edema and suggested that it was related to altitude exposure. Subsequently, several studies appeared in the Peruvian literature describing the essential clinical features of the syndrome. In 1957, Houston published the first report of HAPE in a skier who developed the syndrome in Aspen, Colorado. Houston suggested that deaths in mountaineers, previously ascribed to pneumonia, were probably instances of HAPE (17). A further detailed report of the essential clinical features of HAPE was published in 1961 (25). Since then, many studies have been published concerning this unique altitude illness (19).

ALTITUDE OF OCCURRENCE

Rapid ascent to an altitude exceeding 8000 feet by an unacclimatized person is the usual precipitant for the HAPE syndrome, especially if heavy physical exertion occurs upon arrival. The altitude threshold of 8000 feet refers to the sleeping altitude. Many skiers in the Lake Tahoe area ski at elevations of up to 9000 feet, but their living accommodations are at 6300 feet. Instances of HAPE among skiers in this area are extremely rare. In the Rocky Mountain ski areas where living accommodations are above 8000 feet, many instances of HAPE occur.

CLINICAL PRESENTATION

The first symptoms of HAPE usually begin 24–96 hours after arrival at high altitude and are commonly preceded by heavy physical exertion such as climbing, skiing, or carrying heavy loads. Dyspnea, a persistent nonproductive cough, and notable weakness and fatigue are the most common early symptoms. Headache, nausea, vomiting, or somnolence is often seen in children. As the severity of the pulmonary edema increases, usually during the night, dyspnea at rest becomes severe and the cough may become productive of clear, watery sputum. Rhonchi and gurgling sounds can often be heard without a stethoscope. Hemoptysis, sometimes involving fairly large quantities of blood, is seen in about 20% of severe episodes. The patient becomes apprehensive, fears death, and may become incoherent, irrational, or hallucinatory. Coma may occur and precedes death by 6–12 hours if oxygen is not administered or if the patient is not carried to a lower altitude. In some instances, stupor progressing to coma may occur, with minimal symptoms or signs of respiratory distress, and the clinical features may resemble those of encephalitis or intracranial disease. Central nervous system dysfunction and altered consciousness are probably related to hypoxia or cerebral edema, which may be profound in severe HAPE.

Common clinical signs include cyanosis, hyperpnea, crepitant rales, and rhonchi. The blood pressure is low. In a study of 21 patients in Peru, the mean arterial pressure was 109/69 mmHg. Severe hypoxia induces tachycardia, with heart rates of up to 160 per minute in severe episodes. The mean heart rate in 34 episodes was 122 per minute. The respiratory rate is increased, and a mean value of

32 per minute was observed in Peruvian studies. A typical episode of HAPE is summarized below.

J. W. was a 33-year-old experienced, physically fit mountaineer. He was able to run 100 miles over lowland trails in less than 24 hours. On a climbing trip in the Sierra Nevada range, he went from sea level to 10,000 feet in 1 day without prior acclimatization. He climbed and slept above 10,000 feet for 4 days. He felt well until the third day, when he had trouble sleeping, and his wife noted that he had periodic breathing. The next day he felt weak and short of breath, with a rapid heart rate persistent even at rest. During the night he had a persistent dry cough, which later became productive of clear, watery sputum. He developed orthopnea and noted wheezing and gurgling sounds in his chest. Unable to sleep, he had to sit up to relieve his dyspnea. The next day, he was evacuated to a regional hospital (altitude 4147 feet).

The patient gave a past history of two prior episodes of probable HAPE.

On entry to the emergency room, he was alert, with a blood pressure of 170/80 mmHg, temperature 101.6°F, heart rate 112, and respiratory rate 28. Cyanosis was present, and there was 1+ papilledema. The patient was slightly ataxic. Bilateral rales were present up to the scapulae.

Pertinent laboratory data demonstrated an arterial Po_2 of 25 mmHg, an arterial oxygen saturation of 43%, a Pco_2 of 24 mmHg, and a pH of 7.47 when breathing room air. The white count was 15,000. Microscopic urinalysis was normal, and specific gravity was 1.023. The chest x-ray revealed bilateral infiltrates consistent with pulmonary edema.

The patient responded well to 100% oxygen therapy and bed rest. Arterial blood gases 24 hours later on room air were: Po_2 56 mmHg, arterial oxygen saturation 90%, Pco_2 31 mmHg, and pH 7.45. At his request, the patient was transferred 24 hours after admission to his home at sea level. His recovery there was uncomplicated.

This case report illustrates that pulmonary edema can occur in the physically fit. Recurrent episodes in the same individual are common. The onset of HAPE is usually on the second or third day after arrival at high altitude. Symptoms become worse during the night. Despite the low arterial oxygen saturation, a patient may remain mentally alert. Usually, in other hypoxic settings, markedly diminished mental acuity or coma is present with such degrees of hypoxia. Recovery is prompt after descent and oxygen administration. Table 2 analyzes the clinical and epidemiologic features of 33 cases of HAPE.

LABORATORY STUDIES

Laboratory studies in persons with HAPE show an elevated hematocrit and acidic urine

TABLE 2
Analysis of 33 Instances of HAPE in Climbers

	Mean	Range
Age	30 years	20–43 years
Altitude of occurrence	13,670 feet	8600–24,000 feet
Duration of ascent	3.9 days	1–11 days
Interval before onset of symptoms	3 days	1–11 days
Most common features	Cough[a] Shortness of breath[b] Fatigue[c] Confusion, mental changes[c] Gurgling in chest[d]	
Pulse rate	115 per minute	96–170 per minute
Duration of edema	5.2 days	2–10 days
Previous episodes of HAPE	4 (12%)	
Deaths	9 (27%)	

[a] Reference 24.
[b] Reference 20.
[c] Reference 16.
[d] Reference 14.
Source: From Reference 19.

with high specific gravity, compatible with hemoconcentration. Signs of infection are absent, with only minor temperature elevation, a normal or moderately raised leukocyte count, and a normal erythrocyte sedimentation rate.

Electrocardiograms taken during acute episodes of HAPE display tachycardia and signs of acute right ventricular overload, including right axis deviation, P-wave abnormalities compatible with right atrial strain, prominent R waves in the right precordial leads, and S waves in leads V_5 and V_6. In one instance, transient atrial flutter has been noted. The changes are similar to those occurring during pulmonary embolism or acute cardiogenic pulmonary edema and generally subside during treatment. The electrocardiographic abnormalities are probably best explained on the basis of acute pulmonary hypertension.

Even after a patient is moved to a lower altitude, blood gas studies will show a marked reduction in arterial Po_2, especially in comatose patients. The Pco_2 is usually reduced, while the pH is normal or slightly elevated. Retention of CO_2 or acidosis has not been observed. Table 3 summarizes observations made of arterial blood gases before and after the administration of 100% oxygen by a face mask. A total of 26 patients were studied; 19 had moderate (grades 2 and 3) and seven had severe (grade 4) HAPE (severity classification in Table 4). The mean hospital stay was 3.7 days (range 2–7 days). All patients recovered fully without the use of intubation or positive end-expiratory pressure (PEEP) (27). The oxygen tensions are probably higher than those that were present before hospitalization, since many patients were transported to a lower altitude for hospitalization.

RADIOLOGIC FEATURES

Radiologic studies have been done in many instances of HAPE, and the extent of the edema shown on films of the chest roughly parallels the clinical severity. In mild episodes, single or several small, patchy infiltrates are present. In severe forms, the infiltrates may nearly fill both lung fields. The infiltrates are rarely confluent and clear spaces of aerated lung are usually present, especially at the lung bases. The edema is more severe and common in the right midlung field. The usual symmetrical batwing distribution of edema commonly seen in cardiogenic pulmonary edema or uremia is rare (Figure 4). The central branches of the pulmonary artery are prominent, but the overall heart size is not increased. Left atrial enlargement and pulmonary venous congestion are absent. Kerley lines of pulmonary venous hypertension are absent. Pleural effusion is rare.

In the presence of unilateral pulmonary edema, consideration should be given to unilateral pulmonary atresia as a source of HAPE. A lung perfusion scan may confirm the diagnosis by revealing unilateral blood flow (44).

Serial x-ray films of the chest during recovery from HAPE show clearing of the infiltrates and a decrease in prominence of the pulmonary arteries, but no consistent change in heart size. The radiologic features of HAPE are illustrated in Figure 4.

In persons with severe HAPE, especially when treatment has been delayed or recovery has been slow, infiltrates may persist for many days, or even for up to 2 weeks after clinical recovery, as noted on chest films. For this reason, it is advisable that chest films be done

TABLE 3
Arterial Blood Gases in 26 Patients with HAPE while Breathing Room Air and after Receiving 100% Oxygen by Face Mask

	Age (years)	Po_2 (mmHg)		Pco_2 (mmHg)	
		Room Air	100% O_2	Room Air	100% O_2
Mean	29	42	57	28	28
Range	19–56	23–56	45–115	21–32	27–36

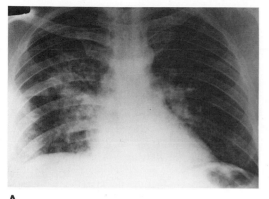

A

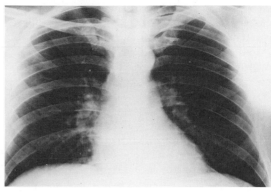

B

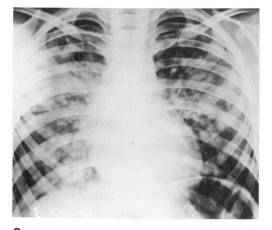

C

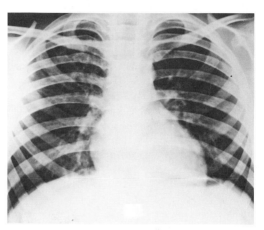

D

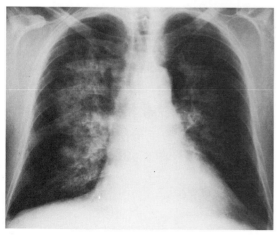

E

FIGURE 4 (*A*) Typical mild high-altitude pulmonary edema (grade 1) with infiltrate in right middle lung field. (*B*) Same patient 3 days later. (*C*) Moderately severe pulmonary edema in a 12-year-old boy. Bilateral infiltrates (grade 3). (*D*) Same patient 2 days later. Note absence of cardiac enlargement, clear spaces above diaphragms and between patchy infiltrates, and predilection for infiltrate to involve the right middle lung field. (*E*) Cardiac pulmonary edema in a patient with chronic renal disease. Note cardiac enlargement, bat-wing distribution of edema, and fine, granular appearance of infiltrate.

on any person who may have had an episode of HAPE, even though clinical recovery has occurred. Films showing a slowly clearing residual pulmonary infiltrate may confirm the diagnosis of suspected HAPE even after a return to sea level.

SEVERITY

In evaluating the treatment and prognosis, objective assessment of the severity of HAPE is important. In evaluating therapy for HAPE in prior studies, a simple method of severity grading has been used based on clinical features and x-ray films of the chest (Table 4). Grade 1 cases are very mild and usually do not come to a physician's attention. Most patients who seek medical attention are grades 3 and 4. Grade 4 cases are severe and characterized by stupor or coma. Arterial Po_2 values of less than 33 mmHg may be observed. General experience indicates that such patients will die within 6–12 hours unless prompt therapy or rapid descent to a lower altitude is initiated. The grading system must be modified for younger people. Children have higher heart rates and respiratory rates than adults.

In addition, some patients may present without dyspnea, and the initial symptoms may be somnolence or coma. At high altitude, cases of grades 2 and 3 can progress within a few hours to grade 4, particularly during sleep.

The mortality of HAPE is variable and depends on many factors. Studies of large population groups at risk indicate a mortality of 0.5–12.0%.

The chance of developing HAPE upon ascent to high altitude depends on the altitude attained, speed of ascent, altitude at which the individual sleeps, degree of physical exertion after arrival, age, and a history of prior episodes of HAPE. Let us consider a single ascent from sea level to 12,000 feet in 1 day, sleeping at that altitude, moderately heavy daily physical exertion upon arrival, and no prior history of HAPE. In such a situation, adults over the age of 21 years will have a low incidence, about 0.5%. In 200 trekkers evaluated at 14,000 feet by Hackett and Rennie, pulmonary rales were present in 23% and the incidence of HAPE was 4.5% (14). In children and adolescents ages 10–18, the incidence is higher, about 6% (23). HAPE rarely

TABLE 4
Severity Classification of HAPE

	Clinical Signs or Symptoms	Heart Rate (beats/minute)	Respiratory Rate (breaths/minute)	Chest Films
1. Mild	Minor symptoms only. Dyspnea on moderate or heavy activity. Rales may be present.	<110	<16	Minor infiltrates of <25% in one lung field.
2. Moderate	Symptoms of dyspnea, weakness, and fatigue on ordinary effort. Headache and dry cough. Rales usually present.	110–120	16–30	Infiltrate involving 50% of one lung field, usually the right mid-lung field.
3. Serious	Symptoms of dyspnea and weakness, and headache at rest. Anorexia common. Persistent loose, productive cough. Rales easily heard.	121–130	31–40	Bilateral infiltrates involving at least one-half of each lung field.
4. Severe	Stupor or coma. Hallucinations may occur. Inability to stand or walk. Severe cyanosis. Prominent rales heard. Copious sputum present, often bloody.	>130	>40	Bilateral exudates involving >50% of each lung field.

occurs in children under the age of 2 years. In neither children nor adults does there appear to be a sex preference.

SUBCLINICAL HAPE

The data described refer only to obvious HAPE severe enough to require medical attention. If one includes subclinical HAPE, the true incidence is substantially higher than indicated. Houston and Dickinson (18) have made observations of climbers before and after the ascent of Mount Rainier, Washington (14,408 feet). Of 140 subjects, 15% had pulmonary rales after descent, suggesting the presence of mild pulmonary edema. Singh *et al.* noted that about one-third of patients with severe AMS had pulmonary rales (45). Subclinical pulmonary edema, therefore, can be estimated to occur much more frequently than more severe forms.

SUSCEPTIBLE PERSONS

Some persons are susceptible to HAPE and may have recurrent episodes when reascending to high altitude. In one study, 20% of patients with HAPE had experienced at least one previous episode (23). Physiologic studies have indicated that in persons with a history of HAPE, there is an abnormal rise in pulmonary arteriolar resistance and an impaired oxygen exchange during acute altitude exposure (22). In susceptible persons, there is also a more pronounced rise in pulmonary artery pressure and arteriolar resistance during low oxygen breathing (29). Pulmonary artery wedge pressure remains normal.

Persons with congenital absence of the right pulmonary artery appear to be predisposed to pulmonary edema at moderate (9900 feet; 3000 m) altitudes.

HAPE DURING REASCENT

In fully acclimatized persons who descend to sea level and then return to high altitude, HAPE may develop on reascent. HAPE during reascent is rare when the sea-level sojourn is less than 10–14 days. Recent studies of Leadville, Colorado (altitude 10,300 feet), residents have shown that a descent to Denver

(altitude 5400 feet) or lower for as little as 3–5 days may be followed by HAPE upon return to Leadville (43). Pulmonary edema during reascent may occur more frequently than pulmonary edema during initial ascent to high altitudes, but further data are needed to settle this point.

TREATMENT

Prompt recognition of early signs and symptoms, bed rest, descent to a lower altitude, and oxygen administration are the principal methods of treatment of HAPE. Drug therapy is of limited or doubtful value.

Severe HAPE and fatalities have occurred largely because early signs and symptoms were ignored or concealed, as when pneumonia has been erroneously diagnosed. Early recognition of HAPE is important to permit prompt treatment and to prevent progression to a more serious stage. Trip leaders should be aware of the younger members of the party who are not acclimatized, who ascend rapidly, and who carry out heavy physical work during the first 2–3 days after arrival at high altitude. Fatigue, weakness, dyspnea, cough, mental confusion, loss of appetite, and inability to keep up with the other party members should lead to the presumptive diagnosis of HAPE. Such individuals should be examined after 15–20 minutes of bed rest. One should check mental acuity, heart rate, and respiratory rate and listen to the chest for rales even if a stethoscope is not available. Mental confusion, a heart rate of more than 110 beats per minute, a respiratory rate greater than 16 per minute, and rales indicate the presence of HAPE. Ataxia may occur and can be evaluated by asking the subject to walk a straight line on a level surface.

BED REST

Absolute bed rest is extremely important. Physical exercise will aggravate HAPE by increasing pulmonary artery pressure and reducing arterial oxygen saturation. Mild cases of HAPE can be treated with bed rest alone at high altitude, without oxygen administration or descent (33). Recovery is slower with bed rest therapy than when oxygen is used.

monary artery pressure during exercise and with acute hypoxia has been greater than that in normal persons. Subjects with a history of HAPE, when rapidly exposed to high altitude, have shown an abnormal increase in pulmonary artery pressure at rest and during exercise. This was not observed in normal controls. Pulmonary artery wedge pressures were normal (22).

Arterial oxygen saturation is decreased with HAPE, often to very low levels. The CO_2 pressure is decreased or normal, and the pH is normal or slightly elevated. In victims of HAPE, exercise or induced hypoxia results in an increase in pulmonary arterial oxygen saturation, but normal values are usually not attained; this suggests that there is intrapulmonary shunting. Oxygen administration will rapidly lower pulmonary artery pressure, but usually not to normal levels (19).

PATHOLOGIC CONDITIONS

Autopsy findings in fatal cases of HAPE have been reported by several workers (2,26). Severe, confluent pulmonary edema is present, with a protein-rich exudate filling the alveoli. In some cases, fibrinous intra-alveolar exudates or hyaline membranes are present, resembling those seen in patients with mitral stenosis and influenza pneumonia. Such deposits are usually found when very high capillary pressures occur or when capillary injury is present with increased permeability to protein. Hemorrhage into the alveoli may occur. Pronounced capillary congestion and distention of capillaries by erythrocytes are commonly found. Obstruction of capillaries and arterioles by thrombi consisting of platelet aggregates, leukocytes, red cells, and fibrin strands or clumps has been described. Numerous megakaryocytes may be present in such aggregates. Notable dilatation of preterminal arterioles, capillaries, and small pulmonary veins has also been observed.

Pneumonitis is rare. In one patient with this condition, the clinical history suggested that a viral respiratory infection existed before HAPE occurred. Pneumonitis may have facilitated HAPE; pneumonia in experimental animals increases capillary permeability and susceptibility to pulmonary edema.

The right atrium, right ventricle, and large pulmonary arteries are usually distended, and hepatic congestion may be present. Signs of left ventricular failure are absent. The left ventricle, left atrium, and pulmonary veins are not distended. Underlying cardiac or pulmonary disease is absent.

Cerebral edema related to severe hypoxia may occur.

CAUSES

The causes of HAPE must be considered within the framework of the following well-established features of this unusual form of pulmonary edema: (1) a rapid rise in pulmonary artery pressure due to high-altitude ascent, with a low pulmonary artery wedge pressure and left atrial pressure; (2) acute hypoxic pulmonary arteriolar vasoconstriction, which is reversed by breathing oxygen; (3) absence of left ventricular failure or pneumonia; (4) pronounced pulmonary capillary congestion and the presence of capillary and arterial thromboses in many fatal cases; and (5) harmful effect of heavy exercise, but improvement with bed rest.

In 1966, the author proposed the following concept of the etiologic factors in HAPE (24): The primary cause of HAPE is nonpatterned obstruction, with varying severity, of the pulmonary vascular bed by hypoxic vasoconstriction and possibly intravascular thromboses. During periods of exercise and increased pulmonary blood flow, unobstructed areas of the pulmonary circulation are subjected to high pressure and flow. The precapillary arterioles become dilated, permitting the high pulmonary artery pressure to be transmitted directly to the capillary bed, with resulting interstitial and alveolar edema. With dilatation of arterioles and capillaries, pulmonary veins may then become the site of resistance to flow, which would also result in a high capillary pressure. Therefore, an important mechanism of HAPE is failure of hypoxic vasoconstriction, along with dilatation of nonconstricted vessels in local areas of the lung (19). A similar concept has been proposed for the mechanism of hypertensive encephalopathy in systemic hypertension: In this condition, cerebral edema is due to failure of cerebral vasoconstriction, permitting a high arterial pressure to be transmitted to the capillary bed, with resultant edema. Failure of vasoconstriction seems to occur when a very high arterial pressure is present. The high degree of pressure elevation is thought to be the cause. Clinical and experimental evidence supporting this concept is available (28).

High-Altitude Encephalopathy (HAE)

In 1959, Chiodi described a patient who had predominantly neurologic signs and symptoms during exposure to high altitude in the Andes (7). Occipital headaches were intense and associated with cervical pain; tinnitus was troublesome. Areas of anesthesia and paresthesia, particularly in the arms and legs, as well as hemiplegia, occurred. There was severe pain in the limbs, joints, and lumbar region. Examination demonstrated cervical rigidity, ankle clonus, an abnormal Babinski sign, localized areas of cutaneous anesthesia, and dilatation of retinal veins. On lumbar puncture, the spinal fluid was bloody, but the dynamics were normal. The signs and symptoms disappeared promptly on return to sea level. There was no evidence of unusual polycythemia or alveolar hypoventilation. A cerebral arteriogram and cerebral blood flow studies were normal. The usual increase in cerebral blood flow in response to low-oxygen breathing was absent. Chiodi suggested that this may have been a factor in the development of the clinical features.

Subsequently, many instances of illness characterized by cerebral neurologic symptoms and signs associated with confusion, stupor, or coma have been observed at high altitudes (7,18,45,53). Findings from autopsies have shown cerebral edema. Because the syndrome has sometimes occurred without the signs and symptoms of HAPE, it is likely that HAE represents another manifestation of high-altitude exposure. Cerebral edema is believed to be present in most cases. Data from a small number of patients have shown that papilledema, retinal hemorrhages, and increased cerebrospinal fluid pressure are present. In one instance, the symptoms were so suggestive of a subdural hematoma or neoplasm that a craniotomy was done. Cerebral edema was noted, and a biopsy of the brain confirmed the gross diagnosis (42).

A possible mechanism is the effect of severe hypoxia on the brain, with inhibition of the sodium pump and resultant intracellular edema. Cerebral edema has been observed in monkeys subjected to an altitude of 28,000 feet in a low-pressure chamber. It has been shown that hypoxia results in cerebral edema in humans. Prompt removal to a low altitude and the use of oxygen therapy will usually result in complete recovery. Late neurologic complications are rare, and mental processes appear to recover completely in most cases.

HAE may be an example of a high-altitude illness still in search of an appropriate name. In previous reports, the term *high-altitude cerebral edema* was employed since clinical and experimental evidence indicated that cerebral edema was probably present in most cases and because severe cerebral hypoxia may result in brain edema. However, cerebral edema may be a consequence of hypoxia and not necessarily a cause of the many clinical manifestations of this syndrome. For example, while it is attractive to attribute the headache of AMS to brain edema, this may not be accurate. In patients with brain tumors, headache was observed as frequently in those without a raised intracranial pressure as in those with a normal pressure. In addition, of seven patients without headache, three had a raised intracranial pressure (8). The intracranial pressure can be raised by intrathecal infusions to over 50 cm H_2O without the onset of headaches (30). It is well known that removal of cerebrospinal fluid is commonly followed by headache. For these reasons, the term *high-altitude encephalopathy* may be more suitable. Cerebral dysfunction due to hypoxia differs from that due to ischemia or vascular obstruction and generally carries a better prognosis than the latter. A typical example of severe encephalopathy is presented.

S. L. was a 29-year-old mountain climber who left Los Angeles on February 9, 1980, to climb Mount Aconcagua (altitude 22,824 feet) in Argentina. On February 11, he and his companion arrived at Mendoza (altitude 2700 feet), where they stayed for 4 days. During this period, S. L. developed diarrhea three to four times daily without fever or abdominal pain. Diphenoxylate (Lomotil) provided no relief. On February 15, S. L. traveled by bus to 9000 feet and on the following day began climbing with an 80 pound pack. On February 18, he reached 13,000 feet, where his diarrhea continued. On February 19, he reached 15,000 feet, where he and his companion spent the night. On February 21, they reached 17,000 feet, where they again spent the night. During the night, S. L. had frequent violent jerking movements of his arms and hands, but his mental state was clear. On the following day, he felt ill and spent the day in the tent. His companion noted that S. L. had a slow, garbled speech, but that his mental state was clear. On February 23, they descended to 15,000 feet, where they spent the night. The following morning, S. L. had gross ataxia and difficulty with speech, and was unable to walk without assistance. With the help of another party of climbers, he was able to descend to 13,000 feet. He was evacuated by helicopter to a military hospital in Mendoza. Skull films, an electroencephalogram (EEG), and a lumbar puncture were reported to be normal. On March 11, 1980, S. L. was transferred to a hospital in the United States, where a thorough history revealed that he had had episodes of nausea, headache, confusion, and drowsiness on prior climbs to high altitude.

On March 12, examination revealed a patient lying nearly motionless in bed with a glassy stare. He was unable to speak (marked expressive aphasia) and could not control movements of his tongue. He appeared to be able to mouthe words such as his name with difficulty. He was unable to phonate except for a weak grunting sound on forced expiration. He appeared to understand what was said to him and could follow simple commands. Cranial nerve function was intact. There was marked dysdiadochokinesia; truncal ataxia was present, and the patient had difficulty in sitting up. He could not stand without assistance. The right upper extremity appeared weaker than the left. Plantar reflexes were equivocal bilaterally. A speech pathology consultant stated that the patient was nonverbal, with marked apraxia of the muscles of phonation. There appeared to be deficits in visual perception, comprehension, and memory.

Acquired studies revealed a normal chest x-ray and electrocardiogram. The vital capacity was 3 liters. A lumbar puncture and computed tomographic (CT) brain scan were normal. The EEG on March 13 demonstrated abnormal θ activity bilaterally; a repeat study a few days later was normal. A skull series was normal. Routine laboratory tests including a blood count, urinalysis, and serum electrolytes were normal. An echocardiogram was normal.

On April 23, S. L. was improved. His mental state was clear and indicative of full comprehension. He was able to speak but still had some difficulty in expression. Gait ataxia was present, but he could ambulate with moderate assistance. He had difficulty in feeding himself properly, due to a secondary tremor and weakness in his arms.

On September 15, he was still receiving rehabilitative therapy. His coordination remained poor, with a bilateral stance of 15 seconds and a unilateral stance of 5 seconds. He was able to walk only with a walker or assumed a four-stance gait with crutches.

Clearly, this is an example of severe anoxic encephalopathy with prolonged truncal ataxia. There was no evidence of cerebral edema or pulmonary edema. The patient's history of cerebral symptoms at high altitude suggests an individual susceptibility to cerebral anoxic injury. No report is available regarding a fundoscopic examination, so that it is not possible to determine if retinal hemorrhages were present. There was no history of visual difficulties. A less severe example is described:

T. K. was a 21-year-old climber who was climbing Mount McKinley until he reached an altitude of 15,000 feet on June 24, 1970. The following day, he climbed to a camp at 17,400 feet, where he had a headache and noted unusual fatigue.

On June 26, he climbed higher to Denali Pass and then returned to his 17,400 foot camp. He vomited on the return trip and spent a restless night. Early on June 27, he noted dyspnea, occipital and nuchal headache, substernal tightness, and pleuritic chest pains, without cough or sputum production. He was given 80 mg of furosemide (Lasix), with considerable diuresis but no relief of symptoms. In 2 days he was slid down to 15,000 feet in a make-shift sled and evacuated by helicopter to an Anchorage hospital.

Physical examination was normal except for bilateral retinal hemorrhages and a grossly ataxic gait that prevented him from walking a straight line. Finger-to-nose and heel-to-shin tests, deep tendon reflexes, and the Romberg test were normal. There was no papilledema. A lumbar puncture was not performed. On June 30, the neurologic examination was unchanged. Truncal ataxia was present without nystagmus. Laboratory studies, chest film, and the electrocardiogram (ECG) were normal, with the exception of a hematocrit of 57%. Improvement was rapid, and he was discharged from the hospital on July 1. There were no sequelae. The discharge diagnosis was hypoxic midline cerebellar cell damage and bilateral retinal hemorrhages. In retrospect, prompt removal to a lower altitude and air evacuation to a hospital probably prevented more serious neurologic damage or death.

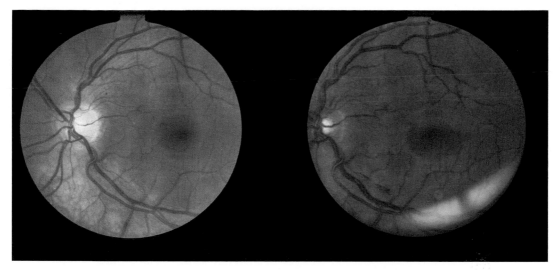

Plate 1   The normal fundus at sea level (*left*). The same fundus at 5400 m (*right*). Note the vascular engorgement and tortuousness at altitude. (Retinal photographs courtesy of Dr. M. McFadden, U.B.C., Vancouver, B. C., in association with Dr. C. Houston, Burlington, Vermont; Dr. G. Gray, D.C.I.E.M., Toronto, Ontario; and Drs. J. Sutton and P. Powles, McMaster University, Hamilton, Ontario.)

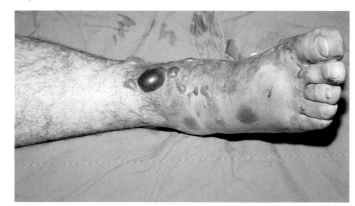

Plate 2A   Edema and blister formation 24 hours after frostbite injury occurring in an area covered by a tightly fitted boot.

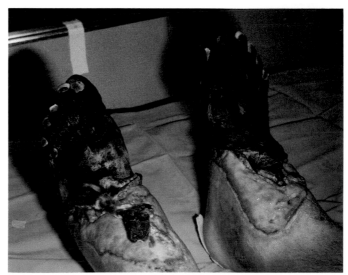

Plate 2B   Gangrenous necrosis 6 weeks after frostbite injury shown in Plate 2A.

Plate 3   Deadly stonefish (*Synanceia horrida*). (Photo by Carl Roessler.)

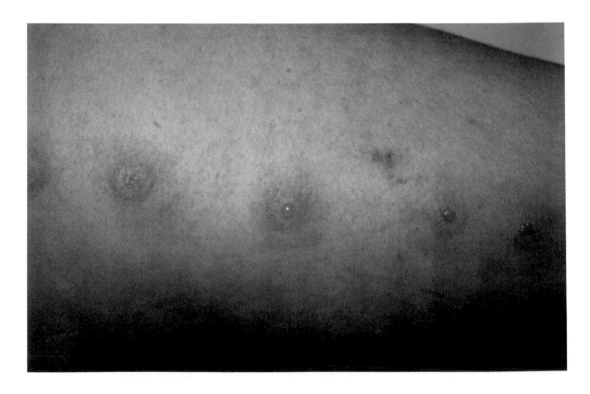

Plate 4   Typical linear pattern of triatomid bites on the forearm.

Trip leaders and physicians should be aware of the early symptoms and signs of HAE. Ataxia, a staggering gait, severe headache, mental confusion, and somnolence are common early manifestations. Physical examination may reveal neurologic deficits or abnormal reflexes such as upgoing toes. Papilledema and retinal hemorrhages are common. Increased resting heart rate and respiratory rate, rales, and cyanosis may indicate the presence of HAPE, which occasionally accompanies central nervous system signs and symptoms. Fortunately, the treatment for HAE is similar to that for HAPE: prompt descent, high-flow oxygen, and bed rest. Acetazolamide (Diamox) may be helpful. Descent is usually the only method available in the field, and litter transport is usually necessary. The most severe instances of central nervous system damage have occurred when descent was not possible and oxygen was unavailable. The use of mannitol, glycerol, and other such medications is of doubtful value. Such measures may be of value in ischemic encephalopathy or other conditions associated with severe cerebral edema. However, in the absence of cerebral edema, such interventions may cause harm by reducing cerebral blood flow. Steroids may be helpful and will not reduce cerebral blood flow. Patients with cerebral or central neurologic dysfunctions which persist after descent should be hospitalized.

The incidence of HAE is probably lower than that of HAPE. Encephalopathy frequently occurs in association with HAPE. In 40 accidents or deaths occurring on Mount McKinley in 1976, there were five associated cases of HAPE, five cases of HAPE combined with anoxic encephalopathy, and one case of anoxic encephalopathy without HAPE (54). Anoxic encephalopathy appears to occur at higher altitudes than does HAPE.

Venous Thrombosis and Pulmonary Embolism

The mountaineering literature contains many references to episodes of thrombophlebitis, pulmonary embolism, and cerebrovascular accidents which were presumably of thrombotic origin. Increased blood viscosity due to polycythemia and dehydration is probably an important factor. In addition, several studies have shown that high-altitude exposure in certain subjects results in alteration of blood coagulation factors, which may facilitate thromboses. In fatal cases of HAPE, thrombotic lesions of arterioles and capillaries have been observed.

Prevention of venous thrombosis by regular limb exercises, even in the restricted confines of a shelter during a storm, is important. Constrictive clothing that may impede venous return should be avoided. Adequate fluid intake to prevent hemoconcentration is essential. In the event of obvious venous thrombosis, thrombophlebitis, suspected pulmonary embolism, or cerebral thrombosis, immediate removal to a lower altitude and a medical facility is indicated. The use of anticoagulants under field conditions is hazardous and should be avoided.

Acute Mountain Sickness

The rapid exposure to high altitude of unacclimatized persons commonly results in a group of symptoms generally known as *acute mountain sickness (AMS)*. Severe symptoms rarely occur below 8000 feet. In most persons, some symptoms will be present at 10,000–12,000 feet. AMS is the most common high-altitude illness. Excellent descriptions of AMS have been published by De Acosta and Barcroft (5). De Acosta's description is one of the earliest published records of AMS (1589). Barcroft's report describes symptoms affecting passengers on a train trip from Lima to Cerro de Pasco, Peru (altitude 14,200 feet).

The most common initial symptom consists of headache, which may vary in severity from a mild feeling of light-headedness or dizziness to severe, prolonged, and incapacitating pain. Lassitude, anorexia, drowsiness, a general feeling of malaise, weakness, and dyspnea on exertion are common. A reduced urine output may occur. During ascent, somnolence, chilliness with pallor of the face, and cyanosis of the lips and nail beds are frequently noted. Nausea and vomiting may occur, especially in children.

After arrival, a feeling of warmth and flushing of the face may be noted for the first 24–48 hours. These symptoms may persist for several days, although in most instances they disappear within 24–48 hours. Sleep, especially for the first few nights, is difficult, with frequent periods of wakefulness and strange dreams. Slight physical effort may produce troublesome weakness and dyspnea, often requiring considerable rest until the respiratory distress has ceased. Palpitations and tachycardia may be present. A common complaint is dull pain or discomfort in the muscles of the posterolateral chest wall. Cheyne-Stokes respiration may be experienced above 8000 feet and occurs in nearly all persons at altitudes above 13,000 feet. It appears most frequently during the night and is a major factor in preventing sound, restful sleep. If present during the day, it does not appear to be related to activity or eating. It is rarely continuous, but appears and disappears, lasting for minutes to hours.

Neurologic and cerebral symptoms may be experienced, including a reduced capacity for sustained mental work, memory defects, auditory and visual disturbances, vertigo, and tinnitus. Ataxia may occur and may be progressive. This symptom is a clear indication for descent or bed rest and oxygen therapy. Irritability may be noted. Appetite may remain poor, with marked weight loss. In some persons, symptoms may persist throughout the stay at high altitudes and may result in an inability to work efficiently; in some cases, a return to sea level may be necessary.

Headache is the most severe and disabling symptom of AMS. In a series of 200 trekkers studied at Pheriche, Nepal (altitude 14,000 feet), 22% reported headaches. In subjects who flew to 9300 feet, the incidence of AMS was 49% compared to 31% in those who walked up; 16.5% of subjects had such severe symptoms that they were unable to continue the trek or had to descend to a lower altitude, while 3% had to be carried down (14). It has been suggested that headache is due to cerebral edema; however, cerebral edema in other clinical conditions is not regularly associated with headache. A more plausible explanation is spasm or dilatation of cerebral blood vessels related to hypocapnia (which causes cerebral vasoconstriction) or to hypoxia (which causes cerebral vasodilatation).

AMS may not be evident during the first 24 hours of altitude exposure; the symptoms are usually most severe on the second and third days. More rapid ascent to higher altitudes is occasionally associated with more severe AMS, but this is not without variation. The altitude at which one sleeps is more important than the altitude attained during a climb. On Mount Whitney (altitude 14,495 feet), for example, AMS occurs less frequently in climbers who make the ascent in 1 day from Owens Valley than in those who spend the night at Mirror Lake (altitude 10,640 feet).

TREATMENT

Mild or moderately severe AMS is best treated by rest, light diet, increased fluid intake, and symptomatic measures to relieve headache [aspirin, acetominophen (Tylenol), or acetominophen plus codeine]. Smoking and the use of alcohol should be avoided. Voluntary hyperventilation every 10–15 minutes may be helpful. Excessive hyperventilation may result in symptoms of hypocapnea, including dizziness and paresthesias of the hands and lips. Barbiturates may make rest and sleep possible, but are also associated with an intensification of symptoms upon awakening. Oversedation may mask incipient HAE, so that the use of narcotics should be discouraged. Diazepam (Valium) occasionally causes hypoxia, disorientation, and hallucinations. For severe episodes of AMS, descent or the administration of oxygen is indicated. Continuous oxygen administration (1–2 liters/minute) with a plastic face mask or nasal prongs during sleep may be very helpful, not only in relieving symptoms but also in facilitating restful sleep. Lightweight oxygen tanks are now available, providing 247 liters of oxygen (about a 12 hour supply) with a variable-flow regulator and a carrying weight of only 6.5 pounds (Erie Manufacturing Company, 4000 S. 13th Street, Milwaukee, WI 53221). Acetazolamide may be helpful.

PREVENTION

The most effective method of preventing AMS is by acclimatization. For those persons susceptible to AMS, the administration of acetazolamide is useful (6,9,11,15). Acetazolamide may be given in a dose of 125 or 250 mg once or twice a day, beginning on the day of ascent and continuing for 2–5 days after arrival. Acetazolamide is a carbonic anhydrase inhibitor that increases the urinary excretion of bicarbonate, sodium, and potassium. A metabolic acidosis is produced, which diminishes the diuretic effect. Carbonic anhydrase inhibitors are felt to stimulate respiration and ventilatory exchange via a number of possible mechanisms. These include augmentation of peripheral oxygen-sensitive chemoreceptors and stimulation of central nervous system medullary chemoreceptors by reducing alkaline inhibition. Promotion of bicarbonate excretion anticipates the normal renal adaptation to the respiratory alkalosis induced at altitude. Side effects, such as tingling of the lips and fingertips, alteration in the taste of beer, and myopia usually occur only if acetazolamide administration is continued for more than 5 days. Known contraindications are conditions of preexisting metabolic acidosis. Field studies of troops have shown that AMS at 14,200 feet can be ameliorated by staging for 4 days at 5300 feet and administering acetazolamide (125–250 mg twice a day) for the last 2 days of staging and the first 2 days at high altitude. Persons treated at high altitude had a higher arterial oxygen tension (PaO_2), a lower arterial carbon dioxide tension ($PaCO_2$), and a lower pH than control subjects (6). The dosage of acetazolamide in these studies was high, usually 250 mg twice a day. A higher staging altitude of 6000–7000 feet may be preferable. In a randomized study of 64 climbers who ascended Mount Rainier (4394 m) with an average ascent time of 33.5 hours, the prophylactic administration of acetazolamide (250 mg every 8 hours beginning 1 day prior to ascent) was seen to have significant effects. Minute ventilation and expired vital capacity were improved, and the overall incidence and severity of AMS was markedly decreased. The beneficial effects of acetazolamide were postulated to be due to increased ventilation at altitude, increased alveolar oxygen tension, and possible improved sleep patterns. The theoretical possibility that acetazolamide prevented or reduced the increase in intrathoracic fluid volume associated with high altitude suggests an application to the amelioration or prevention of the HAPE syndrome, but warrants further clinical evaluation prior to a recommendation (30a).

Furosemide (Lasix) is of no value in preventing AMS (1,20). Physical conditioning before ascent does not appear to reduce the incidence or severity of AMS, but it will permit more effective climbing. Alkalinization of the blood by the use of antacids is of no value. Even the ingestion of 50 g of sodium bicarbonate per day for 3 days resulted in no major effect upon the respiratory response to hypoxia (10).

Symptoms of AMS usually disappear in 2–6 days. In rare instances, symptoms may persist for weeks or months. Major problems may consist of anorexia with weight loss, insomnia, and mental and physical fatigue. Symptoms will disappear upon descent to a lower altitude.

Chronic or Subacute Mountain Sickness

Subacute mountain sickness (SAMS) is similar to high-altitude deterioration except that it may occur at lower altitudes. In employees of mining industries in the central Peruvian Andes, several episodes were observed at 12,000 feet. Symptoms were so severe and persistent that return to a lower elevation was necessary.

A typical case study from the United States described a 45-year-old male seen in referral for an elevated hematocrit. A longtime resident at 10,200 feet, he had been disturbed during the previous year by restless sleep, memory loss, and lack of interest in his work. Physical examination, chest x-ray, and spirometry were within normal limits. The hematocrit was 67%. Cutaneous oximetry performed at 10,200 feet during sleep showed prolonged periods of arterial oxygen desaturation to a low of 65%. Treatment with medroxyprogesterone resulted in a drop in hematocrit to a value of 55% and improvement in symptoms (43).

Typically, male highland dwellers are most vulnerable to SAMS, with complaints of headache, lethargy, and sleep disturbance and elevations of hematocrit to a value greater than 60%. Although traditional therapy has included phlebotomy, the respiratory stimulant drug medroxyprogesterone acetate (Provera) has shown promise by improving ventilation and oxygenation during sleep. Thus, the hypoxemia-stimulated erythropoiesis and sleep disturbance are ameliorated. The recommended dosage is 20 mg orally three times a day. Avoidance of sedatives, barbiturates, and codeine is essential. Low-flow oxygen during sleep may be of use.

High-Altitude Deterioration (HAD)

This problem usually occurs at extreme altitudes (greater than 18,000 feet) and is manifested by a deterioration in physical and mental performance. While it may occur in the absence of heavy physical activity, it is usually more severe in individuals who carry out daily heavy physical work. During rapid (alpine-style) ascents, deterioration may be severe and life-threatening. Causative mechanisms are probably multifactorial and include chronic hypoxia, inadequate nutrition, and inadequate fluid intake, with a decrease in plasma volume and hemoconcentration. Hypothermia and frostbite may be complicating factors. Treatment consists of (1) rest days at a lower altitude; (2) low-flow oxygen during sleep; (3) an adequate diet, preferably high in carbohydrates; and (4) optimal fluid intake to maintain a daily urinary output of at least 1 liter/day. Since hemoconcentration and hyperviscosity may be aggravated by hypothermia and frostbite, infusions of saline or Ringer's lactate may be beneficial therapeutic measures. The role of acetazolamide or medroxyprogesterone acetate is unknown, but these may be helpful. Sedative drugs such as diazepam, barbiturates, or codeine should not be used.

High-Altitude Systemic Edema (HASE)

Asymptomatic edema of the face, hands, and feet, associated with a weight gain of 4–12 pounds in 4–10 days at high altitudes, is most common in women. Puffiness of the face and eyelids in the morning after sleep may be troublesome and unsightly. Edema may occur in the absence of other symptoms of altitude illness. In susceptible persons, repeated episodes during each exposure to altitude are common. Upon return to sea level, diuresis with weight loss occurs. Edema may persist for 1–3 days after return to a lower altitude. The cause is not clear. There appears to be no relation to the menstrual cycle or to the use of birth control pills. In 200 trekkers at 14,000 feet, 18% had some peripheral edema. Peripheral edema was twice as common in females as in males (14). It is possible that sodium and water retention is stimulated by the decrease in plasma volume that occurs during high-altitude exposure. Published data regarding this syndrome are minimal, and the need for studies of etiologic mechanisms is clearly indicated.

Prevention and cautious treatment by the use of furosemide or other diuretic agents are usually effective. Salt intake should be reduced to less than 2 g/day. HAPE should be excluded by physical examination. The necessity for treatment of an essentially nonharmful condition with diuretics must be weighed against the possible induction of potentially harmful dehydration.

High-Altitude Retinal Hemorrhage (HARH)

Retinal hemorrhages related to high-altitude exposure were first noted in 1968 in subjects studied at an altitude of 17,500 feet on Mount Logan. In 1969, a study on Mount Logan revealed that 9 of 25 subjects had retinal hemorrhages. Since then, systematic examinations of the fundus at high altitude have revealed asymptomatic hemorrhages in 30–60% of subjects sleeping above 17,000 feet (34,47,55). The incidence is substantially less at 14,000 feet and need not be associated with symptoms of AMS.

The normal retinal response to altitude includes vascular engorgement, tortuousness, and disk hyperemia (34). High-altitude retinal hemorrhage (HARH) is typified by multiple flame-shaped hemorrhages, although cotton-wool spots and macular hemorrhages are occasionally observed (see Figure 5; Plate 1). Visual disturbance is rare, and even careful testing of visual fields tends to be normal. Follow-up visual field testing has failed to show

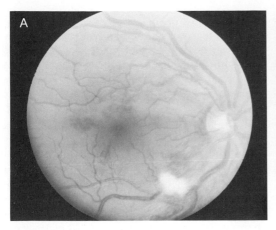 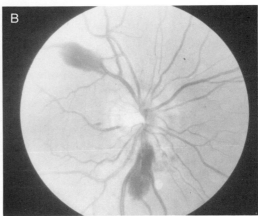

FIGURE 5 (*A*) An example of the most severe retinopathy. This subject, although symptomatically well, developed multiple cotton-wool spots as well as hemorrhages. The cotton-wool spot shown here corresponds to a permanent arcuate scotoma. Cotton-wool spots represent areas of microinfarction of the nerve fiber layer. (Subject female, aged 25.) (*B*) Demonstrates moderate sized superficial retinal hemorrhages and small flame-shaped hemorrhages close to the disk. (Subject male, aged 25.) (Retinal photographs courtesy of Dr. M. McFadden, U.B.C., Vancouver, B.C., in association with Dr. C. Houston, Burlington, Vermont; Dr. G. Gray, D.C.I.E.M., Toronto, Ontario; and Drs. J. Sutton and P. Powles, McMaster University, Hamilton, Ontario.)

defects except in those with macular hemorrhage.

The mechanism of retinal hemorrhage is unclear. Hypoxia is a probable cause, as retinal hemorrhages have been noted in other hypoxic states such as congenital cyanotic heart disease, chronic pulmonary disease, and carbon monoxide poisoning. Increased retinal blood flow, increased retinal capillary pressure, hyperemia of the optic nerve head, and changes in capillary permeability may be involved. Heavy physical exercise with repeated Valsalva maneuvers during isometric exercise may transiently elevate retinal vein pressures and predispose to bleeding. Although repeat episodes may occur during reascent, no subjects showed increased susceptibility, nor was there a predilection for HARH in newcomers, in returnees to altitude, or in men versus women. HARH seems to be related to strenuous exercise and occurs less often in those acclimatized to altitude. Acetazolamide offers no protective effect.

It is generally accepted by climbers that asymptomatic retinal hemorrhages are not an indication for descent. There is no evidence that the typical flame-shaped hemorrhage will worsen with ascent or result in any permanent visual sequelae. Hemorrhages which are large

or involve the macula and which interfere with visual acuity are an indication for descent. Oxygen therapy is recommended if descent is not possible, although its efficacy has not been proven. Any decision regarding descent in the presence of HARH should be made jointly by the physician and the patient after a discussion of the possible consequences.

High-Altitude Flatus Expulsion (HAFE)

High-altitude flatus expulsion (HAFE) is the unwelcome spontaneous passage of colonic gas at altitudes above 11,000 feet (4). The mechanism has been postulated to relate to the expansion of intraluminal bowel gas at the decreased atmospheric pressure of altitude. It has been likened to the gastrointestinal barotrauma sustained by deep sea divers on ascent from a dive. Other etiologies include intestinal hypermotility or a high-fiber flatogenic backpacker's diet. While no serious sequelae have been noted to date, HAFE nonetheless can prove to be a disconcerting affliction for members of trekking parties. Stricken individuals may benefit from the oral administration of digestive enzymes or simethicone.

Ultraviolet Keratitis (Snow Blindness)

Excessive ultraviolet radiation exposure of wavelengths 2900–3200 nm to the unprotected eye causes damage to the cornea and conjunctiva, in effect creating a sunburn of the surface of the eye. Because of the high level of transmitted ultraviolet radiation at high altitude, snow blindness is much more likely to occur than at lower elevations, where the radiation is diminished by the atmosphere, smog, and shade. During the period of exposure, there is little or no sensation of ocular damage except for the brightness of the light, which should serve as a warning to the climber. Symptoms usually appear 6–12 hours later. At this time, the eyes feel dry and painful, and there is a sensation of grittiness. Eye movements, blinking, or further exposure to light are painful. Chemosis, conjunctivitis, and excessive lacrimation develop. Symptoms may persist for several days and may be completely incapacitating.

Protection of the eyes by appropriate ultraviolet radiation-filtering goggles or sunglasses is essential at high altitude. Glasses should have darker lenses than are generally used at beach resorts, transmitting less than 10% of ultraviolet light in wavelengths below 3200 nm. A tint containing yellow or orange is useful for visibility in snow or overcast. The glasses should be curved and have side shields as well. Goggles are more effective, but may steam up during heavy exertion. Spare glasses or goggles should be carried in the event that one pair is lost or broken. In an emergency, a cardboard lens with a slit glued into the eyeglass frame will provide protection. A visor or wide-brim hat will further shield the eyes. Sunscreen ointment, with a rating above no. 10 para-aminobenzoate (PABA), may be applied to the eyelids. Snow blindness may occur with only a 1 hour exposure to bright sunlight, and may also occur in the presence of a cloud cover.

Treatment consists of a fluorescein corneal examination, if feasible, to determine the extent of injury and exclude a foreign body; a one-time dose of topical anesthetic; and the instillation of mydriatic-cycloplegic agents and antibiotic drops. Persistent infusion of anesthetic drops or the use of steroid-containing antibiotics is not recommended, for reepithelialization of the cornea will be impaired. The eyes should be firmly patched and the victim given bed rest. Complete resolution can be expected in 24–48 hours.

Altitude Throat

Physical exertion at very high or extreme altitudes induces an increase in pulmonary ventilation and the use of accessory muscles of respiration. Mouth breathing is necessary to reduce airway resistance. Because of the very low humidity at such altitudes and the high flow of dry air passing over the mucus membranes of the throat and upper airways, drying and thickening of the mucus will occur. Inflammation and pain without evidence of exudates, adenopathy, or infection are present. In severe cases, an "altitude throat" may persist for days or weeks and may be partially incapacitating.

Unfortunately, little can be done for this condition. Adequate fluid intake and the use of saline or bicarbonate gargles and medicated lozenges are helpful. A few rest days at a lower altitude with hot steam inhalations may provide temporary relief. Low-flow oxygen breathing during sleep, which will reduce ventilation, may be helpful. Local anesthetics should be avoided, since epithelial injury and infection may occur unnoticed. If evidence of bacterial infection is present in the form of fever, adenopathy, or exudate, throat and sputum cultures and appropriate antibiotic therapy are indicated.

Chronic Mountain Polycythemia

Permanent residents at high altitudes may have asymptomatic polycythemia. The normal hematocrit at 12,000 feet is 54%, while the reading at 14,900 feet is 59%. Some otherwise healthy individuals may record readings of 60–70%. Erythropoiesis is probably stimulated by a decrease in arterial oxygen saturation during sleep, which is more severe in polycythemic than in normal persons. One study showed a 79% arterial oxygen saturation in polycythemic persons at 10,152 feet, compared to 88% in normal persons at the same altitude (25).

Pulmonary Hypertension at High Altitudes

There is a moderate increase in pulmonary artery pressure and arteriolar (precapillary) resistance in persons living at high altitudes. The normal mean pulmonary artery pressure is 22 and 30 mm Hg at 12,000 and 14,900 feet, respectively. Very high pulmonary artery pressures are occasionally found, especially in children. Signs of pulmonary hypertension, such as an accentuated second heart sound, right heart strain on electrocardiogram, and prominent pulmonary arteries on chest x-ray are observed. Persons with these findings are usually asymptomatic, however, and continued residence at high altitude does not appear to be harmful. It is noted that pulmonary artery pressure will return to normal when residents are transported to sea level.

References

1. Aoki, A., Robinson, S. Body hydration and the incidence and severity of acute mountain sickness. *J Appl Physiol,* **31**(Sept. 1971), 363–366.
2. Arias-Stella, J., Kruger, H. Pathology of high altitude pulmonary edema. *Arch Pathol,* **76**(Aug. 1963), 147–157.
3. Åstrand, P. O., Saltin, B. Plasma and red cell volume after prolonged severe exercise. *J Appl Physiol,* **19**(Sept. 1964), 829–832.
4. Auerbach, P., Miller, E. High altitude flatus expulsion (HAFE) (correspondence). *West J. Med,* **134** (Feb. 1981), 173–174.
5. Barcroft, J. Respiratory functions of the blood, in *Lessons from High Altitudes,* Vol. I (London: Cambridge University Press, 1925).
6. Carson, R. P., Evans, W. O., Shields, J. L., et al. Symptomatology, pathophysiology and treatment of acute mountain sickness. *Fed Proc,* **28**(May–June 1969), 1085–1091.
7. Chiodi, H. Mal de montana a forma cerebral: Posible mechanismo etiopatogenico. *An Fac Med Lima,* **43** (2nd trimestre 1960), 437.
7a. Cox, R. E. Splenic infarct in a white man with sickle cell trait. *Ann Emerg Med,* **11**(Dec. 1982), pp. 668–69.
8. Dalessio, D. *Wolff's Headache and Other Head Pain* (New York: Oxford Press, 1980), p. 288.
9. Evans, W. O., Robinson, S. M., Horstman, D. H., et al. Amelioration of the symptoms of acute moun-

10. Falchuk, K., Lamb, T., Tenney, S. Ventilatory response to hypoxia and CO_2 following CO_2 exposure and $NaHCO_3$ ingestion. *J Appl Physiol,* **21**(Mar. 1966), 393–398.
11. Forwand, S. A., Landowne, M., Follansbee, J. N., et al. Effect of acetazolamide on acute mountain sickness. *N Engl J Med,* **279**(Oct. 1968), 839–845.
12. Gray, G. W., Bryan, A. C., Frayser, R., et al. Control of acute mountain sickness. *Aerosp Med,* **48**(Jan. 1971), 81–84.
13. Grover, R. F., Lufschanowski, R., Alexander, J. K. Alterations in the coronary circulation of man following ascent to 3100 meters altitude. *J Appl Physiol,* **41**(Dec. 1976), 832—838.
14. Hackett, P., Rennie, D. Rales, peripheral edema, retinal hemorrhage and acute mountain sickness. *Am J Med,* **67**(Aug. 1979), 214–218.
15. Hackett, P., Rennie, D. The incidence, importance and prophylaxis of acute mountain sickness. *Lancet,* **2**(Nov. 1976), 1149–1154.
16. Hecht, H. H. A sea level view of altitude problems. *Am J Med,* **50**(June 1971), 703–708.
17. Houston, C. Acute pulmonary edema of high altitude. *N Engl J Med,* **263**(Sept. 1960), 478–480.
18. Houston, C., Dickinson, J. Cerebral form of high altitude illness. *Lancet,* **2**(Oct. 1975), 758–761.
19. Hultgren, H. N. High altitude pulmonary edema, in Staub, N. (ed.), *Lung Water and Solute Exchange* (New York: Marcel Dekker, 1978), pp. 437–469.
20. Hultgren, H. N. High altitude medical problems. *West J Med,* **113**(July 1979), 8–23.
21. Hultgren, H., Grover, R. circulatory adaptation to high altitude. *Ann Rev Med,* **19**(1968), 119–152.
22. Hultgren, H., Grover, R., Hartley, J. Abnormal circulatory responses to high altitude in subjects with a previous history of high altitude pulmonary edema. *Circulation,* **44**(Nov. 1971), 759–770.
23. Hultgren, H., Marticorena, E. High altitude pulmonary edema: Epidemiologic observations in Peru. *Chest,* **74**(Oct. 1978), 372–376.
24. Hultgren, H., Robinson, M., Wuerflein, R. Overperfusion pulmonary edema. *Circulation,* **34**(Suppl 3) (Oct. 1966), 132 (abstract).
25. Hultgren, H., Spickard, W., Hellriegel, K., et al. High altitude pulmonary edema. *Medicine,* **40**(Sept. 1961), 289–313.
26. Hultgren, H., Spickard, W., Lopez, C. Further studies of high altitude pulmonary edema. *Br Heart J,* **24** (Jan. 1962), 95–102.
27. Hultgren, H., Wilson, R. Blood gas abnormalities and optimum therapy in high altitude pulmonary edema. *Clin Res* (in press).
28. Johansson, B., Strandgaard, S., Lassen, N. On the pathogenesis of hypertensive encephalopathy: The hypertensive "breakthrough" of autoregulation of cerebral blood flow with forced vasodilatation, flow increase, and blood-brain-barrier damage. *Circ Res,* **34**, **35**(Suppl 1) (May 1974), I-167–I-171.
29. Kleiner, J., Nelson, W. High altitude pulmonary edema—A rare disease?" *JAMA,* **234**(Nov. 1975), 491–495.
30. Kunkle, E. C., Ray, B. S., Wolff, H. G. Experimental

studies on headache: Analysis of the headache associated with changes in intracranial pressure. *Arch Neurol Psychiat,* **49**(Mar. 1943), 323–358.

30a. Larson, E. B., Roach, R. C., Schoene, R. B., Hornbein, T. F. Acute mountain sickness and acetazolamide. Clinical efficacy and effect on ventilation. *JAMA,* **248**(3), 328–32, 1982.

31. Lenfant, C., Sullivan, K. Adaptation to high altitude. *N Engl J Med,* **284**(June 1971), 1298–1309.

32. Lenfant, C., Torrance, J. D., Reynafarje, C. Shift of the O₂-Hb dissociation curve at altitude: Mechanism and effect. *J Appl Physiol,* **30**(May 1971), 625–631.

33. Marticorena, E., Hultgren, H. Evaluation of therapeutic methods in high altitude pulmonary edema. *Am J Cardiol,* **43**(Feb. 1979), 307–312.

34. McFadden, D., Houston, C., Sutton, J. R. High altitude retinopathy. *JAMA,* **245**(6) (Feb. 1981), 581–586.

35. Ou, L. C., Tenney, S. M. Properties of mitochondria from hearts of cattle acclimatized to high altitude. *Respir Physiol,* **8**(Jan. 1970), 151–159.

36. Pugh, L. Blood volume changes in outdoor exercise of 8–10 hour duration." *J Physiol* (London), **200**(Feb. 1969), 345–351.

37. Pugh, L. Physiological and medical aspects of the Himalayan Scientific and Mountaineering Expedition 1960–61. *Br Med J.* **5305**(Sept. 1962), 621–627.

38. Pugh, L., Gill, M., Lahiri, S., et al. Muscular exercise at great altitudes. *J Appl Physiol,* **19**(May 1964), 431–440.

39. Ravenhill, T. Some experiences of mountain sickness in the Andes. *J Trop Med Hyg,* **16**(1913), 313–320.

40. Read, W., Morrissey, J., Reichardt, L. American Dhaulagiri Expedition 1969. *Am Alpine J,* **17**(1970), 19–26.

41. Reed, D. J., Kellogg, R. H. Changes in respiratory response to CO₂ during natural sleep at sea level and at altitude. *J Appl Physiol,* **13**(Nov. 1958), 325–330.

42. Roy, S., Singh, I. Acute mountain sickness in Himalayan terrain: Clinical and physiological studies, in Hegnauer, A. (ed.), *Biomedical Problems of High Terrestrial Elevations* (Natick, Mass.: U.S. Army Research Institute of Environmental Medicine, 1969).

43. Scoggin, C., Hyers, T., Reeves, J., et al. High altitude pulmonary edema in children and young adults of Leadville, Colorado. *N Engl J Med,* **297**(Dec. 1977), 1269–1272.

44. Scoggin, C., Miller, Y., Tate, R. Getting high: The pathophysiology of high altitude. *Top Emergency Med,* **2**(3) (Oct. 1980), 53–61.

45. Singh, I., Kapila, C., Khanna, P. K., et al. High altitude pulmonary edema. *Lancet,* **1**(Jan. 1965), 229–234.

46. Surks, M., Chinn, K., Matoush, L. Alterations in body composition in man after acute exposure to high altitude. *J Appl Physiol,* **21**(Nov. 1966), 1741–1746.

47. Sutton, J., Gray, G., et al. Retinal hemorrhage at altitude. *Am Alpine J,* **22**(1980), 531–518.

48. Sutton, J. R., Houston, C. S., Mansell, A. L., et al. Effect of acetazolamide on hypoexemia during sleep at high altitude. *N Engl J Med,* **301**(Dec. 1979), 1329–1331.

49. Tenney, S. M. Physiological adaptations to life at high altitude. *Mod Concepts Cardiovasc Dis,* **31**(Mar. 1962), 713–718.

50. Tenney, S. M., Rahn, H., Stroud, R. S., et al. Adaptation to high altitude: Changes in lung volumes during the first 7 days at Mt. Evans, Colorado. *J Appl Physiol,* **5**(Apr. 1953), 607–613.

51. West, H., Lahiri, S., Gill, M., et al. Arterial oxygen saturation during exercise at high altitude. *J Appl Physiol,* **17**(July 1962), 617–621.

52. West, J. B. Gas diffusion in the lung at high altitude, in Margaria (ed.), *Exercise at Altitude* (New York: Excerpta Medica Foundation, 1967).

53. Wilson, R. Acute high altitude illness in mountaineers and problems of rescue. *Ann Intern Med,* **78**(Mar. 1973), 421–428.

54. Wilson, R., Mills, W. J., Jr., Rogers, D. R., et al. Death on Denali: Fatalities among climbers in Mount McKinley National Park from 1903 to 1976—Analysis of injuries, illnesses and rescues in 1976." *West J Med,* **128**(June 1978), 471–476.

55. Zink, R. "Hämodilution bei hochgebirges expeditionen als ertrieruns prophylaxe." *Artzliche Praxis,* **29**(1977), 873–874.

Recommended Readings

Bert, P. *Barometric Pressure: Researches in Experimental Physiology,* translated from the French by M. A. Hitchcock and F. A. Hitchcock (Columbus, Ohio: College Book Co., 1943).

Hackett, P. *Mountain sickness: Prevention, recognition and treatment* (New York: American Alpine Club, 1980).

Heath, D., Williams, D. *Man at High Altitude* (Edinburgh: Churchill Livingstone, 1977).

Houston, C. *Going High.* (New York: American Alpine Club, 1980).

Mosso, A. *Life of Man on the High Alps,* translated from the second Italian edition by E. Lough Kiesow (London: T. Fisher Unwin, 1908).

Steele, P. *Medical Care for Mountain Climbers* (London: Heineman Medical Books, 1976).

Ward, M. *Mountain Medicine* (London: Crosby-Lockwood-Staples, 1975).

2 | HYPOTHERMIA AND COLD INJURIES

Cameron Bangs, M.D.
Murray P. Hamlet, D.V.M. *

Historically, cold injuries have been most important during times of war or great social upheaval. Recently, severe winter weather and increasing winter wilderness recreation have caused an apparent increase in the incidence of cold weather injuries.

A better understanding of the pathophysiology of cold injuries and a scientific approach to their management are emerging through the study of surgically induced hypothermia, animal models, and human volunteers and the evaluation of clinical incidents.

Historical Aspects

Many armies exposed to cold environments have suffered serious numbers of cold injuries. Although it is difficult to differentiate among trench foot, frostbite, and hypothermia in these descriptions, some numbers appropri-

ately define the problem for the modern audience. During the winter of 400 B.C., in subzero temperatures, Xenophon led his Greek army of 10,000 through the deep snows of the Armenian mountains, where they suffered many severe cold injuries. In 218 B.C., Hannibal started with an army of 46,000 to go over the Pyrenees Alps in northern Italy. In 15 days, he lost approximately 20,000 men to the cold. In 1812, Napoleon left France with 250,000 men and returned in 6 months with 350 effective soldiers, the remainder having been killed or injured by cold or starvation. During the Crimean War, 300,000 French troops suffered more than 5000 cases of frostbite and 1000 deaths. The number of cold casualties sustained during World War I by the British, French, and Italian forces was 115,000, 80,000, and 38,000, respectively. In World War II, U.S. forces suffered 90,000 cold injuries. The Germans suffered 100,000 cold

* The authors wish to thank William Mills, Jr., M.D., for his generosity in the preparation of this chapter.

TABLE 1
Factors that Predispose to Urban Hypothermia

Decreased heat production	Increased heat loss
Myxedema	Erythrodermas
Hypopituitarism	Malnutrition
Adrenal insufficiency	Anorexia nervosa
Hypoglycemia	Environmental exposure
Malnutrition	Immersion
Neuromuscular disorders	Ethanolism, barbiturate ingestion
Immobilization	
Drug overdose	
Obtundation	

Disorders of impaired thermoregulation

Central thermoregulatory failure	Mechanism unknown
Hypothalamic infarction	Congestive heart failure
Cerebral thrombosis/hemorrhage	Acute myocardial infarction
Subarachnoid hemorrhage	Pulmonary embolism
Subdural hematoma	Mesenteric vascular occlusion
Brain contusion or laceration	Portal vein thrombosis
Postcardiac arrest anoxic	Severe pancreatitis
encephalopathy	Pneumonia
Carbon monoxide poisoning	Tracheobronchitis
Uremia	Urinary tract infection
Phenothiazine ingestion	Peritonitis
Wernicke's encephalopathy	Sepsis
Diabetic ketoacidosis	

Peripheral thermoregulatory failure

Cervical spinal cord transection
Diabetes mellitus
Neuropathies
Anorexia nervosa

casualties, requiring 15,000 amputations in November and December 1942 (205). Of the total U.S. casualties (9000) in Korea, 10% were cold injuries (157).

Epidemiology

To date, the United States has not provided any good statistical data on the incidence of cold injuries. The Royal College of Physicians in London surveyed 10 English and Scottish hospitals during the 3 winter months of 1965 and found that 0.68% of all patients and 1.2% of patients over age 65 who were admitted to the hospital were hypothermic (174). In 1975, another British survey found that 3.6% of all patients older than 65 were hypothermic on hospital admission (56). In 1973, a survey

of elderly British home dwellers showed that 10% were hypothermic, as measured by urine temperature (43).

Based on these and other statistics, it has been estimated that there are between 20,000 and 100,000 cases of hypothermia annually in England (198).

Many predisposing factors are associated with urban hypothermia (Table 1). In many reports, alcohol seems to be the predominant cause (30). This has been attributed to cutaneous vasodilatation, loss of shivering, hypothalamic dysfunction, and lack of concern regarding the environment.

Classification

Cold injuries are defined as follows:

ACCIDENTAL HYPOTHERMIA

This is the clinical condition in which body temperature has accidentally dropped to 35°C (95°F) or below.

Immersion or Acute Hypothermia: This is rapid onset of hypothermia caused by prolonged immersion in cold water [exposure usually less than 6 hours in duration in water with a temperature of 21°C (70°F) or less].

Chronic Hypothermia: This form of hypothermia results from nonimmersion exposure to cold, usually 6 hours in duration or longer.

1. *Exposure hypothermia.* Hypothermia in an otherwise healthy individual that results from prolonged accidental exposure to the cold.
2. *Urban hypothermia.* Hypothermia that occurs within the urban setting, predisposed to by aging, debilitation, drugs, and alcohol.

FROSTNIP

This is superficial, reversible ice crystal formation associated with intense vasoconstriction.

FROSTBITE

This is the actual freezing of water in the skin and subcutaneous tissues, which results in tissue morbidity or loss.

TRENCH FOOT OR IMMERSION FOOT

In this condition, neurovascular damage results from prolonged exposure to moisture and cold, without ice crystal formation.

Physiology

THERMAL REGULATION

Humans are homeothermic, warm-weather, tropical animals who neither tolerate nor adapt well to the cold (14,162). Until humans developed a microclimate of clothing, shelter, and fire to keep their skin temperature close to 32.8°C (91°F), they could not survive at temperatures much below 21°C (71°F) (17). Anecdotal evidence suggests that long-term cold exposure reduces the discomfort of the cold, but there is little evidence that humans have any significant physiologic adaptation to cold with respect to survival. The shivering

response may be reduced by repeated cold exposure; repeated hand cooling changes cold-induced vasodilatation.

Body temperature is regulated by a "thermostat" in the hypothalamus, which is responsive to changes in blood temperature as little as 0.5°C (1°F) and, in a less sensitive fashion, to impulses received from nerve endings in the skin. There is usually a diurnal variation, causing a 1°F temperature rise by later afternoon. Normal body temperature is maintained through a balance of heat production and heat loss (17).

HEAT PRODUCTION

Heat is produced by the metabolism of food, muscular work, and shivering, and by chemically produced energy within the organs of the body. The percentage of heat produced by each organ is shown in Figure 1.

At the basal metabolic rate, heat is produced at approximately 50 kcal/m² of body surface area per hour, or roughly 100 kcal/hour for the average-sized person.

SHIVERING

In response to a cold stress, heat production is increased 50–100% by a thermomuscular, or preshivering, tone (48). Further cold stress results in visible shivering, which can maximally increase heat production by 500% (82). Gross limb movements are avoided during shivering by the synchronous contraction of the small groups of motor units, which contract out of phase with alternate antagonistic muscle groups (116). Maximum heat production from shivering is limited to a few hours because of glycogen depletion and fatigue. Shivering is abolished by physical activity (116), and is also suppressed by hypoglycemia, hypoxia, and fatigue (17,40). Some drugs, including phenothiazines, barbiturates, and probably alcohol, may also suppress shivering (73,126,128). Shivering induces vasodilatation and thereby decreases natural insulation by up to 25% (17).

HEAT LOSS

At least 95% of daily heat production must be lost to the environment. The prime physio-

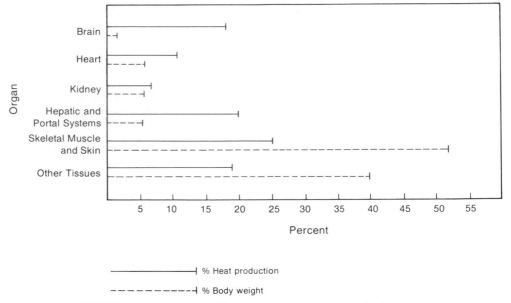

FIGURE 1   Percentage of heat produced by various body organs.

logic regulator of this loss is the variability of the skin or surface temperature, as influenced by vasodilatation and vasoconstriction (173,176).

Under basal euthermic conditions, total blood flow to the skin represents 5% of the cardiac output, or 300–500 ml/minute. With heat stress and maximum vasodilatation, cutaneous blood flow may reach a maximum of 3000 ml/minute. With maximal vasoconstriction, total blood flow to the skin can be reduced by a remarkable degree, to as little as 30 ml/minute (173). Heat is lost to the environment by four mechanisms:

Conduction

The transfer of heat from warm to cold media may be through direct contact. This method of heat loss normally provides very little loss (2%), but during contact with cold ground, snow, or water, it may result in overwhelming losses (fivefold in wet clothes, 25-fold in cold water immersion) (106).

Convection

Heat may transfer through air movement. Air in close proximity to the body is heated

by conduction. The amount of heat lost by convection is variable, depending on wind velocity and protective clothing.

Radiation

Heat can be transferred indirectly via infrared radiation. Heat loss is influenced by the temperature gradient between the body and the environment and the surface area available for radiation. Approximately 85% of the naked body surface area is available for radiation. This surface area may be voluntarily increased or decreased by varying apposing surfaces. Radiation normally accounts for about 65% of body heat loss.

Evaporation

Evaporation is the conversion of water from the liquid phase to the gaseous phase. A total of 0.58 kcal is required to convert 1 g of water from a liquid to a gas. At least 20% of body heat is lost via this mechanism, with tremendous potential for increased losses associated with sweating. Evaporative heat losses are influenced by humidity. Two-thirds of normal evaporative heat loss occurs on the skin surface and one-third from the respiratory tract. About 25% of evaporative heat loss comes from insensible perspiration. A significant increase in evaporative heat loss occurs from wet or damp clothing.

Physiology of Acute Immersion

The effects of sudden immersion into cold water should be considered in terms of two time categories: (1) the first 15–20 minutes, during which the core temperature remains normal and the effects result from reflex responses to the cooling of the skin; and (2) the later period, when the core temperature starts to decline and the effects are caused by hypothermia.

The initial response to immersion is a dramatic increase in total ventilation, or the so-called gasp response (129). If the face is immersed during this period, there is a danger of aspiration of water, laryngospasm, and asphyxiation. This may account for sudden and unexplained deaths after cold water immersion. Expired air volume immediately rises from resting levels of 5 liters/minute to nearly 50 liters/minute (24). This hyperventilation, with respiratory rates of 60–70 per minute, causes a drop in arterial carbon dioxide pressure (Pco_2), causing cerebral vasoconstriction and a reduction in cerebral blood flow (24). This, coupled with hypothermia, results in clouding of judgment, confusion, and ultimate loss of consciousness (69,90,91). The respiratory alkalosis induced by hyperventilation may lead to tetany and the inability to swim (53).

A vagus nerve-induced bradycardia occurs when the face is immersed in cold water. Frequent premature ventricular contractions (PVCs) may be observed during sudden cold water immersion, raising the possibility of other ventricular arrhythmias, such as ventricular tachycardia or fibrillation (22–24). Atrial fibrillation in the absence of core hypothermia may result from immersion incidents. Cooling of the peripheral muscles and nerves occurs at a rate that is dependent on fat insulation and water temperature. This results in a loss of muscle strength and a decrease in nerve conduction velocity in both large fibers and peripheral nerves. This decreased strength may result in an inability to swim or remove oneself from cold water (53).

EFFECTS OF PROLONGED IMMERSION

After immersion, there is an initial increase in heat production. Oxygen consumption rises from 0.3 liter/minute before immersion to 0.8 liter/minute immediately following immersion. After 15–20 minutes, heat loss exceeds heat production and the core temperature begins to fall. The rate of decline in core temperature depends on water temperature, insulation from clothing, body size, fat, sex (males cool 0.84 times faster than females), movement in the water, and other behavioral variables (69). Alcohol and fatigue also influence survival time. Survival time in cold water has been calculated (70) (Figure 2). Swimming increases the rate of heat loss by two mechanisms. Vasodilatation increases heat flow to the skin, where it may be lost. This, in effect, increases the exposed surface area. The cooling rate is about 35–50% higher in swimmers than in subjects who remain still (90,91). Heat loss may be decreased by 12% by assuming a knee-chest or huddle position to insulate the high heat loss areas, including the inguinal area, lateral chest, head, and neck (69) (see Figure 4, Chapter 7).

GENERAL OVERVIEW OF COLD CHALLENGE

The first response of the body immersed in a cold environment is to conserve core heat by peripheral vasoconstriction (213). There are initial increases in sympathetic discharge, respiration, heart rate, basal metabolic rate, and shivering (24,127,130). At approximately 35°C (95°F), the metabolic rate may be increased three to six times above the basal rate. As body core temperature decreases, there is a decrease in respiration, heart rate, and blood pressure.

If cooling persists, a cold-induced diuresis occurs, which, combined with the usual decrease in fluid intake, results in volume depletion. There is a plasma shift away from the circulation; viscosity of the blood increases, flow decreases, platelets decrease, and the oxyhemoglobin dissociation curve shifts to the left (8,9,26,88,132). The oxygen supply to the tissues fails to meet even the reduced demand,

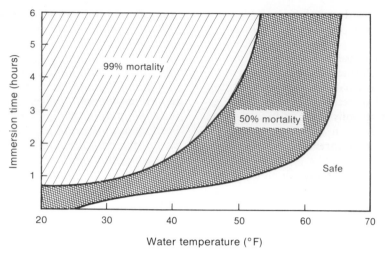

FIGURE 2 Survival in cold water.

resulting in metabolic acidosis without respiratory compensation.

Cardiac stroke volume decreases and peripheral vascular resistance increases (67). Electrical conduction through the heart is altered, which may result in diverse arrhythmias (84,117,201). Liver metabolism is decreased, and pancreatic function is altered; the insulin effect is diminished (34,170). Circulating corticosteroids are increased. The most important of these changes will be discussed in detail.

SPECIFIC CHANGES BY ORGAN SYSTEM

Central Nervous System

As hypothermia develops, there is deterioration in mental function and judgment. In the early stage of hypothermia, with core temperatures above 32°C (90°F), the victim becomes apathetic, lethargic, and withdrawn. In the field, observers note that the hypothermic victim talks less, perhaps complains more, and is less apt to get involved in activities. When hiking or climbing, the victim may fall behind and make less effort to contribute or keep up (75).

With urban hypothermia, the elderly patient may be more cantankerous, senile, and forgetful, and perhaps more confused than usual. He is less coordinated, has more difficulty in walking, and may perhaps stumble. As hypothermia progresses to a core temperature below 32°C (90°F), the victim becomes more confused, lethargic, and disoriented. He may lapse into periods of total withdrawal. Lethargy progresses to intermittent stupor, ultimately to be followed by complete coma. Complaints of loss of vision and notably slurred speech are not infrequent, but in our observation, these are end-stage symptoms followed by complete coma within 30 minutes. A peculiar flattened affect gives the impression that the patient refuses to cooperate or understand.

Inappropriate behavior may occur, with the victim refusing to protect himself from the environment, neglecting to button a jacket, replace dropped mittens, put on a hat or hood, or cover up with blanket. Victims have frequently been observed to urinate in their clothing. Paradoxical undressing may occur, leading to the erroneous conclusion that hypothermia victims found dead may have been sexually assaulted (207).

Serious errors in judgment made by hypothermia victims have led to further tragedy (100). Medicolegal problems have arisen following boating accidents in cold water because of confusion and conflicting observations of hypothermic victims.

Deep hypothermia (28°C; 82.4°F) is manifested by weak pulse and respirations, complete unresponsive coma, and absent corneal, pupillary, and deep tendon reflexes. The presentation of coma, fixed and dilated pupils, flat EEG, and rigid muscles, could lead to the erroneous and premature diagnosis of death.

Less than 5% of patients who are stuporous or comatose on the basis of hypothermia alone will have focal neurologic findings on physical examination that resolve upon rewarming. Computed tomography of the brain performed on such individuals in quest of a surgically correctable lesion is unremarkable.

Circulatory Effects of Hypothermia

The overall effect of hypothermia on the circulation is to decrease the circulating volume and flow rate while increasing peripheral resistance and viscosity. This results in poor blood flow, sludging, and an inadequate oxygen supply (67).

Hematocrit is invariably elevated as a result of fluid loss, plasma shifts, and splenic contraction (88). Decreased numbers of circulating platelets and white corpuscles have been attributed to sequestration in the spleen, liver, and splanchnic vasculature. Coagulopathies are not infrequent, particularly in the alcoholic victim, and correlate with more serious outcomes. Blood viscosity studied in dogs cooled to 25°C (77°F) has been shown to be increased to 173% of normal (26,71). This is attributed to the direct effect of low temperature on plasma viscosity, as well as to hemoconcentration and the low sheer state induced by the hypothermia (26,88). The oxyhemoglobin dissociation curve is shifted to the left, causing decreased release of oxygen to the tissues (132). During cardiopulmonary bypass for surgery, a functional hemoglobin value as low as 4.2 g per 100 ml of blood has been calculated (41). The shift in the oxyhemoglobin dissociation curve may in part be counterbalanced by the increased oxygen actually dissolved in blood because of the decreased temperature. There is a 19% increase in the amount of oxygen in physical solution in the blood at 30°C (86°F) and a 33% increase at 25°C (77°F). At 16°C (60.8°F), dissolved oxygen may be sufficient to meet tissue requirements (133).

Cold Diuresis

Cold diuresis occurs with a drop in the deep body temperature but also results from mere inactivity in a cold environment (116). The cold diuresis, combined with decreased fluid intake, may reduce the measured total blood volume to as low as 68% of the predicted value (67). The diuresis is a manifestation of the production of large quantities of dilute urine of low specific gravity (1.002) (176). Parenthetically, it should be noted that oliguria or anuria is not uncommon following recovery from frank hypothermia (132).

There are multiple probable causes of cold diuresis. The peripheral vasoconstriction results in increased filling of deep-capacitance vessels, which causes an indirect suppression of antidiuretic hormone (ADH) release (74). Cold causes a depression in oxidative renal tubular activity, which results in reduced sodium and water reabsorption (144).

Cardiac Changes

Hypothermia decreases heart rate, cardiac output, and arterial blood pressure (101). One cardiac catheterization study of six accidental hypothermia victims demonstrated a decreased heart rate and cardiac index, with a stroke index at the lower limit of normal and systemic arterial resistance slightly increased (67).

The effects of pH, electrolyte imbalance, hypoxia, and cold on myocardial conduction fibers result in multiple cardiac arrhythmias. There may be a prolongation of all electrocardiogram intervals, including P-R, QRS, and Q-T. P waves may be diminished or absent, and T waves may be inverted or elongated. A positive deflection in the R-T segment, called a *J* or *Osborne wave,* is pathognomonic for hypothermia (Figure 3) (33,117,201,208). Atrial fibrillation is common and generally converts spontaneously to sinus rhythm after rewarming (90,91). Bradycardia may occur with severe hypothermia (33,177).

Ventricular fibrillation and asystole are the two most frequent life-threatening arrhythmias. Asystole was more prevalent in patients with a mean age of 15 years versus a mean age of 39 years for those who suffered ventricular fibrillation. Patients with asystole had mixed metabolic and respiratory acidoses, whereas ventricular fibrillation was associated with mixed metabolic and respiratory alkaloses. This may reflect the observation that

if not corrected for temperature (92,199). All three measurements are best corrected by using the nomograms shown in Figure 4.

There is no evidence that the sodium, potassium, or chloride concentration is altered by hypothermia itself. Sodium and potassium levels have been found to be elevated, depressed, or normal, seemingly at random. In one review of the literature, there was no correlation between core temperature and electrolyte balance (187). Electrolytes may be dramatically altered iatrogenically during rewarming therapy (160). Severe hypophosphatemia has been reported in at least one case of rewarming, with the serum level dropping from 5.1 to 0.9 mg/dl (107). This was attributed to the intracellular shift of phosphorus attendant to accelerated glycolysis.

Blood Sugar

Glucose utilization is decreased during hypothermia, which frequently leads to hyperglycemia. Explanations for the altered glucose utilization include decreased break-down of hepatic glycogen (105), decreased peripheral utilization of glucose, the influence of increased circulating catecholamines, and the effects of acute pancreatitis. There is a significant correlation between high blood glucose levels and elevated serum amylase levels (120).

Hypoglycemia may occur secondary to glycogen depletion caused by shivering. This may be more common after acute immersion hypothermia. Because alcohol blocks gluconeogenesis, ingestion may predispose the individual to hypoglycemia, cessation of shivering, and a shortened survival time (65).

Autopsy Findings

Hirvonen has concluded that "the statement that there is no single sign of hypothermia in necropsy is perhaps still valid, but the combined macroscopic and biochemical changes in the cadaver justify the diagnosis with reasonable certainty" (76). He found that the two most specific changes were in the gross appearance of the skin and the microscopic degeneration in the myocardium. Roughly one-half of the victims had skin changes, including red or purple discolorations, swelling of the ears and hands, frostbite, violet patches

over pressure points (elbows and knees), and dilated superficial veins. The red discoloration may be as vivid as that occasionally associated with carbon monoxide intoxication and is perhaps due to increased oxygen binding by cold hemoglobin or to late-stage dilatation of venous plexuses (97).

Macroscopically, the heart appeared normal, but there were microscopic foci of myocardial degeneration which were not present in control sections taken from victims of murder, rapid suicide, or shock.

In 10 autopsies performed on relatively young victims of exposure hypothermia, the most conspicuous changes were in the lungs (79–81). These changes consisted of pulmonary edema; intra-alveolar, intrabronchial, and interstitial hemorrhages; focal emphysema with ruptured alveolar walls; and vascular engorgement (76,124).

The hemoconcentration, sludging, and stagnation of blood led to generalized visceral congestion and tissue edema (45). Microinfarction and thrombosis in large and small vessels were diffusely present. Gross changes in the pancreas occurred in 80% of cases and included fat necrosis, aseptic pancreatitis, and hemorrhage (34,124).

The most conspicuous but less specific findings were those of gastric erosion and hemorrhage, found in 45–86% of cases (124).

General Principles of Treatment

Hypothermia is an easy diagnosis to reach when a lost mountaineer is found frozen in a block of ice, but it is frequently missed apart from its usual presentation. It is confused with senility, stroke, drug overdose, metabolic coma, and near-drowning. Rectal temperatures should be routinely recorded with a low-reading thermometer or thermocouple (e.g., Yellow Spring) in all patients with any alteration of sensorium.

SUBDIVISION OF CASES

There are several practical reasons for the arbitrary classification of hypothermic victims as mild or severe, with a boundary core temperature of 32°C (90°F). At core temperatures below this figure, the metabolic changes are profound. With severe cold illness, hypothermia itself is a major contributor to the patient's symptoms, and mortality is considerable. At this severe level, the management of hypothermia should take priority.

During the prehospital field management and evacuation of victims, the mild-severe classification is very useful. Mild hypothermics need to be kept from getting any colder, with higher priorities safely assigned to other injuries or other victims. Severe hypothermia, in contrast, should be treated as a life-threatening emergency, with full attention given to rapid and careful early management and evacuation. These priorities are particularly important in a mass-casualty situation or a military setting. Some controversy exists regarding the role of prehospital rewarming. Most authorities, including the authors, believe that with deep hypothermia there will be less mortality if victims are not rewarmed in the field, but rather kept in a "metabolic icebox" until complete physiologic monitoring and control are available (209).

In the hospital, hypothermic victims should be handled emergently, utilizing the team approach, with a supervising physician, an anesthesiologist, and other physicians skilled at handling fluid-electrolyte and metabolic problems. They should be assisted by a respiratory therapist and critical care nurses. All rewarming should be done in a critical care area, emergency department, or intensive care unit. A prearranged protocol should be used, if at all possible.

A simplistic, but useful, approach in the treatment of severe hypothermics is to realize that the goal is to rewarm the victim while preventing ventricular fibrillation or respiratory distress. One should always follow the adage that victims of severe hypothermia are never dead until they are warm and dead. Even with prolonged cardiac arrest, resuscitation is possible (182)

Acute immersion hypothermia and chronic hypothermia should be treated similarly.

BASELINE STUDIES

Minimal initial baseline laboratory determinations should include a complete blood count, blood glucose, electrolytes, and arterial blood gases (corrected for temperature). These should be obtained initially and repeated during rewarming as indicated, every 20–30 minutes or with each 2–5°F rise in temperature. An initial 12-lead electrocardiogram should be obtained, and the patient should have continual cardiac monitoring. A chest x-ray should be obtained as early as possible. Foley catheterization may be of value to monitor urine output and to obtain specimens. Central venous pressure or Swan-Ganz monitoring is useful to avoid overexpansion of the circulating volume. Blood cultures should be obtained prior to the administration of prophylactic antibiotics.

VOLUME EXPANSION

It is the authors' opinion that the most valuable modality of therapy is early and rapid volume expansion. The rationale for this profound statement is threefold:

1. Hypothermic victims are severely volume-depleted and vasoconstricted. Release of vasoconstriction during rewarming increases relative volume depletion.
2. Catheterization studies of hypothermic victims before and after intravenous volume expansion have shown marked improvement in cardiovascular parameters after volume expansion (67).
3. The only known prospective controlled clinical studies of hypothermic neonates showed that administration of intravenous saline prior to rewarming reduced mortality from 75 to 16.7% (195).

Blood volume should be expanded using a crystalloid solution, such as dextrose in saline. Ringer's lactate may also be acceptable, bearing in mind that at extremely low temperatures, lactate may not be metabolized by the liver (170). In adults, 300–500 ml should be given rapidly as a fluid challenge, with the subsequent rate of infusion adjusted according to the blood pressure and urine output (2,44). Ideally, intravenous administration should be started in the field prior to transportation. The solution should be at least at room temperature and, if convenient, may be warmed to 45°C (115°F) (2). The number of calories transferred in 1 liter of heated intravenous fluid is relatively small (Table 2).

The use of military antishock trousers

TABLE 2
Estimated Heat Gain from Endogenous and Exogenous Sources

Heat Source	Calories Provided at Core Temp. of 28°C[a]
Normal metabolic rate	70 kcal/hour
Maximal shivering	350 kcal/hour
Heated (45°C) humidified O_2 at 20 liters/minute	30 kcal/hour
Heated (45°C) IV (1 liter)	17 kcal
Heated (45°C) peritoneal dialysis; 1 liter	17 kcal;
flow rate at 5 liters/hour	85 kcal/hour
Cardiopulmonary bypass at 45°C; 1 liter	17 kcal;
flow rate at 28 liters/hour	476 kcal/hour
Trunk immersion in hot water at 45°C	
Vasoconstriction	600 kcal/hour
Vasodilatation	2400 kcal/hour

[a] A 70 kg human requires a gain of 60 kcal of heat to increase body temperature 1°C.
Source: Adapted from Reference 148.

(MAST) has been suggested to increase the effective circulating volume. This would increase the return of cold blood from the extremities, which could decrease the core temperature and lead to cardiac complications. The use of MAST with hypothermic victims has not been methodically studied and should, at this point, be considered potentially harmful.

With regard to mild hypothermia, one should assume that otherwise healthy individuals who are exposed to the cold are volume-depleted. Forced drinking in the absence of thirst is recommended for individuals who work in the cold. Coffee, tea, and cocoa have xanthine diuretic effects and should be avoided. Water and warm fruit drinks are the most effective.

ELECTROLYTES, pH, AND GLUCOSE

During rewarming, changes in serum potassium must be anticipated and corrected. An initial normal serum potassium level may decline as acidosis and hyperglycemia are corrected. As peripheral warming and vasodilatation occur, there may be an influx of potassium that leads to hyperkalemia, which may require clinical intervention (160). If heated peritoneal dialysis is used, the potassium in the dialysate solution should be adjusted to the patient's needs.

Hypophosphatemia may occur during rewarming (107). Serum phosphate levels should be checked and corrected.

If the pH, corrected for temperature, is 7.1–7.2, then cautious use of sodium bicarbonate is indicated. Overcorrection leads to alkalosis, with increased risk of ventricular fibrillation. Theoretically, the leftward shift in the oxyhemoglobin dissociation curve caused by hypothermia may be partially reversed by acidosis. Rapid correction of pH prior to rewarming may decrease the amount of oxygen released to the myocardium, causing an increase in hypoxia and a heightened danger of ventricular fibrillation. In the absence of cardiac arrest, little if any bicarbonate is usually needed, as pH will be corrected with rewarming.

Shivering and heat production are diminished by hypoglycemia. Low blood glucose should be corrected with intravenous dextrose, with the rapidity and the solution dependent on estimated needs.

Hyperglycemia is of less concern and generally responds to rewarming. Insulin is usually not necessary if the blood sugar is less than 400 mg/dl, but the possibility of antecedent diabetes should always be considered and treated appropriately. Insulin administered during hypothermia will have little effect until rewarming occurs. Overzealous use may cause hypoglycemia and lower the serum potassium level. The safe approach is to follow the blood sugar frequently and use insulin only if blood sugar measurements do not drop during rewarming.

In the absence of Addison's disease or myxedema, there is no evidence that steroids or thyroid extracts are of any value (38,115,119). Conversely, in the appropriate settings, these disorders should always be suspected. If hypothyroidism is suspected, 500 μg of sodium levothyroxine (T_4) is administered intravenously.

AIRWAY MANAGEMENT

Supplemental oxygen is necessary to decrease hypoxia, reduce the risk of ventricular fibrillation, and treat pulmonary edema. The use of 100% oxygen in hypothermic dogs has caused isolated microvascular damage in the cerebral circulation (151,169). In normothermic patients, pure oxygen administration has been shown to cause depression of ciliary activity and increased mucous plugs (72). Based on these studies, the use of 50% oxygen may be indicated. Arterial blood gases should be used as the guideline for oxygen concentration. Patients who are not mechanically ventilated should be observed closely because of depression of the CO_2-sensitive respiratory center caused by hypothermia. Correction of hypoxia could cause a decrease in ventilatory effort (175).

Acute noncardiogenic pulmonary edema has been successfully treated with digitalis, diuretics, morphine sulfate, and positive end-expiratory pressure (PEEP) (156). The authors recommend judicious digitalization in the presence of heart failure. Continuous positive airway pressure (CPAP) or PEEP deserves further study in the treatment of this disorder.

Intubation may be indicated to allow adequate control of ventilation, to provide good tracheal toilet in the presence of bronchorrhea and pulmonary edema, and to act as a route for the administration of heated, humidified oxygen. Failure to clear the thick, copious tracheobronchial secretions can result in the immediate problem of an obstructed airway or the delayed problem of bronchopneumonia (160,209).

Intubation can trigger ventricular fibrilla-

tion and should be done skillfully, preferably by an anesthesiologist. In two series, hypothermic patients were nasotracheally intubated without adverse effects (266,137). Rough handling should be avoided. Topical anesthesia should be used even in a comatose patient (90,91). The patient must be well oxygenated prior to intubation (112,114). Rigidity of the oropharynx, secondary to cold, may necessitate nasotracheal intubation.

Overventilation should be avoided, as it may cause respiratory alkalosis and trigger ventricular fibrillation (90,91). Serial PCO_2 measurements, corrected for temperature, should be used to determine the proper ventilatory rate.

Techniques of Rewarming

The two general techniques of rewarming, passive (slow) and active (rapid), are further subdivided into external and internal (86). Passive rewarming is the prevention of heat loss by effective insulation (28). This allows spontaneous metabolic heat slowly to rewarm the body. If the core temperature is 23.8°C (74.8°F) or higher, shivering should be present to produce heat (17). Active rewarming involves the internal or external addition of heat to the body.

All methods have been used and reported extensively in the literature, each with varying degrees of success. There has been no randomized prospective series of note to compare one rewarming technique with another. Retrospective analysis is difficult because of the many variables and deaths due to underlying pathology. The principles and problems of each technique will be presented, along with the authors' personal preferences.

Regardless of which method is used, all patients should be carefully evaluated, monitored, and controlled.

PASSIVE SPONTANEOUS REWARMING

With this technique, the patient is covered with one to two blankets and rewarmed in bed at a room temperature of 25–32.9°C (77–90°F). The recommended increase in core temperature varies from 0.5 to 2°C (1–4°F) per hour, so that 24 hours may be required to achieve normal temperature (116). The theoretical advantages obtained from slow, passive rewarming are avoidance of the rewarming temperature "afterdrop" and hypotension (associated with cutaneous vasodilatation) and the slow resolution of spontaneous fluid shifts.

Slow, passive rewarming is a safe and simple method for mild hypothermia, and frequently is the only available method for field management. Most authorities currently do not recommend this method for use with severe hypothermia.

ACTIVE REWARMING

Active rewarming is the addition of exogenous heat to the hypothermic body. The rate of rewarming depends upon the amount of heat and the rate of administration. The heat may come from one or multiple sources. This is the technique most preferred for treatment of the well-monitored, severely hypothermic victim (62,209).

Active rewarming may be necessary for victims with a core temperature below 23.8°C (74.8°F) and at any temperature during cardiopulmonary arrest. This method minimizes the time that the heart is exposed to the risk of a dangerous arrhythmia. Afterdrop may be decreased or avoided by the overwhelming addition of heat.

External rewarming is used, so that the skin is warmed to a level above the victim's core temperature. This may be accomplished by immersion in heated water, body-to-body contact in a sleeping bag, or the addition of hot water bottles, heating pads, heated stones, or warm garments.

Physiologic changes that occur during external rewarming can lead to undesirable complications. Peripheral cutaneous vasodilatation may shunt the already reduced circulating volume from the core to the periphery, causing severe hypotension (90,91). This increased peripheral flow may cause liberation of acidotic blood (139). Also, the increased skin temperature may cause shivering to cease, decreasing endogenous heat production to the point where rewarming may actually be slowed (24,68). These complications may be ameliorated by adding heat only to the trunk while keeping the extremities unheated.

Internal Rewarming

Heat may be added internally via many sources, including heated intravenous solutions, extracorporeal circulation, heated humidified oxygen or air, heated peritoneal dialysate, and warm gastric, colonic, or pleural irrigations. The combination of any of these will increase the rate of rewarming. Advantages include the avoidance of peripheral vasodilatation and its complications; the vital internal organs, such as the liver and heart, will be rewarmed early.

Heated Humidified Inhalation

Heated, humidified air or oxygen may be safely administered at temperatures up to 47°C (116°F) (1,64,71). The heat is transferred to the pulmonary and bronchial circulations and thus delivered directly to the atria, coronary circulation, and myocardium. This technique warms the lungs and heart first, causing thermal stimulation of cilia and curtailing respiratory heat loss (10% of body heat loss). How much heat exchange actually occurs beyond the carina is a matter of some dispute.

In a study of healthy volunteers cooled in cold water to a core temperature of 35°C (95°F), heated humidified oxygen produced less afterdrop during rewarming than did heating pads or warmed garments (68).

The method is safe, simple, and relatively inexpensive. Apparatus may be made of lightweight, easily transportable equipment which requires no external power source (137). This method is applicable with or without endotracheal intubation and does not rely on spontaneous respiration (Figure 5) (112–114).

The number of calories supplied by heated humidified inhalation (HHI) is relatively small. The overall gain, utilizing HHI at 40°C (104°F) at 3 liters/minute is 9.4 kcal/hour and at 10 liters/minute is 23.7 kcal/hour (64). About 60 kcal/hour are required to raise the core temperature by 1°C in a 70-kg human (mean specific heat of body tissue equals 0.8 kcal/kg). Therefore, HHI should be accepted only as an adjunct to active rewarming. Its benefits derive not from total calorie delivery but from the fact that the lungs and heart receive the heat directly.

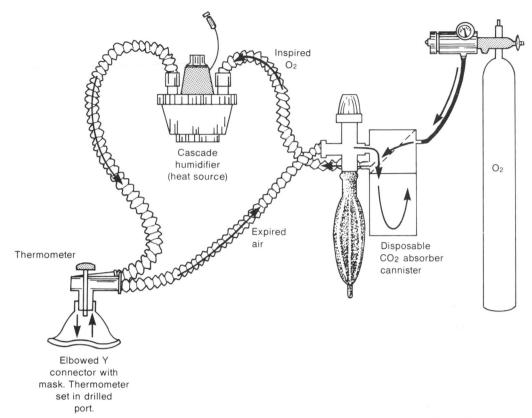

Inspired
O₂

Cascade
humidifier
(heat source)

O₂

Expired
air

Thermometer

Disposable
CO₂ absorber
cannister

Elbowed Y
connector with
mask. Thermometer
set in drilled
port.

FIGURE 5 Technique for heated humidified oxygen. Tubing should be kept short to minimize heat loss.

One method of delivering HHI is shown in Figure 5.

Intravenous Solutions

Intravenous solutions are heated to 45°C (115°F) in a water bath or in a blood-warming coil. They provide 17 kcal of heat per liter to a body with a core temperature of 28°C (82.4°F). The total amount of heat delivered is obviously limited by fluid requirements.

Extracorporeal Blood Rewarming

Extracorporeal rewarming, which utilizes cardiac bypass or hemodialysis, has been reported quite extensively (23,29,83,200,202). The advantages are that relatively large amounts of heat are added rapidly and that the heat added provides early rewarming of the heart. The disadvantages are that it requires specialized equipment, considerable medical and surgical expertise, anticoagula-

tion, and physical stimulation associated with an invasive procedure.

Peritoneal Dialysis

Peritoneal lavage, which uses standard peritoneal dialysis technique and solutions heated to 45°C (115°F), provides an effective, safe method for heating the core (32,63,87,99,167). This technique is readily adapted to emergency department or intensive care unit use. In addition to providing heat, it offers some control over pH and electrolytes. By using two trochars (one for infusion and one for drainage; placed through an infraumbilical incision, one into each peritoneal gutter), a flow rate in excess of 4–6 liters/hour can be achieved (87). With solutions at 45°C (115°F), 68–102 kcal/hour can be provided, resulting in a 1–2°C temperature rise in a 70-kg human.

Dialysate is commercially available, and should contain 1.5% glucose with potassium added as needed. Normal saline and Ringer's lactate have been successfully used (27). Solutions can be preheated in a water bath or warmed through a 44 foot blood-warming coil submerged in water heated to 48–54.4°C (121–130°F). The temperature of the solution which infuses into and drains from the peritoneal cavity may be checked by detaching the plastic adaptor, running some fluid into a Styrofoam cup, and measuring the temperature with a candy thermometer. Because of the resistance of the blood-warming coil, the flow will be slow, unless pressure in the dialysate bottle is increased by pumping air through the vent, using a sphygmomanometer bulb (2) (Figure 6).

Microwave Irradiation

Microwave irradiation has been used to rewarm hypothermic infants in the People's Re-

public of China. In 1976–77, 19 infants were rewarmed without a microwave adjunct and had a mortality of 63.2%. In 1978, 28 infants were rewarmed utilizing microwave irradiation and had a mortality of 28.6%. No complications from the microwave irradiation were reported. The rewarming rate was 1°C every 6–7 minutes (216). This appears to be a promising technique.

Treatment of Arrhythmias

During the past 10 years, we have developed a therapeutic armamentarium which allows us to keep the pulse, cardiac output, and blood pressure within narrow confines.

With good justification, clinicians abhor deviations from cardiac normalcy and strive to correct them. When dealing with the hypo-

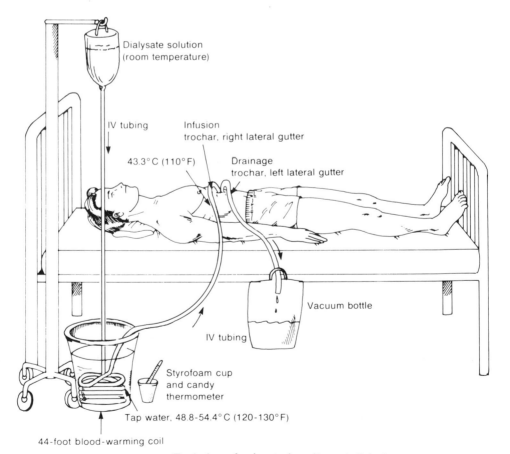

FIGURE 6 Technique for heated peritoneal dialysis.

thermic heart, this attitude must be tempered by the following facts:

1. Some of the arrhythmias of hypothermia (e.g., bradycardia) are physiologic.
2. The hypothermic heart does not respond to therapeutic intervention as predictably or as rapidly as does the normothermic heart (5,166).
3. The metabolism of most drugs is altered by hypothermia (102,103,166).
4. Most arrhythmias of hypothermia spontaneously convert during rewarming (90,91,166).
5. The ventricular fibrillation threshold is decreased in hypothermia.
6. Ventricular fibrillation is triggered by multiple peripheral stimuli.
7. Ventricular fibrillation will usually not convert until some rewarming has occurred (54).
8. In addition to the direct effects of cold on the heart, hypothermia causes indirect insult through changes in pH, electrolytes, and blood viscosity, volume depletion, shift in oxyhemoglobin dissociation, and hypoxia.
9. The ultimate goal in the management of the hypothermic victim is to rewarm him while preventing ventricular fibrillation and pulmonary complications.
10. Asystole may be a correctable arrhythmia after rewarming has occurred.
11. To some degree, hypothermia protects the central nervous system against hypoxic damage (58,59).

MANAGEMENT OF NON–LIFE-THREATENING ARRHYTHMIAS

These arrhythmias include bradycardia, atrial fibrillation, "asymptomatic" AV block, and premature atrial beats. They are best handled by the correction of circulating volume, pH, electrolytes, and oxygenation. Atrial fibrillation will usually convert to sinus rhythm spontaneously within 24 hours of rewarming (90,91). Lidocaine may be safe to use for ventricular irritability, but its necessity has not been proven (166,172). Until evidence appears, ventricular irritability should be managed in a standard fashion.

MANAGEMENT OF CARDIAC ARREST

Cardiac arrest manifested as either asystole or ventricular fibrillation is the gravest complication of hypothermia. The most important point to be made is that *cardiac arrest associated with hypothermia is reversible, and resuscitation should be continued until normothermia has been achieved.* There are numerous reports in the literature of successful resuscitaton without neurologic damage, in one case even after 3.5 hours of cardiac arrest. Successful resuscitation requires the following:

1. Continuous cardiopulmonary resuscitation (CPR)
2. Active rapid rewarming
3. Careful attention to physiologic needs

After cardiac arrest from either asystole or ventricular fibrillation, it is obvious that cerebral perfusion will cease unless CPR is performed. If resuscitation is to be attempted and anoxic brain damage avoided, CPR is necessary. There is some controversy among hypothermologists about how CPR should be performed after hypothermic cardiac arrest. The controversy stems from some of the following facts and opinions:

1. In the field without cardiac monitoring, the misdiagnosis of asystole is possible.
2. External cardiac massage may trigger ventricular fibrillation.
3. Rewarming alone may revive subjects with asystole. This is highly controversial.
4. Hypothermia protects the brain from anoxic damage (Figure 7) providing a "safe period" for total circulatory arrest (58).
5. Because external cardiac massage may trigger ventricular fibrillation, some authors have assumed that CPR is detrimental to the already fibrillating myocardium. There is no evidence in the literature to support this assumption.

All cases reported in the literature in which resuscitation included neurologic success involved CPR. Because the hypoxic brain requires less oxygen (7), it might be assumed that cardiac compressions should be performed at a slower rate than usual. However, this protection may be offset by the increased viscosity of hypothermic blood, which produces a decreased flow rate. At this point, there is no evidence to support any deviation from the CPR standards advocated by the American Heart Association (131).

It has been suggested that a delay in instituting CPR might be indicated "in the field when one has rescued an apparently dead person,

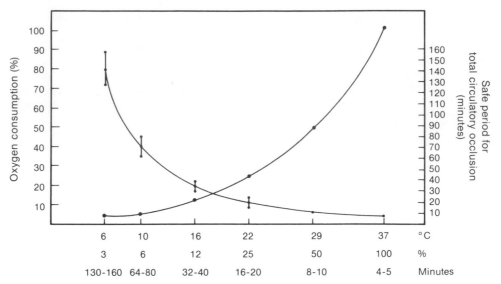

FIGURE 7 Relationship between body temperature, oxygen consumption, and the safe period for total circulatory occlusion. (After Reference 58.)

and is faced with 15 to 30 minutes of travel time to the hospital" (125). This position creates medicolegal problems that are best avoided.

The many drugs that have been used during successful resuscitation after hypothermia-induced cardiac arrest include atropine, epinephrine, dopamine, isoproterenol, lidocaine, steroids, and calcium chloride. There is little clinical evidence to confirm or deny their effectiveness or complications, as they are never withheld during therapy and the immediate response is not reported. Most authorities suggest that such drugs should be used with caution during the treatment of profound hypothermia or cardiac arrest (166,189). Without double-blind evaluation, conclusions are anecdotal.

In animal experiments, the core temperature at which fibrillation occurred was significantly lowered by bretylium. In control dogs, when fibrillation did occur during hypothermia, bretylium was successful 50% of the time in the conversion to an effective rhythm (15,154). At least one successful chemical defibrillation utilizing bretylium has been reported in management of the severely hypothermic victim (26a).

The use of open-chest cardiac massage for resuscitation has been advocated by some to be efficacious for the preservation of myocardial and cerebral blood flow, and for rapid rewarming of the myocardium, using direct mediastinal lavage. Such techniques cannot be advocated until formal prospective evaluation confirms improved survival. It can be argued that the application of heated fluid directly to the heart might create temperature gradients across the myocardium that alter normal cardiac conduction, and which predispose to chaotic ventricular contraction.

After Care

Problems that develop after core temperature and circulatory volume are normal may be due to underlying pathology (209). Hypothermia may mask many other disease states, including sepsis, stroke, myocardial infarction, and endocrinopathy. Most series indicate that approximately 40% of hypothermic victims are septic at the time of presentation. If fever occurs, pneumonia or sepsis should be considered. Oliguria is not uncommon; hypovolemia should be ruled out before using diuretics. If hypotension persists after rewarming, hypovolemia or a primary cardiac problem may be present. Mental function should be normal; if it is not, neurologic disorders may exist.

If the patient fails to maintain normal body temperature, hypothalamic dysfunction or endocrinopathy must be suspected.

After rewarming, the patient should have 24–48 hours of continuous cardiac and temperature monitoring. Careful observation with physical examinations and chest x-rays is needed for early diagnosis of the frequent pulmonary complications.

The list of complications that follow rewarming from deep hypothermia is long. Some have only recently been observed, and more will become apparent as hypothermic victims are further studied. The list includes:

1. Pneumonia (160,209)
2. Pancreatitis (120,122,147,163,166)
3. Intravascular thrombosis with myocardial infarction and cerebrovascular accidents (116,209)
4. Pulmonary edema (156,160)
5. Acute tubular necrosis (39,78,101)
6. Kaliuresis and metabolic alkalosis
7. Hemolysis (101,160)
8. Depressed bone marrow (160)
9. Disseminated intravascular coagulation (118, 121,122,187)
10. Hypophosphatemia (107,147)
11. Seizures (155)
12. Hematuria (13)
13. Myoglobinuria (13)
14. Simian-type deformity of the hand (13)
15. Temporary adrenal insufficiency (38)
16. Gastric erosion and hemorrhage (78,123)

Suggested Protocol for Severe Hypothermia

PREHOSPITAL CARE

1. Handle the victim gently to avoid physical trauma to the chest or heart (54).
2. Do not allow the victim to ambulate or use his extremities.
3. Place a large-bore intravenous line. Administer 50 ml 50% dextrose and 0.8 mg naloxone, followed by D_5 normal saline, 300–500 ml, as rapidly as possible; administer a total of 1000 ml over 60 minutes. If possible, do not move the victim until 300 ml has been given.
4. Carefully remove all of the victim's wet clothing, apply dry clothing or waterproof cover, and protect the victim from further heat loss and wind.
5. Do not immerse the victim in hot water or cover him with heated blankets. Do not massage the victim.

EMERGENCY DEPARTMENT

The initial history should analyze the cold exposure: duration, ambient temperature, wind chill, insulation, and moisture. It should also focus on underlying diseases: hypothyroidism, diabetes, cerebrovascular accident, blood loss, fracture, head injury, or previous cold injury. Finally, one must inquire about medications and drugs, particularly alcohol.

OBJECTIVE EVALUATION

Perform a brief examination to rule out life-threatening problems: airway obstruction, bleeding, and head and neck trauma.

The secondary evaluation should be done as soon as it is practical. Handling the patient very gently, remove his clothing.

1. Rectal temperature should be measured with a cold-recording thermocouple placed 15 cm into the rectum. Care should be taken not to injure the bowel with the rigid thermometer. This temperature should be continually monitored.
2. Place a cardiac monitor.
3. Obtain a 12-lead electrocardiogram. If muscle tremor obscures the recording, repeat the tracing when shivering ceases.
4. Obtain venous blood for stat complete blood count, electrolytes, and glucose.
5. Obtain arterial blood gases, corrected for temperature.
6. Depending on experience and need, measure central venous or pulmonary artery wedge pressure. (Exercise caution when passing central monitoring lines due to the tendency to induce heart block.)

THERAPY

1. If not already placed in the field, one or more large-bore intravenous catheters should be inserted. Administer 100 mg of thiamine (Wernicke's encephalopathy may predispose to hypothermia in the chronic alcoholic), 50 ml of 50% dextrose and 0.8 mg of naloxone (Narcan), infuse 300–500 ml of D_5 normal saline rapidly, and then adjust the rate to the blood pressure and urine output. From 1000 to 2000 ml may be needed during the first few hours. Heat intravenous fluid to 45°C (115°F) if this can be done rapidly, but *do not delay volume expansion to heat the fluid.* The second liter can be heated as the first is running in.

2. Intubation should be performed only if airway problems exist. If possible, delay intubation until 300 ml of intravenous solution has been given. The patient should be preoxygenated prior to intubation. A trained anesthesiologist or skilled emergency room clinician should use topical anesthesia to perform the procedure.

3. Place a Foley catheter.

4. Start HHI at 45°C (115°F) with 50–100% oxygen. Do not overventilate the victim. Check the Po$_2$ after 5–10 minutes and adjust the ventilation accordingly.

5. Peritoneal dialysis
   a. Assemble the fluid, tubing, and other equipment. Attach the infusion line to a 44 foot blood-warming coil. Submerge the coil in a large bucket of water, 48–54.4°C (121–130°F), and flush the tubing.
   b. Prepare the lower abdomen and infiltrate it with lidocaine even in a comatose patient. Make a midline 2 cm incision two fingers' breadth below the umbilicus.
   c. Insert one standard peritoneal dialysis trochar into the peritoneal cavity and advance it into one peritoneal gutter.
   d. Check the temperature of the dialysate before starting the infusion. Infuse 2 liters of 1.5% dextrose, potassium-free dialysate solution at 45°C (115°F). Normal saline or Ringer's lactate may be substituted.
   e. After infusion of 1000 ml, insert a second trochar through the same incision and advance it to the opposite gutter. Attach this trochar to a drainage (vacuum) bottle.
   f. Infuse 2 liters before draining the fluid. Check the drainage temperature, and if it is not at least several degrees cooler than the infusion, slow the drainage rate.
   g. Keep a careful record of dialysate input and output. The output may safely lag 2–5 liters behind the input.
   h. Frequently check the temperature of the water surrounding the blood-warming coil, and add hotter water as needed.
   i. Continue peritoneal dialysis until the core temperature reaches 36°C (97°F).
   j. Monitor blood pressure frequently. A Doppler transducer may be necessary. Hypotension should respond to an increased rate of intravenous infusion.
   k. During peritoneal dialysis, keep the patient covered with insulating blankets to prevent further heat loss.

6. Sodium bicarbonate should be used only if the corrected pH is very low (≤ 7.2) or if the pH does not rise with rewarming (35).

7. Insulin should be given only if the blood sugar is over 400 mg/dl and does not drop during rewarming. Insulin has little effect at a core temperature of less than 30°C (86°F) (209).

8. Repeat arterial blood gas, glucose, and potassium measurements with each 3–6°F temperature rise or until these parameters are stable.

9. During rewarming, a more complete examination should be performed, including chest x-ray, blood tests for cardiac and hepatic enzymes, toxic screening, and blood alcohol. A lactate level should be obtained if the anion gap is greater than 15.

10. If extremities are frozen on admission, keep them frozen by gently packing them in ice until the core temperature is near normal; then rapidly thaw them (see the protocol for frostbite).

11. Draw aerobic and anaerobic blood cultures. Perform spinal fluid examination if meningitis is suspected.

12. Begin administration of prophylactic broad-spectrum antibiotics.

AFTERCARE

1. Continue cardiac and temperature monitoring for at least 24 hours.

2. Carefully monitor the chest with serial examinations and chest x-ray to detect early pneumonia.

3. Repeat blood studies as indicated, including amylase and thyroid function tests.

4. Be suspicious about the presence of uremia, sepsis, aspiration, and substance abuse (ethanol, barbiturates, phenothiazines, tricyclic antidepressants). Also consider the possibility of hypopituitarism, Wernicke's encephalopathy, exfoliative dermatitides, and malnutrition.

5. Consider CT brain scan to rule out the presence of space-occupying lesions in patients who appear to have focal neurologic signs.

TRENCH FOOT (IMMERSION FOOT)

Trench foot, or immersion foot, is a disease of the sympathetic nerves and blood vessels in the hands or feet that results from prolonged exposure to cold and wet environments. These injuries do not require freezing temperatures.

Trench foot is produced by standing or sitting for long periods in water or with wet extremities and dependent limbs. Poor nutrition, inadequate clothing, and constriction of blood flow by shoes, socks, and other garments are predisposing factors.

Historically, trench foot has played a major role in various combats, including the Crimean War, World War I, World War II, and the Korean War. That freezing temperatures are not required has been demonstrated by the significant number of immersion injuries incurred in South Vietnam.

Immediate symptoms include numbness and tingling pain with itching. These progress to leg cramps and complete numbness. The skin appears initially reddened, later becoming progressively pale and mottled and then gray or blue. There are three stages in the progression of this injury. The first is a prehyperemic phase, lasting for a few hours to a few days, in which the limb is cold, slightly swollen, discolored, and possibly numb. Major pulses are poorly palpable. The second or hyperemic phase lasts from 2 to 6 weeks. Tingling pain, significant temperature differentials on the skin, swelling, blister formation, ulceration, and gangrene are involved. The third or posthyperemic phase lasts for weeks to months. The limb may be warm, but increased sensitivity to cold is noted; when the limb cools, the patient describes various degrees of pain, itching, and paresthesias. This injury often produces a moist, liquefaction gangrene quite dissimilar to the dry, mummification gangrene that occurs with severe frostbite.

TREATMENT

The management of this injury entails careful washing and drying of the feet, gentle rewarming, and slight elevation of the extremities. Intra-arterial reserpine (0.5 mg) has been found in certain cases to be effective in alleviating the vasospasm.

This topic is discussed further in the section on frostbite. Early physical therapy is essential. The victim should be warned that subsequent chilling will affect previously injured areas preferentially.

Chilblains appear to be a variation of the same syndrome, and involve the upper extremities with lesser degrees of vasospasm.

FROSTBITE

Frostbite is a cold injury that occurs almost exclusively in humans. Animals such as the moose, wolf, and polar bear evolved in the cold and are not susceptible to frostbite even while walking on snow or ice at $-70°C$

(17,184). Frostbite occurs when tissue temperature drops below its freezing level. Tissue temperature in cold is controlled by two opposing factors: the external temperature, or cold insult, and the internal heat flow. Cold-adapted animals apparently provide their extremities with enough blood and heat flow to prevent freezing. Because of vasospasticity and shunting, humans do not always allow adequate heat to flow into the extremities to prevent freezing.

At least 1 million cases of frostbite were incurred during World Wars I and II and the Korean War. Frostbite is not confined to the military setting. Mills collected 500 cases in Alaska by 1963; Cook County Hospital in Chicago recorded 143 cases, and Maria Hospital in Helsinki, Finland, noted 110 cases in 1968 and 1969 (10,98,139).

Frostbite is more common in the lower extremities. Only 2.5% of Korean War victims had hand involvement alone, while only two of the 110 cases in Helsinki did not involve the feet. In an indigent Chicago population, 48% of the cases involved the upper extremities. Frostbite can involve the ears, face, or knees, but only 0.5% of Korean War victims were affected in this manner (157).

The incidence of frostbite is influenced by two factors: the cold stress and the internal heat flow or vascularity. The cold stress is affected by low ambient temperature, wind chill, moisture, insulation, and contact with metal or supercooled liquids. Heat flow into an extremity is altered by constricting garments, cramped position, local pressure, and vasospastic conditions which result from such factors as previous cold injuries, cigarette smoking, Raynaud's phenomenon, and collagen-vascular disease (193,204). There are no data to suggest any influence of age or sex on the incidence of frostbite, but blacks seem slightly more susceptible than whites (136,153), perhaps because of the sickle cell trait (165).

Cutaneous Circulation

The cutaneous circulation plays an important role in the genesis of frostbite (173). Because of its role in thermoregulation, the skin normally has a blood flow far exceeding its nutritional requirements. The skin has a dense system of capillary loops which empty into a large subcapillary venous plexus that contain the majority of the cutaneous blood volume. Under normothermic conditions, 80% of the blood volume in a limb is in the skin and muscle veins. Blood volume is dramatically influenced by vascular tone. Under basal conditions, a 70 kg human has a 200–500 ml/ minute total cutaneous blood flow. With heat stress, this can maximally increase to 7000–8000 ml/minute, and with extreme cold stress, it can decrease to a mere 20–50 ml/minute (173).

Blood flow through apical structures (nose, ears, hands, and feet) is most variable because of the richly innervated arteriovenous (AV) anastomoses. The blood flow to the skin of the hand can be increased from a basal flow of 3–10 ml/minute per 100 g of tissue to a maximum of 180 ml/minute per 100 g of tissue. Cutaneous vascular tone is controlled by direct local effects, as well as by the reflex effects of both central and peripheral heating or cooling. Indirect heating (warming a distant part of the body) causes a reflex-mediated cutaneous vasodilatation, whereas direct warming results in vasodilatation dominated by local effects. When both types of heating or cooling are present, the effects are summated.

The cutaneous vessels are innervated by tonically active sympathetic adrenergic vasoconstrictor fibers. Vascular smooth muscles have both α and β receptors, although the significance of the β receptors is unknown. Vasodilatation in the hands and feet, but not in the forearm, is passive, so that maximal reflex vasodilatation occurs after sympathectomy. After sympathectomy, residual local control of vascular tone persists, so that direct heat or cold continues to alter blood flow (6).

Cold-Induced Vasodilatation

When the hand or foot is cooled to 15°C (59°F), maximal vasoconstriction and minimal blood flow occur. If cooling continues to 10°C (50°F), the vasoconstriction is interrupted by periods of vasodilatation and an associated increase in blood and heat flow. This cold-induced vasodilatation (CIVD), or "hunting response," recurs in 5–10 minute cycles to provide some protection from the cold (110). There is considerable individual variation in the amount of CIVD, which might explain some of the variation in susceptibility to frostbite (110). Prolonged, repeated exposure to cold will increase CIVD and offer some degree of acclimatization (152). Eskimos, Lapps, and Nordic fishermen have a very strong CIVD response and very short intervals between dilatations, which may contribute to the maintenance of hand function in the cold environment.

PATHOLOGY OF FROSTBITE

The pathologic changes of frostbite may be subdivided into four phases (97). These phases are not completely distinct, and some overlapping may occur. The changes during each phase vary with the rapidity of freezing and the duration and extent of the injury.

1. *Prefreeze phase.* This results from changes that occur secondary to chilling, prior to ice crystal formation. Changes are caused by vasospasticity and transendothelial plasma leakage.
2. *Freeze-thaw phase.* This results from actual ice crystal formation.
3. *Vascular stasis phase.* This involves changes in the blood vessels, which include spasticity and dilatation, and induce plasma leakage, stasis coagulation, and shunting.
4. *Late ischemic phase.* This is a result of thrombosis and AV shunting, ischemia, gangrene, and autonomic dysfunction.

Prefreeze Phase

This phase has been studied in the ears of laboratory mice kept at 3–10°C (37.9–50°F) for several days (97). Initially, there was generalized constriction of all vessels, followed by disproportionate dilatation of veins. After 2–4 days, there was leakage of fluid and injected dye from the veins. Red blood cells were blocked in minute venules, which led to stagnation and swelling. Capillary walls were eroded, presumably secondary to ischemia, which allowed red cell extravasation. Finally, the swollen, pale ears became bright red due to AV shunting and bypass of the obstruction.

Freeze-Thaw Phase

Ice crystal formation may occur within tissues in a few minutes or over several days (138). In Korea, 80% of frostbite incidents occurred after exposures of 12 hours or less (157). Ambient temperatures generally have to be about −6°C (21°F) and frequently −10 to −15°C (14 to 5°F) or less to freeze subcutaneous tissue (212). Skin must be supercooled to temperatures of −3 to −4°C to freeze (60). Wet skin freezes at a higher temperature than does dry skin (143). Wind increases the rate of freezing dramatically (212). The temperature temporarily remains at the freezing level because of the exothermic latent heat of crystallization (143). When freezing is complete, the temperature rapidly drops to ambient levels (109,134,146).

Intracellular crystallization and mechanical damage from ice crystals, which may cause irreversible damage, does not invariably occur (77,184). Irreversible damage may be due to the 10-fold increase in the extracellular concentration of sodium chloride, which is caused by the intracellular transfer of water as it contributes to ice formation (184). Ultrastructural studies performed on tissue after rapid freeze-thaw injury have shown drastic degenerative changes in muscle, mitochondria, and capillaries. These changes included ruptured cell membranes, fragmentation of cells in the capillary lumen, and general loss of cellular integrity (12).

Tissues vary in their susceptibility to freezing, with endothelial cells being the most sensitive, followed in decreasing order by bone marrow, nerve, muscle, bone, and cartilage (20). In spite of the complexity of the changes associated with freezing, the damage is usually reversible. Weatherly-White has shown that a button of frozen rabbit ear in the freeze-thaw stage will survive when transplanted to the contralateral healthy ear (206). This leads one to conclude that the permanent changes of frostbite result from the third and fourth phases.

Vascular Stasis Phase

Immediately after thawing, the combination of venous dilatation, arterial spasm, and slow flow of cold hypercoagulable viscous blood leads to stasis (96). Proteinaceous emboli and packed red blood cells are noted in both arteries and veins (97,191). Histamine release contributes to the stasis and capillary permeability, which may progress to involve larger areas (146). Finally, AV shunting bypasses the involved areas, leading to tissue hypoxia (97,164).

Microangiography of cold-injured rabbit ears demonstrates severe defects in arterial lumina, with total reversibility by 43 days (4). Human angiograms also demonstrate the reversibility of some lesions (61). Following the thaw of a mild frostbite, there exists a hyperdynamic state of maximal vasodilatation, as shown by digital plethysmography. More severe frostbite blunts or obliterates vasodilatation, which reflects the continuation of arterial spasm or obstruction (165).

Late Ischemic Phase

The late changes, morbidity, and tissue loss are due primarily to vascular occlusion and hypoxia (97,164). Direct cold injury to nerves, muscles, cartilage, and bones may also play a minor role. In amputated specimens, ischemic gangrene with vascular thrombi is a constant finding (1570). Neural damage is consistent with circulatory or ischemic neuritis. Axonal degeneration is associated with secondary degeneration in the spinal cord and sympathetic ganglia. Anterior horn cell changes correspond to the segments which innervate the injured limb (159,194).

CLINICAL PRESENTATION

It is difficult to predict the extent of frostbite damage from the initial examination (95,140). Therefore, any classification should be retrospective. Most authorities currently use two simple classifications: mild (without tissue loss) and severe (with tissue loss) (138). Historically, frostbite has been classified into four degrees of clinical severity (157). All may be present in a single extremity.

1. First degree—numbness, erythema, swelling, and desquamation
2. Second degree—vesiculation of the skin

3. Third degree—involves the entire thickness of the skin and extends into varying depths of subcutaneous tissue
4. Fourth degree—involves the entire thickness of the part, including the bone, with resultant loss of the part

SYMPTOMS

There are many descriptions of frostbite symptoms in the literature (194). The symptoms generally increase in incidence and severity in direct proportion to the severity of the cold injury.

Numbness

The initial symptom, which follows the uncomfortable coldness, is numbness (76.5%). The extremity has been described as feeling "like a stump," "like a block of wood," or "clublike" (157). Anesthesia is attributed to ischemia secondary to intense vasoconstriction.

Pain

Pain is present in 76% of all patients and in 97% of those who lose tissue. Throbbing pain usually starts 2–3 days after exposure and continues for a variable period even after the line of demarcation appears (22–45 days). Pain is caused by inflammation.

Paresthesias (Tingling)

Tingling is present in 72% of victims. This sensation does not appear until a week after exposure, but it tends to persist longer than other symptoms. Of those who lost tissue, 30% experienced this symptom even after apparent clinical recovery; many were disabled for up to 6 months. Tingling subsided after a month in those without tissue loss. Paresthesias are intensified by a warm environment (157). This sensation is probably caused by neuropathologic changes, such as ischemic neuritis (159).

Electric Currentlike Sensation

An electric currentlike sensation that passes through the affected area is present in 50% of all victims and 97% of those with tissue loss. It is very unpleasant and occurs frequently at night. The sensation has a delayed onset of 2 days, lasts for an average of 42 days, and is similar to paresthesias associated with tabes dorsalis. It has been speculated that it may originate from lesions in the posterior root ganglion.

Spontaneous Burning Sensation

The initial burning sensation in most patients (69%) subsides within 2–3 weeks, but may return with the resumption of normal activities and the wearing of boots. This sensation is not present in those with tissue loss.

Sensory Deficit

All victims experience some sensory deficit of touch, pain, or temperature. The involved areas vary but may extend to 4 cm proximal to the line of demarcation. Some degree of sensory loss can be expected to persist for at least 4 years, and perhaps indefinitely (9).

Late Symptoms

From 40 to 80% of Korean War victims studied after 4 years had late symptoms of cold feet, pain, excessive sweating, numbness, abnormal color, and joint discomfort. These symptoms were more severe during the winter.

Following recovery from frostbite, an exaggerated cold pressor response is present (149,150), which probably increases the susceptibility to frostbite (9). Years after frostbite, particularly in children, epiphyseal destruction and osteoarthritis may occur (18,19,-36,52,111,178). Epidermoid carcinoma of old frostbite scars has been reported (89). Extensor tenosynovitis from cold injury has occurred (50).

Clinical Appearance

Only a small number of victims with frostbite present to the hospital with tissue still frozen (12% in urban Chicago, 2.1% in Korea) (10,157). A frozen extremity appears waxy white, yellow-white, or mottled blue-white; hard, cold, and insensitive; and gives the illusion of being frozen solid. Even a rela-

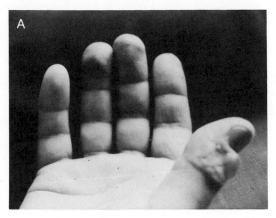
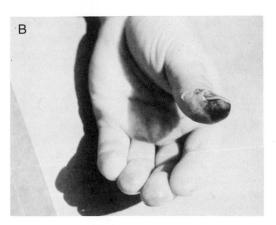

FIGURE 8   Demonstration of progression from early vesiculation (*A,* 24 hours) to eschar (*B,* 4 weeks) formation with frostbite injury. Cold sensitivity has persisted for 1 year.

tively shallow freeze may give this appearance, which precludes any judgment of its severity at the time (138–140,157). As thawing occurs, flushing progresses distally along the extremity and results in erythema or a more ominous purple or burgundy hue. Even with severe frostbite, there will be immediate hyperemia and warmth after thawing which subside in 2–3 days (157). If rapid warming is used, sensation returns when thawing is complete, and will persist until blebs appear (138).

Edema appears within 3 hours (157). It persists for less than 5 days with mild frostbite, but may last longer with severe frostbite (85). Vesicles and bullae form 6–24 hours after thawing. If left intact, they are reabsorbed in 5–10 days (138,157).

Favorable prognostic signs during early treatment include sensation to pin pricks, good color, warmth, and large, clear blebs that appear early and extend to the tips of the digits (138). Poor prognostic signs include small, dark blebs which appear late and do not extend to the digit tips, the absence of edema, and the presence of cyanosis which does not blanch with pressure (85,138). During the first 9–15 days, severely frostbitten skin forms a black, hard, and usually dry eschar, whether vesicles are present or not (157). The mummification forms an apparent line of demarcation in 22–45 days (157) (Figure 8). Wet, soft, purulent gangrene is most likely to occur only when the injury extends proximally to the web spaces between digits (157). Mummification and demarcation may take 6 weeks to 6

months to complete (see Plates 2*A* and 2*B*) (98,138).

EVALUATION

The clinical evaluation or early prediction of the severity of frostbite remains an inexact science. Analysis of the cold stress may provide some hint of the expected damage, bearing in mind the multiple variables (95). Temperature is modified by wind chill, moisture, duration, insulation, and contact with heat or conductors. *Frostbite injury is greatly increased when refreezing occurs after thawing.*

The early clinical appearance of the affected area, as previously discussed, allows only a gross judgment (50% accuracy) of the expected damage (93,94,135,138,192). Accurate, early determination of tissue damage is necessary to evaluate the effectiveness of therapeutic measures, and would be of value in the triage of casualties. Some useful indicators are enumerated below.

Kettelkamp was able to predict tissue loss in experimental frostbite (rabbit paws) with 80–100% accuracy utilizing intravenous radioisotope (RISA) [131]I (93,94). With severe frostbite, extravasation and entrapment of the isotope in the injured extremity led to a diagnostic pattern.

Using a ^{133}Xe clearance technique to study blood flow in 20 severely frostbitten human extremities, an accuracy rate of 75–97% in predicting tissue loss was obtained (94).

Technetium   methylene   disphosphonate

(^{99m}Tc MDP) soft tissue and bone scintiscanning can predict tissue loss, but not until 5 days after the injury (135). To date, no good prospective study with isotope evaluation has been recorded.

Angiography has limited use in the early evaluation of frostbite (185). Arteriograms taken at early stages show a marked decrease in circulation which may spontaneously reverse. Angiography after the administration of vasodilators may delineate their effects (61). Angiograms taken 3 weeks after injury may assist in making the decision for surgical excision (37).

X-rays of involved extremities are usually negative during the first 3 months. Between the third and sixth months, there may appear fine, irregular, lytic, and punctate lesions which often involve the articular surfaces (138).

Digital plethysmography performed after thawing allows classification for prognostication and can measure the response to vasodilators. Patients who exhibit a hyperdynamic digital pulsation do not lose tissue and do not improve after administration of intra-arterial reserpine, a sympathetic blocker and vasodilator. Patients with a digital pulsation equal to that of normal controls, or with an absent or severely blunted pulsation, may respond to intra-arterial reserpine. This latter group may progress to some tissue loss (165).

THERAPY

The goal in frostbite therapy is primarily to prevent or decrease tissue loss and secondarily to diminish discomfort, shorten hospitalization, and prevent late sequelae. Therapeutic modalities include a wide variety of scientific and not-so-scientific remedies.

Little controversy remains about the value

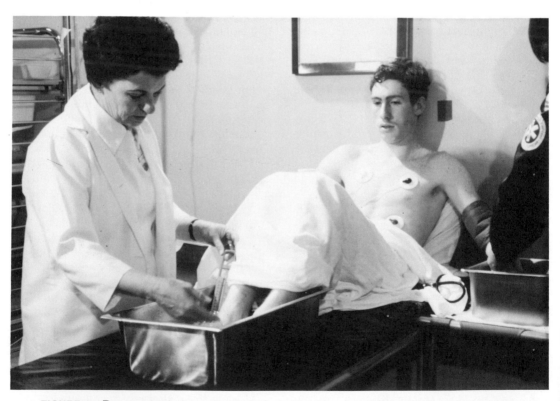

FIGURE 9 Recommended position for thawing all four extremities simultaneously. With the patient sitting, the hands and feet may be submerged in hot water without cramming the digits. The water temperature is 104–110°F, monitored by a thermometer and circulated manually. Thawing is complete in 25–30 minutes, when the extremities are pliable and color and sensation have returned.

of rapid thaw, whirlpool baths, and late amputation. The use of anticoagulants and antisludging agents, sympathectomy (medical or surgical), and vasodilators continues to be explored and debated.

Therapy can be divided into local (skin) and systemic treatment. The latter ameliorates vasospasticity, ischemia, and inflammation.

Rapid Thaw

Most of the damage from freezing occurs during the transition from the liquid to the solid state or vice versa (134). Rapid thaw decreases the injury by decreasing the time that the cells are exposed to the most damaging electrolyte and temperature conditions (190). Experimentally, the most effective thawing temperature is 42°C (46). In humans, thawing temperatures above 42.8°C cause increased discomfort (138). The ideal thawing temperature is somewhere between 37.8 and 43.3°C, never to exceed 44.4°C.

Temperature should be carefully monitored with a thermometer; if none is available, water at 43.3°C (110°F) may be estimated as the temperature at which most people can submerge their hand with only slight discomfort. Water at 44.4°C is decidedly uncomfortable. Most heated tap water is between 54.4°C and 60°C (130–140°F).

Boots or mittens are occasionally frozen to the extremities and have to be thawed with hot water prior to removal. This should be done as rapidly as possible to avoid slow rewarming.

Extremities should be completely submerged in large vessels of water, with the water circulated manually or mechanically (Figure 9). The digits should not be crammed into the sides of the vessel. Water cools quite rapidly; the temperature should be maintained by adding hot water. One must carefully avoid direct contact between the hottest water and the frozen part. The thawing process requires 30–40 minutes and should not be prolonged after complete rewarming. Thawing is judged to be complete when the part is pliable and color and sensation have returned (3).

If the extremity has previously been thawed prior to hospital admission, reapplication of heat may be harmful and should be avoided (46,138). If profound hypothermia with a core temperature of less than 32°C (90°F) coexists, the extremities should not be thawed until the core temperature approaches 35°C (96°F).

Postthaw

After thawing, the extremity should receive protective isolation. For mild frostbite, sterile sheets and a blanket cradle are adequate. Sterile gloves, caps, and masks should be worn when handling extremities. For severe frostbite, complete protective isolation is required. For example, if the patient ambulates on his heels to the bathroom, the toes should be wrapped with a sterile covering. When plastic gloves are worn on the hands, the patient may attend to his personal needs without risk of contamination.

The involved areas should be bathed in a whirlpool two or three times daily for 30 minutes each in water at 32.2–37.8°C (90–100°F) with hexachlorophene or povidone-iodine. These contribute to bacteriostasis and help greatly with debridement. During the whirlpool, the patient should actively exercise the affected parts. If eschar prohibits movement of digits, it should be split laterally to allow movement. Uninfected blebs should be left intact, but if ruptured, they should be debrided.

If major limb damage exists, tissue pressure can be monitored. If a rapid rise to more than 40 mmHg occurs, then distal blood flow should be reestablished with fasciotomies. Tissue cultures are obtained routinely on admission and thereafter as indicated. Antibiotics are used only for specific indications.

Analgesics are frequently necessary. Continuous epidural blockage for up to 48 hours has been used to control severe pain.

With lower extremity involvement, Buergher's exercises (to avoid venous stasis) are utilized. With upper extremity involvement, digital exercises are essential.

All patients should be hospitalized for at least 24–48 hours to determine the extent of damage. If only mild frostbite is present, with absent or minimal blebs, then the individual may be treated as an outpatient with daily whirlpool baths and minimal heel ambulation. If extensive blebs are present, hospitalization should extend for 2–5 days. If deep frostbite without anticipated tissue loss is expected, then hospitalization is extended until demarcation is complete, and amputation and skin grafting are carried out.

Phenoxybenzamine hydrochloride (Dibenzyline), a long-acting α-adrenergic receptor blocking agent, is administered orally to all frostbite patients, starting at 10 mg/day and increased as tolerated to 60 mg/day. This is continued throughout the entire clinical course.

REVIEW OF OTHER MEDICATIONS

Several medical regimens have included anticoagulants, antisludging agents, anti-inflammatory drugs, sympathectomy, vasodilators, and hyperbaric oxygen. There have been few controlled human series to document their effects.

Sympathectomy

Surgical sympathectomy has been used extensively to treat frostbite since the early 1940s (104,180,181). It is reported to cause prompt disappearance of pain, decreased edema, more rapid demarcation, and to decrease the post-frostbite sequelae of autonomic dysfunction. Sympathectomy in rabbits results in a significant decrease in tissue loss if done within 24–48 hours after frostbite occurs (51,55).

Unilateral sympathectomy performed on 10 patients with bilateral frostbite involvement resulted in no difference in clinical course or tissue loss (11). It is interesting to note that one patient suffered a second cold injury, with less severe frostbite on the sympathectomized side.

After extensive experience with both unilateral and bilateral sympathectomy, Mills concluded that sympathectomy led to a smoother early clinical course, but the end results were no better. In fact, the extremity not subjected to ganglionectomy often showed more preservation of tissue (138).

Intra-Arterial Reserpine

Reserpine causes a depletion in arterial norepinephrine, in effect a medical sympathectomy (16,161). When reserpine is injected directly into an artery, its local effects are immediate and last for 2–4 weeks. Spillover effects in distant arteries reach a maximum in 24

hours and lasts for 7 days (161). Experimental frostbite induced in rabbit paws was less destructive, with decreased tissue loss after the administration of intra-arterial reserpine, when the cold injury was thawed slowly. No benefit was derived if the extremity was thawed rapidly and then treated with intra-arterial reserpine. This suggests that intra-arterial reserpine may be of most benefit when used in patients who have thawed slowly (186).

Angiography performed before and after injection of intra-arterial reserpine into five patients with frostbite more than 24 hours old showed resolution of vasospasm and increased blood flow (Figure 10). Patients with post-frostbite pain who were treated subsequently enjoyed relief of pain for as long as 2 years (186).

Frostbite patients with diminished digital pulsations, as shown by plethysmography and Doppler ultrasound, manifest increased blood flow after administration of intra-arterial reserpine (165).

The recommended dosage is 0.5 mg reserpine injected into the femoral, brachial, or radial artery. This should be repeated in 2–3 days. Intraarterial infusion is confirmed by subjective feelings of flushing and warmth in the extremity. No systemic side effects have been observed (2,3).

Dextran

Part of the pathologic process in frostbite is sludging and coagulation of blood, which lead to thrombosis and ischemia. Reversal of this process should decrease ultimate tissue damage (190). Low molecular weight dextran inhibits intravascular cellular aggregation, and improves small vessel perfusion in injured tissue (49,197). This drug has had variable success in the management of frostbite.

In 1963, Mundth showed that continuous infusion of low molecular weight dextran, started early after thawing, improved tissue survival in experimental frostbite. Conversely, experimental frostbite induced in dog paws, when treated with low molecular weight dextran, resulted in increased edema formation and no reduction of tissue loss (158). Dextran was found to be inferior to sympathectomy in preserving tissue in rabbit ears (57). Several

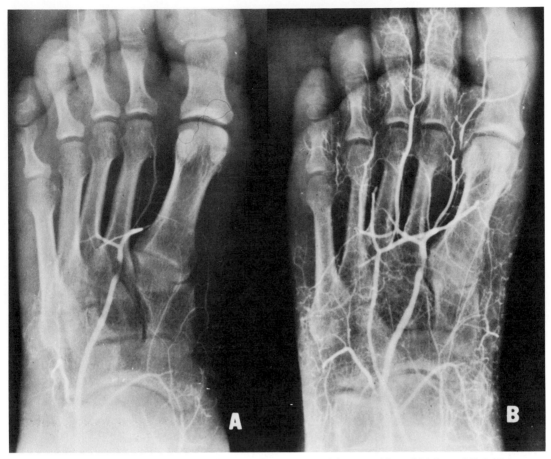

Figure 10 Angiograms of the left foot of a 30-year-old man with cold injury. (*A*) Initial angiogram (*B*) Angiogram taken 2 days after intra-arterial injection of reserpine (From Gralino B. J., Porter J. M., Rosch J., Angiography in the Diagnosis and Therapy of Frostbite. *Radiology,* **19**:301 305, 1976, with permission).

clinical observations in human frostbite have similarly concluded that there is no benefit from the use of low molecular weight dextran (98,138,183).

Heparin

Heparin was found to be effective in decreasing tissue loss in one animal experiment but was of no value in another (108,145). No human use studies are available. In a well-designed rabbit study, ears were frozen (frostbitten), thawed, and then treated 1 hour later with either intra-arterial or systemic heparin. Two other groups were managed with systemic prophylactic heparin or intraperitoneal prophylactic reserpine (medical sympathectomy). Prophylactic anticoagulation and medical sympathectomy appeared to delay the appearance of vascular injury, but did not affect the ultimate vascular or tissue damage. Therapeutic anticoagulation did not have any beneficial effect (101a).

Anti-Inflammatory Agents

Nonsteroidal anti-inflammatory agents, including oxyphenbutazone, indomethacin, and xanthinol nicotinate, have significantly reduced tissue loss in experimental frostbite in rabbit paws (196). Again, reports of human use are anecdotal.

Hyperbaric Oxygen

Hyperbaric oxygen therapy has not been of value in experimental frostbite. However, it has been reported in one human case to have dramatically improved the color of the digits, although it markedly increased the pain (47,211).

α-Blocking Agents

An α-blocking agent, buflomedil hydrochloride (not available in the United States), when given intravenously during thawing, is reported to potentiate the thawing and to decrease tissue loss in humans (42).

Summary of Clinical Management

Early prediction of frostbite severity is inaccurate. Isotope scanning, digital plethysmography, and Doppler ultrasound may help somewhat in prognostication. The best treatment is rapid thaw, followed by sterile isolation and daily whirlpool baths with active exercise. Surgical sympathectomies are no longer advocated, but medical sympathectomies with intra-arterial reserpine may be of value. Vasodilators such as phenoxybenzamine hydrochloride (Dibenzyline) may possibly decrease tissue loss. Heparin and dextran are probably not useful. Anti-inflammatory agents may help to some degree. Surgical intervention should be conservative, with late amputation only.

Suggested Protocol for Frostbite Therapy

Prehospital Care (203)

1. All constricting clothing should be removed. The injured area should be protected by nonconstricting blankets or garments.
2. Do not allow smoking or the ingestion of alcohol. Do not apply topical medications or rupture blebs.
3. If lower extremities are involved, transport the patient by litter. If foot travel is necessary, do not thaw the extremity.
4. Rapidly thaw the injured area in hot water (see later instructions) only if slow thawing would occur before hospitalization and if refreezing can

be absolutely prevented (142). Do not expose the frostbitten area to extreme dry heat (fires or exhaust pipes). Hot water therapy should not be continued after thawing.

Emergency Department

1. Perform a brief examination to rule out other medical problems. Obtain a rectal temperature to rule out hypothermia. If the rectal temperature is less than 32°C (90°F), proceed with a hypothermia protocol.
2. Obtain the exposure history to determine the duration and extent of the cold insult. This may be obtained during treatment.
3. Perform baseline laboratory studies using the hypothermia protocol.
4. For extensive frostbite injury:
   a. Cardiac monitoring must be provided during rewarming.
   b. Pay close heed to the initial serum potassium level and follow serial potassium levels during thawing.
   c. Place an intravenous line to keep open.
5. Rapid thaw: Submerge the extremity in a large bucket of tap water at 40.0–43.3°C (104–110°F). Avoid cramming the digits into the sides of the bucket. Monitor the temperature by placing a candy thermometer in each vessel. Circulate the water manually or with a whirlpool. As the water cools, add hotter tap water to the bucket and bail out the excess. Do not pour hot water directly on the extremity. Each assistant should monitor no more than two buckets. Thaw for 20–45 minutes, until the extremity is pliable and the color and sensation return.
6. Intra-arterial reserpine, 0.5 mg, may be injected into a proximal artery during rewarming. This should be repeated in 3 days.
7. Phenoxybenzamine (Dibenzyline), 10 mg given orally, can be increased by 10 mg/day up to 60 mg/day.
8. After the thaw, wrap the extremity in soft sterile dressing with cotton balls between the digits.

Hospital Orders

1. Sterile sheets and a blanket cradle must be used.
2. Caps, gowns, masks, and gloves must be worn when handling extremities.
3. For extensive frostbite, complete protective isolation is required.
4. Bed rest for 24 hours is necessary. If able, the patient may then walk on his heels to the bathroom after sterile wraps are applied to the extremities.

5. The patient should wear plastic gloves during bowel movements, discarding them afterward.
6. The patient may feed himself unless there is extensive hand involvement.
7. Gowned visitors are permitted.
8. No smoking or chewing is permitted.
9. Whirlpool baths should be taken two or three times a day for 20 minutes with tap water at 32.3–37.8°C (90–100°F), with hexachlorophene (pHisoHex) or povidone-iodine (Betadine) added. The patient should actively exercise the digits while in the bath.
10. Buerger exercises should be done four times a day.
11. Digital finger exercises should be done at least four times a day for 20 minutes.
12. Analgesics should be given as needed.
13. Involved tissues should be cultured on admission.
14. Daily creatinine phosphokinase should be monitored for 4–5 days. (This is an indicator of tissue damage.)

OTHER COLD INJURIES

COLD URTICARIA

Cold urticaria, an allergy to cold, is a quite uncommon phenomenon. Individuals with cold urticaria describe an itching sensation in the skin, rhinitis, and variable degrees of swelling or wheal production associated with the cooled part. They often describe such symptoms after swimming in cold water, putting their hands in cold water, or working with ice. Very little stimulation may be needed to produce the urticarial response, and many individuals who have this affliction do not consider it to be abnormal. A simple test for this condition is to place an ice cube on the forearm for 30 seconds to 3 minutes to elicit the wheal response. Redness without elevation and itching is a negative test. Individuals may or may not have cryoglobulins or cold agglutinins. Symptoms are controlled with antihistamines.

OPHTHALMIC INJURIES

Freezing of corneas has been reported in snowmobilers and cross-country skiers. Individuals who force their eyes open in a high wind chill situation without goggles induce these injuries. Initial corneal flare and pain on rewarming are signs of an injury. Keratitis and corneal opacification may require cornea

transplantation. No known treatment other than rapid rewarming and patching is effective. Corticosteroids are contraindicated.

SNOW BLINDNESS

This injury is produced by reflected ultraviolet solar radiation from snow, ice, or water. It tends to be more common at high elevations, where the air filtration of ultraviolet radiation is diminished. Excess radiation produces corneal pitting and disruption of the epithelium. Retinal damage can also occur. Individuals may be asymptomatic at the time of the injury. Symptoms develop 4–12 hours after exposure and include a painful, dry, granular sensation. The lids and corners of the eye may be swollen and red. Tearing is common and may be the most prominent sign. The treatment involves induced cycloplegia, mydriasis, and patching. Artificial tears and nonsteroidal antibiotic ointments are indicated early in the treatment. Steroid ointments may be indicated only after the corneal epithelium is restored.

REFERENCES

1. Auld, C. D., Light, I. M., Norman, J. N., Accidental hypothermia and rewarming in dogs. *Clinical Science,* **56**(6): 601–606 (June 1979).
2. Bangs, C. C., *Disturbances Due to Cold. In Current Therapy,* Conn, H. F., ed. Philadelphia: W. B. Saunders, 1981, pp. 981–88.
3. Bangs, C. C., Boswick, J. A., Hamlet, M. P., Sumner, D. S., Weatherley-White, R. C. A., When your patient suffers frostbite. *Patient Care,* **11**:132–156. (Feb. 1977).
4. Bellman, S., Strombeck, J. O., Transformation of the vascular system in cold-injured tissue of the rabbit's ear. *Angiology,* **2**:108–125 (1960).
5. Bergh, U. L. F., Hartley, H., Landsberg, L., Ekblom, B., Plasma norepinephrine concentration during submaximal and maximal exercises at lowered skin and core temperature. *Acta Physiologica Scandinavica* **106**:383–384 (1979).
6. Best, C. H., Taylor, N. B., *Physiological Basis of Medical Practice,* 10th ed., Brobeck, J. R., ed. Baltimore: Williams & Wilkins, 1979.
7. Bigelow, W. G., Lindsay, W. K., Harrison, R. C., Gordon, R. A., Greenwood, W. F., Oxygen transport and utilization in dogs at low body temperature. *American Journal of Physiology,* **60**:125 (1950).
8. Blair, E., Physiologic and metabolic effects of hypothermia in man, in depressed metabolism." *Proceedings of the First International Conference on Depressed Metabolism,* Aug. 22–23, 1968. Musacchia,

X. J., Saunders, J. F., eds. New York: American Elsevier, pp. 525–568, 1969.

9. Blair, J. R., Schatski, R., Orr, K. D., Sequelae to cold injury in one hundred patients, follow-up study four years after occurrence of cold injury. *Journal of the American Medical Association,* **163**(14):1203–1208 (Apr. 1957).

10. Boswick, J. A., Thompson, J. D., Jonas, R. A., The epidemiology of cold injuries. *Surgery, Gynecology and Obstetrics,* **149:**326–332 (Sept. 1979).

11. Bouwman, D. E., Morrison, S., Lucas, C. E., Ledgerwood, A. M. Early sympathetic blockade for frostbite. *The Journal of Trauma,* **20**(9):744–749 (Sept. 1980).

12. Bowers, W. D., Jr., Hubbard, R. W., Daum, R. C., Ashbaugh, P., Nilson, E., Ultrastructural studies of muscle cells and vascular endothelium immediately after freeze-thaw injury. *Cryobiology,* **10:**9–21 (1973).

13. Bristow, G., Smith, R., Lee, J., Auty, A., Tweed, W. A., Resuscitation from cardiopulmonary arrest during accidental hypothermia due to exhaustion and exposure. *Canadian Medical Association Journal,* **117:**247–249 (Aug. 1977).

14. Bruck, K., Baum, E., Schwennicke, H. P., Cold adaptive modifications in man induced by repeated short-term cold-exposures and during a 10 day and night cold-exposure. *Pfluegers Archiv. European Journal of Physiology* (Berlin), **363:**125–133 (1976).

15. Buckley, J., Bosch, O. D., Bacaner, M. D., Prevention of ventricular fibrillation during hypothermia with bretylium tosylate. *Anesthesia and Analgesia* (Cleveland), **50:**587–593 (1971).

16. Burns, J. H., Rand, M. J., Noradrenaline in artery walls and its dispersal by reserpine. *British Medical Journal,* **1:**903–309 (1958).

17. Burton, A. C., Edholm, O. G., *Man in a Cold Environment.* London, Edward Arnold (Publishers), Ltd., 1955.

18. Carrera, G. F., Kozin, F., McCarty, D. J., Arthritis after frostbite injury in children. *Arthritis and Rheumatism,* **22**(10):1082–1087 (Oct. 1979).

19. Carrera, G. F., Kozin, F., Flaherty, L., McCarty, D. J., Radiographic changes in the hands following childhood frostbite injury. *Skeletal Radiology,* **6:**33–37.

20. Cavanaugh, D. G., The pathogenesis and treatment of frostbite. *Journal of the Kansas Medical Society,* **71**(1):11–25 (1970).

21. Chen, R. Y. Z., Chien, S. Hemodynamic functions and blood viscosity in surface hypothermia. *American Journal of Physiology,* **235**(2):136–143 (Aug. 1978).

22. Cooper, K. E., *Diving Medicine.* Strauss, R., ed. New York: Grune and Stratton, 1976.

23. Cooper, K. E., Ross, D. N., *Hypothermia in Surgical Practice.* Philadelphia: F. A. Davis, 1960.

24. Cooper, K. E., Sheilagh, M., Riben, P., Respiratory and other responses in subjects immersed in cold water. *Journal of Applied Physiology,* **4**(6):903–910 (June 1976).

25. Coopwood, T., Kennedy, J. H., Accidental hypothermia, *Cardiovascular Research Center Bulletin,* **12**(4):104–111 (Apr.–June 1974).

26. D'Amato, H. E., Hegnauer, A. H., Blood volume in the hypothermic dog. *American Journal of Physiology,* **173:**100–102 (1953).

26a. Danzl, D. F., Sowers, B. M., Vicario, S. J., Chemical ventricular defibrillation in severe accidental hypothermia. (letter) *Annals of Emergency Medicine,* **11:**689–99 (Dec. 1982).

26b. Danzl, D. F., Thomas, D. M., Nasotracheal intubation in the emergency department. *Critical Care Medicine,* **8:**677–82 (1980).

27. DaVee, T. S., Reineberg, E. J., Extreme hypothermia and ventricular fibrillation. *Annals of Emergency Medicine,* **9**(2):100–102 (Feb. 1980).

28. Davidovic, V., Petkovic, M., Petrovic, V. E., The capacity for restitutional thermogenesis—its dependence on the duration of the hypothermic state and catecholamine content of the adrenals. *Resuscitation,* **3:**295–301 (1975).

29. Davies, D. M., Millar, E. J., Miller, I. A., Accidental hypothermia treated by extracorporeal blood-warming. *Lancet,* **1:**1036–1037 (1967).

30. Day, E. A., Morgan, E. B., Accidental hypothermia: Report of a case following alcohol and barbiturate overdose. *Anaesthesia and Intensive Care,* **2**(1):73–76 (1974).

31. Dominguez de Villota, E., Barat, G., Peral, P., Juffe, A., Fernandez de Miguel, J. M., Avello, F., Recovery from profound hypothermia with cardiac arrest after immersion. *British Medical Journal,* **4:**394–395 (1973).

32. Doolittle, W. H., Disturbances due to cold. In *Current Therapy 1977,* Conn, H. F., Philadelphia: W. B. Saunders, 1981.

33. Drake, C. E., Flowers, N. C., ECG changes in hypothermia from sepsis and unrelated to exposure. *Chest,* **77**(5):685–686 (May 1980).

34. Duguid, H., Simpson, R. G., Stowers, J. M., Accidental hypothermia. *Lancet,* **2:**1213–1219 (1961).

35. Dula, D. J., Use of IV bicarbonate in hypothermia. Letter to the editor. *Journal of the American College of Emergency Physicians,* **8**(1):48 (Jan. 1979).

36. Ellis, R., Short, J. G., Simonds, B. D., Unilateral osteoarthritis of the distal interphalangeal joints following frostbite. *Radiology,* **93:**857–858 (Oct. 1969).

37. Erikson, U., Ponten, B., The possible value of arteriography supplemented by a vasodilator agent in the early assessment of tissue viability in frostbite. *Injury,* **6:**150–153 (Nov. 1974).

38. Felicetta, J., Green, W. L., Goodner, C. J., Decreased adrenal responsiveness in hypothermic patients. *Journal of Clinical Endocrinology and Metabolism,* **50**(1):93–97 (1980).

39. Fell, R. H., Gunning, A. J., Bardman, K. D., Trigor, D. R., Severe hypothermia as a result of barbiturate overdose complicated by cardiac arrest. *Lancet,* **1:**32 (1968).

40. Finney, W. H., Dworkin, S., Cassidy, G. J., The effects of lowered body temperature and of insulin on the respiratory quotient of dogs." *American Journal of Physiology,* **80:**301 (1927).

41. Fisher, A., Foex, P., Emerson, P. M., Oxygen availability during hypothermic cardiopulmonary bypass. *Critical Care Medicine,* **5:**154–158 (1977).

42. Foray, J., Baisse, P. E., Mont, J. P., Cahen, C. Treat-

ment of frostbites. Analysis of results in twenty patients with buflomedil chlorhydrate. *Semaine Des Hopitaux de Paris,* **15**(56):490–497 (Mar. 1980).

43. Fox, R. H., Woodward, P. M., Exton-Smith, A. N., et al., Body temperature in the elderly: A national study of physiological, social and environmental conditions. *British Medical Journal,* **1**:200–206 (1973).

44. Frank, D. H., Robson, M. C., Accidental hypothermia treated without mortality. *Surgery, Gynecology and Obstetrics,* **151**:379–381 (Sept. 1980).

45. Fruehan, A. E., Accidental hypothermia. *Archives of Internal Medicine,* **106**:218–229 (1960).

46. Fuhrman, R. A., Fuhrman, G. J., The treatment of experimental frostbite by rapid thawing. *Medicine* (Baltimore) **36**:465–487 (1957).

47. Gage, A. A., Ishikawa, H., Winter, P. M., Experimental frostbite, the effect of hyperbaric oxygenation on tissue survival. *Cryobiology,* **7**(1):1–8 (July–Aug. 1970).

48. Garry, R. C., Control of the temperature of the body. *Medicine, Science and the Law,* **9**:242–246 (1969).

49. Gelin, L. E., Ingelman, B., Influence of low viscous dextran of peripheral circulation on Man. *Acta Chirurgica Scandinavica,* **122**:303–308 (1961).

50. Georgitis, J., Extensor Tenosynovitis of the hand from cold exposure. *Journal of the Maine Medical Association,* **69**:129–131 (Apr. 1978).

51. Gildenberg, P. L., Hardenbergh, E., The effect of immediate sympathectomy on tissue survival following experimental frostbite. *Annals of Surgery,* **160**(1):160–168 (July 1964).

52. Glick, R., Parhami, N., Frostbite arthritis. *Journal of Rheumatology,* **6**(4):456–460 (1979).

53. Golden, F., St. C., Rivers, J. F., The immersion incident. *Anaesthesia,* **30**:364–474 (1975).

54. Golden, F., St. C., Recognition and treatment of immersion hypothermia. *Proceedings of the Royal Society of Medicine,* **66**:1058–1061 (Oct. 1973).

55. Golding, M. R., Mendoza, M. F., Hennigar, G. R., Fries, C. C., Wesolowski, S. A., On settling the controversy on the benefit of sympathectomy for frostbite. *Surgery,* **56**(1):221–231 (July 1964).

56. Goldman, A., Exton-Smith, A. N., Francis, G., et al., A pilot study of low body temperature in old people admitted to hospital. *Journal of the Royal College of Physicians of London,* **11**:291–306 (1977).

57. Goodhead, B., The comparative value of low molecular weight dextran and sympathectomy in the treatment of experimental frost-bite. *British Journal of Surgery,* **53**(12):1060–1062 (Dec. 1966).

58. Gordon, A. S., Cerebral blood flow and temperature during deep hypothermia for cardiovascular surgery. *Journal of Cardiovascular Surgery,* **3**(4):299–307 (Aug. 1962).

59. Gordon, A. S., Meyer, B. W., Jones, J. C., Open heart surgery using deep hypothermia without an oxygenator. *Journal of Thoracic and Cardiovascular Surgery,* **40**(6):787–799 (Dec. 1960).

60. Gracey, L., Ingram, D., The diagnosis and management of gangrene from exposure to cold. *British Journal of Surgery,* **55**(4):302–306 (Apr. 1968).

61. Gralino, B. J., Porter, J. M., Rosch, J., Angiography in the diagnosis and therapy of frostbite. *Radiology,* **19**:301–305 (May 1976).

62. Gregory, R. T., Doolittle, W. H., Accidental hypothermia, Part II, Clinical implications of experimental studies. *Alaska Medicine,* **15**(2):48–52 (Mar. 1973).

63. Grossheim, R. L., Hypothermia and frostbite treated with peritoneal dialysis. *Alaska Medicine,* **15**(2):53–55 (Mar. 1973).

64. Guild, W. J., Rewarming via the airway (CBRW) for hypothermia in the field? *Journal Royal Naval Medical Service,* **64**(3):186–193 (1978).

65. Haight, J. S. J., Keatinge, W. R., Failure of thermoregulation in the cold during hypoglycemia induced by exercise and ethanol. *Journal of Physiology* (London), **229**:87–97 (1973).

66. Hanson, H., Goldman, R. F., Cold injury in man: A review of its etiology and discussion of its prediction. *Military Medicine,* **134**(11):1307–1316 (Oct. 1969).

67. Harari, A., Regnier, B., Rapin, M., Lemaire, F., LeGall, J. R., Haemodynamic study of prolonged deep accidental hypothermia. *European Journal of Intensive Care Medicine,* **1**:65–70 (1975).

68. Harnett, R. M., O'Brien, E. M., Sias, F. R., Pruitt, J. R., Initial treatment of profound accidental hypothermia. *Aviation, Space, and Environmental Medicine,* **51**:680–687 (July 1980).

69. Hayward, J. S., Eckerson, J. D., Collis, M. L., Effect of behavioral variables on cooling rate of man in cold water. *Journal of Applied Physiology,* **38**(6): 1073–1077 (June 1975).

70. Hayward, J. S., Eckerson, J. D., Collis, M. L., Thermal balance and survival time prediction of man in cold water. *Canadian Journal of Physiology and Pharmacology,* **53**(1):21–32 (1975).

71. Hayward, J. S., Steinman, A. M., Accidental hypothermia: An experimental study of inhalation rewarming. *Aviation, Space, and Environmental Medicine,* **46**:1236–1240 (Oct. 1975).

72. Hedley-Whyte, J., Burgess, G. E., III, Feeley, T. W., Miller, M. C., *Applied Physiology of Respiratory Care.* Boston: Little, Brown, 1976.

73. Hemingway, A., The effect of barbital anaesthesia on temperature regulation. *American Journal of Physiology,* **134**:350 (1941).

74. Hervey, G. R., Hypothermia. *Proceedings of the Royal Society of Medicine,* **66**:1053–1057 (Oct. 1973).

75. Hervey, G. R., Physiological changes encountered in hypothermia. *Proceedings of the Royal Society of Medicine,* **66**:1053–1057 (1973).

76. Hirvonen, J., Necropsy findings in fatal hypothermia cases. *Forensic Science,* **8**:155–164 (1976).

77. Holm, P. C. A., Vanggaard, L., Frostbite. *Plastic and Reconstructive Surgery,* **54**(5):544–551 (Nov. 1974).

78. Hudson, L. D., Conn, R. D., Accidental hypothermia. *Journal of the American Medical Association,* **227**(1):37–40 (Jan. 1974).

79. Hunter, W. C., Accidental hypothermia, Part I. *Northwest Medicine,* **67**(6):569–573 (June 1968).

80. Hunter, W. C., Accidental hypothermia, Part II. *Northwest Medicine,* **67**(8):735–739 (Aug. 1968).

81. Hunter, W. C., Accidental hypothermia, Part III. *Northwest Medicine,* 67(9):837–844 (Sept. 1968).

82. Iampietro, P. F., Vaughan, J. A., Goldman, R. F., Kreider, M. B., Masucci, F., Bass, D. E., Heat production from shivering. *Journal of Applied Physiology,* 15(4):632–634 (July 1960).

83. Ionescu, M. E., Wooler, G. H., *Current Techniques in Extracorporeal Circulation.* London: Butterworths, 1976.

84. Jacob, A. I., Lichstein, E., Ulano, S. D., Chadda, K. D., Gupta, P. K., Werner, B. M., A-V block in accidental hypothermia. *Journal of Electrocardiology,* 11(4):399–402 (1978).

85. Jarrett, F., Frostbite: Current concepts of pathogenesis and treatment. *Review of Surgery,* 31:71–74 (Mar.–Apr. 1974).

86. Jessen, K., Immersion and accidental hypothermia. *Acta Med. Port.,* 2:225–237 (1979).

87. Jessen, K., Hagelsten, J. O., Peritoneal dialysis in the treatment of profound accidental hypothermia. *Aviation, Space and Environmental Medicine,* 49:426–429 (Feb. 1978).

88. Kanter, G. S., Hypothermic hemoconcentration. *American Journal of Physiology,* 214(4):856–859 (Apr. 1969).

89. Katsas, A., Agnantid, J., Smyrnis, S., Kakavoulis, T., Carcinoma on old frostbite. *The American Journal of Surgery,* 133:377–378 (Mar. 1977).

90. Keatinge, W. R., *Survival in Cold Water.* Oxford: Blackwell Scientific Publications, 1969.

91. Keatinge, W. R., Accidental immersion hypothermia and drowning. *Symposium on Environmental Problems,* 219:183–187 (Aug. 1977).

92. Kelman, G. R., Nunn, J. F., Nomograms for correction of blood Po_2, pCO_2, pH, and base excess for time and temperature. *Journal of Applied Physiology,* 21:1484–1490 (1966).

93. Kettelkamp, D. B., Walker, M., Radioactive albumin, red blood cells, and sodium as indicators of tissue damage after frostbite. *Cryobiology,* 8:79–83 (1970).

94. Kettelkamp, D. B., Bertuch, C. J., Ramsey, P., Radioisotope (I^{131} RISA) evaluation of damage in frostbite. *Journal of Bone and Joint Surgery,* 51A(4):717–727 (June 1969).

95. Knize, D. M., Weatherley-White, R. C. A., Paton, B. C., Owens, J. C., Prognostic factors in the management of frostbite. *Journal of Trauma,* 9(9):749–759 (1969).

96. Knize, D. M., Weatherley-White, R. C. A., Paton, B. C., Use of antisludging agents in experimental cold injuries. *Surgery, Gynecology and Obstetrics,* 129:1019–1026 (Nov. 1969).

97. Kulka, J. P., Vasomotor microcirculatory insufficiency: Observations on nonfreezing cold injury of the mouse ear. *Antiology,* 12:491–506 (1961).

98. Kyosola, K., Clinical experiences in the management of cold injuries: A study of 110 cases. *Journal of Trauma,* 14(1):32–36 (1974).

99. Lash, R. F., Burdette, J. A., Ozdil, T., Accidental profound hypothermia and barbiturate intoxication, a report of rapid 'core' rewarming by peritoneal dialysis. *Journal of the American Medical Association,* 201:267–670 (1967).

100. Lathrop, T. G., *Hypothermia: Killer of the Unprepared,* 2nd ed. Portland, Oregon, Mazamas, 1975.

101. Laufman, H., Profound accidental hypothermia. *Journal of the American Medical Association,* 147(13):1201–1212 (Nov. 1951).

101a. Lazarus, H. M., Hutto, W., Electric burns and frostbite: Patterns of vascular injury. *Journal of Trauma,* 22(7):581–85 (1982.)

102. Ledingham, I. M., Mone, J. G., Treatment of accidental hypothermia: A prospective clinical study. *British Medical Journal,* 280:1102–1105 (Apr. 1980).

103. Ledingham, McA., Routh, G. S., Couglas, I. H. W., Macdonald, A. M., Central rewarming system for treatment of hypothermia. *Lancet,* 1:1168–1169 (May 1980).

104. LeRich, R. A., A propos des gelured et de leur traitment immediat par infiltration lombaire. *Presse Med.,* 48:75 (1940).

105. LeRoith, D., Vinik, A. T., Jackson, W. P. U., Recovery on rewarming after hypothermic hyperglycaemia. *South African Medical Journal,* 48:1616–1619 (1974).

106. Levinson, R., Epstein, M., Sackner, M. A., Begin, R., Comparison of the effects of water immersion and saline infusion on central haemodynamics in man. *Clinical Science and Molecular Medicine,* 52:343–350 (1977).

107. Levy, L., Severe hypophosphatemia as a complication of the treatment of hypothermia. *Archives of Internal medicine,* 140:128–129 (Jan. 1980).

108. Lewis, R. B., Moen, P. W., Further investigations on the use of heparin in the treatment of experimental frostbite. *Surgery, Gynecology and Obstetrics,* 97:59–66 (1953).

109. Lewis, R. B., Local and cold injury a critical review. *American Journal of Physiological Medicine,* 34:538–578 (1957).

110. Lewis, T., Observations on some normal and injurious effects of cold upon the skin and underlying tissue. III. Frostbite. *British Medical Journal.* 2:869–871 (1941).

111. Lindholm, A., Nilsson, O., Svartholm, F., Epiphyseal destruction following frostbite. *Archives of Environmental Health* (Washington), 17:681–684 (Oct. 1968).

112. Lloyd, E. L., Accidental hypothermia treated by central rewarming through the airway. *British Journal of Anaesthesia,* 45:41–47 (1973).

113. Lloyd, E. L., Conliffe, N. A., Orgel, H., Walker, P. N., Accidental hypothermia: An apparatus for central rewarming as a first aid measure. *Scottish Medical Journal,* 17:83–91 (1972).

114. Lloyd, E. L., Treatment after exposure to cold. *Lancet,* 2:1376 (1971).

115. Maclean, D., Browning, M. C. K., Cortisol utilization in accidental hypothermia. *Resuscitation,* 3(4):257–264 (1974).

116. Maclean, D., Emslie-Smith, D., *Accidental Hypothermia.* Oxford, Blackwell Scientific Publications, 1977.

117. Maclean, D., Emslie-Smith, D., The J loop of the spatial vectorcardiogram in accidental Hypothermia in man. *British Heart Journal,* 36:621–620 (1974).

118. Maclean, D., Goodall, H. B., Todd, A. S., Cryofibrinogenaemia and activation of coagulation/lysis systems in accidental hypothermia of the elderly. *Journal of Clinical Pathology,* 28:758 (1975).

119. Maclean, D., Griffiths, P. D., Browning, M. C. D., Murison, J., Metabolic aspects of spontaneous rewarming in accidental hypothermia and hypothermic myxoedema. *Quarterly Journal of Medicine,* New Series XLIII(171):371–387 (July 1974).

120. Maclean, D., Murison, J., Griffiths, P. D., Acute pancreatitis and diabetic ketoacidosis in hypothermia. *British Medical Journal,* 2:59 (1974).

121. Mahajan, S. L., Myers, T. J., Baldini, M. G., Disseminated intravascular coagulation during rewarming following hypothermia. *Journal of the American Medical Association,* 245(24):2517–2518 (June 1981).

122. Mahood, J. M., Evans, A., Accidental hypothermia, disseminated intravascular coagulation and pancreatitis. *New Zealand Medical Journal,* 87:283–284. (1978).

123. Mann, T. P., Elliott, R. I. K., Neonatal cold injury due to accidental exposure to cold. *Lancet,* 2:229–234 (1957).

124. Mant, A. K., Autopsy diagnosis of accidental hypothermia. *Journal of Forensic Medicine,* 16(4):126–129 (Oct.–Dec. 1969).

125. Marcus, P., The treatment of acute accidental hypothermia: Proceedings of a symposium held at the RAF Institute of Aviation Medicine. *Aviation, Space, and Environmental Medicine,* 50:834–843 (Aug. 1979).

126. Martin, S., Cooper, K. E., Alcohol and respiratory and body temperature changes during tepid water immersion. *Journal of Applied Physiology,* 44(5):683–689 (May 1978).

127. Martin, S., Cooper, K. E., The relationship of deep and surface skin temperatures to the ventilatory responses elicited during cold water immersion. *Canadian Journal of Physiology and Pharmacology,* 56(6):999–1004 (1978).

128. Martin, S., Diewold, R. J., Cooper, K. E., Alcohol, respiratory, skin and body temperature changes during cold water immersion. *Journal of Applied Physiology: Respiratory, Environmental, and Exercise Physiology,* 43:211–215 (1977).

129. Martin, S., Diewold, R. J., Cooper, K. E., The effect of clothing on the initial ventilatory responses during cold-water immersion. *Canadian Journal of Physiology and Pharmacology,* 56:886–888 (1978).

130. Martin, S. M., Bauce, L., Cooper, K. E., Continuous sampling of plasma catecholamines in man during cold water immersion and rewarming. *Federation Proceedings,* 40(3):580 (1981).

131. McIntyre, K. M., Parker, M. R. Standards and guidelines for cardiopulmonary resuscitation and emergency cardiac care. *Journal of the American Medical Association,* 224(5):453–509 (Aug. 1980).

132. McNicol, M. W., Smith, R., Accidental hypothermia. *British Medical Journal,* 1:19–21 (1964).

133. McNicol, M. W., Respiratory failure and acid-base status in hypothermia. *Postgraduate Medical Journal,* 43:674–676 (1967).

134. Merryman, H. T., Mechanism of freezing injury in clinical frostbite. *Proceedings of the Symposium on Arctic Medicine and Biology. IV. Frostbite.* Vierech, E., ed. Ft. Wainwright, Alaska: Arctic Aeromedical Laboratory, 1964, pp. 1–7.

135. Miller, B. J., Chasmar, L. R., Frostbite in Saskatoon: A review of 10 winters. *Canadian Journal of Surgery,* 23(5):423–426 (Sept. 1980).

136. Miller, D., Bjornson, D. R., An investigation of cold injured soldiers in Alaska. *Military Medicine,* 127:247–252 (Mar. 1962).

137. Miller, J. W., Danzl, D. F., Thomas, D. M., urban accidental hypothermia: 135 cases. *Annals of Emergency Medicine,* 9(9):456–461 (Sept. 1980).

138. Mills, W. J., Jr., Clinical aspects of frostbite injury, in *Proceedings of the Symposium on Arctic Medicine and Biology. IV. Frostbite.* Vierech, E., ed. Fort Wainwright, Alaska: Arctic Aeromedical Laboratory, 1964, pp. 149–196.

139. Mills, W. F., Jr., Summary of treatment of the cold-injured patient. *Alaska Medicine,* 15(2):56–57 (Mar. 1973).

140. Mills, W. J., Jr., Frostbite. *Alaska Medicine,* 15(2):27–47 (Mar. 1973).

141. Milner, J. E., Hypothermia (editorial). *Annals of Internal Medicine,* 89(4):565–567 (Oct. 1978).

142. Minor, T. M., Shumacker, H. B., An evaluation of tissue loss following single and repeated frostbite injuries. *Surgery,* 61(4):562–563 (Apr. 1967).

143. Molnar, G. W., Hughes, A. L., Wilson, O., Goldman, R. F., Effect of skin wetting on finger cooling and freezing. *Journal of Applied Physiology,* 35(2):205–207 (1973).

143a. Morris, D. L., Jande, M. A., Diagnosis of sepsis in the hypothermic patient. Abstract. *Journal of Clinical Research,* 30(2):519A (1982).

144. Moyer, J. H., Morris, G. C., de Bakey, M. E., Renal functional response to hypothermia and ischaemia in man and dog, in *The Physiology of Induced Hypothermia,* Dripps, R. D., ed. Washington, D.C., National Academy of Science, National Research Council, Publication Vol. 451, 1956, pp. 199–213.

145. Mundth, E. D., Long, D. M., Brown, R. B., Treatment of experimental frostbite with low molecular weight dextran. *Journal of Trauma,* 4:246–257 (1964).

146. Mundth, E. D., Studies on the pathogenesis of cold injuries. Microcirculatory changes in tissue injured by frostbite. *Proceedings of the Symposium on Arctic Medicine and Biology. IV. Frostbite,* Vierech, E., ed. Fort Wainwright, Alaska: Arctic Aeromedical Laboratory, 1964, pp. 51–59.

147. Murray, B. J., Severe lactic acidosis and hypothermia. *Western Journal of Medicine,* 134(2):162–165 (Feb. 1981).

148. Myers, A. M., Britten, J. S., Cowley, R. A., Hypothermia: Quantitative aspects of therapy. *Journal of the American College of Emergency Physicians,* 8(12):523–527 (Dec. 1979).

149. Nair, C. S., Singh, I., Malhotra, M. S., Mathew, L., Dasgupta, A., Purakayastha, S. S., Shanker, J., Studies on heat output from the hands of frostbite subjects. *Aviation, Space and Environmental Medicine,* 48(3):192–194 (1977).

150. Nair, C. S., Singh, I., Malhotra, M. S., Dasgupta,

A., Dass, S. L., Studies on cold pressor response of subjects who suffered from frostbite at high altitude. *International Journal of Biometeorology*, **21**(4):332–336 (1977).

151. Negovskii, V. A., Restoration of vital functions of the body after 2 hours of clinical death in conditions of deep hypothermia. *Vestnik Akademii Meditsinskikh Nauk SSSR (Moskva)* 15(10):40–44, 1960

152. Nelms, J. D., Soper, J. G., Cold vasodilatation and cold acclimatization in the hands of British fish filleters. *Journal of Applied Physiology*, **17**(3):444–448 (1962).

153. Newman, R. W., Cold acclimation in Negro Americans. *Journal of Applied Physiology*, **27**(3):316–319 (Sept. 1969).

154. Neilsen, K., Owman, C., Control of ventricular fibrillation during induced hypothermia in cats after blocking the adrenergic neurons with bretylium. *Life Sciences*, **7**:159–168 (1968).

155. Nugent, S. K., Rogers, M. C., Resuscitation and intensive care monitoring following immersion hypothermia. *Journal of Trauma*, **20**(9):814–815 (1980).

156. O'Keeffe, K. M., Non-cardiogenic pulmonary edema from accidental hypothermia: A case report. *Colorado Medicine*, **77**(3):106–107 (Mar. 1980).

157. Orr, K. D., Fainer, D. C., *Cold Injuries in Korea during winter of 1950–51.* Fort Knox, Ky.: Army Medical Research Laboratory, 1951.

158. Penn, I., Schwartz, S. L., Evaluation of low molecular weight dextran in the treatment of frostbite. *Journal of Trauma*, **4**:784–790 (1964).

159. Peyronnard, J. M., Pedneault, M., Aguayo, A. J., Neuropathies due to cold: Quantitative studies of structural changes in human and animal nerves. In *Neurology*, Den-Hartog-Jager, W. A., et al., eds. Amsterdam: Experpta Medica, 1978, pp. 308–329.

160. Phillipson, E. A., Herbert, F. A., Accidental exposure to freezing: Clinical and laboratory observations during convalescence from near-fatal hypothermia. *Canadian Medical Association Journal*, **97**:786–792 (Sept. 1967).

161. Porter, J. M., Reiney, C. G., Effect of low dose intra-arterial reserpine on vascular wall norepinephrine content. *Annals of Surgery*, **183**(1):50–55 (July 1975).

162. Post, P. W., Daniels, F., Jr., Binford, R. T., Jr., Cold injury and the evolution of "white" skin. *Human Biology*, **47**(1):65–80 (Feb. 1975).

163. Prescott, L. F., Peard, M. C., Wallace, I. R., Accidental hypothermia, a common condition. *British Medical Journal*, **2**:1367–1370 (Nov. 1962).

164. Rabb, J. M., Renaud, M. D., Brandt, P. A., Witt, C. W., Effect of freezing and thawing on the microcirculation and capillary endothelium of the hamster cheek pouch. *Cryobiology*, **11**:508–518 (1974).

165. Rakower, S. R., Shahgoli, S., Wong, S. L., Doppler ultrasound and digital plethysmography to determine the need for sympathetic blockade after frostbite. *Journal of Trauma*, **18**(10):713–718 (1978).

166. Reuler, J. B., Hypothermia: Pathophysiology, clinical settings, and management. *Annals of Internal Medicine*, **89**:519–527 (1978).

167. Reuler, J. B., Parker, R. A., Peritoneal dialysis in the management of hypothermia. *Journal of the American Medical Association*, **240**(21):2289–2290 (Nov. 1978).

168. Rotth, D. El., Vinik, A. I., Jackson, W. P. U., Recovery on rewarming after hypothermic hyperglycaemia. *South African Medical Journal*, **48**:1617–1619 (1974).

169. Romanova, N. P., Dynamics of histopathologic changes in brain in experimental hypoxia. *Zhurnal Nevropatologii i Psikhiatrii*, **56**(1):49–55 (1956).

170. Rosenfeld, J. B., Acid-base and electrolyte disturbances in hypothermia. *American Journal of Cardiology*, **12**:678–682 (1963).

171. Rosenthal, T. B., The effect of temperature on the pH of blood and plasma in vitro. *Journal of Biological Chemistry*, **173**:25–30 (1948).

172. Ross, D. N., Problems associated with the use of hypothermia in cardiac surgery. *Proceedings of the Royal Society of Medicine*, **50**:76–78 (1957).

173. Rowell, L. R., The cutaneous circulation. In *Circulation, Respiration, and Fluid Balance.* In *Physiology and Biophysics*, Vol. 2, 20th ed., Ruch, T. C., Patton, H. D., eds. Philadelphia, Saunders, 1973.

174. *Report of the Committee on Accidental Hypothermia.* London: Royal College of Physicians of London, 1966.

175. Ruiz, A. V., Carbon dioxide response curves during hypothermia. *Pfluegers Archiv. European Journal of Physiology* (Berlin), **358**:125–133 (1975).

176. Segar, W. E. Effect of hypothermia on tubular transport mechanisms. *American Journal of Physiology*, **195**:91–96 (1958).

177. Sekar, T. S., MacDonnell, K. F., Mansirikal, P., Herman, R. S., Survival after prolonged submersion in cold water without neurologic sequelae. *Archives of Internal Medicine*, **140**:775–779 (June 1980).

178. Selke, A. C., Destruction of phalangeal epiphyses by frostbite. *Radiology*, **93**:859–860 (Oct. 1969).

179. Shanks, C. A., Heat gain in the treatment of accidental hypothermia. *Medical Journal of Australia*, **2**:346–349 (1975).

180. Shumacker, H. B., Jr., Lempke, R. E., Recent advances in surgery. *Surgery*, **30**(5):873–904 (1951).

181. Shumacker, H. B., Jr., Kilman, J. W., Sympathectomy in the treatment of frostbite. *Archives of Surgery*, **89**:575–584 (Sept. 1964).

182. Siebke, H., Breivic, H., Rod, T., Lind, B., Survival after 40 minutes[1] submersion without cerebral sequelae, *Lancet*, **1**:1275–1277 (June 1975).

183. Singer, A., Low-molecular-weight dextran in the treatment of peripheral arterial insufficiency. *Lancet*, **2**:1050–1052 (Nov. 1965).

184. Smith, A. U., *Current Trends in Cryobiology.* New York: Plenum Press, 1970.

185. Smith, S. P., Walker, W. F., Arteriography in cold injuries. *British Journal of Radiology*, **37**:471–474 (June 1964).

186. Snider, R. W., Porter, J. M., Treatment of experimental frostbite with intra-arterial sympathetic blocking drugs. *Surgery*, **77**(4):557–561 (April 1975).

187. Southwick, F. S., Dalglish, P. H., Recovery after prolonged asystolic cardiac arrest in profound hy-

pothermia. *Journal of the American Medical Association,* **243**(12):1250–1253 (Mar. 1980).

188. Spencer, F. G., Bahnson, H. T., The present role of hypothermia in cardiac surgery. *Circulation,* **26**:292–300 (1962).

189. Stine, R., Accidental hypothermia. *Journal of the American College of Emergency Physicians,* **6**(9):413–416 (Sept. 1977).

190. Sullivan, B. J., LeBlanc, M. F., Effect of inositol and rapid rewarming on extent of tissue damage due to cold injury. *American Journal of Physiology,* **189**(3):501–503 (1957).

191. Sullivan, B. J., Towle, L. B., Vascular responses to local cold injury. *American Journal of Physiology,* **189**(3):498–500 (1957).

192. Sumner, D. S., Boswick, J. A., Criblez, T. L., Doolittle, W. H., Prediction of tissue loss in human frostbite. *Surgery,* **69**(6):899–903 (June 1971).

193. Sumner, D. S., Criblez, T. L., Doolittle, W. H., Host factors in human frostbite. *Military Medicine,* **139**:454–461 (June 1974).

194. Suri, M. L., Vijayan, G. P., Puri, H. C., Barat, A. K., Singh, N., Neurological manifestations of frost-bite. *Indian Journal of Medical Research,* **67**:292–299 (Feb. 1978).

195. Tafari, N., Gentz, J., Aspects on rewarming newborn infants with severe accidental hypothermia. *Acta Paediatrica Scandinavica,* **63**:595–600 (1974).

196. Talwar, J. R., Gulati, S. M., Non-steroidal anti-inflammatory agents in the management of cold injury. *Journal of Medical Research,* **60**(11):1643–1650 (1972).

197. Talwar, J. R., Gulati, S. M., Kapur, B. M. L., Comparative effects of rapid thawing, low molecular dextran and sympathectomy in cold injury in the monkeys. *Indian Journal of Medical Research,* **2**:242–250 (Feb. 1971).

198. Taylor, G. F., Old people in the cold. *British Medical Journal,* **1**:428 (1964).

199. Thews, G., Monograms for the consideration of body temperature in blood gas and pH-measurements. *Anaesthetist,* **21**:466–472 (1972).

200. Towne, W. D., Geiss, W. P., Yanes, H. O., Rahimtoola, S. H., Intractable ventricular fibrillation associated with profound accidental hypothermia—successful treatment with partial cardiopulmonary bypass. *Medical Intelligence,* **287**(22):1135–1136 (Nov. 1972).

201. Trevino, A., Razi, B., Beller, B. M., The characteristic electrocardiogram of accidental hypothermia. *Archives of Internal medicine,* **127**:470–473 (Mar. 1971).

202. Truscott, D. G., Firor, W. B., Clein, I. J., Accidental profound hypothermia. *Archives of Surgery,* **106**:216–218 (1973).

203. U.S. Army Research Institute of Environmental Medicine, *Resuscitation of Accidental Hypothermia Victims,* Report No. T 42/76. Natick, Mass., United States Army Medical Research and Development Command, 1976.

204. Varma, R. N., Boparai, M. S., Cold injury as an occupational hazard in the armed forces. *Indian Journal of Medical Research,* **62**(10):1478–1485 (Oct. 1974).

205. Vaughn, P. B., Local cold injury—menace to military operations: A review. *Military Medicine,* **145**(5):305–311 (May 1980).

206. Weatherly-White, R. C. A., Knize, D. M., Geisterfer, D. J., Paton, B. C., Experimental studies in cold injury. V. Circulatory hemodynamics. *Surgery,* **66**(1):208–214 (July 1969).

207. Wedin, B., Vanggaard, L., Hirven, J., "Paradoxical undressing" in fatal hypothermia. *Journal of Forensic Sciences,* **24**(3):543–553 (1979).

208. Welton, D. E., Mattox, K. L., Miller, R. R., Petmecky, F. F., Treatment of profound hypothermia. *Journal of the American Medical Association* **240C**(21):2291–2292 (Nov. 1978).

209. Weyman, A. E., Greenbaum, D. M., Grace, W. J., Accidental hypothermia in an alcoholic population. *American Journal of Medicine,* **56**:13–21 (Jan. 1974).

210. Wickstrom, P., Ruiz, E., Lilja, G. P., Hinterkopf, J. P., Haglin, J. J., Accidental hypothermia. *American Journal of Surgery,* **131**(5):622–625 (May 1976).

211. Wilson, J. A., Wilson, A. N., Cold injury: Report of an unusual case. *Alaska Medicine,* **10**:172–174 (Dec. 1968).

212. Wilson, O., Goldman, R. F., Role of air temperature and wind in the time necessary for a finger to freeze. *Journal of Applied Physiology,* **29**(5):658–664 (1970).

213. Wilson, R. A., Chapman, B. J., Munday, K. A., The effects of hypothermia (25°C) on the circulatory system of the rat. *Comparative Biochemistry Physiology* **54A**:135–139.

214. Witherspoon, J. M., Goldman, R. F., Breckenridge, J. R., Heat transfer coefficients of humans in cold water. *Journal de Physiologie, extrait due Tome* **63**(3):459–462 (1971).

215. Yates, D. W., Little, R. A., Accidental hypothermia. *Resuscitation,* **7**:59–67 (1979).

216. Zhong, H., Qinyi, S., Mingjiang, S., Rewarming with microwave irradiation in severe cold injury syndrome. *Chinese Medical Journal,* **93**(2):119–120 (1980).

HEAT ILLNESS: CURRENT PERSPECTIVES

Charles McElroy, M.D.
Paul S. Auerbach, M.D.

Human core temperature is closely regulated by a host of servoregulatory mechanisms programmed to maintain it at 37°C. Processes, either endogenous or exogenous, which alter this homeostasis beyond a surprisingly narrow range, result in demonstrable pathologic changes in cellular and molecular structure and a cessation of effective thermoregulation. Core temperature, unprotected, rapidly exceeds the "critical thermal maximum" for humans, and irreversible organ system damage results. Without immediate and effective intervention, death quickly follows.

Recognition of heat illness is extremely important, not only for health care personnel but also for the general public (4). Heat stress is often a part of daily life for individuals, and is becoming more important as great numbers of individuals participate in active physical endeavors or live to an advanced age at which defective thermoregulatory systems are

common. Fortunately, data acquired in occupational and military settings have made it possible to understand, recognize, and frequently prevent heat illness. This chapter will detail our current understanding of heat-related disorders as a pathophysiologic state distinct from febrile illness.

Heat illness is understandable and predictable if a few physical principles are recognized. Humans are, among other things, biochemical systems. As such, the reactions upon which life is dependent are possible only when appropriate substrate is present under conditions of compatible temperature. Because of the relatively low temperature under which human biochemistry occurs, most such reactions are facilitated by enzyme systems which act as catalysts. These chemical reactions consume substrate, generate usable energy, and produce by-products which must be eliminated for continued operation of the system. Water and carbon dioxide are produced and eliminated in large quantities, as are urea, sulfates, phosphates, and a variety of other chemical moieties. Excess electrons are handled by the electron transport system, and complex proteins are either broken down and reutilized, excreted, or deposited in "graveyards" which line the vascular beds of elderly humans.

Since all of the reactions outlined above are exothermic in nature, the obligate removal of heat from the microenvironment is a necessary concomitant of continued biochemical success. Indeed, since every beat of the heart or blink of the eye is accompanied by heat production, efficient thermoregulatory systems are critical in human ecology. Failure of any of these systems results in the excessive loss or retention of heat, rendering orderly biochemical activity impossible. Excess exogenous heat is similarly capable of upsetting this delicate energy balance.

The "biochemical pot" in which these reactions occur is also a major factor in establishing limits for the chemicals which can be utilized and the by-products which are tolerable. The cellular architecture of known life forms is remarkably consistent, reflecting evolutionary constraints. Despite its proven utility and undeniable success, limits are apparent in the physical nature of the dynamic structure which is the human cytoarchitecture. Enzymes necessary for the low-temperature biochemical reactions, the protein-lipid cell walls, the DNA "brain," the RNA communication systems, and the proteinacious contractile components conferring shape and motion are all constructed with chemical and thermal design limits. These limits are a reflection of the environmental conditions which have been present throughout evolution and which must be maintained, at least internally, for life's continued success. Thermal stresses which result in excess heat generation or which preclude adequate transfer of heat from the microenvironment into the macroenvironment result in structural damage to the cytoarchitecture.

While the absolute temperature at which these processes occur varies slightly from person to person, and while systems failure is far more likely in the aged, infirm, or ill, few if any individuals can sustain a core temperature of 43°C or greater for any significant period of time without suffering irreversible and usually catastrophic damage.

Endocrine and thermal signals from both the core and peripheral portions of the body are carried via neuronal and circulatory pathways. Peripheral and core temperatures originate in skin, viscera, and nervous tissues. Convergence of these signals in the anterior hypothalamus results in changes in bioamine concentrations, which have been measured in experimental animals. Final common pathway effectors probably include prostaglandins, central nervous system amines, dopamine and its derivatives, various cholinergic agents, and a host of other hypothesized candidates. Aberrations of calcium and sodium balance can also result in ineffective activity of the thermoregulatory control center.

While the chemical nature of thermoregulatory control is still poorly understood, the effector arm of the system has been intensively investigated. The organ systems responsible for the majority of heat loss in humans include the skin, cardiovascular system, and respiratory apparatus. (When skin vessels dilate, blood flow shunted through the area can exceed 4 liters/minute.) Relatively insignificant amounts of heat are lost in the feces and urine. Each component contributes to the total body economy. The cardiovascular system is responsible for conducting heat to the surface of the body, where it can be lost to the environment. This is the major contributor to pathologic states resulting from ineffective heat loss.

Groups who contribute most to the mortality statistics, including the very young and the very old, die in significantly larger numbers during extremes of environmental conditions. During heat waves, death from myocardial infarction, stroke, pneumonia, and renal failure climbs sharply. While these final events are listed on the death certificate, heat stress is frequently the mediator. While such deaths are not the direct result of heat damage, heat nonetheless is the overload which results in the failure of organ systems to meet the demands necessary for survival. Thus, any estimate of the annual contribution of heat to morbidity and mortality is a dramatic underrepresentation of this vector of human disorder.

Disorders affecting the cutaneous structures of the body can also contribute measurably to morbidity and mortality. Because of the rarity of the disorders, they do not contribute in large measure to the overall morbidity and mortality statistics.

Fever versus Hyperthermia

Elevations of body temperature can occur as a result of several different mechanisms. One very important subset of hyperthermia is *fever*. Since the physiology of fever differs from that of other identifiable causes of temperature elevation, it is both diagnostically and therapeutically important to understand fever and to identify those suffering from a febrile as opposed to a hyperthermic state.

Fever is generally caused by pyrogens released by bacteria or viruses, or from cells undergoing autolysis after having participated in phagocytic activity (31,44). These pyrogens reach the region of the thermoregulatory control center in the preoptic area of the anterior hypothalamus through the circulatory system and act there to reset the *thermal set point* at a new level above 37°C, the "normal setting." Considerable evidence suggests that pyrogens act by inducing synthesis of prostaglandins in the region of the thermoregulatory center. These prostaglandins attach to cell surface receptor sites, producing an elevation in the thermal set point (5,31,40,44).

Under most circumstances, the temperature elevation itself is not a significant problem and therapy is directed at the underlying disease state. There is good evidence to suggest that such temperature elevations have not been demonstrated to cause pathologic or physiologic damage to the organism and do not require primary emphasis in the therapeutic regimen designed to manage the patient (44). However, if temperature-related physiologic changes, such as tachycardia in a patient with marginal cardiac reserve, compromise the individual, the temperature must be artificially regulated.

The temperature that the thermoregulatory center is protecting is elevated from that which is normal. Once that temperature is established, the thermoregulatory center utilizes all available heat regulatory servomechanisms to maintain the new temperature. The set point established, as previously mentioned, appears

to be a function of molecular interaction between receptors in the hypothalamic region and effectors generated by the invading organisms.

This definition of fever as a subset of hyperthermia has extremely important physiologic and clinical implications. Because fever is the product of a molecular interaction which establishes a new physiologic thermal set point, therapeutic ministrations which utilize external artificial means to lower temperature are opposed by body mechanisms which attempt to maintain the new set point. Therapy which utilizes agents to block the molecular interaction that establishes a new set point represents the most rational approach and is clinically effective. Aspirin is the time-honored means of combating fever. This agent works in a remarkable fashion, apparently by blocking the action of the pyrogen at hypothalamic receptor sites, either directly or indirectly (44). Whether the action of aspirin is effected by blocking the receptor site directly or indirectly through its action on prostaglandin synthetase activity, the important conclusion, which corroborates clinical and empirical observations, is that aspirin works well to control fever but *does not work and should not be used* to control hyperthermia (7,18,30,40,44). It thus becomes important therapeutically, as well as diagnostically, to discriminate between a febrile state and a hyperthermic state.

A second important category of elevation of body temperature is hyperthermia due to inadequate means of heat dissipation. While a variety of specific pathophysiologic subsets exists in this category, the underlying physiology involves one of two basic causes. When an imbalance between heat loss and heat production exists for any significant period of time, the body temperature will, of necessity, change. Here, the thermal set point remains normal, but the servoregulatory mechanisms designed to defend the set point are incapable of meeting heat dissipation demands. This circumstance arises when (1) environmental conditions overwhelm normal thermoregulatory mechanisms, or (2) thermoregulatory mechanisms are defective. Under extreme circumstances, environmental conditions can overwhelm a perfectly normal individual. More commonly, normal individuals exercise excessively in nonextreme ambient environmental conditions. Joggers' heat stroke and the heat illness encountered during football training exercise are two commonly encountered conditions (1,3,7,18,30,40).

Since peripheral blood flow and sweating are the two primary means of heat dissipation, anything which alters these activities will contribute to the inability of the body to meet heat production demands. Cardiovascular disease, fluid and electrolyte imbalance, dehydration, illnesses affecting sweat production, and a variety of other pathologic states may contribute to an inability to balance heat production with heat dissipation. This mechanism, defective thermoregulation, is commonly encountered in elderly, ill, or debilitated individuals (7,11,13,38,40,46). Therapy designed to reset the thermal set point will have no effect on body temperature in this category of patients, while interventions designed to increase the net loss of heat from the body will succeed (5,7,30,31,40,44).

Syndromes of Hyperthermia

PATHOLOGIC AND PHARMACOLOGIC HYPERTHERMIA

1. Hypothalamic lesions have been reported to causes changes in basal temperature by damaging the control center which establishes the thermal set point for normal body function. Cerbrovascular accidents (e.g., subarachnoid hemorrhage), surgical lesions (in the hypothalamic region), tumor invasion, and a variety of other pathologic conditions may on rare occasions cause damage to the preoptic region of the anterior hypothalamus and, hence, either alter the thermal set point or establish a situation in which no thermal set point mechanism is operant. Such lesions are serious and life-threatening (44).

2. Hyperthermia due to metabolic disorders, such as thyrotoxicosis, diabetic ketoacidosis, and pheochromocytoma, is well described in the literature.

3. *Malignant hyperthermia* is an unusual condition which represents a surprisingly appropriate topic for emergency physicians, who may encounter such a patient in the course of routine emergency activities. Specifically, the utilization of succinylcholine, atropine, and haloperidol is commonplace in emergency departments; these substances are most com-

TABLE 1
Drugs associated with Malignant Hyperthermia

Succinylcholine (77% of all cases)
Halothane (60% of all cases)
Anticholinergics
Atropine
Belladonna alkaloids
Mepivacaine (Carbocaine)
Cyclopropane
Dibenzazepines
Digitalis glycosides
d-Tubocurarine
Enflurane
Ether
Ethyl chloride
Ethylene
Galamine
Isoflurane
Lidocaine
Methoxyflurane
N_2O-meperidine
Phenothiazines
Trichloroethylene

monly mentioned as causal agents (10,25,42) (Table 1).

Malignant hyperthermia is characterized by a rapid rise in body temperature, with muscle rigidity, tachycardia, tachypnea, cyanosis, and severe respiratory and metabolic acidosis. Many of the victims of this disease state, if tested in intercritical periods, are noted to have an elevated resting creatine phosphokinase (CPK) muscle enzyme level. While only one-half of all individuals reported to have suffered this catastrophic disease state can be identified by an elevated resting CPK level, the condition appears to have a genetic basis. The current pathophysiologic hypothesis envisions a defect in muscle membranes which results in aberrant calcium physiology, the uncoupling of oxidative phosphorylation (similar to that seen with aspirin overdose), and a dissociation of the respiratory chain from adenosine triphosphate (ATP) production. The last is corroborated by measurements of low ATP activity in muscle cell membranes and other tissues, such as red blood cells and platelets. As a final part of the pathophysiologic process, there is an uptake of calcium into the mitochondria which causes uncoupling of mitochondrial oxidative phosphorylation and production of heat by the entropy of the contraction (10). ATPase activated by calcium released from skeletal muscle sarcoplasmic reticulum generates ADP, phosphate, and heat. ATP depletion follows, due to both decreased production and increased utilization. This depletion, coupled with the high calcium level in the sarcolemma, leads to membrane instability with leaks of intracellular substances across the sarcolemma, with resultant increases in blood levels of potassium, myoglobin, and CPK. Because of sustained muscle contraction and resultant heat generation, total body temperature rises at a rate in excess of that which can be handled by heat loss mechanisms. Thus, a potentially lethal state is created.

The clinical features of full-blown malignant hyperthermia include a rapid increase of body core temperature, muscle rigidity, tachycardia, bradycardia, arrhythmias, and pulmonary edema. As respiratory embarrassment progresses, cyanosis, tachypnea, and reduced pulmonary compliance supervene. Sweating is observed, and the skin becomes hot and flushed with occasional mottled cyanosis. Coma, mydriasis, and loss of deep tendon reflexes are common, and may progress to convulsions and signs of decerebration complicated by cerebral edema. The condition is characterized by laboratory changes including metabolic acidosis, hypercarbia and hypoxemia, and an increased A-a O_2 gradient with central venous oxygen desaturation. There is consistent hyperkalemia, hypocalcemia, hyperphosphatemia, and elevated lactate and pyruvate levels. Frequently, hyperglycemia is observed, with high serum catecholamine, myoglobin, and CPK levels. There are accompanying elevations of lactic acid dehydrogenase (LDH), serum glutamic oxaloacetic transaminase (SGOT), and aldolase. Occasionally, disseminated intravascular coagulation occurs (10,25,42).

Therapy is directed at early diagnosis and elimination of the agents which have precipitated the condition. If the precipitating agent is stopped promptly upon recognition of the condition, it is unlikely that the patient will suffer the full-blown clinical syndrome (10). Once the syndrome is established, discontinuation of surgery and anesthesia, where appropriate, is imperative. The patient should be hyperventilated with 100% oxygen and the metabolic and respiratory acidoses rapidly corrected. Immediate institution of active and aggressive central cooling techniques must be employed while measures to control hyperkalemia are instituted. Procainamide has been reported to be effective in controlling muscle rigidity and in helping to lower the body temperature (10). The mechanism of action is believed to be mediated by the effect of procainamide on intracellular myoplasmic calcium. As postulated, procainamide accelerates active uptake of calcium into the sarcoplasmic reticulum and blocks calcium release from these same structures. Dantrolene sodium also appears to work in this condition, putatively by inhibition of sarcoplasmic calcium release, with amelioration of excessive heat-generating muscle contraction (25). Used in doses of 1–10 mg/kg slow IV, it is still considered experimental by some clinicians. (Dantrolene has been used to manage heat stroke in at least one instance.) The use of calcium channel antagonists for the management of malignant hyperthermia has not been investigated.

In summary, this unusual condition, with its high morbidity, must be recognized early. The identification of susceptible individuals with baseline CPK levels has not met with widespread enthusiasm, as many patients with this condition do not have elevated levels of CPK. Often, an elevated resting level may be attributed to exercise, alcohol indiscretion, or a variety of other minor problems which do not relate to a predisposition to malignant hyperthermia (42).

4. A variety of drugs has now been reported to cause syndromes accompanied by hyperthermia, which may dominate the patient's clinical course and be the actual cause of death (Table 2). The interaction of monoamine oxidase inhibitors with amphetamines, tricyclic antidepressants, or phenothiazines as a cause of this syndrome is well reported. By ingesting mixtures of routine dosages of these drugs, susceptible patients may develop hyperkinesis and agitation, which gradually result in an elevation of body temperature, probably on the basis of hypothalamic failure, which progresses to malignant temperatures as high as 42.7–43.3°C. Coma, opisthotonic convulsions, and death may follow. The condition is believed to be mediated by accumulation of serotonin or other biogenic amines at critical sites

TABLE 2
Drugs Reported to Cause Fatal Hyperthermia

	Ref. No.[a]
Lithium	16
Haloperidol	17
Chlorpromazine plus benztropine mesylate	14
Lysergic acid diethylamide	21
Phenelzine plus imipramine	43,8
Atropine	37
Tranylcypromine plus dextroamphetamine	26

[a] Complete reference citations are located at the end of this chapter.

in the central nervous system, such as the thermoregulatory centers and the reticular activating system, leading to both increased heat production and failure of thermal regulation. While some individuals develop the syndrome during normal environmental conditions, it also appears that all of these drugs can establish increased sensitivity to environmental stress which would be ordinarily tolerated. Therapy is aimed at identifying the offending agent and instituting active cooling measures. When anticholinergics are the offending agents, physostigmine has been reported to be effective as part of the therapeutic regimen (37).

Other drugs that are associated with hyperthermia include those that induce hypersensitivity or idiosyncratic reactions (e.g., antibiotics, anticonvulsants, antihypertensives), and those that induce direct pyrogenic stimulation (e.g., bleomycin).

Heat Illness

Heat illness ranges from minor aberrations in physiology attended by minimal clinical symptoms to full-blown heat stroke accompanied by major clinical manifestations and occasional death. We will focus upon individual syndromes which possess widely accepted clinical and pathologic substrates, and for which there is an evolving consensus on appropriate management.

Heat Edema

Swelling of the feet and ankles is often reported by nonacclimatized individuals, espe-

cially the aged, who encounter the climatic stress of tropical and semitropical areas. Many such individuals have no underlying cardiac, hepatic, venous, or lymphatic disease to explain this abnormality. They frequently have assumed rigorous schedules with long periods of sitting or standing. The edema is usually minimal, is not accompanied by any significant impairment in function, and often resolves after several days of acclimatization. Since this entity is of inconsequential clinical import, detailed assessment of its pathophysiology is lacking. It is presumed that vasodilatation of the cutaneous and muscular vessels, combined with venostasis, leads to vascular leak and accumulation of interstitial fluid in the lower extremities. Simultaneously, there may be an increase in aldosterone in response to perceived central volume deficit. The most important reason for being aware of this clinical presentation is to prevent overly vigorous diagnostic and therapeutic intervention in patients with this problem. Brief diagnostic evaluation to rule out thrombophlebitis, lymphedema, or congestive heart failure is appropriate, but invasive diagnostic techniques or vigorous pharmacologic therapy are clearly not indicated. There is no evidence that diuretic therapy is appropriate; rather, simple elevation of the legs or support hose should be employed. In the majority of individuals, benign neglect is the order of the day, as the problem will resolve either through adequate acclimatization or with the individual's return to his place of origin.

Heat Syncope

Syncope is a perplexing disorder, because a host of serious and an even larger number of nonserious underlying mechanisms can result in temporary cessation of consciousness. Heat syncope can occur in any individual, but the elderly seem to have a special predilection for this disorder. Individuals adapt to a hot, humid environment by dilating cutaneous and muscular vessels to deliver heat to the surface of the body. Thus, an increased portion of the intravascular pool is located at the periphery at any given time. Individuals who stand for protracted periods of time tend to pool blood in the lower extremities. Combined with volume loss and peripheral vasodilatation, this may result in inadequate central venous return, a concomitant drop in cardiac output, and cerebral perfusion inadequate to maintain consciousness. The disorder is self-limited, since assumption of a horizontal position is the cure. Unfortunately, individuals may injure themselves in a fall. Skull, cervical spine, and hip injuries must be expected in such individuals.

Individuals at risk for heat syncope should be warned to move about, to flex their leg muscles repeatedly whenever standing, to avoid protracted standing in hot environments, and to assume a sitting or horizontal position whenever prodromal warning signs or symptoms occur. Scintillating scotomata, tunnel vision, vertigo, nausea, diaphoresis, and weakness are prodromal symptoms of syncope. Adequate education will prevent many serious injuries. While adequate oral volume replacement may prevent some cases, prophylactic positioning under these conditions is the most important therapeutic measure. Support hose may be of use to prevent peripheral venous pooling.

Heat Exhaustion and Heat Stroke

When the body temperature begins to rise above normal, a continuum of pathologic states results. At one end lies heat exhaustion, a mild to moderate aberration of thermoregulation that results in reproducible symptoms but no lasting pathology. At the other end lies heat stroke, a condition associated with body temperatures of 43°C or greater, accompanied by serious morbidity and occasional mortality. We will discuss human physiology under conditions of extreme stress, the pathophysiologic conditions which predispose to heat exhaustion and heat stroke, the climatic and regional settings, and the individuals at greatest risk.

Heat exhaustion is defined as a derangement of body function encountered when the body temperature is elevated, usually in the 39–41°C range. It is of note that in some persons, body temperature will rise to 38–38.5°C during normal exercise. The syndrome is characterized by minor aberrations in mental status, dizziness, nausea, headache, and temperature elevation. While water deficiency is believed to contribute significantly in some patients, it is clearly not necessary for the development of the syndrome. A clear understanding of heat exhaustion logically evolves from an understanding of heat stroke. The former results from the same conditions and pathophysiologic states that contribute to heat stroke but stops short of significant pathology.

Etiology and Predisposing Factors

Climate

The two major determinants of the impact of heat upon the body are the absolute temperature and the humidity of the atmosphere. A hot, dry climate produces much less stress than a hot, humid one. As the humidity rises, the ability of the body to dissipate heat and moisture into the surrounding environment through radiation and sweating is reduced. Under extremely humid conditions, sweating may cease altogether. At some point, the environment not only ceases to be a reservoir for dissipation but becomes an external source of heat which is added to the body.

The necessity to predict morbidity is encountered in a variety of settings. Armies, explorers, and occupational groups are regularly exposed to dramatic thermal stress and need a way to predict and prevent heat-related disorders. Data from the military show that calculation, memorization, and judgment are all adversely affected by heat stress before the physiologic mechanism shows signs of inadequacy.

The wet bulb globe temperature (WBGT) is the world standard for assessing the probable effect of a hot environment on any given individual. This index takes into consideration the temperature, air movement, and humidity (Table 3). Alternatively, a sling psychrometer, utilizing dry and wet bulb thermometers, may be employed. Dry-air temperature alone, as measured by a regular thermometer, is extremely inaccurate in predicting the potential for heat illness. Oral, axillary, and other surface measures of body temperature are dangerously inaccurate. Devices which can be affixed to the head or worn inside clothing and thermistor probes placed inside the ear canal near the tympanic membrane, in the rectum, or in the distal third of the esophagus are more accurate.

TABLE 3
Wet Bulb Globe Temperature (WBGT) and Recommended Activity Levels

WBGT °C	WBGT °F	Activity
15.6	60	No precautions
19–21	66–70	No precautions as long as water, salt, and food are easily available
22–24	71–75	Lighter practice and work with rest breaks
24	76	Postpone sports practice, avoid hiking
27	80	No hiking or sports
28	82	Only necessary heavy exertion; use caution
30	85	Cancel all exertion for unacclimatized persons; avoid sun exposure at rest
31.5	88	Limited activity for acclimatized, fit personnel only

WBGT index: 70% of the naturally convected wet bulb temperature plus 20% of the black-globe (radiant) temperature plus 10% of the dry bulb temperature (6).
Source: Courtesy of M. Callaham.

Exercise and Acclimatization

Extremes of exercise in inappropriate climatic conditions are risk factors even in normal individuals (5,6,8,9,12,13).

Even well-conditioned athletes may develop untoward consequences of heat retention when proper acclimatization has not been established before beginning vigorous physical activity (3,7,30). Football training programs are notorious for contributing an unreasonable share of heat stroke deaths to annual morbidity and mortality statistics (7,30). In fact, heat illness is second only to head injuries as a cause of death in American football (7,30). The ignorance which still surrounds organized exercise activities, predominantly team sports and endurance events, leads to the development of heat-associated illness. Coaches who labor under the misconception that water should not be provided during exercise, that young individuals can tolerate great excesses of physical exertion without negative effects, and that it is acceptable to utilize occlusive clothing all contribute to this unfortunate circumstance (7,30). With proper acclimatization, conditioning, rational clothing, proper fluid replacement, and education of supervisors and players, the majority of these problems could easily be avoided.

Activities commonly employed in the armed services training program ("boot camp"), in which large numbers of unacclimatized and unconditioned individuals are pushed rapidly beyond their tolerance or physical capability, contribute to the understanding of heat illness (2). The contemporary enthusiasm for jogging has produced another situation which generates large numbers of heat illness victims (3). Trained marathon runners may sport rectal temperatures of 40°C and muscle temperatures of 41°C. Any unacclimatized, unconditioned individual who suddenly undertakes excessive physical activity is especially at risk for heat stroke.

Daily exposure to work and heat causes acclimatization within 10 days. This is best characterized by the early onset of sweating, sweating at lower temperatures, an increase in sweat volume and a lowering of the electrolyte concentration in the sweat. Under ordinary circumstances, an untrained person may lose up to 1 liter of sweat per hour. As acclimatization proceeds, the sweat chloride concentration drops from approximately 40–45 mEq/liter to as low as 15–20 mEq/liter, while the volume increases to as much as 3 liters/hour. This dramatic volume loss must be replaced in order to prevent intravascular volume depletion.

The cardiovascular system plays an important role in acclimatization (41). Peripheral vasodilatation occurs earlier and in greater magnitude in trained individuals. Heart rate is lower and associated with a higher stroke volume; an increase in cardiac output may occur. Aerobic metabolism is enhanced as glycogen storage and utilization are improved. Other physiologic changes include the earlier release of aldosterone from the adrenal cortex, with an increase in distal tubular resorption of sodium and water. Concomitantly, there is a potassium depletion of up to 20% (500 mEq) by the third to fourth week of acclimatization. This has been reputed to contribute to a form of anhidrotic heat exhaustion, which is believed by some to respond to potassium repletion.

To maintain heat acclimatization, individuals must initiate moderate work for 10 days, followed by a continuation of the regimen for at least 1 day/week. Interestingly enough, after the initial acclimatization has been successfully completed, further work need not take place constantly in a hot environment.

The duration of physical exercise should be adjusted on the basis of conditioning and climate. It is a common misconception that fluid ingestion before or during physical exercise results in stomach cramps. To the contrary, water must be provided and occlusive clothing must not be utilized. The death toll in organized football has been reduced dramatically in the last few years by the widespread utilization of fishnet-type clothing, restriction of practice to tolerable environmental conditions, progressive acclimatization and conditioning prior to extreme exercise, and the repletion of adequate amounts of fluid and electrolytes.

Age

Both infants and the elderly are at greatest risk (46). Since heat illness in children is especially difficult to recognize, the circumstances contributing to its development must be understood. The relatively small surface area of the child's body is conducive to the early development of heat illness, especially when heat loss is prevented by placing the child in an extremely hot environment or wrapping in occlusive clothing, particularly when the child is febrile. Mild diarrhea, failure to feed, irritability, hypotonia or hypertonia, and a progressive elevation of body temperature are signs of hyperthermia in infants and young children.

The aged are at great risk for developing heat illness under conditions which are ordinarily safe (46). Underlying heart failure, minor neurologic aberrations, the utilization of multiple drugs, and general frailty all contribute to the propensity for older individuals to suffer from heat stroke (40).

Heart Failure

Individuals suffering from active or latent myocardial dysfunction may be unable to adapt to changes in environmental or physical stress, and are clearly at increased risk for developing heat stroke (40).

Obesity

Whether obesity per se or the accompanying lack of physical conditioning establishes this as a risk factor for developing heat stress is not clear from an evaluation of the available literature. Individuals with extremely high body weight should be viewed as being more at risk than individuals of normal weight.

Drugs

A variety of medications has been directly or indirectly associated with the development of heat stroke. Some of these drugs affect the ability to sweat and/or to vasodilate peripherally; others increase metabolic activity. Some may have additional effects on central thermal regulatory activity. The following drugs have been reputed to contribute to the development of hyperthermia: cocaine, salicylates, antihistamines, phencyclidine, alcohol (withdrawal), anticholinergics, phenothiazines, tricyclic antidepressants, monoamine oxidase inhibitors, glutethimide, lyseric acid diethylamide, lithium, amphetamines, nitrous oxide, halothane, ethylene, ethyl chloride, pancuronium bromide, and succinylcholine (40). It is important to note that even though phenothiazines are listed as causally related to the development of heat stroke, this should not preclude their use in a full-blown case of heat stroke for the control of shivering, which may develop in the course of therapy. Although phenothiazines have been reported to alter the hypothalamic control of temperature regulation, when a patient is being cooled by artificial means and has been removed from ambient climatic conditions or from the circumstances which generated intolerable heat production, phenothiazines would not be expected to potentiate the persistence or aggravation of hyperthermia. Phenothiazines have been used successfully on repeated occasions to block shivering, and hence are listed as agents of choice for this special circumstance.

Alcohol

Alcohol, through a complex set of mechanisms, has been said to predispose most individuals toward heat illness (40). Interestingly, it also predisposes toward hypothermia.

Special Clinical States

Excessive utilization of sauna baths, hot tubs, and Turkish baths followed by exceptionally vigorous physical activity, incarceration in the "Black Hole of Calcutta," and other similarly unusual circumstances have been reported to generate large numbers of heat casualties. In addition, anhidrosis, ectodermal dysplasia, mucoviscidosis, exfoliative dermatitides, Riley-Day syndrome, the myopathy associated with malignant hyperthermia, and a variety of other unusual illnesses have all been associated with an increased risk of developing heat illness.

Prior Heat Illness

It has long been debated whether individuals who have suffered from heat stroke are at greater risk for repeat episodes. Evaluation of many individuals has indicated that some persons, for reasons which are not clear, are at increased risk of developing heat stroke under circumstances which will not simultaneously precipitate the same condition in other individuals (38). Persons with a history of heat stroke, with or without an inherent aberration which has established their susceptibility to develop that condition, are at increased risk of a repeat episode. Current evidence suggests that any physiologic aberration predisposing these individuals to heat stroke was preexisting rather than induced by damage related to the heat stroke (38). The observation is

that victims of heat stroke may exhibit labile thermoregulation for months afterward.

Fatigue and Lack of Sleep

Evaluations by the army have clearly pointed out that there is an association between these conditions and the predisposition toward development of heat stroke.

Febrile Illness

As would be expected, febrile illness carries with it a variety of risk factors (e.g., dehydration, pulmonary dysfunction, dermatitis) which predispose an individual to heat stroke under appropriate circumstances.

Increased Biologic Susceptibility

As indicated in many portions of the preceding discussion, there does appear to be biologic variation which makes certain individuals more susceptible to the development of heat stroke. Unfortunately, under most circumstances, this biologic variation has not been succinctly identified and thus has little predictive value.

Muscle Cramps

The problem of muscle or heat cramps is extremely common in hot climates and is believed to be primarily due to a rapid change in extracellular fluid osmolarity resulting from salt and water losses, which may occur rapidly under the circumstances described. Muscle cramps can be easily treated, as in the heat exhaustion syndrome, with appropriate salt and water replacement. Products such as Gatorade (a relatively balanced salt solution) and other similar fluids available for oral volume replacement are effective in both the prevention and therapy of this problem in victims of mild heat illness. Salt and electrolyte tablets swallowed whole are gastrointestinal irritants and should be avoided. Intravenous fluid replacement is reliable but rarely necessary.

HEAT STROKE

DEFINITION AND PATHOPHYSIOLOGY

Heat stroke is the syndrome which occurs when the body temperature results in cell death and physiologic collapse. It results when heat loss mechanisms are either overwhelmed or deficient in meeting environmental demands. In humans, temperatures above 42°C are almost universally associated with the heat stroke syndrome, while temperatures in the 40–42°C range are less frequently productive of the full-blown disorder (5,40). A temperature of 42°C is fairly well established. Humans undergoing experimental temperature elevation in an attempt to control cancer by enhancing target cell destruction were demonstrated to tolerate temperatures of up to 41.8°C. Nonetheless, occasional individuals develop full-blown heat stroke at lower temperatures, while others tolerate temperatures of up to 42°C. Above 42°C, and certainly in the 43–46°C range, enzymes denature, membranes liquefy, mitochondria become nonfunctional, coding of proteins becomes disrupted, and the coordination of physiologic processes ceases. Thus, the concept of a critical thermal maximum has evolved to allow a definable standard for the diagnosis of heat stroke. Amazingly, one victim has survived with no permanent residua after reaching a core temperature in excess of 46.5°C (115.7°F) (41a).

In many discussions of heat illness, it has been stated that heat stroke occurs either with destruction of sweat glands or when sweat glands undergo temporary dysfunction because of sensory input overload. It is quite clear that this is not always true and that continued sweating is quite possible. Similarly, while cardiovascular disease certainly predisposes to the development of heat stroke, because of the inability of the cardiovascular system to maintain adequate blood flow through the periphery to maximize heat loss, heat stroke is nonetheless possible with optimal cardiac function. Dehydration, often an accompanying parameter of heat stroke, is similarly not necessary for the development of overt heat stroke.

The temperature achieved by the body is apparently the culprit in the cytolysis and disruption of servomechanisms. Other proposed etiologies include hypoxia, intravascular coagulation, electrolyte abnormalities, and severe acidosis (28,40). While any of these physiologic aberrations may accompany heat

stroke, it is apparent that temperature itself is the primary pathologic force (3).

DIFFERENTIAL DIAGNOSIS

While obvious cases of heat stroke are easy to diagnose, one must frequently rule out other diseases which might mimic this condition. Meningitis, encephalitis, malaria, typhoid fever, typhus, delirium tremens, and hypothalamic hemorrhage have all been reported to cause syndrome complexes similar to heat stroke (7,40). The occasional drug-related case must be identified to be appropriately managed. When a difficult differential diagnosis defies precise definition on purely clinical grounds, measurement of SGOT, serum glutamic pyruvic transaminase (SGPT), and LDH may be useful in defining heat stroke. In most febrile states which present with mental aberration or coma, these enzymes will be normal or only minimally elevated, while they are routinely significantly elevated early in the course of heat stroke (19). While this is not pathognomonic, it may help in confirming a presumed case of heat stroke.

Presentation

CENTRAL NERVOUS SYSTEM

Disturbances of the central nervous system often dominate the early course of heat stroke. Confusion, irrational behavior, and a sudden change or loss of consciousness are characteristic. Convulsions are not uncommon and may present early or in a delayed fashion. Early seizures may not be as ominous prognostically as late seizures, perhaps because delayed seizure activity often reflects an underlying structural abnormality such as *in situ* thrombosis, frank hemorrhage, or cytopathologic damage resulting in loss of neuronal structure and function. Hemiplegia, ataxia, and permanent dementia have all been reported as residua of heat stroke (36,40,46).

HYPOTENSION

Hypotension, which may progress to frank shock, is a common early manifestation of heat stroke. The mechanism of this aberration is complex and includes the conditions discussed below.

Volume Depletion: This has been repeatedly shown to be at least a minor component of hypotension (6,36,40). Since both water and sodium chloride are lost during sweating, at rates of up to 3 liters/hour under special circumstances, large volume loss may occur rapidly (7). In one dramatic case, a football player reportedly lost 22 pounds during one early-season game, with resultant confusion, hypotension, and signs of heat exhaustion (30).

Peripheral Vasodilatation: Peripheral vasodilatation with resultant peripheral pooling of intravascular contents is both a mechanism of heat loss and a contributor to hypotension. Furthermore, when lactic acidosis supervenes, peripheral pooling is enhanced, thereby augmenting any hypovolemia or decrement in myocardial performance which may be simultaneously present.

Myocardial Dysfunction: Myocardial dysfunction plays a role in the development of hypotension and/or shock (6,22,33,34,40). Most often noted in the elderly, pulmonary edema with high central venous pressure and pulmonary artery wedge pressures in the 25–40 mmHg range is frequently reported. Heart failure uncommonly presents in younger individuals. Myocardial infarction and death from heart failure or arrhythmias have been repeatedly reported in the setting of heat stroke (22,34). At post mortem and in those cases in which cardiac catherization was performed, coronary arteries were usually completely normal or demonstrated insignificant atherosclerotic change (22,34). Pathologic section of the hearts of heat stroke victims has shown mild to moderate hemorrhage into various areas of the myocardium, cellular degeneration, and spotty inflammatory infiltration of the heart muscle (34). While such pathologic changes have often been demonstrated, the extent of the pathologic change was not sufficient to explain the incidence or degree of cardiac dysfunction and did not provide a cardiac etiology for the demise of the individual. Nonetheless, aberrations in myocardial performance are certainly frequent and can contribute to the development of hypotension and/or shock.

Thus, care must be taken to avoid overly vigorous volume restoration.

Disseminated Intravascular Coagulation: Local areas of intravascular coagulation or disseminated intravascular coagulation leading to *in situ* thrombosis further contribute to multiple organ dysfunction and pulmonary and cardiac insufficiency (9,39). These aberrations and occasional episodes of massive gastrointestinal hemorrhage combine to present numerous etiologies for hypotension and shock (9,22,27,40).

RESPIRATORY DYSFUNCTION

As mentioned, pulmonary edema is not uncommon and reflects both myocardial dysfunction and intravascular coagulation, with resulting *in situ* vascular thrombosis. This triad, plus local cytolysis and concomitant systemic acidosis, generally leads to tachypnea, hypoxemia, and hypercarbia (6,22,33,40). Occasionally, hyperventilation can cause initial respiratory alkalosis and the traditional tetanic syndrome.

GASTROINTESTINAL DYSFUNCTION

Gastrointestinal dysfunction is often present and reflects poor perfusion, electrolyte abnormalities, and intravascular coagulation. These processes may lead to gastroparesis, ileus, frank gastrointestinal ulceration, and massive bleeding (28). Alternatively, diarrhea and vomiting may be noted.

ADRENAL FUNCTION

Adrenal function appears to be well maintained during the course of heat stroke despite frequent pathologic findings, including hemorrhage and an inflammatory infiltrate. There have been no reported cases of adrenal insufficiency secondary to heat stroke (40).

RENAL DYSFUNCTION

The renal system is reportedly one of the most commonly involved organ systems in heat stroke (20,22,32,40,45). Aberrations in renal function are secondary to hypovolemia and hypoperfusion due to all of the conditions listed above. Prerenal dehydration may lead only to transient renal function embarrassment or to frank acute vasomotor nephropathy, which may require temporary dialysis for maintenance of the patient. Under these circumstances, the urine has occasionally been described as looking like machine oil, with a low specific gravity due to an inability of the kidneys to concentrate. Red and white cells, white cell, hyaline, and granular casts, and mild to moderate proteinuria are commonly seen. The urine is usually dipstick positive for ketones, reflecting fat mobilization.

HEPATIC DYSFUNCTION.

The liver is usually injured in cases of significant heat stroke (9,19,27,28,32). Frank jaundice may occur due to hepatocellular dysfunction. Rarely, edema of the head of the pancreas may cause obstructive jaundice. Frank pancreatitis is only rarely reported, even though pathologic sectioning routinely discloses local intravascular coagulation and an inflammatory infiltrate, or hemorrhage into the substance of the pancreas (40). The liver is frequently enlarged and tender on physical examination. Laboratory evaluation usually shows elevation of SGOT and SGPT, with minimal elevation of alkaline phosphatase and mild to marked increases in bilirubin, LDH, and gammaglutamyltranscarbamylase (GGT) (19). All of these hepatocellular enzymes reflect hepatocellular death, which on pathologic evaluation is corroborated by occasional centrilobular necrosis, dropping out of heptocytes, diffuse monocellular infiltrates, and widespread membrane damage (27). Early (<24 hours after onset of hyperthermia) jaundice may portend a worse prognosis than does the delayed (48–72 hours) onset of manifest hyperbilirubinemia.

Laboratory Findings

CLOTTING DISORDERS

Hemostasis is routinely abnormal during heat stroke. Clotting disturbances, believed to be mediated by a drop in the platelet count, hypoprothrombinemia (decreased production), hypofibrinogenemia (increased consumption), and increased capillary fragility are hallmarks of this disorder (39,40). Liver

dysfunction is certainly contributory, along with diffuse intravascular coagulation. Direct thermal damage to cells and protein has been postulated to play a role in the dysfunctional clotting system, but the evidence favors the other mechanisms as the major factors.

ELECTROCARDIOGRAM (ECG)

The ECG may show conduction disturbances and/or nonspecific ST-T wave changes. On occasion, patterns suggestive of true myocardial infarction may appear. Cross-correlation with pathologic findings compatible with coronary artery disease does not usually substantiate a diagnosis of true myocardial infarction. In most cases, the arteries are normal or are only minimally compromised by atherosclerotic change (9,28,34,40). The cause of cardiac damage is not clearly established and probably is the result of many combined factors.

WHITE BLOOD CELL COUNT

The white blood cell count is routinely elevated and may be in the range of 20,000–30,000 per cubic millimeter. Indeed, white counts in the 40,000–50,000 range with a marked left shift are not uncommon with marked hyperthermia (40). These findings do not represent infection, but simply the stress of the heat stroke.

POTASSIUM VALUES

Potassium values are routinely quite low. This condition is believed to be mediated by renal losses incurred when renal regulatory mechanisms are shifted toward sodium retention via the renin-angiotension-aldosterone axis, resulting in sodium-potassium exchange (24). Potassium is also lost in the sweat, but calculated losses do not explain total body deficits; hence, the complete explanation remains in question (24).

HYPOPHOSPHATEMIA

Hypophosphatemia is frequently described (42). This results from a respiratory alkalosis which accompanies early heat stroke or heat exhaustion. Indeed, even in normal subjects serum phosphate concentrations may be depressed to levels as low as 0.3 mg/dl with hyperventilation (23). A state of accelerated cellular uptake of phosphorus coincident with respiratory alkalosis, with alkalinization of intracellular contents, may contribute to hypophosphatemia.

HYPOCALCEMIA

Hypocalcemia is commonly seen on the second or third day of heat stroke (23). Although this condition is not perfectly elucidated, it has been proposed that hypocalcemia is the result of calcium phosphate and calcium carbonate deposition in the skeletal muscle which has undergone rhabdomyolysis. This is a self-limited problem; overzealous attempts to normalize calcium measurements early in therapy will result in increased muscle deposition.

HYPERKALEMIA

Although most patients are hypokalemic in the setting of heat stroke, occasional patients rapidly develop hyperkalemia. This is believed to be due to rhabdomyolysis with the release of potassium into the bloodstream, often coupled with renal insufficiency, thereby minimizing renal excretion. Such patients must be managed with great caution; early dialysis is indicated. Emergency therapy with glucose, insulin, bicarbonate, and calcium will be effective for short-term management but must be followed by definitive procedures to eliminate potassium from the body. Sodium polystyrene sulfonate (Kayexalate) enemas and dialysis should be arranged with the utmost speed.

THERAPY

Immediate therapy of heat illness involves the usual ABCs of emergency management, plus energetic and definitive control of body temperature.

The ABCs

As is always the case, airway management is critical in the immediate resuscitation of seriously ill patients. Since pulmonary edema is commonly reported, oxygen is always provided, and intubation with positive-pressure breathing is indicated for patients with pulmonary edema. Pulmonary edema occurring in heat stroke may be the result of the capillary leak syndrome and/or myocardial dysfunction (6,22,23,36,40,43). Because of this, insertion of a Swan-Ganz pulmonary artery catheter is indicated to confirm the diagnostic category and to aid in patient management. In individuals with a low central venous pressure, cautious fluid administration, averaging 1.0–1.5 liters of Ringer's lactate or saline is appropriate to restore intravascular volumes which were depleted during the stress which caused the heat stroke (6,40). It is surprising that volume deficits are frequently smaller than might be expected, and caution is indicated in avoiding overly vigorous volume replacement. Fluid challenge should be given in 250 ml increments. In individuals with a high Swan-Ganz pressure reading in the pulmonary edema range, digitalization and/or isoproterenol (Isuprel) administration have been recommended to improve cardiac output and tissue perfusion (22,36,40). If pulmonary edema is found with central venous pressure or Swan-Ganz readings in the low to normal range, then the primary management modality of choice is positive end-expiratory pressure (PEEP) therapy with volume replacement.

Rhythm monitoring is routinely indicated, since patients have been reported to incur ECG changes suggestive of myocardial infarction, with ischemia and dysrhythmias.

Cooling

This therapeutic modality is of primary importance and must be initiated as early as possible (7,18,30,40). Cooling efforts should precede any time-consuming search for the etiology. The patient should be removed from the initiating environment, clothing removed when appropriate, and any of a variety of cooling measures instituted. Modalities which have been reported to be effective are listed in Table 4.

Of these modalities, only aspirin is clearly contraindicated, since it not only fails to correct the temperature elevation but also has the potentially negative effect of aggravating any underlying abnormality of hemostasis (40,44). Most importantly, the temperature should be lowered as quickly as possible to

TABLE 4
**Agents Reported to be Effective in
Lowering Body Temperature**

Alcohol sponge baths (*caution*)
Ice packs (*caution*)
Large circulating fans
Immersion in a tub of cold water (*caution*)
Cooling blankets
Peritoneal lavage
Rectal lavage
Cardiopulmonary bypass
Gastric lavage
Phenothiazines (*caution*)
Aspirin (*caution*)
Acetaminophen

39°C, as measured by a rectal thermometer or thermistor probe placed in the colon or the esophagus (5,35). When the temperature reaches 39°C, the cooling measures should be modified to avoid a hypothermic overshoot. Careful, continued monitoring is then necessary to avoid rebound hyperthermia and to maintain a core temperature of 37–38°C.

If shivering develops during the course of temperature lowering, then chlorpromazine (Thorazine), 10–25 mg by slow intravenous (IV) push, has been recommended (18,36, 40,46). The wisdom of utilizing Thorazine to block shivering has been questioned, but on grounds which seem unreasonable. As discussed previously, Thorazine has been implicated as a possible cause of heat stroke by interfering with normal thermoregulatory mechanisms (14,37). Despite this, once a patient has suffered heat stroke, and is in the hands of competent medical managers who are utilizing external means of temperature lowering, phenothiazines are not contraindicated. Thorazine effectively stops shivering and helps block further heat production. It should be noted that phenothiazines are α-adrenergic blockers and therefore may potentiate hypotension. They have been reported to cause life-threatening arrhythmias and also may lower the seizure threshold. For these reasons, phenothiazines should be utilized only when effective temperature control cannot be obtained because of excessive shivering.

When circumstances dictate more heroic means of heat management, peritoneal dialysis using a cold dialysate has been described (15). The authors of one report described a maximum exchange of 17.5 kJ/minute when 2 liters of cold dialysate was instilled and allowed to equilibrate for 10 minutes and then removed. We favor infraumbilical placement of adjacent peritoneal dialysis catheters ("in" and "out") directed at opposite pelvic gutters. In this way, iced dialysate can be rapidly infused through one and drained from the other. We have successfully resuscitated patients with core temperatures in excess of 42.7°C with such techniques. It is unlikely that such heroic modalities are necessary except in cases of malignant hyperthermia or cases of temperature elevation caused by certain drug interactions, including monoamine oxidase inhibitors with tricyclic antidepressants or amphetamines. Under such circumstances, the heat generated can cause a temperature rise which is uncontrollable using conventional means. The employment of dialysis, utilizing refrigerated or iced dialysate, can be undertaken and is quite safe when the technical details are assiduously adhered to. Of less use are cold inhaled mists and ice water enemas. *Extreme caution* must be exercised when ice water immersion is used. This may cause rapid peripheral vasoconstriction, with shunting of hyperthermic blood to the core, transiently raising the central temperature. A preferred technique is the constant application of cooled water, evaporated by large circulating fans.

It is important to note that the topical application of isopropyl alcohol is especially dangerous in children and may result in deep coma (29). Coma results from the rapid absorption of the alcohol through the skin and dilated superficial blood vessels, which may produce toxic blood levels.

Central Nervous System Abnormalities

The level of consciousness is routinely depressed in victims of acute heat stroke (7, 18,30,40,46). While this is expected, it is important to assess carefully for the presence of cerebral edema, which would dictate the need for mannitol and steroid administration. If cerebral edema is diagnosed, 1 g/kg IV of mannitol should be given over 15–20 minutes (36,40). Dexamethasone, 10 mg IV stat and 4 mg IV every 6 hours, is also indicated. If focal neurologic deficits are found, the patient should have an emergency computed tomography (CT) scan to rule out the presence of an intracerebral hemorrhage which might be amenable to neurosurgical decompression.

Seizures should be treated with IV diazepam (Valium) or barbiturates in conventional dosages (36,40,46). Phenytoin (Dilantin), although effective, is more difficult to administer and should be reserved for patients with demonstrable intracranial pathology, which will require chronic medication for seizure control.

Renal Dysfunction

Of all the organ systems involved in heat stroke, the kidneys may deserve the greatest emphasis. Renal failure, both transient and permanent, is commonly reported. Victims of heat stroke almost always have demonstrable urine abnormalities and routinely demonstrate a rise in blood urea nitrogen (BUN) and creatinine (6,20,22,40,45). The management regimen commonly reported to minimize the pathology includes the early and vigorous use of mannitol. In oliguric individuals who do not respond appropriately to IV crystalloid expansion, 0.25 g/kg IV of mannitol should be delivered in an attempt to reestablish urine flow.

Rhabdomyolysis leading to myoglobinuria may be of significant importance to the production and propagation of renal failure (20,45). For this reason, maintenance of rapid (at least 50 ml/hour) urine output and alkalinization of the urine are indicated as soon as myoglobinuria is documented.

Patients may require acute dialysis. The necessity for this therapy does not carry an ominous prognosis of protracted renal failure. Many patients will eventually regain normal or near-normal renal function.

Miscellaneous Therapeutic Principles

Nasogastric Aspiration

Nasogastric aspiration is routinely required to prevent regurgitation of gastric contents and concomitant pulmonary aspiration. Hypokalemic ileus may be induced, leading to gastric atony and a high risk of pulmonary aspiration. Gastric contents should be tested for the presence of blood, since gastrointestinal bleeding may complicate the heat stroke

sydrome (40,46). Neutralization of gastric contents with antacids to a pH greater than 4 should be undertaken. Intravenous cimetidine may be employed, 300 mg IV every 6 hours.

Steroid Utilization

As is almost always the case in a serious illness, steroids have been used in the therapeutic management program; however, they are of no proven benefit (6,36,40). Addisonian crisis secondary to adrenal apoplexy has not been reported in this syndrome.

Antibiotic Administration

There are no special circumstances in heat stroke that justify the routine prophylactic administration of antibiotics.

Disseminated Intravascular Coagulation

This syndrome has been frequently reported to accompany heat stroke. Although heparin and clotting factor replacement have been reported to be effective management, there is no evidence that such intervention is in fact therapeutically effective in improving morbidity and mortality. The standard management principle of eliminating the underlying cause of intravascular coagulation should be followed.

Suggested Laboratory Parameters

1. Complete blood count
2. Sodium, potassium, bicarbonate, and chloride
3. Urinalysis
4. Phosphate and calcium
5. BUN and creatinine
6. CPK (MM and MB fractions)
7. Arterial blood gases
8. SGOT, LDH, SGPT, bilirubin, and alkaline phosphatase
9. Prothrombin time, partial thromboplastin time, platelet count, and fibrinogen levels
10. Serum and/or urinary amylase
11. Chest x-ray
12. ECG
13. Stool for guaiac
14. Lumbar puncture and electroencephalogram are not generally helpful and are not routinely indicated unless neurologic syndromes develop

15. Central venous pressure and Swan-Ganz catheterization when necessary

FLUID REPLACEMENT—MILD CASES

In cases of heat exhaustion that do not appear severe enough to warrant aggressive cooling and supportive measures, fluid may be replaced by the oral or parenteral route. Cool liquids in sufficient volume (500 ml) and proper tonicity (<200 mOsmol/liter) sufficient to promote gastric emptying may be ingested; D_5 half-normal saline, D_5 normal saline, and Ringer's lactate are appropriate IV solutions. Prophylactic ingestion of at least 1 liter/hour of water is absolutely necessary during vigorous exercise. Salt supplements (particularly sodium) are rarely necessary, and may actually stimulate hypernatremia/hypokalemia. Daily dietary sodium ingestion of 8–14 g and 80–100 mEq of potassium are well tolerated in the absence of underlying cardiovascular or renal disease.

CONCLUSION

With appropriate management, most victims of even serious heat stroke survive to return to normal life. The probability that they are at increased risk for a repeat attack must be explained to the patient. There are no other consistent sequelae.

REFERENCES

1. Andrews, J. R., Massey, M., Mullins, L., et al: Heat illness in athletes. *J. Med Assoc State Ala,* **45**(2):29–32, August 1975.
2. Bartley, J. D.: Heat stroke: Is total prevention possible? *Milit Med,* **142**(7):528, 533–535, July 1977.
3. Beard, M. E. J., Hamer, J. W., Hamilton, G., et al: Jogger's heat stroke. *NZ Med J,* **89**(631):159–161, March 1979.
4. Bridger, C. A., Ellis, F. P., Taylor, H. L.: Mortality in St. Louis, Missouri, during heat waves in 1936, 1953, 1954, 1955, and 1956—coroner's cases. *Environ Res,* **12**:38–48, 1976.
5. Bynum, G. D., Pandolf, K. B., Schuette, W. H., et al: Induced hyperthermia in sedated humans and the concept of critical thermal maximum. *Am J Physiol,* **235**(5):R228–R236, November 1978.
6. Clowes, G. H. A., O'Donnell, T. F.: Heat stroke. *N Engl J Med,* **291**(11):564–567, September 1974.
7. Collins, K. J.: Heat illness: Diagnosis, tretatment and prevention. *Practitioner,* **219**:193–198, August 1977.
8. Cooper, R. A.: Heat and neuroleptics: A deadly combination. *Am J Psychiatry,* **136**:466–467, April 1979.
9. Costrini, A. M., Pitt, H. A., Gustafson, A. B., et al: Cardiovascular and metabolic manifestations of heat stroke and severe heat exhaustion. *Am J Med,* **66**:296–320, February 1979.
10. Demeyere, R.: Malignant hyperthermia. *Acta Anaesthesiol Belg,* **1**:101–120, March 1978.
11. Ellis, F. P.: Heat illness. I. Epidemiology. *Trans R Soc Trop Med Hyg,* **70**(5/6):402–411, 1976.
12. Ellis, F. P.: Heat illness. II. Pathogenesis. *Trans R Soc Trop Med Hyg,* **70**(5/6):412–418, 1976.
13. Ellis, F. P.: Heat illness. III. Acclimatization. *Trans R Soc Trop Med Hyg,* **70**(5/6):402–411, 1976.
14. Forester, D.: Fatal drug-induced heat stroke. *JACEP,* **7**(6):243–244, June 1978.
15. Gjessing, J., Barsa, J., Tomlin, P. J.: A possible means of rapid cooling in the emergency treatment of malignant hyperpyrexia. *Br J Anaesthesiol,* **48**:469–473, 1976.
16. Granoff, A. L., Davis, J. M.: Heat illness syndrome and lithium intoxication. *J Clin Psychiatry,* **39**:103–107, February 1978.
17. Greenblatt, D. J., Gross, P. L., Harris, J., et al: Fatal hyperthermia following haloperidol therapy of sedative-hypnotic withdrawal. *J Clin Psychiatry,* **39**:673–675, August 1978.
18. Hamilton, D.: The immediate treatment of heatstroke. *Anaesthesia,* **31**:270–272, 1976.
19. Kew, M., Bersohn, I., Seftel, H.: The diagnostic and prognostic significance of the serum enzyme changes in heatstroke. *Trans R Soc Trop Med Hyg,* **65**(3):325–330, 1971.
20. Kew, M. C., Abrahams, C., Levin, N. W., et al: Effects of heatstroke on the function and structure of the kidney. *Q J Med,* **New Series XXXVI**(143):277–300, July 1967.
21. Klock, J. C., Boerner, U., Becker, C. E.: Coma, hyperthermia, and bleeding associated with massive LSD overdose: A report of eight cases. *West J Med,* **120**:183, 1974.
22. Knochel, J. P., Beisel, W. R. Herndon, E. G., et al: The renal, cardiovascular, hematologic and serum electrolyte abnormalities of heat stroke. *Am J Med,* **30**(2):299–309, February 1961.
23. Knochel, J. P., Caskey, J. H.: The mechanism of hypophosphatemia in acute heat stroke. *JAMA,* **238**(5):425–426, August 1977.
24. Knochel, J. P., Dotin, L. N., Hamburger, R. J.: Pathophysiology of intense physical conditioning in a hot climate. I. Mechanisms of potassium depletion. *J Clin Invest,* **51**:242–255, 1972.
25. Krakowiak, F. J., Vatral, J. J., Moore, R. C. et al: Malignant hyperthermia—Report of two cases. *Oral Surg,* **47**(3):218–222, March 1979.
26. Krisko, I., Lewis, E., Johnson, J. E.: Severe hyperpyrexia due to tranylcypromine-amphetamine toxicity. *Ann Intern Med,* **70**(3):559–564, March 1969.
27. Kew, C., Minick, O. T., Bahu, R. M., et al: Ultrastructural changes in the liver in heatstroke. *Am J Pathol,* **90**:609–618, 1978.
28. Malamud, N., Haymaker, W., Custer, R. P.: Heat stroke—A clinicopathologic study of 125 fatal cases. *Milit Surgeon,* **99**:397–449, November 1946.
29. McFadden, S. W., Haddow, J. E.: Coma produced by topical application of isopropanol. *Pediatrics,* **43**:622–633, April 1969.

30. Murphy, R. J.: Heat illness. *J Sports Med*, 1(4):26–29, 1973.
31. Musacchia, X. J.: Fever and hyperthermia. *Fed Proc*, 38(1):27–29, January 1979.
32. O'Donnell, T. F. Jr.: Acute heat stroke—epidemiologic, biochemical, renal and coagulation studies. *JAMA*, 234(8):824–828, November 1975.
33. O'Donnell, T. F., Clowes, G. H. A.: The circulatory abnormalities of heat stroke. *N Engl J Med*, 287(15):734–737, October 1972.
34. Pal, A. K., Chopra, S. K.: The cardiopathology of heatstroke. *Indian J Med Sci*, 29(12):299–304, December 1975.
35. Pandolf, K. B., Goldman, R. F.: Convergence of skin and rectal temperatures as a criterion for heat tolerance. *Aviat Space Environ Med.*, 49(9):1095–1101, September 1978.
36. Proulx, R. P.: Heat stress disease, in Schwartz, G. R. (ed): *Principles and Practice of Emergency Medicine*, Vol. 1. Philadelphia, W. B. Saunders Company, 1978, pp. 815–822.
37. Rumack, B. H.: Anticholinergic poisoning: Treatment with physostigmine. *Pediatrics*, 52(3):449–451, September 1973.
38. Shapiro, Y., Magazanik, A., Udassin, R.: Heat intolerance in former heatstroke patients. *Ann Intern Med*, 90(6):913–916, June 1979.
39. Shibolet, S., Fisher, S., Gilat, T., et al: Fibrinolysis and hemorrhages in fatal heatstroke. *N Engl J Med*, 266(4):169–173, January 1962.
40. Shibolet, S., Lancaster, M. C., Danon, Y.: Heat stroke: A review, *Aviat Space Environ Med*, 47(3):280–301, March 1976.
41. Shvartz, E., Shibolet, S., Meroz, A., et al: Prediction of heat tolerance from heart rate and rectal temperature in a temperate environment. *J Appl Physiol*, 43:684–688, 1977.
41a. Slovis, C. M., Anderson, G. F., Cosolaro, A., et al: Survival in a heat stroke victim with a core temperature in excess of 46.5 C. *Ann Energ Med*, 11:269–71, May 1982.
42. Sonnenklar, N., Krasna, I. H.: Clinical management of malignant hyperpyrexia. *J Pediatr Surg*, 11(5):617–623, October 1976.
43. Stanley, B., Pal, N. R.: Fatal hyperpyrexia with phenelzine and imipramine. *Br Med J*, 2:1011, 1964.
44. Stitt, J. T.: Fever versus hyperthermia. *Fed Proc*, 38(1):39–43, January 1979.
45. Vertel, R. M., Knochel, J. P.: Acute renal failure due to heat injury. An analysis of ten cases associated with a high incidence of myoglobinuria. *Am J Med*, 43:435–451, September 1967.
46. Wheeler, M.: Heat stroke in the elderly. *Med Clin North Am*, 60(6):1289–1296, November 1976.

4 | WILDERNESS RESCUE AND PREPARATION

Warren D. Bowman, M.D.
Charles Farabee
Jacques Foray, M.D.

As ever-increasing numbers of hikers, campers, and climbers turn to our wildlands for recreation, the medical community and search and rescue (SAR) organizations will have to contend with a growing number of lost, sick, and injured persons. The decade of the sixties witnessed 756 North American climbing accidents which resulted in 209 deaths. There are 300–350 fatalities each year in the European Alps among both climbers and casual hikers.

Wilderness rescue and medical intervention are unique in several ways. All aspects of the rescue are enormously time-consuming. Simply getting messages out of a wilderness area concerning an injury may take days. Organizing a team, equipment, and transportation requires a variable amount of time depending on the level of preparedness of the rescue organization. To find, gain access to, and then transport the victim to definitive care completes a lengthy process.

Due to the large number of people involved (six to eight people are required to carry adequately a single Stokes litter), logistical problems of food, shelter, and transport are multiplied.

Rescuers are subjected to the same risks and environmental stresses that compromise the victims. To obviate further tragedy, a heightened awareness of potential danger and adverse conditions is required among rescue personnel. In addition to Basic and Advanced Life Support training, rescuers must have extensive wilderness experience, combining practicality with creativity and resourcefulness. Many interventions, such as cardiopulmonary resuscitation (CPR), tube thoracostomy, and intubation, are difficult, if not entirely precluded, in the wilderness setting. Examinations may be hampered by bulky clothing necessary to keep the victim warm. Medications and equipment are subject to extremes of temperature and abuse and may be rendered ineffective, unsterile, or inoperative (Appendix A provides drug stability information).

Finally, decision making that optimizes patient care, while not unduly risking the well-being of the crew, requires experienced leadership grounded in both common sense and technical skill.

A review of statistics from the Hospital Chamonix-Mont-Blanc serves to illustrate the nature of the problems encountered in mountain environments. There were 1616 climbing and hiking accidents from 1972 to 1980 on the Mont Blanc massif, resulting in 289 deaths. More than two-thirds of all accidents occurred above 3000 m, suggesting that the environmental stresses of high altitude, cold exposure, and fatigue played a significant role in morbidity. A statistical breakdown supports this notion: 68% were victims of trauma, often the result of a slip or fall (20% resulting in multisystem injury); 24% suffered from exposure, hypothermia, and frostbite; 7% had high altitude–related illnesses; and 1% (16 people) were struck by lightning.

Most wilderness accidents are the result of inexperience or lack of preparation, often aggravated by fatigue, rather than the direct result of natural phenomena such as avalanche, lightning, or high-altitude exposure.

This chapter is intended as a primer to introduce medical professionals to the unique rescue and medical problems encountered in wilderness situations. The rudiments of SAR organization and specialized aspects, such as mountain, oversnow, avalanche, water, and cave rescue, are discussed. A section on cold weather survival outlines current recommendations for existence in this extreme condition.

Wilderness Search and Rescue

It is impossible to estimate the exact number of wilderness SARs that occur each year. In the United States, there is no federal agency charged with gathering these data; it is probable that local registries maintain this inventory to some degree. Consolidation of this vital information would be useful in the initiation of preventive education. In 1979, the National Association of Search and Rescue initiated a major program to obtain SAR statistics from its membership. This information will greatly aid the understanding of SAR.

PARTICIPATING SAR ORGANIZATIONS

Wilderness SAR personnel, in whatever geographic setting, are by and large enthusiasts and active participants in the recreational environments which prove perilous to the unwary. Such paramedical expertise creates a comaraderie unique to the wilderness community which gives support to what can be an extraordinarily complex, frustrating, and exhausting task.

The SAR organizational framework is poorly defined, with a matrix of national, regional, and local organizations. The diffuse nature of individual SAR operations and their respective geographic spread has to date precluded a tighter structure. It is to be hoped that the 1980s will see a national effort to coordinate these units. Until that time, the following list should assist the entry-level rescuer to identify some of the major and more visible components of the SAR community. For a more detailed list of "Who's Who in SAR," the reader is directed to Rick LaValla's *Resources Guide for Search and Rescue Training Materials.*

AIR FORCE RESCUE COORDINATION CENTER (AFRCC)

The Aerospace Rescue and Recovery Service (ARRS) operates the AFRCC, which is the single federal agency responsible for coordinating military and civilian SAR activities in the 48 contiguous states. The AFRCC is located at Scott Air Force Base in Illinois. It is a 24 hour operation staffed by personnel experienced in land SAR operations. This agency maintains a comprehensive SAR resource file with a detailed compilation of all federal, state, local, and volunteer organizations capable of conducting or assisting an SAR operation. Access to this service can be obtained only by certain authorities: state offices of Emergency Services, sheriff's offices, National Park Services, and so on. Standard and specialized manpower, advanced equipment, and transportation can be identified and procured through the AFRCC. For example, the AFRCC can redirect an airborne military transport aircraft to carry personnel, animals, or vehicles to a search or rescue scene.

If the search or rescue requires a tremendous amount of overhead illumination, the AFRCC can request an 8,000,000 candlepower "Night Sun" from the U.S. Coast Guard. This semiportable lamp, carried aboard a large aircraft, was developed for rescues at sea; it has been recently used for land operations as well. If the operations leader wishes to employ aerial mapping and infrared sensors to locate moving objects such as lost hikers or to assist in the identification of downed or snow-covered aircraft, the AFRCC can provide this assistance. The U.S. Navy, under the auspices of the AFRCC, has participated in such operations by deploying its Aerial Interpretation Section from San Diego. The Rescue Center makes every effort to coordinate with local authorities in an attempt to be a secondary source for assistance. The address is: Air Force Rescue Coordination Center, Scott Air Force Base, Illinois 62225 (telephone number: 1–800–851–3051).

AMERICAN RESCUE DOG ASSOCIATION (ARDA)

ARDA was formed in 1972 in order to link the numerous German shepherd handlers and to provide uniform standards of training and expertise for both dogs and trainers. The group assists those interested in training dogs for operation during SAR missions. Official agencies using this adjunct are assured of excellent service.

Search dogs have been successfully used to locate victims of avalanche, collapsed buildings, flood, and rock slide, as well as in the open countryside. Although the ARDA is willing to consult, in an actual emergency they prefer to be alerted through the proper state and federal coordinating agencies. Their address is: American Rescue Dog Association, 10714 Royal Springs Drive, Dallas, Texas 75229.

CIVIL AIR PATROL (CAP)

The CAP is a private, nonprofit volunteer corporation dedicated to the development of aviation education for an emergency assistance to private citizens. An official auxiliary of the Air Force, the CAP effectively conducts approximately three-fourths of all aerial search activity in the contiguous 48 states.

While the administrative support originates from the Air Force, most members are private citizens whose avocations are flying and SAR. Aircraft may be owned by the CAP or by members and are equipped with special equipment to assist in locating downed aircraft.

Their address is: Civil Air Patrol National Headquarters, Maxwell Air Force Base, Alabama 36112 (telephone number for SAR: 1–205–293–7467).

EXPLORER SEARCH AND RESCUE (ESAR)

ESAR is a formal arm of the Boy Scouts of America. It began in 1955 in Washington state and has grown to include more than 25 teams, predominantly in the Pacific Northwest.

Its dedicated young members train diligently and are subject to 24 hour call. They conduct a great deal of valuable research, as well as contribute thousands of hours to actual SAR. Their efforts have inspired a number of excellent books and manuals on search statistics and team organization and control. Particularly noteworthy is Jon Wartes' *Explorer Search and Rescue Team Member and Team Leader Training Manual.*

ESAR groups are well organized, motivated, and disciplined. Their address is: Western Region, Explorer Search and Rescue, 790 Lucerne Drive, Sunnyvale, California 94086 (telephone number: 1–408–735–1201).

INTERNATIONAL ASSOCIATION OF DIVE RESCUE SPECIALISTS (IADRS)

IADRS is a relatively recent addition to the SAR community, created to fill a void in the training and coordination of rescue related to diving and whitewater boating. The initial thrust was to standardize training for law enforcement agencies in body recovery, physical evidence searches, and whitewater survival. This has expanded to cover dive rescue, marine law enforcement, and self-contained underwater breathing apparatus

(SCUBA) instruction. Specialty diving courses, such as ice diving, are proposed.

IADRS is also a resource for specialty pieces of rescue diving equipment, such as swift water body harnesses, retrieval nets, and lift bags.

Their address is: International Association of Dive Rescue Specialists, 2619 Canton Court, Fort Collins, Colorado 80525 (telephone number: 1–303–482–0887).

MILITARY ASSISTANCE TO SAFETY AND TRANSPORTATION (MAST)

The MAST program was created by Public Law 93–155 in November, 1973. Under this law, the Army and Air Force have identified certain units to assist local governments in maintaining an effective emergency service. The MAST program is a temporary measure to fill local needs in areas where civilian assets are insufficient or nonexistent. MAST units are authorized in direct coordination with local governments, medical facilities, and law enforcement agencies. After approval for mobilization, MAST units are directed to conduct specific missions. When MAST units are used on SAR missions, as opposed to local medical evacuations, they are recruited and controlled by the AFRCC. The Washington state response to the Mount St. Helens eruption exemplifies this process.

The MAST program is also recognized for other humanitarian efforts. The northwestern United States utilizes MAST outfits for such tasks as helicopter transportation of premature infants to neonatal care facilities, the transfer of critically burned patients to burn centers, and the air evacuation of traffic victims.

There is no central office or address for these units. Indeed, not all Army and Air Force operations have a MAST program. In those areas where there is adequate private helicopter assistance, the MAST units will not be visible.

MOUNTAIN RESCUE ASSOCIATION (MRA)

The MRA is composed of more than 50 specialized teams, mostly located in the western states. This highly trained and superbly skilled volunteer paraprofessional group physically performs mountain rescues.

Some teams may be involved in up to 100 SARs a year and have gained international recognition. Each member team must meet standard entrance requirements. Conditioning, teamwork, discipline, and ingenuity are stressed. In the wilderness setting, these teams are expected to be totally self-sufficient for up to 3 days. Several MRA teams, which have large expanses of desert in their areas, have perfected the art of tracking. With instruction from the U.S. Border Patrol, trackers are able to follow man-made trails across solid rock for hundreds of yards. Other teams are heavily involved with Preventive Search and Rescue (PSAR). This program, now mandatory for elementary school children in parts of Oregon, Washington, and California, is an effort to teach wilderness users of tomorrow about the problems they may face.

Their address is: Mountain Rescue Association, P.O. Box 396, Altadena, California 91001 (telephone number: 1–213–791–1731).

NATIONAL ASSOCIATION FOR SEARCH AND RESCUE (NASAR)

The NASAR is a private, nonpolitical, nonprofit group dedicated to the advancement of SAR. It provides a forum for the crystallization of ideas and the interaction of many SAR organizations and nonaffiliated individuals. The latter includes hundreds of people who represent SAR at a grass-roots level: jeepers, alpinists, cavers, snowmobilers, amateur radio operators, and so on. Additionally, there are liaisons with the Federal Emergency Management Agency, various military SAR organizations, and land management agencies such as the Forest Service, Park Service, and Bureau of Land Management.

NASAR hosts an annual conference to update and refine present SAR theory. The Satellite communication used during the Mount St. Helens operation is one example of the efforts of NASAR. The group is active in data collection regarding SAR operations so that the nature and extent of SAR may be accurately interpreted.

Their address is: National Association for Search and Rescue, P.O. Box 2123, La Jolla,

California 92038 (telephone number: 1–714–268–3611).

NATIONAL CAVE RESCUE COMMISSION (NCRC)

The NCRC is the offspring of the National Speleological Society and consists of members highly qualified in technical rock rescue and underground search.

The problems encountered in cave rescue are unique to the SAR community and include poor communications, difficult lighting problems, and cramped, wet spaces. Cave rescue, like other contemporary rescue problems, has inspired unique solutions. A rubberized and SCUBA-equipped exposure suit has been developed to take injured or trapped cavers through water-filled passages. To assist with communications, the NCRC has several sophisticated radio systems, which are available through the AFRCC.

Their address is: National Cave Rescue Co-ordinator, c/o National Speleological Society, Cave Avenue, Huntsville, Alabama 35810 (telephone number: 1–205–852–1300 or through the AFRCC).

SURVIVAL EDUCATION ASSOCIATION (SEA)

The SEA is composed of writers, lecturers, and survival instructors who believe that education saves lives. They continually research and develop visual aids, texts, and course outlines at the secondary and collegiate levels which encompass emergency procedures and preparedness, preventive SAR, and survival education. In addition, the association is a resource center for information about workshops, seminars, reference material, and college credit courses.

Their address is: Survival Education Association, 9035 Golden Given Road, Tacoma, Washington 98445 (telephone number: 1–206–531–3156).

Responsibility, Authority, and Mobilization

The first concern of any individual, team, or agency should be the identification of the individual with authority in a particular incident or area. Despite the variety and often bizarre disorganization of wilderness catastrophes, the organization of authority and jurisdiction should be preplanned.

The official response to the call for a wilderness rescue is usually delegated to a political subdivision within the state. This subdivision normally is a county, and the agent would then be the County Sheriff. When the need arises within an incorporated city, the city has the primary responsibility. This may be handled by the local fire department, police department, or emergency services department. On federal lands, the general rule is that inside national parks, the National Park Service has primary jurisdiction, while in the forests and lands administered by the Bureau of Land Management, the county probably has authority. However, it should be noted here that jurisdiction and ultimate responsibility vary nationwide, and thus cause confusion. Fortunately, most states have either a Search and Rescue Coordinator or a Division of Emergency Services Department. Every Emergency Physician and Rescue Group should be thoroughly familiar with their area and support systems (Figure 1).

The state of Colorado serves to illustrate the sophistication and refinements of authority for wilderness SAR. The Colorado system is outlined to demonstrate the components of a well-functioning agency with regard to authority and jurisdiction, standards, liability, and training. These are stated briefly:

1. The Division of Emergency Services is assigned the authority and responsibility for action in an emergency and must continuously maintain and improve readiness in this field.
2. All search, rescue, and recovery missions and training must be under the direction and control of the appropriate authority. This authority can originate only from the following: the governor, the Director of the Division of Emergency Services, the SAR Coordinator of the Division of Emergency Services, the County Sheriff, or the appropriate official of the political subdivision affected.
3. All SAR individuals and teams must be registered with the appropriate County Emergency Service and the State Division of Emergency Services.
4. All SAR and training missions must have a state SAR Coordination Center mission number if

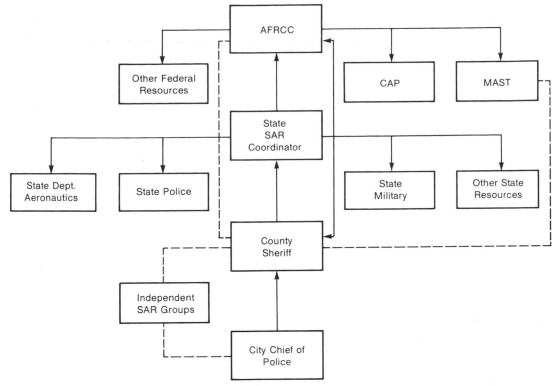

FIGURE 1 Search and rescue (SAR) request and communication channels. The dotted lines show the channel for communication and information; the solid lines show the channel for requesting SAR mutual aid and assistance (AFRCC, Air Force Rescue Coordination Center; CAP, Civil Air Patrol; MAST, Military Assistance to Safety and Transportation).

they are to be covered for legal liability, compensation benefits, and reimbursement for expenses incurred during the mission or training event.

5. All SAR units and individuals are required to meet SAR training and proficiency standards before they are registered locally or with the State SAR Coordinator. All qualified people will be issued an Emergency Services identification card.

6. Expenses incurred as a result of participation in SAR operations are borne by the respective state and federal agencies assigning personnel and equipment in support of such an operation.

7. Training programs are established, with annual team and individual recertification examinations administered by the county emergency services or Sheriff's Department.

AIR SEARCH AND SUPPORT

In most states, the responsibility for disabled civilian aircraft searches falls to the SAR Coordination Center for the state. This center, whether it is called the Office of Emergency Services or the Department of Aeronautics, works closely with county and state aircraft-oriented teams and agencies. Some Sheriff's Departments, especially in the larger counties of the West, have Aero Squadrons specially equipped to search for downed aircraft.

Other agencies lend their expertise to the operation. The Federal Aviation Administration (FAA) is particularly important, providing weather advisories, radar plotting, communications, and historical perspective. This agency has developed an adjunct consisting of a radar backtrack coordinated with a weather map; a computer plots the probability of where aircraft has gone down. This system, coupled with knowledge of the terrain and altitudes involved, has been responsible for the prompt location of several aircraft.

Additional groups providing service are CAP, AFRCC, MAST, and the National Safety Transportation Board.

ORGANIZATION

Although every SAR is different, there are common organizational themes and delegations of responsibility that must structure each

event. Every team has its own idiosyncrasies and needs time as a unit to function smoothly. The organizational components (Figure 2) are discussed below.

Agency Coordinator

This public official represents the jurisdictional region in which the operation is taking

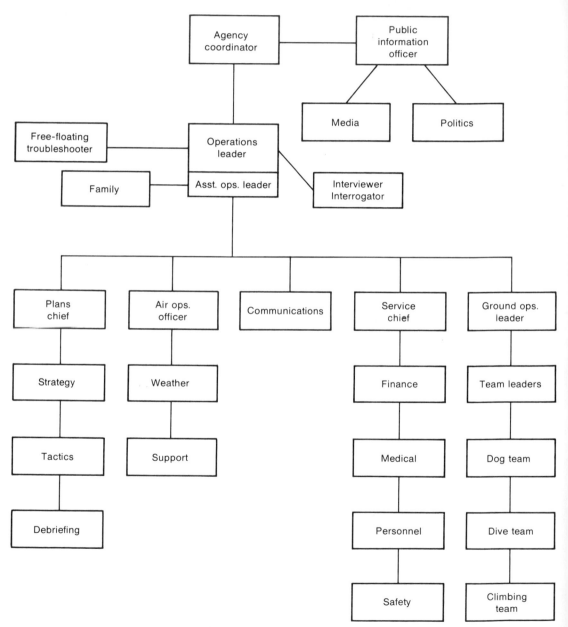

FIGURE 2 Search and rescue (SAR) organization.

place. It is his task to establish liaison with various groups and run interference for the people in the field. This includes keeping the Public Information Officer (PIO) advised of the operation's status.

Public Information Officer

This person handles all media relations and attempts to separate implied or direct political pressures from the rescue operation. People in the field should direct all media inquiries to this person and concentrate on the matter at hand.

Operations Leader

This person is the mastermind of the SAR operation and generally is responsible for strategy decisions. As a rule, he is the most experienced or senior leader. On a large or long operation, he should engage an assistant. The Operations Leader should assign appropriate interrogation agents, troubleshooters who act to sample SAR efforts, effectiveness, and conditions.

Plans Chief

The Plans Chief is second in command to the Operations Leader and is responsible for obtaining adequate personnel, special teams, and equipment. Some searches have employed more than 1000 searchers for a period of up to 10 days, requiring a tremendous effort by the Plans Chief. With his supervisor, he correlates available information into strategy. A good Plans Chief and his Operations Leader do not get much sleep.

Air Operations Officer

When aircraft are engaged for search or support, an Air Operations Officer coordinates the aerial activity. This individual needs to be cognizant of limitations for flying as well as of various aircraft.

Communications Officer

This person coordinates communications, utilizing an appropriate and adequate mainte-nance staff. Malfunctions of communications can be fatal. Large geographic areas require a sophisticated network; a standard police dispatch center is seldom capable of providing it.

Services Chief

The Services Chief keeps track of the numbers of an operation: rescuers, equipment, and finances. The provision of medical services and the physical camp of operations are his responsibility. He maintains an orderly and secure base camp.

Ground Operations Officer

This person actively controls the field teams. The Ground Operations Officer or Leader knows the location, capabilities, and limitations of each team. On a large search, he deploys the field teams according to their area of expertise. This control is exercised down to the individual team leader and team member.

On smaller operations with limited needs or with a smaller initial organization, one person may perform several different functions.

For a more thorough discussion of the organization of an SAR, the reader is directed to NASAR Publication 77–1001, *Pre-Planning the Land Search Organization,* edited by Lois McCoy.

INITIATION AND TERMINATION OF THE SAR

Initiation

Sizeup is fundamental to every SAR. Someone needs to decide who, what, why, how many, the seriousness of the situation, and where the victims are. The call for assistance may come from a friend or family member. It is imperative to interview this reporting party to determine how serious the incident is, how speedy the response must be, and what resources will be required.

These questions, coupled with other variables of time, weather forecasts, historical perspective, resources, and manpower, combine to form an alert and initiation of an SAR.

There should not be a stereotypical response to any given situation. The details of a particular SAR may vary with the experience of the Operations Leader; however, the decision to embark or to wait must be made early.

Termination

Terminating an operation can clearly be a very delicate decision. Considerations include family and political pressures, hazards to the rescue teams, the lack of clues or tangible results, fatigue, and insurmountable weather problems.

At the initiation of the mission, it is important to establish a strong working liaison with any family members or friends of the victims. This relationship will prove valuable when it comes time to terminate an unsuccessful search or rescue. Empathy and compassion early in the operation will allow family members to know that a genuine effort has been made and everything possible has been done.

Political considerations often extend an operation. Honest dialogue with the media and others involved will help mitigate against such influence.

In most SARs, there is a hazard to personnel. Terrain, dangerous techniques, marginal weather, and risk to helicopters may each cause the operation to be terminated as too risky. These considerations are magnified as the search continues without results. The Operations Leader must keep the safety of his crews uppermost in his mind.

If all the strategies and techniques available to the Operations Leader have been attempted, the mission may be terminated. Similarly, a search which has been lengthy or tiring may be ended. If all available resources have been expended, the Operations Leader will have to modify or suspend the operation.

A predicted and extended meteorologic storm pattern in the SAR area adds to the urgency of locating the lost person. However, the Operations Leader should not jeopardize his rescuers needlessly, or he may create additional victims.

The Operations Leader needs to articulate the reasons for terminating an operation in order to provide both moral and legal protection for the SAR team.

Equipment in SAR

The rescue of persons in hazardous wilderness circumstances is often referred to as *technical rescue* and involves the use of specialized equipment. Training and total familiarity are mandatory for the proper and safe use of the equipment discussed. Contemporary SAR technology is well refined, but the elements of a successful rescue are still basic and utilitarian. A recommended SAR equipment list is provided in Appendix C.

Rope

The most essential piece of equipment is the rope. This is particularly useful in vertical rescue but is also the construct of horizontal safety lines used in river rescue. There are several different kinds of rope, each with certain properties.

Dynamic or stretching rope, which has springiness as its chief virtue, may stretch as much as 50% of its length. Rock climbers use this type of rope to help absorb the shock from a fall. Most dynamic ropes are not as abrasion resistant as are other ropes.

Static or nonstretch rope is used by cavers, because they travel up the rope more often than do rock climbers and do not need a springy rope. Static rope is important to the rescuer when long vertical or horizontal distances may be involved. When one is raising or lowering a stretchered victim and an attendant, springiness and stretch may pose a hazard. A hoisting or lowering operation of more than 200 feet necessitates a static rope. Static rope is also more abrasion resistant than dynamic rope, an important consideration in a cave or on ground which is gritty and sharp.

Never trust a life to anything but a nylon rope. Nylon has a great capacity for shock loading and rot resistance and a good weight-to-strength ratio. Manila, hemp, and other synthetic ropes should by used only for securing loads and equipment and not for climbing aids or rescue operations.

Ropes are also categorized as either laid or kernmantle. Laid rope is the common twisted type. These ropes tend to spin when used to raise or lower an object. They permit easy inspection for small breaks and damages and are moderately abrasion resistant.

A kernmantle rope has a core of fibers surrounded by a woven sheath. The external sheath protects the load-bearing core from abrasion. This type of construction does not permit easy inspection of the weight-bearing core. Kernmantle has less tendency to spin and comes in many colors; this is important when there is a need for identifying a rope during a rescue.

Carabiners

Another very common and important tool for rescue is a metal ring-shaped device called a *carabiner* (Figure 3). This 3–4 inch item is a securing mechanism which can be used to descend ropes, to lock into a safety line, or to clip onto objects for protection. Carabiners are generally made of an aluminum alloy, with a maximum breaking strength of 5000 pounds, and come with an opening gate which may or may not have a lock on it. The locking ring prevents the carabiner from opening unexpectedly.

Descending Devices

Additional specialized tools may be required to drop down a vertical face. All such adjuncts generate friction on a rope to permit a safe and orderly descent. The carabiner, when wrapped in a particular way with a rope, will perform this function. This is not a suggested method, however, as the rope may force the carabiner's gate open, permitting a fall.

FIGURE 4 Descending devices.

There are two common devices for descent or rapelling. The first is called the *Six-biner Brake,* which is a combination of at least six carabiners positioned so as to allow a maximum amount of friction and control. A virtue of this system is that it does not require any special equipment. The second, and newer, form of rapelling device, is called the *Figure-Eight* (Figure 4). This is a 6–8 inch ring shaped in a figure eight. These devices are expensive but are increasing in popularity. Descent devices such as the Six-biner Brake and the Figure-Eight can also be used at the top of a cliff to lower weight through this friction-bearing mechanism. In one case the system becomes a "traveling system"; in the other it is a "stationary system," secured at the top.

Ascent Devices

To ascend a rope, mechanical ascenders are necessary (Figure 3). These are metal camlike devices which grip the rope either with teeth or by being clamped under the weight of the user's body so that it will move in only one direction. There are two popular models. The first is the Gibbs Ascender, designed to deal with the adverse conditions found in caves. It is made of rolled aluminum shaped like a clam shell. It is very rugged and, since the cam uses pressures to grip, does not slip on icy or muddy rope. It can be used on horizontal and oblique angles with safety.

The second model is the Jumar Ascender. It is made of cast metal and is shaped like a

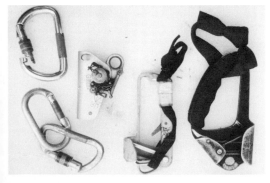

FIGURE 3 Carabiners (*left*) and ascending devices (*right*).

FIGURE 5   Two-person litter.

large letter D. It is not as rugged as the Gibbs Ascender and uses teeth on a cam for gripping. These teeth can become clogged with mud and ice. The Jumar Ascender cannot be used on anything but a vertical rope. The Gibbs is more popular with the caver and the Jumar with the rock climber.

Both of these ascent devices, as well as other gripping mechanisms, can be employed in other capacities during a vertical rescue. They may be used as a "safety" or backup for a lowering. They are placed on the rope in such a manner as to ensure that the rope cannot run free or dangerously fast. A good caver or rock climber can ascend extremely rapidly. With the right system, 100 feet of rope can be climbed in less than 10 seconds. This time can be further reduced on a static rope.

Several safety considerations must be kept in mind. Rope that is laid and stored should not be stepped on or exposed to corrosives and petroleum products. One must be cognizant of what stresses the rope is placed under and over what sharp corners it runs. After suffering a great drop or being exposed to a severe shock of any kind, the rope should be retired and never again used for a lifeline. A well-organized rescue team will maintain histories and records on ropes and other pieces of equipment.

Carabiner gates occasionally need to be lu-

bricated with graphite, and the locking gates need to be cleaned with a brush to rid them of grit. Carabiners should be marked by paint or tape for ready identification. The same maintenance is required for ascent devices. A careful periodic check should be made of the camming portions of the devices for function and proper lubrication.

Other rescue aids, such as a Stokes or Two-Man Liter (Figure 5), are burdensome to carry but may provide the only means of transporting the victim. For anticipated spinal trauma (falls, head injuries, avalanche victims), short or long backboards are recommended to stabilize the spine during extrication and transport. Hare traction devices may relieve considerable deformity, muscle spasm, and pain related to fractures of the femur. The newly developed Reel splint offers an adjustable, lightweight, and collapsible alternative to the Hare device (Figure 3, Chapter 5).

Cave SAR

The National Speleological Society estimates that there are more than 100,000 known solutionally formed caves in the United States. The sport of cave exploring, spelunking, has generated a specialized need for SAR expertise.

PROBLEMS

Total darkness can be overwhelming to both the novice caver and the inexperienced cave rescuer. One of the most common emergencies of caving is created by "flashlight cavers." Ill-equipped and inexperienced, they enter caves without adequate light sources and power supplies. Experienced cavers and rescuers should never enter a cave without at least three independent sources of light.

Reduced visibility mandates lighting the rescue scene beyond the normal limits of a flashlight. The vastness of some passages and rooms necessitates large beams for searching. A water cave, or *live cave,* involves a moisture range inside the cave from mud to rivers. Western caves are generally drier than eastern caves. The humidity and wetness in caves, along with the temperature, create a potential for hypothermia greatly underestimated by the average caver.

Flooding in caves is often a great problem. Both novice and experienced cavers die because of inattention to the weather on the outside. In many caves, the openings are natural drains for streams. This may seriously hamper exit by the caver or entrance by the rescuer.

Cave diving is a popular sport in the southeastern United States. It has already claimed the lives of several hundred cave divers. Novices rarely seem to prepare themselves properly for these water-filled passages.

Wind and temperature are underestimated problems associated with caving emergencies. It is not unusual for streams of air to blow along cave passages; these caves are commonly called *blowing* or *breathing caves.* This wind may intensify chilling conditions.

Most caves maintain a constant temperature year round; often it is much lower than the outside ambient temperature. The rescuer needs to dress accordingly.

UNIQUE CHARACTER OF CAVE RESCUE

Route finding in caves is a great challenge. Aboveground, there are clear landmarks; belowground, the landmarks are appreciated only by experienced cavers. Passages and scenes seem to change appearance constantly. Some caves are characterized by linear development with minimal branching, while others are developed along straight lines with a great deal of branching. This organization is characterized by high variability.

Climbing underground must be done with greater care. The principal matrix, limestone or dolomite, is often covered with calcite or mud, forming a treacherous and deceptive layer upon which to work. Pitons and expansion bolts may not work well here.

Confined passages, low crawls, and squeezes pose unique problems for the rescue of injured cavers. The use of standard items, such as stretchers, backboards, and splints, may not be possible in such places. Confined passages also occasionally lead to hypoxic states for victims and rescuers.

The humidity and dampness create treacherous handholds and awkward footing. Many cavers explore in wet suits; although they are more restrictive, they ensure better temperature regulation.

PERFORMING CAVE SAR

Cave rescue must involve people experienced in and familiar with the particular cave. In areas with a lot of caves, this precaution will prove invaluable. Maps of many caves can be procured from these caving groups. With the aid of cave diagrams, fast-moving teams may sweep through the main passages and move to the prominent features of the cave. Although echoes and the muffling effect of falling water can confuse sounds underground, whistles and shouts can be helpful in many situations to locate lost people in side passages. The pattern of discarded equipment may indicate to experienced rescuers the likely location of a lost victim.

The search for a lost but uninjured person may prove exasperating, but hardly as difficult and dangerous as that for an injured caver. Raising and lowering skills are essential prior to the extrication of victims from a cave. Many eastern caves are honeycombed with vertical pits that are often several hundred feet deep. Ingenuity and creativity are necessary to remove people through talus slopes, rockfalls, tight passages, waterfalls, and vertical areas. Lighting equipment is of paramount importance. Handheld lights and generator-powered equipment, familiar to aboveground operations, are dangerous and inadequate underground. Headlamps, carbide lamps, and electric lights are most often used. Exposure suits or wet suits may be mandatory. Individual ascent and descent devices are required for even short raisings and lowerings. Static non-stretch rope is essential for vertical extrication.

Communication is a matter of gravest concern. Frequently, men in plain sight below a party cannot communicate due to poor acoustics, falling water, moving air currents, or confusion caused by the talking of others. This problem may be partially solved by using pre-arranged whistle or voice commands, runners, and, at the most sophisticated level, by the field telephone.

For a more thorough discussion of the unique aspects of a cave SAR, the reader is directed to NASAR Publication 77–1019, *Hazards and Rescue Problems in the Cave Environment,* by Barlow and Vines of the Appalachian Search and Rescue Conference, Inc.

Technical Rock Rescue

Mountaineering, rock climbing, and casual scrambling have created the need for specialized SAR expertise. Each year in Yosemite National Park there are approximately 75 technical rock rescues.

Individuals and groups involved in rock rescue have refined and developed techniques for most situations. The hallmark of a technical rock rescuer is the ability to extemporize and modify his tools and techniques to meet any crisis. He must be comfortable using climbing gear and being exposed to height.

PROBLEMS

Once the victim has been located and the situation surveyed, it will become necessary to gain access to this person. Local groups familiar with a particular well-known area will have already solved this problem.

The solution will involve either climbing to or dropping down to the victim. Safety for all persons involved is paramount; an accident during the rescue is catastrophic.

Climbing up to the victim requires a knowledge of contemporary rock-climbing techniques. Proper equipment and familiarity with its use are critical. The reader should contact local outing clubs or mountaineering stores for more detailed assistance.

Specialized technical rock rescue teams, such as the MRA, routinely practice climbing techniques and the solving of vertical rescue problems. For example, the face of Yosemite Valley's El Capitan, an 800 m unbroken vertical face of granite, has been climbed in 15 hours.

The decision to go up or down may depend on accessibility to either the top or the bottom. A river at the bottom may preclude an approach from below. Conversely, a brush-filled approach to the top may preclude going in from above. The availability of a helicopter and adequate landing sites may provide easy access to the top. Suitable anchor sites or easier climbing at the top favor a superior approach.

Going down necessitates good descent techniques and proper anchors. The Figure-Eight and Six-biner Brake are two methods of rappelling to the victim. Rappelling allows more control by the descending rescuer but "ties up" his hands. The Operations Leader may elect to lower the rescuer rather than allow him to rappel. This necessitates greater communication between the top and the rescuer but allows the hands to be free.

The rescuer needs to prepare for all eventualities. The Operations Leader needs to have solutions for potential complications which may occur during the lowering.

On a cliff more than 200 feet high, it is probably easier to go down to the victim rather than up. A long enough rope is required for the initial lowering, with a second long rope available if complications occur. If the victim is able to assist himself, it may only be necessary to lower him to the bottom. If the victim cannot assist himself and needs to be placed on a stretcher, others must be present at the accident site. This is a complicated but not impossible task.

Whitewater River Rescue

Sports involving swift-moving water, such as tubing, canoeing, kayaking, and rafting, are important forms of recreation. Inherent in these endeavors is the risk that the vessel will be stuck in midstream or the occupants will be thrown out on a rock or log. A similar problem is created by vehicles going over an embankment into a river, with the occupants scrambling to the roof of the partially submerged vehicle.

PROBLEMS

The single greatest problem associated with this type of emergency is that the rescuer may underestimate the seriousness of the situation. Foolhardy heroics and overzealous enthusiasm frequently lead to further tragedy.

Cold water, coupled with the wind generated by its motion, may predispose persons to hypothermia. Low ambient temperatures, wet clothing, darkness, and injury escalate the insult.

Noise associated with the moving water may obviate clear communications. Poor contact between the victim and rescuers and between rescuers is confusing and dangerous.

Lack of proper equipment and adequately trained rescuers is hazardous to all involved. The forces encountered upon entering the water are tremendous and deceiving. Thorough training and experience are paramount.

PERFORMING WHITEWATER RIVER RESCUE

The rescuer needs to be cognizant of all variables: lack of access to both sides of the river, rapids above and below the victim, the width of the river, the location of the victim, the ability of the victim to assist himself, the presence of darkness, and the equipment available.

Depending on the initial assessment, there may be several solutions. The first entails putting a boat, fixed hull or rubber, into the water. Ropes, strategically placed from the bank to the boat, may prove effective for stabilization in rough water. Occupants of the boat must wear wet suits and/or flotation devices. A motorized vessel may be necessary. This is a highly specialized form of rescue which requires great skill and caution. A river may be so small or rocky that the use of any boat will be impossible.

When the victim is unreachable by boat, a rescuer may have to go into the rapids or between the rocks without this aid. Flotation devices are again essential. If a rope is being taken to the victim, it should not be tied to the rescuer. If the rescuer is forced underwater by a swift current, it is very possible that he will drown if tied to the rope. Quick-release buckles, similar to those on a parachute, will give a rescuer a safer journey in the rapids. Once the rescuer has reached the victim, they may both be pulled to shore. If the victim is to be pulled to shore, he should wear a flotation device.

A third way to reach the victim is by a *tyrolean traverse,* in which the rescuer travels along a rope suspension in order to reach the victim. In a narrow river, the use of this method may be limited by the length of rope available. Rope that stretches will dip the rescuer into the river. The longer the traverse, the higher the anchors need to be on both banks. The author has set up one traverse of 300 feet. This is not a technique which can be used without prior practice and/or experience.

A fourth method of extraction from the middle of a river employs a helicopter coupled with either a hoisting device or a length of line with a basket attached to the end. The pilot must be alert to rotor clearance and may need to watch for tall trees to attain vertical accessibility. With adequate maneuvering space, this is a quick and relatively safe method.

Oversnow SAR

Oversnow rescue is a special subdivision of back-country and mountain rescue that involves cold weather, frequently at high altitude, and utilizes items of equipment designed to move the victim over the snow and to protect him and his rescuers from cold and wind. The medical care of such victims is no different from the care of any victim, but it must frequently be rendered under adverse weather conditions. The victim may be isolated by many miles from a doctor or hospital, and evacuation may have to be performed without communication over difficult and hazardous terrain. The complicating effects of cold, wind, and altitude may modify the course of the victim's illness. Ski patrollers and others engaged in oversnow rescue in the back country are given special training in the techniques of extended first aid. They need to be in good physical condition, expert in skiing and other techniques of oversnow travel, good snow campers, and winter survival experts. The National Ski Patrol System, Inc., and mountain rescue groups have special training courses in these disciplines.

Persons who need oversnow rescue include patrons of downhill and ski touring areas, skiers who wander off-area, lost hunters, injured ski mountaineers, winter climbers and back-country skiers, and survivors of downed aircraft.

Leaders of SAR parties have an obligation to conduct an efficient search, but *their first duty is to ensure the safety of the members of the rescue party.*

The worldwide proliferation of ski areas is now associated with more than 500,000 ski-related injuries per year. Large, complicated organizations have been developed to give first aid to injured downhill skiers. In the United States, the National Ski Patrol System, Inc., has more than 24,000 members. The recent

expansion of nordic skiing has stimulated the growth of nordic ski patrols. In many cases, these patrols make themselves available to perform other types of oversnow back-country rescue.

First aid and transportation facilities at commercial ski areas are highly organized. Transportation is usually accomplished by a toboggan handled by patrollers on skis or pulled by a snow machine (Figures 6, 7, 8). Large oversnow vehicles, such as Sno-Cats and Thiokols, are sometimes used to transport victims directly.

Groups who perform back-country oversnow rescue work at the request of the National Park Service, Forest Service, State Police, County Sheriff, or other legally constituted authority. Group members carry a backpack with equipment adequate to maintain the individual in the winter environment for at least 48 hours. First aid supplies, rescue and transportation equipment, radios, and supplies to sustain the victim during rescue are also carried. Sample SAR plans are prepared and rehearsed beforehand.

When a missing person is reported at a

FIGURE 6 Cascade toboggan of the type used at many downhill ski areas. It is handled by two skiers, one in front holding on to the handles and a safety person in back holding on to the tail rope. (Photo courtesy of Steve Reisman.)

FIGURE 7 Lightweight toboggan suitable for Nordic and backcountry oversnow rescue. The front poles are attached by a standard pack-frame waist belt, freeing the hands for poling. Can be handled by one person, but has attachments for rear and belaying ropes for safety in steep terrain. (Photo courtesy of Mountain Man, Bozeman, Montana.)

suming line searches requiring large numbers of persons are employed to cover every square foot of the area in question. Reliable radio communication between search parties and their base and between the search teams is essential. Search paths and important clues must be marked conspicuously with flagging. At the end of the search, all searchers must be accounted for.

Where large areas must be searched, as is the case with lost hunters and downed aircraft, several types of search methods are employed simultaneously. If weather permits, helicopters and fixed-wing aircraft are very useful. Ground vehicles can be used to patrol roads and snow machines to patrol trails where lost persons may come out. At the same time, ground parties on skis or snowshoes are sent out.

Once the victim has been located, he is taken to a shelter and given first aid. Further evacuation is not started until his condition is stabilized, even if this means spending a night outdoors. Rather than subject the victim to a long, uncomfortable toboggan ride, it may be better to wait for clear weather so that a helicopter can be brought in.

Parties engaging in multiday, back-country ski tours or winter climbs should have self-help capacity in the event of an illness or injury. First aid kits should be carried. (Appendix E) Evacuation sleds can theoretically be improvised by lashing the victim's skis to a frame of small poles and ski poles or a pack-frame, but it cannot be relied on for long-distance transportation, especially in deep, soft snow. A lightweight (less than 5 pounds) kit can be carried which uses the victim's skis and a piece of aluminum sheeting to make a rescue toboggan.* At the time of this writing, the best arrangement seems to be a lightweight (less than 30 pounds) fiberglass toboggan, one per party. This is easier to handle on skis than a 50 pound pack and can be used to haul up to several hundred pounds of payload while being available to serve as a rescue sled. Some brands can be worn as backpacks for short distances by means of detachable shoulder straps; others have attachments so that they can be pulled by a dog or snowmobile.

downhill ski area, the informant must be detained so that all necessary information can be obtained and recorded. The missing person's name, age, physical condition, equipment, clothing, skiing ability, last known location, and survival experience are important. A necessary job is the "bastard search," in which local bars and friends' houses are checked before a full-scale back-country search is mounted. In many cases, the actual search requires no more than following a set of tracks in the snow until the victim is found. In other instances, complex patterns of search are necessary. For example, in a perimeter search, rescue teams ski the boundaries of the ski area looking for tracks leading away from the area. In the scratch, or hasty, search, a small team searches the last seen point and the most logical path the missing person might have taken while the main search team is being assembled. The main team conducts a thorough search of the area where the missing person is presumed to be, paying particular attention to trails, high points, stream bottoms, old cabins, and danger areas. If this search fails, then complicated and time-con-

* Available as the Hall-U from Ski Treads, P.O. Box 1127, Hamilton, Montana 59840.

FIGURE 8   Use of a 4½ foot Nordic sled during mountaineering operations on Mount McKinley. (Photo courtesy of Mountain Smith, Golden, Colorado.)

Snow Avalanche

Snow avalanches are frightening and powerful natural phenomena (Figure 9) which have been responsible for the loss of many lives and much property. It is estimated that 10,000 avalanches occur yearly in the United States. Fortunately, the great majority of these fall in isolated or uninhabited areas, so that the yearly toll averages seven lives and $300,000 in property damage. As population pressures, winter sports activity, and mining activity increase, the persons and property exposed to avalanche danger will increase.

In this section, we will deal with the recognition of dangerous avalanche conditions and with the rescue of persons caught in avalanches. Interested readers may consult the Recommended Reading at the end of this chapter for in-depth discussions of snow physics and avalanche control. In order to understand the behavior of snow, however, it is useful to know its unique characteristics.

Snow is one of the solid forms of water,

the only substance able to exist in all three physical states at the natural temperature ranges present at the earth's surface. Water has a very high heat of fusion (80 kcal/g), seven times that of iron and 13 times that of lead. This means that the vast amounts of snow and ice in polar and subpolar areas can exert profound effects on the earth's climate, because they represent the investment of enormous amounts of heat and require such large amounts of heat to cause melting.

Snow has very low heat conductivity, ranging from 0.0001 to 0.0007 cal/cm per second per degree Celsius, about 1/10,000 that of copper or about the same as that of wool felt. This explains why snow shelters can be so comfortable and partly accounts for snow's resistance to melting. Snow is a viscoelastic substance, tending to be more brittle at lower temperatures and more plastic at higher temperatures. As new-fallen snow ages, it undergoes a process called *destructive* or *equitemperature metamorphism,* whereby the flakes become smaller and denser, causing the snow to settle and become stronger and more com-

FIGURE 9 Avalanche.

pact. This process is more rapid at higher temperatures. Another type of metamorphism, called *constructive* or *temperature-gradient metamorphism,* is important because of its contribution to snowpack instability and slab avalanche formation. It occurs when marked temperature differences between the snow surface and the ground surface set up currents of water vapor within the snowpack, leading to the formation of scroll or cup-shaped ice crystals called *depth hoar,* which are weak and poorly bonded to each other and to adjacent snow layers. Temperature-gradient metamorphism is more common at high altitudes, on north-facing slopes and shaded areas, and in early winter when the snowpack is shallow and unconsolidated. It is seen in the Rocky Mountains and other inland ranges, and less frequently in coastal ranges.

Snow deposited on a slope tends to flow slowly downhill under the influence of gravity. This process, known as *creep,* depends on the plastic properties of the snow, which are more pronounced at higher temperatures. Creep can produce tensile and sheer stresses in a snow slope and is a major contributor to avalanche formation; it can also relieve these stresses and, together with equitemperature metamorphism, can act as a strengthening and stabilizing factor. Since creep and equitemperature metamorphism are more active at warmer temperatures, avalanche conditions tend to stabilize rapidly at higher temperatures and persist much longer at lower temperatures.

When snow is disturbed mechanically, as by wind action, skiing, or foot packing, and then allowed to set, it becomes progressively harder over a period of several hours. This process, called *age hardening,* is more active the lower the temperature, and explains the increase in hardness associated with wind-drifted snow.

The two basic requirements for a snow avalanche are snow and a slope for it to slide on. Most large avalanches occur on slopes with inclinations of 25–60°, with 30–45° being the most dangerous range. Slopes steeper than 60° will rarely retain great quantities of snow, and slopes of less than 25° are not steep enough to generate enough sheer stress. Most avalanches (90%) fall during or shortly after a storm.

TYPES OF AVALANCHES

The two main types of avalanche are *loose snow* and *slab.* A loose snow avalanche occurs when the steepness of the slope exceeds the

FIGURE 10   Loose snow avalanche. (Photo by Ross Gregg.)

angle of repose of unconsolidated snow (Figure 10). There is a local loss of cohesion at one small point of the slope, and the falling snow disturbs snow below it so that the avalanche fans out below this point. When seen from above, a loose snow avalanche is wedge-shaped and seems to start at a single point. These avalanches occur frequently throughout the winter, from early fall to late spring, and may be dry, moist, or wet. They range in size from harmless "sluffs" to large, dangerous, wet loose snow avalanches seen in maritime climates. Most are small, and their danger consists more of knocking mountaineers or skiers from safe perches than of actually causing burial.

The slab avalanche is the most dangerous type of avalanche and occurs when a large, cohesive slab of snow, usually shaped roughly like an oblong dish, breaks loose from its attachments and begins to slide all at once (Figure 11). A well-defined fracture line is characteristically visible where the slab has broken away from the snow above it. The slab immediately breaks up into many small blocks

which tumble downhill. Softer slabs (with a density less than 300 kg/m³) may disintegrate entirely into a jumble of loose snow. Slab avalanches are responsible for the majority of avalanche accidents and in most cases are triggered by the victims themselves (Figure 12).

Much research has gone into studying the conditions which result in slab formation, and the following generalizations can be made:

1. Most slabs consist of snow with densities between 100 and 400 kg/m³. There is no consistent type of snow form and no visible characteristic of the snow cover which can be correlated with slab formation.
2. In most cases, the bed on which the slab slides is weaker than the undersurface of the slab. This can be due to such weak snow forms as *graupel* (a type of rimed crystal resembling a soft shotgun pellet which bonds poorly) or depth hoar, to an ice crust, or to grass on the ground surface. Meltwater percolating through a slab can run along an ice crust and lubricate the sliding surface.
3. Wind-drifted snow frequently forms slabs, particularly on the lee slopes of ridges, but wind

FIGURE 11 Slab avalanche. (Photo by André Roch.)

is neither a necessary nor a sufficient cause alone. Wind speeds of 15–60 mph, when combined with heavy snowfalls of 0.5–1.0 inch/hour, frequently cause widespread slab avalanche formation.

4. A slab avalanche is released when the forces which attach it at its top (crown), flanks, bottom, and bed are exceeded by the forces which tend to make it fall down the mountainside. The most important attachment is at the top (potential fracture line), where the snow is subjected to tensile stress. Sudden forces which trigger a slab avalanche usually act in this area. Common factors which cause slab avalanche release include:

   a. Increased weight on the surface by heavy snowfall or wind-drifted snow.

   b. Sudden shock due to fall of a cornice, explosive blast, loose snow avalanche, and so on.

   c. Skier, climber, or snowmobiler traversing the slab.

   d. Weakening of the bed surface by meltwater, metamorphism, or creep.

   e. Increased tension at the top resulting from stretching forces when a slab builds up on a *convex* slope.

   f. Temperature changes which weaken critical attachments.

5. Dangerous slab avalanches rarely occur in deep timber, but can take place in sparse timber and are common on bare slopes. Avalanches rarely occur unless the snow depth is adequate to cover

FIGURE 12 Slab avalanche released by a skier. (Photos by Rudolf Ludwig.)

smoothly natural irregularities and protrusions of the ground surface.

6. Slabs rarely form on wind-packed windward sides of ridges.

7. Persons intending to travel into mountainous back-country areas during the snow months should be able to identify avalanche-prone topography and climatic conditions producing great hazard, and areas of little danger where travel is relatively safe. Dangerous areas may

be easy to identify at certain times and difficult at others. *Cirques, bowls* and *gullies, lee slopes of ridges,* and *open or sparsely timbered slopes of 25–60° inclination* are dangerous. During the summer, avalanche slopes stand out because of the abrupt change of vegetation where large evergreens have been replaced by small and limber deciduous trees, such as alders and aspens. Larger trees which remain may be bent over or may have lost their uphill branches. Piles of logs and other avalanche debris may be seen at the bottom of these slopes.

TRAVEL IN AVALANCHE COUNTRY

Skiers, mountaineers, and others who elect to travel through avalanche country can minimize the hazard by proper route finding. Parties should be of sufficient size (minimum, four persons), and each member should carry a shovel and a collapsible avalanche probe or ski poles which can be joined to form a probe. Avalanche cords have been widely used in the past but are probably not as useful as formerly thought. These are colored nylon cords 30 m in length which are tied securely around the waist and trailed out behind in areas of high hazard. Theoretically, if the wearer is caught and buried in an avalanche, part of the cord may remain on the snow surface and will aid rescuers in locating him. The best insurance for a speedy location and rescue, however, is for each member of the party to carry an electronic transceiver (Pieps, Skadi, Echo II) which must be attached securely to the body. These transceivers are turned to "send" during travel and, if a party member is buried, the rest of the party will turn their units to "receive" and dig where the signal is loudest.

When traveling up a valley, one should stay in the middle and as far from avalanche path runouts as possible (Figures 13 and 14). When traveling along a ridge, one should stay below the crest on the windward side of the ridge and avoid cornices. Camp should be made as far as possible from avalanche starting zones and runouts. One should camp and travel in heavy timber when possible and should *never* travel alone.

If dangerous slopes must be crossed, they should be crossed as low as possible in the valley or as high as possible above likely avalanche starting zones. Only one person should

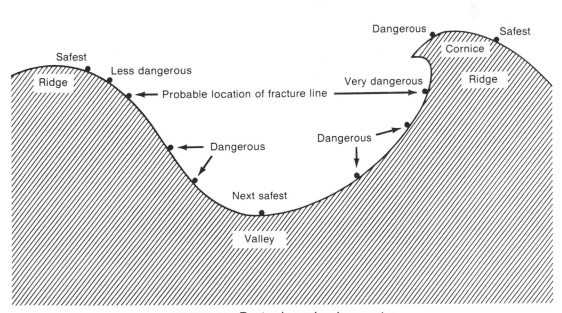

FIGURE 13 Routes in avalanche country.

FIGURE 14 Four ski-tour areas showing the safer (dashed lines) and the more dangerous routes (dotted lines). Arrows indicate areas of wind loading. (Reprinted with permission from the *Avalanche Handbook,* Agricultural Handbook 489, USDA Forest Service. Photo by Alexis Kelmer.)

cross at a time, the rest of the party remaining out of danger. In very hazardous areas, belaying may be advisable. Before crossing a slope, one should remove his ski pole wrist straps from his wrists, zip up his parka, undo his ski safety straps, put on his mittens and parka hood, undo his pack waist strap, carry his pack by one shoulder strap if feasible, and move as quickly and quietly as possible. He should take advantage of natural protection by skiing between rock outcrops, ridges, or clumps of trees. Parties should move downhill so that there is a chance of skiing out of the way if an avalanche starts.

If an avalanche path must be ascended or descended, it should be done without skis, straight up or straight down without undercutting the slope, and as far to the side as possible, since snow at the sides of an avalanche tends to be deposited on top of snow in the center and one has a better chance of getting to the side out of the avalanche path. Whenever one is considering travel on an avalanche path, he should think of what may happen if the snow does slide. Slopes which funnel in a narrow gulley where one may be buried deeply, over cliffs, or into crevasses are especially hazardous.

In many instances, it may be better to make a long detour or even call off the trip rather than continue over hazardous slopes or travel during times of high hazard.

Signs of Danger and Instability

1. Fracturing of the snow under the skis, with the fracture line propagated away from the skis.
2. Crunching or "whumping" noises in the snow underneath or nearby.
3. A hollow sound when hard snow is tapped with a ski pole.
4. Very hard snow in a lee area.
5. Avalanching nearby on similar slopes.

One should avoid travel during and immediately after storms when avalanche danger is likely to be the highest, and in early winter when the snow pack is unconsolidated. Danger after a storm may persist for many days on north-facing or shaded slopes. The safest time of the year for ski touring is in the late season after the snowpack has compacted and become isothermal. At this time, slab avalanche danger exists for only a few days following a fresh snowfall.

Avalanche Control at Downhill Ski Areas

Most ski areas have ski patrollers on duty who have been trained in avalanche recognition, control, and rescue. Rehearsal for the rescue and resuscitation of avalanche victims permits mobilization of a large group of rescuers within minutes. The necessary equipment should be cached in a place where all parts of the avalanche area can be reached rapidly. At ski areas with high avalanche hazard, avalanche control work is performed daily and consists of (1) disturbing dangerous slopes with explosives so that the snow will either stabilize in place or slide in a controlled manner, (2) control skiing, or the testing of small, representative slopes by men on skis to check on snow stability, and (3) evaluation of the condition of the snowpack by snow pit analysis and the use of the ram penetrometer, a device which quantitates the relative hardness of successive snow layers. Dangerous areas which cannot be stabilized are closed to the public. No skier should be allowed to ski in a closed area.

Helicopter skiing, a relatively new sport which allows skiers to ski hitherto inaccessible, untracked slopes in the high mountains, has also opened up new areas of avalanche hazard. It should not be done without electronic transceiver protection and the services of a guide familiar with local conditions.

Conduct When Caught in an Avalanche

A person caught in an avalanche can increase his chances of survival if he keeps his wits about him. He should call out immediately to alert his companions. If he is close to the edge, he may be able to ski out of the way. If he can grab a tree or branch, he may avoid being carried away. Otherwise, his best chance is to discard his skis, poles, and pack and try to stay on top of the snow by vigorous swimming motions. If he is buried, as soon as he feels the snow stop, he should move his head vigorously back and forth to make a breathing space, get one hand in front of his face to protect it, and thrust the other vigorously straight over his head (it will occasionally break the snow surface, where it can be seen). He then should try to relax, since struggling uses up precious oxygen. Shouting is of little value because of poor transmission of sound through the snow.

AVALANCHE RESCUE

Most avalanche deaths are due to suffocation, either from failure of air to penetrate the dense snow or from respiratory embarrassment due to obstruction of the respiratory passages or to the pressure of the snow on the chest. Accident analysis shows that 50% of victims die within the first half hour of burial. Therefore, a successful rescue depends on location of the buried victim and rapid extrication. The victim has a 10-fold chance of being found alive if he is buried where an organized rescue group can reach him quickly. Observers of an avalanche accident have two urgent and sometimes conflicting duties: to conduct a search for the victim and to mobilize organized rescue groups. Victims have died when witnesses left to seek help instead of researching obvious clues which would have led to discovery of the victim within a few minutes. In a party of several people, one can usually be spared to go for help while the others start searching, but in the back country where help may take many hours to arrive, it is usually best to make a thorough search with all available personnel before going for help. Victims have survived burial for several hours (Figure 15).

If one witnesses an avalanche accident, he must avoid being included in the avalanche, while making a mental note of the point where the victim was last seen. After the avalanche has stopped, this point should be marked with a branch or ski pole. The victim often lies somewhere below, usually in the debris at the toe of the avalanche; at other times, he lies near natural features such as trees, boulders, benches, bends in the gulley, or other obstacles which slow the snow. A rapid search should be made of the most likely areas for clues, such as parts of the victim's body or equipment protruding above the snow. Likely areas are probed with ski poles or avalanche probes. If the search is unsuccessful, the party should

FIGURE 15 Avalanche victim rescued after 4 hours. (Photo courtesy of J. Foray.)

be organized into a probe line, keeping in mind the possibility that other avalanches may occur down the same track. If enough manpower is available, guards should be posted to sound a warning if another avalanche starts. Probing should be conducted in silence so that the victim's cries or the start of a second avalanche can be heard. Probers should occasionally shout the victim's name and then listen for a possible reply.

Probing Technique

Probing is easiest and most efficient when the line is moving uphill. Formal probing should start at the toe of the avalanche and advance uphill. As long as there is any chance of finding the victim alive, *coarse* probing should be conducted (Figure 16). This gives a 70% chance of finding the victim and takes only one-fourth the time of more meticulous *fine* probing. Probers are spaced along a line with their feet comfortably apart (20 inches) and 10 inches from the next man. The probe pole is inserted in front of the prober midway between his feet. On a signal, the probers withdraw their probes, move forward one step, and reinsert them. Probing should be done silently, rhythmically, and with military precision. Shovelers should follow the probe line and dig whenever the probers discover any

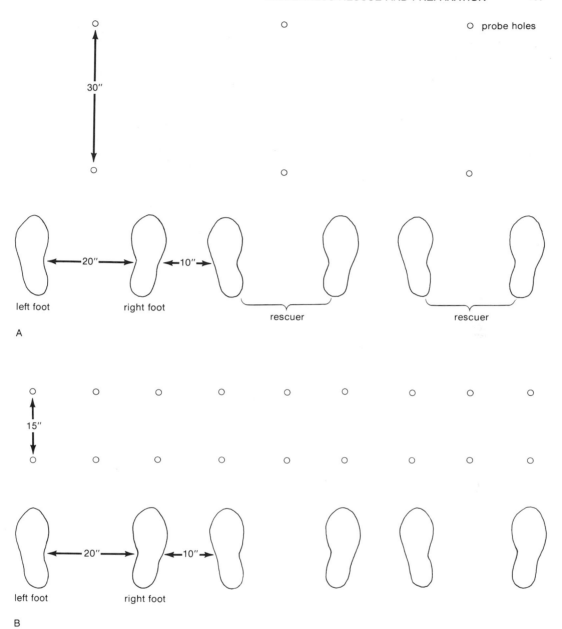

FIGURE 16 Coarse (*A*) and fine (*B*) fine avalanche probing.

unexplained obstacle to their probes. Coarse probing should be repeated several times if it is unsuccessful. Fine probing is utilized when coarse probing is unsuccessful and the chances of a live recovery are unlikely.

If a party is equipped with electronic transceivers, all members should operate on the same frequency (2275 hz). Searchers should switch their units to "receive" and move over the avalanche debris in a pattern to locate the point where the transmitted signal is loudest; the victim is most likely directly below this point.

Trained avalanche dogs can search an avalanche rapidly by scent and have been used extensively in the Alps with considerable success. Their use has caught on more slowly in North America, partly because of the greater distances involved and the greater time lags before dogs can reach accident scenes. A suitable dog must have a strong constitution and a keen sense of smell; German shepherds seem to be the best choice.

First Aid and Transportation of the Victim

Victims of avalanche burial suffer from hypothermia and hypoxia, and may also have frostbite, mechanical injuries, and shock. The most urgent requirement is restoration of breathing, which requires mouth-to-mouth or bag-mask resuscitation and should be started as soon as the victim's head is uncovered. Oxygen is added if available, and if appropriate, CPR is given. The upper respiratory passages may be blocked by snow or vomit and have to be cleared by the best available method. Most rescue groups carry foot- or vacuum-operated pumps for this purpose.

The victim should be extricated with care and the neck splinted with a cervical collar if cervical spine injury appears likely. This is followed by backboard immobilization.

Hypothermia is invariably present and must be treated by the usual methods (see Chapter 2), which include providing insulation and wind shelter and adding heat by the best available means. Fractures and other injuries are treated by splinting, immobilization, and traction as needed.

Trained avalanche rescue groups should carry bag-mask resuscitators, oral airways, suction equipment, oxygen, selected drugs, intravenous (IV) solutions, airway rewarming and other special warming devices, tents, sleeping bags, stoves, radio, and toboggans.

Helicopters in SAR

No one technique or instrument has done more to change SAR operations than the helicopter. It is mandatory that those involved with this machine know its capabilities, limits, hazards involved, and safety requirements.

Safety Rules

1. All personnel should stay at least 100 feet from small models and 150 feet from larger models (unless they are part of the authorized crew).

2. All personnel should approach or leave the helicopter from the front, where they can be seen by the pilot.

3. One should keep his head down at all times. The slower the rotor is moving, the lower it will dip.

4. One should never approach or leave a helicopter from any side where the ground is higher than it is where the helicopter is standing, or he may walk into a rotor.

5. No one should smoke within 100 feet of a helicopter.

6. Under many circumstances of visibility and viewpoint, a helicopter tail rotor cannot be seen due to its high speed. All personnel should maintain a wide clearance from the tail area and not stoop or walk under the tail boom.

7. Personnel working with a helicopter should wear hardhats with chin straps, goggles, and bright jackets or vests.

8. Passengers should wear hard hats and seat belts.

9. Long-handled tools, ice axes, skis, litters, radio antennas, and other similar items should be kept low and parallel to the ground when one is approaching or leaving the helicopter.

10. Ropes should be coiled and secured. Loose, light items, such as sleeping bags and parkas, should be secured in packs or bags.

11. One should not load a helicopter without the pilot's supervision. Tie-down straps are kept short to eliminate loose ends which might get tangled in control cables or the motor. Tie-downs should be resecured after unloading.

12. Passengers should not enter the helicopter until the pilot gives the signal.

13. Passengers should not leave the helicopter until the pilot gives the signal. Ground personnel should not approach the helicopter until the engine is off and the rotors have stopped or until the pilot gives the signal. After touchdown, the pilot may want to shift a helicopter's position.

14. One must never stand directly beneath the helicopter in its takeoff or landing pattern unless directly authorized to hook sling loads.

15. At takeoffs and landings, all personnel should be well away from helicopter. Main rotors may dip to one side or the tail rotor may swing around as the craft moves.

Landing Zones

A good landing zone or helipad is an area cleared to accommodate safely the ship on the ground, as well as provide a clear landing and takeoff lane (Figure 17). The best helipads are located on exposed areas, such as ridge

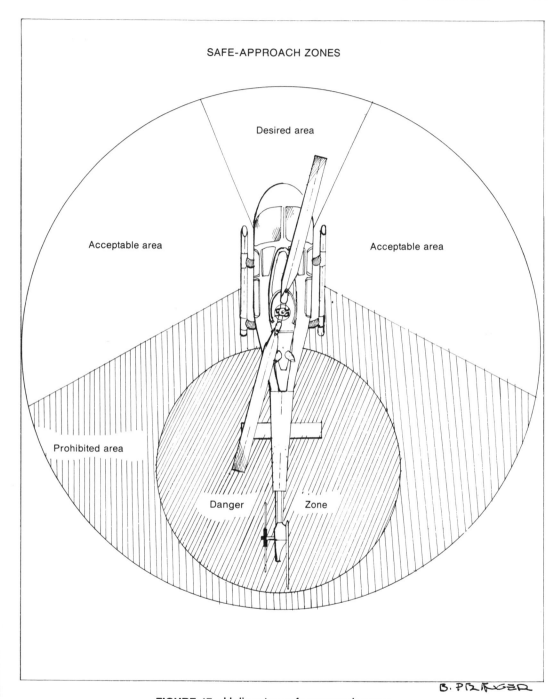

FIGURE 17 Helicopter safe-approach zones.

tops. This allows a 360° choice of landing and take-off directions. Dropoffs allow the cleanest takeoffs. The higher the elevation, the more important the dropoff becomes. Helipads should be situated so that the ship can land and take off into the prevailing wind. All obstacles, such as brush and trees, should be cleared to a diameter of at least 50 feet for small models and 100 feet for larger ones. The touchdown pad should slope as little as possi-

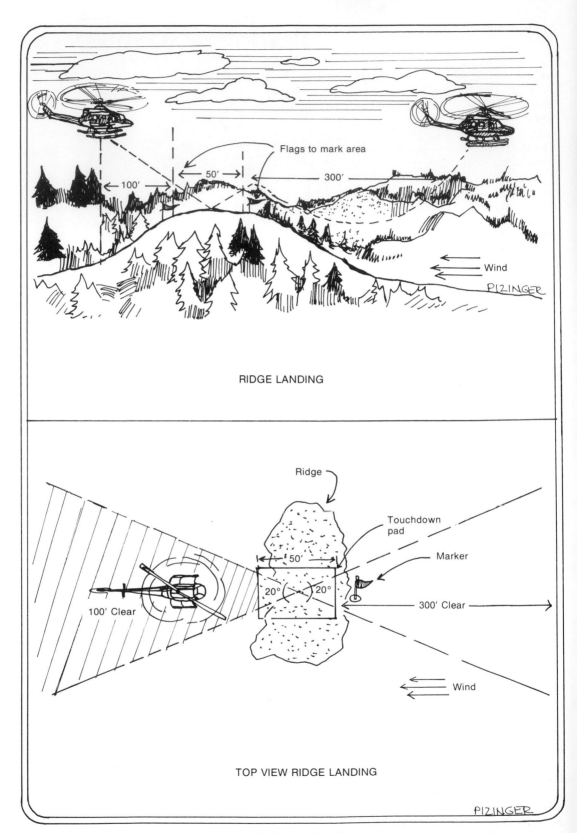

FIGURE 18 Helicopter landing zones.

ble, not to exceed an 8% grade (Figure 18).

On level or bottom lands, a truly vertical takeoff should not be considered safe at any elevation. A small helicopter must have at least 300 feet of altitude to autorotate safely. The pilot will avoid "dead air" or downdraft spots, such as might occur on the lee side of a ridge. The helicopter must have a place to go when it gains forward flight at the end of the takeoff path.

Landing zones in a canyon bottom are acceptable if there are no dead air holes caused by downdrafts from neighboring ridges. If the canyon is deep, the helicopter needs a long forward run to pull out or a wide area in which to circle to gain elevation.

When landing in snow or on glaciers, depth perception is often poor. Helipads must be marked clearly with objects which will not blow away. In deep snow, the ship may come to rest on its belly rather than on the skids or wheels. If the area is icy, a landing on a grade may allow the machine to slide at rest. In icy areas, the torque from the tail rotor may pull the ship around. Loose-blowing snow causes a "whiteout," with visibility for pilot and ground crew virtually zero.

A helicopter landing at night requires more room for error. Depth perception can be very poor for both the pilot and the ground crew. Lights should not be shined into the helicopter, but rather toward the ground. All hazards should be marked with lights and the landing pad identified with a circle or triangle of lights. All pedestrians must be acknowledged by the pilot.

BOARDING AND EXITING

Ideally, the ship is completely idle when injured parties are boarded. However, this is often impossible, and the loading has to be done with the machine running. This requires the utmost cooperation and safety orientation.

The victim must be briefed and reassured. This is particularly important when the victim is winched into the ship from above (Figure 19). While smaller ships are seldom adequate for such a maneuver, the military helicopters commonly used on rescues very often have this capability. However, most military units will not casually use a hoist/winch except in life-and-death emergencies. One U.S. Naval

FIGURE 19 Hoisting the victim into the helicopter. (Photo courtesy of J. Foray.)

Helicopter Rescue Unit, Lemoore Naval Air Station, is capable of extricating someone from a vertical face while the helicopter is 500 feet above the victim. This is the exception rather than the rule.

Many evacuations will be performed by a *one-skid* landing (Figure 20). This method requires extreme coordination with the pilot so that the exiting weight will not unbalance the machine.

One should never leave a ship and then go immediately uphill (Figure 21). Rather, one should squat downhill within sight of the pilot. The same considerations are true when boarding a helicopter while it is resting on one skid. Ambulatory victims should be escorted and guided through the boarding procedure.

Occasionally, rescue personnel will have to exit a helicopter while it is in a low hover because the ship cannot land. The risks are obvious, and the need for caution is extreme. Seldom does anyone jump from a distance of more than 4 feet. In jumping, it is important not to push off from the helicopter, as this may upset the balance of the ship. Occasionally, the reverse is necessary, as the rescuer may have to climb onboard while the ship is hovering. This is a very calculated risk and is almost never called for.

For a definitive discussion of helicopter use,

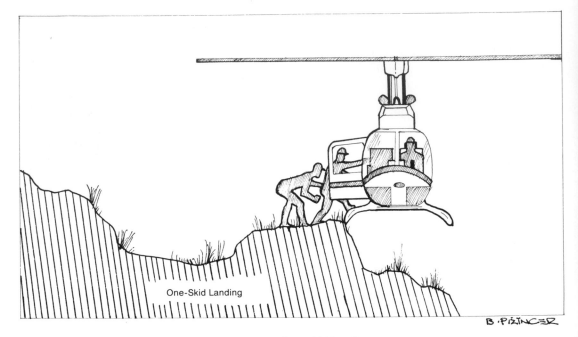

FIGURE 20 One-skid landing.

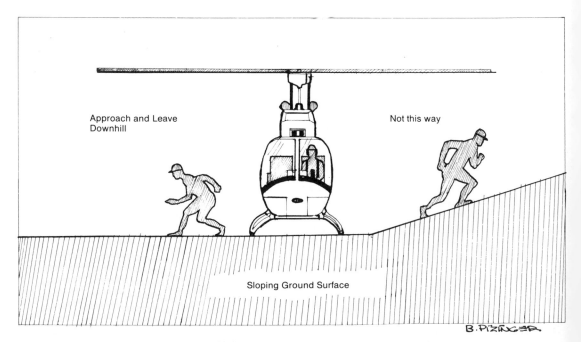

FIGURE 21 Helicopter approach on sloping ground.

the reader should consult *Helicopter Operations and Personnel Safety,* by John Dalle-Molle, available through the Survival Education Association.

Cold Weather Survival

This section examines the basic requirements of the human body and how they can be supplied in the high mountains and in cold weather. Emphasis is placed on the anticipation and prevention of cold weather environmental emergencies rather than on improvisation after the emergency has begun. The authors draw from personal experience and the analysis of actual survival situations. The reader already has an advantage over the ill-clad hiker caught in an unseasonable storm, having given forethought to the unexpected and having approached the elements of survival in an orderly fashion. A few emergency items placed in a day pack before setting out on a day-long ski tour can turn an injury-forced bivouac into more of an inconvenience than a life-threatening ordeal.

The serious mountaineer spends significant time in regions where winter exists all year round and where it is difficult to supply the body's requirements for oxygen. Physicians who participate in such sports or treat such individuals need to be aware of the impacts of environmental stresses on the human body and how their deleterious effects can be prevented and treated.

For survival, the body requires a constant supply of oxygen; a core temperature between the relatively narrow limits of 75–107°F (24–42°C); a supply of water; food to provide adequate calories as protein, fat, and carbohydrates; vitamins and minerals; and a generous amount of faith and the will to live. It also requires a minimum amount of physical integrity and conditioning, and preferably the absence of sickness and injury. In the winter setting, a very important requirement is *warmth* and *shelter,* since hypothermia contributes to most deaths in the back country in cold weather. Injuries and the effects of high altitude, dehydration, starvation, and exhaustion accelerate the development of hypothermia and contribute independently to back-country morbidity and mortality.

OXYGEN

As a human ascends from sea level, he is subjected to increasing cold, decreasing oxygen, increasing solar radiation, and decreasing atmospheric pressure. For every 1000 feet of altitude gain, the temperature drops by about 4°F (6°C/km), the barometric pressure drops by about 20 mmHg (0.1 mb/m), and the amount of ultraviolet radiation increases by about 5%. The percentage of oxygen in the atmosphere remains constant, but the absolute amount diminishes as the air thins, so that at 10,000 feet only two-thirds of the sea-level value remains and at 18,000 feet only one-half remains (1).

In acute exposure to high altitude, the direct and indirect effects of hypoxia can lead initially to symptoms of fatigue, weakness, headache, loss of appetite, nausea, vomiting, shortness of breath on exertion, insomnia, and Cheyne-Stokes respirations (7). These symptoms are probably present to some degree in everyone who goes suddenly from sea level to 8000 feet or above. The clinical effects of hypoxia are often difficult to separate from those of cold, high winds, dehydration, and exhaustion. Serious degrees of acute mountain sickness are unusual below 12,000–14,000 feet but have been reported in trekkers as low as 7500 feet. Anyone who intends to attain these altitudes should be familiar with diseases of altitude. The major preventive measure for these diseases is *slow* ascent to altitude to allow time for acclimatization. It is usually safe to ascend to 10,000 feet in 1 day, but altitude gains above 10,000 feet should be limited to 1000 feet/day. The use of acetazolamide (Diamox), 250 mg by mouth every 12 hours for 36 hours beginning the morning of ascent, may prevent acute mountain sickness. It must be emphasized that the routine use of acetazolamide is a poor substitute for slow ascent to altitude. A detailed discussion of the physiologic effects and process of adaptation to altitude may be found in Chapter 1.

At any altitude, oxygen in ambient air may be prevented from reaching the cellular level because of interruption of the normal transport pathways, generally by illness or injury. Common examples of this in the back country include:

1. Insufficient oxygen in the inspired air, as from suffocation in avalanche burial, near drowning, or living in a poorly ventilated snow cave
2. Upper airway obstruction, as in a facial injury or aspiration with blockage of the respiratory passages
3. Interference with respiratory control, as in injury to the respiratory center from brainstem trauma or hyperviscosity-induced infarction
4. Interference with proper lung function, as in pneumonia, pulmonary edema, pulmonary hemorrhage, atelectasis, hemothorax, or pneumothorax
5. Circulatory insufficiency, as in myocardial infarction, pericardial tamponade, hemorrhagic shock, or pulmonary embolism
6. Interference with the oxygen-carrying capacity of the blood, as in anemia or carbon monoxide poisoning

The first aid and medical treatment of each of these conditions follows standard techniques and includes the use of medical oxygen if available. Carbon monoxide poisoning is probably more of a hazard than is generally appreciated. Many tales are told of arctic explorers who became very ill or died because of stoves operated in tightly closed areas.

WARMTH AND SHELTER

Humans are called *homeotherms* because they, along with other warm-blooded creatures, maintain a body temperature which varies within very narrow limits despite changes in the temperature of the environment. *Poikilotherms,* or cold-blooded animals, vary their body temperature with that of the environment. Homeothermy is necessary because the speed of chemical reactions varies with temperature and the enzyme systems of the human body function best at 98.6–100.5°F (37.0–37.5°C). *In vitro,* the speed of enzymatic reactions tends to double for each 10°C rise in temperature until the enzyme starts to denature. It is useful to conceive of the body as composed of a *core,* which includes the brain, heart, lungs, liver, adrenals, and other vital organs, and a *shell* composed of the skin, muscles, and extremities.

Addition of heat to the body can be accom-

plished by *internal* and *external* means. Internally, basal heat production occurs at a rate of about 50 kcal/m² per hour. This can be increased by muscular activity, both involuntary (shivering) and voluntary (by eating), developing fever, and responding to exposure to cold. Shivering can increase heat production by up to five times that of the basal rate and vigorous exercise by up to 10 times. Cold exposure appears to increase hunger, the secretion of epinephrine, norepinephrine, and thyroxin, and semiconscious activity such as foot stamping and dancing in place. The *specific dynamic action (SDA)* of food refers to the temporary increase in basal metabolic rate which occurs during the assimilation of various types of foods into the body; the SDA of protein is five to seven times higher than that of fat and carbohydrate. However, the onset of the SDA is much faster with carbohydrate than with protein or fat.

Externally, heat can be added to the body by close approximation to a fire or other heat source, by sunlight exposure, and by ingesting hot food and drink.

Heat is lost from the body by conduction, convection, evaporation, radiation, and respiration.

Conduction refers to the transfer of heat from a warm body by contact with a cooler object, the amount of heat transferred dependent on the temperature difference and the rapidity with which the two conduct heat.

Convection refers to the transfer of heat from a warm body when air with a temperature lower than that of the body moves across its surface, the amount of heat transferred dependent on the speed and temperature of the air.

Radiation refers to the loss of heat from a warm body by infrared emissions to the cooler environment.

Evaporation refers to the loss of heat from a warm body when water or another liquid on the body surface is transformed into vapor. The high latent heat of vaporization of water (540 cal/g) has a potential for considerable heat loss.

Respiration refers to the loss of heat from a warm body in expiration, the amount of heat loss dependent on the outside temperature and the rate and depth of breathing (4).

The relative importance of these mechanisms depends on such variables as temperature, humidity, wind velocity, cloud cover, insulation, contact with cold objects, sweating, and muscular exercise. For the purpose of illustration, in still air at a temperature of 70°F, radiation, conduction, and convection together account for 70% of total heat loss, evaporation accounts for 27%, and urination, defecation, and respiration for only 3%. During work, however, evaporation may account for up to 85% of heat loss.

When exposed to cold, the body reduces perspiration and gradually reduces circulation to the shell; the individual curls into a ball to present the smallest surface area to the cold. If protective mechanisms fail, insufficient heat to parts of the shell may allow these parts to freeze, or the body core temperature may fall to seriously low levels (see Chapter 2).

The importance of seeking shelter during periods of high wind and extreme cold cannot be overemphasized. Wind chill charts are available (Figure 22) which show the relationship between actual temperature, wind velocity, and "effective" temperature at the body surface. *Wind chill* refers to the *rate* of cooling only; the actual temperature reached is no lower than it would be if wind were absent. The increase in heat loss as the wind rises is not linear; rather, it is a function of the *square root* of the wind speed.

Methods for Maintaining Body Temperature

Body temperature in adverse environments is maintained by increasing body heat production, decreasing body heat loss, and adding external heat. The most efficient of these methods is conservation of body heat by decreasing heat loss, generally by using clothing and shelter.

In order to obtain maximal heat production, the body should be kept in the best possible physical condition. This is particularly important for persons with sedentary jobs who participate in vigorous outdoor sports and for rescue personnel. A suitable physical conditioning program should develop both *aerobic* and *motor* fitness. The goal of aerobic exercise is the efficient extraction of oxygen from alveolar air ($Vo_{2,max}$). This skill is best developed by rhythmic endurance exercises, such as run-

ning, cross-country skiing, cycling, and long-distance swimming, with the highest $Vo_{2,max}$ produced by activities which exercise both lower and upper extremities simultaneously. Exercise should be vigorous enough to produce a heart rate of 75% of the age-related maximum (75% of 220 minus the participant's age) for at least 15 minutes 4 days/week.

Motor fitness, which includes strength, power, balance, agility, and flexibility, is developed by vigorous competitive team sports, selected calisthenics, and weight exercises.

Heat loss from conduction and convection can be prevented by interposing substances of low thermal conductivity between the body and the outside air. Clothing creates a microclimate of warmed, still air next to the surface of the body. Its value is dependent upon how well it traps the air and prevents its motion, how thick the layer of air is, and whether wetting reduces its effectiveness (Table 1). Traditional insulating materials are wool, down, foam, and the older synthetics, such as Orlon and Dacron. Wool retains warmth when wet because of its moderately low wicking action and its unique ability to suspend water vapor within its fibers without affecting its low thermal conductance. It can absorb a considerable amount of water without feeling wet, but it is heavier than synthetics and harder to dry. Cotton, particularly denim and corduroy, becomes wet easily because of its low evaporative ability; its high thermal conductance is further increased by water. Cotton has no place in the back country. Orlon and acrylic were developed in an attempt to duplicate the properties of wool without its high cost and are used in hats, sweaters, and long underwear. They are almost as warm and not as itchy as wool, and evaporate moisture better. Olefin and polypropylene are two new fibers which have the lowest thermal conductance and the highest insulating ability and are able to wick moisture away from the skin quickly. Other new insulating materials include Thermolactyl, a combination of acrylic and polyester; Hollofil II, a hollow synthetic fiber designed according to the principle of reindeer hair; polyester pile, which is light, dries easily, and is supposed to stay warm when wet because its fibers do not absorb water; and Thinsulate, which is said to have increased insulating value for its thickness be-

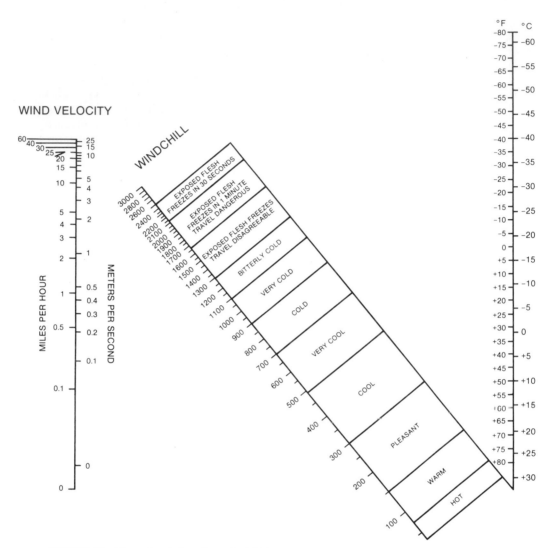

FIGURE 22 Line chart showing windchill and state of comfort under varying conditions of temperature and wind velocity. The numbers along the right margin of the diagonal center block refer to the *windchill factor*—the rate of cooling in kilogram-calories per square meter per hour of an unclad, inactive body exposed to specific temperatures and wind velocities. Windchill factors above 1400 are most hazardous. [Reproduced with permission from Robert E. Johnson, in Consolazio *et al.* (eds.), *Metabolic Methods.* C. V. Mosby and Company, St. Louis, 1951, p. 389, Figure 62.]

cause it consists of very small, finely divided fibers which trap more air than similar materials. The use of the new materials will depend on their effectiveness, cost, weight, and durability.

Outdoorsmen should use the "layer princi-ple" of clothing, which is effective in prevent-ing overheating or chilling. One or more layers of clothing may be added or subtracted as necessary, avoiding excessive perspiration and the saturation of clothing with moisture. In this way, loss of heat from conduction and

TABLE 1
Fiber Characteristics

	Specific Gravity[a] (Ratio to Water)	Thermal Conductance[b] (Calories/M²)	Evaporative Ability[c]	Wicking Ability	Moisture Regain[d]
Wool	1.32	2.10	Low	Moderate	17
Cotton	1.54	6.10	Low	High	7.9
Nylon	1.14	2.40	High	Low	4
Polyester	1.38	2.40	High	Low	1
Acrylic	1.15	2.40	High	High	1
Olefin (Polypropylene)	0.91	1.20	High	High	5

Source: Adapted with permission from Ann K. Davis.
[a] The lower the specific gravity, the better the insulating ability.
[b] The lower the thermal conductance, the slower the flow of heat away from the body.
[c] The higher the evaporative ability, the shorter the amount of time a fiber will be wet, i.e., in a reduced insulative state.
[d] Moisture regain is the amount of moisture a fiber can absorb before feeling wet.

evaporation is avoided. Since water conducts heat 32 times faster than does air of the same temperature, exertion leading to sweating and wetting of clothing should be avoided. Clothing should be easily adjustable, sweaters should be of the zipper or cardigan type, and outer layers should be cut full enough to allow expansion of inner layers to their full thicknesses.

The loss of heat from convection can be prevented by wearing windproof outer garments of nylon, tightly woven cotton/nylon (60–40 cloth), Gore-Tex, etc. Typical examples include a fingertip-length parka with a hood and a pair of wind pants or ski warmup pants.

The loss of heat from infrared radiation can be prevented by insulation, emphasizing proper coverings for body parts with a large surface area. A source of considerable heat loss is the uncovered head, which can dissipate up to 70% of total body heat production at ambient temperatures of 5°F (−16°C), partly because the body does not reduce the blood supply to the head and neck as well as it does to the extremities. High heat loss by radiation during cold nights can be decreased by sleeping in a tent or under a tarp instead of in the open. Coverage for the head, ears, hands, and feet should not be tight enough to restrict circulation. Spare socks and mittens should always be carried.

Heat loss from the respiratory tract can be diminished by avoiding overexertion and over-heating with excessive heavy breathing. When it is extremely cold, the inspired air can be warmed by pulling the parka hood out in front of the face to form a "frost tunnel."

Heat loss from conduction occurs when the body comes in contact with a colder object. Sitting down in the snow or on a cold rock is not as good as sitting on a pack, log, or other object of lower heat conductivity. At low temperatures, bare skin will freeze to metal. This can be avoided by wearing light gloves. Gasoline or other liquids with freezing points lower than that of water can cause frostbite if accidently poured on the skin at low temperatures. During bivouacs in a snow trench or snow hole, contact with the snow can be avoided with the use of a mattress of evergreen boughs or dry leaves. Rescuers must remember that a cold, injured person needs insulating material between him and the snow or cold ground as well as over him.

Heat loss from conduction and evaporation can be lessened by drying out quickly if one gets wet. Ideally, outer clothing should be windproof, should not collect snow, and should shed water but not be waterproof, since waterproof garments prevent the evaporation of sweat. Gore-Tex and Stormshed are two recent fabrics which do this reasonably well and are desirable for maritime climates and summer storms. In areas of heavy rainfall, it is probably best to have separate sets of outer garments, one waterproof and the other windproof.

METHODS FOR INCREASING HEAT PRODUCTION

Heat production can be increased by raising the level of muscular activity. A cold person should loosen his boots, walk around, stamp his feet, jump in place, swing his arms, and wiggle his fingers and toes. Shivering is involuntary and generates heat.

The ingestion of foodstuffs provides calories and the SDA of the food. It is preferable to eat often in cold weather, at least every 2 hours on the trail. Meals should not be skipped. Because alcohol may lower blood sugar and invariably increases peripheral vasodilatation, it should be avoided outdoors in cold weather. Nicotine-induced peripheral vasoconstriction may predispose the individual to frostbite.

SAMPLE COLD WEATHER CLOTHING

Anyone who ventures outdoors in cold weather should carry clothing for the most extreme environmental conditions which are likely to be experienced.

Underwear

Underclothing can be made of 85–100% wool. If considerable exertion and sweating are anticipated, polypropylene or Olefin may be preferable because of their superior ability to wick moisture away from the skin. Duofold and other fabrics containing cotton should be avoided for reasons mentioned previously. Net underwear is preferred by some, but should be made of wool.

Other synthetics, such as polyester, Orlon, and Dacron, are satisfactory.

Shirt

Shirts should be made of light, soft wool. Large breast pockets with buttons are handy to carry items such as sunglasses and a compass.

Pants

Wool is best, in knickers or long pants. Army surplus wool pants are inexpensive and durable.

Sweater

Sweaters should be woolen, preferably with a zipper front or cardigan style. Sweaterlike jackets of polyester pile are preferred by some and are lighter than wool. A turtleneck feature adds protection.

Parka

The parka can be a standard ski or mountaineering jacket or vest, filled with down, Dacron, Hollofil II, or Thinsulate. A good combination is a medium-weight down or Dacron jacket covered by a windshell or mountaineering parka. The latter should be long enough to protect the hips and have a hood with a drawstring, a two-way zipper with an overlying weather flap closed with Velcro or snaps, hand-warmer pockets, and a cloth flap to protect the chin from the metal zipper pull.

Windpants or Warmup Pants

Windpants should be light and windproof, with leg openings that permit easy removal and pockets or slits for access to the inner pants pockets.

Socks

For socks, wool of the Ragg variety is excellent. At least one spare set should be carried. A light pair of Olefin socks worn underneath the wool socks next to the skin may be preferable, especially for those with hyperhidrosis.

Hat

A hat should be of the stocking variety, made of wool, Orlon, or polypropylene, and large enough to cover the ears, with a face mask or balaclava feature to protect the face from wind. A mask which covers only the lower part of the face can be used conveniently with glasses or ski goggles.

Hand Gear

Mittens are warmer than gloves and should be made of heavy, oiled wool (Dachstein or Ragg) with windproof leather or nylon outer shells. Light wool gloves can be carried for delicate tasks.

Foot Gear

Sturdy boots should be designed for climbing or heavy-duty backpacking, made of full-thickness leather, 6–8 inches in height with rubber lug soles, and roomy enough to accommodate two to three pairs of heavy wool socks. They must be long enough so that the toes do not impact against the front of the boot when walking downhill. To avoid circulatory restriction, boots should be laced firmly enough so that the heel does not move, but not so tightly that the toes cannot be wiggled easily.

Double winter mountaineering boots, the Canadian type of shoe-pak with removable inner felt liners (Sorel), or vapor barrier boots, such as U.S. Army Korean boots, are preferred by some. Most of these boots can be used with snowshoes. For ski touring and ski mountaineering, special boots may be necessary, depending on the type of binding that is used. Similarly, high-altitude and/or winter mountaineering boots depend on the type of binding that is used. For high-altitude and/or winter mountaineering, special overboots or felt-lined gaiters are desirable. Gaiters should be used to keep snow out of the tops of the boots.

Rain Gear

In moderate climates or in spring conditions in which rain or wet snow may be encountered, outer garments of Gore-Tex, Stormshed, or a separate set of waterproof rain garments should be carried.

Shelter

Every outdoorsman should practice the construction of several types of emergency survival shelters. The function of a shelter is to provide an extension of the microclimate of still, warm air furnished by clothing and to contain heat generated by a fire or other heat source. A properly designed shelter can be constructed easily and rapidly with simple tools and will give good protection from wind, rain, and snowfall. The type and size of shelter will depend on the presence or absence of snow cover and its depth, on natural features of the landscape, and on whether firewood or a stove and fuel are available. If external heat cannot be provided, a shelter must be small and windtight to preserve body heat.

Advantage can be taken of small trees, branches, leaves, small caves, and snow holes under downed trees or dense evergreens. If possible, a shelter should be constructed in the timber. Generally, shelters partway up the side of a ridge are warmer than those in a valley, since cold air tends to collect in valleys and basins during the night. Exposed, windy ridges above the timberline are quite cold. Areas exposed to rockfall and avalanches or under dead trees and large, dead limbs should be avoided. If open water is available, one may wish to camp close to it. To avoid drifting snow, tents and shelters should be located with the entrance at right angles to the prevailing wind. Snow is a very good insulator, with heat conductivity 1/10,000 that of copper and about the same as wool felt, so that snow shelters may be warmer than other types of constructed shelters so long as the inhabitants remain dry. Contact with the snow or cold ground is avoided by constructing a bed of evergreen boughs or dry leaves.

Types of Shelters

Natural Shelters

Caves and alcoves under overhangs are good shelters and can be improved by building wind walls with rocks or snow blocks. A fire should be built so that heat from it will reflect onto the occupant. This can be accomplished by positioning it 5–6 feet from the cliff, with a reflector wall of logs or stones on the side of the fire opposite the cliff; the occupant should sit between the fire and the cliff (Figure 23).

In deep snow, large fallen logs and bent-over evergreens frequently have hollows under them which can be used as small caves. Cone-shaped depressions in the snow around the trunks of evergreens ("tree wells"), already quite deep, can be improved by digging them out and roofing them over with evergreen branches or a tarp. If one cannot build a fire, the shelter should be small in order to retain

FIGURE 23   Natural shelter.

body heat. A fire can be built to one side of such a shelter, and the heat will reflect off the snow toward the occupant.

ARTIFICIAL SHELTERS

When no snow is available, shelters can be constructed of small trees, branches, brush, and boughs. A tarp can be rigged into a lean-to type of shelter. In cold weather, the most satisfactory form is a lean-to closed on three sides, with a fire in front of the open side and a reflector wall to direct heat into the lean-to (Figure 24).

Snow Shelters: Although a small snow cave large enough for one person can be dug with a ski or cooking pot as a shovel, larger ones take several hours to dig with good shovels and will usually cause the digger to become quite wet (Figure 25). Igloos are very comfortable but require time, experience, and engineering skill. They are not recommended to the novice.

A snow trench is the easiest and quickest shelter. It can be dug wherever the snow is

3 feet or deeper or can be piled to that depth. A 4 × 6 foot trench can be dug in 20 minutes, one end roofed over with a tarp or boughs, with a fire built at the opposite end (Figure 26).

If one has a large tarp and a stove, a trench can be dug which is as comfortable as a snow cave and will hold three people. The trench is dug 4 feet wide and 8 feet long at the surface, and then undercut at the back and sides so that the bottom is 6–7 feet wide and 9–10 feet long (Figure 27). The entrance is made narrow so that it can be closed with a small plastic sheet or a pack. Four or more skis or branches are laid from side to side over the top of the trench, with ski poles or branches interwoven at right angles. A tarp is then laid on top of these, and snow is piled around the edges to hold it down. When the entrance is closed, a small stove plus the body heat of the occupants will raise the interior temperature up to 25–30°F. Higher temperatures should be avoided, lest clothing and bedding become wet from melting snow.

Above the timberline in deep, wind-packed

FIGURE 24 Lean-to shelter.

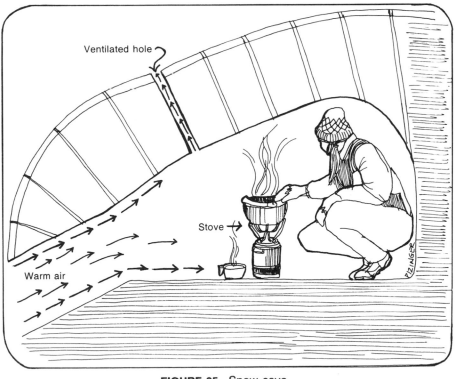

FIGURE 25 Snow cave.

FIGURE 26 Snow trench.

snow, a similar trench can be roofed with snow blocks (Figure 28). A good design is a T shape with a central cooking area at the entrance.

Tents and Bivouac Sacks: Tents are generally comfortable and dry, but in very cold weather they are not as warm as snow shelters. They are preferable to snow shelters only at mild temperatures and with damp snow conditions. Tube tents and bivouac sacks are emergency shelters which hold one to two persons and are usually waterproof and windproof. Bivouac sacks and various types of hammock-tent combinations are popular with climbers who may have to bivouac on a long route. Gore-Tex bivouac sacks are a recent improvement.

Vehicles: Persons stranded in their cars or in downed airplanes can survive using the equipment in the vehicles. It is best to stay with the vehicle rather than to go for help, because the vehicle is more visible than a person. In winter, survival equipment should be carried in the vehicle. Although cars can be quite comfortable, in very cold weather one may do better to construct a shelter adjacent

to the car so that a fire can be built. Running the car motor and heater or using a stove in a car is dangerous unless proper ventilation is provided. The fusilage of a downed aircraft can be very cold; one is usually better off outside but near the aircraft. Batteries and cigarette lighters can be used as fire starters, with oil and gasoline as fuel.

FIRE BUILDING

The ability to build a fire under adverse conditions is an essential skill which should be practiced by every outdoorsman (Figure 29). Necessary equipment includes a sturdy knife, a candle, and waterproof matches. For wet climates, some sort of fire starter is needed. Dry wood can be found in the form of small twigs on the lower (dead) branches of evergreens (squaw wood) or the inner bark of birches, or can be produced by shaving off the wet outer wood of dead branches or splitting them lengthwise with a knife. The dry tinder is arranged out of the wind in lean-to form by placing it against a larger branch,

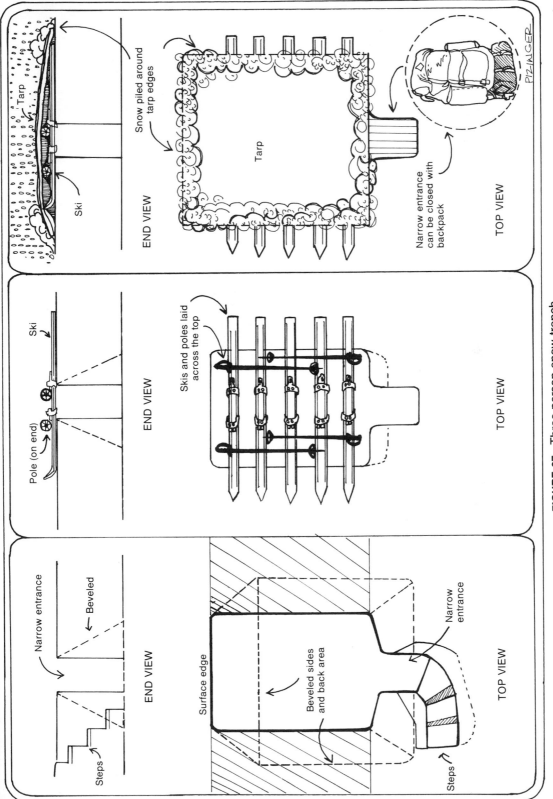

FIGURE 27 Three-person snow trench.

123

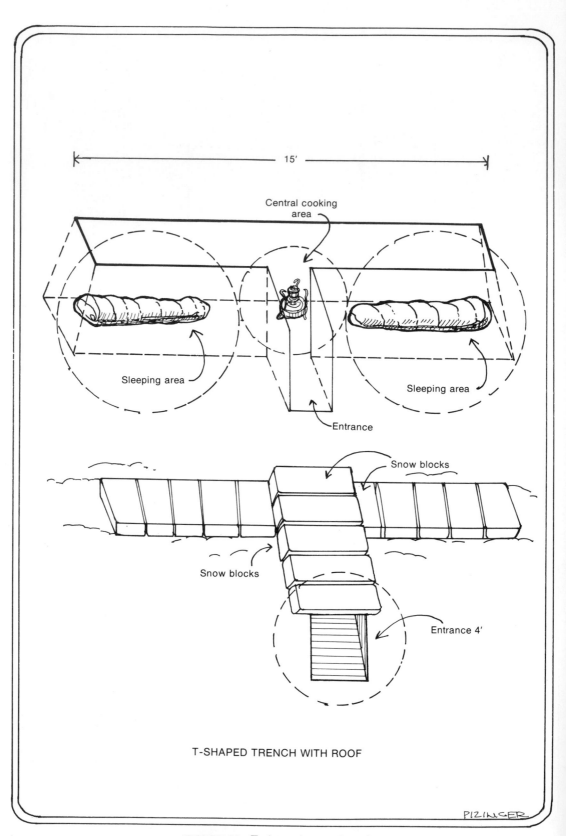

FIGURE 28 T-shaped snow trench.

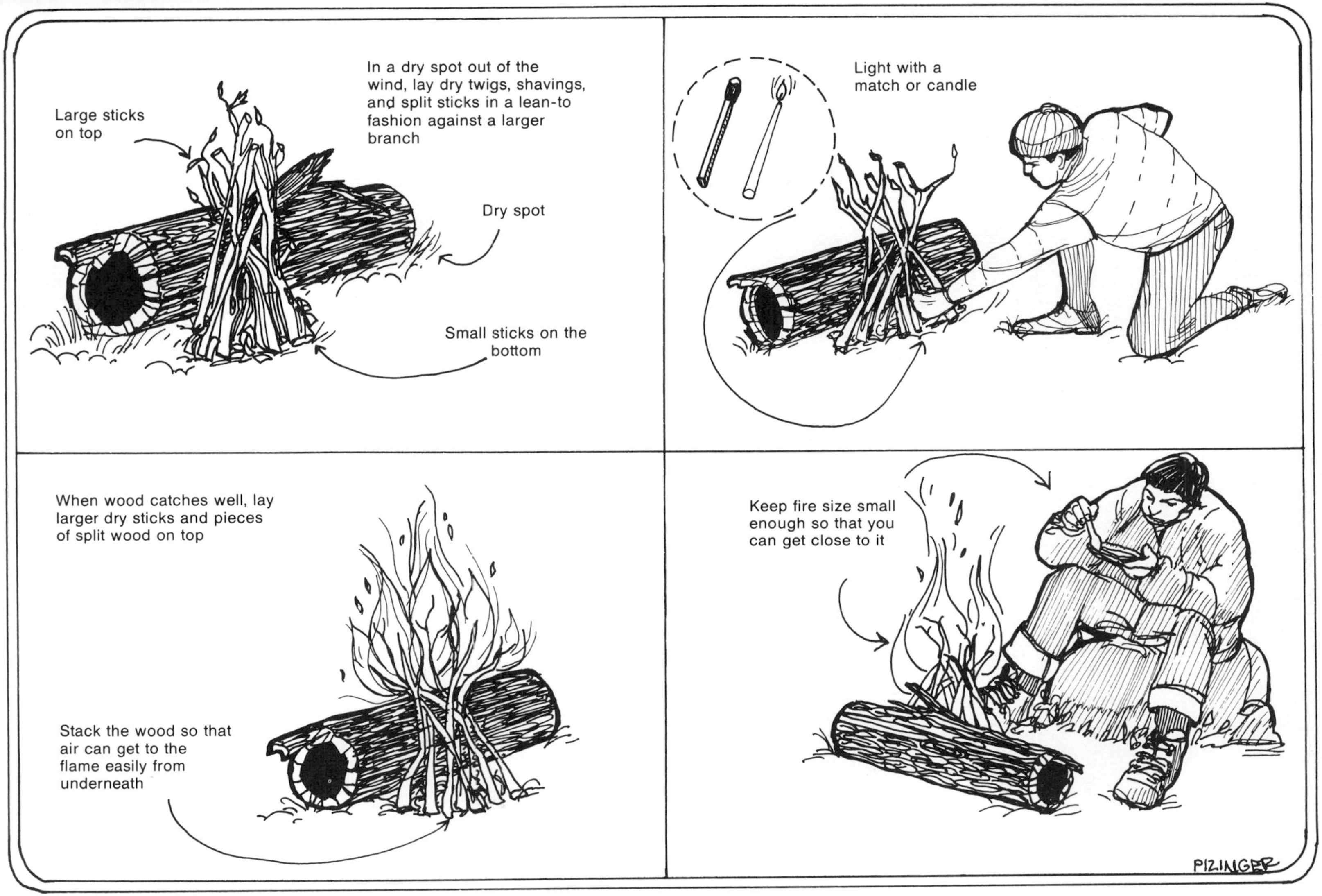

Light with a
match or candle

Keep fire size small
enough so that you
can get close to it

In a dry spot out of the
wind, lay dry twigs, shavings,
and split sticks in a lean-to
fashion against a larger
branch

Dry spot

Small sticks on the
bottom

Large sticks
on top

When wood catches well, lay
larger dry sticks and pieces
of split wood on top

Stack the wood so that
air can get to the
flame easily from
underneath

FIGURE 29 Building a fire.

small sticks on the bottom and larger ones on top, so that air can reach each piece of tinder. Once the flame has caught well, larger pieces of wood are added. To avoid having the fire sink into the snow, it should be built on a platform of green logs or directly on the ground. One should collect twice as much wood as one estimates will be needed. If no ax or saw is available, it is wise to build the fire next to a large downed log which will catch and burn for several days. Otherwise, fires should be kept small, both to conserve wood and to allow them to be approached closely.

A fire can be started without matches by using an automobile cigarette lighter, or batteries and steel wool. A "wire" can be made by twisting and pulling out a fine grade of steel wool. This will catch fire if the ends are touched to the terminals of an automobile battery or to the positive and negative terminals of two fresh C or D batteries in tandem. A fire starter can be made by wrapping a wire 7 to 10 times around a dry stick. If the two ends of the wire are touched to the terminals of an automobile battery, the wire will become red hot and the stick will ignite. Oil or gasoline can be used as fuel if it is poured over a container full of dirt or sand.

Food

The human body requires a daily supply of calories, carbohydrate, protein, fat, minerals, and vitamins. Carbohydrates supply calories and are essential for replacement of muscle glycogen. If a diet is inadequate, body stores of fat and protein will be depleted to provide calories. A sedentary 70 kg man requires the food equivalent of 2800 kcal/day, but if he is exercising in cold weather, he may require more than twice this amount. Protein intake should be at least 65 gm/day, and carbohydrates should make up 60–70% of the diet.

Although most persons in a survival situation worry more about food than anything else, food is usually less important than water or shelter, as one can survive for weeks without food even in cold weather. However, there must be enough water, and energy expenditure must be kept to a minimum. Most ski mountaineering or climbing parties carry adequate supplies of food; problems arise if food is exhausted, lost, or contaminated. In most cases, the amount of wild food found by an untrained individual will provide barely enough calories to replenish the energy expended in searching for it. Bare ridges, high mountains above the timberline, and dense evergreen forests are difficult places to find wild food, especially in winter. Success is more likely along river and stream banks, lake shores, margins of forests, and natural clearings.

Here are a few general rules about wilderness edibles (2,8):

1. All wild foods except fruits and berries should be cooked. This will make them more palatable, digestible, and safer to eat. (For a detailed discussion of poisonous plants, see Chapter 13.)
2. One should know the edible plants and animals of the area. Similar life forms are often found in other similar areas.
3. No one should eat large quantities of a strange food without first testing it and waiting a few hours to see whether it induces illness.
4. All land mammals, birds, and birds' eggs can be eaten. The entire carcass, both fat and lean, should be eaten, except for seal and polar bear livers. Crustaceans, mollusks, insects, some amphibians (except for toads), and some reptiles can be eaten. Salamanders should be skinned. Fish, crustaceans, and mollusks should be eaten promptly because they spoil quickly. Fish and meat can be preserved by drying. One should avoid black mussels, Pacific reef fish, "puffers," and any fish which looks ugly.
5. Edible parts of wild plants include roots and young curled fronds of ferns; nuts (including pine nuts); grass seeds; inner barks of aspen, cottonwood, birch, willow, lodgepole pine, and scotch pine; many roots; berries (except water hemlock and baneberry); aspen and poplar buds; spruce and tamarack shoots; leaves of mountain sorrel, young willows, and fireweed (if boiled).
6. Certain types of lichen can be eaten. Iceland moss should be boiled for an hour, reindeer moss boiled or roasted, and rock tripe dried and then boiled.
7. Mushrooms, buttercups, and any unknown plant with milky sap should be avoided.

There are many exceptions to the above rules. (Refer to Chapter 13 for known toxic species.) If in doubt, one should not eat foods from unfamiliar sources except in extreme circumstances.

WATER

Water comprises about 60% of the body weight of an average young adult male; the value in a female is slightly lower. The percentage of water tends to decrease with age. Daily water excretion includes 1200 ml of urine, 1000 ml through the skin and lungs, and 300 ml in the stool. Thus, in a temperate climate at sea level, a minimum intake of 2500 ml of fluid per day is required to avoid dehydration. In a hot, dry climate, at high altitude, or with exertion, insensible losses are increased considerably. Up to 1 liter/hour can be lost during very hard exercise. In cold weather there is decreased thirst, so that an individual may not replete fluids adequately. At subfreezing temperatures and in locations above the snow line, the lack of liquid water and the effort required to melt snow compound the problem.

Active efforts must be made to prevent fluid deficit. Whenever open water is encountered, one should drink heartily and fill all empty canteens. Each morning, enough snow should be melted to provide everyone with at least a canteenful for the day. At night, no one should go to bed thirsty. Melting ice or hard snow is more efficient than melting light, powdery snow. On warm, sunny days, snow can be spread on a dark plastic sheet to melt.

At high altitudes, at least 3–4 liters of water per day should be ingested. If intake is adequate, one should excrete 1.0–1.5 liters of light-colored urine per day. Adding fruit flavors or making hot drinks will make water more palatable. Electrolyte drinks (Gatorade) and salt tablets are generally unnecessary in cold weather, since the electrolytes lost in sweat are easily replaced by a normal diet. When fuel is exhausted and snow must be melted, trekkers must descend below the timberline to seek open water. When water supplies are limited, overexertion should be avoided ("ration your sweat").

Water contaminated with human or animal wastes may carry disease and must be avoided or purified. Small streams and springs descending from high, uninhabited areas at right angles to the main valley drainage pattern are more apt to be safe than larger streams running parallel to the valley's long axis. Contaminated water can be purified by boiling for 5 minutes plus 1 minute for each 1000 feet of altitude above sea level, or by adding four drops of iodine tincture per quart and letting it stand for half an hour. Alternatively, iodine crystals can be used to fill a 1 ounce bottle, and a saturated solution can be made by filling the bottle with water. The supernatant is then added to a quart of water and allowed to stand for half an hour. It must be cautioned that the 4–8 g of crystalline iodine carried by the hiker represents two to four times the lethal dose. This danger could be obviated with the use of a Teflon filter, but these are expensive and not readily available (9). In comparison, a bottle of 50 tetraglycine hydroperiodide tablets contains a sublethal (one-fifth the lethal dose) amount (0.4 g) of iodine. There is some recent evidence that the effectiveness of iodine, especially against *Giardia,* is lowered if the water is quite cold. Most chemical methods of purification require a water temperature of at least 20°C (68°F) to be effective. The only easily available substance which is reputed to be effective in clear water at 3°C is tetraglycine hydroperiodide, which must be fresh. The dose is one or two tablets added to 1 liter of water and allowed to stand for half an hour before drinking (6).

Preparing for a Possible Survival Situation

Basic survival equipment and skills for anyone interested in mountaineering, winter or high-altitude backpacking, back-country skiing, or hunting in cold weather should include:

1. Physical conditioning and healthful habits.
2. The ability to swim well.
3. Expertise in the use of map and compass, and in finding directions without a compass. One should be able to identify the Big Dipper and follow the "pointers" (farthest stars on the bowl of the Dipper) to the North Star (Polaris). On a sunny day, a watch set to standard time can be used to find direction. When the hour hand is pointed toward the sun, south will be one-half of the shorter of the two distances between the hour hand and 12 o'clock.
4. The ability to build a fire under adverse conditions.
5. A working knowledge of local weather patterns. The back country should be avoided dur-

ing times of high hazard. The best source of weather information is the National Weather Service, which broadcasts on a 24-hour basis at frequencies of 162.40 or 162.55 MHz VHF-FM. Many multichannel radios will receive this frequency; there are also inexpensive, light radios which receive this frequency only. In evaluating avalanche conditions, it is necessary to know what the weather conditions have been over the *previous few days.*

6. Familiarity with special medical problems of cold and high altitude, such as hypothermia, frostbite, and acute mountain sickness. Basic principles of first aid and how to improvise splints and bandages are crucial. Unless one has had special training in first aid, he should not assume that a medical or other professional degree confers expertise in this area.

7. A cold weather survival kit (Appendix B).

8. The ability to construct several different types of survival shelters.

9. A working knowledge of the characteristics of natural hazards, and of how to predict and avoid them. These include forest fire (see Chapter 16), lightning strike (see Chapter 18), snow avalanches, rockfall, cornice falls, flash floods, deadfalls, blizzards, and other severe storms, undercut snow banks of streams, and hazardous insects, animals, and plants.

10. Reading and analyzing accounts of survival experiences. The American Alpine Club's *Accidents in North American Mountaineering* and the U.S. Forest Service's accounts of avalanche accidents are excellent examples. Common mishaps that lead to survival situations are listed in Appendix D.

11. One should be aware of the psychological aspects of a survival situation, and of errors in judgment which can lead one into a survival emergency, such as continuing a preestablished journey despite conditions which dictate a prudent bivouac or return.

    Many anxieties may appear in a survival situation which paralyze action (3). These include:

    a. Fear: of the unknown, being alone, wild animals, darkness, weakness, personal failure, discomfort, suffering, and death.

    b. Surrender: which results in chaotic thought, inactivity, and loss of the will to live.

    c. Panic: the uncontrolled urge to run from the situation. Useless flight exhausts available energy; exhaustion and death are inevitable. One must have faith in his abilities and equipment and in the likelihood that rescuers will find him.

12. Never skiing, climbing, hunting, or backpacking alone, and never failing to let others know where one is going and when one expects to return.

Faith and the Will to Survive

A person faced with a survival emergency who has adequate oxygen, warmth, shelter, water, and food may still die if he is unable to withstand the psychological stress. Conversely, persons have survived amazing hardships with little more than a strong determination to live. If one possesses the necessary skills and has minimal survival equipment (Appendix E), the odds are strongly in his favor. Medical personnel have the advantage of being trained by and large to suppress panic. Fear and surrender are normal reactions that must be opposed by whatever psychological tools are available. In some cases, religious faith and the desire to rejoin loved ones have been credited with survival. No one can predict what his own reactions will be. Groups faced with emergencies testify that courage and leadership appear in unexpected places.

One of the hardest decisions is whether to stay put and wait for rescue or try to "walk out." In general, it is better to use the time to prepare a snug shelter and conserve strength so long as there is any chance of rescue. Travel should never be attempted in severe weather or in deep snow without snowshoes or skis. If there is no chance of rescue, one should prepare as best possible, wait for good weather, and then travel in the most logical direction.

Appendix A: Drug Stability Information

Stability data on drug products are nearly always based on studies done in controlled environmental conditions. It is often difficult to ascertain whether a drug product can be safely used after storage under conditions other than those specified by the manufacturer.

The question of stability of drug products pertains not only to the drug itself, but also to the container in which it is packaged. If, for example, a parenteral drug packaged in a syringe for ready use is frozen, the drug itself may be fully potent, but the sterility of the product may be lost. Hairline cracks in the syringe may have occurred secondary to freezing.

Thus, for most of the drug products listed, stability or sterility or both cannot be guaranteed if stored under conditions other than those recommended by the manufacturers.

Mannitol injection 25%. Stable at higher air temperatures. Crystallizes out at lower temperatures, but will resolubilize when warmed. Sterility *cannot* be guaranteed if frozen.

Lidocaine 1% injection. Lidocaine is a relatively stable drug, but excessive heat or cold will decrease shelf life. May be used after thawing, provided that the container is completely intact and the solution remains clear.

Sodium bicarbonate injection, 50 ml. The manufacturer specifically states "Do not freeze." If frozen, this product should not be used.

Naloxone hydrochloride, 0.4 mg/ml. Protect from light during storage. Should *not* be used after being frozen.

Diphenhydramine injection, 10 mg/ml. Drug is stable after freezing. Container should be checked for cracks or leakage.

Dexamethasone injection, 4 mg/ml. Sensitive to light and extremes of temperature. Do not store at high temperature for long periods. Do not use after freezing.

Tetanus toxoid, 0.5 ml. Do *not* use after freezing. Should be refrigerated; however, remains stable for months when stored at room temperature.

Meperidine hydrochloride, 100 mg/ml. May be used after thawing if the solution shows no signs of precipitation or cloudiness and if the ampules or vials show no signs of cracking or leaking.

Calcium chloride 10% ml. May be used after freezing, barring obvious damage such as cracks or leaks.

Penicillin GK injection. Stable in powder form for 2 to 3 years if stored at no greater than 30°C; higher temperatures will cause potency to decrease.

Procaine penicillin G injection. Should be refrigerated; however, is stable at room temperatures for 6 months. Higher temperatures would increase hydrolysis and decrease potency.

Furosemide injection. May be used after freezing, barring evidence of cracking, leaking, or other damage to glass. All intact ampules or syringes when returned to room temperature should be vigorously shaken to redissolve any constituents that may have crystallized out of solution.

Gamma benzene hexachloride lotions. Not stable after freezing. Effect of high temperatures unknown. Protect from light.

Glucagon injection. In powder form, should be refrigerated, but is stable at room temperature for several weeks. When diluent is added to powder, resulting solution may be used for up to 3 months, if refrigerated. Effects of high temperature or freezing are unknown.

Intravenous solutions (D5W, D5NS, etc.). Effects of freezing these solutions are unknown. Incomplete resolubilization, especially with electrolyte solutions, seems a real danger.

Thanks to Robert J. Matutat, Pharm.D., from the UCLA Drug Information Services Center, for his help in preparing this appendix.

Appendix B: Sample Cold Weather Survival Kit

BASIC ITEMS

Waterproof matches	Flashlight
Knife	Metal pot with bale
Candle (add fire starter in wet climates)	Plastic or nylon tarp
Whistle	First aid kit
Signal mirror	Toilet paper
Card with ground-to-air signals	Sunglasses
Four dimes for phone	Sunburn cream
Fishline or parachute cord (¼-inch nylon cord)	Snow shovel*
Compass	Map

Emergency food and spare clothing adequate for the most severe climatic conditions likely to be experienced.

Source: Reprinted from "Mountain Rescue and Preparation," by E. Geehr, by permission of Aspen Systems Corporation, © October, 1980.

* An excellent snow shovel is an aluminum "car shovel." It looks like a small grain scoop with a wooden handle and a wooden or plastic D-shaped hand grip. The handle can be detached from the scoop for packing. This model will move a lot more snow in less time than more expensive shovels available at mountaineering stores.

OPTIONAL ITEMS

Piece of ensolite, sleeping bag, Gore-Tex bivouac sack, stove and fuel, fishhooks, collapsible saw, light ax.

Appendix C: Equipment List for SAR

It is important that members of a rescue team have their equipment in good repair and in a ready state. The equipment lists provided are generalized and without great detail. Equipment preferences cover a broad spectrum.

GENERAL OPERATIONS*

Required Equipment

Rescue pack	Can opener
Ground sheet	Bandana
Bivouac shelter	Food for 3 days
Ground pad	Water (2 quarts)
Whistle	Carabiners (three)
Signal mirror	Nylon slings (two)
Flashlight	Rain parka
Extra batteries and	Mountain boots
bulb	Wool socks
Compass and map	Helmet
Notebook and pencil	First aid kit
Sunglasses	Sunscreen
Matches	Salt
Knife	Toilet paper
Nylon cord	Mountain pants
Rope	Spoon, fork, utensils
Ascenders	

Recommended

Day/night flare	Wool sweater
Rappel Seat	Gaiters
Insect repellent	Heavy clothing
Fire starter	Ruler
Headlamp	Short backboard
Prusik slings (three)	Litter (Stokes or Two-man)
Waist sling	
Leather gloves	Hare Traction device
Cotton underwear	or Collapsible Reel splint

* These items are tailored to weather and altitude.

Optional

Sleeping bag	Food, extra
Binoculars	Rescue pulley
Watch	Long-sleeve shirt
Camera	Wool hat
Lip balm	Down jacket
Stove and fuel	Nylon rope
Cook kit	
Cup and bowl	

MOUNTAIN OPERATIONS

In addition to items mentioned under General Operations, there are a few specialized pieces essential for a specific emergency.

Nylon rope, long	Wire saw
Carabiners, extra	Sheath knife
Helitac goggles	Belt
Nylon cord, extra	Aerial flare kit
Rescue pulley, extra	

CAVE/MINE OPERATION

Light, three independent sources	Batteries and bulb, extra
Coveralls	Rescue pulley, extra
Wet suit (depends on wetness)	Cotton gloves
	Piton hammer
Cave ladder	Pitons
Gibbs ascenders	Expansion bolts
Carabiners, locking	Body harness

Do not make up a separate survival kit. All survival equipment should be with the rescue pack.

Place everything inside the rescue pack. Avoid tying items on the outside.

Keep the rescue pack completely packed and handy for a call-out. Items not normally stored in the pack, such as food and water, should be stored nearby.

Constantly check all equipment. Repair and replace items as necessary.

Mark all equipment with some personal identification, especially rescue gear such as carabiners. Use color coding if possible.

Appendix D: Some Examples of Mishaps that May Lead to a Survival Situation

LOSS OF VITAL EQUIPMENT

Tent catches fire
Sleeping bag blows off cliff
Ski breaks
Cooking pot blows away

Gas tin leaks
Food lost or contaminated as by gas leak
Radio malfunctions

UNANTICIPATED OR EXTREME ENVIRONMENTAL STRESS

Extreme heat or cold
High wind
Getting wet in very cold weather; falling through ice

Severe storm
Inadequate clothing

ILLNESS OR INJURY

Snow blindness
Sunburn
Hypothermia
Frostbite

Acute mountain sickness
Gastroenteritis
Trauma

LACK OF SPARE PARTS OR TOOLS

Spare parts for stove or packframe
Ski repair kits
Batteries for radio

MISCALCULATIONS

Not enough food or fuel
Getting lost
Caught by dark

Pinned down by storm
Climb takes longer than expected

INATTENTION TO HYGIENE

Eating native food without proper preparation

Drinking contaminated water
Improper waste disposal

MISCELLANEOUS

Climbing, skiing, or hiking alone
Inexperience
Inadequate equipment
Ignorance
Sleeping in a poorly ventilated shelter

Poor judgment
Climbing above abilities
Climbing without a hard hat
Not letting someone know where one is going and when one expects to return

Appendix E: Sample Survival First Aid Kit

One cravat
One roll of Kling or 2-inch gauze
One roll of 2-inch adhesive tape
Six Bandaids
Six butterflies
Four nonadhering sterile gauze pads
Two sterile compresses
One steel sewing needle
One single-edged razor blade
One low-reading thermometer
One 2-inch rubberized bandage (Ace)
Aspirin or acetaminophen, 0.3-g tablets, no. 12
    codeine tablets, 30 mg, no. 12
    diphenhydramine (Benadryl) capsules, 25 mg, no. 12
One small bottle of hexachlorophene (pHisoHex) scrub or povidone-iodine (Betadine) solution

Splinting materials can usually be improvised, using ski poles, ice axes, piton hammers, branches, etc.
Physicians and other medical personnel may wish to take an injectable narcotic such as morphine or meperidine.

References

1. Bowman, W. D., Jr. *Winter First Aid Manual,* 2nd ed. National Ski Patrol System, Inc., Denver, 1976, p. 15.
2. Craighead, Frank C., Jr., and Craighead, John J. *How to Survive on Land and Sea.* U.S. Naval Institute, Annapolis, Md., 1956, pp. 51–105.
3. Fear, Gene. *Surviving the Unexpected Wilderness Emergency.* Survival Education Association, Tacoma, Wash., 1975.
4. Ganong, W. F. Respiratory adjustments in health and disease, in *Review of Medical Physiology,* 7th ed. Lange Medical Publications, Los Altos, Calif., 1975, p. 505.
5. Geehr, E. C. Mountain rescue and preparation, in *Environmental Medical Emergencies,* Auerbach, P. S.,

and Geehr, E. C. (eds.). 1980, vol. 2 (no. 3), p. 127. Aspen Systems Corp., Rockville, Maryland.

6. Jarroll, E. L., Jr., Bingham, A. K., and Meyer, E. A. *Giardia* cyst destruction: Effectiveness of six small-quantity water disinfection methods. *Am. J. Trop. Med. Hyg.*, **29**:8, 1980.

7. Miller, A. T., Jr. Altitude, in *Environmental Physiology*, Slonin, N. B. (ed.). C. V. Mosby Co., St. Louis, 1974, p. 351.

8. Nesbitt, P. H., Pond, A. W., Allen, W. H. *The Survival Book*. Funk & Wagnalls, New York, 1959, pp. 42–66.

9. Zemlyn, S., Wilson, W. W., Hellweq, P. A. A caution on iodine water purification (Information). *West. J. Med.*, **135**:166–167, 1981.

Recommended Reading

SEARCH AND RESCUE

Austin, C. G. *A Manual of Mine Search and Rescue*. Naval Weapons Center, China Lake, Calif., May 1968.

Barlow and Vines. Hazards and Rescue Problems in the Cave Environment. NASAR Publ. No. 77–109.

Dalle-Molle, J. *Helicopter Operations and Personnel Safety*. Survival Education Association, Tacoma, Wash., 1978.

Fear, G. *Surviving the Unexpected Wilderness Emergency*. Survival Education Association, Tacoma, Wash., 1979.

Kelley, D. *Mountain Search for the Lost Victim*. Dennis E. Kelley, Publisher, Montrose, Calif., 1973.

LaValla, R. *Resources Guide for Search and Rescue Training Materials*. Survival Education Association, Tacoma, Wash., 1975.

Lewis, T. *Organization, Training, Search and Recovery Procedures for the Underwater Unit*. Tom Lewis, Publisher, Littleton, Colo., 1974.

MacInnes, H. *International Mountain Rescue Handbook*. Scribner's, New York, 1972.

May, W. G. *Mountain Search and Rescue Techniques*. Rocky Mountain Rescue Group, Inc., Boulder, Colo., 1972.

L. McCoy, ed. *Pre-Planning the Land Search Organization*. NASAR Publ. No. 77–1001.

Setnicka, T. *Wilderness Search and Rescue*. Appalachian Trail Club, Boston, 1980.

Smith, D. I., ed. *Handbook of Cave Rescue Operations*. Daniel Smith, Publisher, Petaluma, Calif., 1978.

Stoffel, R. *Emergency Preparedness Today*. Department of Emergency Services, Olympia, Wash., 1976.

Wartes, J. *Explorer Search and Rescue Team Member and Team Leader Training Manual*. Glover Park Education Center, Tacoma, Wash., 1975.

SURVIVAL

American Alpine Club, *Accidents in North American Mountaineering*. Published yearly by the AAC.

Brown, T., and Hunter, R. *Concise Book of Survival and Rescue*, Gage Publishing, Agincourt, 1978.

Craighead, F. C., Jr., and Craighead, J. J. *How to Survive on Land and Sea*. U.S. Naval Institute, Annapolis, Md., 1956.

Fear, G. *Surviving the Unexpected Wilderness Emergency*. Survival Education Association, Tacoma, Wash., 1975.

Ganong, W. F. *Review of Medical Physiology*, 7th ed. Lange Medical Publications, Los Altos, Calif., 1975.

Greenbank, A. *The Book of Survival*. Harper & Row, New York, 1967.

Lansing, A. *Endurance*. Avon Publications, New York, 1976.

Nesbitt, P. H., Pond, A. W., and Allen, W. H. *The Survival Book*. Funk & Wagnalls, New York, 1959.

Olsen, L. D. *Outdoor Survival Skills*. Brigham Young University Press, Provo, Utah, 1973.

Ormond, C. *Complete Book of Outdoor Lore*. Harper & Row, New York, 1964.

Patterson, C. E. *Mountain Wilderness Survival*. And/Or Press, Berkeley, Calif., 1979.

Petzoldt, P. *The Wilderness Handbook*. Norton, New York, 1974.

Riley, M. J. *Don't Get Snowed: A Guide to Mountain Travel*. Great Lakes Living Press, Matteson, Ill., 1977.

Rutstrum, C. *Paradise Below Zero*. Collier Books, New York, 1968.

Slonim, N. B., ed. *Environmental Physiology*. C. V. Mosby Co., St. Louis, 1974.

Tejada-Flores, L., and Steck, A. *Wilderness Skiing*. Sierra Club, San Francisco, 1972.

Troebst, C. C. *The Art of Survival*. Doubleday, Garden City, N.Y., 1965.

Whelen, T., and Angier, S. *On Your Own in the Wilderness*. Stackpole Co., Harrisburg, Pa., 1958.

OVERSNOW SAR

Bowman, W. *Extended Out of Ski Area First Aid for Ski Mountaineers and Nordic Ski Patrollers*. National Ski Patrol System, Inc., Denver, 1976.

Bowman, W. *Winter First Aid Manual*, 3rd ed. National Ski Patrol System, Inc., Denver, 1981.

Brower, D., ed. *Manual of Ski Mountaineering*. Sierra Club, San Francisco, 1969.

Grand Teton Natural History Association, *Mountain Search and Rescue Operations*, Grand Teton National Park, 1958.

MacInnes, H. *International Mountain Rescue Handbook*. Scribners, New York, 1972.

Manning, H., ed. *The Freedom of the Hills*, 3rd ed. The Mountaineers, Seattle, 1974.

Mariner, W. *Mountain Rescue Techniques*. Frohnweiler, Innsbruch, 1963.

May, W. G. *Mountain Search and Rescue Techniques*. Rocky Mountain Rescue Group, Inc., Boulder, Colo., 1973.

Roder, H. *NSPS Ski Mountaineering Manual*. National Ski Patrol System, Inc., Denver, 1980.

AVALANCHE HAZARD MANAGEMENT

Diltz-Siler, B. *Understanding Avalanches, a Handbook for Snow Travellers in the Sierras and Cascades*. Signpost Publications, Lynnwood, Wash., 1977.

Fraser, C. *The Avalanche Enigma*. John Murray, London, 1966.

Gallagher, D., ed. *The Snowy Torrents: Avalanche Accidents in the United States 1910–1966.* U.S. Department of Agriculture, Forest Service, Wasatch National Forest, 1967.

LaChapelle, E. R. *Field Guide to Snow Crystals.* University of Washington Press, Seattle, 1969.

LaChapelle, E. R. *The ABC of Avalanche Safety.* The Mountaineers, Seattle, 1978.

Perla, R. I., and Martinelli, M., Jr. *Avalanche Handbook.* U.S. Government Printing Office, Washington, D.C., 1975.

U.S. Department of Agriculture, Forest Service. *Snow Avalanches: A Handbook of Forecasting and Control Measures.* U.S. Government Printing Office. Washington, D.C., 1961.

Williams, K. *The Snowy Torrents: Avalanche Accidents in the United States, 1967–1971.* U.S. Government Printing Office, Washington, D.C., 1975.

| ALPINE AND NORDIC SKI INJURIES

Wade R. Eckert, M.D.
Jan Stehlik, M.D.

Skiing is a thrilling and beautiful sport of ever-growing popularity. However, the combination of speed, human error, bad luck, and the long lever of arms, skis, and poles gives the sport a predictable morbidity. Although permanent disabilities are infrequent, injuries are reported at a rate of 6 to 10 per 1000 skier days (4,5,24). This is probably an underestimate, since some skiers may bypass the local emergency room. Nine out of ten ski racers will suffer a major injury during their career, but few are permanently disabled or removed from further competition (20). Over the past 15 years, accident rates have decreased by 50%. At Mammoth Mountain, California, one of the largest ski areas in the United States, injury rates have dropped from 0.032 per skier day in 1965 to 0.016 in 1980 (28). The primary cause of the few fatal accidents in skiing is collision with other skiers or obstructions (28).

Most ski injuries fall in predictable patterns, the knowledge of which offers a more precise diagnosis and leads to better treatment. Common mechanisms and causative factors will be explored before individual injuries are discussed. The two basic types of accidents are collisions and falls. Avalanche danger and falls from heights will not be discussed. The rise of collision incidence is attributable to crowding of the slopes. The major contributing factor in a skier-skier or skier-obstacle accident is recklessness. Collisions that result in significant injury are caused almost exclusively by young adult males. Patrol of the popular slopes is designed to prevent their occurrence (28). Numerous factors are responsible for the decreasing incidence of injuries from falls. Slope grooming is now common in the United States and greatly improves the snow conditions. Better release bindings help prevent the ski forces, which act as a lever, from injuring the lower extremities, and high-top boots and better skis increase skier efficiency and the ability to recover from near-fall situations. Finally, the snow quality itself (deep snow versus hard, icy snow) influences the type of injury

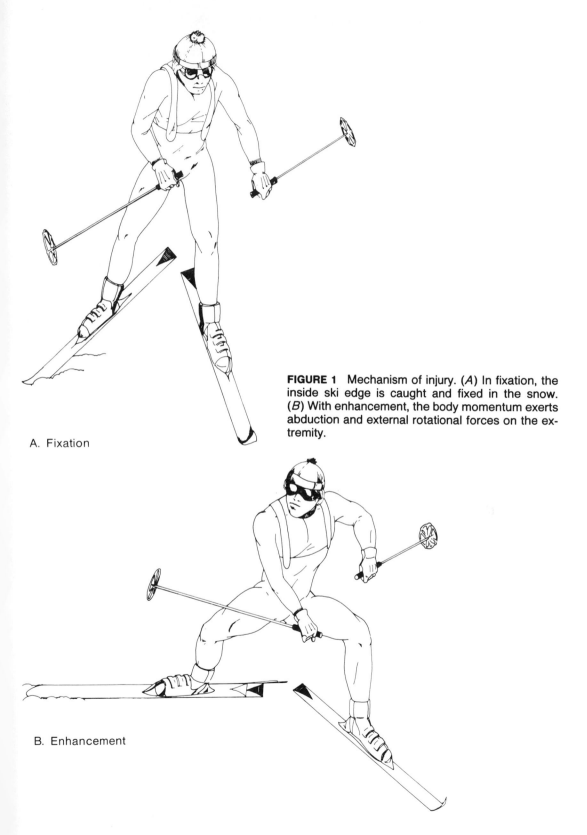

A. Fixation

B. Enhancement

FIGURE 1 Mechanism of injury. (*A*) In fixation, the inside ski edge is caught and fixed in the snow. (*B*) With enhancement, the body momentum exerts abduction and external rotational forces on the extremity.

seen. Skis and poles tend to get fixed in deep snow. The falling body torques around the fixed extremity, commonly causing knee ligament sprains, tibial fractures, and shoulder dislocations. On the other hand, hard, icy conditions produce direct impact trauma such as bruises, lacerations, shoulder separations, and a variety of upper extremity injuries (32,33).

Mechanism of Injury

Dr. John Moritz filmed and studied more than 2000 falls which produced lower extremity injuries and concluded that the mechanism responsible for producing injuries was the fixation and enhancement principle (21). In brief summary, when the ski encounters an obstruction in the snow, it fixes the foot and exposes the leg to pathologic forces, a process called *fixation*. Unless the binding releases, the body momentum can exert angular or rotating forces on the leg, a process called *enhancement* (Figures 1 and 2).

The three basic forces that produce injuries in the lower extremities are (1) forward fall (Figure 2), (2) internal rotation and adduction, and (3) external rotation and abduction (Figure 1). In a forward fall, a ski tip is dug into a snow obstruction, the foot becomes fixed, and body momentum angulates the lower leg over the boot top, creating a tibial fracture. Internal rotation and adduction stresses occur when the skier catches the outside ski edge in a turn. The body continues to rotate around the fixed ski, causing a spiral fracture or knee ligament strain. Abduction-external rotation is the most common pathologic force in skiing. As the inside ski edge becomes caught and fixed in the snow, the body momentum exerts abduction and external rotation forces, commonly injuring the ankle, tibia, or knee. Pure rotational forces applied to the ankle or knee rarely cause injury in skiing. It is only when abduction or adduction is added or present as an isolated force that injury to the ligaments results.

FOOT INJURIES

Foot injuries are usually uncomplicated and simple to treat, but are a major cause of dis-

comfort and spoiled ski vacations. It is not an overstatement to say that the perfectly fitting ski boot is yet to be made. The two major causes of foot pain are foot sprains and pressure problems. Even though the foot is well protected inside a rigid ski boot, sprains are still occasionally seen.

Mechanism of Injury

During a forward fall after digging the ski tip into the snow, the foot can be hyperflexed, leading to a midfoot sprain.

ASSESSMENT

Pain and tenderness over the dorsum of the foot can usually be elicited by motion and direct pressure. These sprains usually involve little or no swelling. Radiographic evaluation of the foot includes anteroposterior, lateral, and oblique projections. Avulsion fractures of the fifth metatarsal head, metatarsal fractures, and dislocation must be ruled out. These are uncommon due to protection of the foot in the rigid boot.

TREATMENT

Foot injuries are treated by rest, crutches if necessary, Acc bandages, and analgesics. Treatment of nondisplaced metatarsal fractures is symptomatic, with optional referral to an orthopedist. A short-leg walking cast allows early weight bearing, but is not essential for proper healing.

Pressure Injury

MECHANISM OF INJURY

Many areas of the foot are subject to pressure inside the unyielding boot. Pressure reduces circulation and predisposes to cold injuries. Short footwear causes subungual hematomas, which often result in loss of the great toenail. This injury is not usually noted until after the boot is removed or after a 24 hour delay. The first and fifth metatarsal heads, the bony prominence of the fifth metatarsal base, the medial arch, the superior-lateral border of the calcaneus, the malleoli, and

A. Fixation

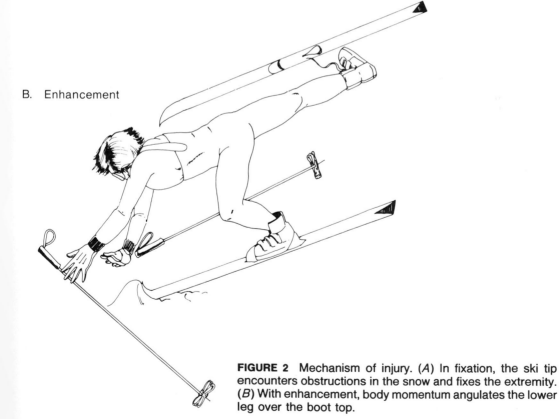

B. Enhancement

FIGURE 2 Mechanism of injury. (*A*) In fixation, the ski tip encounters obstructions in the snow and fixes the extremity. (*B*) With enhancement, body momentum angulates the lower leg over the boot top.

the anterior tibia are all exposed to boot insult. With repeated insult, some pressure areas, specifically the anterior distal tibia and the head of the fifth metatarsal, may form chronic bursae. This is seen in the professional skier (instructor and patrolman) and is not unlike the "surfer's knot."

ASSESSMENT

Due to local pressure anesthesia, the symptoms of tingling and burning pain often do not appear until after the boot is removed. This is particularly true of the area high on the proximal medial arch. Examination reveals painful erythema in areas of pressure points.

TREATMENT

The boot needs to be modified in the pressure area, which usually requires overstretching of the plastic shell, since this material has "memory" and to some extent resumes its original shape.

Persistent anesthesia over the dorsum of the foot may be caused by pressure injury to the superficial peroneal nerve. Recovery occurs in 1–3 days but can take several weeks and is usually complete. Rubber donuts are helpful in the treatment of chronic bursae. Occasionally, surgical resection of an underlying bony prominence may be needed.

The skier will usually request to have something done about his painful foot. He must be reminded that it is better to alter the boot than the foot. The problem is pressure; the treatment is to remove it.

Ankle Sprains and Fractures

Ankle injuries are not peculiar to skiing. In fact, their incidence has declined due to the use of high-top ski boots. The modern ski boot restricts foot eversion and inversion and protects the ankle in these modes of motion to some extent. The ankle is not protected, however, from rotational forces. These forces, when combined with even limited abduction or adduction in the best ski boots, can result in severe injury.

MECHANISM OF INJURY

Anatomy

The ankle mortise consists of the medial and lateral malleoli, encompassing the talus, which is stabilized by the deltoid ligament medially, the anterior and posterior talofibular ligaments, and the fibulocalcaneal ligaments laterally. The tibia and fibula are united by the interosseous membrane and the tibiofibular ligaments. The ankle, for ski injury purposes, can be thought of as a structure consisting of three bones: the talus and the two malleoli.

Mechanical Forces and Pathophysiology

In most sports, the vast majority of ankle sprains are produced by inversion forces that injure the fibulotalar and fibulocalcaneal ligaments as the lateral surface of the talus is brought away from the fibula. The vast majority of sprains about the ankle which are caused by skiing mishaps are also lateral, but for a distinctly different reason. Approximately 85% of these sprains occur as the inside edge of the ski is caught, causing the foot to be abducted and externally rotated. This forces the talus against the fibula, while the body weight tends to bring the tibia medially. The result is some widening of the distal tibiofibular joint. The force is rotatory, which tends to rotate externally the lateral malleolus. This stresses the anterior tibiofibular ligament more than the posterior one and produces the most common ankle sprain in skiing. Forcing the foot further may totally disrupt the tibiofibular ligaments as well as the deltoid ligament, creating an unstable ankle.

A very similar force may create an oblique fracture of the lateral malleolus and further separate the medial malleolus at the angle of the ankle mortise. Should the foot rotate even further, the posterior malleolus will fracture. The reverse mechanism of inversion with medial rotation of the foot in the ankle mortise will produce a near-transverse fracture of the lateral malleolus. This is associated with a fracture of the medial malleolus, which extends proximally from the angle of the mortise.

Associated Injuries

Knee sprains commonly accompany ankle injuries. Medial collateral ligament sprains are frequently seen with lateral ankle fractures. The aware physician always examines the whole extremity.

ASSESSMENT

The extremity is first observed carefully for evaluation of swelling, ecchymosis, and deformity. The ski boot is not removed until the patient reaches the examining room. This prevents the occurrence of gross generalized swelling and facilitates examination. Injured ligaments cause bleeding and swelling in their respective anatomic locations: the deltoid ligament distal to and around the tip of the medial malleolus and the lateral ligaments around the distal fibula. The often missed anterior tibiofibular ligament tear is associated with sausagelike longitudinal swelling at the anterolateral portion of the ankle just anterior and proximal to the lateral malleolus. Early ankle swelling over the anterior portion of the joint may indicate a capsular tear or a fracture caused by forces capable of displacing the ankle mortise. This may result in an unstable joint.

Displaced fractures usually produce deformity and malalignment. The ankle should be palpated and areas of tenderness carefully localized. Pain over ligament structures points to their injury. Crepitus is often appreciated in unstable fractures. Undisplaced fractures are tender but may cause little or no swelling.

Stress testing of the ankle is the most important and difficult part of assessment. The ankle is tested for stability in inversion, eversion, rotation, and anterior direction. Combined instability, i.e., abduction-external rotation and adduction-internal rotation are likewise investigated. The degree of displacement is compared to the uninjured side. An unstable ankle joint is a clinical diagnosis, with a stress x-ray used as a graphic record.

If more than several hours have elapsed since the injury occurred, the swelling will become diffuse and generalized, making localization of the injured structures more difficult. This is particularly true if use of the limb continues after injury. Extensive swelling will distend and tighten tissues around the joint. This not only obscures the anatomic landmarks but may also give a false impression of stability.

Radiographic evaluation of ankle injuries includes anteroposterior, lateral, and 25° oblique (mortise) views. Stress x-rays are obtained when clinically indicated. A special lateral oblique view tangential to the neck of the talus is indicated if talar fracture is suspected.

The nondisplaced fracture of the neck of the talus is of special note. This injury occurs when the skier digs a tip, particularly when the body weight comes down and forward. The tibia forces the trochlear portion down, while the forefoot in the boot fixes the head of the talus. If the fracture is not displaced, the usual findings are notable absence of swelling, with mild to moderate pain and tenderness medially and laterally over the head of the talus, which is just anterior to the medial and lateral malleoli. The diagnosis can be confirmed with a lateral ankle x-ray supplemented by a tangential view through the neck of the talus with the foot placed flat on the x-ray cassette. This view is not routinely used in ankle injuries and should be specified if a talar injury is suspected.

TREATMENT

Prehospital care is aimed at minimizing movement, further injury, and pain. This is accomplished by splinting the extremity. In most circumstances, it is proper to splint the joints above and below the injury as well. Cardboard splints, inflatable air splints, and other commercially available devices are adequate. The ski boot remains in place. It splints the ankle and provides compression, thus preventing edema. The patient is transported with the limb elevated.

Emergency Department Care

The task of the primary physician is threefold: (1) to establish the adequacy of the neurovascular status of the extremity, (2) to reduce dislocations, and (3) to refer appropriate injuries for treatment.

Although dislocations and neurovascular

injuries occur infrequently as a result of ski trauma, their treatment must not be delayed. Gentle manipulation and realignment of the ankle reduce the dislocation and will usually reestablish circulation. Ankle injuries are often undertreated, and we recommend that all but the most trivial ones (i.e., grade 1 sprains) be referred to an orthopedist. General treatment guidelines are discussed below.

Treatment of Sprains

Treatment of ligament sprains depends on the severity of the injury. A grade 1 sprain, the mildest ligament injury associated with minimal symptoms and swelling, is treated with rest and a compression bandage until symptoms subside. A grade 2 sprain consists of partial ligament tears without demonstrable instability. It is immobilized for 3–4 weeks in a short-leg walking cast and then protected by taping for 2–3 months. Sports are prohibited for about 6 weeks. A complete ligament tear which produces an unstable ankle (grade 3) requires a minimum of 6 weeks of immobilization and often surgical repair as well. The sequelae of a severe unimmobilized sprain are gross instability and reduced function.

Treatment of Ankle Fractures

Treatment of ankle fractures is guided by the principle of anatomic reduction of the talus in the ankle mortise and congruity of joint surfaces. Unless these criteria are met, traumatic arthritis is inevitable. Nondisplaced and stable fractures can be treated by cast immobilization alone. A period of 4 to 6 weeks in a short-leg cast and guarded weight bearing until the eighth to tenth week produces the best results. Innate stability of the fracture is determined by the initial displacement at the time of injury. Careful judgment must be used to evaluate this stability and thence the amount and nature of the support needed to treat the fracture adequately by closed reduction and cast immobilization. We emphasize that the maintenance of anatomic reduction requires close follow-up, patient cooperation, and critical assessment. The talus must align under the tibial plafond. The medial clear space (the distance between the lateral border of the medial malleolus and the medial wall of the talus)

must not be larger than that on the normal side. Reduction of fractures requires a knowledge of the mechanism of injury so that in manipulation, the reverse forces may be applied. For example, the common external rotation abduction injury (oblique fracture of the fibula and medial malleolus avulsion or deltoid ligament tear) should be reduced in internal rotation and adduction. Most ski injuries are seen early, before extensive swelling occurs; immediate application of a cast and elevation of the extremity control subsequent swelling and promote healing. The patient must be instructed to check for circulatory embarrassment. The structures most sensitive to circulatory changes are the sensory nerves. Reduced sensation and/or slight tingling is common and should be expected in the first few days. Near-total or total loss of sensation demands immediate attention. The elevated exposed extremity is frequently rather pale and cool. The overly-restricted dependent covered (i.e., warmed) extremity is usually dusky or even cyanotic.

Displaced and unstable fractures are treated by open reduction and internal fixation.

Pitfalls of diagnosis and treatment of ankle injuries are numerous. The cavalier attitude toward sprains should be avoided either in evaluation or treatment. If in doubt, support and reevaluate. Overly conservative treatment in the form of casts and restricted weight bearing will at worst slow the recovery of the limb; however, undertreatment can result in permanent damage. Anatomic reduction and maintenance of ankle fractures, with proper positioning of the talus in the ankle mortise, deserves reemphasis. Indeed, the primary reason for reducing malleolar fractures is to position and stabilize the talus.

Associated and commonly missed injuries are (1) sprain of the medial collateral ligament of the knee, which accompanies lateral ankle sprains or fractures, (2) fracture of the proximal fibula, which accompanies rotational ankle injuries, and (3) tibiofibular diasthesis. The most commonly overlooked ligament injury is the anterior tibiofibular ligament sprain. This is due to both lack of awareness and a failure to evaluate the ankle with stress in external rotation. Similarly, stressing the ankle in inversion may not reveal talar tilt unless the foot is plantar flexed. This is the case in an isolated rupture of the anterior talofibular ligament with the calcaneofibular ligament intact.

Achilles Tendon Rupture

MECHANISM OF INJURY

Achilles tendon rupture occurs in a straightforward fall which is checked by forceful contraction of the posterior calf muscles, with the knee in forceful extension.

ASSESSMENT

The injury is most common in the 30- to 50-year-old male. The history is of a forward fall with a popping or snapping sound at the heel, associated with sharp, severe pain which almost instantly lessens. When the patient is first examined while sitting with the leg hanging free, the foot assumes a neutral position compared to the usual resting position of plantar flexion. The tear is most commonly 1.5 inches above the insertion into the calcaneus, where a defect is palpable. Partial tears can be analyzed by the Thompson test (calf squeeze technique). The test is performed with the patient sitting or lying face down. If one cannot achieve plantar flexion by squeezing the calf, complete tendon rupture is likely. A word of caution is in order: The foot is flexed by five muscles other than the triceps surae. Although the patient has a complete Achilles tendon rupture, he may be able to flex his foot actively, but without most of his flexion power, a handicap not generally appreciated by skiers.

TREATMENT

Patients with Achilles tendon injury are best transported in a simple long-leg splint for comfort. Treatment should be provided by an orthopedist. For complete tendon ruptures, open repair is preferable (23). Partial tears are best treated by immobilization of the ankle in plantar flexion and the knee in 30° of flexion, using a long-leg cast. After 6 weeks, a heel lift is worn and the triceps surae are gradually stretched to their normal length (13).

Closed treatment in a short-leg cast for 8 weeks with the foot in plantar flexion has been reported as successful, but is still considered controversial (16,17). Rerupture occurs more often after closed treatment (9).

Peroneal Tendon Dislocation

This is a common ski injury which is seen only sporadically in other sports.

MECHANISM OF INJURY

This injury occurs when the foot is forced into dorsiflexion and eversion. The peroneal tendons forcefully contract to counteract foot hyperextension, tearing the peroneal retinaculum and allowing the tendons to dislocate anteriorly.

ASSESSMENT

There are tenderness and swelling posterior to the lateral malleolus. The swelling is longitudinal, and the tenderness is localized precisely on the posterior border of the lateral malleolus at its widest point. Pain is usually mild, and the ambulatory patient will describe a slipping sensation over the lateral malleolus. The tendons are either dislocated anteriorly or can be dislocated on active dorsiflexion and eversion of the foot. X-ray evaluation of the ankle occasionally reveals a small avulsion fracture of the posterior border of the lateral malleolus. This bone fragment is the attachment of the peroneal retinaculum and should be distinguished from avulsion of the distal malleolar tip which bears the attachment of the collateral ligament.

TREATMENT

Suspected cases should be referred to an orthopedist. Early surgical repair yields better results than late reconstruction of the retinaculum (3). In a recent series, in which 37 of these injuries were treated conservatively, 28 resulted in instability of the tendons (6). Conservative treatment, using a short-leg walking cast for 4 weeks, should be considered only if the examiner is unable to demonstrate instability of the peroneal tendons.

Fractures of the Fibula

The fibula is fractured in combination with fractures of the tibia, either as part of an ankle sprain or as an isolated injury. An oblique or spiral fracture signifies rotational stress and is usually part of ankle ligament injury. Tibiofibular fractures are described below. Transverse isolated fibular shaft fracture is very common in skiing and results from direct compression by the top of the boot during a fall to the outside or back.

ASSESSMENT

The diagnosis is suspected if there is tenderness over the fibula at boot-top height level. There is usually little swelling or ecchymosis. Displaced fractures are easily seen on x-ray, but over 30% of these fractures are hairline and appear only on close inspection. A magnifying glass is invaluable.

TREATMENT

Therapy of isolated nondisplaced fibular shaft fractures is symptomatic. The use of a compression bandage and protected ambulation with crutches or a cane are frequently sufficient. Displaced fractures are best treated by a short-leg walking cast for a period of 1 month. Return to athletic activities is possible after 1–2 months.

Fibular head dislocation is a relatively uncommon but well-recognized ski injury. It is caused by the forceful pull of the biceps femoris tendon during knee flexion, usually with the skier in a tuck position. It can be confused with a lateral collateral ligament sprain, but careful examination will demonstrate localized mild to moderate tenderness distal to the ligament itself. Posteriorly directed pressure on the fibular head will displace it and again produce pain. The therapy for acute injury is rest, ice, and a compression bandage.

Fractures of the Tibia

In spite of a marked decline in lower extremity injuries secondary to the use of release bindings, tibial fractures continue to be common serious ski injuries. The use of the high, rigid ski boot has shifted the stresses from the ankle and distal tibia to a more proximal area. Tibial fractures are usually sustained by indirect rotational and levering forces. Ski-related tibial fractures tend to involve less violence and less soft tissue trauma and have better prognoses for healing without complications than do fractures resulting from motor vehicle accidents or gunshot wounds (31).

MECHANISM OF INJURY

Pure forward or backward falls which lever the tibia over the boot top result in transverse or short oblique fractures, with comminution of the cortex opposite to the fracture apex. Rotational forces produce spiral fractures. The common external rotation and abduction force is responsible for the largest number of tibial fractures. The degree of displacement, comminution, and soft tissue damage is directly proportional to the magnitude of the trauma. Most fractures are closed, but occasionally the sharp bony spike can break the skin and create an open fracture. The compound site is usually on the anterior surface, at or just inside the boot top.

ASSESSMENT

The diagnosis of tibial fractures is not difficult. Attention to displacement, soft tissue injury, shortening, stability, and comminution is necessary for a rational approach to reduction and immobilization. Assessment of soft tissue injury is also essential for the evaluation and treatment of possible complications of a compartment syndrome. Direct trauma and vascular compromise cause swelling inside tight muscle compartments of the lower leg. Increased pressure is poorly tolerated by tissues and can lead to compartment syndrome with myonecrosis, ischemic contractures, and permanent nerve damage. Muscles and nerves are sensitive to ischemic injury and can be damaged even in the face of an apparently normal pulse because capillary perfusion ceases prior to obstruction of large arteries. Careful and sequential neurovascular examination is mandatory. Numbness, increasing rest pain, and pain on passive stretching of muscles indicate increased intracompartmental pressure, which demands hospital admission for observation and possibly fasciotomy.

Direct measurement of compartment pressures is possible, but the mainstay of early diagnosis is clinical assessment and a high index of suspicion. Fortunately, this is not a frequent complication of ski-related tibial fractures. When examining the extremity, attention must be paid to the proximal joints; associated serious knee and ankle trauma can be masked by a tibial fracture.

Children under 10 years of age with sudden onset of pain in the shin area after a fall have a tibial fracture until proven otherwise. Ligament sprains and muscle strains are extremely uncommon in children, due to the relative strength of these structures in early life. Tenderness near an epiphysis must always lead the clinician to suspect an epiphyseal fracture. Diagnosis is often obscured by the fact that epiphyseal fractures are often undisplaced and cause little swelling.

Radiographic evaluation of tibial fractures consists of anteroposterior and lateral views. Diagnosis is difficult only in cases of nondisplaced fractures of the shaft and epiphysis. If doubt exists, it is better to immobilize the extremity and obtain repeat x-rays in 10 days. Healing evidenced by callus formation reveals the diagnosis at that point.

TREATMENT

Prehospital Care

General principles of fracture care are applied. Treatment instituted by trained paramedical personnel consists of maintaining gross alignment of the extremity, splinting (including the joint above and below the injury), and transportation. Padded cardboard splints are inexpensive and efficacious. The newly designed Reel splint (Figure 3) or the Hare traction splint (Thomas type) provides excellent immobilization.

Emergency Department Care

The primary physician must establish whether the fracture is open or closed and whether vascular injury has occurred. Open fractures and vascular compromise are orthopedic emergencies which demand immedi-

ate treatment. Patients with open fractures should receive intravenous broad-spectrum antibiotics and open debridement with irrigation of fracture ends. Vascular insufficiency demands immediate attention by qualified surgeons.

Reduction of closed fractures with immediate cast immobilization should not be delayed. It reduces pain, minimizes soft tissue injury, and helps control swelling, which is beneficial for healing. If early reduction is not possible, the extremity should be well splinted and the patient transferred to the care of an orthopedist.

Reduction of Tibiofibular Fractures

Reduction is best done with the leg hanging over the edge of the table, allowing its weight to apply traction. From x-ray analysis, a plan is formulated for the manipulation and reduction of bone fragments, using intact periosteal and soft tissue hinges when present (2). Manipulation is done with whatever anesthesia is adequate to relax the muscles. After reduction, cast padding is wrapped snugly and the cast is applied and molded to obtain three-point fixation reproducing forces used for reduction manipulation (2). Satisfactory reduction requires at least partial bony apposition, less than 5° of posterior angulation, no anterior angulation, less than 10° of valgus or 5° of varus angulation, and minimal shortening (23). The anterior tibial border is subcutaneous, and a bony prominence after healing may be cosmetically objectionable or uncomfortable in a hard boot. Rotation of the foot with respect to the knee must be checked clinically and corrected with respect to the contralateral side.

Primary open reduction and internal fixation of tibial fractures is advocated by many traumatologists in Switzerland and Germany (15). Their advantages are anatomic restoration, rapid healing, and preservation of joint and muscle function. Most orthopedists in the United States believe that the risks of infection and nonunion outweigh the advantages in routine primary treatment (23). Open reduction and internal fixation are reserved for displaced intra-articular fractures, nonunions, and other selected cases, such as unstable short oblique midshaft fractures. Before beginning any pro-

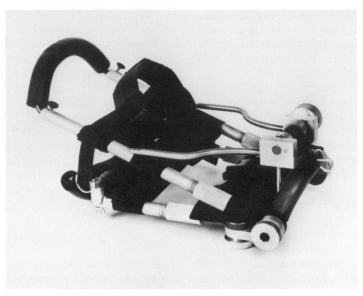

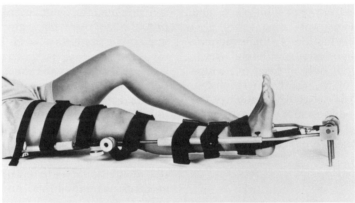

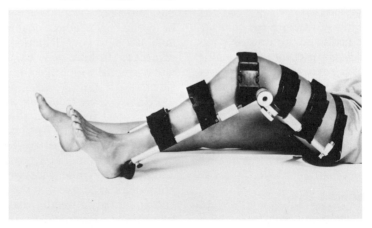

FIGURE 3 Reel Splint traction device can be used to secure and immobilize an upper or lower extremity in any position. It is lightweight and collapsible, making it ideally suited for ski patrol or mountain rescue activity.

144

cedure, a surgeon should ask himself if healing and function will be adequate if little or nothing is done, such as closed reduction.

Specific Fractures

TIBIAL SPIRAL AND LONG OBLIQUE FRACTURES

These fractures pose little problem because they expose large areas of bone to healing and require little manipulation, and because the associated fibular fracture will be at a different level, which provides some splinting through the interosseous membrane. Simple alignment of the limb with application of a cast, which is molded to prevent angulation, will suffice. If more than 2 cm of shortening occurs, external fixation or pins-in-plaster technique gives excellent control. With the latter, the pins may be removed after 6 weeks, at which time a weight-bearing cast is applied. Tibial fractures become solid in 3–4 months, but mature healing as evidenced by reformation of the medullary canal takes 8 months or longer. It is important to appreciate this end point. The hardened cortical bone accepts stress, with a softer center to absorb the impact. It is only after the callus matures that the limb can again be expected to absorb all types of stress.

TRANSVERSE FRACTURES

Transverse fractures in skiing usually cause little soft tissue injury, as they are caused primarily by levering of the bone over the boot top, with little displacing force. They are most often treated with closed manipulation and casting, followed by early weight bearing. Reduction is accomplished by increasing the deformity and then bringing the distal portion in an arc over the proximal fracture end. This fracture can rarely be reduced by traction alone. If the associated fibular fracture reduces easily, this may be done. However, one should not compromise the soft tissue or the tibial reduction by vigorous attempts at fibular reduction. In our experience, distraction of the tibial fracture by reduction of the fibula has not been a problem. The proximal and distal tibiofibular joints easily accommodate a small length discrepancy when a weight-bearing cast is used.

SHORT OBLIQUE FRACTURES

These fractures are difficult to reduce and to maintain in reduction. In the presence of an intact fibula, the fracture tends to angulate toward it. Because of its shape, even minimal shortening results in a large offset at the fracture site. The short oblique line offers neither the bone apposition of the spiral fracture nor the stable reduction of the transverse fracture. In this case, the intact or reducible fibula may be used to maintain the length of the limb. Prevention of shortening will decrease the amount of offset. If this course of treatment is taken, the orthopedist must be skilled in the application of a well-molded cast to prevent angulation of the tibia toward the fibula. It will be necessary to cast the limb with the knee flexed at least 25° and the foot in approximately 15° of plantar flexion to prevent anterior angulation caused by the deforming force of the gastrosoleus musculature. Anterior displacement or angulation at the fracture site does not preclude bone healing, but may make it impossible to fit a ski boot and is cosmetically objectionable. In skiers, the offset skin is unacceptable and may demand internal fixation to achieve proper alignment.

Patients treated by closed reduction and cast immobilization must have frequent x-ray follow-up to ensure that reduction is maintained. Repeated manipulation or open reduction may be required later on.

TRANSVERSE FRACTURES OF THE PROXIMAL THIRD OF THE TIBIA

These fractures almost always result from a direct blow inflicted during collisions. Due to extensive soft tissue trauma, these fractures are associated with a high incidence of compartment syndrome and should be observed closely. Reduction is ordinarily not difficult. Rapid union can be expected, thanks to the superior blood supply of the metaphysis as compared to the tibial shaft.

TIBIAL PLATEAU FRACTURES

Treatment of these fractures is predicated on principles which apply to all intra-articular fractures: (1) Precise anatomic restoration of joint surfaces is essential in the prevention of degenerative osteoarthritis. (2) Prolonged immobilization of injured joints leads to stiffness secondary to arthrofibrosis. According to these principles, all displaced fractures are anatomically reduced and rigidly fixed internally. Knee motion is encouraged immediately, but weight bearing is allowed only after fracture union, which takes approximately 3 months.

Stable, nondisplaced fractures are immobilized in a non–weight-bearing cast brace with a knee hinge. This protects against angulation and displacement but allows knee flexion and extension. An excellent discussion of tibial plateau fractures by Mason Hohl can be found in Reference 23 (p. 1158).

Pilon-Plafond Fractures

These fractures were a more common injury in times of low-cut, rigid boots. They are caused by anterior angulation of the distal tibia over the boot tops during a forward fall after digging the ski tip. The comminuted intra-articular fracture that results is a serious injury which often leads to painful ankle arthritis in spite of expert treatment. Anatomic reduction should always be sought. Closed manipulation is attempted by distraction of the fracture site using intact soft tissue and the periosteum as a hinge to bring the fracture fragments into alignment. The fibula is often fractured about 2 inches proximal to the ankle and can be reduced and used as a fulcrum for reduction of the tibia. Fractures which cannot be reduced by closed methods should be operated upon. Severely comminuted fractures may not lend themselves to internal fixation. In these cases, reduction with traction through the os calcis is the method of choice. Ankle motion without weight bearing is encouraged as early as possible (3–4 weeks). Pain and stiffness are to be expected.

A final note concerns tibial fractures which do not involve a joint surface. Any of these fractures can be treated by early weight bearing in a cast brace if the patient is ready to accept small amounts of shortening and possibly some cosmetic defect. This method is strongly recommended, as bone healing is stimulated by use of the limb; nonunion or delayed union is rare, and the extremity is

not predisposed to trophic changes of disuse (26).

KNEE INJURIES

Ligament Sprains

Sprains of the medial collateral ligament (MCL) make knee injuries extremely common problems which bring the skier to medical attention. Modern high-top ski boots protect the foot, ankle, and lower tibia and transfer stress proximally to the knee. While 90% of knee sprains are mild and pose no long-term problems, the serious injury may lead to permanent instability and disability if not properly diagnosed and managed.

Mechanism of Injury

Four common mechanisms of knee sprain will be discussed. These are (1) abduction-external rotation, (2) adduction-internal rotation, (3) hyper-extension, and (4) a direct blow to the anterior tibia. The principles of fixation and enhancement are involved with the first three mechanisms.

With the first mechanism, during a forward fall with the inside ski edge fixed in the snow, the extremity is forcefully abducted and externally rotated by the continuous momentum of the body mass. The medial joint stabilizers, MCL, and medial capsule can be torn in this fashion. Forces sufficient to rupture the MCL also stress the anterior cruciate ligament (ACL), which is often torn in combination with the MCL.

Adduction and internal rotation are exerted on the knee when the outer ski edge becomes caught and fixed in the snow, resulting in a fall to the side. The lateral collateral ligament (LCL) and the ACL are both exposed to trauma by this mechanism.

Hyperextension of the knee can occur in a straightforward or tumbling fall. Since the ACL, posterior cruciate ligament (PCL), and posterior capsule are at maximum tension in full extension, hyperextension leads to sprains of any or all of these structures, most commonly the ACL. Extensive ligament and capsule rupture can lead to frank knee dislocation, which is associated with a high incidence of injury to the popliteal artery and the tibial and peroneal nerves. Knee dislocations are fortunately uncommon in skiers.

A direct blow to the anterior tibia sustained in collision accidents displaces the tibia posteriorly on the femur, causing stress to the PCL. The posterior capsule is lax in flexion and escapes injury.

ASSESSMENT

The aim of diagnosis is to identify the structures involved and the extent of injury. The major stabilizers of the knee are the MCL, LCL, ACL, and PCL, as well as the joint capsule. The three grades of sprain are (1) mild stretch of fibers, (2) partial tear without instability, and (3) complete tear with instability. These all dictate different specific treatments.

Specific points in the history can provide clues to the diagnosis. The skier who sustains a mild (grade 1) ligament sprain may not recall a specific accident and often does not stop skiing. He presents to the physician the following day with symptoms of pain. Pain is due to edema of the ligament, which takes 8–18 hours to develop. Grade 2 sprains are quite painful from the onset of injury and prevent the patient from skiing. Patients with grade 3 sprains complain of instability (inability to support weight on the extremity), and they recall popping or snapping accompanied by severe pain which gradually subsides. Curiously, complete ligament tears are less painful than partial ones in the first hours, as there is no tension left on the injured structure.

Systematic, thorough examination of the completely exposed extremity is essential (12). If possible, one should observe the patient's gait and examine the knee in flexion, extension, and in comparison to the uninjured limb. Acute accumulation of fluid inside the joint represents bleeding from a ruptured ligament or capsule or a fracture. It can be detected by the loss of joint contour, palpation of the distended capsule, and ballottement of the patella. Substantial effusion will prevent full flexion and extension. It should be noted that the tibial attachment of the MCL and the fibular attachment of the LCL are extra-articular,

and their detachment will not necessarily cause hemarthrosis. This demonstrates the existence of a grade 1 or 2 sprain ligament without joint effusion. The knee should be supported in some flexion with a pillow to maximize comfort. Palpation is initiated away from any suspected area of pathology, with slow, gentle motion. Knowledge of the anatomy and precise location of tenderness will localize injured structures. The femoral attachments of both collateral ligaments are confined to a small area, as is the fibular attachment of the LCL. The MCL has a wide, broad origin from the tibia. A midsubstance tear will cause the most tenderness along the course of the ligament, while avulsion produces tenderness at the ligament attachment to bone. Tenderness at the joint line may signify meniscus injury. This is difficult to diagnose in acute knee trauma, but it can accompany any ligament sprain. One must have a high index of suspicion.

Determination of instability is the most important and difficult part of the evaluation. Muscle splinting and guarding of the painful joint can mask serious instability. It is important to reassure the patient, to relax his muscles, and to proceed gently with the knee in some flexion if extension is painful. Local anesthetic administration may be used, but the most important factor, other than the examiner, is the cooperative patient. If pain and muscle splinting preclude satisfactory examination, it should be repeated in 2 days. Examination under anesthesia must be done if satisfactory examination is not otherwise possible. This should be performed by a qualified orthopedist capable of rendering definitive treatment.

The collateral ligaments are tested by varus and valgus stress with the knee in 20° of flexion and in full extension. Most normal knees are stable in extension, while 5–10° of motion is allowable in 20° of flexion. Because of individual variation, comparison with the other extremity is always necessary. The ACL is tested by anterior drawer and Lachman tests. The anterior drawer test is performed by applying anterior force to the tibia with the knee flexed and the foot firmly fixed. The Lachman test consists of anterior displacement of the tibia on the femur with the knee in 20° of flexion. More than 5° of displacement indicates definite ligament rupture (14). Integrity of the PCL is tested by a posterior drawer test, the reverse of the anterior drawer test. Careful observation usually reveals a posterior sag of the tibia on the femur in PCL insufficiency. Any suggestion of straight instability demands further tests for combined rotary instability (29). The anteromedial rotary instability due to MCL and ACL tear is a common result of ski accidents (abduction-external rotation injury). Combined rotary instabilities comprise a complex topic hotly debated by orthopedic surgeons. Their consultation is mandatory in any case of unstable knee injury.

All injured knees require an x-ray evaluation. Ligaments are commonly avulsed with a piece of bone, which must be reattached if displaced. If instability is suspected, it should be documented by a stress view. This is particularly important in the immature skeleton, where epiphyseal fractures occur more commonly than ligament ruptures. Stress must be applied gently to a relaxed extremity and only after a review of the routine roentgenogram; excessive use of force can lead to unnecessary displacement and further injury.

The lateral x-ray should be examined for the fat-fluid level. The fat comes from bone marrow, and its presence signifies an intra-articular fracture.

Special studies, such as arthrography and arthroscopy, are useful tools to confirm intra-articular pathology such as meniscal and cruciate ligament tears. These tools complement a careful clinical assessment. Arthrocentesis is performed to relieve painful effusions, to differentiate between acute and chronic conditions, and to identify fat globules, hemarthrosis, crystals or organisms.

PREHOSPITAL CARE

If an injury is too painful for weight bearing, the extremity should be splinted and the patient transported.

EMERGENCY DEPARTMENT CARE

The role of the primary physician is to distinguish grade 1 sprains from the more severe injuries which require orthopedic consultation.

TREATMENT

Treatment of knee sprains is guided by the degree of ligament damage. Grade 1 sprains (no ligament tear) resolve within 1–3 weeks with local care and restriction of activity. Cooling with ice for 48 hours, followed by heat, is recommended. Athletics are permitted as symptoms allow. Grade 2 sprains (partial tears without instability) should be immobilized in a splint or cast for 2–4 weeks. Isometric exercises can be started right away, but full athletic activity is disallowed until after muscle strength and coordination are regained following removal of the cast. Unstable ligament injuries, grade 3, should be treated by a qualified orthopedist. In most cases, surgical repair is preferred to conservative treatment, particularly in cases of ligament avulsion from bone (23, p. 1247).

Controversy surrounds the treatment of isolated anterior cruciate tears, which are now commonly diagnosed through clinical evaluation and arthroscopy. Substantial evidence supports the theory that the anterior cruciate-deficient knee loosens with time, leading to instability and degenerative arthritis (8). While repairs of avulsed ligament attachments yield predictably good results, there is no reliable way of repairing the common midsubstance tears. Many authors now advocate substitution or augmentation of the midsubstance tear with a tendon graft in the young athletic patient. Results of these procedures are based on limited follow-up; firm conclusions cannot be drawn at this time.

Meniscal Injuries

Meniscal injuries are relatively less common in skiing than in other sports. The possible explanation for this is comparative lack of axial loading forces in ski accidents. Meniscal tears nevertheless do occur, both as isolated problems and in combination with ligament tears. Unless a high index of suspicion exists, the diagnosis is missed or delayed. A history of specific trauma may not be elicited. Patients classically complain of intermittent pain, locking, clicking, giving way, and effusions. In all acute knee injuries, meniscal tear should be suspected.

MECHANISM OF INJURY

The menisci are injured in one of two ways. They can be torn from their attachment during a ligament sprain or become trapped and crushed between the tibial and femoral condyles. The latter usually occurs in two stages. First, the cartilage becomes trapped between the joint surfaces during hyperflexion, hyperextension, or other uncoordinated motion. The opposite movement of the knee crushes and tears the meniscus. Axial loading (weight bearing) is usually involved.

ASSESSMENT

A comprehensive knee examination, as described in the discussion of ligament injuries, should be carried out (12). Specific findings associated with meniscal tears are (1) joint line tenderness, (2) positive McMurray test, (3) positive Appley test, and (4) inability to fully extend the joint, so-called locked knee. Joint line tenderness is the most common finding in peripheral tears, but it may not be present in tears confined to the substance of the meniscus. The examiner must be sure of the location of the joint, which is easily identified anteriorly above the tibial plateau and becomes less prominent peripherally and posteriorly.

The McMurray test, when positive, is pathognomonic for torn meniscal cartilage. It is performed by internal and external rotation of the joint in maximum flexion, which tends to trap the loose cartilage fragment between the condyles (12). Subsequent extension leads to a painful click or snap of the displaced fragment in a positive test. The maneuver should be performed with external rotation and valgus as well as internal rotation and varus stress to test both the medial and lateral menisci.

The Appley test is performed with the patient prone and the knee flexed to 90°. Compression and rotation are applied to the joint through the foot (12). Pain with this maneuver suggests meniscal pathology.

Torn fragments of cartilage tend to become trapped between the condyles, causing a mechanical block to motion. This is manifested by lack of complete flexion or extension. Unlike the limitation of motion caused by effu-sion, the locked knee has a firm end point. The fragments can often be reduced, or "unlocked," by gentle skillful manipulation.

A simple test which eliminates the possibility of minimal tear is the ability to perform a full squat. The patient who is able to do a deep knee bend probably does not have a torn meniscus, and another diagnosis should be sought.

Arthrographic or arthroscopic examination confirms the diagnosis of meniscal tear.

TREATMENT

Treatment of symptomatic meniscal tears is excision via open arthrotomy or by a skilled arthroscopist. Neglected tears can lead to early degenerative joint arthritis.

Patellar Dislocations

Patellar dislocations are a regularly seen ski injury. The senior author treats about 8–10 each year in a major ski area. The acute dislocation should be distinguished from the more common problem of chronic dislocation or subluxing patella. Although the etiologic factors show similarities, the two entities require different treatment. The following discussion emphasizes the diagnosis and treatment of the acute injury.

MECHANISM OF INJURY

Patellar dislocation occurs in the patient who is susceptible to it. The predisposing factors are increased q angle, shallow, flat lateral femoral condyle, weak vastus medialis muscle and patellofemoral ligament, patella alta, valgus knee, recurvatum, and general ligamentous laxity. The mechanism of injury is a forceful quadriceps contraction on a flexed knee with the leg abducted and externally rotated. It involves catching the inside ski edge in snow, which abducts and externally rotates the leg. Powerful quadriceps contraction forces the patella laterally out of the femoral groove. A direct blow incurred by falling on the medial side of the patella can contribute to the dislocation. Most of these injuries occur in females.

ASSESSMENT

Many patients relate a history of the patella popping or going out of the joint at the time of the accident, often twice (once when it goes out and once again when it spontaneously reduces with extension). In cases of unreduced dislocation, the diagnosis is obvious by the displaced prominence of the kneecap laterally. Spontaneous reduction makes the diagnosis more difficult and easy to confuse with other knee derangements, such as meniscal tear. The knee may be swollen, with bloody effusion and tenderness. Occasionally, a defect can be palpated medial to the patella. Pressure directed laterally on the kneecap produces pain and may reproduce a dislocation. In the chronic dislocation or subluxing patella, the so-called apprehension sign may be present. The patient will resist lateral displacement of the patella even in the absence of pain. Compression of the patellofemoral joint is painful, as is palpation of the lateral femoral condyle and the medial patellar facet (12).

X-ray evaluation, including sunrise and lateral views, must be performed, even in the obvious dislocation. Osteochondral fractures of the lateral femoral condyle and medial patellar facet can be easily overlooked, causing problems with posttraumatic arthritis or with an unrecognized loose body.

PREHOSPITAL CARE

This consists simply of transporting the patient, with the extremity splinted in a long-leg splint.

TREATMENT

Reduction often occurs spontaneously before the patient reaches his physician. It can otherwise be accomplished by gradual full, passive knee extension. If the patella does not relocate spontaneously with full extension, gentle pressure medially against the lateral border of the patella can be applied. Patient relaxation is the key. When the patella is tilted and wedged in the femoral notch, pressure on the proximal pole directed distally will disengage it and facilitate reduction. Immobilization for 4–6 weeks in a molded cylinder cast is necessary for soft tissue healing. Surgical repair, advocated by O'Donahue, is usually not necessary in the first episode of dislocation. Surgery is indicated for removal or fixation of osteochondral fractures and in recurrent cases. Rehabilitation of quadriceps strength is essential for stability of the patella and can be started as soon as symptoms permit, even with a cast still in place. Chronic dislocation demands orthopedic consultation and surgical intervention.

Femur Fractures

Femur fractures in skiing are usually the result of direct-impact trauma, the offending agents being hard snow and other obstacles encountered in collisions. Direct blows produce transverse or short, oblique fractures of the shaft. Peritrochanteric fractures are occasionally seen due to falls directly onto the hip, and are among the most difficult fractures to treat in the young adult. The long spiral fracture is caused by forces which rotate the torso on an extended leg. This mechanism more commonly results in knee or tibial trauma, making spiral femur fractures a rare ski injury.

ASSESSMENT

Diagnostic clues to femur fractures are pain, deformity, shortening, and malposition of the distal portion of the extremity. The knee or hip is occasionally injured in combination with femur fractures. These injuries deserve particular attention on physical and x-ray examination. It is always difficult to examine the hips and knee in an ipsilateral femur fracture, and one cannot rely on pain, tenderness, effusion, and x-ray evaluation for diagnosis. Many unstable knees, as well as acetabular fractures and even hip dislocations, have been discovered too late for effective treatment because symptoms and findings were masked by displaced femoral fractures. Neurovascular examination of the limb must always accompany the initial evaluation.

PREHOSPITAL CARE

Femur fractures are difficult to immobilize in regular splints due to lack of purchase on the proximal fragment. A portable traction apparatus, consisting of a frame with a groin ring and foot traction mechanism, is necessary for adequate immobilization during transport. If this is not available, the patient's leg and torso can be strapped to a backboard.

TREATMENT

Treatment of femur fractures falls into the realm of orthopedic surgeons. The initial management is immobilization by traction and debridement of open fractures. Many fractures are amenable to internal fixation. Others require skeletal traction, followed by cast bracing. Associated complications are primarily blood loss and fat embolism (7). Rarely, the sciatic nerve is damaged or a major vessel is lacerated. It is not uncommon to lose 2 units of blood into the thigh, which will be manifested by a tense swelling. The peak incidence of fat embolism is at 24–48 hours postaccident. This is heralded by altered sensorium, fever, tachypnea, and less commonly by petechial hemorrhages. These symptoms warrant early medical consultation. Neurologic deficits are rarely missed if looked for. Vascular deficits may be missed initially and are usually worse than the first evaluation would suggest. Even though vascular deficits are not common in ski injuries, they must be carefully investigated at an early period. Small lacerations of arteries are difficult to recognize early, as the adjacent fracture may leave the area painful and swollen, with a pulse distal to the injury. Persistent or recurring pain at the site, particularly with a burning quality, should alert the physician to listen for a bruit and palpate for the expanding false aneurysm.

Posterior Hip Dislocation

This injury is only occasionally seen as a result of ski trauma. However, its severity and need for immediate treatment warrant attention in this chapter. The reader is referred to Reference 23 for discussion of anterior and central hip dislocations.

MECHANISM OF INJURY

The classic mechanism of posterior hip dislocation is an anterior blow to the flexed knee on a flexed femur, which forces the hip out posteriorly. Internal rotation and adduction contribute to the ease of dislocation and are often involved in ski falls which lead to dislocations. The posterior wall of the acetabulum is frequently fractured in this injury.

ASSESSMENT

In a posterior hip dislocation, one finds the extremity short, internally rotated, flexed, and adducted. Motion of the limb is limited and painful. Neurovascular examination often reveals sciatic nerve involvement. X-ray evaluation consists of anteroposterior and Johnson lateral projections, neither of which requires moving the affected extremity. Oblique projections (Judet views) help define acetabular fractures. These are obtained by rolling the patient 45° to either side.

PREHOSPITAL CARE

This involves transporting the patient with minimal movement of the limbs, which are best strapped on a backboard.

TREATMENT

Emergency Department Care

Hip dislocation is an orthopedic emergency demanding prompt reduction. The vascular supply to the femoral head is compromised, and delay in reduction is associated with an increased incidence of avascular necrosis. If an orthopedist is not available, the patient should be transferred to an appropriate trauma facility, but under no circumstances should treatment be delayed for more than 24 hours.

Definitive Treatment

Closed reduction of simple dislocations is performed by traction in flexion, with muscle relaxation under spinal or general anesthesia. Major acetabular fractures require open reduction and fixation to provide stability to the hip. The joint must be debrided of all intra-articular bone fragments. If closed treatment is undertaken in the face of an acetabular fracture, absence of intra-articular debris must be established by tomograms or computed tomography (CT) scan.

Follow-Up Care

The reduced hip is immobilized in balanced suspension for 2–3 weeks and then protected from weight bearing for 3 months by the use of crutches. Radioisotope scanning is helpful in following vascularity and healing of the femoral head. Patients should be under the close observation of an orthopedist. Physical therapy, such as passive range-of-motion exercises and splinting, may be needed in patients with sciatic nerve palsy.

UPPER EXTREMITY INJURIES

Although no fractures or dislocations are unique to skiing, some typical injuries are seen with predictable frequency. Injuries due to direct impact prevail in hard-pack snow conditions. The most common ones are fractures of the clavicle, acromioclavicular (AC) separations, proximal humerus fractures, tuberosity avulsions, and thumb sprains. Shoulder dislocations are frequent in soft snow conditions, and Colles fractures usually occur in the walking skier who falls after slipping on ice.

Clavicle Fractures

Mechanism of Injury

The clavicle is commonly fractured in ski falls on the shoulder. Force applied laterally compresses the S-shaped bone and tends to produce breaks in the middle of the clavicle. Blows to the superior aspect of the shoulder depress the acromion and result in distal clavicular fractures. The same mechanism is responsible for AC joint sprains.

Assessment

The diagnosis is revealed by the tenderness and deformity of the clavicle. The patient usually supports the affected arm on his chest to protect against motion of the shoulder, which causes pain. Nondisplaced fractures may be overlooked unless proper x-rays are taken. Associated neurovascular injuries can

result from massive trauma uncommon to skiing. Careful examination must nevertheless be performed. X-ray evaluation consists of anteroposterior and 45° oblique cephalad projections. Distal clavicle fractures should be checked for ligament tears with stress x-rays (see Acromioclavicular Joint Sprains).

Prehospital Care

This consists of immobilizing the shoulder girdle with a sling and swath and transporting the patient.

Treatment

Most clavicle fractures can be treated by the emergency department physician by snug application of a figure eight splint. This pulls the shoulder girdle up and back, tends to decrease displacement, and provides immobilization. The patient is instructed to keep the splint tight. Healing occurs in 6–8 weeks in an adult and in 3–4 weeks in a child. Immobilization should be continued for the same amount of time. Anatomic alignment is very difficult to achieve and is not necessary for satisfactory function. Surgical treatment is reserved for rare nonunions and some distal clavicle fractures. Fractures of the distal clavicle deserve orthopedic consultation. They are commonly associated with injury to the coracoclavicular joint and are treated accordingly with AC splints or surgical fixation (see Acromioclavicular Joint Sprains).

Acromioclavicular Joint Sprains

Mechanism of Injury

This is a common ski injury caused by a superior blow to the shoulder in a fall. The acromion is pressed downward and separated from the clavicle, which rides superiorly. In severe injuries, the coracoclavicular (CC) ligaments are torn as well. The severity of the sprain is designated by three grades to facilitate rational choice of treatment. The structures involved are the AC and CC ligaments. Grade 1 is a sprain of the AC ligament only, without displacement or frank tear. Grade 2 is a partial tear of the AC and CC ligaments, causing mild AC joint widening and distal clavicle elevation. Grade 3 is a complete AC separation caused by rupture of all concerned ligaments.

ASSESSMENT

The diagnosis is suspected when there is tenderness, swelling, and deformity in the area of the AC joint. Clinical findings range from mild tenderness without deformity in a grade 1 sprain to a widely gaping AC joint with a high-riding distal clavicle in a grade 3 sprain. Integrity of the ligaments should be tested by gentle traction on the arm, documented by stress x-rays. These are obtained by suspending 5–10 pound weights from the arm and obtaining anteroposterior projections of the clavicle.

TREATMENT

Prehospital Care

This consists of simple immobilization of the arm in a sling.

Emergency Department Care

The emergency department physician should attempt to diagnose the grade of AC sprain, apply an AC splint, and refer grades 2 and 3 to an orthopedist for follow-up.

Definitive Treatment

Grade 1 sprains are treated symptomatically, with a sling for 2–3 weeks and ice for 48 hours, followed by heat and gradual resumption of activities as symptoms subside. Some pain may persist for several months. Grade 2 sprains are treated by closed means by most physicians. Treatment is directed at relief of symptoms, with rest to allow healing. Various methods of immobilization have been used, including sling, tape, straps, cast, and harness. In all methods the clavicle is pulled down, while the acromion is elevated by upward pull on the elbow. The commercially available AC splint has the advantage of tension adjustment, which must be done daily by the patient. Skin irritation and breakdown over the two pressure points (the clavicle and the olecranon) are common problems. The

splint is used for 3–6 weeks, and the shoulder is protected from reinjury for another 6 weeks. Good results are obtained as a rule, but occasional traumatic arthritis occurs due to derangement of the AC joint. Treatment of this complication, if symptoms demand, consists of resection of the joint and the distal end of the clavicle.

Treatment of the complete AC separation is controversial. Good results are obtained by both closed and surgical means. Numerous operative techniques have been described which reduce the AC joint, repair or substitute the CC ligaments, and internally fix the clavicle to the acromion or coracoid process. The major advantage is anatomic reduction; some of the disadvantages are scar, wound infection, pin migration, recurrence of separation, and painful AC arthritis. Closed methods of treatment also have drawbacks; the harness or strapping must be used continuously for 6 weeks, skin irritation occurs, and mild residual subluxation and deformity are common. Nevertheless, the functional results are quite satisfactory (23).

Sternoclavicular Joint Sprains

MECHANISM OF INJURY

Sprain or dislocation of this joint can result from a lateral blow to the shoulder and is seen occasionally in skiers.

ASSESSMENT

Swelling, tenderness, and deformity in cases of dislocation are apparent in the anatomic location of the joint. Manipulation of the shoulder girdle, particularly compression, reproduces pain and may reveal subluxation or dislocation. Neurovascular examination is essential, particularly in cases of rare posterior dislocation.

TREATMENT

Stable injuries are treated with analgesics, ice for 48 hours, and a sling until symptoms subside. Unstable injuries and dislocation should be treated by an orthopedist. A figure eight dressing applied snugly pulls the shoulder and clavicle backward and tends to reduce the dislocation. Direct pressure on the proximal clavicle with local anesthesia may be used. Incomplete reduction is compatible with full function, but occasional painful joint derangement requires surgical intervention (23).

Shoulder Dislocation

MECHANISM OF INJURY

Anterior shoulder dislocation is a frequently seen ski injury which results from a fall on the abducted, externally rotated arm. The ski pole extends the arm lever and predisposes the person to this injury, especially in deep snow conditions. The humeral head is usually rotated out of joint. In extremely rare cases, it is knocked out of joint by a direct blow. Posterior shoulder dislocations are rare due to inherent posterior stabilization of the joint.

ASSESSMENT

The diagnosis is obvious on physical examination. The acromion is prominent, giving the shoulder a squared-off appearance, and there is a hollow in the place of the humeral head, which can be palpated in the anterior axilla. Range of motion is painful and restricted. The arm is carried slightly forward and to the affected side. When the dislocation is very low, the patient may present with the shoulder in high abduction, even holding the hand on the top of his head. The classic finding in posterior dislocation is the lack of external rotation. Careful neurologic examination is important and frequently reveals decreased sensation over the lateral aspect of the deltoid. An anteroposterior x-ray reveals a subcoracoid anterior shoulder dislocation, and a trans-scapular or transaxillary projection confirms the anterior position of the humeral head. Posterior dislocations are frequently missed on the anteroposterior view. The lateral x-ray is essential in this instance. The x-ray must be scrutinized for associated fractures. Minimally displaced tuberosity fractures are common and usually reduce spontaneously with relocation. Associated humeral neck fractures are infrequent, but if they are present, they must be diagnosed to avoid displacement and unnecessary further injury by injudicious closed manipulation.

TREATMENT

Prehospital Care

This consists of immobilizing the arm in a sling and swath and transporting the patient.

Emergency Department Care

Dislocations should be reduced promptly. Reduction decreases pain and is easier to perform before muscle spasm occurs. Every emergency department physician ought to be skilled in reduction of uncomplicated shoulder dislocations. Orthopedic consultation should be sought in case of fracture dislocations.

Methods of Reduction

No matter which method is chosen, complete muscle relaxation is essential. This makes it possible to use minimum force and prevent further unnecessary soft tissue injury.

Longitudinal traction on the arm with countertraction in the axilla provided by the physician's foot was devised by Hippocrates. This method is still widely used, but an assistant holds a sheet through the axilla to substitute for the foot countertraction. Gentle rotation may help to disengage the head from the glenoid.

Stinson advised placing the patient prone on a table and suspending a weight from the wrist, pulling the arm at 90°. Reduction usually occurs within 20 minutes (23).

The Kocher maneuver involves traction, external rotation-adduction, and internal rotation. It has fallen into disfavor, since excessive use of force can fracture the humerus or glenoid or cause capsular or brachial plexus damage (23).

The authors find the following method of gentle manipulation both expedient and atraumatic. No analgesics are required if the patient is seen early after the injury and given verbal reassurance. With the elbow flexed at 90°, the arm is brought into full abduction and external rotation. One proceeds gently to avoid painful muscle spasm. The shoulder is then brought slowly back into adduction and internal rotation. No force or levering should or need be used. Reduction occurs spontaneously, usually after the arm reaches full abduction and external rotation. The position of the humeral head is confirmed by two-plane x-ray examination, and the arm and shoulder are immobilized in a sling and swath or a Velpeau's bandage. External rotation and abduction is prevented for 6 weeks and heavy activity for another 6–8 weeks. This time is used to regain shoulder motion. It is well to advise the patient of the high recurrence rate, which is significantly higher under the age of 25. Some authors believe that absolute immobilization for 3–6 weeks is essential if the dislocation is primary; whether this decreases the incidence of subsequent dislocations is controversial.

Soft tissue interposition which prevents reduction, displaced tuberosity, or glenoid fracture requires surgical treatment.

Fractures of the Proximal Humerus

It is beyond the scope of this chapter to explore the entire subject of proximal humeral fractures. Fractures of the greater tuberosity and the surgical neck are common in skiers. The incidence of these fractures is highest in the skeletally immature patient with open epiphyses and in the over-50 population with osteoporotic humeri.

MECHANISM OF INJURY

The forces responsible for causing proximal humeral fracture are (1) direct impact on the shoulder, (2) fall on the abducted arm, and (3) reactive forceful rotator cuff contracture, which causes avulsion of the greater tuberosity. Proximal humerus fractures sometimes accompany shoulder dislocations.

ASSESSMENT

The diagnosis is suspected when there is tenderness, deformity, and painful rotation of the shoulder. It is established by anteroposterior and trans-scapular or transaxillary lateral x-rays of the humerus. Nondisplaced tuberosity fractures are often overlooked unless internal and external rotation views of the shoulder are taken. Neurovascular injury, particularly to the axillary nerve, is not infrequent and prompts a careful physical examination.

TREATMENT

Prehospital Care

This consists of sling and swath immobilization and transportation to a medical facility.

Emergency Department Care

Nondisplaced fractures are treated in a sling for 3–4 weeks. Protected shoulder motion is allowed from the onset, but regular activity is prohibited until full healing occurs, usually in 6 weeks. Displaced fractures should be referred to an orthopedist. Displaced surgical neck fractures are usually reduced by closed manipulation, while displaced tuberosity fractures often require open reduction and internal fixation (23, p. 598).

Rotator Cuff Injuries

Rotator cuff tears occur regularly in skiers. The tendinous cuff is ruptured by forces which result from a fall on the lateral aspect of the shoulder and forceful contraction of the rotator muscles, mainly the supraspinatus. Complete tears are more common in the male patient over 55 years of age.

ASSESSMENT

Patients with complete tears present with a painful shoulder and an inability to initiate arm abduction. Tenderness can usually be localized to the precise anatomic location of the tear just distal to the acromion. Swelling is commonly absent. In partial tears, the ability to abduct the arm is preserved.

Internal and external rotation x-rays should be obtained to demonstrate the integrity of the greater tuberosity to which the tendons attach. If the diagnosis is in question, an arthrogram can be performed. It is particularly useful in the diagnosis of chronic tears.

TREATMENT

The emergency department physician should be able to diagnose this condition and distinguish between partial and complete tears. Symptomatic management, which consists of sling, ice, analgesics, and restricted activity, is advised for a partial tear. Complete ruptures and questionable cases should be evaluated by an orthopedist. Most require surgical repair.

Thumb Injuries

Ulnar collateral ligament sprain of the metacarpophalangeal joint and metacarpal base dislocation or fracture dislocation are two classic skiing thumb injuries. The former injury is seen several times a day in any busy ski area. Dislocation of the first metacarpal base is relatively uncommon except in skiers.

MECHANISM OF INJURY

Both injuries result from a fall on a fist-clenched pole, which levers the proximal phalanx or the metacarpal base in a radial direction. Depending on the amount of force involved, mild sprain, partial tear, or complete rupture of the ligament with joint capsule tear occurs as the proximal phalanx is displaced radially on the metacarpal. Sprains are classified as grade 1, 2, or 3. Grades 1 and 2 show no instability and are distinguished by the amount of swelling and hematoma, while grade 3 refers to an unstable joint.

In the carpometacarpal dislocation, the base of the metacarpal is forced radially and dislocated if the radial joint capsule and ligaments rupture. The ulnar aspect of the metacarpal base is held in place by a strong collateral ligament, which is responsible for causing a fracture instead of a simple dislocation. This is referred to as a *Bennett fracture.*

ASSESSMENT

Examination of the thumb reveals tenderness, swelling, hematoma, and sometimes deformity of the carpometacarpal or metacarpophalangeal joints. The area of maximum tenderness should be localized carefully because it corresponds to the injured anatomic structures.

X-rays in anteroposterior and lateral projections are obtained and scrutinized for avulsion fractures, dislocations, and fracture dislocations.

In the absence of an avulsion fracture, the metacarpophalangeal joint is stressed by exerting radial pressure on the proximal phalanx. The instability is compared to the uninjured side and documented by stress x-rays. A word of caution: Nondisplaced ligament avulsion fractures treatable by closed means can be displaced by excessive force, committing the patient to an open reduction.

TREATMENT

Emergency Department Care

It is essential that the complete tear of the ulnar collateral ligament be treated adequately, as severe chronic instability (so-called gamekeeper's thumb) is painful, disabling, and more difficult to treat than an acute injury (30). The primary physician should recognize this injury, temporarily immobilize the thumb in a short arm splint, and refer the patient to an orthopedist. Carpometacarpal dislocations and Bennett fractures should be treated by specialists.

Definitive Treatment

Treatment of a partial tear of the ulnar collateral ligament is cast immobilization for 3–6 weeks depending on the severity of the injury. Complete ruptures have been treated with a cast alone, but the results are unpredictable compared to open treatment (1). Stener (23, p. 333) documented infolding of the torn ligament in 25 of 39 operative cases in which proper healing of the structure would be impossible. We prefer surgical repair of unstable injuries and displaced fractures.

Treatment of a Bennett fracture requires anatomic reduction of the intra-articular components, which can be accomplished by either closed or open reduction and percutaneous pin fixation. Carpometacarpal dislocations are usually easy to reduce by closed manipulation but difficult to maintain without redisplacement. Close follow-up by an orthopedist is necessary.

Spinal Trauma

The incidence of spinal trauma increased somewhat in the last decade, paralleling the popularity of "hot dog" skiing and jumping. More skiers fall onto their head and back in uncontrolled accidents. Trauma to the spine can result in many types of fracture dislocations, accompanied by various degrees of instability and neurologic deficit. Because of the nature of ski falls and the commonly resulting vertical compression and flexion forces, compression fractures of the low cervical spine and fractures at the thoracolumbar junction are the most common spinal injuries seen in skiing. Compared to highway accidents, spinal trauma from skiing involves less violence; therefore, neurologic involvement is less frequent and profound.

APPROACH TO TREATMENT

Management of spinal trauma is directed at minimizing cord injury, providing spinal stability and preventing late pain syndrome. Certain fracture dislocations are notoriously unstable, threaten damage to neurologic elements, and require prolonged immobilization or surgical intervention. This is unnecessary in injuries in which stability can be established. Fracture stability is usually not immediately apparent and must be deduced from all available information derived from the history, physical examination, and x-ray examinations. Information must include the degree of violence and the forces involved, as well as the immediate posttraumatic neurologic status. In examining the patient, the location of pain and tenderness points to the damaged structures and the degree of guarding and spasm helps to determine the extent of injury. Complete neurologic examination and sequential reevaluation are essential. Progressive neurologic involvement secondary to bony encroachment is an absolute indication for surgical intervention (22,27).

ANATOMY AND PATHOMECHANICS

Knowledge of pathomechanics and anatomy is necessary for intelligent interpretation of x-rays. Spinal stability depends on integrity of the anterior and posterior bony elements and adjoining ligaments. The anterior stability is provided by the vertebral bodies joined by disks and the anterior and posterior longitudinal ligaments. Posterior elements, the pedicles, facets, pars interarticularis, and the spinous processes are joined together by interspinous ligaments and the ligamentum flavum. Stability is determined by damage to these structures. Isolated mild compression fractures are stable unless they are associated with damage to posterior bony or ligamentous structures. Deciding on the degree of stability is often difficult. Damage to ligaments can be assessed only by bony displacement, which may not be apparent if a dislocation reduces spontaneously. Knowledge of the mechanism of injury is helpful. For example, the anterior teardrop fracture is caused by forward sliding of the superior vertebra and combined compression and avulsion of the inferior vertebra. Considerable ligamentous damage is necessary to allow this displacement, making this a clearly unstable situation.

X-RAY EVALUATION

Initial anteroposterior and lateral views are obtained without moving the patient to prevent any possible spinal displacement. X-rays are scrutinized for alignment, fractures, and soft tissue swelling. Good alignment at the time of x-ray may be deceptive. Attention must be paid to soft tissue swelling, frequently seen anterior to the spine. This prevertebral edema signifies anterior longitudinal ligament damage. Special views and techniques may be necessary to define the extent of the injury. The pars interarticularis can be seen on the oblique projections, tomograms are often helpful in defining displaced comminuted fractures, and flexion-extension views can be used to rule out ligamentous damage but should not be done in the presence of fractures or significant pain. Flexion and extension should be done actively by the patient and must be supervised by the physician. A myelogram often is necessary in evaluation of the patient with neurologic deficit. CT scanning is the newest addition to diagnostic technology. The full scope of its use is being investigated.

Neck Trauma

Although various injuries can result from ski falls, by far the most common significant trauma is the low cervical spine compression fracture. Mild compression fractures, anterior teardrop fractures, and burst compression fractures with fragments extruded into the spinal canal all fall into this category.

MECHANISM OF INJURY

The accident always involves a fall on the vertex of the skull or occiput, creating vertical compression and flexion forces, sometimes combined with rotation, which may cause facet fracture or dislocation. A severe flexion component may result in disruption of the interspinous ligament or create a spinous process fracture.

PREHOSPITAL CARE

Initial management of spinal trauma consists of immobilization on a backboard, preventing motion by strapping the body and head, and immobilization with sandbags and a collar. Basic cardiopulmonary resuscitation is provided as necessary. When stabilized, the patient is transported to the nearest medical facility.

EMERGENCY DEPARTMENT CARE

Prior to moving the patient, a lateral x-ray is obtained. The shoulders are pulled down to visualize the C-7, T-1 level. If this does not reveal a fracture, the series may be continued.

The occurrence of paresis, shooting electrical sensations, apnea, loss of bladder control, and loss of bowel control are investigated. Neck tenderness, guarding, and spasm are noted, and the complete neurologic examination is recorded. The initial neurologic examination should include muscle function, sensory function with regard to dermatomes, perirectal sensation, and sphincter tone and strength, as well as reflexes such as deep tendon, anocutaneous, and Babinski (12).

X-ray evaluation is completed by taking anteroposterior and oblique spine projections. An assessment of spinal stability is made.

Unstable fractures require immobilization in the emergency department prior to any further manipulation of the patient. Halo traction provides better immobilization than tongs. If these are not available, a well-fitted cervical collar and sandbags can be used. Caution, awareness, and close supervision are more important than the method used.

DEFINITIVE CARE

Isolated, mild compression fractures are generally stable. They are treated by a short period of immobilization in halter traction for pain control, followed by a soft cervical collar until symptoms subside. Unstable cervical spine fractures require surgical stabilization. Progressive neurologic involvement caused by displacement of fracture fragments into the spinous canal demands early surgical intervention, but stable neurologic deficits may be worsened by operating, as hemorrhage and swelling increase the degree of trauma to the spinal cord. Immediate and complete paralysis does not benefit by surgery either. High doses of steroids [6α-methylprednisolone (Solu-Medrol), 100 mg/day] are helpful in combating cord edema, if started early.

Comprehensive care of quadriplegic patients includes bladder-bowel training, skin care, and psychosocial rehabilitation. This should be started as early as possible and is best done in spinal cord centers.

Thoracolumbar Fractures

MECHANISM OF INJURY

The other common area of spinal trauma is the thoracolumbar junction. Vertical loads from impact on the buttocks or vertex of the skull in a fall cause compression fractures of the low thoracic and high lumbar vertebrae. Anterior compression fractures result from vertical loads with the spine in flexion. Increased magnitude of trauma will cause posterior ligament rupture, posterior bony element fracture, and possible dislocation. Lateral compression fractures usually result from violent contracture of the lumbar and paraspinous musculature. A history of loss of balance and sharp pain prior to the fall can usually be elicited.

ASSESSMENT

Patients with fractures in this area complain of back pain radiating anteriorly to the abdomen. Muscle spasm, tenderness, and sometimes deformity can be appreciated in the back at the level of trauma. Neurologic evaluation must include motor, sensory, and reflex examinations as well as rectal tone, sphincter strength, and perineal sensation.

Sequential examination to document neurologic status and its progression is necessary for treatment decisions and the prognosis for recovery. Nerve root lesions are distinguished by loss of power, sensation, and reflexes at the affected levels; distal and contralateral neural segments remain intact. Cord lesions, on the other hand, display motor and sensory deficits at all levels distal to the injury, as well as hyperactive peripheral reflexes and pathologic reflexes due to release of central inhibition. Absence of hyperreflexia during the initial 24–72 hours may be due to spinal shock rather than interruption of the reflex arc (22).

Cord lesions are more serious than root lesions and carry a poor prognosis for recovery.

The importance of examination for perineal sensation, rectal sphincter tone, and anocutaneous and bulbocavernosus reflexes must be reemphasized. This information reveals the status of the distal end of the spinal cord, conus medullaris, and sacral roots, which are essential for bowel and bladder function.

Anteroposterior, lateral, and oblique roentgenograms are essential in arriving at the diagnosis, mechanism of injury, and degree of stability. The extent of fragment displacement, particularly into the spinal canal, may require conventional or CT scan to be fully appreciated.

Prehospital Care

The initial management in the field consists of basic cardiopulmonary resuscitation, immobilization on a full-length backboard, and transportation.

Emergency Department Care

The importance of complete initial neurologic evaluation cannot be overstressed because treatment decisions often rest on the sequential progression and development of neurologic findings. Movement of a patient with a back injury must be minimized until spinal stability can be established. Orthopedic and neurosurgical consultations should be sought liberally and promptly.

Treatment Guidelines

Treatment of fractures in the thoracolumbar region is dictated by the degree of instability. Minor compression fractures, under 15% of vertebral body height without ligament damage, are treated by bed rest and log rolling for several days, followed, when the patient is comfortable, by careful ambulation and hyperextension exercises. Corsets and braces may be helpful but are not often necessary. Neurologic involvement and late collapse are rare. Ileus commonly accompanies thoracolumbar trauma and must be treated appropriately. More severe burst fractures, particularly when accompanied by posterior element fractures or ligament damage, are unstable and require either prolonged bed rest or surgical stabilization. This is often accomplished by Harrington Rod instrumentation. Cord and root damage is proportionately more frequent with severe injuries.

Miscellaneous Injuries

Lacerations to the face and extremities are common injuries inflicted by ski edges. This usually happens after the ski is released in a fall and windmills around the skier, attached by safety straps to his leg. In rare collisions, the other skier's ski edge may be the culprit. Runaway skis can reach high speeds and pose a significant hazard, but the recent use of stoppers is becoming popular and effective in preventing this occurrence. The common areas of laceration are the back of the scalp, face, orbital ridges, wrists, forearms, and shins. Treatment involves the general surgical principles of repair of injured structures. Perineal injuries caused by the ski tail after the ski tip has been dug in have been encountered. They include scrotal avulsions and urethral and rectal tears (10). Lacerations by ski poles are common. Heart puncture by a skier's pole has been reported (28). Collisions produce a variety of injuries, including skull fractures. Blunt abdominal trauma is relatively rare, but rib fractures from falls on poles, fists, or other hard objects are rather common.

CROSS-COUNTRY SKI INJURIES

Cross-country skiing is an ancient sport with roots in the stone age. In Norway, skis were used for transportation in every facet of life. There are reports of wars fought on skis in Scandinavia and Russia as early as the fourteenth century (19). The first recorded ski competition took place in Norway in 1767. Cross-country skiing gained popularity in the United States when Bill Koch won the silver medal in the 1976 winter Olympics.

Compared to its downhill counterpart, cross-country skiing is a much safer sport, with the reported injury rates being three to seven times lower. According to Eriksson (5), fractures caused by cross-country skiing make up only 12% of all ski-related fractures. This is in spite of the high popularity of this sport in Sweden. Skiing across flat land has few hazards. These are likened to the risks of hiking in snow or running. Both recreational and competitive skiers are plagued by overuse syndromes, such as sprains, pulls, and muscle soreness (25). These will be explored in some detail.

In spite of the relative safety of the sport, severe injuries do occur. In 1978, Lyons (18) reported 11 cross-country injuries in the 1976–77 season in a small area in New Hampshire. They included two femur fractures, a hip dislocation, ankle fracture, patellar dislocation, and severe ligament injuries to the knee. All of the reported injuries occurred during the downhill portion of cross-country skiing, which exposes the skier to speed, collisions, falls, and torquing forces. Cross-country skis are less controllable than downhill skis due to the free heel pin binding and ski construction. Consequently, difficult terrain is harder to negotiate, and falls are more frequent. The cross-country skier is also less familiar with the techniques of turning and stopping during the downhill phase of this sport than is the alpine skier.

Lower Extremity Injuries

Since the leg is not attached to the ski in a rigid manner, the pathologic torquing forces associated with falls are smaller. This explains the lower rate of tibial fractures and severe knee ligament sprains. At the same time, the low-cut, flexible shoe used with pin bindings offers little protection to the foot and none to the ankle. As a result, foot sprains and ankle sprains occur commonly. The reader is referred to the previous discussion of foot and ankle problems for details of diagnosis and treatment. The topics of lower extremity fractures and ligament sprains explored in the section on downhill skiing likewise will not be repeated.

Muscle and Tendon Strains and Overuse Syndrome

Cross-country skiing involves a prolonged, vigorous effort in a cold environment and is likely to precipitate injury to muscles and tendons. Muscle strains, pulls, cramps, and spasms are somewhat obscure topics, poorly understood by many physicians.

Muscle soreness and cramps which occur as a result of exercise are often due to an accumulation of irritating metabolites. The accompanying cycle of spasm causes capillary constriction, ischemia, and further painful spasm, which aggravates the symptoms. This syndrome is easily confused with muscle strain, but can be distinguished by the prompt relief produced by stretching alone.

Shin splints is a painful condition caused by microscopic tears of the attachments of the anterior and posterior tibial muscles from the bone. This occurs typically in the untrained person who neglects preexercise stretching. Pain and tenderness along the medial or lateral tibial borders (posterior and anterior muscles, respectively) are related to exercise and often persist with rest or walking in severe cases. Repeated injury elicits periostitis, seen on x-ray as fuzzy, hypertrophic periosteal bone formation. This finding should not be confused with the periosteal reaction of neoplasms. Treatment consists of rest, cold packs, and a gradual stretching program. Symptoms can be disabling for several months. This problem can be eliminated by proper conditioning and skiing techniques.

Tendinitis, whether Achilles, patellar, or

hamstring, is relatively common in cross-country skiers (19). Its onset is usually gradual, and point tenderness incriminates the tendon in question. Bursae at and near the insertion of the hamstrings may also become inflamed. The most common site is at the lateral surface of the knee, just distal to the joint level. This pain and tenderness are of gradual onset, are aggravated by continual activity, persist for days to weeks after cross-country skiing, and rarely cause swelling or erythema. Rest, including cast immobilization in severe cases, ice application, oral anti-inflammatory agents, and passive stretching to tolerance, are the mainstays of therapy. Steroid injections into tendons should be avoided. Their use, particularly if repeated, leads to tendon weakening and rupture. Injection of steroids into bursae, however, may result in dramatic improvement. Chronic recalcitrant cases have been reported to respond to resection of diseased portions of the tendon.

Muscle strains are various degrees of muscle fiber and fascia tears and form the bulk of muscle syndromes. They are caused by forceful, often uncoordinated, contraction heralded by either immediate or delayed pain which worsens with the development of edema and spasm. All lower extremity and back muscles are predisposed to strains in the cross-country skier.

Physical examination shows tenderness and occasionally a defect in the muscle and loss of function which are usually proportional to the amount of pain. Palpation of the affected tendon, ligament, or muscle often reveals increased turgor even when swelling is not visible. Treatment is aimed at pain relief and the promotion of healing. Rest, ice, occasional aspiration of hematoma, and compressive dressing are used initially. Depending on the severity of the injury, active contraction, passive stretching, and massage can be started hours to days following the insult. This regimen combats painful spasm, controls edema, and provides motion that is beneficial for the organization of strong scar tissue. (Muscle does not regenerate, but rather heals by scar formation.)

It is difficult to determine when and how vigorously active therapy should be administered. Symptoms should serve as a guideline,

and adjustments should be made accordingly to prevent further muscle injury. A program of muscle strengthening before resumption of full athletic activity is mandatory, as strong musculotendinous units are less susceptible to injury than are weak ones. Complete muscle tears are relatively infrequent and best treated by surgical repair.

Low Back Strains

Low back strains are common in cross-country skiers. The obscure topic of low back pain is better understood and treated when one is familiar with the complex muscle and ligament structures in the spine. The latissimus dorsi, serratus anterior and posterior, iliocostalis, longissimus multifidus, rotator spinae, and many ligaments, aponeuroses, and fasciae support the back through short, mechanically disadvantaged lever arms, which predisposes them to strain. The twisting action during diagonal stride and flexion-extension of the lumbar spine in the double poling used in cross-country skiing greatly stresses the musculotendinous supports of the spine. Diagnosis of low back strain rests on a history of exertion-related pain and is often not clear-cut. Irritation of lumbar muscles, due either to accumulated metabolites or mild strain, may cause sudden spasm with a minor fall, sneeze, cough, or lift. Even the mildly inflamed muscle is prone to overreact to subsequent use. If the examiner does not obtain a history of prior exertion or fall, then the cause of sudden onset of recent pain may be overlooked. A history of previous backache not related to activity, radiation of pain particularly below the knee, and neurologic findings prompt further investigation. The skier is not immune from other back problems, such as a herniated nucleus pulposus. The differential diagnosis of low back pain is protean, and the patient who does not respond to rest and simple therapeutic measures must be worked up thoroughly for both intra- and extraspinous causes.

Treatment of low back strain consists of rest, pain relief with analgesics, and local heat, wet or dry. As soon as it is tolerated, a stretching and strengthening exercise program should be initiated. This includes flexion of the lumbar spine, pelvic tilt, and partial sit-ups. The intensity of the exercises is increased gradually as symptoms permit. Cross-country skiing should not be attempted before the patient is able to perform other less stressful athletic activities, such as jogging, swimming, and bicycle riding. Initially, it is generally best to advise the patient with back pain resulting from low back strain to do less than he thinks he can do.

Frostbite, Hypothermia, and Exhaustion

Frostbite, hypothermia, and exhaustion (11) are all potentially serious hazards of cross-country skiing. The cross-country skier keeps clothing to a minimum due to its weight and in order to dissipate body heat associated with strong physical efforts. Perspiration, inadequate spare clothing, exhaustion, and cold-weather clothing changes contribute to hypothermia.

The hands, feet, and face are exposed to direct cold injury due to the peripheral vasoconstriction which accompanies the cold response, as well as to the lack of awareness of frostbite caused by cold-induced numbness. In adverse weather conditions, the skier must conscientiously check for numbness in the toes and fingers and on the face. These signify decreased circulation and impending frostbite. The topic of cold injury is explored in detail in Chapter 2.

References

1. Browne, E. Z., H. K. and Snyder, C. C.: Ski pole thumb injury. *Plast. Reconstr. Surg.,* **58**(1):17–23, July 1976.
2. Charnley, J.: *The Closed Treatment of Common Fx.* Churchill Livingstone, Edinburgh, 1976.
3. Eckert, W. R., and Davis, E. A., Jr.: Acute rupture of the peroneal retinaculum. *J. Bone Joint Surg.,* **58A**:670–672, July 1976.
4. Ellison, A. E.: Skiing injuries. *Ciba Clin. Symp.,* **29**:1–40, 1977.
5. Eriksson, E.: Ski injuries in Sweden: A one year survey. *Orthop. Clin. North Am.,* **7**:3–9, 1976.
6. Escalas, F., Figueras, J. M., and Merino, J. A.: Dislocation of the peroneal tendons. *J. Bone Joint Surg.,* **62**(3):451–453, Apr. 1980.
7. Evarts, C. M.: The fat embolism syndrome: A review. *Surg. Clin. North Am.,* **50**:493–507, 1970.
8. Fetto, J. F., and Marshall, J. L.: The natural history and diagnosis of anterior cruciate ligament insufficiency. *Clin. Orthop.,* **147**:29, 1980.
9. Forste, R. L., Ritter, M. A., and Young, R.: Rerupture of a conservatively treated Achilles tendon rupture. *J. Bone Joint Surg.,* **56A**:174, Jan. 1974.
10. Hildreth, T. A., Cass, A. S., and Kahn, A. V.: Winter sports—related urological trauma. *J. Urol.,* **121**(1): 62–63, January 1979.
11. Hoffman, A., Herold, G., and Minder, E.: Internal medical accidents during cross country skiing. Deaths and hospitalizations in the upper Engadine. *Schweiz. Med. Wochenschr.,* **108**(29):1126–1128, June 1978.
12. Hoppenfeld, S.: *Physical Examination of the Spine and Extremities.* Appleton-Century-Crofts, New York, 1976.
13. Jamieson, E.: Injuries to tendo calcaneus. *J. Bone Joint Surg.,* **58B**:384, Aug. 1976.
14. Kochan, A., Markolf, K. L., Amstutz, H. C., and Marquette, S. H.: Measurement of AP stability in patients with documented absence of the anterior cruciate ligament. In press.
15. Laros, G. S., and Spiegel, P. G., editors: Rigid internal fixation of fractures. *Clin. Orthop.,* **138**:2, 1979.
16. Lea, R. B., and Smith, L.: Rupture of the Achilles tendon, non-surgical treatment. *Clin. Orthop.,* **60**:115, Sept. 1968.
17. Lea, R. B., and Smith, L.: Non-surgical treatment of tendo Achilles rupture. *J. Bone Joint Surg.,* **54A**:1399–1407, Oct. 1972.
18. Lyons, J. W., and Porter, R. E.: Cross-country skiing, a benign sport? *J.A.M.A.,* **239**:344, 1978.
19. Lyons, J. W.: Cross country ski injuries. *Physician Sports Med.,* **8**:65, Jan. 1980.
20. Margreiter, R., Raas, E., and Lugger, L. J.: The risk of injury in the experienced alpine skier. *Orthop. Clin. North Am.,* **7**:51, 1976.
21. Moritz, J. R.: Ski injuries. *Am. J. Surg.,* **98**:493, 1959.
22. Norell, H. A.: Fractures and dislocations of the spine, in Rothman, R. H., and Simone, F. A. (eds.): *The Spine.* W. B. Saunders Co., Philadelphia, 1975, pp. 529–566.
23. Rockwood, C. A., and Green, D. P.: *Fractures.* J. B. Lippincott Co., Philadelphia, 1975.
24. Reqva, R. K., Toney, J. M., and Garrick, J. G.: Parameters of injury reporting in skiing. *Med. Sci. Sports,* **9**(3):185–190, Fall 1977.
25. Sandelin, J., Kivilvoto, O., and Santauirta, S.: Injuries of competitive skiers in Finland: A three year survey. *Ann. Chir. Gynaecol.,* **69**:97–101, 1980.
26. Sarmiento, A.: Functional bracing of tibial fractures. *Clin. Orthop.,* 105, 105–202, Nov. 1974.
27. Schneider, R. C.: Trauma to the spine and spinal cord., in Kahn, E. A. (ed.): *Correlative Neurosurgery.* C. C. Thomas, Springfield, Ill., 1971, p. 597.
28. Ski Patrol, Mammoth Mountain ski area, personal communication.
29. Slocum, D., and Larson, R.: Rotatory instability of the knee. Its pathogenesis and a clinical test to demonstrate its presence. *J. Bone Joint Surg.,* **50A**:211–225, Mar. 1968.
30. Smith, R. J.: Post-traumatic instability of the meta-

carpophalangeal joint of the thumb. *J. Bone Joint Surg.,* **59A:**14–21, Jan. 1977.

31. Van DerLinden, N., Sunzel, H., and Larson, K.: Fractures of the tibial shaft after skiing and other accidents. *J. Bone Joint Surg.,* **57A:**321–327, Apr. 1975.

32. Westlin, N. E.: Factors contributing to the production of skiing injuries. *Orthop. Clin. North Am.,* 7:45–49, 1976.

33. Westlin, N. E.: Injuries in long distance, cross country, and downhill skiing. *Orthop. Clin. North Am.,* 7:55–58, 1976.

Jefferson C. Davis, M.D.

The expansion of industrial exploration and recreation in recent years has made it imperative that all physicians become familiar with medical emergencies peculiar to the underwater environment. Until relatively recently, undersea medicine was limited to physician support for naval diving, caisson work in bridge or tunnel building, and commercial diving. The development of a self-contained underwater breathing apparatus (scuba) during the 1950s ushered in a period of rapid expansion of scientific and sport diving during the following two decades. Presently, the worldwide energy crisis has driven humans to the oil-rich sea bed in the search for new sources of petroleum. The requirement for divers to construct, inspect, and maintain offshore systems at increasing depths and in hostile waters has spurred advances in technology to provide environmental support for and emergency care of diving accident victims. Our increasing awareness of the importance of protecting the marine environment from the ravages of pollution, as well as the oceanic potential for food

and other needed resources, has led to extensive studies by university, government, and private foundation scientific divers.

In general, scuba divers of the 1950s were "water people"—well-trained athletes experienced in breath-hold diving and competitive swimming. To don a scuba tank, regulator, mask, fins, and snorkel was a natural extension to those people already at home in the aquatic environment. Thus, they seldom encountered problems which required the attention of the general medical community.

Modern diving technology introduced reliable and readily available scuba diving equipment to an affluent, mobile, and adventure-minded public during the 1960s and 1970s, opening a new world of beauty and weightless experience to millions of new divers. This vast expansion of sport diving induced participation by people who often possessed little physical training or experience in water sports, with varying levels of health and sometimes advanced ages.

Today, almost every physician will find

scuba divers among the patient population and should be prepared to answer questions on fitness for diving as well as to handle diving emergencies. Because scuba diving is conducted not only in salt water but also in inland freshwater lakes and quarries, every emergency facility must be ready to provide immediate care and transportation to compression chambers for victims of pulmonary overpressure accidents and decompression sickness.

To understand the pathophysiology and clinical manifestations of barotrauma, certain historical and physical aspects of the underwater environment must first be considered.

Brief Historical Review

People have been diving under the sea for more than 2000 years, but until the seventeenth century they were limited by the ability to breath-hold while swimming to depth. In the seventeenth century, primitive bells containing air carried from the surface and compressed by pressure at depth allowed Swedish divers to salvage cannons from the Stockholm harbor (18). In 1690, Sir Edmund Halley, of astronomy and comet fame, devised a leather tube to carry surface air from barrels, which resupplied air to manned bells at a depth of 60 feet. These barrels were submerged, and the air they contained was compressed (8). The first practical diving suit was fabricated by Augustus Siebe in 1837 (1,8,18). Atmospheric air was supplied to the man in the suit by compressed air from a pump on the surface. By 1841, French engineers had developed the technique of using compressed air to keep water and mud out of caissons sunk to the bottom of riverbeds for bridge footings and tunnels. It was soon recognized that people working in this compressed air environment suffered joint pain, paralysis, and other medical problems after decompression to the surface. This was the introduction of *caisson disease,* now known as *decompression sickness.*

Beginning in the early 1930s and continuing into World War II, it became necessary to train men to escape from submarines disabled at depth. Exhaling during ascent through the column of water was usually successful, but the problem of pulmonary overpressure accidents with the syndrome of dramatic and life-threatening cerebral air embolism now came to the fore.

In 1865, Rouquayrol and Denayrouse developed a unit that supplied air on demand underwater at appropriate breathing pressure, but it required a surface connection (1). The 1943 development of a demand valve for a scuba apparatus by Cousteau and Gagnon opened the way for World War II underwater breathing devices, such as closed (Lambertsen's amphibious respiratory unit) and semiclosed systems (3). While open-circuit scuba with a demand valve provides the breathing gas as needed, exhaled gas is wasted into the water. Closed and semiclosed systems conserve breathing gas by "scrubbing" CO_2 and recirculating all or part of each exhalation. Following the war, open-circuit scuba equipment opened the underwater world to millions of recreational and scientific divers. This population will be emphasized in this chapter because of its importance to the emergency physician.

The Underwater Pressure Environment

Separate chapters in this book deal with other aspects of the underwater environment (hazardous marine life, cold water immersion, near-drowning); hence, this section is limited to the pressure environment and its hazards.

DEFINITIONS AND TERMINOLOGY

Atmospheric pressure is the pressure exerted by the atmospheric air above the earth's surface and varies with elevation or altitude. At sea level, atmospheric pressure is 760 millimeters of mercury (mmHg) or 14.7 pounds/in.² (psi). Another commonly used term for barometric pressure at sea level is *1 atmosphere (atm).*

With pressure gauges calibrated to read zero at sea level, *gauge pressure* is the amount of pressure greater than atmospheric pressure. *Absolute pressure* is the total barometric pressure at any point (gauge plus atmospheric pressure).

It is always important to specify whether one is expressing pressure in terms of gauge or absolute pressure. Except in situations which require laboratory precision, units commonly used to express water pressure are:

Pounds per square inch gauge (psig)
Pounds per square inch absolute (psia)
Feet of sea water (FSW)
Feet of fresh water (FFW)
Atmospheres absolute (ATA)

Each foot of sea water depth exerts a force of 0.445 psi, so it follows that the 14.7 psi pressure of 1 atm divided by 0.445 psi/foot of sea water equals 33 FSW. Thus, each 33 feet of depth adds an additional atmosphere of pressure. Hence, the gauge pressure at 33 FSW is 14.7 psig (in excess of atmospheric pressure), and adding atmospheric pressure gives an absolute pressure of 29.4 psia at 33 FSW depth. Because of the weight of solutes in sea water, it is a bit heavier than fresh water. In fresh water, 34 feet equals the additional atmosphere of pressure. Pressure change with increasing depth is linear; thus, a simple table of units (Table 1) will clarify units of pressure in sea water.

When a diver submerges, the tremendous weight of the water above him is exerted over the entire body. Except for air-containing spaces such as the lungs, paranasal sinuses, and middle ears, the body is a fluid. The law that describes the behavior of pressure in liquids is named for Pascal (1623–62). Pascal's law states that a pressure applied to any part of a fluid is transmitted equally throughout the fluid.

TABLE 1
Commonly Used Units of Pressure in the Underwater Environment

Depth (FSW)	psig	psia	ATA	mmHg (absolute)
Sea level	0	14.7	1	760
33	14.7	29.4	2	1,520
66	29.4	44.1	3	2,280
99	44.1	58.8	4	3,040
132	58.8	73.5	5	3,800
165	73.5	88.2	6	4,560
198	88.2	102.9	7	5,320
231	102.9	117.6	8	6,080
264	117.6	132.3	9	6,840
297	132.3	147	10	7,600

Thus, when a diver reaches 33 FSW, the pressure on the surface of the skin and throughout the body tissues is 29.4 psia or 1520 mmHg (Figure 1). The diver is generally unaware of this pressure, except in air-containing spaces of the body. The gases in these spaces obey Boyle's law (Figure 2), which states that the pressure of a given quantity of gas whose temperature remains unchanged varies inversely with its volume. Hence, air in the middle ear, paranasal sinuses, lungs, and gastrointestinal tract will be reduced in volume during compression or descent through the column of water. Inability to maintain gas pressure in these body spaces equal to the surrounding water pressure leads to the mechanical effects of pressure changes, which will be discussed later. Because of the weight of water exerting pressure over the chest wall, humans can breathe surface air through a snorkel or tube to a surprisingly shallow depth of only about 1 or 2 feet. Attempts to breathe at greater depth through the tube are not only impossible but dangerous, because the diver augments his physiologic negative-pressure breathing. In other words, in air at sea level, when muscles of respiration are relaxed, alveolar pressure is equal to surrounding air pressure. At a depth of 1 foot, the total water pressure on the chest wall is nearly 200 pounds (0.445 psi)! Because of the loss of normal chest expansion and the pressurization of intra-alveolar air, the diver has to "suck" or use negative-pressure breathing to draw surface air into the lungs through the tube. Even at a depth of 1 foot, the great respiratory effort required is rapidly fatiguing and becomes impossible at further depths of only a few inches. Forced negative-pressure breathing will ultimately result in pulmonary capillary damage, with intra-alveolar edema or hemorrhage. Symptoms include dyspnea and hemoptysis. Therapy is supportive.

Diving Equipment and Techniques

In general, two methods are used to supply compressed breathing gas to the diver. Air, helium-oxygen, or nitrogen-oxygen mixtures other than air can be supplied by hoses from the surface or from a diving bell at a pressure equal to water pressure. In the other method,

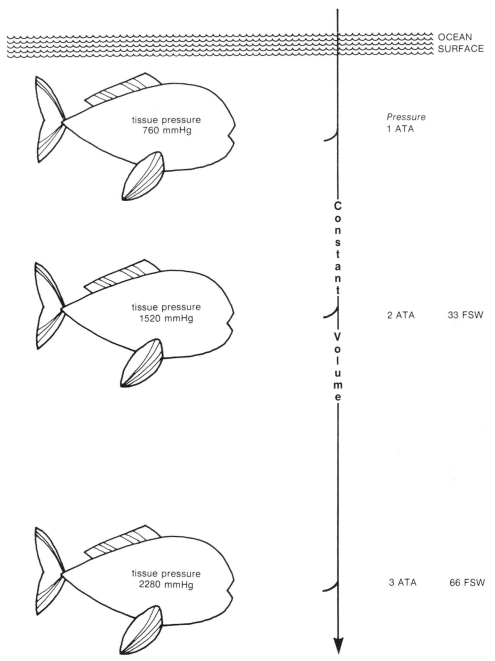

FIGURE 1 Pascal's law. Pressure applied to any part of a fluid is transmitted equally throughout the fluid.

scuba tanks with regulators supply diver-carried compressed air at a pressure balanced with water pressure. In either event, because of the problem of central nervous system oxygen toxicity and possible underwater seizures, 100% oxygen is not breathed underwater, except in specialized situations such as decompression stops in professional diving. An inert gas diluent is required to provide oxygen partial pressures adequate for respiration, but be-

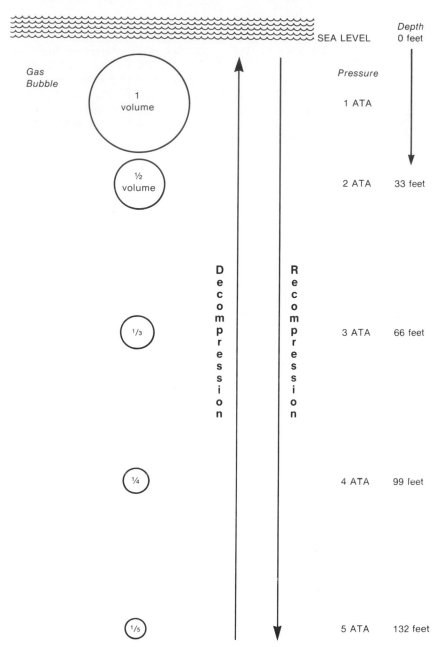

FIGURE 2 Boyle's law. The pressure of a given quantity of gas at constant temperature varies inversely as its volume: $P_1V_1 = P_2V_2$.

low the threshold for any danger of oxygen poisoning. In sport scuba diving this is usually compressed air, while in commercial and scientific work at greater depths, mixtures of helium and oxygen are commonly used to avoid the problem of nitrogen narcosis.

Standard equipment includes a scuba tank, usually pressurized to about 2400 psig with carefully filtered, oil-free compressed air. A first-stage regulator is attached to the tank to reduce pressure to a lower pressure second-stage regulator, which is attached to the diver's mouthpiece. The diver wears a face mask covering the mouth and nose to allow underwater vision; fins for propulsion; a snorkel for surface swimming; a buoyancy-compensating vest or weight belt to adjust for neutral buoyancy underwater and for flotation in case of an emergency; a watch and depth gauge to track time and depth; and a tank pressure gauge to monitor air consumption. Because of the high thermal conductivity of water, divers wear wet suits, which maintain a layer of water, warmed by body heat, between the skin and the suit.

Mechanical Effects of Pressure Changes

PROBLEMS DURING COMPRESSION OR DESCENT IN THE WATER

Barotitis

Referred to by the diver as "ear squeeze," barotitis is the most common medical problem in scuba diving. The physics and physiology of the problem are straightforward, but too easily forgotten by the diver who jumps from a boat, eager to explore the beauty beneath him. The problem centers on the structure of the eustachian tube and the application of Boyle's law (Figure 3). As previously explained, this law relates pressure to volume in an inverse fashion and dictates that the greatest volume change for a given depth increase is near the surface. Thus, with an unequalized descent of 2.5 feet (each foot of sea water exerts a pressure of about 23 mmHg), the diver develops a relative vacuum in the middle ear as the pressure effect generates a volume contraction. He notices this relative vacuum in the middle ear as the 60 mmHg pressure differential between air in the middle ear and external ambient water pressure causes the tympanic membrane to stretch and bulge inward, causing pain. At a depth of 4 feet, a 90 mmHg pressure differential is generated. At this depth, the nonsupported, flutter-valve medial one-third of the eustachian tube collapses and becomes obstructed. Therefore, attempts at the Valsalva or Frenzel maneuver to autoinflate the middle ear are usually not successful.

The Valsalva maneuver involves blowing with an open glottis against closed lips and nostrils to increase pressure in the nasopharynx in order to inflate the middle ear through the eustachian tubes. The Frenzel maneuver is performed by a swallowing movement with a closed glottis while the lips are closed and the nostrils are pinched. When the differential pressure reaches 100–400 mmHg, at depths of 4.3–17.4 feet, the pressure imbalance will be unsatisfactorily solved by perforation of the tympanic membrane (13). The problem for the diver is now the admission of cold water to the middle ear, with attendant severe vertigo. Prior to this event, serum may have been drawn into the middle ear by the relative vacuum, with resultant serous otitis.

Prevention is the key element in dealing with barotitis. If divers are made aware of the above sequence, they can inflate the middle ear prior to submerging and avoid the entire sequence as they descend in the column of water. If the middle ear pressure is kept equal to or greater than the water pressure, no problems will ensue.

Once serous otitis has occurred, nasal vasoconstrictor drops or spray (phenylephrine) and repeated Valsalva or Frenzel maneuvers will displace the fluid through the eustachian tube. Once the tympanic membrane has ruptured, diving must be suspended until it is fully healed or a repair is successful.

Barosinusitis

Barosinusitis, or "sinus squeeze," results from the same mechanism as does barotitis, but is much less common. If there is an inability to maintain and balance the air pressure in any paranasal sinus with the external water pressure during descent, a relative vacuum in the sinus cavity develops. This initially produces intense pain and then structural damage to the sinus wall mucosa, with bleeding into the sinus. Less commonly, a "reverse sinus squeeze" can occur on decompression or ascent in the water. In this condition, pain is produced by relatively high air pressure in the sinus as compared to decreasing external water pressure.

Prevention of barosinusitis mandates avoidance of diving with an upper respiratory infection or while allergic rhinitis is causing edema of the mucosa about the sinus orifices. Treat-

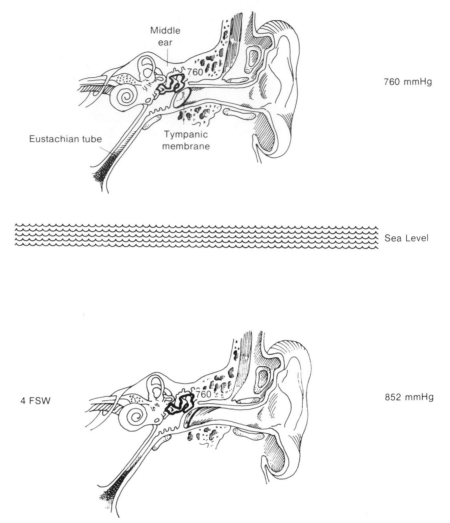

FIGURE 3 Middle ear trauma. Symptoms include fullness and pain due to stretching of the tympanic membrane.

ment involves the use of systemic (pseudoephedrine) and local (phenylephrine) vasoconstrictors, and occasionally antibiotics (penicillin) in the event of severe squeeze with bleeding into the sinus cavity.

Labyrinthine Window Rupture

The sudden onset of persistent, severe vertigo with tinnitus during attempts to clear the ears forcibly by the Valsalva maneuver during descent should raise the suspicion of round or oval window fistula. The mechanism (11) is thought to be transmission of Valsalva-in-

duced elevation of cerebrospinal fluid pressure to intracochlear fluid at a time when there is a relative vacuum in the middle ear. A forcible Valsalva attempt results in "explosion" of the labyrinthine window. When the diver reaches the surface, deafness may be noted in the affected ear. Immediate treatment is bed rest with head elevation, avoidance of straining, and prompt referral to an otolaryngologist. There is controversy as to management of these cases. Some otolaryngologists recommend immediate exploratory tympanotomy and repair if a fistula is found. Others advocate surgery only for those people who do not improve after several days of bed rest and symptomatic care for vertigo.

Mechanical Effects of Pressure Changes Related to Breath-Hold Diving

Despite the scuba diving emphasis of this chapter, this often discussed aspect of diving medicine must be included. Simplistic definitions of "lung squeeze" often imply our full appreciation of this complex problem, which is actually not fully understood at present. Based on classic teaching, the depth of a breath-hold dive should be limited to the depth predicted by the ratio of total lung volume (TLV) to residual volume (RV). According to this theory, a breath-hold dive to a depth greater than that where the resultant lung volume (Boyle's law) is less than the RV would cause a greater transpulmonic pressure than intra-alveolar pressure. Subsequent transudation of fluid or frank blood from the rupture of pulmonary capillaries would lead to massive pulmonary edema and hypoxemia—lung squeeze. According to this theory, a breath-hold diver with a TLV of 6000 ml and an RV of 1200 ml could dive to only 6000/1200, or 5 ATA or 132 FSW, before lung squeeze would ensue.

Another factor, that of central blood pooling by breath-hold divers, was reported by Schaefer et al. (19) in 1968. They reported that a diver can accumulate an increase of as much as 1047 ml in central blood volume at 90 FSW. If it is assumed that this adjustment in pulmonary blood volume partly reduces the RV, it is theoretically possible for the diver with the 6000 ml TLV to breath-hold to 6000/1200 minus 1047, or almost 40 ATA (2). In 1976, the world record breath-hold dive of Mayol to 316 FSW added credence to the latter theory. However, the lung-squeeze controversy is not settled. Cases continue to occur which seem to be due to lung squeeze, in which the breath-hold diver arrives at the surface dyspneic and coughing up bloody froth. Whether some of these latter cases are in fact near-drowning or lung squeeze is academic because the treatment is essentially the same: oxygenation with positive end-expiratory pressure (PEEP) ventilation and the management of acidosis.

PROBLEMS DURING DECOMPRESSION OR ASCENT IN THE WATER

The most important mechanical effects of trapped gas expansion during decompression involve the lungs.

Mechanism

It must be recalled that the basic principle of all diving regulators is to maintain breathing gas pressure. This keeps intrapulmonic pressure close or equal to surrounding water pressure, thus avoiding negative-pressure breathing. So long as these pressures are equal, the diver is relatively unaware of the crushing water pressure surrounding his body and no problems occur. In this regard, it is important to review three factors of great clinical importance:

There is significant change in barometric pressure in shallow water. Boyle's law dictates greater volume changes for a given change in depth near the surface than at greater depths. Hence, shallow depths are most dangerous for breath-holding ascents.

A pressure differential of only 80 mmHg (alveolar air above ambient water pressure on the chest wall), or about 3–4 feet of depth, is adequate to force air bubbles across the alveolar-capillary membrane.

Pulmonary overpressure accidents have occurred during breath-holding during ascent from depths of as little as 6 feet of water.

If a given intrapulmonic gas volume is trapped by forcible breath-holding or a closed glottis, or even in a small portion of the lung by bronchospasm during ascent, the intrapulmonic volume will increase, according to Boyle's law, until the elastic limit of the chest wall is reached. After that, the intrapulmonic pressure will rise until, at a positive differential pressure of about 80 mmHg, air will be forced across the pulmonary capillary membrane. This air will usually enter either the pulmonary interstitial spaces or the pulmonary capillaries.

Pneumothorax and Mediastinal Emphysema

Rarely, the air will be vented through a path of greater resistance, i.e., the visceral pleura, to produce a pneumothorax. This is treated in standard fashion with chest tube placement, if indicated. If air enters the pulmonary interstitial spaces, it can dissect along bronchi to the mediastinum or superiorly to the subcutaneous tissue of the neck, where it can be felt as subcutaneous crepitus. Treatment of these events is conservative, with bed rest, observation, and supplemental oxygen administration.

Arterial Gas Embolism (AGE)

The major life- and function-threatening introduction of air into the pulmonary capillaries, producing AGE, requires expeditious treatment in a compression chamber. When air is arterialized into the pulmonary capillary blood, frank gas bubbles are showered into the left atrium, to the left ventricle, and subsequently into the aorta, where occasional bubbles are scavenged by coronary arteries and can produce myocardial infarction or cardiac

arrest secondary to occlusive bubble emboli. Gas embolization to the coronary arteries may induce arrhythmias which may be exacerbated or independently stimulated by central nervous system stimulation from cerebral air embolism. Commonly, bubbles pass up the carotid arteries to embolize the cerebral circulation.

Clinical manifestations of cerebral air embolism are sudden, dramatic, and life-threatening. Because of the rapid onset of seizure activity or unconsciousness while in the water, the cited cause of death is frequently drowning in a diver actually incapacitated by cerebral air embolism. The neurologic pattern may be confusing, as showers of bubbles randomly embolize the brain, producing involvement of diverse brain regions. Commonly, the first manifestation is seizure activity, either focal or generalized (Table 2). The patient may suddenly be rendered blind or may develop visual field defects. Some patients demonstrate confusion, along with variable sensory and motor deficits. The differential diagnosis between cerebral air embolism and decompression sickness is made by the sudden onset noted in air embolism. In general, it may be said that symptoms which have their onset later than 10 minutes after surfacing from a dive are not due to air embolism.

IMMEDIATE CARE OF AGE

The primary concerns at the accident site are providing immediate care, contacting the nearest compression chamber, and transporting the patient.

Animal studies and clinical experience have demonstrated the value of placing the victim in the Trendelenburg position as soon as possible after the embolic event. In 1963, Kruse (16) reported anecdotal evidence of the value of the Trendelenburg position in a scuba diving-induced air embolism case. He observed the patient carried into his office in a head-low position; later neurologic improvement in that position was lost when the patient was placed supine. The patient improved again when the Trendelenburg position was resumed. This led to studies of cerebral AGE through a calvarial window in anesthetized cats. Photographs showed full clearing of arterial air bubbles in the Trendelenburg position,

TABLE 2
Pulmonary Overpressure Accident: Common Symptoms and Signs

Arterial Gas Embolism	
Symptoms	*Signs*
Seizure (focal or general)	Hemiplegia
Unconsciousness	Disturbed level of
Confusion	consciousness
Headache	Blindness
Visual disturbances	Visual motor deficit
Bloody sputum	Focal motor or sensory
	losses

Mediastinal-Subcutaneous Emphysema	
Symptoms	*Signs*
Substernal pain	Subcutaneous crepitus
"Brassy voice"	Gas patterns on x-ray,
Neck swelling	mediastinum, neck
Dyspnea	
Bloody sputum	

Pneumothorax	
Symptoms	*Signs*
Chest pain	Loss of breath sounds
Dyspnea	Hyperresonant percus-
Bloody sputum	sion
	Tracheal shift

presumably as the weight of the column of blood forced bubbles through the capillary bed. Unfortunately, these studies, performed at the University of Washington, were not published.

In the pulmonary overpressure accident, as soon as normal breathing resumes at the surface of the water, the pressure differential, which drives air bubbles into the pulmonary capillaries, is equalized. From this point on, there is usually no further introduction of intra-arterial air.

In the Trendelenburg position, the weight of the column of blood from feet to head may induce the transfer of bubbles from the arterial side through the capillary beds to the venous side. Additionally, the increased intracranial pressure caused by the weight of spinal fluid may help compress bubbles somewhat.

Because the event is so often acutely enacted in the water, the victim frequently suffers concurrent near-drowning. Accordingly, the rescuer must be ready to provide cardiopulmonary resuscitation and to protect the airway from the aspiration of gastric contents. Immediate care should also include 100% oxygen inhalation by mask. Bicarbonate treatment for the hypoxemia and acidosis of near-drowning, in the nonarrest setting, is reserved for the emergency department.

While these lifesaving measures are instituted, a member of the diving or rescue team should telephone the nearest civilian or military compression chamber and contact an air ambulance operation if air evacuation is required. Aircraft selection is crucial because the stricken diver *must not be exposed to significant cabin altitude.* Ideally, the diver should be transported by aircraft pressurized to sea level so that existing intra-arterial bubbles do not further expand. In the case of helicopter evacuation or in the event that an unpressurized aircraft is required, the flight altitude must be maintained as low as possible, never to exceed 1000 feet above sea level. An intravenous infusion of lactated Ringer's solution should be started and urine output maintained at 1–2 ml/kg per hour. Because of the occasional occurrence of both decompression sickness and AGE in the same patient, it is important to maintain an adequate intravascular volume. Unless adequate capillary perfusion is maintained, inert gas cannot be effectively eliminated from tissues or from intravascular bubbles at the arteriolar-capillary level.

There must never be a delay in transportation to a compression chamber. The *one* determining factor that correlates consistently with the outcome in such cases is the delay between the onset of symptoms and compression treatment. Every minute lost decreases the chances of complete recovery. Delay prolongs cerebral ischemia and cellular hypoxia, resulting in significant cerebral edema, and leads to a difficult course of therapy. On the other hand, remarkable improvement has been seen in cases in which treatment was delayed for more than 24 hours after the onset of neurologic manifestations. This reemphasizes the need for persistent efforts to move the victim to a compression chamber for a therapeutic trial.

DEFINITIVE CARE OF AGE

Definitive treatment of AGE is compression in a compression chamber (Figure 4) to at least 6 ATA, equivalent to a pressure of 165 FSW. The minutiae of compression chamber treatment are beyond the scope of this chapter, but we will review the general principles. Treatment consists of rapidly increasing ambient pressure (recompression) to reduce intravascular bubble volume and restore tissue perfusion; using oxygen-enriched breathing mixtures to enhance bubble resolution and to supply oxygen to partially ischemic and hypoxic nervous tissue; and providing slow decompression calculated to avoid the reformation of bubbles.

Hyperbaric chamber treatment of air embolism should be performed only by fully trained diving medicine physicians or, in their absence, by trained divers skilled in hyperbaric chamber treatment. Treatment of AGE has encompassed various methods during the past 40 years. These include treatment according to the 38 hour U.S. Navy Treatment Table 4, which was generally used until 1968. This treatment began with the diver breathing chamber air at 6 ATA for 30–120 minutes and then progressed through a slow, staged decompression, preferably with oxygen breathing by mask at the shallower stops. Details will not be presented because this treatment has been largely abandoned in favor of newer methods.

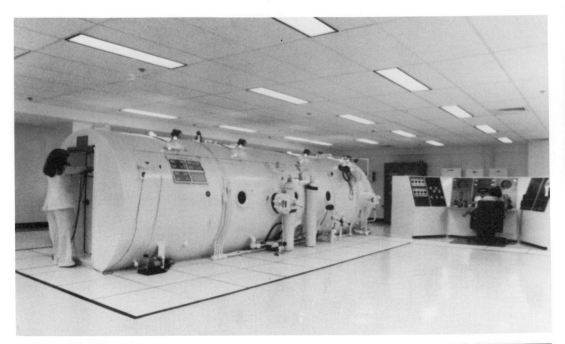

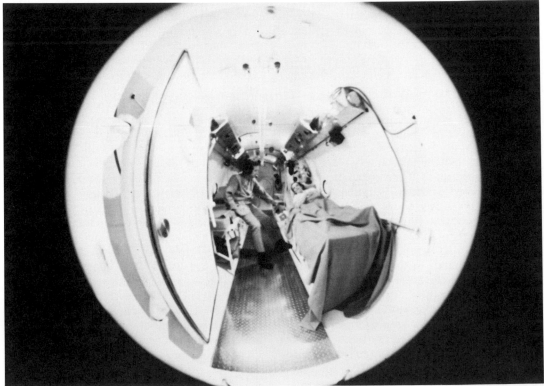

FIGURE 4 An adequate compression chamber for treating decompression sickness or arterial gas embolism should have a pressure capability of at least 6 ATA (165 FSW). It must have space for an attendant to provide ongoing care and repeated neurologic examinations. It must have provisions for supplying 100% oxygen and other gases for treatment of the stricken diver.

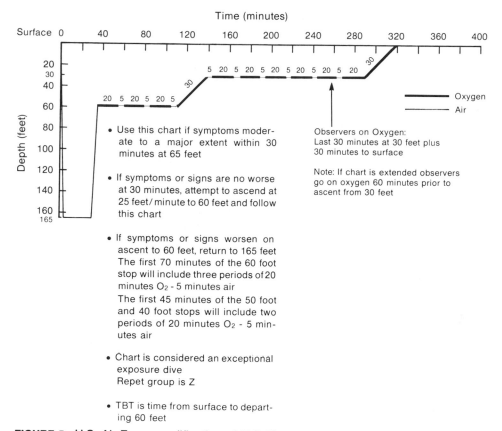

Time (minutes)

Surface 0   40   80   120   160   200   240   280   320   360   400

Depth (feet)
20
30
40
60
80
100
120
140
160
165

5 20 5 20 5 20 5 20 5 20 5 20 5 20

20 5 20 5 20 5

30

30

Oxygen
Air

- Use this chart if symptoms moderate to a major extent within 30 minutes at 65 feet

- If symptoms or signs are no worse at 30 minutes, attempt to ascend at 25 feet/minute to 60 feet and follow this chart

- If symptoms or signs worsen on ascent to 60 feet, return to 165 feet The first 70 minutes of the 60 foot stop will include three periods of 20 minutes O_2 - 5 minutes air The first 45 minutes of the 50 foot and 40 foot stops will include two periods of 20 minutes O_2 - 5 minutes air

- Chart is considered an exceptional exposure dive Repet group is Z

- TBT is time from surface to departing 60 feet

Observers on Oxygen:
Last 30 minutes at 30 feet plus 30 minutes to surface

Note: If chart is extended observers go on oxygen 60 minutes prior to ascent from 30 feet

FIGURE 5 U.S. Air Force modification of U.S. Navy treatment table for the management of arterial gas embolism.

Since 1968, most treatment of AGE begins with compression to 6 ATA (165 FSW) breathing air; after 30 minutes at that depth, decompression is effected over 4 minutes to 2.8 ATA (60 FSW). Then 100% oxygen is administered by mask according to a 20 minutes oxygen/5 minutes chamber air breathing schedule for at least three oxygen periods at 2.8 ATA. Ascent to 1.9 ATA (30 FSW) is at a rate of 1 foot/minute, whereas U.S. Navy Treatment Table 6A calls for two 15 minutes air/60 minutes oxygen periods and the U.S. Air Force modification (Figure 5) gives the same number of oxygen and air minutes on a 5 minutes air/20 minutes oxygen schedule as a further precaution against pulmonary oxygen toxicity. In 1977, Hendricks et al. (15) published results of their studies indicating significant extension of pulmonary safety limits by intermittent exposure on this schedule.

Decompression to the surface while breathing 100% oxygen is at a rate of 1 foot/minute.

This appears to be a straightforward prescription for treatment of AGE, and indeed, victims treated immediately by this method usually respond and remain free of neurologic deficit. The requirement for the experienced diving medicine physician, however, is mandated by the fact that some cases, especially those in which there is a long delay in reaching the chamber, may require other treatments. These options have been set forth in the report of a workshop on the treatment of difficult cases (9). For example, the patient who fails to respond, or who responds only partially after 30 minutes at 6 ATA, may be held there breathing air and managed by other methods of saturation treatment. These methods use exceedingly slow decompression rates and a reduction in the percentage of chamber environmental oxygen according to depth, to avoid oxygen poisoning in the patient as well as in his tenders.

PREVENTION OF PULMONARY OVERPRESSURE ACCIDENTS

Divers must be warned of the great intra-thoracic volume changes that occur in shallow depths. An open airway must be maintained during ascent through the last 10 feet to the surface. If an equipment malfunction or deple-tion of the air supply at depth makes this im-possible, the diver must make every attempt to exhale continuously during "emergency swimming ascent." This is an attempt to vent the increasing volume of air in the lungs. With a satisfactory air supply, the diver should sim-ply breathe normally on ascent to the surface.

Effects of Alterations in Gas Partial Pressures

DALTON'S LAW OF PARTIAL PRESSURES

This law states that the total pressure ex-erted by a mixture of gases is the sum of the pressures that would be exerted by each of the gases if it alone were present and occupied the total volume. The partial pressure of a gas in a mixture is the pressure exerted by that gas alone. The symbols for partial pres-sure of oxygen, nitrogen, carbon dioxide, and water vapor are P_{O_2}, P_{N_2}, P_{CO_2}, and P_{H_2O}, respectively. Dalton's law states that in an air mixture, the total pressure $(P_T) = P_{N_2} + P_{O_2} + P_{CO_2} + P_{H_2O} + P$ other. The partial pres-sure of each gas in the mixture is found by multiplying the percentage of that gas present by the total pressure. In Figure 6, we assume a mixture of air with nitrogen 78%, oxygen 21%, CO_2 0.03%, and the balance composed of water vapor and other trace gases.

The partial pressure of inspired gases—not their percentage—in a gas mixture is of prime importance in diving. For example, it will be shown that in compression chamber treatment of decompression sickness, 100% oxygen can be safely used at depths to 60 FSW (2.8 ATA) for 20 minute periods with the subject at rest in the dry chamber. On the other hand, even with 21% oxygen in a helium-oxygen mixture, at 600 FSW (20 ATA) the diver would be breathing 0.21×20 or 4.2 ATA of oxygen, which would soon produce central nervous system oxygen poisoning. This is avoided in deep diving by reducing the oxygen percentage in the gas mixture to maintain P_{O_2} of 0.35–0.50 ATA of oxygen (266–380 mmHg) for prolonged exposures.

The scuba diver who uses open-circuit com-pressed air is the central concern in this chap-ter. The principles of partial pressures in div-ing must be firmly remembered as we consider each medical problem of the scuba diver. Even though the gas mixture is compressed air with constant *percentages* of oxygen and nitrogen, the increases in partial pressures, along with multiplication of even trace contaminants at sea level, represent the first potential problems we consider.

NITROGEN NARCOSIS

During the 1930s, Behnke et al. (4) sus-pected that the mood changes at 200 FSW described by divers breathing compressed air was due to the high inspired P_{N_2}. The term *nitrogen narcosis* is generally used to describe this effect, although Cousteau's term *rapture of the deep* is most descriptive.

The complete compilation of data on inert gas narcosis (covering not only nitrogen but other inert gases) was provided by Bennett (5,6). Decrements in performance and behav-ior have been noted at depths as shallow as 66 FSW (3 ATA), but significant symptoms usually develop as the diver exceeds 100 FSW (4 ATA) while breathing compressed air. Sub-stitution of helium for nitrogen as the inert gas diluent avoids these effects and is generally required by professional divers for diving deeper than 180 FSW. Nitrogen narcosis, with its attendant euphoria and impairment of judgment, is one of the factors which has led to a recommendation that sport divers should never exceed a depth of 130 FSW.

There is considerable day-to-day variation in susceptibility to euphoria, as well as a signif-icant experience factor. In hyperbaric cham-ber work, it is common to see student divers laughing and seemingly unable to obey in-structions at 165 FSW in the compressed air chamber, while the experienced observer looks on and calmly completes a checklist. At about 250–300 FSW there may be depression and

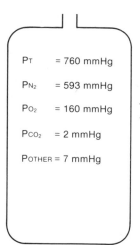

P_T = 760 mmHg

P_{N_2} = 593 mmHg

P_{O_2} = 160 mmHg

P_{CO_2} = 2 mmHg

P_{OTHER} = 7 mmHg

Tank at Sea Level, Equilibrated with Ambient Air Pressure

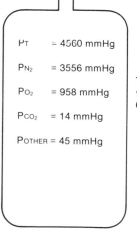

P_T = 4560 mmHg

P_{N_2} = 3556 mmHg

P_{O_2} = 958 mmHg

P_{CO_2} = 14 mmHg

P_{OTHER} = 45 mmHg

Tank Pressurized with Compressed Air to 6 ATA (165 FSW)

FIGURE 6 Dalton's law of partial pressure. The total pressure exerted by a mixture of gases is the sum of the pressures that would be exerted by each of the gases if it alone were present and occupied the total volume.

loss of neuromuscular control and, by 300–350 FSW, loss of consciousness. The treatment is to decompress to a depth shallower than 100 FSW, where immediate clearing of the sensorium is seen. The problem can be prevented by using helium-oxygen mixtures for deep diving.

OXYGEN POISONING

Retrolental fibroplasia in premature infants and pulmonary oxygen toxicity in adults are problems well known in sea-level administration of therapeutic oxygen. From the discussion of gas partial pressures in diving, it can be seen there are two ways in which high in-

spired P_{O_2} can be found in diving. Obviously, breathing 100% oxygen in the water or in compression chambers is the first. The second manner is not so obvious and could go unrecognized. Even though a normal 21% oxygen gas mixture is breathed, 300 FSW (10 ATA) will provide an inspired P_{O_2} of 2.1 ATA, equivalent to breathing 100% oxygen at 33 FSW (2 ATA).

Pulmonary Oxygen Toxicity

Pulmonary oxygen toxicity is thus induced by a relatively low P_{O_2} for prolonged exposures. It is generally considered that the limit for indefinite exposure without demonstrable lung damage is a P_{O_2} of about 0.5–0.6 ATA (380–450 mmHg), and that on a time-dose curve, it is safe to breathe 100% oxygen at 1 ATA for up to about 20 hours or at 2 ATA for up to 6 hours. This time can be lengthened significantly by intermittent exposures, such as a 5 minute air break between every 20 minutes of oxygen breathing, as demonstrated by Hendricks (15). At 2.8–3.0 ATA (60–66 FSW), where 100% oxygen is used to treat decompression sickness and gas gangrene, pulmonary oxygen toxicity is rarely a problem because central nervous system manifestations intervene before adequate time elapses to induce pulmonary damage. A complete review is that of Clark and Lambertsen (7).

Central Nervous System Oxygen Toxicity

During the 1880s, the French physiologist Paul Bert described convulsions in animals breathing 100% oxygen at elevated chamber pressures. This work was confirmed by Behnke and others in human studies during the 1930s. The classic human observations on divers by Donald (10) in 1947 provided much of our current knowledge on predisposing factors and clinical manifestations. He found that the diver in the water was more susceptible to a given time and pressure of oxygen than the same diver in a warm, dry hyperbaric chamber. This observation called for the limit of 25 FSW for special operations dives while breathing 100% oxygen from closed-circuit oxygen diving rigs. Most people can tolerate 100% oxygen breathing for 30 minutes at rest in a dry chamber. Common symptoms and signs of central nervous system oxygen poison-

ing are shown in Table 3. Unfortunately, there may be none of the early warning symptoms, so that the first manifestation may be a grand mal seizure.

Treatment for central nervous system oxygen toxicity in a hyperbaric chamber is as follows:

1. Remove the oxygen mask.
2. Do not change the chamber depth for fear of a pulmonary overpressure accident with breath-holding on ascent.
3. Protect the convulsing patient from head or other injuries in the steel chamber. Use a bite block.
4. Protect the airway.

After a postictal period the patient will recover, and standard decompression sickness treatment tables allow a return to oxygen breathing in a few minutes. We rarely see recurrent seizures. Although diphenylhydantoin and diazepam used in prophylaxis will suppress oxygen-induced seizures, anticonvulsant drug therapy is not used because raising the seizure threshold might allow high-dose oxygen brain damage to occur. Removing oxygen at the first sign of central nervous system manifestations has to date prevented any documentation of permanent central nervous system damage after an oxygen-induced seizure.

CONTAMINATED BREATHING GAS

As breathing gas cylinders are pressurized or filled, the sea-level partial pressure of each gaseous component is multiplied. Thus, any contaminant can become dangerous to the diver. Compressor motors must be free of oil which could be pumped into tanks; otherwise, they will induce an oil mist pneumonitis. The siting of compressed air inlets to avoid engine exhaust from the compressor, parking lots, or other sources is crucial in avoiding carbon monoxide inhalation. With tank pressurization and multiplication, even small amounts of carbon monoxide could produce significant poisoning. Since carbon monoxide is odorless and tasteless, the diver could detect it only if it was accompanied by other contaminants. The first warning might be headache, nausea, or dizziness during the dive. Examination at the surface might show mental dullness and specific neurologic deficits which could be con-

---

TABLE 3
Common Manifestations of Central Nervous System Oxygen Poisoning

Apprehension
Feeling of air hunger
Sweating
Nausea
Focal muscle twitching
Isolated jerking of a limb
Auditory changes (e.g., "bells ringing")
Tunnel vision
Diaphragmatic flutter
Convulsion

fused with decompression sickness or air embolism. The cherry red skin color is rarely observed in carbon monoxide poisoning. Fortunately, the treatment of choice for carbon monoxide poisoning, decompression sickness, and air embolism is compression in a hyperbaric chamber with an oxygen treatment.

UNDERWATER UNCONSCIOUSNESS

Causes of underwater unconsciousness include the factors shown in Table 4. *Shallow water blackout* is a term originally used by the British to describe the unexplained loss of consciousness in divers using a closed-circuit rebreathing apparatus at shallow depth. Edmonds et al. (12) point out the confusion which has been generated by the term because of its recent use to describe underwater unconsciousness due to hypoxia after hyperventilation prior to the dive. Miles and Mackay (17) describe this latter problem as "latent hypoxia." Without further confusing the issue (we hope), we present in Table 4 an expansion of Edmonds' "Commonest Causes of Unconsciousness in Divers" followed by a description of shallow water blackout as it is commonly taught.

SHALLOW WATER BLACKOUT

In what is commonly described as *shallow water blackout,* the diver hyperventilates prior

TABLE 4
Causes of Unconsciousness in Divers

Breath-hold diving
  Underwater hypoxemia following hyperventilation
    prior to the dive
  Near-drowning

Compressed-gas equipment
  Hypoxic breathing gas
  Contaminated breathing gas (e.g., carbon monoxide)
  Equipment failure or exhaustion of breathing gas
  Near-drowning
  Inert gas narcosis
  Oxygen poisoning
  Pulmonary overpressure accident with AGE

Rebreathing equipment
  Carbon dioxide toxicity
  Oxygen poisoning

to starting the dive, thus driving his alveolar P_{CO_2} down to 20–30 mmHg. However, because hemoglobin is almost saturated with oxygen during normal respiration, there is little gain in arterial P_{O_2}. In an underwater swim, even in a shallow swimming pool, exercise-induced hypoxia of a degree sufficient to cause unconsciousness may occur before the arterial P_{CO_2} reaccumulates to provide a stimulus indicating the need to breathe. In a deep breath-hold dive, the problem is compounded when hyperventilation precedes the dive. Besides the starting depression of arterial CO_2 secondary to hyperventilation, the elevated alveolar and arterial P_{O_2} seen initially at depth are noted. During the dive, these serve to suppress the respiratory response to hypercarbia. During the descent in the water, PaO_2 increases due to compression, but after oxygen consumption at depth, decompression toward the surface causes a dramatic drop in alveolar and arterial P_{O_2}. Even if P_{CO_2} rises to the stimulatory breakpoint during ascent, hypoxemia may cause unconsciousness and resultant drowning.

DECOMPRESSION SICKNESS

In the mid-nineteenth century, decompression sickness was first described as *caisson disease* or *compressed air illness.* Bridge and tunnel workers labored in caissons pressurized with compressed air and were afflicted with symptoms we recognize today in recreational divers. Because of its ubiquity, decompression sickness remains the subject of continued research in pathophysiology and treatment.

Symptoms and signs during or following decompression from water, caisson, or chamber pressures greater than those at sea level may be seen in commercial divers who breathe helium and oxygen mixtures for deep work. However, the following discussions will concentrate more on deep and shallow compressed air diving situations encountered by scuba divers.

Etiology

As previously discussed, the mechanical effects of pressure necessitate the interposition of the diving regulator, which maintains intrapulmonic pressure equal to the surrounding water pressure at any depth. Decompression sickness introduces the concepts of tissue uptake and the elimination of inert gases supplied in the gas mixture breathed by a diver. If it were possible for a diver to breathe 100% oxygen during the dive, there would be no problems on decompression. Oxygen is rapidly metabolized and, for practical purposes, does not contribute to bubble formation on ascent. Pure oxygen administration is unsafe, however, because of the central nervous system oxygen toxicity previously described.

The mandatory inert gas diluent represents the basic problem in decompression sickness. As the alveolar air pressure increases at depth, the partial pressures of inspired gases increase. At 99 FSW (4 ATA), the absolute pressure is 3040 mmHg (Table 1). Seventy-nine percent of this pressure is nitrogen (2400 mmHg, as compared to 600 mmHg PN_2 breathing air at sea level). Accounting for water vapor and carbon dioxide, this results in an alveolar partial pressure of nitrogen (PaN_2) of about 2360 mmHg. This PaN_2 is rapidly reflected across the alveolar-capillary membrane to the arterial blood, where, according to Henry's law, nitrogen is physically dissolved in the blood. Henry's law states that the amount of any given gas that will dissolve in a liquid at a given temperature is a function of the partial pressure of that gas in contact with the liquid and the solubility coefficient of the gas in the particular liquid. As this nitrogen-laden blood is presented to tissues at the capillary level, a complex set of variables, dictated by perfusion, diffusion, and nitrogen solubility, results in a family of uptake curves throughout the body. For practical purposes, tissue nitrogen saturations on a given dive are a function of depth and time.

The navies and diving companies of the world have developed decompression schedules based on calculations and testing to avoid exceeding safe rates of decompression after a given dive profile. Even at this date, however, conflicting theories and philosophies prevail, and studies continue to define the best methods.

Most current tables are based on the following concept: The tissues can tolerate some degree of inert gas supersaturation, but if barometric pressure is lowered too quickly beyond the critical level at which tissue supersaturation occurs, then inert gas separates from solution as bubbles in the blood, lymph, or other tissues. The physiologic sequelae are multitudinous, and include mechanical stretching of tendons or ligaments with resulting pain; intravascular occlusion in the venous circulation; and congestive infarction with platelet aggregation invoked at the bubble-blood interface with activation of coagulation mechanisms. Other manifestations are nervous tissue ischemia, hypoxia, and edema and pulmonary arterial bubble embolism as gas evolved in the venous blood is swept to the pulmonary artery. The resulting symptoms and signs constitute the disorder known as *decompression sickness*.

Clinical Manifestations of Decompression Sickness

The arbitrary division of clinical manifestations into type 1 or "minor" (limb bends, cutaneous changes, and fatigue) and type 2 or "serious" (chokes, neurologic forms, shock) is losing favor. There is growing awareness that all decompression sickness must be considered serious and treated vigorously. For example, when gas presumably separates in tendons and ligaments to produce joint pain (limb bends), Doppler-detected central venous gas emboli indicate gas separation throughout the body simultaneously.

LIMB-BENDS

Limb-bends is defined as mild to severe deep tendinitis or bursitislike pain in or about joints that occurs within minutes to hours of a compressed gas dive. The term *bends* originated with caisson workers on the Brooklyn Bridge, who were noted to suffer from this affliction. The descriptions of their posture, induced by multiple joint pains, portrayed the victims as fashionable bustled ladies of the day who were said to be doing the "bend."

Any joint may be involved, and the pain may radiate to surrounding areas. Lymphedema and paresthesias may be associated. Palpable tenderness may or may not be present. Frequently, the differential diagnosis between limb bends and trauma may be established by the application of a sphygmomanometer cuff, which can relieve the pain of the bends by reducing the gas volume in tendons and ligaments. This relief suggests that the mechanism of pain is gas-induced microseparation in tendons and ligaments with stretching of nerve endings. Limb-bends pain itself is not life- or function-threatening, but it indicates that bubbling may be occurring in venous blood. Often, patients who begin with limb-bends pain and are left untreated progress to more serious manifestations of decompression sickness.

FATIGUE

Fatigue, profound and out of proportion to the activity performed, may be a significantly early manifestation of decompression sickness. While its etiology is unknown, fatigue demands careful observation for the development of more severe manifestations.

SKIN MANIFESTATIONS

Skin manifestations, such as *mottling* and *itches,* are uncommon but significant indications of decompression sickness. Mottling or marbling of the skin is considered important and may herald the delayed onset of serious problems. The exact physiologic basis of the mottled skin lesion is unknown. Itches, the creeps, or skin bends, a pruritic skin reaction, is seen during decompression in compression chamber workers when the skin is exposed to the high partial pressure of nitrogen in compressed air. The concentrations of dissolved gases in ocean water are essentially constant at all depths, so that underwater the skin is not exposed to elevated partial pressures of inert gases. It is thought that in chambers, inert gas from the external environment is absorbed directly into skin; the itches represent bubble formation in the skin itself during decompression. It is rarely followed by serious manifestations and does not require compression treatment.

CHOKES OR PULMONARY DECOMPRESSION SICKNESS

The *chokes* is a serious form of decompression sickness characterized by burning substernal pain, cyanosis, dyspnea, and nonproductive cough. Animal studies have demonstrated gas bubbles or foam in the pulmonary arteries, right atrium, and right ventricle following unsafe decompression. Most likely, chokes represents massive pulmonary gas embolism with mechanical obstruction of the pulmonary bed by bubbles, accompanied by pulmonary vasoconstriction and bronchospasm induced by vasoactive substances released at the blood-bubble interface. Chokes patients can progress rapidly to profound shock or neurologic decompression sickness.

NEUROLOGIC DECOMPRESSION SICKNESS

Neurologic decompression sickness may occur as an isolated manifestation or as part of a progression from limb bends to chokes to neurologic patterns. Any level of the central nervous system may be involved, although in divers the most common involvement is the spinal cord, specifically the lower thoracic and upper lumbar segments. The mechanism is considered to be that of inert gas bubble formation in the epivertebral venous system, with resulting congestive infarction of the spinal cord (14). The most common presentation is the onset of low back pain with girdling abdominal pain within minutes to hours after the offending dive. This is followed by variable degrees of subjective "heaviness," weakness, and sensory loss in the lower extremities, with ominous bladder and anal sphincter paralysis. Absence of the bulbocavernosus reflex, elicited by gently squeezing and pulling the glans penis to seek reflex contraction of the anal sphincter, often foretells a poor prognosis. If left untreated or even with prompt treatment, permanent neurologic deficit may occur.

VASOMOTOR DECOMPRESSION SICKNESS

The extremely rare but life-threatening picture of shock with decompression sickness is still poorly understood. Bubble embolization, ischemia, hypoxia, and blood-bubble interface interactions can result in a rapid shift of fluid from intravascular to extravascular spaces. Hypotension may also occur as a result of massive sudden embolic pulmonary obstruction. Despite adequate intravenous fluid replacement, hypotension in decompression sickness may respond poorly until compression treatment is undertaken. The most common symptoms and signs are summarized in Table 5.

TABLE 5
Decompression Sickness (DCS): Common Symptoms and Signs

Limb-Bends

Symptoms	*Signs*
Awareness of severe tendinitis-quality joint pain	Absence or presence of tenderness
Single or multiple joints involved	May be temporarily relieved by local pressure
Paresthesias over joint	
Lymphedema (uncommon)	
Grating sensation on joint motion	

Neurologic DCS

Symptoms	*Signs*
Spinal cord	Spinal cord
Back pain	Hyper- or hypoesthesia
Girdling abdominal pain	Paresis
Extremity heaviness or weakness	Anal sphincter weakness
Paresthesias of extremities	Loss of bulbocavernosus reflex
Fecal incontinence	Urinary bladder distention
Urine retention	
Paralysis	
Brain	Brain
Scotomata	Visual field deficit
Headache	Spotty motor or sensory deficits
Dysphasia	Disorientation or mental dullness
Confusion	

Fatigue

Symptoms	*Signs*
Profound generalized heaviness or fatigue	May precede signs of other forms

Cutaneous Manifestations

Symptoms	*Signs*
Itches	Itches
Intense cutaneous pruritus	No visible signs
Mottling	Mottling
Pruritus possible	Local or generalized hyperemic ischemic marbled skin

Chokes

Symptoms	*Signs*
Dyspnea	Cyanosis
Substernal pain—worse on deep inhalation	Tachypnea
Nonproductive cough	Tachycardia

Vasomotor DCS

Symptoms	*Signs*
Weakness	Hypotension
Sweating	Tachycardia
Unconsciousness	Pallor and/or mottling
	Hemoconcentration
	Decreased urine output

Treatment of Decompression Sickness

One must have a high index of suspicion for and awareness of the often diverse and confusing clinical manifestations of decompression sickness. The history of the dive profile is helpful if the diver clearly violated decompression procedures, but for reasons not fully understood, decompression sickness may occur on dives that appear to be safe according to current decompression schedules. Of course, there could have been an error in the reported depth and time of the dive, or for inexplicable reasons the patient may be unduly susceptible to decompression sickness. The most common differential diagnosis to be made is between limb-bends and joint trauma. As mentioned previously, sometimes an inflated sphygmomanometer placed over the painful joint will relieve the pain of bends; sometimes only a trial of treatment in a compression chamber will make the definitive diagnosis.

IMMEDIATE CARE

In sport divers, who are usually far from a compression chamber, immediate and definitive en route management must be instituted. First, 100% oxygen should be administered by double-seal oronasal mask to provide a favorable gradient for nitrogen washout. Second, of equal importance is the maintenance of intravascular volume to ensure good capillary perfusion for elimination of microvascular inert gas bubbles and for the oxygenation of tissues. An intravenous infusion of lactated Ringer's solution sufficient to maintain urine output at 1–2 ml/kg per hour is recommended. With spinal cord involvement, an indwelling urinary catheter may be needed because of sacral nerve root dysfunction. For intractable vomiting or vertigo, parenteral diazepam is preferred by otolaryngologists experienced in treating divers. Doses of 5–15 mg given intramuscularly (smaller doses intravenously) have been effective in the relief of vertigo associated with labyrinthine decompression sickness when other agents have failed. Some physicians administer 0.5–1.0 g of oral salicylate for its antiplatelet activity.

While these measures are being undertaken, someone should be arranging for transportation to the nearest compression chamber. Because of the large number and frequently changing status of compression chambers, a listing is not provided. Instead, the 24-hour telephone number of the United States National Diving Accident Network (DAN), located at Duke University, should be readily available to all divers and medical facilities. Help with the treatment of dive-related incidents may be obtained by dialing 1–919–684–8111 and requesting DAN. Diving medicine experts will provide help with diagnosis, immediate care, and the location of the nearest chamber.

It is imperative to contact the chamber immediately to determine its availability. If evacuation by aircraft is required, it is critical to obtain an aircraft which can maintain sea-level cabin pressurization at flight altitude. Examples of such aircraft are the C-130 Hercules, Learjet, and Cessna Citation. If the patient is to be moved by helicopter, the crew must maintain the lowest possible flight altitude, but never greater than 1000 feet above the starting elevation. All resuscitative measures must be maintained in flight.

DEFINITIVE CARE

At the compression chamber, one of several standard treatment profiles will be followed. One is a double-lock, compressed air chamber in which the patient and an attendant can be pressurized with compressed air and the patient given therapeutic breathing gas, usually beginning with 100% oxygen at 60 FSW (2.8 ATA). Like the treatment tables for AGE, hyperbaric chamber treatment of decompression sickness has undergone significant evolution during the past 2 decades. At present, the diving medicine community is actively evaluating the results of previous treatment methods and seeking improvements. In one series of 92 sport scuba divers treated after a significant delay between the offending dive and the start of compression treatment, 85% had good results using standard U.S. Navy Treatment Tables (9). Such treatment is usually given according to U.S. Navy tables 5 and 6 (Figure 7). The U.S. Air Force modification of U.S. Navy tables 5 and 6 is identical to table 6A (Figure 5) without the excursion to 6 ATA used for air embolism. Some centers

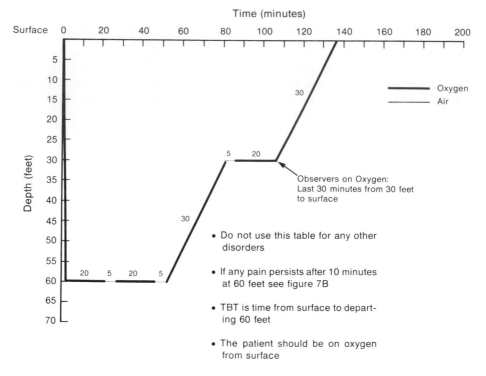

Time (minutes)

- Do not use this table for any other disorders

- If any pain persists after 10 minutes at 60 feet see figure 7B

- TBT is time from surface to departing 60 feet

- The patient should be on oxygen from surface

Observers on Oxygen: Last 30 minutes from 30 feet to surface

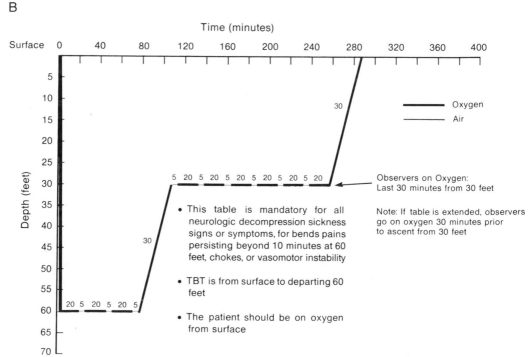

Time (minutes)

- This table is mandatory for all neurologic decompression sickness signs or symptoms, for bends pains persisting beyond 10 minutes at 60 feet, chokes, or vasomotor instability

- TBT is from surface to departing 60 feet

- The patient should be on oxygen from surface

Observers on Oxygen: Last 30 minutes from 30 feet

Note: If table is extended, observers go on oxygen 30 minutes prior to ascent from 30 feet

FIGURE 7 U.S. Air Force modification of U.S. Navy decompression tables for management of bends pain only (A) and decompression sickness (B).

advocate table 6A for serious decompression sickness also, but whether this affects the outcome remains unproved. When the patient with apparent limb-bends arrives at the hyperbaric chamber, a detailed neurologic examination is performed to document any subtle changes. If only limb-bends is confirmed, the chamber is pressurized to 2.8 ATA (60 FSW) and the patient is given 100% oxygen by mask. If pain is totally relieved by 10 minutes, it is possible to complete the treatment on table 5 (Figure 7A), which has only two 20 minute oxygen periods at 2.8 ATA, a 30 minute oxygen-breathing ascent to 1.9 ATA (30 FSW), and one 5 minute air/20 minute oxygen cycle at 1.9 ATA, followed by a 30-minute oxygen-breathing ascent to the surface. Recurrence of pain at any point calls for return to 2.8 ATA and use of table 6 (Figure 7B). Many experienced diving medicine physicians prefer liberal use of the longer table 6 (Figure 7B) in limb-bends, especially if there has been a significant delay between the onset of symptoms and arrival at the chamber.

Any limb-bends case which does not clear by 10 minutes at 2.8 ATA and any cases with neurologic decompression sickness or chokes require at least a table 6 (Figure 7B) protocol. Some diving medicine physicians proceed with table 6A (Figure 5) for spinal cord decompression sickness or chokes.

The current emphasis (9) is to turn to other options, such as deep saturation treatment for any decompression sickness case which does not respond to standard tables. A significant problem in spinal cord decompression sickness is the high incidence of residual neurologic deficits after apparently adequate treatment. While experimental proof of its efficacy is lacking, dexamethasone, 10–20 mg intravenously, is given initially, followed by 4–6 mg intravenously or intramuscularly every 6 hours to possibly reduce spinal cord edema. One or two daily repetitive hyperbaric oxygen treatments using table 5 (Figure 7A) can be given until no further improvement is seen during each treatment.

Prognosis

Because the outcome is influenced most significantly by the time lapse from the onset of symptoms to the start of the recompression treatment, every emergency department physician and diver should know the location of the nearest compression chamber. Persons treated early generally respond well. Spinal cord decompression sickness treated after hours of delay may result in residual deficits ranging from mild weakness or sensory changes to permanent paraplegia. On the other hand, dramatic results have been seen even in persons arriving at a chamber days after the insult. It is never too late to attempt a cure.

Training and Selection of Divers

A diver should be the graduate of a recognized scuba training agency course. These courses are taught by certified instructors who conduct intensive classroom, pool, and open-water training. Under direct supervision, students learn the physics and physiology of diving, aquatic skills, and the proper use of scuba equipment.

Physical Standards for Diving

Specific physical examination forms and standards have been established by the navies of the world and commercial diving concerns. Because the reader of this book will have greatest contact with sport divers, guidelines for decisions on fitness to dive will be limited to that group. The physician's natural desire to allow each candidate to pursue the activity of his choice must be balanced against the threat to the diver's life and the lives of buddy divers. Harsh and unpredictable environmental factors interact unfavorably with existing medical or psychological disabilities. Thus, recommendations are often based on reasoning rather than on a rigid set of standards.

The following considerations represent the opinion of the author with respect to some common disorders. The following conditions are considered to be absolute disqualifications:

1. History of seizure disorder or after head injury: Diving should not be allowed during the time when the patient is at risk of posttraumatic seizures.

2. Insulin-dependent diabetes mellitus: The risk of a hypoglycemic insulin reaction underwater is increased by the possibility of a need for sudden bursts of energy expenditure in

emergencies. Underwater incapacitation not only endangers the life of the individual but may cause multiple drownings during rescue attempts. With adult-onset diabetes that can be controlled by rigid diet and exercise programs, sport diving may be allowed.

3. Coronary artery disease: In addition to the need for cardiac reserve in an in-water emergency, the carrying of tanks, donning of equipment, and swimming against a current represent significant stresses. A history of myocardial infarction is considered a disqualification even for sport diving, except in the most unusual case of exceptional rehabilitation.

4. Sickle cell disease or trait: The possibility that the sport diver will breathe a hypoxic gas mixture is remote, but it certainly is present. Another concern is heavy exertion in cold water or local compromise of microvascular blood flow by bubble evolution during decompression, which could lead to sickling and a vicious cycle of hypoxia with further sickling.

5. A history of unexplained syncopal episodes, whether cardiovascular or neurogenic, precludes diving.

6. Inability to equalize pressure in the middle ear by autoinflation: This may be due to a correctable problem, such as polyps, allergic rhinitis, nasal septal deviation, or coryza, in which case the diver can be reevaluated after correction or desensitization.

7. Air-containing pulmonary blebs or cysts, which can trap air and lead to local pulmonary overpressure accidents during decompression: If a ball-valve or flutter-valve effect allows such a bleb or cyst to equalize with the elevated breathing pressure during compression or descent but blocks the escape of air during decompression, rupture could cause air embolism, mediastinal emphysema, or pneumothorax.

8. Significant obstructive pulmonary disease disqualifies a candidate for diving.

9. No individual who is a chronic alcoholic or who abuses any other substance should dive.

The following disorders require special consideration or represent subjects of controversy among diving physicians:

1. Bronchial asthma: Because of the risk of local air trapping and pulmonary overpressure accidents during decompression, one rec-

ommendation is disqualification for a patient with any history of asthma since childhood. It is generally true that scuba air is free of pollens, but other stresses in diving, i.e., cold water, heavy exertion, or psychic stress, could cause bronchospasm at depth, with resultant local air trapping during ascent. If there is any suggestion of bronchospastic tendencies, pulmonary function studies should be performed. Mild airway trapping at sea level takes on greater significance at depth. It is true that some asthmatic people are presently diving successfully, but the author believes that they do so at increased risk.

2. Pneumothorax: Even without the pressure variations of diving, a history of previous spontaneous pneumothorax carries a high incidence of recurrence, and the candidate must be advised against compressed-gas diving. A pneumothorax that occurs while still at pressure underwater or in a compression chamber can become a life-threatening tension pneumothorax as the pleural cavity air expands (Boyle's law) during progressive ascent. In the case of previous traumatic or surgical pneumothorax, especially in an already trained diver, combined clearance from a diving physician, chest surgeon, and pulmonary disease specialist may allow continued diving.

3. Migraine headaches: Diving does not seem to precipitate attacks of migraine. The concern is that scintillating scotomata and severe headache can be symptoms of decompression sickness, and a migraine episode following diving could be misinterpreted, initiating compression treatment to avoid the sequelae of decompression sickness. The author does not consider this problem severe enough to prohibit diving by migraine patients. However, commercial diving requires constant readiness to dive; hence, migraine is generally a disqualification.

4. Middle ear surgery with placement of a prosthesis in the conduction chain: This requires consultation between the diving physician and the otolaryngologist to determine the risk of displacement during pressure changes and ear clearing.

5. History of pulmonary overpressure accident in previous diving: The circumstances of the offending dive weigh heavily in the decision. For instance, in a "physiologically undeserved" episode (i.e., asthma), a diver can

breathe normally to the surface, yet suffer air embolism; furthermore, the risk of recurrence is great because of underlying small airway disease. On the other hand, a diver who suffers a pulmonary overpressure accident which is considered "physiologically deserved" (i.e., ignorance of the rules of ascent) could be considered for a return to diving after full neurologic recovery and with the determination of normal pulmonary function. Some argue that even this diver, who may have suffered the accident during straining, lifting an anchor during ascent, or struggling with another diver during a rescue attempt, is at greater risk because of potential pulmonary damage with scarring and an inability to detect small airway air trapping.

6. Hypertension: The decision is based upon the therapy required for control. Diving has little effect on blood pressure, but when a regimen in excess of weight control, diet, and mild diuretics is required for control, the unknown effects of antihypertensive agents during the stresses of diving represent a contraindication.

7. Visual acuity: In sport diving, corrective lenses can be mounted in scuba face masks or contact lenses can be worn. Soft contact lenses are preferable.

8. Perforation of the tympanic membrane: Until this has fully healed or has been successfully repaired, diving is contraindicated.

The following disorders are temporary disqualifications for diving:

1. Coryza or bronchitis: Either may cause an inability to equalize pressure in the ears, sinuses, or lungs due to mucous plugs or bronchospasm.

2. Pregnancy: While studies continue, the author advises a female who is or may be pregnant to suspend compressed-air diving until after delivery. Animal studies are conflicting in different species and different laboratories, but the possibility of bubble formation in fetal tissues, even on a dive safe for the mother, should suggest a conservative approach.

3. Inguinal hernia: This presents a risk of trapped gastrointestinal gas expansion in a herniated loop of bowel during ascent. All types of diving should be suspended until surgical repair is completed.

4. Physical fitness: Sport scuba diving is deceptively easy until an emergency occurs and long, heavy swimming against a current or the rescue of a buddy diver is required. The diver should be capable of performing representative strenuous activity before entering the water. Regular swimming or other exercise programs to ensure cardiovascular fitness are encouraged.

Conclusion

The rapid growth of recreational scuba diving is expected to continue in the years ahead. The underwater world is vast, beautiful, and hospitable. A well-trained, physically fit, properly equipped and disciplined diver incurs no greater risk during a scuba dive than in playing a round of golf. It is noted that the rare decompression accidents in diving are unique in their manifestations and treatment. To be effective, the clinician must be astute in his observations and be prepared to respond decisively to the situation.

References

1. Bachrach, A. J., A short history of man in the sea. In *The Physiology and Medicine of Diving and Compressed Air Work.* (2nd ed.), P. B. Bennett and D. H. Elliott (Eds.), Baltimore, Williams and Wilkins, 1975, pp. 1–10.
2. Bayne, C. G., Breath-hold diving. In *Weekly Update: Hyperbaric and Undersea Medicine.* J. C. Davis (Ed.), Princeton, N.J., Biomedia, Inc., vol. 4, 1978, pp. 1–7.
3. Behnke, A. R., The history of diving and work in compressed air. In *Weekly Update: Hyperbaric and Undersea Medicine.* J. C. Davis (Ed.), Princeton, N.J., Biomedia, Inc., 1978, pp. 1–7.
4. Behnke, A. R., Thomson, R. M. and Motley, E. P. Psychological effects from breathing air at four atmospheres pressure. *Am. J. Physiol.,* **112:**554, 1935.
5. Bennett, P. B., Inert gas narcosis. In *The Physiology and Medicine of Diving.* (2nd ed.), P. B. Bennett and D. H. Elliott (Eds.), London, Baillier Tindall, 1975, pp. 207–230.
6. Bennett, P. B., The physiology of nitrogen narcosis and the high pressure nervous syndrome. In *Diving Medicine.* R. H. Strauss (Ed.), New York, Grune and Stratton, 1976, pp. 157–181.
7. Clark, J. M. and Lambertsen, C. J., Pulmonary oxygen toxicity: A review. *Pharmacol. Rev.,* **23:**37–133, 1971.
8. Davis, R. H., *Deep Diving and Submarine Operations.* (6th ed.), London, Siebe Gorman, 1955, pp. 8–9.
9. Davis, J. C. (Ed.), *Treatment of Serious Decompression Sickness and Arterial Gas Embolism.* Undersea

Medical Society Publication No. 34, WS (SDS), Bethesda, Maryland, November 1979.

10. Donald, K. W., Oxygen poisoning in man. *Br. Med. J.,* **1:**667–72, 1947.

11. Edmonds, C., Freeman, P. and Tonkin, F., Fistula of the round window in diving. *Trans, Am. Acad. Ophthalmol. Otolaryngol.,* **78:**444–447, 1974.

12. Edmonds, C., Lowry, C. and Pennefather, J. In *Diving and Subaquatic Medicine.* Mosman, N.S.W., Australia, Diving Medical Centre, 1976, p. 318.

13. Farmer, J. C. and Thomas, W. G. Ear and sinus problems in diving. In *Diving Medicine.* R. H. Strauss (Ed.), New York, Grune and Stratton, 1976, pp. 109–133.

14. Hallenbeck, J. M. Cinephotomicrography of dog spinal vessels during cord-damaging decompression sickness. *Neurology,* **26:**190–199, 1976.

15. Hendricks, P. L., Hall, D. A., Hunter, W. L., Jr., and Haley, P. J., Extension of pulmonary oxygen tolerance in man at 2 ATA by intermittent oxygen exposure. *J. Appl. Physiol.,* **42:**593–599, 1977.

16. Kruse, C. A., Air embolism and other skin diving problems. *Northwest Med.,* **62:**525–529, 1963.

17. Miles, S. and Mackay, D. E., In *Underwater Medicine.* (4th ed.), Philadelphia, J. B. Lippincott, 1976, pp. 109–113.

18. Peterson, M. Underwater archeology. In *Exploring the Ocean World.* C. P. Idyll (Ed.), New York, Thomas Y. Crowell, 1977, pp. 196–231.

19. Schaefer, K. E., Allison, R. D., Doutherty, J. H., et al., Pulmonary and circulatory adjustments determining the limits of depths in breath-hold diving. *Science,* **162:**1020–1023, 1968.

7 | SUBMERSION INCIDENTS: DROWNING AND NEAR-DROWNING

Ronald D. Stewart, M.D.

> *Death may usurp on nature many hours,*
> *And yet the fire of life kindle again*
> *The o'erpress'd spirits.*
> Shakespeare, *Pericles,* III:ii, 82

The earliest records of humans' perception of life in and under the water indicate both their fascination and their fear. Quick to explore its mysteries and to use it for recreation and transportation, humans soon began to learn the dangers of the aquatic environment.

In eighteenth-century England, commercial water transportation was crucial to the nation's economic survival. Incidents of drowning were widely reported, and deaths were not uncommon. While the actual incidence of drowning is unknown, the interest shown by the society of the day indicates that the problem was a significant public issue (3). In response to this fashionable humanitarian cause,

the Society for the Recovery of Persons Apparently Drowned was formed in 1774. Their activities included research, public education, and treatment of unfortunate victims. The organization survives today as the Royal Humane Society (36).

Techniques for resuscitation of drowning victims developed rapidly during the early years that followed the establishment of special-interest groups; mouth-to-mouth ventilation was described, as well as what may have been the first defibrillation (37,67). Only recently, however, have practical methods of artificial ventilation, circulation, and defibrillation become widely accepted (70).

In the past decade, a greater understanding of the pathophysiology and natural history of submersion incidents has allowed revised approaches to therapy and the adoption of more optimistic attitudes toward outcomes (9, 51,69).

The Problem

It is difficult to estimate accurately the total number of submersion incidents which occur, since such accidents are not reportable and very little has been written about the incidence of morbidity in patients following submersion. Retrospective studies are beginning to allow quantification of the problem and to suggest directions for prevention and management. At present, it is estimated that there are more than 140,000 annual deaths worldwide from drowning (58). At least 8000 of these occur in the United States (59). The statistics underestimate the problem, since many drownings go unreported and others are classified in other categories, e.g., motor vehicle accidents.

Drowning kills mainly the young; 64% of all victims are younger than 30 years of age, and 26% are under the age of 5 (20,64). In areas where there are abundant recreational waterways, the problem is magnified, with almost as many fatalities in children caused by drowning as by motor vehicle accidents (37 versus 32%) (60).

Risk Factors

The problems of drowning and near-drowning can often be related to predictive risk factors which are valuable in the planning and institution of preventive practices.

AGE

Age appears to be an indicator of risk (4). Toddlers are especially vulnerable, as are teenage males (60,64). When incidents of submersion are considered, it has been estimated that 10% of children under the age of 5 experience a near-drowning episode in 1 year, as do 22% of those in the age group 15–24. Twelve percent of persons between the ages of 25 and

TABLE 1
Factors Common to Drowning Incidents

Age—toddlers, teenage boys
Location—home swimming pools
Gender—males predominate
Race—black children (64)
Drugs—particularly alcohol (41,58)
Trauma—secondary to diving, falls, horseplay

64 experience a near-drowning incident, whereas the lowest risk appears to be among those more than 65 years of age (64).

Toddlers are at risk due to their inquisitive nature and the fact that they are often unsupervised, especially at home. The high risk of a submersion incident among teenage boys represents their mobility, their adventuresome nature, and the absence of adult supervision. The lowest risk of a serious submersion incident in the elderly reflects their decreased exposure to water environments, increased experience, and mature judgment.

LOCATION

Drowning, or death by submersion, is not necessarily a recreational accident. Incidents and deaths occur in locations as far removed as the backyard swimming pool, the ocean, the unsupervised bath, and even the lowly cleaning bucket (55,63). The location of the submersion incident is often determined by the geography and social aspects of the community. In water-oriented areas such as Florida, California, and Australia, submersion incidents are common year round, and often occur in home swimming pools. It appears that the great majority of deaths which occur in children under the age of 4 take place at home (60).

Domestic swimming pools are especially dangerous, particularly for young children. More than one-half of all drownings in this age group occur in swimming pools. Black children tend to drown in lakes, canals, and quarry sites; white children have more incidents in swimming pools (60). Public or motel swimming pools are not often implicated. Despite ordinances defining the safe operation of a swimming pool, records demonstrate that safety features were either ignored or were faulty. Although all but 3% of home swimming pools in a Florida community were properly fenced and protected, 70% of the locks were found to be unfastened or nonfunctioning (60). In an Australian study of drowning incidents, only 1 of 66 swimming pool barriers was considered to be adequate, and in 76% of the incidents no fence existed at all (58).

The level of water in the pool may be of importance in the etiology of some deaths. The average distance from the water to the poolside lip is 12–14 inches. This distance provides a significant barrier to young children who have fallen into a pool. They may reach the side but be unable to pull themselves out of the water. It is recommended that the water level in swimming pools be raised (60).

While the incidence of drownings tends to be greater in coastal communities oriented to large bodies of water, most surveys indicate that drownings in salt water are relatively rare. This is particularly true in Australia and, in the author's experience, in California. This is due, in part at least, to effective surveillance of public beaches by lifeguards and Surf Lifesaving Societies.

Males predominate among the victims of drowning. In all age groups, males account for more than one-half of the cases (58,60).

The reasons for this predominance are presumed to include the traditional roles assumed by males in our culture: assertive, outgoing, and inquisitive behavior, which often is manifested by exploration, risk taking, and bravado.

RACIAL STATISTICS

Considerable evidence suggests that race may be a factor in the increased risk of exposure to submersion incidents, particularly in children. The incidence of both drowning and near-drowning episodes appears to be greater in black children. The drowning rate of black male children has been estimated to be as much as three times that of white males of the same age (64).

In incidents of drowning reported in the United States, unsupervised swimming or accidental falls into unattended canals or quarries accounted for a large percentage of deaths in black males (60).

ABILITY TO SWIM

The ability to swim does not appear to be consistently related to drowning rates unless gender differences are considered. White males have a higher incidence of drowning than do white females, yet have a reported better swimming ability. On the other hand, black females are reported to have the lowest swimming ability but a very low rate of drowning (64). In Florida, nonswimmers or beginners accounted for 73% of the drownings in home swimming pools and 82% of the incidents in canals, lakes, and ponds (60).

Parental example is an important determinant of whether children can swim. Children whose parents can swim are most likely to be strong swimmers; those with parents who cannot swim are likely to be nonswimmers. Parents of white children are much more likely to be swimmers than parents of black children.

DRUGS

Alcohol is the chief drug implicated in submersion incidents; the danger of its use in the aquatic environment cannot be overemphasized (41). An Australian study reported that 64% of males who drowned had measurable levels of alcohol in blood samples taken post mortem, and 53% of those over the age of 26 had blood alcohol levels greater than 100 mg% (58). While it cannot be stated definitively that alcohol was the *cause* of these tragedies, the common association of intoxication with drowning argues against the use of alcohol near the water (15).

The loss of judgment associated with the use of intoxicants is most likely the reason for their frequent association with drowning incidents. Drugs such as phencyclidine (PCP), lysergic acid diethylamide (LSD), and marijuana alter the sensorium; their use undoubtedly increases the risk of accidents in the water. Up to 30% of adult drownings occur because of boating accidents in which occupants demonstrated poor judgment: overcrowding, speeding, use of boats for purposes for which they were not intended, failure to wear life jackets, and reckless handling of the craft. The incidence of drug use in these episodes is not known, but it can be assumed that intoxicants play a role in many such accidents (41,58).

UNDERLYING INJURY OR DISEASE

Underlying injury or illness can account for loss of life in the water. Hypoglycemia, myocardial infarction, cardiac arrhythmias, and syncope predispose to the drowning incident. A search for an underlying cause of the tragedy should be made, particularly in persons who are evaluated in the hospital following rescue.

Cervical spine injuries and head trauma should be suspected in all unwitnessed incidents, particularly in surfers and in victims found near diving boards or rafts in shallow water. Possible damage to the cervical spine should be a consideration in both immediate on-scene care and emergency department management.

CHILD ABUSE

Attention has been drawn to the problem of submersion incidents as a manifestation of child abuse. All suspicious incidents must have thorough legal investigation (38,39).

Prevention

A broad approach to the problem of drowning must include not only effective therapy but prevention as well. Public education is the cornerstone of prevention and should include the hazards of unsupervised children or poorly conditioned adults in the water, boating and diving safety, and training in first aid and basic life support.

The active presence of adequate local emergency medical services, staffed by well-trained paramedical personnel, has been cited as being a determinant of the overall outcome of submersion incidents. The quality of on-scene resuscitation often determines the ultimate fate of the patient.

Since many of these tragedies occur in the home, attention must be paid to reducing the hazard of the swimming pool and the risk of leaving children unattended. Measures proposed include secure barriers with locked access doors, education of the family in safety and swimming techniques, higher pool water level, and "drownproofing" of young children. This last technique involves teaching methods of floating and swimming to very young children and attempting to instill confidence in their aquatic ability. Although it is controversial, drownproofing is popular in areas where water sports and recreation place toddlers at risk.

Learning to swim, although no guarantee of safety, can protect most older children. The high incidence of drowning in unsupervised swimming areas, such as quarries and ponds, indicates a need for supervised areas in which swimming and water recreation can more safely take place.

Terminology

Drowning has been defined as death following submersion, while *near-drowning* is a term introduced by Modell to indicate submersion with at least temporary survival (47). Recent resistance to these terms has developed because of growing knowledge of the pathophysiology of drowning and the success of many resuscitation efforts (22,35,69). The terms *drowning* and *near-drowning* depend upon the ultimate outcome and therefore are of little immediate clinical value. Obviously, it is often impossible to predict at the scene whether a patient will survive, particularly in light of advances in cerebral resuscitation and the management of hypothermia.

Use of these terms may create confusion both in the immediate-care period and ultimately in the medical record. A patient who dies within 24 hours, according to a modification of the terms recently introduced, is a victim of drowning, while a patient who dies after the first 24 hours is said to be near-drowned (64).

To clear up the confusion, a somewhat complicated classification has been proposed in which a scoring system based on the organs adversely affected and the pathophysiologic problems more accurately define the condition of the victim (32). However, this is unwieldy and cumbersome, and is unlikely to be accepted.

Most recently, it has been proposed that *drowned* be used for patients who suffocate by submersion and that *near-drowned* be reserved for those who survive, at least temporarily, a submersion episode.

The use of a more neutral term without the implication of time or retrospective analysis is necessary to avoid confusion and to simplify classification. Essentially, a person who is adversely affected by being submersed in water has, simply put, suffered a *submersion incident.* The term is descriptive, does not imply a prognosis, and can therefore be used in immediate care without the considerations of time or outcome.

Special Considerations

HYPOTHERMIA

Drowning may result directly from hypothermia (7,31). Experience with persons shipwrecked in relatively warm water has shown that the body temperature of victims can be lowered to the point where hypothermia endangers survival. Thermal conductivity of cold water is approximately 32 times that of air (31,39). Thus, in very cold water, hypothermia may ensue rapidly and proceed to drowning. This is particularly true in children who have less subcutaneous fat and a relatively greater body surface area compared to adults (39).

Survivors of a Canadian boating tragedy painted a vivid picture of the effects of hypothermia, which resulted in the deaths of an instructor and 12 of his students (72):

Gradually we could feel the sensation going out of our limbs, and we heard some of the boys starting to get paranoid about being in the water. Some started to talk nonsense and then, one by one, their voices faded away as they lost consciousness.

Death in submersion-associated hypothermia can be attributed to three basic mechanisms:

1. *The immersion syndrome.* This is defined as cardiac arrest secondary to massive vagal stimulation (39).
2. *Excessive fatigue and confusion.* The combination of hypothermia, exertion, panic, and confusion leads to poor judgment, which causes the victim to endanger himself further by swimming

away from help, leaving an overturned canoe, or misjudging the distance to shore.
3. *Direct Hypothermia.* At or below a core temperature of 28°C (82.4°F), ventricular fibrillation is a real risk (68). It has been estimated that at a water temperature of 0°C (32°F), the victim of submersion cannot survive for more than 1 hour; at a water temperature of 15°C (59°F), survival is not common after 6 hours (6).

In those victims who are kept afloat by life preservers or other means, death may be due directly to hypothermia. Although some people may appear to be dead after rescue, efforts to resuscitate and rewarm them may be rewarded with recovery.

In certain cases, hypothermia may be protective, particularly in children (31,68). One fascinating report recorded a normal recovery in a child submerged in cold water for 40 minutes before resuscitation efforts were applied.

Further documentation that hypothermia may be protective is provided by the work of Modell, Conn, and others (7,38,51,76). Data which document outcomes in submersion cases associated with hypothermia are confusing. Some reports suggest that hypothermia is associated with poorer outcomes, but this is attributed to the fact that most of these patients had longer submersion times (7,51,57). Little information concerns the initial resuscitation measures and the time to reversal of the hypoxic state.

Laboratory studies suggest that hypothermia decreases cerebral blood flow and oxygen consumption, which may lead to a protective effect (65). Reduction of oxygen consumption is significant only below a temperature of 32°C (89.6°F). The mammalian *diving reflex* may be activated in children. This slows the heart rate, shunts blood to the brain, and closes the airway (23). There is accumulating evidence that hypothermia below 32°C (89.6°F) is protective, providing that hypoxia is rapidly reversed and any increase in intracranial pressure is properly managed (7,8). Many clinicians use hypothermia as a therapeutic measure in children who present in coma (8, 31,73).

In contradistinction to the cerebral protective effect, hypothermia can create grave problems for the exposed victim. Specific patterns of heat loss from the body can be demon-

until an appropriate body temperature is reached (13). No decision on survival should be made until the patient is normothermic, unless it is decided to maintain an appropriate level of hypothermia for therapeutic reasons. The management of hypothermia is well delineated by Bangs and Hamlet in Chapter 2.

Type of Water

Much discussion has been generated concerning the importance of the type of water in which the patient is submersed (44,62,71). Most victims of submersion injury aspirate impurities or foreign materials, including algae, bacteria, sewage, chemicals, and sand (31). The osmolality of the water has been shown, in animal experiments, to cause biochemical changes in nonsurvivors (46,47). While the difference between saltwater and freshwater submersion is not of immediate clinical importance, a knowledge of the effect of aspiration of both fluids will help in the interpretation of findings seen in some patients (14).

Theoretically, the changes which occur following aspiration of salt water and fresh water should be different, and the biochemical abnormalities secondary to such aspiration should play a role in management. This has not been the case, however. Work done by Modell *et al.* demonstrates convincingly that it is the *amount* of water aspirated, rather than the type, that is of prime importance (49).

FRESHWATER ASPIRATION

Fresh water is hypotonic to plasma and passes readily out of the alveolus into the circulation. If a sufficient volume is aspirated (more than 22 ml/kg), blood volume can increase and hemolysis can result (45). The hemolysis, along with the hypoxia, can lead to hyperkalemia, higher levels of circulating free hemoglobin, and a lowered hematocrit. Expansion of blood volume due to the fluid shift from the alveoli to the intravascular compartment lowers the concentrations of serum sodium, chloride, calcium, and magnesium (46,47).

Despite these expected changes, few near-

drowning victims (survivors) present with electrolyte abnormalities serious enough to warrant therapy. In survivors of a submersion injury, biochemical and blood volume changes are autogenously corrected quickly and should be considered transient (49). Management efforts in both freshwater and saltwater submersion should be directed primarily toward the effects of aspiration on the lungs.

The aspiration of fresh water induces pulmonary changes, the most important of which is the "washout" of surfactant (48). This leads to atelectasis, with consequent ventilation-perfusion imbalance and hypoxia (31,49). In addition, direct destruction of alveolar cells may lead to accumulation of fluid within the lung and a decrease in compliance. Thus, the overwhelming insult which the clinician faces in the initial management of submersion injury is hypoxia.

SALTWATER ASPIRATION

Seawater has an osmolality three to four times greater than that of blood. The effect of aspiration of this hypertonic fluid is the rapid outpouring of fluid from the plasma into the alveoli and interstitial spaces of the lung parenchyma (39). Theoretically, the loss of such fluid from the circulation should produce a decrease in blood volume and a rise in serum electrolytes because of the high concentrations of sodium, potassium, chloride, calcium, and magnesium in seawater. However, as with freshwater aspiration, electrolyte changes do not appear to be important in the early management of submersion victims (16,17,50).

Once again, the main problem is hypoxia. Pulmonary edema results quickly, with an outpouring of protein-rich fluid into the alveoli and interstitium, reduction of compliance, and direct parenchymal damage (48). The resulting hypoxia and metabolic acidosis are of immediate concern to the emergency physician.

CONTAMINANTS

Most water in which submersion incidents occur contains chemicals, contaminants, or particulates which may produce further injury to the lung (31). Pool water containing chlorine or water contaminated with chemical wastes, cleaning solvents, detergents, or disinfectants irritates the tracheobronchial tree and the alveoli, leading to further fluid accumulation in the already wet lung (44,63). Inhalation of mud, sand, and other particulates may require bronchoscopy to cleanse the airway of such debris. Although uncommon in survivors, *sand bronchograms* have been described on chest films of surfers and others who aspirated radiopaque calcium carbonate sand (5).

Trauma

Part of the initial resuscitation and evaluation of any patient must include a complete examination for obvious trauma, with appropriate stabilization. Repeated examination, combined with an understanding of the mechanisms of injury in cases of submersion, must be fundamental to the approach of every clinician. A thorough evaluation of each patient should minimize death from unrecognized trauma, such as a ruptured spleen or fractured cervical spine. Neither a fall nor the subsequent submersion injury need be fatal if both are properly dealt with. Catastrophic injury must be assumed until ruled out in all patients. Appropriate intensive care monitoring should be a part of the management routine.

Classification and Types

Death by submersion, or drowning, has historically been classified according to the pathophysiology of the process. Such classifications are usually made after the fact and are of little use in the immediate period of management. However, the terms can be related to the underlying physiology of submersion and, as such, are in common medical use.

Wet versus Dry Drowning

The term *wet* drowning refers to the great majority of patients who aspirate water; hence, the lungs are wet, with pulmonary derangements resulting from the effect of the fluid. It is estimated that 85–90% of patients fall into this category (31). The remaining 10–15% do not aspirate to a significant degree and their lungs, consequently, are dry. Such *dry* drowning cases represent those patients who develop laryngospasm in response to the cold water stimulus, mechanical irritation of swallowing water, or initial inhalation of fluid (20,62). Although it might be reasonable to assume that patients who do not aspirate will respond better to resuscitation measures, there is no real evidence to support this. The response to resuscitation depends more on the rapid reversal of hypoxia than on the type of submersion injury that has occurred. The acute and chronic responses of the lungs to various amounts and types of fluids may range from mild to very severe, as will be discussed. Patients with preexisting pulmonary disease are at greater risk for decompensation if they suffer a submersion incident.

Shallow Water Blackout

The phenomenon known as *shallow water blackout* predisposes to drowning in those swimmers who hyperventilate prior to entering the water for an endurance underwater swim. Hyperventilation substantially reduces the CO_2 pressure (P_{CO_2}). Vigorous underwater muscular activity engenders hypoxia before enough CO_2 reaccumulates to provide a stimulus to return to the surface to breathe. Without sufficient hypercapnia to stimulate breathing, consciousness can be lost due to the hypoxia and the victim may drown. A recent case of apparent shallow water blackout is recorded in which the author of the report was the victim of the submersion incident and spent several days in his own intensive care unit. His observations are well worth noting (74).

Immersion Syndrome and the Diving Reflex

Immersion syndrome is sudden death following contact with very cold water, presumably due to vagal stimulation and resultant cardiac arrest (33).

Investigation into the nature of the mammalian diving reflex was reported in the early 1960s. Cold water stimulation of cutaneous receptors appears to trigger shunting of blood to the brain and heart from the skin, gastrointestinal tract, and extremities. Bradycardia results from the reflex vagal response to increased central volume. This *diving reflex* may account for survival after relatively long periods of submersion in cold water. If it is overwhelming, it may play a role in the immersion syndrome.

POSTIMMERSION SYNDROME

This unsatisfactory term refers to the delayed development of the adult respiratory distress syndrome (ARDS), which is preceded by a relatively asymptomatic interval of several hours to several days (19,22). This *secondary drowning syndrome* necessitates close observation and evaluation of all patients who present with a history of even a minor submersion incident.

Pathophysiology

MECHANICS OF DROWNING

The effects of submersion on mammals were first reported in the scientific literature in the late 1800s. Findings in animals were consistent with drowning episodes later observed in humans (31). The initial response in humans to submersion, particularly in cold water, includes a period of panic, followed by violent struggling accompanied by hyperventilation due to stimulation of thermal receptors in the skin. Breath-holding may be attempted, but the hyperventilation is usually uncontrollable by the victim and can result in aspiration of significant quantities of water. Water may also be swallowed in large quantities, resulting in vomiting and subsequent aspiration (39). It is this occurrence that may present difficulties to initial rescuers; gastric distention may make ventilation more difficult, and regurgitation is an ever-present danger (18).

In most victims of submersion, violent struggling occurs prior to the loss of consciousness and the exercise-induced acidosis leads to even more hyperventilation and greater risk of aspiration of water. Laryngospasm may ensue in some victims.

The common denominator of submersion is hypoxia due to either laryngospasm or the aspiration of water. Once the victim is unconscious, all airway reflexes are abolished and fluid can be passively introduced into the airway. Cardiac arrest follows this sequence of

events. Hypoxia and acidosis lead to derangements in many organ systems in those who have suffered a serious incident (39).

PULMONARY SYSTEM

The target organ in episodes of submersion is the lung. In cases of freshwater aspiration, fluid moves quickly across the alveolar-capillary membrane into the microcirculation, surfactant washout occurs, and high surface tensions in the lung lead to reduced compliance and atelectasis with resultant ventilation-perfusion mismatching (31,46,48). Seawater aspiration produces rapid outpouring of protein-rich fluid into the alveoli and pulmonary interstitium, a reduction in compliance, and direct damage to pulmonary capillaries (49).

The inhalation of particulate matter, contaminants, bacteria, or chemicals found in some water can produce chemical or mechanical irritation, which results in more deposition of fluid in the tracheobronchial tree and may lead to the destruction of alveoli (5). Despite the absence of direct evidence in humans, it is suspected that direct damage to the alveolar-capillary membrane may be produced by coagulation defects, the breakdown of platelets, microembolization, and other adverse effects initiated by fluid aspiration or hypoxia.

Hypoxia in humans following submersion incidents is the result of fluid in the alveolar and interstitial spaces, loss of surfactant, proteinaceous material in the alveoli and tracheobronchial tree, damage to the alveolar-capillary membrane and small pulmonary vessels, and hypoxia-initiated central nervous system (CNS) reflex mechanisms (31,39,49).

Acute respiratory failure follows, with a reduction in compliance and an increase in ventilation-perfusion mismatching, resulting in an enhanced shunt (31,46,75). The difference in oxygen tension between the alveoli and the arterial blood is increased in pulmonary failure following submersion. In normal subjects breathing 100% oxygen, the difference is about 35 torr; in human victims of submersion, differences as high as 600 torr with 100% oxygen have been reported (31).

In cases of prolonged submersion or significant aspiration, pulmonary derangements occur rapidly. In lesser insults, the onset of symptoms may be delayed for as long as 24 hours. This *secondary drowning* most likely represents a delayed onset of the manifestations of the initial insult (53).

The effect of the inhalation of fluid or asphyxia on the function of the lungs will often be the first consideration of initial management. In addition, efforts to correct hypoxia must be vigorous and sustained, directed toward reversing the underlying defects and sustaining pulmonary function until healing takes place.

CARDIOVASCULAR SYSTEM

Cardiovascular derangements in cases of serious submersion injury are usually secondary to hypoxia, acidosis, or other indirect causes, rather than due to the actual fluid aspiration. In the past, death was thought to be due to the induction of ventricular fibrillation by electrolyte changes, but this is now known not to be the case. Cardiac dysrhythmias and depression of myocardial function are due to acidosis and hypoxia resulting from pulmonary changes (31).

Management requires close observation of the cardiovascular system. A delicate balance is often struck between pulmonary function and oxygenation versus cardiac output and right heart return. This has particular relevance to those cases in which positive end-expiratory pressure (PEEP) is used to improve oxygenation.

CENTRAL NERVOUS SYSTEM

The endpoint of successful resuscitation of victims of submersion incidents has heretofore been the restoration of adequate perfusion and pulmonary function. With the development of more sophisticated monitoring capabilities, attention is now being directed toward preserving central nervous system function and preventing further damage once vascular perfusion has been restored.

Insults to the central nervous system can include not only hypoxia but also trauma to the spine and spinal cord. The search for other causes of CNS dysfunction is mandatory in those who remain comatose following submersion incidents.

The initial insult to delicate brain tissue is hypoxia and ischemia, but there is ample evidence to suggest that tissue damage can continue after the restoration of cerebral blood flow (9,61). Dysfunction of the central nervous system occurs rapidly following the onset of hypoxia; flattening of the electroencephalogram (EEG) takes place within 20 seconds of total cerebral ischemia. Continuing insult to the brain following resuscitation results from elevated intracranial pressure (ICP) and edema, and increased cerebral vascular resistance, which compromise oxygenation of the cells (31,61). Hyperpyrexia can accompany drowning and increases cerebral oxygen consumption. This, in turn, can lead to increased tissue insult (8,9).

Methods to monitor ICP are being promoted as guides to the success of measures directed toward cerebral resuscitation. Experimental and clinical evidence demonstrate that attempts to prevent postresuscitation cerebral injury will play a prominent role in the management of patients who remain in coma following serious submersion accidents (9,51,52).

All patients should be investigated for expanding intracranial lesions secondary to trauma or damage to the spinal cord which may occur in platform diving accidents or during horseplay.

RENAL SYSTEM

Acute renal failure is not common in victims of submersion incidents. When it occurs, it may be due to several factors. The most frequent cause is the destruction of tubules secondary to hypoxia. Reduced blood flow secondary to shock and acidosis increases the incidence of renal failure (31,39).

METABOLIC CHANGES

Electrolyte changes in a survivor of a submersion incident do not appear to be either consistent or important in management. Elevations of potassium levels in freshwater aspiration have been theoretically ascribed to hemolysis. Few patients who survive aspirate sufficient water to pose any problem; aspiration of quantities which would cause serious electrolyte imbalance usually results in death (19). This applies equally to electrolyte changes in the aspiration of fresh and salt water (49). Postmortem measurements of electrolytes in experimental animals have uncovered increases in serum sodium, chloride, calcium, and potassium, presumably due to the high concentrations in the seawater within the alveoli. Again, these problems are not seen consistently in survivors of submersion incidents.

Respiratory acidosis is the main *immediate* problem in patients (30). In most patients, a severe metabolic acidosis develops, due in part to pulmonary failure with resultant cellular anaerobic metabolism. Persistence of acidosis depresses myocardial function and leads to the development of lethal dysrhythmias.

Hematologic Changes

Hemolysis has been described in both freshwater and saltwater aspiration, more commonly in the former, with levels of circulating free hemoglobin ranging from 8 to 500 mg% (44). There appears to be no consistent change in the level of hemoglobin or hematocrit following submersion in humans. Low values should initiate a search for underlying trauma with hemorrhage or a bleeding disorder.

Disseminated intravascular coagulation has been described with submersion and aspiration (10,31). Contributing to the genesis of this disorder are hypoxia, acidosis, sepsis, hemolysis, and low perfusion states.

MANAGEMENT

Introduction to Immediate Care

The scene of a submersion incident is usually chaotic. Early considerations must include the safety of rescuers and retrieval of the patient. Well-intentioned but ill-advised heroic efforts can create additional victims.

Initial observations are quite important. Circumstances which suggest trauma, as well as the temperature of the water and the environment, should be noted. There is always an underlying *cause* of the patient's predicament; hypothermia, trauma, seizures, and hypoglycemia should all be considered.

The appropriateness of instituting life-support measures in victims of submersion must be considered (57). Until there is evidence that aggressive on-scene resuscitation does not help

in the prevention of loss of life, no efforts should be withheld. The decision to withhold or cease resuscitation attempts is *not* a field decision.

Estimation of submersion times may be misleading. Observations of time underwater are notoriously inaccurate when made by bystanders, parents, or even trained rescuers (52). Thus, rescuers should begin resuscitative measures and present the patient to the in-hospital team, who can decide on continuing therapy. In the event of prolonged transport, cardiopulmonary resuscitation should be performed for no less than 30 minutes.

Specific Therapy

Patients generally may be classified into one of four groups:

1. The asymptomatic patient
2. The symptomatic patient
3. The patient in cardiopulmonary arrest
4. The obviously dead or still submerged patient

The Asymptomatic Patient

The history is of prime importance. A description of the incident, the estimation of submersion time, and the past health of the patient should be obtained. All patients with any conceivable history of submersion who manifest shortness of breath (however slight) should be considered hypoxic; oxygen by simple face mask at 8–10 liters/minute should be administered. This author goes a step further and believes that any patient seen in the field with a history of submersion, regardless of the time or the absence of presenting symptoms, should be given oxygen. Significant hypoxia can exist in these patients without symptoms, and oxygen administration carries little risk (31). A cardiac monitor should be placed and an intravenous (IV) line started with 5% dextrose in water (D_5W) at a keep-open rate for the administration of medications. The patient must then be transported to an emergency facility.

In the hospital, the patient will be reexamined, have baseline arterial blood gases drawn, and a chest x-ray taken. Patients with a confirmed history of submersion will be ad-

TABLE 2
Field Approach to the Asymptomatic Patient

History	Baseline Examination	Intervention
Time submerged	Appearance	Oxygen by simple mask, 8–10 liters/minute
Description of incident	Vital signs	IV D_5W at keep-open rate
Complaints	Chest examination	Reexamine patient
Past health	Electrocardiogram	Transport patient

mitted for 12–24 hours of observation (Table 2).

The Symptomatic Patient

Discounting hysteria, any patient who shows signs of distress (persistent anxiety, tachypnea, dyspnea, syncope, persistent cough, or vital sign changes) at the scene has potentially suffered a significant submersion injury. The two immediate problems are hypoxia and acidosis (31,39). Correction involves respiratory manipulation. The airway must be kept patent, which can be a problem in patients who are vigorously vomiting. Emesis is frequent in submersion victims, especially in those who have swallowed large amounts of sea water. If the transport time is long, diarrhea due to the laxative effect of swallowed sea water may add insult to injury.

NECESSITY OF SUPPLEMENTAL OXYGEN

If the victim is breathing spontaneously, high flow rates (10 liters/minute) should be provided by simple face mask (12–15 liters/minute with a nonrebreathing face mask) or by demand valve, which gives 100% oxygen at the valve opening. Maintaining a positive pressure in the airway during expiration can be of value in the management of submersion injury of the lung (17,31). In patients who are spontaneously breathing and are able to hold a mask, continuous positive airway pressure (CPAP) can be used with beneficial effect (21,25,31). Experience is growing with this method, which represents an attempt to raise oxygen tensions (PaO_2) in patients with compromised pulmonary function.

In selected patients in the intensive care unit, the use of CPAP by mask has delayed or eliminated the necessity of intubation (25).

In experienced hands, it is an acceptable adjunct to emergency department therapy. Most would agree that an inability to maintain a PaO_2 of greater than 55 torr with an inspired oxygen concentration of 50% is one of the criteria for the use of this method (31). In addition, the patient must be able to respond normally to a command, control his own airway, and be nonhypercarbic ($PaCO_2$ less than 45 torr). Pressures used within the system, as well as forced inspiratory oxygen (FiO_2), will vary according to the clinical and arterial blood gas response of the patient. Pressures may range from 0 to 4 cm H_2O on inspiration to 4 to 14 cm H_2O on expiration (25). At present, a definitive recommendation concerning the use of CPAP by mask at the scene of a submersion incident must await further experience in the prehospital setting.

Any decrease in body temperature in these patients, particularly if accompanied by shivering, is important. All wet clothing must be removed and the patient wiped dry. If the patient continues to shiver, carefully wrapped hot packs should be placed in the axillae and inguinal areas and near the scalp and neck.

In advanced life support systems, a cardiac monitor is placed on the patient and an intravenous line is established with D_5W at a keep-open rate.

Attention to potential metabolic acidosis can be given following establishment of a patent airway, oxygenation, and access to the intravascular space. Metabolic acidosis exists in even relatively asymptomatic victims of submersion (31). The administration of sodium bicarbonate has been advocated in those patients with adequate circulation who are tachypneic or dyspneic with cyanosis (43). Although controversial, the administration of bicarbonate on a empiric basis at the scene of the incident in a dose of 1 mEq/kg may be

TABLE 3
Field Approach to The Symptomatic Patient

History	Examination	Intervention
Description of incident	General appearance	Oxygen mask (10 liters/minute) or demand valve
Time submerged	Level of consciousness	IV D_5W at keep-open rate
Past health	Chest examination	Consider sodium bicarbonate, 1 amp (or 1 mEq/kg) if patient is tachypneic/dyspneic with cyanosis
Symptoms	Vital signs	Transport patient
	Electrocardiogram rhythm	

Note: Be prepared for vomiting.
Take precautionary measures to prevent hypothermia/shivering.
Use lidocaine if ventricular irritability persists after initial oxygen therapy.

warranted. It must be noted that the primary problem is with ventilation; appropriate respiratory management takes priority over the administration of exogenous bicarbonate.

For the most part, the use of other drugs should await evaluation in the hospital. Cardiac irritability usually responds to the reduction of hypoxia and acidosis. If evidence of significant ventricular irritability persists, the judicious field use of lidocaine by multiple-bolus technique, using an initial dose of 1 mg/kg over 2 minutes and 0.5 mg/kg every 5–10 minutes as necessary, not to exceed a total dose of 225 mg, is justified (Table 3).

The Patient in Cardiopulmonary Arrest

Vigorous cardiopulmonary resuscitation measures must be initiated immediately, even with the patient in the water. Mouth-to-mouth ventilation may be attempted during extrication procedures, but this is difficult. As soon as shore, jetty, shallow water, or a boat is reached, mouth-to-mouth ventilation should begin in earnest.

A recent suggestion has been to perform closed-chest compressions while the patient is still in the water (42). Trials in which a recording manikin was ventilated and compressed, using a modified ventilator and posterior-grasp position, demonstrated adequate chest compression and ventilation. However, these trials could not take into account the problems of blood flow achieved when the "patient" was held in an almost upright position. The likelihood of keeping a victim afloat in the circumstances described should be analyzed. Other factors which would obstruct or preclude in-water cardiopulmonary resuscitation include an inability to ascertain pulselessness, frigid water and rescuer fatigue, waves-surge-current, wet suits/scuba apparatus obstruction, and the delay to definitive out-of-water cardiopulmonary resuscitation (37). Until more experience with this technique is gained, it must be considered experimental.

As soon as the patient has been extracted from the water, he should be placed on a firm surface (float board, backboard, jetty, or boat deck) and appropriate resuscitation measures continued. Basic care given at the scene is the most important factor in the survival of the patient (38,57). If rescue is performed on a sloping beach, the patient should be placed parallel with the water's edge (neither head up nor head down) in order to prevent gravity from reducing carotid blood flow during compressions and to prevent an undue increase in intracranial pressure in a head-down position.

If advanced airway control devices for ventilation (endotracheal tube, esophageal airway) are available, these should be inserted after good initial ventilation. When only tank oxygen with a delivery hose, nasal cannula, or face mask is available, mouth-to-mouth ventilation may be supplemented with oxygen by applying the nasal prongs to the rescuer (at 6–8 liters/minute) or by placing the oxygen tube into the patient's mouth and setting the flow rate at 2–3 liters/minute. The latter method is occasionally complicated by stomach insufflation. Hand-triggered devices or proper mouth-to-mask ventilation are preferable to other methods (1). Bag-valve-mask ventilators should have an oxygen reservoir in order to increase the percentage of oxygen delivered to the patient. Bag-valve-mask devices are not the preferred method of applying positive pressure in a field setting without endotracheal tubes in place because of the difficulty in achieving a mask seal and operator fatigue, which inevitably reduce tidal volume (1).

LUNG DRAINAGE

Frequent clearing of the airway is necessary, since vomiting and copious drainage from the lungs and stomach are common. The issue of lung drainage is both of past and present interest. Draining the lungs of water may improve the chances of survival, although this recommendation may be limited to seawater incidents, in which pulmonary water is increased and is sometimes seen to froth from the trachea.

The concept of draining water from the lungs dates back to the seventeenth and eighteenth centuries. The Dutch method consisted of rolling the victim over a barrel; another method advised flinging the victim over the back of a horse, which was then made to trot about (1). In 1975, Dr. H. Heimlich introduced an abdominal compression maneuver (Heimlich maneuver), advocated for victims of food choking (26). In the initial and later reports, he suggested its use in the victims of drowning (27,28,29). Evidence for the effectiveness of the maneuver in drowning is anecdotal. It remains unclear whether the maneuver was clearly responsible for the outcome. The use of abdominal compression in victims of fresh or seawater submersion may predispose to pulmonary aspiration due to induced emesis of large amounts of swallowed water.

Evidence that greater survival rates occur in animals subjected to drainage techniques is based on experiments with dogs (48). In these studies, drainage was performed on the animals by placing them in a head-down (Trendelenburg) position. It is to be noted, however, that these dogs did not apparently require cardiopulmonary resuscitation with

closed-chest compression. It was concluded that drainage techniques were of use in those subjected to seawater aspiration.

No human studies are reported in the literature, and the descriptions of drainage procedures in the most recent works are in reference to *gastric* drainage (61). The technique in these cases was to place the patient on the side and compress the abdomen, or to place the patient in a prone position, grasp him about the abdomen, and lift (*breaking* the victim, in older lay language). Whether these maneuvers may lead to drainage of water from both the stomach and lungs is not clear. A study underway at the University of Pittsburgh will seek to compare survival rates in animals subjected to various methods of lung drainage.

Gastric drainage may be required in patients who have swallowed large amounts of water, since gastric distention may interfere with ventilation. If gastric distention is a problem, abdominal compression with adequate suction (or gravity drainage in breaking the victim) may suffice. Abdominal compression accomplishes drainage without the need to interrupt cardiac compressions or ventilation for as long a time as other methods. Whatever the method, it must be performed quickly so that basic life support can continue. Suction apparatus, if available, must be used as needed. A nasogastric tube is preferable to all other methods.

None of the methods suggested for lung or gastric drainage should take precedence over initial ventilation. When, as in the case of seawater aspiration, the need for lung drainage is evident, it is recommended by the author that the abdominal thrust maneuver be performed several times in quick succession, with attention being paid to suction and positioning in order to remove both lung water and gastric contents from the oropharynx. Any delay in initial ventilation to apply the maneuver as an immediate first step in airway control is inappropriate.

ENDOTRACHEAL INTUBATION AND PEEP

Endotracheal intubation facilitates control of the airway by reducing dead space, providing protection against aspiration, and facilitating pulmonary toilet. PEEP has been demonstrated to be of use in victims of submersion (17,31). Although there is no decrease or even an increase in total lung water, PEEP acts in several ways to improve ventilation patterns in the noncompliant lung:

1. By shifting interstitial pulmonary water into capillaries
2. By increasing lung volume via prevention of expiratory air space collapse
3. By increasing the diameter of large and small airways to improve ventilation distribution
4. By decreasing alveolar capillary blood flow and providing better alveolar ventilation, and hence an improved ventilation-perfusion ratio and PaO_2

The use of PEEP in the field situation has been made possible with the development of a small apparatus adaptable to manual self-inflating bag ventilation devices (40). Experience with field PEEP is limited, and clinicians must be thoroughly familiar with its benefits and drawbacks: these include reduction of right heart return, increase in fluid retention

---

TABLE 4
Field Intervention in Patients with
Cardiopulmonary Arrest

Begin ventilation and compression
1. Use mouth-to-mouth, mouth-to-mask, or oxygen-powered resuscitator valve (bag-valve-mask an alternative)
2. Use supplemental oxygen

Endotracheal intubation
1. PEEP at 5 cm H_2O may be useful
2. IV D_5W at "keep-open" rate
3. Rapid transport to ALS facility

Drain lungs if needed by abdominal thrust, suction, and gravity if:
1. Seawater aspiration has occurred with copious drainage
2. Marked gastric distention interferes with ventilation

Sodium bicarbonate
1. 1 mEq/kg IV initial bolus; repeat one-half dose every 10 minutes while spontaneous circulation is absent
2. Treat dysrhythmias in standard fashion
3. If cervical spine injury is suspected, use collar/sandbags, etc.

---

in an already stressed lung, increase in pulmonary artery pressure, decrease in cardiac output, and, at high levels, increased intracranial pressure (2,12).

Effective cardiac compression remains mandatory in all pulseless patients. Interruption of compressions to effect drainage should be undertaken only if ventilation appears inadequate and frothy drainage is evident from the mouth or endotracheal tube.

DRUGS

Standard drug therapy indicated in cardiopulmonary resuscitation emphasizes prompt attention to the administration of sodium bicarbonate. A severe metabolic acidosis exists in these patients, due not only to circulatory arrest but also to preceding vigorous muscular activity in the struggle for survival (43,46). Doses of 1 mEq/kg can be given on an empiric basis in the field, and should be repeated at one-half of this initial level every 10 minutes while spontaneous circulation is absent. Cardiac dysrhythmias are managed in a standard fashion (Table 4).

The Obviously Dead or Still Submerged Patient

The term *obviously dead* refers to any patient who has a normal temperature and who demonstrates asystole, absent respirations, postmortem lividity, or rigor mortis. In cases in which rescue operations have been in progress for more than 30 minutes, those victims who are retrieved from the water during the summer months or in warm southern waters should be considered dead-on-scene. It should be remembered that cold water submersion for up to 40 minutes has been associated with neurologic survival (33,66,68).

In these tragic cases, the rescue team must comfort the family or friends and participate in recovery of the body. The victim's body, once retrieved, should be covered immediately and treated with proper dignity. Family members and friends should be escorted from the scene, if possible, prior to recovery of the body.

Most drownings are medical examiner cases, as foul play is frequently suspected and must be investigated.

In-Hospital Management

Therapeutic decisions in the emergency department will depend upon the extent of field intervention, the response of the patient, presenting complaints, and the physical examination.

Asymptomatic Patients

Patients may present with little or no evidence of submersion injury. They should be admitted for observation for 12–24 hours. In the secondary drowning syndrome, pulmonary failure ensues after a latent period of up to 36 hours.

Auxiliary data should include arterial blood gas, chest x-ray, and baseline studies: complete blood count, electrolytes, blood urea nitrogen, platelet count, partial thromboplastin time, prothrombin time, and urinalysis.

RADIOLOGIC STUDIES

X-ray examination of the chest is performed on all patients with a history of submersion. The findings vary widely with the severity of the incident and other less well identified factors. The usual pattern seen in patients suffering from significant insult is similar to that of pulmonary edema. In mild cases, fine alveolar infiltrates are seen predominantly in the peripheral areas. Such findings may be quite subtle. Patients who become symptomatic often demonstrate changes consistent with diffuse or localized intra-alveolar or interstitial infiltrates, segmental atelectasis, or "shock lung." Air bronchograms are frequently seen in severely affected patients, and the lungs may appear opaque. An initial normal chest x-ray does not rule out a significant pulmonary insult. Depending upon the severity of the submersion, findings are usually seen within several hours of the incident, but changes have been delayed for as long as 12–24 hours after the patient became symptomatic (34).

Spinal injury should be suspected in patients who have been platform diving or surfing or who may have fallen from a height into the water. A full radiographic series of all seven cervical vertebrae is standard prior to neck manipulation.

The patient who remains asymptomatic may need attention because of the psychologic trauma of the near-tragedy. This is frequently important when others have been involved in the incident, particularly if fatalities resulted.

Symptomatic Patients

Patients will complain of combinations of sore throat, burning in the chest, and dyspnea. Patients who are dyspneic are almost always hypoxic and, if severely affected (with cyanosis), acidotic as well. Intervention must be aggressive and planned. Initial blood gases and chemistries should be drawn. A chest x-ray may be taken by a portable machine, unless an x-ray is done in the emergency department or the patient is accompanied to the x-ray department and receives priority.

Blood gas determinations can be carried out rapidly in most modern emergency departments, and in almost all cases these should guide therapy. Oxygen is administered by demand valve (100%) or through a nonrebreathing mask at a rate of 12–15 liters/minute. The use of CPAP by mask may be helpful in patients who are sufficiently alert to protect their own airways, who can follow commands, who have adequate alveolar ventilation ($PaCO_2$ less than 45 torr), and who appear to be in distress (25). Pressures used with CPAP by mask will vary according to the blood gas determinations; initial pressures should be low (e.g., 2/5 cm H_2O inspiratory/expiratory ratio) and may be increased or decreased according to the patient's response to and tolerance of the procedure.

The decision to perform endotracheal intubation in patients is made on the basis of blood gas determinations and the following (39):

1. Comatose patients unable to handle secretions
2. Comatose patients who require nasogastric intubation
3. Patients with a PaO_2 of 90 torr or less on high-flow oxygen administered by nonrebreathing mask at 12–15 liters/minute *or* a $PaCO_2$ of more than 45 torr

An intravenous line should be in place, as well as a cardiac monitor, an indwelling urinary

dobutamine) used to support myocardial function (31). Whenever barbiturate therapy is considered, mass intracranial lesions should be ruled out by computed tomography (CT) scan. Sudden increases in ICP can be managed by hyperventilation and the use of mannitol (0.5–1.0 g/kg in an IV bolus).

Steroids are given in the form of dexamethasone (1 mg/kg IV initial dose, 0.2 mg/kg every 6 hours for 2–5 days), or methylprednisolone (5 mg/kg IV initial dose, then 1 mg/kg every 6 hours IV for 2–5 days). Most workers advise prompt institution of this therapy once it has been decided upon (31,61).

Muscular Activity

Complete muscle paralysis is advocated by Conn *et al.* and is maintained in order to prevent increased intracranial pressure induced by muscular rigidity, as well as to enable complete control of ventilation. Muscle paralysis is achieved with pancuronium (0.1 mg/kg IV) hourly or as needed (8,9).

The value of any one of these modalities is not documented by Conn or any other investigator, and most would recommend careful clinical trials. However, Conn and his colleagues report "significant improvement in cerebral salvage" (9). Adjunctive measures include ICP monitoring to ensure an ICP below 15 mmHg, daily EEGs, and the availability of computed tomography (CT) in case of a sudden, unexplained rise in ICP.

Results in patients who were comatose on admission (category C patients) indicate a difference in the incidence of complete cerebral recovery in a partially treated group (35.7%) and a fully treated group (90.0%). Morbidity (neurologic deficit) was correspondingly reduced from 42.8 to 9.0% (9).

The use of these measures in both adults and children deserves investigation. Certainly, caution must be observed in adults with preexisting cardiovascular disease, particularly in the case of barbiturate use, since these drugs act to depress myocardial function (Table 7).

Conclusion

The science and art of dealing with submersion incidents has seen significant progress in the past several years. Recent improvements in the understanding and therapy of this entity hold great hope for the future.

References

1. American Heart Association, National Research Council. Standards for cardiopulmonary resuscitation and emergency cardiac care. *JAMA* (suppl), 227(7):833–68, 1974.
2. Ashbaugh, D. G., Petty, T. L. Positive end-expiratory pressure—physiology, indications and contraindications. *J Thorac Cardiovasc Surg*, 65(1):165–70, 1973.
3. Bartecchi, C. E. Cardiopulmonary resuscitation—an element of sophistication in the 18th century. *Am Heart J*, 100(4):580–81, 1980.
4. Battaglia, J. D., Lockhart, C. H. Drowning and near drowning. *Pediatr Ann*, 6(4):97–106, 1977.
5. Bonilla-Santiago, J., Fill, W. L. Sand aspiration in drowning and near-drowning. *Radiology*, 128:301–2, 1978.
6. Collis, M. L. Survival behaviour in cold water immersion. In: Proceedings of the Cold Water Symposium, Royal Life Saving Society of Canada, Toronto, 1976.
7. Conn, A. W. The role of hypothermia in near-drowning. In: Proceedings of the Cold Water Symposium, Royal Life Saving Society of Canada, Toronto, 1976.
8. Conn, A. W., Edmonds, J. F., Barker, G. A. Cerebral resuscitation in near-drowning. *Pediatr Clin North Am*, 26(3):691–701, 1979.
9. Conn, A. W., Montes, J. E., Barker, G. A., Edmonds, J. F. Cerebral salvage in near-drowning following neurological classification by triage. *Can Anaesth Soc J*, 27(3):201–10, 1980.
10. Culpepper, R. M. Bleeding diathesis in fresh water drowning. *Ann Intern Med*, 83(5):675, 1975.
11. Department of Transportation, U.S. Coast Guard. *Hypothermia and Cold Water Survival*, 1979.
12. Dick, W., Lotz, P., Milewski, P., Schindewolf, H. The influence of different ventilatory patterns on oxygenation and gas exchange after near-drowning. *Resuscitation*, 7:255–62, 1979.
13. Dominquez de Villota, E., Barat, G., Peral, P. Recovery from profound hypothermia with cardiac arrest after immersion. *Br J Med*, 4:394, 1973.
14. Donaldson, J. C., Royall, J. D. Drowning and near-drowning—pathophysiology and therapy. *Postgrad Med*, 64(1):71–9, 1978.
15. Drinking and drowning (editorial). *Br Med J*, 2:1284, 1978.
16. Fandel, I., Bancalari, E. Near drowning in children: Clinical aspects. *Pediatrics*, 58:573–79, 1976.
17. Fine, N. I., Myerson, D. A., Myerson, P. J. Near-drowning presenting as the adult respiratory distress syndrome. *Chest*, 65:347–49, 1974.
18. Fleetham, J. A., Munt, P. W. Near-drowning in Canadian waters. *Can Med Assoc J*, 118:914–17, 1978.
19. Fuller, R. H. Drowning and the postimmersion syndrome: A clinicopathologic study. *Milit Med*, 128:22, 1963.
20. Giammona, S. T. Drowning: Pathophysiology and management. *Curr Probl Pediatr*, 1:1, 1971.

21. Glasser, K. L., Civetta, J. M., Flor, R. J. The use of spontaneous ventilation with constant positive airway pressure in the treatment of salt water near-drowning. *Chest,* **67**(3):355–57, 1975.

22. Golden, F. St. C., Rivers, J. F. The immersion incident. *Anaesthesia,* **30**:364–73, 1975.

23. Gooden, B. A. Drowning and the diving reflex in man. *Med J Aust,* **2**:583–87, 1972.

24. Grausz, H., Amend, W. J. C., Jr., Earley, L. E. Acute renal failure complicating submersion in sea water. *JAMA,* **217**:207, 1971.

25. Greenbaum, D. M., Millen, J. E., Eross, B. Continuous positive airway pressure without tracheal intubation in spontaneously breathing patients. *Chest,* **69**:615, 1976.

26. Heimlich, H. J. A life-saving maneuver to prevent food-choking. *JAMA,* **234**:398–401, 1975.

27. Heimlich, H. J., Hoffman, K. A., Canestri, F. R. Food choking and drowning deaths prevented by subdiaphragmatic compression. *Ann Thorac Surg,* **20**:188, 1975.

28. Heimlich H. J., Uhley, M. H. The Heimlich maneuver. *Ciba Clin Symp,* **31**(3):1–31, 1979.

29. Heimlich, H. J. The Heimlich maneuver: First treatment for drowning victims. *Emerg Med Services,* **10**(4):58–61, 1981.

30. Hermann, L. K. Drowning, a common tragedy. *Rocky Mountain Med J,* **76**(4):169–73, 1979.

31. Hoff, B. H. Multisystem failure: A review with special reference to drowning. *Crit Care Med,* **7**(7):310–20, 1979.

32. Hoff, B. H. Drowning and near-drowning (letter). *Crit Care Med,* **8**(9):530, 1980.

33. Hunt, P. K. Effect and treatment of the "diving reflex." *Can Med Assoc J,* **111**:1330–31, 1974.

34. Hunter, T. B., Whitehouse, W. M. Fresh-water near-drowning: Radiological aspects. *Radiology,* **112**:51–6, 1974.

35. Jacobsen, J. B., Neilsen, H., Ringsted, C., Andersen, P. K. Drowning and near-drowning (letter). *Crit Care Med,* **8**(9):529–30.

36. Julian, D. G. Cardiac resuscitation in the eighteenth century. *Heart Lung,* **4**(1):46–9, 1975.

37. Kite, C. *An Essay on the Recovery of the Apparently Dead.* London, 1788.

37a. Kizer K. W. Aquatic rescue in-water CPR. *Ann Emerg Med,* **11**:3, 166–67, 1982.

38. Knopp, R. Near drowning. *JACEP,* **7**(6):249–54, 1978.

39. Levin, D. L. Near drowning. *Crit Care Med,* **8**(10):590–95, 1980.

40. Lilly, J. K. An inexpensive portable positive end-expiratory pressure system. *Anesth Analg,* **58**(10):53–5, 1979.

41. Mackie, I. Alcohol and aquatic disasters. *Med J Aust,* **12**:652, 1978.

42. March, N. F., Matthews, R. C. New techniques in external cardiac compressions: Aquatic cardiopulmonary resuscitation. *JAMA,* **244**(11):1229–32, 1980.

43. Medical news. *JAMA,* **210**(9):1683, 1969.

44. Modell, J. H., Moya, F. Effects of volume of aspirated fluid during chlorinated fresh water drowning. *Anesthesiology,* **27**(5):663–72, 1966.

45. Modell, J. H., Moya, F. The effects of fluid volume in seawater drowning. *Ann Intern Med,* **67**:68–79, 1967.

46. Modell, J. H., Davis, J. H., Giammona, S. T. Blood gas and electrolyte changes in human near-drowning victims. *JAMA,* **203**(5):99–105, 1968.

47. Modell, J. H. *Pathophysiology and Treatment of Drowning and Near-Drowning.* Springfield, Ill.: Charles C Thomas, 1971.

48. Modell, J. H., Calderwood, H. W., Ruiz, B. C. Effects of ventilatory patterns on arterial oxygenation after near-drowning in sea water. *Anesthesiology,* **40**(4): 376–84, 1974.

49. Modell, J. H., Graves, S. A., Ketover, A. Clinical course of 91 consecutive near-drowning victims. *Chest,* **70**:231–38, 1976.

50. Modell, J. H. Near-drowning. *Int Anesthesiol Clin,* **15**(1):107–15, 1977.

51. Modell, J. H., Conn, A. W. Current neurological considerations in near-drowning, (editorial). *Can Anaesth Soc J,* **27**(3):197–98, 1980.

52. Modell, J. H., Graves, S. A., Kuck, E. J. Near-drowning: Correlation of level of consciousness and survival. *Can Anaesth Soc J,* **27**(3):211–15, 1980.

53. Modell, J. H. Drown versus near-drown: A discussion of definitions (editorial). *Crit Care Med,* **9**(4):351–52, 1981.

54. Orlowski, J. P. Prognostic factors in pediatric cases of drowning and near-drowning. *JACEP,* **8**(5):176–79, 1979.

55. Pearn, J., Nixon, J. Bathtub immersion accidents involving children. *Med J Aust,* **1**:211, 1977.

56. Pearn, J. H., Bart, R. D., Yamaoka, R. Neurologic sequelae after childhood near-drowning: A total population study from Hawaii. *Pediatrics,* **64**(2):187–91, 1979.

57. Peterson, B. Morbidity of childhood near-drowning. *Pediatrics,* **59**(3):364–70, 1977.

58. Plueckhahn, V. D. Drowning: Community aspects. *Med J Aust,* **2**:226–28, 1979.

59. Press, E., Walker, J., Crawford, I. Interstate drowning study. *Am J Public Health,* **58**:2275, 1968.

60. Rowe, M. I., Arango, A., Allington. Profile of pediatric drowning victims in a water-oriented society. *J Trauma,* **17**(8):587–91, 1977.

61. Safar, P. *Cardiopulmonary Cerebral Resuscitation.* Stavanger, Norway: A. S. Laerdal, 1981.

62. Schaeffer, Y., Cot. Asphyxia from drowning: Treatment based on experimental findings. *Bull Acad Natl Med* (Paris), **105**:758, 1931.

63. Scott, P. H., Eigen, H. Immersion accidents involving pails of water in the home. *J Pediatr,* **96**(2):282–84, 1980.

64. Schuman, S. H., Rowe, J. R., Glazer, H. M., Redding, J. S. Risk of drowning: An iceberg phenomenon. *JACEP,* **6**(4):139–43, 1977.

65. Shapiro, H. M., Wyte, S. R., Loeser, J. Barbiturate-augmented hypothermia for reduction of persistent intracranial hypertension. *J Neurosurg,* **40**:90, 1974.

66. Siebke, H., Breivik, H., Rod, T. Survival after 40 minutes' submersion without cerebral sequellae. *Lancet,* **1**:1275, 1975.

67. Society for the Recovery of Persons Apparently Drowned. *Report.* London, 1775.

68. Southwick, F. S., Dalglish, P. H. Recovery after pro-

longed asystolic cardiac arrest in profound hypothermia. *JAMA,* **243**(12):1250–53, 1980.

69. Stewart, R. D. Drowning and near-drowning. *Top Emerg Med,* **2**(3):63–76, 1980.

70. Stewart, R. D. Prehospital emergency care: Historical foundations. *Top Emerg Med,* **1**(2):11–15, 1979.

71. Swann, H. G., Spafford, N. R. Body salt and water changes during fresh and sea water drowning. *Tex Rep Biol Med,* **9**:356, 1951.

72. *Toronto Sun,* June 16, 1978, p. 2.

73. Wegener, F. H., Edwards, R. M. Cerebral support for near-drowned children in a temperate environment. *Med J Aust,* **2**:135–37, 1980.

74. Westacott, P. A most unlikely patient. *Med J Aust,* **2**:157, 1980.

75. Williams, J. New thoughts on breathing. Presented at the annual conference, British Association of Immediate Care Schemes, Southampton, September 1979.

76. Young, R. S. K., Zalneraitis, E. L., Dooling, E. C. Neurological outcome in cold water drowning. *JAMA,* **244**(11):1233–35, 1980.

8 | # HAZARDOUS MARINE LIFE*

Paul S. Auerbach, M.D.
Bruce W. Halstead, M.D.

The expanses of ocean and fresh water that cover this earth are unquestionably the greatest wilderness. Seventy-one percent of the earth's surface is composed of ocean, the volume of which exceeds 325 million cubic miles. Within this realm exists four-fifths of all living organisms. A large percentage of this aquatic life presents a hazard to humans, and it is the purpose of this chapter to classify and to describe some of these unpleasant interactions.

The opportunity for direct encounters with marine organisms statistically increases with greater numbers of recreational, economic, and military oceanic activities. The world population is increasing, by some estimates, at a rate of 1 million per day, a rate which will overwhelm existing land-based food and energy resources. Presently, 200–240 million tons of fish are harvested each year, with 50% of that coming from coastal regions (17). Of the 25,000 classified species of fish, fewer than 15 species have heretofore provided the bulk of the world's catches, and this number is likely to increase dramatically. It is becoming increasingly clear that the ocean is our last great untapped resource, and thus will begin the large-scale agricultural and industrial exploitation of the sea.

For this and other reasons, the year 2000 will see approximately 80% of the world's population living in coastal regions (12). A significant proportion of this population will be directly involved as entrants into the aquatic world: industrial, military, scientific, agricultural, and recreational divers; swimmers, boaters, and fishermen. It is imperative that clinicians be familiar with those hazards unique to the marine environment, and not rely on diagnostic and therapeutic folklore, myth, and misinformation.

* We would like to thank J. K. Sims, M.D., for his gracious review and abundant suggestions in the preparation of this chapter.

Although the concentration of noxious marine organisms is predominantly in warm temperate and tropical seas, particularly in the Indo-Pacific region, they may be found as far north as latitude 50°. The increasing number of salt water aquaria in private homes and public settings has created additional risks. The ubiquity of hazardous creatures and their propensity to appear at inopportune times make it imperative to be intelligently aware of them, to respect their territorial rights, and to avoid needless unpleasant contact with them.

Divisions and Definitions

Dangerous marine animals will be divided into four groups: (1) traumatogenic, (2) stinging, (3) poisonous on ingestion, and (4) shocking. Plants are discussed in detail in Chapter 9, but are mentioned here briefly. Freshwater hazards, which are in large measure a study in parasitology, will be discussed in one example only. Each section will elucidate the pertinent biology, physical diagnosis, and treatment.

Prior to the individual discussions, definitions and the concepts of biotoxicity will be presented.

Biotoxicity: Poisons, Venoms, and Defense

The science of poisons, *biotoxicology,* is divided into plant poisons, or *phytotoxicology,* and animal poisons, or *zootoxicology* (3). Naturally occurring marine zootoxins may be further designated as:

1. *Oral toxins*—poisonous to eat; include bacterial poisons and products of decomposition
2. *Parenteral toxins*—venoms produced in specialized glands and injected mechanically with traumatogenic devices (i.e., spines, teeth, fins)
3. *Crinotoxins*—venoms produced in specialized glands and administered *without* the aid of traumatogenic devices (i.e., slime, gastric secretion)

Within these three subdivisions, further classifications are by phylogeny, chemical structure, and clinical syndrome.

It is important to specify that although all venoms are poisons, not all poisons are venoms (16). If one adheres to the theory that offensive venoms are generally associated with the oral (mouth, teeth) pole and defensive venoms with the aboral (tail, sting) pole or dermal tissues (barbs, secretions), then one must classify the majority of marine venoms as defensive (34).

In snakes, the latency, toxicity, and duration of a venom effect are related to the route of administration, with intravascular injection being significantly more lethal, as determined by the measured lethal dose for 50% survival of the group (LD_{50}), than intraperitoneal or transcutaneous injection (34). The application of this principle to marine venoms is direct, albeit of limited frequency, as few encounters involve direct intravascular invasion.

Generally, venoms are of large molecular weight and are composed of multifarious vasoactive amines, proteolytic enzymes, and

TABLE 1
A Brief Comparison of the Features of Venoms and Poisons

Poison (Oral)	Venom (Parenteral)
Toxin or poison produced in skin, muscle, blood, and/or inner organs	Venom produced in venom gland and associated with a traumatogenic device
Ingestion	Envenomation or parenteral application to skin/mucous membranes
Heat (115–120°F)/gastric acid stable	Heat/gastric acid labile
No well-defined biologic function	Conquest and defense
No individual protection; possible evolutionary advantage to species	Self-protection
(±) seasonal toxicity; not released	Constant toxicity; can be released in varying amounts

other biogenic compounds (33). These and other more or less well-defined substances denature membranes, catabolize cyclic 3', 5'-adenosine monophosphate (cyclic AMP), degranulate mast cells, provoke histamine release, interfere with cellular transport mechanisms, disrupt metabolic pathways, impede neuronal transmission, and otherwise wreak havoc with cascades of anaphylaxis and shock. It is a continuing frustration that although many marine venoms are composed of protein and polypeptide subunits, for some reason they lack sufficient immunogenicity to foster the development of antitoxins or antivenins (23).

Poisons represent metabolic by-products produced in animals or plants, and are usually of smaller molecular weight (14). It is curious to note that although radiation exposure is not known to induce the production of new marine poisons, the ingestion of radioactive fish poses a potential radiation hazard (22). In the evolutionary scheme, it appears that venomous fish seek specific self-defense, whereas poisonous fish are noxious in a non-specific manner (Table 1).

In Defense of the Fish

Before discussing the individual groups of biologic marine hazards, a word in defense of the fish: As it is in all of nature (except for humans), there is little aggression involved when injuries are inflicted (40). Most injuries are gestures of warning or self-defense; with the exception of some sharks, few aquatic creatures attack humans without provocation (36). Attacks are made in the defense of young, in territorial disputes, or to provide food. It is hoped that a better understanding of the dangers of the deep will foster respect and add caution to what otherwise might become catastrophic curiosity.

Traumatogenic Marine Hazards

SHARKS

Myth and folklore surround sharks, the most sinister of all sea creatures (Figure 1). These savage and highly feared animals are the subject of many ongoing behavioral inves-

FIGURE 1 Great white shark. This animal has been implicated in many attacks on humans; the most dangerous of all sharks, it may attain a length of 20 feet.

tigations, but until there are more reproducible data, some degree of mystery will remain. The Shark Attack File, maintained at the Mote Marine Laboratory in Sarasota, Florida, is currently the most authoritative collection of data available, containing a series of 1165 case histories. Although feared, sharks are among the most magnificent denizens of the deep.

Life and Habits

Some 32 out of the 250 species of sharks have been implicated in the 50–100 shark attacks reported annually worldwide (Table 2). In the United States, the most frequently im-

TABLE 2
Representative Traumatogenic Marine Animals

Phylum Chordata
Class Chondrichthyes, subclass Elasmobranchii
Order Squaliformes: sharks
Family Carcharhinidae
  Carcharhinus melanopterus: black-tip reef shark
  Galeocerdo cuvieri: tiger shark
Family Isuridae
  Carcharodon carcharias: white shark
Family Sphyrnidae
  Sphyrna diplana: hammerhead

Class Osteichthyes
Order Anguilliformes: true eels
Family Muraenidae
  Gymnothorax javanicus: moray eel
Order Belonidormes: needlefish, halfbeaks, flying-fishes
Family Belonidae
  Strongylura gigantea: needlefish
Order Perciformes: perchlike fishes
Family Serranidae
  Promicrops lanceolatus: giant grouper
Family Sphyraenidae
  Sphyraena barracuda: great barracuda

Class Mammalia
Order Cetacea: whales, dolphins, porpoises
Family Delphinidae
  Orcinus orcus: killer whale
Order Carnivora: carnivores
Family Ursidae
  Thalarctos maritimus: polar bear
Order Pinnipedia: seals, sea lions, walruses
Family Phocidae
  Neophoca cinerea: Australian sea lion

plicated offenders are the great white, blue, mako, and grey reef sharks. Sharks are carnivorous, ranging in size from 18 inches in some species to the 50 foot giant whale shark (which, fortunately, eats tiny marine organisms). The danger to humans is a combination of size, aggression, and dentition. Some sharks, such as the giant whale shark, are plankton eaters and use their teeth as filters (33). It is axiomatic that even small sharks can be destructive.

Although sharks are not highly intelligent, they are endowed with remarkable sensory systems. Their color vision is poor, but well compensated for by the acute perception of motion; the eye musculature is adapted for fixation with any body motion. Keen olfactory and gustatory chemoreceptors permit taste and the recognition of blood, urine, or peritoneal fluid in the water. Additionally, the shark possesses skin chemoreceptors which detect chemical irritants. Perhaps the most important series of telereceptors is within the hearing apparatus (ampullae of Lorenzini), which is extremely sensitive to vibration and low-frequency sound waves. This allows the shark to home in on struggling fish, swimmers, or distressed divers. Current research is directed to delineation of the piscine ability to recognize electric fields.

Shark Feeding and Attack

Sharks feed in two basic patterns: (1) normal or subdued, with slow, purposeful group movements, and (2) frenzied or mob, as the result of an inciting event. The latter is precipitated by the sudden presentation of commotion or food-blood in the water. In a frenzy, sharks become fearless and savage, snapping at anything and everything, including each other.

It is very difficult to generalize about shark attacks on humans. While it has been previously assumed that attack motivation is related to hunger, current explanations favor aggression directed at the frightened victim. This may be aggravated by purely anomalous behavior, the violation of courtship patterns, or territorial invasion (4).

Shark attacks have occurred from the upper Adriatic Sea to southern New Zealand, with most between latitudes 46° N and 47° S (Fig-

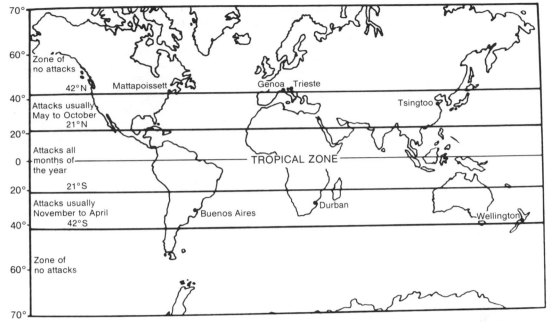

FIGURE 2 Shark attack zones. [From Coppleson, V. M. (1950). A review of shark attacks in Australian waters since 1919. *Med. J. Aust.,* **2**:680–87.]

ure 2). The odds of being attacked by a shark along the North American coastline is approximately one in five million (11a). The danger is greater in recreational areas, during late afternoon and nighttime feeding, and in murky warm (68°F or 20°C) water. Although most attacks occur within 100 feet of shore, it is believed that the danger is greater further out, in deep channels or dropoffs. Because of their ability to detect contrasts, sharks have a predilection to attack bright, contrasting, or reflective objects. Movement is an added attraction to sharks, who have been known to bite surfboards, boats, and buoys.

Most victims are attacked by single sharks, violently and without warning. In the majority of attacks, the victim does not see the shark prior to the attack. The first contact may be a "bumping," or an attempt by the shark to wound the victim prior to the definitive strike. Severe skin abrasions from the shark skin denticles can be engendered in this manner. It is difficult to postulate hunger as the sole motive, since more than 70% of victims are bitten only once or twice (43). Usually, the lower teeth are used first in feeding; solitary upper-tooth slashes might indicate attacks unrelated to feeding.

Clinical Aspects

The jaws of the shark are crescent-shaped and contain rows or series of razor-sharp ripsaw teeth, which are replaced every few months by advancing the inner rows. Incredibly, the biting force of some sharks is estimated at 18 tons/square inch. Severe shark bites result acutely in massive tissue loss, hemorrhage, shock, and death. The potential for destruction is unparalleled in the animal world.

Treatment

In most cases, the immediate threat to life is hypovolemic shock. Thus, it is occasionally necessary to compress wounds or manually to constrict arterial bleeding while the victim is in the water. As soon as the victim is out of the water, all means available must be used to ligate large, disrupted arteries or to apply compression dressings. If at all possible, the injudicious use of tourniquets should be avoided. If volume must be replaced in large quantities, at least two large-bore (12 or 14 gauge) intravenous (IV) lines should be inserted in the uninvolved extremities, to deliver crystalloid (normal saline or lactated Ringer's solution) and blood products. Central venous cannulation should be reserved for the emergency department, unless there will be inordinate delay in transport. A dopamine infusion may be required after the repletion of intravascular volume. Some authors recommend the immediate administration of colloid (albumin or plasmanate), which is used until more specific blood products are available. This is controversial in the literature. Fluorinated hydrocarbon blood substitutes are experimental. If necessary, a three-piece MAST (Military Antishock Trouser) suit should be applied, provided there will be no excessive hemorrhage from areas not covered by the suit.

The patient should be kept well-oxygenated and warm, while being transported to a facility equipped to handle major trauma. He should be thoroughly examined for evidence of cervical, intrathoracic, and intraabdominal injuries. Tetanus toxoid, 0.5 ml intramuscularly (IM), and tetanus immune globulin (Hyper-Tet, Cutter), 250–500 units IM must be given. The administration of prophylactic antibiotics is more controversial. The consensus presently is to place victims on moderate to high doses of IV prophylactic penicillin. The rationale is that shark wounds are prone to heavy contamination with sea water, beach sand, debris, shark teeth, and shark mouth flora, which occasionally includes *Clostridia*. Wounds should be cultured for aerobes and anaerobes only after a clinical infection is recognized, by inserting sterile swabs deeply into available lesions. Marine organisms can be virulent and difficult to identify. For instance, at least one dolphin bite has been implicated in a *Mycobacterium marinum* infection (13). Many marine infections result from *Erysipelothrix* species, which induces "fish handler's disease," an indolent cellulitis of the hands that responds best to outpatient doses of penicillin or erythromycin. The authors are presently conducting an investigation to identify the microorganisms that initiate infections which complicate marine wounds.

Immediate transport to a trauma center for proper operative intervention is mandatory. It is inappropriate to attempt emergency department exploration of what often prove to be extensive and complicated wounds. Follow-up for infection is mandatory.

TABLE 3
Supplies for a Shark Pack

Lactated Ringer's solution or normal saline: 3 liters
20, 18, 16, and 14 gauge IV catheters: three each
Vented IV administration sets: three
Adhesive tape: two rolls (1 and 2 inch)
Sterile gauze, 4 by 4 inches, and rolled bandages: 10 packages each
Abdominal pads, 8 by 10 inches, sterile: eight
1 ml syringe with 25 gauge needle
5 ml syringe with 21 gauge needle
Elastic wraps: two
Peripheral tourniquets: two
Epinephrine, 1:1000, 1 ml vial: two
Morphine sulfate, 10 mg vial: two
Blood pressure cuff
Stethoscope
MAST suit
Portable oxygen tank with nasal cannula: optional
Cervical collar
Traction splint

A reasonable "shark pack" should be available in emergency facilities near shark-infested waters. This must be portable and should include those items listed in Table 3.

Prevention

Every precaution should be taken to avoid shark attack, beginning with an intimate knowledge of the local waters. The following is precautionary advice and a list of alternatives for action in the event of a confrontation:

1. Shark-infested water should be avoided, particularly at dusk and at night. This fundamental rule is disregarded amazingly often. There is nothing romantic about losing life or limb to a shark.
2. Swimmers should remain in groups. Isolation creates a primary target and eliminates companion surveillance. When diving, vigilance must be constant.
3. Turbid water, dropoffs, deep channels, and sanitation waste outlets are areas frequented by larger sharks and should be avoided.
4. Blood and other body fluids attract sharks. Women should not be in shark waters during menstruation (controversial) and no one should be in shark waters with open wounds.
5. Brightly colored swimwear or diving equipment and shiny snorkling gear attract sharks and should not be worn.

6. Captured fish must be tethered at a distance from any divers.
7. *If a shark appears* in shallow water, swimmers should leave the water with slow, purposeful movements, facing the shark if possible and avoiding erratic behavior that could be interpreted as distress. If a shark approaches in deep water, the diver should remain submerged, rather than wildly surface to escape. He should move to defensive terrain with posterior protection in order to fend off, as best as possible, a frontal attack. It is inadvisable to trap a shark, so that it must attack to obtain freedom. Fighting sharks is very difficult; they are best repulsed with blunt blows to the snout, eyes, or gills. Spears, knives, and powerheads will worsen the situation if their application promotes frenzy in a school of sharks.
8. Shark avoidance techniques and repellants are in constant evolution. Experimental devices include chain mesh suits, inflatable plastic protective bags, acoustical and electrical field repellants, and chemical repellants (Moses sole, firefly extract). There is no question that shark avoidance is the most reliable maneuver. The recent shark attacks in northern California coastal waters involved swimmers on surfboards (black on white) who entered migratory elephant seal (shark food) habitats.

BARRACUDA

Life and Habits

Of the 22 species of barracuda, only the great barracuda (*Sphyraena barracuda*) has been implicated in human attack. This fish is encountered in all tropical seas and can grow to 10 feet and 100 pounds, but is rarely sighted at a size greater than 5 feet. It is a solitary swimmer and is extremely swift. The barracuda possesses a large mouth filled with enormous knifelike teeth (Figure 3).

Although great barracudas seldom attack divers, they do so rapidly and fiercely, often out of confusion in murky waters (33). Considering the frequency with which they are encountered and the number of reported attacks, they do not pose nearly the hazard of sharks. They are distributed in the Atlantic Ocean

FIGURE 3 Jaws of the great barracuda. Note canine-type teeth. (Photo courtesy of Stephen Dresnick, M.D.)

from Brazil north to Florida, and in the Indo-Pacific area from the Red Sea to the Hawaiian Islands.

Clinical Aspects

Barracuda jaws contain two nearly parallel rows of teeth, which produce straight or V-shaped lacerations, in contradistinction to the crescent-shaped bite of the shark. Except for this difference and the magnitude of injury, the medical problems engendered by the barracuda do not differ from those of the larger denizen. The clinician will encounter tissue loss, hemorrhage, and hypovolemic shock.

Treatment

Barracuda bites are treated in a manner analagous to that of shark bites.

Prevention

Barracudas are attracted to turbid waters, irregular motion, surface splashing, bright objects, and tethered fish. These should all be avoided.

MORAY EELS

Life and Habits

Moray eels are found in tropical, subtropical, and some temperate waters. In the family Muraenidae, some individuals of the larger species may attain lengths of 10 feet. They are muscular, powerful, and savage bottom dwellers, residing in holes or crevices or under rock and coral (Figure 4). The skin of the moray eel is leathery and not easily lacerated with a knife. Fortunately, the eel will usually evade confrontation unless cornered or provoked. Bites usually occur when a diver accidentally reaches into a coral bed or fishing net and offers his hand to a feeding moray eel, probes into a cave that is home for the eel, or removes an eel from a fishing net (33). Elderly blind eels may strike out without specific provocation.

Clinical Aspects

Morays are powerful and vicious biters that can inflict severe lacerations with their nar-

FIGURE 4 Spotted moray eel, with good illustration of biting potential. (Photo courtesy of Carl Roessler.)

row, vicelike, muscular jaws, which are equipped with long, sharp, fanglike teeth. What is worse, a moray has the tenacity of a bulldog and will hold on to the victim, rather than strike and release.

Treatment

Moray bites are treated in a manner analagous to that of barracuda bites. If the eel remains attached to the victim, the jaws may need to be cracked to effect release. Follow-up for infection is mandatory.

Prevention

It is unwise for a snorkeler or diver to place his hand in unexplored coral or rock holes unless he has probed or otherwise searched first specifically for an eel.

GIANT GROUPER

Life and Habits

Some of the larger species of sea bass or grouper (family Serranidae) may grow to 12 feet and 1000 pounds (Figure 5). Distributed in both tropical and temperate seas, they are curious, pugnacious, and voracious feeders.

FIGURE 5 Diver alongside giant grouper.

They are not aggressive, like sharks, but are to be feared for their boldness, bulk, and cavernous jaws. Indeed, it has been suggested that perhaps a giant grouper swallowed Jonah, because no whale has a mouth configuration that would admit a man (33). Groupers can be found frequenting old wrecks, swimming in caverns, and lurking behind rocks.

Clinical Aspects and Treatment

Grouper bites are treated in the same manner as shark bites.

SEA LIONS

Sea lions (family Phocidae) are mild-mannered mammals, except during the mating season, at which time the males may become aggressive. Divers have been seriously bitten and therefore should avoid ill-behaving animals. There is nothing unique about the clinical aspects or treatment of these injuries, except for the posttraumatic infections.

KILLER WHALES

Orcinus orca, or the killer whale, is probably not the ferocious killer it is reputed to be. The largest of the living mammalian dolphins, these magnificent animals grow to 30 feet and are found in all oceans. They usually travel in pods of up to 40 individuals. Swift and enormously powerful creatures, they feed on a remarkable array of fauna, including squid, fish, birds, seals, walrus, and even other whales. Their powerful jaws are equipped with

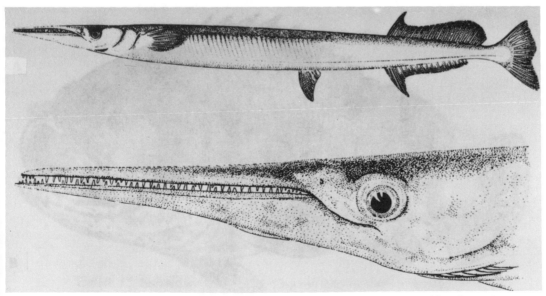

FIGURE 6 Needlefish, with enlarged rendition of needle-like beak, capable of causing a penetrating injury.

awesome cone-shaped teeth that are directed back into the throat, designed to grasp and hold food. The killer whale can generate enough crushing power to bite a seal or porpoise in two in a single snap.

In captivity, they are playful creatures and do not seem as primal as do sharks. Nonetheless, although it is believed that killer whales do not prey on humans, they should be regarded respectfully and at a distance. A human, mistaken for a sea lion, would be a nice snack for a killer whale.

NEEDLEFISH

Marine needlefish (family Belonidae) are slender, lightning-quick surface swimmers found in tropical seas (Figure 6). They resemble, but are not related to, the freshwater gar, and may attain lengths of up to 2 m. Possessed of an elongated pointed snout (hence their name), they move rapidly, often leaping out of the water. On occasion, they have flown into people, spearing them in the chest, abdomen, extremities, head, and neck, in one case causing brain injury (25). Treatment is according to the nature of the injury; in particular, all wounds should be debrided and irrigated, followed by a search for foreign material. Chest wounds can be complicated by pneumothorax.

GIANT CLAM

Although many adventure stories describe divers being caught in the clamp of a giant clam (family Tridacna), there are no verifiable reports of such a calamity (39). These clams can weigh as much as 250 pounds and pose a hypothetical hazard to divers.

TABLE 4
Representative Sponges Hazardous to Humans

Phylum Porifera
Class Demospongiae: sponges
Family Desmacidonidae
  Microciona prolifera: red sponge
Family Spirastrellidae
  Spheciospongia vesparia: loggerhead sponge
Family Tedaniidae
  Tedania ignis: fire sponge

Stinging Animals

The second class of marine organisms in this discussion is that of stinging animals. This large group contains vertebrates and invertebrates, and both primitive and extremely sophisticated organisms. We shall deal first with invertebrates.

INVERTEBRATES

SPONGES (Table 4)

Life and Habits

There are approximately 4000 species of the phylum Porifera, or sponges, which are composed of horny but elastic skeletons of spongin, some forms of which we use as bath sponges. Embedded in the connective tissue matrices are spicules of silica or calcium carbonate. Sponges are the subject of ongoing research to investigate the possibility that they harbor various biodynamic substances, with antitumor, antibacterial, growth-stimulating, antihypertensive, neurotropic, and antifungal actions (16). In general, they are stationary animals that attach themselves to the sea floor and may be colonized by other sponges, hydrozoans, mollusks, coelenterates, annelids, crustaceans, echinoderms, fishes, and algae. Indeed, these secondary coelenterate inhabitants are responsible for the dermatitis and local necrotic skin reactions termed *sponge diver's disease* (23,39).

Clinical Aspects and Treatment

Two general syndromes, with minor variations, are induced by contact with sponges. The first is a pruritic dermatitis similar to plant-induced allergic dermatitis, although the dermatopathic agent is not defined. Rarely, an erythema multiforme or anaphylactoid reaction may be present. Topical steroids may be helpful in treating the secondary inflammation, but do not appear to be good initial detoxicants. A typical offender is the fire sponge (*Tedania ignis*), a brilliant yellow-vermilion-orange organism found off Hawaii and the Florida Keys. The reactions are characterized by itching and burning, which may progress to local joint swelling, vesiculation, and stiffness, particularly if small pieces of broken sponge are retained in the skin near the finger joints. Spicules should be removed, if possible, and dilute (5%) acetic acid soaks applied. The second syndrome is an irritant dermatitis and involves the penetration of small spicules of silicon dioxide or calcium carbonate into the skin. If this is suspected, the particles should be removed with adhesive tape and isopropyl alcohol applied to the skin (12). Most sponges have spicules; "toxic" sponges may possess toxins which enter microtraumatic lesions caused by the spicules.

Severe reactions resemble erythema multiforme. Although steroid lotions may help to relieve the secondary inflammation, they are of no value as an initial decontaminant; in some cases, they appear to worsen the primary reaction. Severe secondary reactions may require the administration of systemic corticosteroids. Delayed (ten days to two months) surface desquamation may occur. Other anecdotal remedies that have been suggested for management of sponge envenomation include antiseptic dressings, broad-spectrum antibiotics, promethazine HCl, topical carbolic oil, zinc oxide cream, phenobarbital therapy, and diphenhydramine therapy (36a).

As mentioned previously, sponge diver's disease is not due to any toxin produced by the sponge, but rather is a stinging syndrome related to contact with the tentacles of the small coelenterate anemone *Sagartia rosea*, which attaches itself to the base of the sponge. Treatment is as for coelenterate envenomation.

COELENTERATES (CNIDARIA)

Coelenterates are an enormous group, comprising approximately 9000 species, at least 100 of which are dangerous to humans (Table 5). Those coelenterates possessed of the venom-inducing stinging cells called *nematocysts* are cnidaria; those without nematocysts are acnidaria. For practical purposes, the cnidaria can be divided into three main groups: (1) hydrozoans, i.e., Portuguese man-o-war; (2) scyphozoans, i.e., true jellyfish; and (3) anthozoans, i.e., alcyonarians or soft corals, stony corals, and anemones (23). Before dis-

TABLE 5
Representative Coelenterates Hazardous to Humans

Phylum Coelenterata
Class Hydrozoa: Hydroids
Family Corynidae
  Sarsia mirabilis (also *Sarsia tubulosa* or *Syncoryne mirabilis*): stinging hydroid
Family Milleporidae
  Millepora alcicornis: fire coral
Family Olindiadidae
  Olindias singularis: stinging medusa
Family Physaliidae
  Physalia physalis: Atlantic Portuguese man-o-war, bluebottle
  Physalia utriculus: Pacific Portuguese man-o-war, bluebottle
Family Plumulariidae
  Lytocarpus philippinus: feather hydroid

Class Schyphozoa: jellyfishes
Family Carybdeidae
  Carybdea rastoni: sea wasp
  Tamoya haplonema: sea wasp
Family Chirodropidae
  Chironex fleckeri: sea wasp or box jellyfish
  Chiropsalmus quadramanus: sea wasp
Family Cyaneidae
  Cyanea capillata: sea nettle, hairy stinger, sea blubber
  Cyanea lamarcki: blue jellyfish
Family Pelagiidae
  Chrysaora quinquecirrha: sea nettle
Family Ulmaridae
  Aurelia aurita: moon jelly

Class Anthozoa: corals, sea anemones
Family Acroporidae
  Acropora palmata: elk horn coral
  Astreopora spp.: stony coral
Family Actinodendronidae
  Actinodendron plumosum: stinging anemone
Family Sagartiidae
  Sagartia elegans: rosy anemone
Family Activiidae
  Anemonia sulcata: European sea anemone

cussing the individual groups, we will consider coelenterates in general.

MORPHOLOGY, VENOM, AND VENOM APPARATUS

Coelenterates are predators and feed upon other fish, crustaceans, and mollusks. They are radially symmetrical animals of simple structure and exist in two predominant life forms, either as sedentary, asexual polyps (hydroids) or as free-swimming, sexual medusae. As a general rule, the polyps are saclike creatures with a single orifice or mouth at the upper end surrounded by stinging tentacles. This form predominates in the hydrozoans and anthozoans. The medusa is a bell-like creature, with a floating gelatinous umbrella from which hang an elongated tubular mouth and nematocyst-bearing tentacles (Figure 7). This form predominates in the scyphozoans.

The stinging organelle, or nematocyst, is located on the outer surface of the tentacles or near the mouth and is triggered on contact with the victim's body surface. The nematocyst is contained within an outer capsule called the *cnidoblast,* to which is attached a single pointed "trigger" or *cnidocil.* The nematocyst is fluid (venom) filled and contains a hollow, sharply pointed and coiled thread tube (Figure 8). This tube may attain lengths

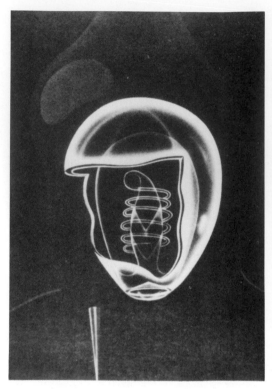

FIGURE 8 Nematocyst, undischarged.

FIGURE 7 Portuguese man-o-war, Atlantic variety (*Physalia physalis*). (Photo courtesy of Larry Madin and the Woods Hole Oceanographic Institution.)

of 200–400 μm and is sufficiently hardy to penetrate a surgical glove. When the cnidocil is stimulated, either by physical contact or by a chemoreceptor mechanism, it causes the opening of a trap door (operculum) in the cnidoblast, and the venom-containing thread tube is everted (Figure 9). The sharp tip of the thread tube enters the victim's skin, and envenomation occurs. The severity of envenomation is directly related to the number of nematocysts triggered and the inherent toxicity of the venom. A human encounter with a large Portuguese man-o-war could conceivably trigger the release of several hundred thousand stinging cells (Figure 10).

The nematocyst venom, to which there is only one specific antivenin, contains various fractions. Some of those which have been isolated are listed in Table 6. Before discussing the general and specific clinical syndromes induced by these components, we will consider the life and habits of each major group in turn.

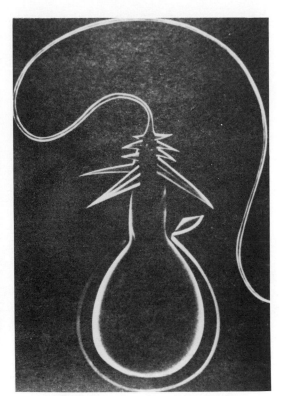

FIGURE 9   Nematocyst, discharged.

FIGURE 10   Tentacles of Portuguese man-o-war. Nematocysts may number in the hundreds of thousands. (Photo courtesy of Larry Madin and the Woods Hole Oceanographic Institution.)

TABLE 6
Components and Activities Present in Nematocyst Venom

Serotonin
ATPase
RNase
DNase
Aminopeptidase and other proteolytic enzymes
Fibrinolysin
Hyaluronidase
Acid phosphatase
Alkaline phosphatase
Histamine and histamine liberators
Kinins
Catecholamines
Phospholipases
Peripheral calcium antagonists
Membrane-depolarizing agents
Cardiotoxic fractions
Hemolytic fractions
Dermatonecrotic fractions

Source: From References 6, 7, 14, and 16.

HYDROZOA

Life and Habits

The hydrozoans range in spectrum from the sedentary *Millepora* hydroid coral to the free-floating colonial siphonophore *Physalia* (Portuguese man-o-war). As opposite ends of the same spectrum, they serve as perfect examples.

Millepora (Fire Coral)

The stony, hydroid, corallike *Millepora*, or fire corals, are not true corals. They are widely distributed in shallow tropical waters. Sessile creatures, they are found attached to the bottom in depths of up to 1000 m. Often, they may be mistaken for seaweed in their attachment to pilings, rocks, shells, or coral. Although they typically resemble little Christmas trees or bushes 3–4 inches in height, they may attain lengths of 2 m (33). Their color ranges from white to yellow-green, and they are possessed of a razor-sharp lime carbonate exoskeleton, which is an important factor in the development of coral reefs. They assume upright, clavate, bladelike, or branching calcareous growth structures which form encrus-

FIGURE 11   Fire coral. (Photo courtesy of Dee Scarr.)

tations over other corals and objects (Figure 11).

From numerous minute surface gastropores protrude tiny nematocyst-bearing tentacles, wherein lies the stinging apparatus.

Physalia

The Atlantic Portuguese man-o-war, or *Physalia physalis,* is a pelagic (open sea) polymorphic colonial siphonophore that inhabits the surface of the open sea. It is constructed of a floating sail, or nitrogen- and carbon monoxide-filled pneumatophore, up to 30 cm in length, from which are suspended multiple nematocyst-bearing tentacles, which may measure up to 30 m in length (33) (Figure 10). The smaller Pacific version, *Physalia utriculus,* or bluebottle, usually has a single fishing tentacle which attains lengths of up to 15 m.

The Physaliae depend upon the winds, currents, and tides for their movements, traveling as individuals or in floating colonies. They are widely distributed but seem to abound in tropical waters and in the semitropical Atlantic Ocean, particularly off the coast of Florida and in the Gulf of Mexico.

As with an iceberg, the scene above water does not fully tell the story. Because the tentacles may reach lengths of 30–100 feet and are nearly transparent, they pose a definite hazard to the unwary. As the animal moves in the ocean, these tentacles constantly undergo a rhythmic contraction, sampling the water for potential prey. If the tentacle strikes a foreign object, the nematocysts are stimulated and discharge their contents into the victim. Amazingly, each tentacle may house more than 750,000 nematocysts (Figure 10). To increase the intensity of the response, the remainder of the tentacle shortens in such a way as to create loops and folds, presenting a greater surface area and number of nematocysts for offensive action in what are called *stinging batteries.*

Broken-off tentacles contain live nematocysts capable of firing for months. Theoretically, indirect dermatitis can result from contact with certain sea slugs (nudibranchs) that ingest nematocysts or tentacle fragments, or from water containing venom that has already been released from stimulated nematocysts (12). The loggerhead turtle, *Caretta caretta,* reportedly feeds on *Physalia.* This is a gastronomic feat which, to the authors' knowledge, has not been purposefully duplicated by any cerebrating creature.

SCYPHOZOA

Life and Habits

This group of animals comprises the larger medusae or jellyfish, including the deadly sea wasps and other larger species (*Chironex, Cyanea, Chiropsalmus*). Jellyfish are mostly free-swimming pelagic creatures; however, some can be found at depths of more than 2000 fathoms. They may be transparent or multicolored, and range in size from a few millimeters to more than 2 m in width across the bell, with tentacles of up to 40 m in length. Like Physaliae, the scyphozoans depend on the wind, currents, and tides for transport and are widely distributed, Some vertical motion may be produced by rhythmic contractions of the gelatinous bell, from which originate the feeding tentacles.

Miraculously, some jellyfish have been measured to have less than 5% solid organic matter. They can withstand remarkable temperature and salinity variations, but do not fare well with violent activity and thus may descend to the depths in stormy surface weather. Some scyphozoans avoid sunlight; others follow opposite patterns.

The sea wasp, *Chironex fleckeri* (box jellyfish), is the most venomous sea creature in existence and can induce death in 30 seconds with its lethal sting. Like all other scyphozoans, it is a carnivore, and is adapted to deal rapidly with prey. It is a member of the group of Cubomedusae jellyfish and ranges in size from 2 to 10 cm across the bell. Although these creatures seem to prefer quiet, protected, shallow areas, chiefly in the waters off northern Queensland, Australia, they can be found in the open ocean. They are fragile and photosensitive, and thus will be found submerged in bright sunlight, seeking the surface in the early morning, afternoon, and evening. They are swift and graceful travelers, capable of sailing along at a steady 2 knots.

Sea nettles (*Cyanea, Chrysaora*) are considerably less lethal animals and can be found in both temperate and tropical waters, particularly in Chesapeake Bay.

ANTHOZOA

Life and Habits

The group Anthozoa includes the sea anemones and stony or true corals (Zooantharia), and the soft corals (Alcyonaria). We will consider the anemones here because they envenomate, and the corals later, because they do not.

Anemones

Actinarians, or sea anemones, are abundant (1000 species), multicolored animals with sessile habits and a flowerlike appearance. They are composed of stalked, fingerlike projections capable of stinging and paralyzing passing fish (16,20,21,33). Their size ranges from a few millimeters to more than 0.5 m; they are found at depths of up to 2900 fathoms. The insides of some anemones can be eaten after they are dried.

They are attractive creatures and are often found in tidal pools, where the unwary will brush up against them or inquisitively touch them (Figure 12). Like other coelenterates,

FIGURE 12 Sea anemone (*Stoichactis helianthus*) coexisting with fire coral. (Photo courtesy of Dee Scarr.)

they possess tentacles loaded with their own form of nematocysts, called *sporocysts,* which wreak havoc upon stimulation by an unfortunate victim. The reason for the name *Hell's fire sea anemone* (*Actinodendron plumosum*) becomes readily apparent.

Sponge diver's disease, a typical coelenterate envenomation, is a dermatitis caused by contact with *Sagartia.* In this case, the flower-shaped *Sagartia* attaches itself symbiotically to the base of a sponge, where it is handled by fishermen who harvest the host sponge (12).

Clinical Aspects

Coelenterate nematocyst envenomations vary in their toxicity in relation to the type of organism involved, the biogenicity and amount of the toxin, the site and surface area afflicted, and the underlying physical condition of the victim (24). Milder envenomation may result only in an annoying dermatitis, whereas severe envenomation can progress rapidly to involve virtually every organ system, resulting in significant morbidity and mortality. For the sake of convenience, we will describe the clinical picture by severity, with the understanding that there is a fair degree of overlap.

Mild Envenomation

In general, the stings caused by the hydroids and hydroid corals, along with lesser envenomations by *Physalia,* scyphozoans, and anemones, result predominantly in skin irritation. There is usually an immediate pricking or stinging sensation, accompanied by pruritus, paresthesias, burning, throbbing, and radiation of the pain centrally from the extremities to the groin, abdomen, and axillae. The area involved by the nematocysts will become red-brown-purple, often in a linear whiplike fashion, corresponding to "tentacle prints." Other features are blistering, local edema, and wheal formation, as well as violaceous petechial hemorrhages (16,23,33). The papular inflammatory skin rash is strictly confined to the areas of contact and may persist for up to 7 days. If the envenomation is slightly more severe, then the aforementioned symptoms, which are evident in the first few hours, can

progress over a course of days to local necrosis, skin ulceration, and secondary infection. This is particularly true of certain anemone stings (*Sagartia, Actinia, Anemonia, Actinodendron, Triactis*) (20).

Moderate and Severe Envenomation

The prime offenders in this group are the anemones, *Physalia* species, and scyphozoans. The skin manifestations remain similar, but are compounded by the onset of systemic symptoms, which may appear immediately or be delayed:

1. Neurologic—malaise, headache, aphonia, diminished touch and temperature sensation, vertigo, ataxia, spastic or flaccid paralysis, delirium, loss of consciousness, convulsions, coma, death
2. Gastrointestinal—nausea, vomiting, dysphagia, thirst
3. Musculoskeletal—abdominal rigidity, diffuse myalgia and cramping, spasm, back pain
4. Cardiovascular—anaphylaxis, hemolysis, hypotension, bradyarrhythmias, tachyarrhythmias, ventricular fibrillation
5. Ocular—conjunctivitis, chemosis, corneal ulcers, lacrimation
6. Respiratory—bronchospasm, laryngeal edema, cyanosis, respiratory failure
7. Other—chills, fever, sialorrhea

The extreme example of envenomation occurs with *Chironex fleckeri,* the dreaded sea wasp, which is located chiefly in the waters off Australia. Larger individuals are capable of injecting venom that has been estimated to exceed 10 ml, and death can occur in less than 1 minute. There is an overall mortality of 15–20%. *Physalia* and anemone stings, although extremely painful, are rarely fatal.

Treatment

Therapy is directed at stabilizing major systemic decompensation, opposing the venom's multiple effects, and alleviating pain.

Pain Control

If there is no contraindication (head injury, altered mental status, respiratory depression, allergy, profound hypotension), then the administration of narcotics (morphine SO$_4$, 2–

10 mg IV; nalbuphine HCl, 2–10 mg IV or IM; meperidine HCl, 50–100 mg, with hydroxyzine HCl, 25–50 mg IM) is often indicated. If severe muscle spasm is in evidence, then trials of 10% calcium gluconate (5–10 ml IV slow push) or methocarbamol (1 g, no faster than 100 mg/minute through a widely patent IV line) are indicated.

DERMATITIS

If a person is stung by a jellyfish or other coelenterate, then the following steps should be taken:

1. Immediately *rinse the wound with sea water,* not fresh water. Fresh water will stimulate any nematocysts that have not already fired.
2. *Topical alcohol is the treatment of choice* to inactivate the toxin. This should be used in any form available: isopropyl alcohol (40%), perfume, aftershave lotion, high-proof liquor (40). It should be applied continuously for at least 30 minutes or until there is no further pain. Other substances reputed to be effective as alternatives are organic solvents such as formalin, ether, and gasoline (*all to be condemned*), dilute ammonium hydroxide, sodium bicarbonate, olive oil, sugar, urine, and papain (papaya latex or meat tenderizer). The last is supposed to work by cleaving active polypeptides into nontoxic amino acids. Acetic acid (vinegar), 5%, is an effective alternative to alcohol, and is the decontaminant of choice for some researchers. There is recent evidence that alcohol may stimulate the discharge of nematocysts *in vitro;* the clinical significance is as yet undetermined.
3. No oral drugs other than antihistamines are of verifiable use. Ephedrine, atropine, calcium, methysergide, and hydrocortisone have all been touted at one time or another, but there is no proof that they help. The administration of epinephrine is appropriate in the setting of anaphylaxis only.
4. Immersing the area involved into hot water to tolerance *may* be of some benefit, particularly in anemone envenomations. If it increases the pain, it should be discontinued. Hot water therapy should always follow alcohol or acetic acid decontamination. Remove the gross tentacles using forceps.
5. Once the wound has been rinsed and soaked with alcohol or vinegar, the remaining nematocysts must be removed. The easiest way to do this is to apply shaving cream or a paste of baking soda, flour, or talc and to shave the area with a razor or reasonable facsimile. If sophisti-cated facilities are not available, the nematocysts should be removed by making a sand or mud paste with sea water and using this to help scrape the victim's skin. The rescuer must take care not to become envenomated in the process; bare hands must be frequently rinsed.
6. Local anesthetic ointments (lidocaine HCl, 2.5%) or sprays (benzocaine, 14%), antihistaminic creams (diphenhydramine or tripelennamine HCl) or mild steroid lotions (hydrocortisone, 1%) may be soothing. They are to be used *after* the toxin is inactivated. It should be noted that occasional *paradoxical* reactions are noted with benzocaine.
7. All patients should receive standard tetanus prophylaxis.
8. There is no justification for the use of prophylactic antibiotics. Wounds which become secondarily infected should be Gram-stained and cultured so that antibiotics can be chosen appropriately. Generally, the wounds should be checked at 3 days and 7 days post injury for infection.

SYSTEMIC

Generally, only severe *Physalia* or Cubomedusae stings will result in rapid decompensation. In both cases, supportive care is based on the presenting signs and symptoms.

Chironex fleckeri, the box jellyfish or sea wasp, produces the only coelenterate venom for which there is a specific antidote. To date, the venoms of *Physalia* and *Chrysaora* species have not been sufficiently purified as antigens to permit the production of an antitoxin. Sea wasp antivenin is prepared by hyperimmunizing sheep with Cubomedusae venom. Antivenin administration may be lifesaving and should accompany the following first aid protocol:

In the case of known sea wasp envenomation, if an extremity is involved, the immediate application of a loose tourniquet, which impedes the lymphatic and superficial venous return, should be enacted. This tourniquet is loosened for 90 seconds every 10 minutes and should be removed after 1 hour. Alcohol or vinegar should be applied in any form to all suspected areas of contact. No attempt should be made to remove any remaining tentacles until *after* alcohol or vinegar is applied, or the envenomation may be worsened.

Sea wasp antivenin is administered IV as soon as possible. The IM route is less preferred. The antivenin is supplied in ampules of 20,000 units by Commonwealth Serum Laboratories, Parkville, Victoria, Australia. The dose is one ampule over

5 minutes or three ampules IM. The risk of acute or chronic serum sickness is the same as for equine hyperimmune globulin preparations. Premedication with antihistamines should be used appropriately.

Prevention

If jellyfish are sighted, they should be given a wide berth, as their tentacles may trail great distances from the body. All swimmers and divers in hazardous areas should wear protective clothing and should be on constant alert. In areas inhabited by anemones and hydroid corals, protective gloves should be worn when handling specimens. Beached dead jellyfish or tentacle fragments washed up after a storm can still inflict serious stings. Any person stung by a jellyfish should leave or be assisted from the water because of the potential risk of drowning. As soon as possible, alcohol or vinegar should be applied to any adherent tentacles and areas of stings. The rescuer must take care not to use bare hands to touch tentacles or sting sites.

CORAL

The anthozoan Madreporariae, or true (stony) corals, exist in colonies that possess calcareous outer skeletons with razor-sharp edges. They live in waters at temperatures of 20°C or higher, generally at depths of up to 20 fathoms. Rarer species have been noted at depths of more than 6000 fathoms. Snorkelers and divers frequently handle or brush against these living reefs, inflicting superficial cuts on the extremities. These wounds are notoriously slow healers and result in prolonged morbidity.

Clinical Aspects

The initial reaction to a coral cut is "coral poisoning," consisting of red, raised welts and local pruritus. With or without prompt treatment, this may progress to a cellulitis with subsequent ulceration and tissue sloughing.

Treatment

Coral cuts should be scrubbed vigorously with soap and water, and then irrigated copi-

ously to remove all foreign particles and obviously devitalized tissue. It is occasionally helpful to use hydrogen peroxide to bubble out coral dust (23). Any fragments that remain can become embedded and increase the risk of an indolent infection or foreign body granulomas.

Tetanus prophylaxis is provided in the usual fashion. There are two approaches to take with regard to antibiotics. The first, favored by us, is to manage wounds with sterile wet-to-dry dressings, dilute antiseptics (povidone-iodine solution, 1–5%), or nontoxic topical antibiotics (polymyxin B-bacitracin-neomycin), dealing with secondary infections as they arise. The second approach, favored by others, is to apply full-strength antiseptic solutions, followed by powdered topical antibiotics, such as tetracycline. Neither method has been supported by any prospective controlled data.

Prevention

When exploring near coral reefs, every care must be taken to avoid coral cuts. Protective clothing and gloves should be sufficiently heavy to prevent penetration. Wounds should be treated promptly with irrigation and thorough debridement.

MOLLUSKS

The phylum Mollusca (comprising 45,000 species) encompasses a group of unsegmented, soft-bodied invertebrates, many of which secrete calcareous shells (12). Generally, a muscular foot is present, with various modifications. There are five main classes, of which three predominate in their hazard to humans: the pelecypods (scallops, oysters, clams, mussels); the gastropods (snails, slugs); and the cephalopods (squids, octopus, cuttlefish). Mollusks are often implicated as the transvectors in poisonous ingestions; these are mediated by dinoflagellates and will be discussed separately. In this section, we will be concerned predominantly with the venomous cone shells and octopus.

Cone Shells: Life and Habits

There are about 400 species of these beautiful, yet potentially lethal, univalve, cone-shaped shelled mollusks of the genus *Conus*

FIGURE 13 Cone shells. External appearance is deceiving; a nasty sting awaits those without caution.

(Figure 13). Most of these contain a highly developed venom apparatus, and about 18 species have been implicated in human envenomations (Table 7), with occasional fatalities. These include *Conus aulicus, C. geographus, C. gloria-maris, C. omaria, C. striatus, C. textile,* and *C. tulipa.*

Most harmful cone shells are creatures of shallow Indo-Pacific waters; the variance in feeding habits and venom production accounts for the varying toxicity (1). Apparently, cones which feed upon fish or mollusks seem to be the most dangerous (16). Less toxic stings are attributed to cones that feed upon marine worms. Predominantly nocturnal creatures, cones burrow in the sand and coral during the daytime, emerging at night to feed.

Venom and Venom Apparatus

Cone shells are predators that feed by injecting venom by means of a detachable, dart-

TABLE 7
Representative Mollusks Hazardous to Humans

Phylum Mollusca
Class Gastropoda: snails, slugs
Subclass Prosobranchia
Order Archaeogastropoda

Family Conidae
   Conus aulicus: court cone
   Conus geographus: geographer cone
   Conus gloria-maris: glory of the sea
   Conus omaria: marbled cone
   Conus striatus: striated cone
   Conus textile: textile cone
   Conus tulipa: tulip cone

Class Cephalopoda: cuttlefish, squids, octopuses
Order Octopoda
Suborder Cirromorpha

Family Octopodidae
   Octopus maculosus: spotted octopus
   Octopus lunulatus: blue-ringed octopus

like, radular tooth. In order to do this, the head of the animal must extend out of the shell. The venom apparatus is composed of a set of minute, harpoonlike, radular teeth associated with a venom bulb, duct, and radular sheath (Figure 14). The teeth are housed within the radular sheath. The act of envenomation is performed by the release of a radular tooth from the sheath into the pharynx, where it is "charged" with venom from the venom duct, and then transferred to the extensible proboscis. This appendage grasps the venom-impregnated, barbed radular tooth and thrusts it into the flesh of the victim. This represents quite an aggressive action.

The venom itself interferes with neuromuscular transmission, may have a curariform effect, and is otherwise poorly characterized.

Clinical Aspects

Mild stings are of the puncture wound variety and may resemble bee or wasp stings (23). The initial symptoms may be localized ischemia, cyanosis, and numbness in the area about the wound but more often consist of sharp stinging or burning. More serious envenomations induce paresthesias at the wound

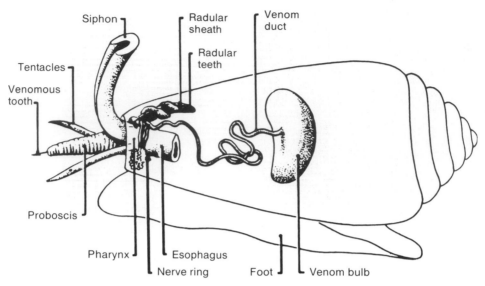

FIGURE 14   Venom apparatus of the cone shell. (B. Halstead)

site, which rapidly become perioral and then generalized. Although bronchospastic respiratory distress is not commonly seen, generalized muscular paralysis may lead to respiratory failure. Coma has been observed, and death is based on cardiac failure. Other symptoms include dysphagia, syncope, weakness, areflexia, aphonia, diplopia, blurred vision, and pruritus. To recapitulate, the bite of *C. geographus* may be rapidly toxic, with a progression to cerebral edema and coma, respiratory arrest, disseminated intravascular coagulation, and cardiac failure within a few hours (23,32).

Treatment

There is no antivenin for cone shell envenomations. Apply a venoconstrictive tourniquet and mildly promote bleeding from a scalpel blade incision. Inject local anesthetic (without epinephrine), administer an IV naloxone-reversible narcotic (if not contraindicated, and if needed for pain), and place into hot water at 45–50°C until pain is relieved. All wounds should be irrigated vigorously and rinsed with a mild antiseptic. Cardiovascular and respiratory support are the usual priorities in severe poisoning. IV naloxone (2–4 mg) may be of use to block the β-endorphin vasodepressor response. Tetanus prophylaxis is standard.

Prevention

Cone shells should be handled only with the proper gloves; if the proboscis protrudes, the cone should be dropped. If the animal must be carried, it should always be lifted by the large posterior end of the shell.

Octopuses: Life and Habits

Octopuses and cuttlefish are cephalopods, usually harmless and retiring. True octopuses are inhabitants of warmer waters, with little tolerance of extremes in salinity. They prefer rocky bottoms and rock pools in the intertidal zones. The entertainment media have created the image of a giant creature that envelops its victim in a maze of tentacles and suction cups. The truth is that the most dangerous creatures are smaller than 6 inches and do not squeeze their victims at all.

Octopus bites are rare but, in certain cases, can result in severe envenomations. Fatalities have been reported from the bites of the Australian spotted and blue-ringed octopuses, *Octopus (Hapalochlaena) maculosus* and *O. (H.) lunulatus.* These are small creatures that rarely exceed 20 cm. The blue-ringed octopus is an attractive creature found in Australian waters in rock pools and shallow waters, posing a threat to curious and unwary divers (11).

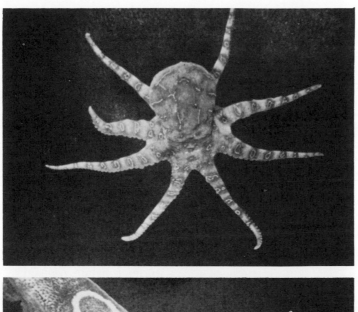

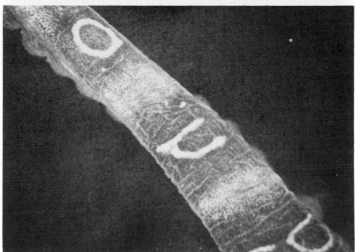

FIGURE 15 Blue-ringed octopus. When excited, the markings glow iridescent peacock blue.

At rest, it is covered with dark brown to ochre bands over the body and arms with superimposed blue circles. When the animal is angered, the entire body darkens and the blue rings glow irridescent peacock blue (41) (Figure 15).

Venom and Venom Apparatus

The venom apparatus of the octopus consists of the anterior and posterior salivary glands, salivary ducts, buccal mass, and beak. The mouth is located centrally at the base of the arms or tentacles and is surrounded by a circular lip fringed with fingerlike papillae. The mouth leads into a muscular pharyngeal cavity. This entire complex is the buccal mass, concealed by the base of the tentacles. The buccal mass is fronted by two parrotlike, powerful, chitinous jaws, which bite and tear with great force at food held by the suckers. The salivary glands, particularly the posterior ones, secrete the toxic venom (maculotoxin) into the pharynx via the salivary ducts. The venom is injected into the victim under considerable pressure, with tissue destruction noted through the dermis down to the muscle fascia (41).

The toxin contains a fraction similar to tetrodotoxin (discussed later) in that it is a potent biotoxin which apparently blocks conduction in peripheral nerves by preventing sodium conductance that normally accompanies neuronal excitation (16). The venom is of low molecular weight and is active on ingestion or by parenteral administration, the later being much more effective. It is interesting to note that most venoms and toxins with molecular weights greater than 30,000 are reasonable antigens. Octopus venom has a molecular weight of less than 5000 and, as predicted, elicits no good antivenin (14,41).

Clinical Aspects

Octopus bites usually consist of two small puncture wounds produced by the chitinous jaws. The bite site is initially numb, followed in 5–10 minutes by a stinging, burning, or pulsating sensation that may spread to involve the entire limb, persisting for up to 6 hours. Local urticarial reactions occur variably, and profuse bleeding at the site is a harbinger of coagulation abnormalities (12). Within 30 minutes, there is considerable erythema, swelling, tenderness, heat, and pruritus.

More serious symptoms are related predominantly to the neurotoxic properties of the venom. Voluntary and involuntary musculature are involved, and envenomation may progress to total flaccid paralysis and respiratory failure. Other symptoms include perioral and intraoral anesthesia, blurred vision, aphonia, dysphagia, ataxia, myoclonus, a sense of detachment, nausea, vomiting, and peripheral neuropathy.

Treatment

Treatment is based on the symptoms and is supportive. Provided there is no period of profound anoxia, mentation is usually normal. Prompt mechanical respiratory assistance has by far the greatest influence on the outcome.

Some authors recommend the immediate wide circular excision of bite wounds down to the deep fascia, with either primary closure or immediate full-thickness free skin grafts (12,33). As mentioned previously, there is no good antivenin.

Prevention

All octopuses, particularly those less than 6 inches in length (including *Octopus joubini* of the Caribbean), should be handled with gloves. Divers need to be familiar with the lethal creatures in their domain. Giving an octopus a "ride" on your back, shoulder, or arm is not recommended.

ANNELID WORMS

There are 6200 species of segmented marine worms (phylum Annelida; class Polychaeta), either free-moving or sedentary. Some members of the former group are considered to be toxic and may attain 1 foot in length. The worms are predominantly carnivorous and exist in the tidal zone to depths of 5000 m, mostly as bottom feeders (Figure 16). Each segment of the worm possesses paddlelike appendages, or parapodia, for locomotion. From these project numerous bristlelike setae, which are capable of envenomating the victim.

Functionally, these chitinous bristles are arranged in soft rows about the body. When a worm is stimulated, its body contracts and the bristles are erected. Easily detached, they penetrate skin like cactus spines and are difficult to remove (12). Additionally, some marine worms possess strong chitinous jaws and are able to inflict painful bites.

Clinical Aspects

Annelid bites or stings may induce intense inflammation, with erythema, pruritus, swelling, and paresthesias. Secondary infections and cellulitis are not uncommon.

Treatment

There are no specific antidotes. The spines should be removed with adhesive tape, taking care not to embed them further in the skin by scraping. Alcohol or dilute ammonia should then be applied for pain relief. Tetanus prophylaxis is standard.

FIGURE 16 Bristleworm eating fire coral. (Photo courtesy of Dee Scarr.)

ECHINODERMATA

The phylum Echinodermata has five classes: sea lilies, brittle stars, starfish, sea urchins, and sea cucumbers (14). We will consider the last three (Table 8).

Starfish

Starfish are simple, free-living, stellate echinoderms covered with simple thorny spines of calcium carbonate ($CaCO_3$) crystals held erect by muscle tissue (12). The creatures move about over the ocean floor by means of tube feet located under the arms or rays. They eat other echinoderms, mollusks, and worms, and often ingest poisonous shellfish.

Glandular tissue interspersed in the epidermis produces a slimy venomous substance that causes a contact dermatitis. The "crown-of-thorns sea star" (*Acanthaster planci*) is a particularly venomous species found from the Polynesian waters to the Red Sea (Figure 17). It attains sizes of up to 60 cm in diameter, with 5–21 arms. The venomous aboral spines of this animal often grow to 4–6 cm and are covered with a thin layer of integument. Envenomation can induce acute systemic reactions that include paresthesias, nausea, vomiting, and muscular paralysis. In some cases, chronic granulomatous lesions may develop.

TABLE 8
Representative Echinodermata Hazardous to Humans

Phylum Echinodermata
Class Asteroidea: starfishes
Family Solasteridae
　Solaster papposus: sun-star, rose star

Class Echinoidea: sea urchins
Family Diadematidae
　Diadema setosum: needle-spined urchin, black sea urchin
Family Echinidae
　Echinus esculentus: edible sea urchin
Family Strongylocentrotidae
　Strongylocentrotus drobachiensis: green urchin
Family Toxopneustidae
　Toxopneustes elegans: sea urchin
　Tripneustes ventricosus: white sea urchin

Class Holothurioidea: sea cucumbers
Family Cucumariidae
　Pentacta australis: sea cucumber
Family Holothuriidae
　Actinopyga agassizi: sea cucumber
　Holothuria argus: sea cucumber, tiger fish

Treatment

The dermatitis component should be treated in standard fashion. A useful topical solution is calamine with 0.5% menthol. One author

FIGURE 17 Crown-of-thorns sea star. This creature has been responsible for large areas of destruction in the Great Barrier Reef, Australia. (Photo courtesy of Carl Roessler.)

has suggested that the immediate application of hot water may be helpful in a crown-of-thorns sea star envenomation (33). Systemic therapy is supportive. Granulomas may require excision. Starfish that have ingested poisonous shellfish are themselves toxic on ingestion.

Sea Urchins: Life and Habits

Sea urchins are free-living enchinoderms that have an egg-shaped, globular or flattened body. A hard shell, or test, surrounds the viscera and is covered by regularly arranged spines and triple-jawed pedicellariae. Urchins are omnivorous eaters, yet are shy, nonaggressive, slow-moving animals that are found on rocky bottoms or burrowed in sand and crevices (12). Their bathymetric range extends from the intertidal zone to great depths. A fair number of urchins are nocturnal feeders. The gonads of several species can be eaten either raw or cooked by humans.

Venom and Venom Apparatus

The venom apparatus of sea urchins consists of the hollow, venom-filled spines and the triple-jawed, globiferous pedicellariae. Gener-

ally, only one or the other is present in a single species.

The spines of sea urchins may either be non–venom-bearing, with solid blunt and rounded tips, or venom-bearing, with hollow, long, slender, sharp needles. These are extremely dangerous to handle; such spines are very brittle and break off easily in the flesh, lodging deeply and making removal very difficult. They are keen enough to penetrate rubber gloves and flippers. *Diadema* spines may exceed 1 foot in length (Figure 18). The aboral spines of *Asthenosoma* have developed into special venom organs enveloped by a single large glandular covering. The sharp point serves as a means of introducing the venom.

Pedicellariae are small, delicate seizing organs scattered among the spines. One type are the globiferous pedicellariae, typified by *Toxopneustes pileolus,* which have globe-shaped heads, and serve as venom organs. The terminal head, with its calcareous pincer jaws, is attached by the stalk to the shell plates of the sea urchin. The outer surface of each jaw is covered by a large venom gland, which, with the jaw, is triggered to contract upon contact.

When the sea urchin is at rest in the water, the jaws are extended, slowly moving about. Anything that comes into contact with them

FIGURE 18 Black sea urchin (*Diadema setosum*). Long spines can penetrate into joints easily.

is seized. As long as the object is moving, the pedicellariae hang on. They will be torn from the shell rather than release, and continue to bite and envenomate. Detached pedicellariae may remain active for several hours.

The venom of echinoderms is said to contain various toxic fractions, including steroid glycosides, serotonin, and cholinergic substances (23). One urchin, *Tripneustes,* found in the Pacific Ocean, has a neurotoxin with a predilection for facial and cranial nerves.

Clinical Aspects

Venomous spines inflict immediate and intense burning stings, which are followed by redness, swelling, and aching. Frequently, the spines will break off and lodge in the victim. However, it should be noted that some sea urchin spines contain dye, which may give a false impression of spines left in the skin. Soft tissue density x-ray techniques for foreign body calcification may be diagnostic in these cases (12). Systemic reactions to spine injuries include numbness and muscular paralysis,

particularly if there are multiple puncture wounds. Secondary infections are common (22).

The stings of pedicellariae are often of greater magnitude, causing immediate intense radiating pain, local edema and hemorrhage, faintness, numbness, generalized muscular paralysis, loss of speech, respiratory distress, and occasionally death (12,14,16,22). In some cases, the pain may disappear over 1 hour, while the paralysis persists for up to 6 hours.

Treatment

Treatment is based on the symptoms and is supportive. There are no specific antivenins. Hot water may provide pain relief.

Any detached pedicellariae that are still attached to the skin must be removed mechanically or envenomation will continue (33). Embedded spines should be removed with care, as they are easily fractured. If the spines are removed and purplish discoloration surrounds the wound, this is most often merely spine dye and of no consequence. Although some thin venomous spines may be absorbed within 24 hours to 3 weeks, the consensus is to remove those that are easily reached and leave the remainder for resorption. All thick calcium carbonate spines should be removed due to infection and foreign body granuloma risk. On histologic examination, these granulomas demonstrate focal necrosis with a granulomatous foreign body reaction (12). After a period of months, these foci are best removed surgically or injected with intralesional steroids. If the spines have acutely entered into joints or are closely aligned to neurovascular structures, the surgeon should take advantage of an operating microscope (in an appropriate setting) to remove all the spine fragments.

Sea Cucumbers

Sea cucumbers are free-living worm or sausage-shaped bottom feeders that are essential scavengers (Figure 19). They are cosmopolitan in distribution and may be found in both shallow and deep waters. They produce a visceral liquid toxin called *holothurin* that induces a contact dermatitis and an intense inflammatory reaction that can lead to blindness if the corneas are involved (12,14,33). Holothurin is concentrated in the tentacular organs of Cuvier, which can be projected and extended anally when the animal mounts a defense. Some cucumbers actually dine on nematocysts and thus can secrete coelenterate venom as well. For this reason, the initial treatment should include the topical application of alcohol or vinegar for detoxification, followed by standard therapy for chemical irritant derma-

titis. Ingestion of sea cucumbers can result in fatality, attributed to holothurin, a toxic cardiac glycoside.

VERTEBRATES

STINGRAYS

The stingrays make up one of the largest and most important group of venomous marine animals, and are the most commonly incriminated group of fishes involved in human envenomations (Table 9). They have been recognized as venomous since ancient times, known as *demons of the deep* and *devil fishes* (12). Aristotle (348–322 B.C.) made reference to their stinging ability (5).

There are 11 species of stingrays found in U.S. coastal waters, 7 in the Atlantic and 4 in the Pacific (26). It is estimated that there are more than 1500 stingray injuries per year in this country.

Life and Habits

Stingrays are usually found in tropical, subtropical, and warm temperate oceans, generally in shallow water areas, such as sheltered bays, shoal lagoons, river mouths, and sandy areas between patch reefs (23). Rays can enter brackish and fresh waters as well. Although

FIGURE 19   Brown sea cucumber.

TABLE 9
Representative Stingrays Hazardous to Humans

Phylum Chordata
Class Chondrichthyes
Order Rajiformes: rays
Family Dasyatidae
  Dasyatis americana: southern stingray
  Dasyatis pastinaca: European stingray
  Dasyatis dipterurus: diamond stingray
Family Gymnuridae
  Gymnura marmorata: California butterfly ray
Family Modulidae
  Mobula mobular: horned ray
Family Myliobatidae
  Aetobatus narinari: spotted eagle ray
  Myliobatis californicus: California bat stingray
Family Rhinopteridae
  Rhinoptera bonasus: cownose ray
Family Urolophidae
  Urolophus halleri: round stingray

FIGURE 20 Southern stingray nestles in sand until disturbed. (Photo courtesy of Dee Scarr.)

rays are generally considered swimmers of moderate depth, at least one deep-sea species has been reported.

Rays are small (several inches) to large (up to 12 by 6 feet) creatures that are observed lying on top of the sand or partially submerged, with only the eyes, spiracles, and part of the tail exposed (10) (Figure 20). Their flattened bodies are round, diamond, or kite-shaped, with wide pectoral fins that look like wings (26). Rays are nonaggressive scavengers and bottom feeders that burrow into the sand or mud to feed upon worms, mollusks, and crustaceans.

Venom and Venom Apparatus

The venom organ of stingrays consists of one to four venomous stings on the dorsum of an elongate, whiplike caudal appendage (31). There are four different anatomic types of stingray venom organs, based upon their adaptibility as a defense organ. These are typified by the families Gymnuridae, Myliobatidae, Dasyatidae, and Urolophidae, with the first owning the most weakly developed organ and the last possessing the most muscular and highly developed striking weapon. The efficiency of the apparatus is related to the length and musculature of the tail and to the location and length of the sting.

In all cases, the venom apparatus of stingrays consists of a bilaterally retroserrate den-

tinal spine and its enveloping integumentary sheath (5,16). The elongate, tapered vasodentine spine is firmly attached to the dorsum of the tail by dense collagenous tissue and is edged on either side by a series of sharp retrorse teeth. Along either edge, on the underside of the spine, are the two ventrolateral glandular grooves, which house the soft venom glands. The entire spine is encased by the integumentary sheath, which also contains some glandular cells (14).

The venom contains various toxic fractions, including serotonin, 5'-nucleotidase, and phosphodiesterase (16). Russell and his associates investigated the pharmacologic properties of stingray venoms. In animal studies, they demonstrated significant venom-induced peripheral vasoconstriction, bradycardia, first-, second-, and third-degree atrioventricular block, ischemic ST-T wave changes, asystole, central respiratory depression, seizure activity, ataxia, coma, and death. The venom does not seem to affect neuromuscular transmission.

Clinical Aspects

Stingray "attacks" are purely defensive gestures. They occur when an unwary individual steps on a camouflaged creature while wading in shallow waters. The tail of the ray reflexly whips upward and, with amazing accuracy, thrusts the caudal spine into the victim, producing a puncture wound or laceration (12,33) (Figure 21). The integumentary sheath covering the spine is ruptured, and venom is released into the wound.

Thus, a stingray wound is both a traumatic injury and an envenomation. The former involves the physical damage caused by the sting itself. Because of the retrorse serrated teeth and powerful strikes, significant lacerations can result. Secondary bacterial infection is common. The lower extremities, particularly the ankle and foot, are involved most often, followed by the upper extremities, abdomen, and thorax. Fatalities have been reported secondary to intra-abdominal and thoracic trauma (10,23).

The envenomation itself classically demonstrates immediate (onset in less than 10 minutes) local intense pain, edema, and bleeding. The pain may radiate centrally and last for up to 48 hours. The wound is initially dusky

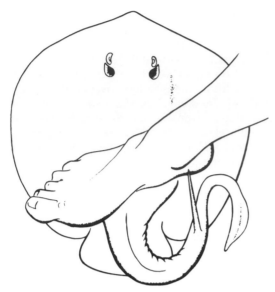

FIGURE 21 The stingray lashes its tail upward into the leg and generates a deep puncture wound. (R. Kreuzinger)

or cyanotic and rapidly progresses to erythema and hemorrhagic discoloration (15). Systemic manifestations include weakness, nausea, vomiting, diarrhea, diaphoresis, vertigo, tachycardia, headache, syncope, muscle cramps, fasciculations, paralysis, hypotension, arrhythmias, and death. It has been suggested that the paralysis represents spastic muscle contractures induced by pain.

Treatment

The success of therapy is largely related to the rapidity with which it is undertaken. Treatment is directed at combating the effects of the venom, alleviating pain, and preventing infection.

The wound should be irrigated *immediately* with whatever cold diluent is at hand. If no sterile saline is available, sea water does nicely. This removes some venom, provides mild anesthesia, and induces local vasoconstriction, possibly retarding the absorption of the toxin. Local suction, if applied in the first 15–30 minutes, may be of some value, as may a loose tourniquet which occludes only superficial venous and lymphatic return. This should be released for 90 seconds every 10 minutes in order to preserve circulation (12).

As soon as possible, the wound should be explored and debrided of any pieces of the sting's integumentary sheath which continue to envenomate the victim. After the wound is thoroughly irrigated and cleansed, it should be soaked in hot water to tolerance (115–120°F or 45–50°C) for 30–90 minutes (33). This relieves pain and attenuates the venom. There is no indication for the addition of ammonia, potassium permanganate, or formalin to the soaking solution. In these circumstances, they are tissue toxic and/or obscure visualization of the wound. Cryotherapy is disastrous, and there are no data to support the use of antihistamines or steroids.

If there is no contraindication, pain control should be initiated during the first debridement or soaking period. Narcotics may be necessary. Local infiltration of the wound with 1–2% lidocaine (Xylocaine) without epinephrine may be very useful.

After the soaking procedure, the wound should be reexplored and, after sterile preparation, debrided. Wounds should be closed loosely with drainage. Tetanus prophylaxis is standard. Prophylactic antibiotics are controversial but are frequently used because of the high incidence of secondary infection and subsequent necrosis. Penicillin or a broad-spectrum cephalosporin, such as cefaclor (250 mg orally three times a day) is sufficient for this purpose.

All victims with significant envenomations should be observed for a period of hours for systemic side effects and supported appropriately.

Prevention

The stingray spine can penetrate rubber boots and even the side of a wooden boat; therefore, a wet suit or pair of sneakers is not adequate protection (10). One must shuffle along through shallow waters known to be frequented by stingrays and create enough disturbance to frighten off any nearby animals.

CATFISH

Life and Habits

Approximately 1000 species of catfish are in existence, inhabiting both fresh and salt wa-

TABLE 10
Representative Catfish Hazardous to Humans

Phylum Chordata
Class Osteichthyes
Order Cypriniformes
Suborder Siluroidei: catfishes
Family Ariidae
   Bagre marinus: sea catfish
Family Icraluridae
   Ictalurus catus: white catfish
   Ictalurus nebulosus: brown bullhead
   Noturus furiosus: Carolina mudtom
Family plotosidae
   Plotosus lineatus: oriental catfish

ters; many of these are capable of inflicting serious stings (Table 10). They are fascinating animals, valuable as a food source and the origin of many amazing tales. For example, the South American astroblepins have flattened suctorial lips that allow them to scale cliffs, while the small Amazonian barb-headed "candiru" can enter the human urethra and may require surgical removal (35). Freshwater catfishes of North America include the brown bullhead, Carolina mudtom, channel, blue, white, and so on.

The catfish derives its name from the well-developed sensory barbels or "whiskers" surrounding the mouth. Catfish possess a slimy skin without any true scales (38). Marine forms include schools of the *Plotosus lineatus,* or oriental catfish, which lurk in tall seaweed and can inflict extremely painful stings. Marine catfish, as opposed to freshwater catfish, frequently travel in large schools. Most catfish are bottom feeders noted for their junkyard diet. They are poor swimmers and are not very evasive.

Venom and Venom Apparatus

The venom apparatus of catfish consists of the dorsal and pectoral fin spines, or "stings," and the axillary venom glands. Both the dorsal and pectoral spines are exquisitely sharp and can be locked into an extended position by the fish when it is handled or becomes excited (12,15,35,38). The spine is enveloped in an integumentary sheath; some spines have sharp retrorse teeth.

The toxin, which is poorly antigenic, probably contains vasoconstrictive, dermatonecrotic, and other biogenic fractions (9). It behaves *in vivo* much as a milder version of stingray venom.

Clinical Aspects

Most stings are incurred when the fish are handled, and thus involve the hands and forearms. The envenomation is purely a defensive maneuver and creates an injury out of proportion to the mechanical laceration (27). When the stinger penetrates the skin, the integumentary sheath is damaged and the venom gland exposed. Catfish stings are described as instantaneously stinging, throbbing, or scalding, with central radiation up the affected limb. Normally, the pain subsides within 30–60 minutes, but in severe cases it can last for up to 48 hours. The area about the wound is quickly ischemic, causing initial pallor with a progression through cyanosis to redness and swelling. Edema can be severe, and secondary infections are frequent; gangrenous complications have been reported. Common side effects include local muscle spasm and fasciculation. Less common sequelae are peripheral neuropathy, lymphedema, adenopathy, weakness, syncope, hypotension, and respiratory distress (15). Death is rare.

Treatment

There are no specific antidotes. Essentially, the treatment is the same as that for stingray envenomations, namely, local anesthesia without epinephrine, narcotics when necessary, irrigation, hot water, debridement, appropriate antisepsis, and follow-up for infection. It is believed that hot water relieves pain in part by reversing local toxin-induced vasospasm (29). As previously mentioned, there is no justification for irrigation with bicarbonate, vinegar, or potassium permanganate. In catfish envenomations, as opposed to those of stingrays, tourniquets have not been shown to be of value. All wounds must be carefully observed until healed for signs of secondary infection.

Prevention

Catfish should be handled without grabbing the dorsal or pectoral fins, preferably by using a large instrument. If possible, *Plotosus lineatus* should not be handled at all.

WEEVERFISH

Life and Habits

The weeverfish is the most venomous fish of the temperate zone (19). It is found in the Mediterranean Sea, eastern Atlantic Ocean, and European coastal areas. Common names for the weeverfish include the *adderpike, sea dragon, sea cat,* and *stang* (Table 11). Weeverfish are small (up to 46 cm) marine creatures that inhabit flat, sandy, or muddy bays, usually burying themselves in the soft sand or mud with only the head partially exposed

TABLE 11
Representative Weeverfish Hazardous to Humans

Phylum Chordata
Class Osteichthyes
Order Perciformes
Suborder Percoidei: perchlike fishes
Family Trachinidae
   Trachinus araneus: araneus weeverfish, dragonfish
   Trachinus draco: greater weeverfish, sea cat
   Trachinus radiatus: weeverfish
   Trachinus vipera: lesser weeverfish, adder pike

(Figure 22). They lead sedentary lives but, when provoked, can strike out with unerring accuracy. Weevers are a terror to fishermen working in shallow, sandy areas.

Venom and Venom Apparatus

The venom apparatus consists of dorsal and opercular dentinal spines, associated glandular tissue, and the enveloping integumentary sheath. When excited, the fish extends the dorsal fin and expands the operculum, projecting the opercular spine out to a 40° angle.

One name for the venom is *ichthyoacanthotoxin,* which is known to have various toxic fractions and appears to be heat inactivated.

Clinical Aspects

Weeverfish stings usually occur in professional fishermen or in vacationers who wade or swim along sandy coastal areas. The force of the sting is sufficient to penetrate a leather boot and creates substantial puncture wounds. The onset of pain is instantaneous. It is described as intensely burning or crushing, spreading to involve the entire affected limb. The pain usually peaks at about 30 minutes and generally subsides within 24 hours, but can last for days. Its intensity can induce irrational behavior and syncope; even narcotics are poorly effective. The wound itself is of the puncture variety, bleeds little, and usually becomes pale and edematous early on, with

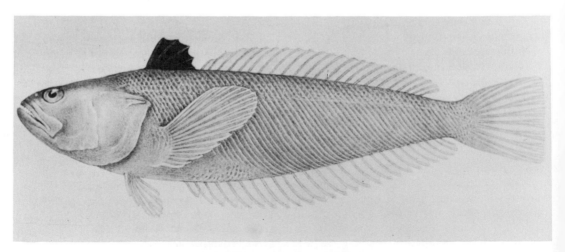

FIGURE 22 Lesser weeverfish.

a progression to erythema, ecchymosis, and warmth. Edema may progress for up to 10 days. Secondary infections are common, and gangrene has been reported. Total healing may take months, depending on the severity of the injury.

Systemic symptoms associated with weeverfish envenomations include headache, delirium, aphonia, fever, chills, dyspnea, diaphoresis, cyanosis, nausea, vomiting, seizures, syncope, hypotension, and cardiac arrhythmias.

Treatment

There are no specific antidotes. Treatment is similar to that of stingray envenomations, with the application of heat, presumably to help denature the protein venom and to reverse local vasospasm (28). Pain control is notoriously difficult, and if there are no contraindications, the liberal use of narcotics is often required.

Prevention

Weeverfish, similar to stingrays, hide themselves in bottom sand; thus, persons must shuffle along with adequate footwear. These fish are easily provoked and should be avoided by skin divers. They should *never* be handled alive and treated with extreme caution when dead, as the poison is well maintained, particularly in refrigerated fish (37). Weeverfish survive for hours out of the water, and careless handling of a seemingly dead fish may result in an envenomation.

SCORPIONFISH

Scorpionfish are members of the family Scorpaenidae and follow stingrays as perpetrators of piscine stings (Table 12). Distributed in tropical and less commonly in temperate oceans, several hundred species are divided into three groups on the basis of venom organ structure: (1) zebrafish (*Pterois*), (2) scorpionfish (*Scorpaena*), and (3) stonefish (*Synanceja*) (12). All have a bony plate, or stay, which extends across the cheek from the eye to the gill cover. Each group contains a number of different genera and species.

TABLE 12
Representative Scorpionfish Hazardous to Humans

Phylum Chordata
Class Osteichthyes
Order Perciformes
Suborder Cottoidei: scorpionfishes, sculpins, and so on
Family Scorpaenidae
　Pterois volitans: zebrafish, lionfish, tigerfish, turkeyfish, scorpionfish, firefish
　Scorpaena guttata: California scorpionfish, sculpin
　Synanceja horrida: stonefish, star-gazer, warty-ghoul

Life and Habits

Their concealment in bottom structures and protective coloration make them difficult to visualize. Some species bury themselves in the sand, and most dangerous types lie motionless in such concealment. In many regions, they are valuable as a food fish. In the United States, they are found in greatest concentration about the Florida Keys and the Gulf of Mexico, off the coast of southern California, and in Hawaii.

Zebrafish, or turkeyfish, are beautiful, graceful, and ornate coral reef fish which are generally found as single or paired free swimmers or hovering in shallow water (22). The venom organs consist of long, slender, delicate dorsal, pectoral, pelvic, and anal spines, with associated venom glands.

Scorpionfish proper (*Scorpaena*) dwell on the bottom, in shallow water, bays, and coral reefs, and along rocky coastlines to a depth of 50 fathoms. Their shape and coloration provide excellent camouflage, allowing them to blend in with the ambient debris, rocks, and seaweed (see Plate 3). They can be captured by hook and line, and serve as important food fish in many areas. Their venom organs include stout spines.

Stonefish live in shallow waters, often in tide pools and among reefs. They frequently poise motionless and absolutely fearless under rocks, in coral crevices or holes, or buried in the sand or mud. Their spines are very heavy and are covered with a thick, warty integumentary sheath. They are so sedentary that algae frequently take root on their skin.

When any of these fish are removed from the water, handled, stepped on, or otherwise threatened, they erect the spinous dorsal fin and flare out the armed gill covers and pectoral and anal fins. If provoked while still in the water, they will actually attack.

The venom is injected in a manner analagous to that of a stingray envenomation (33). The venom apparatus consists of 12 or 13 dorsal spines, 3 anal spines, and 2 pelvic spines. Scorpionfish venom contains multiple toxic fractions and, in the case of stonefish venom, has been likened in potency to cobra venom.

Clinical Aspects

Scorpionfish stings vary according to the species. It is the consensus that stings of the stonefish inflict the most serious envenomations. Pain is immediate and intense, with radiation centrally. In the case of the stonefish, the pain may be severe enough to cause delirium and, unfortunately, may persist at high levels for days. The wound and the surrounding area are initially ischemic and then cyanotic, with more broadly surrounding areas of erythema, edema, and warmth. Rapid tissue sloughing and close surrounding areas of cellulitis, with anesthesia adjacent to peripheral hypesthesia, are not uncommon. Systemic side effects include maculopapular skin rash, nausea, vomiting, diarrhea, diaphoresis, pallor, restlessness, delirium, seizures, limb paralysis, peripheral neuritis or neuropathy, lymphangitis, arthritis, fever, hypertension, respiratory distress, bradycardia, tachycardia, atrioventricular block, ventricular fibrillation, congestive heart failure, hypotension, and death (12,16,38). Delayed secondary infection with abscess formation and tetanus are possible complications. Healing may require up to 6 months (22).

Therapy

A stonefish antivenin is manufactured by the Commonwealth Serum Laboratories, Melbourne, Australia (16,38). It can also be used in the treatment of other scorpionfish stings. The antivenin is supplied in ampules containing 2 ml of hyperimmune horse serum, with 1 ml capable of neutralizing 10 mg of dried venom. After appropriate skin or conjunctival

tests to establish hypersensitivity to equine sera, it is administered as a 2 ml dose IM, or in severe cases IV, with a repeat dose as needed. Roughly one vial should be able to handle two significant stings. The frequency of resultant serum sickness has not been quantified in the literature.

The remainder of the treatment is the same as that for stingray envenomations, using vigorous irrigation and hot water. Local lidocaine (Xylocaine) anesthesia or nerve blocks are particularly appropriate with these injuries. It must be reiterated that to date, there are no data to support the topical administration of any empirical remedies, such as ground liver or formalin. Cryotherapy is absolutely contraindicated.

VENOMOUS (HORNED) SHARKS

Horned sharks are those species which possess dorsal fin spines. In the United States, this is essentially limited to the spiny dogfish (*Squalus acanthias*). These and other similar animals are distributed throughout subarctic, temperate, tropical, and subantarctic seas (Table 13).

The fish are sluggish, and prefer cooler water and shallow protected bays. They are erratic in their migration and may be found singly or in schools. Voracious feeders, they eat other fishes, coelenterates, mollusks, crustaceans, worms, and fishing gear.

The venom apparatus consists of two dorsal fin spines and the associated venom glands.

Clinical Aspects

As with other vertebrate stings, there is immediate, intense stabbing pain which may last

TABLE 13
Representative Venomous (Horned) Sharks Hazardous to Humans

Phylum Chordata
Class Chondrichthyes
Order Squaliformes: sharks
Family Heterodontidae
  Heterodontus francisci: hornshark
  Heterodontus portusjacksoni: Port Jackson shark
Family Squalidae
  Squalus acanthias: spiny dogfish
  Squalus fernandinus: spiny dogfish, spiky jack

---

for hours and is accompanied by erythema and edema. Although systemic side effects are rare, fatalities are possible.

Treatment

The treatment is the same as that for stingray envenomation. Generally, the severity of the injury is mild in comparison.

OTHER VENOMOUS FISH

Other venomous fishes include ratfish, dragonfish, toadfish, surgeonfish, rabbitfish, stargazers, carangids, scats, moray eels, squirrelfish, butterflyfish, tigerfish, sculpins, sea robins, flying gurnards, and goosefish, to name a few. Stings from this group pose no special problems and should be treated by the principles previously outlined.

SEA SNAKES

Life and Habits

Sea snakes are true reptiles; indeed, they are probably the most abundant reptiles in the world (18). There are at least 52 species, all of which possess a venom apparatus. At least six species have been implicated in human fatalities (Table 14).

The snakes are distributed in the tropical and warm temperate Pacific and Indian oceans, with the highest number of envenomations occurring along the coast of southeast Asia, in the Persian Gulf, and in the Malay Archipelago. No sea snakes live in the Atlantic Ocean or in the Caribbean Sea. Hawaii is the only state that has sea snakes (*Pelamis platu-*

rus) (33). The Pacific snakes usually inhabit sheltered coastal waters and congregate about river mouths, but occasionally migrate far out to sea (*Pelamis platurus* is pelagic).

Sea snakes have no limbs, ear openings, sternum, or urinary bladder. Most species of sea snakes are 3–4 feet long, but some attain lengths of up to 9 feet. They are sinuous scaled creatures whose bodies are compressed posteriorly into a flat, paddle-shaped tail designed for marine locomotion. They swim in an undulating fashion and, incredibly, can move backward or forward in the water with equal speed (Figure 23). On land, however, they are awkward and do not readily survive.

Sea snakes can remain submerged in the water for hours, using an air retention mechanism in the lung to control buoyancy. Their food, small fish swallowed whole, is captured underwater, usually around bottom rocks and coral.

In general, sea snakes are docile creatures and will flee when approached. However, when provoked, they become aggressive and strike out. During the reproductive season,

TABLE 14
Representative Sea Snakes Hazardous to Humans

Phylum Chordata
Class Reptilia
Order Squamata: snakes and lizards
Family Hydrophiidae
  Enhydrina schistosa: sea snake
  Hydrophis ornatus: spotted sea snake
  Lapemis hardwicki: sea snake
  Pelamis platurus: yellow-bellied sea snake
  Thalassophina viperina: sea snake

FIGURE 23 Sea snake (Coral Sea). (Photo courtesy of Carl Roessler.)

certain males will adopt more irritable attitudes.

Venom and Venom Apparatus

The well-developed venom apparatus consists of two to four hollow maxillary fangs and a pair of associated venom glands. Fortunately, because the fangs are short and easily dislodged from their sockets, many bites do not result in envenomation.

The protein venom is very toxic and includes neurotoxins more potent than those of terrestrial snakes (16). Neuromuscular transmission is thought to be blocked at the presynaptic membrane. Among other fractions of the venom are hemolytic and myotoxic compounds, which result in skeletal muscle necrosis, intravascular hemolysis, and renal tubular damage.

Clinical Aspects

Bites are usually the result of accidental handling of snakes snared in the nets of fishermen, or of wading and accidentally stepping on a snake. Thus, nearly all bites involve the extremities.

The diagnosis of snake bite is based on the following:

1. Location. One must have been in the water with a sea snake to have been bitten.
2. Absence of pain. Initially, sea snake bites do not cause great pain.
3. Fang marks. These are characterized by multiple pinhead-sized hypodermic-like puncture wounds, usually one to four, but potentially up to 20. Fang marks may be difficult to detect because of the lack of a localized reaction.
4. Identification of the snake. Snakes should be carefully killed with a blow to the head and retained for identification.
5. Development of characteristic symptoms. These include painful muscle movement, lower extremity paralysis, trismus, and ptosis. If symptoms do not develop within 6–8 hours, there has been no sea snake envenomation.

In greater detail, envenomation by sea snakes characteristically shows an evolution of symptoms over a period of hours, with the latent period being a function of venom volume and patient sensitivity. The onset of symptoms can be as rapid as 5 minutes or as long as 8 hours (38). There is no appreciable local reaction to a sea snake bite other than the initial pricking sensation. The first complaint may be one of euphoria, malaise, or anxiety. Gradually, classic muscle aching and stiffness develop, along with a "thick tongue." An ascending flaccid or spastic paralysis follows shortly, beginning in the lower extremities; speech and swallowing are impaired, and deep tendon reflexes diminish and may disappear after an initial period of spastic hyperactivity. Nausea, vomiting, and the pulmonary aspiration of gastric contents are frequent. Diffuse muscle twitching, myoclonus, and spasm develop, along with ptosis, facial paralysis, and trismus. Occasionally, a bilateral painless swelling of the parotid glands will develop.

Severe envenomations are marked by progressively intense symptoms. Patients become cool and cyanotic, begin to lose vision, and lapse into coma. Failing vision is reported to be a preterminal symptom. Pathognomonic myoglobinuria becomes evident about 3–6 hours after the bite and may be accompanied by albuminuria and hemoglobinuria. Cerebrospinal fluid is normal. Respiratory distress and bulbar paralysis, aspiration-related hypoxia, electrolyte disturbances, and acute renal failure all contribute to the ultimate demise, which can occur hours to days after the untreated bite occurs. The mortality is 25% in patients who do not receive antivenin and 3% overall (22).

Treatment

The therapy is identical to that for terrestrial snakebite. Since venom is absorbed rapidly, incision and suction are of value, and at that with considerable controversy, only in the first 5 minutes. This is performed by making incisions 0.5 cm long by 0.125 cm deep in parallel directly through the deepest two or three puncture wounds. Criss-cross incisions are of no value. It is preferable to use a suction cup provided in a snakebite kit rather than one's mouth.

The affected limb should be immobilized and maintained in a dependent position. The patient must be kept as still as possible. If transport to an appropriate facility is delayed for more than 30 minutes, a loose tourniquet which constricts only the superficial venous and lymphatic flow may be applied. This is released for 90 seconds every 10 minutes and should be completely removed after 4 hours. If the bite is older than 30 minutes, a tourniquet is of questionable value. Ice should not be applied to the wound.

In transport, the patient should be kept warm and calm. If possible, the offending snake should be collected for identification, taking care not to increase the number of victims.

One should be able to tell if envenomation has occurred within 2 hours of the purported sea snake bite, with the onset of early clinical symptoms. If there is no early evidence of envenomation, the victim must be observed for at least 8 hours prior to release.

With any evidence of envenomation, polyvalent sea snake antivenin (Commonwealth Serum Laboratories, Melbourne, Australia) prepared from the venom of *Enhydrina schistosa* or polyvalent elapidae antivenin should be administered, after appropriate skin or conjunctival testing for serum sensitivity. Sensitivity testing to equine hyperimmune globulin and the control of hypersensitivity reactions are well described in Chapter 12. It should be reemphasized that antivenin is both specific and absolutely indicated in cases of envenomation; supportive measures, while critical in management, are no substitute. The administration of antivenin should begin as soon as possible, and is most effective if initiated within 8 hours. The minimum effective adult dosage is one ampule, which neutralizes 10 mg of *E. schistosa* venom. The proper administration of antivenin is described in Chapter 12 in the discussion of terrestrial envenomations and is clearly described on the antivenin package insert.

Prevention

Sea snakes may attack when provoked, but most species tend to be docile. Every attempt should be made to avoid encounters while in infested waters. Handle sea snakes with discretion. Large numbers may be taken in fishing nets; the utmost caution must be exercised in their disposal.

Poisonous on Ingestion

A third form of biologic marine hazard is offered by marine animals that are poisonous to eat. The creatures involved include dinoflagellates, coelenterates, mollusks, echinoderms, crustaceans, fishes, turtles, and some mammals. In this section, the major intoxications and health dangers will be considered.

It is clear that population growth will necessitate the development of marine fisheries as food resources for the production of harvestable protein, including fish, invertebrates, and plants (3). As these endeavors involve tropical waters, marine biotoxins will become an increasing concern to the health care community.

Ingestible toxins may be classified by specific toxin or by the donor organ of origin, that is, that which is ingested by the victim. *Ichthyosarcotoxin* is a general term that refers to poison derived from the fresh flesh (i.e., muscle, viscera, skin, or slime) of any fish (3,30). This can be further broken down by specific organ system.

ICHTHYOCRINOTOXICATION

Ichthyocrinotoxic fish poisoning is induced by glandular secretions not associated with a specific venom apparatus and usually involves skin secretions, poisonous foams, or slimes. Examples are certain filefish, pufferfish, porcupine fish, trunkfish, boxfish, cowfish, lampreys, moray eels, and toadfish (Table 15, Figure 24).

Clinical Aspects, Treatment, and Prevention

Gastrointestinal distress, which is evident within a few hours, is characterized by nausea, vomiting, dysenteric diarrhea, tenesmus, abdominal pain, and weakness. Toxic slimes can induce a contact irritant dermatitis. Recovery is evident in 1–3 days. Cyclostome poisoning, which involves lampreys and hagfish, is of the ichthyocrinotoxic category.

Therapy is symptomatic and supportive. All suspicious fish should be washed carefully with water or brine solution and skinned before they are eaten. Puffer skin is extremely

TABLE 15
Representative Ichthyocrinotoxic Fish Hazardous to Humans

Phylum Chordata
Class Agnatha
Order Myxiniformes: hagfishes, lampreys
Family Myxinidae
　Myxine glutinosa: Atlantic hagfish
　Petromyzon marinus: sea lamprey, large nine-eyes

Class Osteichthyes
Order Anguilliformes: eels
Family Muraenidae
　Muraena helena: moray eel

Order Perciformes: perchlike fishes
Family Serranidae
　Grammistes sexlineatus: golden striped bass
　Rypticus saponaceus: soapfish

Order Tetraodontiformes: triggerfishes, puffers, trunk-
　fishes, and so on
Family Canthigasteridae
　Canthigaster jactator: sharp-nosed puffer
Family Diodontidae
　Diodon hystrix: porcupinefish
Family Ostraciontidae
　Lactoria diaphana: trunkfish
　Lactoria fornasini: trunkfish, boxfish
Family Tetraodontidae
　Arothron hispidus: puffer, toadfish, blowfish, rabbit-
　fish
　Fugu xanthopterus: puffer

Order Batrachoidiformes: toadfishes
Family Batrachoididae
　Opsanus tau: oyster toadfish
　Thalassophryne maculosa: toadfish

FIGURE 24 Trunkfish. (Photo courtesy of Carl Roessler.)

toxic. Care must be taken to avoid toxin contact with the eye.

ICHTHYOHEMOTOXICATION

Ichthyohemotoxic fish are possessed of "poisonous blood," the toxicity of which is usually inactivated by heat and gastric juice. Examples are various eels, such as morays, anguilliformes, and congers. Symptoms are predominantly gastrointestinal and should be treated symptomatically. Hematologic complications are rare.

ICHTHYOHEPATOTOXICATION

Ichthyohepatotoxic fish house their toxin predominantly in the liver. The remainder of the fish may be nontoxic. Some authors believe that the toxicity may be partially due to hypervitaminosis A, with seasonal variation. Fish that are always toxic fall into two basic groups: Japanese perchlike fish (i.e., mackerel, sea bass, porgy, and sandfish) and tropical sharks (i.e., requiem, sleeper, cow, great white, cat, hammerhead, angel, greenland, and dogfish) (30). Additionally, some skates and rays harbor ichthyohepatotoxins.

Clinical Aspects, Treatment, and Prevention

Ingestion of the Japanese perchlike fish group causes an onset of symptoms in 1–7 hours. These include nausea, vomiting, headache, flushing, rash, fever, and tachycardia. No fatalities have been reported. Delayed necrodermolysis is rare.

Ingestion of the tropical shark liver and occasionally of the musculature results in elasmobranch poisoning (Table 16) (3). Symptoms are noted within 30 minutes and include nausea, vomiting, diarrhea, abdominal pain, malaise, diaphoresis, headache, stomatitis, esophagitis, muscular cramps, arthralgias, paresthesias, hiccoughs, trismus, hyporeflexia, ataxia, incontinence, blurred vision, blepharospasm, delirium, respiratory distress, coma, and death. Usually, if only the flesh is eaten, the symptoms are mildly gastroenteritic and resolve spontaneously. It is unlikely that the intoxication induced by ingesting shark liver is purely that of hypervitaminosis A.

Therapy is symptomatic and supportive.

TABLE 16
Representative Poisonous Sharks (Elasmobranchs) Hazardous to Humans

Phylum Chordata
Class Chondrichthyes
Order Squaliformes: sharks
Family Carcharhinidae
   Carcharhinus melanopterus: black-tip reef shark
   Carcharhinus menisorrah: gray reef shark
   Galeocerdo cuvieri: tiger shark
   Prionace glauca: great blue shark
Family Dalatiidae
   Somniosus microcephalus: Greenland shark, sleeper shark, nurse shark
Family Hedanchidae
   Hexanchus griseus: cow shark, gray shark, mud shark
Family Isuridae
   Carcharodon carcharias: white shark
Family Scyliorhinidae
   Scyliorhinus caniculus: dogfish, lesser-spotted cat shark
Family Sphyrnidae
   Sphyrna diplana: hammerhead
Family Squatinidae
   Squatina dumeril: monk-fish, angel shark
Family Triakidae
   Triaenodon obesus: white tip, houndshark

Fish liver should not be eaten; indeed, nor should any shark viscera. Drying the flesh properly may minimize the toxicity.

ICHTHYOOTOXICATION

Ichthyootoxic fish carry ingestible toxin in their gonads and may vary in toxicity with the reproductive cycle. The musculature is generally nontoxic. Examples are the sturgeon, alligator gar, salmon, pike, minnow, carp, catfish, killifish, perch, and sculpin. Sea urchins and coelenterates may be toxic during the reproductive period; they have been used for criminal purposes in the South Pacific (3).

Clinical Aspects, Treatment, and Prevention

Symptoms generally begin within an hour of ingestion and include nausea, vomiting, diarrhea, headache, dizziness, fever, thirst, xerostomia, bitter taste, tachycardia, seizures, migraine, paralysis, hypotension, and death. Treatment is symptomatic and supportive.

The roe of any fish should not be eaten during the reproductive season. Heat will not inactivate the toxin.

ICHTHYOALLYEINOTOXICATION

Ichthyoallyeinotoxic fish induce hallucinogenic poisoning. They are predominantly fish of the tropical Pacific and Indian reefs, which carry toxins mainly in their head parts, brain, and spinal cord, and in lesser amounts in their bodies. Typical species include surgeonfish, chup, mullet, unicornfish, goatfish, sergeant major, grouper, rabbitfish, rock cod, drumfish, rudderfish, and damselfish.

Clinical Aspects, Treatment, and Prevention

Symptoms can develop within 5–90 minutes of ingestion, and include dizziness, circumoral paresthesias, diaphoresis, weakness, incoordination, auditory and visual hallucinations, nightmares, depression, dyspnea, bronchospasm, brief paralysis, and pharyngitis (3, 23,38).

Therapy is symptomatic and supportive, and may include the administration of antipsychotic medications. One should not eat the heads, brain, or spinal cord of any tropical fish. Heat will not inactivate the toxin.

CIGUATOXICATION (CIGUATERA FISH POISONING)

Ciguatoxin derives its name from the word early Spanish settlers used to call poisoning from ingestion of a Caribbean marine snail (*cigua*) (23). It involves almost exclusively tropical and semitropical marine reef fish and probably is a direct function of the food chain, as initiated by the toxic dinoflagellate *Gambierdiscus toxicus.* Ciguatoxic fish feed on certain plants or bottom fish, implicating specific species of algae (30). No plankton feeders have been reported as ciguatoxic.

As mentioned, the food chain originates in certain sessile algae or microbial heterotrophs (*G. toxicus,* which elaborates ciguatoxin and maitotoxin), which are consumed by herbivorous fishes, which in turn are ingested by carnivorous fishes. It has been suggested that the proliferation of toxic algae may be triggered by contamination of the water by industrial wastes, metallic compounds, ship wreckage, or other pollutants (17). As the feeding progression develops, the toxin appears to accumulate in the fish, rendering larger (greater than 6 pounds) and elderly fish more toxic (16,30).

More than 400 species of benthic fish have been implicated, with the greatest concentration in the Caribbean Ocean, the Indo-Pacific islands, and along the continental tropical reefs. More than 75% of reported cases (except in Hawaii) involve the barracuda, snapper, jack, or grouper. Hawaiian carriers include the parrot-beaked bottom feeders, particularly those that inhabit areas of high dinoflagellate population, such as disturbed coral reef waters. The remaining culprits are listed in Table 17.

Ciguatera fish poisoning is associated with more than five toxins, including a fat-soluble quaternary ammonium compound (ciguatoxin) and a water-soluble component (maitotoxin) with anticholinesterase and cholinomimetic activity. (This is the subject of some controversy.) One mode of action may be the false occupation by the toxin of calcium receptor sites that modulate the sodium pore permeability in neural and myocardial membranes

(38). This allows increased permeability to sodium, and causes sustained depolarization. All toxins identified to date are heat, cold, and gastric acid stable, and do not affect the odor, color, or taste of the fish.

Clinical Aspects

The onset of symptoms is generally within 15–30 minutes of ingestion, with an increase in severity over the ensuing 4–6 hours (3,23). Rarely, the onset of symptoms may be delayed for up to 24 hours. Symptoms include abdominal pain, nausea, vomiting, diarrhea, paresthesias, pruritus, tongue and throat numbness, odontalgia, dysphagia, tremor, fasciculation, athetosis, meningismus, aphonia, ataxia, visual blurring, hyporeflexia, tremor, seizures, coma, conjunctivitis, maculopapular rash, bullae, sialorrhea, arthralgias, myalgias, weakness, and central respiratory failure, with an overall death rate of 0.1–12.0%. A pathognomonic symptom is the reversal of hot and cold perception, which may last for months (22).

It appears that the toxin can accumulate in humans as well as in fish, so that prior illness places a person at greater risk for a severe reaction upon consumption of fish. Immune sensitization may play a role. Consumption of alcoholic beverages may also produce an exacerbation, by an unknown mechanism.

Treatment

Therapy is symptomatic and supportive. Gastric emptying and the administration of activated charcoal (100 grams) may be of limited value if instituted within the first 5 hours after ingestion. It has been suggested that the administration of magnesium-based cathartics may augment a calcium-channel blockade. Some investigators recommend the administration of calcium gluconate (1–3 grams intravenously over 24 hours) for the management of hypotension, although clinical hypocalcemia is not a diagnostic standard. Bradyarrhythmias and cardiac insufficiency are managed with atropine, monitored volume resuscitation, and dopamine or dobutamine. Other drugs that have been advocated include edrophonium, neostigmine, corticosteroids, pralidoxime, ascorbic acid, and vitamin B complex. These do not have scientific support.

TABLE 17
Representative Ciguatoxic Fish Hazardous to Humans

Barracuda	Halfbeak	Scorpionfish
Batfish	Hawkfish	Seabass
Bigeye	Hogfish	Seahorse
Bonefish	Jack	Sea trout
Bonito	Ladyfish	Silverfish
Butterflyfish	Lizardfish	Snake eel
Cardinalfish	Mackerel	Snapper
Combtooth blenny	Milkfish	Soldierfish
Cowfish	Mojarra	Squirrelfish
Conger eel	Moonfish	Surgeonfish
Croaker	Moray eel	Sweeper
Damselfish	Mullet	Tang
Drumfish	Needlefish	Tarpon
Flounder	Parrotfish	Toadfish
Flyingfish	Pipefish	Triggerfish
Frogfish	Pompano	Trumpetfish
Garfish	Porgy	Trunkfish
Boatfish	Rabbitfish	Wahoo
Goosefish	Rudderfish	Wrasse
Grouper	Sailfish	and *many* others
Grunt	Scat	

Because of the accumulation of toxin, all oversized fish of any likely predacious reef species, i.e., jack, snapper, barracuda, grouper, or parrot-beaked bottom feeder, should be suspected. Never eat the viscera of any tropical marine fish. Moray eels should never be eaten. If possible, a small portion of the fish in question should be fed to a sacrificial small animal, which is then observed for 12 hours. Ordinary cooking procedures afford no protection. A ciguatoxin radioimmunoassay is now available, and can be used to test small portions of the suspected fish. The RIA does not identify a clinical syndrome in humans; the diagnosis of ciguatera poisoning is made on clinical grounds.

CLUPEOTOXICATION

Clupeotoxic fish poisoning, as opposed to ciguatera fish poisoning, involves plankton-feeding fish, which ingest planktonic blue-green algae and surface dinoflagellates rather than benthic organisms. These fish are also found in tropical Caribbean, Indo-Pacific, and African coastal waters. Examples are herring, sardines, anchovies, ladyfish, bonefish, and slickhead (3,30). Toxicity is reported to increase during the warm summer months.

Clinical Aspects

Clupeotoxic poisoning is rapid and violent, with nearly immediate onset of symptoms and a mortality of up to 45%. Initial signs are a marked metallic taste, xerostomia, nausea, vomiting, diarrhea, and abdominal pain. These are followed shortly by chills, headache, severe paresthesias, muscle cramps, vertigo, hypertension, seizures, paralysis, coma, hypotension, and death, often within 15 minutes.

Treatment

Therapy is supportive and based on symptoms. Aggressive management and early intensive care are mandatory.

Prevention

Like ciguatera fish poisoning, clupeotoxic food poisoning should be suspected, especially during summer months, in fish indigenous to the Caribbean, African coastal, or Indo-Pacific waters. The viscera of suspicious fish should be fed to experimental animals. It is again noteworthy that the toxin is heat stable.

GEMPYLOTOXICATION

Gempylotoxic fishes are the pelagic mackerels, which produce an oil with a pronounced purgative effect. The "toxin" is contained in both the musculature and the bones. The syndrome is one of diarrhea unassociated with abdominal pain. No specific therapy is recommended.

TETRODOTOXICATION

Tetrodotoxin is one of the most potent nonprotein poisons found in nature and is characteristic of the order Tetraodontiformes, which includes pufferfish (toadfish, blowfish, globefish, swellfish, balloonfish, toado), porcupine fish, and sunfish. These are tropical and subtropical fish, some of which ("fugu") are prepared as delicacies in Japan by specially licensed and trained chefs (3,22). Pufferfish are distinguished by the ability to inflate their bodies to a nearly spherical shape using air or sea water (Table 15).

The ichthyosarcotoxin is distributed throughout the entire fish, with the greatest concentrations in the liver, gonads, intestine, and skin. There is some variability in toxicity with reproductive or feeding cycles and among species.

Tetrodotoxin has been fully characterized and synthesized, and is believed to be chemically identical to toxins isolated from certain North American newts and the Australian blue-ringed octopus (3,38). Structurally, it is aminoperhydroquinazolone ($C_{11}H_{17}N_3O_3$), a water-soluble and heat-stable compound (30,42). The poison interferes with central and peripheral neuromuscular transmission by altering sodium conductance. Although it is not a depolarizing agent, in animals it causes depression of the medullary respiratory mechanism, intracardiac conduction, myocardial contraction, and skeletal muscle contractility (16).

Clinical Aspects

The onset of symptoms can be as rapid as 10 minutes or can be delayed for up to 4 hours.

Initially, patients develop oral paresthesias, with rapid progression to light-headedness and generalized paresthesias. The following symptoms develop with moderate rapidity: hypersalivation, diaphoresis, headache, nausea, vomiting, diarrhea, abdominal pain, weakness, ataxia, tremor, paralysis, cyanosis, aphonia, dysphagia, seizures, dyspnea, bronchorrhea, bronchospasm, respiratory failure, coma, and hypotension. Early miosis may progress to mydriasis with poor pupillary light reflex. A disseminated intravascular coagulation-like syndrome presents with petechial skin hemorrhages, which may progress to bullous desquamation, along with hematemesis and diffuse stigmata of prolonged coagulation. Sixty percent of victims will die, most of these within the first 6 hours. Survival past 24 hours is a good prognostic sign.

Treatment

Early treatment is directed at eliminating the gastric acid-stable toxin, which is partially inactivated in alkaline solutions. If the patient is received at an emergency facility within an hour or two of ingestion, induced emesis or gastric lavage (using 2% sodium bicarbonate) is indicated, followed by intragastric placement of activated charcoal. Further therapy is supportive and usually involves advanced cardiac and respiratory life support. There is no specific antidote.

Prevention

Although the toxin is water soluble, it is very difficult to remove from the fish, even by cooking. It is wisest to avoid all puffers, even when prepared by an expert.

PARALYTIC SHELLFISH POISONING

Paralytic shellfish poisoning is induced by ingesting any of a variety of filter-feeding organisms. These include familiar mollusks (clams, oysters, mussels), chitons, limpets, murex, starfish, and sandcrabs (22). The origin of their toxicity is the biologic chemical toxin they accumulate and concentrate by feeding upon various planktonic dinoflagellates and protozoan organisms (17).

The unicellular phytoplankton are the foundation of the food chain, and in warm summer months are noted to "bloom" rapidly in nutrient-rich coastal temperate and semitropical waters (23,30). These free-living aquatic microorganisms belong to the phylum Protozoa. Marine protozoa poisonous to humans are largely of the class Mastigophora, order Dinoflagellata. They rank second in abundance to diatoms and are extremely important producers of marine carbohydrates, fats, and proteins.

If a single organism predominates, it can discolor the water, creating a black, blue, pink, red, yellow, brown, or luminescent "tide." These plankton can release massive amounts of toxic metabolites into the water and, with great rapidity, cause enormous mortality in various bird and marine populations. Indeed, large numbers of dead animals on the beach suggest a colored tide. Kills by the dinoflagellate *Gymnodinium* (now *Ptychodiscus*) *breve* are estimated at 100 tons of fish per day (16). To date, the magnitude of destruction has prompted at least two international congresses.

Many genera of microorganisms have been implicated in toxic syndromes. Paralytic shellfish poisoning can be linked to the dinoflagellate *Gonyaulaux,* species *catenella* (U.S. Pacific coast) and *tamarensis excavata* (U.S. Atlantic coast) (2,16,22). These creatures are relatively fastidious and prefer warm, sunlit water of low salinity in which to bloom. They release a number of toxic metabolites, including saxitoxin, into the water, where they are filtered through resident bivalves, which are subsequently ingested by humans (39). In mollusks, the greatest concentration of toxin is found in the digestive organs, gills, and siphon.

Saxitoxin ($C_{10}H_{17}N_7O_4$) takes its name from *Saxidomus giganteus,* the Alaskan butter clam (23). *S. giganteus* and the Washington clam (*S. nutalli*) may carry the toxin in their neck parts for periods of up to one year; however, there is no physical characteristic which distinguishes the carrier animal. A toxin concentration of greater than 75–80 micrograms/100 grams foodstuff is considered hazardous to humans. Unfortunately, a direct assay is not as yet readily available to the clinician. The toxin is a water-soluble, heat-stable compound that is stable in an acid environment; like tetrodotoxin, it can be destroyed in an alkaline medium, but not by ordinary cooking. The toxin appears to block sodium conductance, inhibiting neuromuscular transmission at the axonal and muscle membrane levels. It suppresses atrioventricular nodal conduction, depresses the medullary respiratory center, and progressively reduces peripheral nerve excitability.

Clinical Aspects

Three types of illnesses can be related to the ingestion of shellfish: allergic or erythematous, bacterial choleratic or viral gastroenteritic, and paralytic. In this discussion, we shall address only the last.

Within minutes of ingestion of contaminated shellfish, there is the onset of intraoral and perioral paresthesias, notably of the tongue and gums. These progress rapidly to involve the neck and distal extremities. The following symptoms soon follow: light-headedness, incoordination, weakness, hyperreflexia, incoherence, salivation, dysphagia, thirst, diarrhea, abdominal pain, headache, diaphoresis, loss of vision, a sensation of loose teeth, chest pain, and tachycardia. Mental status is not altered, and a patient may develop flaccid paralysis and respiratory failure while still awake. From 10 to 25% of victims expire in respiratory arrest within the first 12 hours.

As mentioned previously, *Ptychodiscus breve* is a toxic dinoflagellate that can "bloom" and create a colorful tide. Ingestion of shellfish contaminated with *P. breve* can induce a milder version of paralytic shellfish poisoning, known as "neurotoxic shellfish poisoning," with a delayed onset of up to 3 hours. The condition resembles ciguatera toxin poisoning in symptomatology. Thus, calcium infusions may be of value in the rare severe case. Confirmation of this will require clinical investigation.

A curious phenomenon occurs when large blooms of *P. breve* occur near the shore. If sea breezes blow the aerosolized toxin onshore, then rapidly reversible rhinorrhea and respiratory distress can be expected to occur in local inhabitants. A certain sophistication is required to consider this diagnosis.

Treatment

Treatment is symptomatic and supportive. Some authors suggest the use of neostigmine to counteract the curarelike effects. There are no good data to support or refute this proposal. If the victim is received within the first few hours after ingestion, the stomach should be emptied and lavaged with 2% sodium bicarbonate. The use of activated charcoal and catharsis makes empirical sense but is not documented in the literature. There is no reason not to follow recommended guidelines for the management of poison overdose. Some authors advise against the administration of magnesium-containing solutions, such as cathartics, on the rationale that hypermagnasemia can contribute to nerve conduction suppression. Calcium supplementation is as yet experimental. Alcohol ingestion appears to increase toxicity (2).

Prevention

Although leeching of shellfish in fresh water for several weeks, followed by vigorous cooking, may remove up to 70% of the toxin, such procedures are recommended only for persons stranded on desert islands. To the old axiom "Don't eat shellfish in the Northern Hemisphere in months that contain the letter *r*" should be added "However, it doesn't matter how you spell the month if the shellfish have been dining on *Gonyaulaux*." Outbreaks of shellfish poisoning have been reported in North America, Europe, Africa, Asia, and the Pacific islands, the last linked to certain Pacific crabs and lobster (3).

OTHER SHELLFISH POISONING

CALLISTIN SHELLFISH POISONING

The Japanese *Callista* clam (*C. brevisiphonata*) is toxic during the spawning months of May to September, at which time there are increased cholinergic compounds in the ovaries. The intoxication resembles cholinergic crisis, with both muscarinic and nicotinic components. Within an hour of ingestion of the heat-stable toxin, the victim presents with generalized pruritus, urticaria, erythema, facial numbness and paralysis, hypersalivation, diaphoresis, fever, chills, nausea, vomiting, diarrhea, and constrictive dyspnea. Therapy is supportive, and recovery is usually complete within 2 days.

VENERUPIN SHELLFISH POISONING

The Japanese lake-harvested oyster (*Crassostrea gigas*) and clam (*Tapes semidecussata*) occasionally feed on toxic dinoflagellate species of the genus *Prorocentrum* and pose the greatest risk during the months of December through April (3,16). The heat-stable toxin induces the rapid onset of gastrointestinal distress, headache, and nervousness, which evolve over 48 hours to hepatic dysfunction, as manifested by the elevation of liver enzymes, leukocytosis, jaundice, and profound coagulation defects. Delirium and coma may ensue, with death occurring in 33% of victims. Therapy is symptomatic and supportive.

TRIDACNA CLAM POISONING

These giant clams are found in French Polynesia and contain a poorly characterized toxin in the mantle and viscera that induces paresthesias, gastrointestinal hyperactivity, tremor, ataxia, and incoordination. Therapy is supportive, and recovery is usually complete.

POISONING BY DECOMPOSITION: SCOMBROID POISONING

Fish of the family Scombridae include the bluefin and yellowfin tuna, mackerel, sauries, wahoo, skipjack, and bonito (Table 18). Non-scombroid fish which produce scombroid poisoning include mahi-mahi, sardines, anchovies, and the Australian ocean salmon. These dark-fleshed or red-muscled fish are subject, by delayed refrigeration, or improper preservation, to bacterial decomposition of the fish muscle (2,16,30). The bacteria *Proteus morganii, Klebsiella pneumoniae, Aerobacter aerogenes,* and others have been implicated in the putrefaction, which breaks down histidine to histamine and saurine (histamine PO_4 and histamine HCl) (22,38). Histamine levels of greater than 20–50/100 gm are noted in the toxic fish. Affected fish typically have a sharply metallic or peppery taste; however, they may be normal in appearance, color, and flavor.

Symptoms occur within minutes of inges-

TABLE 18
Representative Scombridae Hazardous to Humans

Phylum Chordata
Class Osteichthyes
Order Belonidormes: needlefishes, sauries, and so on
Family Scomberesocidae
　Cololabis saira: saury
Order Perciformes
Suborder Scombroidei: tuna and related species
Family Scombridae
　Euthynnus pelamis: skipjack tuna
　Sarda sarda: Atlantic bonito
　Scomber japonicus: Pacific mackerel
　Scomber scombrus: Atlantic mackerel
　Scomberomorus cavalla: kingfish
　Scomberomorus maculatus: Spanish mackerel
　Thunnus alalunga: albacore
　Thunnus albacares: yellowfin tuna, ahi
　Thunnus thynnus: bluefin tuna, aku

tion and are mediated by histamine and its analogs. These include flushing, pruritus, urticaria, angioneurotic edema, bronchospasm, nausea, vomiting, diarrhea, epigastric pain, dysphagia, headache, thirst, pharyngitis, palpitations, and hypotension. This syndrome may mimic that of monosodium glutamate (MSG) sensitivity. Death is unusual.

Therapy is directed at reversing the histamine effect and is essentially the medical response to anaphylaxis. Minor intoxications can be treated with intravenous diphenhydramine or hydroxyzine, supported as necessary with epinephrine, bronchodilators, steroids, and pressor agents. Persons on isoniazid (isonicotinic acid hydrozide, INH) have severe reactions due to INH blockade of gastrointestinal tract histaminase. If large quantities of the tainted fish have been consumed within an hour of the patient presentation to an emergency facility, it may be of value to empty the stomach, and then to administer activated charcoal with a cathartic. It has been observed recently that the histamine antagonist cimetidine (300 mg IV) may be rapidly efficacious in alleviating symptoms in patients who do not respond to diphenhydramine (5a).

Scombroid poisoning, ptomaine (*Staphylococcus, Streptococcus*) poisoning, enterotoxic poisoning, and botulism can all be avoided with the proper refrigeration, preservation, and preparation of fish. No fish should be consumed if it has been handled improperly.

VIBRIO PARAHEMOLYTICUS

Vibrio parahemolyticus is a halophilic gram negative rod to which is attributed a gastroenteritic syndrome that has been reported in the United States, Japan, Great Britain, and Australia. Ingestion of contaminated shrimp, oysters, or fish is followed in 12–24 hours by explosive diarrhea, nausea, vomiting, abdominal pain, fever, and prostration. The stools may contain blood and classically demonstrate leukocytes on methylene blue staining. The syndrome generally resolves spontaneously in 24–48 hours, but may be of a severity sufficient to cause significant fluid and electrolyte depletion. Stool cultures should be obtained prior to the initiation of antibiotic therapy. The laboratory should be alerted to the necessity for special culture media (TCBS with 0.5% NaCl). A course of oral tetracycline may shorten the course of severe gastroenteritis.

VIBRIO VULNIFICUS

Vibrio vulnificus is a halophilic gram negative bacillus to which is attributed a syndrome of septicemia that occurs following a period of 7–10 days after the ingestion of raw oysters. The classic syndrome evolves rapidly after the initiation of symptoms, and has been noted most frequently in victims with preexisting hepatic dysfunction or leukopenia, although it has been reported in young, previously healthy individuals. It consists of fever, chills, hypotension, and early skin vesiculation which evolves into necrotizing dermatitis, with vasculitis and myositis. Gastroenteritis is unusual.

The explosive nature of the syndrome can lead to sepsis and death. Appropriate antibiotics include ampicillin, tetracycline, carbenicillin, chloramphenicol, tobramycin, and gentamicin. The laboratory must be cautioned to use culture media with a high salt content (3% NaCl) for proper identification. Suggestive features include positive fermentation of glucose, oxidase test, positive reaction for both lysine and ornithine decarboxylase, hydrolysis of orthonitrophenylgalactoside, and inability to ferment sucrose (20a).

FISH TAPEWORM

In the United States, there is increasing popularity in the consumption of raw fish ("sushi"), which has led to more frequent recognition of infestation with the fish tapeworm, *Diphyllobothrium latum*. Classic symptoms include subacute abdominal pain, nausea, vomiting, diarrhea, and weight loss. Chronic *D. latum* infestation may induce megaloblastic anemia. The diagnosis can be made by examination of the stool for typical operculate egg forms, which measure 60–75 microns in length. Proper identification of the eggs is important in the differentiation from the ova of trematodes endemic in southeast Asia, which may be carried by refugees to the United States. For documented *D. latum* infestation, treatment is initiated with niclosamide, which is provided by the Centers for Disease Control, Parasitic Disease Drug Service, Atlanta, Georgia.

AMEBIC MENINGOENCEPHALITIS

Amebae of the genera *Naegleria* and *Acanthamoeba* are freeliving, freshwater organisms found in warm coastal waters of the United States (42a). They have been implicated as the perpetrators of primary amebic meningoencephalitis, with a predilection for infectious involvement of the frontal areas of the brain and olfactory bulb neuroepithelium (35a). Victims likely to acquire the organism include those with upper respiratory tract infections or with immunosuppression; however, the majority of reported *Naegleria* infections have been in healthy people (25).

The diagnosis is made by cerebrospinal fluid (CSF) culture and observation of motile organisms in fresh CSF. Therapy must be aggressive and requires the administration of amphotericin-B and miconazole, intravenously and intrathecally (35a). Delay or lack of treatment culminates in death within 5–8 days.

POISONING BY ENVIRONMENTAL CONTAMINATION

In the process of concentrating fish proteins as a food source, a variety of protein-bound, non-water–soluble, or non-alcohol–soluble toxic compounds may be passed on (17). These include organic mercurials, hydrocarbons, and some heavy metals (antimony, arsenic, cadmium, chromium, cobalt, lead, phosphorus, mercury, nickel, and zinc). Toxic chemical spills and petroleum by-products will certainly continue to expand the list of potential carcinogens to which humans are becoming exposed through the marine environment. Divers are exposed to a variety of environmental contaminants while exploring polluted waters. These hazards include solvents, nuclear wastes, herbicides, chemical effluents, and sewage.

CHELONINTOXICATION

A variety of tropical Pacific, particularly Japanese, marine turtles are toxic upon ingestion (Table 19). These include the green, leatherback, hawksbill, loggerhead, and softshell. All portions of the turtle are toxic; freshness of the meat is irrelevant. Symptoms develop in 1–48 hours of ingestion and include ulcerative stomatitis, pharyngitis, salivation, nausea, vomiting, diarrhea, abdominal pain, vertigo, icterus, desquamative dermatitis, hepatosplenomegaly, hepatic necrosis with fatty degeneration, renal failure, somnolence, and hypotension. There is a 28–44% mortality. Therapy is symptomatic and supportive. Prevention is afforded by feeding potential turtle dinners to sacrificial small animals, which are observed for 24–48 hours.

TABLE 19
Representative Marine Turtles Hazardous to Humans

Phylum Chordata
Class Reptilia
Order Chelonia: turtles
Family Cheloniidae
  Caretta caretta gigas: Pacific loggerhead turtle
  Chelonia mydas: green turtle
  Eretmochelys imbricata: hawksbill turtle
Family Dermochelidae
  Dermochelys coriacea: leathery turtle
Family Thionychidae
  Pelochelys bibroni: soft-shell turtle

POLAR BEAR LIVER POISONING

The ingestion of polar bear (*Thalarctos maritimus*) liver causes a syndrome related to hypervitaminosis A. This also occurs with the ingestion of the livers of certain seals, seal lions, whales, dolphins, walruses, husky dogs, and Pacific sharks. A typical ingestion involves the administration of more than 3–8 million IU of vitamin A and results in the following symptoms: formication, headache, apathy, drowsiness, giddiness, irritability, photophobia, nausea, vomiting, diarrhea, polyarthralgia, seizures, desquamative dermatitis, and raised cerebrospinal fluid pressure with a pseudotumor cerebri-type presentation. Although extremely distressing, the syndrome is rarely fatal and resolves in less than 2 weeks (3,38).

Shocking Marine Animals

Only two groups of electric fish are marine; the remainder are freshwater animals. They rarely pose a health hazard, but are rather curious creatures surrounded by superstition and folklore. The marine electric fish include the stargazers (*Astroscopus*) and the electric rays (*Torpedo*). The electric eel is a freshwater Amazonian animal (33).

Electric rays are found in temperate and tropical oceans. They swim slowly and sluggishly, and are usually found partially buried in bottom mud and sand. The externally visible electric organs are located on each side of the anterior part of the disk between the anterior extension of the pectoral fin and the head, extending from above the level of the eye backward past the gill region. They are composed of a honeycomb network of columnar prismlike structures and connective tissues.

Generally, the ventral surface of the ray is negative, whereas the dorsal side is positive. An electrical discharge is reflexly produced on contact, often in a series exhaustive for the fish. This necessitates a period of recharging. Electricity is delivered in doses of 8–220 V (12). Although the shock is of low amperage, it can be enough to stun a grown man and induce drowning. Recovery from the shock itself is usually uneventful.

Hazardous Marine Plants

There is little collected knowledge of hazardous marine plant life, except for the dinoflagellates. In these cases, it has been demonstrated that toxicity may vary according to the location and season, and that the danger lies in bioaccumulation in higher life forms.

The biogenesis of marine phytotoxins is unclear. In most cases, it is not apparent wherein the evolutionary advantage lies.

SEAWEED DERMATITIS

Seaweed dermatitis is almost always secondary to irritation from algae, of which there are more than 3000 species. These range from microscopic diatoms (1 μm long) to kelp plants of 100 m in length (12). Algae can be found in all marine environments and are extremely adaptive to temperature and depth variation. For instance, one form of blue-green algae thrives at hot spring temperatures of 160°F, while others dwell in frigid arctic water. Although sunlight can penetrate only to a depth of 900 feet, some blue-green algae exist at depths of up to 12,000 feet.

The blue-green algae *Lyngbya majuscula* (now *Microcoleus lyngbyaceus*) has strains of varying toxicity. It is a fine, hairlike plant that occurs in abundance at depths of up to 100 feet. Documented outbreaks of *Lyngbya*-induced dermatitis occur from May to September throughout Hawaiian and Floridian waters. Typically, a victim swimming in water infested with plant life does not remove his wet bathing suit for a while after leaving the water. In minutes to hours, a pruritic, burning, erythematous rash develops in a bathing suit distribution, followed by bullous desquamation in the scrotal, perineal, and perianal regions. The treatment is vigorous irrigation with soap and warm water, followed by isopropyl alcohol rinses and topical steroid application.

DOGGER BANK ITCH

Dogger Bank itch is an eczematous dermatitis induced by a bryozoan or moss animal, the sea chervil *Alcyonidium hirsutum,* which forms a seaweedlike colony on the Dogger Bank between Scotland and Denmark. It presents like poison ivy and is treated in a similar fashion.

Detailed discussions of aquatic skin disorders may be found in Chapter 9.

References

1. Abbott, R. T.: Mollusks dangerous to scuba divers. *Del. Med. J.,* **45**(6):161–64, June 1973.
2. Acres, J., and Gray, J.: Paralytic shellfish poisoning. *Can. Med. Assoc. J.,* **119**(10):1195–97, Nov. 1978.
3. Bagnis, R., Berglund, F., Elias, P. S. *et al.:* Problems of toxicants in marine food products. *Bull. WHO,* **42**:69–88, 1970.
4. Baldridge, H. D., Jr., and Williams, J.: Shark attack: Feeding or fighting? *Milit. Med.,* **134**(2):130–33, Feb. 1969.
5. Bitseff, E. L., Garoni, W. J., Hardison, C. D., and Thompson, J. M.: The management of stingray injuries of the extremities. *South. Med. J.,* **63**(4):417–18, Apr. 1970.
5a. Blakesly, M. L.: Scombroid poisoning: prompt resolution of symptoms with cimetidine. *Ann. Emerg. Med.,* **12**:104–106, 1983.
6. Burnett, J. W., and Calton, G. J.: The chemistry and toxicology of some venomous pelagic coelenterates. *Toxicon,* **15**(3):177–96, 1977.
7. Burnett, J. W., and Calton, G. J.: Sea nettle and man-o'war venoms: A chemical comparison of their venoms and studies on the pathogenesis of the sting. *J. Invest. Dermatol.,* **62**(4):372–377, April 1974.
8. Calton, G. J., and Burnett, J. W.: The assessment of pain following coelenterate envenomations. *Toxicon,* **16**(6):679–82, 1978.
9. Calton, G. J., and Burnett, J. W.: Catfish (*Ictalurus catus*) fin venom. *Toxicon,* **13**(6):399–403, Dec. 1975.
10. Cross, T. B.: An unusual stingray injury—the skindiver at risk. *Med. J. Aust.,* **2**(5):947–48, Dec. 1976.
11. Edmonds, C.: A non-fatal case of blue-ringed octopus bite. *Med. J. Aust.,* **2**(12):601, Sept. 1969.
11a. Davies, D. H., and Campbell, G. D.: The aetiology, clinical pathology and treatment of shark attack. J. Roy. Nav. Med. Serv., **3**:110–36, 1962.
12. Fisher, A. A.: *Atlas of Aquatic Dermatology.* Grune and Stratton, New York, 1978.
13. Flowers, D. J.: Human infection due to *Mycobacterium marinum* after a dolphin bite. *J. Clin. Pathol.,* **23**(6):475–77, Sept. 1970.
14. Freyvogel, T. A.: Poisonous and venomous animals in East Africa. *Acta Trop.* (Basel), **29**(4):401–51, 1972.
15. Halstead, B. W., Kuninobu, L., and Hebard, H.: Catfish stings and the venom apparatus of the Mexican catfish, *Galeichthys felis* (Linnaeus). *Trans. Am. Microsc. Soc.,* **4**:297–314, 1953.
16. Halstead, B. W.: *Current Status of Marine Biotoxicology—An Overview.* International Biotoxicological Center, World Life Research Institute, Colton, Calif., 1980.

17. Halstead, B. W.: Marine pollution and the pharmaceutical scientist. *Am. J. Pharmacol. Ed.*, **37**:267–75, 1973.

18. Halstead, B. W., Engen, P., and Tu, A.: The venom and venom apparatus of the sea snake *Lapemis hardwicki* (Gray). *Zoo. J. Linnean Soc.*, **63**:371–96, 1978.

19. Halstead, B. W., and Madglin, R. F.: Weeverfish stings and the venom apparatus of weevers. *Z Tropenmed. Parasitol.*, **9**:129–46, 1958.

20. Hansen, P. A., and Halstead, B. W.: The venomous sea anemone *Actinodendron plumosum* (Haddon) of South Vietnam. *Micronesia*, **7**:123–36, 1971.

20a. Kelly, M. T., and McCormick, W. F.: Acute bacterial myositis caused by *Vibrio vulnificus. J.A.M.A.*, **246**(1):72–73, 1981.

21. Levy, S., Masry, D., and Halstead, B. W.: Report of stingings by the sea anemone *Triactis producta* Klunziger from Red Sea. *Clin. Toxicol.*, **3**(4):637–43, Dec. 1970.

22. Linaweaver, P. G.: Toxic marine life. *Milit. Med.*, **131**(6):437–42, June 1967.

23. Manowitz, N. R., and Rosenthal, R. R.: Cutaneous-systemic reactions to toxins and venoms of common marine organisms. *Cutis*, **23**(4):450–54, Apr. 1979.

24. Marr, J. J.: Portuguese man-of-war envenomation. A personal experience. *J.A.M.A.*, **199**(5):337–38, Jan. 1967.

25. McCabe, M. J., Hammon, W. M., Halstead, B. W., and Newton, T. H.: A fatal brain injury caused by a needlefish. *Neuroradiology*, **15**:137–39, 1978.

25a. McCool, J. A., Spudis, E. V., McLean, W., et al.: Primary amebic meningoencephalitis diagnosed in the emergency department. *Ann. Emerg. Med.*, **12**:35–37, 1983.

26. Mullanney, P. J.: Treatment of sting ray wounds. *Clin. Toxicol.*, **3**(4):613–15, Dec. 1970.

27. Pacy, H.: Australian catfish injuries with report of a typical case. *Med. J. Aust.*, **2**(2):63–5, July 1966.

28. Patkin, M., and Freeman, D.: Bullrout stings. *Med. J. Aust.*, **2**(1):14–16, July 1969.

29. Patten, B. M.: More on catfish stings (letter), *J.A.M.A.*, **232**(3):248, Apr. 1975.

30. Pepper, S. J., and Smith, H. M.: *Toxic Fish and Mollusks.* Information Bulletin No. 12, Air Training Command/Experimental Information Division, Maxwell A.F.B., Alabama.

31. Rathjen, W. F., and Halstead, B. W.: Report on two fatalities due to stingrays. *Toxicon*, **6**:301–2, 1969.

32. Rice, R. D., and Halstead, B. W.: Report of fatal cone shell sting by *Conus geographus* (Linnaeus), *Toxicon*, **5**:223–24, 1968.

33. Rosco, M. D.: Cutaneous manifestations of marine animal injuries including diagnosis and treatment. *Cutis*, **19**(4):507–10, Apr. 1977.

34. Russell, F. E.: *Snake Venom Poisoning*, J. B. Lippincott Co., Philadelphia, 1980.

35. Scoggin, C. H., Catfish stings. *J.A.M.A.*, **231**(2):176–77, Jan. 1975.

35a. Seidel, J. S., Hormatz, P., Visvesvara, G. S., et. al.: Successful treatment of primary amebic meningoencephalitis. *N. Engl. J. Med.*, **306**:346–48, 1982.

36. Shattock, F. M.: Injuries caused by wild animals. *Lancet*, **1**(539):412–15, Feb. 1968.

36a. Sims, J. K., and Irei, M. Y.: Human Hawaiian marine sponge poisoning. *Hawaii Med. J.*, **38**(9):263–70, 1979.

37. Skeie, E.: Weeverfish stings. Frequency, occurrence, clinical course, treatment and studies on the venom apparatus of the weeverfish, the nature of the toxin and immunological aspects. *Dan. Med. Bull.* **13**(4):119–21, Aug. 1966.

38. Southcott, R. V.: Australian venomous and poisonous fishes. *Clin. Toxicol.*, **10**(3):291–325, 1977.

39. Southcott, R. V.: Human injuries from invertebrate animals in the Australian seas. *Clin. Toxicol.*, **3**(4):617–36, Dec. 1970.

40. Strauss, M. B., and Orris, W. L.: Injuries to divers by marine animals: A simplified approach to recognition and management. *Milit. Med.*, **139**(2):129–30, Feb. 1974.

41. Sutherland, S. K., and Lane, W. R.: Toxins and mode of envenomation of the common ringed or blue-banded octopus. *Med. J. Aust.*, **1**(18):893–98, May 1969.

42. Torda, T. A., Sinclair, E., and Ulyatt, D. B.: Puffer fish (tetrodotoxin) poisoning: Clinical record and suggested management. *Med. J. Aust.*, **1**(12):599–602, Mar. 1973.

42a. Wellings, F. M., Amuso, P. T., Chang, S. L., et al.: Isolation and identification of pathogenic Naegleria from Florida. *Appl. Environ. Microbiol.*, **34**:661–67, 1977.

43. White, J. A. M.: Shark attack in Natal. Injury. *Br. J. Accident Surg.*, **6**(3):187–94, 1974.

Recommended Reading

Arnold, H. L., Jr.: Portuguese man-of-war ("bluebottle") stings: Treatment with papain. *Straub Clin. Proc.*, **37**:30–3, 1971.

Bagnis, R., Kuberski, T., and Langier, S.: Clinical observations on 3009 cases of ciguatera fish poisoning in the South Pacific. *Am. J. Trop. Med. Hyg.*, **28**:1067–73, 1979.

Bagnis, R., et al.: Origins of ciguatera fish poisoning: A new dinoflagellate *Gambierdiscus toxicus* Adachi and Fukuyo, definitively identified as a causal agent. *Toxicon*, **18**:199–208, 1980.

Cleland, J. B., and Southcott, R. E.: *Injuries to Man from Marine Invertebrates in the Australian Region.* Canberra: A. J. Arthur, Commonwealth Government Printer, 1965.

Cousteau, J., and Cousteau, P.: *The Shark: Splendid Savage of the Sea. The Undersea Discoveries of Jacques-Yves Cousteau.* New York: A and W Publishers, Inc., 1970.

Dunson, W. A.: *The Biology of Sea Snakes.* Baltimore: University Park Press, 1975.

Edmonds, C.: *Dangerous Marine Animals of the Indo-Pacific Region.* Newport, Australia: Wedneil Publications, 1975.

Foo, L. Y.: Scombroid poisoning. Isolation and identification of "saurine." *J. Sci. Food Agric.*, **27**:807–10, 1976.

Halstead, B. W.: *Poisonous and Venomous Marine Ani-

mals of the World. Washington, D.C., U.S. Government Printing Office. Vol. 1, *Invertebrates,* 1965; Vol. 2, *Vertebrates,* 1967; Vol. 3, *Vertebrates,* 1970.

Halstead, B. W.: *Poisonous and Venomous Marine Animals of the World.* Abridged edition (updated). Princeton, N.J., Darwin Press, 1976.

Hartwick, R., Callanan, V., and Williamson, J.: Disarming the box-jellyfish. *Med. J. Aust.,* **1:**15–20, 1980.

Hokama, Y., Banner, A. H., and Boylan, D. B.: A radioimmunoassay for the detection of ciguatoxin. *Toxicon,* **15:**317–25, 1977.

Kim, R.: Flushing syndrome due to Mahi mahi (scombroid fish) poisoning. *Arch Dermatol.,* **115:**963–65, 1979.

Rayner, M. D.: Mode of action of ciguatoxin. *Fed. Proc.,* **31:**1139–45, 1972.

Roessler, C.: *The Underwater Wilderness—Life Around the Great Reefs.* New York: Chanticleer Press, Inc., 1978.

Russell, F. E.: Stingray injuries: A review and discussion of their treatment. *Am. J. Med. Sci.,* **226:**611–22, 1953.

Russell, F. E.: Marine toxins and venomous and poisonous marine animals. In Russell, F. S., ed., *Advances in Marine Biology,* Vol. 3. New York: Academic Press, Inc., 1965.

Sims, J. K., and Irei, M. Y.: Human Hawaiian marine sponge poisoning. *Hawaii Med. J.,* **38**(9):263–70, 1979.

Sims, J. K., and Zandee Van Rilland, R. D.: Escharotic stomatitis caused by the "stinging seaweed" *Microcoleus lyngbyaceus* (formerly *Lyngbya majuscula*): Case report and literature review. *Hawaii Med. J.,* **40:**243–48, 1981.

Turner, B., Sullivan, P., and Pennefather, J.: Disarming the bluebottle. *Med. J. Aust.,* **2:**394–95, 1980.

| AQUATIC SKIN DISORDERS

Gail E. Drayton, M.D.

Dermatitis Caused by Sponges (Phylum Porifera)

Sponges are plantlike sea animals with a porous structure and a tough, fibrous skeleton. They grow in fixed colonies on the ocean bottom. Both freshwater and marine animal sponges can cause contact dermatitis.

Two sponges are of particular interest to dermatologists: the fire sponge, *Tedania ignis,* and the poison bun sponge, *Fibula nolitangere.*

FIRE SPONGE DERMATITIS

Tedania ignis, the fire sponge, is most abundant in the Miami area and near the shore along the Florida Keys (Figure 1). The nickname is appropriate from the standpoint of both color and stinging properties. It is brilliant vermilion or reddish orange and grows as a bunch of branches or "fingers" extending upward from a main base. When the fingers are broken or detached, the fire sponge is capable of producing a severe dermatitis, which resembles poison ivy dermatitis. The sting initially causes an itching or prickling sensation, followed in a few hours by swelling, stiffness, and pain. If the patients' fingers are stung, they become almost immovable within a day. The symptoms usually subside in 2 days.

Treatment of fire sponge dermatitis is the same as for severe poison ivy dermatitis. Compresses or soaks with a solution of dilute acetic acid are effective to lessen the pruritus and minimize crusting. Severe dermatitis should be treated with potent topical fluorinated corticosteroids and, if necessary, with systemic corticosteroids (prednisone, 30 mg daily, tapered over 2 weeks). Severe pruritus may be controlled with oral antihistamines (diphenhydramine hydrochloride 50 mg three times a day.

The fire sponge can also produce an erythema multiforme type of eruption 10 days postexposure (6).

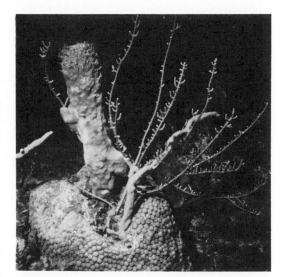

FIGURE 1 *Tedania ignis,* the fire sponge, is the most prevalent hazardous sponge along the shore of the Florida keys.

POISON BUN SPONGE DERMATITIS

Fibula nolitangere, the poison bun sponge, is found in somewhat deeper water and produces a more violent reaction than the fire sponge (Figure 2).

The poison bun sponge is not easy to recognize, as it resembles a number of other common sponges. It generally grows in small masses, and the oscula (holes) are large enough to admit a finger. Brownish on the outside and drab on the inside, it has a soft

FIGURE 2 *Neofibularia nolitangere,* the poison bun sponge, produces a violent reaction.

"bready" texture. When one touches the surface or breaks the sponge, the skin is exposed to the toxic substance. Burning and pruritus are pronounced. Systemic symptoms may include formication and cramps.

Treatment is the same as for severe poison ivy dermatitis.

RED SPONGE DERMATITIS

Microciona prolifera, the red sponge, may produce erythema and edema of the hands in those who handle it, particularly oyster fishermen. Joint stiffness and bullae subsequently develop. If not properly treated, the bullae may become purulent, and the eruption may persist for several months.

Treatment is the same as for severe poison ivy dermatitis.

SPONGE SPICULE DERMATITIS

Some sponges can produce traumatic injuries via their spicules. These sponges are equipped with a skeletal matrix which contains silicon dioxide or calcium carbonate spicules. Either may produce irritation when broken off in the skin. Both are very difficult to remove once they have penetrated the skin. Adhesive tape may be used to strip off some of the spicules. Isopropyl alcohol should be applied after the tape is removed. Surgical exploration of these wounds without visible targets is not warranted.

Those who handle living sponges that can cause injuries should wear canvas gloves.

Dermatitis Caused by Seaweed

Seaweed dermatitis can be divided into two types: the animal plant variety, including sea moss or sea mat dermatitis, and the marine plant variety, including Hawaiian dermatitis due to algae (6).

SEA MOSS DERMATITIS (DOGGER BANK ITCH)

An eczematous dermatitis termed Dogger Bank itch is caused by the sea-chervil, *Alcyondium hirsutum,* a seaweedlike animal colony. North Sea fishermen come in contact with these sea mosses, or sea mats, when they are drawn up in the fishing nets. Large quantities of sea-chervil are sometimes landed and then thrown back into the sea.

The dermatitis, understandably, first appears on the hands and clears when the fisherman goes ashore. However, with increasing exposure, more severe attacks occur, characterized by a blistered, edematous eruption of the hands, arms, face, and legs.

It is not clear whether this is an allergic dermatitis, borne out by positive patch test reactions with an extract from the causative marine animals and negative reactions in controls, or an irritant dermatitis, supported by the fact that frequently all on board, save the cook, acquire the dermatitis (17).

Treatment is the same as that for a mild poison ivy dermatitis. Calamine lotion is used, as well as 20% alcohol, which acts as a cooling agent. Potent fluorinated topical corticosteroids may be employed.

Proper protective clothing usually prevents recurrence of the eruption.

Seaweed Dermatitis Due to Algae

To the nonbotanist, the algae are a mystery. Most observers may know that seaweeds and pond "blooms" are algae, but are not aware of the universal distribution of these complex organisms in moist environments. The algae are difficult to classify and even to define. Approximately 30,000 species have been identified. *Algae* may be loosely defined as chlorophyll-bearing organisms (and their colorless relatives) which are thalloid (have no true roots, stems, or leaves).

Algae vary in size, shape, and color. Some are equipped with flagella and propel themselves through water very much like animals (19). The smallest, such as the diatoms, are microscopic, while the giant kelp may attain lengths of 300 feet.

The blue-green algae, *Lyngbya majuscula,* is of particular medical importance. Not all strains are toxic. One area may breed a toxic strain, while the algae just a few miles away are nontoxic. *Lyngbya* occurs abundantly from the intertidal zone to a depth of 100 feet.

Grauer and Arnold reported a seabather's dermatitis in Hawaii following contact with *Lyngbya* (8). The 125 cases were all from windward beaches. The following pattern emerged during this epidemic:

1. The patient had been swimming, often in water made turbid by suspended fragments of seaweed.
2. He continued to wear the wet swimsuit after leaving the ocean.
3. A few minutes to a few hours after emerging from the ocean, itching and burning occurred.
4. After 3–8 hours, a visible dermatitis occurred.

Blisters and deep desquamation followed the initial symptoms. There were moist, bright red, painful areas on the scrotum, perineum, or perianal area. The eruption affected the parts of the body covered by the bathing suit.

There have also been occasional reported outbreaks of skin reactions to fresh water blue-green algae (5,11).

A number of similarities exist between seaweed dermatitis and seabathers' eruption. Both occur in the same body region after swimming in salt water at a time when large amounts of seaweed are in the water or on the beach; both have a seasonal incidence in the spring and summer (March–September in Florida and June–September in Hawaii); and both are characterized by a pruritic eruption which occurs within a few hours of swimming, persists for a few days, and spontaneously subsides. Differentiating between the two conditions may be difficult.

Treatment for severe algae dermatitis is systemic corticosteroids, (prednisone, 20–40 mg daily initially and tapered over 2 weeks). Less severe cases will respond to medium to high-potency topical corticosteroids. The most effective measures are prophylactic. Patients who swim in algae-abundant areas should shower with soap and water and wash their bathing suits immediately after their swim.

Infections Caused by Achloric Algae (Protothecosis)

Human and animal infections have been caused by achloric mutants of the green algae, *Chlorella.* Species of *Prototheca* have been found in the fresh and marine water and in sewage treatment systems (20). Both *Prototheca segbwema* and *P. wickerhamii* have been demonstrated as pathogens in humans (13). The condition is most likely to occur as a result of barefoot walks in swampy areas, work with aquariums, or exposure of the skin to water from contaminated water supply systems. Although widespread visceral disease has been noted in animals, infections in humans have been limited to the skin, subcutaneous tissue, and regional lymphatics.

The initial lesion is a nodule or tender red papule which enlarges, becomes pustular, and ulcerates. A purulent, malodorous, blood-tinged discharge is present. Satellite lesions usually develop and frequently become confluent. The lesions may become verrucous and resemble chromomycosis. Regional lymph nodes may develop metastatic granulomas. Most patients have a history of exposure to water which could have been contaminated with the organism, but the portal of entry is unknown.

Diagnosis is made through histologic sections and culture. The organisms are spherical and vary in diameter from 2 to 11 μm. They are basophilic, Gram-positive, and stain well with Grocott's methenamine silver stain, colloidal iron stains for acid mucopolysaccharides, and the periodic acid-Schiff reaction. The larger organisms have thick walls and characteristic internal septations. *Prototheca* grows on Sabouraud's agar, blood agar, or brain-heart infusion agar at an optimum temperature of 30–32°C. The colonies are cream-colored and yeastlike (16).

The disease is chronic and progressive. Early excision may be curative.

Dermatitis Caused by Schistosomes and Other Marine Worms

SCHISTOSOMIASIS

There are two types of human schistosomiasis: (1) a cutaneous affliction due to nonhuman schistosomes for which humans are abnormal hosts, and (2) visceral schistosomiasis, or bilharziasis, a serious systemic disorder due to the human blood flukes *Schistosoma mansoni, S. japonicum,* and *S. haematobium.* This chapter will discuss only the first. However, when human blood flukes penetrate the skin during the invasive stage of visceral schistosomiasis, an eruption is occasionally provoked, which mimics the purely cutaneous schistosomiasis.

Cercarial dermatitis is an infestation that results from penetration of the skin by the cercariae of schistosomes. The cercariae are an immature larval form, usually microscopic, of these parasitic flatworms.

The geographic distribution of schistosome cercarial dermatitis is worldwide, occurring in arctic, temperate, and tropical zones and in both fresh and salt water.

Although serious schistosomal infestation is uncommon in North America, cercarial dermatitis is a vexing problem on certain freshwater and even saltwater beaches. Snails and birds which inhabit the lakes of Wisconsin, Michigan, Manitoba, and neighboring North Central states are the intermediate hosts.

Ecologic Cycle

Cercarial dermatitis results when humans become unwitting interlopers in this rather complex cycle. The adult schistosomes are blood parasites of birds or mammals. The schistosome eggs are present in the droppings of infested animals. Certain species of snails become infested upon contact with the miracidia hatched from the eggs. Snails then serve as an intermediate host. After an incubation period in the snail, hundreds of fork-tailed cercariae are released into the water. A specific warm-blooded host is found, and the parasites mature in its vascular system, unless humans accidently intrude into this normal life cycle. When the adult worms produce eggs, the cycle restarts.

Terminology

Various synonyms, including *clam diggers' itch, swimmers' itch, collectors' itch,* and *sea bathers' eruption,* have been used interchangeably with cercarial dermatitis. Many observers insist on a clear distinction between *swimmers' itch* and *sea bathers' eruption,* limiting the former to eruptions on exposed areas and the latter to a dermatitis which results from ocean bathing.

Clinical Manifestations

Schistosome cercarial dermatitis is a skin infestation caused by an immune response in the human, an unnatural host. The cercariae are walled off and destroyed in the epithelial layers of the skin. The dead cercariae then elicit an allergic reaction.

Although penetration of cercariae may take place in the water, it usually occurs as the film of water evaporates on the skin. The cercariae are unable to penetrate beyond the papillary dermis. Histologic examination reveals intraepithelial burrows and abscesses surrounded by an infiltrate of eosinophils, polymorphonuclear leukocytes, and lymphocytes (22). Cercariae themselves are not seen in serial sections unless the biopsy is taken within 24 hours of penetration, as the parasite is quickly destroyed by the inflammatory reaction.

The patient initially experiences a prickling sensation. Itching occurs 4–10 minutes after the cercariae reach the skin; they evoke an acute inflammatory response with erythema and edema. The initial urticarial reaction subsides, leaving erythematous macules which become papular and more pruritic over the next 10–15 hours. Discrete, highly pruritic papules surrounded by a zone of erythema are typical of this disorder. Vesicles, which may become pustules, frequently form a day or two later. Excoriation often leads to pustulation, crusting, and secondary infection.

The eruption occurs primarily on exposed areas of the body. The inflammatory response reaches its peak within 3 days and subsides slowly over 1–2 weeks. The reaction is more severe in those patients who have had a previous attack, suggesting acquired sensitivity.

Treatment

Brisk rubbing with a rough, dry towel upon leaving the water is helpful, as it removes the water droplets which harbor the cercariae. Children, in particular, should be reminded to dry themselves each time they leave the water.

In mild cases, application of rubbing alcohol or equal parts of rubbing alcohol and calamine lotion will control the itching. Severe cases may require systemic corticosteroids (prednisone, 30 mg tapered over 10–14 days). Secondary bacterial infection may necessitate the use of topical antibacterial ointments or the appropriate systemic antibiotics (erythromycin, 250 mg four times a day for 8–10 days).

Control of the parasite in limited water areas may be achieved by adding a mixture of two parts copper sulfate and one part copper carbonate to the water, using 3 pounds to each 1000 square feet (15). To destroy cercariae in larger lakes, the surface of the area in use may be sprayed each morning with formaldehyde.

SEA BATHERS' ERUPTION

The term *sea bathers' eruption* is often erroneously used to describe cercarial dermatitis (Table 1). Properly used, it refers to a dermatitis which results from contact with sea water but is not traceable to cercarial penetration. It resembles cercarial eruptions and seaweed dermatitis. Cercarial dermatitis, frequently called *swimmers' itch,* occurs predominantly in fresh water and involves uncovered areas of the body. Sea bathers' eruption occurs in salt water and involves covered areas of the body. It appears that sea bathers' eruption is caused by some organism that can be brushed off before it penetrates the skin and frequently is synonymous with seaweed dermatitis.

TABLE 1
Contrast between Swimmers' Itch and Sea Bathers' Eruption

Factor	Swimmer's Itch	Sea Bathers' Eruption
Type of water	Predominantly fresh	Salt
Part of body involved	Uncovered	Covered
Locale	Northern United States, Canada	Florida, Cuba, Gulf Coast
Cause	Schistosome	Unknown
Lesion	Vesicle-topped papules	Wheal

The eruption ensues within a few hours after bathing and consists of pruritic, erythematous wheals or papules which last a few days and involve spontaneously. Individual lesions closely resemble insect bites. In children with extensive eruptions, fever of 101–102°F is common.

The disorder is self-limited and rarely persists for more than 7–10 days. Therapy is palliative and consists of calamine lotion with 1% menthol, along with parenteral antihistamines. Systemic corticosteroids are rarely needed.

LEECHES

Leeches are classified in the phylum *Annelida* (segmented worms), in which they constitute the class *Hirudinea.* These blood-sucking animals secrete an anticoagulant, hirudin.

Most species inhabit fresh water, although there are both marine and terrestrial types. Leeches attach themselves to the skin, feed until engorged, and then fall off.

The wound bleeds freely and heals slowly in unsensitized individuals. Lesions frequently become secondarily infected. If sensitization has developed, the reaction to the bite may be urticarial, bullous, or necrotic. The bite of a leech can cause a serious allergic reaction, including anaphylaxis (12).

The usual victims of leech bites are persons walking through streams or marshes. In some areas of the world, leeches are still used medicinally. Allergic reactions may complicate treatment in such areas.

Removal of leeches may be facilitated by application of a few drops of brine, alcohol, or strong vinegar, or a match flame near the site of attachment (6). The leech should never be pulled off the skin, as the jaws may remain and induce phagedena. Bleeding from the bite may be staunched with a styptic pencil. Wounds should be cleansed several times daily with a mild antiseptic lotion to prevent infection.

MARINE ANNELID DERMATITIS

A number of marine organisms can produce an irritant dermatitis or wound by contact with their bristles or by a bite from their jaws.

Bristle Worm Dermatitis

Certain sea worms of the family *Amphinomidae* are equipped with tufts of chitinous bristles arranged in rows around their bodies. When the worm is touched or stimulated, the bristles are raised and the body of the worm contracts, thus presenting a defensive armor of bristles (Figure 3). The bristles detach easily and penetrate the skin. The spines, like cactus spines, are difficult to remove, and each must be extracted individually.

The common bristle worm of Florida's lower east coast, *Hermodice carunculata,* is nearly 1 inch wide and can attain a length of 1 foot (6). This species is usually found on coral, rock slabs, and sponges, and in porous rock. The body is green with reddish markings along the sides; the white bristles are tipped with dull red. The bristle tufts appear small when the worm is not in a defensive pose, but raise impressively when *H. carunculata* is disturbed.

Hermodice is a sea bottom worm. There are also free-swimming worms, such as *Chloeia euglochis ehlers.* These worms are often found near the water surface and have even been caught on a hook as they attempt to settle on the bait (Table 2).

CLINICAL MANIFESTATIONS

Contact with a bristle worm produces an intense burning sensation. Moderate edema and papules ensue. Occasionally, the lesions are necrotic. Frequent symptoms include pain, paresthesias, and pruritus.

FIGURE 3 Bristle worm. This animal induces a dermatitis with its spiny bristles.

TABLE 2

Bristleworm	Geographic Location
Chloeia flava	Malayan coast
Chloeia viridis	West Indies, Gulf of California, Gulf of Mexico south to Panama
Euythoe complanata	Australia and tropical seas
Hermodice carunculata	Tropical eastern America and eastern Gulf of Mexico

TREATMENT

The bristles should be carefully removed with forceps. Scraping usually breaks the bristles and leaves many embedded in the skin. Sometimes the bristles may be extracted with adhesive tape. Rubbing alcohol may be applied after removal to soothe the wounds.

Worm Bites

Certain segmented worms with chitinous jaws produce painful bites. Stinging pain is followed by edema and pruritus. Cool compresses or alcohol may be soothing. One should not handle sea worms unless gloves are worn.

Dermatitis Caused by Other Macroscopic Organisms

SEA LOUSE DERMATITIS

Sea lice are actually small marine crustaceans of the order *Isopoda,* suborder *Cymothoidra.* Water skiers, skin divers, and swimmers who frequent the shore waters of temperate and tropical seas may encounter these active, free-swimming crustaceans (2). The creatures frequently bury themselves in the sandy bottom below the water level. They are equipped with powerful biting parts and will quickly attach themselves to fish, feet, or searching inquisitive hands (2). Sea lice bites are common along the Southern California coast. The bite is rapid and sharp, causing punctate hemorrhage. The lesions gradually clear over a 5–7 day period.

The lesion should be cleansed with hydro-

gen peroxide. An antibiotic ointment may then be applied.

CREEPING ERUPTION

Cutaneous larva migrans is a cutaneous eruption caused by the larvae of various nematode parasites for which humans are an abnormal final host. The following are the more common species responsible: *Ancylostoma braziliensis* in the central and southeastern United States, *A. caninum, Uncinaria stenocephala* (hookworm), and *Bunostomum phlebotomum* (hookworm of cattle). However, a transient creeping eruption also results from the larvae of the human hookworms, *A. duodenale* and *Necator americanus.*

The ova are deposited in the soil and hatch into larvae, which then penetrate human skin. Sandy, warm, and shady areas are favorable. People exposed most often to the larvae are sea bathers, children, gardeners, farmers, and those who work under buildings.

In humans, the larvae penetrate the skin but are unable to penetrate through the dermis. The larvae migrate between the dermis and the epidermis, producing superficial serpiginous tunnels. The feet and buttocks are most commonly involved. Some larvae remain quiescent for a few weeks or months, after which migration is manifested by a wandering, thin, linear, raised, and tunnellike lesion 2–3 mm wide. Older lesions become dry and crusted. Pruritus may be pronounced. The larvae move a few millimeters to a few centimeters per day. Larva migrans may be associated with eosinophilia (10–35%) and Loeffler's syndrome.

Larva currens is a special form of cutaneous larva migrans caused by *Strongyloides sterocoralis.* Usually, the eruption is associated with intestinal strongyloidiasis and begins in the perianal skin. It may involve the buttocks, thighs, back, and shoulders, but the genitalia are spared. Pruritus is intense, and the lesions spread as rapidly as 5–10 cm/hour. The larvae leave the skin, enter the blood, and later settle in the intestinal mucosa, while the rash fades.

Treatment of larva migrans may include cryotherapy with ethyl chloride for very mild infestations, topical thiabendazole in more stubborn cases, and oral thiabendazole (25–50 mg/kg) for 2–4 days in more severe cases.

Secondary infection of the skin is not uncommon. It may require incision and drainage of pustules or furuncles and the use of topical or systemic antibiotics.

In endemic areas, the following precautions may be taken:

1. Avoid sitting or lying on damp soil or sand, especially during rainy seasons.
2. Do not walk barefoot.
3. Drape the ground with impenetrable material prior to doing any work which requires crawling under buildings.
4. Cover sandboxes with a tarpaulin when not in use to prevent contamination by prowling cats.

SOAPFISH DERMATITIS

The soapfish, *Rypticus saponaceus,* family Grammistidae, receives its name from the soapy mucus it releases when handled or disturbed. Fishermen in the Virgin Islands and Puerto Rico are aware that a soapfish kept in a restricted volume of sea water with other fishes often causes the death of the other fish (10). Human contact with a soapfish, however, results only in a dermatitis. The skin irritant in the soapfish mucus is called *grammistin.* Similar irritant substances have been isolated from certain species of boxfish and sea bass (3,10).

Treatment consists of cold compresses of Burow's solution to allay the burning and itching.

Dermatitis and Infections Caused by Marine Bacteria

"SWIMMING POOL" GRANULOMAS

Skin granulomas caused by *Mycobacterium marinum* were first described in 1954 by Linell and Norden (14). The lesions resembled tuberculosis verrucosa cutis.

M. marinum, a so-called atypical (anonymous or unclassified) mycobacterium, differs from the typical ones in certain culture characteristics and in its *in vivo* resistance to standard antituberculous chemotherapeutic agents. Typical mycobacteria are animal pathogens which cannot multiply outside their animal host, while atypical mycobacteria are free-living soil and water saprophytes and only occasional pathogens.

M. marinum is an acid-fast, rod-shaped bacillus. By Runyon's classification, it is a group 1 photochromogen that produces yellow-orange pigment after exposure to light. It grows optimally at 31–33°C (typical mycobacteria are grown at 37°C). Correspondingly, in humans, *M. marinum* infections are limited to the cooler acral skin and rarely involve deeper, warmer lymphatic and lymph node structures (7).

Infections may occur after exposure in either fresh or salt water to aquariums, fish bites, or swimming pools. *M. marinum* invades the tissue through a preexisting skin lesion. Chlorinated swimming pools provide little protection, as the organism is relatively resistant to chlorine.

Within 3–4 weeks of the abrasion, a red papule develops, which slowly increases in size to become a hard purple nodule, frequently verrucous, with a violaceous base. The lesion may enlarge to 6 cm in diameter, although 1–2 cm is more common. New lesions may occur in a pattern which resembles sporotrichosis, with spaced dermal granulomas in a linear distribution along the superficial lymphatics. The granuloma may become secondarily infected, resulting in cellulitis or lymphangitis. Many *M. marinum* granulomas undergo spontaneous healing within 2 years, with scarring and pigmentation.

The diagnosis of *M. marinum* granuloma is confirmed bacteriologically by isolation of the organism from a homogenized skin biopsy specimen on standard mycobacterial culture medium, but at 31–33°C rather than the standard 37°C. Acid-fast bacilli are visualized in less than 10% of biopsies.

Treatment should be conservative, as most lesions heal spontaneously within 2–3 years. Some small lesions are easily excised. Minocycline hydrochloride (100 mg twice a day) for 2–3 months has been effective. Ethambutol hydrochloride and cycloserine may afford symptomatic relief, but before initiating antituberculous chemotherapeutic agents, drug sensitivities of the isolated *M. marinum* should be determined, because of the high rate of drug resistance.

ERYSIPELOTHRIX DERMATITIS

Erysipeloid is an acute infection of traumatized skin caused by a slender Gram-positive rod, *Erysipelothrix insidiosa.* It occurs in fishermen, butchers, and others who handle raw fish, poultry, or meat products. Also called *speck finger* or *blubber finger,* the condition is common on the Atlantic Coast in workers who handle crabs and live fish (6).

The bacillus is microaerophilic and nonmotile, and does not have spores or capsules. It is hardy enough to survive drying, putrefaction of tissue, and saltwater or freshwater exposure. Closely related bacteriologically to *Listeria monocytogenes,* the organisms may be confused with streptococci or diphtheroids.

Erysipelothrix enters the skin through a puncture wound or abrasion, usually on the finger. Within 2–7 days a violaceous, raised area appears and enlarges, accompanied by pain and itching. Low-grade fever and malaise are not uncommon; bacteremia and endocarditis are rare (9).

The distinctive lesion, usually on the finger or hand, is violaceous, warm, and tender, with a sharply defined, raised margin. The lesion characteristically progresses up the edge of the finger into the web and descends along the adjoining finger. Frequently, as the lesion advances peripherally, the central area clears without ulceration or desquamation. It seldom affects the palm. Rarely, dissemination results in multiple lesions distant from the original site.

Erysipeloid usually runs its course within 1–3 weeks. Penicillin, 2–3 million units daily for 7–10 days, is effective. Erythromycin may be used as an alternative. If arthritis, septicemia, or endocarditis is present, the dose of penicillin should be raised to 2–4 million units every 4 hours intravenously (7).

Dermatitis Caused by Aquatic Equipment

HOT TUB DERMATITIS

Several cases of *whirlpool dermatitis* have recently been described (4,18,21). The eruptions occurred following the use of motel whirlpools. *Pseudomonas aeruginosa,* a nonfermentative, obligately aerobic, gram-negative bacillus, has been implicated as the causative agent. This organism has the ability to infect healthy but moistened skin. The high whirlpool temperature, high humidity, high concentrations of organisms, and the chemical irritants in the water all contribute to this dermatitis. Deficiencies in disinfecting equipment have been found in several outbreaks of whirlpool dermatitis.

The rash appears within 8–48 hours after exposure and resolves within 7 days without treatment. The eruption is most pronounced in areas covered by bathing garments and spares the head and neck. The erythematous, maculopapular, vesiculopustular eruption is accompanied by pruritus.

As the eruption is self-limited, treatment should be conservative. Alleviation of the pruritus may be accomplished by drying lotions such as calamine or by oral antihistamines. In severe cases, a course of antibiotic therapy may be warranted.

REACTIONS TO SNORKEL AND DIVING EQUIPMENT

Allergic reaction to underwater masks and mouthpieces is another common equipment-related dermatologic problem (1).

Mask burn may range from a minor reddish imprint of the mask on the face to a full-blown, severe, vesicular, weeping eruption. Mouthpieces similarly may produce minor to severe intraoral inflammation and ulceration. Chemical constituents in the equipment may be the causative allergens (1). Rubber mouthpieces and masks contain antioxidants similar to those that cause contact dermatitis in some surgeons who wear rubber gloves. Mercaptobenzothiazol is commonly implicated. Both irritant and allergic reactions to diving equipment may occur (6).

Acute facial dermatitis may be treated with cold compresses of Burow's solution and systemic corticosteroids (prednisone, 30 mg daily tapered over 7–10 days). In serious intraoral reactions, a mouthwash of equal parts of antihistamine elixir (diphenhydramine) and milk of magnesia is efficacious. For those with frequent severe reactions, a hypoallergenic mask is mandatory.

References

1. Alexander, J. E.: Allergic reactions to mask skirts, regulator mouthpieces, and snorkel mouthpieces. *Pressure,* **5:**10, Feb. 1976.

2. Best, W. C., Sablan, R. G.: Cymothoidism (sea louse dermatitis). *Arch. Dermatol.,* **90:**177–179, 1964.
3. Boylan, D. B., Scheuer, P. J.: Pahutoxin: A fish poison. *Science,* **155:**52, Jan. 1967.
4. Center for Disease Control: Pool-associated rash illness—North Carolina. *Morbidity Mortality Weekly Rep.,* **24:**349, 1975.
5. Cohen, S. G., Reif, C. B.: Cutaneous sensitization to blue-green algae. *J. Allergy,* **24:**452, 1953.
6. Fisher, A. A.: *Atlas of Aquatic Dermatology.* San Francisco, Grune and Stratton, 1978, p. 46.
7. Fitzpatrick, T. B.: *Dermatology in General Medicine.* San Francisco, McGraw-Hill Book Company, 1979, p. 1506.
8. Grauer, F. H., Arnold, H. L.: Seaweed dermatitis. *Arch. Dermatol.,* **84:**720, Nov. 1961.
9. Grieco, M. H., Sheldon, C.: *Erysipelothrix rhusiopathiae. Ann. N.Y. Acad. Sci.,* **174:**523, 1970.
10. Hashimoto, Y., Kamiya, H.: Occurrence of a toxic substance in the skin of a sea bass *Pogonoperca punctata. Toxicon,* **7:**65–70, 1969.
11. Heise, H. A.: II. Microcystis: Another form of algae producing allergenic reactions. *Ann. Allergy,* **9:**100, 1951.
12. Heldt, T. J.: Allergy to leeches. *Henry Ford Hosp. Med. J.,* **9:**498, 1961.
13. Klintworth, G. K., Fetter, B. F., Nielsen, H. S. Jr.: Prototheocosis, an algae infection: Reports of a case in man. *J. Med. Microbiol.,* **1:**211, 1968.
14. Linell, F., Norden, A.: *Mycobacterium Balnei. Acta Tuberc. Scand.,* suppl. **33:**1–84, 1954.
15. McMullen, D. B., Brackett, S.: Distribution and control of schistosome dermatitis in Wisconsin and Michigan, *Am. J. Trop. Med.,* **21:**725, 1941.
16. Moschella, S. L., Pillsbury, D. M., Hurley, H. J.: *Dermatology.* Philadelphia, W. B. Saunders Company, 1975, pp. 704–5.
17. Newhouse, M. D.: Dogger Bank itch: Survey of trawlermen. *Rehabilitation,* **60:**941, 1967.
18. Sausker, W. F., et al.: Pseudomonas folliculitis acquired from a health spa whirlpool. *J.A.M.A.,* **239:**2362, 1978.
19. Tiffany, H. L.: *Algae, the Grass of Many Waters.* Springfield, Ill., Charles C Thomas, Publisher, 1968.
20. Tindall, J. P., Fetter, B. F.: Infection caused by achloric algae (prototheocosis). *Arch. Dermatol.,* **104:**490, 1971.
21. Washburn, J., Jacobson, J. A., Marston, E., Thorsen, B.: *Pseudomonas aeruginosa* rash associated with a whirlpool. *J.A.M.A.,* **235:**2205, 1976.
22. Wood, M. G., Srolovitz, H. Schetman, D.: Schistosomiasis: Paraplegia and ectopic skin lesions as admission symptoms. *Arch. Dermatol.,* **112:**690, 1976.

CHAPTER 10

ARTHROPOD ENVENOMATION

Sherman A. Minton, M.D.

The phylum Arthropoda contains about four-fifths of the known animals of the world (900,000 species), and insects compose the largest group of arthropods. Insects are an important part of the biota of all terrestrial and freshwater environments that support life; only in marine environments are they relatively unimportant. Insects are the most common form of multicellular life, and they may well exceed all other land animals in biomass. There are very few substances of plant or animal origin that cannot be utilized by some insects as food, and in their feeding, insects play a vital role in recycling organic compounds. They compete with other organisms for the world's food supply and, in turn, are a major food source for many forms of life. Additionally, they are essential for the pollination of many plants.

Insect life cycles are diverse and often complex, involving developmental and sexual stages that are widely different in morphology and life style. Although sexual reproduction is the rule, parthenogenetic (asexual) and pedogenetic (larval) reproduction occur. Some groups, such as ants, bees, and termites, have

developed a high degree of social organization.

During at least part of their life cycle, insects have a body divided into three distinct regions (head, thorax, abdomen) and have three pairs of legs, all attached to the thorax. Except for a few primitive or parasitic groups, most adult insects have wings.

More deaths occur annually in the United States because of arthropod envenomation than any other variety of envenomation. This is no doubt more a function of the number of incidents than of the relative toxicity (49). With respect to insects, the greatest direct medical importance is associated with their feeding on human blood and tissue fluids. In doing so, they usually inject salivary secretions. This is a highly effective method of transmitting pathogenic microorganisms; moreover, the secretions are often allergenic and sometimes toxic. Other insects may carry pathogens passively on their feet or mouthparts or in their digestive tracts. Arthropods serving as biologic vectors of human disease and the diseases that they transmit are listed in Table 1.

Table 1 does not include purely mechanical

TABLE 1

Arthropods Serving as Biologic Vectors of Human Disease, and the Diseases They Transmit

Arthropod Vector	Disease Transmitted	Geography	Pathogen	Clinical Manifestations	Treatment
Mosquitoes (Culicidae)	Chik-ung-unya, O'Nyong Nyong, Uruma, equine encephalitis (2)	Tanzania; Uganda Congo, South Africa, Thailand; East Africa; Trinidad, Brazil, and Bolivia; worldwide	Arbovirus A	Fever, rash, arthralgias, encephalitis	None
	Yellow fever, dengue, viral encephalitis, West Nile fever (2)	Central Africa, South Central America; worldwide, especially Puerto Rico; worldwide; Egypt, Israel, South Africa, Uganda, and India	Arbovirus B	Fever, icterus, hemorrhagic diathesis, headache, arthralgias, rash	None
	Malaria (10)	South and Central America, Africa, Asia	Protozoa of genus *Plasmodium*	Fever, anemia, hepatomegaly, acute renal failure	Chloroquine and primaquine; for drug-resistent *P. falciparum*, use quinine, pyrimethamine, and sulfonamide
	Lymphatic filariasis (Bancroftian and Malayan) (10)	China, Korea, Philippines, Southeast Asia, India, Japan	Nematodes: *Brugia malayi* and *Wuchereria bancrofti*	Lymphadenopathy, edema secondary to lymphatic obstruction	Diethylcarbamazine
Biting midges (Ceratopogonidae)	Dipetalonemiasis (12)	Tropical Africa and South America	Nematodes: *Dipetalonema perstans* and *D. streptocera*	Fever, rash, subcutaneous swelling, abdominal pain	Diethylcarbamazine
	Mansonelliasis Ozzardi (12)	South America	Nematode: *Mansonella*	Fever, lymphadenopathy, hydroceles	None

(continued)

TABLE 1. (*Continued*)

Arthropod Vector	Disease Transmitted	Geography	Pathogen	Clinical Manifestations	Treatment
Sandflys (Psychodidae)	Leishmaniasis (9)	Asia, Africa, southern Europe, South and Central America	Protozoa of genus *Leishmania*	Fever, organomegaly, pancytopenia, mucocutaneous lesions, lymphadenopathy	Sodium antimony gluconate
	Phlebotomus fever (1)	Middle East, Central Asia, South and Central America	Arbovirus	Fever, facial rash, conjunctival injection, leukopenia, muscular and abdominal pain, photophobia, relative bradycardia	None
	Bartonellosis (carrion's disease) (7)	Peru, Ecuador, Colombia	Gram-negative bacillus: *Bartonella bacilliformis*	Fever, anemia, rash	Chloramphenicol or tetracycline
Blackflies (Simuliidae)	Onchocerciasis (river blindness) (13)	Mexico, Guatemala, Colombia, Venezuela, Surinam, Brazil, and tropical Africa	Nematode: *Onchocerca volvolus*	Subcutaneous nodules, keratitis, iridocyclitis, chorioretinitis	Local excision, diethylcarbamazine or suramin
Deerflies (Tabanidae)	Loiasis (14)	West and Central Africa	Nematode: *Loa loa* (eye worm)	Calabar swellings, endomyocardial fibrosis	Diethylcarbamazine
	Tularemia (Ohara's disease) (5)	United States	Bacteria: *Pasturella* (*Francisella*); a gramnegative bacillus	Localized skin or mucosal lesion with regional adenopathy, pneumonia, fever, splenomegaly, and evanescent rash	Streptomycin
Tsetse flies (Gloss)	African trypanosomiais (sleeping sickness) (11)	Africa	Hemoflagellate: *Trypanosoma brucei*	Fever, lymphadenopathy, meningoencephalomyelitis	Suramin or pentamidine before central nervous system (CNS) involvement; melarsoprol if CNS involved

Vector	Disease	Etiologic agent	Geographic distribution	Clinical features	Treatment
...dae)	(Chagas' disease) (11)	...soma cruzi	and southern United States	inflammatory reaction at inoculation site (chagoma); conjunctivitis, palpebral edema, and preauricular adenopathy (Romaña's sign); fever, hepatosplenomegaly, myocarditis, meningoencephalitis, rash; megacolon and megaesophagus	Primaquine or Bayer 2502 (Lampit)
Fleas (Siphonaptera)	Plague (bubonic) (6)	Bacteria: gram-negative bacillus (*Yersinia pestis*)	United States, western Canada, and western Mexico	Fever, suppurating lymphadenopathy, pneumonia, intravascular coagulopathy	Streptomycin or tetracycline
	Murine (endemic) typhus fever (17)	*Rickettsia mooseri*	United States	Maculopapular rash, fever, headache, myalgias; positive Weil-Felix reaction (*Proteus* OX-19)	Chloramphenicol or tetracycline
Lice	Epidemic typhus fever and Brill-Zinsser disease (18)	*Rickettsia prowazekii*	Worldwide	Macular and petechial rash, neurologic and cardiovascular disturbances, thrombosis and azotemia; positive agglutinins to *Proteus* OX-19	Chloramphenicol or tetracycline
	Relapsing fever (8)	Spirochete: *Borrelia recurrentis*	Ethiopia, South America, Far East	Fever, macular and petechial rash, myalgias, arthralgias, headache, vomiting, jaundice, hemorrhagic diathesis; relapse in 1–2 weeks; routine Weil-Felix reaction to *Proteus* OX-K	Penicillin or chloramphenicol
	Trench fever (20)	*Rickettsia quintana*	Mexico, Tunisia, Poland, Soviet Union	Fever, arthralgias, myalgias, macular rash; relapses; negative Weil-Felix reaction	Broad-spectrum antibiotics

(continued)

TABLE 1. (*Continued*)

Arthropod Vector	Disease Transmitted	Geography	Pathogen	Clinical Manifestations	Treatment
Hard ticks (Ixodidae)	Spotted fever group (Rocky Mountain spotted fever, Boutonneuse fever, Queensland tick typhus, north Asian tick-borne rickettsiosis) (16)	United States, Canada, Mexico, Colombia, Brazil for Rocky Mountain spotted fever, Eastern Hemisphere for others	*Rickettsia rickettsii, R. coronii, R. autralis, R. sibirica*	Fever, headache, characteristic maculopapular and ecchymotic rash, azotemia; positive Weil-Felix reaction (*Proteus* OX-2 and OX-19)	Chloramphenicol or tetracycline
	Q fever (19)	United States, North Africa, Europe	Rickettsia: *Coxiella burnetii*	Fever, headache, interstitial pneumonitis, hepatitis, endocarditis; negative Weil-Felix reaction	Chloramphenicol or tetracycline
	West Nile fever; louping ill disease, central European and tick-borne encephalitis, Onisk hemorrhagic fever, Colorado tick fever, Kyasanur forest disease (3)	Egypt, Uganda, South Africa, Israel, India; England and Ireland; central Europe and Soviet Union; Soviet Union; Western United States except Pacific Coast; India	Arbovirus	Fever, meningoencephalitis, hemorrhagic diatheses	None
	Tularemia (Ohara's disease) (5)	United States	Bacteria (gram-negative bacillus): *Pasturella (Francisella) tularensis*	Localized skin or mucosal lesion with regional adenopathy, pneumonia, fever, splenomegaly, evanescent rash	Streptomycin
	Babesiosis (16)	Ireland, United States	Protozoan: *Babesia* species	Fever in splenectomized persons, red blood cells parasitized	Chloroquine or pentamidine
	Tick paralysis (4)	United States, Australia, South Africa, Canada	Neurotoxin in tick saliva	Paralysis	Removal of tick
	Lyme disease (15)	United States, Europe	Unknown	Erythema chronicum migrans, fever, head-	Penicillin or tetracycline

	Disease (ref.)	Distribution	Agent	Clinical features	Treatment
Soft ticks (Argasidae)	Relapsing fever (8)	Worldwide	Spirochete: *Borrelia recurrentis*	Fever, macular and petechial rash, myalgias, arthralgias, headache, vomiting, iridocyclitis, repeated mild relapses; negative Weil-Felix reaction	Tetracycline
Mites Trombiculidae	Scrub typhus (19)	Southeast Asia, India, Northern Australia	*Rickettsia tsutsugamushi*	Fever, headache, lymphadenopathy, maculopapular rash, myocarditis, positive Weil-Felix reaction to *Proteus* OX-K	Chloramphenicol or tetracycline
Meso-stigmatidae	Rickettsial pox (17)	United States, western Soviet Union	*Rickettsia akari*	Fever, headache, myalgias, photophobia, maculopapular and vesicular rash; negative Weil-Felix reaction	Chloramphenicol or tetracycline

[1] Andrews, C., *Viruses of Vertebrates*. Bailliere, Tindall, and Cassell, London, 1964, p. 88.
[2] Casals and Clarke, in Horstall F. L. and Tamm I. (Eds.), *Viral and Rickettsial Infections of Man*, 4th ed., Lippincott, Philadelphia, 1965, pp. 586, 590, 608, 615, 633.
[3] Casals and Clarke, in Horstall F. L. and Tamm I., *loc. cit.*, pp. 633, 636, 641–43, 671.
[4] Cherington, M., Lynder, R. D., Tick paralysis: Neurophysiologic studies. *New England Journal of Medicine*, **275**:95, 1968.
[5] Cluff, L. E. in Thorn G. W. *et al.* (Eds.), *Principles of Internal Medicine*, 8th ed. McGraw-Hill, New York, 1977, p. 858.
[6] Johnson, J. E., in Thorn, G. W. *et al.*, *loc. cit.*, p. 860.
[7] Plorde, J. J., in Thorn, G. W. *et al.*, *loc. cit.*, p. 1071.
[8] Plorde, J. J., in Thorn, G. W. *et al.*, *loc. cit.*, pp. 934–36.
[9] Plorde, J. J., in Thorn, G. W. *et al.*, *loc. cit.*, p. 1075.
[10] Plorde, J. J., in Thorn, G. W. *et al.*, *loc. cit.*, p. 1071.
[11] Plorde, J. J., in Thorn, G. W. *et al.*, *loc. cit.*, pp. 1079–82.
[12] Plorde, J. J., in Thorn, G. W. *et al.*, *loc. cit.*, p. 1102.
[13] Plorde, J. J., in Thorn, G. W. *et al.*, *loc. cit.*, p. 1104.
[14] Plorde, J. J., in Thorn, G. W. *et al.*, *loc. cit.*, p. 1105.
[15] Steere, A. C. *et al.*, Antibiotic therapy in lyme disease. *Annals of Internal Medicine*, **93**:1, 1980.
[16] Voge, M. and Markell, E. K., *Medical Parisitology*. W. B. Saunders, Philadelphia, 1971, p. 148.
[17] Woodward, T. E., in Thorn, G. W. *et al.*, *loc. cit.*, pp. 957–61.
[18] Woodward, T. E., in Thorn, G. W. *et al.*, *loc. cit.*, pp. 962–63.
[19] Woodward, T. E., in Thorn, G. W. *et al.*, *loc. cit.*, pp. 964–65.
[20] Woodward, T. E., in Thorn, G. W. *et al.*, *loc. cit.*, p. 966.

Source: Courtesy Richard P. Kaplan, M.D.

transmission, such as that of enteric pathogens by houseflies and the trachoma agent by eye gnats. Vector transmission may be human-to-human or animal-to-human; it may also involve transmission to progeny of the vector. To be an effective vector, an arthropod must permit appropriate multiplication or growth of the microorganism without loss of infectivity and without serious immediate pathogenicity for itself. The vector must be anthropophilic in its feeding and be able to maintain itself close to human populations. In most of the groups listed, only a few species meet these requirements.

Venoms have evolved in several insect groups, and venomous insects may attack humans, sometimes with lethal results. Skins, hairs, and secretions of insects may be irritant or allergenic, producing cutaneous and respiratory syndromes. Finally, insects have a high annoyance potential. Their mere presence, especially in large numbers, may be detrimental to health and well-being.

Venomous Insects

HYMENOPTERA (BEES, WASPS, AND ANTS)

By far the most important venomous insects are the bees, wasps, and ants, all members of the order Hymenoptera. Stinging hymenoptera occur throughout most of the world and often live in close association with humans. Four main venomous families affect humans: the Apidae, or honeybees; the Bombidae, or bumblebees; the Vespidae, or wasps, hornets, and yellow jackets; and the Formicidae, or ants (Figure 1). The honeybee (*Apis mellifera*) is one of the few domesticated insects and is maintained in hives of up to 50,000 members in many countries. Smaller feral colonies usually nest in hollow trees or crevices in rocks but may also utilize the walls of occupied houses. Paper wasps (*Polistes*) suspend their nests in shaded locales, often in shrubbery near houses or below eaves, window frames, or gutters. The large paper nests of the white-faced hornet (*Dolchiovespula maculata*) may be plastered to buildings but are more often hung from the branches of trees. Yellow jackets (*Vespula* sp.) and bumblebees make underground nests in burrows of mammals or in rotted tree stumps. Fire ants (*Solenopsis*) and harvester ants (*Pogonomyrmex*) often build their mounds in cultivated fields or pastures. Mud daubers (e.g., *Sceliphron caementarium*), solitary wasps which rarely sting, may plaster their nests on house walls or under bridges.

The general appearance of these insects is familiar to most persons. The abdomen and thorax are connected by a slender pedicle that may be quite long in some wasps and ants. Bees and most wasps are winged as adults; ants are wingless except for sexually mature adults during part of their life cycle. Mouthparts are basically adapted for chewing but in some species are modified for sucking. The life cycle includes egg, larva, and pupa stages prior to the emergence of adults. Immature insects are usually protected and provided with food by the adult. Both animal and plant foods are utilized. Many species are parasitic on other arthropods. A high degree of social organization is characteristic of ants and of many species of bees and wasps. Colonies range in size from a few dozen to many thousands of individuals. In cold climates, most individuals die in the autumn, leaving the fertilized females to overwinter and found new colonies in the spring.

Killer Bees

Some concern has been expressed, particularly in the mass media, over the "Brazilian killer bees." This African race of the honeybee (*A. mellifera adansoni*) was introduced into Brazil because it was a more efficient honey producer. The first escape occurred in 1957, and the form spread northward at a rate of about 320 km/year until 1971. It has most recently been reported near Caracas, Venezuela. While no geographic or climatic barrier seems likely to stop it before it reaches the southern United States, it seems that its progress has been slowed and its aggressive behavior diluted by hybridization with domestic bees of Latin America. The African bees are characterized by frequent swarming, large populations, and mass attacks following minimal provocation. Although the toxicity of their venom is reported to be no greater than that of other forms of *mellifera*, there have been fatalities from multiple stings (17,44).

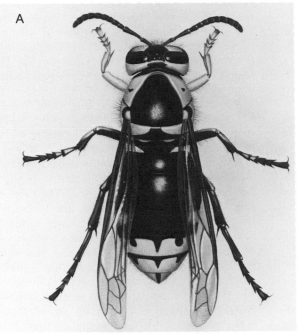

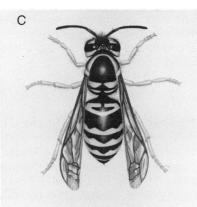

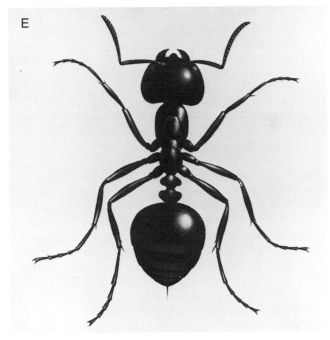

FIGURE 1 Representative venomous hymenoptera: (*A*) hornet (*Vespula maculata*); (*B*) wasp (*Chlorion ichneumerea*); (*C*) yellow jacket (*Vespula maculiforma*); (*D*) honey bee (*Apis mellifera*); and (*E*) fire ant (*Solenopsis invicta*). (Reproduced by permission of Merck Sharpe & Dohme, Division of Merck & Co., Inc.)

Fire Ants

South American fire ants (*Solenopsis richteri* and *S. invicta*) were introduced to the southern United States in the 1920s (50a). Since that time, they have spread their infestation to include 13 southern states and millions of acres of farmland. They are prolific, becoming adaptable to climate, and resistant to many insecticides. Worker colonies reach maximum size in two years, and have been known to "march" into neighborhoods rapidly, often in days. Possessed of a foul disposition, tenacious jaws, and a striking abdominal stinger, they inflict both bites and stings with little provocation.

Stinging Patterns

Multiple stings often result from the disturbance of an insect nest. The first insects encountered release alarm odors, or pheromones, that incite aggressive behavior in other members of the colony. With large species, such as the white-faced hornet, 40–50 stings may represent a life-threatening injury.

In the United States and other Western nations, the incidence of serious insect stings is higher in adults than in children and higher in males than in females. Most persons are stung while engaged in outdoor work or recreation. Beekeeping is a high-risk occupation; however, many bee keepers seem to develop considerable immunity as the result of frequent stings.

Other relatively high-risk occupations are those of farmer, house painter, carpenter, and bulldozer operator. Wasps and bees frequently are swept into the interior of moving automobiles, exposing the occupants of the car to the risks of both a sting and a highway accident. Many foods, particularly ripe fruits or fruit syrups, attract yellow jackets, hornets, and paper wasps; flowers and some perfumes attract bees. In temperate zones, the incidence of hymenopteran stings is highest in late summer and early fall, since insect populations are highest during these seasons.

Venom and Venom Apparatus

Venom is present in many hymenopteran species and is used for both defense and the subjugation of prey. The stinging apparatus is a modified ovipositor located at the posterior end of the abdomen. It consists of venom glands, a reservoir, and structures for piercing the integument and injecting the venom. In many cases, it can be withdrawn into the abdomen when not in use.

Venoms of most medically important hymenoptera are mixtures of protein or polypeptide toxins (mellitin in bee venoms, kinins in wasp venoms), enzymes (phospholipases, hyaluronidase), and pharmacologically active low molecular weight compounds (histamine, serotonin, acetylcholine, dopamine). The active components of fire ant venoms are alkaloids. Paper wasp, honeybee, and hornet venoms contain 9–13 antigenic proteins, some of which are species specific and others of which are shared among species. Some, e.g., phospholipase A in honeybee venom and protein 5 in *Polistes* venom, appear to be more important than others in producing sensitization (63). Some low molecular weight compounds, such as the alkaloids of fire ant venoms, may act as haptens in producing sensitivity. Hundreds of allergic reactions to fire ant stings, some of them fatal, have been reported in the southern United States (27,56,75).

Clinical Aspects

The most common site of the sting is the head and neck region, followed by the foot, leg, hand, and arm. Single wasp, bee, or ant stings in unsensitized individuals usually cause instant pain, accompanied by a wheal and flare reaction with a variable amount of edema. Individuals with milder reactions to hymenopteran stings typically develop hives, nausea, and wheezing. These symptoms may subside in a short time without treatment but are a warning of a dangerously allergic state. With the more venomous species, pain and swelling may extend well beyond the site and persist for as long as 4 days. Stings of the imported fire ants, *Solenopsis invicta* and *S. richteri,* produce multiple vesicles that become sterile pustules, which are prone to secondary bacterial infection (Figure 2). Clear vesicles appear at 2–4 hours, with a pustular evolution over 12–24 hours.

Severe individual stings can induce flushing of the skin with pruritus and fever, followed

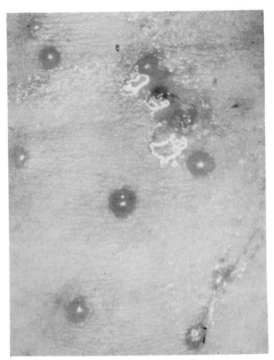

FIGURE 2 Vesicles produced by fire ant stings, about 2 hours after injury. These subsequently become sterile pustules. (Photo courtesy of Cameron Smith.)

by pronounced dyspnea, cyanosis, and collapse. With multiple hymenopteran stings there may be vomiting, diarrhea, generalized edema, oliguria, and hypotension. Widespread necrosis of skeletal muscle, acute tubular necrosis, and hyperkalemia have been reported following multiple hornet stings (62). Myocardial infarction in previously healthy individuals may follow multiple hymenopteran stings (31). Bee stings of the esophagus may result from the inadvertent ingestion of bees while consuming beverages.

About 85% of systemic allergic reactions to insect stings occur within the first 15 minutes, and nearly all occur within 6 hours. Fatalities are more common in adults than in children. They occur most often within the first hour as a result of airway obstruction or primary hypotension. In 69% of fatal cases, obstruction of the respiratory tract by edema or secretions was the principal finding at autopsy; in 12%, vascular pathology was the principal finding; and in 7%, primary central nervous system involvement occurred (3).

Delayed atypical reactions (10–14 days) to insect stings occur in a small number of patients. These include the Arthus reaction, serum sickness, arthralgia, fever, nephrotic syndrome, acute glomerulonephritis, hepatorenal syndrome, necrotic angiitis, thrombocytopenic purpura, transverse myelitis, Guillain-Barré syndrome, brain infarct, lymphadenopathy, and birth defects. Most appear to be immunologically mediated. In one series, elevated immunoglobulin E (IgE) to bee or yellow jacket venom was observed in 6 of 13 patients (36).

Therapy

Treatment of acute reactions to insect stings follows conventional lines for the treatment of acute allergic emergencies. Aqueous epinephrine 1:1000 should be administered subcutaneously at the first indication of serious hypersensitivity. The dosage is 0.3–0.5 ml in adults and 0.01 ml/kg in children. An alternative administrative route for epinephrine in cases of profound hypotension or extremis is sublingually as the 1:1000 solution; the drug may also be delivered as a 1:10,000 preparation in an adult dose of 2–5 ml via an endotracheal tube or slow intravenous push. Doses should be repeated as necessary every 20–30 minutes.

In the event of hypotension, volume replacement and pressor agents, such as dopamine, may be required. If airway obstruction ensues, some patients will require intubation and mechanical respiratory assistance. Antihistaminics are of little value in the acute severe reaction but may prove useful in lesser envenomations. The dose of diphenhydramine is 50–100 mg in an adult and 1 mg/kg in a child by the slow intravenous route. In cases of full-blown anaphylaxis, an intravenous corticosteroid, such as 2 mg/kg hydrocortisone, is indicated, remembering that there is a delay of hours in the onset of action. Intravenous calcium gluconate (10%, 5–10 ml), in conjunction with parenteral antihistaminics and corticosteroids, may be used to relieve the pain, edema, vomiting, and diarrhea accompanying envenomation. Propranolol augments the hypotension caused by the administration of large doses of bee venom to animals and may be contraindicated in humans (30).

Individuals who have been stung by more than 10 hornets or paper wasps, or by large numbers of fire ants, harvester ants, or honeybees, should be observed for delayed reactions for 12–24 hours. Urinary output must be monitored and the urine tested frequently for hemoglobin and myoglobin as a measure of rhabdomyolysis. Serum potassium levels should also be monitored, as cases of acute renal failure in response to nephrotoxicity and hypotension have been reported. Oliguria with myoglobinuria, azotemia, and hyperkalemia are indications for starting hemodialysis.

Stings or fragments left in the skin should be scraped or brushed off, not removed with forceps. Only the honeybee leaves its stinger and venom sac at the site of envenomation. The barbed stinger hooks into the skin and causes the bee to be fatally disemboweled when it flies off. The detached venom sac continues to contract for a period of minutes, injecting more venom into the wound.

In mild hymenopteran stings, application of ice packs often gives relief. The wound should be washed with soap and water. Some authorities suggest that topical papain, as contained in meat tenderizer, may be of use. Local application of antihistamine lotions or creams, such as tripelennamine, may also be helpful. This should be followed by an oral antihistaminic, e.g., diphenhydramine, 25–50 mg every 6 hours. Tetanus prophylaxis is standard. Baking soda paste is a harmless but ineffective home remedy for insect stings, especially those of ants. It may date back to the days when formic acid was considered the principal toxin in insect venoms.

Sensitization and Desensitization

Anaphylaxis and other syndromes associated with hymenopteran stings are relatively common outdoor emergencies. It has been estimated that about 0.4% of the U.S. population, or 1–2 million people, shows some degree of clinical allergy to insect venoms, and 40–45 deaths are reported annually (3,35). Indeed, allergy to hymenopteran venom accounts for more deaths in the United States than does any other envenomation.

The interval between the first known sting and the reaction-producing sting is usually less than 5 years but may be as long as 48 years. Some patients give a history of increasingly severe local reactions preceding a sting with a systemic reaction. About 15% give a personal or family history of insect sting allergy (45). A prior history of sting or sensitivity may be absent, leading some authors to believe that airborne sensitization may be possible (32).

Identification of the individual with a potentially dangerous allergy to insect stings is not always possible, despite new immunologic techniques, such as radio-allergoimmunoassay (RAST) and the measurement of histamine release by leukocytes. In one study, IgE antibody to hymenopteran venoms was found in sera of 71 of 109 individuals with a history of systemic insection sting reaction. Some had antibody to all three of the venoms tested, others to only one or two (54). In another study, IgE to bee venom was found in 70% of patients with insect sting allergy, 40% of beekeepers, and 12% of blood donors. There was no correlation between the antibody level as determined by RAST and the severity of sting reactions (46). IgE levels often fall virtually to zero 3–18 months following a sting reaction, and clinical sensitivity is lost. The venom skin sensitivity test is reported to be about 95% reliable in identifying individuals who should receive immunotherapy (34,55).

Desensitization with freeze-dried, purified insect venoms produces an excellent blocking antibody response, lowering of venom-specific IgE, and resistance to natural stings in a majority of patients who have had systemic reactions to insect stings and who have a positive RAST or skin test (33,34,55). These products are marketed under the trade name Pharmalgen (Pharmacia Diagnostics). It should be noted that these venom antigens are expensive, and some are not generally available; moreover, some reactions do not seem to be IgE mediated. With proper indications, however, these substances are a valuable addition to the allergist's armamentarium. Venoms used for skin testing and immunotherapy are those of the honey bee, yellow jacket, yellow hornet, white-faced hornet, wasp, and mixed vespid. Some studies have shown that immunotherapy provides complete protection for 70% of treated individuals and partial protection for the other 30% (26). The Food and Drug Administration suggests that immunotherapy be used only for patients with a history of life-threatening reaction who remain hypersensitive on the basis of skin testing. Desensitization with insect whole-body extracts is of little value and should not be considered.

There is no consensus on the best regimen for desensitization to hymenopteran venoms. The best of three programs used in one clinical study involved subcutaneous injections of 1, 5, and 10 μg of venom at 30 minute intervals on the first day of therapy. This was followed in 2 weeks by a dose of 30 μg, and in 4 weeks by 60 μg. Doses of 100 μg each were given on weeks 6, 8, 11, 15, and 19. With all of the regimens used, large local reactions occurred in about one half of the patients. Systemic reactions occurred in 16%; one-third of these were severe enough to require administration of epinephrine. Most systemic reactions occurred early in the course of therapy. When a systemic reaction occurred, the next dose was held at the same level or reduced, depending on the severity of the reaction. Starting therapy with very small doses (0.01 μg) and giving doses at more frequent intervals did not reduce either local or systemic reactions (21). A program beginning with a 10 μg dose and increasing to 100 μg with twice-weekly doses achieved maximal desensitization in 5 weeks. Maintenance doses of 100 μg were given monthly thereafter. Most patients had local reactions early in the program, and 5 of 40 had systemic reactions (1).

It is not known how frequently desensitization must be repeated. Because of the relatively high incidence of systemic reactions, desensitization should be undertaken in the hospital or another appropriately prepared facility.

Prevention and Preparedness

The frequent cleaning of garbage cans and the disposal of decaying fruit will make premises less attractive to bees and wasps. The hymenoptera are highly susceptible to many insecticides, and their control around dwellings and other inhabited buildings is rarely difficult. It is safer to spray the nests after dark.

Many hymenoptera are economically valuable as pollinators of plants or as predators on other insects; hence, their control on a wide scale is rarely desirable. The fire ant in the southern United States has been the target of massive control campaigns that have been marginally effective and have had undesirable effects on local ecosystems.

Patients known to be sensitive to insect stings should carry an emergency kit, such as Ana-Kit (Holister-Stier) or Epi Pen (Center Laboratories), containing a preloaded syringe of epinephrine, and should be instructed in its use. Kits should also be available in work or recreation areas where there is a high risk of insect stings. Allergic individuals should wear medical identification badges.

LEPIDOPTERA (CATERPILLARS)

Lepidoptera commonly cause envenomation in humans, although it is generally less serious than that caused by hymenoptera. It usually results from contact with caterpillars and, less frequently, from the cocoon or adult stage. The larval lepidopteran (caterpillar) is usually free-living and moderately active and feeds on plants, although a few species are parasites of insect nests or eat other food of animal origin. The pupal stage may be encased in a silk cocoon; overwintering in cold climates usually occurs in the pupal stage. Adults (butterflies and moths) are nearly always winged and have their wings covered with microscopic scales. While most butterflies feed largely on nectar and other plant juices, some feed on semiliquid mammalian feces and urine, and one genus of tropical moths feeds on ocular secretions. There is no care or protection of immature stages by the adult, nor is there true social organization, although the larvae and adults of some species assemble in large aggregations.

Venomous Species

Venomous species occur in at least 10 families of lepidoptera, and there are no general rules for their recognition. Many venomous caterpillars are broad, flat, and sluggish. Some have the dorsal surface densely covered with long hairs. Others are markedly spiny and may have bright, conspicuous colors and markings that probably serve a warning function. Still others are highly cryptic.

Venomous lepidoptera occur on all continents, but the greatest concentration of species causing clinical envenomation occurs in the American tropics. Some of the most important belong to the genus *Megalopyge*. These are large, stout caterpillars, often densely covered with hair that accounts for such local names as *perrito* (little dog). Caterpillars of the genus *Automeris* are large (80–100 mm) and often brightly colored. *Dirphia* is a third important genus, characterized by long-branched spines. Several other genera are of minor or local importance. Moths of the genus *Hylesia* have a tuft of venomous spines at the posterior end of the abdomen. They occur throughout much of tropical South America.

Probably the most important venomous caterpillar in the United States is the puss caterpillar, or wooly slug (*Megalopyge opercularis*), which occurs from the southern states west through most of Texas, and north to Maryland and Missouri. This hairy, flat, ovoid caterpillar reaches a length of 30–35 mm and feeds on a wide variety of shade trees, including elm, oak, and sycamore. In some years, it may be plentiful enough to be an unpleasant nuisance. In southeastern Texas in 1958, at least 2130 persons were treated for stings, with eight hospitalizations (42). A related species, the flannel moth caterpillar (*Lagoa crispata*), occurs in the middle eastern states north to New England. Its sting is less severe than that of *M. opercularis*. The large, spiny caterpillar of the io moth (*Automeris io*) is pale green with red and white lateral stripes. It is widely distributed in the eastern United States but is rarely plentiful. The saddleback caterpillar (*Sibine stimula*) and the oak slug (*Euclea delphinii*) are flat and almost rectangular. All these species can deliver a painful injury. The tussock moth caterpillars (*Hemerocampa* spp.) and range caterpillar (*Hemileuca oliviae*) are the other common nettling species.

The proliferation of the gypsy moth caterpillar (*Lymantria dispar*) in the northeastern United States has brought with it thousands of cases of a pruritic dermatitis characterized by blotchy redness, erythematous and urticarial papules, and linear streaks. Histamine has been extracted from the hairlike setae of the older caterpillars, which have been implicated

as the organ of envenomation (4a, 61a). The diagnosis may be confirmed in some cases by the application of clear adhesive tape to the affected area; the setae are visible on microscopic examination.

In Europe, the processionary caterpillars (*Thaumatopoea* spp.), some of the tussock moth caterpillars (e.g., *Euproctis*), and the devil's ring caterpillar (*Lasiocampa quercus*) are important venomous species. Venomous caterpillars occur in Africa, Asia, and Australia but do not seem to represent a serious or widespread problem. Envenomation from about 20 species of caterpillars and four species of moths has been reported from Japan, chiefly from the southern Nansei Islands. Many of these species almost certainly occur on the Asian mainland as well (29).

Venom and Venom Apparatus

Venoms in lepidoptera serve purely for defense. The venom apparatus is simple, consisting of hollow, brittle spines with venom-secreting glands at their bases. The spines may be simple or branched, and may be widely scattered over the surface of the insect or arranged in clumps. They are often intermixed with nonvenomiferous hairs or spines. No muscles or other special structures for expelling the venom have been described. Little is known of the chemistry of caterpillar venoms. They are heat labile and, in at least one species, have been shown to be proteins. Histamine and serotonin have been found in a few caterpillar venoms but are not of general occurrence.

Stinging Patterns

Caterpillar envenomation usually occurs when the insects are touched as they cling to vegetation. Persons cutting branches, picking fruit, or climbing trees are likely to be stung. Caterpillars may also be found on clothing, in bedding left outdoors, or on outdoor furniture. In some species, the spines of dead caterpillars, detached spines, and spines woven into cocoons may retain their stinging property for a long time. In temperate regions, caterpillar stings are most frequent from August to early November. In the American tropics, envenomation is most prevalent during the rainy season. Heavy infestations with *Megalopyge* and other caterpillars seem to be related to favorable weather and sporadic decreases in the populations of parasites that serve as natural controls.

Clinical Aspects

Contact with a venomous caterpillar results in instant nettling pain, followed by redness and swelling, occasionally in a gridlike pattern. With such species as *M. opercularis,* the pain is very severe, with central radiation. This may be accompanied by lymphadenopathy, nausea, headache, and low-grade fever. Convulsions and hypotension have been reported. In the more usual cases, however, there are no systemic manifestations, and the pain and redness are followed by a pruritic papular rash that may persist for 3–4 days. A hemorrhagic syndrome with petechiae, melena, and bleeding from the ears, nose, and vagina has been reported following the sting of a large caterpillar in Venezuela (2). Ophthalmia from detached spines lodging in the eye has been reported. In rare cases, this has been serious enough to require enucleation. Irritation of the respiratory tract, stomatitis, and pharyngitis have been ascribed to inhaled or ingested caterpillar spines. Acute anaphylactic reactions, so common after hymenopteran stings, have not been reported following lepidopteran stings. Residents of the Peruvian jungle often appear to develop some immunity to caterpillar stings with regular and repeated exposure (51). However, a chronic granuloma of the hands of Brazilian rubber workers, known as *pararama,* is reported to result from repeated contact with caterpillars and cocoons (11).

Therapy

Treatment of lepidopteran envenomations is symptomatic. Patients with local symptoms generally get relief from antipruritic lotions and creams. Antihistaminics and corticosteroids are not markedly better than simpler preparations, such as calamine lotion with phenol. Prompt application of adhesive or Scotch tape to the site of the sting may remove many spines. Codeine, meperidine, oxymorphone, or morphine may be needed to control the severe pain, nausea, and vomiting in severe

envenomation. Intravenous calcium gluconate has been reported by some to be effective in the control of pain and muscle spasm. Tetanus prophylaxis is standard. Some authors recommend tolmetin sodium (400 mg orally three times a day) as an analgesic and anti-inflammatory agent.

Prevention

Trees on which the caterpillars feed should be sprayed with appropriate insecticides to control outbreaks of the puss caterpillar and other venomous species when they become annoyingly plentiful. Screens on windows and doors protect against moths with toxic spines.

HEMIPTERA (SUCKING BUGS)

The Hemiptera are a large order of insects characterized by sucking mouthparts, generally in the form of a beak. Their life cycle has no well-demarcated larval and pupal stages, but rather is a gradual transition from the hatchling nymph to the adult. Most hemiptera are winged as adults, with the anterior wings generally divided into a chitinized and a membranous section. Most feed on plant juices, but several families are predators, and two feed on the blood of humans and other vertebrates.

The assassin bugs (Reduviidae) are generally recognizable by the long, narrow head, stout three-jointed beak, long antennae, and typical hemipteran wings. Most have a dark color, but a few are brightly marked. Some species attach fragments of their prey, sand grains, or other debris to their backs. The family occurs on all continents. They frequent a variety of habitats and are often nocturnal.

Venomous aquatic species include the giant waterbugs (Belostomatidae), back-swimmers (Notonectidae), and water scorpions (Nepidae). Waterbugs can be distinguished from aquatic beetles by their beak and hemipteran wings; the back-swimmers have a much elongated hind pair of legs; and the water scorpions have a slender body with long terminal breathing tubes.

The bloodsucking hemiptera include the triatomids (e.g., *Triatoma protracta,* alias assassin, western conenose, or kissing bug), which are a subfamily of the Reduviidae, and the Cimicidae, or bedbugs. The latter are flat, ovoid, reddish-brown insects whose wings are reduced to a pair of functionless pads. The lack of large terminal claws distinguishes them from lice. The triatomids are primarily a neotropical group, with some species ranging northward in the United States to Utah and southern Indiana. The bedbugs are cosmopolitan.

Triatomids feed on a wide range of mammals and often live in their nests or burrows. Armadillos and pack rats are common hosts in the southwestern United States. Some triatomids adapt readily to life in human dwellings, particularly those of adobe construction. Two bedbugs, *Cimex lectularius* and *C. hemipterus,* feed primarily on humans and live in dwellings where they hide in bedding, under wallpaper, and behind baseboards and window frames. The homes of the economically and socially disadvantaged are most likely to be heavily infested, but the insects are also known to reside in well-appointed residences, hospitals, and hotels. Other species of *Cimex,* normally parasitic on bats and swallows, occasionally attack humans.

Venom and Venom Apparatus

The hemipteran venom apparatus consists of two or three thoracic pairs of glands, whose secretions are ejected through one-half of a double tube formed by the interlocking of very elongate maxillae and mandibles. The distal tip of this apparatus is modified for piercing. Few hemipteran venoms have been studied. Those of the African reduviid *Platymeris rhadamanthus* and the Middle Eastern *Holotrichius innesi* contain several enzymes, as well as some nonenzymatic protein toxins. Venom is used primarily for the subjugation and digestion of prey, but may also be used for defense. Salivary secretions of the bloodsucking hemipterans presumably serve an anticoagulant and vasodilating function. They are toxic to some extent and are potent allergens.

Biting Patterns

Triatomids usually bite at night on exposed parts of the body. Their predilection for biting the face accounts for the common names *kissing bug* and *barbero.* Entomologists and small children are the groups most frequently bitten by assassin bugs, for it usually takes rather rough handling of the insect to induce it to bite. Bites by aquatic hemiptera apparently are much like those of assassin bugs; few cases have been described in detail. The suspicion of this author is that some midwestern bites attributed to water moccasins are more appropriately characterized as aquatic hemipteran envenomations.

Clinical Aspects

Triatomid bites are painless in most individuals, and are usually followed by the development of an erythematous, itching papule that may persist for up to a week. Bites are often multiple and grouped in a cluster or line (see Plate 4). Hypersensitivity develops in many persons, and the bites may be accompanied by giant urticarial wheals, lymphadenopathy, and hemorrhagic bullae (25). Anaphylactoid reactions have been described (38).

The multiple, red, edematous, and pruritic lesions characteristic of bedbug bites are probably the result of delayed sensitization. Anaphylaxis from bedbug bites has been reported (50).

The bites of several species of domestic assassin bugs, such as the wheel bug (*Arilus cristatus*), the black corsair (*Melanolestes picipes*), and the masked bedbug hunter (*Reduvius personatus*), have been described to be as painful as the sting of a hornet and are accompanied by local swelling that lasts for several hours. Bites of the African *Platymeris* have been followed by local necrosis; moreover, this species can eject its venom as a spray, causing irritation to the eyes and nasal mucous membranes.

Aquatic hemipteran stings demonstrate local pain and swelling, and may be accompanied by diaphoresis, weakness, nausea, and regional lymphadenitis.

Therapy

Treatment is symptomatic and not particularly effective. Various antipruritic preparations are helpful in mild cases. The use of steroids as local applications or injected into lesions has been generally disappointing. Immobilization and elevation of the extremities are helpful in severe cases.

Prevention

Triatomids and bedbugs are more resistant than many insects to the common insecticides suitable for household use. Benzene hexachloride has been effective against triatomids in Latin America.

COLEOPTERA (BEETLES)

Beetles (Coleoptera) are the largest order of insects, with at least 250,000 species. The prothorax of beetles is generally very distinct, while the two posterior thoracic segments are more or less fused to the abdomen. In most beetles, the anterior pair of wings are heavily chitinized, acting as covers for the posterior membranous wings, which are used in flight. Mouthparts are of the chewing type. The life cycle involves larval and pupal stages prior to emergence of the adult. Many beetles feed on plants throughout their life cycle, many are predators or scavengers, and a few are parasitic. No beetles are known to have a bite or sting venomous to humans, but several families have toxic secretions that may be deposited on the skin.

Blister Beetles

The blister beetles (Meloidae) are a cosmopolitan group well represented in deserts and semiarid regions. In these areas, a species may suddenly appear by the thousands, particularly after rain storms, persist for a few days, and just as rapidly disappear, to be replaced by another species. The majority are of medium size (about 15 mm) and usually have soft, leathery forewings or elytra. Some are brilliantly colored. They are plentiful on vegetation, and some species are attracted to lights. A low molecular weight toxin, cantharidin, is present in the hemolymph and in most of the insect's tissues. If the beetle is gently pressed or otherwise injured, the toxin exudes from multiple sites.

Blister beetle dermatitis is not uncommon. In the eastern United States, it is usually caused by species of *Epicauta,* which occur on many garden plants. The initial contact with the beetle is painless and seldom remembered by the patient. Blisters first appear 2–5 hours after contact and may be single or multiple. They are ordinarily 5–50 mm in diameter and thin-walled. Unless broken and rubbed, they are not painful. Cantharidin nephritis has been reported following unusually heavy vesication, but more frequently it is the result of using cantharidin preparations as aphrodisiacs (8).

Rove Beetles

Another type of beetle vesication is caused by small rove beetles. These are slender insects with elongate abdomens and very short rectangular elytra. Most of the vesicating species belong to the genus *Paederus* and occur in many tropical and warm temperate regions, almost never in the United States. They usually fly during the evening in hot, humid weather. The vesicant substance of these beetles is not cantharidin. It is present in greatest concentration in the hemolymph, but does not exude spontaneously as does cantharidin in blister beetles. If the beetles are crushed or rubbed on the skin, local erythema appears after a period of several hours and is followed by a crop of small blisters that persist for 2–3 days. Conjunctivitis results if the secretion is rubbed into the eyes.

Darkling Ground Beetles

The darkling ground beetles are moderately large, dark, and heavily chitinized beetles. When disturbed, they assume a characteristic posture with the head down and the tail up. They are typically found in arid regions throughout the world, where they live under stones and other cover and crawl about at night. Most species can spray irritant secretions, mostly benzoquinones, from the tip of the abdomen to a distance of 30–40 cm. These are generally harmless to humans, but blistering of the skin has been reported in some cases, and eye injury is possible.

Therapy

There is no special treatment for beetle vesication. The injuries are best treated as partial-thickness chemical burns. Local preparations containing corticosteroids and antihistamines are not particularly effective and may actually worsen the situation. In cases of systemic cantharidin poisoning from ingestion, standard methods of gastric emptying and supportive care are indicated. The acute nephritis usually responds to conventional management.

DIPTERA (BLOODSUCKING FLIES, MOSQUITOES, GNATS, AND MIDGES)

The order Diptera contains most of the insects that serve as vectors of human disease. Most of these insects are cosmopolitan in distribution, exceptions being the tsetse flies that are restricted to Africa and the sandflies that are tropical and subtropical. Some species of mosquitoes and blackflies are adapted to cold temperate, subarctic, and alpine environments, where they may occur in such numbers and intensity as to make the areas virtually uninhabitable. Other mosquitoes and biting midges are equally abundant and annoying

in coastal areas and on islands. A list of the major groups of biting dipterans, their principal features of recognition, and the habitat of the larval and pupal stages is given in Table 2.

Clinical Aspects: Bloodsucking Flies

These insects feed on blood, and in doing so inject salivary secretions that are vasodilatory and anticoagulant. In most cases, these substances do not seem to be intrinsically toxic, but rather are potent allergens. Experimentally, it has been shown that children under 1 year of age rarely show a skin reaction to mosquito bites, but by age 5 nearly all react. Both the immediate and delayed types of hypersensitivity are induced, with the latter being more prolonged and troublesome. Paradoxically, prolonged natural exposure to bites

TABLE 2
Major Groups of Biting Flies (Diptera), Their Principal Recognition Features, and the Habitat of the Larval and Pupal Stages

Insect	Recognition Features of the Adult	Larval and Pupal Stages
Mosquitoes (Culicidae)	Prominent proboscis, wings with scales; palps of the female much shorter than the proboscis; usually rest with body parallel to substrate	Aquatic in a great variety of habitats; both larval and pupal stages motile
Mosquitoes (Anophelidae)	Prominent proboscis, wings with scales and often with dark mottling; palps of the female about as long as proboscis; usually rest with head down and body held at an angle to the substrate	Same as above
Blackflies, buffalo gnats (Simuliidae)	Stout, humpbacked, short antennae, wings broad with most of veins faint, body length <2.5 mm	Sessile in flowing water; usually attached to rocks, logs, etc., and sometimes to crustaceans
Sandflies (Phlebotomidae)	Small (usually <2 mm body length), hairy, wings with rather straight, prominent veins	In damp crevices, animal burrows, leaf litter
Biting midges, sandflies, no-see-ums (Ceratopogonidae)	Small (<2 mm body length), wings often mottled, most of wing veins faint	In mud, wet sand, rotting vegetation; larvae very motile
Horseflies, deerflies (Tabanidae)	Large (5–25 mm body length), with large eyes usually brilliantly colored; body stout; wings with prominent veins	In mud or damp soil
Stable flies *Stomoxys* (Muscidae)	Similar to housefly in size and general appearance; sharp-pointed proboscis projects downward and backward.	In dung, urine-soaked straw, or decaying vegetable matter
Tsetse flies (Glossinidae)	Large (6–14 mm); proboscis projects foreward; wings fold scissorlike over back	Larvae complete most of development in female; pupate in soil a few hours after birth
Snipe flies (Rhagionidae)	Long legs, relatively slender body, large eyes, wings with prominent veins	Aquatic or in moist soil or rotten wood

produces a loss of sensitivity in some individuals. Despite this observation, medical desensitization procedures have not been successful.

Serious reactions of an anaphylactoid nature have been reported following the bites of mosquitoes, tabanids, sandflies, and midges. Immunologic injury resulting from antigen-antibody complexes is known (43,73). Blackfly bites may be accompanied by hemorrhage, swelling, fever, malaise, and leukocytosis. In parts of Quebec, most children develop induration of the lymphatics and display lymphadenopathy as a result of these bites (43).

Therapy

Treatment of dipteran bites is symptomatic and not particularly effective. Local applications containing antihistamines or corticosteroids are not clearly superior to calamine lotion or aluminum acetate (Burow's solution). In the case of generalized illness, a trial of oral or parenteral corticosteroids is not contraindicated.

Prevention

The use of protective clothing and repellents, such as diethyltoluamide (*N,N*-diethyl-*m*-toluamide) or dimethylphthalate will often allow reasonably normal activity in the presence of large numbers of biting flies. However, protective clothing may become uncomfortably hot, and repellents do not always repel. Large-scale control measures usually are necessary in areas of permanent settlement.

Other Insects

Other types of insect envenomation occur sporadically. Many insects, such as leaf-hoppers and thrips that normally feed on plant juices, occasionally inflict annoying bites. This behavior may be initiated by dehydration of the insect or by unknown factors. The stick insect, *Anisomorpha buprestoides,* a common species in Florida and adjacent states, ejects a noxious fluid from its thoracic region that deters birds and other predators. According to regional folklore, this secretion can be directed toward human eyes, with painful consequences.

Arachnids

The arachnids are a large and diverse group of organisms found mostly in terrestrial environments, where they have been nearly as successful as insects in exploiting a variety of ecologic niches.

Among the arachnids, a number of ticks and mites parasitize humans, and in doing so may transmit pathogenic microorganisms (Table 1). Others inject secretions that cause local irritation or systemic illness. Venoms for killing prey and deterring predators occur in spiders, scorpions, and a few other groups. Some of these venomous arachnids represent a danger to humans. Mites sometimes proliferate in enormous numbers in stored foods or other organic substances. Dried bodies of certain mites are said to be the principal inhalant allergen in house dust, while other mites cause allergic dermatitis.

Arachnids may show marked segmentation of the body (e.g., scorpions) or very little (e.g., ticks), but they do not show the three distinct body regions characteristic of insects. Except for a few aberrant groups, adult arachnids have four pairs of legs. There are no winged arachnids.

A typical arachnid life cycle involves sexual reproduction with the deposition of eggs that hatch into an immature stage resembling the adult. However, there are numerous departures from this norm. Females sometimes defend and care for eggs and young. A high proportion of arachnids are predators or parasites; a low proportion feed directly on plants or act as scavengers.

SPIDERS

Spiders are a highly successful group of arachnids, with 100,000 species that have a virtually worldwide distribution. Of these, approximately 20,000 species are found in the United States. They are ubiquitous creatures that vary widely in habitat, and are considered to be great travelers. By some estimates, there are 10,000 to 2 million spiders per acre of grassy land and 265,000 spiders per acre of forested land. They are strict carnivores and may ingest up to 2000 insects in a lifetime.

Some large species may prey to an appreciable extent on small vertebrates such as frogs, lizards, and fish.

Most spiders in their natural habitat live for 1–2 years, with some tarantulas known to survive for 20 years in captivity. Some are nocturnal, while others are diurnal. They are generally shy and run from large animals. Spiders molt 5–10 times during their lifetime and are vulnerable to attack during these periods, when they cannot run. Their natural enemies are wasps, birds, reptiles, parasites, and other spiders.

Although the great majority of spiders are harmless to humans, it is likely that any species with fangs strong enough to pierce human skin can cause at least local envenomation (6,40). In the United States, only about 50 species have fangs sufficiently long to penetrate the human epidermis (78). Serious and fatal poisonings have been associated with a few species. Table 3 lists representative spiders that cause human envenomation.

Venom and Venom Apparatus

All spiders have hollow fangs, and all but one family have venom glands as well. Venom is used primarily for killing or subduing prey and secondarily for defense. The release of venom is under neurologic control of the spider, and thus is not necessarily an all-or-none phenomenon. The venom apparatus is contained in two jaws (celicercae) that connect via a duct to venom glands.

Spider venoms contain protein and polypeptide toxins, enzymes (proteases, lipases, phosphodiesterase, hyaluronidase), and low molecular weight compounds such as serotonin. They are designed to be rapid paralytic agents and are incredibly efficient (78). The venom of the black widow spider, for example, produces an adrenergic-cholinergic clinical syndrome, presumably by the rapid, sustained depletion of peripheral catecholamines. No doubt, a fair number of cases of necrotic arachnidism attributed to the venom of the brown recluse spider are induced by similar venoms from other spiders. Some of the components of these venoms are collagenase, deoxyribonuclease, ribonuclease, and the other mentioned fractions (67).

BLACK WIDOWS AND OTHER LACTRODECTUS

Spiders of the genus *Lactrodectus* occur on all continents, tending to be more plentiful in temperate and subtropical regions. They are moderate-size spiders, the dangerous females having a body length of 12–18 mm, with males about one-half this size, too small to cause injury to humans. They are smooth, shiny spiders, usually black or brown with red, orange, or yellow markings. There is considerable confusion regarding the number of valid species in the genus, with some authorities recognizing as many as 21 and others as few as five. In North America and much of South America, the black widow, *Lactrodectus mactans,* is the important species. It is found in every state except Alaska. Typical adult females are black with a red hourglass mark on the underside of the abdomen and often two or three additional red marks along the midline (Figure 3). The form *tridecimguttatus* is most important in the Mediterranean region, the Middle East, and parts of the Soviet Union. This creature may show numerous red or orange spots or may be almost entirely black, being known as *kara kurt* (black wolf) in parts of Russia. The red-backed spider (*hasselti*), with a broad red or orange dorsal band, is medically important in Australia, New Zealand, and parts of southern Asia. A similar form (*indistinctus*) in South Africa has a narrow or broken dorsal band and may be entirely black. *L. geometricus,* which is brown with black, red, and yellow markings, is common in southern Africa and also occurs in warmer parts of the Americas. Other species or subspecies are of localized distribution and minor medical significance.

In undisturbed areas, *Lactrodectus* spiders typically are found under stones, logs, and pieces of bark and around clumps of vegetation. They may infest grain fields and vineyards. They are rarely found in occupied dwellings but may be plentiful in barns, privies, other outbuildings, stone walls, and trash heaps. A few species, such as *L. variolus* of the eastern United States, are arboreal. Females make a strong irregular web in which they suspend their egg sacs and may react aggressively to disturbance of them. In some

TABLE 3
Representative Spiders that Cause
Human Envenomation

Species Known to Cause Human Deaths

Species[a]	Distribution
Black widow and related species (*Latrodectus mactans complex*)	Cosmopolitan
Brown recluse and related species (*Loxosceles reclusa, L. laeta,* possibly others of the genus)	North and South America, Middle East, South Africa
Wandering spider (*Phoneutria nigriventer*)	Southern South America
Sydney funnel-web spider (*Atrax robustus*) and probably others of the genus	Eastern Australia

Spiders Known to Cause Nonfatal Human Envenomation

Baboon spiders (*Harpactirella* spp.)	Southern Africa
American tarantulas (*Aphonopelma* spp., *Dugesiella* spp.)	Southwestern United States and Mexico
Trap-door spiders (*Bothriocyrtum, Ummidia*)	Southern United States and Mexico
Bird spiders (*Pterinochilus, Lampropelma, Avicularia*)	Circumtropical
Florentine spider (*Segestria florentina*)	Mediterranean area
Comb-footed spiders (*Steatoda* spp.)	Cosmopolitan
Orb-weavers, writing spiders (*Argiope* spp., *Araneus* spp.)	Cosmopolitan
Cat-head spider (*Mastophora gasteracanthoides*)	South America
Grass spiders (*Agelena* spp., *Coelotes* spp.)	Cosmopolitan
European water spider (*Argyroneta aquatica*)	Europe
Wolf spiders (*Lycosa* spp.)	Cosmopolitan
Parson spider (*Herpyllus vasifer*)	Eastern United States
Pallid spiders (*Chiracanthium* spp.)	Cosmopolitan
Giant crab spider (*Heteropoda venatoria*)	Circumtropical
Huntsman spiders (*Olios* spp., *Polybetes* spp.)	Australia, South America
Green lynx spider (*Peucetia viridens*)[b]	Southern United States
Jumping spider (*Phidippus formosus*)	Western United States (genus cosmopolitan)
Sac spiders (*Clubiona* spp., *Trachelas* spp.)	Cosmopolitan
Rock spiders (*Ixeuticus* spp.)	Australia

[a] With spiders, species identification is difficult, and even experts do not always agree. In clinical situations, generic identification is often sufficient. Whenever possible, spiders responsible for serious envenomation should be sent to specialists for identification.
[b] Including one case report of venom ejection into the eye.
Sources: References 6, 40, 41, 48; Levi *et al.* (Recommended Reading); Oehlar, C., The medical significance of spiders at Cincinnati, *Ohio. J. Cincinnati Mus. Nat. Hist.,* **23:**1–11, 1974; Trestrail, J. H., *Poisonous Spiders and Spider Bite Poisonings.* Western Michigan Poison Center, Grand Rapids, May 1979.

FIGURE 3 Black widow spider (*Lactrodectus mactans*). Adult female showing the red hourglass ventral mark characteristic of the species in North America.

regions such as the Mediterranean basin, southern Russia, and South Africa, *Lactodectus* bites are associated with grain harvesting and threshing and with grape picking. In the United States, most bites occur in rural and suburban areas of the southern states, with no special age, sex, or occupational predilection.

Clinical Aspects

Black widow bites are not particularly painful, and the local lesion is insignificant. Bites on the buttocks have been a source of outdoor humor since the invention of the outhouse, but are less common in modern times. A pinprick sensation may be noted, with slight redness and swelling. Symptoms of general toxemia begin after a latent period of 10–60 minutes. Muscle spasm and cramps are characteristic and may result in marked truncal and abdominal rigidity without true palpable tenderness. More frequently, however, pain is intense and often accompanied by a high de-

gree of anxiety. Paresthesia, frequently described as a burning sensation, may affect the entire body but is often most intense in the soles of the feet. Headache, dizziness, dysphagia, nausea, vomiting, diaphoresis, facial edema, and ptosis are frequent. Blood pressure is normal or elevated; the electrocardiogram may show abnormalities. Hypertensive crises may be precipitated. Temperature is slightly to moderately elevated, deep tendon reflexes hyperactive, spinal fluid pressure increased, and urine output decreased. Leukocytosis and albuminuria are common laboratory findings. Complete recovery after a few days is the rule. Those at greatest risk for morbidity are the very young, the aged, and those with hypertension.

The clinical picture of *Lactrodectus* poisoning is much the same in other parts of the world. Bites of the red-backed spider in Australia and New Zealand characteristically show more pain, redness, and swelling than are seen with black widow bites. About one-half of the cases have regional lymphadenopathy (72). Patients bitten by *tridecimguttatus* show more spasm of facial muscles, swollen eyelids, lacrimation, and photophobia, producing the characteristic "facies lactrodectisima." A rash may appear 2–11 days after envenomation (41).

Therapy

Immediate measures include local cleansing, the intermittent application of ice, sedation, and standard tetanus prophylaxis. Intravenous calcium gluconate (10 ml of a 10% solution, slowly) has long been the treatment of choice for *Lactrodectus* envenomation. It usually relieves the muscle cramps, headache, and paresthesias promptly, but repeated doses at 2–4 hour intervals often are necessary. Good results can also be obtained with the administration of methocarbamol (1 g or 10 ml intravenously, no faster than 100 mg/minute in a widely patent line). The initial dose can be followed with an intravenous infusion at a rate of 200 mg/hour or with 500 mg orally every 6 hours (59).

Equine *Lactrodectus* antivenin (e.g., Lyovac; Merck, Sharp, and Dohme) is available in several nations, and its use is indicated when there is severe envenomation. It is used more extensively in Australia and Europe than in the United States. After conjunctival or skin testing for hypersensitivity, one ampule (2.5 ml) is given in 10–50 ml of normal saline as a slow intravenous infusion. Narcotics may be used if necessary for pain control. Moist heat may be of use to control muscle spasm.

Patients should be observed for 8–12 hours, as relapses are not uncommon. All patients younger than 14 years of age, over 65, with a history of end-organ hypertensive disease, or with early signs of significant envenomation should be hospitalized.

Prevention

Prevention of bites involves wearing protective clothing and frequent clearing of areas known to be routinely inhabited by spiders. Insecticides may be useful.

RECLUSE SPIDERS (LOXOSCELES)

Spiders of the genus *Loxosceles* are an important cause of arachnidism in the Americas. The brown recluse spider (*L. reclusa*) is probably the most common cause of serious spider bites in the United States. It is most abundant in the mid-South and southern Midwest, which probably represents its original range; however, it is readily transported by humans, typically in freight shipments, and has been reported from most of the states. In the western and southern parts of South America, *L. laeta* is the most important species, with *L. rufipes* of some significance in Peru. Colonies of *L. laeta* have been found in southern California; to date, no bites have been reported. *L. rufescens,* originally native to the Mediterranean region, has become established in a number of other parts of the world, including the southern United States. *L. spinulosa* is of some importance in South Africa (48).

Loxosceles spiders have a body length of 9–14 mm and long, slender legs that may span 2–4 cm. Their general color is pale brown to reddish. Many species show a dark, violin-shaped mark on the cephalothorax (Figure 4). They have three pairs of eyes, in contrast to the two or four pairs of most spiders. Unlike *Lactrodectus,* the sexes are nearly equal in size and danger.

Loxosceles spiders are secretive and live un-

FIGURE 4 Brown recluse spider (*Loxosceles reclusa*). This is the most important member of the genus in the United States. The dark violin-shaped mark on the cephalothorax is seen in most North American species. (Photo courtesy of IUMC.)

der stones or bark in relatively dry environments. They adapt readily to living in houses and other buildings, where they may be found under boxes, behind furniture, curtains, or pictures, and in other sheltered situations. In Chile, *L. laeta* was found in 41% of urban homes and 24% of rural homes (61). These spiders are not aggressive but will bite if squeezed, threatened, or restrained, as may happen when they are trapped under clothing or bedding. Both sexes can inflict dangerous bites.

Clinical Aspects

In the United States, *Loxosceles* bites usually occur indoors during the warmer months of the year. Only *L. reclusa,* the brown recluse or fiddleback, seems to cause systemic manifestations along with major necrotic ulceration. Children are bitten more frequently than adults and adult females more frequently than males. Effective bites are usually inflicted where the skin is thin, for the spiders have short, comparatively weak fangs. The immediate pain of the bite may be fairly sharp or so trivial as to go unnoticed. In severe bites, after a latent period of 1–4 hours, a painful reddish blister surrounded by a blue-white halo appears at the site of the bite. This may be further encircled by a small ring of extravasated blood, creating a "bull's eye" lesion (Figure 5). At the same time, there may be chills, malaise, and a scarlatiniform rash.

During the next 3–6 days, the local lesion becomes hemorrhagic and spreads irregularly. There may be extreme erythema, regional lymphadenitis, and early prostration. In some cases, the lesion resolves; in others, most of the area becomes necrotic, with destruction of skin and subcutaneous fat. The indurated ulcer classically presents as a central ulceration surrounded by a firm plaque and cellulitis. The destruction is the result of toxin-induced endothelial damage with arteriolar and venular thrombosis, leading to local infarction and secondary necrosis. Healing is slow and results in an extensive scar.

A few persons, most of them children, develop massive intravascular hemolysis after *Loxosceles* bites before the local lesion has progressed to necrosis. This is accompanied

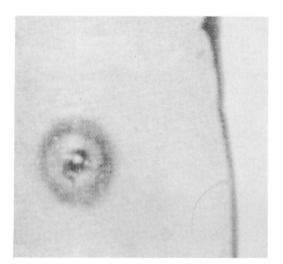

FIGURE 5 Appearance of an early brown recluse spider bite (4–8 hours), a hemorrhagic vesicle surrounded by a pale zone. This is the "bull's eye" lesion. It may resolve without further evidence of envenomation, or it may progress to ulceration.

by hemoglobinuria, headache, fever, chills, weakness, petechiae, jaundice, and hypotension. Such cases have a grave prognosis, with death resulting from renal failure, pulmonary edema, disseminated intravascular coagulation, and diffuse hemorrhage. A case fatality rate of 30% has been reported for Latin America, and there have been several deaths in the United States (60,74,76). The pathogenesis of these severe hemolytic reactions is not well understood. They are unrelated to the severity of the local lesion. There is evidence that some component of *Loxosceles* venom, probably an enzyme, alters the surface of human erythrocytes, so that they are lysed by complement and an unidentified factor in human serum. Erythrocytes of most laboratory animals are not lysed (19). Examination of blood for spherocytosis should be done, for this is reported to be a warning of impending hemolytic crisis (9).

Immunologic studies have shown that mild and subclinical *Loxosceles* envenomation is common in regions where these spiders are plentiful and apparently confers a significant degree of protection (5).

Loxosceles bites can pose a vexing problem in differential diagnosis if the offending arthropod is not available. Bites by other spiders with necrotizing venom, those of *Ornithodorus* ticks, and bites of reduviid bugs may be impossible to differentiate from *Loxosceles* bites. Bedbug, triatomid, flea, and mite bites are usually multiple; spider bites are rarely so. Stasis ulcers may be confused with necrotizing spider bites, and vice versa. In the absence of a history of arthropod bite, the diagnosis rests on clinical judgment. Bacterial infections such as streptococcal cellulitis, anthrax, and some rickettsial diseases may be ruled out by cultures and serologic tests. An immunologic test for detection of *Loxosceles* venom in blister fluid has been described but is not yet in general use (15).

Therapy

Treatment of *Loxosceles* envenomation is far from satisfactory. Early excision of the bitten area has been suggested when the spider is definitely identified. Some say that this is needlessly drastic therapy for mild bites and that its value in severe ones is unproved. The problem, of course, is that there is no good way to predict which bites will fall into which category. Often, moderate bites may progress to significant ulceration and systemic reactions.

Until there are more controlled data, the recommendation is to excise the necrotic area when it approaches a diameter of 1 cm, extending the debridement into the indurated subcutaneous tissue. Further areas of involvement are debrided continuously as they present. As soon as the wound shows no further progression, all efforts are directed to expeditious split-thickness skin grafting. Some physicians have reported success with enzymatic or mechanical (wet to dry) debridement. Intralesional steroids wax and wane in popularity. These should be used only if the decision is made to forego excision and watch the mild bite.

Despite some difference in opinion and variable clinical experiences, corticosteroids appear to be the most effective systemic medication. They appear to help control inflammation, but have no documented beneficial effect on the necrotic component. A dose of 40–60 mg of oral prednisone or 4–10 mg of oral or intramuscular dexamethasone should be given as soon as there are definite signs of envenomation. This level of dosage is maintained for the first few days, tapering off gradually, depending on the response. Steroid therapy should not be initiated if the bite is older than 72 hours. *Loxosceles* antivenins, monovalent or polyvalent against other spiders, are produced by laboratories in Latin America; they are not available in the United States. Their therapeutic value is questionable. Patients with hemolytic crises require careful surveillance and supportive therapy. Whole blood transfusions and maintenance of alkaline urine are beneficial; heparin has been administered with variable success. Tetanus prophylaxis is standard. Hyperbaric oxygen therapy may promote wound healing by inducing capillary proliferation and epithelialization.

Prevention

Prevention of *Loxosceles* bites involves the careful inspection of clothing, bedding, and shipping cartons. Insecticides may be useful. Elimination of roaches, silverfish, and other spider food makes houses less attractive to spiders.

TARANTULAS

The largest spiders belong to the suborder Mygalomorphae. Many of them are known as *tarantulas,* although this term has no zoologic meaning and may be applied to any big spider (Figure 6). It seems to have been first used for *Lycosa tarantula,* the largest spider of Europe, although the tarantism of southern Europe in the sixteenth to nineteenth centuries probably had its factual basis in *Lactrodectus* poisoning (41).

Most, but not all, are large spiders. They occur on all continents, but most are native to tropical and warm temperate regions. The common large mygalomorphs, or tarantulas of the southwestern United States, belong to the genera *Dugesiella* and *Aphonopelma.* Size alone (body length 40–60 mm) will distinguish adults from other U.S. spiders, except for some of the large trap-door spiders; however, these are very rarely encountered. The American tarantulas are regularly active on warm nights and are found by day under stones and other ground cover. Sometimes, especially on warm overcast days, they may be seen by the dozens moving about in the open. They do not live in houses or other buildings. They are mild-tempered; instances of their biting humans are almost unknown.

Mygalomorph spiders are characterized by fangs that move vertically and more or less parallel to one another, in contrast to the majority of spiders, whose fangs are opposed and move toward each other (Figure 7). Mygalomorphs also have two pairs of book lungs, while other spiders have one pair. Some species have irritant hairs on the dorsal surface of the abdomen.

The largest mygalomorph spiders (60–90 mm in body length) are found in tropical Africa, America, and Asia. Although some of these spiders are found in banana and cacao plantations and have been popular in the U.S. pet trade, there are few reports of bites. Those that have been reported resulted in comparatively mild, brief envenomation with mostly local symptoms (18,37,48). There is no specific treatment for bites by these spiders.

FIGURE 6 A large tarantula from the state of Guerrero, Mexico.

The most dangerous mygalomorphs are the funnel-web spiders (*Atrax* spp.) of southeastern Australia. The best-known species and the one most often implicated in serious poisonings is *A. robustus,* which is fairly plentiful in the suburbs of Sydney. These are large spiders, generally black but sometimes with a purplish-brown abdomen. They are found in relatively cool, damp places such as hollow logs, where they make dense tubular webs. They occasionally enter houses and will also crawl into clothing or bedding left outdoors. They are irritable and aggressive if disturbed, often erecting their large fangs in a threat gesture.

Clinical Aspects

Bites by funnel-web spiders are unique in several respects. All fatal and near-fatal bites, when the spider was available for examination, have been caused by male spiders. Although the spiders have large fangs and can bite with great force, a fair percentage of bites are not accompanied by significant envenomation. Local pain is intense, but necrosis does not occur. Serious poisoning sometimes runs a biphasic course. The onset is rapid, with nausea, vomiting, diaphoresis, salivation, violent muscle twitching, and mental confusion that may progress to coma. Early hypertension may be

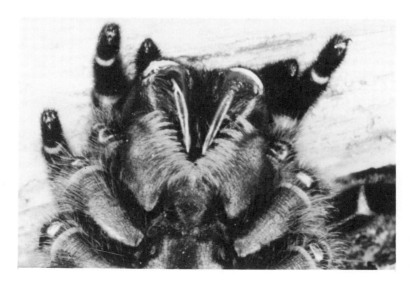

FIGURE 7 Head of a mygalomorph spider (*Atrax* sp.) showing obliquely oriented fangs.

followed by hypotension and hypothermia. There is severe dyspnea. Small children may die 15–90 minutes after being bitten. In some patients, there may be a remission of most symptoms for 14–48 hours, with persistent muscle twitching, followed by a relapse, which is heralded by the sudden onset of confusion and hyperactivity. This is shortly followed by coma and cardiopulmonary failure. In one case, fatal cardiac arrest occurred 48 hours after the bite (68).

Therapy

Prompt application of a snug elastic bandage over the bite with immobilization of the extremity has been recommended as a first aid measure for funnel-web spider bites (71). It is *not* recommended for *Lactrodectus* and *Loxosceles* bites. Patients bitten by funnel-web spiders should be hospitalized and treated symptomatically. Complications, such as pulmonary edema and cardiac failure, must be managed along conventional lines. A funnel-web spider antivenin will probably be available for general use in 1983 (70).

OTHER VENOMOUS SPIDERS

The small, nondescript spiders of the genus *Chiracanthium* are widely distributed, chiefly in temperate regions. The two common species in the midwestern United States, *C. inclusum* and *C. mildei,* are 7–10 mm in body length and have a white to greenish-yellow abdomen, with a pale brown cephalothorax. They often enter houses, where they make dense tubular or saccate webs in crevices. Members of this genus are a common cause of spider bites in the mainland United States and in Hawaii. Other species are medically important in southern Europe, South Africa, and Japan. They have proportionately large fangs, and both sexes are venomous. *Chiracanthium* bites are acutely painful and frequently followed by local swelling, redness, and lymphadenopathy that may persist for several days. Rarely, there may be local necrosis. Systemic symptoms, such as fever, vomiting, and hypotension, are unusual with the U.S. species.

The wolf spiders (*Lycosa* and related genera) are large brown or gray spiders that are often seen running about on the ground. They do not make webs. They may enter houses, especially with the onset of cold weather. They will bite if injured or restrained. Bites by U.S. species produce only local transient symptoms. *Lycosa raptoria* of South America is reported to cause deep ulcers.

Phoneutria nigriventer, the wandering spider, is a large, aggressive species found in southern Brazil, Uruguay, and northern Argentina. Its bite causes intense pain, followed by cutaneous hyperesthesia, diaphoresis, and sometimes muscle spasm with convulsions. Other systemic symptoms may include hypothermia, arrhythmias, hypertension, and tachypnea. Fatalities have been reported, most of them among children (20).

The large orb-weaving spiders, whose conspicuous webs are constructed in shrubs and trees, very rarely bite humans. The few bites that have been reported have produced only minor local envenomation.

Wolf spider and *Chiracanthium* bites seldom require treatment other than reassurance and mild analgesics. Systemic corticosteroids may be of value in the exceptional patient with severe symptoms. An antivenin is produced in Brazil for *P. nigriventer* bites.

SCORPIONS

Scorpions are an ancient, but not particularly large (650 species), group of arachnids. They occur on all continents but are confined mostly to tropical and warm temperate regions. They are characteristic of deserts and semiarid grasslands but are not restricted to such habitats.

Most scorpions are nocturnal, secretive crevice dwellers that live under stones, bark, and rubbish. However, a number of species are somewhat arboreal, and some desert species burrow well. Scorpions often enter houses to feed on cockroaches and other insects and to seek shelter from extremes of temperature. They possess the ability to fast for long periods and to conserve body water. Some scorpions are plentiful in cane fields and cacao and banana plantations. Scorpions give birth to soft white young that, during the early days of their lives, are carried on the back of the female. Females carrying young seem no more aggressive or prone to sting than other adult scorpions.

Identification of scorpions as a group is easy, but species identification is difficult. The family Buthidae, which contains most of the world's dangerous scorpions, has a roughly triangular sternum that is longer than wide. In other families, the sternum is pentangular, square, or triangular (wider than long) (Figure 8). The dangerous scorpions of Mexico and the United States belong to the genus *Centru-*

roides. In addition to the triangular sternum, they have slender, graceful pinchers and usually have a tubercle under the sting. Most of the dangerous species are slender and predominantly yellow or yellow with dark longitudinal stripes, but so are some species that are practically innocuous. *C. sculpturatus* is 2.0–7.5 cm in length, and is yellow and without other coloration.

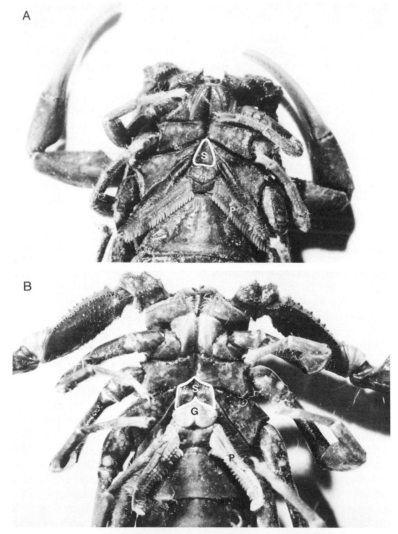

FIGURE 8 (*A*) Anterior ventral aspect of a scorpion of the family Buthidae showing the characteristic triangular sternum (*S*). Also identified are the genital plate (*G*) and pecten or comb (*P*). Nearly all dangerous scorpions belong to this family. (*B*) Similar view of a scorpion of the family Vejovidae showing the more or less pentagonal sternum. Several common North American scorpions belong to this family; they are not dangerous. (Photos courtesy of Illustration Department, Indiana University Medical Center.)

Most of the other common U.S. scorpions belong to the family Vejovidae, in which the sternum is pentagonal and there is no tubercle under the sting. This family includes the large, hairy scorpions of the genus *Hadrurus,* which is native to the southwestern United States. Scorpions of the family Diplocentridae are widespread in Mexico and reach the southwestern United States. They have unusually large, heavy pinchers and a tubercle under the sting.

Scorpion stings are a significant medical problem in North Africa and the Middle East (*Leiurus, Androctonus, Buthus,* and so on); western Mexico (*Centruroides* spp.); Brazil and Trinidad (*Tityus* spp.); southern and western India (*B. tamulus, Palmneous*). Serious and sometimes fatal scorpion envenomation is known in many other parts of the world, but is infrequent. In the United States, the dangerous species of scorpion, *C. sculpturatus,* is restricted to Arizona and small sections of adjoining states. There have been very few fatalities from its sting in the last decade.

Venom and Venom Apparatus

The venom apparatus of scorpions is located in the last segment of the tail (actually, the last of the five abdominal segments), called the *telson,* which terminates in a hollow curved sting and contains a pair of venom glands. Scorpions feed mostly on insects and other terrestrial invertebrates; large species occasionally eat small vertebrates. Prey is usually grasped in the chelicerae, or pinchers, where it is crushed and torn apart. In order to sting a victim, the scorpion must arch its pseudoabdomen over its head. Venom may be used to subdue or kill prey, but for many species it seems to be more important in defense. Species with large, powerful chelicerae tend to have relatively weak venoms and vice versa, although there are exceptions. Some African scorpions eject venom in a spray as a defensive tactic.

Venom is designed to immobilize the victim, as the scorpion dines on its vital fluids. The principal toxins of scorpion venoms are polypeptides and low molecular weight proteins, some of which are toxic primarily for invertebrates and others for mammals. Enzymes are present in the venoms of several species of scorpions; their role in toxicity is unknown. Histamine and indole compounds, including serotonin, have been reported in some scorpion venoms. In some manner, the venom acts to induce the release of endogenous neurotransmitters at the presynaptic terminal. The mechanism of action is overwhelmingly one of catecholamine-induced sympathetic storm.

Stinging Patterns

In arid and semiarid regions, the incidence of scorpion stings is usually highest at the onset of the rains. May through August are the peak months for stings in Arizona (63,64). Scorpions hibernate in the winter.

Persons are most frequently stung in or close to their homes, especially those made of adobe, while putting on clothing, walking barefoot in the dark, picking up objects lying on the ground, or tending to animals. From 70 to 90% of stings occur on the hands. Infants may be stung while in their beds. In a few countries e.g., Trinidad, the incidence of stings is greatest in agricultural occupations (77). Small children appear to be stung more frequently than are adults and older children, but this may reflect the higher percentage of serious stings in the younger age group.

Clinical Aspects

Stings by the dangerous *Centruroides* of Mexico and the southwestern United States are acutely painful. A zone of hyperesthesia soon develops around the site. Lightly tapping the area causes immediate pain and withdrawal, a pathognomonic response not usually seen with stings by insects and less dangerous scorpions (65). Characteristic later manifestations are salivation, diaphoresis, perioral paresthesias, dysphagia, gastric distention, hyperactivity, diplopia, nystagmus, visual loss, incontinence, penile erection, exaggerated reflexes, opisthotonus, seizures, hypertension, pulmonary edema, and respiratory arrest.

There are some regional differences in scorpions and the effects of their stings. Stings by *Leirurus quinquestriatus* may be accompanied by peripheral vascular collapse, tachycardia, and congestive heart failure, with electrocardiographic patterns simulating early myocardial infarction (23). Abdominal pain and vomiting, with laboratory indices compatible with acute pancreatitis, are seen with many cases of scorpion poisoning in Trinidad (4). Coagulopathies, including a disseminated intravascular coagulation (DIC) syndrome, have been reported following scorpion stings in southern India (10). Hemoglobinuria, followed by oliguria, jaundice, edema, and renal failure, has been reported following stings in southern Iran (39).

Stings of less dangerous scorpions, which include the vast majority seen in the United States, usually cause transient local pain, sometimes with edema. Its severity is equal to that of a bee sting. Rarely, there may be paresthesias, mydriasis, salivation, sweating, nausea, generalized muscular pains, and weakness. Occasional reports of fatal or life-threatening reactions may represent anaphylaxis or some idiosyncratic response to the venom. Because of the problems of scorpion identification, scorpions involved in stingings should be preserved whenever possible and sent to specialists for identification.

Therapy

The first treatment consists of immobilization of the affected body part and the intermittent local application of ice packs. Tourniquets are of little value. Tetanus prophylaxis is standard.

Diazepam or phenobarbital is effective in controlling excitability and seizures. Phentolamine or other sympatholytic antihypertensives should be used to control blood pressure. Atropine may be useful if there are profound parasympathomimetic effects. Opiates such as meperidine and morphine are contraindicated, as they seem to potentiate toxicity. Intravenous fluids should be given with caution because of the propensity to develop pulmonary edema. Methocarbamol or calcium gluconate should be used to control muscle spasm.

Scorpion antivenins are available in most countries where dangerous scorpions are plentiful. In cases of severe poisoning, they should be administered intravenously, as are snake antivenins. The dosage depends upon the nature of the product and the response of the patient. Although some degree of cross-protection has been demonstrated in animal experiments between antivenins designed for different parts of the world, this should not be relied upon if a local antivenin is available. In the United States, antivenin against *C. sculpturatus* is produced by the Poisonous Animals Research Laboratory of Arizona State University for local use.

Prevention

Scorpions are difficult to eradicate from dwelling sites, since they can hide for a long time in inaccessible places. The most effective pesticides appear to be a 3% solution of chlordane or a 0.15% solution of pyrethrum in kerosene (66). Better construction of dwellings and destruction of roaches and other household pests make residences less attractive to scorpions. Natural enemies such as cats, ducks, solfugids, and some lizards should be encouraged.

SCORPIONLIKE ARACHNIDS

Arachnids of several other groups are sometimes believed to be venomous. The large whip scorpion, *Mastigoproctus giganteus,* often called the *vinegaroon* or *grampus* in the southern United States, is somewhat scorpionlike in general form, but the tail is a long, slender filament with no terminal sting. The animal can eject a fine spray of acetic and caprilic acids from the base of this filament. This is an antipredator defense and could be irritant to human eyes at sufficiently close range. The amblypygids resemble large, flat spiders, with an extremely long, threadlike first pair of legs and a segmented abdomen. They are widely distributed in the tropics and subtropics. The solfugids, or weirds, are moderate to large arachnids with huge jaws, large pedipalps that resemble a fifth pair of legs, and a soft segmented abdomen. They occur in the southwestern United States, Mexico, Africa, and western Asia, chiefly in deserts. They are active nocturnal predators, hiding by day in burrows or under stones. Their bite can be painful but is not accompanied by venom injection.

The pseudoscorpions are small (2–5 mm) arachnids with claws and a body much like those of a scorpion, but without a segmental tail. They are cosmopolitan, plentiful, and sometimes found in houses, where they may be mistaken for hatchling scorpions.

TICKS

Ticks belong to the large arachnid order Acarina. In common with other members of the order, they have a body divided into two regions: the head, or gnathosoma, and body, or idiosoma. Their life cycle begins with an egg that hatches into a six-legged larval stage, followed by nymphal and adult stages with eight legs. A characteristic feature of the mouthparts of ticks is a toothed hypostome.

Two major subgroups are recognized. The Ixodidae, or hard ticks, are characterized by a chitinous plate, or scutum, that covers the entire dorsum of the male but only a small anterior portion in the gravid female. The mouthparts project and are visible from above. The Argasidae, or soft ticks, have no scutum. The mouthparts are ventral and not visible from above except in young larvae.

Ticks are cosmopolitan in distribution and are ectoparasites of vertebrates. They are vectors of many diseases of medical and veterinary importance. Moreover, a true envenomation may accompany their bites as a result of the injection of salivary secretions as the tick is feeding on blood. The venomous property of the secretion apparently affords the tick no advantage in defense or food getting.

Tick Paralysis

A paralytic syndrome associated with the attachment of ticks was first described in domestic animals about a century ago. It is caused in the western United States by *Dermacentor andersoni* (Figure 9); however, the disease is unknown in some areas where the tick is common. There is no correlation with the incidence of Rocky Mountain spotted fever transmitted by the same tick. Cases of tick paralysis due to *D. variabilis* have been reported from about a dozen of the eastern states, and *Amblyomma americanum* and *A. maculatum* have been incriminated in a few cases in the southeastern states. *Ixodes holocyclus* appears to be the only species that causes tick paralysis in Australia, but several species have been incriminated in South Africa. Female ticks cause the great majority of cases, but a few have been caused by males and nymphs.

The nature of the paralytic toxin in tick

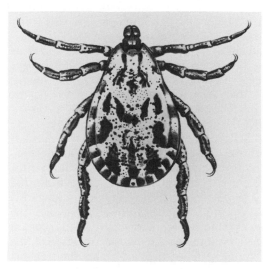

FIGURE 9 Rocky Mountain wood tick (*Dermacentor andersoni*), responsible for tick paralysis in the western United States. (Reproduced by permission of Merck Sharpe & Dohme, Division of Merck & Co., Inc.)

saliva is obscure. The toxin isolated from *I. holocyclus* of Australia appears to be a protein (28). Attempts to isolate a similar toxin from North America's *D. andersoni* have been unsuccessful, and it has been suggested that a totally different low molecular weight toxin may be involved (47). The progressive neurologic defect induced by the toxin is presynaptic and due to a failure in acetylcholine release, affecting both central and peripheral nerve transmission.

In North America, tick paralysis is much more common in children and in females. This may merely mean that ticks in girls' hair are more likely to be overlooked, rather than to suggest an age and sex difference in susceptibility to the toxin. Most cases occur between the months of March and August (57). Persons living in or visiting rural areas are usually the victims.

Clinical Aspects

Ticks causing paralysis have usually been found on the scalp or neck and sometimes in the groin or axilla or under the breast. There is reason to believe that they must be attached for 4–5 days before symptoms of paralysis develop. Illness may begin with a few hours of anorexia, irritability, and lethargy. This is followed by ataxia and weakness of the legs. Flaccid paralysis involves the legs, trunk, and arms in that order, and is followed by cranial nerve involvement and respiratory paralysis, similar to that seen with Guillain-Barré syndrome. The reflexes are greatly decreased or absent; sensory changes are minimal or lacking. There is little or no fever, and the spinal fluid is normal; these characteristics help to differentiate the syndrome from acute poliomyelitis. Reported case fatality rates have been 10–12%, chiefly ascribed to failures in diagnosis (7). In the Australian form of the disease, the onset is more acute, and vomiting is a common early symptom. As previously mentioned, the absence of fever, negative spinal fluid abnormalities, and the lack of any characteristic sensory involvement differentiate tick paralysis from infections of the central nervous system, myelitis, polyneuritis, and similar conditions.

Therapy

Removal of the tick is curative. In North American cases, improvement may begin within an hour and be complete in 48 hours; Australian cases run a longer course. Canine immune serum is used to treat severe cases in Australia, but not in North America (69). An open airway must be maintained, and respiratory assistance may be required temporarily. Evidence from veterinary practice and animal experiments indicates immunity following Australian tick paralysis; this does not seem to apply to the American forms of the disease.

Prevention

Prevention of tick paralysis and most tick-borne microbial diseases involves regular inspection of the body for ticks when one is in a country where they are prevalent. Adult ticks, at least, usually wander about for an hour or two before attaching. Immature ticks are hard to find and often are not noticed until they have attached and local itching calls attention to their presence.

Ticks can best be removed by grasping them as closely as possible to the mouthparts with splinter forceps and pulling them free. The wound should be superficially explored and all retained mouthparts removed. Touching the tick with a hot object or applying substances such as mineral oil, petroleum jelly, chloroform, or nail polish to its body may be effective. However, these result in agonal struggling, with the probable injection of additional saliva and stomach contents. Insect repellents may provide effective protection when applied to clothing.

Other Tick-Related Disorders

Argasid ticks of the genus *Ornithodorus* have toxic saliva. The *pajaroello* (*O. coriaceus*) of Mexico and the southwestern United States inflicts a painful bite, sometimes accompanied by a pruritic maculopapular lesion or small necrotic ulceration that persists for up to 4 weeks. In a few cases, the swelling may involve an entire extremity and be accompanied by general malaise, lymphadenitis, and other systemic symptoms (14). Similar symptoms have been reported following bites by species of the *O. moubata* complex, which frequently infest native dwellings in Africa and the Middle East. These ticks do not attach and usually bite at night. Larvae and nymphs of *O. stageri,* which frequent bat caves in Texas and northern Mexico, bite viciously, leaving a welt that persists for several days (12). The cosmopolitan ticks of the genus *Ixodes* can inflict painful bites, occasionally accompanied by fever, vomiting, and local ulceration. There is no specific treatment for this type of tick envenomation.

A granuloma that histologically resembles malignant lymphoma may develop at the site of tick bites as much as 6 weeks after removal of the tick, and may persist for several months if not excised. It is believed to be due to a toxin or virus in tick saliva (22). A possible variant of this condition is erythema chronicum migrans of Afzelius. Here, the tick bite becomes surrounded by a slightly elevated ring of erythema that spreads, reaching a diameter of 50 cm or more. Most cases are seen in northern Europe and are associated with the bite of *I. ricinus* (16). Patchy alopecia in children has been reported following bites by *D. variabilis,* and a papular eruption of 6 month's duration was documented in a patient bitten repeatedly by *A. integrum* (58,79).

Lyme disease (arthritis) is a syndrome, heralded by erythema chronicum migrans, that has been linked to the arthropod tick vector *I. dammini* and related species. Spirochetes that bind specific antibodies have been isolated in the gastrointestinal tracts of adult *I. dammini.* These organisms may prove to be related to the transmission of the disease. First noted officially in Lyme, Connecticut, cases have been clustered in New England, but have appeared worldwide. The violaceous, annular, expanding skin discoloration precedes by 1–30 days a constellation of symptoms that include arthralgias (large joints), spinal or cranial neuropathies, fever, chills, malaise, headache, aseptic meningitis, arrhythmias, and congestive cardiomyopathy. Treatment is supportive, with anti-inflammatory agents; some authors have suggested the efficacy of penicillin or tetracycline, particularly if used in the early phases of the disease.

Centipedes

Centipedes are elongate, flattened arthropods with one pair of legs for each of the typical body segments, which may number from 15 to more than 100. The first segment bears a pair of curved hollow fangs with venom glands in their bases. The last segment bears a pair of filamentous to forcepslike caudal appendages not associated with the venom apparatus. The largest species reach a length of almost 30 cm. Most centipedes live beneath objects resting on the ground or in crevices. Some are burrowers, while others are able to climb quite well. Many are nocturnal. *Scutigera coleoptrata,* with a body length of about 25 mm and very long, thin legs, is a common house arthropod in much of the United States. Other species enter dwellings occasionally. Centipedes are predators on invertebrates, and the large species occasionally eat small vertebrates. Female centipedes of some species curl around their egg clusters and newly hatched young, and may actively defend them.

Centipede bites have been reported from numerous subtropical and tropical regions, but never as a serious medical problem. Most have been ascribed to species of the genus *Scolopen-*

FIGURE 10 Anterior end of large *Scolopendra* (centipede) showing fangs.

dra, which has a wide distribution with several species in the southern United States (Figure 10).

Centipedes use their venom primarily to kill prey, and only secondarily for defense. The venom may also have a digestive function. The chemistry of centipede venom has not been well elucidated.

As with spiders, it is likely that any centipede whose fangs can penetrate human skin can cause local envenomation. Contrary to popular folklore, they do not inject venom with their feet, or caudal appendages. Burning and local swelling are the common manifestations of centipede bites. There may be lymphangitis, lymphadenopathy, and superficial necrosis at the site of the two fang punctures. Swelling and tenderness may persist for up to 3 weeks or may disappear and recur (24). There are a few reports of bites with severe systemic reactions.

Treatment of centipede envenomation is symptomatic. Infiltration of the bitten area with lidocaine (Xylocaine) or another local anesthetic promptly relieves the pain. This can be followed with oral analgesics. Tetanus prophylaxis is standard.

Millipedes

Millipedes differ from centipedes in having two pairs of legs per body segment and in being without structures for injecting venom (Figure 11). Some species are broad and short and will roll into a ball when disturbed. Millipedes are generally ground-dwelling and se-

FIGURE 11 Large millipede (*Spirobolus* sp.) photographed in central Arkansas.

cretive. Occasionally, they aggregate in enormous numbers. They generally feed on decaying vegetation.

Millipedes are exceptionally well endowed with defensive chemical secretions that include hydrogen cyanide, organic acids, phenol, cresols, benzoquinones, and hydroquinones (13). These effectively deter most predators. Some large millipede species can eject their secretions for distances of up to 80 cm.

Human injury from millipede secretions has been reported from a number of tropical regions. The most common injury is a dermatitis that begins as a brown-stained area with some burning. This may blister and exfoliate. Millipede secretions in the eyes cause immediate pain, lacrimation, and blepharospasm. This may be followed by chemosis, periorbital edema, and corneal ulceration. A few instances of blindness have been reported (52,53).

There is no specific treatment. Prompt irrigation with water or saline should be followed by analgesics, antimicrobials, and other measures appropriate for chemical burns. Proper ophthalmologic evaluation is mandatory.

References

1. Abkiewicz, C., Lomnitzer, R., and Rabson, A. R.: Desensitization of patients with bee sting allergy using pure bee venom. *S. Afr. Med. J.,* **55:**285–87, 1979.
2. Arocha-Pinago, C. L., and Layrisse, M.: Fibrinolysis produced by contact with a caterpillar. *Lancet,* **2:**810–12, 1969.
3. Barnard, J. H.: Studies of 400 *Hymenoptera* sting

deaths in the United States. *J. Allergy Clin. Immunol.,* **52:**259–64, 1973.
4. Bartholomew, C.: Acute scorpion pancreatitis in Trinidad. *Br. Med. J.,* **1:**666–68, 1970.
4a. Beaucher, W. N., and Farnham, J. E.: Gypsy-moth-caterpillar dermatitis. Occasional notes. *N. Engl. J. Med.,* **306**(21):1301–2, 1982.
5. Berger, R. S., Millikin, L. E., and Conway, F.: An *in vitro* test for *Loxosceles reclusa* spider bites. *Toxicon,* **11:**465–70, 1973.
6. Bettini, S., and Brignoli, P. M.: Review of the spider families with notes on the lesser known poisonous forms. *Handbook Exp. Pharmacol.,* **48:**101–20, 1978.
7. Biery, T. L., and Mosely, J. C.: Venomous arthropods in the United States: A review. *J. Assoc. Milit. Dermatol.,* **2:**8–18, 1976.
8. Brown, S. G.: Cantharidin poisoning due to a "blister beetle." *Br. Med. J.,* **2:**1290–91, 1960.
9. Chu, J. Y., Rush, C. T., and O'Conner, D. M.: Hemolytic anemia following brown spider (*Loxosceles reclusa*) bite. *Clin. Toxicol.,* **12:**531–34, 1978.
10. Devi, C. S. *et al.:* Defibrination syndrome due to scorpion venom poisoning. *Br. Med. J.,* **1:**345–47, 1970.
11. Dias, L. B., and Azevedo, M. C.: Pararama doenca causada por larvas de Lepidoptero. *Bol. Of. Sanit. Panam.,* **75:**3, 1973.
12. Eads, R. B., Menzies, G. C., and Hightower, B. G.: The ticks of Texas with notes on their medical significance. *Tex. J. Sci.,* **55:**7–24, 1956.
13. Eisner, T. *et al.:* Defensive secretions of millipedes. *Handbook Exp. Pharmacol.,* **48:**41–72, 1978.
14. Failing, R. M., Lyon, C. B., and McKittrick, J. E.: The pajaroello tick bite—the frightening folklore and the mild disease. *Calif. Med.,* **116:** 16–19, 1972.
15. Finke, J., Campbell, B. J., and Barrett, J. T.: Serodiagnostic test for *Loxosceles reclusa* bite. *Clin. Toxicol.,* **7:**375–82, 1974.
16. Flanigan, B. F.: Erythema chronicum migrans Afzelius in Americans. *Arch. Dermatol.,* **71:**410–11, 1962.
17. Frazier, C. A.: Brazilian honey bee. *Ann. Allergy,* **32:**146–50, 1974.
18. Freyvogel, T. A., Honegger, C. G., and Maretic, Z.: Zur Biologie und Giftigheit der ostafrikanischen Vogelspinne *Pterinochilus. Acta Trop.,* **25:**217–55, 1968.
19. Furtell, J. M., Morgan, B. B., and Morgan, P. N.: An *in vitro* model for studying hemolysis associated with venom from the brown recluse spider (*Loxosceles reclusa*). *Toxicon,* **17:**355–62, 1979.
20. Gajardo-Tobar, R: El araneismo en el mundo tropical y subtropical. *Mem. Inst. Butantan Simp Int.,* **33:**45–53, 1966.
21. Golden, D. B. K. *et al.:* Regimens of hymenoptera venom immunotherapy. *Ann. Intern. Med.,* **92:**620–24, 1980.
22. Goldman, L.: Tick bite granuloma: Failure of prevention of lesion by excision of tick bite area. *Am. J. Trop. Med. Hyg.,* **12:**246–48, 1963.
23. Gueron, M., and Yarom, R.: Cardiovascular manifestations of severe scorpion sting. *Chest,* **57:**156–62, 1970.
24. Haneveld, G. T.: Beten door reuzenduizendpoten

van Niew-Guinea (*Scolopendra morsitans* en *Sc. sub-spinipes*). *Ned. Tiljdschr. Geneeskd.*, **100**:2906–9, 1956.

25. Hunt, G. R.: Uncommon insect bites: The reduviid bite. *Tex. Med.*, **73**:45–50, 1977.

26. Hunt, K. J. *et al.*: A controlled trial of immunotherapy in insect hypersensitivity. *N. Engl. J. Med.*, **299**:157, 1978.

27. James, F. K. *et al.*: Imported fire ant sensitivity. *J. Allergy Clin. Immunol.*, **58**:110–16, 1976.

28. Kaire, G. H.: Isolation of tick paralysis toxin from *Ixodes holocyclus*. *Toxicon*, **4**:91–7, 1966.

29. Kano, R.: Leipidoptera. In *Animals of Medical Importance in the Nansei Islands of Japan*. M. Sasa, H. Takahashi, R. Kano, and H. Tanaka (eds.). Shinjuku Shobo, Tokyo, 1977, pp. 117–22.

30. Kaplinsky, E. *et al.*: Effects of bee (*Apis mellifera*) venom on the electrocardiogram and blood pressure. *Toxicon*, **15**:251–56, 1977.

31. Levine, H. D.: Acute myocardial infarction following wasp sting. *Am. Heart J.*, **91**:365–74, 1976.

32. Lichtenstein, L. M.: Allergic responses to airborne allergens and insect venoms. *Fed. Proc.*, **36**(5):1727, 1977.

33. Lichtenstein, L. M., Valentine, M. D., and Sobotka, A. K.: A case for venom treatment in anaphylactic sensitivity to *Hymenoptera* sting. *N. Engl. J. Med.*, **290**:1223–27, 1974.

34. Lichtenstein, L. M., Valentine, M. D., and Sobotka, A. K.: Insect allergy· The state of the art. *J. Allergy Clin. Immunol.*, **64**:5–12, 1979.

35. Light, W. C., and Reisman, R. E.: Stinging insect allergy: Changing concepts. *Postgrad. Med.*, **59**:153–57, 1976.

36. Light, W. C. *et al.*: Unusual reactions following insect stings. *J. Allergy Clin. Immunol.*, **59**:391–97, 1977.

37. Lim, B. L., and Davies, C. E.: The bite of a bird-eating spider *Lampropelma violaceopedes*. *Med. J. Malaya*, **24**:311–13, 1970.

38. Lynch, P. J., and Pinnas, J. L.: "Kissing bug" bites. *Cutis*, **22**:585–91, 1978.

39. Malhotra, K. K. *et al.*: Acute renal failure following scorpion sting. *Am. J. Trop. Med. Hyg.*, **27**:623–26, 1978.

40. Maretic, Z.: Toxicity of "non-venomous" spiders. *Arachnolog. Cong. Internat.* V., pp. 201–6, 1971.

41. Maretic, Z., and Lebez, D.: *Araneism with Special Reference to Europe*. Molit, Belgrade, 1979.

42. McGovern, J. P. *et al.*: *Megalopyge opercularis*, observations on its life history, natural history of its sting in man, and report of an epidemic. *J.A.M.A.*, **175**:737–40, 1961.

43. McKiel, J. A., and West, A. S.: Nature and causation of insect bite reactions. *Pediatr. Clin. North Am.*, **8**:795–816, 1961.

44. Michner, C. O.: The Brazilian honeybee—possible problems for the future. *Clin. Toxicol.*, **6**:125–27, 1973.

45. Mueller, H. L., Schmid, W. H., and Rubinsztain, R.: Stinging insect hypersensitivity: A 20-year study of immunologic treatment. *Pediatrics*, **55**:530–45, 1975.

46. Muller, U., Spiess, J., and Roth, A.: Serological investigation in hymenoptera sting allergy: IgE and hemagglutinating antibodies against bee venom in patients with bee sting allergy, bee keepers, and nonallergic blood donors. *Clin. Allergy*, **7**:147–54, 1977.

47. Murnaghan, M. F., and O'Rourke, F. J.: Tick paralysis. *Handbook Exp. Pharmacol.*, **48**:419–64, 1978.

48. Newlands, G.: Review of the medically important spiders in southern Africa. *S. Afr. Med. J.*, **49**:823–26, 1975.

49. Parrish, H. M.: Death from bites and stings of venomous animals and insects in the United States. *Arch. Intern. Med.*, **104**:198, 1959.

50. Parsons, D. J.: Bedbug bite anaphylaxis misinterpreted as coronary occlusion. *Ohio Med. J.*, **51**:669, 1955.

50a. Patterson R., and Valentine, M.: Anaphylaxis and related allergic emergencies including reactions due to insect stings. *J.A.M.A.* **24B**:2632–36, 1982.

51. Pesce, H., and Delgado, A.: Lepidopterismo y erucismo. *Mem. Inst. Butantan Simp. Int.*, **33**:829–34, 1966.

52. Radford, A. J.: Giant millipede burns in Papua New Guinea. *Papua New Guinea Med. J.*, **18**:138–41, 1975.

53. Radford, A. J.: Millipede burns in man. *Trop. Geogr. Med.*, **27**:279–87, 1975.

54. Reisman, R. E., Wypych, J., and Arbesman, C. E.: Stinging insect allergy: Detection and clinical significance of venom IgE antibodies. *J. Allergy Clin. Immunol.*, **56**:443–49, 1975.

55. Reisman, R. E., Arbesman, C. E., and Lazell, M.: Observations on the aetiology and natural history of stinging insect hypersensitivity: Applications of measurements of venom-specific IgE. *J. Allergy Clin. Immunol.*, **59**:303–11, 1979.

56. Rhodes, R. B. *et al.*: Hypersensitivity to the imported fire ant. *J. Allergy Clin. Immunol.*, **56**:84–93, 1975.

57. Rose, I.: A review of tick paralysis. *J. Can. Med. Assoc.*, **70**:175, 1954.

58. Ross, M. S., and Friede, H.: Alopecia due to tick bite. *Arch. Dermatol.*, **71**:524–25, 1955.

59. Russell, F. E.: Muscle relaxants in black widow spider (*Lactrodectus mactans*) poisoning. *Am. J. Med. Sci.*, **243**:159–61, 1962.

60. Schenone, H., and Prats, F.: Arachnidism by *Loxosceles laeta*. *Arch. Dermatol.*, **83**:139–42, 1961.

61. Schenone, H. *et al.*: Prevalence of *Loxosceles laeta* in houses in central Chile. *Am. J. Trop. Med. Hyg.*, **19**:564–66, 1970.

61a. Shama, S. K., Etkind, P. H., Odell, T. M. *et al.*: Gypsy-moth-caterpillar dermatitis. Occasional notes. *N. Engl. J. Med.*, **306**(21):1300–1, 1982.

62. Shilkin, K. B., Chen, B. T., and Khoo, O. T.: Rhabdomyolysis caused by hornet stings. *Br. Med. J.*, **1**:156, 1972.

63. Sobotka, A. K. *et al.*: Allergy to insect stings, II. Phospholipase A: The major allergen in honeybee venom. *J. Allergy Clin. Immunol.*, **57**:29–40, 1976.

64. Stahnke, H. L.: The Arizona scorpion problem. *Ariz. Med.*, **7**:23–9, 1950.

65. Stahnke, H. L.: Arizona's lethal scorpion. *Ariz. Med.*, **29**:504–7, 1972.

66. Stahnke, H. L.: The genus *Centruroides* (Buthidae) and its venom. *Handbook Exp. Pharmacol.*, **48:**277–307.

67. Stochosky, B.: Necrotic arachnidism. *West. J. Med.*, **131:**143–48, 1979.

68. Sutherland, S. K.: The Sydney funnel-web spider (*Atrax robustus*) 3. A review of some clinical records of human envenomation. *Med. J. Aust.*, **2:**643–46, 1972.

69. Sutherland, S. K.: Treatment of arachnid poisoning in Australia. *Aust. Fam. Physician*, **5:**305–12, 1976.

70. Sutherland, S. K.: Antivenom to the venom of the male Sydney funnel-web spider *Atrax robustus*. Preliminary report. *Med. J. Aust.*, **2:**437–41, 1980.

71. Sutherland, S. K., and Duncan, A. W.: New first-aid measures for envenomation. *Med. J. Aust.*, **1:**378–79, 1980.

72. Sutherland, S. K., and Trinca, G. F.: Survey of 2144 cases of red-back spider bites in Australia and New Zealand. *Med. J. Aust.*, **2:**620–23, 1978.

73. Suzuki, S. *et al.:* A case of mosquito allergy. *Acta Allerg.*, **2:**245–67, 1976.

74. Taylor, E. H., and Denny, W. F.: Hemolysis, renal failure and death presumed secondary to bite of brown recluse spider. *South. Med. J.*, **59:**1209–11, 1966.

75. Triplett, R. F.: The imported fire ant: Health hazard or nuisance? *South. Med. J.*, **69:**258–59, 1976.

76. Vorse, H. *et al.:* Disseminated intravascular coagulopathy following fatal brown spider bite. *J. Pediatr.*, **80:**1035–40, 1972.

77. Waterman, J. A.: Some notes on scorpion poisoning in Trinidad. *Trans. R. Soc. Trop. Med. Hyg.*, **31:**607–24, 1938.

78. Wingert, W. A.: Poisoning by animal venoms. *Top. Emerg. Med.*, **2**(3):89–118, 1980.

79. Yersudian, P., and Thambiah, H.: Persistent papules after tick bites. *Dermatologica*, **147:**214–16, 1973.

Recommended Reading

Bettini, S. (Ed.): *Arthropod Venoms,* vol. 48, *Handbook of Experimental Pharmacology.* Springer-Verlag, Berlin, 1978.

Biery, T. L.: *Venomous Arthropod Handbook.* U.S. Government Printing Office, Washington, D.C. (no date).

Bücherl, W., Buckley, E. E., and Deulofeu, V. (Eds.): *Venomous Animals and Their Venoms.* 3 vols. Academic Press, New York, 1968. (Material on arthropods in vol. III.)

De Vries, A., and Kochva, E. (Eds.): *Toxins of Animal and Plant Origin.* 3 vols. Gordon and Breach, New York, 1971–73.

Frazier, C. A.: *Insect Allergy: Allergic Reactions to Bites of Insects and Other Arthropods.* Warren H. Green, St. Louis, 1969.

Harves, A. D., and Millikin, L. B.: Current concepts of therapy and pathophysiology in arthropod bites and stings, *Int. J. Dermatol.*, **14:**543–62, 621–34, 1975.

James, M. T., and Harwood, R. F.: *Herm's Medical Entomology,* 6th ed. Macmillan, London, 1969.

Levi, H. W., Levi, L. R., and Zim, H. S.: *Spiders and Their Kin.* Golden Press, New York, 1968.

Minton, S. A.: *Venom Diseases.* Charles C Thomas, Springfield, Ill., 1974.

Reid, H. A.: Bites and stings in travellers. *Postgrad. Med. J.*, **51:**830–37, 1975.

Rhoades, R. B.: *Medical Aspects of the Imported Fire Ant.* University of Florida Press, Gainesville, 1977.

Rosenberg, P. (Ed.): *Toxins: Animal, Plant and Microbial.* Pergamon, Oxford, 1978.

Russell, F. E.: Venomous animal injuries. *Curr. Probl. Pediatr.*, **3**(9):1–47, 1973.

Smith, K. G. V.: *Insects and Other Arthropods of Medical Importance.* British Museum (Natural History), London, 1973.

PROTECTION FROM BLOOD-FEEDING ARTHROPODS

Richard P. Kaplan, M.D.

There are basically three ways by which humans can protect themselves from insects: (1) insecticides, (2) topical application of repellents or toxicants, and (3) proper clothing that acts as a physical barrier. Insecticides (DDT or dichlorodiphenyl trichlorethane; malathion) are generally used for agricultural purposes (protecting crops from destruction) or for protecting large populations (from diseases such as malaria, onchocerciasis, and filariasis).

For wilderness travel, a discussion of repellents, toxicants, and protective clothing is relevant.

A *repellent* is defined as a chemical which causes insects to redirect their path. Repellents are of two classes. One is a vapor or olfactory type, which is a volatile chemical (such as N,N-diethyl-m-toluamide, or Deet) that keeps flying insects at a distance. The other is a contact or gustatory type (such as butyl 3,4-dihydro-2,2-dimethyl-4-oxo-2H-pyran-6-carboxylate, or Indalone), in which a crawling insect is repelled when actually on the skin surface. An effective repellent is one that can rebuff the ectoparasite over a period of time. Ideally, a repellent should be chemically stable, effective against many insects, nonirritating to skin and mucous membranes, and cosmetically pleasing.

There are a number of techniques for evaluating insect repellents (12). The most common test method is *in vivo*, in which insects are placed in a cage with a volunteer's forearm, which has the repellent applied; protection time is measured in hours. A minimum effective dose (MED, in milligrams per square centimeter) of repellent is determined *in vivo* and refers to the least amount of chemical needed to inhibit biting. Apparently, there is little correlation between MED and protection time (6). *In vitro* testing requires the use of an olfactometer, in which an air stream containing repellent enters through a port into a cage containing mosquitoes; insect avoidance is quantitated (13). Inanimate attractants, such as light for ticks or warm, moist air for mosquitoes, can be used for *in vitro* testing. Animals and field testing can be used for testing repellents against crawling insects.

A repellent which is effective for one species of insect may not be effective for another variety of ectoparasite. It is not completely known how repellents work, but they are probably more than chemicals that smell or taste bad. Wright is of the opinion that, in the case of the mosquito, the insect's sensors are essentially jammed, so that it is unable to follow the warm, moist currents given off by a warm-blooded host (16). Hairs on insect antennae sense the carbon dioxide (CO_2) concentration, heat, and moisture in the environment. The CO_2 directs the insect toward the host, and the final approach is guided by warmth and humidity receptors. Repellents interfere with the sensor reception, so that when the chemical comes in contact with the antennae, the insect's movement becomes nondirected.

Certain physical properties of repellents bear mentioning. Compounds with low boiling points vaporize too rapidly, and those with high boiling points fail to vaporize sufficiently to provide a repellent atmosphere. A boiling point range of 230–260°C at atmospheric pressure is desirable. The better repellents are highly fat and water soluble. Repellents absorb in the far infrared spectra; this phenomenon may interfere with the heat sensors' (on the insect's antennae) function, causing the ectoparasite to avoid the host (1). Optimal molecular weight is 200–210, reflecting the optimal vapor pressure. Repellents appear to be longer-lasting if applied to clothing rather than directly to the skin, because a number of factors remove the chemical from the skin. Abrasion is the single greatest source of loss, particularly with physical exertion. Evaporation is augmented when the repellent has a low boiling point. Most vapor-type repellents are effective at a distance of 4 cm from the skin. Compounds with high boiling points act as contact repellents. With regard to temperature, for every 10°C rise, protection time may be halved. Under windy conditions, repellents become less effective. Insect repellents can be washed off; consequently, perspiration decreases the protection time of Deet, dimethyl phthalate (DMP), and ethyl hexamediol but, interestingly, increases the protection time of Indalone (5). For these reasons, insect repellents must be applied frequently (every few hours) and over all exposed surfaces. There may be a significant loss of chemical through the skin.

Spherical or oval molecules are thought to be more effective blockers of receptors on the sensory hairs of antennae than are long and flat molecules (2). Some amides and alcohols are repellent to yellow fever mosquitoes but not to malaria mosquitoes. Adding oxygen to hydrocarbons increases their repellency. As a class of organic compounds, only amides and imides are more repellent than alcohols and phenols. A glycol with good efficacy is 2-ethyl-1,3-hexanediol (Rutgers 612). The amide that is the standard for comparison is Deet. Other effective amides are the cyclohexanealkanoic carboxamides for mosquito repellents and 1-acetyl-1,2,3,4-tetrahydroquinoline, which appears to be effective against flies, ticks, gnats, and mosquitoes (7). Aminoacetals exhibit a high degree of repellency, and benzylic ethers have a long protection time (3). Natural repellents may have useful application. Vapors of nepetalactone (catnip) from the plant *Nepeta cataria* repel many species of insects; pyrethrum, derived from chrysanthemum, has marked repellent properties toward mosquitoes.

There are very few side effects with repellent use, and they occur infrequently. Dimethyl phthalate can irritate mucous membranes. Immediate hypersensitivity to Deet, which is manifested as contact urticaria, has been reported. Open patch tests are positive within a half hour (4). In the rabbit ear model, repeated applications of Deet and dimethyl phthalate produce irritation (15). In contrast, patch-testing human subjects repeatedly with up to 100% Deet produces no irritant or allergic contact dermatitis (8). Aside from mucocutaneous reactions, two cases of toxic encephalopathy associated with exposure to Deet are mentioned in the literature (17).

The common available and effective insect repellents generally are composed of four chemicals: Deet, Indalone, Rutgers 612, and dimethyl phthalate. These repellents are made by McKesson (Mosquitone), Johnson Wax (OFF), Cutter, and Union Carbide (6-12). Generally the liquid forms (lotions) have the highest concentration of the active ingredients and are probably more efficacious than the towelette, spray, and stick forms. Other active chemicals have been added to these preparations in small amounts; *N*-octyl bicycloheptene dicarboximide, 2,3,4,5-*bis*(2-butylene) tetrahydro-2-furaldehyde, and di-*n*-propyl isocinehomeronate are examples. For a single 1 ounce insect repellent container (towelette, lotion, spray, or stick), the cost runs from $1 to $3. As mentioned previously, applying repellent to clothing will increase the protection time because the chemical remains on the garment longer than on the skin. One such preparation is M-1960, used by the U.S. military on combat fatigues; it consists of 30% 2-butyl-2-ethyl-1,3-propanediol for protection against mosquitoes and biting flies, 30% benzyl benzoate for chiggers and fleas, 30% *N*-butylace-

tanilide for ticks, and 10% nonionic emulsifier (11).

Another way that an individual can rid himself of biting arthropods is to apply a topical toxicant. Toxicants are substances that act as poisons, killing rather than repelling; they are used for prophylaxis, unlike insecticides, which are used for fumigation and crop dusting. One of the advantages over repellents is that the toxicant removes the attacking arthropod from the local environment (9). Resmethrin, a synthetic pyrethroid, is an effective toxicant when applied to clothing. Resmethrin offers greater protection to exposed skin than does a clothing-applied repellent. It is speculated that a combination of toxicant-treated clothing with repellent-treated exposed skin might extend the protection time afforded by repellent use alone. Another effective toxicant is Permethrin, also a synthetic pyrethroid (10).

Clothing is protective because it maintains a distance between the insect and the host. Rip-stop weave nylon used for backpacking clothing, tents, and boat sails has a slick surface to which bees, wasps, and other insects find it difficult to cling. This type of clothing is excellent when one is outdoors in infested areas (14).

References

1. Cohen, G.: Behavior of mosquitoes and the infrared spectrum *Nature* (Paris), **3333**:34–6, 1963.
2. Garson, L. R., and Winnike, M. D.: Relationships between insect repellency and chemical and physical parameters—a review. *J. Med. Entomol.,* **5**:339–52, 1968.
3. Gualtieri, F. *et al.:* Topical mosquito repellents IV: Alicyclic, bicyclic, unsaturated acetals, aminoacetals and carboxamide acetals. *J. Pharm. Sci.,* **61**:577–79, 1972.
4. Maibach, H. I., and Johnson, H. L.: Contact urticaria syndrome. *Arch. Dermatol.,* **111**:726–30, 1975.
5. Miabach, H. I.: Use of insect repellents for maximum efficacy. *Arch. Dermatol.,* **109**:32–5, 1974.
6. Maibach, H. I. *et al.:* Insects, topical insect repellents. *Clin. Pharmaceut. Ther.,* **16**:970, 1974.
7. McGovern, T. P. *et al.:* Mosquito repellents: Cyclohexanealkanoic carboxamides as repellents for *Aedis egypti, Anopheles quadrimiculatus* and *Anopheles albimanus. Mosquito News,* **40**:394–99, 1980.
8. *Public Health Letter,* Los Angeles County Department of Health Services, vol. 3, 1981, p. 19.
9. Schreck, C. E. *et al.:* Chemical treatment of wide-mesh net clothing for personal protection against

blood-feeding arthropods. *J. Econ. Entomol.,* **71:**397–400, 1978.

10. Schreck, C. E. *et al.:* Durability of Permethrin as a potential clothing treatment to protect against blood-feeding arthropods. *J. Econ. Entomol.,* **71:**397–400, 1978.
11. Schreck, C. E. *et al.:* Repellents vs. toxicants as clothing treatments for protection from mosquitoes and other biting flies. *J. Econ. Entomol.,* **71:**919–22, 1978.
12. Schreck, C. E.: Techniques for the evaluation of insect repellents: A critical review. *Ann. Rev. Entomol.,* **22:**101–19, 1977.
13. Smith, C. N. *et al.: Factors Affecting the Protection Period of Mosquito Repellents.* Technical bulletin 1285, U.S. Department of Agriculture, Washington, D.C.
14. Wagner, R. E., and Reierson, D. A.: Clothing for protection against venomous hynenoptera. *J. Econ. Entomol.,* **68:**126–28, 1975.
15. Wong, M. H., and Yew, M. H.: Dermatotoxicity of mosquito repellent related to rabbit ears. *Acta Anat.,* **100:**129–31, 1978.
16. Wright, R. H.: Why mosquito repellents repel. *Sci. Am.,* **233:**104–11, 1975.
17. Zadikoff, C. M.: Toxic encephalopathy associated with use of insect repellent. *J. Pediatr.,* **95:**140–42, 1979.

MITES AND LICE

Richard P. Kaplan, M.D.

Mites

Mites rarely transmit disease (scrub typhus); nevertheless, their dermatologic manifestations should be briefly mentioned. Infestation with and sensitization to the itch mite, *Sarcoptes scabiei* var. *horminis,* causes scabies (1). The mite has four pairs of legs, transverse corrugations, and bristles on its dorsal aspect. The adult female mite measures 0.3 by 0.4 mm. In this common dermatosis, the mites live in epidermal burrows which are a few centimeters in length. The female mite lives 1–2 months, traveling 2 mm/day, laying a total of 10–25 eggs. The eggs mature in 3 weeks. Most infected hosts harbor 10 adult mites. Scabies are acquired through close personal contact, with an incubation period of 1–2 months.

The infested patient itches intensely, particularly at night. The interdigital folds, flexor aspects of the wrists, extensor surfaces of the elbows and knees, anterior axillary folds, periareolar (breast) region, waistline, penis, lower buttocks, and outer aspects of the feet are all areas of frequent involvement. The primary lesion (the burrow) is often obscured by secondary eczema and impetigo. A rare variant, called *Norwegian scabies,* in which large number of mites infest the individual, occurs primarily in the mentally retarded; extensive crusting exists over widespread regions, including the palms, soles, and head. The diagnosis of scabies can be made positively by scraping the burrows and examining the preparation under the microscope to identify the ectoparasite, eggs, and feces.

Other mites can cause acute eczematous reactions. Glyciphagus (grocery mite) and acarus (cheese mite) are examples of food mites. *Demodex folliculorum* (follicle mite) parasitizes pilosebaceous structures. The *Dermanyssidae* family (murine and fowl mites) can cause dermatitis as well. The grain mite (*Pyemotes ventricosus*) and the harvest mite (the chigger, *Thrombicula alfreddugesi*) may cause intense pruritus.

The treatment of choice for mite infestation is γ benzene hexachloride (Kwell, Gamene) (2). The cream or lotion should be applied to the body from the neck down, and should be washed off in 24 hours. Clothing, linens, and towels should be washed in hot water or dry-cleaned. Twenty-four hours after treatment, transmission is unlikely. One should re-apply the medication 1 week later to destroy larvae or nymphs. Alternative treatments are available. Crotamiton [10% *N*-ethyl-o-croto-notoluide (Eurax)] cream is applied twice to the body over a 48-hour period. Precipitated sulfur (6–10%), applied for 3 nights, is the treatment of choice for very young children and pregnant women. Benzoyl benzoate (20–25%) can also be used daily for 2–3 days. Head lice may be treated with 0.5% malathion lotion, applied to the scalp for 12 hours (3).

References

1. Orkin, M., and Maibach, H. I.: Scabies, a current pandemic. *Postgrad. Med.,* **66**:52–65, 1979.

2. Orkin, M. *et al.:* Treatment of today's scabies and pediculosis. *J.A.M.A.,* **236**:1136–39, 1976.
3. Taplin, D. *el al.:* Malathion for treatment of *Pediculus humanus* var. *capitis* infestation. *J.A.M.A.,* **247**(22):3103–5, 1982.

Lice

Lice are known to transmit disease (trench fever and epidemic typhus); thus, they merit some discussion. Pediculosis is produced by two species specific for the human host: *Phthirus pubis* and *Pediculus humanus*. The adult *P. humanus* louse is 2–4 mm long, has three pairs of legs with delicate hooks at the tarsal extremities, and is gray-white. The *P. pubis* louse is only 1–2 mm long and broad, with the first pair of legs shorter than the clawlike second and third pairs. The lice that inhabit the head or body interbreed. Lice are transmitted by close personal contact and sharing of

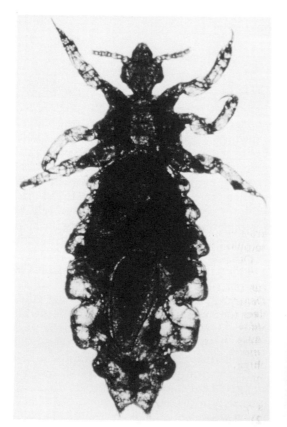 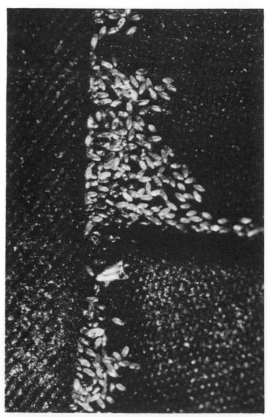

FIGURE 12 *Pediculus humanus* (body lice) (*left*) spend little time on the skin and much time on clothing (*right*) laying eggs (nits) in seams. (Photos courtesy of Dr. Victor Newcomer.)

clothing, bedding, or towels. The adult female lives for 1 month, depositing 10 eggs per day (Figure 12). The ova (nits), which are attached to the base of the hair, hatch and mature in 1–2 weeks. Except for situations of overcrowding and poor sanitation, pediculosis capitus is the most common variety seen in women. Usually, mature insects are present on the scalp (occiput and temples). Secondary infection with cervical lymphadenopathy may occur. Body lice are found in clothing, feeding only transiently on the interscapular, shoulder, and waist regions; urticarial or eczematous changes are evident there. Pubic lice can be found in the axillae and eyelashes, as well as the groin. Maculae caeruleae are gray-blue, purpuritic macules seen on the thighs of infected persons. Treatment for infestation is essentially for head, body, and pubic lice. For pediculosis capitus or pubis, γ benzene hexachloride (Gamene, Kwell) shampoo is applied for 5 minutes. After rinsing, the hair is cleaned with a fine-toothed comb to remove the nits. For pediculosis corporis, the same medication is applied in cream or lotion form. An alternative treatment for pediculosis is copper oleate-tetrahydronaphthalene lotion (Cuprex), which is applied for 15 minutes to the head and pubis prior to rinsing. Eyelash infestation may be treated by applying 0.025% physostigmine ophthalmic ointment with a cotton-tipped applicator.

Recommended Reading

Derbes, V. J.: Arthropod bites and stings. In Fitzpatrick, T. B. (ed.), *Dermatology in General Medicine.* McGraw-Hill, New York, 1979, pp. 1661–63.

Arndt, K. A.: *Manual of Dermatologic Therapeutics.* Little, Brown, Boston, 1978, p. 127–34.

Carslow, R. W.: Skin infestation. *Practioner,* **216:**154–58, 1976.

Orkin, M., and Maibach, H. I.: Scabies, a current pandemic. *Postgrad. Med.,* **66:**52–65, 1979.

Orkin, M. *et al.:* Treatment of today's scabies and pediculosis. *J.A.M.A.* 1976, **236:**1136–39.

11 | DOMESTIC AND FERAL MAMMALIAN BITES

Michael L. Callaham, M.D.

Mammalian bites possess few unique presentations with which to distinguish them from all of the other assorted bruises, abrasions, lacerations, and punctures that are suffered by human victims. The combinations of tearing, cutting, and crushing are not remarkably different from those inflicted by any moderately sharp object. While it is true that animal* bites may become infected, this complication is hardly unique; many of the offending bacteria are ubiquitous in the environment.

The apparent uniqueness of mammalian bites is attributed to three factors. First, the event is frightening, and many victims are understandably terrorized by an attacking animal. Second, animals are capable of transmitting a wide variety of systemic diseases, many of which have substantial morbidity and mortality, in addition to the transmission of common bacterial pathogens. Finally, and perhaps most important, in marked contrast to the large, detailed, and scientific literature related to traumatic injuries incurred with inanimate objects, the literature on animal bites is sparse, largely unscientific, and often simply anecdotal. As a result, rational treatment decisions must be made without an overwhelming data base. However, we shall interpret and revise the present state of knowledge in order to present fairly specific recommendations.

Incidence of Bites

The true incidence of animal bites is essentially unknown and probably will always remain so. Neither the number of bites that occur annually nor the base population at risk has been estimated with consistent accuracy or reliability. The world supports approximately 4400

---

* Throughout this discussion, *animal bites* will be used to refer specifically to mammalian bites, although most of the statements are applicable to bites inflicted by birds and reptiles as well.

species of mammals, 8600 species of birds, 6000 species of reptiles, and 35–40 species of domestic animals (44). None of these species is subject to any sort of census. The actual number of wild animals in the world can only be estimated, but it is in the billions. There are estimated to be 3 billion domestic animals worldwide, with an estimated 25 million dogs and 25 million cats in the United States in 1968 (98). The only animal population figures that are anything more than a guess are those for dogs and cats. However, even these are strongly suspect, since there is no method of enumeration in the United States other than county pet license statistics, which are known to be incomplete. It is even impossible to obtain accurate information on the number of animals in species as well tabulated as the purebred dogs, as the only available figures come from the registry of the American Kennel Club (AKC). In 1976, this totaled only 386,000 dogs, obviously a very small proportion of the total population.

Accurate figures for the total number of bites inflicted in any given year are unavailable. For one thing, many people who suffer relatively minor injuries from pets or laboratory and farm animals do not seek medical attention unless infection or some other complication occurs. Familiarity breeds a fairly stoic attitude and indifference toward much more severe injuries than are tolerated by the nonprofessional. Additionally, animal bites are generally not a reportable condition. In cities such as New York, Los Angeles, and Baltimore, where animal bite is a reportable condition, the incidence of dog bites has tended to run between 300 and 700 per 100,000 population (9,56,104). In rural Ohio, the rate was 271 per 100,000 in 1966, as compared with a rate of 2059 per 100,000 in West Texas in 1977 (69,98). The 1970s witnessed a dramatic increase of up to 186% in the reported incidence of urban dog bites, although this seems recently to have leveled off. Using available data to extrapolate to the entire United States, there is an annual incidence of at least 1.5 million dog bites. Furthermore, 1 of 17 dogs bites someone in the United States each year, while the average dog bites a human only once in its life.

Fairly extensive information is available regarding the incidence of animal bites by species in the United States (Table 1). In New York City, as illustrated, dogs accounted for 89% of all animal bites; cats, 4.6%; humans, 3.6%; rodents, 2.2%; and the other species listed for very small percentages (77). Since there are supposedly as many cats in the United States as there are dogs, it is surprising

TABLE 1
Incidence of Bites by Species (%)

Species	Ref. 77	Ref. 98	Ref. 36	Ref. 1	Ref. 106	Ref. 69
Dog	89	91.6	63	50	83	
Cat	4.6	4.5	15	14	1	
Human	3.6	0.03	15	23	0	
Rodent	2.2	3	0.6	12	3.4	65
Monkey	0.1[a]	0.2	2.4		2.2	15
Skunk		0.02			2.2	
Lagomorph	0.2	0.5	0.6			
Horse	0.1	0.06				6
Large mammal	0.03[b]	0.01[c]		1.2		3[d]
Reptile	0.1				8	
Bat		0.004	0.6			6
Raccoon		0.08	0.7			3[e]
Total no. of cases	24,790	24,003	321	160	88	34

[a] Includes 21 monkeys, four raccoons, three ferrets, one weasel, one coati mundus, one skunk, and one goat.
[b] Includes three lions, one ocelot, one leopard, one polar bear, and one anteater.
[c] Includes one goat, one ocelot, one jaguar. Also includes one groundhog, which inflicted a bite on Groundhog day, of course.
[d] One coyote.
[e] One kinkajou.

to note the low percentage of the total number of bite wounds attributed to cats. It is also surprising that rodents, which are ubiquitous in city, country, pet, and laboratory environments, produce very few treatable bites. By contrast, mandatory reporting in a largely rural area of Ohio demonstrated that dogs accounted for 91.6% of all bites; cats for 4.5%; rodents for 3%; skunks, rabbits, horses, bats, and raccoons for less than 1% each; and humans for only 0.03% (98). Presumably, the figure for human bites represents either different methods of handling aggression in a rural population or a greater reluctance to report such incidents. In every statistical series, very small numbers of exotic animals such as ocelots, jaguars, lions, leopards, polar bears,

anteaters, ferrets, and weasels are represented. It must be reemphasized that these figures represent reported bites. Doubtless, many bites occur in homes, barns, zoos, and laboratories which the victims do not report and which, therefore, are never reflected in these data. Therefore, the apparent incidence of infection and other complications from animal bite wounds, as suggested by the available data, is significantly less than the true incidence.

The cost of all these bites in time, money, and disability is very great. Modern laboratory, zoo, and farm workers receive such injuries fairly frequently in the course of their work, while in many underdeveloped countries, animals remain the daily threat to health and existence that they were in prehistoric

TABLE 2
Human Deaths from Animal Attacks

Species	Annual Estimated Deaths	Annual Estimated Attacks	Predominant Area	Comments
Homo sapiens	200,000		Worldwide	Individual murders—excludes 1,000,000 per year by war in recent decades
Snake	50,000		Worldwide	
Crocodile (niloticus)	1000		Africa	Man eating predominant
Domestic horses, cattle, pigs	800	39,549	Europe alone	Mostly accidental
Tiger	600–800		India	Frequently man eaters
Lion	300–500		Africa	Frequently man eaters
Leopard	400		Africa, India	Frequently man eaters
Elephant	200–500		Central Africa, India	Frequently rogue man killers
Hippopotamus	200–300		Africa	Unpredictable; bites and tramplings
Buffalo	20–100		Africa	Only if cornered or wounded
Hyena	10–50	Hundreds	Africa	Frequently bites off face of sleeper; frequent man eater
Wolf	20–50	200–500	Eurasia (none in North America)	Hundreds per year in previous centuries
Domestic dog	10	1,500,000	United States only	
Indian sloth bear	5–10	50?	India, Ceylon	Severe facial injuries common
Gorilla	Ø	2–3	Africa	Only if cornered; injuries usually not severe
Baboon	Ø	1–2	South Africa	Usually pets
Ostrich	1–2		South Africa	Disembowelment or kick to head
Grizzly bear	Rare	<1	North America	Occasionally unprovoked attacks on campers; aggravated by campfires?
Black rhinoceros	<1		Africa	Easily provoked

Source: From Reference 24.

times. On a rubber plantation in Sumatra, animal (including nonmammalian) -inflicted injuries regularly accounted for 1–2% of hospital admissions annually (99). Dog bites account for 1% of all the emergency department visits made in the United States (36). Of these patients, 10% require suturing and 1% require hospitalization (9). In 1974, the average outpatient charge for a dog bite wound was $38, a cost which has risen drastically with inflation (9). It is thus clear that the financial burden of dog bites alone is very great, as is the amount of time lost from work and other pursuits.

Fatal attacks on humans are a major problem (Table 2). Several thousand people a year are killed by mammalian bites, most of these inflicted by man-eating lions and tigers in Africa and Asia. However, these figures must be kept in perspective. The World Health Organization estimates that roughly 60,000 people a year are killed by snakes and that additional millions are killed by insect-borne diseases (24). It would be unfair to the animals not to point out that in World War II, humans killed 22 million of their own kind, including 6 million in programs of genocide. Individual acts of murder account for more than 200,000 annual worldwide deaths and suicide for almost 400,000. In the United States alone, more than 50,000 people a year are killed in traffic accidents. One can only conclude from these figures that although death from animal attack has at times been a major problem, we shall be lucky indeed if we can deal as effectively with our own instinct to kill.

Circumstances and Prevention: Animal Behavior

The prevention of animal bites requires a thorough knowledge of the behavior, personalities, and patterns of the various species of animals. In general, this sort of information is available more in the forms of verbal instruction, folk wisdom, and personal experience than as published information or instructional texts. Newspaper and magazine articles are invariably based on anecdotal experience and not on anything approaching a statistical survey. A person wishing to avoid the bite of a particular species usually will be able to gain expertise

about that species' behavior only from those who work regularly with it. In effect, this means that there is no reliable information about the behavior of lions, tigers, elephants, and other exotic animals except that derived from persons working in zoos, and the behavior of animals in zoos may not be at all typical of their behavior in the wild. Similarly, experience with rats, mice, hamsters, and other rodents is usually gained either by ownership of a pet or by laboratory work. Once again, the personality and behavior of domesticated and laboratory animals in no way resemble those of the wild creatures. Finally, the behavior of domestic farm animals is best learned from farm workers and veterinarians. Such information can be critical. For example, horses bite frequently, cattle almost never. Horses tend to kick backward with both rear feet; cows tend to kick forward with only one foot. Some small species of deer have large canines and bite; most do not. The various attack and defense patterns of animals are well described in Fowler's text (45). Detailed information on behavior and attack patterns of animals in the wild (particularly African and Asian animals) is available in Clark's text (24). Readers are directed to the Suggested Reading list.

Basic Principles

Recognition of a few simple principles may help avoid animal bites. In fact, animals rarely attack people without provocation. Exceptions are those creatures clinically infected with rabies and large carnivores, whose predatory nature may lead them to be relatively unafraid of humans. However, it is still relatively uncommon for these carnivores, such as the lion and tiger, to hunt humans as preferred prey. Details of man eating are discussed in the sections on the relevant species, since patterns of behavior and attack differ.

Thus, in the vast majority of cases involving both domestic and wild animals, bite injury is provoked, although the animal's perception of provocation may differ from that of the human being.

Most species have a strong sense of territoriality (2,65). Individuals, pairs, or larger groups stake off territory that ranges in size from square feet to square miles and will aggressively prevent any intrusion into that territory, particularly by members of their own species. During the mating season, this drive may stimulate even small animals to threaten or attack humans, particularly in protection of the nest and young. Some species, such as dogs, are well known and even chosen for their willingness to defend their territory against human beings.

A major principle of animal attack and defense behavior is that actual physical attack is often the animal's last resort. This may not be obvious in some of the spectacular fights that occur in the wild. However, elaborate rituals and rules exist in these confrontations that encourage a nonviolent solution, so that the victor may successfully defend his territory and himself with little or no injury. For the human encountering animals, successful interpretation of these visual, auditory, and olfactory warning signs can facilitate complete avoidance of attack and injury.

Animals generally give ample warning of their intentions, which are to repel the intruder or to permit its escape, rather than to inflict damage. If a human slowly and carefully backs off without making sudden or threatening gestures, usually no harm will be done. The ideal reaction may depend on the particular species. For example, man-eating lions and tigers have been turned from a full charge by an angry human being who attacked or advanced rather than fled (24). Given a choice of victims, such a predator will choose the fleeing, panicky victim who demonstrates the expected flight behavior rather than the unexpected. Nonpredator species such as cattle and deer are extremely susceptible to human intimidation, while dogs can be provoked to attack by a direct stare, which is regarded as a challenge. It becomes clear that the nature of the species and even of the individual must be well known.

Humans may provoke attack by attempting to capture or to corner an animal. Even the most timid creature will kick, bite, or scratch if cornered in a small space or if physically restrained. This desperate behavior should be expected when an animal is inadvertently trapped. If the creature is allowed to escape without threat, the human should usually not anticipate any injury or attack. If, for some

reason, it is essential physically to capture an animal, very detailed preparation and precautions should be undertaken. For smaller animals, it is advisable to use nets or heavy cloth and to wear extremely heavy gloves with other protective clothing. Desperate animals can bite with tremendous force; large carnivores can easily amputate a gloved digit. A wolf can tear apart a stainless steel bowl with its teeth, while a hyena can bite through a 2-inch plank (24). Four men are needed to subdue an adult chimpanzee; an orangutan can maintain a one-fingered grip that an adult man cannot break (45). A camel can break a 4 by 4 inch wooden beam with one kick (45).

Larger animals will generally require a team approach, nets, barriers, cages, and immobilizing drugs. Ideal immobilization techniques for various species have been detailed in several veterinary texts (45,46).

Domestic animals, under the proper circumstances, can easily turn on their owners. Far and away the most common offenders are dogs, which bite at least 1.5 million people per year in the United States and attack untold millions more. Details of such attacks are presented in the section on the appropriate species.

Prehospital Considerations

Important local treatment can be initiated at the scene of the bite. This is often more important in determining the course of healing than any later maneuvers. Medical personnel should be aware of the usefulness of simple first aid measures, which must be initiated immediately unless definitive or better treatment is available within a short period of time.

Bites and clawings rarely result in major injuries. Domestic and farm attacks are fairly predictable and preventable. Unfortunately, in the wilderness, this is often not the case, as has been shown by grizzly bears' behavior in Glacier and Yellowstone national parks. In other countries, life-threatening attacks by large animals such as water buffalo, lions, tigers, and elephants are common. The medical literature on such attacks is extremely sparse, so that there are insufficient data on which to base accurate generalizations about the specific complications that may ensue.

Attacks by larger animals should be considered as blunt and penetrating trauma, with possible major arterial blood loss, airway damage, broken ribs, pneumothoraces, intraperitoneal bleeding, and so on (99). Victims of such attacks should be managed the same way as any other trauma victim. The airway should be protected and its patency ensured, and significant bleeding should be promptly controlled. The victim's condition at the time and the availability of rapid evacuation will determine whether further treatment should be attempted in the field. In many situations in which wild animals are encountered, there are no medical personnel or supplies on the scene. Thus, the patient should be moved to a hospital or clinic as soon as possible.

If the victim is more than an hour from treatment, the wounds should be cleansed at the scene as soon as the ABCs of resuscitation are completed. It is adequate to use potable water, preferably boiled or treated with germicidal agents. The use of ordinary hand soap will add some bactericidal, virucidal, and cleansing properties. When there are delays of more than 1–2 hours in providing definitive treatment, such wound irrigation may determine the whole course of the patient's recovery. Early cleansing reduces the chance of wound infection. Additionally, it can kill rabies and other viruses. The wound should be gently but thoroughly irrigated with about a pint of water and soap and then gently debrided of dirt and foreign objects, using a soft, clean cloth or sterile gauze. (Irrigation with a syringe is much better, but syringes are seldom available.) Simple irrigation without actual swabbing of the wound edges will not remove rabies virus (67). After the wound has been cleansed thoroughly, it should be covered with sterile dressings or a clean, dry cloth. If a 1 or 5% providone-iodine solution (Betadine) or similar antiseptic agents, such as 1% benzalkonium (Zephiran), are available, they should be used as irrigants. However, alcohol, hydrogen peroxide, and other disinfectants, which in concentration are harmful to normal tissue, should be avoided. Ordinarily, disinfectants are not often available at the scene of an injury, and the mechanics preempt chemical therapeutics. If available, topical external antibiotic ointments such as gramicidin-neomycin-bacitracin (Neosporin) may be helpful

(96). Pressure on the wound or pressure points will control most bleeding; tourniquets are to be avoided unless blood loss cannot be otherwise controlled. Wounds of the hands or feet should be cleansed, and then the limb should be immobilized. If the wounds are substantial, treatment is hours away, and antibiotics such as penicillin, cephalexin, or erythromycin are available, it is reasonable to start immediate treatment with a large oral dose (0.05–1.0 g). Ideally, this should be done within an hour of wounding to be most effective in preventing subsequent wound infection. However, with severe wounds, it is worth doing even many hours later.

In addition to treating the bite victim, rescuers should try to capture the offending animal for examination, if this can be done without risk of further injuries. Unusual behavior, such as unprovoked attack by a wild animal in broad daylight, should raise the suspicion of rabies. Attempts to capture such animals should emphasize protection for the capturers. Live capture is optimal, but freshly killed animals are usually satisfactory for examination for fluorescent rabies antibody (FRA). Damage to the head and brain should be avoided, as brain tissue is needed. The availability of the animal can eliminate the need for costly and uncomfortable rabies prophylaxis. If more than an hour will elapse before the animal can be transported to a hospital or public health department, the body should be refrigerated or frozen. Use of preservatives should be avoided, as is discussed in the section on rabies.

Examination of the animal is not useful for most other diseases and will not help predict local wound infections. Therefore, judgment must be used in deciding how much time and energy to expend on its capture.

Wound Care

The principles of wound care used in the treatment of injuries caused by inanimate objects apply to bite wounds as well. Many bite injuries are simple contusions that do not break the skin. The infection potential of these injuries is low; superficial wound cleansing and symptomatic treatment of the pain and swelling are all that are needed (Figure 1). In the

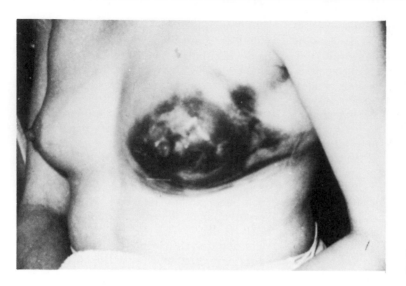

FIGURE 1 Soft tissue injury after horse bite.

case of the large herbivores, most of the injury may consist of severe contusions. Treatment should include prompt and liberal application of ice or other cold packs during the first 24 hours; this will substantially reduce the duration of the injury (M. E. Fowler, personal communication, 1981).

TABLE 3
Summary of Animal Bite Wound Treatment

A. Mandatory
1. Ensure appropriate tetanus immunization.
2. Irrigate wound thoroughly for 3–5 minutes with 100–200 ml. of 1% povidone-iodine solution, using a 12 ml syringe and a 19-gauge needle.
3. Debride all crushed and devitalized tissue.
4. If the animal is suspected to be rabid (shows atypical behavior, appears ill, belongs to a species with a high incidence of rabies), infiltrate wound with 1% procaine hydrochloride, swab the wound surface with cotton swabs and 1% benzalkonium chloride solution, and then rinse out with saline.
5. Assess risk factors (See Table 4).

B. Optional
1. Suture skin wounds in the usual fashion anywhere *except the hand.*
2. Do not culture a fresh wound.
3. Culture infected wounds only if they fail to respond to initial treatment or carry a very high risk.
4. Prophylactic antibiotics (cephalexin or dicloxacillin, 500 mg four times a day for 5 days) in high-risk wounds are logical but of unproven value.

When the skin is broken, the risks of local wound infection or the transmission of systemic disease are incurred. Such infection can be caused by organisms carried in the animal's saliva or nasal secretions, by organisms present on the victim's skin which are carried into the wound, or by environmental organisms which enter the wound during or after the attack. Thus, virtually any bacterium, virus, or fungus can become a contaminant in bite wounds. Fortunately, most wounds do not become infected, and the observance of a few general principles of wound care can significantly reduce infection rates (Table 3). Unfortunately, the topic is so undramatic that it is universally ignored.

MANDATORY BASIC WOUND CARE

Soaking the Wound

It is common practice in most emergency departments to soak fresh traumatic wounds in basins of fluid (usually containing povidone-iodine solution) with the intention of cleansing and disinfecting them. The effectiveness of this practice remains completely untested and unproven. Some surgeons believe that it is actually harmful, claiming that it breaks down the skin's protective mantle (38). It is possible that wound soaking washes large numbers of transient microflora off the skin, suspends them in solution, and redistributes them throughout the wound. In one study of 80 traumatic wounds treated in an emergency department, it was found that although 57% of the wounds had a decrease in bacteria after being prepared with povidone-iodine, hexachorophene (pHisoHex), or green soap solution, 25% showed no change and 18% had an increase in the number of bacteria per gram of wound tissue (37). This last parameter is the only accurate predictor of wound infection (71). (In this study, however, the method of wound preparation was not specified.)

Normal skin contains both a resident and a transient bacterial flora. The transient flora reflects a continuous exposure to the various environmental microorganisms. Healthy skin is quite efficient at ridding itself of this transient flora, and bacteria planted on normal skin rapidly disappear. The resident flora consists of very few species, chiefly aerobic *Staphylococcus epidermis* and *Micrococcus* species, as well as anaerobic *Propionobacterium acnes*, which may outnumber the aerobic flora by 10 to 1 over most surfaces (8). These resident bacteria, which inhabit the sweat and sebaceous glands, persist even when the surface of the skin is sterile. Pathogenic *Staphylococcus aureus* and occasionally *Streptococcus pyogenes* can be recovered from normal skin at the site of fresh wounds and are often the offending organisms in local wound infection. Thus, elimination of the patient's resident flora would be desirable (66). However, an isolated single, very thorough, although traditional 2 minute surgical scrub of the hands does not reduce the number of bacteria significantly (73). In a single scrub, almost all of the benefit occurs in the first 30 seconds. By contrast, repeated scrubs, performed several times a day over a period of days, can markedly reduce, but not eliminate, the resident flora of the hands. Thus, a single superficial hand or wound scrub is not very helpful, and simple rinsing of the hands with antiseptic preparations has no effect whatsoever (73). Scrubs with 0.5% chlorohexidine, 1% iodine, or 5% laurolinium were all equally effective, although laurolinium was particularly toxic to skin cells in tissue culture. All of these agents were applied in 70% ethyl alcohol, which has its own tissue toxicity.

Soaking and the typical halfhearted scrubbing are unlikely to have a significant effect on the bacterial population or even to remove much dirt or debris (29). Such treatment should be entertained only as a maneuver to keep the patient occupied until definitive preparation begins. An acceptable procedure would be to scrub the surrounding skin gently with a surgical sponge and normal saline or a 1% povidone-iodine solution (see the section on irrigation). *The wound itself should not be scrubbed,* and contamination of the wound with scrub solution should be minimized.

Irrigation

Irrigation of nonbite traumatic wounds has been extensively studied in the surgical literature and has consistently been shown to decrease substantially infection [other techniques which have been used in the past, such as sponge scrubbing, are sufficiently damaging to tissues so that they actually increase infection (27,92,102)]. In a dog bite study, an infection rate of 12% in irrigated wounds was noted as compared to 69% of those that were not irrigated (18). Irrigation is clearly a useful technique.

Irrigation functions by removing bacteria, debris, and soil which have been introduced into the wound. The latter two are deleterious to tissue healing even when they are sterile (92). Irrigation cannot remove devitalized tissue; this must be carried out by debridement. The ideal irrigation method should produce enough pressure to dislodge the bacteria and debris without inducing tissue damage.

At 90 pounds/square inch, irrigation fluid applied to a skin wound on the back of an experimental animal disseminates into the pleural and peritoneal cavities (34). At 70 pounds/square inch, irrigating fluid spreads into surrounding soft tissue for distances of up to 14 mm from the wound edge, but the bacteria in the wound are not disseminated out into the tissues along with the fluid (113). High-pressure irrigation used on the wound before contamination by bacteria may greatly increase the incidence of infection, and some authors recommend that it be used only in heavily contaminated wounds.

At the low end of the scale, there is essentially little or no benefit from irrigation of less than 5 pounds/square inch. This includes gravity and bulb syringe techniques, which generate about 0.05 pound/square inch (92).

A pressure of 10 pounds/square inch removes approximately 80% of the soil in a wound and lowers the infection rate from 100% at 1 pound/square inch to 21% at 10 pounds/square inch and 7% at 15 pounds/square inch. At any given pressure, pulsatile jet irrigation has no advantage over a steady-stream application (92).

A 19-gauge needle on a 12 ml syringe will deliver a pressure of approximately 20 pounds/square inch (103). Using a smaller-size syringe increases the pressure but is impractical for delivering irrigating quantities of 100 ml or more. A 19-gauge needle or plastic intravenous (IV) catheter on a 35 ml syringe delivers approximately 7–8 pounds/square inch and decreases the infection rate of lacerations fivefold. The author recommends this for general use unless a wound is heavily contaminated, in which case the 12 ml syringe will generate higher pressures and thus remove more bacteria and soil. This technique will not damage tissues or increase the likelihood of infection in relatively clean wounds. In addition, it has the advantage of using equipment which is extremely inexpensive, disposable, and readily available. Even greater convenience at low cost is offered by 12 ml ring-handle syringes with built-in one-way valves, IV tubing, and blunt irrigating tips (Travenol Pressure Irrigation Set, Code No. 2D2113). These irrigate with fluid from standard IV bags.

The optimal quantity of irrigation fluid appears to be between 100 and 200 ml for most wounds. Greater quantities do not appear to be of added benefit (39,92). When antibacterial agents are added, the duration of application is also important. A 1% povidone-iodine (Betadine) solution requires 5 minutes to kill all bacteria, although most are killed within 30 seconds (61). Weaker solutions are not advised, since they require contact times in excess of 10 minutes.

The irrigating fluid must not be toxic to the tissues. Normal saline functions well as such an irrigant and is widely used. Because it possesses no bactericidal or surfactant cleansing properties, it functions chiefly as a mechanical dislodger of particles. Normal saline irrigation effectively reduces infection, and there is no evidence that it injures tissues or increases inflammation (13,39,41,103). However, *scrubbing* a contaminated wound with a surgical sponge and irrigating with normal saline may result in more infection than irrigation alone (91). If a scrubbing technique is used, a nonirritating detergent (pluronic F-68) is more effective than normal saline. Presumably, the ill effect is due to the scrubbing technique, as it seems fairly certain that saline itself does not damage tissues.

It would be ideal if the irrigating fluid possessed inherent antibacterial and detergent properties. Pluronic F-68 is a nonirritating surfactant which is very effective in removing debris from wounds and decreasing infection, despite the fact that it completely lacks intrinsic antibacterial activity (91). It appears to be completely nontoxic to tissue, leukocytes, and red blood cells. However, this is a new agent which has had only a few clinical trials upon which to judge effectiveness.

There are many other agents which possess antibacterial activity and reduce wound infection when used for irrigation. These include tincture of iodine, povidone-iodine, 20% hexachlorophene solution, benzalkonium chloride solution, Dial soap, green soap, 70% ethyl alcohol, quaternary ammonium compounds, chlorhexidine, hydrogen peroxide, and hand soap (39,53,102). Unfortunately, most of these are tissue toxic (13). Treatment of wounds with any of these agents causes almost immediate abnormality of vascular flow on the edge of the wound and a complete standstill of blood in the microvascular bed of the tissue exposed to a depth of 300–400 μm, as well as extensive local hemolysis and intravascular disruption of granulocytes. This is followed by endothelial leakage with edema, hemorrhage, and deposits of fibrin microthrombi. Eventually, due to the disruption of nutrition, cells in the immediate region exhibit different stages of cellular damage. In most cases, the tissue does not regain normal function within the first 6 hours. Hydrogen peroxide is particularly destructive to tissues, does not penetrate well, and is a weak germicide (57). Silver nitrate is also extremely damaging to tissues; it almost universally causes infection in treated wounds (39). Agents which contain detergents, such as povidone-iodine *scrub* solution or 3% hexachlorophene solution, cause significant damage when injected into joint spaces (41). Povidone-iodine *preparation* solution, however, causes only minimal damage. A 1% chlorhexidine/gluconate (Hibiclens) solution also may have significant harmful tissue effects (91). Thus, many agents which are clearly bactericidal are also so damaging to open tissue and the wound-healing process that their routine use is contraindicated.

The one solution which has been proven to be both bactericidal and nondamaging to tissues is povidone-iodine *solution* (*not* the surgical scrub), which is supplied in a stock concentration of 10%. This is an excellent bactericidal, fungicidal, and virucidal agent to which few bacteria develop resistance (61). The 1% solution (dilution of the stock solution in a ratio of 1 to 10 with normal saline) has been proven to have no ill effects on wound healing, but the number of studies documenting its effectiveness against wound infection is very limited (110). Five and 10% solutions of povidone-iodine (Betadine) have been much better studied and have been proven effective. The bulk of evidence suggests that these concentrations have no deleterious effect on tissue, wound healing, or wound strength (39,41, 82,101). One study found the higher concentration to be harmful to wound healing (110). In very clean wounds and those in which cosmetic considerations are extremely important (such as on the face), it is wisest to use a 1% solution. Because of the bactericidal effect, this solution is preferable to saline. In wounds thought to be heavily contaminated with soil or bacteria, a 5 or 10% solution should be used. It must be emphasized once again that povidone-iodine solution must not be confused with surgical scrub solution, which contains a detergent and actually doubles the infection rate (27). A further caution is that 1% povidone-iodine solution has not been proven effective against rabies virus. Until further studies are done, 1% benzalkonium chloride should be used to cleanse wounds inflicted by animals suspected of being rabid. Finally, prolonged application of high concentrations of povidone-iodine to wounds results in systemic absorption of iodine. This has been a problem only with repeated applications in burns and peritonitis involving a large percentage of the external body or peritoneal surfaces (57,

86,111). Systemic effects of one-time use in lacerations are unknown, due to the brevity of application and the relatively small surface area.

Irrigation of experimental wounds with antibiotic solutions such as kanamycin, neomycin, vancomycin, ampicillin, tetracycline, and streptomycin has generally been more effective than irrigation with saline (14,28,62,102). However, there has been much variation in techniques of irrigation, concentration of antibiotics, and type of wounds. Most antibiotics are absorbed systemically through the wound; systemic toxicity from the use of aminoglycoside antibiotics has been reported. Bacteria easily become resistant to topical antibiotics. Although the use of agents such as ampicillin in low concentrations seems quite rational, normal saline or povidone-iodine has been proven effective and safe. Thus, recommendations for antibiotic irrigation await further study.

Debridement

Debridement is a well-proven means of reducing infection in all types of wounds (62,102). It has been proven particularly effective in dog bites, in which it decreased infection 30-fold (17). Dog and other animal bites are not clean lacerations but crush injuries. Adult dog teeth are not very sharp, but can exert 200–400 pounds/square inch of pressure, enough to perforate sheet metal (83). Debridement removes bacteria, clots, and soil far more effectively than does irrigation. No other technique removes the crushed or torn, devitalized tissue present in animal bites, which so greatly increases infection. Although irrigation can remove surface bacteria, it cannot remove organisms embedded in dead tissue. Additionally, debridement creates a clean new surgical wound edge which is easier to repair, heals faster, and produces a smaller scar. Once the physician becomes adept at using a scalpel to debride several millimeters of tissue from all wound edges, debridement actually becomes a time-saving procedure. The only limitations of this technique are those imposed by anatomy, where skin tautness (such as on fingers or the pretibial region) or the presence of vital structures (such as tendons, nerves, and vessels) precludes debridement. In such cases, the wound should first be very well irrigated and debrided with great care so as not to injure uninvolved tissues. In the author's opinion, good debridement is the treatment of choice for all bite wounds; prophylactic antibiotics are an adjunct, not a substitute.

Tetanus Prophylaxis

Recently, more cases of tetanus from animal bite have occurred in the United States than have cases of human rabies (104). The spores of *Clostridia* species are ubiquitous in the soil, on the teeth, and in the saliva of animals. Therefore, the risk of tetanus may be present from any animal injury that penetrates the skin. Prophylaxis is administered in standard fashion (Table 4). In the case of a clean wound which contains little devitalized tissue and which can be easily irrigated and debrided, a previous full course of immunization plus a booster within the last 10 years is sufficient. In deep punctures or wounds with much devitalized tissue that are difficult to irrigate and debride (predisposing to anaerobic growth), a full series of previous immunizations plus a booster within the last 5 years is sufficient. Multiple and extensive, deep lacerations with much devitalization of tissue are high-risk wounds. Regardless of the patient's prior immunization status, he should receive an intra-muscular injection of 250–500 units of tetanus human immune globulin, as well as 0.5 ml of diphtheria tetanus (DT) toxoid. The latter contains one-twentieth the amount of diphtheria toxoid contained in the pediatric version and elicits a good booster response with few local reactions. Diphtheria immunization is recommended every 10 years throughout life.

Because many patients do not have full prior immunization for tetanus, it is critically important to question the patient thoroughly. If a history cannot be elicited, the patient must be treated with 250–500 units of human tetanus immune globulin intramuscularly in one arm and 0.5 ml of the adult diphtheria tetanus toxoid in the other. Booster doses of tetanus toxoid are administered at 30 and 60 days after the initial injection to complete the course of immunization.

Topical Antibiotics

Topical antibiotic ointments, such as neomycin-bacitracin-polymixin, have been demonstrated to be highly effective in preventing infections and promoting healing in minor skin wounds (48a,72a). The latter action may not be related solely to antibacterial activity. Silver sulfadiazene cream minimizes tissue loss in ischemic flaps (78a). Povidone-iodine ointment has no effect, and nitrofurazone ointment slows healing (48a). Despite the widespread belief, based on early reports, that

TABLE 4
Tetanus Prophylaxis

| History of Immunization (Dates) | Clean Minor Wounds | | Major and Dirty Wounds | |
	Toxoid[a]	TIG[b]	Toxoid	TIG
Unknown	Yes	No	Yes	Yes
None–one	Yes	No	Yes	Yes
Two	Yes	No	Yes	No (unless wound older than 24 hours)
Three or more				
Last booster within 5 years	No	No	No	No
Last booster within 10 years	No	No	Yes	No
Last booster more than 10 years ago	Yes	No	Yes	No

[a] Toxoid: Adult: 0.5 ml DT   IM.
            Child less than 5 years old: 0.5 ml DPT IM.
            Child older than 5 years: 0.5 ml DT   IM.
[b] Immune globulin (TIG): 250–500 units IM in limb contralateral to toxoid.

neomycin is highly sensitizing, at least one recent evaluation recorded sensitivity to this agent in only 2 of 2,175 subjects (72a).

SELECTIVE FURTHER WOUND TREATMENT

Suturing

GENERAL CONSIDERATIONS AND RISK FACTORS

In recent years, the consensus has changed from that of never suturing animal bite wounds to that of closing them with good surgical technique. Adequate data exist only for dog bite wounds, and this discussion will center on that species. The study cited by opponents of suturing was a small one based exclusively on atypical wounds thought to be heavily contaminated (72). Two large studies of typical emergency department dog bite wounds have shown a lower infection rate in wounds sutured than in those left open, even though all wounds were irrigated with saline and all puncture wounds were excluded (17,18). As in other studies reporting less infection in larger dog bite wounds, these results were attributed to the better surgical wound toilet received by the larger (and sutured) wounds (106).

Three major considerations govern the decision on whether to suture: cosmetics, function, and risk factors. Cosmetic appearance virtually mandates suturing all facial wounds, which are low risk anyway. Similar reasons may dictate closure of wounds elsewhere on visible portions of the body. Function is of critical importance in wounds of the hand and foot, which are high risk areas where infection has disastrous consequences. Thus, wounds of the hand should be left open. Risk factors are many and complex (Table 5). Risk factors for infection are an age less than 2 or greater than 50 years, deep puncture wounds, treatment delay of 12 hours or more, hand bites, chronic alcoholism, asplenia, corticosteroid therapy, and the presence of diabetes or an immune disorder (18). Uncomplicated facial wounds are at low risk of infection. Certain species seem to have a propensity for inflicting infection-prone wounds. Although the evidence is not incontrovertible, human and other primates, domestic and wild cats, pigs, and all large, wild carnivores should be consid-

TABLE 5
Animal Bite Risk Factors

High risk	
Location:	Hand
	Wrist
	Foot
Type of wound:	Punctures
	Much crushing which cannot be debrided
Type of patient:	Age less than 2 or more than 50 years
	Asplenic
	Chronic alcoholic
	Altered immune status
	Diabetic
	Peripheral vascular insufficiency
	Corticosteroid therapy
Biting species:	Humans and primates (anecdotal evidence only)
Low risk	
Location:	Face
	Scalp
Type of wound:	Clean, large laceration, easy to cleanse—the larger the wound, the better
Biting species:	Rodents

ered sources of high-risk wounds. Cases must be assessed individually; the presence of one or more risk factors may preclude suturing or mandate the use of prophylactic antibiotics. However, most simple bites of most species, including dogs, can be safely sutured after proper wound preparation.

BITES OF THE HAND

Bites of the hand are common, and infection in them can be disastrous. In lacerations of the hand not caused by animal bites, infection rates vary from 1.1 to 8.5%, not significantly different from that of other areas of the body. Sutured nonbite lacerations of the feet and legs are even more likely than hand and arm wounds to become infected (64,94). The response of hand wounds to suturing is variable, with a suggestion that there is an increase in infectious complications (54,58,95).

Human bites of the hand are discussed elsewhere. For animal bites specifically, data have been collected only for dog bites. Although dog bites in general have an infection rate of 6–13%, typical dog bite wounds of the hand show a rate of 30–36%, even in promptly treated wounds (1,17,18,91). The hand contains many poorly vascularized structures and tendon sheaths which poorly resist infection and which physically aid in its spread. The various spaces of the hand communicate with each other; movement of the structures within them seals off the puncture wound from external drainage and spreads bacteria and soil throughout the space. Infection spreads through fascial spaces, tendon sheaths, and lymphatics. One-half of infections are cellulitis or lymphangitis, about 10% are tenosynovitis, and the remainder are fascial-space infections or felons (78).

Due to the unique anatomy, it is often impossible to irrigate adequately wounds of the hand. The laceration may be irrigated or debrided to the subcutaneous level, but deeper layers are already sealed and cannot be entered. Considering the high morbidity and permanent residual impairment that characterize hand infections, it is best to take the most conservative route. Hand wounds should be irrigated, debrided if possible, and left open. The hand should be immobilized with a bulky mitten dressing and elevated, and the patient should be started on antibiotics, as discussed later. Patients with an established infection should be admitted to the hospital and started on intravenous antibiotics (78,84). Signs of localized pus, devitalized tissue, joint penetration, or foreign body necessitate incision and drainage. Repeat incision and drainage with irrigating catheters are needed in about 10% of established infections (78). Patients not hospitalized should be rechecked daily until signs of infection clear. In the patient without initial evidence of infection, 5–7 days of splinting and oral antibiotics should suffice if no complications develop.

PUNCTURES

Up to one-half of dog bite wounds are puncture lacerations (18). Puncture wounds carry an infection rate of about 20–25% (17,18). This presumably stems from the fact that they are very difficult to irrigate properly. The larger the wound, the lower the infection rate, presumably due to the greater ease and thoroughness of good wound toilet (17,18,106). Total excision is time-consuming, expensive, often prohibited by anatomy, and has not been proven to be of any benefit. Suturing is often proscribed for such wounds, although the only study that specifically addressed this issue did not support such a ban (17). Such wounds should be irrigated or debrided as well as possible, sutured only if cosmetic or functional considerations require it, and treated as having a high potential for infection. Since these wounds carry a high risk, prophylactic antibiotics may be considered.

Indications for Cultures

The specific bacteriology of bites has been well studied only in dog bites and is discussed in that section and in the one on antibiotics. Cultures of fresh bite wounds are an utter waste of time. All fresh lacerations of any kind contain bacteria (71). Cultures of fresh wound surfaces have been shown to be useless as predictors of infection whether judged quantitatively or qualitatively (17,39,74,89). Only homogenized tissue sample cultures are useful in this regard; this is an unwieldy procedure done in few institutions (71). Once infection is established, cultures are indicated only when there is a failure of initial antibiotic therapy or in very high-risk wounds, such as those of the hand. Only about 5% of infecting organisms in dog and cat bites will fail to respond to initial treatment with a penicillinase-resistant penicillin, cephalexin, or erythromycin; thus, at least 95% of cultures taken at the time of initiating antibiotic therapy will be useless (18). Gram stains of pus (or, better yet, aspirated fluid) from an established infection are useful only if one predominant bacterial type is seen. The Gram stain appearance of common pathogens is described in Table 9.

Both aerobic and anaerobic cultures should be obtained when cultures are indicated. Many of the bacterial species in animal mouths are anaerobic, and some of these (such as *Bacteroides*) have caused fatal sepsis (42). Although locally infected wounds produced no purely anaerobic cultures, 75% of wounds contained anaerobes in combination with aerobes (50, 51).

Prophylactic Antibiotics

In bite wounds, treatment can begin only *after* wounding and bacterial inoculation; thus, in a sense, it is never prophylactic. Prophylactic antibiotics are a controversial form of therapy. In major surgery, they are of proven value only in carefully selected high-risk procedures and only if begun *before* the surgery (74). In nonbite outpatient lacerations, prophylactic antibiotics either demonstrated no benefit or actually increased the infection rate, even in wounds of the hand (31,54,58, 64,81). In one controlled study of outpatient dog bite wounds, all irrigated by syringe-and-needle technique, prophylactic penicillin V-K was useful in trunk, limb, and particularly hand wounds, but not in low-risk facial and scalp wounds (17). A similar study using oxacillin, however, found no benefit (40). A very large Russian study of severe wounds found prophylactic ampicillin and oxacillin helpful (79).

Surgical wound toilet remains the most important factor in decreasing infection. The weight of the evidence at this time supports the judicious use of prophylactic antibiotics in high-risk wounds, particularly since the protocols used in the studies cited tended to decrease the likelihood of reliable and early serum antibiotic levels. The use of antibiotics is particularly advisable in wounds of the hand. The cost and side effects of such focused use of antibiotics are relatively small, and the infection potential of hand wounds is great. The speed of development, frequency, and severity of hand wound infections can be impressive; in this application, the cost-benefit ratio justifies antibiotic use. Patients with other risk factors, particularly asplenia or immune deficiency, may benefit from judicious prophylactic antibiotics. There is no indication for their use in ordinary animal bites in normal patients. Although only dog bites have been studied, it is reasonable to extrapolate these recommendations to other species until new data suggest otherwise. Primate bites (including humans) are considered high risk, rodent bites low risk. Cat bites have the reputation of being high risk, but this is based on a very

biased literature and is discussed elsewhere.

Prophylactic antibiotics must be given early to be effective. The offending bacteria are already present in the wound when the patient is first seen. Three hours is generally considered the maximum acceptable delay, although treatment should not be withheld because more time has elapsed (3). Oral administration is markedly less efficacious than parenteral, taking several hours to demonstrate a useful

TABLE 6
Aerobic Bacteria in Dog Bites[a]

	Percentage Normal Flora in[b]	Percentage of Infected Wounds[c]
More than one species		20
Gram positive		
Micrococcus spp.	32	5, 0
Staphylococcus aureus	72	10, 30
Staphylococcus epidermidis	64	10, 30
Streptococcus spp., groups D, G, M, F, E	92	15, 23
Bacillis subtilis	22	0
Corynebacterium spp.	68	7.6
Gram negative		
Pseudomonas spp.	36	10, 7.6
Brucella canis	4	
Bordetella bronchiseptica	6	
Neisseria spp.	68	0
Moraxella spp.	60	5, 0
Acinetobacter calcoaceticus	16	
Escherichia coli	28	
Enterobacter spp.	8	5, 23
Serratia marcescens	2	
Proteus mirabilis	2	
Aeromonas hydrophila	4	
Pasteurella multocida	66	15
Pasteurella pneumotropica	4	
Pasteurella spp.	28	
Eikenella corrodens	18	
Gram-negative rods		10, 7
Hemophilus aprophilus	12	7.6
CDC Alphanumeric		
IIj	90	
EF-4	82	0
M-5	12	3

[a] Partial listings only. Compiled from References 7, 16, and 50.
[b] Normal flora of healthy dogs' mouths.
[c] More than one figure indicates results of separate studies.

serum level. Intravenous administration is 4–12 times faster than intramuscular administration in developing a useful wound fluid antibiotic concentration, although intramuscular doses are effective in maintaining a sustained level (4). Antibiotics differ in the speed with which they enter the wound; ampicillin is the fastest, exceeding the serum concentration within 1 hour (4). Oxacillin, penicillin, and the cephalosporins are also rapid. Erythromycin and gentamycin take 2–4 hours for wound concentration to match serum concentrations, while tetracycline and clindamycin never reach serum levels. The bite victim needing

prophylactic antibiotic treatment should be identified early, preferably during triage on entry to the emergency department, and should receive immediate intravenous or intramuscular antibiotics by protocol. A wait of more than 15 minutes should not be tolerated. Drugs that produce very slow therapeutic wound levels, such as tetracycline and clindamycin, should not be used. The drugs of choice are cephalosporins or penicillinase-resistant penicillins.

The bacteriology of bite wounds is discussed in more detail in the section on dog bites. The summaries in Tables 6 and 7 are applica-

TABLE 7
Anaerobic Bacteria Isolated from Infected and Noninfected Animal Bite Wounds

	DB		OB[a]	
Bacterium	Infected	Non-infected	Infected	Non-infected
Bacteroides melaninogenicus subsp. intermedius		2		
Bacteroides melaninogenicus spp.				
Bacteroides asaccharolyticus		2		
Bacteroides pneumosintes			1	
Bacteroides bivius			1	
Bacteroides spp.		1		
Fusobacterium nucleatum		2	1	
Fusobacterium russii		1	1	
Fusobacterium spp.	1	1		
Peptococcus prevotii	1			
Peptococcus magnus	1	1		
Peptostreptococcus spp.		1		
Veillonella parvula	1			1
Propionibacterium acnes		2		1
Propionibacterium granulosum		1	1	1
Propionibacterium spp.	1			2
Eubacterium spp.	1	1		
Leptotrichia buccalis	1	1		

[a] Includes cat, squirrel, snake, and rat bites.
Source: Reference 50.

TABLE 8
Oral Antibiotic Prophylaxis in Bite Wounds (Minimum Treatment Period is 5 Days)

	Child	70 kg Adult
First choice		
Cephalexin	50–100 mg/kg per day in four divided doses	500 mg orally four times a day
or		
Dicloxacillin	50–100 mg/kg per day in four divided doses	500 mg orally four times a day
Penicillin-allergic		
Erythromycin	30–50 mg/kg per day in four divided doses	500 mg orally four times a day

ble to most species. No one antibiotic is effective against all bacteria. However, a cephalosporin such as cephalexin, or a penicillinase-resistant penicillin such as dicloxacillin, given orally for 5 days, will be effective against the great majority of organisms. Erythromycin can be used in persons allergic to penicillin, although it is less likely to be effective against *S. aureus* (Table 8).

Septic Complications

Immense numbers of bacteria inhabit animals' mouths and can be inoculated into a bite wound. The major aerobic and anaerobic species are listed in Tables 6 and 7. If inoculated in sufficiently large numbers, these bacteria can cause localized cellulitis and abscess formation, the most common forms of infection, with occasional lymphadenitis and lymphangitis. Bacteremia and sepsis, although theoretical risks with any of the bacteria found, have so far been reported with only a limited number of species (Table 9).

Many uncommon septic complications have been reported. Shock, disseminated intravascular coagulation (DIC), symmetrical peripheral gangrene, and adult respiratory distress syndrome have been attributed to Gram-negative bacillemia due to CDC alphanumeric strain DF-2 in an asplenic woman following a dog bite (43). More than 12 similar cases

have been identified so far (22). Meningitis caused by CDC alphanumeric group II-J occurred in a 5-year-old girl 3 days after she was bitten by a dog about the head and neck (12). A case of fatal *Bacteroides* sepsis accompanied by coagulopathy and renal thrombotic microangiopathy after a dog bite occurred in an alcoholic patient (42). A generalized Schwartzman reaction secondary to dog bite and sepsis has been reported (80). *Pasteurella multocida* was cultured from a brain abscess in a 19-month-old girl bitten 3 weeks earlier by a dog, with perforation of the skull not observed at the initial presentation (70). *Pasteurella* has also been responsible for inoculation osteomyelitis, which does not present with the fever and toxicity of Gram-positive hematogenous osteomyelitis of childhood (105).

Special consideration must be given when sepsis or shock is potentially related to an animal bite. Such a patient must be treated aggressively. The wound discharge and the blood should be cultured for aerobes and anaerobes. Tender, inflamed lymph nodes should be aspirated and cultured. If there is no obvious source of culture material, normal saline can be injected into areas of cellulitis and then aspirated for culture, although it is often difficult to get fluid back (109). The same material should be examined by Gram stain in an effort to identify the offending organism. The typical Gram stain appearance and the indicated antibiotics for selected pathogens are described in Table 9. If one predominant type of organism is identified, the indicated antibiotics for that specific organism should be begun. However, in most cases, organisms will not be found, will be mixed, or will be difficult to identify. In such cases, the optimal adult antibiotic therapy is a combination of a cephalosporin, such as cephalothin or cephazolin, plus gentamycin (68). Although cephalothin alone is not the drug of choice for any of these organisms, it provides effective coverage against *S. aureus* and is effective against *Pseudomonas*. Gentamycin covers many of the coliforms, *Klebsiella, Pseudomonas, Aeromonas,* and *Eikenella corrodens.* There are two important exceptions to this approach. If *Pseudomonas* is very strongly suspected, then the drugs of choice are tobramycin plus ticarcillin or gentamycin plus carbenicillin. If *Bacteroides* is sus-

TABLE 9
Potential Bacterial Pathogens in Sepsis from Dog Bites

Species	Gram Stain Appearance	Drug of Choice	Drug for Penicillin-Sensitive Patients	Other Useful Drugs	Resistant to:
Aeromonas hydrophila	G⁻ bacillus	Gentamycin		Kanamycin Chloramphenicol Tetracycline	Penicillin Ampicillin Cephalosporins
Bacteroides[a]	Pleomorphic, usually G⁻ rods, branching forms	Clindamycin		Chloramphenicol Cefoxitin Metronidazole	Tetracycline
CDC Alphanumeric: IIj[a]	Long, thin G⁻ rods, thin centers, and bulbous ends	Penicillin	Erythromycin	Cephalothin Gentamycin Tetracycline	Polymixin
DF-2[a]	Non-spore–forming G⁻ rods	Penicillin	Erythromycin	Virtually all except gentamycin Kanamycin Colistin	Gentamycin Kanamycin Colistin
EF-4[a]	Small G⁻ coccoid and long rods, chains of 4–7	Penicillin	Erythromycin	Chloramphenicol Tetracycline Ampicillin	Clindamycin Methicillin
M-5	G⁻ rods, coccoid or diplococcoid, some filamentous				
Eikenella corrodens	Small G⁻ rod	Penicillin		Ampicillin Cephalosporin	Oxacillin Methicillin Nafcillin Clindamycin
Enterbacter spp.[a]	Non-spore–forming G⁻ rod	Kanamycin	Gentamycin	Carbenicillin	
Klebsiella spp.	Short G⁻ rods, occurring in chains, large capsule	Gentamycin		Cephalothin Cefazolin Kanamycin	
Pasteurella[a]	Ovoid, plump G⁻ rods	Penicillin	Erythromycin	Tetracycline Cephalothin Aminoglycosides	
Proteus mirabilis	G⁻ rod	Ampicillin	Gentamycin	Kanamycin Cephalothin Gentamycin	
Pseudomonas	Small G⁻ rod	Tobramycin plus ticarcillin	Tobramycin plus cephalosporin	Gentamycin plus carbenicillin	
Staphylococcus aureus[a]	G⁺ cocci, often in clusters	Methicillin	Cephalothin or erythromycin		
Streptococcus pyogenes[a]	G⁺ cocci, singly and in chains	Penicillin	Erythromycin	Cephalothin	

[a] Proven cause of sepsis.

TABLE 10
Parenteral Antibiotics in Bite Sepsis

Initial coverage
Cephazolin	25–100 mg/kg per day IV in four divided doses
plus	
Gentamycin (normal renal function)	3–5 mg/kg per day IV in four divided doses

Species-specific
Pseudomonas:
Tobramycin	3–5 mg/kg per day IV in three divided doses
plus	
Ticarcillin	200–300 mg/kg per day IV in four to six divided doses
or	
Gentamycin (normal renal function)	3–5 mg/kg per day IV
plus	
Carbenicillin	500–600 mg/kg per day IV in 6–12 divided doses

Bacteroides:
Clindamycin	25–40 mg/kg per day IV in four divided doses
or	
Chloramphenicol	50–100 mg/kg per day IV in four divided doses

pected, the drugs of choice are clindamycin or chloramphenicol. The doses are summarized in Table 10. Within 24 hours, preliminary identification by culture should be possible, and the patient can be switched to optimal antibiotic therapy. In every regard, the treatment of the patient in septic shock from animal bite is the same as that for shock from other sources.

Transmitted Systemic Diseases

Approximately 150 systemic diseases of mammals can be transmitted in some fashion to humans. However, relatively few of these have been documented to occur by the bite or scratch route. The list includes pasteurellosis, leptospirosis, rat-bite fever, cat-scratch fever, tularemia, erysipelothrix, bubonic plague, tetanus, gas gangrene, rabies, sporotrichosis, and *Bacteroides* and other Gram-negative anaerobic infections (69). It is theoretically possible

for almost any systemic disease of mammals to be transmitted. Pathogens may be secreted in saliva, nasal secretions, or tears or reach the animal's mouth through cleaning activities. In parts of the world, many exotic diseases are endemic in domestic and wild animal populations. However, there is no proof that they are transmitted by bite, they occur rarely in humans, and it is beyond the scope of this chapter to attempt a discussion of them.

Table 11 lists most of the diseases theoretically transmitted by lick, bite, or scratch. For example, tularemia is almost invariably contracted by the skinning of infected rabbits, not by bites. Similarly, leptospirosis is usually transmitted through the urine of infected animals. Some of the really rare diseases, such as simian herpes, foot-and-mouth disease, lymphocytic choriomeningitis, simian hepatitis, and Rio Bravo infection, are completely limited to the occupational exposures of laboratory workers handling animals, to pet owners, and to veterinarians. Excluding *Clostridia, Staphylococcus, Streptococcus,* and *Bacteroides* infections, cat-scratch fever is by far the most frequent disease, yet only a few hundred cases have been reported. Thus, although systemic disease is a valid consideration, 99% of all mortality and morbidity arises from local wound infection, including rabies and tetanus.

With the exception of unusual entities such as rat-bite fever and cat-scratch fever, most diseases do not present to medical care with animal bite as one of the chief complaints. Generally, the animal bite is completely forgotten by the patient or overlooked by the physician in the history and examination. This being the case, workups proceed in standard fashion for fevers, rashes, and other systemic complaints. If animal disease transmission is entertained, the differential diagnosis is usually very extensive and diagnostic tests are not readily available in the emergency department.

RABIES

Rabies occurs in wild and domestic animals, in which migrating cyclic epidemics alternate with periods of endemicity. There is no true reservoir host for rabies; that is, there is no species in which latent and nonfatal infection occurs. An animal stricken with rabies is con-

TABLE 11
Summary of Diseases Transmitted from Mammals to Humans by Bite, Scratch, or Lick

Disease	Organism	Proven Trans.	Poss. Trans.	Dog	Cat	Rodents	Lagomorphs	Horse
Gram-negative bacteria								
Bacteroides infection (B)	Bacteroides spp.	x						
Brucellosis (C)	Brucella spp.	x		x	x	x	x	x
Melioidosis (C)	Pseudomonas pseudomallei		x	x				
Glanders (C)	Pseudomonas mallei		x			x		x
Pasteurellosis (B, C)	Pasteurella multocida	x		x	x			
	Pasteurella hemolytica		x					
	Pasteurella pneumotropica	x		x	x	x		
Plague (C)	Yersinia pestis		x		x	x	x	
Yersiniosis (B)	Yersinia enterocolitica							
	Yersinia pseudotuberculosis	x		x				
Rat-bite fever (B)	Spirillum minus	x			Very rare	x		
	Streptobacillus moniliformis	x				x		
Tularemia (C)	Francisella tularensis	x		x	x	x	x	
Gram-positive bacteria								
Tetanus (B, C)	Clostridium tetani	x		x	x	x	x	x
Corynebacterium infections (C)	Cornybacterium spp.	x						x
Erysipeloid (B, C)	Erysipelothrix rhus	x		x	x			
Staphyloccus infections (B)	Staphylococcus aureus	x						
Streptococcus infections (B)	Streptococcus	x						
Tuberculosis (C)	Mycobacterium spp.		x					x
Rickettsia								
Q fever (C, A)	Coxiella burnetii		x					
Murine typhus (A, C)	Rickettsia typhi		x			x		
Spirochetes								
Leptospirosis (B, C)	Leptospira interrogans	x		x		x		

Cow	Goats, Sheep	Fox, Coyote	Pig	Rac-coon	Bat	Mon-key	Other
							All species—normal oral flora
x	x	x	x	x			Proven only in dog bite
x							Virtually all species
							Virtually all species except cows and pigs
							Virtually all species
							Virtually all species
							Skinning infected rabbits
							All mammals; rare
							Also carnivores
							Rats only
x	x						
x	x	x		x			All species and soil contaminants
x	x						Bites rare
			x				Especially pigs
							All species normal human skin flora
							All species
x	x						Dogs and cats resistant; monkeys have highest rate
x	x						All species; rarely, through abrasion
							Rare
x							

(continued)

TABLE 11 (*Continued*)

Disease	Organism	Proven Trans.	Poss. Trans.	Dog	Cat	Ro-dents	Lago-morphs	Horse
Virus								
Simian herpes (B)	Herpes viruses B and T	x						
Foot-and-mouth disease (C)	Virus		x					x
Rabies (B)	Virus	x		x	x	x	x	x
Cat-scratch disease (B)	Unknown	x		x	x			
Lymphocytic chorio-meningitis (C)	Arenavirus		x	x		x	x	
Simian hepatitis (C)	Virus		x					
Rio Bravo infection (B)	Arbovirus B	x						
Fungi								
Sporotrichosis (B)	*Sporothrix schenckii*	x				x		
Blastomycosis	*Blastomyces dermatitidis*	x		x				

Key:
A = Normally transmitted from animal to human by *arthropod vector.*
B = Normally transmitted from animal to human by *bite,* scratch, or abrasion with saliva contact.
C = Normally transmitted from animal to human by nontraumatic *contact* with excretions, etc.

demned to death. In the United States, Europe, and Canada, wild animals are the main vectors of rabies. Foxes are the primary offenders in Europe, skunks and foxes in Canada and the United States, and the mongoose in Puerto Rico. In Africa, Latin America, and most of Asia, dogs are the principal vector. In South America and Mexico, rabid vampire bats cause heavy losses of livestock and occasional infection of humans. In India and Israel, wolves and jackals are the chief vectors. In the United States (and most other countries), cases of rabies in various species are tabulated annually by local county health departments and by the Centers for Disease Control in Atlanta. Such local incidence figures are a valuable resource for the physician assessing the risk of a particular exposure. Over the last two decades in the United States, the number of cases in dogs and domestic animals has steadily declined while the number of cases in wild animals has increased (100). Table 12 lists the confirmed rabies cases by species of

animals in the United States in 1979. Of all of the cases, 80% occurred in wild animals, with skunks, bats, foxes, and bobcats being the worst offenders. Human cases of rabies in recent years have numbered only one or two a year, most of which originated outside of the United States.

Rabies virus is excreted in the saliva of infected animals. Direct bite wounds account for virtually every human and animal case recorded. It is also possible for infection to occur when saliva or other infected tissues make contact with fresh, open wounds or mucosal membranes, although this risk is estimated at only 0.1% (5). Rabies can be transmitted by aerosol, which was the case in persons who contracted the disease after visiting a cave full of infected bats (100).

Not every animal that has rabies can transmit it. From 50 to 90% of animals dying of rabies excrete virus in the saliva (100); bites by a proven rabid animal carry a risk of transmission which ranges from 5 to 80% (5). The

Cow	Goats, Sheep	Fox, Coyote	Pig	Rac-coon	Bat	Mon-key	Other
							Monkey bites; usually fatal
x	x		x				Low infectivity
x	x	x	x		x		Excreted in saliva 50–90%
							Low infectivity; monkey also
							Low infectivity
							Monkey only; unproven
					x		Rare; laboratory acquired
							All species; common in nature

titer of virus in the saliva also varies greatly, and this determines infectivity. Skunks tend to emit more virus than other species for a longer period of time, and they also tend to bite readily (45). Although rodents are quite susceptible to rabies infection, they virtually never excrete the virus in their saliva; therefore, the Centers for Disease Control rates a rodent bite as carrying extremely low risk. Although the amount present in the saliva is the chief concern, the virus replicates in kidneys, mammary glands, nasal mucosa, and muscle and has been shown to be present occasionally in maternal milk.

Animals vary a good deal in their susceptibility to infection. Extremely susceptible species are foxes, coyotes, jackals, wolves, kangaroo rats, cotton rats, and common field voles (field mice). Highly susceptible species are hamsters, skunks, raccoons, domestic cats, bats, bobcats, ferrets, mongooses, guinea pigs, other rodents, and rabbits. Moderately susceptible species are cattle, sheep, goats, horses, dogs, and subhuman primates. The animal least susceptible to rabies is the opossum (100). In recent years in the United States, 50% of skunks tested for rabies have been found to be positive, along with 30% of foxes, 11.7% of bats, 12% of livestock, and only 4.9% of dogs and 3.8% of cats (100).

An extremely important factor in the transmission and severity of disease is the location of the wound. Rabies virus ascends to its target organ, the central nervous system, by traveling up peripheral nerves. The farther the location of the bite from the brain, the longer the victim has to develop antibodies in response to a course of vaccination. Wounds of the face have a 20 day incubation period, with an ultimate mortality of 1 in 160, whereas wounds to the leg have a 60 day incubation period with an ultimate mortality of one in 6670 (100). Thus, a facial wound carries the highest risk and should receive much more aggressive treatment. In a typical clinical situation, it is impossible to know whether virus was secreted in saliva and in what titers. Thus, all wounds at high risk for rabies should receive special wound care.

The judgment of risk rests on several other factors. The incidence of rabies in local species is important; in the United States, urban dogs

TABLE 12
Reported Cases of Rabies in Animals by State and By Species of Animal, United States, 1979

Area	Total	Domestic				Wild				
		Cats	Cattle	Dogs	Other Domestic[a]	Bats	Foxes	Raccoons	Skunks	Other Wild[a]
United States	5119	154	228	194	56	756	140	543	3031	17
New England	50	—	—	—	1	23	26	—	—	—
Maine	31	—	—	—	1	4	26	—	—	—
N.H.	5	—	—	—	—	5	—	—	—	—
Vt.	1	—	—	—	—	1	—	—	—	—
Mass.	9	—	—	—	—	9	—	—	—	—
R.I.	2	—	—	—	—	2	—	—	—	—
Conn.	2	—	—	—	—	2	—	—	—	—
Mid. Atlantic	77	—	3	1	—	62	8	—	3	—
N.Y.	48	—	3	1	—	34	8	—	2	—
N.J.	12	—	—	—	—	12	—	—	—	—
Pa.	17	—	—	—	—	16	—	—	—	—
E.N. Central	470	23	33	22	4	49	9	1	329	—
Ohio	41	3	1	—	—	13	3	—	21	—
Ind.	68	—	4	1	1	6	—	1	55	—
Ill.	226	14	12	5	1	10	5	—	179	—
Mich.	16	2[b]	1	—	1	11	—	—	1	—
Wis.	119	4	15	16	1	9	1	—	73	—
W.N. Central	1059	45	111	37	22	26	4	10	801	3
Minn.	172	6	21	8	4	3	—	—	130	—
Iowa	206	13	39	7	10	8	1	2	126	—
Mo.	307	10	18	13	4	7	2	5	247	1
N. Dak.	99	3	9	3	1	—	1	2	79	1
S. Dak.	143	8	17	3	1	2	—	—	111	1
Nebr.	4	1[b]	1	—	—	—	—	—	2	—
Kans.	128	4	6	3	2	6	—	1	106	—
S. Atlantic	688	21	2	9	2	125	26	482	18	3
Del.	2	—	—	—	—	2	—	—	—	—
Md.	39	—	—	—	—	39	—	—	—	—
D.C.	—	—	—	—	—	—	—	—	—	—
Va.	19	—	—	—	—	10	—	4	4	1
W. Va.	12	1	—	—	—	—	—	8	2	—
N.C.	26	—	1	—	—	25	—	—	—	—
S.C.	173	7	—	3	—	19	6	137	—	1
Ga.	338	8[b]	1	3	1	19	15	279	11	1
Fla.	79	5	—	3	1	10	5	54	1	—
E.S. Central	327	1	4	19	3	31	17	37	210	5
Ky.	138	—	3	12	—	2	14	—	107	—
Tenn.	109	—	1	4	2	8	3	—	91	—
Ala.	73	1	—	3	1	14	—	37	12	5
Miss.	7	—	—	—	—	—	7	—	—	—
W.S. Central	1857	62	70	95	21	144	29	13	1418	5
Ark.	332	3	8	3	2	14	1	—	301	—
La.	41	—	—	1	1	7	—	1	31	—
Okla.	292	11	28	8	3	8	—	4	229	1
Texas	1192	48	34	83	15	115	28	8	857	4

(continued)

TABLE 12 (*Continued*)

Area	Total	Domestic				Wild				
		Cats	Cattle	Dogs	Other Domestic[a]	Bats	Foxes	Raccoons	Skunks	Other Wild[a]
Mountain	**117**	**1**	**2**	**8**	**—**	**118**	**1**	**—**	**46**	**1**
Mont.	21	—	—	—	—	14	—	—	7	—
Idaho	—	—	—	—	—	—	—	—	—	—
Wyo.	12	—	—	—	—	7	—	—	5	—
Colo.	51	—	—	—	—	51	—	—	—	—
N. Mex.	49	1	—	8	—	13	—	—	27	—
Ariz.	27	—	2	—	—	17	1	—	7	—
Utah	11	—	—	—	—	10	—	—	—	1
Nev.	6	—	—	—	—	6	—	—	—	—
Pacific	**414**	**1**	**3**	**3**	**3**	**178**	**20**	**—**	**206**	**—**
Wash.	21	—	—	—	—	20	—	—	1c	—
Oreg.	17	—	—	—	—	16	—	—	1c	—
Calif.	357	1	3	2	3	142	2	—	204	—
Alaska	19	—	—	1	—	—	18	—	—	—
Hawaii	—	—	—	—	—	—	—	—	—	—
Guam	—	—	—	—	—	—	—	—	--	—
P.R.	26	2	—	2	—	—	—	—	—	22
V.I.	—	—	—	—	—	—	—	—	—	—

[a] Other domestic: 44 equine, 7 ovine, and 5 porcine; other wild: 8 coyotes, 3 rodents, 2 bobcats, 1 buffalo, 1 lagomorph, 1 ringtail, and 1 moose.
[b] Vaccine-associated (Mich. 2, Nebr. 1, Ga. 2).
[c] Pet skunk.
Source: From Reference 19.

and cats and domestic ferrets, rodents, and lagomorphs (rabbits and hares) are at low risk. The behavior of the animal is sometimes helpful. This is easily evaluated in wild animals, since most tend to shun humans. The urban appearance of a skunk, fox, or bat in broad daylight, showing no fear of human beings, is very abnormal and should raise the index of suspicion. Classic rabies, with unprovoked attack, foaming at the mouth, and laryngospasm, is seldom seen in developed countries. Assessing provocation and unusual behavior in domestic species, such as dogs under crowded urban conditions, is often impossible.

Local Treatment

Local wound treatment is extremely important in rabies prophylaxis. Rabies virus is easily killed by sunlight, ultraviolet radiation, air, drying, heat, formalin, and strong acids and bases. In addition a 20% soap solution or 2% benzalkonium chloride reduces ultimate mortality by about 50% (67). However, simple flushing of the wound is not in itself very protective, regardless of the solution used. True protection is provided only by swabbing of the wound, such as with cotton applicators inserted into and rotated against the edges of the wound. The effectiveness of syringe-needle irrigation remains completely untested. Antirabies gamma globulin is also useful as a swabbing solution but is more effective when infiltrated locally around the wound. The best location for infiltration is proximal to the wound, which presumably blocks migration of the rabies virus to the central nervous system. A 1% procaine hydrochloride infiltration of the wound (especially proximally) also provides some protective effect against the rabies virus (67). Presumably, this also relates to inhibition of peripheral nerve virus travel. Substances which have not been found to be useful in killing rabies virus are a 5% Lugol's aqueous iodine solution, 7% tincture of iodine, and 1:1000 tincture of thimerosal. No one has studied the effectiveness of iodine or povidone-iodine as swabbing solutions or for syringe irrigation; both have excellent virucidal qualities (57,61).

There is almost complete protection when effective agents are applied within 1–3 hours after inoculation. Experimental mortality increases markedly when treatment is delayed, going from 10% at 3 hours to 60% at 6 hours and 100% at 24 hours (32). Other agents which are effective when used with the scrubbing technique include warm tap water, 20% soap solution, 1% aqueous benzalkonium chloride, and Ivory soap. Equine rabies immune globulin is most effective when administered within the first 6 hours of infection. Benzalkonium chloride 1–2% equals or outperforms the rabies antiserum but may produce severe local tissue reactions in deep puncture wounds.

In conclusion, thorough and rapid early treatment of wounds from animals suspected of being rabid is mandatory. The wound should be washed out in the first 3 hours with whatever solution is at hand. Plain tap water or hand soap and water are effective, readily available, and not damaging to tissue. In the hospital, the wound should be anesthetized with 1% procaine hydrochloride, which exerts a protective effect. Unfortunately, studies have not been done on lidocaine and other local anesthetics, and their efficacy remains unproven. A 1% benzalkonium chloride solution should then be used as a scrub and rinsed from the wound. It is extremely important to scrub to the depths of puncture wounds by rotating cotton swabs against the wound surfaces. This is not the treatment one would prefer for plastic results, since it is irritating and mildly damaging to tissues. However, since there is no proof that high-pressure irrigation is effective against rabies virus, high-risk wounds should continue to be treated in this fashion. If rabies immune globulin is available and can be used to irrigate and swab the wound, all the better.

If certain risk factors are present, the physi-cian must decide whether to proceed further with immune globulin and rabies vaccine. If the animal is a normal-appearing domestic pet and is captured or its location known, treatment is normally not commenced while the animal is observed for a period of 10 days. Most animals infected with rabies at the time of a bite will become clinically ill or die within this time period. Treatment then commences. If the animal's initial behavior is remarkably abnormal or if it appears ill, it should be sacrificed and submitted for laboratory examination, as should any wild animal which is captured.

If the animal is not captured, particularly if it is wild, then a judgment must be made on the advisability of treatment. This is based on the local incidence of rabies and the behavior of the animal. Unfortunately, it is usually very difficult to determine whether a domestic animal acted normally or was provoked, since it is almost always possible to conceive of some way in which the animal might have perceived an act as provocation. If a wild animal was involved, treatment of any penetrating wound must be begun.

If the animal is captured and sacrificed, the brain tissue must be preserved for examination. It is possible to examine the salivary glands, muscle, lung, kidney, pancreas, and adrenals, but brain tissue is ideal. The optimal methods of preservation are refrigeration, freezing, or preservation in 50% neutral glycerol saline solution. The latter two are optimal for fluorescent rabies antibody (FRA) testing or for mouse inoculation to determine infectivity. Traditionally, brain tissue has been examined for Negri bodies; for this purpose, refrigeration is preferable to freezing. However, if delay is necessary, preservation in 50% neutral glycerol saline solution is acceptable. Paraffin sections can also be stained for Negri bodies, but tissue embedded in paraffin cannot be used for the FRA test.

The FRA test is the most sensitive and accurate means of examination. It can be performed overnight by the public health department and has a reliability of greater than 99.9% (63). While the presence of Negri bodies has been traditionally believed to be pathognomonic of rabies, a substantial proportion of specimens (10–20%) found to be non-rabid by FRA have demonstrated Negri bodies (33). Treatment should not be initiated on the basis of Negri bodies without a positive FRA.

Until very recently, further treatment for rabies prophylaxis presented a truly agonizing decision. Previously, the immune globulin was derived from equine sera. Its use was associated with an extremely high incidence of serum sickness and anaphylactoid reactions, which guaranteed that most of the recipients would be ill from the globulin itself. Fortunately, in the last 10 years, human rabies immune globulin (HRIG) has become readily available, although it is quite expensive. HRIG is essentially without side effects other than local tenderness and inflammation. It is administered in a dose of 20 IU/kg at the time that the patient is first seen. One-half of this dose should be infiltrated locally around the wound, and the remaining half should be given intramuscularly. It is recommended that HRIG and human diploid cell vaccine neither be mixed in the same syringe nor be administered at the same site. Larger doses are harmful, since they interfere with the acquisition of active immunity (26).

The original Pasteur vaccine was a neural tissue vaccine which was administered in large volumes with multiple painful injections. Sensitization to the patient's own myelin could occur, causing a postvaccine meningoencephalitis. In the 1950s, duck embryo vaccine (DEV) was developed, which was the vaccine of choice in the United States until recently. It contains significant amounts of duck embryo tissue and therefore can produce a wide range of allergic and hypersensitivity reactions. Anaphylactic episodes are estimated to occur at a rate of five per 100,000 vaccinees, and the incidence of life-threatening reactions is approximately 1%. Various neurologic "accidents," such as Guillain-Barré syndrome, occur at a rate of 1 per 25,000. The vaccine has a very low antigenic value which is not standardized and requires a minimum of 23 injections. Of all recipients, 23% fail to develop adequate antibody titers after a full course of vaccine plus antiserum (88).

This situation has changed with the recent introduction of the first rational antirabies vaccine, human diploid cell vaccine (HDCV).

HDCV has a standardized antigenicity which is 20 times greater than that of DEV. Furthermore, it is developed in human cells and has induced essentially no significant neurologic or allergic reactions. From 10 to 20% of recipients will have minor local reactions of redness, tenderness, and itching to the HDCV injections, while minor symptoms such as nausea, vomiting, diarrhea, or joint pains are seen in 1–2%. No major reactions have been attributed to the vaccine (5). It is very effective, and no failures to develop good antibody titers have yet been reported. However, it is not so effective that the initial dose of HRIG can be omitted; such an omission may have resulted in the development of fatal rabies in an otherwise properly treated person (33a). To administer HDCV, doses of 1 ml each are given on days 1, 3, 7, 14, and 28. HDCV is so superior to DEV and neural tissue vaccines that there is no justification for their use. HDCV is now in commercial production and is readily available. At the end of the series of injections an antibody titer may be drawn and sent to the health-department laboratory to document adequate antibody levels. These have been so uniformly high after HDCV use, however, that the Centers for Disease Control no longer considers this mandatory.

HDCV can be administered intradermally to provide preexposure rabies prophylaxis (15a). Three 0.1 ml doses should be injected into the dermis on days 1, 7, and 28 to produce antibody titers in excess of 0.50 international units/ml. Subcutaneous or intramuscular injections require greater volumes of the expensive vaccine. At this time, there are no recommendations available concerning the timing and effectiveness of booster vaccinations, although it appears that an adequate anamnestic response can be initiated with low-dose intradermal or subcutaneous injections of HDCV.

CAT-SCRATCH DISEASE

Cat-scratch disease is not common but, after rabies, accounts for more wound infections than most of the other diseases listed in Table 11. It is reputed to be caused by a virus, although this has not been proven. Of all cases, 90% are caused by cat scratch, but dog and monkey bites, as well as thorns and splinters, have also been implicated (85). Most cases occur in children. The average incubation period is 3–10 days. The characteristic feature is regional lymphadenitis, usually involving the lymph nodes of the arm or leg. Often only one node is involved. The nodes are often painful and tender, and about 25% of them suppurate (112). Adenopathy may spread proximally; occasionally, cervical adenopathy is mistaken for Hodgkin's disease. In most cases, a characteristic raised, erythematous, slightly tender, nonpruritic papule with a small central vesicle or eschar which resembles an insect bite is seen at the site of primary inoculation. Constitutional symptoms are mild, with approximately two-thirds of patients manifesting fever, which is rarely greater than 102°F. Chills, malaise, anorexia, and nausea are common. Infrequent evanescent morbilliform and pleomorphic skin rashes lasting for 48 hours or less have been reported. Parinaud's oculoglandular syndrome of granulomatous conjunctivitis and an ipsilateral, enlarged, tender preauricular lymph node occurs frequently. Serious complications are rare and include encephalitis, osteolytic bone lesions, and thrombocytopenic purpura. Routine laboratory studies, including urinalysis and complete blood count, are normal, although mild leukocytosis may be seen. An intradermal skin test of 0.1 ml of cat-scratch disease antigen is positive in approximately 95% of victims, although 10% of the population react in a false-positive fashion. In dubious cases, lymph nodes can be biopsied for characteristic findings. However, in most situations, the diagnosis is made on the basis of a history of contact with a cat, painful lymphadenopathy in one limb, and the presence of the characteristic primary papule.

The workup should exclude other causes of regional lymphadenopathy, such as tuberculosis, tularemia, lymphogranuloma venereum (LGV) lymphoma, brucellosis, and sporotrichosis. In general, only sporotrichosis and lymphogranuloma venereum will demonstrate localized unilateral lymphadenopathy, and LGV usually occurs in the groin. Cat scratches are normally found on the upper extremities. Skin tests, cultures, serologic tests, or biopsies are available for the differentiation of these other diseases.

There is no known treatment for cat-scratch disease, and it usually resolves in a period of weeks to months. There are no known sequelae other than the rare complications mentioned.

RAT-BITE FEVER

Rat-bite fever is an acute illness caused by *Streptobacillus moniliformis* or *Spirillum minus,* which are part of the normal oral flora of rodents. It may also result from bites by wild and domestic carnivores, which may have been infected by hunting rats and mice. Carrier rates among rats vary from 0 to 25% (10). Fewer than 70 cases have been reported in the American-Canadian literature (49). The disease seems to affect lower socioeconomic groups with poor sanitation and heavy rodent populations. The streptobacillary form is an occupational hazard of laboratory workers.

Streptobacillary Variety

Streptobacillary rat-bite fever is caused by *S. moniliformis,* an aerobic, nonmotile, Gram-negative bacillus. The onset usually occurs within a week of the bite, but the incubation period may extend to several weeks, during which time the original wound often heals. Initial symptoms consist of fever, chills, cough, malaise, headache, and, less frequently, local lymphadenitis. This is followed by a nonpruritic morbilliform or petechial rash, which frequently involves the palms and soles. Approximately 50% of patients develop a migratory polyarthritis. Generalized lymphadenitis may be present; splenomegaly and hepatomegaly are rare. Of all victims, 25% develop a false-positive VDRL. Leukocytosis with a left shift is common, and agglutinating antibodies for the bacillus appear during the course of the disease. When a history of animal bite is lacking, the differential diagnosis must include rickettsial and viral infections. Definitive diagnosis requires demonstration of rising antibody titers or isolation of the bacillus from the blood, joint fluid, pustules, or the original bite location. The untreated mortality of this disease is 10%, with most deaths due to endocarditis and pneumonia. The drug of choice is procaine penicillin in a dose of 8000–16,000 IU/kg per day, given in two divided intramuscular injections. Effective alternatives for penicillin-allergic patients are tetracycline, 30 mg/kg per day orally in four divided doses, or streptomycin, 15 mg/kg per day intramuscularly in two divided doses. Complications such as endocarditis should be treated with high-dose intravenous potassium penicillin G.

Spirillar Variety

Spirillar rat-bite fever is caused by *Spirillum minus,* a Gram-negative, tightly coiled, spirillar microorganism. This is usually transmitted by infected rats, although cats have also been implicated. The general setting of socioeconomic deprivation in which this disease occurs is the same as in the streptobacillary form. Reported cases are rare. The incubation period is between 7 and 21 days, during which the bite lesion heals. The onset of illness is heralded by chills, fever, lymphadenitis, and a dark red macular rash. Myalgias are common, but arthritis is absent, which helps in the differentiation from streptobacillary fever. Leukocytosis and a false-positive VDRL are often present. The disease is episodic, with a 24–72 hour cycle. The differential diagnosis includes rickettsial and viral diseases when the history of animal bite is not present. Definitive diagnosis rests on demonstrating the presence of *S. minus* in a dark-field preparation of exudate from an infected site. The patient's blood can be inoculated into mice, which may be tested for subsequent infection. The mortality of this disease when untreated is considerably lower than that of streptobacillary fever. The antibiotic therapy is the same (49).

TULAREMIA

Tularemia represents a variety of syndromes caused by *Francisella tularensis,* a small, Gram-negative coccobacillus. This bacterium normally parasitizes about 100 different mammals and arthropods, most commonly cottontail rabbits, rodents, hares, moles, beavers, muskrats, squirrels, rats, and mice. The primary mode of transmission to humans is via a bloodsucking arthropod, such as a tick, or by skin or eye inoculation resulting from skinning, dressing, or handling diseased animals. Other routes of infection include ingestion of water contaminated by urine or feces and inhalation of dust. Infection following bites or scratches from dogs, cats,

skunks, coyotes, foxes, and hogs has been reported, although it is rare. The disease is an occupational hazard of hunters, butchers, cooks, campers, and laboratory technicians. Humans are quite susceptible to the disease, and several hundred cases a year are reported in the United States (60).

Tularemia is manifested by an abrupt onset of fever, often with chills and temperatures of up to 104–106°F. Headache is common and may mimic meningitis in severity. Hepatomegaly and splenomegaly are present in most patients. Of all cases, 80% take the ulceroglandular form, in which the skin is ulcerated at the point of entry, and regional lymph nodes are enlarged. Bacteremia, pneumonitis, and, more rarely, meningitis, osteomyelitis, and endocarditis may occur. The oculoglandular form occurs in 1% of cases and is marked by extreme ocular pain, photophobia, itching, lacrimation, and mucopurulent discharge. Ulceration and corneal perforation may occur. When pneumonia occurs, mortality increases from 5 to 30%.

Diagnosis is keyed to a thorough history eliciting contact with infected animals. Patients usually present with a fever of unknown origin. The differential diagnosis of regional lymphadenopathy must be entertained. *Salmonella typhosa,* if present, is cultured from blood, feces, or urine. Extremely rare diseases that are introduced by travelers from areas remote from the United States are melioidosis and glanders. The cutaneous ulcers seen in these diseases can mimic tularemia. Neither has been reported to be transmitted by animal bite directly, and diagnosis rests on culture of the offending organism (Table 11). The accurate diagnosis of tularemia depends on a positive skin test, which is usually not commercially available, and rising agglutination titers. The treatment of choice is streptomycin 30–40 mg/kg per day, given intramuscularly in two divided doses. Kanamycin or gentamycin should be equally effective, although they have not been used extensively. Chloramphenicol and tetracycline are not effective in eradicating the organism.

LEPTOSPIROSIS

Leptospirosis is caused by *Leptospira icterohaemorrhagiae,* an organism which infects virtually every wild and domestic species at some time and is shed in large quantities in the urine. Among pets, the disease is common in dogs but rare in cats. The vast majority of cases are transmitted by contact or ingestion of material contaminated by urine. Transmission by inoculation by bite has occurred in dogs, mice, and rats but is extremely rare, since leptospires are not secreted in the saliva; therefore, the mouth would have to be contaminated with urine (35). Farm workers and slaughterhouse workers have traditionally been at high risk of occupational exposure, but the disease now occurs more commonly in children, students, and housewives.

The disease has both the anicteric form and the more severe icteric form (Weil's disease). The latter carries a mortality of 20% or more in patients who have severe renal and hepatic involvement (35). The illness is characterized by an initial phase of high fever, headache, myalgia, and prominent conjunctival injection, apparent recovery for a few days, followed by the return of fever associated with meningitis. In Weil's disease, jaundice, petechial hemorrhages, and renal insufficiency are noted. Most cases are initially interpreted as septic meningitis, infectious hepatitis, or fever of unknown origin (35). Elevated blood urea nitrogen (BUN), hematuria, and proteinuria occur in about 20–25% of patients, 28% have elevated cerebrospinal fluid (CSF) protein, and 44% have increased white cells in the cerebrospinal fluid.

In the early stages of leptospirosis, other infectious causes of fever, such as malaria, typhoid, typhus, and brucellosis, should be suspected. Diagnosis rests on the demonstration of antibodies by the microscopic slide agglutination test, which is rapid and simple but not of high specificity. If positive results are obtained, more refined tests should be conducted at the Centers for Disease Control. Rising agglutination titers are seen after the first week.

The efficacy of specific antibiotic treatment has not been proven, although treatment within the first few days seems to reduce the severity of the disease. Procaine penicillin G, 50,000 units/kg per day in four divided doses intramuscularly, is preferred and is continued for 7–10 days. Tetracycline, 20 mg/kg per day in four divided oral doses, is used as an alternative.

BRUCELLOSIS

Brucella infection is caused by a number of species of *Brucella,* a small, Gram-negative bacterium. The disease usually results from the ingestion of contaminated milk or milk products or by direct skin contact. *Brucella* organisms are chiefly carried by swine, cattle, goats, and sheep, and may be recovered from almost all tissues. Most animals used as livestock are susceptible to brucellosis, while the occurrence in wild animals is rather small. Infection may occur accidentally in the laboratory or occupationally. A proven case of transmission by dog bite has been reported (90).

The incubation period in humans is 1–15 weeks. The disease ranges from mild to severe; it is frequently recurrent and can persist for years. There are no specific symptoms or signs; hence, the illness has been nicknamed *mimic disease* (59). The most characteristic clinical manifestation is undulating fever (59). Others include fever, chills, weakness, malaise, headache, muscle and joint pains, backache, and loss of weight. There is almost always a bacteremia in the early stages which may induce lesions of the viscera, bones, and joints. Due to the nonspecific clinical syndrome, diagnosis rests on demonstrating rising agglutination titers.

The treatment is oral tetracycline, 50 mg/kg per day in four divided doses for 21 days. In very severe cases, streptomycin, 20–40 mg/kg intramuscularly once a day for 1 week, is added to this regimen. The next week, streptomycin is continued at a level of 15 mg/kg. The prognosis is generally excellent.

PLAGUE

Plague is caused by the bacterium *Yersinia pestis.* With a dreaded reputation in history, it has persisted in recent centuries at a much less deadly level. Wild plague is endemic in many parts of the world, chiefly among rats, mice, moles, marmots, squirrels, hares, cats, and mongooses. More than 200 species of rodents and lagomorphs are naturally infected. Major plague areas include parts of China, Afghanistan, and South Africa. One of the larger areas of endemic plague is the western United States, where voles, field mice, ground squirrels, prairie dogs, and pack rats carry the infection. The infection is usually transmitted to humans by the bite of arthropods from infected animals. Handling infected animals can allow *Yersinia pestis* to enter cuts and abrasions, which has been reported in hunters who skin and clean infected rabbits (30). Transmission by actual bite or scratch has never been reported. The disease is mentioned here because of its historic significance and the frequency of occurrence in wild animal reservoirs.

Dog Bites

Dogs are the only species whose bites have been well studied in large numbers. They account for about 90% of all reported bites. In essence, dogs are hunting carnivores and pack animals, categorizations which are frequently inconsistent with peaceful human cohabitation. Instinctively, they are prone to attack and bite, which they do liberally to friend and foe alike. Indeed, the majority of cases occur when a dog bites someone it knows or lives with (Table 13). At the turn of the century, stray dogs were greatly feared due to the high incidence of rabies in them. Bounties were offered for hunting and slaughtering such strays (56). Such procedures are not warranted today, as stray dogs account for only 15–20% of all bites.

Large dogs (weighing more than 50 pounds) account for about 43% of all bites, medium-sized dogs (15–50 pounds) for about 26%, and small dogs (less than 15 pounds) for only about 5% (56). There is a substantial increase in the incidence of biting during the warm

FIGURE 2 Typical mechanism of dog bite injury to the hand and arm.

summer months. Most bites occur between the hours of 1:00 and 9:00 P.M., which is probably related to the number of people on the street at those hours (56). The majority of bites occur in children when they are coming home from school or playing outdoors. It is estimated that 1% of all children are injured by dog bites each year; animal bites are the fourth leading cause of accidents in children (69). The increased susceptibility of children is due to their smaller size, their relative inability to defend themselves, their interest in animals, and their frequent abuse of these animals due to inexperience. Children, more than adults, are bitten when they try to separate fighting animals. Hand and arm bites are the most common, although facial wounds are frequent in smaller children (9,19,60) (Figure 2).

TABLE 13
Relationship of Biting Animal to Victim

Relationship	Dog[a]	Dog[b]	Dog[c]	Cat[c]	Misc.[c]
Victim's or family pet	16%	18%	30%	60	38
Friend's pet	0	42	55	20	40
Stranger's pet	62	22	0	0	0
Stray	22	17	} 15	20	22
Wild	—	—			
Total no. of cases	1868	214	189	34	32

Sources: [a] References 56.
 [b] Reference 9.
 [c] Reference 69.

Fatal Attacks

Fatal attacks by dogs in the United States cause many more deaths than rabies. There were at least 51 such cases in the years 1975–80 (87,114). During this same period, only one person acquired rabies from a dog bite in the United States. The incidence is estimated at one fatal attack per 5 million dogs per year. None of these fatal attacks were caused by stray dogs; most dogs were owned either by the victim's family or by an immediate neighbor or friend. Many of the dogs had previously been friendly and without a history of attacks. Ten of the cases involved attacks by three or more dogs, including one attack by 20–40 dogs. The victims ranged in age from infancy to old age, and most expired at the scene of the attack. Injuries were markedly concentrated about the head and neck, as opposed to the extremity distribution usually seen in nonfatal dog bites. This suggests that the triggering and intent of these attacks differ in some critical fashion from the usual nonfatal biting episode. The beginning of the attack was unwitnessed in most cases, which makes it impossible to determine the provocation or attack behavior.

Fatal attacks cannot be predicted from a dog's prior behavior, and most offending dogs revert to normal, friendly behavior after the episode. The most obvious conclusion is that infants, small children, and the disabled should *never* be left alone with a dog regardless of the dog's prior reputation and behavior. The only other predictive information comes from examining the incidence of bites by particular breeds (Table 14). When viewing these numbers, it must be remembered that only 4% of the total dog population, all purebred, are registered. In almost all series, German shepherds were responsible for the largest proportion of bite wounds, both fatal and nonfatal. In the latter category, they contributed more than their share. Contrary to their reputation for viciousness, Dobermans contributed only a very small number of nonfatal attacks and 2.4% of fatal attacks. This may reflect precautions taken on the basis of their reputed behavior. The category of sporting dogs, which includes the golden and Labrador retrievers, known for their unaggressive nature, represents 17% of total AKC registration but contributed only 0.4% of nonfatal bites and 5% of fatal bites. In contrast, the St. Bernard and Great Dane represent only 4.4 and 5%, respectively, of AKC registration, but they contribute 10 and 7.4%, respectively, of fatal attacks. Although none of these data are comprehensive or incontrovertible, they do suggest

TABLE 14
Incidence of Dog Bites by Breed

	% of Total AKC Registrations, 1976	Reference 9		Reference 69	Reference 87[b]
		Bites	% of All Licensed Dogs[a]		
Mixed	0	37	28.0	31	12.3
German shepherd	19	44	44.0	28	20.0
Terrier	5.4			5	8.6
Cocker spaniel				4	
Doberman	19	1.0	1.7	4	2.4
St. Bernard	4.4			4	10.0
Great Dane	5			4	7.4
Poodle				4	
Collie	6	2.6			2.4
Sporting dogs[c]	17	0.4			5.0
Other		13.6	18.6	16	
Total no. of cases	386,000	2921		135	81

[a] Percent of total Baltimore dog license registrations, by breed, 1976.
[b] All fatal attacks.
[c] Golden and Labrador retrievers.

that some breeds of purebred are more prone to attack behavior.

Overall infection rates for dog bites vary in the literature from 2 to 2.9% (17,18,36, 52,72,107). The latter rate was reported only in atypical, heavily contaminated wounds (72). In typical outpatient-treated dog bite wounds which are managed properly with irrigation and debridement, a wound infection rate of 5–10% is typical, which compares favorably with the 5% infection rate reported for clean, nonbite lacerations repaired in the emergency department (48).

The bacteriology of dog bite wound infections is complex. More than 64 species of bacteria are part of the normal flora of a dog's mouth (7). Cultures of fresh wounds have no predictive value, since all wounds contain bacteria. Most wound infections are due to organisms (Tables 6 and 7) which originate in the dog's mouth, not on the patient's skin (50). One-quarter of wound infections culture out more than one species; no single organism accounts for more than 15% of infections (17). Although *Pasteurella multocida* is commonly mentioned in the literature, only 22% of dogs carry this organism (97). It may cause 10–20% of infections and is sensitive to common antibiotics (16,47). *Pseudomonas* and *S. aureus* are each seen in 10% of infections. Many anaerobic species are commonly present (Table 6) but are invariably mixed with aerobic species (50). Whether they cause wound infection in pure culture is not known, but both aerobic and anaerobic species should be sought in culture. This is important in the setting of sepsis. At least one case of human blastomycosis following a dog bite has been reported (51a). *Blastomyces dermatitidis* was demonstrated in the poorly-healing wound, and therapy was successfully undertaken with ketaconazole.

Bites of the Cat Family

DOMESTIC CATS

Domestic cat bites have been reported in large enough numbers for researchers to reach sound conclusions. Their bites tend to be wounds of the hand (few cats attack passers-by by biting them on the legs). Because they have small, sharp fangs and do not slash, their bite is much more likely than that of a dog to produce a small, deep puncture wound, often involving joint spaces and tendons (1). As a result, the infection rate ranges from 29 to 50% (1,36,69). This rate is comparable to that of dog bite puncture wounds but much higher than the rate for dog bites in general.

Cats get much undeserved bad press. There are just as many cats as dogs in the United States, yet dogs account for 80–90% of bites seen by physicians, while cats account for 5–15%. Cats either inflict fewer bites and scratches on their owners, or else the vast majority of these wounds are relatively minor and cause no sequelae. Treatment of cat bite wounds is the same as for dogs. *P. multocida* seems to be a more frequent cause of infection, but this organism is very sensitive to most antibiotics. Cat bite puncture wounds of the hand should be considered in the same high-risk category as those of other species and should receive prophylactic antibiotics. Cat bites and scratches elsewhere on the body have not been proven to carry a high risk and should receive standard wound care. The possibility of transmission of cat-scratch disease should be recalled, although there is no antibiotic treatment for this infection.

BIG CATS

Most of the information about bites from the large feline carnivores is anecdotal. Tiger bites, for example, seem commonly to become infected with *Pseudomonas* (M. E. Fowler, personal communication, 1980). Wound care should be the same as for other species, with attention paid to the occurrence of major internal injury.

Tigers

The big cats are a major threat to humans in their native regions due to their regular killing of humans (24). Although the number of tigers in the world is dwindling rapidly, they still remain the number one human killer (Table 2). Adult tigers often weigh 500–700 pounds; they are so powerful that the victim is often killed instantly. It is not unusual for the head or a limb to be severed with a single bite. A tiger subsisting solely upon human meat would have to kill approximately 60 adults a year, and documented cases in selected regions have approached this rate over periods of up to 8 years. However, unlike lions, tigers do not become exclusive man eaters. Over the last 4 centuries, an estimated 1 million people have been eaten by tigers. Entire districts have been depopulated and villages abandoned. In the nineteenth century, the tigers' toll in India averaged 2000 victims a year. From 1930 to 1940, the annual number never dropped below 1300. In the late 1940s, this rate dropped to about 800 a year, where it now remains. At the same time, approximately 17,000 people per year are killed in India by other wild beasts, which include non-mammalian species. The tiger problem used to exist in China, Manchuria, and Korea, but the creature is now extinct in these regions.

Lions

Despite their appearance and reputation, lions are not greatly feared or respected by experienced hunters. A threatening gesture or shout may be enough to repel a lion, although a lioness guarding her cubs may well attack. It is usually safe to walk unarmed in lion country; the majority of hunters who succumb to lions are killed by wounded or sorely provoked animals, usually in dense brush. Many who survive the initial mauling die later of infection. Details of their treatment are not available. Persons who have survived attacks state that it is unwise to struggle and that the cat should be allowed to chew on an arm or other extremity. Hopefully, it will then often lose interest and leave. Experienced hunters find that when a charging lion is faced head on and confronted, it will often turn tail and run (24). If the intended victim flees, he is most likely to be attacked.

Occasionally, man-eating lions appear, particularly in Central Africa. Lions are estimated to eat 300–500 Africans a year, causing them to be ranked second among man eaters after the tigers. Conversion to man eating has been blamed on drought, famine, and human epidemics in which large numbers of corpses are abandoned in the bush. Lions which become man eaters and which subsist exclusively on human flesh need approximately 40 victims a year to stay alive. They usually kill with one bite in the head or neck, which kills instantly, or with a swipe of the paw, which can break an ox's neck. Lions have tremendous strength and can easily carry victims for a mile with no rest. Although most lions in captivity become passive and dull, circus and zoo lions periodically kill attendants. Many such deaths have occurred when keepers accidentally backed into an animal or trod upon its tail or foot.

Leopards

The leopard, when wounded, trapped, or cornered, is irrational and ruthless, always attacking the first person to come within striking distance. Unmolested and in normal health, it is a shy, nervous animal with a marked fear of humans. Unlike a lion or tiger, which often kills by cuffing a victim with a tremendous blow, the leopard relies upon fast clawwork and biting. In addition, the leopard seems inclined to retreat when much resistance is put up, even in encounters with baboons. There are well-documented instances of an unarmed man fighting and killing an attacking leopard. Before the days of antibiotics, three-quarters of people mauled by leopards died from subsequent wound infection, but today morbidity is estimated to be less than 10% (24). Mauling is much more common than killing; estimated casualties are 400 a year, mostly in Africa.

Most leopards are provoked by wounds or by a dog attack. The leopard does not often turn man eater; when it does, it attacks mainly children or sick adults. In the state of Bihar in India, leopards ate 300 people in 1959 and 1960 (24). Like man-eating lions, man-eating leopards completely change their normal hunting pattern when their prey becomes exclusively human.

Others

The jaguar is a shy animal that avoids humans and has rarely, if ever, killed them. The puma (mountain lion) is a clever cat and is the most widely distributed large animal on the American continent. There has been only one alleged report of it as a man eater. The only authenticated report of an unprovoked fatal human attack occurred in 1949. The cheetah is the most amiable of all the large cats and has never killed a human. There are a few cases of attacks, but never with severe effects.

Rodents

Rodents do not tend to bite unless severely provoked; their bites are usually small and do not cause much disability. The exact number of rodents in the world is not known, but they probably number in the hundreds of millions, with 1500 species of laboratory and pet rodents. Despite these numbers, they account for only 3–10% of animal bites brought to medical attention. The reasons for poor reporting may be that such bites are infrequent in occurrence, seldom cause any problems for the victim, or often occur among lower socioeconomic groups who do not have good access to medical attention. Rat bites show about a 10% infection rate (69). The various systemic diseases transmitted by rats are summarized in Table 11. Rat-bite fever was discussed in an earlier section. Sporotrichosis has been reported (93). Although rodents can become infected with rabies, they virtually never secrete this virus in their saliva; therefore, they inflict extremely low-risk bites for transmission of the disease.

Human Bites

Although humans do not properly fall into the category of domestic or feral animals, human bite injury certainly can occur in the wild environment. Human bites account for 3.6–23.0% of all bites seen by urban physicians (Table 1). By contrast, in a rural population, only 0.03% of bites are human (98).

Human bite wounds have long had a very bad reputation for infection (55,76). In most of the cases reported over the years, they involved the hand and their treatment was markedly delayed (24 hours to 6 days) (76). Both of these factors dramatically increase the risk of infection in any wound.

With aggressive treatment, such morbidity need not occur. Treatment should optimally be initiated as soon as possible and no later than 12 hours after injury (108). In a number of recent large studies, up to one-half of pa-

tients were treated within 12 hours of injury as outpatients and developed no complications (23,75). Human bites in locations other than the hand do not have an unusually high infection rate (75).

From 60 to 80% of the bite wounds are seen in males, and most occur in the dominant fist as a result of the fist's striking an opponent's tooth. In this position, the extensor tendon and its underlying bursa are pulled distally over the metacarpophalangeal joint. The result is a deep laceration which can disrupt superficial and deep fasciae, the extensor tendon and its bursa, and the joint capsule. When the fingers are extended, the skin and tendon retract proximally, sealing off the contaminated wound. These anatomic relationships set the stage for the characteristic spread of infection. The sites of infection in order of frequency are the subcutaneous space of the dorsum of the hand, the fascial space of the dorsum of the proximal phalanx, the metacarpophalangeal joint, the palmar fascial spaces, and the flexor tendon sheaths.

Of all human bite wounds, 60% are uninfected when originally seen; 21% are superficially infected with local tenderness or inflammation; 15% are moderately infected with a stiff, swollen, tender finger or hand, cellulitis, lymphangitis, and purulent drainage; and only 1% are severely infected, with inability to move a hand or fingers and involvement of deep hand structures (75). Tenosynovitis and septic arthritis are serious complications.

At least 42 different species of bacteria have been reported in human saliva (76). Of all human bite infections, 31% are due to Gram-negative organisms, and 43% are due to mixed Gram-positive and Gram-negative organisms. The single most frequent organism is *Streptococcus,* and the next most frequent is *S. aureus,* which is usually resistant to penicillin. *S. aureus* is cultured from 50–80% of hand infections due to human bites and has been most strongly associated with the major infectious complications (75). A variety of other organisms have been seen in smaller numbers, including *Eikenella corrodens, Bacteroides,* and *Peptostreptococcus* (50). Transmission of actinomycosis, syphilis, tuberculosis, and hepatitis B has been documented by this route.

Any penetrating injury in the vicinity of the metacarpophalangeal joint should be con-

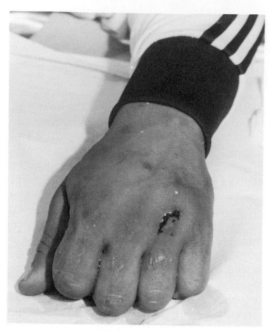

FIGURE 3 Typical human bite wound to the dorsum of the hand caused by striking a person's mouth.

sidered a human bite wound until proven otherwise (Figure 3). X-rays should be obtained to look for foreign bodies, fractures, and air in joints. Treatment of such hand wounds should be very aggressive. Although it is generally not possible to debride them significantly, they should all be thoroughly irrigated with 1% povidone-iodine solution and *should not be sutured.* Soaks and compresses of 1% povidone-iodine solution three to four times a day are useful adjuncts for particularly large, open wounds. The affected extremity should be elevated with a sling and immobilized by packing the palm of the hand with bulky gauze and wrapping the hand in a mitten-type dressing. Wounds seen less than 24 hours after injury and with no overt signs of infection can be treated on an outpatient basis. Patients presenting with any degree of infection beyond very limited local wound cellulitis should be hospitalized with the same treatment plus intravenous antibiotics. In particular, redness, swelling, and tenderness of large areas of the hand, as well as pain on passive range of motion, indicate the need for admission.

Controlled studies of prophylactic antibiotics in nonbite wounds of the hand show no benefit (54,58,81). However, no controlled studies have been done in human bites of the hand, and all authors are unanimous in recommending prophylactic antibiotics. Since *Staphylococcus* and *Streptococcus* account for most of the infections, cephalosporins are a rational initial antibiotic choice for outpatients; they cover many Gram-negative bacteria as well. The oral dose of cephalexin is 500 mg by mouth four times a day for at least 5 days. An initial loading dose of 1 g will help provide prompt and effective plasma and tissue levels, particularly if given intravenously.

Considering the high-risk potential of the hand and the disastrous consequences if infection does not respond to initial treatment, it is a wise idea to culture all infected human bite injuries of the hand. When infection is already established, it is important to get a specimen from deep within the wound, lymph nodes, or cellulitis, since contamination with many other organisms will occur in more superficial specimens. Aerobic and anaerobic cultures should be obtained and sensitivity tests performed.

Human bite injuries in locations on the body other than the hand are no more likely to become infected than are animal bite injuries. Treatment includes aggressive debridement, irrigation, and suturing if anatomy permits and cosmetic considerations are important. Antibiotics are indicated for the same risk factors as in animal bites.

Primates

Monkeys and other primates have an informal reputation for inflicting vicious bites, which virtually always become infected (M. E. Fowler, U. C. Davis, personal communication, 1981). Monkeys often bite the hands and have been known to amputate parts of fingers. Unfortunately, the published reports cover only 13 patients, 15% of whom became infected (36,69). Infecting organisms have not been reported (99). It is advisable at the present time to consider these bites as relatively high risk. Victims should, therefore, be placed on prophylactic antibiotics when bites occur in high-risk areas and should be treated in the same fashion as for human bites.

The wild gorilla, despite its reputation and appearance, is very shy and will take any opportunity to avoid humans. Although it may charge in defense, it seldom attacks and can be easily confronted and forced to retreat. When a gorilla attacks, it takes one bite and runs. In Africa, gorillas are responsible for two to three attacks per year, none of which are fatal and few of which are severe. Chimpanzees occasionally attack humans, usually only if provoked or cornered. Rare instances of chimpanzees eating children and women have been reported. The baboon is responsible for one to two attacks per year, almost all in South Africa; these are usually by pets. Occasional man eating has been reported. The incidence of hunting and meat eating by these animals has increased over the last century, perhaps paralleling the evolution of humans into hunters and meat eaters (24).

Skunks

Skunks bite readily when captured and are frequent carriers of rabies (45). No data exist on the likelihood of other wound infections after skunk bite. Their most frequent means of defense, spraying the secretions of anal sacs, warrants discussion.

A skunk ready to spray directs its hindquarters to the enemy, feet firmly planted and tail straight in the air, often stamping the front feet in warning. The spray is accurate to 13 feet and can be discharged when the animal is lifted by the tail, contrary to popular belief.

Skunk musk causes skin irritation, keratoconjunctivitis, temporary blindness, nausea, and occasional convulsions and loss of consciousness (45). The chief component of the musk is butyl mercaptan. This can be neutralized by strong oxidizing agents, such as sodium hypochlorite in a 5.25% solution (household bleach), further diluted 1:5 or 1:10 with water. The chlorine forms odorless sulfate or sulfone compounds by oxidizing the mercaptan and breaking the sulfur free from the carbon chain. This solution can bleach clothes. The eyes should be rinsed copiously with water or saline. The skin can be cleansed with a tincture of green soap, followed by a dilute bleach rinse. Tomato juice shampoo has been advocated for deodorizing hair, which can also be washed and mildly bleached or cropped short.

Cattle and Other Large Herbivores

Domestic animals, such as cows, bulls, horses, and dogs, are now estimated to kill 800 people a year in Europe alone (24,45). Cattle are usually docile but are capable of inflicting a variety of injuries. Accidental trodding upon the human victim or butting can cause major crush injuries and fractures (99). The horns are used in an inward hooking motion to butt and fling the victim, or the horn tip can be used for goring. Goring injuries seen in bullfighting are penetrating injuries which can cause major internal injuries of the chest and abdomen. Deer, gazelle, and antelope are also capable of delivering damaging kicks. The horse is inclined both to bite and to kick, whereas cattle virtually never bite, since they lack upper incisors. The soft tissue contusions inflicted can be very severe (Figure 1). A death has been reported from fat embolism due to fractures after a donkey bite (11). Pigs have a reputation for inflicting bites of high infection risk (M. E. Fowler, personal communication, 1980).

The African buffalo is a threat only when provoked. Left alone, it does not attack, but when shot or cornered, it will charge and is difficult to avoid or stop. It hooks the victim 10 feet into the air with its horns. If the victim is prostrate, the buffalo gores him into the ground with its horns and the heavy buttress across its forehead and then tramples him. Such brutality is estimated to be responsible for 20–100 deaths per year, mostly in Africa. The horns are always covered with mud, so goring wounds must be laid open and cleansed. However, the patients generally do well (99). The North American bison and the musk ox have been responsible for only very occasional accidental deaths.

Camels have a bad reputation as foul-tempered animals that work up a deep hatred for persons who overload them; they have bitten several handlers to death (24). Unlike most other herbivores, the camel has canines, and its bite can sever a man's limb (25). The camel can also use a biting technique in which it lifts its head up and back, whipping the victim about strongly enough to break his neck (M. E. Fowler, personal communication, 1980).

Other wild species, such as the giraffe, can occasionally turn rogue, but this is exceedingly rare. The black wildebeest has killed one or two zookeepers, as has the spiral-horned kuda and the bushbuck. Other antelopes have killed or wounded hunters or zookeepers with their sharp horns.

There is no literature substantial enough to warrant specific recommendations in treating any of these injuries.

Elephants, Rhinoceroses, and Hippopotamuses

The elephant is one of the most dangerous of wild animals and is probably the greatest killer of hunters. Statistics are hard to come by, but the annual death toll in Central Africa is probably between 200 and 500 (24). Elephants turn rogue from time to time, deliberately attacking and killing humans. Death is by trampling, goring with the tusks, or striking or throwing with the trunk. Elephants frequently rip the victim's body apart and scatter the pieces. Another elephant tactic is to toss the victim into the trees or straight over the pachyderm's back; a number of victims have survived this experience. Some hunters pursued by elephants have diverted them by throwing off items of clothing. Many rogues seem to be injured; others have become intoxicated by eating fermenting marula berries. Persistent hunting has made the elephant more wary and irritable than it was 100 years ago. There are a few rare stories suggesting that an elephant may actually be a man eater; one of these occurred in 1944 at the Zurich zoo. A person with a special relationship with an elephant, who actually slept in the room next to its stall, disappeared; all that was found was a human hand and toe. Considering the legendary truthfulness of the Swiss, it is hard to discount this story. Elephants captive in zoos and circuses may cause deaths while temporarily insane. Man killing in trained work elephants in India is frequently tolerated, since there are only approximately 7000 trained elephants in India, while elephant handlers are plentiful (24). Indian elephants tend to be more docile than African ones, but they, too, occasionally turn rogue. An estimated 50 people annually die in India due to elephant attacks. Elephants have been used extensively in the past as war machines; this period reached its golden age under the Romans, who, after consolidating their victories, insisted on international elephant disarmament. Having made sure that all war elephants in neighboring countries were eliminated, they then retired their own. As history shows, this rational gesture did not affect their ultimate destiny.

The black rhinoceros is one of the meanest animals in Africa and has been known to charge any moving object, including trains. The click of a camera, a gentle movement, or a scent is enough to induce a charge. Contrary to the popular belief that, due to its near-sightedness, it can be easily sidestepped, it can turn on a dime (24). At the end of its charge, it usually hooks right and left with its horns and is generally satisfied with tossing the victim high (12 feet) in the air. By contrast, the white rhinoceros is extremely docile and has killed few, if any, people.

The hippopotamus is a substantial killer in Africa. It is unpredictable and bad-tempered, and will attack boats and people in the water without provocation. Despite its peculiar and ineffective-looking teeth, it is capable of chopping people in half. Hippopotamuses habitually run along established narrow tracks back to the river at night. They will not change course for anything, and humans who make the mistake of staying in the tracks may be trampled.

Vampire Bats

Vampire bats are a vector of rabies in Central and South America, inducing one to two deaths per year in those regions. They feed at night on animal blood, including human, by making an incision in the skin to lap up the blood on the lips, the earlobes, the forehead, the fingers, or between the toes. One bat can eat a maximum of 1 ounce of blood per night, which is clearly not enough to cause death. However, a cave of 1000 bats needs 15 gallons per night, which amounts to more than 5750 gallons per year (24,46).

Other species of bats are noteworthy chiefly for the high risk of rabies transmission. Most bats have very small teeth which often cannot penetrate human skin.

Wolves, Hyenas, and Bears

As a predator on humans, the wolf has a contradictory history. There have been no significant problems or killings in North America, where wolves are traditionally timid. However, throughout Europe and Asia, the wolf has a well-documented history of cunning behavior, pack attacks, and human killing. Wolves tend to hunt in packs and attack women and children. In the year 1712, 100 Frenchmen were killed by wolves, a typical toll for the time. In December 1927, the Siberian village of Pilovo was besieged by hundreds of starving wolves that not only attacked and ate all the human beings and animals found outdoors but actually broke down doors of homes to attack and kill humans in their cottages. Only the arrival of the army prevented total extermination of the inhabitants. In a single year in the previous decade, wolves killed 10,000 horses, 35,000 head of livestock and 26,000 poultry in Russia. That same year, 168 people were attacked, 11 of whom were killed (24). In 1968, in one winter week in Iran, 18 people were eaten by hungry wolves. Rabid wolves are still seen; a substantial number of attacks by rabid wolves in Iran in the last 10 years provided the clinical population on which the new human diploid cell vaccine for rabies was tested (6).

Two other canines which traditionally hunt in packs are the cape hunting dog of Africa and the Indian "devil dog." Although both are feared in their respective environments, they are not deliberate attackers of humans.

The hyena frequently attacks humans in Africa. In certain areas, it is an African habit to leave the dead or dying in the bush for predators (hyenas) to eat, which accustoms the animals to the taste of human meat. Hyenas forage around campsites and villages and are quite wary of awake people. During the summer months when Africans sleep outside their huts, many of them are assaulted with one clean, massive bite that removes the face and/or head. Hyenas have tremendously strong jaws and can leave teeth marks in forged steel. In a circus act, a hyena was able to chew up and eat a 2 inch wooden plank covered with horse fat (24). As with other species, an occasional hyena will become a man eater. In some parts of Africa, the hyena is a more consistent man eater than the leopard or the lion.

The North American grizzly bear, although possessed of a fearful reputation, in fact attacks humans very seldom and usually with provocation. Serious maulings are much more common than killings, and no man eater has ever been recorded in Canada. Occasional rogues have been reported. Apparently unprovoked attacks by grizzlies on sleeping campers have occurred in Yellowstone and Glacier national parks in the last decade, but these have been few, considering the number of humans in grizzly territory. Some species of carnivores regard campfires as a threat and are not afraid of them (24). The North American black bear is responsible for very few attacks, most of them not serious, involving captive bears. The polar bear will stalk humans but often does not attack; when it does, it may abandon the victim, whom it perhaps mistook for another species. Rare cases of man eating have been reported. The Indian sloth bear of India and Ceylon perhaps kills the most people. While not a man eater, it has an irritable nature. Most attacks occur when humans unsuspectingly walk right into bears while they are feeding. The bear slashes at the face with 3 inch claws; 50% of survivors lose facial parts.

A bear does not hug the victim, but tears and bites with claws and teeth. To do this, it pulls the victim up against its own body. As with wounds from other carnivores that feed on decaying meat, there is significant contamination that requires thorough surgical debridement.

Venomous Mammals

There are only two known types of venomous mammals. The short-tailed shrew (*Blarina brevicauda*) of the northeastern United States secretes a protein venom from its maxillary gland and injects it with the lower incisors. The venom may cause edema, a few days of burning sensation, and pain lasting up to 2 weeks (20). There is no specific antivenin, and treatment is symptomatic. No reports of bites have been made since the 1930s. A similar venom is possessed by the European water shrew (*Neomys fidiens*) and the primitive Cuban insectivore (*Solenodon paradoxus*) (15). Documented bites are exceedingly rare, so that a physician should consider reporting them.

The other type of venomous mammal is the male platypus (*Ornithorhynchus anatinus*), which injects a venom from a hollow spur in its hind leg. This appears to resemble viperine snake venom and causes local pain, edema, and lymphangitis (15). Again, reports of such injuries are exceedingly rare. The echidna, or spiny anteater, possesses a similar spur and venom, but envenomation has not been reported (45).

Nonmammalian Species

The ostrich is responsible for one to two deaths a year, mostly in Africa where it is raised commercially (24). Most of the fatal attacks are kicks to the head and abdomen. The ostrich can only kick forward, but when it does, a sharp toenail flicks out like a switchblade, which can penetrate the abdomen. Since the ostrich can easily outrun any human being, the only protection is to lay prone, protecting oneself against disembowelment, and to cover the neck to protect against pecks. Eventually, the ostrich will lose interest and allow the victim to escape.

The Nile crocodile accounts for 1000 human deaths a year in Africa (24). Individual crocodiles have been responsible for up to 400 deaths. Most attacks take place in the water, where crocodiles are accustomed to scavenging for the dead, sick, and deformed babies that are tossed into the water to be disposed of by these reptiles. The crocodile has tremendous grip strength and locks this grip by slotting two lower teeth into holes in the upper jaw. When unable to drag the victim completely underwater, it may grip a limb and then spin over until the limb is detached. Happily, the American crocodile has not been documented to be responsible for any cases of man eating, and the American alligator has also caused few problems.

References

1. Aghababian, R. V.; Conte, J. E.; Mammalian bite wounds. *Ann Emerg Med,* **9**:79–83, February, 1980.
2. Alcock, J.; *Animal Behavior: An Evolutionary Approach* (Second Edition); Sinauer Association, Sunderland, Massachusetts, 1979.
3. Alexander, J. W.; Alexander, N. S.; Influence of route of administration on wound fluid concentration of prophylactic antibiotics. *J Trauma,* **16**:488–95, 1976.
4. Alexander, J. W.; Sykes, N. S.; Mitchell, M. M.; Concentration of selected intravenously administered antibiotics in experimental surgical wounds. *J Trauma,* **13**:423–34, 1973.
5. Anderson, L. J.; Winkler, W. J.; Hafkin, B.; *et al.;* Clinical experience with a human diploid cell rabies vaccine. *JAMA,* **244**:781–84, 1980.
6. Bahmanyar, M.; Fayaz, A.; Nour-Salehi, S.; *et al.;* Successful protection of humans exposed to rabies infection. *JAMA,* **236**:2751–54, 1976.
7. Bailie, W. E.; Stowe, E. C.; Schmitt, A. M.; Aerobic bacterial flora of oral and nasal fluids of canines with reference to bacteria associated with bites. *J Clin Microbiol,* **7**:223–31, February, 1978.
8. Barry, A. L.; Clinical specimens for microbiologic examinations, in Hubbert, W. T.; McCulloch, W. F.; Schnurrenberger, P. R., editors; *Diseases Transmitted from Animals to Man* (Sixth Edition); Charles Thomas, Springfield, Illinois, 1975.
9. Berzon, D. R.; DeHoff, J. B.; Medical costs and other aspects of dog bites in Baltimore. *Public Health Rep,* **89**:377–81, July–August 1974.
10. Biberstein, E. L.; Rat bite fever, in Hubbert, W. T.; McCulloch, W. F.; Schnurrenberger, P. R., editors; *Diseases Transmitted from Animals to Man* (Sixth Edition); Charles Thomas, Springfield, Illinois, 1975.
11. Bloch, B.; Fatal fat embolism following severe donkey bites. *J Forensic Sci,* **16**:231–33, 1977.
12. Bracis, R.; Seibers, K.; Julien, R. M.; Meningitis caused by group II-J following a dog bite. *West J Med,* **131**:438–40, 1979.
13. Branemark, P. I.; Ekholm, R.; Tissue injury caused by wound disinfectants. *J Bone Joint Surg,* **49A**:48–62, 1967.
14. Bröte, L.; Elfström, J.; Höjer, H.; Treatment of *Pasteurella multocida* infection after dog bite by ampicillin wound irrigation. *Acta Chir Scand,* **143**:485–87, 1977.
15. Bucherl, W.; Buckley, E. E.; Deulofeu, V., editors; *Venomous Animals and Their Venoms;* Academic Press, New York, 1968.
15a. Burridge, M. J.; Baer, G. M.; Sumner, J. W.; Sussman, O.: Intradermal immunization with human diploid cell rabies vaccine. *JAMA* **248**:1611–14, 1982.
16. Callaham, M.; Emergency medical management: Dog bite wounds. *JAMA,* **244**:2327–28, 1980.
17. Callaham, M.; Prophylactic antibiotics in common dog bite wounds: A controlled study. *Ann Emerg Med,* **9**:410–14, 1980.

18. Callaham, M.; Treatment of common dog bites: Infection risk factors. *JACEP,* 7:83–7, 1978.

19. Center for Disease Control; Annual summary, 1979. *Morbidity Mortality Weekly Rep,* 28:47–68; September, 1980.

20. Chadwick, J. B.; New England's venomous mammals. *N Engl J Med,* 281:274, July, 1969.

21. Chambers, G.; Payne, J.; Treatment of dog bite wounds. *Minn Med,* 52:427–30, 1969.

22. Check, W.; An odd link between dog bites, splenectomy. *JAMA,* 241:225–27, 1979.

23. Chuinard, R. G.; Ambrosia, R. D.; Human bite infections of the hand. *J Bone Joint Surg,* 59A:416–18, 1977.

24. Clarke, J.; *Man Is the Prey;* Andre Deutsch, Ltd., London, 1969.

25. Consul, B. N.; *et al.;* Orbital fracture due to camel bite. *J All India Ophthal Soc,* 16:245–48, December, 1968.

26. Corey, L.; Hatwick, M. A. W.; Baer, G. M.; *et al.;* Serum neutralizing antibody after rabies postexposure prophylaxis. *Ann Intern Med,* 85:170–76, 1976.

27. Custer, J.; Edlich, R. F.; Prusak, M.; *et al.;* Studies in the management of the contaminated wound. *Am J Surg,* 121:572–75, 1971.

28. Cutwright, D. E.; Bhaskar, S. N.; Gross, A.; *et al.;* Effect of vancomycin, streptomycin, and tetracycline pulsating jet lavage on contaminated wounds. *Milit Med,* 20:810–13, October, 1971.

29. Dagher, F. J.; Cutaneous wounds. *Contemp Surg,* 17:73–85, 1980.

30. Davis, D. H. S.; Hallett, A. F.; Isaacson, M.; Plague, in Hubbert, W. T.; McCulloch, W. F.; Schnurrenberger, P. R., editors; *Diseases Transmitted from Animals to Man* (Sixth Edition); Charles Thomas, Springfield, Illinois, 1975.

31. Day, T. K.; Controlled trial of prophylactic antibiotics in minor wounds requiring suture. *Lancet,* 4:1174–76, December, 1975.

32. Dean, D. J.; Baer, G. M.; Thompson, W. R.; Studies on the local treatment of rabies-infected wounds. *Bull WHO,* 28:477–86, 1963.

33. Derakhshan, I.; Bahmanyar, M.; Fayaz, A.; *et al.;* Light-microscopical diagnosis of rabies: A reappraisal. *Lancet,* 1(1):302–3, February, 1978.

33a. Devriendt, J.; Staroukine, M.; Costy F.; Vanderhaeghen, J.: Fatal encephalitis apparently due to rabies. *JAMA* 248:2304–6, 1982.

34. Dhingra, J.; Schauerhamer, R. R.; Wangenstein, O. H.; Peripheral dissemination of bacteria in contaminated wounds: Role of devitalized tissue. *Surgery,* 80:535–43, 1976.

35. Diesch, S. L.; Ellinghaufen, H. C.; Leptospirosis, in Hubbert, W. T.; McCulloch, W. F.; Schnurrenberger, P. R., editors; *Diseases Transmitted from Animals to Man* (Sixth Edition); Charles Thomas, Springfield, Illinois, 1975.

36. Douglas, L. G.; Bite wounds. *Am Fam Physician,* 11:93–9, 1975.

37. Duke, W. F.; Robson, M. C.; Krizek, T. J.; Civilian wounds, their bacterial flora and rate of infection. *Surg Forum,* 23:518–20, 1972.

38. Dushoff, I.; Handling the hand. *Emerg Med,* 8:26–52, October, 1976.

39. Edlich, R. F.; Custer, J.; Madden, J.; Studies in management of the contaminated wound, III—Assessment of irrigation with antiseptic agents. *Am J Surg,* 118:21–30, 1969.

40. Elenbaas, R. M.; McNabney, W. K.; Robinson, W. A.; Prophylactic oxacillin in dog bite wounds. *Ann Emerg Med* 11:248–51, 1982.

41. Faddis, D.; Daniel, D.; Boyer, J.; Tissue toxicity of antiseptic solutions. *J Trauma,* 17:895–97, 1977.

42. Fiala, M.; Bauer, H.; Khaleel, M.; *et al.;* Dog bite, *Bacteroides* infections, coagulopathy, renal microangiopathy. *Ann Intern Med,* 87:248–49, 1977.

43. Findling, J. W.; Pohlmann, G. P.; Rose, H. D.; Fulminant gram-negative bacillemia (DF-2) following a dog bite in an asplenic woman. *Am J Med,* 60:154–56, 1980.

44. Fowler, M. E.; Diseases of children acquired from nondomestic animals. *Curr Probl Pediatr,* 4:1–45, August, 1974.

45. Fowler, M. E.; *Restraint and Handling of Wild and Domestic Animals;* Iowa State University Press, Ames, Iowa, 1978.

46. Fowler, M. E., editor; *Zoo and Wild Animal Medicine;* W. B. Saunders Co., Philadelphia, 1978.

47. Francis, D. P.; Holmes, M. A.; Brandon, G.; *Pasteurella multocida* infections after domestic animal bites and scratches. *JAMA,* 233:42–5, July, 1975.

48. Galvin, R. J.; Desimon, D.; Infection rate in simple suturing. *JACEP,* 5:332–33, 1976.

48a. Geronemus, R. G.; Mertz, P. M.; Eaglstein, W. H.: Wound healing: the effects of topical antimicrobial agents. *Arch Dermatol* 115:1311–14, 1979.

49. Goldstein, E.; Rat-bite fever, in Hoeprich, P. D., editor; *Infectious Disease: A Modern Treatise of Infectious Processes* (Second Edition); Harper and Row, Hagerstown, Maryland, 1977.

50. Goldstein, E. J. C.; Citron, D. M.; Wield, B.; *et al.;* Bacteriology of human and animal bite wounds. *J Clin Microbiol,* 8:667–72, 1978.

51. Goldstein, E. J. C.; Citron, D. M.; Firegold, S. M.; Dog bite wounds and infection: A prospective clinical study. *Ann Emerg Med,* 9:508–12, 1980.

51a. Gnann, J. W.; Bressler, G. S.; Bodet, C. A.; Avent, D. K.: Human blastomycosis after a dog bite. *Ann Intern Med* 98:48–49, 1983.

52. Graham, W. P.; Calabretta, A. M.; Miller, S. H.; Dog bites. *Am Fam Physician,* 15:132–37, 1977.

53. Gross, A.; Cutwright, D. E.; Larson, W. J.; *et al.;* Effect of antiseptic agents and pulsating jet lavage on contaminated wounds. *Milit Med,* 21:145–47, April, 1972.

54. Grossmann, J. A. I.; Adams, J. P.; Kurec, J.; Prophylactic antibiotics in simple hand lacerations. *JAMA,* 245:1055–56, 1981.

55. Guba, A. M.; Mulliken, J. B.; Hooper, J. E.; Selection of antibiotics for human bites of the hand. *Plast Reconstr Surg,* 56:538–42, 1975.

56. Harris, D.; Imperato, P. J.; Oken, B.; Dog bites—an unrecognized epidemic. *Bull NY Acad Med,* 50:981–1000, 1974.

57. Harvey, S. C.; Antiseptics and disinfectants; fungicides; ectoparasiticides, in Gilman, A. G.; Goodman, L. S.; Gilman, A., editors; *The Pharmacologi-*

cal Basis of Therapeutics (Sixth Edition); Macmillan, New York, 1980.

58. Haughey, R. E.; Lammas, R. L.; Wagner, D. K.; Use of antibiotics in initial management of soft tissue hand wounds. *Ann Emerg Med,* **10:**187–92, 1981.

59. Hendricks, S. L.; Meyer, M. E.; Brucellosis, in Hubbert, W. T.; McCulloch, W. F.; Schnurrenberger, P. R., editors; *Diseases Transmitted from Animals to Man* (Sixth Edition); Charles Thomas, Springfield, Illinois, 1975.

60. Hornick, R. B.; Tularemia, in Hoeprich, P. D., editor; *Infectious Disease: A Modern Treatise of Infectious Processes* (Second Edition); Harper and Row, Hagerstown, Maryland, 1977.

61. Houang, E. T.; Gilmore, O. J. A.; Reid, C.; Absence of bacterial resistance to povidone-iodine. *J Clin Pathol,* **29:**752–55, 1976.

62. Howes, E. L.; Topical use of streptomycin in wounds. *Am J Med,* **3:**449–56, 1947.

63. Humphrey, G. L.; Rabies, in Hoeprich, P. D., editor; *Infectious Disease: A Modern Treatise of Infectious Processes* (Second Edition); Harper and Row, Hagerstown, Maryland, 1977.

64. Hutton, P. A. N.; Jones, B. M.; Law, D. J. W.; Depot penicillin as prophylaxis in accidental wounds. *Br J Surg,* **65:**549–50, 1978.

65. Johnsgard, P. A.; *Animal Behavior* (Second Edition); William C. Brown Co., Dubuque, Iowa, 1972.

66. Johnson, J. E.; Wound infections. *Postgrad Med,* **50:**126–32, November, 1971.

67. Kaplan, M. M.; Cohen, D.; Koprowski, H.; *et al.;* Studies on local treatment of wounds for the prevention of rabies. *Bull WHO,* **26:**765–75, 1962.

68. Kirby, W. M. M.; Chemotherapy of infection, in Isselbacker, K. J.; Adams, R. D.; Braunwald, E.; Petersdorf, R. G.; Wilson, J. D., editors; *Harrison's Textbook of Medicine* (Ninth Edition); McGraw-Hill, New York, 1980.

69. Kizer, K. W.; Epidemiologic and clinical aspects of animal bite injuries. *JACEP,* **8:**134–41, April, 1979.

70. Klein, D. M.; Cohen, M. E.; *Pasteurella multocida* brain abscess following perforating cranial dog bite. *J Pediatr,* **49:**588–89, 1970.

71. Krizek, T. J.; Robson, M. C.; Evolution of quantitative bacteriology in wound management. *Am J Surg,* **130:**579–84, November, 1975.

72. Lee, J. L. H.; Buhr, A. J.; Dog bites and local infection with *pasteurella septic. Br Med J,* **2:**169–71, 1960.

72a. Leyden, J. J.; Sulzberger, M. B.: Topical antibiotics and minor skin trauma. *Amer. Fam. Prac.* **23**(1):121–25, 1981.

73. Lowbury, E. J. L.; Lilly, H. A.; Bull, J. P.; Methods for disinfection of hands and operation sites. *Br Med J,* **2:**531–76, August, 1964.

74. Maki, D. G.; Lister revisited: Surgical antisepsis and asepsis. *N Engl J Med,* **294:**1286–87, June, 1976.

75. Malinowski, R. W.; Strate, R. G.; Perry, J. F.; *et al.;* Management of human bite injuries of the hand. *J Trauma,* **19:**655–59, 1979.

76. Mann, R. J.; Hoffeld, T. A.; Farmer, C. B.; Human bites of the hand: Twenty years of experience. *J Hand Surg,* **2:**97–104, 1977.

77. Marr, J. S.; Beck, A. M.; Lugo, J. A.; An epidemiologic study of the human bite. *Public Health Rep,* **94:**514–21, 1979.

78. McConnell, C. M.; Neale, H. W.; Two-year review of hand infections at a municipal hospital. *Am Surg,* **45:**643–46, October, 1979.

78a. McGrath, M. H.: How topical dressings salvage "questionable" flaps: experimental study. *Plast Reconstr Surg* **67**(5):653, 1981.

79. Mederbekov, B. I.; Antibacterial therapy of wounds after animal bites. *Antibiotiki,* **25:**44–8, January, 1980.

80. Meyers, B. R.; Hirschman, S. Z.; Sloan, W.; Generalized schwartzman reaction in man after a dog bite. *Ann Intern Med,* **73:**433–38, 1970.

81. Morgan, W. J.; Hutchinson, D.; Johnson, H. M.; Delayed treatment of wounds of the hand and forearm under antibiotic cover. *Br J Surg,* **67:**140–41, 1980.

82. Mulliken, J. B.; Healey, N. A.; Glowacki, J.; Povidone-iodine and tensile strength of wounds in rats. *J Trauma,* **20:**323–24, 1980.

83. Parks, B.; Hawkins, L.; Horner, P.; Bites of the hand. *Rocky Mt Med J,* **71:**85–8, 1974.

84. Peeples, E.; Boswick, J. A.; Scott, F. A.; Wounds of the hand contaminated by human or animal saliva. *J Trauma,* **20:**383–89, 1980.

85. Petersdorf, R. G.; Cat-scratch disease, in Isselbacker, K. J.; Adams, R. D.; Braunwald, E.; Petersdorf, R. G.; Wilson, J. D., editors; *Harrison's Textbook of Medicine* (Ninth Edition); McGraw-Hill, New York, 1980.

86. Pietsch, J.; Meakins, J. L.; Complications of povidone-iodine absorption in topically treated burn patients. *Lancet,* **1:**280–82, February, 1976.

87. Pinckney, L. E.; Kennedey, L. A.; Violent deaths from dog attacks in the United States, in press.

88. Plotkin, S. A.; Rabies vaccination in the 1980s. *Hosp Pract,* **10:**65–71, November, 1980.

89. Pollack, A. V.; Kroome, K.; Evans, M.; Bacteriology of primary wound sepsis in potentially contaminated abdominal operations. *Br J Surg,* **65:**76–80, 1970.

90. Robertson, M. G.; *Brucella* infection transmitted by dog bite. *JAMA,* **225:**750–51, 1973.

91. Rodeheaver, G. T.; Kurtz, L.; Kircher, B. J.; *et al.;* Pluronic F-68: A promising new skin wound cleanser. *Ann Emerg Med,* **9:**572–76, 1980.

92. Rodeheaver, G. T.; Pettry, D.; Thacker, J. G.; *et al.;* Wound cleansing by high pressure irrigation. *SGO,* **141:**357–62, 1975.

93. Rugiero, J. R.; Gonzalez, C. E.; Yerga, M.; *Rev Asoc Med Argent Microbiol,* **75:**491–94, September, 1961.

94. Rutherford, W. H.; Spence, R. A. J.; Infection in wounds sutured in the accident and emergency department. *Ann Emerg Med,* **9:**350–52, 1980.

95. Samson, R. H.; Altman, S. F.; Antibiotic prophylaxis for minor lacerations. *NY State J Med,* **77:**1728–30, September, 1977.

96. Sande, M. A.; Mandell, G. L.; Antimicrobial agents: The aminoglycosides, in Gilman, A. G.; Goodman, L. S.; Gilman, A., editors; *The Pharmacological Basis of Therapeutics* (Sixth Edition); Macmillan, New York, 1980.

97. Saphir, D. A.; Carter, G. R.; Gingival flora of the dog with special reference to bacteria associated with bites. *J. Clin Microbiol,* **3:**344–49, March, 1976.

98. Scarcella, J. V.; Management of bites. *Ohio State Med J,* **65:**25–31, January, 1969.

99. Shattock, F. M.; Injuries caused by wild animals. *Lancet,* 412–15, February, 1968.

100. Sikes, R. K., Sr.; Rabies, in Hubbert, W. T.; McCulloch, W. F.; Schnurrenberger, P. R., editors; *Diseases Transmitted from Animals to Man* (Sixth Edition); Charles Thomas, Springfield, Illinois, 1975.

101. Sindelar, W. F.; Mason, R. J.; Irrigation of subcutaneous tissue with povidone-iodine solution for prevention of surgical wound infections. *Surg Gynecol Obstet,* **148:**227–31, 1979.

102. Singleton, A. O.; Julian, J.; An experimental evaluation of methods used to prevent infection in wounds contaminated with feces. *Ann Surg,* **151:**912–16, 1960.

103. Stevenson, J.; Thatcher, J. G.; Rodeheaver, G. T.; *et al.;* Cleansing the traumatic wound by high pressure irrigation. *JACEP,* **5:**17–21, 1976.

104. Strassburg, M. A.; Greenland, S.; Marron, J. A.; *et al.;* Animal bites: Patterns of treatment. *Ann Emerg Med,* **10:**193–97, 1981.

105. Szalay, G. C.; Sommerstein, A.; Inoculation osteomyelitis secondary to animal bites. *Clin Pediatr,* **11:**687–89, 1972.

106. Thomson, H. G.; Svitek, V.; Small animal bites: The role of primary closure. *J Trauma,* **13:**20–23, 1973.

107. Tindall, J. P.; Harrison, C. M.; *Pasteurella multocida* infections following animal injuries, especially cat bites. *Arch Dermatol.,* **105:**412–16, March, 1972.

108. Tomasetti, B. J.; Walker, L.; Gormley, M. E.; *et al.;* Human bites of the face. *J Oral Surg,* **37:**565–68, 1979.

109. Uman, S. J.; Kunin, C. M.; Needle aspiration in the diagnosis of soft tissue infections. *Arch Intern Med,* **135:**423–34, 1973.

110. Viljanto, J.; Disinfection of surgical wounds without inhibition of normal wound healing. *Arch Surg,* **115:**253–56, 1980.

111. Vorherr, H.; Vorherr, ULFL; Mehta, P.; *et al.;* Vaginal absorption of povidone-iodine. *JAMA,* **244:**2628–29, 1980.

112. Warwick, W. J.; Cat scratch disease, in Hubbert, W. T.; McCulloch, W. F.; Schnurrenberger, P. R., editors; *Diseases Transmitted from Animals to Man* (Sixth Edition); Charles Thomas, Springfield, Illinois, 1975.

113. Wheeler, C. B.; Rodeheaver, G. T.; Thacker, J. G.; *et al.;* Side effects of high-pressure irrigation. *SGO,* **143:**775–78, 1976.

114. Winkler, W. G.; Human deaths induced by dog bites, United States, 1974–75. *Public Health Rep,* **92:**425–30, September–October, 1977.

CHAPTER 12

VENOMOUS SNAKE BITES

Willis A. Wingert, M.D.

Poisoning by animal venoms differs from simple chemical poisoning because of the complex composition of venom. Where an industrial chemical may exert a pharmacologic action on only one or two organ systems, a venom usually contains many enzymes and proteins which simultaneously damage local tissues, blood vessels, cellular blood elements, the conduction system of the heart, and myoneural junctions. The 20 or 30 different components in venom may act independently or in synergism. Physiologic chain reactions and occasional immunologic sequelae follow, such as renal insufficiency due to circulatory failure, to the tubular precipitation of liberated hemoglobin, or to serum sickness. The physician confronted with an envenomated patient must therefore be prepared not only to neutralize the animal toxin by means of an antivenin but also to counter many physiologic dysfunctions involving circulation, respiration, and coagulation.

Snakes are found from below sea level to above the timberline. While most snakes prefer the ground, some climb trees or swim. Although the natural habitat of all venomous reptiles is rural, in sparsely inhabited areas such as deserts and swamps, no clinician dealing with emergencies is immune to treating envenomation, even in a large urban emergency department. City dwellers in increasing numbers venture into the reptiles' habitats and frequently collect these poisonous animals for display in their homes or as pets. Furthermore, foreign or exotic snakes are smuggled illegally into the United States, apparently in large numbers. Collectors of these often brightly colored and attractive reptiles may handle the animals carelessly and sometimes mistake venomous for nonvenomous species. The venomous coral snake, for example, has many mimics.

Complicating the problem of envenomation is the application of ill-advised, empirical, and sometimes mutilating therapy, much of which has no pharmacologic or scientific basis and, indeed, may be based on folklore. Examples are the traditional internal use of alcohol ("snake bite medicine"), extolled widely by lay people; the wide surgical incisions of bitten extremities; the use of steroids and antihistamines; and the use of cryotherapy, which imposes frostbite on already damaged tissues. Envenomation should be approached as scientifically as are all other poisonings. One should:

1. Identify the toxin
2. Determine the severity of the poisoning
3. Neutralize the poison with a specific antidote as completely as possible
4. Support all physiologic body functions until the poison has been chemically neutralized or metabolized and excreted
5. Restore functional joint patterns by physiotherapy
6. *Primum non nocere!*

Epidemiology

Each year in the United States, approximately 7000 patients are treated for snake venom poi-

soning, an incidence of about 3.74 bites per 100,000 population (24). From 9 to 14 deaths result annually; therefore, the case fatality rate is less than 0.5% (17). Nineteen species of poisonous snakes account for these envenomations (Table 1):

1. The Crotalidae, or pit vipers, of which three genera inhabit the United States: *Crotalus,* or rattlesnakes, which includes 15 species; *Agkistrodon,* which includes the cottonmouth moccasin (*A. piscivorus*) and the copperhead (*A. contortrix*); and *Sistrurus,* including the pigmy rattlesnake (*S. miliaris*) and the massasauga (*S. catenatus*).
2. The Elapidae, or coral snakes, which are limited geographically to the southern and southwestern states. Only 20–25 persons suffer bites by these dangerous snakes each year, accounting for less than 0.5% of all envenomations (21).

The highest bite rates are found in southern states: North Carolina (18.79 per 100,000 population per year), Arkansas (17.19), Texas (14.70), Mississippi (10.83), and Louisiana (10.25). The southwestern deserts also have

TABLE 1
Major Venomous Snakes of North America

Area	Common Name	Scientific Name	Usual Habitat and Characteristics
Northeastern states	Cottonmouth	*Agkistrodon piscivoris*	Average adult length 30–45 inches (maximum 6 feet). Semiaquatic: swamps, lakes, sluggish streams. Swims and crawls with head raised at an angle of 45°. Pugnacious.
	Copperhead	*A. contortrix*	Average adult length 24–36 inches (maximum 4 feet). Wooded mountains, damp meadows, along old stone walls, near abandoned buildings. May climb bushes and low trees in search of food. Usually docile.
	Timber rattlesnake	*Crotalus horridus horridus*	Average adult length 36–48 inches (maximum 6 feet). Wooded, mountainous areas, usually in second-growth timber. May stray into farmlands in harvest season. Basks and hibernates in rocky bluffs and ledges. Usually retreats if disturbed.
Southeastern states	Cottonmouth	*Agkistrodon piscivoris*	Lagoons, sluggish waterways. Basks by day on logs, stones, or branches near water. When disturbed, vibrates tail and opens mouth wide to reveal white lining.
	Copperhead	*A. contortrix*	Frequents both lowland swamps and uplands.

(Continued)

TABLE 1 (*Continued*)

Area	Common	Scientific Name	Usual Habitat and Characteristics
	Eastern diamond back rattlesnake	*Crotalus adamanteus*	Average adult length 42–66 inches (maximum 8 feet). Low coastal areas, scrub palmetto, low brush, and dry pine woods, often close to water. Sometimes found in farmlands. Largest and most dangerous rattler. Usually does not retreat when disturbed.
	Canebrake rattlesnake	*C. horridus atricaudatus*	Average adult length 36–48 inches (maximum 6 feet). Lowlands, swamps and cane thickets. Related to northern timber rattlesnake. Mild-mannered.
	Pigmy rattlesnake	*Sistrurus miliaris*	Average adult length 15–22 inches (maximum 31 inches). Usually found near water: lakes, rivers, flood plains, swamps, and marshes. Alert and bad-tempered, but rarely inflicts serious bites.
	Eastern coral snake	*Micrurus fulvius fulvius*	Average adult length 23–32 inches (maximum 4 feet). Grasslands and dry open woods, sometimes along streams or in piles of garden compost. Usually docile and seldom bites unless handled roughly. Diurnal.
Central states	Cottonmouth	*Agkistrodon piscivoris*	See above.
	Copperhead	*A. contortrix*	See above.
	Massasauga rattlesnake	*Sistrurus catenatus*	Average adult length 18–28 inches (maximum 3 feet). Prairie regions, dry wooded land, grasslands, in woodpiles and cellars, under steps, in hay fields. Bogs and marshes in northeastern region. Secretive, not usually aggressive, but bites readily if cornered.
	Timber rattlesnake	*Crotalus horridus horridus*	Wooded rocky hills, basking on ledges.
	Prairie rattlesnake	*Crotalus viridis viridis*	Average adult length 36–48 inches (maximum 5 feet). Dry grasslands, rocky hills, on open mountain slopes to 9000 feet. Diurnal, but avoids intense light and heat. Irritable.
	Great Basin rattlesnake	*C. viridis lutosus*	Average adult length 24–35 inches (maximum 4 feet). Arid to semiarid rocky areas.
Southwestern states	Cottonmouth	*Agkistrodon piscivoris*	Near water in central and western Texas.
	Copperhead	*A. contortrix*	Wooded hills in central Texas.
	Pigmy rattlesnake	*Sistrurus miliarsis*	Grasslands in southeast Arizona; New Mexico to southern Texas.
	Massasauga rattlesnake	*S. catenatus*	Prairie lands, Texas and Arizona.
	Northern black-tailed rattlesnake	*Crotalus molossus*	Average adult length 36–48 inches (maximum 5 feet). Southern regions of southwestern states, extending into Mexico. Characteristic solid black tail.

(*Continued*)

TABLE 1 (*Continued*)

Area	Common	Scientific Name	Usual Habitat and Characteristics
	Prairie rattlesnake	*C. viridis viridis*	Dry hills and grasslands.
	Sidewinder	*C. cerastes*	Average adult length 18–25 inches (maximum 30 inches). Desert areas, sandy flats, sand dunes, arid rocky hillsides. Rests with body buried in the sand. Has elevated hornlike scale above the eye. Not highly irritable.
	Mojave rattlesnake	*C. scutulatus*	Average adult length 30–40 inches (maximum 4 feet). Lowlands, in southeastern Arizona and northern Mexico (desert and arid areas). Moderately irritable. Highly toxic venom.
	Western diamond back rattlesnake	*C. atrox*	Average adult length 36–66 inches (maximum 7 feet). Lowlands and rocky hillsides. Diurnal. Large, bold, and aggressive snake often found in open and cultivated areas and near farm buildings. Raises head and loop of neck high above coils in striking.
	Red diamondback rattlesnake	*C. ruber ruber*	Average adult length 40–50 inches (maximum 5 feet). Similar to Western diamondback. Hisses loudly when disturbed. Less irritable than Western diamondback.
	Texas coral snake	*Micrurus fulvius tenere*	Average adult length 23–32 inches (maximum 4 feet). See Eastern coral snake.
	Sonoran coral snake	*M. euryxanthus*	Average adult length 12–16 inches (maximum 20 inches). Limited to Arizona and New Mexico. Smaller than *M. fulvius*. Antivenin not available for this species.
Pacific coast	Northern Pacific rattlesnake	*Crotalus viridis oreganus*	Average adult length 36–48 inches (maximum 5 feet). Semiarid areas from sea level to 11,000 feet. Avoids extremes of heat and moisture. May be found in suburban areas and farmlands. Northern California, Washington, and Oregon. Highly toxic venom.
	Southern Pacific rattlesnake	*C. viridis helleri*	Same as above, except found in southern California.
	Great Basin rattlesnake	*C. viridis lutosus*	Arid and semiarid areas in eastern Oregon.
	Western diamond-back rattlesnake	*C. atrox*	Confined to narrow zone of dry, rocky hills and sandy desert in southwestern California and Baja California. Active during the day in cool weather.
	Red diamondback rattlesnake	*C. ruber ruber*	Same as above.
	Sidewinder	*C. cerastes*	See above.
	Mojave rattlesnake	*C. scutulatus*	Mojave Desert area in southern California.

Note: A complete listing of all poisonous snakes and their distribution may be found in *Snake Venom Poisoning*, by F. E. Russell, M.D. (Reference 25).

a respectable incidence: Arizona (7.83) and New Mexico (7.47) (18).

About 90% of envenomations occur between April and October, as may be expected, since the snake is a cold-blooded animal (25). One-half of all bites occur from 3 to 9 P.M. (18). The incidence is higher in males than in females (4:1), and more than 50% of all bites occur in children and in young adults less than 20 years old (20,21). Almost all bites are on the extremities, with the majority (65%) on the hand and arm (7). Up to one-third of all bites occur when snakes are purposefully handled.

Characteristics of Poisonous Snakes

The major offenders belong to the family Crotalidae, or pit vipers, so-called because of a depression or pit in the maxillary bone. This is located midway between and below the level of the eye and the nostril on each side of the head. This organ is believed to be a sensory heat-detecting organ, which enables the snake to sense and locate warm-blooded prey or enemies even in absolute darkness (16). It serves to guide the direction of the strike and possibly to determine the amount of venom to be released from the venom gland, according to the size or heat emission of the prey (2). These thermal receptors are exquisitely sensitive to infrared radiation and can detect changes in temperature as little as 0.003°C. (14). However, the maximal range of this organ is believed to be only 14 inches (8). Snakes are deaf to most airborne sounds, since they lack an external ear; they are similarly blessed with very poor vision. However, their sense of smell is keen. The major component of olfaction is Jacobson's organ in the roof of the mouth, to which stimuli in the form of volatile chemical substances are brought by the protruding forked tongue. Snakes are very sensitive to ground-conducted vibrations, probably by conduction through the stapes of the middle ear (8).

Rattlesnakes, like most reptiles, are relatively inactive animals when compared to mammals. Snakes generally do not travel long distances in search of prey, nor can they sustain maximal physical activity for a prolonged period. Muscular energy is limited by a single functional lung and a three-chambered heart with a pulmonary shunt due to an incomplete vertricular septum. Therefore, blood in the dorsal aorta has a reduced oxygen content; oxygenation of peripheral tissue and the augmented elevation of blood pressure are limited (8). In addition, snake skin lacks integumentary glands with which to eliminate excess body heat produced by excessive muscular activity. The rattlesnake's top speed of travel is 3 mph, equivalent to a human's moderate walking pace. When a human appears, snakes do not give chase.

Habits and Habitats

Snakes lack internal means for the regulation of body temperature. Thus, environmental temperature variations influence their activity. Snakes become immobile at temperatures below 8°C and cannot survive for more than 12 minutes at temperatures above 42°C. Their optimal temperature range is 27–32°C, which occurs in evenings and at night in southern states and southwestern deserts. Therefore, snakes are nocturnal feeders and are winter hibernators, usually in rocky dens. Snakes mate in the spring, and in most cases the young are born between August and October. Influenced by temperature and by food supply, they grow to maximal size in 2 years. The life span of some captive snakes has exceeded 30 years.

Snakes are strict carnivores and are venomous at birth. Their food consists largely of small nocturnal mammals, especially rodents, birds and bird eggs, frogs, lizards, and other snakes. The copperhead's diet includes a high proportion of insects (25). Snakes secure prey by lying coiled and immobile beside animal trails or burrows. Aided by a keen sense of smell and by its heat receptors, the snake detects and locates a passing mammal. When the prey comes within striking range, which is usually a distance half the length of the snake, the snake opens its mouth wide, erects its fangs, and lunges forward, briefly burying its fangs into the prey in order to inject a lethal dose of venom. The amount of venom released is based on the snake's estimate of the victim's size (8). The speed of the strike is extremely rapid, approximately 8 feet/second (36). The strike is usually directed slightly downward, but rattlesnakes may strike horizontally or even upward at a 45° angle. Although the strike is usually single and from a coiled position, rattlesnakes may strike from almost any position, and may strike several times. The strike is more an injection than a bite, so that the fragile fangs and jaw articulation are less at risk. The potent venom is designed to immobilize the prey rapidly, so that it cannot escape beyond the snake's area of sensory apprehension (about 20 feet), and to prevent a retaliatory struggle which would injure the snake. After the victim is subdued, the snake swallows it head first. This is facilitated by a loose muscular (rather than connective tissue) articulation between the upper and lower jaws, which permits the ingestion of amazingly large prey. However, these articulations have a disadvantageous lack of rigidity and strength, so that a large struggling rodent can readily break a rattlesnake's jaw.

CROTALIDAE

Characteristics

Four distinguishing characteristics of the Crotalidae are facial pits, vertical elliptical pupils ("cat's eye"), a triangular head distinct from the remainder of the body, and a single row of subcaudal scutes or scales (Figure 1). The genus *Crotalus* is further characterized by rattles, which are interlocking horny segments formed on the tail as the snake periodically sheds its skin during growth (Figure 2). The age in years of the snake is *not* determined by the number of rattles, since molting occurs from one to four times annually, depending on temperature, food, moisture, age, health, and possibly other factors. Rattles are commonly missing as a result of injury. The characteristic buzz occurs when the tail vibrates from 20 to 85 cycles per second, in direct relation to the environmental temperature (8). *Strikes may occur without a preliminary warning buzz.*

Venom Apparatus

The venom apparatus of Crotalidae consists of a gland, duct, and one or more fangs on each side of the head (Figure 3). The venom glands are located at the outer edge of the upper jaw, immediately below the eye, and are homologous to the human parotid. Each secretory cell synthesizes all components, both toxic peptides and digestive enzymes (31). The gland is contracted by an external jaw muscle to discharge the venom. Since these muscles have an innervation separate from that of the biting mechanism, the snake can control the amount of venom to be discharged and injected. This is quantitated by the weight and size of the victim. Therefore, discharge is not an all-or-none phenomenon, and pit vipers rarely discharge the full contents at a single bite. A high-speed sensory feedback in the heat-detecting pit enables the snake to make split-second adjustments in the force and direction of the strike, as well as in the quantity of venom injected. Most rattlesnakes discharge between 25 and 75% of their venom when they bite a human (26). After discharge, the venom is completely replenished in as few as 21 days. Lethal peptides appear first, probably as a defense mechanism (7).

The venom glands are connected by ducts to two elongated hollow upper maxillary teeth or fangs which have a slitlike opening near the tip. The ducts empty into the fang sheath, which itself contains venom in a small pocket. When not in use, the fangs are folded against the upper jaw, along the roof of the mouth. During the strike, the fangs rotate down and forward so that their base is at a right angle to the jaw. In adult snakes, the fangs vary from 8 to more than 20 mm in length. Fangs of large snakes may penetrate to the muscles of humans and may perforate rubber or even leather boots (13). The fangs are deciduous, being shed and replaced every 6–10 weeks in the adult snake (8). Reserve fangs may move into position before the functional fang is shed. Therefore, a victim may demonstrate from one to four fang marks at the site of a single bite.

Venom

Crotalus venom is a complex substance with two functions: to immobilize and kill prey, and to aid in digestion. The venom of old snakes appears to be less lethal than that of younger snakes, although the former is present in greater quantity. Venom does not act in humans as a single chemical poison, but affects almost every body tissue and organ system either primarily or secondarily. Treatment of envenomation is similar to that of poisoning by many drugs or chemicals simultaneously.

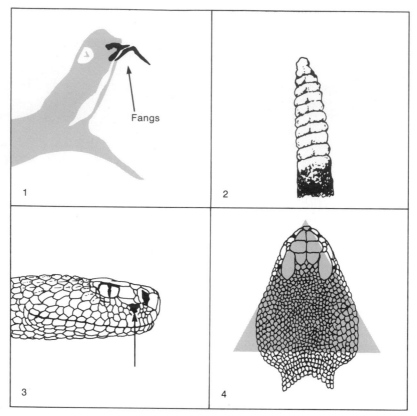

FIGURE 1 Identification of venomous pit vipers. (1) Two hinged fangs in front part of jaw. (2) Rattles on tail (baby rattlers only have "buttons" but are still dangerous). (3) Heat-sensory facial pits on sides of head near nostrils. (4) Triangular head.

FIGURE 2 Northern Pacific rattlesnake (*Crotalus viridis oreganus*).

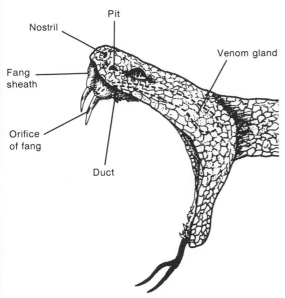

FIGURE 3 Anatomy of the poison apparatus of pit vipers.

Chemically, venom consists of 90% water, 5–15 enzymes, 3–12 nonenzymatic proteins and peptides, and at least six as yet unidentified substances.

The lethal components, responsible for the immediate death of the prey, are low molecular weight peptides and polypeptides (20–82 amino acid chains, molecular weight 4800–100,000) (22). These components appear to alter the endothelial cells of vascular walls, producing transient microangiopathic vascular permeability to both plasma proteins and often to red blood cells. This is manifested by the loss of fluid into the "third space." The results are hemoconcentration, lactic acidosis, and hypovolemic shock. Tissue destruction is local and diffuse, caused by various enzymes designed by nature to aid in and hasten the digestion of prey. The more important enzymes and their actions are:

1. *Proteolytic enzymes or proteases.* Trypsinlike action damages muscle and subcutaneous tissues, leading to necrosis (27).
2. *Hyaluronidase.* Cleavage of internal glycoside bonds of various acid mucopolysaccharides decreases the viscosity of connective tissue and allows other fractions of venom to spread through involved tissues.
3. *Phospholipase A_2.* This is an esterolytic enzyme which specifically catalyzes the hydrolysis of the ester bond at the C-2 position on lecithin. This

action releases a molecule of fatty acid and lysolecithin. The latter substance damages most cells and provokes histamine release. Since red blood cell membranes contain lecithin, the normal permeability of the cell wall may be altered, allowing water to enter the cell without regulation. This may lead to hemolysis.

4. *L-Amino acid oxidase.* This enzyme causes tissue destruction by catalyzing the oxidation of amino acids.
5. *Thrombinlike enzymes and amino acid esterases.* These enzymes act as defibrinating anticoagulants, promoting fibrinogen clot formation by incompletely splitting fibrinopeptide A or B from the fibrinogen molecule. Factor XIII is not activated. The result is formation of an unstable fibrin clot, readily lysed by both plasmin and other enzymes in the venom. Afibrinogenemia and thrombocytopenia follow.
6. *Other enzymes.* Other enzymes, whose pharmacologic actions have not been fully determined, include collagenase, RNase, DNase, and arginine ester hydrolase.

Physiologic Venom Effects

The components of venom differ in relative amounts among species of pit vipers. Therefore, the toxic effects of venom remain multiple but vary with the offending species. The major toxic effects are:

1. *Cardiovascular.* Alteration of vessel permeability with loss of plasma and blood into tissues; local edema and ecchymosis; decrease in circulating blood volume; hypotension; hypovolemic shock.
2. *Hematologic.* Prolongation of bleeding and coagulation times; spherocytosis; hemolysis; hematuria; hematemesis; melena; hemoptysis; epistaxis; hemorrhage at the site of the bite; thrombocytopenia may be seen in 25–40% of victims within 12 hours (9).
3. *Pulmonary.* Pulmonary hemorrhage and intraalveolar edema due to capillary damage. This has been a consistent finding at autopsy and may be an immediate cause of death (28).
4. *Renal.* Acute tubular necrosis; renal failure. This may occur because of the decreased perfusion seen with hypotension or may be due to the precipitation of hemoglobin from lysed red blood cells in the renal tubules.
5. *Local.* Enzyme-induced tissue necrosis, including skin, muscle, and subcutaneous tissue. Some believe that if venom is injected into a muscle sheath, a "compartment syndrome" or marked rise in tissue pressure beyond the normal 8 mmHg will occur, thus restricting circulation to the muscle, with resulting ischemic tissue ne-

crosis. However, Russell, on the basis of experiments in dogs and observations of humans, believes that muscle necrosis is caused by proteolytic enzymes in the venom, rather than by pressure-induced compartment tamponade. Thus, the incision of fascia (fasciotomy) to relieve pressure not only is valueless but may be dangerous in the face of a potential coagulopathy and enzymatically compromised host defense (5). This will be reemphasized in the section on management.

ELAPIDAE

Two members of the coral snake family, Elapidae, occur in the United States: the western coral snake (*Micrurus euryxanthus*), found in Arizona and New Mexico, and the eastern coral snake (*M. fulvius*), distributed from coastal North Carolina through the Gulf states to western Texas (Figure 4). Elapids favor dry, open, brushy or sandy ground near rivers or lakes. Sometimes they may be found in loamy soil under leaf accumulations (35). The elapids differ from pit vipers in having very short fangs fixed at the anterior part of the maxilla, round pupils, and subcaudal scales in a double row. The color pattern is characteristic, with red, black, and yellow or white bands completely encircling the body. The snout is completely black. Since many nonpoisonous mimics occur in coral snake territory, the rule of thumb for identifying the coral is by the sequence of colors: red bands bordered by yellow (or white) indicate a venomous animal—"Red on yellow, kill a fellow; red on black, venom lack."

The coral snake is slender, ranges in length from 50 to 110 cm (20–44 inches), feeds chiefly on small lizards and other snakes, and is diurnal. Most coral snakes are shy, docile animals and seldom bite unless handled roughly or deliberately provoked. The small mouth and fangs make it difficult for the snake to bite anything larger than a finger, toe, or fold of skin. The coral snake tends to hang on and chew, rather than to strike and release like the rattlesnake.

The coral snake's bite produces little or no pain and no local edema or necrosis. The venom is primarily neurotoxic. Paresthesias and muscle fasciculations are common at the site of the bite. Flaccid paralysis and respiratory failure develop over a course of several hours. The incidence of envenomation is lower than that of rattlesnakes, with only about 40% of coral snakebites resulting in significant envenomation (25).

Signs and Symptoms of Envenomation

Not all victims of a venomous snakebite receive a significant amount of venom. Bites by nonpoisonous snakes are more common and often terrorize the victim. Since the treatment itself may be hazardous, it is important to distinguish the bites of venomous from those of nonvenomous snakes (Table 2).

Signs and symptoms are dependent upon a number of factors. As previously noted, pit vipers rarely discharge the full content of their venom glands at a single bite. Although the heat-detecting pit organ is believed to regulate the amount of venom discharged, according to the size of the animal bitten, these heat receptors appear to be unable to cope with the large amount of heat radiated by a human mass. Consequently, on any given strike, the snake may release a quantity of venom varying from little or none to almost the entire content

FIGURE 4   Coral snake (*Micrurus fulvius*).

TABLE 2
Signs and Symptoms of Envenomation in 100 Patients

Symptoms	Frequency (%)	Signs	Frequency (%)
Pain	65	Fang marks	100
Weakness	70	Swelling	74
Paresthesia	63	Blood pressure changes	54
Loss of consciousness	12	Ecchymosis	51
Blurred vision	12	Vesiculation	40
		Nausea, vomiting	42
		Swollen regional lymph nodes	40
		Fasciculations	41
		Necrosis	27
		Increased salivation	20
		Cyanosis	16
		Hematemesis, hematuria, or melena	15

of the glands. Russell estimates that about 20% of all bites do not end in envenomation, either because the strike is too superficial or because the snake does not inject venom (25).

Other important factors include the age, size, and species of snake (Table 3). As noted in Table 3, the venom glands of the eastern diamondback (*Crotalus adamanteus*) contain a large amount of very potent venom, compared to what is contained in the glands of the sidewinder (*C. cerastes*) or the copperhead (*Agkistrodon contortrix*). Pit vipers are poison-

TABLE 3
Comparative Toxicity of Snake Venoms

Species of Rattlesnake (Crotalus)	Average Length of Adult (Inches)	Approximate Yield, Dry Venom (mg)	Intra-Peritoneal LD_{50} Mice (mg/kg)	Intra-Venous LD_{50} Mice (mg/kg)
Eastern diamondback (*C. adamanteus*)	32–65	370–700	1.89	1.68
Western diamondback (*C. atrox*)	30–65	175–320	3.71	4.20
Prairie (*C. viridis viridis*)	32–46	35–100	2.25	1.61
Southern Pacific (*C. viridis helleri*)	32–48	75–150	1.60	1.29
Mojave (*C. scutulatus*)	22–40	50–90	0.23	0.21
Sidewinder (*C. cerastes*)	18–30	18–40	4.00	—
Moccasins (*Agkistrodon*)				
Cottonmouth (*A. piscivorus*)	30–50	90–145	5.11	4.00
Copperhead (*A. contortrix*)	24–36	40–70	10.50	10.92
Coral snakes (*Micrurus*)				
Eastern Coral (*M. fulvius*)	16–28	2–6	0.97	

Source: Modified from Russell, F. E., and Puffer, H. W.: Pharmacology of snake venoms. *Clin. Toxicol.,* **3:**433, 1970. Copyright Marcel Dekker, Inc., New York.

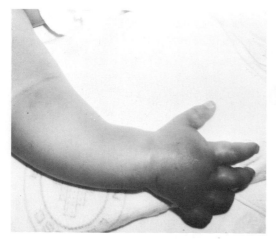 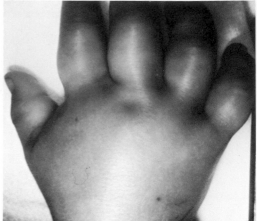

FIGURE 5 Moderate rattlesnake envenomation, 18-month-old male, 12 hours after bite, showing fang mark and fang scratch on wrist with ecchymosis and edema of extremity to axilla. The patient required 25 vials of antivenin.

ous at birth, but their glands do not contain as much venom as do the glands of an adult. The age, size, and health of the victim, along with the nature, location, depth, number of bites, and length of time the snake holds on determine the severity of envenomation and must be considered early in the management of the poisoning. Finally, clothing and shoes may decrease the penetration of the fangs or may totally deflect the strike.

CROTALIDAE

Crotalid envenomation is characterized by the presence of one or more fang marks. The distance between the marks varies from 0.5 to 4.0 cm and the depth of the puncture wounds from 1 to 8 mm (25). Because of their superficial nature, almost all bites deposit venom only into the subcutaneous tissues, not into the muscles. Immediately following the bite, most victims experience a local burning pain which usually is not overly severe. Progressive local swelling appears within 5 minutes. Without treatment, the edema may progress rapidly and involve an entire injured extremity within 1 hour. Generally, however, the edema spreads more slowly over a period of 6–8 hours. This edema is soft, pitting, and limited to the subcutaneous tissues (Figure 5). It is most marked after bites by the eastern diamondback and least marked after bites by the copperhead, pigmy rattler, massasauga,

and the dangerous Mojave rattlesnake. In bites by the last rattlesnake, the severity of the local reaction should not be relied upon as a measure of potential lethality.

Ecchymosis due to the destruction of blood vessels and red blood cells may occur within several hours. Hemorrhagic blebs and bullae develop at the site of the bite within 6–36 hours and may progress up the involved extremity (Figures 6 and 7).

Paresthesias of the scalp, face, and lips, along with perioral and periorbital muscle fasciculations, indicate that a significant envenomation has occurred. Some patients complain

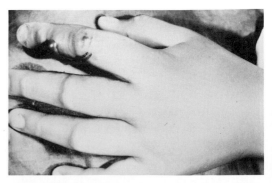

FIGURE 6 Mild rattlesnake envenomation, right index finger, 4 hours after bite. Note hemorrhagic bleb at the site of the bite, subcutaneous hemorrhage, and swelling of the hand. All laboratory values were within normal range.

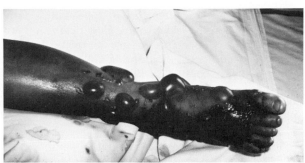

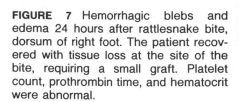

FIGURE 7 Hemorrhagic blebs and edema 24 hours after rattlesnake bite, dorsum of right foot. The patient recovered with tissue loss at the site of the bite, requiring a small graft. Platelet count, prothrombin time, and hematocrit were abnormal.

of a metallic taste in the mouth. Bites by the eastern diamondback and the Pacific and timber rattlesnakes cause these early symptoms.

General symptoms include weakness, sweating, nausea, and faintness. The regional lymph nodes enlarge and become tender. Hemorrhage may occur throughout the body as soon as 6 hours after envenomation. This is manifested as epistaxis, hematemesis, hematuria, skin petechiae, and melena. If untreated, the patient may develop hypovolemic shock and severe pulmonary edema.

The bite of the Mojave rattlesnake, while causing a minimal local reaction, may produce neuromuscular blockade leading to respiratory paralysis.

ELAPIDAE

Elapid bites cause moderate pain at the bite site which sometimes radiates up the extremity. Fang marks may be difficult to find. Within 90 minutes, the extremity may feel weak or numb. Several hours later, systemic symptoms appear; these include tremors, drowsiness or euphoria, and marked salivation. After 5–10 hours, slurred speech and diplopia herald the onset of cranial nerve palsies and a bulbar paralysis manifested as dysphagia and dyspnea (14). The curarelike effect of the venom may cause total flaccid paralysis. Death is associated with respiratory and cardiac failure.

Management

Snake venom poisoning is a medical emergency that requires immediate and adequate neutralization of as much of the venom as possible, prevention or reduction of the effects of the venom already absorbed, and prevention of complications, such as tetanus, infection, and contractures.

TREATMENT IN THE FIELD (FIRST AID)

First aid measures are *never* a substitute for definitive treatment with the specific poison antidote, antivenin. Many of the recommended historical procedures have never been proven to be of value in controlled studies. Such procedures as incision and suction, and application of tourniquets, complicate management by creating devitalized tissue or secondarily infected wounds. Although time-honored, these modalities are no longer acceptable therapies. Only the following procedures are necessary:

Avoid panic. Excitement and hysteria result in nausea, faintness, dizziness, hyperventilation, and other stress reactions which obscure the differentiation between bites by poisonous and nonpoisonous snakes. The victim may run hysterically from the area or move about in an agitated state. Studies on experimental animals indicate that the LD_{50} (median lethal dose) of venom can be decreased significantly by increasing the envenomated animal's activity (37).

The victim should retreat out of the snake's striking range, which is less than the length of the snake. Since snakes are defensive animals and rarely actually attack, they will remain immobile or attempt to retreat if given the opportunity. Second bites occur primarily in small children who are paralyzed with fright within 2 or 3 feet of the snake or in individuals who persist in harassing the snake in spite of the first bite.

Locate the snake. After this is done, kill it with a blow on the neck from a *long,* heavy stick. This is not done as a gesture of cruelty, but to avoid adding victims during collection of the animal. The snake's head should not be crushed or multilated, since it is a great aid to species identification. Identification of the snake species is imporant because of the variation in venom toxicity among species, which in turn influences the amount of antivenin required for treatment of a bite.

If several persons are present, the victim should retreat and lie down while another person searches for the snake. Most snakes have a limited range of activity and can be found within 20 feet of the site of the accident, even after several hours.

The snake must not be directly handled, but should be transported in a cloth bag or carried on a long stick to the closest available herpetologist or other person trained in identification. Decapitated head reactions persist for 20–60 minutes (8).

Immobilize the bitten extremity. This is performed by splinting as if for a fracture. Experiments with crotalid venom in rabbits and with elapid venom in monkeys indicate that local tissue necrosis is diminished by immobilization and that systemic absorption of elapid venom is delayed (30,34). For the same reason, the victim should reduce physical activity to a minimum.

Obtain medical assistance. Transport the victim to the nearest medical facility, either on an improvised stretcher or by ambulance if circumstances permit (many bites occur in urban areas, often in the patient's home or garage). If the victim is alone, he should walk slowly, resting periodically, until help is reached. Again, activity should be kept to a minimum.

If the victim is many hours away from medical care, i.e., backpacking in a wilderness area, or if severe symptoms develop rapidly, the following measures *may* be of value:

First, apply a constricting band—not a tourniquet—above the first proximal joint or 2–4 inches proximal to the bite. This band should occlude only lymphatic and superficial drainage. It should be released every 10–15 minutes for 60 seconds and should be moved proximally as the swelling advances. These bands are of no value in coral snake bites.

Alternately, if an Ace bandage or similar wrap is available, apply it firmly but at a pressure less than venous blood pressure (e.g., 50 mmHg.) to the bitten extremity. Wrap from proximal to distal. Australian physicians (34) report that lymphatic compression prevents a rapid rise of venom plasma levels following elapid snake envenomation. Whether this is applicable to North American rattlesnake poisoning is undetermined.

Immobilize the extremity by splinting. Place the victim at rest and keep activity to a minimum. The victim should drink as much fluid as possible, preferably at least two liters in 24 hours, in frequent small increments.

Evacuation to a medical facility depends upon the number of rescuers, the distance involved, the ruggedness of the terrain, and the transportation facilities available in the region.

The classic recommendation to incise the fang puncture wound, making ⅛–¼ inch linear incisions through the fang marks with a sterile instrument, has become highly controversial. Most experience indicates that cruciate or multiple wide incisions are inadvisable, as they frequently result in devitalized tissue flaps or gaping wounds which leave a wide scar.

Unquestionably, the procedure is of little value if delayed for more than 5 minutes after envenomation, since snake venom is rapidly absorbed from the bite area. McCullough and Gennaro found that suction removed over 50% of radioisotope-labeled crotalid venom injected into canine subcutaneous tissue if the suction was instituted within 3 minutes of injection (15). However, the data have not been verified in humans. Incision is of no value for coral snake bites.

Cryotherapy of any sort is mentioned only for condemnation. There is no experimental evidence that vasoconstriction by cold affects morbidity or mortality favorably. Freezing the already compromised tissues may contribute to necrosis. There is no well-controlled in vitro data or prospective human observation to support the contention that low temperatures induced by cooling diminish the envenomation. Although the hypothesis that snake venom enzyme activity diminishes with tissue cooling is attractive, it remains to be confirmed.

HOSPITAL MANAGEMENT

Treatment of envenomation in a medical facility may be carried out in 11 steps, the sequence of which depends somewhat on the presenting condition of the patient (39).

Step One: Establish a Physiologic Baseline

1. *Identify the species of the offending snake,* if possible with the aid of a herpetologist (29). Time will usually permit at least the differentiation between a venomous and a nonvenomous species. If expert consultation is not available, observe the size of the snake, since large snakes potentially cause more serious bites due to the amount of toxic venom they contain.

2. *Perform a rapid evaluation of the presenting signs and symptoms.* Inquire about the time of the envenomation, the first aid methods applied, a previous history of snakebite treatment, and any known allergies, especially sensitivity to horse serum and antibiotics. Ask the patient about tingling or numbness about the mouth and scalp. Vital signs should be recorded carefully.

3. *Draw blood* for the following determinations: complete blood count and differential, peripheral blood smear (note spherocytosis), platelet count, thrombin time, prothrombin time, partial thromboplastin time, fibrinogen, fibrin split products, type and crossmatch, total protein, albumin, electrolytes, blood urea nitrogen, and creatinine. Obtain urine for urinalysis (note hematuria).

4. *Measure and record the circumference of the injured extremity* at the level of edema and approximately 4 inches proximal to this level.

Step Two: In Cases of Pit Viper Bites, Determine the Severity of the Envenomation

This factor determines the amount of antiserum to be administered or, indeed, whether antiserum is required at all. The severity of the poisoning is dependent upon a number of variables: the genus, species, and size of the snake; the size of the patient; the amount of venom injected; the consequent activity of the patient; and the type of first aid rendered.

At Los Angeles County, University of Southern California (LAC/USC) Medical Center, a grading system is used that is based on the local and systemic reactions, available knowledge of the species and size of the snake, and circumstances of the bite. Reactions are graded as follows:

No envenomation—No local or systemic reactions
Minimal—Local swelling but no systemic reactions
Moderate—Swelling, which progresses beyond the
   site of the bite, together with a systemic reaction

and/or laboratory changes, such as a fall in hematocrit
Severe—Marked local reaction, severe symptoms, and laboratory abnormalities

Step Three: Perform Skin Tests for Sensitivity to Horse Serum

This is done by the intradermal injection of 0.02 ml of a 1:10 dilution of antivenin, with 0.02 ml of normal saline injected in the opposite extremity as a control. The development of erythema and pseudopodia at the small test wheal within 15–30 minutes is a positive test. If the patient gives a history of past sensitivity to horse serum, a conjunctival test may be done, although it probably offers no advantage over intradermal testing. One drop of a 1:100 dilution of serum is instilled into one conjunctival sac and a control drop of normal saline into the other sac. A positive reaction occurs within 5 minutes and consists of itching with occasional swelling of the eyelids, as well as dilatation of the superficial conjunctival vessels. If this occurs, the eye should be treated immediately with one or two drops of 1:1000 epinephrine. *Neither of these tests has proven to be infallible.* Specifically, they do not reliably predict which patients may have the delayed reaction of serum sickness. It must be emphasized that skin testing should *only* be performed if the physician intends to use antivenin.

Step Four: Obtain Access to the Circulation with an Intravenous Infusion in Two Extremities

One line is primarily for cardiovascular support. Blood products, crystalloid, pressor agents, and epinephrine (in case of an anaphylactic reaction to antivenin) may be administered if necessary. If the patient is hemodynamically unstable, a central venous line or right heart catheter may be placed. The second line is for the administration of antivenin.

Step Five: Administer an Adequate Amount of Antivenin Intravenously

Antivenin is the single most important therapeutic measure responsible for the decrease in fatalities in recent years. The use of antiserum is directed at the neutralization of venom at the local wound site before it or its toxic by-products can be absorbed into the systemic circulation. Antivenin should be administered at the earliest possible moment after a snake bite occurs and only under the supervision of a physician.

One commercial pit viper antivenin is available in the United States: *Antivenin (Crotalidae) Polyvalent, North and South American antisnakebite serum,* produced by Wyeth Laboratories. Since the venoms of all pit vipers, including rattlesnakes, copperheads, and moccasins, share some common basic antigens, Wyeth has manufactured an antivenin from a formula containing four snake venoms: *Crotalus atrox, C. adamanteus, C. terrificus,* and *Bothrops atrox.* This antivenin is standardized by its ability to neutralize the toxin of a specific quantity of venom injected intravenously into mice. Wyeth also manufactures a commercial antiserum against the venom of the eastern coral snake (*Micrurus fulvius*). This antivenin is *not* effective for bites of the Arizona coral snake (*Micruroides euryxanthus*), whose venom is less toxic than that of its eastern relative.

Both antisera are prepared by the immunization of horses. Horse serum is inherently highly antigenic; McCullough and Gennaro reported a 75% incidence of serum sickness to some degree after the administration of snake antiserum (15). Wainschel has observed that patients who receive more than 70 ml of the antivenin usually develop some degree of serum sickness (39).

In serum-sensitive patients who risk death unless given antivenin, desensitization can be carried out according to the outline in the brochure accompanying the antivenin. The antivenin gradually complexes with the patient's antibodies to horse serum so that anaphylaxis is less likely to occur.

A technique has recently been developed by Russell and Sullivan in which nearly all sensitizing proteins are removed from antivenin. However, this improved product is not yet commercially available (29a).

PROTECTION OF THE SENSITIZED INDIVIDUAL

Unfortunately, in severe envenomations, when time is an important factor in the neutralization of toxins, only a small quantity of antivenin can be administered by the desensitization method to a critically ill patient. A procedure used at LAC/USC Medical Center is to begin therapy with the administration of 50–100 mg of diphenhydramine hydrochloride (Benadryl) intravenously, followed by a slow intravenous administration of antivenin for 15–20 minutes, while closely observing the patient for signs and symptoms of anaphylaxis. If anaphylaxis does not occur, the antivenin is continued at a faster rate while still closely observing the patient.

Patients who require antivenin, but who develop signs of impending anaphylaxis in spite of this procedure, present a problem in clinical judgment and in the design of therapy. A method used successfully by Wainschel at LAC/USC Medical Center, which requires considerable clinical acumen by an experienced observer, is the intravenous injection of the antivenin with epinephrine (34). A solution of 1:10,000 epinephrine is attached "piggyback" to an intravenous crystalloid solution in another extremity; 0.3–1.0 ml of epinephrine, enough to produce an increase in the pulse rate, is given first. Then, 0.1–0.2 ml of antivenin is injected into the second intravenous line. The physician observes the patient closely for signs of anaphylaxis and continues to alternate epinephrine with the serum slowly as necessary. Eventually, the patient may not require epinephrine with each dose of antivenin. However, these patients frequently develop serum sickness within a week.

ROUTE AND DOSAGE OF ANTIVENIN

The most effective and rapid route of administration is intravenous. Gennaro reported that antivenin labeled with radioactive iodine accumulated at the site of the bite significantly faster after intravenous than after intramuscular or subcutaneous injection (36). Furthermore, in severe envenomations, the systemic circulation may already be compromised and the antivenin will be picked up too slowly from intramuscular or intracutaneous sites. Antivenin should never be injected into a finger or toe.

The dose is based on the severity of the envenomation. Adequate dosage, particularly in children, cannot be overemphasized. Children receive more milligrams of toxin per kilogram of body weight than do adults, have less body water with which to dilute the venom, and have less inherent resistance to its effects. Therefore, children generally require larger doses per unit of body weight than do adults to prevent convulsions, shock, and death. The following amounts of crotalid antivenin should be administered *initially,* according to the estimation of the patient's total reaction to the bite:

No envenomation: no antivenin
Minimal: 5 vials (50 ml)
Moderate: 10 vials (100 ml)
Severe: 10–15 vials (100–150 ml)

Patients bitten by the Mojave rattlesnake (*Crotalus scutulatus*) require careful evaluation since the venom, while very lethal, may cause only moderate swelling and the symptoms of poisoning are frequently delayed (37). If the offending snake is identified as *C. scutulatus,* the initial dose of antivenin should be 10 vials.

Bites by coral snakes require 3–6 vials of *M. fulvius* antivenin. This amount generally neutralizes the maximal dose of venom that a coral snake can deliver (35).

Poisoning by larger snakes and in smaller persons requires greater percentage doses of antivenin. *Children may require larger doses than adults.*

To be most effective, antivenin should be given within 4 hours after the bite. It is of less value as time passes, but it is not known exactly how long after envenomation antivenin can be given and still be effective. Our experiments with the injection of radioisotope-labeled venom in rabbits indicate the presence of some circulating venom component at least 96 hours after the injection. Russell has observed the efficacious administration of antivenin a full 26 hours after an eastern diamondback bite (8). It is possible that a symptomatic patient, i.e., one having coagulation defects with active hemorrhage, may benefit from antivenin administered up to 72 hours after envenomation.

Step Six: Prevent Secondary Infection by Administering an Appropriate Antibiotic

Pathogenic bacteria, predominantly Gram negative, often exist in snakes' mouths and in their venoms (10,38). A broad-spectrum antibiotic such as ampicillin, amoxicillin, or a cephalosporin is indicated. Later in the course, wound cultures may be necessary to determine the antibiotics to be used. Antibiotics should not be used for trivial bites, which rarely are secondarily infected.

Step Seven: Prevent Tetanus

Snakes' mouths do not harbor clostridial organisms. The organism is carried into the fang puncture wound by contamination with the soil, from dirt on the skin, or from nonsterile first aid procedures. If the patient has been immunized adequately in the past, administer 0.5 ml of tetanus toxoid. If the status of immunity is questionable, also administer 250 units of hyperimmune tetanus globulin along with the toxoid, in the opposite extremity. Gas gangrene is a rare complication.

Step Eight: Support the Circulatory, Respiratory, and Hematologic Systems

A decrease in red cell mass, as evidenced by a progressively falling hematocrit (either from red cell lysis or active bleeding), should be treated by the infusion of packed red cells or typed and cross-matched whole blood. In a rabbit model for the consumption (platelets, fibrinogen) coagulopathy that accompanies the western diamondback rattlesnake (*C. atrox*) bite, antivenin resulted in some amelioration of the coagulopathy, and steroid administration tended to worsen it. Interestingly, most platelet consumption occurred at the site of the injury (32a). A decrease in circulatory volume, with perfusion defects due to the loss of plasma and serum proteins into the tissues, as indicated by arterial hypotension and hemoconcentration, may be restored by the infusion of plasma, albumin, or other plasma expanders (39). Crystalloid solutions, such as normal saline or lactated Ringer's solution, have been relatively contraindicated early in the management of envenomation, thus far having failed to prevent shock in envenomated experimental animals (32,39). This may prove to be more a function of the delay in administration of antivenin than in the choice of volume expanders. Until further notice, the logical physiologic supplement is a plasma expander. The debate between colloid and crystalloid infusion in the management of hypovolemic shock is ongoing. Vasopressor drugs should not be used unless the intravascular volume has been restored. In severe envenomations in small children, rapid transfusion of fresh whole blood is preferred.

Respiratory failure may occur with coral snake and Mojave rattlesnake bites. At the first sign of distress, oxygen should be given by those methods indicated by the degree of dysfunction. An anesthesiologist should be aware of the patient. Equipment for endotracheal intubation and a cricothyrotomy set should be kept at the bedside of any patient displaying early signs of respiratory distress (cyanosis, trismus, laryngeal spasm, excessive salivation).

Electrolyte imbalance occurs because of the loss of blood and intracellular fluid associated with venom-damaged tissues. Progressive changes in water and electrolyte concentrations should be monitored and corrected as required by the appropriate parenteral administration of fluid and electrolytes (6).

Renal shutdown may occur as a result of shock or red cell lysis with the liberation of hemoglobin. Measurement of urine output and central pressures are critical in the assessment of renal status. Renal dialysis may ultimately be necessary in critically ill patients.

Pit viper venom stimulates the smooth musculature of the gastrointestinal tract, causing nausea, vomiting, and diarrhea. For the first 24 hours, the patient should receive fluids intravenously and only be allowed sips of oral liquids. Thereafter, the diet may be advanced as tolerated.

Pain varies in intensity according to the degree of envenomation. Acetaminophen (325–650 mg) or codeine (30–60 mg) can be used safely to alleviate pain in adults. Mild sedation with small doses of diazepam (2–10 mg) may be used in severe bites if respiratory failure is not a problem. Repeated verbal assurance is helpful in allaying some of the patient's apprehension.

Step Nine: Monitor the Physiologic Status of Severely Envenomated Patients Carefully to Determine Further Requirements for Antivenin, Fluids, or Electrolytes

1. Monitor the progress of swelling every 20 minutes by measuring the circumference of the af-

fected extremity at the previously defined landmarks. Give 50–100 ml (5–10 vials) of antivenin intravenously every 1–2 hours until no further progression of the swelling is seen and no generalized symptoms appear.
2. Monitor hemoglobin and hematocrit levels. If they are falling, give transfusions of fresh whole blood or packed cells.
3. Obtain serial platelet counts. Severe envenomation depresses the platelets. The mechanism appears to be related to peripheral destruction or consumption rather than due to damage to marrow megakaryocytes. If active hemorrhage occurs, transfuse with platelets. It should be noted that clinically significant bleeding usually does *not* occur, despite the thrombocytopenia, and the number of platelets usually returns spontaneously to normal within 7 days.
4. Monitor respiration, pulse rate, and blood pressure. Changes portend impending shock and the need for more aggressive cardiovascular support.
5. Obtain serial electrolyte measurements. There is a frequent transient hyperkalemia secondary to fluid shifts and hemolysis. Dialysis may be required.
6. Serial electrocardiograms are necessary for victims over the age of 40 and for all victims of severe envenomations during the first 48 hours. Myocardial ischemia has been reported following an envenomation.
7. The urine should be monitored with respect to volume and hemoglobin/cellular content. Treatment is directed at maintaining a urine output of 30–50 ml/hour unless there is evidence of renal failure.

Step Ten: Care for the Wound

The extremity should be well immobilized in a position of function on a splint padded to prevent pressure necrosis. The extremity should be maintained at or slightly below heart level (30).

Between the third and fifth days, the hemorrhagic blebs, vesicles, and superficial necrotic tissue should be debrided surgically (Figure 8). Most tissue necrosis occurs during the first 3 days, and premature disruption of vesicles or damaged tissue during this initial period results in further tissue injury and bleeding. Debridement should not be delayed beyond the seventh day, since the injured tissues and blood will begin to organize, making surgical removal more difficult.

After debridement, the envenomated area should be cleansed gently with hydrogen per-

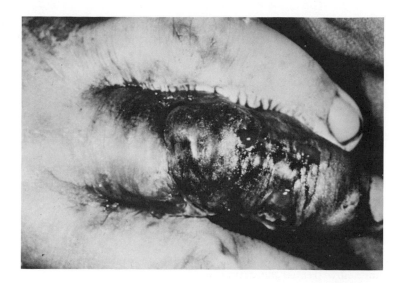

FIGURE 8 Debridement of a large hemorrhagic bleb on the fourth day after the bite. The area is now the equivalent of a second degree burn. Active physiotherapy was begun on the sixth day. The wound healed completely within 30 days, with no loss of function.

oxide solution three times a day. If extensive tissue destruction has occurred, a plastic surgeon should be consulted for the consideration of early skin grafting.

It is worthwhile to discuss fasciotomy briefly once again. There is nothing beyond empirical reports to support its use, and extremely poor results have been described. Until a well-controlled study is performed that can manometrically demonstrate raised intracompartmental pressures in bite-affected limbs and poor outcomes with nonsurgically treated limbs, fasciotomy cannot be recommended. One surgeon has discussed his success with hydrocortisone sodium succinate and surgery for bite wounds believed to be intra-articular or intramuscular. This has been reported to be lifesaving; cosmetic results are still at issue (6a). Another interesting parallel has been drawn between the pressure-immobilization techniques to retard the venom spread of the funnel web spider bite and that which may prove effective for the bite of the elapid snake (34). This technique has been previously mentioned.

Step Eleven: Be Prepared to Treat Serum Sickness within the Next 24 Days

This reaction is caused by the production of immunoglobulin (IgG) antibodies in response to an antigen, in this case a foreign protein, in the patient's serum, with the formation of immune complexes circulating in anti-gen excess. Localization of these antigen-antibody complexes in parts of the vascular bed increases vascular permeability through the local release of vasoactive amines. The complexes also activate complement and chemotactic factors, attracting neutrophils, which release proteolytic enzymes and basic proteins, which in turn cause local tissue destruction. Finally, the complexes induce histamine release from mast cells, which further increases capillary permeability.

Symptoms include malaise, fever, arthralgias and swollen joints, generalized urticaria, lymphadenopathy, and occasional peripheral neuritis, manifested by pain and weakness in the extremities. Serum sickness should always be anticipated if 70 ml or more of antivenin has been administered.

Corticosteroids are the drugs of choice for the treatment of serum sickness. In severe adult cases, one should administer 10 mg of dexamethasone intravenously or intramuscularly at the onset of symptoms, followed by 4–10 mg every 4–6 hours by any route, depending on the progress of symptoms. If the presenting symptoms are not severe, the equivalent of 10 mg of prednisone orally every 6 hours may be preferred. For children, the equivalent of prednisone, 2–5 mg/kg per day by any route, not to exceed 60 mg, may be administered according to the severity of symptoms. The corticosteroids should be administered until all signs and symptoms have subsided, and then gradually tapered while observing the patient closely for recurrence or adrenal insufficiency.

Antihistamines seem to be of little value in the suppression of serum sickness, except for their sedative and antipruritic effects (24).

Prognosis

Death is uncommon if antivenin is given without delay and in adequate amounts. The fatality rate in treated cases is less than 1%. No deaths have been reported from coral snake bites in Florida since 1959 (30). Permanent disability and amputation are less frequent since cryotherapy has fallen into disuse. We have now treated more than 816 patients at LAC/USC Medical Center, and no deaths or amputations have occurred that can be attributed to venom poisoning. However, several amputations were necessitated by frostbite induced by cryotherapy.

Prevention

The best method of avoiding snakebite poisoning is to avoid poisonous snakes (39). The rule to remember is that snakes generally are afraid of humans and will retreat to safety if given some chance. Therefore, unless accidentally and suddenly confronted at very close range, a snake is unlikely to strike at his relatively huge human adversary.

The rules to follow when in snake-infested territory are:

1. Avoid the known habitats of snakes, which are generally areas in which the snake seeks protection: swamps, rocky ledges, wood, stone, and rubbish piles, caves and deserted mines, and deserted buildings, especially in rural areas.
2. Do not put any part of your body, especially hands and feet, into places where you cannot look. Snakes often lie next to a fallen tree or under a rock. Do not sit on or step over a log if the other side is not visible. Walk on clear paths as much as possible. Carry a walking stick to prod logs and rocks before stepping over them.
3. Wear adequate protective clothing. The majority of bites are on the hands and lower legs; this speaks for the value of boots and gloves in avoiding serious envenomation.
4. Avoid hiking alone in snake-infested areas. Include an elastic pressure wrap in your backpacking equipment if medical care is more than 4 hours away.
5. Avoid walking at night in snake-infested areas, especially in the southwestern deserts and mountains. If you must walk, wear boots and carry a flashlight and walking stick. Most venomous snakes avoid direct sunlight and are more active during the moderate temperatures of the night.
6. Finally, do not handle snakes unless you are an experienced herpetologist or at least familiar with the identification and habits of snakes. Many victims are bitten every year because they handled a snake carelessly, attempted to pick up a freshly killed rattlesnake, or went out of their way to kill snakes without knowledge of their habits and habitats.

Gila Monster

The only indigenous venomous reptiles in the United States, other than pit vipers and coral snakes, belong to the lizard family Helodermatidae. Two species, the Gila monster (*Heloderma suspectum*) (Figure 9) and the beaded lizard (*H. horridum*), possess venom glands and grooved teeth which are capable of envenomating humans.

These lizards are found only in the Great Sonoran Desert area in southern Arizona and northwestern Mexico. However, human envenomations are not restricted to these geographic areas, since bites are incurred during careless handling of captive specimens by amateur collectors (25).

The Gila monster is a large (300–400 cm), slow-moving reptile with a large flat head, bulging mandibular muscles, and a relatively long, round, thick tail. The limbs are short and stubby. The color of the thick skin ranges from pink or orange to black.

Venom and Venom Apparatus

The venom apparatus consists in part of paired inferior labial glands located on either side of the lower jaw. Each gland contains several lobes with separate ducts that carry the venom to the mucous membrane between the lower lip and the lower jaw, close to the base of the teeth. The teeth are solid, lance-

FIGURE 9 Gila monster (*Heloderma suspectum*).

shaped, and sharp, recurved and grooved on the anterior and posterior surfaces. Each half of the jaw has nine or 10 teeth, the largest and most deeply grooved located nearest the discharge orifice of the venom glands (1).

Human envenomation occurs when venom is drawn into puncture wounds through capillary action along the grooved surface of the teeth, especially when the lizard retains its grasp and chews for an extended period of time. All bites do not result in envenomation, since the lizard may only nip the victim, may bite without chewing, or may not expel venom from the glands to the infralabial area during a bite. Russell has noted that of 15 cases observed, only 9 involved envenomation (25).

The venom is a complex mixture of enzymes, including amine oxidase, phospholipase A, protease, hyaluronidase, kallikrein, and serotonin (11,12,40). The lethal dose for humans is estimated at 5–8 mg; Russell estimates that an animal's venom glands contain approximately 17 mg of venom (25). The major pathophysiologic actions in experimental animals are systemic hypotension and respiratory arrest (4,23,25).

Medical Aspects

Heloderm wounds usually are simple punctures, although teeth may break off or be shed during the bite and remain in the wound. Pain, often severe burning, appears at the wound site within 5 minutes and may radiate up the extremity (25,33). Intense pain may last from 3–5 hours and then subside after 8 hours. Edema occurs at the wound, usually within 15 minutes, and progresses slowly in variable degrees up the extremity (1,25,33). Cyanosis or blue discoloration may appear around the wound (1). The victim may feel weak and faint, while becoming diaphoretic. The wound site may remain tender 3 or 4 weeks after the bite (25). Usually, little tissue necrosis occurs. In humans, severe hypotension is rarely observed and no coagulation defects have been noted (25).

Gila monsters may hang on tenaciously during a bite, and mechanical means may be required to loosen the grip of the jaws; rescuers have used pliers, chisels, crowbars, or incision of the jaw muscles with a sharp knife (33).

Treatment

The wound should be cleansed thoroughly with a soap or iodophore solution. Russell advises infiltration of the teeth puncture wounds with lidocaine, using a 25-gauge needle, in addition to probing the wounds gently with the needle to detect the presence of shed or broken teeth (25). Intense pain may require analgesics in doses appropriate for the patient's age and weight. The vital signs, especially blood pressure, should be monitored closely for at least 24 hours. The extremity should be immobilized in a functional position near heart level. The circulating blood volume should be maintained by intravenous crystalloid or colloid solutions, as indicated by laboratory determinations. Tetanus prophylaxis is standard. The wound should be observed for secondary infection, although antibiotics usually are not required (25).

Follow-up care is the same as for any penetrating reptilian wound: dry sterile dressings, along with daily soaks in 1:20 aluminum acetate solution, dilute hydrogen peroxide scrubs, or wet-to-dry saline advancement. Physical therapy may be necessary to prevent contractures and restore function.

Envenomation by Exotic Snakes

Many species of exotic snakes are housed in scientific collections, in zoos, and in the private collections of amateur herpetologists and nonprofessional snake fanciers. Annually, about 75,000 snakes, including more than 6800 belonging to venomous species, are legally imported into the United States, and an additional number are smuggled in which may fall into the collections of individuals who are skilled snake handlers (3). Of all snake envenomations, the proportion due to exotic snake bites is reported to be 4–13% (19,25). Consequently, a physician occasionally may be confronted with the management of a bite by a king cobra, a mamba, or a fer-de-lance.

Signs and symptoms vary with the family of snake involved. As a general rule, crotalid envenomation usually causes a severe reaction with swelling and ecchymoses, followed within an hour by damage to multiple organ systems: hemolysis, generalized capillary damage, coagulopathy, vesiculation, paresthesias, hypovolemic shock, and pulmonary edema (3). Viperid venom poisoning is characterized by coagulopathy and severe hemorrhage from mucous membranes. Elapid envenomation produces predominantly neurologic symptoms involving cranial nerve and peripheral nerve deficits. Envenomation by rear-fanged colubred snakes causes local pain, progressive swelling and hemorrhage, malaise, and fever, all lasting 4–7 days.

Table 4 describes the major common venomous species, which may be found in pet stores, collections, houses, garages, and public zoos. The animals are listed according to the area or origin.

Management of Exotic Snakebites

Antivenins for the management of envenomation by almost all poisonous snakes are available. Confronted with a patient possibly envenomated by a nonnative snake, the physician should proceed as follows:

1. Identify the species of snake if possible. Usually, a herpetologist may be consulted, either through a local zoo, educational institution, or government agency. Identification by the inexperienced examiner's description on the basis of color or markings is deceptive.
2. Be sure that the patient has been envenomated. The bite of a venomous snake is identified by the presence of one or more distinct fang marks. Teeth puncture wounds of nonpoisonous snakes usually are multiple, shallow, and arranged in a semicircle.
3. Note local and systemic reactions and establish a physiologic baseline. Remember that a patient may be severely envenomated even in the absence of local swelling or hemorrhage, especially with bites by elapid snakes.
4. Obtain a specific antivenin and follow the directions on the enclosed brochure regarding the route of administration and the quantity of antivenin required.

Since antivenins for foreign snakes are not stocked routinely in most medical centers, the material usually must be obtained as follows:

a. Zoological parks and aquariums generally stock antivenin for all the exotic snakes in their collections and possibly for other species. Furthermore, many antivenins are polyvalent and will neutralize the venoms of additional species. The zoo will usually release sufficient antivenin for emergency treatment. Therefore, the closest zoo should be contacted.
b. A *National Antivenin Index* is maintained by the Oklahoma Poison Control Center in Oklahoma City. The *Index* lists all the antivenins available in the United States, their location, and a 24 hour telephone number for the resource. *Index* information is accessible at telephone number (405) 271–5454.
5. Be prepared to support compromised respiration, circulation, and metabolism until the antivenin has been administered. This management has been outlined previously. All envenomated patients should be observed in an intensive care setting.

TABLE 4
Poisonous Exotic Snakes

Area	Common Name	Family and Scientific Name	Description	Habitats	Signs and Symptoms of Envenomation
South America	Urutu	Crotalus: *Bothrops alternatus*	Length 3–5 feet. Brown head with distinct marking on crown; brown with light brown round lateral markings shaped like a cradle telephone.	Found along water-course.	Severe local tissue necrosis; rarely lethal.
	Jaracara	Crotalus: *B. jaracara*	Length 3–4 feet. Olive green, brown-blotched, long head with short snout.	Common in grass-lands and open country.	Similar to Crotalidae
	Fer-de-lance	Crotalus: *B. lanceo-latus*	Length 4–5 feet. Brown lance-shaped head; gray, olive, or brown body with hour-glass-shaped blotches down the back.	Forests of Martinique.	Usually severe local pain and ecchymo-sis; red blood cell ly-sis, thrombocytope-nia; marked systemic hemor-rhage.
	Cascabel	Crotalus: *Crotalus durissus terrificus*	Length 4–6 feet. A true rattlesnake; stout brown or olive body with 18–35 darker rhomb-shaped markings down the back.	Dry areas, grasslands extending into Mex-ico; venom usually highly toxic.	Minor local but severe systemic effects: blindness, paralysis of neck muscles, ptosis; facial muscle and tongue fascicu-tions; apnea; asys-tole; myoglobinuria.
Mexico and Central America	Barba amarilla	Crotalus: *Bothrops atrox*	Length 4–6 feet. A true rattlesnake, stout brown or olive body with 18–35 darker rhomb-shaped markings down the back.	Widespread in forest areas, along streams, often in plantations; long fangs and highly toxic venom; ag-gressive if disturbed and may strike re-peatedly.	Usually severe local pain and ecchymo-sis; red blood cell ly-sis, thrombocytope-nia; marked systemic hemor-rhage.
Mexico and Central America	Bushmaster	Crotalus: *Lachesis mutus*	Length 5–12 feet. Tan or brown body with black rhombs; a burr of pointed spines on the tail is character-istic.	Rain forests, near coasts, and in river basins; large snake with long fangs and large amounts of toxic venom; strictly nocturnal.	Severe local pain, lo-cal swelling, and edema, ecchymo-sis, weakness, par-esthesias, ptosis, blurring of vision, re-spiratory distress.

(*Continued*)

TABLE 4 (*Continued*)

Area	Common Name	Family and Scientific Name	Description	Habitats	Signs and Symptoms of Envenomation
Africa	Cobra	Six spp. of Elapidae; genus *Naja*	Length varies with species: 4–9 feet (king cobra up to 14 feet). Colors extremely variable, characterized by rearing up and spreading a hood when disturbed; *N. nigrallis* "spits" venom at the eyes of aggressors with accuracy from approximately 6–8 feet.	Range throughout Africa except Sahara sands, in tropical rain forests, savannahs, and newly cleared areas.	Approximately 50% of bites do not end in envenomation; venom sprayed in eyes causes severe pain and conjunctivitis; corneal ulceration, anterior uveitis, and blindness if eye is not irrigated promptly; bites cause local swelling and necrosis in 35% of patients; neurologic signs and symptoms appear in 1–4 hours; bilateral ptosis (initial), other cranial nerve palsies, flaccid paralysis, convulsions, shock, cardiac arrest, and coma.
Africa	Vipers, especially saw-scaled	Viperidae: *Echis carinatus*	Length 15–32 inches. Short head with light trident or arrowhead mark on top, blunt snout, tan or olive body; when disturbed, body inflates and hissing sound is produced by rubbing saw-edged lateral scales against one another.	Found in deserts and scrub forests; usually nocturnal; may climb into bushes; alert and irritable, striking quickly and repeatedly; venom highly toxic.	Immediate severe radiating pain, local swelling, ecchymosis, bleb formation, and necrosis; fang marks commonly bleed; severe hemorrhage and disseminated intravascular coagulation with bleeding from all mucous membranes, especially gums; fibrinogen markedly decreased; may develop central nervous system hemorrhage, convulsions, and shock.

(*Continued*)

TABLE 4 (*Continued*)

Area	Common Name	Family and Scientific Name	Description	Habitats	Signs and Symptoms of Envenomation
Africa	Boomslang	Colubridae: *Dispholidus typus*	Length 4–6 feet. Black to green without spots; a colubrid snake with long rear fangs.	Tree dweller, usually not agressive; inflates neck when cornered; highly toxic venom.	Severe internal hemorrhage with bleeding from every mucous membrane.
Africa	Mambas	Elapidae: *Dendroapsis* spp. Black: *D. polylepsis* Green: *D. angusticeps* *D. jamesoni* *D. viridis*	Very long (6–9 feet, green species, 9–14 feet, black species), slender, bright green to very dark olive brown snake, very fast-moving (up to 7 mph); lining of mouth is characteristically black in *D. polylepis*.	Usually arboreal; green species are shy and venom is only moderately toxic; black species will fight if disturbed and may strike out quickly for 40% of its length (5–6 feet); amount of venom secreted by one snake may be lethal to 5–10 humans; the world's most dangerous snake.	Minimal location reaction; dyspnea, dysphagia, slurred speech, muscle spasms and fasciculation; marked weakness, paralysis, respiratory distress, hypotension, and shock.
Africa	Puff adder Gabon viper Horned puff adder	Viperidae: *Bitis arietans* *B. gabonica* *B. caudalis*	Large, thick-bodied snakes varying from 1 foot (*B. caudalis* is 6 feet in length); broad head, distinct neck; some species have small "horns" on the head.	Found in deserts (*B. caudalis*), tropical rain forests (*B. gabonica*), and savannah and grasslands (*B. arietans*); nocturnal and generally sluggish; produce large amounts of highly toxic venom; may strike rapidly and with great accuracy, difficult to handle because of sudden jerking.	Similar to *Crotalus* envenomation; local pain, swelling, ecchymosis, tissue necrosis; hemorrhage from mucous membranes, external and internal, resulting in shock.
Southeast Asia and India	Krait	Elapidae *Bungarus* spp.	Length 4–7 feet. Small, flat head, slender body, banded in some species (*B. fasciatus* and (*B. multicinctus*).	Active on humid or rainy nights; often found near human habitations; bites are unusual, but venom is highly toxic.	Little local reaction or pain; intense abdominal pain; slow onset of nerve paralysis follows; cranial nerve palsies, generalized muscle weakness or paralysis, respiratory depression, shock, coma.

(*Continued*)

TABLE 4 (*Continued*)

Area	Common Name	Family and Scientific Name	Description	Habitats	Signs and Symptoms of Envenomation
Southeast Asia and India	King cobra India cobra	Elapidae: *Ophiophagus hannah* *Naja, naja naja*	Length 4–18 feet. Length 4–6 feet. All species are characterized by a hood or a flattening of the neck when alarmed; body color and pattern vary with the species.	Found in all terrain except desert and dense rain forest; common around human habitations; diurnal in India and Pakistan, nocturnal elsewhere; tumid and often bite only as a last resort, sometimes with mouth closed; however, tend to hold on and chew savagely; have large quantities of highly lethal venom.	Varies with the species; generally, local pain followed by slow onset of neurologic symptoms: drowsiness, weakness, facial nerve palsies, flaccid paralysis, and respiratory failure; local necrosis in 35%.
Southeast Asia and India	Russell's viper	Viperdiae: *V. russelii*	Length 40–65 inches. Tan or yellow body with characteristic three rows of large oval, black-bordered spots.	Found in open grassy or brushy country, often near human habitation; slow, phlegmatic snake, mainly nocturnal; hisses when disturbed and strikes with great force and speed; venom of one snake contains enough lethal venom for three humans.	Venom contains both procoagulants (activation of factors V, IX, X) and fibrinolytic components; bleeding from wound site and from all mucous membranes is characteristic (gums, intestine, kidney).
Australia and Pacific Islands	Death adder	Elapidae: *Ocanthophis antarticus*	Length 18–24 inches. Flat, broad triangular head, thick gray, brown, or yellowish body with irregular narrow, dark crossbands; fangs are relatively long for Elapidae.	Widely distributed throughout South Pacific area; mainly nocturnal; defends aggressively with great speed.	Local burning pain and swelling, followed by drowsiness, nausea, vomiting, headache, abdominal pain, cranial nerve palsies: ptosis, visual disturbances, slurring of speech, and generalized muscle weakness and paralysis; hemoglobinuria. (*Continued*)

TABLE 4 (*Continued*)

Area	Common Name	Family and Scientific Name	Description	Habitats	Signs and Symptoms of Envenomation
Australia and Pacific Islands	Tiger snake	Elapidae: *Notechis sculatus*	Length 4–6 feet. Usually brownish-gray, but color varies widely; flat, broad head and short tail.	Occurs in grassy or marshy areas in Australia and offshore islands; nocturnal and not aggressive unless molested; venom is extremely toxic.	Minimal local tissue reactions, but often bleeding from fang marks; in 30–40 minutes, severe abdominal pain and cranial nerve palsies: ptosis, blurring of vision, gradual paresis; skeletal nerve paralysis, respiratory arrest, hemorrhages into internal organs: hematuria, melena, hemoptysis, hematemesis.

Source: Modified from Dowling, H. G., Minton, S. W., and Russell, F. E. (editors): *Poisonous Snakes of the World.* Department of the Navy, Bureau of Medicine and Surgery. Washington, D.C., U.S. Govt. Printing Office, 1965.

6. The incident should be reported to legal authorities. Most areas require licensing in order to collect or house poisonous snakes. If the snake was in the possession of an unlicensed individual, it should be confiscated and the situation investigated through proper legal channels to determine whether additional venomous exotic snakes have been collected and are waiting to bite additional victims.

References

1. Bogert, C. M., and del Campo, R. M.: The gila monster and its allies. The relationships, habitats and behavior of the family Helodermatidae, *Bull. Am. Mus. Natl. Hist.,* **109:**1, 1956.
2. Bullock, T. H. and Diecke, F. P. J.: Properties of an infrared receptor. *J. Physiol.,* **134:**47, 1956.
3. Busack, S. D.: *Amphibians and Reptiles Imported into the U.S.* Wildlife Leaflet 506. U.S. Fish and Wildlife Service, 1974.
4. Cook, E. and Loeb, L.: General properties and actions of the venom of *Heloderma* and experiments in immunization. In Loeb, L. (editor), *The Venom of Heloderma.* Washington, D.C., Carnegie Institute, 1913.
5. Garfin, S. R., Castilonia, R. R., Mubarak, S. J. *et al.:* A clinical and laboratory evaluation of the role of surgical decompression in the treatment of rattlesnake bites. *Surg Forum,* **30:**502, 1979.
6. Gennaro, J. F.: Observations on the treatment of snakebite in North America. In Keegan, H. L., and MacFarlane, W. V. (editors), *Venomous and Poisonous Animals and Noxious Plants of the Pacific Region.* New York, Pergamon, 1963.
6a. Glass, T. G.: Treatment of Rattlesnake bites. Letter. *J.A.M.A.,* **247**(4):461, 1982.
7. Jenkins, M. S. and Russell, F. E.: Physical therapy for injuries produced by rattlesnakes. In Kaiser, E. (editor), *Animal and Plant Toxins.* Nilheim Goldman Verlag, 1973, p. 196.
8. Klauber, I. M.: *Rattlesnakes: Their Habitats, Life Histories and Influence on Mankind,* 2nd ed. Berkeley, University of California Press, Vol. 1., 1972.
9. LaGrange, R. G. and Russell, F. E.: Blood platelet studies in man and rabbits following *Crotalus* envenomation. *Proc. West. Pharmacol. Soc.,* **13:**99, 1970.
10. Ledbetter, E. O. and Kutcher, A. T.: The aerobic and anerobic flora of rattlesnake fangs and venom. *Arch. Environ. Health,* **19:**770, 1969.
11. Mebs, D.: Biochemistry of kinin-releasing enzymes in the venom of the viper *Bitis gabonica* and of the lizard *Heloderma suspectrum.* In Sicuteri, F. (editor), *Bradykinin and Related Kinins. Cardiovascular Biochemical and Neural Actions.* New York, Plenum Press, 1970.
12. Mebs, D. and Raudonat, H. W.: Biochemical investigations on *Heloderma* venom. *Inst. Butantan Simp. Int.,* **33:**907, 1960.
13. Minton, S. A.: Snakebite in the Midwestern region. *Indiana Univ. Med. Center Bull.,* **14:**28, 1952.
14. McCullough, N. C. and Gennaro, J. F.: Evaluation of venomous snakebite in the southern United States. *J. Fla. Med. Assoc.,* **49:**959, 1963.

15. McCullough, N. C. and Gennaro, J. F.: Treatment of venomous snakebites. In *Snake Venoms and Envenomations.* New York, Marcel Dekker, 1971, p. 137.

16. Noble, G. K. and Schmidt, A.: The structure and function of facial and labial pits of snakes. *Proc. Am. Phil. Soc.,* **77**:263, 1937.

17. Parrish, H. M.: Analysis of 450 fatalities from venomous animals in the United States. *Am. J. Med. Sci.,* **245**:129, 1963.

18. Parrish, H. M.: Incidence of treated snakebites. *U.S. Pub. Health Rep.,* **81**:269, 1966.

19. Parrish, H. M.: Ophidiasis. An unusual occupational hazard. *Indust. Med. Surg.,* **27**:63, 1958.

20. Parrish, H. M., Goldner, J. C. and Silverberg, S. L.: Comparison between snakebites in children and adults. *Pediatrics,* **36**:251, 1965.

21. Parrish, H. M. and Khan, M. S.: Bites by coral snakes. Report of 11 representative cases. *Am. J. Med. Sci.,* **253**:561, 1967.

22. Pattabhiraman, T. R., Bufkin, D. C. and Russell, F. E.: Some chemical and pharmacological properties of toxic fractions from the venom of the Southern Pacific rattlesnake. II *Proc. West. Pharmacol. Soc.,* **17**:227, 1974.

23. Patterson, R. A.: Smooth muscle stimulating action of venom from the Gila monster *Heloderma suspectrum. Toxicon,* **7**:321, 1969.

24. Russell, F. E.: Snakebite. In Conn, H. F. (editor), *Current Therapy.* Philadelphia, W. B. Saunders, 1958, p. 830.

25. Russell, F. E.: In *Snake Venom Poisoning.* Philadelphia, J. B. Lippincott Co., 1980.

26. Russell, F. E.: Injuries by venomous animals. *Am. J. Nursing,* **66**:1322, 1966.

27. Russell, F. E.: Snake venom poisoning in the United States. *Med. Arts Sci.,* **23**:3, 1969.

28. Russell, F. E. and Wingert, W. A., Unpublished data.

29. Russell, F. E.: First aid for snake venom poisoning. *Toxicon,* **4**:285, 1967.

29a. Russell, F. E. Personal communication, 1983.

30. Russell, F. E.: Snake venom poisoning in the United States. *Ann. Rev. Med.,* **31**:247, 1980.

31. Schaeffer, R. C., Bernick, S., Rosenquist, T. H. *et al.*: The histochemistry of the venom glands of the rattlesnake *Crotalus viridis helleri. Toxicon,* **10**:295, 1972.

32. Schaeffer, R. C., Carlson, R. W., Puri, V. K. *et al.*: The effects of colloidal and crystalloid fluids on rattlesnake venom shock in the rat. *J. Pharmacol. Exp. Ther.,* **206**:687, 1978.

32a. Simon, T. L., and Grace, T. G.: Envenomation coagulopathy in wounds from pit vipers. *N. Engl. J. Med.,* **305**(8):443–47, 1981.

33. Stahnke, H. L., Heffron, W. A. and Lewis, D. L.: Bite of the Gila monster. *Rocky Mt. Med. J.,* **67**:25, 1970.

34. Sutherland, S. K., Caulter, A. R. and Harris, R. D.: Rationalization of first-aid measures for elapid snakebite. *Lancet,* 183, 1979.

35. U.S. Navy, Bureau of Medicine and Surgery, *Poisonous Snakes of the World* (rev. ed.), Washington, D.C., U.S. Govt. Printing Office, 1968.

36. Van Riper, W.: Measuring the speed of a rattlesnake's strike. *Anim. Kingdom,* **57**:50, 1954.

37. Watt, C. J. and Gennaro, J. F.: Pit viper bites in south Georgia and north Florida. *Trans. South. S.A.* **77**:378, 1966.

38. Wingert, W. A., Pattabirhaman, T. and Russell, F. E.: Unpublished data.

39. Wingert, W. A. and Wainschel, J.: Envenomation by poisonous snakes. *South Med. J.,* **68**:1015, 1975.

40. Zarafonetis, C. J. D. and Kalas, J. P.: Serotonin degradation by homogenates of tissues from *Heloderma horridum,* the Mexican beaded lizard. *Nature,* **195**:707, 1962.

Chapter 13 | TOXIC PLANT INGESTIONS

Edward C. Geehr, M.D.

Within the infant rind of this small flower
Poison hath residence
And medicine power
Romeo and Juliet, Act 2 Scene 3

Plants, as both poisons and medicines, figure prominently in the history of religious ritual, political intrigue, and the healing arts. For centuries, South and Central American Indians evoked mystical visions through the use of mushrooms. North American Indians still employ peyote buttons as part of their magico-religious rites. Socrates succumbed to a fatal draught of hemlock, and Alexander died from the treacherous use of plant poisons. In the eighteenth century, William Withering keenly recognized both the toxic effects of foxglove and its efficacy as a cure for dropsy:

I found him incessantly vomiting, his vision indistinct, his pulse 40 in a minute. Upon inquiry it came out that his wife had stewed a large panful of foxglove leaves in half a pint of water, and given him the liquor, which he drank at one draught. This good woman knew the medicine of her country, but not the dose of it, for her husband narrowly escaped with his life (64).

That it [digitalis] has a power over the motion of the heart, to a degree yet unobserved in any other medicine, and that this power may be converted to salutory ends (57).

Thus, Withering astutely observed that plants bring us the mixed blessing of important therapeutic agents and some of our most dangerous toxins.

Today, toxic plants are ingested mostly by curious children attracted to bright berries or houseplants, by hikers and foragers mistaking poisonous roots and berries for edible fare, by self-taught herbalists looking for natural remedies, and by pleasure seekers discovering natural highs.

Phytotoxicology, the study of plant poisoning, is a field founded in botany, chemistry, and physiology that has not yet achieved a true clinical sophistication. This has much to do with the disparity between botanists, pharmacologists, and physicians; few scholars have interdisciplinary training in all of these fields. Thus, there is generally poor recording and follow-up of plant poisoning, often a result of the improper identification of plants, the use of common names, and the mixing of scientific facts with myth.

About 15,000 Americans are poisoned by plants each year, resulting in 100 deaths (3). Plant poisonings account for 5–6% of toxic ingestions by children less than 5 years of age (44,62). Kingsbury, one of the leading phytotoxicologists, argues that reporting is so inaccurate that the available statistics have little value. He proposes five plants that he believes are most likely to cause human poisoning. These include Jimson weed (*Datura stramonium*), ingested as a tea for mood-altering properties; oleander (*Nerium oleander*), a common roadside plant; jequirty pea (*Abrus precatorius*), with shiny seeds worn in necklaces; water hemlock (*Cicuta maculata*), with roots similar to those of carrots or parsnips; and rhubarb (*Rheum raponticum*) (29).

The author would like to add five additional plants to complete a listing of the 10 most dangerous plants likely to cause significant poisoning in humans. Included are yellow oleander (*Thevetia peruviana*), an attractive flowering plant that commonly causes poisoning in Hawaii; daphne (*Daphne mezerium*), a highly toxic plant with attractive fruits; Jerusalem cherry (*Solanum pseudocapsicum*), with red berries; dieffenbachia (*Dieffenbachia* species), a common houseplant; and black locust (*Robinia pseudoacacia*), a tree with highly poisonous bark, twigs, and seeds.

Although certain mushroom species are highly toxic, little accurate statistical information is available regarding their ingestion. Toxic and commonly ingested mushrooms include the *Amanita, Clitocybe, Lepiota,* and *Chlorophyllum* species, to be discussed in the section on mushrooms.

This chapter focuses on the recognition and treatment of plant poisoning, with emphasis on the known chemistry and physiology. Plants used as herbal remedies or recreational drugs are only briefly mentioned, while those encountered and ingested in their natural form are stressed. With few exceptions, only North American species are considered. It is not the intent of this chapter to provide details of botanical description, since amateur attempts to distinguish poisonous species may lead to disaster. Definitive identification should always be left to a trained botanist. Guidelines are provided, however, to help classify certain categories of ingestions, stressing the unique features of treatment. This will facilitate the institution of appropriate care before absolute identification can be obtained. The two hallmarks of management are that few specific antidotes are available and that one must always pay heed to the patient and his symptoms and not the ingestion. Aggressive supportive care, precise fluid and electrolyte management, and careful monitoring should prevent most fatalities.

The chapter is divided into three major sections: "General Considerations," a discussion of the principles of history taking, physical examination, and management; "Plants: The Toxic Principles," a discussion of the major plant toxins by chemical grouping, which details the physiologic effects and specific treatments; and "Mushrooms: The Toxic Principles," divided into toxic principles and a rationale for treatment.

General Considerations

HISTORY

An accurate history provides the clinician with significant clues about the nature of the plant ingested. The time of the ingestion, amount and number of plants consumed, initial symptoms, and time between ingestion and onset of symptoms are fundamental toxicologic questions. Inquiry should include the method of preparation of the plant, such as drying, cooking, or boiling as a stew or tea, and the number of people who ate the same plant and their symptoms.

Every effort should be made to obtain as much of the original plant or plants as possible. One should not rely on common names as a guide to treatment, but rather should determine the scientific name by taxonomic identification.

Past medical history and current medications are helpful guides to therapy in any symptomatic patient.

PHYSICAL EXAMINATION

The physician should be attuned to certain syndromes which may develop after plant ingestion. Anticholinergic crisis induced by certain alkaloid principles is easily distinguished by the combination of tachycardia, mydriasis, hot dry skin, decreased bowel sounds, altered vision and abnormal mental status. Cholinergic overdrive induced by some mushroom species may also be clear-cut, with bradycardia, miosis, sweating, salivation, hyperactive bowel sounds, and diarrhea. Nicotinic alkaloids may act as stimulants at first, soon followed by depression and weakness. In many cases, there may be a mixture of syndromes, with no definite pattern established. Thus, a rush to therapy using an "antidote" based on inadequate assessment and physical examination may exacerbate a major and unanticipated aspect of the intoxication.

Changes in behavior should not automatically be attributed to plant toxins. Alterations in mental status mandate a thorough neurologic examination. Focal signs may point to an intracranial lesion, the result of a fall or other injury.

MANAGEMENT

After ensuring the basic ABCs of airway, breathing, and circulation, removal of the toxin is the highest priority. If emesis is not a feature of the intoxication, syrup of ipecac, 30 ml for adults and 15 ml for children, is given with copious amounts of warm water. In those patients with a depressed gag reflex, unresponsiveness, or seizures, an endotracheal airway is established before a large-bore Ewald tube is inserted to perform gastric lavage. Following lavage, activated charcoal (50–100 g in 8 ounces of water) should be given in a slurry to adsorb any toxin left in the upper gastrointestinal tract. If diarrhea is not a feature of the poisoning, cathartics are indicated. Magnesium citrate (8–12 ounces) following the activated charcoal is effective and safe.

Dialysis has not yet been shown to be effective in removing any of the plant toxins.

Meticulous attention should be paid to urinary output and specific gravity as measures of the adequacy of hydration and volume replacement.

Baseline laboratory evaluation in symptomatic patients should include urinalysis, complete blood count, electrolytes, blood urea nitrogen (BUN), and glucose. If hepatotoxins or other specific organ toxins are suspected, appropriate laboratory data, as suggested in later sections on management, should be obtained. Samples of the emesis, gastric lavage fluid, and blood should be saved for toxicologic analysis or microscopic examination for the presence of identifiable toxins, characteristic spores, or hyphal forms.

Mixed ingestions require greater vigilance, for confusing physical signs may evolve or earlier mild signs may give way to serious illness. As previously mentioned, it is prudent to treat the patient, not the suspected ingestion. Specific antidotes are few, and may be deleterious as the clinical pattern changes.

Plants: The Toxic Principles

The toxic principles underlying all major poisonous plant ingestions are organized by chemical and physical properties. Although the human physiologic response tends to be fairly consistent within each group of toxic principles, disparities do exist. These will be discussed. Toxic principles and therapeutics are presented in Table 1.

ALKALOIDS

Alkaloids comprise 10% of plant species; about 5000 types are currently known to exist. The alkaloids are principally distributed in the families Apocynaceae (dogbane), Berberidicaea (may apple), Fabaceae (pea), Papaveraceae (poppy) Ranunculaceae (buttercup), and Solanaceae (potato).

Chemical similarities exist among all of the alkaloids. They are nitrogen-containing organic compounds that act as bases and form salts with acids. In plants, the alkaloids are present as soluble organic acid-alkaloid salts (30). These complex structures all contain ni-

TABLE 1
Plants: Toxic Principles and Therapeutics

Common Name	Genus	Species	Poisonous Principle	Toxic Parts	Distribution[a]	Section[b] Therapeutic Reference
Akee	*Blighia*	*sapida*	Hypoglycin	Fruit wall Seeds	II S. Fla. Carib.	Hypoglycemic Agents
Anemone	*Anemonee*		Ranunculin	White aril All parts	II	Irritant and Essential Oils
Angel's trumpet	*Datura*	*sauveolens*	Atropine Hyoscyamine Hyoscine	Leaves, flowers	II, VI, S.E. U.S., Hi.	Tropane Alkaloids
Apple of Peru	*Nicandra*	*physalodes*	Unknown	Leaves, berries	I	General Considerations
Apple seeds	*Malus*	spp.	Cyanogenic glycosides	Seeds	III	Cyanogenic Glycosides
Apricot pits	*Prunus*	spp.	Cyanogenic glycosides	Pits	II	Cyanogenic Glycosides
Arnica	*Arnica*	*montana fulgens*	Unknown	Flowers Roots	II N. U.S., Can.	General Considerations
Autumn crocus Azalea	*Colchicum* (see *Rhododendron*)	*autumnale*	Colchicine	Seeds, corns	II	Amine Alkaloids
Balsam pear	*Mamordica*	*balsimia*	Saponic glycoside	Seeds Wall of fruit	I Coastal Fla. to Tex.	Saponin Glycosides
Baneberry	*Actae*	spp.	Protoanemone Unknown glycosides	Berries Rootstock	I Widely except S.W.	Irritant and Essential Oils
Beech Belladonna	*Fagus* (See deadly nightshade)	spp.	Saponic glycoside	Nuts	III	Saponin Glycoside
Bellyache bush	*Jatropha*	*gossypifolia*	Curcin	Fruit, seeds, sap	I, V	Phytotoxins
Betel nut	*Areca*	*cathecu*	Arecoline Arecaine	Seeds	II, Fla., Hi.	Pyridine-Piperidine Group
Bird of paradise	*Poinciana*	*gillesii*	Unknown	Green seed pods	II	General Considerations
Black cherry	*Prunus*	*serotina*	Cyanogenic glycosides	Bark, leaves, seeds, "tea" of leaves	I, E. N.A.	Cyanogenic Glycosides

Common Name	Genus	Species	Toxic Principle	Toxic Parts	Code	Phytotoxins
Black locust	Robinia	pseudoacacia	Robin Robitin (glycoside)	Inner bark Young leaves, seeds	I, S. Can., E. N.A., Mid. W., road-sides	Phytotoxins
Black nightshade	Solanum	nigrum	Solanine	Unripened fruit	I, Widely, roadsides	Steroid Alkaloids
Black snake root	(see death camas)					
Bleeding heart	(see dicentra)					
Blood root	Sanguinarine	canadensis	Sanguinarine	All parts	I	Isoquinoline and Quinoline Group
Blister bush	Phebolium	anceps	Unknown	Leaves, fruit	I	General Considerations
Blue cohosh	Caulophyllum	thalactroides	Unknown	Seeds, rootstock	I	General Considerations
Boxwood	Buxus	sempervirens	Buxine, volatile oil	Leaves, twigs	II, V	Alkaloids, Irritant and Essential Oils
Brazilian pepper also: pink or red peppercorn Florida holly	Schinus	terebinthifolius	Unknown	Berries, leaves, flowers	I Fla.	General Consideration
Buckeye	Aesculus	spp.	Aesculin	Leaves, flowers, young sprouts, seeds	III, widely	Coumarin Glycosides
Buckthorn	Rhamnus	cathartica frangula	Anthraquinones	Berries, leaves, bark	I, VI	Anthraquinone Glycosides
Burning bush	Eunonymus	spp.	Unknown	Leaves, bark, seeds	III	General Considerations
Bushman's poison	Acokanthera	spp.	Ouabain, G-strophanthin, acokantherin	All	I	Cardiac Glycosides
Buttercup	Ranunculus	spp.	Protoanemonin	All parts	III	Irritant and Essential Oils
Caladium	Caladium	spp.	Oxalates	Leaves	II, IV	Oxalates
Candle nut	(See lumbang nut)					
Caper spurge	Euphorbia	lathyris	Unknown alkaloid	Milky sap through-out plant	II	General Considerations
Carolina jessamine also: yellow jessamine	Gelsemium	sempervirens	Gelsemine Sempervirine	All parts	II	Indole Derivative Group
Cassava also: manioc, tapioca	Manihot	esculenta	Cyanogenic glycoside	Raw root	II, VI	Cyanogenic Glycosides

(Continued)

TABLE 1 (Continued)

Common Name	Genus	Species	Poisonous Principle	Toxic Parts	Distribution[a]	Section[b] Therapeutic Reference
Castor bean	Ricinis	communis	Ricin	Seeds	III	Phytotoxins
Chalice vine	Solandra	nitida	(See trumpet flower)			
Cherry	Prunus	spp.	Cyanogenic glycosides	Pits	II	Cyanogenic Glycosides
Chinaberry tree	Melia	azederach	Unknown resin	Fruit, tea from leaves	III	Resins
Christmas rose	Helleborus	niger	Hellebrin, helleborin, helleborein	Rootstocks and leaves	II	Cardiac glycosides
Clematis	Clematis	spp.	Steroid alkaloids	Seeds, young plants	II, widely	Steroid alkaloids
Coca	Erythoxylon	coca	Ecogonine	Extract of leaves	VI	Psychoactive plants
Coontie	Zamia	floridana	Unknown alkaloid	Fleshy seeds	II, S. U.S., Hi.	General Considerations
Coral plant	Jatropha	multifida	Curcin	Fruit, seeds, sap of all parts	III S. Fla. to Tex., Hi.	Phytotoxins
Corn cockle	Agrostemma	githago	Githagenin, sapogenin	All parts, especially seeds	I	Saponin Glycosides
Cotoneaster	Cotoneaster	spp.	Unknown	Berries	II	General Considerations
Coyotillo	Karwinskia	humboldtiana	Unknown	Fruit, seeds	I, S.W. U.S.	General Considerations
Crape jasmine	Ervatamia	coronaria	Unknown	Leaves, flowers	II	General Considerations
Crownflower	Calotropis	gigantea	Unknown	All parts	II, V	General Considerations
Crown of thorns	Euphorbia	spp.	Unknown alkaloid	Milky sap throughout plant	II, widely	General Considerations
Cup of gold	Solandra	cuttata	Solaninelike alkaloids	Leaves, flowers	II	Steroid Alkaloids
Cycads	(see coontie)					
Cypress spurge	Euphorbia	cyparissias	Unknown alkaloids	Milky sap throughout plant	II	General Considerations
Daffodils	Narcissus	spp.	Lycorine	Bulb	II	General Considerations
Daphne	Daphne	mezereum	Dihydroxycoumarin, diterpene mezerein	Bark, leaves, fruit	II	Coumarin Glycosides
Day jessamine	Cestrum	diurnum	Tropane alkaloids	All parts	III, Fla., Hi.	Tropane Alkaloids
Deadly nightshade	Atropa	belladonna	Atropine	All parts, black berries	I	Tropane Alkaloids
Death camas Also: black snakeroot	Zigadenus	spp.	Zygacine, zygadenine	Bulb	I, widely	Steroid Alkaloids

Common Name	Genus	Species	Toxic Principle	Toxic Part	Distribution	Class
Delphiniums	Delphinium	spp.	Delphinine, ajacine	Seeds, young plants	III	Steroid Alkaloids
Devil's trumpet also: hairy thorn apple	Datura	metel	Atropine, hyoscyamine, hyoscine	Leaves, flowers	II, VI, Coastal Fla. to Tex.	Tropane Alkaloids
Dicentra also: bleeding heart, Dutchman's breeches	Dicentra	spp.	Protopine	All parts	I, widely	Isoquinoline and Quinoline Group
Dieffenbachia also: dumb cane	Dieffenbachia	spp.	Oxalate, asparagine	Leaves	II, IV	Oxalates
Dogbane also: Indian hemp	Apocynum	cannabium	Cymarin	Flowers, seeds, leaves	I, widely, road-sides	Cardiac Glycosides
Duranta	(See sky flowers)					
Elderberry	Sambucus	spp.	Unknown alkaloids	Unripe berries, leaves, wood	III, all N. Am. except Pac. Coast	General Considerations
Elephant ear	Colocasia	antiquorum	Oxalates	Leaves	IV	Oxalates
English bean	(See fava bean)					
English ivy	Hedera	helix	Hederogenin	Berries and leaves	II, IV, V	Saponin Glycosides
False hellebore also: Indian poke	Veratrum	spp.	Veratrim	Leaves	I, E. N.A., Minn.	Steroid Alkaloids
False sago palm	Cycas	circinalis	Alkaloids	Seeds	II, V, S. U.S., Hi.	General Considerations
Fava bean	Vicia	faba	Hemolytic anemia in glucose-6 phosphate deficiency	Seeds	II	General Considerations
Finger cherry	Rhodomyrtus	macrocarpa	Saponin	Fruit	S. Pacific	Saponin Glycosides
Fool's parsley	Aethusa	cynapium	Unknown	Leaves	I	General Considerations
Four o'clock	Mirabilis	jalapa	Unknown	Roots or seeds	II	General Considerations
Foxglove	Digitalis	purpurea	Digitoxin, gitaloxin, gitoxin	Leaves	III, W. U.S.	Cardiac Glycosides
Glory lily	Gloriosa	superba	Colchicinelike alkaloids, superbine	Rhizomes	II	Amino Alkaloids
Golden chain also: golden rain	Laburnum	anagyroides	Cytisine	Flowers, seeds	II, N. U.S., S. Can.	Quinolizidine Alkaloids

(Continued)

TABLE 1 (Continued)

Common Name	Genus	Species	Poisonous Principle	Toxic Parts	Distribution[a]	Section[b] Therapeutic Reference
Golden seal	Hydrastis	canadensis	Steroid alkaloids	Seeds, young plants	I, N.E. U.S.	Steroid Alkaloids
Ground cherry	Physalis	spp.	Unknown	Leaves, unripe fruit	I, widely	General Considerations
Hill gooseberry	Rhodomyrtus	tomentosa	None—N. Am. non-toxic Rhodomyrtus spp.		II, N.Am.	—
Holly	Ilex	spp.	Unknown	Berries	III, V	General Considerations
Horse chestnut	Aesculus	spp.	Aesculin	Sprouts, mature nuts	II	Coumarin Glycosides
Horseradish	Amoracia	rusticana	Mustard oil	Roots	II	Irritant and Essential Oils
Horse bean (See fava bean)						
Horse nettle also: wild tomato	Solanum	carolinense	Solanine	Fruit	I, widely	Steroid Alkaloids
Hyacinth	Hyacinthus	orientalis	Unknown	Bulb	II, IV	General Considerations
Hyacinth bean	Dolichos	lablab	Cyanogenic glycosides	Pods, seeds	II	Cyanogenic Glycosides
Hydrangea	Hydrangea	spp.	Cyanogenic glycoside	Leaves, buds	III	Cyanogenic Glycosides
Inkberry (See pokeweed)						
Jack in the pulpit	Arisema	spp.	Oxalate	Root	I, N.E. U.S.	Oxalates
Jequirty pea also: rosary pea, precatory bean	Abrus	precatorius	Abrin	Beans	I, V	Phytotoxins
Jerusalem cherry	Solanum	pseudocapsicum	Solanine	Fruit	II, V, widely	Steroid Alkaloids
Jessamine (See Carolina jessamine)						
Jessamines	Cestrum	spp.	Tropane alkaloids	All parts	III	Tropane Alkaloids
Jetbead	Rhodotypus	tetrapetala	Cyanogenic glycosides	Berries	II, N. U.S.	Cyanogenic Glycosides
Jimson weed	Datura	stramonium	Atropine, hyoscyamine, hyoscine	Leaves, Flowers	I, VI	Tropane Alkaloids
Jonquil (see daffodil)						
Kentucky coffee tree	Gymnocladus	dioica	Cytisine	Seeds, pulp	III, E. N.A., Okla.	Quinolizidine Alkaloids

Common name	Genus	species	Toxic principle	Plant part	Location/Class	General Considerations
Lantana	*Lantana*	*camara*	Lantanin, lantadene A	Unripe fruit	II, N. U.S., S.E. U.S.	General Considerations
Larkspur	(See delphinium)					
Laurel	(See mountain laurel)					
Lignum vitae	*Guaiacum*	*officinale*	Unknown	Resin in wood and fruit	II, S. Fla., S. Cal., Hi.	General Considerations
Lily of the valley	*Convallaria*	*majalis*	Convallotoxin	Rhizome	II, widely	Cardiac Glycosides
Lobelia also: Indian tobacco	*Lobelia*	spp.	Lobelamine, lobeline	All parts	III, IV	Pyridine-Piperidine Group
Lumbang nut	*Aleurites*	*trisperma*	(See tung oil tree)			
Manchineel tree	*Hippomane*	*mancinella*	Unknown	Milky sap	I	General Considerations
Marijuana also: grass, dope, pot, ganja, pokololo	*Cannabis*	*sativa*	Tetrahydrocannabinol	Leaves	III, VI	Psychoactive plants
May apple	*Podophyllum*	*peltatum*	Podophyllotoxin	All parts except ripe fruit	I, widely	General Considerations
Mescal bean	*Sophora*	*secundiflora*	Unknown alkaloids	Seeds	III, VI	General Considerations
Mexican prickle-poppy	(See pricklepoppy)					
Milk bush	*Euphorbia*	*tirucallii*	Unknown alkaloids	Milky sap throughout plant	I	General Considerations
Mistletoe (American)	*Phoradendron*	*serotinum*	Toxic amines	Berries	I, V	General Considerations
Mistletoe (European)	*Viscum*	*album*	Viscotoxins	Berries	I, V	General Considerations
Monkshood also: aconite, wolfsbane	*Aconitum*	spp.	Aconotine	All parts, especially roots	III	Steroid Alkaloids
Moonseed	*Menispermum*	*canadense*	Dauricine	Berries	I	Isoquinoline and Quinoline Group
Morning glory	*Ipomoea*	*violacea*	D-Lysergic acid amide	Seeds	II, VI	Psychoactive Plants
Mountain ash	*Sorbus*	spp.	Unknown	Berries	I	General Considerations

(Continued)

TABLE 1 (Continued)

Common Name	Genus	Species	Poisonous Principle	Toxic Parts	Distribution[a]	Section[b] Therapeutic Reference
Mountain laurel	Kalmia	latifolia	Andromedotoxin, arbutin	All parts	III	General Considerations, Resins
Narcissus	(See jonquil)					
Night-blooming jasmine	Cestrum	spp.	Tropane alkaloids	All parts	I, S. U.S.	Tropane alkaloids
Nightshade also: woody nightshade, climbing nightshade, bittersweet	Solanum	dulcamara	Solanine	Fruit	I, V, widely	Steroid Alkaloids
Nutmeg	Myristica	fragrans	Myristicine	Nut	VI	Psychoactive Plants
Oak	Quercus	spp.	Tannin, unknown	Acorns	III, S.W.	General Considerations
Ochrosia plum	Ochrosia	elliptica	Unknown	Fruit	II, Fla., Hi.	General Considerations
Oleander	Nerium	oleander	Oleandrin	All parts	II, S. U.S., Cal., Hi., roadsides	Cardiac Glycosides
Peach pits	Prunus	spp.	Cyanogenic Glycosides	Pits	II, widely	Cyanogenic Glycosides
Peyote	Lophophora	williamsii	Mescaline, lophophorine	Seeds, buttons	I, S. Tex.	General Considerations Psychoactive Plants
Philodendron	Philodendron	spp.	Oxalate	Leaves	IV	Oxalates
Physic nut also: purge nut	Jatropha	curcas	Curcin	Fruit, seeds	II	Phytotoxins
Pigeonberry	(See pokeweed)					
Plum pit	Prunus	spp.	Cyanogenic glycoside	Pit	II, widely	Cyanogenic Glycosides
Poinsettia	Euphorbia	pulcherrima	Unknown alkaloid	Milky sap throughout plant	II, V	General Considerations
Poison hemlock	Conium	maculatum	Coniine	Seeds, roots, young leaves	I	Pyridine-Piperidine Group

Common name	Genus	Species	Toxic principle	Part	Class/Distribution	Category
Pokeweed also: pokeberry, Virginia poke, scoke, garget, inkberry, cao-kum, American cancer, cancer jalep	Phytolacca	americana	Triterpene saponins	All parts	I	Saponin Glycosides
Pongam	Pongammia	pinnata	Unknown	Seeds, roots	II, S. Fla., S. Cal., Hi.	General Considerations
Potato	Solanum	tuberosum	Solanine	Unripe tubers	II, widely	Steroid Alkaloids
Prickly poppy	Argemone	spp.	Sanguinarine, berberine, protopine	All parts, especially seeds	III	Isoquinoline and Quinoline Group
Privet	Ligustrum	vulgare, japonicum	Unknown glycoside	Berries, leaves	II, widely	General Considerations
Purge nut (See physic nut)						
Rattlebox also: coffee bean, sesbane, coffeeweed, rattlebrush	Sesbania	spp.	Saponins	Seeds, flowers	III, V, S.E. coastal	Saponin Glycosides
Rayless goldenrod	Haplopappus	heterophyllus	Tremetol	The milk of cows grazing on this plant	I	Irritant and Essential Oils
Rhododendron also: laurel, azalea	Rhododendron	spp.	Andromedotoxin, Arbutin	All parts	III, E. N. Am., Pac. Coast	General Considerations, Resins
Rhubarb	Rheum	rhaponticum	Oxalates	Leaf blades	II	Oxalates
Rock poppy	Chelidonium	majus	Sanguinarine, berberine, protopine	Leaves, seeds	I, E. N.A.	Isoquinoline and Quinoline Group
Rubber vine	Cryptostegia	grandiflora	Unknown	All parts	II, V, S. U.S., HI.	General Considerations
Sandbox tree	Hura	crepitans	Unknown	Milky sap	II, S. U.S.	General Considerations
Sky flower	Duranta	repens	Saponin	Berries	I	Saponin Glycosides
Snow on the mountain	Euphorbia	spp.	Unknown alkaloids	Milky sap throughout plant	II	General Considerations
Spring adonis	Adonis	vernalis	Steroid alkaloids	Seeds, young plants	II	Steroid Alkaloids
Spurge	Euphorbia	spp.	Unknown alkaloids	Milky sap	III	General Considerations (Continued)

389

TABLE 1 (Continued)

Common Name	Genus	Species	Poisonous Principle	Toxic Parts	Distribution[a]	Section[b] Therapeutic Reference
Star of Bethlehem	*Ornithogalum*	*umbellatum*	Cardiac glycosides	All parts	III, V, E. N.A., Mid. W., Hi.	Cardiac Glycosides
Strawberry bush	(see burning bush)					
Sweet Pea	*Lathyrus*	spp.	β (γ-L-glutamyl)-amino-propionitrile, L-α, γ-diaminobutyric acid	Peas	III	General Considerations
Tobacco	*Nicotiana*	*tabacum*	Nicotine	Leaves	II	Pyridine-Piperidine Group
Tomato	*Lycopersicon*	*esculenta*	Solanine	Leaves	II	Steroid Alkaloids
Trumpet flower	*Solandra*	spp.	Solaninelike	Leaves, flowers	II	Steroid Alkaloids
Trumpet lily	*Datura*	*arborea*	Atropine, hyoscyamine, hyoscine	Flowers, leaves	II, VI	Tropane Alkaloids
Tulip bulb	*Tulipa*	*gesnariana*	Unknown	Bulb	II	General Considerations
Tung oil tree	*Aleurites*	*fordii*	Saponins	Seed	II	Saponin Glycosides
Virginia creeper also: woodbine, American ivy	*Parthenocissus*	*quinquefolia*	Unknown	Berries	I, E. N.A., S.W.	General Considerations
Water hemlock	*Cicuta*	*maculata*	Cicutoxin	Roots	I, widely swamps	Resins
White snakeroot	*Eupatorium*	*rugosum*	Tremetol	The milk of cows grazing on this plant	I, N. Car., Ill., Ind., Oh.	Irritant and Essential Oils
Wild balsam apple	*Mamordia*	*charantia*	Saponic glycoside	Seeds and wall of fruit	I	Saponin Glycosides

Common name	Genus	species	Toxic part	Toxic principle	Distribution	Section
Wild cherry	(See black, cherry)					
Wisteria	Wisteria	spp.	Seeds	Unknown	II	General Considerations
Woody nightshade	(See nightshade)					
Yellow alamanda	Allamanda	cathartica	Fruit	Unknown	II, S. U.S., Hi.	General Considerations
Yellow jessamine	(See Carolina jessamine)					
Yellow Nightshade also: Wild allamanda	Urechite	spp.	Seed pods	Unknown	I, S. Fla	General Considerations
Yellow Oleander also: Lucky nut	Thevetia	peruviana	Flowers, seeds, leaves	Thevetin, thevetoxin	II, Hi.	Cardiac Glycosides
Yew	Taxus	spp.	Berries	Taxine	III, V., E. N.A., Pac. coast	Steroid Alkaloids

a Distribution key:

I   Native or naturalized; found in fields, woods, and roadsides.
II Cultivated; found in gardens and yards.
III Found in both I and II.
IV Common houseplants.
V   Found in decorations or as seasonal ornamentals.
VI Found in herbal or folk remedies or used for mood alteration.

b See appropriate section in text.

Minn.	Minnesota	Can.	Canada
N. Am.	North America	Carib.	Caribbean
N. Car.	North Carolina	Coastal Fla. to Tex.	Coastal Florida to Texas
N.E. U.S.	Northeastern United States		
N. U.S.	Northern United States	E. N.A.	Eastern North America
Oh.	Ohio	Fla.	Florida
Pac. Coast	Pacific Coast States	Hi.	Hawaii
Roadsides	Roadsides, waste areas and swamps	Ill.	Illinois
S. Cal.	Southern California	Ind.	Indiana
S. Can.	Southern Canada	Mid. W.	Middle Western States
S.E. Coastal	Southeastern Coastal Plain		
S.E. U.S.	Southeastern United States		
S. Fla.	Southern Florida		
S. Tex.	Southern Texas		
S.W.	South Western States		
Widely	Distributed throughout the United States		

trogen in a heterocyclic and/or aromatic ring structure. Alkaloids are generally distributed throughout the plant, rendering all ingested parts toxic. Most alkaloids are bound by activated charcoal.

The major types of alkaloids can be divided into chemical groups, with physiologic activity based on ring structure.

Pyridine-Piperidine Group

The pyridine-piperidine group (Figure 1) contains the major alkaloids nicotine, coniine, lobeline, arecoline, piperine, and isopelletierine.

Nicotine and lobeline are characteristic of the ganglionic-stimulating agents in this group. The action of nicotine on a variety of neuroeffector junctions is rapid and variable. There is an initial stimulation of most autonomic ganglia, followed by depression of transmission. Nicotine similarly affects the neuromuscular junction with a stimulant phase followed rapidly by paralysis (Figure

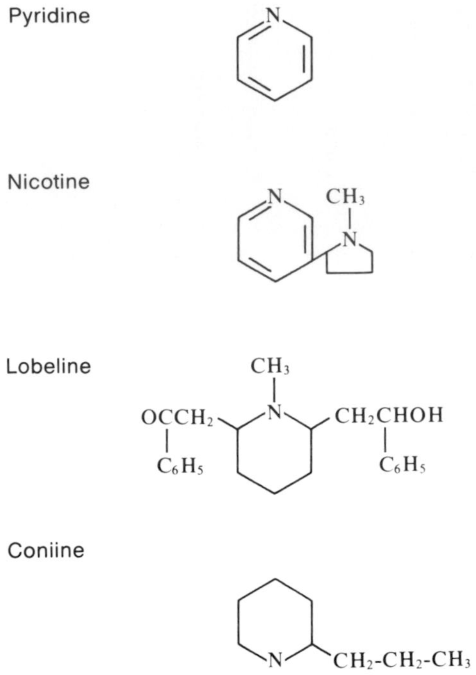

Pyridine

Nicotine

Lobeline

Coniine

FIGURE 1 Pyridine/piperidine alkaloids.

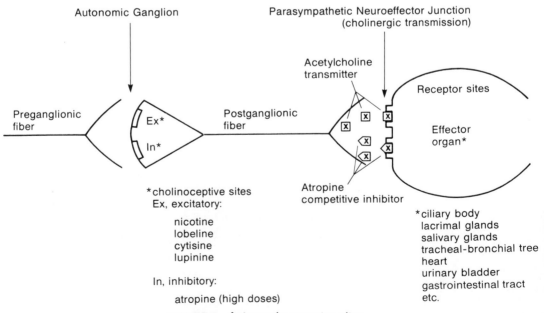

FIGURE 2 Autonomic receptor sites.

2). Although small doses may augment respiration, respiratory blockade ensues after higher doses, secondary to central nervous system depression and peripheral neuromuscular junction paralysis of the muscles of respiration (17).

Coniine (Figure 1), the principal alkaloid in *Conium maculatum* (poison hemlock), is a pyridine derivative similar to nicotine. It also works as a ganglionic stimulating agent, producing a transitory parasympathetic and central nervous system stimulation, followed by mental status depression and respiratory paralysis. The alkaloid is volatile and lost by drying or heating.

The clinical syndromes produced by pyridine-piperidines are mixed, due to the variability of drug effect and dose. Poisoning is heralded by abdominal pain, nausea, and vomiting. Confusion, dizziness, and generalized weakness ensue. Initial parasympathomimetic signs of bradycardia, bowel hyperactivity, salivation, diarrhea, pupillary constriction, and increased respiratory drive change to tachycardia, tachyarrhythmias, hypotension, pupillary dilatation, and respiratory depression. Seizures may occur terminally, along with respiratory failure (17,30). Therapy consists of removing the toxin from the stomach with gastric lavage and instilling activated charcoal. It may be a mistake to treat the initial bradycardia with atropine, due to the natural progression to tachycardia. Temporary cardiac pacing may be preferable to atropine or isoproterenol. These compounds are generally excreted fairly rapidly by the kidneys after biotransformation in the liver and lungs.

Ingestion of as little as 4 mg of nicotine has been fatal, while as much as 2 g has been survived. The average toxic dose of nicotine is 60 mg (17). In the presence of liver and/or renal failure, supportive treatment may be required for days. There is no evidence that dialysis is effective in removing the toxins. Control of the airway with endotracheal intubation and mechanically assisted ventilation are the hallmarks of therapy, and all properly managed patients should survive.

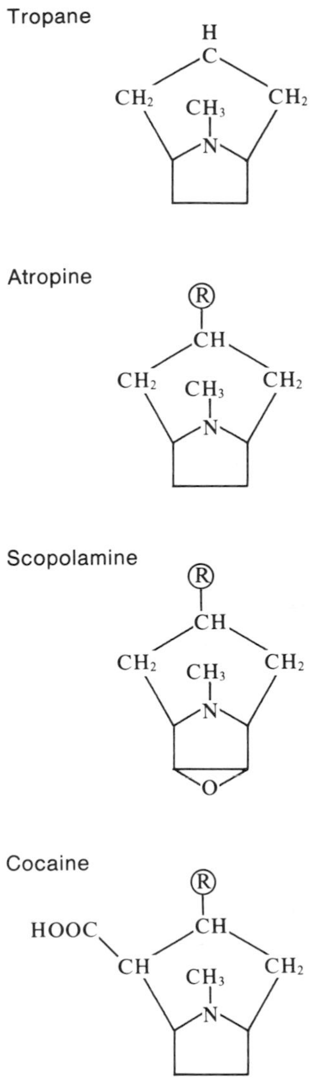

Tropane Alkaloids

The tropane alkaloids often called *belladonna alkaloids* (Figure 3), include atropine

FIGURE 3 Tropane alkaloids.

(hyoscyamine), scopolamine (hyoscine), and ecgonine (cocaine) compounds. This grouping contains the large (75 genera, 2000 species) and commercially important family *Solanaceae*, which includes the medicinal belladonna, the poisonous Jimson weed, and the food staples potato, tomato, eggplant, and pepper.

Ecgonine (cocaine) is mentioned here only to note its structural similarity to atropine. However, it possesses very little antimuscarinic effect, while atropine shows little of the anesthetic effect of cocaine.

Plant sources of atropine and scopolamine

that cause human poisoning are the *Datura* species, including Jimson weed (*D. stramonium*), henbane (*Hyoscyamus niger*), mandrake (*Mandrigora officinarum*), and, rarely, belladonna (*Atropa belladonna*).

The antimuscarinic effects of the tropane alkaloids result from competitive inhibition of acetylcholine at receptor sites in neuroeffector junctions supplied by postganglionic cholinergic innervation. Only at much higher doses does atropine block the nicotinic action of acetylcholine at automonic ganglia (Figure 2). The central nervous system effects are less well understood and generally show predictable dose-response activity. Scopolamine tends to cause more drowsiness and euphoria compared to the agitation, restlessness, and irritability induced by atropine; hence, scopolamine is preferred as a preanesthetic agent and scopolamine-rich plants, such as Jimson weed and henbane, are abused to produce illicit highs.

Most organ systems with parasympathetic innervation demonstrate a dose-related response to atropinic drugs. Low doses suppress secretory function, while higher doses are required for significant cardiac and central nervous system effects.

The tropane alkaloids are rapidly absorbed from the gastrointestinal tract, mucosal surfaces, and respiratory tree. The drugs are hydrolyzed by the liver and excreted in the urine.

The clinical picture is largely dose dependent. At higher doses, the onset of symptoms is rapid, with dry mouth, mydriasis, flushed dry skin, decreased bowel sounds, tachycardia, restlessness, incoordination, and confusion. In a series of 27 cases of Jimson weed poisoning, 100% of the victims had mental status changes and mydriasis (32). In addition, hyperpyrexia, hyperreflexia, bilateral Babinski response, and decerebrate posturing have been described (42). There may be hepatic enzyme and electroencephalogram abnormalities, both of which resolve rapidly with recovery (40). There are few recorded fatalities from belladonna alkaloid poisoning per se, but death has resulted from impaired judgment (18). Children seem to be the most sensitive to atropine poisoning, and most commonly eat the seeds and flowers. Adult poisonings are usually the result of ingesting tea made from the flowers or leaves of the Jimson weed or henbane plant. Of note, pupillary dilatation, or atropine mydriasis, will not reverse after the application of 1% pilocarpine, whereas dilatation of the pupils secondary to a central nervous system mass lesion will usually respond briskly to pilocarpine (59).

The treatment of belladonna alkaloid intoxication requires the removal of the toxin from the gastrointestinal tract via gastric lavage, followed by the instillation of activated charcoal and magnesium citrate. Removal of seeds from the stomach may not preclude serious toxicity, for the alkaloids are rapidly leached into the gastric contents (32). Potassium permanganate is ineffective in detoxifying belladonna alkaloids, and thus should not be added to the gastric lavage solution.

Many authorities recommend treatment of the full-blown anticholinergic syndrome with carefully titrated physostigmine (32,39,40,42). The pharmacology is appealing. By using an anticholinesterase to block acetylcholine degradation, one can override the competitive inhibition of the atropinic agents and rapidly reverse the peripheral and central nervous system effects. Reports of asystole, hypotension, bronchospasm, difficulty in clearing secretions, and seizures after the slow intravenous administration of physostigmine to treat anticholinergic syndromes mandate a reevaluation of the efficacy of this drug compared to supportive treatment (47,60). Propranolol, in carefully titrated 1 mg intravenous doses, is the treatment of choice for the therapy of supraventricular tachyarrthythmias associated with tropane alkaloid ingestion. Isotonic fluid volume replacement is the first-line treatment for hypotension. Vasopressors, such as dopamine, may be used if volume challenge does not reverse hypotension.

Isoquinoline and Quinoline Group

The isoquinoline and quinoline group (Figure 4) contains such divergent species as *Papaver somniferum* (opium poppy), *Cephaelis ipecacuanha* (ipecac), and *Cinchona* species (quinine). A discussion of opium and its many derivatives is beyond the scope of this chapter. The narcotic shares many alkaloids with the toxic plants in this group, including berberine and sanguinarine. The major toxicity is gastrointestinal and mucous membrane irritation,

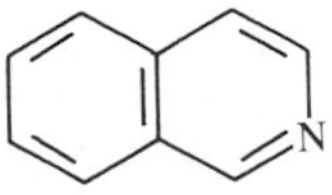

FIGURE 4 Isoquinoline/quinoline nucleus.

with few reported poisonings from plant ingestions in this group. Cardiac toxicity at higher doses has been reported.

The most commonly ingested isoquinoline derivative is emetine in the form of syrup of ipecac. It is mentioned here to highlight the gastrointestinal manifestations of this group of compounds, and may cause myocardial depression and hypotension if absorbed.

Treatment consists of supportive measures only. Mucous membrane irritation may be treated with 2% viscous lidocaine (Xylocaine) and diphenhydramine elixir. Ipecac used in the management of drug ingestions should always be removed by lavage if emesis does not occur.

Indole Derivative Group

Indole derivatives (Figure 5) are the most potent psychoactive compounds in nature. As such, they will be discussed in the section on *psychoactive plants.* The only important toxic alkaloids in this group are gelsemium and sempervine, found in *Gelsemium semperviens* (Carolina or yellow jessamine). These act as neuromuscular blocking agents and can cause death by respiratory paralysis.

The ergots, ergonovine and ergotamine, are indole derivatives, but have little relevance as modern plant poisons. Historically, the fungus *Claviceps purpurea,* the source of ergonovine and ergotamine, infected rye and other grains, which, when consumed, caused a burning sensation in the extremities known as *St. Anthony's fire.* Commercial grains are now inspected for the presence of ergot, and inadvertent poisoning is rare. Ergot derivatives, potent vasoconstrictors and oxytocic agents, are now used

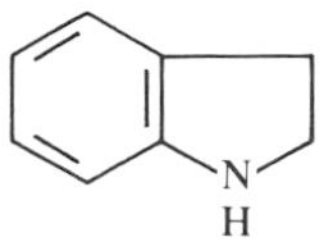

FIGURE 5 Indole nucleus.

in the therapy of vascular headaches and obstetric and gynecologic disorders.

Strychnine, found in the seeds of the tree *Strychnos nux-vomica,* is a powerful central nervous system stimulant and convulsant. The indole derivative is usually ingested accidentally by children who mistakenly consume rat poison.

Treatment consists of supportive measures. Endotracheal intubation and mechanically assisted ventilation may be required, but recovery is expected and mortality is low.

Pyrrolizidine Alkaloids

Ingestion of pyrrolizidine alkaloids usually involves the consumption of mislabeled herbal medicines or teas which contain groundsel (*Senecio longilobes*). Other natural sources are *Amsinckia* (fiddle neck or tar weed) and *Crotalaria* (rattlebox). The principal alkaloids are heliotrine, lasiocarpine, and retrorsine, which may be hepatotoxic and carcinogenic (10). Hepatomas and pancreatic tumors have been produced in rats fed retrorsine. Case reports note deaths from hepatic failure in a person who consumed large amounts of matté tea and acutely in a child who drank groundsel tea (34,58).

The mechanisms of carcinogenesis and hepatotoxicity are unknown; young victims seem to be more susceptible than adults to the effects of acute ingestions (33, p. 120).

Treatment is supportive.

Quinolizidine Alkaloids

The quinolizidine alkaloids, cytisine and lupinine (Figure 6), act much like nicotinic ganglionic stimulating agents (Figure 2). Initial effects of agitation, nausea, vomiting, and delirium give way to weakness, incoordination, seizures, coma, and respiratory arrest (30). Bradycardia may accelerate to tachycardia and tachyarrhythmias.

Common toxic plants in this group include golden chain (*Laburnum anagyroides*), Kentucky coffee tree (*Gymnocladus dioica*), and lupine (*Lupinus* species). Treatment, as with the pyridine-pyrimidine group, is symptomatic only. One must not aggressively treat the initial parasympathomimetic effects,

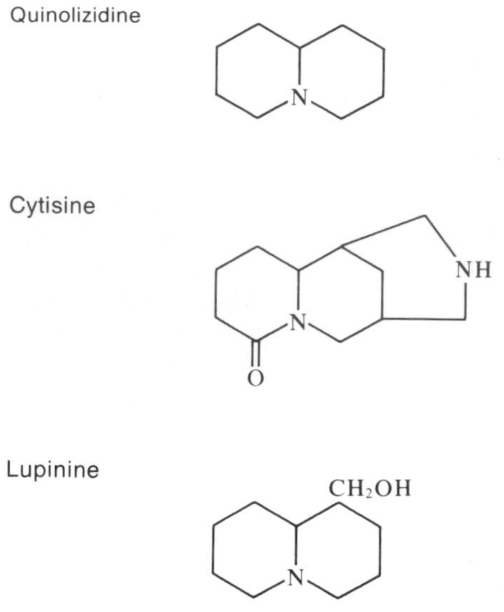

Quinolizidine

Cytisine

Lupinine

FIGURE 6   Quinolizidine alkaloids.

which may unpredictably change to sympathomimetic effects.

Steroid Alkaloids

Steroid alkaloids form the principal toxic component of several common plant poisons: American hellebore (*Veratrum viride*), death camus (*Zigadenus* species), monkshood (*Aconitum* species), and *Solanum* species, including black nightshade (*S. americum*) [not to be confused with deadly nightshade (*Atropa belladonna*)]. Horse nettle (*S. carolinense*) and Jerusalem cherry (*S. pseudocapsicum*) are responsible annually for considerable morbidity and mortality (30).

The plant-derived toxic steroid alkaloids are composed of several distinct glycoalkaloids. Upon hydrolysis, the glycoalkaloids yield a sugar and an alkamine. The intact glycoalkaloid is a severe irritant to the mucous membranes and gastrointestinal tract, while the alkamine accounts for the effects on multiple organ systems, principally cardiovascular and central nervous system. The glycoalkaloids cause burning of the mouth and throat, nausea, vomiting, abdominal pain, and diarrhea. The alkamines' cardiovascular effects include hypotension and bradycardia, probably mediated through stimulation of afferent nerve fibers (the Bezold-Jarisch reflex) (17). The bradycardia can be reversed by atropine, but the hypotension is refractory to vagal blockade, probably due to direct effects on the carotid sinus. Digitalized patients may be at increased risk for cardiac arrhythmias (17). Chest pain, paresthesias, muscle cramps, sweating, salivation, headache, hallucination, and altered mental status have been observed. Pupils may or may not be dilated (30,33).

Veratrum alkaloids are of interest because of their once widespread medicinal use as antihypertensives. Previously restricted to use in preeclampsia, veratrum alkaloids have a narrow therapeutic margin, and severe gastrointestinal side effects preclude their continued use. Plant poisonings are rare.

Death camus and monkshood are especially toxic; the latter, often found as a garden ornamental, may cause death in a few hours by arrhythmias. A fairly constant pattern of mucous membrane and gastrointestinal irritation, followed by progressive systemic symptoms of chest pain, paresthesias, muscle cramps, headache, and altered mental status is observed (30).

The *Solanum* species comprise the largest group of steroid alkaloid-containing plants. Symptomatology depends on the balance between the glycoalkaloid irritant effects and the alkamine systemic effects.

Treatment is supportive. Atropine may be helpful for bradycardia. Spontaneous recovery usually occurs in 2–3 days.

Purine Alkaloids

The purine alkaloids, caffeine and theobromine, are found in a variety of plants. The derivative beverages and stimulants, not the plants themselves, represent a toxic risk. The caffeine content of typical beverages is found in Table 2. A discussion of caffeine and theo-

TABLE 2
Caffeine Content of Common Beverages

Product	Caffeine (mg)
Cup of coffee	75–155
Cup of tea	9–50
12-ounce cola drink	30–65
Cup of cocoa	2–40
1 ounce of milk chocolate	6
Over-the-counter stimulant tablet	100–200

bromine ingestions is beyond the scope of this chapter.

Amine Alkaloids

The amine alkaloids are important for the medicinal derivatives ephedrine and colchicine. Plant ingestions occur from the intentional use of peyote (*Lophophora williamsii*), to be discussed under "Psychoactive Plants," and the accidental ingestion of the garden ornamental autumn crocus, which contains colchicine. Although accidental plant poisoning is rare, a brief discussion of colchicine and its toxicity illustrates its unique biochemical effect. Colchicine directly affects cell mitosis by arresting cell division in metaphase and dissolving the microtubular system necessary for cell division and polymorphonuclear mobility. Acute poisoning may manifest itself after a latent period of several hours. Initial effects are gastrointestinal, with severe abdominal pain, nausea, vomiting, and diarrhea. The diarrhea may induce volume depletion and shock. Terminally, muscular weakness and ascending paralysis culminate in respiratory arrest which may occur in the presence of a clear sensorium.

Treatment is symptomatic and supportive. Parenteral analgesics may be given to relieve severe abdominal pain, keeping in mind that the patient is sensitized to central nervous system depressants by colchicine. Early and vigorous fluid replacement with monitoring of central venous pressure and urine output is essential. Pulmonary function tests should be used to monitor respiratory function, particularly fatigue and ascending paralysis. Assisted ventilation should be employed as long as necessary, for spontaneous resolution may occur. There is a reversible malabsorption of cyanocobalamine (vitamin B_{12}) which is of no clinical significance for acute ingestion.

Glycosides

The glycoside-producing plants constitute a second major group of poisonous principles consisting of cardioactive, cyanogenic, saponin, anthraquinone, and coumarin glycosides. Upon hydrolysis, the glycosides yield sugars (glycones) and aglycone compounds. The aglycone moiety accounts for the major toxic effects of the group.

Cardiac Glycosides

Digitalis is the most famous member of this group, a pharmaceutical of extraordinary medical significance. Its parent plants, *Digitalis purpurea* and *Digitalis lantana,* grow wild in parts of the United States and are cultivated as garden ornamentals and for commercial production. Digitalis is rarely a problem as a plant ingestion, although children have been poisoned by sucking the leaves or seeds. The highly toxic oleander (*Nerium oleander*), which grows in abundance along highways and in gardens, yellow oleander (*Thevetia peruviana*), the principal cause of plant poisoning in Hawaii, and lily of the valley (*Convallaria majalis*), an attractive garden plant, are more commonly implicated in poisoning and death in this country than is foxglove. *N. oleander* is believed to contain at least five potent glycosides, including oleandrin, digitoxigenin, and nerium. Cross-reactivity of the digoxin antibodies between oleander extracts and digoxin in the digoxin radioimmunoassay has been documented (45a).

The clinical signs of acute digitalis ingestion, first described by Withering in 1785, consist of gastrointestinal disturbance with nausea and vomiting, alteration of vision, changes in mental status, and symptomatic bradycardia. The onset of action is well known for certain glycoside preparations, such as digoxin, digitoxin, and ouabain, but may be highly variable following plant ingestions, depending on the species. The clinical signs and symptoms, however, are quite similar for all cardiac glycosides ingested in their natural form.

The aglycones are released by acid and enzymatic hydrolysis. The attached sugar moiety has no inherent cardiac action but may enhance the solubility, absorption, and toxicity of the aglycone.

The mechanism of toxicity is incompletely understood. It is believed to be associated with inhibition of a sodium- and potassium-stimulated, magnesium- and adenosine triphosphate (ATP)-dependent, sodium-potassium transport enzyme complex. As a result of inhibition of this transport mechanism, the extracellular potassium and intracellular sodium concentrations rise. The enzyme complex appears to be protected by high concentrations of potassium and transiently by magnesium. High concentrations of calcium and low serum potassium levels enhance the toxicity of the cardiac glycosides (17).

Cardiac effects on rate and rhythm are potentially the most dangerous sequelae and tend to fall into one or a combination of the following: extrasystoles, tachyarrhythmias, and varying degrees of atrioventricular block.

Central nervous system effects tend to be minimal until late in the course, when dizziness, disorientation, and stupor may occur.

Factors which may enhance systemic and cardiac toxicity include hypokalemia, hypomagnesemia, hypoxia, hypercalcemia, renal insufficiency (most cardiac glycosides are excreted in the urine; a notable exception is the digitalis preparation digitoxin, which is largely metabolized by the liver), hypothyroidism, recent myocardial infarction, reserpine, and old age.

Therapy is directed at removal of the toxin and control of the cardiac arrhythmias. Although gastrointestinal absorption is usually complete in 2 hours, every effort should be made to recover the toxin by the use of gastric lavage, activated charcoal, and cathartics. Cholestyramine may help block enterohepatic recirculation. Dialysis is probably ineffective in removing the highly protein-bound aglycone.

Careful potassium administration is warranted if hypokalemia is accompanied by tachyarrhythmias or extrasystoles. Potassium should not be given with existing atrioventricular block or hyperkalemia. As with digitalis toxicity, parenteral diphenylhydantoin may be effective in controlling arrhythmias from plant cardiac glycoside ingestion. Magnesium infusion has also been advocated, due to its transient protection of the sodium-potassium transport enzyme complex. There are no published reports concerning the effective use of digitalis antibodies used to detoxify nondigitalis cardiac glycosides. Digoxin assays may help to confirm the diagnosis of oleander ingestion in persons not taking digitalis preparations.

Cyanogenic Glycosides

Glycosides which yield hydrocyanic acid upon hydrolysis are known as the *cyanogenic glycosides.* Toxicologically, the only impor-
tant glycoside in this group is amygdalin, abundant in the Rosaceae family. The seeds of apples (*Malus* species) and the pits of the *Prunus* species, including cherries, peaches, plums, and apricots (the commercial source of laetrile), are rich in amygdalin. The black or wild cherry (*P. serotina*) is considered the most dangerous of the group. Deaths have been reported from the ingestion of apricot, apple, cherry, and other fruit seeds (33,53). Poisonings have resulted from milkshakes that included apricot kernels (58). Chronic cyanide toxicity causing goiter, ataxia, and amblyopia has been reported from the ingestion of cassava (*Manihot esculenta*) (58).

After ingestion, hydrocyanic acid is liberated from amygdalin by enzymatic action (β-glucosidase) or mild acid hydrolysis in a two-step process (Figure 7). Cyanide readily combines with the trivalent ion of the cytochrome oxydase in mitochondria, blocking the supply of oxygen for metabolic respiration and causing cytotoxic hypoxia (Figure 8).

The body is normally capable of liberating cytochrome oxidase from the cyanide-cytochrome oxidase complex through the action of the mitochondrial enzyme rhodanese. Rhodanese provides sulfur from endogenous thiosulfate to cyanide, releasing cytochrome oxidase. The resulting thiocyanate ion is relatively nontoxic and readily excreted in the urine. However, the body's ability to handle cyanide is limited by the rate of cleavage of the sulfur-sulfur bond in thiosulfate and the available supply of the thiosulfate, a system which may be rapidly overwhelmed (17).

The clinical signs of cyanide poisoning appear within minutes and include agitation, excitement, gasping, hyperpnea, dyspnea with cyanosis, rapid decline in mental status, and death. There may be a characteristic breath odor of bitter almonds, attributed to the benzaldehyde breakdown product (30).

Treatment must be prompt and is based on the principal that cyanide preferentially combines with methemoglobin, breaking up the dissociable cyanide-cytochrome oxidase complex, liberating the respiratory enzyme (Figure 8). Methemoglobin is rapidly formed upon administration of sodium nitrite and, after combining with cyanide, forms cyanomethemoglobin. Exogenous thiosulfate is then administered to complete the detoxification.

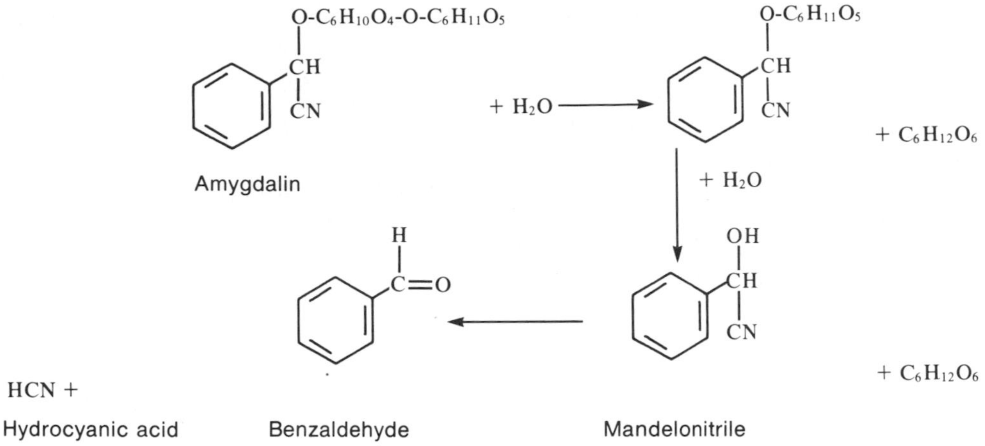

FIGURE 7 Hydrolysis of amygdalin: hydrocyanic acid production.

(1) $\text{Cyt-Fe}^{3+} + \text{HCN} \rightleftharpoons \text{Cyt-FeCN}$

(cytochrome oxidase) + (hydrocyanic acid) ⇌ (cytochrome oxidase-cyanide complex)

(2) $\text{Hb-Fe}^{2+} + \text{NaNO}_2 \rightleftharpoons \text{Hb-Fe}^{3+}$

(hemoglobin) + (nitrites) ⇌ (methemoglobin)

(3) $\text{Hb-Fe}^{3+} + \text{Cyt-FeCN} \rightleftharpoons \text{Hb-FeCN} + \text{Cyt-Fe}^{3+}$

(methemoglobin) + (cytochrome oxidase-cyanide complex) ⇌ (cyanomethemoglobin) + (cytochrome oxidase)

(4) $\text{Na}_2\text{S}_2\text{O}_3 + \text{CN} \underset{\text{SCN}^- \text{ - oxidase}}{\overset{\text{rhodanese}}{\rightleftharpoons}} \text{SCN}^- + \text{Na}_2\text{SO}_3$

(sodium thiosulfate) + (cyanide) ⇌ (thiocyanate) + (sodium sulfate)

FIGURE 8 Principal steps in hydrocyanic acid poisoning and detoxification. (1) Breakdown of cellular respiration resulting from the binding of cyanide to cytochrome oxidase. (2) Conversion of the ferrous (Fe^{2+}) form of hemoglobin to the ferric (Fe^{3+}) form (methemoglobin) by the use of nitrites. (3) Preferential binding of cyanide with methemoglobin, liberating cytochrome oxidase and restoring cellular respiration. (4) Providing exogenous thiosulfate to aid in the formation of nontoxic thiocyanate via the enzyme rhodanese. Thiocyanate is then excreted from the body. The reaction is slowly reversible via the enzyme SCN^--oxidase, so rebound may occur if inadequately treated.

The oxygen-carrying capacity of blood is not affected by cyanide, and the Po_2 may remain normal in the face of marked cyanosis. Oxygen should be administered, however, because cellular hypoxia and the induced methemoglobinemia shift the oxygen-dissociation curve to the left, further impairing cellular oxygen delivery (17).

The cyanide treatment kit by Eli Lilly and Company should be available in all primary care centers and emergency departments. Treatment begins with inhalation of vials of amyl nitrite while the intravenous line is being placed. Sodium nitrite in a 3% solution is given intravenously based on hemoglobin and weight. Methemoglobin levels and clinical response should be monitored to prevent treatment excess.

In the face of persistent cyanosis, a methemoglobin level should be obtained. A solution of 1% methylene blue should be administered by slow intravenous infusion, 0.2 ml/kg, in those patients with methemoglobin levels greater than 30% (16).

Saponin Glycosides

The saponin glycosides are found throughout the plant kingdom, contained within English ivy (*Hedera helix*), pokeweed (*Phytolacca americana*), tung tree (*Aleurites* species), ginseng (*Panax ginseng*), and licorice (*Glycyrrhiza glabra*). Following hydrolysis, saponin glycosides yield an aglycone (sapogenin), which is responsible for the toxicity, and a sugar, usually glucose, galactose, rhamnose, or arabinose, which may enhance the solubility and absorption of the aglycone (30).

Saponins may induce lysis of erythrocytes, causing hemolytic anemia. In addition, they are gastrointestinal irritants which appear to facilitate their own intestinal absorption. Most saponins are found in combination with other toxins, including gastrointestinal irritants and phytotoxins, which contribute to a widely varying clinical picture.

A unique feature of licorice is that chronic excessive ingestion can cause a type of pseudoaldosteronism, with hypertension and hypokalemic alkalosis. Glycyrrhizinic acid may mimic the action of aldosterone, leading to the retention of sodium and free water and the excretion of potassium. Heart failure and cardiac arrest have been attributed to licorice root ingestion (58).

Treatment consists of removing the offending agent from the diet.

Anthraquinone Glycosides

The aglycone moiety of this group is anthraquinone, known to have cathartic activity. Buckthorn (*Rhamnus frangula*) is the only significant toxin in natural form, although herbal teas that contain senna leaves, flowers and bark (*Cassia senna*), aloe leaves (*Aloe barbadensis*), and buckthorn bark have caused severe diarrhea (58).

Treatment is supportive, emphasizing adequate volume and electrolyte replacement.

Coumarin Glycosides

Coumarin glycosides act much the same as the irritant glycoalkaloids of the steroid-alkaloid group. The only plant of significance is the daphne (*Daphne mezereum*), with its fragrant, succulent berries. The fruits contain a coumarin glycoside and a diterpene mezerein that cause burning of the mucous membranes, with swelling of the tongue and lips. Severe gastroenteritis with gastrointestinal bleeding may eventuate in progressive weakness, paralysis, seizures, and coma. Blisters will form if the berries are rubbed on the skin (1).

The widely cultivated daphne represents a significant risk to curious children, in whom only a few ingested berries may be lethal (33).

No antidote is known; treatment is supportive.

Oxalates

Oxalates occur naturally in plants in the form of soluble (sodium and potassium) or insoluble (calcium) oxalates or acid oxalates (Figure 9). Their toxicity is related to their corrosive effects and their ability to bind serum calcium, with resultant hypocalcemia. Insoluble calcium oxalate crystals (raphides) are abundant in the leaves of common houseplants (*Dieffenbachia* species) and *Caladium* species. Biting into the leaves induces a mechanical and chemical injury, with severe burning of the mouth and throat and occasional marked

Oxalic acid

COOH
|
COOH

Potassium oxalate

COOK
|
COOH

Sodium oxalate

COONa
|
COONa

FIGURE 9 Oxalates.

swelling of the lips, mouth, and tongue. Airway obstruction may result (3).

Soluble oxalates found in the leaves of the common garden plant rhubarb (*Rheum rhaponticum*) are rapidly absorbed through the gastrointestinal tract and cause a prompt drop in the serum ionized calcium level. There appears to be a generalized disturbance of monovalent and divalent cation metabolism. Weakness, tetany, hypotension, and seizures may develop.

Acute renal failure may occur if calcium oxalate precipitates in the urine and obstructs the renal tubules. Adjacent epithelial cells become necrotic on contact with the precipitate. Ureteral calculi may be formed (30).

Treatment consists of removal of stomach contents and gastric lavage with a 0.15% calcium hydroxide solution to precipitate the soluble oxalates. Sodium bicarbonate should not be used in the lavage fluid, due to formation of sodium oxalate, a toxic compound which may be rapidly absorbed.

The resulting hypocalcemia is often refractory to parenteral calcium gluconate (30). However, intravenous calcium gluconate is indicated in the face of tetany, a prolonged QT interval on an electrocardiogram, or depressed serum ionized calcium levels. From 10 to 20 ml of 10% calcium gluconate should be given intravenously over 10–15 minutes, followed by additional doses titrated to blood levels and symptoms.

Every effort should be made to maintain a brisk diuresis to prevent the deposition of calcium oxalate crystals in the renal tubules.

Topical measures for the severe burning associated with oral-pharyngeal contact include cold compresses and a mixture of 2% viscous lidocaine (Xylocaine) and diphenhydramine elixir.

Resins

Resins are a group of highly toxic compounds of diverse chemical and plant origin. They are united by their physical characteristics of insolubility in water, absence of nitrogen, and solid or semisolid state upon extraction at room temperature.

Resins are usually found in a mixture with other compounds, such as volatile (essential) oils (oleoresins), gums (gum resins), and sugars (glycoresins) (30).

Water hemlock (*Cicuta maculata*) and chinaberry (*Melia azedarach*) are two of the most toxic resin-containing plants. *Cicuta* contains an unsaturated aliphatic alcohol called cicutoxin. Each has a characteristic and dramatic physiologic action, starting in 15 to 60 minutes with initial muscarinic effects of salivation, abdominal pain, vomiting, and diarrhea, followed by central nervous system depression and respiratory distress. Seizures may be a prominent feature of water hemlock poisonings.

Treatment is symptomatic and supportive. Parenteral short-acting barbiturates are recommended for control of seizures, although no good evidence exists to favor their use over diazepam or phenytoin (3,41). Bowel wall edema and gastrointestinal fluid losses from cicutoxin may require vigorous fluid replacement to maintain adequate blood pressure (2).

PHYTOTOXINS

Phytotoxins are among the most toxic substances of plant origin, ranking with the toxins of *Clostridium tetani* and *botulinum* and *Corynebacterium diphtheriae* (60). It is estimated that 1 kg of ricin, the phytotoxin of the castor bean, could kill more than 3.6 million people (4).

Composed of large protein molecules, phytotoxins resemble bacterial toxins in structure and in their ability to act as antigens, eliciting an antibody response. Unlike bacterial toxins, phytotoxins are readily absorbed in the gastrointestinal tract. The true mechanism of their toxicity is unknown, although it has been suggested that they function as proteolytic enzymes (30).

The phytotoxins are grouped exclusively in the families Fabacae, including jequirty bean (*Abrus precatorius*) and Euphorbiaceae, including castor bean (*Ricinus communis*) and purging nut (*Jatropha curcas*). Poisoning results from eating or chewing on the nut or seed. Castor oil, made from pressing castor beans at temperatures less than 50°F, is a nontoxic cathartic (57).

Local effects are prompt and include burning of the mouth and throat with abdominal pain. Hours later, nausea, vomiting, diarrhea, and hemorrhagic gastritis occur. The seeds are highly allergenic and may cause urticaria, dermatitis, or anaphylaxis secondary to contact alone (37). Systemic effects may be delayed as much as a day or more, and are principally cardiac and central nervous system in origin. Tachyarrhythmias and hypotension may be features of the clinical course. Alterations in mental status are characterized by stupor and coma. Seizures may occur. Terminally, liver enzyme abnormalities may arise, indicating hepatic necrosis and liver failure (45). Although the mechanism is unknown, renal failure is often present (3,33).

Treatment is supportive. Every effort should be made to remove the seeds from the stomach. If swallowed intact, the seeds are often harmless, due to their thick coat, which allows them to pass undigested. It has been suggested that alkalinization of the urine may help promote excretion of the toxin, although this is anecdotal advice (3).

IRRITANT AND ESSENTIAL OILS

Irritant oils are a problem only to livestock and to those who overindulge at the delicatessen. Various mustards (*Brassica* species), horseradish (*Amoracia lapathifolia*), and pro-

Salicylic acid

Methyl salicylate

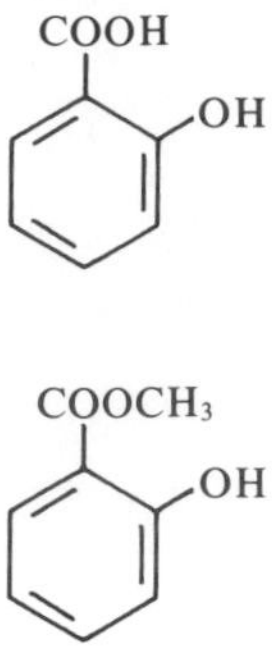

FIGURE 10   Salicylates.

toanemonin from the buttercup family (*Ranunculaceae*) induce gastroenteritis.

Essential oils, often found in combination with resins (oleoresins), are extracted commercially for use as rubifacients, salves, and liniments. Essential oils are mentioned here to warn of their extreme toxicity and to condemn their use as folk medicines.

Methyl salicylate, or wintergreen, is the methyl ester form of salicylic acid, derived from *Gaultheria procumbens* (Figure 10). It was widely used as an antirheumatic agent in the nineteenth century but fell into disfavor because of its extreme side effects and the evolution of the more effective acetysalicylic acid. Poisoning now occurs most often in children who are attracted to the color, smell, and flavor of the wintergreen oil. In addition to the usual symptoms of salicylism, high doses may cause central nervous system excitation, hyperventilation, and hyperthermia.

Pulegone, an essential oil, is the primary component in pennyroyal oil derived from *Hedeoma pulegioides*. As an herbal medicine, it is available as an over-the-counter abortifacient. The author observed a patient in the emergency department who ingested 1 ounce of pennyroyal oil. Initial signs of urticaria, bronchospasm, and delirium progressed to disseminated intravascular coagulation, hepatic necrosis and death within 4 days (56).

ELEMENT AND NITRATE ABSORPTION

Many plants absorb or accumulate metallic compounds (selenium, molybdenum, arsenic, lead, cadmium), nitrites, and nitrates. They are of little importance in humans and constitute a danger only to grazing livestock.

HYPOGLYCEMIC AGENTS

Eating the unripe Caribbean akee fruit produces a unique metabolic effect. Hypoglycin A, the toxic component, blocks hepatic gluconeogenesis, resulting in hypoglycemia. It also interferes with long-chain fatty acid oxidation (28). The latter is mediated by the metabolite MCPA (methylenecyclopropylacetyl-coenzyme A) and results in the accumulation of short-chain fatty acids, which is thought to contribute to the observed central nervous system depression (8).

Vomiting and mental status depression are the principal clinical features; this accounts for the early designation *Jamaican vomiting sickness* (8,43). Onset begins promptly after ingestion, and deaths are frequent without adequate supportive care. Mortality ranges from 40 to 80%.

Treatment consists of activated charcoal to adsorb the toxin, intravenous fluid replacement, frequent blood glucose determinations, and serum electrolyte measurements. Two 50 ml boluses of 50% dextrose are given, followed by a 10% dextrose infusion until repeated blood glucose evaluations show normalization. Glycine has recently been advocated as effective in treating akee poisoning (55). The mechanism of action is thought to be inhibition of the long-chain fatty acid oxidation blockade. Glycine therapy must be considered experimental at this time.

PSYCHOACTIVE PLANTS

In this section, a few common plants that are ingested for intentional mood alteration are mentioned.

Scopolamine-rich plants of the tropane alkaloid group, including henbane (*Hyosyamus niger*), Jimson weed, (*Datura stramonium*), trumpet lilly (*Datura arborea*) and mandrake (*Mandragora officinatum*), have depressant and/or euphoric effects. A tea may be made from leaves, flowers, or roots. Eating the flowers and seeds directly may induce similar effects, occasionally resulting in anticholinergic crisis (see the section on tropane alkaloids) (38,39,51).

Ingestion of large amounts of the common household spice, nutmeg (*Myristica fragrans*), may mimic the anticholinergic crisis seen with tropane alkaloids. Dry mouth, thirst, tachycardia, and hot, dry skin are typical clinical signs. Ten grams or more will produce a brief euphoria followed by a floating, dreamlike sensation, hallucinations, and drowsiness. The psychoactive component is thought to be the aromatic fraction containing myristicin, elemicin, and safrole (33).

Marijuana (*Cannabis sativa*) is one of the few psychoactive plants that possess nitrogen-free compounds. The active ingredients are derivatives of tetrahydrocannabinol (THC). L-Δ ^{9}Tetrahydrocannibol (Δ ^{9}-TCH) is believed to be the most psychoactive isomer (Figure 11). Much is known about the behavioral, systemic, and neurophysiologic effects of Δ ^{9}-THC. The drug is found in abundance in the flowering tops, or "buds," of the plant. The THC concentration may range from less than 1% in homegrown varieties, with mild mood-altering qualities, to 10% in Hawaiian, South American, and Southeast Asian varieties, with powerful psychoactive and hallucinatory effects. This depends on the growing season, climate, soil, cultivation, and other agricultural factors.

THC is easily volatilized and may be inhaled with prompt effect. The drug may also be ingested, with a delay in effect of 30–40 minutes. The effective dose upon smoking is 200–250 μg/kg and on ingestion is 300–480 μg/kg (33, p. 427).

THC is known to alter brain levels of 5-hydroxytryptamine (serotonin) and norepinephrine, although the true mechanism of its toxicity is unknown.

Observed effects are mood alteration with either euphoria or depression, a sense of dissociation from one's surroundings, and altered perceptions of time and distance, combined with atropinelike effects of dry mouth, thirst, and tachycardia. Toxic psychosis and panic reactions are occasionally seen, probably representing the major known risks. Clinical cases of pulmonary aspergillosis have been ascribed to smoking contaminated marijuana (27).

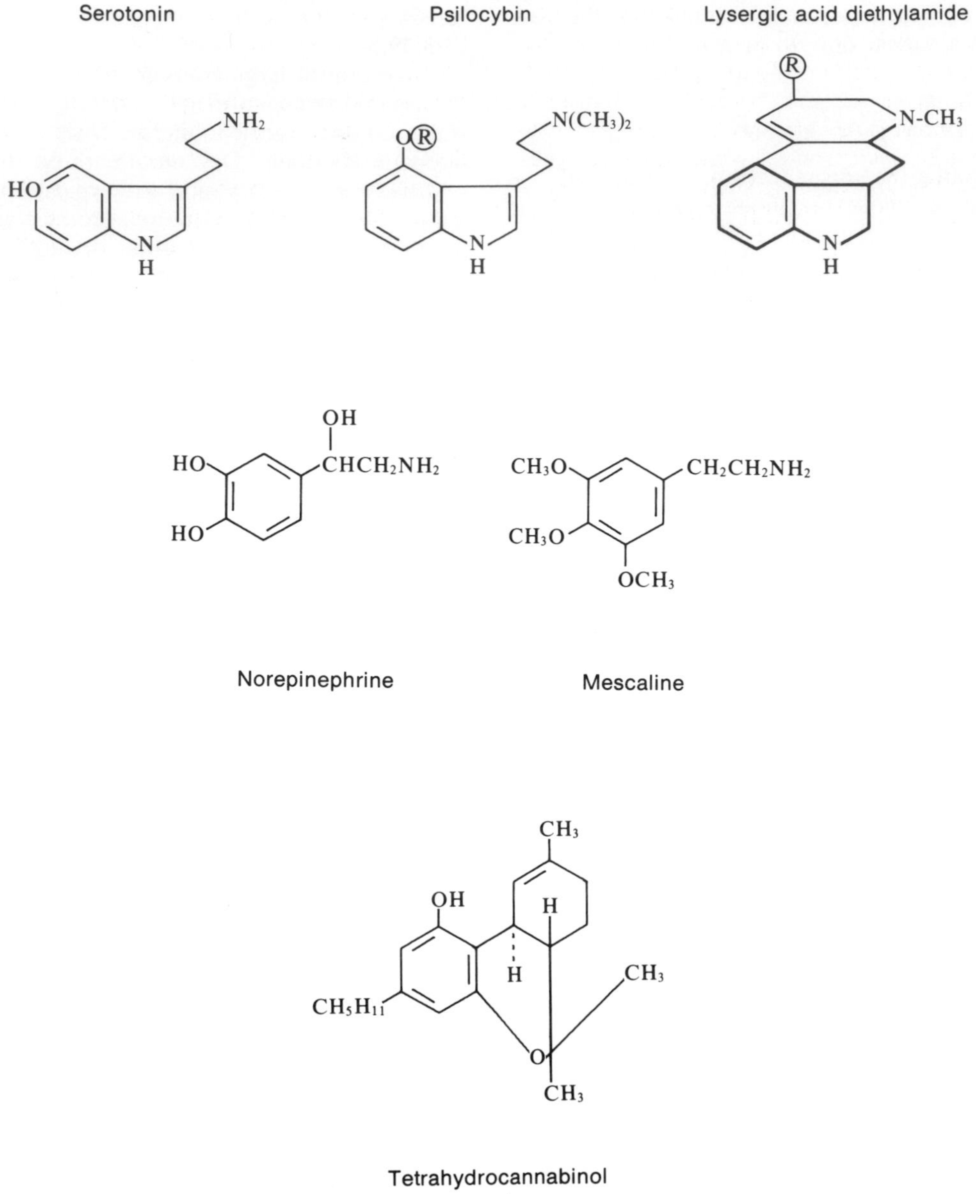

Serotonin   Psilocybin   Lysergic acid diethylamide

Norepinephrine   Mescaline

Tetrahydrocannabinol

FIGURE 11 Chemical similarities between hallucinogens and neurotransmitters.

Striking structural similarities exist between the most potent psychoactive plant compounds and biochemically important neurotransmitters. Chemical relationships exist between serotonin, psilocybin (*Psilocybe* species), and *d*-lysergic acid diethylamide (*d*-LSD) (Figure 11) (54). LSD is synthesized from ergometrine, one of the ergot alkaloids derived from *Claviceps purpurea.*

A less powerful hallucinogen which occurs naturally in the seeds of the morning glory (*Ipomoea violacea*) is ergine, or *d*-lysergic acid amide. About 300 seeds, or enough to fill a cupped hand, are the equivalent of 200–300 μg of *d*-LSD, with similar systemic and hallucinatory effects.

Another striking chemical similarity exists between the phenylethylamine derivative mescaline (*Lophora williamsii*) and the neurotransmitter norepinephrine (Figure 11). At a dose of about 5 mg/kg, mescaline induces sympathomimetic effects, followed by marked visual hallucinations. Thus, those compounds which cause marked perceptual alterations tend to resemble structurally important neurohumoral substances, while non-nitrogen–containing derivatives, such as the tropane alkaloids and Δ ⁹-THC (Figure 11), have less specific depressant or euphoric effects.

Extensive discussions of psychoactive plants may be found in the work of Schultes and Hofmann (54).

Mushrooms: The Toxic Principles

For centuries, mushrooms have provided delicacies for the gourmet's table and poisons for the careless gatherer. It is generally believed that most toadstools (from the German *todesstühl,* or death's stool) are poisonous. Fortunately, few species are highly toxic and a single genus, *Amanita,* accounts for 90–95% of all deaths from mushroom ingestion (36). However, would-be mycologists armed with field guides and a sense of adventure are finding and eating toxic species with increasing frequency. Many poisonous species are mistaken for look-alike edibles (Table 3). From 1957 to 1964, there were 30 deaths from mushroom ingestions in the United States. From 1964 to 1974 there were 57 hospitalizations and eight deaths in California alone (5). A tabulation of case reports for 1979 at the Rocky Mountain Poison Center shows 405 telephone

TABLE 3
Poisonous Mushrooms Resembling Edible Species

Poisonous	*Edibles*
Cyclopeptides	
Amanita phalloides	*Amanita fulva*
	Agaricus spp.
	Lepiota procera
	Trichomola flavovirens
Amanita verna/verosa group	*Amanita vaginata*
	Agaricus spp.
Amanita brunnescens	*Amanita rubescens*
Galerina autmnalis	*Pholiota mutabilis*
Galerina marginata	*Armillariella mellea*
Monomethylhydrazine	
Gyromitra esculenta	*Morchella esculenta*
Coprine	
Coprinus atramentarius	*Coprinus micaceus*
Muscarine	
Clitocybe dealbata	*Marasmius oreades*
Inocybe spp.	*Marasmius oreades*
Ibotenic acid/muscimol	
Amanita muscaria	*Amanita caesarea*
	Amanita rubescens
Amanita pantherina	*Amanita rubescens*
Psilocybin	
Panaeolus foeniscii	*Psathyrella candolleana*
	Agrocybe pediades
Panaeolus spp.	*Coprinus* spp.
Gastrointestinal irritants	
Chlorophyllum molybdites	*Lepiota* spp.
	Leucoagaricus rachodes
	Leucoagaricus procerus

Source: Adapted with permission from Rumack, B. H., Salzman, E., eds., *Mushroom Poisoning: Diagnosis and Treatment.* CRC Press, Inc., West Palm Beach, Florida, 1978, pp. 208–9. © The Chemical Rubber Co., CRC Press, Inc.

consultations for mushroom ingestions (48).

This section focuses upon the toxicology of the poisonous mushroom species and principles of treatment, including controversies in management. Rudiments of mushroom recognition are offered so that the primary care physician will understand the importance of obtaining adequate specimens. Excellent discussions of mushroom identification may be found in Miller's *Mushrooms of North America,* Lincoff's *The Audubon Society Field Guide to North American Mushrooms,* and Rumack and Salzman's *Mushroom Poisoning, Diagnosis and Treatment,* cited in the references (34a,40a,52).

Mushrooms are plant fungi (*Eumycophyta*). Major poisonous species are found in two families: Basidiomycetes and Ascomycetes. Possessing no chlorophyll, they must live on decayed organic matter. Some exist as saprophytes or parasites, while others form a unique and mutually beneficial relationship with higher plants called a mycorrhiza.

The mushroom we see is only the reproductive tip of an extensive network of hyphae, or filaments, that permeate the soil. Collectively, the hyphal network is called the *mycelium,* which often exists in a symbiotic relationship with the ultimate rootlets of trees, to form a joint structure, the mycorrhiza.

Mycelia may live for many years, extending for hundreds of feet in search of organic nutrients. The reproductive fruit or mushroom emerges from a small clump of hyphae, growing to form a fleshy button. In the *Amanitas,* as the fruit grows it bursts from a thick membrane called the *universal veil,* leaving a characteristic jagged cup, or volva, at the base of the stalk or stipe. (Figure 12). A second membrane, the *partial veil,* protects the gills on the underside of the cap, or pilus, and later peels away to form a ringlike skirt, or annulus. In the *Basidiomycetes,* the surfaces of the gills are covered with spore-forming cells called the *basidia.* One to four spores are produced on each basidium. The counterpart of the basidium in the *Ascomycetes* is the *ascus,* a sacklike cell which extrudes spores through a small lid, or operculum.

Spores vary in size and shape but are usually unicellular, 5–10 μm in length. They show species variation in color and in their reaction with a chemical solution of iodine and chloral hydrate, called *Melzer's reagent,* which aids in species identification. Spores which turn blue in this reagent are called *amyloid,* indicating the presence of certain starch components in their walls. Unreactive spores are called *nonamyloid.*

The natural color of the spores may be determined by the use of a spore print. The print is made by cutting the stipe close to the cap and resting the cap on a white sheet of paper for several hours. The spores left on the paper are a characteristic color, ranging from white to pink or green.

Mature mushrooms eject spores which are dispersed by the wind to establish new mycelium. Some species form exclusive mycorrhizal associations with certain tree species. Other mushrooms, such as the *Amanitas,* are not so selective and can be found among both hardwoods and firs.

The mycologist has several ways to identify a particular mushroom species: size, shape, and color of the fruit, mycorrhizal associations, season of appearance, volva, annulus, gills, the spore color, and Melzer's reaction. Often, a microscopic examination is essential to distinguish the toxic species, particularly if the fruit is unavailable and one has only a gastric aspirate. Identifiable spores, hyphal cells, and the presence of basidia or asci may be found in the gastric aspirate or prepared fresh specimens. Recently, thin-layer chromatography has emerged as the gold standard for the identification of toxic species, with standardized "prints" available for comparison.

To obtain the best specimen for mycologic identification, provide as many entire specimens as possible. One must exercise extreme caution in their handling, taking care not to brush off identifying features such as scales, volva, or annulus. A record is kept of the initial color and whether color change or "bruising" occurs with handling. The specimen is placed in a paper bag (not plastic) and refrigerated. Refrigerated samples of vomitus or gastric lavage fluid are held for spore identification.

The toxic species are generally divided into seven groups, based on the onset of symptoms, and the chemistry and qualities of the toxins (Tables 4, 5). It is therefore essential to obtain an accurate history, as well as an adequate

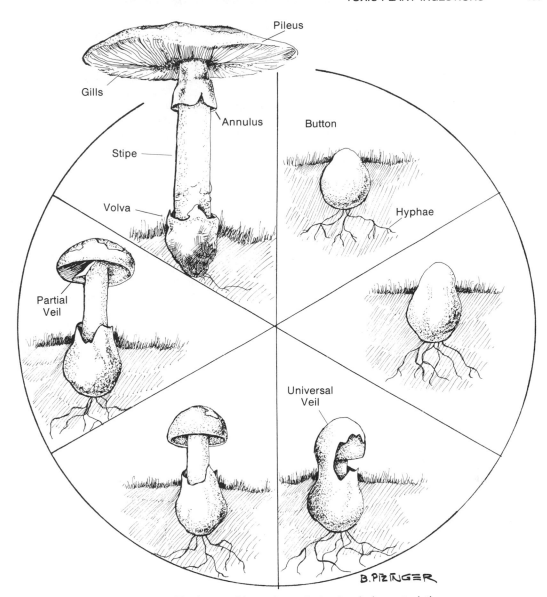

FIGURE 12 Mushroom life cycle and structural characteristics.

specimen. Important facts to be obtained include the number and kind of mushrooms consumed, where they were found, the length of time and method of storage before eating, how the mushrooms were cooked or prepared, when they were eaten, the time of onset of symptoms, and the consumption of alcohol within 1 day of eating the mushrooms.

GROUP I—THE DEADLY CYCLOPEPTIDES

Group I, the deadly cyclopeptides, includes species of the genera *Amanita* and *Galerina*.

The group has generated a large share of the mushroom literature, due to its extraordinary toxicity and controversies about chemical structure and clinical management.

Lynen and U. Wielend in 1937 first isolated a toxic substance from *Amanita,* which they named *phalloiden.* Later, H. Wielend and Hallermayer discovered a more toxic constituent, which they named *amanitin.* Subsequent investigation by T. Wielend and associates succeeded in fractionating phalloiden into six cyclopeptides, called *phallotoxins,* and amani-

TABLE 4
Mushrooms: Toxic Principles

Genus and Species	Distribution[a]	Season[a]	Pileus	Spore Print	Amyloid Reaction[a]
Group I. Cyclopeptide Poisoning					
Amanita					
A. bisporigera	E. NA, Pac. Coast (rare)	Sp., S., F.	White	White	Positive
A. virosa (destroying angel)	E. NA, Pac. Coast (rare)	Sp., S., F.	White	White	Positive
A. verna (death angel)	E. NA, Pac. Coast (rare)	Sp., S., F.	White	White	Positive
A. phalloides (death cap)	Rare—E. NA, PNW, Pac. Coast	S., F.	Pale yellow green to green	White	Positive
A. brunnescens	E. NA	S., F.	Brown with white margin	White	Positive
A. pantherina (see also Group V)	Common; widely, esp. RM, PNW	Sp., S., F.	Light brown to brown with buff or yellowish margin	White	Negative
Galerina					
G. autumnalis	Common, widely	Late F., early Sp.	Dark brown to leathery light tan	Rust brown	Negative
G. venenata	Rare—PNW	Late F., W.	Cinnamon brown	Rust Brown	Negative
Group II. Monomethylhydrazine Poisoning					
Gyromitra					
G. californica	Common, RM, PNW, PSW	Early Sp.	Tan to red-brown	Brown	Negative
G. brunnea	Common, E. NA	Early Sp.	Chocolate brown, white beneath	Brown	Negative
G. esculenta	Common, widely, esp. RM, PNW	Late Sp.	Brown to red-brown	Brown	Negative
Group III. Disulfiramlike Poisoning					
Coprinus					
C. atramentarius	Common, widely	S., F.	Light gray-brown (exhibits deliquescence)	Black	Negative
Group IV. Muscarine Poisoning					
Inocybe					
I. napipes	Common, widely, woodlands	S., F.	Brown to dark brown	Brown	Negative
I. fastigiata					
I. patouillardic					
I. interaria					
I. lanuginose					
I. geophylla			White to lilac	Clay brown	Negative
Clitocybe					
C. dealbata	Common, widely	S., F.	Dull white	White	Negative
C. rivulosa					
C. trunicola					
Paneolus					
P. separatus	Common, widely	Sp., S. F.	Light gray to dull gray-white	Black	Negative

(Continued)

TABLE 4 (*Continued*)

Genus and Species	Distribution[a]	Season[a]	Pileus	Spore Print	Amyloid Reaction[a]
Gymnopilus					
G. spectabilis also:	Common, widely	Sp., S., F., early W.	Buff yellow to yellow-orange	Rusty orange	Negative
G. luteus					
G. decurrens					
G. valipides					
G. aeruginosus					
G. viridans also reported:					
G. stropharia					
G. copelandia					
G. conocyte					
G. pholiotina					

Group V. Isoxazole Derivatives: Ibotenic Acid and Muscimol Poisoning

Genus and Species	Distribution[a]	Season[a]	Pileus	Spore Print	Amyloid Reaction[a]
Amanita					
A. muscaria	Common, widely, esp. N. Eng., Pac. Coast, RM	Sp., S., F.	Orange or straw yellow (N. Eng.) to bright red (Pac. Coast) (often with pileal warts)	White	Negative
A. pantherina	Common, widely, esp. RM, PNW	Sp., S., F.	Light brown to brown with buff or yellowish-white margin	White	Negative

Group VI. Hallucinogens

Genus and Species	Distribution[a]	Season[a]	Pileus	Spore Print	Amyloid Reaction[a]
Psilocybe*					
P. cubensis	Rare, Florida	Late W. to F.	Whitish to pale yellow	Purple-brown	Negative
P. balocystis	Oregon, Washington	W. to F.		Purple-brown	Negative
P. semilanceata	PNW, Britain	F., W.	Buff-gray to gray-green	Purple-brown	Negative
P. stuntzii also:	PNW	F., W.	Brown to ochre	Dark-purple	Negative
P. venenosus					
P. mexicana					
P. quebecensis					

* (The stalks of hallucinogenic *Psilocybe* species stain blue with bruising)

Genus and Species	Distribution[a]	Season[a]	Pileus	Spore Print	Amyloid Reaction[a]
Paneolus					
P. campanulatus	Common, widely	Sp., S., F.	Gray, speckled dark purple-brown	Black	Negative
P. foenisecii	Common, widely	Sp., S., F.	Dark brown or reddish brown to tan or light gray-brown	Purple-brown	Negative

Group VII. Gastrointestinal Irritants

Genus and Species	Distribution[a]	Season[a]	Pileus	Spore Print	Amyloid Reaction[a]
Agaricus					
A. hondensis	Common, widely	S., F.	White-brown, gray-brown	Chocolate brown	Negative

(*Continued*)

TABLE 4 (*Continued*)

Genus and Species	Distribution[a]	Season[a]	Pileus	Spore Print	Amyloid Reaction[a]
Boletus					
B. luridus	Rare, N.E., S.E., Mid W.	S., F.	Mixed, many colors	Olive-brown	Negative
B. eastwoodiae	Rare, Pac. Coast	F.	Dark to red-brown	Olive-brown	Negative
B. satanas	Rare, Pac. Coast		Olive, buff	Olive-brown	Negative
B. sensibilis				Olive-brown	Negative
Chlorophyllum					
C. molybdites	Common, widely	Sp., S., F.	White with buff scales	Green	Negative
Entoloma					
E. lividum	Common, widely	S., F.	Tan	Salmon-pink	Negative
Gomphus					
G. floccosus	Common, widely			Smoky-gray to black	Negative
Hebeloma					
H. crustuliniforme	Rare, widely	F.	Brown to cream at margin	Yellow to olive-brown	Negative
H. mesophaeum	Common, widely	Sp., S., F.	Brown	Yellow to olive-brown	Negative
Lactarius species*	Common, widely	Sp., S., F.	Variable	White to yellow	Positive

* (Beware of all *Lactarius* species that stain lilac when bruised and emit latex from the gills.)

Genus and Species	Distribution[a]	Season[a]	Pileus	Spore Print	Amyloid Reaction[a]
Marasmius					
M. ureus	Common, widely	S., F.		White	Negative
Naematoloma					
N. fasciculare	Common, esp. PNW, S.E.	Sp., F., W.	Yellow to orange-yellow	Purple-brown	Negative
Omphalatus					
O. olearius	E. NA, S. U.S., Pac. Coast	S., F.	Yellow-orange to bright orange	White	Negative
Paxillus					
P. involutus	Common, widely	S., F.	Red-brown	Clay-brown, yellow-brown	Negative
Ramaria (coral fungus)					
R. formosa	Common, widely	F., W.	Pink to light orange (coral branches)	Red-brown	Negative
Rhodophyllus (*R. sinuatus;* see *Entoloma lividum*—same species)					
Russula					
R. emetica	Common, widely	S., F.	Bright red	White	Negative
R. densifolia	Common, widely, esp. E. NA	S., F.	White to gray	White	Positive

(*Continued*)

TABLE 4 (*Continued*)

Genus and Species	Distribution[a]	Season[a]	Pileus	Spore Print	Amyloid Reaction[a]
Scleroderma (puffball fungi) species	Common, esp. E. NA	S., F.	Gleba (spore mass) purple to purple-brown; surface tan to white	Brown	Negative
Tricholoma species	Common, widely, esp. N.E., RM, PNW, and Mid W	F.	Gray-brown	White	Negative

[a] Key:
E. NA, Eastern North America
Mid W, Middle Western States
N. Eng., New England
N.E., Northeastern States
Pac. Coast, Pacific Coast
PNW, Pacific North West
RM, Rocky Mountain States
S.E., Southeastern States
Widely, Distributed throughout North America
Common, Found in abundance during the fruiting season
Sp., Spring
S., Summer
F., Fall
W., Winter
Positive, Spores turn blue in Melzer's reagent
Negative, Spores do not turn blue in Melzer's reagent

tin into five or more compounds, called *amatoxins* (63).

The phallotoxins have been found experimentally to have profound effects on liver cell morphology, with disruption of plasma membranes, massive efflux of calcium and potassium ions, and lysosomal rupture. However, a number of studies indicate that the phallotoxins are nontoxic by the oral route and play no role in human poisoning (36,52).

The amatoxins are felt to be the lethal component of the *Amanita* and *Galerina* species and account for the rapid onset of hepatic cellular destruction after ingestion. The exact mechanism of hepatic injury is unclear, although inhibition of RNA polymerase has been postulated (52). α-Amanita, one of the five amatoxins, is filtered in the kidney by the glomerulus and causes direct damage to the proximal tubules, allowing reabsorption of the toxin. The amount of urinary excretion in humans is unknown, although in dogs, 85% of the administered dose of α-amanita is found in the urine after 6 hours (21).

It is not known if amatoxins undergo bio-transformation or if major bioactive metabolites exist. Though amatoxins are excreted in bile, enterohepatic circulation reduces their gastrointestinal excretion (21, 52).

Cooking, steaming, and drying do not materially affect the toxins of *Amanita* or *Galerina*.

A helpful but not completely reliable field method for detecting amatoxins is called the *Meixner spot test.* A piece of the fruit is rubbed on newsprint, allowed to dry, and 1 drop of 36–38% HCl in water is applied. Formation of blue color indicates the presence of amatoxin.

Clinical Picture

The classic clinical picture of *Amanita* poisoning includes the delayed (6–12 hours) onset of severe gastrointestinal symptoms leading to a latent period of well-being, followed in 24–48 hours by abdominal pain, hepatic necrosis, renal failure, and altered mental status. Mortality ranges from 50 to 90%, usually secondary to hepatic and/or renal failure (5,12).

Initial fluid and electrolyte losses may be

TABLE 5
Mushroom Poisoning: Symptoms and Treatment

Group	Clinical Features	Treatment
Group I: cyclopeptide poisoning	Delayed symptoms, 6–12 hours (range 2–36 hours) Abdominal pain Nausea, vomiting Diarrhea (may be bloody) Hypotension Fever Tachycardia	Removal and adsorption of toxin Activated charcoal slurry 100 g in 8 ounces of water orally (PO) or via nasogastric (NG) tube Repeat charcoal slurry every 6 hours
	Variable latent period, 24–48 hours postingestion Abnormal liver function studies Elevated blood urea nitrogen (BUN), creatinine	Baseline laboratory values Urinalysis Complete blood count (CBC) with platelet count BUN, creatinine Glucose Electrolytes Liver function tests—serum glutamic-oxaloacetic transaminase (SGOT), serum glutamic-pyruvic transaminase (SGPT), alkaline phosphate, and bilirubin Serum protein and albumin Amylase Prothrombin time (PT), partial thromboplastin time (PTT), fibrinogen level Extra red-top tube for radioimmunoassay (RIA) Emesis for spore analysis Repeat daily: Random blood sugar every 6 hours with Dextrostix Clotting studies if indicated LFTs Monitor: Input and output Central venous pressure (CVP) if indicated
	Terminal phase Increase in abdominal pain Adynamic ileus Altered mental status Jaundice Coma, seizures Marked elevation of liver function studies, bilirubin Prolonged PT, PTT Renal failure Death from renal or hepatic failure (Recovery in more than 60% of cases)	Supportive treatment Hepatic failure: Lactulose, 2–3 tablespoons PO or via NG tube, qid Restrict dietary protein to <20 g/day Add thiamine, 100 mg first day and multivitamins every day (qd) to intravenous (IV) fluid Give vitamin K and fresh frozen plasma as indicated Renal failure Peritoneal dialysis or hemodialysis, as indicated Charcoal hemoperfusion not recommended

(Continued)

TABLE 5 (*Continued*)

Group	Clinical Features	Treatment
Group I (*cont.*)		Thioctic acid 　Administer under experimental protocol only; notify Regional Poison Control Center
Group II: 　monomethylhydrazine poisoning	Delayed symptoms, 6–12 hours (range 2–24 hours) 　Bloating, cramping, abdominal pain 　Nausea, vomiting 　Watery diarrhea (may be absent) 　Headache 　Weakness 　Cyanosis	Removal and adsorption of toxin 　Activated charcoal slurry: 100 g in 8 ounces of water PO or via NG tube 　Gastric lavage if no emesis
	Usually self-limited, with resolution in 2–6 days	Baseline laboratory values 　Urinalysis; urine for free hemoglobin 　CBC 　LFTs 　Electrolytes 　Glucose 　BUN 　Creatinine 　Serum for free hemoglobin, haptoglobin If cyanotic: 　Methemoglobin level
	Progression of illness 　Persistent abdominal pain 　Jaundice 　Hepatomegaly 　Fever 　Altered mental status 　Fatalities rare—delayed 　Resolution without sequelae	Treatment of progressive illness 　Pyridoxine HCL 25 mg/kg IV qd titrated to symptoms 　Maintain adequate urine output (>30 ml/hour) in face of hemoglobinuria
Group III: 　disulfiramlike poisoning	Ingestion of alcohol (or tinctures) elixirs, cough or cold medicines 24–48 hours after eating *Coprinus atramentarius*	Removal and adsorption of toxin 　Activated charcoal slurry: 50 g in 8 ounces of water PO or via NG tube if alcohol consumed within 2 hours
	Onset of symptoms in 20 minutes–2 hours after alcohol ingestion 　Flushing—face and neck 　Macular rash—torso, extremities 　Nausea, vomiting 　Chest pain, palpitations 　Paresthesias—hands and feet 　Sweating 　Severe headache	Baseline laboratory values 　CBC 　Electrolytes 　Glucose 　BUN 　Cardiac monitor 　Follow urine output

(*Continued*)

TABLE 5 (*Continued*)

Group	Clinical Features	Treatment
Group III (*cont.*)	Severe cases 　Cardiac arrhythmias 　Hypotension 　Altered mental status	For tachyarrhythmias 　Propranolol, 1 mg slow IV push every 　five minutes; up to 6 mg for sympto- 　matic tachyarrhythmias For hypotension Elevate legs Fluid challenge with normal saline or 　Ringer's lactate Dopamine if fluid challenge does not 　raise pressure For rash Parenteral antihistaminics may be of 　value *Note:* It is important to rule out an aller- 　gic reaction. Epinephrine, effective for 　sensitivity reactions, is *contraindi-* 　*cated* in the treatment of disulfiramlike 　reactions. Other treatments Ascorbic acid, 2 g qd in IV fluid, recom- 　mended.
Group IV: 　muscarine poisoning	Onset of symptoms within 2 hours, 　usually within 15–30 minutes Sweating—most common Abdominal pain Nausea, vomiting Salivation Wheezing Bradycardia	Removal and adsorption of toxin 　Gastric lavage if no emesis 　Activated charcoal, 100 g in 8 ounces 　of water PO or via NG tube
	Severe intoxications 　Miosis 　Blurred vision 　Runny nose 　Respiratory distress 　Diarrhea 　Hypotension	Indications for atropine 　Bradycardia: <50 bpm 　Hypotension: systolic <100 mm Hg 　　diastolic <60 mm Hg (with symptoms) 　Bronchospasm (may require epineph- 　　rine, 0.3 ml SC to start) 　Excessive salivation with difficulty in 　　clearing secretions 　Severe gastrointestinal effects—persis- 　　tent vomiting and diarrhea 　Dose:　Initial 1 mg IV slowly for adults; 　　　　0.02 mg/kg for children 　　　　Give additional half-doses ti- 　　　　trated to response

(*Continued*)

TABLE 5 (*Continued*)

Group	Clinical Features	Treatment

Group V (*cont.*)	Resolution of symptoms in 6–24 hours without sequelae
	Less than 5% mortality
	    Secondary to respiratory distress or cardiovascular collapse
		Endpoint of treatment
		    Stable vital signs—normal sinus rhythm, normotension
		    Bronchospasm resolved—normal peak flow
		    Systemic symptoms resolved
		    Note: Do not treat miosis! Atropinization until pupillary size is normal will result in severe anticholinergic poisoning.

Group V:
    Isoxazole derivatives: ibotenic acid and musci-mol poisoning
	Onset 30 minutes–2 hours
	    Dizziness
	    Ataxia
	    Drunken appearance
	    Euphoria
		Removal and adsorption of toxin
		    Emesis indicated (vomiting uncommon with isoxazole derivatives)
		    Ipecac, 30 ml PO with 32 ounces of water, or gastric lavage if indicated
		    Activated charcoal, 100 g in 8 ounces of water PO or via NG tube
		    Magnesium citrate, 8 ounces PO or via NG tube

	Severe intoxication
	    Visual disturbances
	    Mydriasis
	    Agitation
	    Myoclonus
	    Seizures
	    Coma
		Collect urine for qualitative analysis

	Usually self-limited; resolution in 6–10 hours without sequelae	Seizures:
		    Diazepam, up to 10 mg IV for adults, 0.1 to 0.3 mg/kg for children
		    Note: The respiratory depressant effects of phenobarbital and diazepam may be potentiated by isoxazole derivatives.

	May have mixed cholinomimetic and anticholinergic signs	Atropine contraindicated

Group VI:
    hallucinogens
	Onset up to 30 minutes
	    Nausea
	    Abdominal discomfort
	    Dizziness
	    Weakness
	    Anxiety
		Removal and adsorption of toxins
		    Emesis if vomiting has not occurred: ipecac, 30 ml PO with 16 ounces of water, or gastric lavage if indicated
		    Activated charcoal slurry: 100 g in 8 ounces of water PO or via NG tube
		    Magnesium citrate, 8 ounces PO or via NG tube

(*Continued*)

TABLE 5 (*Contined*)

Group	Clinical Features	Treatment
Group VI (*cont.*)	Up to 1 hour Visual disturbances Euphoria Dissociation Ataxia	Supportive environment Quiet surroundings Reassurance Companion to accompany
	1–2 hours Hallucinations Impaired time/space perception	Toxic psychosis chlorpromazine, 50–100 mg IM or haloperidol, 5 mg IM
	2–4 hours Resolution of symptoms Self-limited without sequelae Mortality less than 1%	Seizures diazepam, 0.1 to 0.3 mg/kg IV for children
	In severe reactions, toxic psychosis may appear but is usually self-lim- ited	Hyperpyrexia Cooling measures *Aspirin contraindicated*
	In children, seizures, hyperpyrexia may occur	
Group VII: gastrointestinal irritants	Onset 30 minutes–2 hours Nausea Vomiting Diarrhea (may be bloody) Abdominal pain	Removal and adsorption of toxins Activated charcoal slurry: 100 g in 8 ounces of water PO or via NG tube
	Volume depletion Large fluid and electrolyte losses from diarrhea	Monitor: Input and output Serum electrolytes
	Hypersensitivity reactions[a] Wheezing Urticaria or rash Hypotension Hemolysis [a] Note: Be certain to distinguish from disulfiramlike reaction	Hypotension: IV replacement with Ringer's lactate or normal saline
	Neurologic Paresthesias Tetany	Mixed ingestions: Baseline urinalysis, CBC, LFTs Observation or close follow-up for de- layed symptomatology
	Resolution in 3–4 hours	

profound, resulting in tachycardia and hypotension. Liver function tests and clotting parameters become abnormal after 24–48 hours, although the patient may feel somewhat better. The final, often fatal phase of the illness is characterized by hepatic failure with jaundice, coagulopathy, altered mental status, and renal compromise with oliguria, increased blood urea nitrogen, and serum creatine. Intestinal pseudo-obstruction with adynamic ileus may be a feature (20). Hepatorenal syndrome has been observed in about 10% of the cases reviewed (52). Central nervous system effects are secondary to the acute liver and renal failure (52).

Histologic examination of the liver in survivors has shown centrilobular necrosis with a significant inflammatory response, in contrast to postmortem examination, which has shown extensive parenchymal degeneration, steatosis, obliteration of portal triads, and diffuse hemorrhage (52). Survivors show complete reversal of hepatic histologic defects, although renal histology and function may return more slowly.

Treatment

EXPERIMENTAL

Considerable research on the treatment of *Amanita* poisonings has yielded some confusion and no clear-cut therapy. Hemodialysis has been advocated, although no controlled studies exist to recommend its use, other than in the management of associated renal failure.

Compounds such as penicillin or phenylbutazone have been used with anecdotal success to displace amatoxins from serum proteins and enhance their excretion. Amatoxins do not seem to bind to serum albumin, however, so another mechanism of action must be proposed (13).

Promising work indicates that cytochrome C, alone or in combination with penicillin, improves survival in laboratory animals poisoned with α-amanitin (14). The protective mechanism is unknown; cytochrome C may function as a free radical scavenger.

Thioctic acid (α-lipoic acid) therapy was first proposed in the late 1950s following several successful treatments using the drug (46,52). Since then, anecdotal reports in the United States have attested to the therapeutic efficacy of thioctic acid (5,12). However, some authors dispute the efficacy of thioctic acid in controlled animal models (15). The hallmark of successful treatment in all the cases reviewed seems to be aggressive, supportive treatment, not the use of thioctic acid or other experimental agents.

RECOMMENDED THERAPY

The delayed onset of gastrointestinal symptoms following mushroom ingestion strongly suggests *Amanita* or *Galerina* poisoning. Despite delayed symptomatology, every effort should still be made to limit absorption from the gastrointestinal tract, particularly in the face of possible enterohepatic recirculation of the toxin (52). Gastric lavage and activated charcoal are recommended acutely (cathartics are generally not necessary), followed by 4–6 hour doses of activated charcoal.

Baseline laboratory data should be obtained, including urinalysis, complete blood count, serum electrolytes, blood urea nitrogen, creatinine, glucose, liver function tests [serum glutamic oxaloacetic transaminase (SGOT), serum glutamic-pyruvic transaminase (SGPT), alkaline phosphatase, bilirubin], amylase, prothrombin time and partial thromboplastin time, platelet time, and fibrinogen level. The SGPT is often the most sensitive monitor of hepatocellular injury and tends to peak at 60 hours (52). Serum should be saved and sent for radioimmunoassay of amatoxins at an appropriate referral center. Strict monitoring of fluid input and output and placement of a central venous line are essential. Frequent blood sugar determinations should be made with Dextrostix or serum measurements. Urine output should be maintained at more than 30 ml/hour.

If hepatic failure, abnormal liver function tests, rising blood urea nitrogen, and mental status changes ensue, then oral lactulose (30–45 ml) every 6–8 hours is recommended to acidify the intestinal contents. Neomycin is not recommended due to the associated renal damage of amatoxins. Dietary protein should be restricted and parenteral vitamin K and fresh frozen plasma provided as necessary. Thiamine and multivitamins are added to the intravenous fluids.

Thioctic acid should be given only under experimental protocol through a poison control center. Controlled studies will determine its efficacy.

GROUP II—MONOMETHYLHYDRAZINE POISONING

Description

The genus *Gyromitra* belongs to the family Ascomycetes, which contains the most sought-after of all edible fungi, the true morels. The morels have a cap, resembling a pine cone, which is composed of ridges and pits and is attached at the base. *Gyromitra* species are false morels with a wrinkled or saddle-shaped cap unattached at the base. The distinction between true and false morels is often difficult and may result in poisoning for the amateur collector.

Gyromitra species are frequently eaten in Europe, where most poisonings have occurred, including the largest series to date of 151 cases with 59 deaths (9). Seven fatalities have been reported in North America from eating *Gyromitra esculenta* (52).

The chemical structure of the principal toxic component, gyromitrin, was elucidated in the late 1960s (52). Upon hydrolysis, gyromitrin yields monomethylhydrazine (MMH), a competitive inhibitor of pyridoxal phosphate (Figure 13). Pyridoxal phosphate serves as a coenzyme for many enzyme systems, including decarboxylases, deaminases, and transaminases. As a result, several organ systems are adversely affected by MMH poisoning.

Erythrocyte hemolysis occurs acutely, and free hemoglobin can be detected early in the course of the illness (35). The mechanism of hemolysis is unknown (52). Oxygen-resistant cyanosis from methemoglobinemia has been observed, but the physiology is not well understood.

Gastrointestinal effects include an initial irritation phase, followed by direct hepatotoxic effects. Recent studies indicate an effect on the drug-metabolizing mixed-function oxidase systems in the liver. Thus, the kinetics of the drugs potentially used in the treatment of monomethylhydrazine poisoning, such as phenobarbital, are altered (7). It is unknown if toxic metabolites, such as those seen in "fast acetylators" with isoniazid hepatitis, are responsible. Other research has implicated the hydrazine compounds isolated from *G. esculenta* in the induction of liver tumors (61).

It is not known if gyrometrin or its metabolites have a direct central nervous system effect or if altered mental status results from prior metabolic imbalances, such as methemoglobinemia or hypoglycemia. Industrial exposure to hydrazine (H_2N-NH_2) resulted in headache, facial dysesthesia, muscular twitching, hyperactive reflexes, and coma (31). As with isoniazid toxicity, peripheral neuropathy could theoretically develop with chronic ingestion of *Gyromitra,* although this has not been described.

Renal toxicity always accompanies significant hemolysis or hypotension and is probably not due to direct effects of gyrometrin.

Gyrometrin and monomethylhydrazine are not present in significant amounts in dried, boiled, or steamed mushrooms, although severe intoxication may result from eating the accompanying soup or stew (52).

Clinical Features

Delayed (6–12 hours) gastrointestinal symptoms are the rule, although the onset may range from 2 to 24 hours. Most patients com-

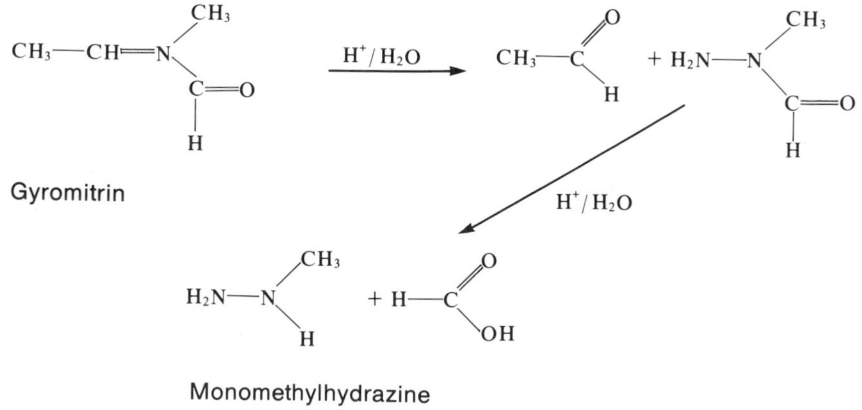

FIGURE 13 Hydrolysis of gyromitrin.

plain of bloating, cramping abdominal pain, nausea, and vomiting. Watery diarrhea is variably present. Headache, weakness, and lassitude are early features. Cyanosis may be found if significant methemoglobinemia exists. Generally, the illness is self-limited, resolving in 2–6 days. Progression is a bad sign, for it usually indicates hepatic involvement. There may be persistent abdominal pain, jaundice, and hepatomegaly. Fever and altered mental status may progress to seizures, delirium, coma, and death. Mortality ranges from 14 to 35%. (35).

Treatment

Treatment involves the use of parenteral pyridoxine hydrochloride (vitamin B_6) as a specific physiologic monomethylhydrazine antagonist. Pyridoxine provides additional pyridoxal phosphate, the essential coenzyme.

Initial steps should be taken to adsorb any remnants in the gastrointestinal tract with activated charcoal. Baseline studies include urinalysis, complete blood count, urine and serum free hemoglobin, blood urea nitrogen, creatinine, liver function tests, glucose, electrolytes, arterial blood gas, and a methemoglobin level in the presence of oxygen-resistant cyanosis. Emesis should be saved for toxicologic study.

For persistent or progressive systemic symptoms or altered mental status, pyridoxine hydrochloride, 25 mg/kg, should be given. It is recommended that one-third of the total dose be given intramuscularly and two-thirds intravenously over 3 hours. There is no known adverse affect from large parenteral doses of pyridoxine (31). If hepatic failure ensues, oral lactulose and a low-protein diet are indicated, as with group I ingestions. In the presence of increased serum or urine free hemoglobin, maintenance of adequate (more than 30 ml/hour) urine output is recommended. Dialysis is not recommended, except for frank renal failure.

Valium is recommended for control of seizures due to the altered kinetics of phenobarbital metabolism.

GROUP III—COPRINE OR DISULFIRAMLIKE POISONING

Coprinus species, of the class Basidiomycetes, are gilled fungi with conical caps that are often folded in umbrellalike fashion over the stipe. At maturity, many species undergo a process called *deliquescence,* whereby the gills dissolve into an inky black fluid. This enzymatic process may be arrested by cooking the plant. Coprine poisoning results from the ingestion of alcohol within 24–72 hours after consuming the common North American mushroom. *C. atramentarius.* It is an otherwise safe and palatable species.

The toxic constituent, coprine, or perhaps the active derivative, L-aminocyclopropanol, acts like the drug disulfiram (Antabuse) by inhibiting acetaldehyde dehydrogenase. This prevents the metabolism of acetaldehyde to acetate, allowing a toxic concentration of acetaldehyde to accumulate in the blood. Acetaldehyde may exert its vasomotor effects by stimulating β receptors.

Clinical Features

Generally, the patient has eaten a meal containing *C. atramentarius.* From 20 minutes to 2 hours after consuming alcohol or alcohol-containing tinctures, elixirs, or cold remedies, the patient develops facial flushing, nausea and vomiting, chest pain, palpitations, paresthesias in the hands and feet, diaphoresis, and severe headache. Cardiac arrhythmias (atrial fibrillation) and hypotension have been reported in several cases. Interestingly, simultaneous ingestion of *C. atramentarius* and alcohol produces no symptoms, although toxic reactions have occurred by drinking alcohol as little as 2 hours after ingesting the fungus (11,52).

Most symptoms resolve spontaneously within 3–6 hours.

Treatment

Treatment is symptomatic and supportive. The most dangerous side effects are the tachyarrhythmias which may cause hypotension or myocardial ischemia in persons with underlying heart disease. Propranolol has been recommended for treatment of symptomatic tachyarrhythmias because of its β blockade effect (35). Vasopressors may be required to support blood pressure if fluid challenge is unsuccessful. A disulfiramlike blockade of norepinephrine synthesis may be a factor; thus, dopamine is recommended should vasopressors be required.

Other treatments, such as intravenous ascorbic acid or parenteral antihistaminics, have had anecdotal success.

GROUP IV—MUSCARINE POISONING

Inocybe and *Clitocybe* species are gilled fungi, members of the class Basidiomycetes. *Inocybe* thrive in woodlands as small brown mushrooms with conical caps, which leave brown spore prints. Virtually all species are poisonous. *Clitocybe* are widely distributed plants with large, fleshy bodies and gray to white caps. The striking clinical picture produced by their ingestion is attributed to muscarine.

Muscarine is a natural parasympathomimetic alkaloid, first isolated from *Amanita muscaria* in 1869. Since then, several species have been shown to contain much greater quantities of muscarine, including *Inocybe* and *Clitocybe* species. *A. muscaria* contains about 0.0002% muscarine (dry weight) compared to 0.7–3.0% (dry weight) for *Inocybe napipes*. Thus, even large quantities of *A. muscaria* produce clinically insignificant amounts of muscarine.

Muscarine stimulates cholinergic postganglionic autonomic effector cells (Figure 2), such as sweat, salivary and lacrimal glands, and smooth muscle of the bronchi, intestines, ureter, and bladder. The cardiovascular system is extremely sensitive to muscarine, exhibiting marked bradycardia and hypotension. The direct central nervous system effects are minimal due to the nondiffusable quaternary ammonium configuration.

The toxin is not heat labile, so that boiling or steaming will not effect the toxicity.

Clinical Features

The clinical course of muscarine poisoning is heralded by potent cholinergic activity within 15 minutes to 2 hours that lasts for 6–24 hours. The most common feature is diaphoresis, accompanied by abdominal pain, nausea, vomiting, salivation, miosis, blurred vision, bronchospasm, bradycardia, and hypotension (52). Mortality is about 5% and tends to occur within 10 hours, secondary to respiratory distress or cardiovascular collapse (21).

Treatment

If emesis has not occurred, syrup of ipecac should be given to empty the stomach. Induced emesis and gastric lavage may further exacerbate the existing vagal effects of muscarine. Activated charcoal will help to adsorb the toxin. Cathartics are not indicated if the bowel is hyperactive.

Atropine provides a prompt and specific treatment for muscarine poisoning. The dose is 1 mg intravenously in adults and 0.01–0.02 mg/kg in children, with additional fractional doses adjusted to the clinical response. The cessation of sweating, salivation, and bronchospasm and the return of normal sinus rhythm and normal blood pressure are endpoints of treatment. However, miosis may last for many hours after adequate therapy has been given. Treating the miosis when systemic symptoms have resolved may result in excessive atropinization with tachyarrhythmias, delirium, and hyperthermia.

GROUP V: ISOXAZOLE DERIVATIVES— IBOTENIC ACID AND MUSCIMOL

Description

A. muscaria (fly agaric) and *A. pantheria* (the panther) are common mushroom species in North America that have been ingested intentionally for their psychoactive properties and are occasionally mistaken for edible species. The fruiting bodies usually have the distinctive annulus and volva of the *Amanita* species, along with heavily warted caps, remnants of the universal veil. *Amanita* has been exalted for centuries in India as the magical soma and is employed in shamanistic rites in contemporary northern Asia and Central America (50).

Chemistry

The active compounds are the isoxazole derivatives, ibotenic acid and muscimol. Muscimol is several times more active than ibotenic acid and is formed by decarboxylation of ibotenic acid. A third compound, muscazone (Figure 14), has limited biologic activity. Clinically insignificant amounts of muscarine are

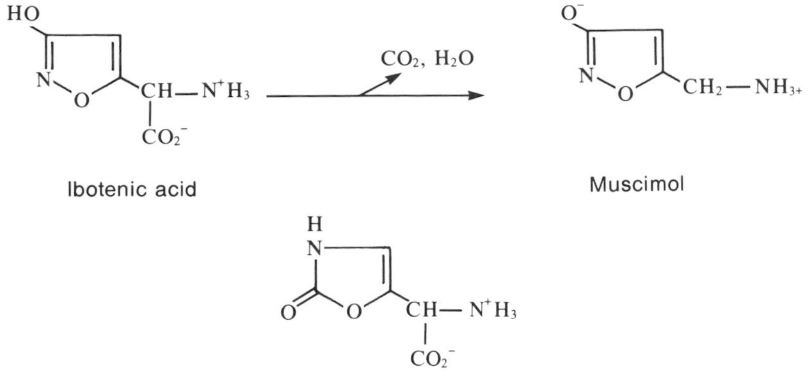

FIGURE 14 Isoxazole derivatives.

found in *A. muscaria*. The concentration of isoxazole derivatives ranges from 0.17 to 1.0% in *A. muscaria* and 0.02 to 0.53% in *A. pantheria* (21). Dried mushrooms and teas made from the fruit are psychoactive, although the potency diminishes with time.

Central nervous system activity is felt to be mediated through γ-aminobutyric acid (GABA) receptors (52). As little as 10 mg of *A. muscaria* produces a slight intoxication with dizziness, ataxia, and mood elevation. A 15 mg dose produces gross ataxia, incoordination, and visual disturbances within 40 minutes (21,38). The potentiation by muscimol of short-acting hypnotics in animals has been described (21). Flaccid paralysis and apnea may result from therapeutic doses of phenobarbital or diazepam (Valium) given in the treatment of seizures.

Both isoxazole derivatives can be detected in the urine within 1 hour of ingestion, but the true extent of their distribution and metabolism is unknown.

Clinical Picture

Symptoms occur in 30 minutes to 2 hours and include euphoria, dizziness, ataxia, and a drunken appearance. Nausea, vomiting, and dysarthria are absent.

With severe intoxications, visual disturbances, mydriasis, agitation, myoclonus, seizure activity, and coma may occur. Visual disturbances are characterized by alteration of perception rather than by frank hallucination. No clear-cut pattern of cholinergic or anticholinergic effects is observed, although both patterns have been described. Children may develop fever.

Mortality is rare, and recovery in 6–10 hours is routine.

Therapy

Treatment is supportive. Vigorous efforts should be made to empty the stomach, since vomiting is not a clinical feature of the intoxication. Activated charcoal is useful.

Atropine is not indicated; ibotenic acid and muscimol potentiate the effects of atropine (21). Care must be taken when phenobarbital or diazepam is used to control seizure activity, since these drugs are potentiated by isoxazole derivatives.

A urine sample should be saved and screened for isoxazole derivaties.

GROUP VI—HALLUCINOGENIC MUSHROOMS

Ethnomycologic explorations in the 1950s by Wasson, Heim, and others uncovered several psychotropic mushrooms species in Central America from the genera *Paneolus* and *Psilocybe. P. campanulatus,* called *teonanacatl* (God's flesh) by the ancient Nahuatl Aztec Indians, used to evoke mystical revelations during festivals and religious ceremonies (50).

In the late 1950s, Hofman et al. isolated the psychotropic principle from *P. mexicana,* which they called *psilocybin* (23). Subsequent discoveries in North America, frequent accidental ingestions, and the drug revolution of 1960s identified many native psychoactive species, resulting in "an epidemic of voluntary cerebral mycetismus" (19,22,26,49,50).

The principal hallucinogenic mushrooms come from three genera, found largely in the Pacific Northwest, Florida, and Hawaii. As a group, *Psilocybe* species have small conical caps and long thin stalks and leave purplebrown to chocolate brown spore prints. Notably, the stalks of all hallucinogenic psilocybin stain blue when bruised, hence the familar name *blue legs* for *P. cubensis.* Of 18 species of psilocybin, 7 are found in North America and, although widely dispersed, are encountered infrequently.

Paneolus species are common mushrooms that are widely distributed, with conical caps, thin stalks, and purple-brown to black spore prints. *Gymnopilus* species have broad yellow to orange caps, thick stalks, and rusty orange spore prints. Although described for years as a hallucinogenic, *Gymnopilus* was not known to contain psilocybin until the compound was isolated from this genus in 1978 (22).

Chemistry

Psilocybin is the principal psychoactive ingredient in *Psilocybe, Paneolus,* and *Gymnopilus* species. Psilocybin resembles 5-hydroxytryptamine and lysergic acid diethylamide in chemical structure: All are tryptamine derivatives with basic indole nuclei. A related substance, psilocin, can be found in trace quantities in some species but is unstable. Psilocybin is quite stable, so that dried plants and boiled extracts retain potency. Two other compounds, baeocystin and nor-baeocystin, have been isolated from *P. baeocystis.* These analogs of psilocybin are not known to possess pharmacologic activity.

Clinical Features

Many volunteers have been willing to ingest psilocybin in controlled experiments; thus, the dose-response relationship and clinical course of psilocybin intoxication have been well studied.

About 5 mg of psilocybin, equal to about 10 g of fresh *P. cubensis,* induces euphoria, while 10 mg, or about 30 g fresh weight, induces more intense psychoactive effects. After an oral dose of 150 μg/kg of pure psilocybin, 84% of those exposed note dizziness, 70% note weakness, drowsiness, difficulty in focus, visual and mood changes, and 50% note paresthesias, altered perception, and dissociation from the surroundings. Only 37% have true visual hallucinations (52).

Clinical Course

Patients note feelings of tension, dizziness, and weakness 30 minutes after ingestion. Within 60 minutes, euphoria and a dreamlike state predominate, with visual distortions. For 1–2 hours, there is an increase in visual effects, hallucinations, and space-time disorientation. Most symptoms resolve within 4 hours (24,25). A poignant description of the visual effects induced by psilocybin is provided by Pollock (50):

. . . the intensity of the intoxication induced by the tropical hongos I had eaten was so great that it became a major decision whether to sit in the sun or the shade. The phantasmagoria of color flashes superimposed on a panorama of solar diffraction produced by clouds blowing over the mighty Amazon was awesomely beautiful. After four and a half hours of a pleasant psychedelic experience, the tremendous exaltation passed as quickly as it had appeared.

Toxic psychoses have been known to occur in persons with underlying psychiatric disorders. Children may be particularly susceptible to the toxin, with hyperpyrexia and seizures described. Death in a child who ate *P. baeocystis* has been reported (42).

Treatment

Therapy is supportive. An effort should be made to remove the toxin with emesis and cathartics, since vomiting and diarrhea are not part of the clinical picture.

Those patients with extreme agitation and paranoia may benefit from a quiet, supportive environment and the company of friends. True psychoses with panic reactions or self-destructive behavior may require sedation with chlorpromazine (50–100 mg intramuscularly) or haloperidol (5 mg intramuscularly) (35). Diazepam (0.1 mg/kg in children and up to 10 mg intravenously in adults) may be required to control seizures. Cooling measures, not aspirin, are recommended in the control of fever, should it occur.

GROUP VII—GASTROINTESTINAL IRRITANTS

Undoubtedly, the most common adverse reaction to eating mushrooms is gastrointestinal irritation in the form of nausea, vomiting, diarrhea, and abdominal pain. Of only a few species, principally *Chlorophyllum molybdites, Gomphus floccosus,* and *Lactarius* species, is there any knowledge about the chemistry of the toxic principles (35). By and large, the toxins are unknown. They do appear to be destroyed by heating; raw mushrooms more frequently produce symptoms than do prepared ones. However, cooking does not ensure safety.

Clinical Features

The onset of symptoms is usually within 2 hours of ingestion, heralded by nausea and vomiting. Mild to severe cramping abdominal pain are features in a highly variable clinical picture. Watery diarrhea may lead to significant volume and electrolyte losses. Fecal blood loss may be occult or dramatic (6). Peripheral paresthesias and tetany have been described, probably secondary to electrolyte losses (52).

The illness is self-limited. Most symptoms resolve in 3–4 hours, with complete recovery in 24–48 hours. Very young and debilitated patients are more vulnerable to the fluid and electrolyte shifts and should be monitored more closely.

Hypersensitivity reactions constitute a dangerous but atypical reaction to mushroom ingestion. Bronchospasm, wheezing, urticarial skin reactions, tachycardia, and hypotension may be seen. Hemolytic anemia has developed in sensitized patients who ate *Paxillus invollutus* (21).

One of the greatest dangers from mixed mushroom ingestions is that early gastrointestinal symptoms may lead to a false sense of security, as one may mistakenly rule out the group I and group II poisonings. In mixed ingestions, early symptoms do not preclude monomethylhydrazine or cyclopeptide poisoning.

Treatment

Treatment is supportive. Activated charcoal may be of benefit in limiting gastrointestinal absorption. Patients should be observed for hypersensitivity reactions and treated appropriately. Bronchospasm and wheezing may require epinephrine or parenteral aminophylline. Epinephrine and/or antihistamines are helpful for urticarial reactions. Hypotension should be managed by isotonic fluid volume replacement. Vasopressors are indicated only if the latter measures are inadequate. Abnormal red blood cell morphology may be the first sign of hemolysis; serial blood counts and blood cell morphology should be followed. Electrolyte replacement is supportive.

In mixed ingestions of unknown mushrooms in areas endemic for group I and group II mushrooms, baseline complete blood count, liver function tests, and urinalysis will be of great value if the patient subsequently develops the classic delayed symptoms of monomethylhydrazine or cyclopeptide poisoning.

References

1. Alpin, T. E. H. *Poisonous Garden Plants and Other Plants Harmful to Man in Australia.* Western Australia Department of Agriculture. Perth, Australia, 1976.
2. Applefeld, J. J. A case of water hemlock poisoning. J.A.C.E.P., **8**(10), October, 1979, pp. 401–43.
3. Arena, J. M., Hardin, J. W. *Human Poisoning from Native and Cultivated Plants,* 2nd ed. Duke University Press. Durham, North Carolina, 1974.
4. Balint, G. A. Ricin: The toxic protein of castor oil seeds. *Toxicology,* **2,** March, 1974, pp. 77–102.
5. Becker, C. E., Tong, T. G., Boerner, U., *et al.* Diagnosis and treatment of *Amanita phalloides*-type mushroom poisoning—use of thioctic acid. *West. J. Med.,* **125**(2), August, 1976, pp. 100–9.
6. Blayney, D., Rosenkranz, E., Zettner, A. Mushroom poisoning from *Chlorophyllum molybdites. West. J. Med.,* **132**(1), January, 1980, pp. 74–7.
7. Braun, R., Greeff, U., Netter, K. J. Liver injury by the false morel poison Gyromitrin. *Toxicology,* **12**(2), February, 1979, pp. 155–63.

8. Bressler, R. The unripe akee—forbidden fruit. *N. Engl. J. Med.,* V. **295**(9), August, 1976, pp. 500–1.
9. Buck, R. W. Mushroom toxins—a brief review of the literature. *N. Engl. J. Med.,* **265**(14), October, 1961, pp. 681–86.
10. Buel, L. B., Culvenor, C. J., Dick, A. T. *The Pyrrolizidine Alkaloids—Their Chemistry, Pathogenicity and Other Biologic Properties.* North Holland Publishing Company. Amsterdam, 1968.
11. Caley, M. J., Clark, R. A. Cardiac arrhythmia after mushroom ingestion. *Br. Med. J.,* **2**(6103), December, 1977, p. 1633.
12. Finestone, A. J., Berman, R., Widmer, B., *et al.* Thioctic acid treatment of acute mushroom poisoning. *Pa. Med.,* **7**, July, 1972. pp. 49–51.
13. Fiume, L., Sperti, S., Montanaro, L., *et al.* Amanitins do not bind to serum albumin. Letter. *Lancet,* **4**, May, 1972, p. 1111.
14. Floersheim, G. L. Cytochrome C as antidote in mice poisoned with the mushroom toxin alpha-*Amanitin.* In *Clinical and Experimental Aspects of Fungal Poisoning.* Bertelli, A., ed. Hans Huber Publishers, Bern, 1977.
15. Floersheim, G. L. Treatment of experimental poisoning produced by extracts of *Amanita phalloides. Toxicol. Appl. Pharmacol.,* **34**, 1975, p. 499.
16. Geehr, E. C. Management of hydrocarbon ingestions. *T.E.M.,* **1**(3), October, 1979, pp. 97–110.
17. Goodman, L. S., Gilman, A. *The Pharmacological Basis of Therapeutics,* 4th ed. The Macmillan Company. New York, 1970.
18. Gowdy, J. M. Stramonium intoxication—review of symptomatology in 212 cases. *J.A.M.A.,* **221**(6), August, 1972, pp. 585–87.
19. Guzman, G. Description and chemical analysis of a new species of hallucinogenic *Psilocybe* from the Pacific Northwest. *Mycologia,* **68**(6), November–December 1976, pp. 1261–67.
20. Hanelin, L. G., Moss, A. A. Roentgenograhic features of mushroom (*Amanita*) poisoning. *Am. J. Roentgenol. Rad. Ther. Nucl. Med.,* **125**(4), December, 1975, pp. 782–87.
21. Hatfield, G. M. Toxins of higher fungi. *Lloydia,* **38**(1), January–February, 1975, pp. 36–55.
22. Hatfield, G. M., Valdes, L. J. The occurrence of psilocybin in *Gymnopilus* species. *Lloydia,* **41**(2), March–April, 1978, pp. 140–44.
23. Hofmann, A., Heim, R., Brack, A., *et al.* Psilocybin ein psychotropen Winkstoff aus dem Mexikanischen Rauschpilz Psilocybe Mexicana Heim. *Experientia,* **14**, 1958, pp. 107–9.
24. Hollister, L. E. Clinical, biochemical and psychological effects of psilocybin. *Arch. Int. Pharmacodyn. Ther.,* **130**(1–2), February, 1961, pp. 42–52.
25. Hollister, L. E., Prusmack, J. J., Paulsen, J. A. Comparison of three psychotropic drugs (psilocybin, JB-329, and IT-290) in volunteer subjects. *J. Nerv. Ment. Dis.,* **131**(5), November, 1960. pp. 428–34.
26. Hyde, C., Glancey, G., Omerod, P., *et al.* Abuse of indigenous psilocybin mushrooms: A new fashion and some psychiatric complications. *Br. J. Psychiatry,* **132**, June, 1978, pp. 602–4.
27. Kagen, S. L. *Aspergillus:* An inhalable contaminent

of marijuana. Letter. *N. Engl. J. Med.,* **304**(8), February, 1981, pp. 483–84.
28. Keeler, R. F. Toxins and teratogens of higher plants. *Lloydia,* **38**(1), January–February, 1975, pp. 56–86.
29. Kingsbury, J. M. Phytotoxicology I. Major problems associated with poisonous plants. *Clin. Pharmacol. Ther.,* **10**(2), March–April, 1969, pp. 163–69.
30. Kingsbury, J. M. *Poisonous Plants of the United States and Canada.* Prentice-Hall, Inc. Englewood Cliffs, N.J., 1964.
31. Kirklin, J., Watson, M., Bondoc, C. C. Treatment of hydrazine induced coma with pyridoxine. *N. Engl. J. Med.,* **294**(17), April, 1976, pp. 938–39.
32. Levy, R. Jimson seed poisoning—a new hallucinogen on the horizon. *J.A.C.E.P.,* **6**, February, 1977, pp. 58–61.
33. Lewis, W., Elvin-Lewis, M. P. F. *Medical Botany: Plants Affecting Man's Health.* John Wiley and Sons. New York, 1977.
34. Lewis, W. H. Reporting adverse reactions to herbal ingestants. Letter. *J.A.M.A.,* **240**(2), July, 1978, pp. 109–10.
34a. Lincoff, G. *The Audubon Society Field Guide to North American Mushrooms.* Alfred A. Knopf. New York, 1981.
35. Lincoff, G., Mitchell, D. H. *Toxic and Hallucinogenic Mushroom Poisoning.* Van Nostrand Reinhold Company. New York, 1977.
36. Litten, W. The most poisonous mushrooms. *Sci. Am.,* **232**, March, 1975, pp. 90–101.
37. Lockey, S. D. Anaphylaxis from an Indian necklace. Letter. *J.A.M.A.,* **206**(13), December, 1968, pp. 2900–1.
38. Mendelson, G. Datura intoxication. Letter, *Med. J. Aust.,* **3**, July, 1976, p. 163.
39. Mendelson, G. Treatment of hallucinogenic plant toxicity. Letter. *Ann. Intern. Med.,* **85**(1), July, 1976, p. 126.
40. Mikolich, J. R., Paulson, G. W., Cross, C. J. Acute anticholinergic syndrome due to Jimson seed ingestion. *Ann. Intern. Med.,* **83**(3), September, 1975, pp. 321–25.
40a. Miller, O. K. *Mushrooms of North America.* E. P. Dutton. New York, 1979.
41. Mitchell, M. I., Routledge, P. A. Poisoning by hemlock water dropwort. Letter. *Lancet,* **1**(8008), February, 1977, pp. 423–24.
42. Morton, Julia F. *Plants Poisonous to People in Florida and Other Warm areas.* Hurricane House. Miami, Florida, 1971.
43. Mutter, L. Poisoning by western water hemlock. *Can. J. Pub. Health,* **67**(5), September–October, 1976, p. 386.
44. *National Clearinghouse Poison Control Centers— bulletin. Top Five Categories of Products Ingested by Children Under Five Years of Age.* U.S. Government Printing Office. Washington, D.C., April, 1977, pp. 1–2.
45. Niyogi, S. K. Elevation of enzyme levels in serum due to *Abrus precatorius* (Jequirty bean) poisoning. *Toxicon,* **15**, 1977, pp. 577–80.
45a. Osterloh, J., Herold, S., Pond, S. Oleander interference in the Digoxin radioimmunoassay in a fatal

ingestion. *J.A.M.A.,* **247**(11), March, 1982, pp. 1596–97.

46. Paaso, B., Harrison, D. C. A new look at an old problem: Mushroom poisoning. *Am. J. Med.,* **58**, April, 1975, pp. 505–9.

47. Pentel, P., Peterson, C. Asystole complicating physostigmine treatment of tricyclic antidepressant overdose. *Ann. Emerg. Med.,* **9**(11), November, 1980, pp. 588–90.

48. Personal communication. Rocky Mountain Poison Control Center. October, 1980.

49. Pollock, S. H. Liberty caps: Recreational hallucinogenic mushrooms. *Drug Alcohol Depend.,* **1**(6), October, 1976, pp. 445–47.

50. Pollock, S. H. The psilocybin mushroom pandemic. *J. Psychedelic Drugs,* **7**(1), January–March, 1975, pp. 73–84.

51. Quek, K. C., Cheah, J. S. Poisoning due to ingestion of *Datura fastuosa. J. Trop. Med. Hyg.,* **77**, May, 1974, pp. 111–12.

52. Rumack, B. H., Salzman, E., eds. *Mushroom Poisoning: Diagnosis and Treatment.* CRC Press, Inc. West Palm Beach, Florida, 1978.

53. Sayre, J. W., Kaymakcalan, S. Cyanide poisoning from apricot seeds among children in central Turkey. *N. Engl. J. Med.,* **270**, May, 1964, pp. 1113–15.

54. Schultes, R. E., Hofmann, A. *The Botany and Chemistry of Hallucinogens.* Charles C. Thomas. Springfield, Illinois, 1973.

55. Sherratt, H. S. A., Al-Bassam, S. S. Glycine in Akee poisoning. Letter. *Lancet,* **2**, December, 1976, p. 1243.

56. Sullivan, T., Rumack, B., Thomas, H., *et al.* Pennyroyal oil poisoning and toxicity. *J.A.M.A.,* **242**(26), December, 1979, pp. 2873–74.

57. Taylor, N. *Plant Drugs That Changed the World.* Dodd, Mead and Company. New York, 1965.

58. Abramowicz, M., ed. Toxic reactions to plant products sold in health food stores. *Med. Lett.,* **21**(7), April, 1979, pp. 29–32.

59. Thompson, H. S. Cornpicker's pupil: Jimson weed mydriasis. *J. Iowa Med. Soc.,* **61**, August, 1971, pp. 475–78.

60. Tong, T. G., Benowitz, N. C., Becker, C. Tricyclic antidepressant overdose. *Drug Int. Clin. Pharmacol.,* **10**, 1976, pp. 711–12.

61. Toth, B., Patil, K., Erickson, J., *et al.* False morel mushroom *Gyromitra esculenta* toxin: *N*-methyl-*N*-formylhydrazine carcinogenesis in mice. *Mycopathologia,* **68**(2), September, 1979, pp. 121–28.

62. Verhulst, H., Crotty, J. Survey of products most frequently named in ingestion accidents. *National Clearinghouse Poison Control-Centers*—Bulletin, July–August, 1966, pp. 1–12.

63. Wieland, T. Poisonous principle of mushrooms of the genus *Amanita. Science,* **159**, March, 1968, pp. 946–52.

64. Withering, W. *An Account of the Foxglove and Some of Its Medical Uses.* Robinson. London, 1785.

14 | PLANT DERMATITIS

Don Friday King, M.D.

Plant dermatitis, or phytodermatitis, is caused by a wide range of plants. It occurs by contact with the plant itself or with plant products; the contact may be direct or indirect through fomites, animals, or other persons. For example, poison ivy dermatitis usually results when a sensitive person touches the infamous vine, but it can also erupt after one touches a dog which has brushed against the plant or when one wears clothes contaminated by plant sap. Plants can induce skin eruptions by a variety of mechanisms, which are best classified as allergic contact dermatitis (allergic sensitization), primary irritant dermatitis (chemical irritation), mechanical irritant dermatitis, and phytophotodermatitis (1). The clinical history is always very important in the diagnosis of plant dermatitis. The patient should be questioned about recent exposure to plants either in the home or outdoors. Occupational contact with plants or plant products is common and important (2). A prior episode of a similar eruption may help to pinpoint the causative agent. Seasonal exacerbation or a relationship

to certain geographic locations are both important details. In addition to the history, the distribution and configuration of the skin eruption are helpful in the diagnosis of plant dermatitis. Such eruptions usually occur on exposed skin surfaces, such as the hands or face. The pattern is unusual, with straight lines, acute angles, and sharp margins. These clues and a high index of suspicion will usually enable the clinician to diagnose plant dermatitis.

Allergic Contact Dermatitis

Most cases of plant dermatitis are examples of allergic contact dermatitis, the result of delayed or cell-mediated hypersensitivity. The allergen acts as a hapten which binds to protein in the epidermis and becomes a sensitizing antigen. Once the person is sensitized to the allergen, T lymphocytes migrate into the skin and signal the release of lymphokines, which mediate epidermal cell damage. Histologically, acute allergic contact dermatitis is characterized by spongiosis or edema between the keratinocytes. As the edema increases, vesicles and finally bullae form. Lymphocytes scatter between the epidermal cells and surround the blood vessels in the superficial dermal plexus. When mild, the rash consists of pruritic, erythematous papules and small vesicles. More severe cases are characterized by larger vesicles and bullae, widespread involvement, and edema of the extremities and face. The eyelids may become so swollen that they cannot be opened. Appropriate therapy is discussed at the end of this section.

RHUS DERMATITIS

Rhus dermatitis is an allergic contact dermatitis to poison ivy, poison sumac, and poison oak (3). These plants belong to the genus *Toxicodendron* and are by far the most common cause of plant dermatitis in North America. They are members of the Anacardiaceae plant family, which has a worldwide distribution. This results in cross-reactivity with other seemingly unrelated plants and their products. For example, a person sensitized to poison ivy may develop a similar eruption when exposed to mango rinds, cashew nut shell oil, Indian marking ink, or Japanese lacquer, to name a few. The term *uroshiol* (derived from the Japanese word *kiurushi,* meaning sap) refers to the sensitizing oleoresin produced by the Anacardiaceae plants. In poison ivy, the specific chemicals responsible for the dermatitis are a group of pentadecylcatechols. These are 1,2-dihydroxybenzenes (catechols) with a 15-atom side chain in the third position of the benzene ring. The side chain has zero to three unsaturated bonds. The di-olefin is present in the greatest concentration and is the most sensitizing, whereas the fully saturated molecule is the least reactive. Three heptadecyl catechols (17-carbon side chain), with one to three unsaturated bonds, have been characterized in poison oak. The dermatitis-producing agents in the other Anacardiaceae plants have not been as clearly defined. Despite specific differences, the molecules are similar enough to result in cross-reactivity in sensitized persons.

The dermatitogenic plant sap is found in the resin canals of leaves, stems, berries and roots of the *Toxicodendron* plants. The resin canals do not connect with the surface, and there are no glandular excretory appendages. Hence, the allergen is released only when parts of the plant are bruised or damaged. The milky sap soon dries and darkens to become a black, enamellike stain. This discoloration is a common property of many phenolic compounds, such as the catechols, and is the biochemical basis for the commerical use of the Indian marking nut tree and Japanese lacquer tree. The "black spot test" is one method of recognizing poison ivy and related species (6). Unfortunately, neither blackening of the sap nor death of the plant itself renders the material nonallergenic. Moisture, however, does promote its degradation and loss of allergenicity.

Despite folklore to the contrary, the virulence of the leaf sap does not vary significantly throughout the foliage period (4). The peak incidence of poison ivy dermatitis occurs in the spring, but this is not due to any increased potency of the sap. The leaves are more tender in the spring and more readily bruised, whereas in the summer months they become tough and leathery. The brilliant fall colors of yellow and red also do not diminish the allergenicity of the leaves. However, after the leaves have withered and fallen, they are much less toxic. The roots and stems remain a menace throughout the year; this makes recognition of the plants a challenge during the winter months, when the characteristic leaf pattern is absent (5). The sap is a heavy, nonvolatile, oily material, and no gases are produced to spread the disease. However, smoke from burning plants can carry the allergens in particulate form and induce a severe dermatitis.

Susceptibility to rhus dermatitis depends on a number of factors, which include genetic predisposition, age, and race (7). Approximately one-half of the population of the United States has been sensitized to *Toxicodendron* plants by casual exposure, and another 35% would become sensitized by prolonged exposure. The remaining 15% are tolerant to the offending chemicals and cannot be sensitized. Sensitivity, once attained, usually diminishes and, in rare individuals, even vanishes with increasing age. The steadily declining sensitivity with age is probably a general immunologic tendency and is not due to a lack of exposure. For example, resistance sometimes develops in person such as farmers and foresters who are repeatedly exposed to *Toxicodendron* plants. Newborns are not sensitive to urushiol but readily develop sensitivity when exposed to the allergens by patch testing. Dark-skinned persons are less susceptible to contact sensitization of all types, including rhus dermatitis.

Probably the most important aspect in the management of any allergic contact dermatitis is avoidance of the responsible agent (8). This requires recognition of the plant; often this is not easy, because poison ivy (*Toxicodendron radicans*) is morphologically variable. This has resulted in its division into a number of subspecies. It may grow as a vine, capable of climbing many feet up a pole or the side of a house, or it may appear as a low, erect bush or leaning shrub. It is found throughout the United States, especially the northeast, and in Canada. Poison oak (*Toxicodendron diversiloba*) is confined to the Pacific coast (California, Oregon, Washington, British Columbia,

and Mexico). The leaves of both plants are pinnate with three leaflets, giving rise to the wise adage "Leaves three, let them be." The stalk (petiolule) that holds the terminal leaflet is longer than the others, and the main leaf stalk (petiole) has a groove where it attaches to the branch. Poison sumac (*Toxicodendron vernix*) is a bush in the swamps of the southern and eastern United States. It has seven to 13 leaflets. Leaves of these plants are shown in Figures 1, 2, and 3.

Sensitization

The process of initial sensitization requires 6–25 days. A late reaction may occur after the initial exposure if sufficient allergen remains on the skin to react with the newly sensitized tissue. Subsequent exposure to the allergen will usually induce a skin eruption within 2 days, although in rare cases the onset may be delayed for up to 10 days or occur as soon as 8 hours after contact. These temporal variations are probably dependent on the quantity of oleoresin contacting the skin, individual susceptibility, and regional variations in cutaneous reactivity. For example, the palm and sole are largely resistant to allergic contact dermatitis because the thickened, compact stratum corneum inhibits cutaneous penetra-

FIGURE 1   Poison ivy (*Toxicodendron radicans*). (Reprinted with permission from Michael D. Ellis, *Dangerous Plants, Snakes, Arthropods and Marine Life—Toxicity and Treatment.* Drug Intelligence Publications, Inc., Hamilton, Illinois 62341.)

FIGURE 2   Poison oak (*Toxicodendron diversiloba*). (Reprinted with permission from Michael D. Ellis, *Dangerous Plants, Snakes, Arthropods and Marine Life—Toxicity and Treatment.* Drug Intelligence Publications, Inc., Hamilton, Illinois 62341.)

FIGURE 3 Poison sumac (*Toxicodendron vernix*). (Reprinted with permission from Michael D. Ellis, *Dangerous Plants, Snakes, Arthropods and Marine Life—Toxicity and Treatment*. Drug Intelligence Publications, Inc., Hamilton, Illinois 62341.)

tion by allergens. However, the contactant is easily spread by the hands to other parts of the body, especially the eyelids, genitalia, and scrotum, where an eruption readily occurs.

There is no known topical agent which can prevent rhus dermatitis. Barrier creams and chelating and oxidizing substances are ineffective. The allergens enter the skin very rapidly and form a tightly bound complex with cutaneous proteins, so that the oleoresin must be removed totally within 10 minutes of exposure if the dermatitis is to be averted. It is best to soak with cool water as soon as possible, using a mild soap. A hot shower and brisk rub with harsh soap may only serve to spread the uroshiol to uncontaminated skin surfaces.

OTHER PLANTS

Flowers and decorative plants may also cause allergic contact dermatitis. In the past, primrose (*Primula obconica*) was the major cause of nonoccupational plant dermatitis in Europe, but it has now become less common because florists are reluctant to stock it. Primin (2-methoxy-6-*n*-pentyl-p-benzoquinone) is the sensitizing chemical in primrose. When tulip bulbs are damaged, tulpalin A, a phytoalexin, is produced. Hypersensitivity to this agent results in a condition called *tulip fingers.* Chrysanthemums, philodendron, lilies, and oleander may also induce an allergic contact dermatitis.

Treatment

The treatment of rhus dermatitis and other types of allergic contact dermatitis is similar. Shake lotions such as calamine lotion are soothing, antipruritic, and drying. Steroid creams and ointments are not effective, but betamethasone valerate aerosol spray may be very useful. Pruritus can be treated with ethyl chloride spray. Systemic antihistamines, such as hydroxyzine (Atarax or Vistaril) and diphenhydramine (Benadryl), are both antipruritic and sedative, and help the patient to sleep comfortably. The patient should be warned that the drugs may make him sleepy and that he should take them with caution if he intends to drive.

Large vesicles or bullae should be punctured under sterile conditions and, if possible, the epidermal roof should be preserved. Denuded, oozing skin is best treated with cool compresses of Burow's solution (aluminum acetate). Rags or towels are soaked in a 1:40 dilution and applied to the affected areas for 15–30 minutes. The aluminum acetate is an astringent which precipitates protein. This dries and soothes the skin. However, if excessive water evaporation occurs, the concentration of aluminum acetate will become too high and may irritate the skin. Burows's solution may be used in a tub bath if weeping and oozing skin surfaces are widespread.

Bacteria readily colonize denuded skin. Any purulent exudate should be submitted for bacteriologic culture and Gram stain. If pathogenic organisms are isolated, appropriate systemic or topical antibiotics should be used.

Some topical medications frequently cause allergic contact dermatitis and should not be prescribed. For example, neomycin is responsible for more allergic contact sensitivity than any other topical antibiotic. Benzocaine, a topical anesthetic, is another well-recognized allergic sensitizer and is best avoided.

Severe allergic contact dermatitis can be dramatically improved by systemic corticosteroids. However, therapy must be continued for at least 2–3 weeks. If therapy is stopped after a shorter period of time, a rebound reaction commonly occurs. Initially the dermatitis improves, but if the drug is discontinued while the allergen remains bound to the skin, the dermatitis will recur with its original intensity. When there are no contraindications for the use of corticosteroids, the initial adult prednisone dosage should be 30–60 mg/day, gradually tapered over the next 2–3 weeks. Intramuscular injections of other corticosteroids in equivalent doses are equally effective.

Irritant Contact Dermatitis

Many plants produce fluids or crystals that act as primary irritants to the skin. The dermatitis appears within a short time after contact. Since this is not an immunologic or allergic reaction, all persons are affected, provided the irritant is present in sufficient quantity and for a long enough period of time. The amount of irritant that penetrates the skin, and hence the intensity of the reaction, depends on the anatomic location and cutaneous moisture. As is the case with allergic contact dermatitis, the palms and soles are more resistant because the thick, compact stratum corneum inhibits cutaneous penetration by the chemical irritants. A humid climate and perspiration cause the skin surface to be moist, which augments penetration. Clinically, the lesions are indistinguishable from those induced by an allergic contactant (9). Initially there is erythema and edema of the skin, followed by vesicles and, rarely, bullae. Histologically, irritant contact dermatitis can be differentiated from allergic contact dermatitis by the presence of necrotic keratinocytes, ballooning of the epidermal cells (intracellular edema), and a neutrophilic infiltrate. Irritant contact dermatitis usually follows a short clinical course and is best treated topically, as described for allergic contact dermatitis. Systemic corticosteroids are only rarely indicated.

Plants produce irritant contact dermatitis via a wide range of chemical agents. For example, the buttercup produces photoanemonin, an unsaturated lactone, which causes an irritant contact dermatitis. Daisies induce an irritant eruption when crushed on the skin. Mustard and radish plants contain sinigrin, a glucoside, which becomes irritative only when exposed to water. Bromelin is a proteolytic enzyme in pineapple juice which induces an irritant contact dermatitis. *Euphorbia* species, such as crown of thorns, snow-on-the-mountain, milkbush, and candelabra cactus contain an irritating milky sap. The peels of lemons and other citrus fruits have oils which can induce an irritant contact dermatitis.

Crystallization of the irritant, as well as skin-piercing structures of the plant itself, are important features of irritant contact plant dermatitis. For example, varieties of *Narcissus,* such as daffodil and jonquil, and hyacinth contain tiny, needle-shaped calcium oxalate crystals in the outer layer of the bulbs. The crystals penetrate the skin and cause "lily rash" or "hyacinth itch." The pruritus can be alleviated by a dilute acetic acid wash.

Members of the Urticaceae, Loasaceae, Euphorbiaceae, and Hydrophyllaceae plant families have stinging nettles. These sharp, hairlike structures prick the skin and inject a toxin. The initial pain is due to the mechanical penetration of the skin, but the subsequent dermatitis is due to the irritant chemicals. *Mucuna pruriens* (itch plant) and other *Mucuna* species have barbed spicules, called *trichomes,* on their seed pods. Mucunain is a proteolytic enzyme on the exterior surface of the trichomes that is responsible for the severe pruritus and dermatitis produced by this group of tropical plants.

Mechanical Irritant Dermatitis

Plants equipped with protective organs, such as sharp spines, thorns, hairs, and bristles, cause a mechanical irritant dermatitis. Bacterial or fungal infections may directly result from the wounds. For example, sporotrichosis is a well-recognized hazard for rose gardeners. The leaf of the dogwood (*Cornus sanguinea*) is covered with T-shaped hairs, which cause erythema and urticaria. Many cereal grasses, such as barley, millet, and rice, have sharp trichomes which act as mechanical irritants. Prickly pear cacti (*Opuntia ficus-indica* and *Opuntia cochinillifera*) produce an occupational dermatitis, called *sabra dermatitis,* when the pears are harvested. The eruption is induced by small, barbed bristles, called *glochidia,* which are found in the areoles of the cacti. Removal of the embedded barbs is a difficult task. Peeling agents such as salicylic acid are useful.

Phytophotodermatitis

Certain chemical agents will induce a dermatitis if the areas which they have contaminated are subsequently exposed to light. Phototoxic contact dermatitis is not based on an immunologic mechanism, since it occurs upon first exposure to the agents, provided the light is intense enough and the photosensitizing material is present in sufficient quantity. Photoallergic contact dermatitis, on the other hand, is a delayed hypersensitivity reaction. Photosensitive eruptions are limited to skin areas exposed to light, such as the face, the V of the neck, and the dorsa of hands, whereas the scalp, upper eyelids, skin folds of the neck, and submental and retroauricular areas are spared.

Phytophotodermatitis is a type of phototoxic contact dermatitis in which a furocoumarin has been contacted from a plant and acts as a primary irritant after photoactivation. Furocoumarins contain psoralen, which is the most active phototoxic agent, as well as the less potent xanthotoxin and bergapten. Besides contact with plant juice containing a furocoumarin, the skin must also be exposed to long wave ultraviolet (UV) light (UVA, 320–400 nm). If the skin is moist, a greater quantity of the furocoumarin will be absorbed into it and thus increase the intensity of the reaction.

Clinically, phytophotodermatitis often resembles a severe sunburn and may sometimes become bullous. The acute stage is typically followed by residual hyperpigmentation, which may persist for months. In the early acute stage, treatment is the same as for any irritant contact dermatitis. The persistent hyperpigmentation will fade with time, but the normalization process can be accelerated by the use of hydroxyquinone (a bleaching agent) and an opaque sun screen. Please refer to Chapter 15 for additional information on phytophotodermatitis, including a list of the plants which can cause it.

References

1. Arndt, K. A. *Manual of Dermatologic Therapeutics.* Second Edition, Little Brown, Boston, 1978, pp. 57–62.
2. Epstein, W. L. Poison oak and poison ivy dermatitis as an occupational problem. *Cutis,* **13**:544–48, 1974.
3. Evans, F. J., Schmidt, R. J. Plants and plant products that induce contact dermatitis. *Planta Medica,* **38**:289–315, 1980.
4. Fisher, A. A.: *Contact Dermatitis.* Second Edition. Lea & Febiger, Philadelphia, 1973, pp. 243–66.
5. Guin, J. D., Beaman, J. H. Recognition of poison ivy during winter with emphasis on Midwestern plants. *Int. J. Dermatol.,* **19**:500–3, 1980.
6. Guin, J. D. The black spot test for recognizing poison ivy and related species. *J. Am. Acad. Dermatol.,* **2**:332–33, 1980.
7. Kligman, A. M. Poison ivy (rhus) dermatitis. *Arch. Dermatol.,* **77**:149–80, 1958.
8. Lampe, K. F., Fagerström, R. *Plant Toxicity and Dermatitis.* Williams & Wilkins, Baltimore, 1968, pp. 184–217.
9. Mitchell, J. C., Rook, A. J. Diagnosis of contact dermatitis from plants. *Int. J. Dermatol.,* **16**:257–66, 1977.

CHAPTER 15 | THE SUN AND THE SKIN

Eric Lewis, M.D.

The sun radiates a full electromagnetic spectrum down to 10 nm. As the earth first evolved, all light from the sun reached it, traveling through a primitive reducing atmosphere. Light rays of short wavelength had an adverse effect on most recognized biologic systems. Therefore, early life evolved in sun-protected areas, such as in the depths of oceans or lakes or in shallower shaded water. Early living organisms metabolized surrounding materials and released molecular oxygen. This oxygen, when exposed to the high-energy, short-wavelength radiation, was converted to ozone (O_3). The ozone ultimately absorbed much of the very damaging light, enabling primitive organisms to live in more exposed areas. As the earth's atmosphere developed, more light of shorter wavelengths was blocked. Presently, the atmosphere absorbs virtually all of the light below 290 nm. Because electromagnetic radiation above 290 nm was

(and still is) damaging, organisms developed a "skin" to protect themselves from it.

Modern Western media dictate that tans are "in," as people equate a tan with health. Actually, the quest for a tan has ancient beginnings. Early civilizations realized the importance of sun to life, and many worshipped the sun. The Egyptians worshipped the sun god Ra and the Peruvians worshipped Kon-Tiki. This popularity declined during the Middle Ages, probably because of church-inspired modesty. A pale complexion denoted nobility, whereas the common laborer was marked by his swarthy complexion.

In modern times, most people work indoors and a tan has become associated with those who have leisure time. Presently, sunbathing has erupted with a cultlike fervor. This is due to many factors, which include (1) increased leisure time, (2) higher economic position, (3) faster means of transportation that can take people to the sun, (4) increased skin surface allowed to be exposed to the sun, (5) increased sun-related activities, and (6) artificial sun exposure (i.e., sun lamps, either privately owned or in tanning salons) (6).

Electromagnetic Radiation

The electromagnetic spectrum ranges from the higher-energy, shorter-wavelength radiation to the lower-energy, longer-wavelength ultraviolet (UV), visual, and infrared radiation (Table 1). As previously mentioned, this radiation is modified by the atmosphere as it passes to the earth. The sun's radiation is nearly a continuous spectrum, but only two-thirds of it reaches the terrestrial surface. The other one-third is absorbed, reflected, or scattered by the atmosphere. The radiation received by the earth is about 50% visible light, 40% infrared light, and 10% ultraviolet light (UVL) (15). About 0.2% of the sun's total radiation is in the ultraviolet B (UVB) (290–320 nm) range (19).

Ozone eliminates the damaging ultraviolet light in the range of 220–290 nm. This is interesting because the total amount of ozone is very small. If it were concentrated into a single

TABLE 1
Classification of Solar Radiation

Radiation	Wavelength Range
Cosmic rays	0.00005 nm
γ rays	0.0005–01.4 nm
X-rays	0.01–10 nm
Vacuum UV	1–200 nm
Ultraviolet C (UVC)	200–290 nm
Ultraviolet B (UVB)	290–320 nm
Ultraviolet A (UVA)	320–400 nm
Visible light	400–740 nm
Near infrared	740 nm–1.5 μm
Middle infrared	1.5–5.6 μm
Far infrared	5.6–1000 μm
Microwaves and radio waves	1000 μ–550 m

Source: From the University of Virginia Burn Center, Charlottesville, Virginia.

layer at standard pressure and temperature, it would be only 3 nm thick. Of major concern is that modern technology is beginning to destroy this ozone layer. Supersonic transports that travel in the stratosphere burn ozone. Chlorofluoromethane propellants (before they were banned) and other fluorocarbons (i.e., Freon) used in air conditioning and refrigeration systems, convert ozone into molecular oxygen. The National Aeronautics and Space Administration (NASA) has reported depletion of about 4% of the ozone over the last 8 years (40). Light of shorter wavelength (<220 nm) is absorbed by other atmospheric gases, especially molecular oxygen and nitrogen.

The atmosphere is filled with particles smaller and larger than the wavelengths of the light which travels through them. The quantity of scatter is inversely proportional to the wavelength of the light. For example, in the visible light range, the shorter-wavelength blue light is scattered more than the longer-wavelength red light. The great amount of blue scatter causes the sky to appear blue. Strictly speaking, any light that is scattered is called *skylight*. Light that passes through the atmosphere without being scattered is called *sunlight*. Probably, most of the ultraviolet light reaching the earth is skylight rather than sunlight.

The spectrum and amount of radiation reaching the earth's atmosphere are constant. However, many factors contribute to the amount and wavelength of light reaching any one point on earth. These include the day of the year, time of day, elevation, latitude, surface reflectivity, and atmospheric conditions. The solar zenith angle is determined by the day of the year, time of the day, and latitude (19). The sun is closest to any one point on earth at 1200 (noon, solar time). Thus, this and the hours on each side (i.e., 0900–1500) witness the transmission of more UVB radiation than at any other time. As the angle from the sun to any one spot becomes more acute (i.e., earlier or later in the day), the light must travel through more atmosphere (and thus ozone). This increased distance through the ozone decreases the amount of UVB that reaches that spot. This same principle also holds for the season of the year (i.e., midsummer receiving the most radiation). Points of higher elevation and lower latitudes receive more radiation. The intensity of ultraviolet energy increases by 5–6% for every 1000 feet of altitude.

Atmospheric conditions, such as smoke, dust, and humidity, also play a role in ultraviolet light exposure. Smoke absorbs ultraviolet light very well and can, on a smokey day, block out UVL completely. Dust and water scatter, rather than absorb, UVL and thus enhance exposure. For this reason, severe acute erythemas may be obtained on dull, hazy days because a person usually underestimates his exposure and the scattering of the UVL "bend" into shaded areas (70).

The terrestrial reflective properties also influence the amount of UVB (at 300 nm) that reaches the skin. Snow reflects about 85% of the ultraviolet rays, dry sand 17%, grass 2.5%, and sandy turf 2.5%. Water reflects 10% in the morning and late afternoon and rises to about 100% at 1200 (at the equator) (8).

Interaction of Light and the Skin

The skin has evolved to protect the underlying tissue. Urocanic acid (oil) acts as a natural sunscreen on the surface of the skin and absorbs UVL in the 300–320-nm wavelength range. To protect the body, the cells of the epidermis reflect, scatter, and absorb light. About 10% of UVL is reflected from the skin. Ultraviolet light is absorbed by different substances in the different layers of the skin. Most substances absorb specific wavelength ranges. The stratum corneum dramatically absorbs light in the UVB (290–320 nm) range and becomes damaged. The damaged stratum corneum cells peel off and are replaced. Only about 20% of UVB light passes to the dermis, which absorbs most of the rest of the light. Although the amount of light passing through to the dermis is small, it causes damage that is cumulative and irreversible. This dermal damage plays an important role in the formation of skin cancers (basal cell and squamous cell). A small amount of light above the 400-nm range reaches the subcutaneous tissue (48). Because of its low energy, minimal or no damage is suspected.

The basal cell layer is the most protected layer of the epidermis. However, the basal cells are affected not only by the light that penetrates but also by substances from the damaged cells above them. This basal cell damage initially causes inhibition and then an increase in mitotic activity. The increased number of epidermal cells produces thickening of the epidermis (48). Loring believes that this thickening of the epidermis produces added protection against further radiation. He has shown that stripping of the stratum corneum from the skin with tape increases the susceptibility of the skin to radiation and thus decreases the person's minimal erythema dose. (MED) (39).

Sunburn

The erythema-producing wavelengths (290–320 nm) are absorbed mostly by the epidermis and to a lesser extent by the dermis. Ultraviolet A (UVA) can augment UVB in producing the delayed erythema (2,73,75). Parrish et al. recently demonstrated that UVA radiation alone has been shown to produce sunburn, although large doses are required (52,72). The damage to the dermis is a combination of the direct light effect and the "dripping-down" effect from the damage to the epidermis. Functional and physiologic changes are noted before any microscopic changes. The function (absorption, degradation) of the skin in regard to clear, soluble, extraneously induced material is drastically reduced immediately following sun exposure. From 1–3 hours following exposure, erythema develops in the exposed skin. If a patient has suffered prolonged exposure, he may feel pain and itching in the involved area (31,54,56,71). The maximum redness of the sunburn is reached about 12–24 hours after exposure. Increased amounts of ultraviolet light above the minimal erythema dose (the lowest dose of UVL in a graduated series which produces erythema 6–12 hours after exposure) raise the intensity and lower the time of onset of the erythema. Severe exposure can produce marked edema and bullae formation one to two days after the exposure (60).

The erythema is caused by dilatation of the blood vessels and increased blood volume to the skin. Prostaglandins have been implicated as mediators of this process (64).

UV radiation will affect different parts of the body in different ways. The trunk reacts consistently in the most sensitive manner. As would be expected with all of the above factors, the time required to obtain a sunburn is variable. For the average Caucasian skin at mid-latitude in the United States during midsummer at noon, about 20 minutes of exposure is required. The variation in normal people can be as much as fivefold. At the same mid-latitude location during midwinter, there is not sufficient UV light to produce erythema, regardless of the exposure time (48).

Windburn, which is well known by the lay community, was never proven until 1973. Owens *et al.* showed that nude mice exposed to wind with UVL sustained increased acute damage over those nude mice exposed only to the UVL. Wind alone had no observable effect on the mice. Thus, windburn is probably sunburn intensified by the wind, (48,51). It has also been shown that wind also increases the chronic effects of UVL in nude mice, such as increased carcinogenesis (49). Heat enhances the injurious effect of UVL in both acute injury and carcinogenesis (14). High humidity, water immersion, and application of wet packs also produce greater ultraviolet radiation damage than maintenance in a dry environment (50). This follows the observation that people have an increased susceptibility to acute erythema after a shower. This may be due to the washing off of urocanic acid, which, as mentioned previously, is considered one of nature's sunscreens (70).

Pigmentation

After the skin has been exposed to ultraviolet radiation, it activates two basic protective feedback mechanisms (25). They are tanning and thickening of the epidermis. Light-induced pigmentation is divided into immediate and delayed types. Melanin exists in two forms, oxidized and reduced. In the resting state, melanin is usually in the lighter reduced form. Immediately following ultraviolet light exposure, especially in the UVA range (peaking at about 365 nm), melanin in the presence of oxygen is oxidized to the darker form. If no further UVL exposure is encountered, the oxidized melanin will slowly be reduced. This rise and fall of the oxidized melanin level takes only a few hours. It provides minimal (if any) protection against further UVL (55).

The delayed pigmentation is a quantitative increase in melanin. This is stimulated by the same wavelength which stimulates most of the acute erythema (290–320 nm), and to a much less extent by wavelengths in the UVA and visible light ranges (53). There are at least two processes involved in forming the delayed hyperpigmentation. UVL seems to decrease the tyrosinase inhibitor function and to stimulate melanocytes indirectly through the release of substances from the sun-damaged keratinocytes. Increased tyrosinase activity is noted in 72 hours and lasts for months (48).

In protecting the skin, melanin is not only an excellent UV light absorber but also acts as a "free radical trap," taking energy from previously radiated and excited molecules and allowing them to return to their ground states without incurring any damage (43). After absorbing enough energy, melanin is converted into an excited state and dissipates heat into the keratinocyte, causing its premature damage and death. Histologically, these cells can be distinguished by their large vacuoles and are called *sunburn cells*. This process is not observed until about 12–24 hours after exposure.

Melanin is pinocytosed by the keratinocytes from the dendrites of the melanocytes as the keratinocytes migrate toward the surface of the skin. The increased quantity of the melanin in the skin is a combination of an increased amount of melanin in each keratinocyte and an increased number of keratinocytes (increased thickness of the epidermis). These contribute to the increased darkness of the skin. Melanin furnishes protection against the damaging UV radiation, but it is by no means complete. Racial pigmentation does not totally protect people with photosensitive diseases such as xeroderma pigmentosa (55).

Effects of Chronic UVL Exposure

Chronic effects of UVL exposure include premalignant and malignant lesions associated with actinic damage, such as actinic keratosis, actinic cheilitis, disseminated superficial actinic porokeratosis, Bowen's disease, basal cell carcinoma, squamous cell carcinoma, and melanoma. Chronic damage also includes uneven pigmentation, solar elastosis, colloid milium, and loss of much of the upper dermal vasculature, while some vessels become dilated and tortuous. Racial pigmentation gives incomplete protection against these changes (33).

Modification of Light by Physical Substances

Electromagnetic radiation is modified by many substances through which it passes. The atmosphere and the skin have been mentioned. Other substances through which light passes are glass, plastic, water, and clothes. Ordinary windowpane glass transmits most of the UVA light above 360 nm and visible light. It transmits much less UVL at lower wavelengths. A thickness of two windowpanes reduces UV light transmission at 320 nm to less than 1%. Pyrex glass transmits more light in the UVB range and Corex D even more; thus, the latter is used to make sunlamps (48).

Because of the wide variation in plastic composition, there are marked variations of UVL transmission. If the plastic is clear, visible light will easily penetrate it. Polymethyl methacrylate will transmit wavelengths below 300 nm; however, when additives are mixed in, the percentage of ultraviolet light transmission is reduced. Lucite, for example, does not transmit wavelengths below 370 nm.

Distilled water will transmit most of the UVL and nearly all of the visible light. Eighty percent of light at 280 nm will pass through 12 inches of distilled water. Fresh and salt water have decreased transmission because of the dissolved particles.

Most clothes, including light cotton and women's hose, absorb or reflect all of the UV light in the UVB range. Wet white cotton, however, transmits much UVB light. Most nylon and white cotton fabrics do not block UVA or visible light, and people who have a photosensitive eruption in this spectrum must avoid these clothes.

Photosensitive Eruptions

Our advanced technology has provided us with magnificent medicines, soaps, cosmetics, perfumes, and numerous industrial chemicals. These chemicals are constantly in contact with our skin, either through systemic administration or topical application. Many of these, in combination with sunlight, produce a severe dermatitis. These are classified into phototoxic and photoallergic eruptions.

PHOTOTOXIC ERUPTIONS

A phototoxic eruption is a well-demarcated sunburnlike reaction. It is confined to skin exposed to the sun. Clinically, erythema and edema are the prominent features; however, in severe reactions, bullae formation can be seen (Figure 1). Increased racial pigmentation helps protect against this type of eruption. The pathophysiology seems to be the absorption of light energy (usually in the UV or visible light range) by the chemical. Each chemical

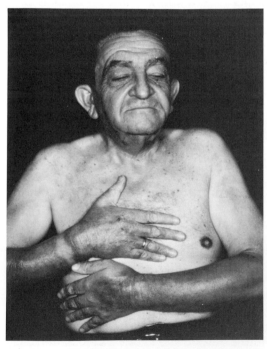

FIGURE 1 Classic phototoxic skin eruption with sharp demarcation of sun-exposed areas.

has its own absorption spectrum. The absorption of a specific wavelength range places the molecule in an excited state, which is unstable and transient. It returns to its ground state by releasing energy in the form of heat, free radical formation, charge transfer, vibration, and fluorescence. Damage to epithelial cellular components, such as the nucleus, cytoplasm, cellular membranes, and endoplasmic reticulum, occurs when a molecule becomes photoexcited and causes oxidation or peroxidation of the adjacent cellular components. Most of the phototoxic drugs are low molecular weight, polycyclic, resonating compounds. If there is a high concentration of a phototoxic compound in the epithelial cells, exposure to the sun should produce a phototoxic reaction in most people whose skin does not adequately block out the sun. This reaction does not require an incubation period; thus, it can occur on the first exposure (21,24).

Histologically, a phototoxic eruption is equivalent to a severe sunburn. There can be vacuolar alteration at the basal cell layer, spongiosis, ballooned or necrotic keratinocytes, and a sparse, superficial chronic inflammatory infiltrate. In severe cases, there can be confluent epidermal necrosis and dermoepidermal separation. These changes are seen 1–2 days after exposure (1).

Rather than mention all of the different chemicals which produce phototoxic and photoallergic reactions, I have modified and added to Demis' extremely complete table (Table 2) (48).

PHOTOALLERGIC ERUPTIONS

The pathogenesis of photoallergy is similar to that of phototoxicity with regard to the absorption of light energy by a chemical in the skin. However, instead of producing an excited state, a new compound (haptene) is formed that binds to a protein to become a haptene-protein complex. This stimulates immunocompetent cell (T lymphocyte) formation, which produces the delayed cell-mediated immune reaction. A person must become sensitized to the haptene-protein complex before a reaction can take place (as with any cell-mediated allergic reaction); thus, there must be an incubation period. Once sensitized,

the reaction occurs 1–2 days after exposure to even a minute quantity of the chemical and sunlight. Only a dilute concentration of the haptene-protein complex is needed to produce a vigorous allergic reaction (depending on the degree of allergy). Photoallergic eruptions are rare. The energy required to produce this type of reaction is usually a higher wavelength than the chemical's absorption spectrum.

Clinically, the photoallergic eruption usually appears as an acute eczema, but it can appear papulovesicular, morbilliform, less commonly lichen-planus-like, and rarely urticarial (22). The dermatitis is usually brief, lasting about 1–2 weeks after the associated chemical has been discontinued. However, on rare occasions the reaction can last for months or years (persistent light reactors). Photoallergic eruptions most commonly involve sun-exposed areas, but can spread to adjacent and even distant areas. This is because of the solubility of the haptene-protein complex and thus dispersion of the molecule away from the photoactivated site. Table 2 enumerates the specific chemicals which produce this photoallergic reaction (19,21).

Histologically, photoallergic dermatitis is identical to an allergic contact dermatitis (9). Intraepidermal vesicles and marked spongiosis (intracellular edema) predominate. If these are severe, reticular degeneration of the epidermis and multilocular bullae result. Throughout this edematous reaction, a chronic inflammatory infiltrate (mononuclear, composed of monocytes, histiocytes, and lymphocytes) is present. Older lesions may contain neutrophils, especially in the stratum corneum, which may demonstrate parakeratosis and aggregates of coagulated plasma (37).

Clinically, the most important factors in all photosensitive eruptions are the history, type, and distribution of the eruption. The history should include the relationship between the covering of clothing and the eruption (inversely related), the time delay between exposure and start of eruption, the amount of light required to produce the eruption, the time of day, the season, a personal or family history of similar reactions, drugs (systemic or topical) which the patient is using, and toiletries, including soap, perfume, shampoo, shaving cream, after-shave lotion, and hair dressing.

TABLE 2
Light Absorbers: Chemicals Involved in Human Light Hypersensitivity Reactions

Chemicals	Reaction to Topical Administration[a] (in nm)				Reaction to Internal Administration[a] (in nm)			
	Photo-toxic		Photo-allergic		Photo-toxic		Photo-allergic	
	<320	>320	<320	>320	<320	>320	<320	>320
Antibiotics								
Sulfonamides								
Sulfacetamide	—	—	×	×	—	—	—	—
Sulfanilamide	—	—	×	×	×	—	—	×
Sulfapyridine	—	—	×	×	—	—	—	—
Sulfathiazole	—	—	×	×	—	—	—	—
Tetracyclines								
Chlortetracycline	—	—	—	—	×	×	—	—
Dimethyl-chlortetracycline	—	—	—	—	×	×	—	—
Oxytetracycline	—	—	—	—	×	×	—	—
Tetracyclines	—	—	—	—	×	×	—	—
Antifungal agents								
Griseofulvin	—	—	—	—	—	—	—	×
"Jadit"	—	—	×	×	—	—	—	—
Anti-insect agents								
Phenothiazine	—	—	—	×	—	—	—	—
Antiseptics								
Bithionol	—	—	×	×	—	—	—	—
Dibromosalicylanilide	—	—	×	×	—	—	—	—
Tetrachlorsalicylanilide	—	—	×	×	—	—	—	—
Tribromosalicylanilide	—	—	×	×	—	—	—	—
Coal tar derivatives								
Acridine	×	—	—	—	—	—	—	—
Acriflavine	×	—	—	—	—	—	—	—
9-Aminoacridine	—	×	—	—	—	—	×	—
Anthracene	×	—	—	—	—	—	—	—
Phenanthrene	×	—	—	—	—	—	—	—
Pitch	×	—	—	—	—	—	—	—

This is a continuation of a tabular listing of photosensitizing agents. The table is printed sideways; the agent names run along the bottom margin and the reaction columns appear as horizontal bands. Reconstructed into standard orientation (× = mark present; — = dash mark):

Agent	1	2	3	4	5	6	7	8	9	10	11	12
Diuretics												
Chlorothiazide	—	×	×	—	—	—	—	—	×	×	—	—
Hydrochlorothiazide	—	×	×	—	—	—	—	—	×	×	—	—
Quinethazone	—	×	×	—	—	—	—	—	—	—	—	—
Dyes												
Eosin	—	—	—	—	×	—	×	—	—	—	—	—
Fluorescein	—	—	—	—	×	—	×	—	—	—	—	—
Methylene blue	—	—	—	—	×	—	×	—	—	—	—	—
Rose bengal	—	—	—	—	×	—	×	—	—	—	—	—
Thionine	—	—	—	—	×	—	×	—	—	—	—	—
Trypaflavin	—	—	—	—	×	—	×	—	—	—	—	—
Essential oils (active ingredients: furocoumarins)												
Lime oil	—	—	—	—	—	—	—	—	—	—	×	×
Oil of bergamot	—	—	—	—	—	—	—	—	—	—	×	×
Oil of cedar	—	—	—	—	—	—	—	—	—	—	×	×
Oil of citron	—	—	—	—	—	—	—	—	—	—	×	×
Oil of lavender	—	—	—	—	—	—	—	—	—	—	×	×
Food additives												
Cyclamates	×	—	×	—	—	—	—	—	—	—	—	—
Saccharine	×	—	×	—	—	—	—	—	—	—	—	—
Furocoumarins												
5-Methoxypsoralen	—	—	—	×	—	×	—	—	—	×	×	×
8-Methoxypsoralen	—	—	—	×	—	×	—	—	—	×	×	×
Psoralen	—	—	—	×	—	×	—	—	—	×	×	×
See Essential Oils	—	—	—	—	—	—	—	—	—	—	—	—
See Plants	—	—	—	—	—	—	—	—	—	—	—	—
Lichens (a symbiotic association between fungi and algae; produce dyes)	—	—	—	—	—	—	×	×	×	×	×	×
Oral hypoglycemics												
Carbutamide	—	—	×	—	—	—	—	—	—	—	—	—
Chlorpropamide	—	—	×	—	—	—	—	—	—	—	—	—
Tolbutamide	—	—	×	—	—	—	—	—	—	—	—	—
Sulfonurea	×	—	×	—	—	—	—	—	—	—	—	—

(continued)

TABLE 2 (continued)

Chemicals	Reaction to topical administration[a] (in nm)						Reaction to internal administration[a] (in nm)					
	Photo-toxic	<320	>320	Photo-aller-gic	<320	>320	Photo-toxic	<320	>320	Photo-aller-gic	<320	>320
Plants (active ingredients: furocoumarins)												
Moraceae family (fig)	×	—	×	—	—	—	—	—	—	—	—	—
Polygonaceae family (buckwheat)	×	—	×	—	—	—	—	—	—	—	—	—
Rutaceae family (bergamot, lime, rue)	×	—	×	—	—	—	—	—	—	—	—	—
Umbelliferae family (parsnip, celery, carrot)	×	—	×	—	—	—	—	—	—	—	—	—
Compositae family (milfoil, mayweed)	×	—	×	×	—	×	—	—	—	—	—	—
Cruciferae family (mustard)	×	—	×	—	—	—	—	—	—	—	—	—
Chenopodiaceae (goose foot)	×	—	×	—	—	—	—	—	—	—	—	—
Ranunculaceae family (buttercup)	×	—	×	—	—	—	—	—	—	—	—	—
Convolvulaceae family (bind weed)	×	—	×	—	—	—	—	—	—	—	—	—
Leguminosae family (scurfy pea)	×	—	×	—	—	—	—	—	—	—	—	—
Hypericaceae family (St. John's wort)	×	—	×	—	—	—	—	—	—	—	—	—
Anacardiaceae (red quebracho)	×	—	×	—	—	—	—	—	—	—	—	—

	Porphyrins											
Hematoporphyrin	−	−	−	−	−	−	×	−	×	−	−	−
Chlorophyll	−	−	−	−	−	−	×	−	×	−	−	−
Sunscreen agents												
Digalloyl trioleate	×	−	×	−	−	−	−	−	−	−	−	−
p-Aminobenzoic acid	×	−	×	×	−	×	−	−	−	−	−	−
Cinnamates	×	−	×	−	−	−	−	−	−	−	−	−
Tranquilizers (phenothiazine)												
Chlorpromazine	−	−	−	×	−	×	×	×	−	×	−	×
Chlorprothixene	−	−	−	×	−	×	×	×	−	×	−	×
Mepazine	−	−	−	−	−	−	−	−	−	−	−	−
Perphenazine	−	−	−	−	−	−	−	−	−	−	−	−
Prochlorperazine	−	−	−	−	−	−	−	−	−	−	−	−
Promethazine	−	−	−	×	−	×	×	×	−	×	−	×
Triflupromazine	−	−	−	−	−	−	−	−	−	−	−	−
Miscellaneous												
Arsenicals	−	−	−	−	−	−	−	−	−	−	−	−
Cadmium sulfide (tattoo)	−	−	−	−	−	−	×	−	×	−	−	−
Gold	−	−	−	−	−	−	−	−	−	−	−	−
Quinine sulfate	−	−	−	−	−	−	×	−	×	−	−	−
Riboflavin	−	−	−	−	−	−	×	−	×	−	−	−
Silver	−	−	−	−	−	−	−	−	−	−	−	−
Triethylenemelamine	−	−	−	−	−	−	−	−	−	−	−	−

a Phototoxic and photoallergic reactions produced by wavelengths greater and less than 320 nm in subjects to whom chemicals were administered topically or internally. These data were obtained from many sources. The mode of action and the wavelengths involved for many of the chemicals listed are unknown; those listed are considered tentative.
Source: From Reference 48.

The most frequent locations for photosensitive eruptions are the head, neck, and dorsa of the hands. The nose, forehead, cheeks, ears (if not covered), chin, back of the neck, and V of the neck are usually involved. On the other hand, the skin under the chin, behind the ears, and around the eyes is usually spared. The exposed skin will be modified according to dress, length and style of hair, and use of shading devices such as hats or umbrellas. If the wavelength of light that causes the photosensitive eruption is in the UVA or visible light range, then thin clothing (e.g., nylon, cotton) will not prevent the eruption.

Phytophotodermatitis

Phytophotodermatitis is a type of phototoxic reaction which develops from contact with one of a number of plants (Table 3) and subsequent exposure of the skin to sunlight. The plants are mainly in the families Rutaceae and Umbelliferae, which include lime, lemon, bergamot, rue, celery, parsnip and carrot (wild and garden (59). All of these plants produce furocoumarins (especially 5-methoxypsoralen and 8-methoxypsoralen), which are well-known phototoxic chemicals. Psoralens attach to the DNA of epidermal cells. When activated by UVL (especially in the UVA range), the psoralens enter an excited state. Energy is released to bring the psoralens back to a ground state, which produces DNA damage and early cell death. The eruption is similar to any other phototoxic dermatitis, except that it usually involves a severe postinflammatory hyperpigmentation.

There is some controversy as to whether or not many members of the Compositae family contribute to allergic dermatitis or photoallergic dermatitis. The means of contact is usually wind-borne and thus would primarily involve the exposed skin in either case. Patch testing has not been conclusive. One opinion is that the dermatitis caused by the weeds of the Compositae family is purely an allergic rather than a photoallergic dermatitis (23). Others have noticed a high association of patients with photosensitive dermatitis to plants in the Compositae family with the actinic reticuloid syndrome (13).

Lichens number about 15,000 species, but are extremely difficult to classify because they are fungi and algae living in a symbiotic association. Presently, they are classified as fungi (11). This group of fungi has no chlorophyll and depends on the algae for organic food. A lichen plant body is called a *thallus*, which grows very slowly and may live for more than 1000 years (4). This longevity may be due to the antibiotic properties of the dyes which are found in the lichens. These dyes produce the lichens' natural colors, which have been used for hundreds of years to dye wool. Lichens are most commonly found in forests and fields, away from the cities that produce pollutants which destroy these organisms. Unlike the above furocoumarin-producing plants, the lichens produce numerous substances which can cause photoallergic and, to a lesser extent, allergic and phototoxic reactions. These include lactones and aromatic compounds such as quinones and derivatives of organic acids: xanthone, dibenzofuran, and diketopiperazine. Ultraviolet light in both the UVA and UVB ranges produces the photosensitive eruptions. To test adequately the allergic or photoallergic nature of these substances, one should follow the protocol established by Thume and Solberg (or a similar one) (69). Lichens can cross-sensitize with the Compositae family of plants (69).

Sunscreens

There are two kinds of sunscreens: Some absorb light of a particular wavelength range, and others are barriers or shades which reflect light. There are various groups of sunscreens (see Table 4).

Each type of absorbing sunscreen has its own absorption spectrum which serves as a crude guide for predicting a wavelength range of topical effectiveness. The spectrum usually broadens as the concentration of the compound is increased. Investigators are attempting to standardize the effectiveness of the sunscreens. The sun protective factor (SPF) is a measurement of the protection of a sunscreen against sunburn. The sun protective factor is a unit value determined by dividing the minimum erythema dose (MED) of protected skin by the minimum erythema dose of unprotected skin. Sunscreens are usually tested on

TABLE 3
Common Plants and Lichens Causing Photodermatitis (11, 47)

Common Name	Botanical Name	Family
Lime	*Citrus aurantifolia*	Rutaceae
Citron	*Citrus medica*	
	(*C. acida*)	
Bitter orange	*Citrus aurantium*	Rutaceae
Lemon	*Citrus limon*	Rutaceae
Bergamot	*Citrus bergamia*	Rutaceae
Gas plant, burning bush	*Dictamnus albus*	Rutaceae
	(*D. fraxinella*)	
Common rue	*Ruta graveolens*	Rutaceae
Persian lime	*Citrus aurantifolia,*	Rutaceae
(Tahitian)	"Persian"	
	Phebalium	
	argenteum	
Cow parsley, wild chervil	*Anthriscus sylvestris*	Umbelliferae
Celery	*Apium graveolens*	Umbelliferae
Giant hogweed	*Heracleum mantegazzianum*	Umbelliferae
	Heracleum maximum	
	(*H. dulce*)	
Parsnip (garden variety)	*Pastinaca sative*	Umbelliferae
	(*P. urens*)	
Cow parsley	*Heracleum sphondylium*	Umbelliferae
Parsnip (wild parsnip)	*Heracleum giganteum*	Umbelliferae
Fennel	*Foeniculum vulgare*	Umbelliferae
Dill	*Anethum graveolens*	Umbelliferae
	Peucedanum ostruthium	Umbelliferae
Wild carrot, garden carrot	*Daucus carota*	Umbelliferae
Masterwort	*Peucedanum ostruthium*	Umbelliferae
	Ammin majus	Umbelliferae
Angelica	*Angelica archangelica*	Umbelliferae
Figs	*Ficus carica*	Moraceae
Milfoil, yarrow	*Achillea millefolium*	Compositae
Stinking mayweed	*Anthemis cotula*	Compositae
Buttercup	*Ranunculus* spp.	Ranunculaceae
Mustard	*Brassica* spp.	Cruciferae
Bind weed	*Convolvulus arvensis*	Convolvulaceae
Agrimony	*Agrimonia eupatoria*	Rosaceae
Goose foot	*Chenopodium* spp.	Chenopodiaceae
Scurfy pea, bavchi	*Psoralea corylifolia*	Leguminosae
St. John's wort	*Hypericum perforatum*	Hypericaceae
	Hypericum crispum	Hypericaceae
	Schinopsis quebracho-	
	colorado	
Red quebracho	(*Schinopsia lorentzii*)	Anacardiaceae
Lichens	*Parmelia* spp.	Lichen (symbiotic
	Hypogymnia spp.	association
		between
	Pseuodovernia spp.	fungi and algae)
	Cladonia spp.	commonly
		grouped
	Platismatia spp.	with fungi
	Physcia spp.	
	Umbilicaria spp.	
	Cetraria spp.	

TABLE 4
Groups of Sunscreens (2)[a]

PABA
    Filtray Lotion
    Pabanol
    Presun
    RVPaba Stick
    Solar Cream
    Supershade
    PABA gel

Glyceryl PABA (Escalol 106)
    Eclipse
    Expose Suntan Liquid
    Negasol
    Sea and Ski Dark Tanning Lotion
    Sea and Ski Suntan Lotion
    Tanfastic Dark Tanning Lotion
    Tanfastic Suntan Lotion with Cocoa Butter

Amyl dimethyl PABA (Escalol 507)
    Ban de Soleil
    Beauty on the Beach
    Block Out
    Bronze Lustre Moon Drops
    California Bronze Suntan Cream
    California Bronze Suntan Oil
    Chap Stick
    Coppertone Baby Tan
    Pabafilm
    Palm Springs Tanning Cream
    Sea and Ski Dark Tanning Foam
    Sea and Ski Dark Tanning Oil
    Skol Regular Lotion
    Skolex Sun Cream
    Suave Suntan Lotion
    Tanfastic Suntan Oil Plus Cocoanut Oil
    UVAL Sun's Wind Stick

Octyl dimethyl PABA (Escalol 507)
    Braggi Sun Block Stick
    Braggi Sun Bronzing Gel
    Braggi Sun Bronzing Oil
    Bronze Lustre Tanning Creme
    Eclipse
    Sundown

Cinnamates
    Full-Filter Sun Creme
    Full-Filter Sun Lotion
    Maxafil
    RVPaque
    Sun Bloc Gel
    Sun Dare Clear Lotion
    Sun Dare Creamy Lotion

Salicylates
    Coppertone Baby Tan
    Coppertone Cream
    Coppertone Lotion
    Coppertone Oil
    Coppertone Royal Blend
    Coppertone Shade Lotion
    QT Quick Tanning Lotion
    SunOff

Anthranilates
    A-Fil
    Maxafil
    Squaw Tan Lotion

Benzophenones
    Pan Ultra
    Solbar
    Sungard
    UVAL
    Block-Aid

Digalloyl trioleate
    Sun Protectol
    Sun Stick Cream
    Sun Swept Cream

Red veterinary petrolatum
    RVP
    RVPaba Stick
    RVPaque
    RVPlus

Physical agents
    A-Fil
    RVPaque
    RVPlus

[a] Many of these have associated SPF numbers (the larger the number, the greater the protection against sunburn).

human backs. The MED is the lowest dose of ultraviolet light in a graduated series which produces erythema 6–12 hours after exposure. First, the MED of unprotected skin is determined for each individual. Then, the sunscreen to be tested is applied, followed by a series of gradually increasing doses of UV light. The SPF does not take into account sweating, bathing, or swimming.

The chemicals which comprise most modern sunscreens include para-aminobenzoic acid (PABA) and its derivatives, cinnamates, anthranilates, benzophenones, and digalloyl triolate (12). Benzylsalicylate became the first commercially available sunscreen in the United States in 1926 (32). This was followed by para-aminobenzoic acid and benzophenones (38).

Para-aminobenzoic acid has peak absorption at 278 nm. In 1949, Rothman and Henningsen used 15% PABA concentrations in ointment and vanishing cream (5%). This provided "complete" protection from UVB light. A 5% solution of PABA in 50–60% ethyl alcohol was said to be the most effective formulation. This formula provided protection from erythema up to 20 times the MED, which could not be improved by increasing the concentration (73). PABA in a 1% concentration absorbs UVL in the 290–320-nm range and expands this range to 360 nm with a 5% concentration (27).

PABA penetrates the stratum corneum and seems to bind to it. Continued application leads to an accumulation of PABA in the skin, giving prolonged protection even after swimming, sweating, or bathing. As with most topical medications, this absorption into the stratum corneum is increased by hydrating the skin prior to application (35). To produce maximal effectiveness, the skin should be kept dry for about 2 hours after application. This allows penetration of the PABA into the stratum corneum and decreases the loss of sunscreen when bathing or sweating occurs (42).

PABA still allows tanning, probably through UVA exposure (36). The PABA esters also give excellent UVB protection, but to a slightly lesser extent than does PABA itself (27). These esters include glyceryl PABA, amyl dimethyl PABA, and octyl dimethyl PABA (74). They are usually found in 2.5% formulations. However, even in 5% concentrations, they are less effective than 5% PABA.

Complications of PABA and PABA ester applications are uncommon. The alcohol bases can sting when placed on broken or very dry skin. PABA can cause yellow staining on clothing because of the photooxidation of PABA (58). These stains usually wash out easily. Allergic contact and photocontact dermatitis are very unusual, and are most frequently encountered with the PABA ester, glyceryl PABA (46,68). More recently, it has been shown that benzocaine may contaminate the sunscreens that contain glyceryl PABA and may actually cause the contact dermatitis in many cases (10). This allergic reaction does not exhibit cross-reaction with other PABA esters, but may cross-react with PABA, sulfa drugs, paraphenylenediamine, benzocaine, and aniline. Photoallergic dermatitis to PABA has also been reported.

Benzoic acid is the nucleus of the PABA family. Substituting side chains produces other sunscreens. 2-Ethoxyethyl-p-methoxycinnamate (cinoxate), methyl anthranilate, tannic acid, and salicylates are derivatives of benzoic acid and are active components of sunscreen preparations. Many of these are combined. All of them protect in the UVB (and may extend into the UVA) range. Their major drawback is that they are easily rinsed off by perspiring or swimming. In volunteer testing, tannic acid was shown to be nearly as protective as PABA, phenyl salicylate less protective, and methyl anthranilate least protective. Combining these agents increased their effectiveness (20). A combination of 4% cinoxate and 5% methyl anthraniline in a cream base absorbed more than 99% of the light in the UVB and UVA ranges (61). This combination may rank second only to PABA, but it provides minimal protection after perspiring or bathing (7). These sunscreens have extremely few side effects. Cinnamates have caused photodermatitis. Benzyl salicylate, a commonly used sunscreen in cosmetics, can cause a contact dermatitis. Tannic acid and anthranilates are rare sensitizers.

In a 6–10% concentration, the benzophenones protect the skin over the entire UVL spectrum. The higher the concentration of benzophenone, the greater the protection (34). Like all sunscreens other than PABA and its derivatives, the benzophenones are surface sunscreens, requiring regular reapplications. Benzophenones are rare sensitizers.

To protect against visible light (400–700-nm range), the compound must be opaque. The upper limit of absorption of clear substances is about 400 nm (28). Titanium dioxide or zinc oxide is effective when applied thickly. Their action is to reflect or scatter, and when used properly, they will block about 99% of ultraviolet and visible light (290–700-nm range). Talc, kaolin, and 2% ichthammol (Ichthyol) are also effective physical barriers (3). Physical sunscreens do not sensitize, but they are occlusive, may be uncomfortable, and are considered by many to be unsightly. In a paste base, these compounds adhere to the skin adequately, but they must be reapplied because they lose their effectiveness rapidly as the thickness of the sunscreen is decreased. Many are incorporated into cosmetics, but are ineffective unless applied generously.

Red veterinary petrolatum is distilled from crude oil and contains a mixture of solids, liquids, and gelling agents. In a 0.03-nm (very thick) layer, it absorbs 100% of UVL between 296 and 302 nm, 98.2% at 313 nm, 84% at 334 nm and 42% at 360 nm (41).

Propyl gallate, used as a preservative in fats and chewing gum, may be the most effective sunscreen, despite its absorption peak of about 275 nm. By increasing its concentration, its spectrum covers the entire UVB (290–320 nm) range. However, this substance is a vigorous sensitizer, which eliminates it for commercial purposes.

Vehicles for sunscreens are very important. For example, many examiners have shown that 50–70% ethyl alcohol produces the most effective base for 5% PABA (18,30,43). This base allows maximal epithelial penetration of the PABA. This does not take into consideration sweating, bathing, and swimming, which wash the alcohol base off the skin if the sunscreen is not given time (about 2 hours) to fix to the stratum corneum. Although PABA penetrates and fixes to the stratum corneum, it should be reapplied for maximal effectiveness.

The thickness and composition are the most important factors in determining the effectiveness of a surface sunscreen (2). If, after applying this type of sunscreen, the person's skin looks naturally oily, the compound's thickness is about 0.002 nm, which increases the tolerance to UVB only about twofold. To maximize the compound's protection, a thickness of about 0.01 nm must be maintained. This is achieved only by frequent application. Vehicles which are nonwater miscible seem to remain on the skin much better than oil-in-water creams (2). If a person wanted to apply a sunscreen immediately prior to engaging in a sweat-producing activity or swimming, an oily or greasy base would adhere to the skin better than an alcohol or oil-in-water base. However, by planning ahead, the alcohol-based PABA will increase penetration if applied at least 1–2 hours in advance. Further protection may be achieved by using the oilier base just prior to and during activities that have a tendency to wash the sunscreens off.

The vehicles can also be sensitizers. The most frequent ones include lanolin, almond oil, and cocoa butter (9). Any cream containing vitamin E can also be sensitizing.

Many "suntan" products do not contain sunscreening substances, but merely lubricating compounds. These provide minimal (if any) protection against sunburn and chronic actinic damage (2).

Selecting the correct sunscreen requires definition of the person's needs. To prevent sunburn and chronic aging of the skin, the person should pick a sunscreen that protects against UVB light. PABA and its derivatives are the most effective. To protect against UVA light (i.e., for a person who has a photosensitive eruption triggered by light in the 320–400-nm range), benzophenones seem to be the most effective. For people who have photosensitivities in the visible light range, an opaque (physical barrier) sunscreen will be needed.

Occasionally, people require absolute protection from the sun. It is recommended that these people avoid sun, use protective clothing, and apply a sunscreen containing titanium dioxide, zinc oxide, kaolin, red ferric oxide, and a benzophenone when exposure cannot be avoided (43).

Anti-Inflammatory Agents

Sunburn and ultraviolet damage to the skin, as discussed, are a combination of reactions, a few of which include lysosomal rupture, vasodilatation, and an increase in the synthesis and release of prostaglandins. Numerous systemic and topical agents, including corticosteroids, indomethacin, and aspirin have been tried with minimal success to diminish the sunburn reaction. Corticosteroids reduce UV erythema by delaying its onset and decreasing its magnitude (29). The stronger the topical steroid, the more blanching of the sunburn that is produced. However, even strong topical steroids have little effect on UVL doses greater than 2 MED. The blanching is produced by vasoconstriction of the superficial cutaneous vessels (26). By stablizing the membranes, steroids have also been shown to decrease the rupture of lysosomes, which contain hydrolytic enzymes. In addition, they inhibit the biosynthesis and release of prostaglandins (16,17,29). Different topical steroids blanch erythema nicely at 1 MED but very little at light exposure greater than 4 MED (67). Strong steroids under occlusion, applied immediately after irradiation, suppress the erythema up to 5 MED (66). However, "Saran Wrap" occlusion is very uncomfortable. There is greater reduction in erythema when the topical steroid is placed after, rather than before, the exposure (67).

Indomethacin may be as effective against sunburn as are corticosteroids (29). Topical indomethacin (2.5%) solution is effective, not only in decreasing erythema but also in reducing the skin temperature and hyperalgesia to near-normal levels (62,63,65). There is no modification of UVL injury, such as keratinocyte cell death and altered DNA synthesis. Indomethacin is approximately 45 times more effective than aspirin.

Treatment For Sunburn and Phototoxic and Photoallergic Eruptions

Protection from sunlight is the most important modality in the control of photosensitive dermatidities. If a person knows that he will have extensive sun exposure, planning is necessary to prevent sunburn. Physical barriers including hats, clothing, and umbrellas are helpful shading devices. However, because of the scattering of UVB light, the burning rays can bend around hats or under trees or umbrellas and reflect off snow, water, sand, and grass. Clothing is a very effective block (except for wet white cotton). Sunscreens, when used properly, can be very useful protection. I recommend a combination of two types of sunscreens. First, a high SPF (14–15) PABA sunscreen in an alcohol base should be placed over *all* possible areas of sun exposure. This should be done at night to allow time for the PABA to penetrate and fix to the stratum corneum. To increase penetration, application should be preceded by a warm shower or warm compresses. People who are in the sun regularly should apply this formula every night, whether or not sun exposure is expected the next day. The PABA will accumulate in the stratum corneum and will provide long-lasting and very effective sun protection.

Sunburn and phototoxic eruptions are very difficult to treat. As has been mentioned, topical steroids, indomethacin, and aspirin are effective for minimal erythema but are ineffective for moderate to severe sunburns. Calamine and strong topical steroids can provide some comfort. Systemic steroids for severe erythema can be helpful (prednisone, 40 mg, tapered over 3 days).

Photoallergic eruptions are treated in the same manner as allergic contact dermatitis. If the eruption is eczematoid with crusting and oozing, the involved areas should be compressed at least three to four times daily until the oozing and crusting have stopped. Warm or cool tap water with or without salts (i.e., Burow's solution or epsom salts) should be used for the compresses. A strong topical steroid (Table 5) in a lotion or cream base should be used after compressing until the wounds begin to dry. If possible, avoid the strong and medium-strength topical steroids on the face or intertriginous areas. If they are needed in these areas, use them for no longer than 1 week. As the wound dries, a cream or ointment base is preferred to cover and occlude the fissures and microfissures that usually result from eczematoid eruptions. Secondary infection is common and should be treated with systemic antibiotics (cephalosporin, erythromycin, dicloxacillin). Topical antibiotics placed on an eczematoid eruption can produce a superimposed contact dermatitis and should be avoided.

TABLE 5
Topical Glucocorticosteroid Preparations

Potency[a]	Ointments	Creams	Gels	Liquids
High	Halcinonide (0.1% Halog) Fluocinonide (0.05% Lidex) Triamcinolone acetonide (Aristocort, 0.5% Kenalog) Betamethasone diproprionate (0.05% Diprosone)	Halcinonide 0.1% Halog Fluocinonide (0.05% Lidex) Triamcinolone acetonide (Aristocort, 0.5% Kenalog) Amcinonide (0.1% Cyclocort)	Fluocinonide (0.05% Topsyn)	Halcinonide (0.1% Halog) Betamethasone diprorionate (0.5% Diprosone)
Medium	Triamcinolone acetonide (Aristocort, 0.1% Kenalog) Betamethasone valereate (0.1% Valisone) Betamethasone benzoate (0.025% Uticort) Fluocinolone acetonide (Synalar, 0.025% Fluonid)	Triamcinolone acetonide (Aristocort, 0.1% Kenalog) Betamethasone valereate (0.1% Valisone) Fluocinolone acetonide (Synalar, 0.025% Fluonid) Flurandrenolide (0.05% Cordran) Clocortolone private (Cloderm 0.1%)	Triamcinolone acetonide (Aristocort, 0.1% Kenalog) Betamethasone benzoate (Flurobate, Benisone, 0.025% Uticort)	Betamethasone valereate (0.1% Valisone) Fluocinolone acetonide (Synalar, 0.01% Fluonid) Triamcinolone acetonide (Aristocort, 0.1% Kenalog) Flurandrenolide (0.05% Cordran) Betamethasone benzoate (0.025% flurobate) (Uticort, Benisone)
Low	Triamcinolone acetonide (0.025% Kenalog) Desonide (0.05% Tridesilon) Flurandrenolide (0.025% Cordran)	Triamcinolone acetonide (Aristocort, 0.025% Kenalog) Desonide (0.05% Tridesilon) Flurandrenolide (0.025% Cordran) Fluocinolone acetonide (Synalar, 0.01% Fluonid)		Triamcinolone acetonide (0.025% Kenalog)
Lowest	Preparations with hydrocortisone, prednisolone, dexamethasone, and methylprednisolone			

[a] Equivalent potency within each group.
Source: From Reference 44.

It is also important to determine the cause of the photodermatitis. As previously mentioned, the history, location, and morphology of the eruption are very important. Photo- patch testing is a helpful adjunct for photoallergic dermatitis. Protection in the proper wavelength range should be provided with the appropriate sunscreen.

References

1. Ackerman, A. Bernard, *Histologic Diagnosis of Inflammatory Skin Diseases,* Lea and Febiger, Philadelphia, 1978, pp. 192–93.
2. Algra, Ronald J.; John M. Knox, Topical photoprotective agents, *Int. J. Dermatol.,* **17,** 628–34, 1978.
3. Boehem, A.; B. Fantus, Evaluation of skin protection against ultraviolet Rays, *Arch. Phys. Med. Rehabil.,* **20:**69, 1939.
4. Bold, Harold C., *Morphology of Plants,* 2nd ed., Harper and Row, New York, 1967.
5. Catalano, P. M.; D. D. Fulghum, A water-resistant sunscreen, *Clin. Exp. Dermatol.,* **2:**127, 1977.
6. Cole, Walter J., Clinical evaluation of a new sunscreen preparation, *Cutis,* 145–98, 1971.
7. Cripps, D. J.; S. Heyedus, Protection factor of sunscreens to monochromatic radiation, *Arch. Dermatol.,* **109:**202, 1974.
8. Daniels, F., Physical factors in sun exposure, *Arch. Dermatol.,* **85:**358, 1962.
9. Fisher, A. A., *Contact Dermatitis,* Lea and Febiger, Philadelphia, 1973, pp. 209–13.
10. Fisher, A. A., The presence of benzocaine in sunscreens containing glyceryl PABA, *Arch. Dermatol.,* **113:**1299–1300, 1977.
11. Fitzpatrick, T. B., *Sunlight and Man,* University of Tokyo Press, Tokyo, 1974, pp. 495–557.
12. Forbes, M. A., Jr.; M. Brannen, and W. C. King, Benzophenone as a sunscreen, *South. Med. J.,* **59:**321, 1966.
13. Frain-Bell, W.; B. E. Johnson, Contact allergic sensitivity to plants and the photosensitivity dermatitis and actinic reticuloid syndrome, *J. Dermatol.,* **101:**503, 1979.
14. Freeman, R. G.; J. M. Knox, Influences of temperature on ultraviolet injury, *Arch. Dermatol.,* **89:**858, 1964.
15. Gates, D., Spectral distribution of solar radiation at the earth's surface, *Science,* **151:**523–29, 1966.
16. Greaves, Malcolm W.; Wendy McDonald-Gibson, Effect of non-steroid anti-inflammatory drugs on Prostaglandin biosynthesis by Skin, *Br. J. Dermatol.,* **88:**41, 1973.
17. Greaves, Malcolm; Wendy McDonald-Gibson, Effect of non-steroid anti-inflammatory and anti-pruritic drugs on prostaglandin biosynthesis by human skin, *J. Invest. Dermatol.,* **61:**121–29, 1973.
18. Groves, G. A., The selection and evaluation of ultraviolet absorbers, *Australas. J. Dermatol.,* **14:**21, 1973.
19. Hanno, R.; Owen, J. Callen, Sunlight and the skin, *Primary Care,* **5:**737–56, 1978.
20. Harber, Leonard C., Clinical evaluation of quantitative differences in ultraviolet absorption of compounds containing the substituted benzoic acid nucleus, *J. Invest. Dermatol.,* **23:**427, 1954.
21. Harber, Leonard C., Drug photosenstivity, *Clinical Dermatology,* Demis, D. J., ed., Harper and Row, Hagerstown, Md., 1981, pp. 2–3.
22. Harber, Leonard C.; Harriet Harris, and Rudolph Baer, Photoallergic contact dermatitis, *Arch. Dermatol.,* **94:**255–62, 1966.
23. Hjorth, Niels; Jytte Roed-Peterson, and Khristian Thomsen, Airborne contact dermatitis from Compositae oleoresins simulating photodermatitis, *Br. J. Dermatol.,* **95:**613, 1976.
24. Jarrett, M., Drug photosensitization, *Int. J. Dermatol.,* **15:**317, 1976.
25. Johnson, B. E., *et al.,* In photophysiology, A. C. Geise, ed., Academic Press, New York, Vol. IV, 1968.
26. Johnson, B. E.; F. Daniels, Jr., Lyposomes and the reactions of skin to ultraviolet Light, *J. Invest. Dermatol.,* **53:**85–94, 1969.
27. Kahn, G.; M. C. Curry, Ultraviolet light protection by several new compounds, *Arch. Dermatol.,* **109:**510, 1974.
28. Kahn, Guinter; M. C. Curry, Ultraviolet light protection by several new Compounds, *Arch. Dermatol.,* **109:**510–17, 1974.
29. Kaidbey, Kays H.; Amalk Kurban, The influence of corticosteroids and topical indomethacin on sunburn erythema, *J. Invest. Dermatol.,* **66:**153–56, 1976.
30. Katz, S. I., Relative effectiveness of selected sunscreens, *Arch. Dermatol.,* **101:**466, 1970.
31. Kestenbaum, Thelda; James Kalivas, Solar pruritus, *Arch. Dermatol.,* **115:**1368, 1979.
32. Klarmann, E. G., *Cosmetic Chemistry for Dermatologists,* Charles C. Thomas, Springfield, Ill., 1962, p. 86.
33. Kligman, A. M., *Sunlight and Man,* Fitzpatrick, T. B., *et al.,* eds., University of Tokyo Press, Tokyo, 1974.
34. Knox, J. M.; J. Guina, and E. Cockerell, Benzophenones: Ultraviolet light absorbing agents, *J. Invest. Dermatol.,* **29:**435, 1957.
35. Langner, A.; A. M. Kligman, Further sunscreen studies of aminobenzoic acid, *Arch. Dermatol.,* **105:**851, 1972.
36. Langner, A.; A. M. Kligman, Tanning without sunburn with aminobenzoic acid type Sunscreen, *Arch. Dermatol.,* **106:**338, 1972.
37. Lever, Walter F.; Gundrita Schaumberg-Lever, *Histopathology of the Skin,* 5th ed., J. B. Lippincott, Philadelphia, 1975, pp. 98–99.
38. Ljunggren, Bo, Psoralen photoallergy caused by plant contact, *Contact Dermatitis,* **3:**85–90, 1977.
39. Loring, A. L., Physiological and pathological changes in skin from sunburn and suntan, *J.A.M.A.,* **173:**1227, 1960.
40. *Los Angeles Times,* August 12, 1981, p. 8.
41. Luckiesh, M.; A. H. Taylor, H. N. Cole, *et al.,* Protective skin coatings for prevention of sunburn, *J.A.M.A.,* **130:**1, 1946.
42. MacLeod, T. M.; W. Frain-Bell, A study of chemical light screening agents, *Br. J. Dermatol.,* **92:**417, 1975.
43. MacLeod, T. M.; W. Frain-Bell, The study of the efficacy of some agents used for the protection of the skin from exposure to light, *Br. J. Dermatol.,* **84:**266, 1971.
44. Mandy, S.; K. Kremer, Topical glucocorticosteroids, *Dermatology,* 55, 1978.
45. Mathias, T. C. G.; Howard I. Maibach, and John Epstein, Allergic contact photodermatitis to para-aminobenzoic acid, *Arch. Dermatol.,* **114:**1665–66, 1978.
46. Meltzer, L.; R. L. Baer, Sensitization to monoglycerol

para-aminobenzoate: A case report, *J. Invest. Dermatol.,* **12**:31, 1949.

47. Moller, Halvor, Phototoxicity of *Dictamnus alba, Contact Dermatitis,* **4**:264–69, 1978.

48. Norins, Arthur L., Effects of light on skin, *Clinical Dermatology,* Demis, D. J., ed., Harper and Row, Hagerstown, Md., 1981, p. 2.

49. Owens, Donald; John M. Knox, H. T. Hudson, Andrew H. Rudolph, and Douglas Troll, Influence of wind on chronic ultraviolet light-induced carcinogenesis, *Br. J. Dermatol.,* **97**:285, 1977.

50. Owens, Donald W.; J. M. Knox, H. T. Hudson, and D. Troll, Influence of humidity on ultraviolet injury, *J. Invest. Dermatol,* **64**:250, 1975.

51. Owens, Donald W.; John M. Knox, Hugh T. Hudson, and Douglas Troll, Influence of wind on ultraviolet injury, *Arch. Dermatol.,* **109**:200–1, 1974.

52. Parrish, J. A., *et al.,* Cutaneous effects of pulsed nitrogen gas laser irradiation, *J. Invest. Dermatol.,* **67**:603, 1976.

53. Pathak, M. A.; T. B. Fitzpatrick, and E. Frenke, Evaluation of topical agents that prevent sunburn: Superiority of para-aminobenzoic acid and its ester in ethyl alcohol, *N. Engl. J. Med.,* **280**:1459, 1969.

54. Ramsay, Colin A., Solar urticaria, *Int. J. Dermatol.,* **19**:233–36, 1980.

55. Ramsay, Colin A., Cutaneous reactions to actinic and ionizing radiations, *Texbook of Dermatology,* Arthur Rook and D. S. Wilkinson, eds., Blackwell, Oxford, 1979, p. 524.

56. Ramsey, Colin A., Solar urticaria treatment by inducing tolerance to artificial radiation and natural light, *Arch. Dermatol.,* **113**:1222, 1977.

57. Rothman, S.; A. B. Henningsen, The sunburn protecting effect of para-aminobenzoic acid, *J. Invest. Dermatol.,* **23**:427, 1954.

58. Rothmann, S; J. Rubin, Sunburn and para-aminobenzoic acid, *J. Invest. Dermatol.,* **5**:445, 1942.

59. Schmidt, Richard J., Fred J. Evans, Plants and plant products that induce contact dermatitis, *J. Med. Plant Res.,* **38**:291–92, 1980.

60. Shelley, Walter B.; Charles L. Heaton, Pathogenesis of solar urticaria, *Arch. Dermatol.,* **112**:850–52, 1976.

61. Smith, E. B.; J. E. Dickson, and J. M. Knox, Protection from sunlight: Evaluation of a new screening agent, *South. Med. J.,* **66**:278, 1973.

62. Snyder, Diane Sekura, Cutaneous effects of topical indomethacin, an inhibitor of prostaglandin synthesis on UV damaged skin, *J. Invest. Dermatol.,* **64**:322–25, 1975.

63. Snyder, Diane Sekura; William Eaglstein, Intradermal anti-prostaglandin agents and sunburn, *J. Invest. Dermatol.,* **62**:47–50, 1974.

64. Snyder, Diane Sekura, William Eaglstein, Prostaglandins and sunburn, Department of Dermatology, University of Miami, Miami, Florida, 33152, Program, p. 110.

65. Snyder, Diane Sekura; William Eaglstein, Topical Indomethacin and Sunburn, *Br. J. Dermatol.,* **90**, 91–93, 1974.

66. Stoughton, R. B., Corticosteroids in psoriasis, *International Symposium on Psoriasis,* Farber and Cox, eds., Stanford University Press, Stanford, Calif., 1971.

67. Sukanto, H.; J. P. Nater, and E. Bleumink, Suppression of ultraviolet erythema by topical corticosteroids, *Dermatologica,* **161**:84–6, 1980.

68. Thompson, Greg; Howard Maibach, and John Epstein, Allergic contact dermatitis from sunscreen preparations complicating photodermatitis," *Arch. Dermatol.,* **113**:1252–53, 1977.

69. Thune, P. O., Y. J. Solberg, Photosensitivity and allergy to aromatic lichen acids, Compositae oleoresins and other plant substances, *Contact Dermatitis,* **6**:64–71, 1980.

70. Tipton, John, The selection of sunblocking topical agents to protect the skin, *Plast. Reconstr. Surg.,* **62**, 223–28, 1978.

71. Waisman, M., Solar pruritus of the elbows, *Arch. Dermatol.,* **98**:481–85, 1968.

72. Willis, I., L. Cylus, UVA erythema in skin: Is it a sunburn?, *J. Invest. Dermatol.,* **68**:178, 1977.

73. Willis, I.; A. Kligman, and J. Epstein, Effects of long ultraviolet rays on human skin: Photoprotective or photoaugmentative?, *J. Invest. Dermatol.,* **59**:416, 1972.

74. Willis, I.; A. M. Kligman, Aminobenzoic acid and its esters, *Arch. Dermatol.,* **102**:405, 1970.

75. Ying, O. Y.; J. A. Parrish, and M. A. Pathak, Additive erythemogenic effects of middle (280–320 nm) and long (320–400 nm) wave ultraviolet light, *J. Invest. Dermatol.,* **63**:273, 1974.

16 | WILDLAND FIRES: DANGERS AND SURVIVAL*

Kathleen M. Davis
Robert W. Mutch

Out of the underbrush dashed a man—grimy, breathless, hat in hand. At his heels came another. Then a whole crew, all casting fearful glances behind them.

"She's coming! The whole country's afire! Grab your stuff, ranger, and let's get outa here!" gasped the leader.
　　　　　　—From *When the Mountains Roared,* stories of the 1910 fire

Magnitude of the Problem

The date was August 20, 1910, in the forest lands of northern Idaho and western Montana, and the vivid history of the 1910 forest fires was recounted by Elers Koch (22):

For two days, the wind blew a gale from the southwest. All along the line from north of the Canadian boundary south to the Salmon River, the gale blew. Little fires picked up into big ones. Firelines which had been held for days melted away under the fierce blast. The sky turned a ghastly yellow and at four o'clock it was black dark ahead of the advancing flames. One observer said the air felt electric, as though the whole world was ready to go up in spontaneous combustion. The heat of the fire and the great masses of flaming gas created great whirlwinds which mowed swaths of trees in

---

* Line drawings on heat transfer and fire behavior are adapted from J. S. Barrows' "Fire Behavior in Northern Rocky Mountain Forests." The booklet "Planning for Initial Attack" by the USDA Forest Service was a helpful reference on fire behavior principles. We thank those who reviewed this chapter and offered helpful suggestions.

FIGURE 1 These burned-over and wind-thrown trees resulted from the 1910 forest fire near Falcon, Idaho. (Courtesy of the USDA Forest Service. Photo by Joe Halm.)

advance of the flames (Figure 1). In those terrible days many fires swept thirty to fifty miles across mountain ranges and rivers.

The town of Wallace, Idaho, lay directly in the path of the fire, and by the evening of the 20th a third of the town lay in ashes (Figure 2). The flames from the Coeur d'Alene fires swept on to Taft, Saltese, DeBorgia and Haugan, crossed the high range to the Clark Fork River, jumped the Clark Fork, and swept on across still another range to the head of the Fisher River, destroying towns, homesteads, lumber camps, everything in their path.

Altogether, 85 lives were lost in the two-day conflagration. Many of the surviving firefighters were terribly burned, and as the pitiful remnants of the crews straggled out of the mountains, the hospitals of Wallace were filled with injured men.

One must ask whether those levels of destruction, injury, and fatality could be repeated today in the face of modern fire suppression technology. The answer requires an analysis of conditions that set up high-intensity fire behavior conditions in the forests of Idaho and Montana in 1910. Numerous conflagrations before and after the 1910 fires provide ample testimony to causative conditions. The Peshtigo, Michigan (1881), Hinckley, Yacoult, and Maine fires burned several million acres and killed more than 2000 people between 1871 and 1947.

On the same day (October 8, 1871) that a fire wiped out the town of Peshtigo, Wisconsin, the great Chicago fire devastated urban Chicago. Comparative statistics for those two fires highlight the destructive potential of wildland fires: The Peshtigo fire covered 518,016 hectares (1,280,000 acres) and killed 1150 people, whereas 860 hectares (2124 acres) burned and 300 lives were lost as a result of the Chicago fire (23).

All these historic wildland fires shared several common elements: many uncontrolled fires burning at one time; prolonged drought, high temperatures, and moderate to strong winds; and mixed conifer and hardwood fuels with slash from logging and land clearing. These large fires primarily occurred in conifer forests north of the 42nd meridian, or roughly across the northern quarter of the contiguous United States (3). One critical element, which is not as likely to occur today as formerly, was the simultaneous presence of many uncontrolled fires. The effectiveness of modern fire suppression organizations has been greatly enhanced by their rapid growth and air deployment of firefighters and retardants of even the remotest wildland locations. Where high-velocity winds and more than 1600 individual fires contributed to the spread of the 1910 fires, it is unlikely that a multifire situation of that magnitude would ever occur today.

Prolonged drought, high winds, and flammable fuel types are as significant to the behavior of high-intensity fires today as previously. In 1967, the Sundance fire in northern Idaho burned more than 22,627 hectares (55,910 acres) and killed two firefighters. In 1970, other fires burned approximately 40,470 hectares (100,000 acres) in the vicinity of Wenatchee, Washington. During the drought-stricken 1977 fire season in California, 21 major fires burned almost 150,000 hectares

FIGURE 2 Burned ruins of the foundry in Wallace, Idaho, furnish mute testimony to the destructive force of the 1910 fires. The cottage on the terrace was the only one left standing in that part of town. (Courtesy of the USDA Forest Service. Photo by R. H. McKay.)

(370,000 acres). The largest of these fires, the remote Marble-Cone, spread through 70,418 hectares (174,000 acres) of flammable chaparral and mixed forest. The Sycamore fire near Santa Barbara, although only 324 hectares (800 acres) in size, destroyed more than 200 homes.

In terms of statistics, the benefits accrued by decreasing the number of uncontrolled fire starts have been offset by the tendency of people to live in fire-prone areas. For example, some of the fires most potentially damaging to human lives and property occur in chaparral shrub fuel types in California. Wilson (23) described the severe 1970 fire year in California, in which official estimates showed that 97% of 1,260 fires that occurred between September 15 and November 15 were held to less than 121 hectares (300 acres). The other 3% of the fires, fueled by a prolonged drought

and fanned by strong Santa Ana winds, produced 14 deaths, destroyed 885 homes, and burned more than 242,820 hectares (600,000 acres). Ten years later, the same situation recurred over 28,330 hectares (70,000 acres) in southern California (Figure 3), resulting in the death of five people and the loss of more than 400 structures.

Wildland fires that threaten human lives and property are not exclusively located in southern California, since the exodus to dwell in wildland regions has become a national phenomenon. Fires burned more than 80,940 hectares (200,000 acres) in Maine in October 1947, killing 16 people; another 80,940 hectares (200,000 acres) burned in New Jersey in 1963. On July 16, 1977, the Pattee Canyon fire in Missoula, Montana, destroyed six homes (Figure 4) and charred 486 hectares (1200 acres) of forests and grasslands in only

FIGURE 3 Fire in southern California in 1980. High-velocity Santa Ana winds pushed the Panorama fire into urban areas of San Bernadino, California, causing extensive property damage.

a few hours (10). Front page stories in the *Missoulian* during the 1979 fire season attested to the routine nature of such fire threats:

Five families near Libby, Montana, fled for safety as the Deep Granite fire approached their homes. The 2,330-acre (943-hectare) fire eventually leveled a house, a barn and two sheds.

Three houses and three other structures were destroyed and about 50 homes threatened when a

800-acre (324-hectare) forest fire burned within two-and-a-half miles (4 kilometers) of Bonners Ferry, Idaho.

The Mill Creek fire west of Lolo, Montana, burned about 600 acres (243 hectares) of forest land and came within one-quarter mile (.4 kilometer) of residences.

Many similar accounts exist from other parts of the United States.

FIGURE 4 A total of six homes in Missoula, Montana were reduced to chimneys and foundations in the 1977 Pattee Canyon fire. (Photo courtesy of William C. Fischer.)

It is becoming increasingly difficult to have a wildland fire situation that does not involve people in some way. In spite of all this, people are not fully aware of their exposure to fire risks and hazards when living and traveling in or near wildland areas. *Risk,* in the jargon of the forest fire specialist, is the probability that a fire will occur. *Hazard* is the likelihood that a fire, once started, will cause unwanted results. Risk deals with causative agents; hazard deals with the fuel complex (10). The results of two recent surveys indicated a general feeling of overconfidence by most residents toward the potential danger of forest fire. Eighty percent of Seeley Lake, Montana, forest residents who were interviewed thought that the forest fire hazard was low to moderate in their

area (9). Seventy-five percent of Colorado residents interviewed by Hulbert thought that the forest fire hazard was low or moderate in mountain subdivisions of Colorado (11). Of course, actual forest fire hazards in these two areas were higher than the public estimates (Figure 5).

Traditional levels of fire-related injuries and fatalities probably will not be attained again, since the numbers of *uncontrolled* fires burning at one time will be substantially less due to improved fire prevention, detection, and suppression techniques. Still, the exposure rate of people and their property to fire risks and hazards will remain high, because easy mobility facilitates life and recreation in wildlands. There is a growing need for the general public,

FIGURE 5 Wildland fuels and homes combine to pose significant fire hazards. (Photo courtesy of June D. Freedman.)

emergency medical personnel, and fire suppression organizations to be well prepared to deal with wildland fire encounters.

The purposes of this chapter are to provide emergency medical personnel with a better understanding of the nature of physical hazards and injuries associated with wildland fires and to suggest safety and survival procedures. These procedures also are applicable to wildland homeowners and recreationists. In addition, wildland fire management programs, fire hazards, and fire behavior principles are discussed.

Wildland Fire Management Programs

Before delving into the subject of wildland fire hazards, some background information on

fire management programs is useful. Since the early 1900s, federal, state, and local fire protection agencies have routinely extinguished wildland fires in order to protect watershed, range, and timber values, as well as human lives and property. Lack of roads has not prevented the application of an increasingly sophisticated technology of fire detection, fire danger rating systems, and fire suppression. The lookout towers and foot trails of the 1930s have gradually been supplanted by patrol planes, some equipped with infrared heat scanners, and other aircraft that can deliver firefighters, equipment, and fire-retarding chemicals to even the most remote fire. It is unlikely, however, that modern fire suppression technology can indefinitely reduce the number of hectares burned. Effective fire suppression in the past has caused wildland fuels to accumulate on a greater amount of contiguous acreage, contributing to present-day fires of unnatural size and intensity. Many agencies are now using prescribed fire, or fire under predetermined conditions, to manage these accumulations of fuels.

We have learned that not all fires are categorically bad. In the United States, many plant communities are highly flammable during certain periods in their life cycles. Annual grasses, ponderosa pine, and chaparral exhibit a flammable condition during almost every dry season. Other species, such as jack pine or lodgepole pine, may remain fuel free during much of their life cycle, eventually becoming predisposed to fire through insects, diseases, and natural mortality.

Thousands of years of evolutionary development in the presence of periodic wildland fires have produced plant species well adapted to recurrent fires. Numerous studies have demonstrated that wildland fires can have a beneficial effect on plant and animal communities. It has been reported that disturbances such as fire tend to recycle ecosystems and maintain diversity (13). Thus, there is an emerging awareness that fire should be returned to wildland ecosystems to perpetuate viable fire-adapted plant and animal communities.

As a consequence of this increasing awareness of the ecologic role and benefits of fire, several agencies are using fire as a resource management tool. A landmark report to the National Park Service by the Advisory Board on Wildlife Management (12) cited several examples of ecosystems that had changed significantly due to human implementation of fire protection:

When the forty-niners poured over the Sierra Nevada into California, those that kept diaries spoke almost to a man of the wide-spaced columns of mature trees that grew on the lower western slope in gigantic magnificence. Today much of the west slope is a dog-hair thicket of young pines, white fir, incense-cedar, and mature brush—a direct function of overprotection from natural ground fires. Not only is this accumulation of fuel dangerous to the giant sequoias and other mature trees, but the animal life is meager, wildflowers are sparse, and to some at least the vegetative tangle is depressing, not uplifting.

The major policy change which we would rec

ommend to the National Park Service is that it recognize the enormous complexity of ecologic communities and the diversity of management procedures required to preserve them. Reluctance to undertake biotic management can never lead to a realistic presentation of primitive America, much of which supported successional communities that were maintained by fires, floods, hurricanes and other natural forces.

PRESCRIBED FIRE

Prescribed fire, or the intentional ignition of grass, shrub, or forest fuels for specific purposes, according to predetermined conditions, has long been a recognized land management practice. Objectives of such burning vary: to reduce fire hazards after logging, expose mineral soil for seedbeds, regulate insects and diseases, and improve range forage and wildlife habitat. In some areas managed by the National Park Service, United States Department of Agriculture (USDA) Forest Service, and Bureau of Land Management, fires may be allowed to burn according to approved prescriptions; fire management areas have been

FIGURE 6 Some lightning fires in wilderness and national parks are now allowed to burn under observation to perpetuate natural ecosystems. This fire covered 1200 acres over a 43 day period in the Selway-Bitterroot Wilderness in northern Idaho before it was extinguished by rain. (Photo courtesy of the USDA Forest Service.)

established in national parks and wildernesses from the Florida Everglades to the Sierra Nevada mountains in California (Figure 6). Fires are not simply allowed to burn; suppression measures, backed by modern fire control technology, are still employed when necessary to protect human life and property or to contain fires within the management unit.

EMERGING PROGRAMS OF MANAGEMENT

Emerging programs for dealing with the overall spectrum of fire are appropriately termed *fire management* (2). They are based upon the concept that fire and the complex interrelated factors influencing fire phenomena can and should be managed. In providing scientifically sound fire management programs that respond to the needs of people and natural environments, we must maintain full respect for the power of fire and the effects of this power on both wildland environments and on the people who live and work in them (2).

Today's wildland fire dilemma is compounded by several factors. Just as resource agencies are attempting to provide a more natural role for fire in wildland ecosystems, the general public is living and recreating in many of these same areas at an ever-increasing rate. Superimposed on this situation is the fact that past fire exclusion practices have contributed to the likelihood of larger fires burning at greater intensities, due to abnormal fuel accumulations in some areas. This combination of events is posing life hazards to the general public as well as to emergency medical and firefighting personnel. Juxtaposition of people, property, and wildland fuel has resulted in the sacrifice of relatively safe perimeter fire suppression strategies in favor of directly protecting people and their possessions (24). Direct suppression actions *within* the fire's perimeter place firefighters at more of a disadvantage from a safety standpoint.

Exposure to wildland fires is increasing for inexperienced people both in the backcountry and near apparently secure residences, recreational homes, and cabins. Thus, what is known of fire behavior and fire survival principles must be readily available to emergency medical personnel, wildland dwellers, and recreationists. It is no longer appropriate that

such information be the exclusive property of those in fire protection agencies.

Wildland/Urban Interface: Nature of the Problem

There is rarely a hot, dry autumn in southern California without severe wind-driven fires that threaten or burn homes in the interface of wildland and urban areas. The news media report startling losses of homes, watersheds, vegetation cover, and, too often, human lives. The costs of property losses, resource losses, and suppression actions are staggering. Sadly, though, too few people learn from the repeated lessons that they must understand wildland fire ecology and fire behavior. Residents need to understand that in some areas fires *are* inevitable, so that they can prepare to protect their lives and property better within a fire-prone environment.

WILDLAND LESSONS

The problems of living in a fire environment are no longer unique to southern California. In recent years, disasters have occurred in Montana, Utah, Colorado, and Oregon. As more people move out of cities and into wildlands, we can expect these tragedies to recur.

Following the Montana Pattee Canyon fire in 1977 (Figure 7), Fischer and Books (8) described three lessons learned from blackened trees and burned homes:

Lesson One: Fire Prevention Is Not Always Effective

The prevention problem goes well beyond fires started by careless smokers, campers, and hunters. Fire prevention specialists must deal with a long list of potential ignition sources, including arsonists. Prevention must be taken more seriously by wildland residents and visitors who do not realize the awesome force of fire.

Lesson Two: Fire Suppression Is Not Always Effective

Weather has a major influence on fire behavior, and under certain conditions no mea-

FIGURE 7 This 1977 forest fire caused many residents of Pattee Canyon to evacuate their homes. Missoula, Montana, is in the foreground.

sures used by trained, well-equipped suppression forces can immediately control a fast, wind-driven fire fed by dry fuels. Such fires are generally suppressed when weather conditions change to benefit firefighters, or when fuels decrease or become less flammable.

Lesson Three: Fire Is Part of the Wildland Environment

Fire is an integral wildland process that rejuvenates vegetation and can be used to regulate fuel at manageable levels. The *natural* interval between fires (i.e., unaltered by humans) depends primarily on the ignition source, favorable weather conditions, and the time required for flammable vegetation to develop and litter to accumulate. Prior to 1900, the average interval between fires was 5–15 years in many ponderosa pine forests, whereas intervals may be more than several hundred years in some wet coastal or mountain forests. Fire history studies of forest, shrub, and grass environments provide basic information to use in

coping with fire in the wildland/urban interface.

Evidence of historic fires in southern California shows they occurred in variable sizes at average intervals of 10–20 years. The pattern of age classes regulated future fire sizes because younger vegetation produced sparse, discontinuous, and less flammable fuel. Humans attempted to exclude fire, and as a result, chaparral plant communities now constitute large areas of hazardous fuels in the wildland/urban interface. Homes are being built where fires burned periodically in the past and where years of suppression have promoted accumulation and continuity of fuels. A logical application of this fire history knowledge is to modify fuels around homesites and subdivisions, using prescribed fire or mechanical treatment to simulate the age class pattern of historic fires.

It is also wise to have sensible land development practices, because tragedies arise not only from ignorance of fuels and fire behavior but also from a greater concern for the esthetics of a homesite rather than for fire safety. Several aspects of development detract from fire safety in the wildland/urban interface (6,8):

1. Lack of access to adequate water sources
2. Firewood stacked next to houses
3. Slash (i.e., branches, stumps, logs, and other vegetative residues) piled on homesites or along access roads
4. Structures built on slopes with unenclosed stilt foundations
5. Trees and shrubs growing next to structures, under eaves, and among stilt foundations
6. Roads that are steep, narrow, winding, unmapped, unsigned, unnamed, and bordered by slash or dense vegetation that makes them virtually undrivable during a fire
7. Subdivisions on sites without two or more access roads for simultaneous ingress-egress
8. Roads and bridges without the grade, design, and width to permit simultaneous evacuation by residents and access by firefighters, emergency medical personnel, and equipment
9. Excessive slopes, heavy fuels, structures built in box canyons, and other hazardous situations
10. Lack of fuelbreaks around homesites and in subdivisions
11. Living fuels that have not been modified by thinning, landscaping, or other methods in order to reduce vegetation and litter on sites that contribute to fire intensity
12. Homes constructed with flammable building materials (wooden shakes, shingles)

Fire Behavior Principles

URBAN AND WILDLAND FIRE THREATS

Safety precautions for wildland firefighting crews are continually upgraded in the light of new knowledge about the behavior of fires. Fire sites where people were injured or killed are visited afterward to assess fuel loading, terrain features, and probable wind movements at the time of the fire (Figure 8).

In reviewing such tragedies, a sobering observation is that crew members are almost always experienced and well equipped firefighters, trained to anticipate "blowup" fire conditions. However, when visibility is lowered to 20 feet, noise levels preclude voice communication, eyes fill with tears, and wind blows debris in all directions, a person's judgment is badly impaired. Too often, previous

training gives way to panic, which can lead to irrational decisions that result in serious injury or death.

This scenario is most evident in urban fires; the pattern is familiar to all fire chiefs when hysteria affects persons trapped in burning buildings. It is informative to review how fire kills in the urban setting and compare this sequence of events with wildland fire. This adaptation from Owen describes what happens (16):

Heat rises rapidly to upper stories when a fire starts in the basement or on the ground floor. Toxic gases and smoke rise to the ceiling and work their way down to the victim—a vital lesson for families planning protective measures. Smoke poses the double problem of obscuring exit routes and contributing to pulmonary injury and oxygen deprivation.

As the fire consumes oxygen, the ambient oxygen content drops, impairing neuromuscular activity. When the oxygen content drops below 16%, death by asphyxiation will ensue unless the victim is promptly evacuated. Asphyxiation, not fire itself, is the leading cause of fire deaths.

Ambient temperatures may rise extremely rapidly from even small fires. Temperatures of 300°F will cause rapid loss of consciousness and, along with toxic gases, will severely damage lung tissues. Warning devices may offer the only possibility for survival due to the rapid onset of debilitating symptoms.

There are some obvious similarities and differences regarding fire threats in urban and wildland situations:

1. Smoke, heat, and gases are not as concentrated in wildland situations as in the confined quarters of urban fires.
2. Flames are not a leading killer in either the urban or wildland situation.
3. Although oxygen levels may be reduced near wildland fires, there is usually sufficient replenishment of oxygen in the outdoor environment to minimize deprivation. Asphyxiation, however, can also be an important cause of death in wildland fires.
4. Inhalation of superheated gases poses as serious a threat to life in wildland fires as in urban fires.
5. Wildland smoke does not contain toxic compounds produced by combustion of plastics and other household materials, but it does impair visibility, contains carbon monoxide, and has suspended particulates that cause severe physical irritation.

FIGURE 8 In an attempt to avoid the intense heat of this brush fire in southwestern Colorado, four firefighters took refuge in the fireline, in the foreground at point A. Affected by intense convective and radiant heat and dense smoke, one individual ran into the fire and died at point B. Another individual ran approximately 1000 feet down the ridge, where his body was found at point C. The third fatality was a person who remained at point A; he died a short time after this position was overrun by fire. The only survivor also remained in a prone position at point A with his face pressed to the ground. At one point he reached back and threw dirt on his burning pants legs. The survivor sustained severe burns to the back of his legs, buttocks, and arms. The death of the other three individuals was attributed to asphyxiation. (Photo courtesy of the USDA Forest Service.)

6. Automatic early-warning devices and sprinkler systems may protect people from serious injury or death in the urban environment, but in the wildland environment, people must rely on their own senses, knowledge, and skills to provide early warning of a pending life threat.

FIRE BEHAVIOR KNOWLEDGE: A WILDLAND EARLY-WARNING SYSTEM

The science of fire behavior describes and predicts the performance of wildland fires in terms of rates of spread, intensity levels, ignition probabilities, spotting, and crowning potentials. (*Spotting* defines a fire spread mecha-

nism resulting from airborne firebrands or embers; *crowning* defines a fire spread mechanism horizontally through the canopies of shrubs or trees, more or less independent of fire burning on the ground.) No two fires are exactly alike, as there is an almost infinite number of combinations of fuel, weather, and topographic factors. Knowledge of current and predicted weather information and fire danger ratings can be obtained from local wildland fire protection agencies.

Experienced firefighters routinely assess the probable behavior of fires under current and expected weather conditions in relation to lo-

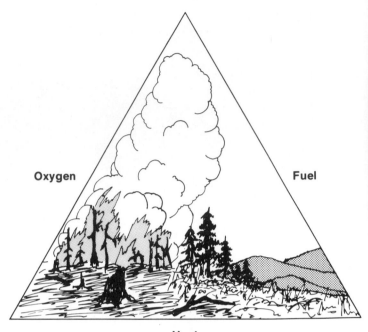

Oxygen

Fuel

Heat

FIGURE 9 Combustion is a process involving the combination of heat, oxygen, and fuel. An understanding of the variation of these three factors is fundamental to an understanding of fire behavior.

cal fuel and topography conditions. It is equally important that the emergency medical person, backcountry recreationist, and wildland homeowner be prepared to apply basic fire behavior principles to provide for adequate personal safety. A cardinal rule of fire safety is to base all actions on current and expected behavior of fires. Attention to simple principles, indicators, and rules should enable wildland users to anticipate and avoid fire threats.

Physical Principles of Heat Transfer

Heat, oxygen, and fuel are required in a proper combination before ignition and combustion will occur (Figure 9) (1). If any one of the three is absent, or if the three elments are not in proper balance, there will be no fire. Fire control actions are directed at disrupting one or more elements of this basic fire triangle. Since heat is critical in fire behavior, it is important to review different heat transfer methods.

With respect to a fire, heat energy is transferred by conduction, convection, radiation, and spotting; generally, only the last three processes are significant in a wildland setting. Although conduction through solid objects is important in the burning of logs, this process

does not transfer much heat outward from a flaming front.

Convection, or the movement of hot masses of air, accounts for most heat transfer outward from the fire. Convective currents generally move vertically unless a wind or slope generates some lateral movement. Convection is responsible for preheating fuels upslope and in shrub and tree canopies, which contributes further to a fire's spread and the onset of crown fires.

Radiation is the process by which heat energy is emitted in direct lines or rays; about 25% of combustion energy is transmitted in this manner. The amount of radiant heat transferred decreases inversely with the square of the distance from a point source. More radiant heat is emitted from a line of fire than from a point source. Radiant heat travels in straight lines, does not penetrate solid objects, and is easily reflected. It accounts for most of the preheating of surface fuel ahead of the fire front and poses a direct threat to people who are too close to the fire (Figure 10). Many organized fire crew members carry aluminized fire shelters in a belt pouch that can be deployed quickly when escape is not possible (Figure 11). These shelters are used as a last resort to protect individuals from radiant heat.

Spotting is a mass transfer mechanism by

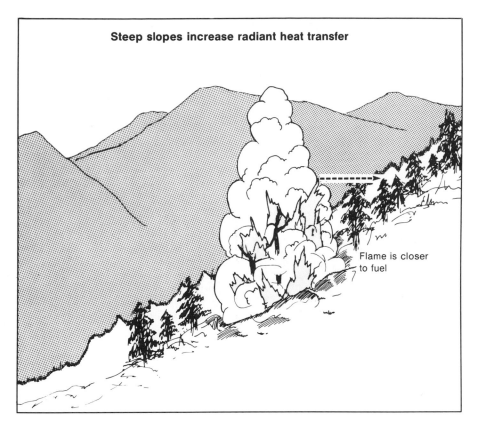

Steep slopes increase radiant heat transfer

Flame is closer to fuel

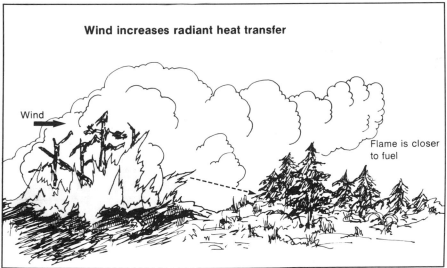

Wind increases radiant heat transfer

Wind

Flame is closer to fuel

FIGURE 10 Fuels and people upslope or downwind from a fire receive more radiant heat than on the downslope or upwind side.

FIGURE 11 An aluminized fire shelter, carried in a waist pouch, is deployed by firefighters as a last resort to provide protection from radiant heat and superheated air. (Photos courtesy of the USDA Forest Service.)

which wind currents carry burning or glowing embers beyond the main fire to start new fires (Figure 12). In this manner, fire spread may accelerate, unexpected fires will occur, and fire intensity and in-draft winds may increase.

A wildland fire behaves according to variations in *fuel, weather,* and *topography.* Interactions among these factors and the fire are characterized as follows:

Fuel—The more fuel that is burning, the hotter the fire will be. Certain types of fuel, such as chaparral, pine, and eucalyptus, burn more intensely because of their fine foliage that contains flammable oils. The size and arrangement of fuel also influence fire behavior. Small, loosely compacted fuel beds, such as dead grass, long pine needles, and shrubs, burn more rapidly than tightly compacted fuel. Large fuels burn best when they are arranged so that they are closely spaced, such as logs in a fireplace. Scattered logs

with no small or intermediate fuel nearby will seldom burn unless they are old and rotten.

Weather—The faster the wind, the more rapidly fire spreads. Drier air and higher temperatures cause fuel to dry out more quickly; fire burns more intensely because drying makes more fuel available to burn. Prolonged drought also makes more fuel available. Fires tend to burn more vigorously when atmospheric conditions are unstable.

The North American continent has been classified into 15 fire climate regions based on geographic and climatic factors (Figure 13) (18). Major fire seasons, or periods of peak fire activity, can be used to forewarn emergency medical personnel and wildland users of the most probable times of the year during which to expect life-threatening situations. Although the fire season for the southern Pacific coast is shown as June through September, critical fire weather can occur year round in the most southerly portion. Fire seasons are most active during spring and fall in the Great Plains, Great Lakes, and North Atlantic regions.

Topography—The steeper the slope, the more rapidly the fire spreads. Fire usually burns uphill, especially in daytime. Changes in the topography will cause changes in the behavior of the fire. Also, on steep terrain, rolling fire brands may cause the fire to spread *downhill.*

EARLY WARNING SIGNALS

Several early warning factors signal the onset of hotter and faster burning conditions within the fire environment:

Fuel
  More fuel
  Drier fuel
  Dead fuel
  Flashy fuel (dead grass, pine needles, and shrubs)
  Aerial fuel (combustible material suspended in crowns of high shrubs and trees, such as branches, needles, lichens, and mosses)

Weather
  Faster winds
  Unstable atmosphere (indicators: gusty winds, dust devils, and good visibility)
  Downdraft winds from dry thunderstorms and towering cumulus clouds (erratic and strong winds)
  Higher temperatures
  Drought conditions
  Lower humidities

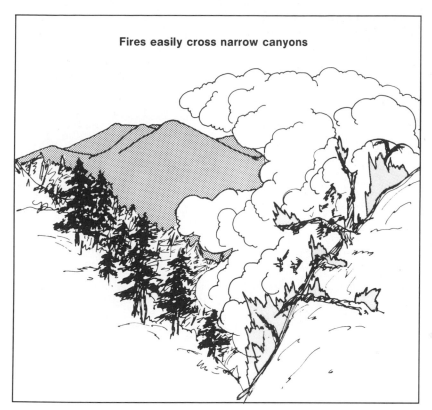

FIGURE 12 Fuels and people on the slope opposite a fire in a narrow canyon are subject to intense heat and spot fires from airborne embers.

Topography
   Steeper slopes
   South and southwest-facing slopes
   Gaps or saddles
   Chimneys and narrow canyons (Figure 14)

Fire behavior
   Rolling and burning pine cones, logs, hot rocks, and other debris igniting fuel downslope
   Spot fires that occur ahead of the main fire
   Individual trees that torch out, or areas of shrubs and trees that burn in a continuous crown fire
   Fires that smolder over a large area
   Many fires that start simultaneously
   Fire whirls that cause spot fires and erratic burning
   Intense burning with flame lengths greater than 4 feet
   Dark, massive smoke columns with rolling, boiling vertical development
   Lateral movement of fire near the base of a steep slope

When a person encounters a wildland fire, the first step should be to review the principles and indicators of fire behavior, sizing up the situation in terms of fuel, weather, topography factors, and observed fire behavior. After making an estimate of the fire's probable direction and rate of spread, travel routes can be planned that avoid life hazards (Figure 15). The direction of the main body of smoke is often a good indicator of the direction the fire will take.

Fire-Related Injuries and Fatalities

Wildland fire disasters that result in injury and death are common to many parts of the world. Most fatalities occur on days of extreme fire danger when people are exposed to abnormally high heat stress caused by weather or proximity to fires. Loss of life is dramatically highlighted under extreme burning conditions; however, many more people are injured than are killed by fires.

One of the worst fire disasters in Australia

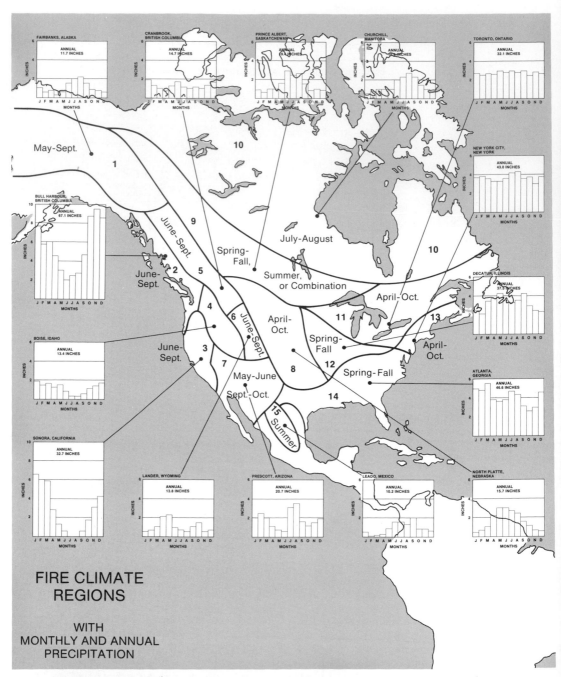

FIGURE 13 Fire climate regions of North America, based on geographic and climatic factors, are as follows: (1) interior Alaska and the Yukon, (2) North Pacific Coast, (3) South Pacific Coast, (4) Great Basin, (5) northern Rocky Mountains, (6) southern Rocky Mountains, (7) Southwest (including adjacent Mexico), (8) Great Plains, (9) Central and Northwest Canada, (10) sub-Arctic and tundra, (11) Great Lakes, (12) Central States, (13) North Atlantic, (14) Southern States, and (15) Mexican Central Plateau. The bar graphs show the monthly and annual precipitation for a representative station in each of the fire climate regions. Months on the map indicate fire seasons. (*Source:* Schroeder, M. J., and C. C. Buck, 1970. *Fire Weather,* USDA Forest Service, Agricultural Handbook 360, 229 pages.)

Fires in a box canyon have an upward draft like a fire in a stove

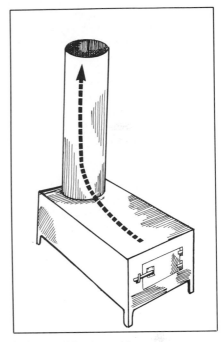

FIGURE 14 Chutes, chimneys, and box canyons created by sharp ridges provide avenues for intense updrafts and rapid rates of spread. People should avoid being caught above a fire under these topographical conditions.

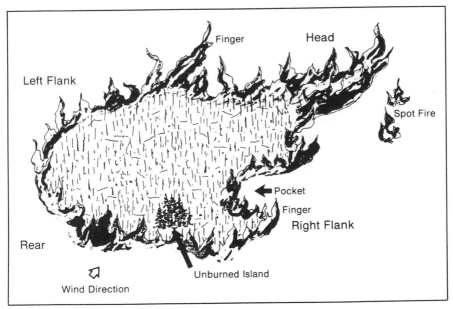

FIGURE 15 The parts of a fire are described in terms of its left flank, right flank, head, and rear. There also may be unburned islands within the fire and spot fires ahead of the fire. The safest travel routes generally involve lateral movement on contours away from the fire's flank or movement toward the rear of the fire. Moving in front of a headfire should be avoided. The burned area inside the fire's perimeter can offer a safe haven, if the flaming perimeter can be safely penetrated by an individual.

TABLE 1
Location of Bodies of 53 Persons Who Died in Tasmanian Fires, February 7, 1967

Location	No. of Deaths
Mustering stock	2
Firefighting	11
Traveling in a vehicle	2
Escaping from and found at some distance from houses	11
Within a few meters of houses	10
Found in houses	11

Source: From Reference 15.

occurred on February 7, 1967, when 62 persons died in Tasmania (14). An analysis of the location and age of 53 of these individuals at the time of their death is instructive (Tables 1 and 2). Most people whose bodies were found within or near houses were old, infirm, or physically disabled. More than one-half of the houses vacated by the 11 people who traveled some distance before being killed were not burned. Most of these victims would probably have survived if they had remained in their homes. Most of the 11 firefighters who died were inexperienced. Many might have survived if they had observed fire behavior and safety rules.

A review of USDA Forest Service records between 1926 and 1976 showed that 145 men died in 41 fires from fire-induced injuries (24). The largest losses occurred in the Blackwater fire in Wyoming in 1937 and in the Rattlesnake fire in California in 1953, with the death of 15 people in each. Wilson's analysis of people lost in fires in areas protected by other federal, state, county, and private agencies indicated 77 fire-induced fatalities in 26 fires.

TABLE 2
Age Distribution of 53 Persons Who Died in Tasmanian Fires, February 7, 1967

Age Group	Number in Group	Average Age
1–25	1	23
26–50	13	38
51–75	26	64
76–88	13	82

Source: From Reference 15.

The 1933 Griffith Park fire in southern California accounted for 25 fatalities and 128 injuries. As a result of his analysis, Wilson (24) identified some common features related to these fatal fires:

1. Relatively small fires or isolated sectors within larger fires seemed associated with most fatal incidents.
2. Flare-ups or blowups of presumed controlled fires seemed to be particularly hazardous. Fatalities occurred in the mop-up stage.
3. Unexpected shifts in wind direction or speed occasionally caused flare-ups in deceptively light fuels.
4. Gullies, chimneys, and steep slopes directed fires to run uphill.
5. The violent wind vortices left by helicopters and air tankers may cause flare-ups in previously controlled areas.

Wilson concluded that the hairline difference between fatal fires and near-fatal fires was determined by the individual's reaction to his suddenly critical situation. Escapes were due either to luck, circumstances, advance planning, a person's ability to avoid panic, or a combination of these factors. Frequently, poor visibility and absence of concise fire information threatened survival opportunities by creating confusion and panic.

Another analysis of 125 wildland fires, which included 236 fatalities and 66 near-fatalities, revealed that the incidents were precipitated by the following basic situations (20):

1. Fire running upslope	29.6%
2. Sudden wind shift	20.8
3. Rapid rate of fire spread	13.6
4. Spot fires	9.6
5. Fire running downslope	6.4
6. Concentrated fuel flare-up	4.8
7. Downdrafts and gusts (overhead cumulus clouds)	4.0
8. Aircraft wake turbulence	0.8
9. Equipment failure	0.8
10. Other (heart attack, electrocution, etc.)	9.6
	100.0%

Fire fatality statistics reported to the National Fire Protection Association reveal that wildland fires have taken the lives of 27 civilians and two firefighters for the period 1971–79 (Table 3). These deaths were attributed to

TABLE 3

Fire Fatalities and Injuries in Open Grass and Brush Areas Reported to the National Fire Protection Association for the Period 1971–79

Year	State	Civilians Killed	Civilians Injured	Firefighters Killed	Firefighters Injured
1971	Alabama	3			
1975	Alabama	1			
	Georgia	1			
	Missouri	1	1		
	Nebraska	1			
	North Carolina	1			
1976	Pennsylvania	1			
1977	California	2		2	
	Hawaii	1			
	Kentucky	1			
	Mississippi	1			
	Ohio	1			
	Pennsylvania	1			
	Tennessee	1			
1978	Alabama	2			
	California	1			4
	Georgia	1			
	New York	1			
	Pennsylvania	1			
1979	California	2			
	Georgia	1			
	Texas	1			
Total		27	1	2	4

Note: One fire in forest fuels over this same period killed two civilians and three firefighters in California in 1973.

fires that occurred in open grass and brush areas. Five fatalities were reported in one forest fire during this same time period. These results supported Wilson's (24) conclusion that fatalities have often occurred in deceptively light but flashy burning fuels. Most reported fatalities in the past decade have been in eastern and southern states rather than in the mountainous western ones.

NATURE OF INJURIES AND FATALITIES

Fire-related injuries and fatalities are a direct consequence of heat, flames, smoke, critical gas levels, or indirect injuries. Injuries and fatalities associated with wildland fires fall into the following categories:

1. Heat
   a. Direct thermal injury
   b. Inhalation
   c. Heat stress disorders: heat cramps, heat exhaustion, heat stroke, dehydration
2. Flames
   a. Direct thermal injury
   b. Inhalation
3. Smoke
   a. Inhalation
   b. Mucous membrane irritation (nasopharyngeal, ocular)
4. Critical gas levels
   a. Oxygen

b. Carbon monoxide
c. Carbon dioxide
5. Indirect effects
a. Acute and chronic medical disability
b. Trauma

These will be discussed briefly. Complete discussions of thermal injury, heat disorders, and smoke inhalation are found elsewhere in this text.

While intense fires do produce very high temperatures, they generally last for only a short time. The duration of intense heat increases with fuel load; thus, the intensity is greater in a forest fire where heavy fuels are burning than in a grass or shrub fire. Temperatures near the ground are lower because radiant heat is offset somewhat by the inflow of fresh air and the fact that gases of combustion rise and are carried away by convection (4,13). Measurements have shown that close to the ground, within a few meters of flames reaching up to 11 m (36 feet), air temperatures were less than 15°C (59°F) above ambient temperature. The breathing of heated air can be tolerated for 30 minutes at 93°C (199°F) and for 3 minutes at 250°C (482°F) (14). Death or severe pulmonary injury is sustained when these limits are exceeded.

Another fire-induced disorder is heat stress (19). This occurs when air temperature, humidity, radiant heat, and poor air movement combine with strenuous work and insulative clothing to raise the body temperature beyond safe limits. Sweating is one mechanism that cools the body as moisture evaporates. When water lost through sweating is not replaced, physiologic heat controls can deregulate and body temperature may rise, leading to heat exhaustion or heat stroke.

Direct contact with flames certainly causes injury, and death is inevitable when exposure is for long periods. Burns may be superficial, partial, or full-thickness. Immediate death is the result of hypotension, hyperthermia, respiratory failure, and frank incineration.

The common cause of asphyxia in relation to fire is suffocation by smoke. Danger increases in locations where smoke accumulates due to poor ventilation, such as caves, box canyons, narrow valleys, and gullies.

Dense, acrid smoke is particularly irritating to the respiratory system and eyes. Excessive coughing induces pharyngitis and vomiting. Keratitis, conjunctivitis, and chemosis may make it impossible to keep the eyes open.

There are concerns about the levels of oxygen, carbon monoxide, and carbon dioxide associated with fire. Critical levels may readily occur in a closed space and near burning or smoldering heavy fuels, but the open space of a wildland fire usually contributes to continual mixing of air. Misconceptions about lack of oxygen or excessive carbon monoxide and carbon dioxide in a wildland fire abound in the lay literature.

Flaming combustion can be maintained only at oxygen levels which exceed 12%, a level at which life can also be supported (4,14). With continued in-drafts of air that feed the

FIGURE 16 Ranger Pulaski led 42 men and 2 horses to this mine tunnel near Placer Creek in northern Idaho to seek refuge from the 1910 fire. One man who failed to get into the tunnel was burned beyond recognition. All the men in the tunnel evidently were unconscious for a period of time. Five men died inside the tunnel, apparently from suffocation. The remainder of the crew was evacuated to the hospital in Wallace, where all recovered. (Photo courtesy of the USDA Forest Service. Photo by J. B. Halm.)

flames, a fresh source of oxygen is usually present. Even mass fires, in which large tracts of land are burning, have rarely been found to reduce oxygen to hazardous levels. Low oxygen levels may occur, however, where there is little air movement, such as in caves (Figure 16) or in burned-over land that continues to smoke from smoldering fuels.

Concentrations of carbon monoxide in excess of 800 parts per million (ppm) can cause death within hours. Most fires produce small quantities; however, atmospheric concentrations rarely reach lethal levels due to air movement. High concentrations appear to be associated with smoldering combustion of heavy fuels, such as fallen trees or slash piles, and carbon monoxide may also collect in low-lying areas or in underground shelters (5). Outdoors, the danger lies in continual exposure to low concentrations that can result in increasing carboxyhemoglobin levels in blood. Prolonged exposure affects the central nervous system, resulting in headache, impaired judgment, progressive lethargy, decreased vision, and other psychomotor deficits (24).

Studies have been conducted to measure levels of carbon monoxide around fires. Levels of 50 ppm were measured close to a prescribed burn in grass (7). In another estimate, concentrations of 30 ppm were found roughly 61 m (200 feet) from the fire front. Studies on the 1974 Deadline and Outlaw forest fires in Idaho showed that firefighters were exposed to levels above the standards proposed by the National Institute of Occupational Safety and Health (35 ppm over an 8-hour period) (21).

Few data are available on levels of carbon dioxide around wildland fires. Although it may be produced in large quantities, it apparently never reaches hazardous concentrations, even in severe fire situations (4,14).

The quantity of burning fuel and the type of topography affect levels of oxygen and toxic gases. Danger is greater in forest fires where heavy fuels burn over long periods of time than in quick-moving grass and shrub fires. Topography has a major influence; caves, box canyons, narrow canyons, gulches, and other terrain features can trap toxic gases or hinder ventilation, thereby preventing an inflow of fresh air. While most fatalities result from encounters with smoke, flames, and heat, critical gas levels can induce handicaps sufficient to render the victim more vulnerable to other hazards.

The strenuous work of fighting or escaping a fire magnifies chronic illnesses, age disabilities, exhaustion, and cardiovascular instability. Common trauma is induced by falling trees or limbs, rolling logs or rocks, vehicular accidents, poor visibility, panic, falling asleep in unburned fuels that later ignite, and leaving the safety of buildings and vehicles. Cuts, scrapes, scratches, lacerations, fractures, and eye injuries (foreign particles, smoke irritation, sharp objects) are other common afflictions. Poison oak, poison ivy, stinging insects, and poisonous snakes are additional sources of trauma during wildland fires. To avoid fire-related injuries and fatalities, one must keep attuned to one's own mental and physical stress levels and be aware of cumulative effects (19). Ignorance of this simple principle is historically disastrous.

Wildland Fire Survival Principles and Techniques

As stated earlier, history has demonstrated repeatedly that individuals simply were not prepared to make correct judgments among survival alternatives under stress situations. Overconfidence, ignorance, bad habits, or panic have quickly led to improper and unsafe actions during fire emergencies. The fact that fatal and near-fatal accidents often have been associated with deceptively simple and easy fire situations reflects overconfidence and inappropriate human behavior patterns (24). "Learning from mistakes" in these settings is not a viable education strategy; second chances are frequently too late.

In order to develop significant safety principles and rules, the USDA Forest Service organized a task force in 1957 to "study how we might strengthen our ways and means of preventing firefighting fatalities." One of the major recommendations of the task force was to adopt Service-wide Standard Firefighting Orders. The task force borrowed the concept of orders from the military's experience:

Military organizations have had long experience in training men to remember certain fundamental instructions and to react even in emergencies in accordance with those instructions. One device by which such discipline is achieved is that of General Orders, which all men of the unit are required to memorize. On some of the fires that the task force reviewed, men who knew better just did not pay adequate attention to good firefighting practices that seem like small details, but could become *the* critical item in an emergency. The use of a form of standard orders starting immediately would be a long step in the direction of assuring attention to the fundamentals.

Ten standard Firefighting Orders were placed into operational practice during the 1957 fire season; later, 13 "watch-out" situations were highlighted. Undoubtedly, these preconditioned responses have saved lives and averted accidents. Almost without exception, when someone is injured or killed during fire suppression actions, it is not because something unexpected happened. Accidents generally result from the violation of one or more of the fundamental principles. The growing opportunity for wildland fire encounters by emergency medical personnel and the public mandates that these people should practice many of the same fire safety principles required of suppression agencies.

Ten Standard Firefighting Orders

Ten Standard Firefighting Orders summarize fundamental principles of safety on the fireline. While the orders were written for firefighters, they apply to all people working, living, or traveling near wildland fires. The orders are adapted below to remind emergency medical personnel, wildland homeowners, and recreationists of safety precautions:

1. Keep informed of fire weather conditions, changes, and forecasts and how they may affect the area where you are located.
2. Know what the fire is doing at all times through personal observations, communication systems, or scouts.
3. Base all actions on the current and expected behavior of the fire.
4. Determine escape routes and plans for everyone at risk and make certain that everyone understands the routes and plans.
5. Post lookouts to watch the fire if you think there is any danger of being trapped, or of increased fire activity or erratic fire behavior.

6. Be alert, keep calm, think clearly, and act decisively in order to avoid panic reactions.
7. Maintain prompt and clear communication with your group, firefighting forces, and command/communication centers.
8. Give clear, concise instructions and be sure that they are understood.
9. Maintain control of the people in your group at all times.
10. Fight fire aggressively, but provide for safety first. (Nonqualified and improperly equipped persons should fight fire only when it is necessary in their mission to assist injured people.)

Thirteen Watch-Out Situations

The 13 watch-out situations are stated below, with a short discussion of their relevance to emergency medical personnel and wildland users.

1. You are moving downhill toward a fire. Fire can move swiftly and suddenly uphill, so that constant observation must be made of fire behavior, fuels, and escape routes when walking downhill toward the fire. Assess the potential for fire to run uphill in every situation.
2. You are on a hillside where rolling, burning material can ignite fuel from below. When on a hillside below a fire, be watchful of burning materials, especially cones and logs, that can roll downhill and start a fire beneath you. Getting caught between two coalescing fires can be deadly.
3. Wind begins to blow, increase, or change direction. Wind has a strong influence on fire behavior, so be prepared to respond to any sudden changes.
4. The weather becomes hotter and drier. Fire activity increases and its behavior changes more rapidly as ambient temperature rises and relative humidity decreases.
5. Dense vegetation with unburned fuel is between you and the fire. The danger in this situation is that unburned fuels can ignite. If the fire is moving away from you, be alert for wind changes or spot fires that may ignite fuels near you. Do not be overconfident if the area has burned once, because it could reignite if sufficient fuel remains.
6. You are in an unburned area near the fire where terrain and cover make travel difficult. The combination of fuel and difficult escape makes this a dangerous situation.
7. Travel or work is in an area that you have

not seen in daylight. Darkness and unfamiliarity are a very poor combination.

8. You are unfamiliar with local factors influencing fire behavior. When possible, seek information on what to expect from knowledgeable people, especially those from the area.
9. By necessity, you have to make a frontal assault on a fire with tankers. Any encounter with an active line of fire is dangerous because of proximity to intense heat, smoke, and flames, along with limited escape opportunities.
10. Spot fires occur frequently across the fireline. Generally, increased spotting indicates increased fire activity and intensity. The danger is that of entrapment between coalescing fires.
11. The main fire cannot be seen, and you are not in communication with anyone who can see it. The danger in this situation is in not knowing the location, size, and behavior of the main fire. Planning becomes guesswork, which is an unfavorable response.
12. An unclear assignment or confusing instructions have been received. Make sure that all assignments and instructions are fully understood.
13. You are drowsy and feel like resting or sleeping near the fireline in unburned fuel. This may lead to fire entrapment. *No one should sleep near a wildland fire.* If it is absolutely necessary to rest, choose a burned area that is safe from rolling material, smoke, reburn and other dangers, or bare ground or rock.

REFUGE IN VEHICLES AND BUILDINGS

As stated previously, much of the heat from a fire is radiant energy. While its intensity at a given location may be very high, it typically lasts for only a short time. Because radiant heat travels in straight lines, does not penetrate solid substances, and is easily reflected, seeking refuge in vehicles and buildings is often lifesaving.

Vehicles

In the United States, there are several accounts of firefighters who have survived severe fire storms or the passage of fire fronts by taking refuge in vehicles. A few case histories follow, serving as examples of intense burning situations in which lives were saved because people stayed inside vehicles when the fire passed. These cases are from a chapter on survival techniques in an international report on fatal and near-fatal wildland fire accidents (20):

1. In 1958, a veteran Field Section Fire Warden and two teenage boys were fighting forest fires that burned in heavy south New Jersey fuels near the Bass River State Forest. A 90° wind shift transformed the flank fire into a broad headfire, with advancing flames of up to 12 m (40 feet). The men entered their vehicle, a Dodge W300 Power Wagon, which stood in the middle of a sand road 4 m (12 feet) wide. Simultaneously, the engine and radio failed.

   The Fire Warden repeatedly admonished the crewmen, who wished to flee, to stay in the truck. Subsequently, the truck was rocked violently by convection currents and microclimatic changes generated by the flames. The men could neither see nor breathe because of smoke, and the cab began to fill with sparks that ignited the seat. The men stayed with the truck for only 3 or 4 minutes during passage of the headfire, but indicated that the interval involved seemed more like 3 or 4 hours.

   At the first opportunity, all of them left the vehicle, on the upwind side, and crouched beside it to escape the searing heat and burning seats. The warden proceeded to burn his hand severely while disposing of a flaming gas can in the truck bed. While the young men escaped virtually unscathed, the older man suffered lung damage and remained on limited duty for 5 years. He has since recovered completely and retired.
2. In 1976, a firefighter died while fighting a grass fire near Buhler, Kansas, in Reno County. A flashover occurred from a buildup of gases on the lee side of a windbreak. A fire truck was caught in the flashover, and the firefighter working from the back of the vehicle ran and was killed. Although the truck burned, the driver was not seriously hurt.
3. In a 1962 California Division of Forestry fire in Fresno County, three men, followed by a flank fire that had turned into a headfire, raced back to their truck only a few feet ahead of the flames. The truck would not restart. After the main body of flames passed over the vehicle, the men jumped out in order to breathe, since the truck was burning. Almost completely blinded by smoke and heat, they stumbled headlong into matted fuels, and two received first- and second-degree burns. One man was not burned, but had to be treated for smoke inhalation. The truck was a loss.

It is often perilous to sit in a vehicle during a passing fire front, but when trapped, it is almost certain doom to attempt escape by running from the fire. These case histories illustrate a few facts that, if remembered, may prevent panic:

1. The engine may stall and not restart.
2. The vehicle may be rocked by convection currents.
3. Smoke and sparks may enter the cab.
4. The interior, engine, or tires may ignite.
5. Temperatures increase inside the cab because heat is radiated through the windows.
6. Metal gas tanks and containers rarely explode.
7. If it is necessary to leave the cab after the fire has passed, keep the vehicle between you and the fire.

The type of vehicle determines the amount of protection provided. Two travelers died in a fire in 1967 in Tasmania, Australia, when they were caught in a canvas-topped vehicle that afforded no protection (14).

A later fire in Australia led to further research on the protection provided by vehicles and the explosiveness of gasoline tanks. In 1969, at Lara, Victoria, Australia, a fast-moving grass fire crossed a four-lane expressway. Several cars stopped on the road in the confusion of smoke and flames. Seventeen people left the safety of their cars and perished. Six people stayed inside their vehicles and survived, even though one car ignited.

Over a period of several years, investigations were carried out by the Forest Research Institute [now the Commonwealth Scientific and Industrial Research Organization (CSIRO), Division of Forest Research] in Canberra, Australia, in an attempt to collect accurate data and to dispel the misconceptions that cause persons to flee a safe refuge if trapped by fire (4). Cars were placed between two burning piles of logging slash to study the ability of a car to shield against radiation. The test was a hotter, longer fire than would normally be encountered by passengers.

Car bodies halved the external radiation transmitted at the peak of the fire, but a person inside would have suffered severe burns to bare skin. Although air temperatures inside the car did not reach hazardous levels until well after the peak radiation had passed, smoke from smoldering plastic and rubber materials would have caused discomfort and made the car un-

inhabitable. In this study, metal gasoline tanks did not explode, whether intact on cars or separated and placed on a burning pile of slash. Apparently, when tanks are sealed, the space above the liquid contains a mixture too deficient in oxygen vapor for an explosion to occur.

Cheney offered the following advice for survival when in a car and trapped by fire (4,5):

1. If smoke obstructs your visibility, turn on the headlights and drive to the side of the road away from the leading edge of the fire. Try to select an area of sparse vegetation offering the least combustible material.
2. Attempt to shield your body from radiant heat energy by rolling up the windows and covering up with floor mats or hiding beneath the dashboard. Cover as much skin as possible.
3. Stay in the vehicle as long as possible. Unruptured gas tanks rarely explode, and vehicles usually take several minutes to ignite.
4. Grass fires create about 30 seconds of flame exposure, and chances for survival in a vehicle are good. Forest fires create higher-intensity flames lasting for 3–4 minutes, lowering your chances for survival. Remaining in your vehicle improves your chances for surviving a forest fire. Remain calm.
5. A strong, acrid smell usually results from burning paint and plastic materials, which is caused by small quantities of hydrogen chloride that are released from the breakdown of polyvinyl chloride. Hydrogen chloride is readily water soluble and discomfort can be relieved by breathing through a damp cloth. Remember that urine is mostly water and can be used in emergencies.

Buildings

Whether people can find refuge in buildings depends on the construction materials and the amount of preparation that has been made to reduce fuels around the structure. A building usually offers protection during the passage of fire even if it ignites later, because it shields against radiant heat and smoke. After fire passes, it may be necessary to exit if the building is burning.

Case history examples from Australia demonstrate that homes do provide safe havens (14). In 1967 in Tasmania, 21 people left their houses as fire approached. All died, and some were within a few meters of the buildings.

Many of the houses did not burn and, therefore, would have been refuges. Most people probably would have survived if they had remained in their dwellings.

When taking refuge in a building, people should be given useful jobs such as filling vessels with water, blocking cracks with wet blankets, and tightly closing windows and doors. If possible, lookouts should keep watch for spot fires on the outside of the building until the last minute. Staying in a house is usually safer than hasty escape. Before fire approaches the house, one should take the following precautions (17):

1. If you plan to stay, evacuate your pets and all family members who are not essential to protecting the home.
2. Be properly dressed to survive the fire. Cotton fabrics are preferable to synthetics. Wear long pants and boots, and carry for protection a long-sleeved shirt or jacket, gloves, a handkerchief to shield the face, water to wet it, and goggles.
3. Remove combustible items from around the house. This includes lawn and poolside furniture, umbrellas, and tarp coverings. If they catch fire, the added heat could ignite the house.
4. Close outside attic, eave, and basement vents. This will eliminate the possibility of sparks blowing into hidden areas within the house. Close window shutters.
5. Place large plastic trash cans or buckets around the outside of the house and fill them with water. Soak burlap sacks, small rugs, and large rags. They can be helpful in beating out burning embers or small fires. Inside the house, fill bathtubs, sinks, and other containers with water. Toilet tanks and water heaters are an important water reservoir.
6. Place garden hoses so that they will reach any place on the house. Use the spray gun-type nozzle, adjusted to a spray.
7. If you have portable gasoline-powered pumps to take water from a swimming pool or tank, make sure that they are operating and in place.
8. Place a ladder against the roof of the house opposite the side of the approaching fire. If you have a combustible roof, wet it down or turn on any roof sprinklers. Turn on any special fire sprinklers installed to add protection. Do not waste water. Waste can drain the entire water system quickly.
9. Back your car in the garage and roll up the car windows. Disconnect the automatic garage door opener (in case of power failure, you cannot remove the car). Close all garage doors.
10. Place valuable papers and mementos inside the car in the garage for quick departure, if necessary. Any pets still with you should also be put in the car.
11. Close windows and doors to the house to prevent sparks from blowing inside. Close all doors inside the house to prevent drafts. Open the damper on your fireplace to help stabilize outside-inside pressure, but close the fireplace screen so that sparks will not ignite the room. Turn on a light in each room to make the house more visible in heavy smoke.
12. Turn off pilot lights.
13. If you have time, take down drapes and curtains. Close all venetian blinds or noncombustible window coverings to reduce the amount of heat radiating into the house. This provides added safety in case the windows give way because of heat or wind.
14. As the firefront approaches, go inside the house. Stay calm; you are in control of the situation.
15. After the fire passes, check the roof immediately. Extinguish any sparks or embers. Then, check the attic for hidden burning sparks. If you have a fire, get your neighbors to help fight it. The water in the pool and in the garbage cans, sinks, toilet tanks, etc., will come in handy now. For several hours after the fire, recheck for smoke and sparks throughout the house.

ENTRAPMENT PROCEDURES

People must recognize that in some instances there may be no chance to escape a fire. When entrapment is imminent, injuries or death may be avoided by following entrapment procedures:

1. *Do not panic.* It is natural for most people to be afraid when trapped by fire. Accept this fear as natural. Once this has been done, clear thinking and intelligent decisions are possible. If fear becomes overwhelming, judgment is seriously impaired and survival becomes a matter of chance.
2. *Do not run blindly or needlessly.* Unless the path of escape is clearly indicated, do not run. Move toward one of the flanks of the fire, traveling downhill where possible. Conserve your strength.
3. *Enter the burned area.* Particularly in grass, low shrubs, or other low fuels, do not delay if escape

means passing through the flame front into the burned area. Move aggressively and parallel to the advancing firefront. Choose a place on the edge of the fire where flames are less than 1 m (3 feet) deep and can be seen through clearly, and where the fuel supply behind the fire edge has been mostly consumed. After covering exposed skin and taking several breaths, move through the flame front as quickly as possible. If necessary, get on the ground to move underneath smoke for improved visibility and to obtain some fresh air for the next move into the burned area.

4. *Burn out.* If you are in dead grass or low shrub fuels and the approaching flames are too high to run through, burn out as large an area as possible between you and the fire edge. Step into the burned area and cover as much of your exposed skin as possible. This action requires time for fuels to burn out, and as a last-ditch effort, it may not be effective. It also does not work well in an intense forest fire.

5. *Regulate breathing.* Avoid inhaling dense smoke. A dampened handkerchief held over the nose will help. Regulate breathing to coincide with the availability of relatively fresh air. If there is a possibility of breathing superheated air, then a dry, not moist, cloth should be placed over the mouth. The lungs are better able to withstand dry heat than moist heat.

6. *Protect against radiation.* Many people who become victims of forest fires actually die before the flames reach them. Radiated heat quickly causes heat stroke, a state of complete exhaustion. Shielding that will reduce the heat rays must be found quickly in any area that will not burn. This may be provided by a shallow trench, crevice, large rock, running stream, large pond, vehicle, building, or the shore water of a lake. Do not seek refuge in an elevated water tank. Wells and caves generally should be avoided because oxygen may be quickly used up in these restricted places. Such refuges might be used as a last resort (Figure 16). For protection against radiation, cover the head and other exposed skin with clothing or dirt.

7. *Lie prone.* In a critical emergency, lie face down in an area that will not burn. A person's chance of survival is greater in this position than if overtaken by fire when standing upright or kneeling.

Arnold "Smoke" Elser, an accomplished Montana outfitter, described how he helped his guests avoid entrapment by a forest fire in this personal communication:

The fire began at the bottom of the canyon and proceeded up canyon as fires do. However, the wind currents carried the smoke to the east and not up the drainage to the north; therefore, we received no warning of the fire. The Monture Creek trail goes through some very old mature timber which was not burning as we approached. As my stock, the guests, and I arrived at the fire site and realized that we were in danger, we felt we should fall back and try to flank the fire to the east. Starting back toward this trail, we found a ground fire that made it very hazardous to travel in this direction. Because of my knowledge of the trail and terrain, I knew that our best bet would be to wet down the stock, guests, saddles and outer clothing and try to break through the head of the fire. We successfully did this, receiving only a few minor burns on the horses and the loss of some apparel tied to the backs of the saddles. Some lessons that I learned in this experience were that in handling livestock in a fire situation you must have a very close, firm hand on them. It is also very important that no one panics or shows any excitement, as this alarms the livestock and begins the panic run that is so well known. I found that by talking in a very low monotone, keeping the pack stock and saddle stock very close together (head to tail), and moving on a good trail, we were able to come through this fire with virtually no harm.

Elser had these additional suggestions for wildland recreationists:

Campers, whether they be livestock oriented, hikers, or boaters, should know where to camp to provide adequate fire barriers around campsites. All campers should consider at least one, and preferably two, safe escape routes and havens (such as rock piles, rivers, and large green meadows) away from heavy fuel areas. Campers should also be alert to canyon air current conditions in critical fire seasons. The safety of many recreationists is threatened by the nylon and other synthetic fabrics used in the manufacture of most backpacking equipment. These materials melt upon contact with heat. The very nature of good horse packing equipment is a deterrent to fire; canvas mantles that cover the gear and the canvas pack saddles are easily wet down. Leather items such as chaps, good saddle bags, and western hats which can shield against heat blasts all provide important protection for the horse user.

PROPER CLOTHING

Clothing provides protection against radiant heat, embers, and sparks, so it is sensible they absorb sweat and aid evaporation, and do not melt, unlike synthetics. Wearing layers of clothing generally contributes to heat stress problems.

As little skin as possible should be exposed to fire. Long trousers and a long-sleeved shirt should be worn. For maximum protection, the shirt should be kept buttoned and the sleeves rolled down.

Brightly colored (yellow or orange) coveralls or shirts are worn by organized firefighting crews. These colors improve safety and communications because they are visible in smoke, vegetation, and blackened landscapes.

Other essential apparel includes a safety helmet (hard hat), gloves (leather or natural fibers), leather work boots, woolen or cotton socks, warm jacket for night wear, goggles, and a handkerchief. Clothing, backpacks, tents, and other camping equipment made of synthetics should be discarded when one is close to a fire.

WATER INTAKE

Sweating, the primary method for body cooling, is an important physiologic function. Exhaling warm air and inhaling cooler air also helps to decrease body temperature. Because the cooling effect of sweat evaporation is essential for thermoregulation, it is important to replace fluids lost during strenuous work. In firefighting, water losses of 0.5 liter per hour are common, with losses of up to 2 liters per hour under extreme conditions (14). Unless water is restored regularly, dehydration may contribute to heat stress disorders, reluctance to work, irritability, poor judgment, and impatience.

The importance of dehydration cannot be overstressed. Thirst is not a good indicator of water requirements during strenuous work, so additional drinking of small quantities of water at regular intervals is recommended. A useful signal of dehydration is dark, scanty urine.

An excessive amount of electrolytes may be lost through sweating, which leads to nausea, vomiting, and muscle cramps. When meals are missed or unseasoned foods are eaten, electrolyte supplements may be necessary to replace lost salts. Sweetened drinks

FIGURE 17 Protective clothing for a firefighter includes hard hat and safety goggles, fire-resistant shirt and trousers, leather boots and gloves, and fire shelter carried in a waist pouch. Firefighters also carry canteens to ensure an adequate water supply in a heat-stressed environment. (Photo courtesy of the USDA Forest Service.)

to dress appropriately (Figure 17). Closely woven material is more resistant to radiation and less likely to ignite than open-weave material. Natural fibers are best. Wool is more flame resistant than cotton, although cotton can be improved by chemical treatment to retard flammability. It must be emphasized that synthetic materials are a poor choice to wear near fire because they readily absorb heat, ignite, or melt.

Because closely woven materials that provide protection also restrict airflow, clothes should fit loosely in order not to interfere with dissipation of body heat. The advantage of cotton longjohns or undergarments is that should be used as a source of energy if solid food is not available.

PERSONAL GEAR

Some rescue and medical missions take a few days. Therefore, it is necessary to be prepared for extended periods and changing conditions in the backcountry. Below is a suggested list of provisions, gear, and personal items.

1. Boots (leather, high top, lace-up, nonslip soles, extra leather laces)
2. Socks (cotton or wool, at least two pairs)
3. Pants (natural fiber, flame-proof, loose fitting, hems lower than boot tops)
4. Belt (suspenders)
5. Shirt (natural fiber, flame-proof, loose fitting, long sleeves)
6. Gloves (natural fiber or leather, extra pair)
7. Hat (hard hat, possibly a bandana, stocking cap, or felt hat)
8. Jacket
9. Handkerchief or scarves
10. Goggles
11. Sleeping bag and ground cover
12. Map
13. Fire shelter
14. Food
15. Canteen
16. Radio (AM radio will receive better in rough terrain; FM is more line-of-sight; emergency personnel should have a two-way radio)
17. Bolt cutters (carried in vehicles to get through locked gates in the escape from fire blowups or in the rescue of trapped people)
18. Miscellaneous items (mess kit, compass, flashlight, extra batteries, toilet paper, pencil, notepaper, flagging tape, flares, matches, can opener, wash cloth, toiletries, insect repellent, plastic bags, knife, first aid kit, and lip balm)

Conclusions

Fire suppression efforts in the late 1800s and early 1900s were largely ineffective due to limited access, absence of trained firefighting organizations, and lack of a fire detection network. During these times, many residents and numerous firefighters died in wildland fires in the United States and Canada. In the recent past, firefighters were more vulnerable to injuries and fatalities from wildland fires than was the general public. Today, with many people living and recreating in wildlands, the odds for serious fire encounters are shifting toward an inexperienced populace. Large property losses and direct injuries are being reported in increasing numbers in the wildland/urban interface. Although wildland fires have not yet posed much of a threat to backcountry recreationists in the United States, the prospect for such confrontations is growing.

Experience with wildland fires allows us to conclude that:

1. Residential shifts to the wildland/urban interface will increase exposures to life-threatening situations.
2. Prescribed fires in national parks and wildernesses will increase the likelihood that people will encounter fires.
3. The general public tends to underestimate existing fire hazards and is usually not experienced in avoiding fire threats.
4. In some instances, past fire suppression actions have contributed to the development of more wildland fuel, setting the stage for greater rates of spread and higher intensity levels.
5. Knowledge of fire behavior principles and survival rules will prepare people to take appropriate preventive measures in threatening situations.

The general public must share responsibility with suppression organizations to minimize fire hazards created by humans. Care with fire, proper cleanup and fuel reduction efforts on wildland property, and application of survival skills will minimize fire threats. Such precautions should become as commonplace in the wildland environment as smoke alarms and fire extinguishers have become in the home.

Wildland fire suppression agencies will continue to provide fast, safe, and energetic initial attack responses to protect human life and property and natural resources. But under conditions of prolonged drought, strong winds, low humidities, and high temperatures, some fires will escape even the very best initial attack efforts, directly threatening human life and property. Emergency medical personnel will probably have increasing exposure to wildland fires and will need to know more about fire-related injuries, fire safety, and fire survival.

How to Report a Wildland Fire to Local Fire Protection Authorities

> A caller should be prepared to provide the following information when reporting a fire:
> 1. Name of person giving the report.
> 2. Where can you be reached immediately?
> 3. Where were you at the time the fire was discovered?
> 4. Location of the fire. It is important to orient the fire to prominent landmarks such as roads, creeks, and mileposts on highways.
> 5. Description of the fire: color and volume of the smoke, estimated size, and flame characteristics if visible.
> 6. Is anyone fighting the fire at this time?

References

1. Barrows, J. S. 1951. Fire behavior in northern Rocky Mountain forests. USDA Forest Srevice. Northern Rocky Mtn. For. and Range Exp. Sta., Station Paper No. 29. 103 pp.
2. Barrows, J. S. 1974. The challenges of forest fire management. *Western Wildlands,* **1**(3):3–5.
3. Brown, A. A., and K. P. Davis. 1973. *Forest Fire: Control and Use,* 2nd ed. McGraw-Hill, New York, 68 pp.
4. Cheney, N. P. 1972. Don't panic—and live. Nat Dev. 1–4.
5. Cheney, N. P. 1981. Senior Research Scientist, Bushfire Research, Division of Forest Research, Commonwealth Scientific and Industrial Research Organization, Canberra, Australia. Personal communication.
6. Colorado State Forest Service. 1977. Wildlife hazards: *Guidelines for Their Prevention in Subdivisions and Developments.* Colorado State University, Ft. Collins, Co. 7 pp.
7. Countryman, C. M. 1971. *Carbon Monoxide: A Firefighting Problem.* USDA Forest Service, Pac. S.W. For. and Range Exp. Sta. 6 pp.
8. Fischer, W. C. and D. J. Books. 1977. Safeguarding Montana homes: Lessons from the Pattee Canyon fire. *Western Wildlands,* **4**(1):30–5.
9. Freedman, J. D. 1980. A fire and fuel hazard analysis in the Seeley Lake area, Missoula County, Montana. M.A. thesis, University of Montana, Missoula. 90 p.
10. Freedman, J. D. and W. C. Fischer. 1980. Forest home fire hazards. *Western Wildlands,* **6**(4):23–6.
11. Hulbert, J. 1972. Fire problems in rural suburbs. *American Forests,* **78**(2):24–47.
12. Leopold, A. S., S. A. Cain, C. M. Cottam, I. N. Gabrielson, and T. L. Kimball. 1963. Wildlife management in the national parks. *Transactions of the American Wildlife and Natural Resources Conference,* **28**:1–18.
13. Loucks, O. L. 1970. Evolution of diversity, efficiency, and community stability. *American Zoology,* **10**:17–25.
14. Luke, R. H. and A. G. McArthur. 1978. *Bushfires in Australia.* CSIRO Division of Forest Research, Australian Government Publishing Service. 359 pp.
15. McArthur, A. G. and N. P. Cheney. 1967. *Report on Southern Tasmania Bushfires of 7 February 1967.* Govt. Printer, Hobart, Australia.
16. Owen, H. R. 1977. *Fire and You.* Doubleday, Garden City, N.Y., 202 pp.
17. Radtke, K. W. H. 1982. *A Homeowner's Guide to Fire and Watershed Management at the Chaparral/Urban Interface.* County of Los Angeles, California. 32 pp. (Available from Santa Monica Mountains Residents Association, 21656 Las Flores Hts. Rd., Malibu, California 90265; cost $0.50).
18. Schroeder, M. J. and C. C. Buck. 1970. *Fire Weather.* USDA Forest Service, Agr. Handbook 360, 229 p.
19. Sharkey, B. J. 1979. *Heat stress.* USDA Forest Service. Missoula Equipment Development Center, Missoula, Mont., 14 pp.
20. Smith, A. *et al.* 1981. Report of U.S.-Canadian task force study of fatal and near-fatal fire accidents. National Wildfire Coordinating Group. 76 pp. (Unpublished report).
21. Tietz, J. G. 1975. *Firefighter's Exposure to Carbon Monoxide on the Deadline and Outlaw Fires.* Ed. T. 2424 (*Smoke Inhalation Hazards*). USDA Forest Service, Equip. Dev. Cent., Missoula, Mont., 8 pp.
22. USDA Forest Service. Undated. *When the Mountains Roared—Stories of the 1910 Fire.* Coeur d'Alene National Forest, Northern Region. 39 pp.
23. Wilson, C. C. 1971. Commingling of urban forest fires (a case study of the 1970 California ncar-disaster). *Fire Research Abstracts and Reviews,* **13**(1):35–43.
24. Wilson, C. C. 1977. Fatal and near-fatal forest fires, the common denominators. *The International Fire Chief,* **43**(9):9–15.

Recommended Reading

Cohen, S. and D. Miller. 1978. *The Big Burn.* Pictorial Histories Publishing Co., Missoula, Mont., 88 pp. (The northwest's forest fire of 1910.)

Gaylor, H. P. 1974. *Wildfires: Prevention and Control.* R. J. Brady Co., Bowie, Md., 319 pp.

Northwest Interagency Fire Prevention Group. 1978. *Fire Safety Considerations for Developments in Forested Areas,* 18 pp. (A guide for planners and developers.)

Northwest Interagency Fire Prevention Group. 1978. *Fire Safety Considerations for Developments in Forested Areas,* 18 pp. (A guide for homeowners and buyers.)

Pringle, L. 1979. *Natural Fire—Its Ecology in Forests.* William Morrow, New York, 63 pp.

Radtke, K. 1981. *Living More Safely at the Chaparral-Urban Interface.* USDA Forest Service and County of Los Angeles Dept. of Forester and Fire Warden. Pacific Southwest For. and Range Exp. Sta., 101 pp.

Note: Copies of publications by the Northwest Inter-agency Fire Prevention Group may be ordered from the following agencies:

Bureau of Indian Affairs
P.O. Box 3785
Portland, OR 97208

Bureau of Land Management
P.O. Box 2965
Portland, OR 97208

Oregon State Department of Forestry
2600 State St.
Salem, OR 97310

U.S. Forest Service
Region 6
P.O. Box 3623
Portland, OR 97208

Washington Department of Natural Resources
Olympia, WA 98504

17 | # BURN WOUNDS

Arnold Luterman, M.D., F.R.C.S., F.A.C.S.
P. William Curreri, M.D., F.A.C.S.

Few areas of medical science have exhibited as radical a change in therapeutic management during the past two decades as has burn medicine. Today, many people with severe burns survive their injury, and most are substantially rehabilitated without permanent, crippling deformities. Despite the increasing medical expenditures required for the treatment of burn victims, the overall cost to society has decreased, since most patients with limited disability may return to a productive occupation.

The more optimistic outlook for the burn victim is attributed to several major improvements in treatment approach. First and foremost has been the development of comprehensive treatment centers throughout the United States, staffed by multidisciplinary teams, to provide the vast array of required specialized therapeutic services. Second, the quality of prehospital care and transport in most areas of the country has been improved with increasing federal and regional reorganization and financial support. Patients now arrive at

the burn centers with emergent complications already treated. Third, there has been growing research interest in the patients' response to major trauma, which has led to better understanding of the pathophysiology of burn injury.

This chapter will summarize currently practiced therapeutic management of burn injuries. Optimal care requires early, effective treatment which is continuous, from emergent procedures at the scene of the accident to definitive care delivered at the specialized burn care facility. A full team approach is required, with the first medical or paramedical person to attend the patient being a vital part of that team. With proper community training, continuing education of paramedics, emergency medical technicians (EMTs), and emergency department physicians, it is possible to broaden the team concept beyond the confines of the hospital. Safe aerotransport by helicopter or fixed wing aircraft into the specialized burn care facility has become feasible. Similarly, upon discharge from the hospital, outpatient physiotherapy, reconstruction, and vocational training are completed by this expanded burn team.

A list of recommended readings has been included at the end of the chapter. Review of this literature will provide a comprehensive summary of the multiple facets of burn care.

Epidemiology of Burn Injuries

Burn injuries constitute a major health problem for this nation. More than 2,000,000 persons suffer thermal injury annually, and 100,000 are hospitalized for a total of 2 million hospital days (16). Like other types of trauma, thermal injuries frequently occur in children and young adults. The prolonged morbidity produced by these injuries results in a staggering economic drain on society.

In children under 3 years of age, contact with hot liquid is the most common etiology of burn injury. (It has been suggested that nearly all scald injuries in children could be prevented by lowering the temperature of water from household heaters to below 130°F) (10a). From 3 to 14 years of age, ignition of clothing is the most frequent cause of burn injury, while from 15 to 60 years, most burn injuries are due to household accidents. For persons over 60 years, most burns are associated with momentary blackouts, smoking in bed, or household fires. It is estimated that 80% of burn accidents occur in the home (2).

Mechanism of Burn Injury

The extent of damage produced by applying a heat source to skin is a function of the intensity of the source, the duration of contact, and the conductivity of the tissues. The two most common heat sources encountered are an open flame and hot liquid. Severe burn injury can also be produced by contact with hot metal, toxic chemicals, or high-voltage electricity.

To produce protein coagulation and cell death, a temperature of 60°C is required. In general, at temperatures below 45°C, no cell damage will occur. Between these two temperatures, the extent of cell damage depends on the duration of exposure to the heat source.

The circulation to the skin helps dissipate the heat from a source applied to the surface. At higher temperatures, this defense mechanism is quickly overwhelmed. At lower temperatures, it is an important asset during brief exposure to heat, but fails when prolonged contact occurs.

Extent of Burn Injury

The burn wound is a three-dimensional wound with length, width, and depth. The severity of a burn injury is a function of a number of variables listed in Table 1. All must be considered to estimate properly the magnitude of damage as well as the ultimate prognosis. Although small in size, certain injuries (of the perineum, eyes, ears, hands, face, feet) may require specialized care facilities for optimal management. Others, although more extensive, may be safely handled in community hospitals without separate burn units. Unlike most types of trauma, guidelines have been developed for the categorization of burn injuries to help the clinician make this distinction. These guidelines will be reviewed in depth in a subsequent section of this chapter.

WOUND DEPTH

The depth of burn injuries is usually described by degree: First-degree burns are the most superficial; second- and third-degree burns are progressively deeper injuries. The major morphologic and clinical features present with each of these degrees of injury are summarized in Table 2. Skin is the body's water, microbial, and thermal barrier (Figure

---

TABLE 1
Severity of Burn Injury

Degree of the burn
Percentage of body surface area involved
Location of the injury
Age of the patient
Past medical history
Associated injuries
General status of the patient

TABLE 2
Burn Injuries: Depth

Degree	Morphology	Appearance
First degree	Devitalized superficial layers of epidermis only Congestion and dilatation of intradermal vessels	Erythema only Blanches on pressure
Second degree	Devitalized deeper layers of epidermis Clefting of epidermis, with fluid collecton (blisters) Congestion and thrombosis to varying degrees in subdermal plexus Retention of some viable skin elements	Erythematous, blistering, weeping wounds in superficial injuries; waxy, white, dry, insensitive wounds in deeper injuries
Third degree	Destruction of all skin elements Coagulation of subdermal plexus	Dry, hard, inelastic wound, with thrombosed veins of subdermal plexus often visible

1). First-degree injuries are distinct from second- or third-degree injuries in that these important properties of the burned skin are not significantly altered. The physiologic and metabolic consequences of a second- or third-degree injury are similar. The main difference between these two types of burns is related to the depth of skin damage, in that third-degree burns cannot regenerate with new skin, and thus heal by the formation of scar tissue unless new skin is grafted to the area. Often, the full physiologic impact of second-degree injury is not fully appreciated by the inexperienced medical or paramedical practitioner.

A first-degree injury usually heals rapidly and rarely produces systemic cardiovascular disturbances. When estimating the percentage of body surface area involved, first-degree injuries are not included in the calculations. Because second- and third-degree injuries are of equal physiologic significance, they are summated in estimating total body surface involvement.

BODY SURFACE AREA

An accurate assessment of the magnitude of a burn injury is important because intravenous fluid therapy and caloric requirements are estimated from this calculation.

The estimation of the percentage of total body surface area involved is best performed with the help of a Lund and Browder chart (Table 3). The percentage of body surface area of different areas of the body varies with age. For example, an injury involving the head in an adult is 7% of the total body surface area. The same injury in a 1 year old involves 19% of the body surface area.

A less accurate estimation of burn wound size, *useful for field assessment,* can be obtained by using the rule of nines (Figure 2, Table 4) or palm of hand rule. This latter technique is particularly helpful for scattered injuries. The palm area of the *patient* is approximately 1.0–1.5% of his total body surface area.

Immediate Therapy at the Scene of the Accident

The initial therapy of a patient with a major burn is directed toward restoration of normal

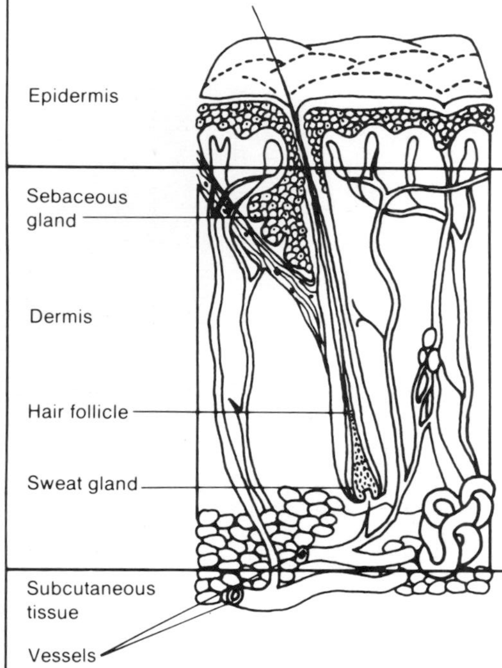

Features of First, Second, and Third Degree Burns

Degree	Appearance	Pain	Histology	Significance
First (partial thickness)	• Pink, dry • No blisters • Slight edema • Elastic	Yes	Epidermis only	• Heals spontaneously • Skin functions (water barrier, thermal barrier, bacterial barrier) intact
Second (partial thickness)	• Pale to red • Weeping, blisters • Marked edema • Elastic	Yes	Epidermis and dermis	• Heals spontaneously • Skin functions lost
Third (full thickness)	• White, black, or red • Thrombosed veins visible • Bullae may or may not be present • Inelastic	No	Full thickness	• Will require grafting • Skin functions lost

Epidermis

Sebaceous gland

Dermis

Hair follicle

Sweat gland

Subcutaneous tissue

Vessels

FIGURE 1 Levels of tissue involvement that correspond with first, second, and third degree burns.

TABLE 3
Lund and Browder Chart: Relative Percentage of Body Surface Area by Age Group

Area	1 Year	1–4 Years	5–9 Years	10–14 Years	15 Years	Adults
Head	19	17	13	11	9	7
Neck	2	2	2	2	2	2
Anterior trunk	13	13	13	13	13	13
Posterior trunk	13	13	13	13	13	13
Right buttock	2½	2½	2½	2½	2½	2½
Left buttock	2½	2½	2½	2½	2½	2½
Genitalia	1	1	1	1	1	1
Right upper arm	4	4	4	4	4	4
Left upper arm	4	4	4	4	4	4
Right lower arm	3	3	3	3	3	3
Left lower arm	3	3	3	3	3	3
Right hand	2½	2½	2½	2½	2½	2½
Left hand	2½	2½	2½	2½	2½	2½
Right thigh	5½	6½	6½	8½	9	9½
Left thigh	5½	6½	6½	8½	9	9½
Right leg	5	5	5	6	6½	7
Left leg	5	5	5	6	6½	7
Right foot	3½	3½	3½	3½	3½	3½
Left foot	3½	3½	3½	3½	3½	3½

physiologic parameters and prevention of life-threatening complications. The burn wound is of secondary importance during the first few hours after injury. The one exception to this rule is a wound caused by a chemical agent. These wounds should be immediately doused with large amounts (i.e., gallons) of water. This immediate dilution of any chemical agent with water is important to prevent further tissue destruction by the agent, and is preferable to a time-consuming search for a specific neutralizing agent.

The steps to be followed at the scene of the accident may be summarized as follows:

REMOVE THE PATIENT FROM THE SOURCE OF INJURY

Smoldering clothing or other materials in contact with the victim must be extinguished. Chemical burns should be doused with gallons of water. In the case of an electrical injury, either the current should be turned off or the patient should be removed from contact with the current by means of a nonconductive implement, prior to implementation of first aid measures.

ESTABLISH AN AIRWAY AND RESTORE CIRCULATION

Cardiopulmonary resuscitation (CPR) may be required at the scene of the accident. The indications for its use and the techniques involved are identical to those for any other injured patient. Patients sustaining electrical injury are more likely to require CPR at the accident scene, since the current interferes with the electrical activity of the heart.

EVALUATE AND TREAT CARBON MONOXIDE POISONING

All patients exposed to smoke should be presumed to have some degree of carbon monoxide poisoning. The symptomatology of carbon monoxide poisoning is characteristic, with low blood levels producing palpitations, muscle weakness, headache, dizziness, and confusion. At higher blood levels, excitement and restlessness are prominent. When the level of carboxyhemoglobin exceeds 40%, collapse and coma occurs (13). Carbon monoxide competitively binds to hemoglobin at the oxygen-carrying sites on the molecule. Carboxyhemo-

Burn Record. Ages 7 to Adult.

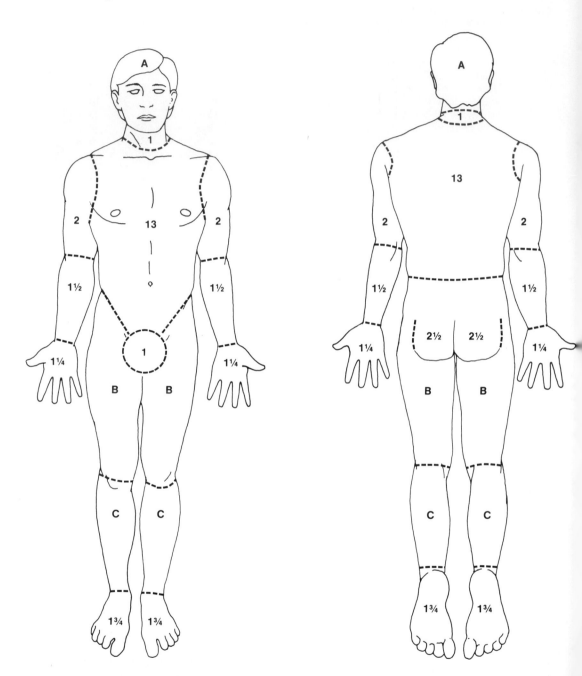

RELATIVE PERCENTAGES OF AREAS AFFECTED BY GROWTH

Area	Age 10	15	Adult
A = ½ of Head	5½	4½	3½
B = ½ of One Thigh	4¼	4½	4¾
C = ½ of One Leg	3	3¼	3-1/3

FIGURE 2 Diagrams used to determine percentage of body surface burned.

Burn Record. Ages—Birth-7½

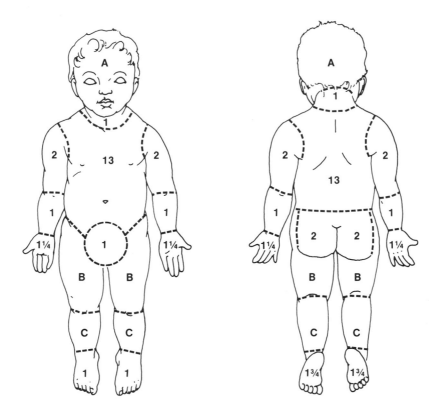

RELATIVE PERCENTAGES OF AREAS AFFECTED BY GROWTH

Area	Age 0	1	5
A = ½ of Head	9½	8½	6½
B = ½ of One Thigh	2¾	3¼	4
C = ½ of One Leg	2½	2½	2¾

FIGURE 2 (*Continued*)

TABLE 4
Rules of Nines for Estimating Body Surface Area Involvement in Adults

Area	% of Body Surface
Head	9
Right upper extremity	9
Left upper extremity	9
Right lower extremity	18
Left lower extremity	18
Anterior trunk	18
Posterior trunk	18
Neck	1

globin is cherry red in color, so that the patient who has inhaled this gas may not be cyanotic, despite dangerously low levels of oxygen carried by hemoglobin in his circulation. Conversely, one must not rely on the red color of the mucous membranes for diagnosis. The treatment for carbon monoxide poisoning is the administration of oxygen. It may take up to 4 hours for a patient spontaneously breathing room air to eliminate one-half of the carbon monoxide in the blood, whereas, treatment with 100% oxygen will effect the same reduction in 40 minutes (20). Please see the excellent discussion in Chapter 21.

ASSESS THE PATIENT FOR OTHER INJURIES

Burn injuries commonly occur in association with other injuries. The burn wound is *not* a contraindication to full examination of the patient. In general, the treatment priorities are similar to those in trauma situation. Burn wounds are not considered to be of immediate danger to life, and thus have a lower priority than wounds capable of causing a threat to life in the early phases of treatment, e.g., airway obstruction, hemorrhage, open chest injuries, and neurologic trauma.

WATCH FOR SIGNS OF IMPENDING UPPER AIRWAY OBSTRUCTION

Upper airway obstruction in burn victims results from edema of laryngeal structures caused by direct exposure to heat. Direct laryngoscopy is the most effective means of diagnosing laryngeal edema. This may be performed rapidly with a laryngoscope or, if available, a fiberoptic flexible nasopharyngoscope. Symptoms and signs suggestive of impending upper airway obstruction are summarized in Table 5. It should be noted that burns of the head and neck, singed nares, and carbonaceous sputum, although suggestive of an inhalation injury, are not indicative of impending upper airway obstruction, and are therefore not indications by themselves for emergency intubation. In the absence of respiratory distress, direct visualization is the standard of care. If intubation is required at the scene of an accident or in the emergency room, the reason for performing the procedure and the condition of the larynx and vocal cords should be noted as a guide for later management. For example, if intubation was carried out to establish an airway during respiratory arrest, and no edema of the cords was noted, extubation could be considered at an earlier time than if severely burned or markedly edematous cords were observed.

QUICKLY ESTIMATE THE EXTENT OF BURN INJURY

The techniques for performing rapid assessment have been described in a previous section. The size of chemical burns is calculated in the same manner as for thermal injuries, although chemical burns are frequently underestimated because the clinical characteristics of the burns develop more slowly. Thus, reestimation of burn size and depth should be performed sequentially during the first 72 hours. The estimation of the damage produced by electrical injuries is more difficult, and will be reviewed in a later section.

TRANSPORT THE PATIENT TO A SPECIALIZED BURN CARE FACILITY OR OTHER EMERGENCY CARE FACILITY

When dealing with a pure burn injury, if a burn center or burn unit is located within 30 minutes of the scene of the accident, the patient should be transported directly to that facility. If the nearest specialized burn care facility is more than 30 minutes away, the patient should be taken to the closest hospital with an emergency department equipped to provide acute care, until arrangements for transportation to a specialized facility can be made. It is important to be familiar with regional protocols for the triage and transport of critically injured patients.

Further Decisions to Be Made at the Scene of an Accident

INTRAVENOUS THERAPY

The factors that must be quickly assessed to decide if intravenous therapy should be started at the scene of an accident are the severity of the injury, how long it would take to start intravenous therapy, and how long it would take to transport the patient to the

---

TABLE 5
**Signs and Symptoms
Indicative of Upper Airway
Obstruction**

Hoarseness
Stridor
Tachypnea
Drooling—inability to swallow
Excessive salivation
Restlessness

nearest medical facility. If the burn injury is greater than 20% of the body surface area, if the patient may require advanced life support, or if the transport time involved is more than 30 minutes, administration of Ringer's lactate solution intravenously is desirable. If the establishment of venous access is difficult, it should be attempted en route.

TREATMENT OF THE BURN WOUNDS

Cool water will reduce pain in limited second-degree burn injuries. Ice directly applied to any wound will add to the tissue damage produced. The benefit obtained by cool, moist dressings is far outweighed by the risks of prolonged cold application, namely, fatal cardiac arrhythmias induced by systemic hypothermia and additional cold thermal injury as a result of exaggerated peripheral vasoconstriction. The patient who has sustained a burn injury should be placed in clean sheets or blankets in preparation for transport and, like any trauma victim, should be kept warm during transport.

USE OF NARCOTICS

Narcotics compound respiratory insufficiency and may interfere with subsequent evaluation of head, abdominal, or chest injuries. *There is (with rare exception) no reason to administer narcotics at the scene of an accident.*

ASSESSMENT OF THE FULL EXTENT OF AN ELECTRICAL INJURY

The damage produced by an electric current may not be estimated by inspection of the surface involvement. Once the current enters the body, it proceeds preferentially along the nerves and blood vessels, producing a core of necrosis deep below the skin. Massive damage may be present deep in viable skin and subcutaneous tissue. These patients must be managed as if they have sustained a major crush injury.

CHEMICAL BURNS OF THE EYES

Chemical burns of the eyes are managed in a similar fashion to chemical burns of the skin. Copious lavage with water is recommended to dilute the agent and decrease the contact time. Continuous irrigation of the eyes should be maintained throughout transport and in the emergency department upon arrival. Two liters is a suggested minimum.

TAR BURNS

Hot tar is used primarily for paving and roofing (10). In terms of its origin and chemical composition, it may be divided into coal tar and petroleum. Roofing asphalt is used at a higher temperature (500°F) than is road tar (300°F), and thus the burn wounds tend to be of greater degree.

The current consensus is to remove tar from the skin as follows (15).

1. The burn site (with adherent tar) should be cooled to prevent tissue injury and to limit the spread of tar. Care must be taken to avoid hypothermia.
2. Tar should not be peeled off in the field, but rather, in an appropriate facility.
3. In the hospital, tar adherent to a vesicle should be excised with the vesicle.
4. Tar adherent to unblistered areas can be covered with a petrolatum or animal fat-based ointment, either alone or in combination with polysorbate. Repeated dressing changes every 1–2 hours will cause dissolution of the tar within 24–72 hours. The addition of antibiotics (bacitracin, neomycin) may decrease the incidence of infection.
5. All organic solvents are generally tissue toxic and should be avoided. In one review, mayonnaise (80% vegetable oil) has been used without toxicity or allergic reaction to rapidly solubilize and remove tar from burned skin (16a).

Emergency Department Management

REASSESS AIRWAY, BREATHING, AND CIRCULATION

At one time, tracheostomy was commonly performed if airway control was required. Since the advent of the "soft cuffed" endotracheal tube, it has replaced tracheostomy as the preferred method of airway control. Tracheotomy, or cricothyroidotomy may be necessary if endotracheal or nasotracheal intubation cannot be performed.

OBTAIN A COMPLETE HISTORY FROM ALL WITNESSES, PARAMEDICAL PERSONNEL, THE PATIENT, AND THE FAMILY

Information concerning previous state of health, drug allergies, circumstances, and mechanism of the burn injury may be vital to management and should be recorded.

CONDUCT A COMPLETE PHYSICAL EXAMINATION

Burn injuries occur in association with other injuries. The burn injury is not a contraindication to performing any maneuver necessary to diagnose an associated injury. Similarly, the management of other injuries *in general* is not modified because of the presence of a surface burn. Two exceptions to this rule are worth noting. Lacerations may be closed primarily. However, careful monitoring of the wound is indicated. The incidence of delayed wound infection is increased. When infection is noted, sutures may have to be removed and the wound allowed to close secondarily. Open fractures are best managed by external traction rather than internal fixation if a surface burn is present over the fracture site.

DETERMINE THE SIZE AND LOCATION OF THE BURN INJURY

An accurate recording of the location and surface area involvement by the burn injury should be undertaken, if it has not been previously performed. Intravenous fluid therapy and, ultimately, caloric requirements will be based on this calculation; therefore, the Lund and Browder chart should be utilized. In general, burn injuries of the hands, feet, eyes, ears, face, and perineum are of particularly high risk and may present difficult management problems.

OBTAIN BASELINE LABORATORY VALUES

Baseline laboratory values should include a complete blood count, serum electrolytes, arterial blood gases, arterial carboxyhemoglobin level, toxicology screen, blood ethanol level, blood urea nitrogen (BUN), blood glucose, creatinine, prothrombin time (PT), partial thromboplastin time (PTT), urinalysis and urine myoglobin, and hemoglobin levels. Blood should also be typed and crossmatched.

ADMINISTER INTRAVENOUS THERAPY

Both plasma and sodium ions are critical in providing early expansion of depleted plasma and extracellular volumes and returning the cardiac output to normal (13). Patients with burn injuries over more than 15–20% of their total body surface area usually require intravenous fluid resuscitation. The preferential site for intravenous catheter insertion is a peripheral vein in an unburned area. If there is no unburned area, the catheter may be inserted through the burn wound. A urinary catheter is also required to allow assessment of renal function, which is a good monitor of the adequacy of fluid resuscitation. Central venous catheters and Swan-Ganz catheters should be reserved for patients in whom hemodynamic stability is not rapidly achieved. The guidelines for their use are identical to those for other victims of severe trauma.

It is recommended that the Parkland formula be utilized to estimate the quantity and appropriate rate of administration of intravenous fluid, since the formula is easily remembered and its use is uncomplicated. It results in complete restoration of the extracellular fluid space and adequate restoration of circulating volume (3,5).

Ringer's lactate solution alone is used. The amount required during the first twenty-four hours is estimated as follows:

4 ml × body weight (kg) × body surface area burned (%) equals the amount of fluid required

for the first 24 hours following injury. One-half of the total calculated fluid volume is delivered during the first 8 hours because extracellular deficits occur most rapidly within the first 6–12 hours after injury. The remainder is administered over the next 16 hours. Frequent evaluation of the patient must be performed to assure adequate resuscitation (Table 6).

Inhalation injury often results in sequestra-

TABLE 6
Signs of Adequate Resuscitation

Clear sensorium
  Normal responses
  No restlessness
  Appropriate pain related to the injury site

Normal pulse rate
  Adult: 80–100 bpm
  Child: 100–200 bpm

Normal to slightly elevated body temperature

Adequate urine output
  Adult: 30–70 ml/hour
  Child (1–3 years): 1 ml/kg per hour
  Child (3–12 years): 15–25 ml/hour

Absence of paralytic ileus or nausea

TABLE 7
Classification of Burn Injuries

Major
  Second-degree burns >25% of body surface area (adult)
  Second-degree burns >20% of body surface area (child)
  Third-degree burns >10% of body surface area
  Inhalation injury
  Electrical injury
  Poor-risk patient, including children <2 years old and adults >50 years old
  All burns complicated by other trauma
  Burns involving eyes, ears, face, hands, feet, perineum

Moderate
  Second-degree burns >15–25% of body surface area (adult)
  Second-degree burns >10–20% of body surface area (child)
  Third-degree burns >2–10% of body surface area not involving eyes, ears, face, hands, feet, perineum

Minor
  Second-degree burns <15% of body surface area (adult)
  Second-degree burns <10% of body surface area (child)
  Third-degree burns <2% of body surface area not involving eyes, ears, face, hands, feet, perineum

tion of fluid in the lungs, which increases fluid requirements. Adjustments in the intravenous flow rates should be made accordingly.

PROVIDE TETANUS PROPHYLAXIS

Unimmunized patients should be given 250–500 units of tetanus immune globulin, plus 0.5 ml of tetanus toxoid intramuscularly. Previously immunized patients (except those who have received tetanus toxoid within the preceding 12 months) should receive 0.5 ml of tetanus toxoid intramuscularly.

DEFINITIVE TREATMENT FACILITY

Burn injuries are classified as being minor, moderate, or major in severity (Table 7). All major and most moderate injuries require treatment in a major burn treatment facility. The remaining injuries may usually be adequately treated in a general hospital.

PREPARE THE PATIENT FOR TRANSFER

The burn unit staff should be consulted prior to transfer. Open communication allows the safe transfer of the severely injured person efficiently and with decreased risk. All information available at the time of transfer, including therapy that has already been insti-

tuted, must be transmitted to the receiving facility.

Further Considerations in the Emergency Department

MANAGING THE BURN WOUND

Burn wounds should be gently washed with an antiseptic solution (e.g., half-strength povidone-iodine). Blisters should be unroofed and loose, dead tissue removed. The wounds then need only be wrapped in clean dressings or sheets while the patient awaits transfer. If a delay in transfer is anticipated, antimicrobial cream (silver sulfadiazine, povidone-iodine, bacitracin) may be applied to make the patient more comfortable. Again, the emergency room physician should be familiar with regional burn center protocols.

MANAGING THE PATIENT WITH AN ELECTRICAL INJURY

The surface burn does not accurately reflect the degree of injury deep to the skin. Ringer's lactate infusion should be started. The rate of administration should be rapid, until a urine output of more than 50 ml/hour (in adults) is established. Thereafter, the fluid rate should be adjusted to maintain urine output at 30–50 ml/hour in adults and 1 ml/kg per hour in children. The electrocardiogram (ECG) and arterial pH must be carefully monitored at the start of the resuscitation and frequently thereafter. Restoration of perfusion to ischemic limbs may result in marked acidosis and hyperkalemia as the products of anaerobic metabolism are returned rapidly into the general circulation. If large amounts of myoglobin or hemochromagens are present in the urine, renal insufficiency may develop from continued exposure of the kidneys to pigment and cell breakdown products. After cardiac output has been restored as indicated by a urine output of 50 ml/hour, 25 g of intravenous mannitol in a 20% solution may be given, followed by 12.5 g every 6 hours, until the urine clears. Pediatric doses are 0.25 g/kg; however, children are less likely to need such support.

MANAGING THE PATIENT WITH A CHEMICAL INJURY

The fluid requirements for a patient who has sustained a chemical burn are identical to those for a patient who has sustained a thermal burn of comparable size.

The following chemicals require unique therapeutic considerations in the emergency department:

1. Strong acids or alkalis. These agents must be diluted promptly and vigorously with copious quantities of water. They should not be "neutralized" with solutions of extreme pH; the resultant reaction is exothermic and worsens the tissue damage.
2. Phosphorus. Yellow or white phosphorus combusts spontaneously on contact with air. Therefore, any chemical that remains on the skin or clothing must be irrigated gently and continuously with water until the phosphorus is removed. If possible, the affected area should be submersed in water. A suspension of 5% sodium bicarbonate and 3% copper sulfate in 1% hydroxyethyl cellulose is used as an irrigant to inactivate the phosphorus, without inducing copper poisoning (5a).
3. Hydrofluoric acid. Fluoride induces liquefaction necrosis of soft tissue, while forming reversible dissociable fluoride salt complexes in the tissue that continue the injury. Calcium and magnesium salt complexes are insoluble and harmless, but formed in small amounts without the administration of exogenous calcium or magnesium. After copious irrigation with water, noninjured areas should be dressed immediately with dressings soaked in calcium gluconate or impregnated with magnesium oxide ointment (8a). Skin that demonstrates burn involvement, generally excruciatingly painful, requires neutralization with intracuticular injections of 10% calcium gluconate. Close attention should be paid to progression of the severity of the injury.
4. Phenol. Phenol is an acidic alcohol that is highly corrosive and causes coagulation necrosis of dermal proteins. After copious irrigation with water, the exposed skin should be washed with polyethylene glycol (PEG), which increases the solubility of phenol and allows more rapid removal with irrigation. If PEG is immediately available, it should be applied full strength prior to water dilution.

NARCOTIC ADMINISTRATION

When fluid resuscitation is underway and the patient is stable, a small dose of morphine (2–6 mg) may be given intravenously. Alternatively, meperidine, 20–25 mg (0.5 mg/kg in children), may be administered intravenously. Before narcotics are given, all other injuries must be fully assessed. The intravenous route is always preferred because absorption may be unpredictable from intramuscular or subcutaneous sites.

USE OF A NASOGASTRIC TUBE

Patients who sustain a burn over more than 20% of their body surface area often develop reflex paralytic ileus with gastric dilatation. A nasogastric tube will obviate the risk of vomiting and pulmonary aspiration in these patients. If transport via air is planned, a nasogastric tube is mandatory because decreasing cabin pressure at elevated altitudes will cause gastric distention and vomiting.

USE OF PROPHYLACTIC ANTIBIOTICS OR STEROIDS

The first invaders of burn wounds are gram-positive (*Staphylococcus, Streptococcus*) organisms. Prophylactic administration of penicillin has been recommended by some authors, with the course of therapy not to exceed 3–4 days. Although the prophylactic administration of penicillin continues to be a common practice, there is evidence that no benefit is derived, and many burn units no longer use prophylactic systemic antibiotics (9). Similarly, steroids, which were commonly used for treating smoke inhalation from about 1955 to 1970, are no longer recommended. There are no benefits to be gained from the administration of steroids; in fact, this practice may result in increased morbidity and mortality (12, 13,17).

USE OF ESCHAROTOMIES

Burned extremities should be elevated and exercised to prevent venous stasis and to minimize edema formation. Increasing fluid accumulation in an extremity can lead to venous congestion within the confinement of inelastic skin. Pressure increases lead to decreased arterial blood flow and venous stasis, with resultant muscle ischemia, necrosis, and fibrosis. For this reason, escharotomies may be required in a patient with circumferential burns of the extremities, particularly if there is an associated significant electrical injury or in the presence of underlying crush injury with or without bone involvement. The indication to perform this procedure is neurovascular compromise in an edematous extremity with a circumferential *third*-degree burn following adequate resuscitation. Ideally, a Doppler ultrasonic device should be used to assess vascular flow at regular intervals. However, if this is not readily available, escharotomy should be performed in the presence of decreased capillary refill, motor or sensory deficits (particularly in digits or in an area of the extremity involved with full thickness), or the development of deep pain beneath the burned surface.

The technique for performing escharotomies is as follows (Figure 3). The overlying skin is surgically prepared. Medial and lateral incisions are made through the third-degree eschar. No anesthetic is required, as the area is already anesthetic. The depth of the incision is only through the eschar, so virtually no blood loss should occur. Vascular flow should be restored immediately after the procedure is completed. Particular care should be taken to avoid transection of major cutaneous nerves and subcutaneous blood vessels; this necessitates surgical experience and a working knowledge of the relevant anatomy.

Rarely, a circumferential injury of the chest may impede normal respiratory excursion. In this situation, incisions are made in the anterior axillary lines to the level of the costal margin, and then brought anteriorly along the costal margin to join in the midline. To avoid major respiratory failure, the physician must heed early warning signs of ventilatory distress, and not rely solely on arterial blood gas determinations.

If escharotomies fail to return vascular flow to an extremity in an otherwise resuscitated patient, fasciotomies should be considered. This situation is most likely to occur in electrical injuries, where most of the damage may be deep to the fascia.

Outpatient Management of Minor Burns

The burn wound should first be cleansed with a dilute antiseptic solution (povidone-iodine) and all loose skin and debris removed. A topical antibacterial cream or ointment, fine-mesh gauze, and a fluffy protective dressing can then be applied. Dressings should be changed daily and checked every 2–3 days. Tetanus toxoid prophylaxis must be administered even with relatively minor burns.

Burn Unit Management

Management of the burned patient in the burn unit requires both general therapeutic measures and specific attention to the burn wound (14). In this section, a brief review of the modalities utilized will be outlined.

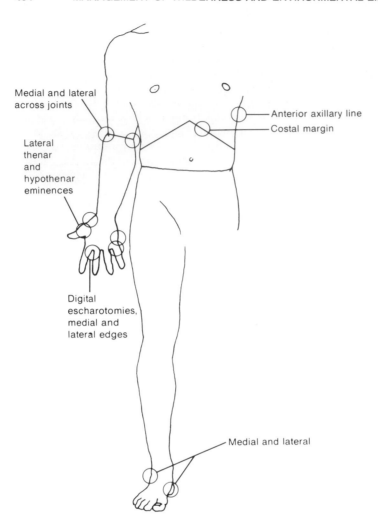

Medial and lateral across joints

Anterior axillary line

Costal margin

Lateral thenar and hypothenar eminences

Digital escharotomies, medial and lateral edges

Medial and lateral

FIGURE 3 Principles of escharotomy: (1) only through third degree eschar; (2) extend until pulses return; (3) not indicated if distal pulses present; (4) medial and lateral incisions on extremities; (5) chest—anterior axillary line, then along costal margins.

GENERAL THERAPEUTIC MEASURES

Fluid Resuscitation: Second 24 Hours

In the second 24-hour period after the burn injury, Ringer's lactate infusion is stopped and 5% dextrose in water infusion is started at a rate sufficient to replace evaporative water loss. The serum sodium ion concentration is monitored, and the rate of infusion of intravenous solutions adjusted to maintain the concentration at approximately 140 mEq/liter. The rate of infusion can be estimated according to the formula:

Water evaporation loss (ml/hour) = (25 ml plus the percentage of total body surface burned) × total body surface area in m^2

Colloid solution (plasma) may also be required during this period to maintain plasma volume in patients with more than 40% second- and third-degree burns. A unit of plasma is administered for each 10% of total body surface area burned over 40%, or approximately 0.3 ml of colloid per kilogram of body weight per percentage of burn per 24 hours.

Red cell destruction from thermal injury seldom exceeds 10% of the red cell mass and rarely becomes manifest at this stage. Therefore, early blood transfusion is usually not required unless the patient was previously anemic, associated injury results in internal or external hemorrhage, or a hemolytic anemia secondary to massive capillary destruction or late sepsis develops. A rapidly falling hematocrit in a patient with only a moderate-sized burn injury should alert the physician that a source of bleeding is present, and should not be attributed to the burn injury.

Nutrition and Metabolism

Major burn injury is characterized by a hypermetabolic response, the level of which is proportional to the magnitude of the surface burn (6,18). The resting metabolic rate may be increased 40–100% above normal in patients with burns exceeding 30% of the total body surface area. These markedly elevated metabolic demands are a consequence of alterations in the neurohormonal control mechanisms which normally regulate energy utilization and substrate flow (19). Simultaneously, severe catabolism is observed during the immediate postburn period. The clinical implication of the hypermetabolic and catabolic response is obvious. Daily energy requirements of up to 5000 kcal may have to be met to delay rapid utilization of endogenous fuel reserves and eventual morbid consequences associated with acute starvation.

The cornerstone of nutritional management is the provision of adequate calories from an exogenous source. Daily caloric requirements of adult patients with burns greater than 20% of the total body surface area may be estimated by the formula:

25 kcal/kg of body weight + 40 kcal per percentage of burn

After caloric requirements are calculated, a dietary program should be designed to provide enough nitrogen to ensure a calories to nitrogen ratio of about 150:1.

A number of auxiliary measures should be simultaneously undertaken to minimize energy demands. Every effort should be made to minimize pain, anxiety, and cold stress, all of which tend to cause the release of catecholamine stores, resulting in an increase of the hypermetabolic response.

Another stimulus to increased metabolic expenditure is infection. Every effort should be made to prevent early colonization of the burn wound. Topical antibacterials may help in this regard. The earliest possible closure of the burn wound by autogenous tissue is highly recommended.

Nutritional supplementation, either by enteral or parenteral routes, should be initiated before the fourth postburn day, and daily caloric intake levels that will satisfy nutritional requirements should be achieved by the end of the first postburn week. A documented weight loss that exceeds 10% of the preburn weight is associated with increased morbidity, and additional efforts to decrease metabolic expenditure and improve dietary intake are indicated.

Physical Therapy, Splinting, and Rehabilitation

A progressive physical therapy program, implemented immediately after hospital admission, will preserve range of motion in joints and minimize contracture formation. Prolonged immobilization is discouraged. In addition, proper positioning during bed rest must be monitored and splints manufactured to maintain an anticontracture position during sleep. This program of exercise, ranging, and antideformity splinting is maintained until the burn wounds are healed and normal range of joint motion can be sustained by the patient.

Scarring

The development of hypertrophic scars may occur after hospital discharge. The resultant scar overgrowth may inhibit function and result in severe disfigurement. Hypertrophic scar formation may be modified by applying conforming elastic garments which exert pressure on the scar, causing better alignment of collagen fibers and a reduction of local interstitial edema (11). A variety of new materials may be inserted deep to the garment to create additional pressure on the scars (1). Such devices are more effective in controlling scar formation in difficult contour areas of the face (bridge of the nose, neck, curve of the chin), chest, axilla, and clavicular areas. In general, these materials and devices must be worn for 6–18 months to gain maximum benefit.

As an adjunctive measure to the compression therapy, intralesional injection of steroids may be indicated. Triamcinolone or other members of the 9,2-hydrocortisone group are the currently preferred agents. They appear to enhance collagen degradation within the treated lesions (1).

Care of the Burn Wound

The principles of managing the burn wound are identical to those for managing any surgical wound, and may be summarized as follows:

Debride dead tissue
Preserve function
Prevent infection
Close the wound

There are two general approaches to management of the wound: nonoperative and operative treatment. There is current enthusiasm for more aggressive operative management, although a large number of major centers still maintain a nonoperative protocol for certain wounds.

NONOPERATIVE MANAGEMENT

The main features of this mode of treatment are:

1. Topical antibacterial application to limit colonization of the burn wound.
2. Repeated biopsy of the wounds with quantitative culture to monitor bacterial growth
3. Subeschar clysis with antibiotics when indicated
4. Daily debridement

FURTHER CONSIDERATIONS

Choice of Topical Antibacterial Agent

Burn wounds treated with topical antibacterial agents are not sterilized. Rather, the bacterial population is suppressed, and bacterial concentration remains below the level at which invasive burn wound sepsis will occur. Conversion of second-degree to third-degree injury is minimized by controlling the rate of bacterial proliferation within the burn eschar.

To be effective as a topical antibacterial agent, the material must possess certain properties (Table 8). No single material fulfills the

TABLE 8
Properties of the Ideal Topical Antimicrobial Burn Agent

Effective against major pathogens
Nontoxic locally and systemically
Readily available
Easy to apply
Rapidly excreted or easily metabolized
No interference with wound healing
Low cost
No emergence of resistant organisms

requirements of an ideal agent. A variety of preparations is available, each with certain advantages and disadvantages. Table 9 summarizes the properties of the currently available topical agents. For optimum results with the use of any of these agents, a number of principles should be adhered to:

1. Avoid the overuse of a single agent; resistant organisms will eventually emerge.
2. Excise dead tissue when feasible.
3. Close the wound as soon as possible.

Monitoring the Burn Wound with Biopsy and Culture

Clinical bacteriologic monitoring of the burn wound is imperative in order to diagnose incipient burn wound sepsis. Cultures taken from the burn wound surface fail to predict accurately progressive bacterial colonization of the deep layers of the eschar. Bacterial growth in burn wounds is best monitored by semiquantitative burn wound biopsy cultures (7). Multiple full-thickness wound biopsies are obtained from representative areas of the burn wound. The tissue is then weighed, homogenized, serially diluted, and inoculated on blood agar and eosin-methylene blue plates. The precise number of viable organisms per gram of tissue is then calculated. When burn biopsy cultures during the first 2 postburn weeks reveal more than 10^5 organisms per gram of tissue or a 100-fold increase in the concentration of bacteria within a 48-hour period, it may be assumed that the organism has escaped effective control by the topical chemotherapeutic agent, and that burn wound sepsis is incipient.

TABLE 9
Topical Antimicrobial Agents for Burn Wound Care

Agent	Supplied	Advantages	Disadvantages
Silver sulfadiazine	1% in water-miscible base	Broad-spectrum bacteriostatic effect; painless on application	Hypersensitivity, neutropenia
Mafenide acetate	10% in water-miscible base	Broad-spectrum bacteriostatic effect; penetrates eschar rapidly	Painful on application; carbonic anyhydrase inhibition; hypersensitivity
Silver nitrate	0.5% solution	Broad-spectrum bacteriostatic effect; painless on application	Poor penetration of eschar; may produce hyponatremia and hypochloremia; requires bulky dressings which may interfere with physiotherapy; discolors wound and environment; may cause methemoglobinemia
Povidone-iodine	Ointment or foam	Broad spectrum; painless; bacteriocidal	(?) Penetration of eschar (?) Iodine toxicity
Gentamycin	0.1% cream or ointment	Broad spectrum; painless; bacteriocidal; active penetration	Rapid development of resistant strains; (?) ototoxicity or nephrotoxicity
Nitrofurazone	0.23% in water-miscible base	Low toxicity; good eschar penetration	No effect on *Pseudomonas*; (?) effect as topical

Use of Subeschar Clysis

This method was introduced by Baxter *et al.* for the treatment of incipient or existing burn wound sepsis (4). It is indicated for cases in which conventional topical therapy has failed to prevent excessive colonization of the eschar and for cases in which delay in onset of treatment has occurred. The maximum daily tolerated dose of an appropriate antibiotic (as determined by biopsy culture and sensitivity) is administered by subcutaneous clysis with multiple needle infusions. The antibiotics are administered in the subeschar tissues in aliquots of 25 ml of fluid in each area of third-degree burn 10 cm in diameter.

Use of Biologic Dressings

Biologic dressings (heterograft and homograft) have become an integral part of the treatment of burn injuries. A summary of their more common uses is presented in Table 10.

For a full discussion of their advantages and disadvantages, the additional readings are recommended. In general, unless one has had experience in using these materials, the majority of wounds are best managed with topical antibacterial agents. The same principle holds for the use of a variety of synthetic dressings that are currently available. These may be applied directly as sheets or sprayed on the burn wound. The wounds must be carefully fol-

TABLE 10
Current Use of Biologic Dressings (Homograft and Heterograft)

Immediate coverage of superficial second-degree burns
Debridement of untidy wounds after eschar separation
Use of test material prior to autografting
Coverage of granulation tissue between crops of autograft in the large burn
Immediate wound coverage following excision

lowed to avoid rapid conversion of second-degree to third-degree injury deep to the dressing.

For clean, superficial second degree burns, heterograft or homograft biologic dressings may be immediately applied to the wounds. Such treatment markedly decreases pain and results in more rapid reepithelialization of the burn. However, one must be certain that the wound is a superficial second-degree burn, since coverage of a full-thickness or deep second-degree injury with contamination deep to the biologic dressings may rapidly precipitate invasive burn wound sepsis. If this type of treatment is chosen, inspection of the dressing at intervals is mandatory. The biologic material must be removed if purulence develops beneath the dressing.

OPERATIVE MANAGEMENT

The operative approach to managing burn wounds involves early tangential or fascial excision of the eschar and closure of the wounds. This has resulted in a dramatic decrease in the length of hospital stay for patients suffering burn injuries (8).

These procedures require the full care of a specialized burn treatment facility to achieve optimum results. Description of the techniques involved is beyond the scope of this text.

Early excision and immediate grafting have been associated with decreased scar formation and improved function. When it is determined that a burn wound is unlikely to heal spontaneously in 3–5 weeks, serious consideration must be given to such procedures.

Stress Gastritis

Gastritis and duodenal ulcers may occur in patients who have sustained major thermal injury. The incidence of this complication has decreased, and is only rarely seen today. This change may be best attributed to three preventive measures that are routinely employed in burn units:

1. Improved nutritional supplementation of burn patients

2. Reduced frequency of major septic complications

3. Maintenance of neutral pH in gastric aspirates with antacids or cimetidine

Septic Thrombophlebitis

Suppurative thrombophlebitis occurs more frequently in patients with thermal injury than in other hospitalized patients with severe illness. This complication follows prolonged ve-

TABLE 11
Survival Probability for Burn Patients

Age	Body Surface Area Burned (%)	Survival Probability (%)
20	20	95+
	40	85
	60	60
40	20	95+
	40	80
	60	50
60	20	80+
	40	40
	60	7

	(Surface Area Burned Producing 50% Survival)	
Age	Body Surface Area Burned (%)	Survival Probability (%)
0–14	62	50
15–40	63	50
40	38	50
65	23	50

Source: From Reference 20.

TABLE 12
Predicted Hospitalization Time (Days) for Surviving Burn Patients

Burn Size (% TBS)	Age (Years)			
	0–14	15–44	45–64	65
10%	16	17	25	33
30%	35	36	37	72
50%	44	56	61	101
70%	103	77	84	131
90%	117	99	102	161

Source: From Reference 20.

nous cannulation for the delivery of intravenous fluids. Most commonly, few physical signs of the problem exist. Instead, the patient presents with bacteremia of unknown origin. Blood cultures often yield *Staphylococcus aureus*.

The diagnosis is confirmed by surgical exploration of all peripheral veins which have been cannulated during hospitalization. The vein is opened and any effluent observed. If pus is found, the diagnosis is confirmed. In the absence of pus, the vein wall is biopsied and examined by frozen section. Bacterial colonization of the intima of the vein strongly suggests the presence of suppurative thrombophlebitis. To avoid this complication, intravenous catheters must be removed at least every 72 hours. Ideally, the site of the cannulation should also be changed at the same time. Should septic thrombophlebitis occur, the offending vein must be excised in its entirety. Failure to employ surgical treatment usually results in fatal bacteremia.

Morbidity and Mortality

The development of multidisciplinary teams to ensure total care of the burn patient has markedly reduced the morbidity and mortality associated with severe burn injuries. Table 11 summarizes the current expected survival with burn injuries of different size in varying age groups. Table 12 summarizes the predicted hospitalization time of surviving burn patients. Most patients can expect to return to an occupation as remunerative as their preinjury employment and will regain self-respect and independence.

References

1. Alston, D. A., Kozerefski, P., Quan, P. E., Luterman, A. Materials for pressure inserts in the control of hypertrophic scar tissue. *Journal of Burn Care and Rehabilitation,* 2:39, 1981.
2. Artz, C. P. Epidemiology: Causes and prognosis. In *Burns: A Team Approach,* Artz, C. P., Moncreif, J. A., Pruitt, B. A. (Eds.), W. B. Saunders, Philadelphia, 1979.
3. Baxter, C. R. Crystalloid resuscitation of burn shock. In *Contemporary Burn Management,* Polk, H. C. Jr., Stone, H. M. (Eds.), Little, Brown, Boston, 1971.
4. Baxter, C. R., Curreri, P. W., Marvin, J. A. The control of burn wound sepsis by the use of quantita-tive bacteriologic studies and subeschar clysis with antibiotics. *Surgical Clinics of North America,* 53:1509, 1973.
5. Baxter, C. R., Shires, G. T.: Early resuscitation of patients with burns. In Welch, C. E. (Ed.), *Advances in Surgery,* Volume 4. Year Book Medical Publishers, Chicago, 1970.
5a. Ben-Hur N., Shani J., Appelbaum, J.: Phosphorus burns in primates: a conclusive experimental study of a new specific therapy. *Burns,* 4:246, 1978.
6. Bradham, G. B.: Direct measurement of total metabolism of a burned patient. *Archives of Surgery,* 105:410, 1972.
7. Curreri, P. W. Burns. In *Principles of Surgery,* Schwartz, S. I., Shires, G. T., Spencer, F. C., Storere, E. H. (Eds.), McGraw-Hill, New York, 1979.
8. Curreri, P. W., Luterman, A., Braun, D. W., Shires, G. T.: Burn injury, analysis of survival and hospitalization time for 937 Patients. *Annals of Surgery,* 192:472, 1980.
8a. Dibbell, D. G., Iverson, R. E., Jones, W., Laub, D. R., Madison, M. S.: Hydrofluoric acid burns of the hand. *Journal of Bone and Joint Surgery,* 52(A), 931, 1970.
9. Durtschi, M., *et al:* Prophylactic penicillin in acute burns. American Burn Association, Twelfth Annual Meeting, San Antonio, Texas, 1980.
10. Halfacre, S., Apesos, J., Rodeheaver, G. T., *et al.:* Hot tar skin burns. *Current Concepts in Trauma Care,* 4(1):18–19, Spring 1981.
10a. Katcher, M. L.: Scald burns from hot tap water. JAMA, 246:1219, 1981.
11. Larson, D. L., Baur, P., Linares, H. A., Willis, B., Abston, S., Lewis, R. R. Mechanisms of hypertrophic scar and contracture formation in burns. *Burns,* 1:119, 1975.
12. Moylan, J. A., Chan, C. K. Inhalation injury—an increasing problem. *Annals of Surgery,* 188:34, 1978.
13. Pruitt, B. A., Jr. The burn patient I. Initial care. *Current Problems in Surgery,* 16(4):1, 1979.
14. Pruitt, B. A. The burn patient II. Later care and complications of thermal injury. *Current Problems in Surgery,* 16:79, 1979.
15. Pruitt, B. A., Edlich, B. F. Treatment of bitumen burns. Letter. *Journal of the American Medical Association,* 247(11):1565, 1982.
16. *Reports on the Epidemiology and Surveillance of Injuries,* No. FY72-R7 DHEW. Publication (HSM) 73–10001, U.S. Department of Health, Education, and Welfare, Health Services and Mental Health Administration, Rockville, Md., July 1972.
16a. Shea, P. C., Jr., Fannon, P.: Mayonnaise and hot tar burns. *Journal of the Medical Association of Georgia,* September, 659–660, 1981.
17. Trunkey, D. D. Inhalation injury. *Surgical Clinics of North America,* 58:1133, 1978.
18. Wilmore, D. W. Nutrition and metabolism following thermal injury. *Clinical Plastic Surgery,* 1:603.
19. Wilmore, D. W., Long, J. M., Mason, A. D., *et al.* Catecholamines: Mediator of the hypermetabolic response to thermal injury. *Annals of Surgery,* 180:653, 1974.
20. Zamen, H. A., *et al.* Carbon monoxide toxicity in human fire victims. *Archives of Surgery,* 107:851, 1973.

CHAPTER 18 | LIGHTNING INJURIES

Mary Ann Cooper, M.D.

Historical Overview

Humans have always viewed lightning with awe and trepidation (76). Priests, the earliest astronomers and meteorologists, became proficient at weather prediction, interpreting changes in weather as omens of good or bad fortune. Lightning as a spectacular celestial event was often depicted in ancient cultures and religions (33).

A roll seal from Akkadian times (2200 B.C.) portrays a goddess holding sheaves of lightning in each hand (33). Next to her, a weather god drives a chariot and creates lightning bolts by flicking a whip at his horses, while priests offer libations. A relief found on a castle gate in northern Syria (900 B.C.) depicts the weather god Teshub holding a three-pronged thunderbolt. (61).

Beginning around 700 B.C., Greek art began to incorporate lightning symbols, representing them as Zeus's tool of warning and vengeance. Aristotle noted that lightning was the result of the ignition of telluric fumes that made up storm clouds.

Thor, of Roman mythology, also utilized thunderbolts. Several of the Roman emperors wore laurel or sealskin to ward off lightning strikes. Important matters of state were often decided on observations of lightning and other natural phenomena. Both Seneca and Titus Lucretius discussed lightning in their treatises on natural events, and Plutarch noted that sleeping persons, having no spirit of life, were immune to lightning strikes (33,48).

In Chinese mythology, the goddess of lightning, Tien Mu, used mirrors to direct bolts of lightning (61). She was one of the five deities of the "Ministry of Thunderstorms" of ancient Chinese religion. Lightning also played a role in Buddhist symbolism and demonstrated the power and omniscience of the god.

Although lightning is most frequently rendered as fire, it has also been represented as stone axes hurled from the heavens. French peasants carry a *pierre de tonnerre,* or lightning stone, to ward off lightning strikes. The Yakuts of eastern Asia regard rounded stones found in fields hit by lightning as thunder axes and often use the powdered stones in medicines and potions. In Africa, the Basuto tribe views lightning as the great thunderbird Umpundulo, flashing its wings in the clouds as it descends to earth.

Incidence of Injury

It is estimated that 2000 thunderstorms are occurring throughout the world at any time. (77) Lightning strikes the earth more than 100 times per second. While lightning strikes humans in only a fraction of these storms, there is a measurable and important number of deaths every year. In a 34-year period ending in 1974, there were 7000 deaths from lightning in the United States (78). Lightning killed 430 persons in 1943.

In 1953, the Public Health Service reclassified the injuries attributed to lightning. It now categorizes separately deaths that are secondarily related to lightning, such as those from forest fires or building fires kindled by lightning. Because of this reclassification, few reliable figures are obtainable for injuries and deaths directly caused by lightning. However, it is estimated that 150–300 persons are killed by lightning annually in the United States (73,76–78). Lightning kills more persons in the United States than any other natural disaster, including volcanic eruptions, blizzards, and earthquakes. It kills 55% more people than tornadoes and 41% more than floods and hurricanes combined (78).

Historically, farmers, sailors, and other people who worked outdoors in isolated areas tended to be the most frequently injured. Today, with the move to urban areas, a larger proportion of the victims are hikers, campers, golfers, and others who are outdoors for recreational purposes (32,60).

Almost 70% of lightning fatalities occur as single deaths from a single discharge (78). However, a significant proportion of deaths occur in multiples. Fifteen percent of victims are killed in groups of two, while the remaining 15% are fatally injured in groups of three or more at a time.

As might be expected, lightning deaths are

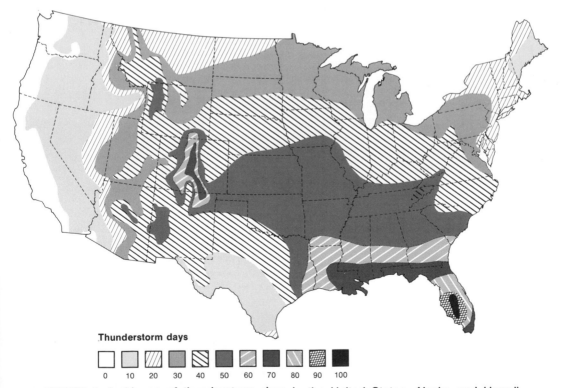

Thunderstorm days

0 10 20 30 40 50 60 70 80 90 100

FIGURE 1 Incidence of thunderstorm days in the United States. Alaska and Hawaii are less than 10.

more frequent during the daytime hours when people are active and outdoors. Seventy percent occur between noon and 6:00 P.M., 20% between 6:00 P.M. and midnight, 10% between 6:00 A.M. and noon, and less than 1% between midnight and 6:00 A.M. Most injuries occur in the summer months of June to September when thunderstorms are most frequent (78).

Although lightning may occur without rain, it does not exist without thunder, so that the number of *thunderstorm days* is an important measure of the number of lightning incidents (76). Belts drawn across the United States according to thunderstorm days (Figure 1) indicate that there are more thunderstorm days in the South than in any other region. Thunderstorms occur five times more frequently east than west of the Rockies, more frequently over high mountains and large plateaus than over coasts, and in low-altitude marsh districts rather than low-altitude dry areas (39).

Because lightning injuries are prevalent in high mountainous areas and around large bodies of water, such as river basins, the states highest in lightning injuries tend to be those of the South, the Gulf Coast, the Rocky Mountain area, and those along the Ohio, Mississippi, and Hudson rivers. However, for some reason, the greatest number of fatalities occur in the Mid-Atlantic states, while the greatest proportionate mortality occurs in Colorado, Wyoming, and Montana (78).

Buildings are susceptible in relation to their size, height, nature of construction, and insulation (40). However, more thickly settled residential areas are five times less likely to be struck by lightning than are rural areas (40). People are better protected in the city, where high buildings have metal frames and lightning protection devices, so that comparatively few injuries are reported in large cities (78).

Myths and Superstitions

The Roman Pliny noted that a man who heard thunder was safe from the lightning stroke. In general, this is true, since the light and strike precede the noise by a measurable amount of time, depending on the distance from the lightning strike. However, some victims of direct hits report a sledgehammerlike effect of the force while seeing a bright light

and occasionally hearing a loud noise (71).

Many myths about lightning still persist today, including the notion that lightning is invariably fatal. It actually carries a mortality of only 30%, while survivors show a morbidity of 70% (18). A recent study demonstrated that a person who receives leg burns is five times more likely to die than one who does not (18). Patients with cranial burns also exhibit a three- to fourfold higher probability of death and are two to three times more likely to suffer an immediate cardiopulmonary arrest. Generally, only victims who sustain immediate cardiopulmonary arrest expire. Those who are only stunned or lose consciousness without cardiopulmonary arrest are highly unlikely to die, although they may still have serious sequelae.

Several booklets listing precautions for personal lightning protection appeared in the late 1700s and early 1800s. One of the superstitions listed was the notion that humans, by their presence, could attract lightning to a nearby object. The "Catechism of Thunderstorms" illustrated other myths (44). Lightning was said to follow the draught of warm air behind a horse-drawn cart, so that coachmen were cautioned to walk their horses slowly through a storm (71). Other precautions listed included seeking shelter away from tall trees and sheaves of corn if caught in the open and directions for installing lightning rods for protection of buildings and ships.

A myth that is still prevalent today is that the victim of lightning retains the charge and is dangerous to touch, since he is still "electrified." This idea has led to unnecessary deaths by delaying resuscitation efforts.

Historically, many remedies for resuscitation of lightning victims have been offered (71). On July 15, 1889, Mr. Alfred West testified in a New York court that he was revived by "drawing out the electricity" when his feet were placed in warm water while his rescuer pulled on Mr. West's toes with one hand and milked a cow with the other (7).

Other early attempts at resuscitation included friction to the bare skin, dousing the victim with a bucket of cold water, and chest compression (71). One of the earliest forms of cardiopulmonary resuscitation as it exists today was given in 1807, when mouth-to-mouth ventilation was used for lightning victims and it was suggested that gentle electric shocks from galvanic batteries passed through the chest might be successful in resuscitating a victim of lightning (11). Prior to this, Benjamin Franklin had electrocuted a chicken and reported successful resuscitation with mouth-to-beak ventilation (29).

A myth in current treatment is the belief that lightning injuries should be treated like other high-voltage electrical injuries. While lightning is an electrical phenomenon and follows the same laws of physics, the injuries seen with lightning are very different from those accompanying high-voltage injuries and should be treated differently if iatrogenic morbidity and mortality are to be avoided. The principles that make the injuries different and the appropriate treatment will be discussed.

Early Scientific Studies and Invention of the Lightning Rod

The beginning of the study of electrical phenoma is often traced to the publication of Gilbert's *De Magnete* in London in 1600. Experiments by members of the Royal Society of London and some experiments in France and Germany led to the invention of the Leyden jar in 1745.

Benjamin Franklin began his scientific studies in America during this period and originated the concept of positive and negative charges (29). He also proved with numerous experiments that lightning was an electrical phenomenon and that thunderclouds are electrically charged, as demonstrated by his famous kite and key experiment (28). He is generally regarded as the father of electrical science and during his lifetime was known as the "American Newton." The lightning rod was invented by Franklin, who announced its use in *Poor Richard's Almanack* in 1753, "How to secure Houses etc. from LIGHTNING":

It has pleased God in his Goodness to Mankind, at length to discover to them the Means of securing their Habitations and other Buildings from Mischief by Thunder and Lightning. The Method is this: Provide a small Iron Rod (It may be made of the Rod-iron used by the Nailers) but of such a Length, that one End being three or four Feet in the moist Ground, the other may be six or eight Feet above the highest Part of the Building. To the upper End of the Rod fasten a Foot of brass Wire the Size of a common Knitting-needle, sharpened to a fine Point; the Rod may be secured to the House by a few small Staples. If the House or Barn be long, there may be a Rod and Point at each End, and a middling Wire along the Ridge from one to the other. A House thus furnished will not be damaged by Lightning, it being attracted to the Points, and passing thro the Metal into the Ground without hurting any Thing. Vessels also, having a sharp pointed rod fix'd on the Top of their Masts, with a Wire from the Foot of the Rod reaching down, round one of the Shrouds, to the Water, will not be hurt by Lightning.

In the 1750s and 1760s, the use of the lightning rod became prevalent in the United States for the protection of both buildings and ships. Some scientists in Europe urged the installation of lightning rods on government buildings, churches, and other high buildings. However, religious advocates maintained that it would be blasphemy to install such devices on church steeples, since they received divine protection (57). For this reason, some towns chose to store munitions in churches, leading on more than one occasion to fantastic fireworks and widespread destruction.

Part of the delay in installing lightning rods in England may have been due to the rivalry between Great Britain and the newly independent United States. It required years and numerous unsuccessful trials with English designs before the Franklin rod became accepted on Her Majesty's ships and buildings (11).

At one time, it was theorized that lightning rods were diffusers of electrical charges and could neutralize a storm cloud passing overhead, thus averting a lightning stroke (71). This theory was in part an outgrowth of the observation of an aura that would appear around the tip of lightning rods and ships' masts (St. Elmo's fire) during a thunderstorm. It has since been shown that lightning rods, properly installed, protect a building from damage by allowing the current to flow harmlessly to the ground (34).

The first Lightning Rod Conference was held in London in 1882. Recommendations from this conference were published that year and again in a revision in 1905. Further progress awaited the technical development of Sir

Charles Vernon Boy's rotating camera and the high-speed cathode ray oscillograph by Dufour, which helped to delineate more of the physical properties of lightning, including the direction and speed of the strokes.

In subsequent years, various countries developed codes of practice for lightning protection (Germany 1924, America 1929, Britain 1943, British colonies 1965). A variety of materials, including copper, aluminum, and iron, are recommended by the various codes, which also specify the measurements and construction of the protective system, depending on the height, location, and construction of the structure to be protected.

Lightning strokes vary in the power and frequency of strikes, depending on the terrain and geographic location. Complicated formulas have been devised to take into account factors which include the relative frequency of strikes in an area; the height, construction, and design of the building; and the degree of protection desirable, depending on whether it is a storage shed, a house, a school, or a munitions factory.

Optimally, a lightning protection system should be designed to take into account all of these factors, plus the economic considerations of construction. It is always easier and less expensive to include a system in the initial design and construction of a building rather than to modify the building after it has been finished. For the design of a lightning protection system for any particular structure, the reader is referred to two excellent texts (33,34).

Physics of Lightning Stroke

THE LIGHTNING DISCHARGE (13,32–34,53,72,75–78)

Warm air can hold more moisture than can cool air, so that when a cold air front (high-pressure system) moves to a warm area (low-pressure system), the warm, moist, low-pressure air rises quickly through the cool, drier, high-pressure air (Figure 2A). As the warm air rises, the moisture condenses into water droplets and a cumulonimbus cloud is formed. As the water vapor condenses, the energy of condensation (or vaporization) is released and the cloud accumulates free energy. Sometimes the rising hot air will "overshoot" the cloud and will be picked up by the strong winds of the upper atmosphere, flattening out into the typical anvil shape of a thundercloud (Figure 2B) (33,76,77).

As the warm air rises, the turbulence and induced friction cause complex redistribution in the charges within the cloud (Figure 2C). The water droplets within the cloud pick up and increase their individual charge as the warm air rises around them. A complex layering of charges with large potential differences between the layers results from the complex interactions between the charged particles and the internal and external electrical fields within the cloud formation.

Generally, the lower layers of the thundercloud become negatively charged relative to the earth, particularly when the storm occurs over a flat plane. The earth, which is normally negatively charged relative to the atmosphere, has a strong positive charge induced in it as the negatively charged thunderhead moves across the earth. The induced positive charge tends to flow as an upward current in trees, tall buildings, or people in the area of the thunderstorm cloud.

Normally, discharge of the potential difference is largely discouraged by the strongly insulating nature of the air. However, when the potential difference between the charges within the clouds or between the thundercloud and the ground becomes great enough, the charge may be dissipated as a display of lightning.

A lightning stroke begins as a relatively weak and slow *leader stroke* from the cloud (Figure 2D). The tip of the leader is very luminous and may travel in irregular strokes and forks ranging from 10 to 200 m in length, with a speed of 10^6 cm/second. It carries a charge of 50,000,000 volts and a current of 500,000 amps. The leader ionizes a pathway that becomes a column of superheated positive and negative ions (plasma) as the leader stroke slowly progresses to the earth (33).

Frequently, as the leader gets close to the ground, a positive *pilot stroke* rises from the ground or a structure to meet the leader stroke (Figure 2E). As the channel of ions is completed by the meeting of the strokes, the resistance falls precipitously. As the resistance drops, the voltage surges and a powerful and

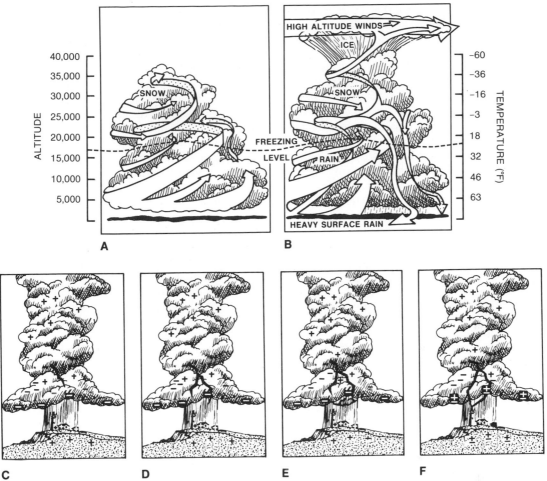

FIGURE 2 (*A*) Warm, low-pressure air rises and condenses into a cumulonimbus cloud. (*B*) Typical anvil-shaped thundercloud. (*C*) Water droplets within the cloud accumulate and layer charges. (*D*) Relatively weak and slow leaderstroke initiates the lightning strike. (*E*) A positive pilot stroke rises from the ground to meet the leaderstroke. (*F*) Return stroke rushes from the ground to the cloud.

much more rapid (10^9 cm/seconds, or 0.7th the speed of light) *return stroke* rushes from the ground to the cloud and serves as the major equalizer of the potential difference (Figure 2*F*).

When a very tall building, such as the Empire State Building, is involved or when high mountains rise into the clouds, the leader stroke may initiate from the building or ground rather than from the cloud. In these cases, a pilot stroke is rarely seen initiating from the cloud. The channel of ions that is formed by the leader stroke continues to be maintained as a *continuous stroke* as the *return*

stroke (misnamed in this instance) travels in the same direction from the ground or building to the cloud, dissipating the charge difference.

The tip of the leader stroke is the most luminous of the sequence of strokes in each lightning discharge, since such a huge amount of energy must be expended to overcome the resistance of the air and ionize a channel. Because of the relative slowness and brilliance of the leader, lightning is perceived as traveling from the cloud to the earth, although the vast majority of the energy is actually dissipated in the opposite direction as the return stroke. The direction of the return stroke is not visually perceived due to its tremendous speed and is recognized merely as an instantaneous brightening of the ionized pathway. Often, a number of brightenings of the pathway will occur as multiple secondary leader and return strokes travel in rapid succession. These may number as many as 40, although the average is four to seven. Lightning may vary in color, either from the excitation of nitrogen molecules in the atmosphere (radiant light energy released as a bluish or reddish afterglow) or because the particles of dust through which it passes are high in ion or mineral content (i.e., smog, mining dust high in coal or iron content) (71).

DIAMETER AND TEMPERATURE OF LIGHTNING (33)

In attempting to measure the diameter or temperature of the lightning stroke, many parameters could be used. All of the measurement techniques have artifact problems. The ionized sheath around the tip of the bright leader stroke has never been measured, but is estimated to be 3–20 m in diameter.

Visual measurement of the stroke, utilizing photography, usually shows the diameter of the main body of the stroke to be about 6–8 cm. The diameter of the arc channel is sometimes measured indirectly, utilizing measure-

ments of holes and strips of damage that lightning produces when it hits aluminum airplane wings, buildings, or trees. Measurements vary from 0.03 to 8.0 cm, depending on the material destroyed, with hard metallic structures sustaining smaller punctures than do soft structures, such as trees.

The temperature of the lightning stroke varies with the diameter of the stroke and has been calculated to be about 8000°C. In a few milliseconds, the temperature falls to 2000–3000°C, that of a normal high-voltage electrical arc.

FORMS OF LIGHTNING (76)

Lightning occurs in many forms. The most common, as described above, is *streak lightning* (Figure 3). *Sheet lightning* is a shapeless flash of light that represents lightning discharges within and between clouds. This may also be seen when lightning occurs over the horizon.

Ribbon lighting is streak lightning driven by the winds of the thunderstorm; the ionized air channel moves so rapidly across the earth that the successive secondary or return strokes seem to parallel one another. *Bead lightning* occurs when different areas of ionization and charge persist longer than others, lending a beadlike appearance to the afterstrokes. Another possible explanation of bead lightning

FIGURE 3 Example of classic streak lightning.

may be the perception of the bright end-on appearance of portions of a very jagged stroke.

The most unusual, least understood, and least predictable type of lightning is *ball lightning*. This takes the form of a softball-sized globe that may enter a door of a house, travel down a hallway and out another door, or exhibit equally bizarre and inexplicable activity (11). Ball lightning has never been photographed, although it has been observed by several reputable scientists.

THUNDER

There are two theories on thunder production. The first attributes thunder to shock waves that result from the instantaneous expansion of air heated and ionized by the lightning stroke (33,76,77).

The second theory, less likely to be true, states that the superheated channel of ions cools rapidly and creates a vacuum. The thunderclap is produced when air rushes back into the vacuum.

A review of the facts and myths about thunder has led to several accepted statements (66):

1. Cloud-to-ground lightning flashes produce the loudest thunder.
2. Thunder is seldom heard over distances greater than 10 miles.
3. The time interval between the perception of lightning and the first sound of thunder can be used to estimate the distance of the lightning stroke.
4. Atmospheric turbulence reduces the audibility of thunder.
5. There is often a heavy downpour of rain immediately after a strong clap of thunder.
6. The intensity of a pattern of thunder in one geographic location appears different from the pattern in another location.
7. The pitch of thunder deepens as the rumble persists.

The thunder clap from a lightning bolt which is close by is heard as a sharp crack. As noted in (7), distant thunder rumbles as the sound waves are refracted and modified by the thunderstorm's turbulence. Utilizing the difference in speeds between light and sound gives an estimate of the distance to the lightning stroke. If one takes the difference in seconds between the perception of the flash and the rumble and divides by 5, the approximate distance to the flash in miles is obtained.

Mechanisms of Injury by Lightning

Lightning is directly dangerous for three reasons: high voltage, secondary heat production, and explosive force. In addition, lightning may injure indirectly by kindling forest fires, house fires, and explosions, and by dropping objects such as trees on occupied homes and automobiles.

Only those injuries that are directly caused by lightning are discussed here. There are four primary mechanisms of injury:

1. Direct hit
2. Splash
3. Step voltage
4. Blunt trauma

A direct strike is most likely to hit a person in the open who has been unable to find shelter. Any conductor that the victim carries, particularly if it is metal and carried above shoulder level, significantly increases the chances of a direct hit (24,58,70).

Perhaps a more frequent cause of injury is that from a *splash*. This occurs when lightning that has hit a tree or building splashes onto a victim who may be seeking shelter nearby (17,22–24,32,69–71). The current, seeking the path of least resistance, may jump to a person whose body has less resistance than the tree or object that the lightning has initially contacted. There are multiple reports of side flashes indoors from metal objects such as plumbing (19,26,40,55,71). Splashes may also occur from person to person when several people are standing close by (2,8,42,49). On occasion, splashes may occur from a fence or other long conductive object that was hit by lightning some distance away. Several groups of animals have reportedly been killed by this mechanism as they were standing in a group near a fence or seeking shelter under trees (32).

Step voltage, also called *stride voltage* and *ground current*, is produced when lightning hits the ground or an object nearby. The current spreads like a wave in a pond, diminishing as the radius from the strike increases.

TABLE 1
Lightning versus High-Voltage Electrical Injury: Mechanism of Injury

Factor	Lightning	High Voltage
Time of exposure	Brief, instantaneous	Prolonged
Energy level	100,000,000 volts, 200,000 amperes	Usually much lower
Type of current	Direct	Alternating
Shock wave	Present	Absent
Flashover	Present	Absent
Cardiac	Asystole	Fibrillation
Burns	Superficial, minor	Deep, with "iceberg" phenomenon
Urinary failure	Rare myoglobinuria and hemoglobinuria	Myoglobinuric renal failure
Fasciotomy and amputation	Rarely if ever necessary	Common, early, and extensive

Resistance may be greater in the ground than between the victim's feet, encouraging the current to pass through the circuit created by his legs. If the victim's feet are at different distances from the origin of the strike, a large potential difference may exist between them, so that they become part of the circuit. Swimmers may also be affected by this mechanism as current passes through them and the water.

Although such ground current is less likely to produce fatalities than are direct hits or splashes, it frequently creates multiple victims and injuries. Large groups have been felled on baseball fields, racetracks, and other sporting arenas. While some of those injured may have suffered direct hits, the vast majority of these victims have shown more direct signs of lightning stroke than would be expected from the explosive blunt force of the strike alone.

Injuries may also occur from blunt trauma related to the electrical effects of lightning. These have been called the *sledgehammer effect* (71). It is not uncommon for a victim to be thrown by opisthotonic contractions initiated by the lightning strike.

Persons who are not affected by the prior three mechanisms may nevertheless be injured by the explosive force of the thunderous shock wave produced as lightning hits nearby. Some have theorized that the person who is struck by lightning may suffer not only from electrical injury but also from implosive forces as the air rushes back into the vacuum caused by the cooling of the superheated plasma channel. This remains to be proven.

DIFFERENCES BETWEEN HIGH-VOLTAGE ELECTRICAL INJURIES AND LIGHTNING INJURIES

One must distinguish between lightning and generator-produced high voltage electrical injuries, since there are significant differences between the mechanisms of injuries (Table 1) and their treatment. While lightning is an electrical phenonomenon and is certainly governed by the laws of electricity, it accounts for a unique spectrum of induced disease that may be better understood in light of specific physical properties of lightning.

Kouwenhoven determined six factors that affect the type and severity of injury encountered with electrical accidents (Table 2): type of circuit, duration of exposure, voltage and

TABLE 2
Factors Affecting Severity of Electrical Burns

AC versus DC
Voltage
Amperage
Resistance
Pathway
Duration

amperage of the current, resistance of the tissues, and pathway of the current (40). The three factors which most clearly distinguish lightning from high-voltage electrical injuries are as follows:

1. Lightning is a direct current.
2. The duration of exposure to the current is almost instantaneous with lightning (1/10,000–1/1000th second).
3. The *flashover phenomenon* pathway characterizes lightning current.

TYPE OF CIRCUIT

Direct current (DC), as occurs with lightning strike, causes only one-third of the damage induced by alternating current (AC) of the same voltage and amperage. Technical electricity usually alternates at about 60 cycles per second, just at the right frequency to cause muscle tetany (21). Because the victim is often working with the electrical source, the hands tend to be the most frequently injured part of the body. The tetanic force triggered by the electricity causes the hand to "freeze to the circuit," since the flexors of the forearm are stronger than the extensors (71). The current will also arc across flexed joints, producing *kissing burns* at each flexion point, including the wrist, elbow, and axilla.

Because the victim clasps the current source in his hand, the exposure is prolonged and the victim's skin breaks down, allowing the current to pass internally through the excellent electrolyte media of the blood and muscles. The external wound may appear to be fairly benign, hiding the extensive damage that may have occurred in the deeper structures. Fasciotomies may be needed with high-voltage injuries in order to maintain the circulation and viability of distal structures. Extensive amputations are not infrequent with high voltage electrical injuries.

Lightning is a direct current which causes a single strong muscle contraction. Exposure to lightning current is instantaneous, so that prolonged contact is not made. Deep burns are infrequent. The neurovascular compromise often seen with lightning injuries usually clears within a few hours, because it is due to transient vascular spasm rather than to the direct thermal injury that is so common in high-voltage electrical accidents. Fasciotomies

and amputations are rarely, if ever, needed with lightning victims.

VOLTAGE, AMPERAGE, AND RESISTANCE

The severity of electrical burns is affected by the voltage, amperage, and resistance. The properties of electrical current are related in Ohm's law:

$$V = I \times R$$
Voltage = amperage × resistance

Lightning, of course, has extremely high amperage and voltage (Table 1).

The heat generated by the sustained current is responsible for the severe tissue damage in high-voltage injuries and is defined by Joule's law:

$$Heat = amperage^2 \times resistance$$

As resistance goes up, so does the heat generated by the passage of the current. In the human, when low energy levels are encountered, much of the electrical energy can be dissipated by the skin, so that superficial burns are often not accompanied by internal injuries. The presence of water or sweat on the skin can lower the resistance as much as 25 times. When the resistance of the dermis is lowered by moisture or diminished skin thickness, the applied energy will be carried preferentially through the inside of the body by the lower-resistance tissues (Table 3). As a result, high-voltage electrical burns are characterized by deep muscle, nerve, and vascular damage, with variable overlying skin damage.

Both entry and exit wounds are usually seen with high-voltage electrical injuries, with diffuse, unpredictable damage occurring in between, similar to that of gunshot wounds.

TABLE 3
Electrical Resistance

Nerves (least resistance)
Blood vessels
Muscle
Skin
Tendon
Fat
Bone (most resistance)

Lightning occasionally shows entry and exit wounds. However, it more commonly causes only superficial streaking burns and seldom shows discrete entry and exit points.

PATHWAY OF THE CURRENT AND THE FLASHOVER PHENOMENON

The pathway of the current defines the damage. In a high-voltage injury, the heart or brain may be traversed, resulting in cardiac arrest from direct myocardial damage, arrhythmias, ventricular hemorrhage, or brain-stem infarction (32). Since burn damage is proportional to the current density, one might expect to encounter more severe burns on fingers traversed by a certain amount of current than if the entire trunk were traversed. It would also be natural to assume from those physical laws governing resistance and pathways that lightning, which has such a tremendously high voltage and amperage (Table 1), would always pass internally and cause massive damage, particularly since it frequently hits a thoroughly rain-soaked victim with lowered skin resistance.

However, the flashover phenomenon usually saves the victim from being fried (32). Electric current travels along the outside of a metal conductor. This is one of the reasons that electrical wiring is made of many small strands, in order to increase the carrying power of the line. Lightning, because of its extremely short duration of contact, seldom causes skin breakdown and thus does not pass internally. In effect, the body acts as a metal conductor, so that the vast majority of the lightning energy flows around the outside of the victim. Usually, only very superficial burns are seen with lightning. As the current flashes over the outside of the body, it often vaporizes the moisture on the skin and blasts apart the clothes and shoes, leaving the victim nearly naked, as noted by Hegner in 1917 (39):

The clothing may not be affected in any way. It may be stripped or burned in part or entirely shredded to ribbons. Either warp or woof may be destroyed leaving the outer garments and the skin intact. . . . Metallic objects in or of the clothing are bent, broken, more or less fused or not affected. The shoes most constantly show the effects of the current. People are usually standing when struck,

the current then enters or leaves the body through the feet. The shoes, especially when dry or only partially damp, interpose a substance of increased resistance. One or both shoes may be affected. They may be gently removed, or violently thrown many feet, be punctured or have a large hole torn in any part, shredded, split, reduced to lint or disappear entirely. The soles may disappear with or without the heels. Any of the foregoing may occur and the person not injured or only slightly shocked.

The amount of damage to the clothing or to the surface of the body is no index to the extent or the severity of the injuries sustained within the body. Either may be disproportionately great or small.

Because of the flashover effect, the victim of lightning experiences far less internal damage than would be expected in a typical high-voltage electrical incident, in which skin integrity is destroyed and resistance is tremendously reduced in the liquid medium of the tissues.

Injuries from Lightning

The overall mortality of lightning injuries is 30%, with a morbidity of 70% in survivors (18). Table 4 lists some of the most common signs and symptoms. Lightning is almost instantaneous in its action, difficult to report accurately, and seemingly unpredictable in its physical effects. Each case report of lightning injury has unique characteristics (31). However, for prognostic reasons, victims can generally be placed in one of three groups.

TABLE 4
Signs and Symptoms of Lightning Stroke

Immediate
  Ventricular standstill
  Chest pain, muscle aches
  Neurologic signs
    Seizures
    Deafness
    Confusion
    Blindness
  Contusions from shock wave
  Tympanic membrane rupture

Late
  Cutaneous burns
  Cataracts
  Myoglobinuria and hemoglobinuria—rare

MINOR

These patients are awake and often report a feeling of having been hit on the head or having been in an explosion. They may or may not have perceived the lightning or thunder. They are often confused and amnesic, with temporary deafness, blindness, or unconsciousness at the scene (11). They seldom demonstrate any cutaneous burns or paralysis, but may complain of paresthesias, muscular pain, and confusion lasting from hours to days. Vital signs are usually stable, although occasional patients demonstrate transient mild hypertension (36,73). Recovery is usually gradual and complete.

MODERATE

These patients may be disoriented, combative, or comatose. They frequently exhibit motor paralysis, with mottling of the skin and diminished or absent pulses, particularly of the lower extremities. Nonpalpable peripheral pulse pressures may indicate arterial spasm and sympathetic instability rather than hypotension. However, the patient should be scrutinized for fractures and other signs of blunt injury, particularly if hypotension persists. Cervical or other spinal fractures, while rare with lightning, may also account for the hypotension.

Occasionally, these victims have suffered temporary cardiopulmonary standstill, although it is seldom documented (71). Spontaneous recovery of a pulse is attributed to the heart's inherent automaticity. However, the respiratory arrest that often occurs with lightning injury may be prolonged and lead to a secondary cardiac arrest from hypoxia. Seizures may also occur.

First- and second-degree burns may not be prominent on admission, but may evolve over the first several hours. Very rarely, third-degree burns may occur. Patients will often have at least one tympanic membrane ruptured as a result of the explosive force of the lightning shock wave. Tympanic membrane rupture or hemotympanum may indicate the presence of a basilar skull fracture.

While these signs often improve within the first few hours, patients are prone to have permanent sequelae such as sleep disorders, irritability, difficulty with fine psychomotor functions, and generalized weakness. A few cases of atrophic spinal paralysis have been reported (8).

SEVERE

These patients may present in cardiac arrest with either ventricular standstill or fibrillation. Cardiac resuscitation may not be successful if the patient has suffered a long period of cardiac and central nervous system (CNS) ischemia. Direct brain damage may occur from the lightning strike or blast effect. Tympanic membrane rupture with hemotympanum and cerebrospinal fluid (CSF) otorrhea are common in this group.

Patients with other signs of blunt injury are likely to be the victims of a direct hit, although sometimes no burns will be noted.

The prognosis is usually poor in this group, and is usually due as much to a delay in cardiopulmonary resuscitation as to the direct lightning damage.

CARDIOPULMONARY ARREST

The most common cause of death in a lightning victim is cardiopulmonary arrest. In fact, a victim is highly unlikely ($p < 0.0001$) to die unless a cardiopulmonary arrest is suffered as an immediate effect of the strike (18). In the past, nearly 75% of those who suffered cardiopulmonary arrest from lightning injuries died, many because cardiopulmonary resuscitation was not attempted.

Lightning apparently acts as a massive DC countershock, causing momentary cardiac standstill (63,73). Because of the heart's inherent automaticity, an organized series of contractions generally ensues within a very short period of time. Unfortunately, respiratory arrest, caused by lightning paralysis of the medullary respiratory center, may last far longer than the cardiac arrest. Unless the victim receives immediate ventilation, the attendant hypoxia may induce arrhythmias and a secondary cardiac arrest.

Both asystole and ventricular fibrillation (45) have been reported with lightning strike. Asystole seems to be both the first response to the strike and the last, as the secondary arrest rhythm of fibrillation deteriorates. Premature ventricular contractions, ventricular tachycardia, and atrial fibrillation have been reported (1,55,83). It is not uncommon to find ST changes consistent with ischemia and damage in subepicardial, posterior, inferior, or anterior patterns (10,36,41,42,45,56,72,73). Creatinine phosphokinase MB isoenzyme elevation has been reported (37,41,72). Elevation of serum glutamic oxaloacetic transaminase and lactic dehydrogenase have been reported, but may also reflect concomitant trauma to other tissues (37,45,83).

Some reports have theorized that vascular spasm is a cause of the cardiac damage (71). However, electrocardiographic changes are not always consistent with vascular supply patterns in the heart (36). They may indicate direct thermal or electrical damage to the myocardium, either from current which passes through the body or from adjacent structures (such as the spine), which are heated and which then radiate thermal energy to the heart. Areas of focal cardiac necrosis have been reported on autopsy (45,49,50,56). Pulmonary edema may accompany severe cardiac damage (41,45). Severe hemoptysis with pulmonary hemorrhage has been reported (8).

NEUROLOGIC INJURIES

The second major cause of morbidity and mortality in lightning injuries is central nervous system damage. When current traverses the brain, there can be coagulation of the brain substance, formation of epidural and subdural hematomas, paralysis of the respiratory center, and intraventricular hemorrhage (55,72). Autopsy findings include extravasation of blood in the meninges and cerebral tissues, petechiae, dural tears, extravasations of blood beneath the scalp, and skull fractures (8, 15,19–21,24,38,43,69). Transient elevation of creatinine phosphokinase BB has been reported (37).

Seizures may accompany the initial cardiorespiratory arrest as a result of hypoxia or direct cerebral damage (51). They are usually transient, although in serious cases, some may recur for the first few days.

Electroencephalogram (EEG) changes may isolate an epileptogenic focus in the acute phase (12,58,59). These patterns may be focal or diffuse, varying with the site and type of injury. However, many patients will not experience seizures during their hospitalization, and most usually have normalization of their electroencephalogram within a few months. One severely injured patient was reported to have continued seizures after discharge to a nursing home (56).

Only 72% of victims suffer loss of consciousness (18). However, of those who do, nearly three-quarters will also suffer a cardiopulmonary arrest (18).

Two-thirds of victims present with some degree of lower extremity paralysis, usually demarcating around the waist or the pelvis. Almost one-third of victims have upper extremity paralysis (18). The affected extremities appear cold, clammy, mottled, senseless, and pulseless (73). This is the result of sympathetic instability and intense vascular spasm, which has been likened to Raynaud's phenomenon, and clears over a period of hours (49). Fasciotomies are almost never indicated. Pulses can sometimes be elicited with a Doppler examination. Atrophic spinal paralysis has been reported, as have persistent paresis, paresthesias, incoordination, hemiplegia, and aphasia (1,47,56,82). There is one report of quadriplegia developing 36 hours after injury and one of progressive muscle atrophy of the upper extremities (4,8).

Whether or not they have suffered loss of consciousness, victims almost universally demonstrate anterograde amnesia and confusion that may last for up to several days. Retrograde amnesia is somewhat less common. Although the patient may be well oriented and remember his actions prior to the strike, he may not be able to assimilate new experiences for several days after the strike, even when there is no external evidence of lightning burns on the head or neck. Patients often act like those who have experienced electroconvulsive therapy.

Victims who survive may sometimes have persistent sleep disturbances, storm neuroses, difficulty with fine mental and motor functions, and headaches (27,56,58).

BURNS

Most people assume that because of the tremendous energy discharge involved, a lightning victim will be flash cooked if a direct hit is sustained (11). However, the flashover phenomenon saves all but a few from more than minor burns. While extensive third- and fourth-degree burns may occur in combination with skeletal disruption, they are very rare (15,27,69).

Discrete entry and exit points are rare with lightning. The burns seen with a lightning accident may be divided into five categories:

1. Linear burns
2. Punctate, full-thickness burns
3. Feathering or flowers
4. Thermal burns from clothing or heated metal
5. Combinations of the above.

Linear burns (Figure 4) often begin at the head and progress down the chest, where they split and continue down both legs. These burns are generally 1–4 cm in width and tend to follow areas of heavy sweat concentration, such as beneath breasts, down the mid-chest and in the mid-axilla (71). They are usually first and second degree burns which may be present initially or develop as late as several hours after the lightning strike.

Punctate burns (Figure 5) are multiple, closely spaced, discrete circular burns that individually range from a few millimeters to a centimeter in diameter. They may be full-thickness, but are usually too small to require grafting.

Feathering burns (Figure 6) are pathognomonic of lightning and are known by such names as *Lichtenberg's flowers, filigree burns, arborescent burns, ferning,* and *kerauno-*

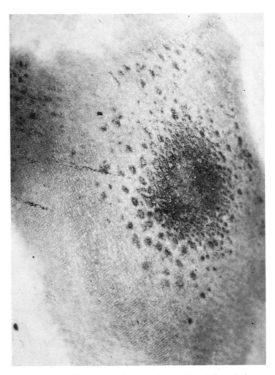

FIGURE 5 Punctate burns from lightning injury. (Photo courtesy of Arthur Kahn, M.D.)

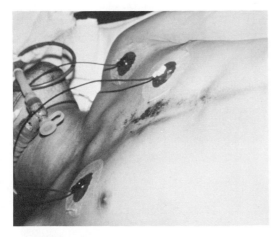

FIGURE 4 Linear burns from lightning injury.

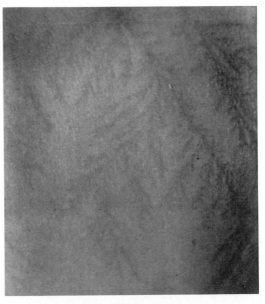

FIGURE 6 Feathering burns.

graphic markings (49). It was once thought that these markings represented a "photographic" imprint of vegetation surrounding the victim (49). It is now known that the markings are not true burns, but rather cutaneous imprints from electron showers which track through the skin, similar to the pattern found on a photographic plate that has been exposed to a strong electric field (5,32).

On rare occasions, clothing may be ignited by lightning and cause severe thermal burns (17,51). If the victim is wearing metal, such as a necklace or belt buckle, or carries coins in his pocket, the metal can be heated enough to cause second- and third-degree burns to the adjacent skin (6,22). Figure 7 shows the burn resulting from a metal belt buckle worn by a young man who was struck while playing softball in the rain.

Victims of lightning may exhibit combinations of burns. The prognosis can be related to the location of the burns. Patients who suffer cranial burns are four times more likely to die than those who do not have cranial burns ($p < 0.25$). Patients with cranial burns are also two and a half times more likely to have a cardiopulmonary arrest than those who

do not exhibit burns around the head and neck ($p < 0.025$). Likewise, those with leg burns are five times more likely to die than those who have no leg burns, probably because of a ground current etiology ($p < 0.05$) (18).

BLUNT AND EXPLOSIVE INJURIES

The victim of a lightning accident may be injured directly from the explosive force of the lightning or from a fall sustained as he is thrown off a horse or mountain ledge, or out of a vehicle, or hurled by his own opisthotonic force (3,6,58). Lightning victims incur a variety of fractures, including those of the skull, ribs, extremities, and spine (4,5,15, 62,72). Occasionally, a bursting injury discloses extensive underlying fractures. Explosive injuries typically occur in the feet, where boots or socks may be blown off (Figure 8) (40).

While blunt injuries may occur, hemoglobinuria and myoglobinuria are seldom reported (83). If they occur, they are usually transient. Myoglobinuric renal failure has not yet been reported in a lightning victim. Persistent hypotension should initiate a search for

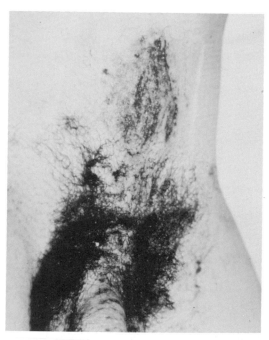

FIGURE 7 Burn resulting from metal belt buckle struck by lightning.

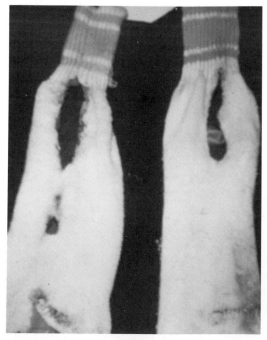

FIGURE 8 Socks blown off during explosive lightning strike.

contusions to the brain, lungs, heart, and intestines (36,49). If not properly managed, these may lead to complications such as prolonged coma, pulmonary compromise, heart failure, and ileus.

EYES

Many types of ocular damage have been reported (11,73). Direct thermal or electrical damage, intense light, contusion from the shock wave, and combinations of these factors have been postulated to contribute to injuries which may occur in as many as 55% of those struck by lightning (12).

Cataracts may be bilateral, and occur as late as 2 years after the strike, although they most commonly present within the first few days (5,16,25,74). Corneal lesions, hyphema, uveitis, iridocyclitis, and vitreous hemorrhage occur with greater frequency than do choroidal rupture, chorioretinitis, uveitis, retinal detachment, and optic atrophy (12,49,64). Diplopia, loss of accommodation, and decreased color sense have been reported (12,46).

Autonomic disturbances of the eye, including mydriasis, Horner's syndrome, anisocoria, and loss of light reflex, may be transient or permanent (12,49). Bilateral blindness is not uncommon initially (24,43). Intense photophobia may be present as the patient recovers.

Dilated or unreactive pupils should never be used as a criterion for brain death in a lightning victim until all anatomic and functional lesions have been ruled out.

EARS

Temporary deafness is not uncommon (5,30,42,73,80). It is postulated that the intense noise and shock wave accompanying the thunder may be responsible for sensorineural loss (6). At least 50% of lightning victims rupture one or both tympanic membranes, which may be the result of a shock wave effect or the accompaniment to a basilar skull fracture (18). Direct nerve damage from the lightning may cause facial palsies (6).

CSF otorrhea or hemotympanum may occur (19). Disruption of the ossicles and mastoid have been reported (6,19). Many cases of permanent deafness are noted in the older literature (68,73).

FETAL SURVIVAL

The fetus of a pregnant woman who has been struck by lightning has an unpredictable prognosis (14,65). Nearly one-half of the pregnancies go on to full-term live births, with no recognizable abnormality in the child (73). One-quarter result in live births, but with neonatal death; the remainder are stillbirths or deaths *in utero* (35,79). There has been one report of a ruptured uterus after a lightning strike (65).

Recognition and Treatment of Lightning Injuries

DIAGNOSIS

The diagnosis of lightning injury is sometimes difficult to make. Often there is a history of a thunderstorm, witnesses who can report having seen the strike, and typical physical findings in the victim.

However, lightning can strike on a sunny day or thunder may not be appreciated. If the victim is struck while working alone in a field, the diagnosis may be initially confused with several other processes, including ruptured cerebral aneurysm or another cerebral vascular accident, seizure disorder, spinal cord injury, closed head injury, Stokes-Adams attack or another arrhythmia, hypertensive crisis with intracerebral hemorrhage, myocardial infarction, or toxic ingestion (particularly of heavy metals).

In the past, persons have been thought to be the victims of an assault, because of the disarray of their belongings and clothing damage (71). The history and a careful physical examination at the earliest opportunity can be very helpful in differentiating the true cause.

Any person found in the open with linear burns and his clothes exploded off should be treated as a victim of lightning strike. Feathering burns are pathognomonic of lightning strike and occur in no other type of injury. Unfortunately, they are not always present in lightning victims. Another complex that is diagnostic of lightning strike includes linear or punctate burns, tympanic membrane rupture, confusion, and being found in the open, whether or not there is a history of a thunderstorm.

INITIAL FIRST AID AND TRIAGE OF VICTIMS

As in any other emergency, the first steps are the ABCs: airway, breathing, and circulation. If the patient has had a cardiac arrest, cardiopulmonary resuscitation should be started immediately and a rescue vehicle called for transportation.

If the strike occurs far from civilization and evacuation, the victim is probably out of luck, unless pulse and respiration resume spontaneously. The heart that has been shocked into asystole will usually resume activity because of the myocardium's property of automaticity, but may slip into a secondary hypoxic arrest from the attendant and more refractory respiratory arrest. If the rescuer is successful at obtaining a pulse with cardiopulmonary resuscitation, ventilation should be continued until spontaneous adequate respirations are obtained.

When a lightning strike involves multiple victims, resources and rescuers may be limited compared to the demand, and triage must be instituted (2,8,73). Normally, the rules of triage in multicasualty situations dictate bypassing dead patients for those who are moderately or severely injured and who can benefit from resuscitation efforts.

However, triage of lightning victims is entirely different. "Resuscitate the dead" is the rule here, since victims who show some return of consciousness or who have spontaneous breathing are generally well on the way to recovery (73). They should be routinely stabilized and eventually transported to the hospital for more thorough evaluation. The most vigorous attempts at resuscitation in the field should be directed to those who appear to be dead, since they may ultimately recover if properly ventilated (71). Certainly, if they do not receive cardiopulmonary resuscitation, they will not survive.

Other first aid, including splinting of fractures and any suspected spinal injuries, should be done prior to transport.

HISTORY AND PHYSICAL EXAMINATION

If witnesses are available, it is very helpful to get a history from them, since the victims are often confused and amnesic. The history should include a description of the event, as well as the patient's responses following the strike. Past medical history, including that of seizures, medications, allergies and cardiac disease, is invaluable.

Like any trauma victim, the patient must be totally undressed in order to facilitate a complete examination. Special note should be taken of the vital signs and level of consciousness. The patient who is awake should be tested for his orientation and short-term memory. The lightning victim typically cannot assimilate information and may keep repeating the same questions. A deteriorating level of consciousness mandates a computed tomography (CT) scan for investigation.

Examination of the eyes to establish their reactivity and any injury is essential. Tympanic membrane rupture is an important indication of lightning strike, and ossicular disruption may be one explanation for a patient's lack of appropriate response to verbal stimuli. It can also indicate a basilar skull fracture.

While the pulmonary system may be affected by a cardiac arrest with complications of pulmonary edema or adult respiratory distress syndrome, it is uncommon to have initial problems. The cardiovascular examination should include qualitation of distal pulses in all extremities, the appreciation of arrhythmias, and evaluation of cardiac damage, including isoenzymatic and electrocardiogram (EKG) changes.

The abdominal examination may occasionally demonstrate absent bowel sounds and, rarely, indicate an acute traumatic injury, including contusion of the liver, bowel, or spleen.

The examiner should document any skin changes. The skin may show mottling, especially below the waist. Burns may be present initially, but usually evolve and mature over a period of hours. Special note of pulses, color, movement, and sensory status of the extremities is essential.

The physical findings and mental state of minimally and moderately injured victims tend to change considerably over the first few hours, and it is essential that careful observation and documentation delineate the patient's course so that therapy can be appropriately planned. The minimally injured patient may require only overnight observation and a few baseline studies, while the severely injured patient may require intensive care with mechanical ventilation, intracranial pressure monitoring, Swan-Ganz catheterization, and antiarrhythmic medications.

LABORATORY AND X-RAY TESTS

The minimum laboratory and x-ray examinations include a complete blood count (CBC), cardiac isoenzymes, electrolyte screen, blood urea nitrogen (BUN), creatinine, and urinalysis (including testing for myoglobin). Additional blood tests are indicated only if the patient's condition warrants them. For example, if the patient is to be placed on a ventilator, blood gases are mandatory; if intracranial pressure monitoring is used, serum osmolalities are required.

A chest x-ray should be obtained. Skull and cervical spine films should be taken if there is any evidence of cranial burns and contusions. The patient in coma or with a deteriorating level of consciousness requires a CT scan. Other x-rays may be ordered as indicated to rule out fractures and dislocations.

An EKG is essential for all lightning victims.

FLUID THERAPY

An intravenous lifeline is mandatory for the patient who shows unstable vital signs, unconsciousness, or disorientation. Generally, this can be run at a keep-open or maintenance rate with any solution desired. Careful intake and output measurements are necessary in the severely injured patient and require the placement of an indwelling urinary catheter. Myoglobinuria is rare and usually transient, so that the standard use of mannitol diuresis and fluid loading, as with other high-voltage electrical burns, is contraindicated (1).

The unconscious patient should not be fluid challenged unless there is some cause to suspect hypovolemic shock, as might occur with the extremely rare case of third- and fourth-degree burns or because of central hypotension. Fluid restriction in normotensive or hypertensive patients is mandatory because of the risk of worsening cerebral edema.

CARDIOVASCULAR THERAPY

The patient who is without spontaneous or adequate respiration should be placed on a ventilator until such time as brain death is determined.

Management of a cardiac arrest is standard, except that normal saline is a more appropriate fluid than 5% dextrose in water because of the possibility of hypotension from accompanying blunt injuries. Because of the vasospastic element in lightning burns, peripheral pulses may be difficult to palpate. Usually, femoral, brachial, or carotid pulses may be found. A Doppler examination may be necessary for locating a peripheral pulse and for reading blood pressure.

If the patient remains hypotensive on Doppler examination, then fluid resuscitation is necessary to establish adequate blood pressure and tissue perfusion. Causes of hypotension, including major fractures, blood loss from abdominal or chest injuries, and spinal shock should be sought. As soon as an adequate central blood pressure is obtained, the patient should be *fluid restricted,* as noted in the previous section, because of the high incidence of cranial injuries and attendant cerebral edema (45). A solution of 5% dextrose in 25% or 50% normal saline is the current neurosurgical recommendation to avoid overhydration and resultant cerebral edema.

All lightning victims, regardless of their presentation, should have an EKG. Cardiac monitoring and serial isoenzymes are indicated if there is any sign of ischemia or arrhythmia on the EKG or if the patient complains of chest pain.

Injury patterns as well as arrhythmias have been reported (45). The indications for use of drugs such as lidocaine, procainamide, bretyllium, propranolol, and pressor agents are the same as for any patient with a suspected myocardial infarction (45).

FASCIOTOMY

The paralyzed and pulseless extremities often seen with lightning injuries should not be confused with those caused by high-voltage injuries. The intense vascular spasm usually is a sequel to sympathetic instability. Most signs and symptoms clear within a few hours, and the extremities should be treated expectantly. Patient observation is required, as steady improvement in the mottled, cool extremity, with the return of pulses in a few hours, is the rule rather than the exception. Fasciotomies are very rarely, if ever, indicated unless the extremity has shown no signs of recovery and raised intracompartmental tissue pressures are measured.

CENTRAL NERVOUS SYSTEM INJURY

Every lightning victim should have a complete neurologic examination. If there is a history of loss of consciousness or if the patient exhibits any confusion, it is necessary to admit the patient for observation.

The patient who has tympanic membrane rupture or a cranial burn should receive skull and cervical spine x-rays. If the patient shows a decreasing level of consciousness or frank coma, a CT scan is indicated. Serial CT scans may be useful in assessing ventricular hemorrhage and edema, particularly in the patient who remains comatose.

In the patient who shows continued loss of consciousness, hyperventilation to maintain a PCO_2 of 25–30 mmHg may be useful in the control of cerebral edema. If there are no other contraindications, the head of the bed should be elevated. Steroids are probably of as little benefit with lightning injuries as they are in other posttraumatic conditions.

Intracranial pressure (ICP) monitoring has never been used with lightning victims, but it may prove to be a useful adjunct in those patients with continued loss of consciousness. If the ICP is elevated, the cerebral edema may be managed with mannitol, furosemide, and fluid restriction (9,52,67). Hypothermia was reported to contribute to a complete recovery after one case of prolonged cardiac arrest prior to resuscitation efforts (63).

Early seizures are probably due to cardiorespiratory insufficiency and anoxia. If there is evidence of central nervous system damage or if seizures continue after adequate oxygenation and perfusion have been restored, then standard pharmacologic intervention with diazepam, diphenylhydantoin, or phenobarbital should be entertained (45,51).

If paralysis does not improve, causes other than lightning, including blunt injury from a fall, may be responsible. Any physical therapy program should be started prior to discharge.

BURNS

Lightning burns may be apparent at the time of admission, but more commonly develop within the first few hours. They are generally very superficial, unlike high-voltage electrical burns, and seldom cause massive muscle destruction, so that vigorous fluid therapy and mannitol diuresis are not indicated. The urine should be tested for myoglobin, although it is infrequently seen (83). In the rare instance of myoglobinuria, intravenous mannitol and alkalinization of the urine with bicarbonate may be used. Overhydration with resultant cerebral edema has probably killed more lightning victims than myoglobinuric renal failure ever will.

The burns are generally so superficial that they require no treatment with topical agents. In the unusual incidence of deep injury, topical therapy should be standard. Only in the very rare instance of third-degree involvement is fasciotomy, amputation, or grafting necessary.

ANTIBIOTICS AND TETANUS PROPHYLAXIS

The use of antibiotics is not indicated until cultures identify a definite organism to be treated. The exceptions are open extremity fractures or open cranial fractures that violate the dura. In the latter case, some neurosurgeons recommend antibiotic prophylaxis.

Tetanus prophylaxis is mandatory if burns or lacerations are present.

EYES

Visual acuity should be measured and the eyes thoroughly examined to establish a baseline. Cataracts are not uncommon. Other eye injuries, as noted in the section on injuries from lightning, should be treated in standard fashion.

EARS

Simple tympanic membrane ruptures are handled conservatively and expectantly, with observation rather than surgical intervention, until after the tissues have returned to normal (6). Sensorineural damage to the auditory nerve and facial palsy are not uncommon. Loss of hearing may require audiograms for evaluation (80). Ossicular disruption or more severe damage may necessitate surgical repair. Otorrhea and hemotympanum are not uncommon and suggest basilar skull fracture.

Injuries to Pregnant Victims

If a pregnant woman is struck, tests should be done to assess the viability of the fetus. These include Doppler location of fetal heart tones, documentation of fetal movement, and serum tests for continued output of fetal modulated products, including estriol levels. Fetal death *in utero* is treated in a standard fashion.

Other Considerations

Gastric irritation may occasionally be seen (51), so that cimetidine and antacid therapy may be indicated after all possibility of blunt abdominal injury has been excluded. A nasogastric tube is appropriate if ileus or gastric irritation occurs (54). Peritoneal lavage may be indicated in the comatose patient who remains hypotensive, since intestinal contusions and hemorrhage have been reported (36).

Pronouncing the Patient Dead

For reasons mentioned in the section on injuries from lightning, dilated pupils should not be taken as a sign of brain death in the lightning victim. Electroencephalograms may also show diffuse damage initially, only to clear with time. However, the patient who shows no response to resuscitative efforts, continues to become more hypothermic, and meets current brain death criteria over a period of several hours to days may be pronounced dead with relative certainty (36).

Precautions for Avoiding Lightning Injury (60,73,76–78)

1. Be aware of weather conditions and predictions before going on excursions and working in the open. Respect thunderstorms and their power. If you cannot avoid being outdoors, carry a small radio to monitor weather reports. Be prepared to seek shelter if a severe thunderstorm watch or warning is announced.

2. If a storm does strike, seek shelter in a substantial building or in an all-metal vehicle, such as a car. Small buildings, especially if they are exposed metal sheds, offer variable protection since side flashes can occur to the occupants, depending on the size and height of the building. Tents offer little protection, since the metal support poles may actually act as lightning rods. Occupants of tents should stay as far away from the poles and the wet cloth as possible.

3. While indoors during a thunderstorm, avoid open doors and windows, fireplaces and metal objects such as pipes, sinks, radiators, and plug-in electrical appliances. Avoid using the telephone. A clothesline pole may act as a lightning rod and transmit lightning energy along the line.

4. Stay away from metal objects such as motorcycles, tractors, fences, and bicycles. Put down metal objects such as umbrellas or golf clubs. Metal cleats in shoes act as excellent grounding agents, and metal objects near the head make a person much more likely to be hit by lightning. Avoid areas near power lines, pipelines, fences, ski lifts, and other structural steel fabrications (73).

5. If you are unable to find shelter, do not stand near tall isolated trees or on hilltops. In the forest, shelter in a low area under a thick growth of saplings or small trees. Seeking a clearing in order to avoid the trees makes one the tallest object in the clearing and more likely to be hit.

6. If you are totally in the open, stay far away from single trees in order to avoid lightning splashes. Crouch down on both feet, kneel, and crouch or roll up in a ball so that if the ground is hit there is the least potential difference between the farthest points on the body and thus the least exposure to the ground current. Avoid seeking shelter in corn stalks, haystacks, or other objects that project above the ground. Caves, ditches, and valleys provide protection unless they are totally saturated with water, which will conduct the current.

7. If you are on the water, seek the shore. Avoid swimming, boating, or being the tallest object near a large open body of water. Lightning is attracted to metal masts and other objects projecting above the surface of the water and flows well through the water to injure swimmers, on the same principles as ground current injuries. Seeking shelter under a bridge or cliff while in the boat may provide some protection. Larger boats should be protected with lightning rods and grounding equipment attached to a metal keel.

8. If you are in an all-metal automobile (as opposed to a cloth-top convertible or jeep), stay in it. The automobile will diffuse the current around you and to the ground. It is a myth that the rubber tires will provide insulation but true that the metal body affords protection.

9. If a group of people are exposed, they should spread out and stay several yards apart, so that in the event of a strike, the least number are injured seriously by ground current and by side flashes between persons.

References

1. Apfelberg, D., Masters, F., Robinson, D.: Pathophysiology and treatment of lightning injuries. *J. Trauma,* **14**:453–60, June 1974.

2. Arden, G. P., Harrison, S. H., Lister, J., Maudsley R: Lightning accident at Ascot. *Br Med J,* **1**:1453, June 1956.

3. Auerbach, P.: Lightning strike. *Top Emerg Med,* **2**:129–35, 1980.

4. Baker, R.: Paraplegia as a result of lightning injury. *Br Med J,* **4**:1464–65, 1978.

5. Barthlome, C. W., Jacoby, W. D., Ramchand, S. C.: Cutaneous manifestations of lightning injury. *Arch Dermatol,* **111**:1466–68, 1975.

6. Bergstrom, L., Neblett, L., Sando, I., Hemenway, W., Harrison, G. D.: The lightning damaged ear. *Arch Otolaryngol,* **100**:117–21, August 1974.

7. Bernstein, T.: Theories of the causes of death from electricity in the late 19th century. *Med Instrum,* **9**:267–73, 1975.

8. Buechner, H. A., Rothbaum, J. C.: Lightning stroke injury—a report of multiple casualties from a single lightning bolt. *Milit Med,* **126**:775–62, 1961.

9. Bruce, D. A.: *The Pathophysiology of Increased Intracranial Pressure.* Upjohn Current Concepts, Upjohn Co., Kalamazoo, Michigan, 1978.

10. Burda, C. D.: Electrocardiographic changes in lightning stroke. *Am Heart J,* **72**:521–24, 1966.

11. Cannel, H.: Struck by lightning—the effects upon the men and the ships of H M Navy. *J R Nav Med Serv,* **65**:165–70, 1979.

12. Castren, J. A., Kytila, J.: Eye symptoms caused by lightning. *Acta Opthalmol,* **41**:139–43, 1963.

13. Chalmers, J. A.: *Atmospheric Electricity,* 2nd ed. Pergamon, London, 1967, p. 515.

14. Chan, Y. F., Sivasamboo, R.: Lightning accidents in pregnancy. *J Obstet Gynecol Br Commonwealth,* **79**:761–62, 1972.

15. Clark, R. O., Brigham, J. K.: Death from lightning. *Lancet,* **2**:77, 1872.

16. Connole, J. V.: Lightning and electric cataract. *Pa Med J,* **38**:939–42, September 1935.

17. Cook, A. H., Boulting, W.: Two cases of injury by lightning. *Br Med J* 2:234–35, 1888.

18. Cooper, M. A.: Lightning injuries: Prognostic signs for death. *Ann Emerg Med,* **9(3)**:134–38, March 1980.

19. Crawford, A. S., Hoopes, B. F.: The surgical aspects of lightning stroke. *Surgery,* **9**:80–6, 1941.

20. Critchley, M.: The effects of lightning with especial reference to the nervous system. *Bristol Med Chir J,* **49**:285–300, n.d.

21. Critchley, M.: Neurological effects of lightning and of electricity. Lancet, **1**:68–72, January 1934.

22. Darling, Frier, Pedlow: Report of cases of lightning stroke. *Br Med J,* **2**:1522, 1905.

23. Dill, A. V.: Notes on a case of death by lightning. *Br Med J,* 426, October 1942.

24. Dunscombe-Haniball, O.: Accidents and injuries caused by lightning. *JMA S Afr,* **1**:1153, 1900.

25. DuToid, J. S.: Bilaterial cataract caused by lightning. *JMA S Afr,* **1**:503, 1927.

26. Edwards, W.: Injuries due to lightning striking a wireless aerial. *Br Med J,* **2**:294, 1925.

27. Elwell, E. G.: Non-fatal lightning burns. *Br Med J,* **2**:771, 1934.

28. Franklin, B.: *Experiments and Observations on Electricity Made at Philadelphia.* E. Cave, London, 1774.

29. Franklin, B.: *The Autobiography of Benjamin Franklin.* Yale University Press, New Haven, Conn., 1973.

30. Gabriell, L.: Unusual clinical picture of intermittent deafness in a subject struck by lightning. *Otorhinolaryng,* **31**:79–90, 1965.

31. Gem, W. Case of lightning stroke followed by recovery. *Lancet,* **2**:288, 1913.

32. Golde, R. H., Lee, W. R.: Death by lightning. *Proc Inst Elec Eng,* **123**:1163–80, October 1976.

33. Golde, R. H.: *Lightning,* Vols. 1 and 2. Academic Press, London, 1977.

34. Golde, R. H.: *Lightning Protection.* Chemical Publishing Co., New York, 1973.

35. Guha-Ray, D. K.: Fetal death at term due to lightning. *Am J Obstet Gynecol,* **134**:103–5, 1979.

36. Hanson, G. C., McIlzoraith, G. R.: Lightning injury: Two case histories and a review of management. *Br Med J,* **4**:271–74, November 1973.

37. Harwood, S. J., Catrov, P. G., Cole, G. W.: Creatinine phosphokinase isoenzyme fraction in the serum of a patient struck by lightning. *Arch Intern Med,* **138**:645–46, 1978.

38. Heffernan, D.: Autopsy in a case of death by lightning. *Lancet,* **2**:266, August 1877.

39. Hegner, C. F.: Lightning—some of its effects. *Ann Surg,* **65**:401, 1917.

40. Jaffe, R.: Electropathology—review of the pathological changes produced by electric current. *Arch Pathol,* **5**:839–69, 1928.

41. Kleiner, J. P., Wilkin, J. H.: Cardiac effects of lightning stroke. *JAMA,* **240**:2757–59, December 1978.

42. Kleinot, S., Lkacko, D., Keeley, K.: The cardiac effects of lightning injury, *S Afr Med J,* **40**:1141–43, 1966.

43. Knaggs, R. H.: Unusual injuries caused by lightning stroke. *Lancet,* **2**:1216, 1894.

44. Kraus, J.: *Gewitterkatechismus, oder Unterricht uber Blitz und Donner, und wie man bey einem Gewitter sein Leben gegen den Blitz schutzen und die vom Blitz getroffenen Menschen retten kann,* 5th ed. Doll, Augsburg, 1814.

45. Kravitz, H., Wasserman, M., Valaitis, J., Anzinger, R. E., Naidu, S. H.: Lightning injury, management of a case with ten-day survival. *Am J Dis Child,* **131**:413–15, 1977.

46. Lea, J. A.: Paresis of accommodation following injury by lightning. *Br J Ophthalmol,* **4:**417, 1920.

47. Leys, K.: Spinal atrophic paralysis case following lightning stroke. *Edinburgh Med J,* **49:**657–62, November 1942.

48. Lucretius, C. T.: *DeRerum Natura.* Gryphium, Lugduni, 1534.

49. Lynch, M. Shorthouse, P.: Injuries and death from lightning. *Lancet,* **1:**473–78, March 1949.

50. Martyak, G. G., Ryan, M. E.: Lightning "deaths" can be reversed. *Emerg Dept News,* 26–8, 1979.

51. McCrady-Kahn, U. L., Kahn, A. M.: Lightning burns. *West J Med,* **134:**215–19, March 1981.

52. McGraw, C. P.: Continuous intracranial pressure monitoring, review of techniques and presentation of method. *Surg Neurol,* **6:**149–55, 1976.

53. Meek, J. M., Craggs, J. D.: *The Lightning Discharge, Electrical Breakdown of Gases.* Clarendon Press, Oxford, 1953, pp. 223–50.

54. Milward, T.: Prolonged gastric dilatation as a complication of lightning injury. *Burns,* **1**(2):175–78, January 1975.

55. Morgan, Z., Headley, R., Alexander, E. A., Sawyer, C. G.: Atrial fibrillation and epidural hematoma associated with lightning stroke. *N Engl J Med,* **259**(20):956–59, November 1954.

56. Myers, G. J., Colgan, M. T., Van Dyke, D. H.: Lightning disaster among children. *JAMA,* **238:**1045–46, 1977.

57. Nollet, J. A.: *Lettres sur l'électricité.* Guérin and Delatour, Paris, 1753.

58. Panse, F.: Electrical trauma. *Handbook Neurol,* **23:**683–729, n.d.

59. Paterson, J. H., Turner, J. W. A.: Lightning and the central nervous system. *J Rl Army Med Corps,* **82:**73–5, 1944.

60. Prentice, S. A.: Death by lightning. *Med J Aust,* **2,** 252, August 1973.

61. Prinz, H., *et al: Feur, Blitz und Funke.* Bruckman, Munich, 1965.

62. Pritchard, E. A. B.: Changes in the central nervous system due to electrocution. *Lancet,* **1:**1163–67, 1934.

63. Ravitch, M. M., Lane, R., Safar, P., Steichen, F. M., Knowles, P.: Lightning stroke. *N Engl J Med,* **264:**36–8, January 1961.

64. Raymond, L. F.: Specific treatment of uveitis—lightning induced: An auto-immune disease. *Am J Allergy,* **27:**242–44, 1969.

65. Rees, W.: Pregnant woman struck by lightning. *Br Med J,* **1:**103–4, 1965.

66. Remillard, W. J.: The acoustics of thunder. Technical Memo No. 44 (unpublished), Acoustic Research Laboratory, Harvard University, Cambridge, Mass., 1960.

67. Shulman, K., Marmarou, A., Miller, J. D., *et al: Intracranial Pressure IV.* Springer-Verlag, Berlin, 1980.

68. Silverman, N.: Unilateral deafness as a sequel to nonfatal lightning trauma. *J Indiana State Med Assoc,* **29:**530–31, 1936.

69. Skan, D. A.: Death from lightning—stroke, with multiple injuries. *Br Med J,* **1:**666, April 1949.

70. Slingerland, I.: Lightning stroke. *New York State Med J,* **14:**466, 1914.

71. Spencer, H. A.: *Lightning, Lightning Stroke and Its Treatment.* Bailliere, Tindall and Cox, London, 1934, p. 91.

72. Strasser, E. J., Davis, R. M., Menchey, J. J.: Lightning injuries. *J Trauma,* **17:**315–19, 1977.

73. Taussig, H.: "Death" from lightning and the possibility of living again. *Ann Intern Med,* **68:**1345–53, 1968.

74. Tiscornia, A.: Bilateral cataract from lightning stroke. *JAMA,* **77:**1930, December 1921.

75. Uman, M. A.: *Understanding lightning.* Bek Technical Publications, Carnegia, Pa., 1971, p. 166.

76. U.S. Department of Commerce: *Lightning,* No. AA-PI 70005. U.S. Government Printing Office, Washington, D.C., 1970.

77. U.S. Department of Commerce: *Thunderstorms,* No. AA-PI 75009. U.S. Government Printing Office, Washington, D.C., 1976.

78. Weigel, E.: Lightning, the underrated killer. *NOAA,* **6:**2, April 1976.

79. Weinstein, L.: Lightning: A rare cause of intrauterine death with maternal survival. *South Med J,* **72:**632, 1979.

80. West, G.: Lightning as a cause of hearing loss. *Md State Med J,* **4:**35–7, 1955.

81. Wilks, G.: Case of lightning stroke. *Lancet,* **2:**655–57, November 1879.

82. Woods, J.: Spinal atrophic paralysis following lightning stroke. *S Afr Med J,* **26:**92–3, 1952.

83. Yost, J. W., Holmes, F. F.: Myoglobinuria following lightning stroke. *JAMA,* **228:**1147–48, 1974.

CHAPTER 19 | AEROSPACE MEDICINE: THE VERTICAL FRONTIER

Charles A. Berry, MD., M.P.H.
Michael A. Berry, M.D.

History

Since its beginning as a separate field of medical endeavor, aerospace medicine has had as its basic premise the maintenance of the health and safety of the flier. In 1918, at the beginning of World War I, it was quickly determined that some medical support for aviation was required to prevent the large number of needless flying accidents. Lt. Col. Theodore C. Lyster was the physician chosen by the Army for this difficult job. The expertise with which he accomplished his goal has since earned him the title "American Father of Aviation Medicine."

Dr. Lyster began this endeavor with the accumulated knowledge and experience of earlier inventors, experimenters, scientists, and physicians. In 1783, the Montgolfier brothers began to launch hot air balloons in France

and quickly captured the interest of the rest of the Western world. In November of that year, Pilatre de Rozier and the Marquis d'Arlandes became the first men to fly. De Rozier, a physician, reported at the end of his maiden flight that it had had no untoward effects on the physical system. He became one of the earliest air travel casualties just 2 years later, when his hydrogen-filled balloon exploded during a flight. As ballooning became more commonplace, the physiologic effects of flight were increasingly studied. At altitudes above 10,000 feet, humans were subjected to decreased oxygen, decreased pressure, and extreme cold. Although not well understood at the time, the effects of these environmental stresses were recorded by those who experienced them and lived to tell about it. One of these early experimenters was an American physician, John Jefferies, who made many of the early inflight observations on barometric

522

pressure, atmospheric composition, and temperature, and their effects on the human body. A Frenchman, Paul Bert, did more than any other investigator to advance knowledge in this new field. In 1878, after 670 separate experiments, many in the world's first pressure chamber, he published *La Pression Barometrique.* This was and is the basis for high-altitude flying as it is practiced to this day. For his monumental efforts, Paul Bert is known to the world as the "Father of Aviation Medicine."

The concept of flight surgeons as special aviation-oriented physicians was realized in 1916, when the Aeronautical Division of the U.S. Army Signal Corps was established. It was during the period 1916–18 that the United States, Germany, Great Britain, France, and Italy first set selection standards for the physical examination of aviation candidates. In 1918, an air service medical research laboratory was established to investigate further the effects of flying; a year later, a special school for flight surgeons was established by Dr. Louis H. Bauer, then director of the medical research laboratory. The earliest arbitrarily established medical standards for pilots were much too restrictive, and disqualified all candidates. Under Bauer's supervision, they were made more realistic. In 1926, Bauer left the military to become the first equivalent of today's Federal Air Surgeon, and began the development of similar standards for civilian fliers. In the same year, he published *Aviation Medicine,* the first such textbook. A system of aviation medical examiners and eventually airline medical directors evolved. Today, medical standards for flying in the civilian and military sectors continue to undergo revision in order to reflect current medical knowledge.

Aviation technology and the skills of the flight surgeon advanced commensurate with the increased speeds and higher altitudes. Oxygen masks were developed to allow function at the higher altitudes. Pressurized cabins followed and allowed even higher altitudes to be attained. Much of the research was accomplished by special balloon flights, both manned and unmanned, such as Explorer I and II in the 1930s (60,000–70,000 feet), Skyhook flights in the 1940s (100,000 feet), Stratolab, and Man High manned flights in the 1950s (75,000–100,000 feet).

Ground-based altitude chambers, similar to those used by Paul Bert, were also utilized. Medical research on animals and humans addressed hypoxia and decompression sickness. Jet aircraft developed after World War II achieved speeds capable of inflicting extreme accelerative forces on their pilots. Ejection seats were developed for rapid escape and introduced further accelerative forces. Centrifuges and rocket sleds were used to delineate the limits of endurance. The research that allowed humans to fly at great speeds and to approach altitudes on the fringes of space served as the core of knowledge upon which later space flights were based.

In the late 1950s, the Space Task Group was formed at Langley Field in Virginia to begin the early planning for the U.S. space effort. The official announcement of Project Mercury came on November 26, 1958, and on April 2, 1959, the United States chose its first seven astronauts. The flight of the Russian cosmonaut, Yuri Gagarin, in April 1961 proved that humans could survive in space. In May 1961, the United States followed with the suborbital flight of Alan Shepard. At the completion of the flights of the Mercury series, it was clear that humans could survive in space if afforded the proper protection. The flight surgeons, working closely with the engineers, assured that this protection was adequate. Project Gemini extended the astronauts' stay in space, revealed some of the physiologic changes of zero gravity, and initiated the engineering and medical groundwork for the Apollo program. On July 20, 1969, men walked on the moon and proved their capability for achievement in this new environment. The Skylab missions increased the space medicine knowledge that in turn will be advanced by the flight surgeons for the Space Shuttle.

The Flight Environment

An understanding of the physiologic effects of flight is based on a thorough understanding of the components of this special flight environment and of the physical laws that govern it. The "natural" environment that will be discussed is a complex of dynamic factors such as pressure, temperature, moisture, gravity, and electromagnetic radiation. The laws of physics which govern atmospheric phenomena are constant and the results are predictable, whether on the surface of the Earth, in the vacuum of space, or anywhere in the continuum between.

BEHAVIOR OF GASES

The gaseous state is one of the simplest forms of matter. Individual molecules of a gas are relatively far apart and continuously move; these properties allow gases to be compressed. When describing a gas in a confined space, the important variables that must be considered are:

1. Pressure
2. Volume
3. Temperature
4. Density

Pressure is defined as force per unit area (pounds/square feet, grams/square centimeters). With respect to a confined gas, the pressure is that force exerted on a specified area of the container due to its bombardment by the moving molecules of the gas.

The *volume* of a confined gas is the space occupied by that gas, expressed in cubic feet or cubic centimeters (cm^3).

The *temperature* of a gas is a measure of the energy content of the moving molecules. It is usually expressed in degrees absolute or degrees Kelvin.

Density is defined as mass per unit volume (g/cm^3).

Four principal gas laws deal with the behavior of gases. The first, *Boyle's law,* states that the pressure (P) of a gas varies inversely with the volume, assuming a constant temperature. *Charles' law* adds temperature to the pressure-volume relationship. When combined with Boyle's law, the result is the general gas law, which states that both pressure and volume increase with an increase in temperature. *Dalton's law* concerning gaseous mixtures states that due to the molecular motion of each separate gas, the mixture is homogeneous and occupies the entire available volume. It also states that the sum of pressures exerted by each gas individually equals the total pressure exerted by the gaseous mixture. The pressure exerted by each gas in the mixture is known

as the *partial pressure* of that gas. The last law, *Henry's law,* states that the amount of gas dissolved in a liquid is proportional to the pressure or partial pressure of that gas above the surface of the liquid (Table 1).

EARTH'S ATMOSPHERE

The atmosphere which surrounds the earth is a mixture of gases, of which oxygen and nitrogen are the primary components. The total chemical composition of the gaseous atmosphere is represented in Table 2. The total mass of this atmosphere is about one-millionth the mass of the earth. It is maintained around the earth by gravitational attraction and by the temperature effect of solar radiation. The density of the atmosphere is greatest at sea level and decreases geometrically with increasing distance from the surface of the earth, due to decreasing gravitational compression. At approximately 18,000 feet (5.5 km) in altitude, one-half of the atmosphere has been passed, and the density and pressure are one-half of those at sea level. At 34,000 feet (10.4 km), three-quarters of the atmosphere is beneath and the density and pressure are one-

TABLE 1
Gas Laws

Boyle's law: $P = C/V$
Charles' law: $P \cdot V = T \cdot C$
Dalton's law: $P = P_1 + P_2 + \ldots$
  where P = pressure, P_1, P_2 = partial pressure,
  T = temperature,
  V = volume, and C = constant

TABLE 2
Chemical Composition of the Earth's Atmosphere (At Sea Level)

Gas	%
Nitrogen (N_2)	78.09
Oxygen (O_2)	20.95
Argon (Ar)	0.93
Carbon dioxide (CO_2)	0.03
Neon (Ne)	0.0018
Helium (He)	0.0005
Krypton (Kr)	0.0001
Hydrogen (H)	0.00005

quarter of those at sea level. At 100,000 feet (30.5 km), approximately 99% of the atmosphere has been left below. The theoretical upper limit of the atmosphere is considered to be 500 miles (700 km). At this altitude, there are no longer any collisions between the molecular constituents.

The variance of physical characteristics at different levels of the atmosphere has given rise to arbitrary nomenclature of different strata, based upon their fairly uniform physical properties (1,10,11,18,20,28). The major demarcation is between the inner and outer atmospheres. The limit of the inner layer is approximately 500 miles, beyond which molecular collisions are so rare that molecules actually leave the influence of Earth's gravity and continue on into space. Molecules within this boundary follow elliptical orbital paths and eventually fall to Earth. The stratification within this inner layer is based primarily on temperature. The atmospheric strata, approximate altitude, and temperature are depicted in Table 3 (1,10,11,18,20,28).

It has been stated that as one ascends in altitude, the pressure and density of the atmosphere or air decrease. A descriptive example is a column of air which extends from sea level to space, with a cross-sectional area of 1.0 square inch. This entire column would weigh 14.7 pounds or would exert a total pressure at sea level of 14.7 pounds/square inch (psi). At the 18,000-foot mark on the column, one-half of the air (atmosphere) is compressed below and each half would weigh 7.35 pounds. Thus, the pressure on 1 square inch at 18,000 feet of altitude is 7.35 psi. This weight of air,

or barometric pressure, is expressed in a variety of units, such as pounds/square inch (psi), millimeters of mercury (mmHg), inches of mercury (in Hg), or millibars. The standard sea level barometric pressure is 14.7 psi or 760 mmHg. The variation of pressure with altitude is shown in Table 4.

From a functional physiologic point of view, it is necessary to know the partial pressure of oxygen (ppO_2). At sea level, oxygen is responsible for one-fifth of the total atmospheric pressure, or has a ppO_2 of 3.1 psi (159 mmHg). For practical purposes, the remaining pressure is made up of nitrogen, where the partial pressure of nitrogen (ppN_2) at sea level is 11.6 psi (601 mmHg). Hypoxia occurs with increase in ambient altitude and will be discussed later.

Temperature variation in the atmosphere is caused by an alteration in the balance between the water vapor in the air and the absorption of the sun's long-wave radiation by the atmosphere. This process is in equilibrium in the stratosphere, where the temperature is a fairly constant −67°F (−55°C). Lower in the troposphere, the greatest temperature variation is seen. Theoretically, if one assumes the standard atmosphere, where the temperature at sea level is considered to be 59°F (15°C), the lapse rate of temperature with increase in altitude is −2°C/1000 feet, until the isothermal layer of the stratosphere is reached at approximately 36,000 feet (11.6 km). Temperature changes are noted as one passes upward through the ionosphere, but for practical purposes, temperature as we know it does not exist due to the scarcity of molecules. The

TABLE 3
Atmospheric Levels

Atmosphere	Level	Altitude (*miles*)	Temperature (*°C*)
Inner atmosphere	Trophosphere	0–7	Variable with season to −55° to +60°
	Stratosphere	7–50	−55° to −70°
	Ionosphere	5–500	−70° to +50°
Outer atmosphere	Exosphere	500–1200	Indeterminate
Free space		1200+	Indeterminate

TABLE 4
Atmospheric Pressure and Temperature

Altitude		Pressure		Temperature	
Feet	Meters	mmHg	psi	°C	°F
0	0.0	760.0	14.69	15.0	59.0
2,000	609.6	706.6	13.67	11.0	51.9
4,000	1,219.2	565.3	12.69	7.1	44.7
6,000	1,828.8	609.0	11.78	3.1	36.6
8,000	2,438.4	564.4	10.91	−0.8	30.5
10,000	3,048.0	522.6	10.11	−4.8	23.3
12,000	3,657.6	483.3	9.35	−8.8	16.2
14,000	4,267.2	446.4	8.63	−12.7	9.1
16,000	4,876.8	411.8	7.96	−16.7	1.9
18,000	5,486.4	379.4	7.34	−20.7	−5.3
20,000	6,096.0	349.1	6.75	−24.6	−12.3
22,000	6,705.6	320.8	6.20	−28.6	−19.5
24,000	7,315.2	294.4	5.69	−32.5	−26.6
26,000	7,924.8	269.8	5.22	−36.5	−33.7
28,000	8,534.4	246.9	4.77	−40.5	−40.9
30,000	9,144.0	225.6	4.36	−44.4	−48.0
32,000	9,753.6	205.8	3.98	−48.4	−55.1
34,000	10,363.2	187.4	3.62	−52.4	−62.3
36,000	10,972.8	170.4	3.30	−55.0	−67.0
38,000	11,582.4	154.9	3.00	−55.0	−67.0
40,000	12,192.0	140.7	2.72	−55.0	−67.0
42,000	12,801.6	127.9	2.47	−55.0	−67.0
44,000	13,411.2	116.3	2.25	−55.0	−67.0
46,000	14,020.8	105.7	2.04	−55.0	−67.0
48,000	14,630.4	96.05	1.86	−55.0	−67.0
50,000	15,240.0	87.30	1.69	−55.0	−67.0
52,000	15,849.6	79.34	1.53	−55.0	−67.0
54,000	16,459.2	72.12	1.39	−55.0	−67.0
56,000	17,068.8	65.55	1.27	−55.0	−67.0
58,000	17,678.4	59.58	1.15	−55.0	−67.0
60,000	18,288.0	54.15	1.05	−55.0	−67.0
62,000	18,894.6	49.2	.951	−55.0	−67.0
64,000	19,567.2	44.7	.864	−55.0	−67.0
			psf[a]		
66,000	20,116.8	40.6	113.2	−55.0	−67.0
68,000	20,726.4	36.9	102.9	−55.0	−67.0
70,000	21,336.0	33.6	93.52	−55.0	−67.0
72,000	21,945.6	30.4	85.01	−55.0	−67.0
74,000	22,555.2	27.7	77.26	−55.0	−67.0
76,000	23,164.8	25.2	70.22	−55.0	−67.0
78,000	23,774.4	22.9	63.8	−55.0	−67.0
80,000	24,384.0	20.8	58.01	−55.0	−67.0
82,000	24,993.6	18.9	52.72	−55.0	−67.0
84,000	25,603.2	17.2	47.91	−55.0	−67.0
86,000	26,212.8	15.6	43.55	−55.0	−67.0
88,000	26,822.4	14.2	39.59	−55.0	−67.0
90,000	27,432.0	12.9	35.95	−55.0	−67.0
92,000	28.041.6	11.7	32.1	−55.0	−67.0
94,000	28,651.2	10.7	29.7	−55.0	−67.0
96,000	29,260.8	9.7	27.02	−55.0	−67.0
98,000	29,870.4	8.8	24.55	−55.0	−67.0
100,000	30,480.0	8.0	22.31	−55.0	−67.0

[a] Pounds/square feet.

temperature experienced at altitudes above 100 miles (160 km) is related to unshielded radiant energy absorbed directly from the sun (20,28).

GRAVITY

The most pervasive environmental factor is gravity. It is ever present and totally independent of other environmental factors. Webster (New International Dictionary, 2d ed.) defines gravity as the acceleration of terrestrial bodies toward the center of the Earth. Newton's law of universal gravitation states that any two bodies attract each other with a force directly proportional to their mass and inversely proportional to the distance between them, as expressed by the equation:

$$F = \frac{GM_1M_2}{r^2}$$

where F is the force, G the universal gravitational constant, M_1 and M_2 the mass of each body, and r the distance between the bodies (28). Physiologically, gravity is more important in its absence than in its presence. This absence is zero G, null gravity, or, more commonly, weightlessness. The force of gravity decreases in inverse proportion to the square of the distance from the Earth's center. At 4000 miles, this force is decreased by one-half, and at 36,000 miles, it is 1/100th of its initial force (1,18,19,20). However, weightlessness can be achieved without traveling this great distance. Weightlessness occurs when the resultant vector of all forces (including gravity) acting on a body is zero. This phenomenon can be achieved in special aircraft which fly parabolic flight paths, achieving 30–45 seconds of zero gravity at the top of the parabola. A spacecraft orbits the Earth in the ionosphere at 100–200 miles, well within the influence of Earth's gravity. Weightlessness during spaceflight does not occur simply because one is in space in an area where gravity is nonexistent. When a spacecraft achieves the orbital velocity of approximately 18,000 miles/hour, the centrifugal force that is generated balances the centripetal force of gravity and creates a state of weightlessness. Orbital velocity usually cannot be achieved until an altitude is reached at which so little atmosphere remains that friction is nonexistent and the velocity

remains fairly constant. To travel to another planet, a vehicle must escape the influence of Earth's gravity by achieving an escape velocity of 25,000 miles/hour. Orbital and escape velocities are illustrated in Figure 1 (18,19).

RADIATION

A common natural component of the atmosphere is radiation, which pervades our environment in a variety of natural forms. This is a potential hazard to high-altitude jet flight and spaceflight, although no ill effects have been noted to date.

The two basic classes of radiation are electromagnetic and particle radiation, originating from the sun and stars both inside and outside of our galaxy. Electromagnetic radiation is wavelike and, in order of decreasing wavelength, is made up of radio waves, microwaves, infrared rays, visible light, ultraviolet (UV) rays, x-rays, gamma rays, and ultra gamma rays (Figure 2). All of these travel at the speed of light, 186,000 miles/second. Particle radiation is composed of subatomic particles, electrons, positrons, protons, neutrons, Pi mesons, and α particles. The speed with which these particles travel varies up to the speed of light (20,27,28).

The radiation which leaves the sun is altered by atmospheric gases, water vapor, and dust before it reaches the surface of the Earth. The less protective atmosphere present between humans and solar radiation, the greater the potential hazard.

As solar radiation reaches the edges of the atmosphere, there are five possible actions. It may travel through unchanged; travel through, but in a different direction; be reflected; be scattered; or be absorbed. When radiation is absorbed, a change, or transformation, of energy takes place and causes the biologic effect. At the atmospheric border of approximately 430 miles in altitude, the solar spectrum is unchanged. The short wavelengths are absorbed by gases in the highest portions of the atmosphere. At slightly lesser altitudes, short UV waves are absorbed by molecular oxygen, forming ozone (O_3). The so-called ozonosphere exists at between 15 and 30 miles of altitude. Ozone is then reconverted to O_2 by the absorption of longer-wave UV, the net effect being the total absorption of the

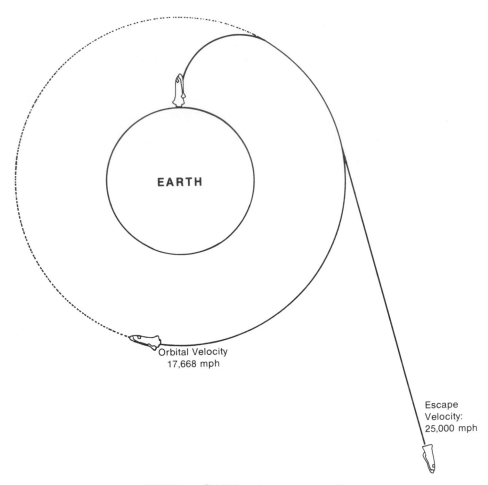

FIGURE 1 Orbital and escape velocity.

biologically harmful UV spectrum. The visible spectrum travels through the gasses unchanged, although absorbed and scattered by the vapors, clouds, and dust. Therefore, daylight is in actuality indirect sunlight. The longwave radiation is absorbed by the gases and water vapor in the lower reaches of the atmosphere. The physiologic effects of this radiation obviously depend upon the altitude and corresponding amount of atmosphere providing protection. At the altitudes reached in standard aviation, radiation poses very little threat. The higher altitudes of some special aircraft and spacecraft are at slightly greater risk. It is of note that the total radiation dose for U.S. astronauts during both orbital and lunar spaceflight has been extremely low (23,24).

Particle radiation within the atmosphere ex-

ists primarily as geomagnetically trapped radiation. The particles are trapped in closed orbital trajectories in the Earth's magnetic field. Two belts of high-intensity radiation, primarily protons and electrons, surround the Earth and are known as the *inner* and *outer Van Allen belts.* The charge on these particles causes a polar alignment with the Earth's magnetic field, as illustrated in Figure 3. These belts can be visualized three-dimensionally as two concentric donuts that surround the Earth, with the inner belt having an asymmetric inner bulge known as the *South Atlantic anomaly.* The inner belt exists between approximately 370 and 6200 miles and the outer belt from 12,000 to 44,000 miles (11,12,20,27). Such radiation, while an early worry for manned spaceflight, has never produced exposure levels of biologic concern. As far as stan-

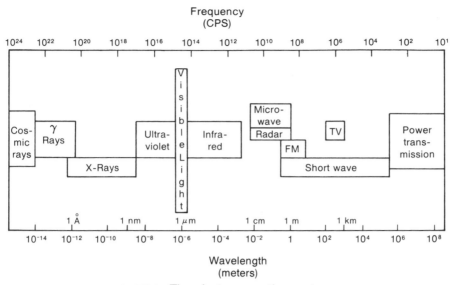

FIGURE 2 The electromagnetic spectrum.

dard aviation is concerned, particulate and electromagnetic radiation is no real problem. Recent concern has been expressed over the effect of very low-dose radiation over long periods, even in aircrews. Data are being collected, but there is no current evidence of a problem.

Special Physiologic Effects of Flight

In this section, we discuss the effects of the aerospace environment on specific physiologic functions. The significant physiologic effects at various altitudes are shown in Figure 4.

Hypoxia

As one ascends in altitude, the *total* barometric pressure decreases; it is one-half that at sea level at 18,000 feet (5.5 km), one-third at 27,000 feet (8.2 km), one-fourth at 33,400 feet (10.2 km), and one-fifth at 38,500 feet (11.7 km). The partial pressure of oxygen is correspondingly reduced. This partial pressure can be determined by multiplying the percentage of oxygen at sea level pressure (20.84) times the pressure at the desired altitude (in mmHg). For example, at 18,000 feet (380 mmHg), $0.2084 \times 380 = 79.5$ mmHg ppO_2. The reduced amount of oxygen available af-

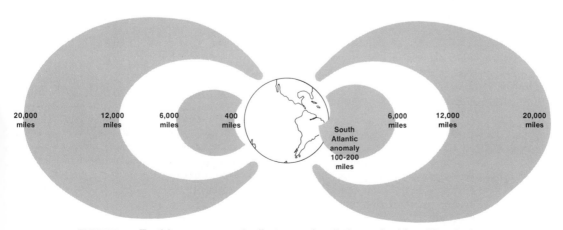

FIGURE 3 Earth's geomagnetically trapped radiation—the Van Allen belts.

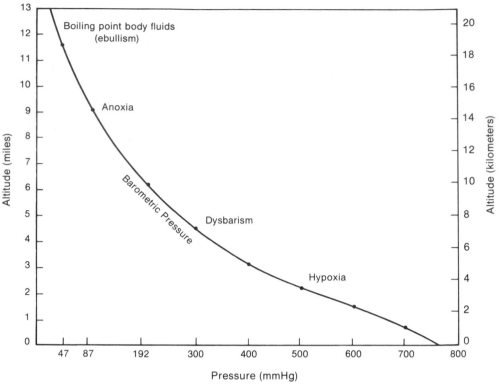

FIGURE 4 Physiologic effects of increasing altitude.

fects the pressure of oxygen in the alveoli at altitude. The partial pressure of inspired oxygen, not the actual concentration of oxygen, is the force that makes oxygen available to hemoglobin. Inspired air becomes saturated with water vapor, which has a constant partial pressure, as does carbon dioxide. Thus, the deficit in oxygen partial pressure can be compensated for by increasing the percentage of oxygen in the inspired air as altitude increases. At 34,000 feet, 100% oxygen must be inspired to provide an alveolar partial pressure of oxygen equal to that at sea level. At 40,000 feet, 100% oxygen can no longer maintain an adequate alveolar oxygen partial pressure, and oxygen must be supplied at increased pressure (10,11,27).

Supplemental oxygen was first supplied to pilots and passengers by "pipe stem," then masks, and now by pressure breathing regulators and full pressure suits. The objective is to prevent *hypoxia,* a condition created by an inadequate supply of oxygen to the cells

of the body. The total absence of oxygen is *anoxia.*

Hypoxia may result from:

1. Reduced oxygen in the inspired air—*hypoxic hypoxia*—as when oxygen is not utilized at altitudes above 10,000 feet or oxygen equipment malfunctions
2. Reduced capacity of the blood to carry adequate inspired oxygen—*anemic hypoxia*—as in anemia or carbon monoxide exposure
3. Reduced blood flow to the cells—*stagnant hypoxia*—as in pain, injury, or shock
4. Reduced ability of cells to utilize oxygen—*histotoxic hypoxia*—as in cyanide or alcohol exposure

Oxygen is essential for human survival. The brain and its sensory organs, such as the retina, are the greatest utilizers of oxygen, exhibit the first signs of decreased supply, and sustain the worst cellular damage if the reduction in supply is prolonged. Anoxia is characterized by immediate loss of consciousness (one circulation time from lungs to brain is roughly 13

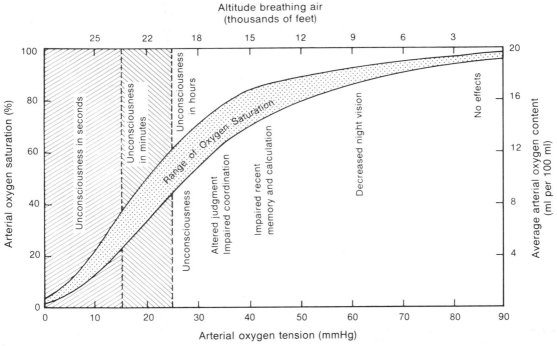

FIGURE 5   Arterial oxygen saturation symptoms in a resting subject.

seconds) and, if prolonged for 90–180 seconds, is usually fatal.

The amount of oxygen available to the cells is dependent on the oxygen saturation of the arterial blood. The blood temperature and level of pH affect the oxyhemoglobin dissociation curve and thus the amount of oxygen available for cellular use.

The arterial blood is usually 95–100% saturated with oxygen at sea level. As the saturation, arterial oxygen tension, and oxygen content decrease with increasing altitude, symptoms of hypoxia develop. The symptoms of hypoxia range from those detectable only by detailed examination of central nervous system functions to unconsciousness. At 10,000 feet, the oxygen saturation has decreased to 90% and a stage of undetectable hypoxia is reached, which is manifested only by decreased night vision. As the saturation decreases from 80 to 70%, the level of handicap in the hypoxic person reaches a serious state, and collapse is imminent near 66% saturation. At 80% saturation, dimming of vision, tremor of the hands, errors in judgment, and

clouding of thought and memory occur. The relationship of arterial oxygen saturation, altitude (alveolar oxygen tension), and symptoms of hypoxia are shown in Figure 5.

A concept which has been helpful in training airmen and spacemen to recognize and correct hypoxia is the *time of useful consciousness,* defined as that period after acute exposure to a hypoxic environment in which the crewman may still perform a purposeful act. For self-preservation, this would include recognizing hypoxia and its cause and taking protective action, such as the use of supplemental oxygen. Studies of airline pilots with decompression training and untrained naive subjects showed similar responses for approximately 50% of each group up to an altitude of 38,000 feet (10 seconds donning time). The training of the pilots became evident by more responses and shorter response times as altitude increased to 48,000 feet. The average time of useful consciousness for persons breathing air prior to decompression is shown in Figure 6.

There are marked individual differences in tolerance to hypoxia, whether acute, inflight,

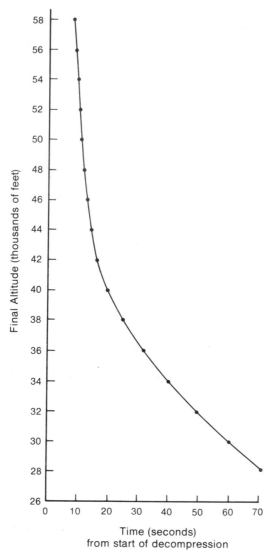

FIGURE 6 Average time of useful consciousness.

or prolonged, as in mountain exposures. Some people note symptoms of shortness of breath, headache, nausea, and decreased ability to concentrate or perform complex tasks at 10,000 feet, while others may not note any symptoms until much higher altitudes are reached. Most persons will develop symptoms after 8–24 hours at 10,000–12,000 feet. Some physiologic adaptation occurs over several days' exposure, but the ability to perform muscular work may be impaired for weeks (10, 11,27).

DYSBARISM

Dysbarism is the complex of symptoms resulting from exposure to reduced atmospheric pressure. The word was developed to indicate painful barometric pressure. Historically, many other names have been used for the different types of dysbarism and have been related to the site of the injury. *Aeropathy, bends, chokes, decompression sickness, itch, prickles, aeroembolism, aerotitis media, barotitis, aerosinusitis,* and *barosinusitis* were all names commonly used and, unfortunately, often interchanged and confused (2). This discussion will clarify the confusion in nomenclature that has previously existed. The two major categories of dysbaric symptoms are those due to trapped gas and those due to evolved gas. The etiology is the difference between the total barometric pressure acting on the outside of the body and the total pressure of the trapped and dissolved gases inside the body.

As the barometric pressure decreases, symptoms result from the expansion of trapped gas (Boyle's law) and from the dissolution (bubbling) of the dissolved gases (Henry's law).

Trapped Gas Syndromes

The trapped gas syndromes are:

Abdominal gas: Decompression causes expansion of abdominal gas bubbles more than two times at 18,000 feet and five times at 34,000 feet. If relief is not obtained by eructation or rectal passage, severe colic-type pain may occur and lead to vasodepressor syncope.

Aerodontalgia (*tooth pain*): Pain in the teeth may occur on ascent to altitudes of 5000–15,000 feet. The victims usually have dental pathology, particularly trapped gas around fillings. Silver-filled teeth seem more susceptible than unfilled or gold-filled teeth.

Aerotitis media (*ear pain*): The escape of expanding gas in the middle ear through the eustachian tube usually occurs rather easily on ascent to altitude. The pharyngeal opening of the tube has a flaplike valve that favors flow from the middle ear to the pharynx. On descent, however, it is more difficult for the air to enter the tube in order to balance the increasing pressure on the outside of the tympanic membrane. The pressure changes are greater at lower altitudes. A negative pressure difference of 15–30 mmHg across the tympanic membrane will produce hemorrhage. With increased pressure difference, a sense of fullness in the affected ear, diminished hearing, and pain may progress to membrane rupture. The process usually stops short of rupture, as either hemorrhage or serous fluid transudation in the middle ear equalizes the pressure. Any process that causes swelling of the nasopharyngeal tissue and eustachian tube opening, such as an upper respiratory infection, is reason to preclude flying temporarily. Slow descent and careful attention to pressure equalization on descent from altitude by swallowing or using the Valsalva maneuver can eliminate this problem.

Aerosinusitis (sinus pain): The sinuses also have to expel the increased gas volume on ascent and pull in additional gas on descent. The mechanism of difficulty is the same, and the formation of a hematoma is more common if the pressure cannot be equalized. Such hematomas may take weeks to resolve and must be watched for the development of infection. Maxillary sinus involvement may produce tooth pain, which could be confused with aerodontalgia. The frontal and maxillary sinuses are most frequently involved.

Evolved Gas Syndromes

Since 1939, investigators have been aware of the similarities between caisson disease, diver's decompression sickness, and evolved gas dysbarism. These are a continuum of the same disorder that results from decreased pressure, whether at altitude or on return to the surface from ocean depths. In fact, the term *decompression sickness* is now widely used for evolved gas symptoms, whatever the decompression source. Chapter 6 should be consulted to understand the continuity between diving and flying syndromes. During World War II, individuals who had recovered from diver's decompression sickness were taken to altitude and developed the recurrent symptoms. Indeed ascent to altitudes as low as 6000 feet immediately after self-contained underwater breathing apparatus (scuba) diving can produce evolved gas symptoms (2).

Gas bubble production on decompression was reported in a viper's eye as early as 1670 by Robert Boyle. In evolved gas dysbarism, nitrogen bubbles, perhaps compounded by water vapor and carbon dioxide, are generally believed to produce many of the symptoms, but there has been great argument over

whether the bubbles act from intra- or extravascular locations. Recent studies, which utilize Doppler devices (ultrasound) over the pulmonary artery (venous circulation), have identified bursts of bubbles in decompressed subjects prior to the development of any symptoms. A system of grading the number of bubbles can provide a prediction of the onset of bends, and the location is predicted by observing which joint is moved when the bubble burst occurs.

Specialists in the field use a numerical system of grading the severity of these syndromes, but for simplicity, a more descriptive method is used here.

Bends (bone and joint pain): This is the most common and frequent evolved gas syndrome. It involves aching pain which can be in any joint, but is most frequent in the shoulders or knees. The pain increases in intensity, spreads along the bone, and may reach an excruciating level. It can be incapacitating and thus simulate a paralysis of the involved extremity. Residual tenderness may last for days.

Chokes: This involves substernal irritation or pain, accompanied by a nonproductive cough and dyspnea. Deep breathing aggravates the symptoms. Chokes frequently lead to circulatory collapse and also have a high association with mottled skin lesions. The evolution of gas bubbles in the pulmonary circulation is the etiology.

Skin reactions: The most common skin reactions are cold or prickling sensations. These are mild and do not usually lead to more severe reactions. Development of mottled skin reactions, however, is usually indicative of progressive, severe dysbarism. These reactions begin as pale, bluish mottling of the skin of the chest, shoulders, upper abdomen, and occasionally the forearms and thighs. The center area may become erythematous and the periphery very blue, giving the appearance of a recent contusion.

Neurologic manifestations: Neurologic manifestations are almost always preceded by bends, chokes, or mottled skin reactions. Almost any part of the central nervous system can be involved, and most fatal cases have some central nervous system findings. The most common of these are scintillating scotomata. Hemiparesis or monoparesis, various sensory disturbances, delirium, convulsions, migrainelike headache, and electroencephalographic abnormalities have been described.

Neurocirculatory collapse: This serious condition has led to a number of fatalities. It is a mixture of neurologic manifestations with hypotension.

Collapse may occur at altitude, disappear on re-compression, and then recur hours later, or it may occur for the first time hours after recompression, when other evolved gas symptoms have disappeared. Thus, all patients must be warned of this possibility and be observed for a sufficient period of time to preclude this development.

Bone lesions: Lesions which involve the femoral heads and infarctlike lesions of the shafts of long bones have been described in caisson workers after years of exposure. Low-pressure chamber workers have been studied; while a U.S. Navy study showed a 17.5% incidence of bone lesions, a U.S. Air Force study showed *no* lesions in 579 low-pressure chamber operators (2,17).

Onset and Frequency of Dysbarism Syndromes

The symptoms usually occur in flight or at altitude in a decompression chamber. In rare cases, they may be delayed for up to 24 hours after exposure.

Actual incidence figures are very difficult to come by because the exposure conditions vary greatly. The most frequent symptoms in low-pressure chamber exposure have been those which involve the ears (49.8%), abdominal gas (19.8%), sinuses (11.7%), bends (10.6%), skin (5.3%), and teeth (2.3%). The frequency of evolved gas syndrome in 61 in-flight cases was as follows: bends (90.1%), central nervous system (54.1%), chokes (45.9%), circulatory collapse (21.3%), and skin reactions (11.4%). A marked difference in the syndromes which result from altitude exposure and caisson or diving exposure is the large number of spinal cord lesions in the latter and their rarity in the former. It has been speculated that this difference may be due to the greater range of pressure changes experienced by divers (6+ to 1 atmospheres) than by fliers (1 to 0 atmospheres) (2,17).

Diagnosis

The most important factor in the diagnosis of any of the dysbarism syndromes is a history of exposure to altitude. The presence of symptoms or findings, coupled with a history of exposure, should invite a high level of suspicion for the diagnosis of evolved gas dysbarism. This is particularly important in view of the large number of people who now participate in scuba diving. Many choice sites for this activity are reached by airplane. The additive effects of decompression from diving, then further decompression, even to a cabin altitude of 8000 feet in an airliner, have produced bends and led to guidelines which dictate avoidance of aircraft flight for 24 hours after scuba diving.

Treatment and Prevention of Evolved Gas Syndromes

Even individuals with minimal symptoms after altitude exposure should be carefully watched for the development of delayed reactions. Initial therapy may be directed at symptoms and findings, such as restoration of blood pressure and reduction of hemoconcentration. Venous access for the initiation of fluid therapy should be obtained early.

The most specific therapy is recompression to more than 1 atmosphere of pressure in a hyperbaric chamber in order to force evolved bubbles back into solution. Specific treatment protocols have been developed for minimum compression time using oxygen breathing. These usually compress the patient to a 60-foot water depth equivalent. If symptoms or findings are not cleared, there is provision to go to a 165-foot water depth equivalent, breathing air. In either case, there is then a stepwise return to 1 atmosphere, with adequate equilibration time en route. The time involved may be 135–319 minutes, depending on the compression table used.

There are a number of hyperbaric treatment facilities available. The U.S. Air Force School of Aerospace Medicine at San Antonio, Texas, maintains a 24-hour hot line to provide treatment information. The telephone number for immediate consultation is 512–536–3278. Duke University provides a similar service through the National Diving Accident Network with a 24-hour telephone number, 919–684–8111.

Prevention depends upon the avoidance of rapid exposure to altitude, especially to 20,000 feet or higher. Adequate cabin pressurization is a key preventive measure. Another commonly used preventive measure for high-altitude and spaceflight evolved gas syndromes is denitrogenation by preflight inhalation of 100% oxygen. The amount of time necessary to wash out the majority of nitrogen from body tissues and fluids can be calculated for various altitudes.

There are a number of risk factors which have been shown to predispose to the development of evolved gas syndromes. These are age (risk increases with age), sex (females appear to be at a higher risk), obesity (fat has large amounts of absorbed nitrogen), exercise or activity at altitude, fatigue, apprehension, rapid rates of ascent, peak altitude, cold, and vibration. Some of these are controversial, and many may be related to blood flow effects, especially the microcirculation (2,17).

NOISE

Noise is of interest to the aerospace medical specialist because of the levels produced by all types of aircraft, the launch of spacecraft, and the hazard of hearing loss to both aerospace and ground crews.

The intensity of sound is measured as sound pressure level (SPL) in decibels (dB). The decibel is based on a reference pressure of 20 micronewtons/m², which is approximately equal to the lowest pressure at a frequency of 1000 Hertz which a young person with normal hearing can detect. Some common sound level pressures are: a business office, 50 dB; approximately 35 feet from a jet aircraft, 130 dB; at the gantry during the Saturn launch, 172 dB.

The frequency of sound is measured in cycles/second or Hertz (Hz), which indicates the pitch or tone of the sound. The speech frequencies are contained in the octave bands 300–600, 600–1200, 1200–2400, and 2400–4800 Hz.

Jet aircraft noise is broad spectrum in frequency (white noise), with some pure tones (concentration of sound energy in one frequency). A pure tone increases the sound level pressure by 10 dB in the octave in which it occurs.

In order to protect hearing, the sound level in decibels must be known; times of safe exposure for these levels are available. For example, the U.S. Air Force limits continuous exposure to 80 dB for 960 minutes but to 115 dB for only 2.2 minutes. The Office of Safety and Health Administration (OSHA) has established permissible daily exposure levels, shown in Table 5.

TABLE 5
Noise Exposure Limits

Duration (Hours)	Sound Level (dB)
8	90
6	92
4	95
3	97
2	100
1.5	102
1	105
0.5	110
0.25	115

Methods of protection are limitation of the duration of exposure, reduction of the decibel level by increasing the distance from the noise source, and best, utilization of earmuffs or earplugs for sound attenuation.

Reciprocating engine noise is generally of greatest intensity in the lower frequencies, 20–600 Hz, while jet engine noise ranges in the higher frequencies, 300–9600 Hz. Aircrews may show low- or high-frequency losses, depending on their exposure to these aircraft (10,11,26).

ACCELERATION AND GRAVITY (G) FORCES

In order to understand acceleration, one must first review some definitions.

Speed is the rate of change in the position of an object (aircraft or spacecraft) determined by distance per unit of time, such as miles/hour.

Velocity indicates both speed and direction of motion. It will change if either speed or direction changes.

Acceleration is a change of velocity in magnitude or direction, expressed in feet or meters/second². The acceleration of gravity is 32.2 feet/second² and is used as the standard–1 G. Acceleration may be linear, radial, or angular and produces forces accordingly.

Linear acceleration occurs when there is an increase or decrease in speed with no change in direction. The G force produced can be determined as follows:

$$G = \frac{V_2{}^2 - V_1{}^2}{32 \times 2d}$$

where V_1 = initial speed in feet/second, V_2 = final speed in feet/second, and, d = acceleration distance in feet.

Radial acceleration occurs with any change in direction while traveling at a constant speed. This is rotation around a distant axis, and the force acts away from the center axis. It is a change in direction only, and the resultant G force can be determined as follows:

$$G = \frac{V^2}{32 \times R}$$

where V = speed in feet/second and R = radius of the turn in feet. This is the most common type of G force in aviation. It can be seen that if the speed is doubled and the turn radius kept constant, the G force will increase four times.

Angular acceleration is a combination of linear and radial acceleration when they occur simultaneously. It involves a change in velocity and direction, as in an uncontrolled maneuver such as a spin. It is usually measured in degrees/second^2 rather than Gs and is complex to calculate.

In the flight environment, it is rare to be exposed to a pure or single acceleration or resultant G force uncomplicated by other forces, vibration, or oscillation. There is a difference in body response to accelerations of less than 0.2 second duration compared to those of greater duration, due to the latent period for developing hydrostatic effects. Therefore, accelerations of less than 0.2 second duration are called *abrupt* and those of longer duration are called *sustained*. We will discuss only sustained acceleration.

Terminology for Direction of G Forces

Several nomenclature systems have been used over the years to try to relate the direction of the accelerative force to the axis of the body and thus to effect and tolerance.

Acceleration in a head-to-foot direction along the long axis of the body is called *positive G*, footward, or eyeballs down.

Acceleration in a foot-to-head direction of the body axis is *negative G*, headward, or eyeballs up.

Acceleration perpendicular to the long axis of the body is either chest-to-back, eyeballs in, or back-to-chest, eyeballs out.

In general terms, the human tolerance (limit) is greatest in transverse G (about 15 Gs), second in positive G (about 4–6 Gs), and least in negative G (about 3 Gs).

These accelerative forces acting along the body axes have been designated in a standard manner, shown in Figure 7 (19,27).

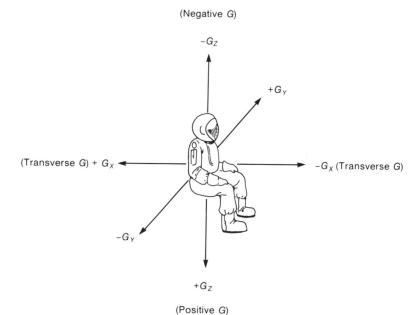

FIGURE 7 Gravity (*G*) nomenclature.

The factors which determine what the G effect will be on humans include the following:

1. The magnitude—number of Gs
2. The duration of the Gs in seconds
3. The direction of the Gs—G_z, G_x, or G_y
4. The body area over which the force is applied; greater area means less effect
5. The rate of application of Gs.

Effects of G Forces

The general body effects are increase in weight, movement of viscera, and cardiovascular responses, which include loss of eye and brain perfusion.

Positive Acceleration: Plus G_z Effects

+1 G_z Equal to upright or seated posture on Earth

+2 G_z Weight doubled; pressure on buttocks; drooping of face and soft body tissues

+2½ G_z Difficult to move body

+3–4 G_z Impossible to raise oneself; difficult to raise arms or legs; progressive dimming of vision after 3–4 seconds, which progresses to tunnel vision

+4½–6 G_z Decreased vision progresses to blackout after 5 seconds; hearing and then consciousness lost if continued; mild to severe convulsions in 50% of persons with unconsciousness; loss of orientation to time and place for 15 seconds after acceleration

Negative Acceleration: Minus G_z Effects

−1 G_z Unpleasant facial congestion

−2–3 G_z Severe facial congestion; throbbing headache; progressive blurring, graying, or reddening of vision after 5 seconds

Transverse Acceleration: Plus G_x Effects

+2–3 G_x Feeling of increased weight and abdominal pressure; progressive slight difficulty in focusing vision; tolerance to +2 G_x–24 hours, +4 G_x–60 minutes, +5 G_x–5 minutes

+3–6 G_x Progressive tightness of chest; difficulty in speaking, or focusing; breathing, blurred vision

+6–9 G_x Chest pain; shallow breathing; more blurred vision with occasional tunnel vision; inability to lift body or limbs at +8 G or head at +9 G

+9–12 G_x Severe difficulty breathing; increased chest pain; loss of peripheral vision

+15 G_x Vicelike chest pain; extreme difficulty in breathing and speaking; complete loss of vision

Note: G_z effects are similar, with variance due only to direction (27)

Protection Against G Effects

Experienced jet pilots and centrifuge subjects can increase their resistance to +G_z by performing what is called an *M-1* maneuver. This is accomplished by bending forward, taking a deep breath, and then exhaling with a grunting sound (partially closed glottis) while fixing the chest. Care must be taken *not* to hold the breath, or one will lose consciousness. This maneuver has been shown to increase tolerance by 1.5–2.0 G.

The common protective device is an anti-G suit, which is a series of bladders that are inflated to put pressure on the calves, thighs, and lower abdomen, thus aiding blood return to the heart and brain. The suit will normally increase tolerance by 1–2 G and generally is automatically inflated in response to the G level. The military antishock trousers (MAST) were based on this device, and in fact, an anti-G suit could be used in shock therapy (10, 11,19).

Body position can obviously be protective. In order to take advantage of the higher tolerances to transverse G, all U.S. spacecraft prior to the Shuttle have positioned the crew on their backs for launch, thus subjecting them to chest-to-back, +G_x, and then back-to-chest, −G_x, on reentry. G levels experienced on Apollo ranged from 3.3 to 7.19 and were well tolerated. Current fighter aircraft designers are trying to take advantage of this information in order to help the pilot keep up with the performance capability of the aircraft by changing the seat back angles and installing hand controls that require no arm movement under high G loads.

The Shuttle is the first spacecraft to expose the crew to +G_z on reentry from orbital flight. Early concern was expressed about +G_z exposure after weightlessness for 3–30 days (the usual Shuttle mission's duration). This concern was based on the cardiovascular system's response to return from weightlessness by pooling blood in the lower extremities. The first Shuttle mission in April 1981 subjected the crew to 1.0–1.5 $+G_z$ for several minutes during reentry. The astronauts did not inflate their anti-G suits, nor did they have any symptoms. Thus, one data point has been obtained, and we look forward to the response after longer zero G exposures.

SPACEFLIGHT—NULL GRAVITY

Spaceflight has long captivated human investigative imagination, and it is based on this stimulus that the special physiologic effects of flight will be completely elucidated. In the face of our accomplishments, we must not forget our first cautious forays into space that have evolved incrementally to 84 days in Skylab. These necessary steps will contribute to longer flight durations, such as the Soviet 6-month flights.

It is well to remember that spaceflight thus far has been an experimental program. All of the medical information gained on early flights was obtained in a research environment heavily oriented toward engineering and safety.

The space medicine community demonstrated a great deal of faith in the human capability to adapt to new environments when they committed astronauts to flights prior to the collection of sophisticated data upon which to base predictions. The problem faced by the flight surgeon in charge was the constant reconciliation of data collection with interest in the success of the operational flight mission. The flight crews desired minimum medical data collection (time-consuming, "unexciting"), while the flight surgeons pushed for such data, to silence the scientific critics who believed that humans were the weak link in spaceflight.

A number of mission difficulties in both the United States and the Soviet Union highlighted this need. The results of the Apollo 15 mission (July 26, 1971) were an anomaly in the U.S. spaceflight program. The most publicized events were short-lived cardiac arrhythmias in two crewmen (bigeminy in one,

multiple premature atrial contractions (PACs) and premature ventricular contractions (PVCs) in the other), which in retrospect were attributed to potassium deficiency coupled with the other operational effects of the mission. It was a unique mission, for it took the crew 21 days to return to the preflight baselines in regard to response to exercise and lower body negative pressure. This was a particular concern, for the findings were reminiscent of the 18-day Soyuz 9 Soviet mission of June 1, 1970. The space medicine community had been greatly surprised that those Soviet crewmen were unable to get out of their spacecraft unaided and required 20–25 days to return to their preflight baselines. They could not believe that a 4-day additional flight exposure over the longest Gemini mission really could be responsible for such effects. The concerns of the more cautious, and thus of the Congress and various consultative scientific committees, were raised further by two other significant events. The biosatellite flight of the monkey, "Bonnie," in June 1969, was an unfortunate occurrence, for it confused many who were honestly trying to evaluate the human capability. The monkey, while programmed to fly for 30 days, flew only for 8, deteriorated during the mission, and died 10 hours after recovery. The animal was completely instrumented in an attempt to acquire the maximum amount of data. Many factors were introduced in both the preflight and flight situations that could have led to the animal's demise. It was unfortunate that the end result was blamed by some of the experimenters entirely on the effects of weightlessness, in spite of the manned flight experience; this led to difficult debate before congressional committees. Shortly after this experience, the Soyuz 11-Salyut mission was flown (June 6-30, 1971). Three cosmonauts perished on reentry as their module suffered a rapid decompression, resulting in severe dysbarism, hypoxia, and virtually immediate death. When this happened, some aerospace medicine scientists blamed the mishap on weightlessness, prior to obtaining the scientific data that proved the deaths to be the result of the rapid decompression.

The above events are important because they influenced the environment in which the decision was made to launch Skylab and in which aerospace medicine was practiced.

Those who were involved in the Manned Space Flight Program were convinced that only the procurement of carefully planned inflight data would answer the question of human durability in space. The ability to run various medical evaluations in flight gave aerospace physicians a large safety edge in such determinations. These data were used to make operational decisions during the Skylab missions. Daily data analyses were performed, along with weekly evaluations of human status. In this way, a conscious decision was made with National Aeronautics and Space Administration (NASA) management on whether we could continue each mission week by week. Consultant groups on the cardiovascular and vestibular systems were also formed and utilized to great advantage during these important decision-making sessions (4).

There is much that could be recounted concerning the dire predictions that were made, the validity of only a few, and finally the flight proof that many were unfounded (Table 6). Thus, we have the great significance of the negative data obtained in the longest flights of humans to date: 28, 59, and 84 days.

The current status of human responses to spaceflight can be summarized in these brief statements. While there has been some individual variability, humans have always been able to perform inflight tasks for short or long durations of up to 175 days. They have suffered no permanent physiologic change after flight, but only time-limited readaptational changes *when* supported with an adequate atmosphere, food and hygiene facilities, exercise and workload planning, rest, time to acclimatize or adapt, and countermeasures if warranted. *When* must be *always,* for the hostile environment must always be considered (5).

Humans have been able to adapt over a period of days to weeks in flight to all of the body systems' physiologic changes, even to the vestibular system aberration that results in motion sickness. Likewise, they have easily readapted to Earth's gravity through a series of physiologic changes on return to Earth. Time phasing of these adaptations is of considerable interest and varies with the individual. There appears to be a general adaptation that starts within the first hours of spaceflight and may be complete in certain systems within hours. The vestibular responses have shown adaptation within a period of 1 week. It appears that the major body system shifts occur within 1 week, and that within 60 days in flight, most of the lability in system response has leveled out. The postflight time to readapt to 1 G on U.S. flights has seemed to decrease with increasing flight duration: 24 days for

TABLE 6
Predicted Effects with Weightlessness

Reduced plasma volume	Decreased exercise capacity
Reduced blood volume	Decreased G tolerance
Electrocardiographic abnormalities	Dysbarism
Syncope after flight	Decreased visual acuity
Tachycardia	Skin infections
Cardiac arrhythmias	Infectious disease
Cardiac failure	Disorientation
Hypertension	Motion sickness
Hypotension	Pulmonary atelectasis
"Break-off" phenomenon	Dehydration
Euphoria	Weight loss
Hallucinations	Anorexia
Impaired psychomotor performance	Nausea
Hyperactivity	Muscular atrophy
Lethargy	Muscular incoordination
Fatigue	Demineralization of bones
Sleepiness	Renal calculi
Sleeplessness	Diuresis
Disruption of circadian rhythms	Urinary retention
	Constipation

a 28-day flight, 5–7 days for a 59-day flight, and 4–5 days for an 84-day flight. Following the Soviet Union's 175-day flight, crews were able to walk immediately and were playing tennis 5 days after landing, thus confirming this trend.

General Weightlessness

Early flights in Mercury, Gemini, Vostok, and Voshkod spacecraft posed the question of whether any of the physiologic changes observed were due to confinement in the small craft or were the result of exposure to weightlessness. Later flights in larger Apollo, Skylab, Soyuz, and Salyut spacecraft confirmed that the observed findings were the result of exposure to null gravity, or weightlessness.

Histories taken from astronauts and cosmonauts have revealed a general sense of enjoyment and well-being in the weightless state. All have been impressed with the reduced effort required for ordinary activity and have used the weightlessness for such conveniences as leaving a camera floating while engaged in another task. There are sensations of fullness in the head due to cephalad shifts of the weightless blood and occasional motion sickness associated with the freedom of movement in this peculiar environment. "Up" and "down" are related only to the placement of objects within the spacecraft.

Cardiovascular System

The first system to evidence physiologic change was the *cardiovascular system*. Early predictions had prophesied that the normal (on Earth) hydrostatic pressure gradients in the vascular system would be severely altered when the body became weightless. Indeed, the first sensation astronauts and cosmonauts have reported on exposure to weightlessness in space has been a feeling of fullness in the head, confirmed by a red facial color, facial edema (particularly of the periorbital areas), and congestion of nasal mucous membranes and of the larynx, which results in voice changes that mimic a cold. Superficial veins of the head and neck were also distended. It is postulated that the cephalad shift in blood volume increases the quantity of blood in the thoracic veins. Inflight measurements of the calf circumferences on Skylab flights confirmed a loss of blood volume in the lower extremities. The average loss measured from both lower extremities was 1500 ml on equilibration to weightless flight in Skylab. This large volume indicates a contribution from areas other than the intravascular volume, such as lymphatic and interstitial spaces.

These fluid shifts undoubtedly initiate reflex actions to produce physiologic compensatory responses. One of these responses is a decrease in plasma volume (from 8% on a 28-day mission to 16% on an 84-day mission), concomitant weight loss (1–2% in the first few days of flight), and total body water loss (mean, 1.5–2.5%).

The hypothesis of stimulation of a diuresis by the cephalad shift of body fluids has not yet been observed in flight, as the urinary output in the first week actually decreased. Measurements of urine output in the first 24 hours have not been obtained; it remains to be seen what combination of sensible and insensible losses exists.

Orthostatic hypotension was noted early in the immediate postflight state, which has been investigated throughout increased flight durations. On the Skylab flights, a lower body negative pressure (LBNP) device was used to measure the orthostatic tolerance before, after, and during the flight. This is a tanklike structure which encases the lower body from the waist down. An airtight seal at the waist allows the pressure to be decreased by 30, 40, and 50 mmHg. This displaces blood to the lower extremities and creates an environment similar to that of standing in 1 G. Inflight responses were helpful in the prediction of the orthostatic response on return to Earth.

Decreased exercise capacity on the bicycle ergometer, coupled with a marked decrease in cardiac output, was also noted after flight. This is related to pooling of blood in the lower extremities which occurs on return to 1 G. During postflight studies on the Skylab 84-day flight, in which echocardiography was coupled with lower body negative pressure, it was demonstrated that the changes were due to decreased blood volume and not to any inherent defect of the myocardium. All of the cardiac electrical activity, measured in detail by vectorcardiography, has shown no significant alteration. There have been minimal episodes of cardiac arrhythmia, with relative bradycardia in Apollo (one of bigeminal rhythm) and some premature ventricular contractions during or following exercise in flight (3–5,24).

Hematology

There is an observed loss of red cell mass. The mean losses after flight were 9.4%, with individual losses as high as 15, 8.6, and 5.9%, respectively, for the 28-, 59-, and 84-day Skylab missions. Reticulocyte counts were also decreased. Chromium 51-tagged red blood cell studies indicate that there is a bone marrow suppression of red cell production that is self-limited so as not to increase with increasing flight duration. In addition, there appears to be a replacement curve which, after about 40 days of zero G exposure, returns the red cell mass toward "normal" for the flight environment (approximately 5% below preflight levels) (4,5,24).

Neurologic Findings

The most important positive findings have involved the development of motion sickness early in flight by four of nine Skylab crewmen. This had been observed earlier in a number of Apollo astronauts and Soviet cosmonauts. Baseline rotating chair studies were done on all the Skylab crewmen to determine the number of head movements they could make prior to the development of early signs of motion sickness. Prediction of inflight difficulty from these studies was never good, as evidenced by one astronaut, very resistant to motion sickness on the ground-based studies, who became the most susceptible in flight. There are no good predictive tests at this time. Several Skylab astronauts developed "stomach awareness," and some individuals vomited in the early inflight period. This problem responded to oral medication, and adaptation occurred within 7–10 days as the crew developed a marked increase in their tolerance to head movements and rotation. It became virtually impossible to create any symptoms in these individuals at the maximum number of rotations and head movements during the time

they were adapted in flight. On return to 1 G, the crewmen had obvious vestibular disturbance, as evidenced by abnormal gait and a sensation of vertigo which lasted for several days after flight. The threshold tolerance to motion sickness on head movements with rotation also gradually decreased to the preflight baseline. The exact mechanism is not clear, but reduced proprioceptive and otolith inputs during multiple physiologic adjustments to weightlessness all seem to be involved.

An immediate postflight deep tendon hyperreflexia was noted in the Skylab crewmen, which was quantitated in the postflight study (24).

Musculoskeletal Status

Muscular strength and tone have been studied on the longer missions; decreases in both have been noted after 7–10 days in flight. As expected, these have particularly involved the body's antigravity muscles. The amount of loss was decreased by the addition of greater exercise loads in flight. The amount necessary to prevent loss of strength and muscle mass has not been determined. This may be a significant operational factor, for 2 hours of exercise per day has not totally prevented decrements. Electrical stimulation of muscles is in experimental use by the Russians.

Moderate losses of calcium, phosphorus, and nitrogen were noted throughout the Skylab flight. The data from these detailed balance studies indicate that the calcium losses are comparable to those observed in bed rest studies and that the trend is related to the increased flight durations. The rate of loss appears to be roughly 6 g, or about 0.5% of total body calcium per month. A loss of 2% of total body calcium is generally necessary to produce osteoporosis; thus, if the rate of loss were sustained for 4 months (as it was through 84 days), osteoporosis would develop. The loss of calcium has also been studied by bone density measurements of the os calcis. The loss is low, but measurable, and may be predictable through a formula which uses the initial bone mineral content and hydroxyproline levels. Soviet scientists have been using os calcis densitometry studies only in the long-duration flights; the trend seems to be the same through 175 days.

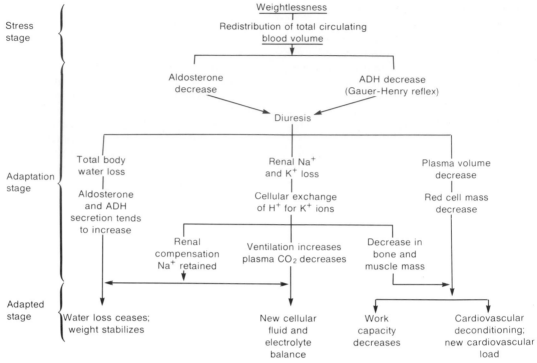

FIGURE 8   Adaptive fluid and electrolyte responses to weightlessness.

Fluid and Electrolytes

It is clear from the Skylab data that there are increases in aldosterone secretion, sodium and potassium excretion, osmolality, and circulating cortisol levels. These changes are consistent in many ways with a hypothesis advanced prior to the skylab flight. This identifies an increase in thoracic blood volume in the weightless state, which acts upon stress receptors in the walls of the great vessels and in the atria (Figure 8). This perceived expansion in blood volume produces a loss of water and electrolytes, particularly sodium. A reduction in blood volume follows, and there is increased secretion of renin, angiotensin, and aldosterone, which leads to the establishment of a new fluid and electrolyte balance, appropriate for the zero G situation. One conflicting data point is that there has been a variable reduction or increase in antidiuretic hormone. Increased inflight excretion of both sodium and potassium occurred, along with absolute increases in aldosterone excretion. The potassium excretion is due to the aldoste-

rone increase; the sodium increase may be due to a functional alteration of the renal tubule proximal to the site of aldosterone action. Increased cortisol levels may reflect stress. All changes in biochemical fluid and electrolyte balance have been well tolerated for the durations of flight thus far undertaken (3–5,18,27).

Psychologic Response

Little has been stated that concerns the psychologic response of space crews. This must be addressed, in view of the public utterances of some of the astronauts. The data show quite clearly that there were no dire effects upon performance; that is, there were no problems with isolation, "breakoff," or boredom. The original crews had strong psyches, good self-images, and great achievement needs and accomplishments. There was some evidence of the development of body consciousness during portions of the Skylab flight, but never to an abnormal degree. Most questions have centered on the Apollo astronauts who visited the moon and then performed activities which appeared out of context with the public's perception of these individuals. In one instance, there was a reactive depression related to demands for public appearances. It was the individual's feeling that the public had reacted in a minor way to an accomplishment of great magnitude. Some astronauts have concentrated on religious pursuits. Another has devoted himself to the study of psychic phenomena and parapsychology. In these instances, the individuals developed their interests prior to flight. It is understandable that an individual who was able to leave Earth's orbit and go to the moon would be greatly affected by the experience. Aerospace scientists who were closely associated with the activity also developed a much deeper concern about the planet Earth, humanity, the space crew, and what could best be done to ensure their future.

The Soviet space medicine scientists have witnessed a definite need by long-duration space crews (175 days) to have contact not only with the flight controllers but also with home, family, and news events on Earth. The cosmonauts have demonstrated the valuable results of such contacts on two prolonged missions.

The almost 80,000 man-hours of null gravity exposure have given us a valuable treasure of negative findings, or lack of adverse effects on many body systems. Table 7 summarizes the significant medical effects of spaceflight.

Emergencies in Space

Possible medical emergencies in space have included symptoms such as nausea and vomiting, diagnoses such as appendicitis, and vari-

TABLE 7
Principal Physiologic Changes in Spaceflight

Body System	Crutch	Countermeasure
Cardiovascular		
Fluid shifts cephalad—sensation of full head and appearance (I)	Exercise	Lower body negative pressure daily for several days before landing
Plasma volume adjustments (I)		
Orthostatic intolerance (P), hypovolemia	Lower extremity positive-pressure garment	
Vestibular		
Otolith disturbance (I)		
Space motion sickness (I)	Medication (Scop-Dex)	None
Disorientation on head movement (P)		
Hematologic		
Decrease in red cell mass (hematocrit) (I)	None	Self-adjusting
Increase toward preflight hematocrit after 40–50 days (I)		
Musculoskeletal		
Decreases in calcium, phosphorus, nitrogen, potassium (I)	Exercise ?"Penguin suit"	? Oral calcium-phosphorus, potassium
Decrease in calf circumference (I)		
Increase in both of the above (P)		
Biochemical		
Aldosterone increase (I)	None	None (adaptive changes)
Sodium increase		
Potassium increase		
Cortisol increase		

I = Inflight.
P = Postflight.

ous injuries. Medication and increased amounts of medical equipment and supplies have been carried as crew size and mission duration have increased. Long-duration crews were given some medical emergency training. Contact with the flight surgeon in the Control Center makes use of the supplies easier when necessary. Although individual reactions to medications have been tested before flight, the physician must always consider the possible changes of medication action in the weightless state and the status of weightless adaptation of the crewman. This would be particularly true should surgery ever be considered in a future space station. Consideration of surgery in weightlessness has led to the development of an enclosure for the patient, with invaginating gloves for the surgeon.

Weightlessness Countermeasures

In spaceflights thus far, we have used preventive measures and devices to protect the crews from adverse system effects which would jeopardize them or the mission. At the same time, data were collected on the extent of physiologic changes with increasing flight durations. Thus, we have basically been using "crutches" rather than true preventive countermeasures.

In order to preclude severe hypotension on standing erect after landing, both U.S. and Soviet crews have effectively used positive-pressure garments on the lower extremities, much like anti-G suits. We have theorized about the use of lower body negative pressure (LBNP) for several days preceding deorbit as a true countermeasure. The Russians have reportedly the successful use of 35 mmHg LBNP for 5 minutes daily several days before deorbit and landing. They have also used salt solution intake (1200–1500 ml of 0.9 normal saline) to increase the circulating fluid volume in the 29 hours prior to return to Earth.

Motion sickness has been treated with a scopolamine (0.35 mg)-dexedrine (5 mg) combination. Transdermal devices can deliver 0.5 mg scopolamine over a 3-day period when the patch is placed on the skin behind the ear. There is no true countermeasure on the horizon.

The calcium loss has been approached by many methods in ground-based studies. The only effective reduction of the loss was an oral combination of calcium and phosphorous. Calcitonin is also being studied. Current work with bed rest patients has shown that etidronate disodium (EDHP) (Didronel, Proctor and Gamble) and dichloromethane diphosphate may possibly prevent osteoporosis over periods of months. The Russians have continued to use a "Penguin" suit in flight. This is a series of bungee cords against which the body must work. It has not been effective in American ground bed rest studies. Skeletal loading by springs and other exercise devices has also been tried. Exercise is probably an effective countermeasure for nitrogen loss. Nearly 2 hours per day seems necessary.

A review of these medical findings and countermeasures (see Table 7) indicates that the significant medical problem for short-duration flights (Shuttle) is space sickness (motion sickness); for long-duration flights (2-year Mars mission), it will be calcium loss.

Early Mars mission plans have called for a 2-year flight duration. The present data on humans in space support the capability to complete such a mission with proper aerospace medical support.

The Space Shuttle cargo bay will carry space laboratories of various types and payloads of up to 33 tons into Earth orbital flight. This vehicle should assist in building orbital operation centers, power plants, and perhaps even colonies where aerospace medicine will become everyday medicine (3–5,27).

Crews, Passengers, and Patients

This section deals with the common aeromedical situations that may be encountered by the primary care or emergency physician.

CREWS

The selection of suitable individuals to fly aircraft is one of the most important tasks of the specialist in aerospace medicine. Presently, this is the responsibility of flight surgeons in the military services, in NASA, and in civil aviation by private aviation medical examiners appointed by the Federal Aviation Administration (FAA).

FAA Classes

There are three classes of civilian airman qualification: class III, student and/or private pilot; class II, commercial (flying for monetary gain other than scheduled passenger airlines); class I, airline transport (scheduled airlines). Of the more than 780,000 active airmen, classes II and III contain approximately 80% of airmen applicants and class I only 20%; 6% of the total population is composed of women (14). In response to the above need, a significant number of physicians are designated as aviation medical examiners (AMEs) by the FAA to perform second- and third-class examinations. They must meet certain training standards and participate in AME continuing medical education seminars at least every 5 years. Some AMEs have volunteered for participation in aircraft accident investigations. A much smaller number of physicians are designated as senior aviation medicine examiners and are qualified to do class I examinations as well as classes II and III. Lists of qualified AMEs in each region, state, and city are available from the FAA Regional Administrators or from the Washington headquarters of the FAA. Each item of pertinent medical history or previous medical treatment may be important in qualifying an examinee, and a physician may be asked for medical documentation on an examinee by an AME for such purposes.

The selection criteria in each of these areas are based on published medical standards (13). Three basic purposes pervade all standards: safety, proficiency, and longevity. Enforcement of physical standards should provide reasonable assurance that qualified candidates have no defects which interfere with their proficiency as safe pilots of either civilian or military aircraft. The selection process should ensure that an individual will be able to pilot an aircraft at peak efficiency under the special stresses of decreased oxygen, changing pressures and temperatures, accelerative forces, and psychologic tension. The physical standards on which selection is based regularly change with the aircraft, the environment, and the expansion of medical knowledge in these areas (6). At one time, it was believed that all cardiac PVCs were indicative of underlying cardiovascular disease and therefore contraindicated a flying clearance. After many years of data collection and experience, it was found that PVCs may be physiologic and are not necessarily a disqualification. In general, physical standards are stricter than necessary in their formulation and become more realistic with use and modification.

Periodic Flying Examination

Selection and annual examinations of airmen are directed at the prediction of incapacitating disease, particularly cardiovascular disease (which accounts for more than 50% of all deaths in the United States). Numerous physiologic risk factors and less well-defined career risk factors may be helpful in predicting and maintaining aircrew health.

The medical examination for flight duty, whether performed for military or civilian pilots, is a standard physical examination. In order of decreasing frequency, the most common causes for disqualification are cardiovascular disease, neuropsychiatric disorders, visual and ophthalmologic disorders, and miscellaneous problems (endocrine or metabolic disorders, medication, general systemic problems, etc. (14).

Many diseases that are innocuous on the ground may become exacerbated in flight and hamper the safe execution of flying duties. The common cold can cause edematous mucous membranes which prevent pressure equalization in the sinuses and middle ears. The pain from a sinus or ear block, barosinusitis, or barotitis could easily cause a pilot to lose control of an aircraft. Even if the pain of a barotitis is tolerable, the pressure differential may cause vertigo and loss of aircraft control. Certain respiratory illnesses are well tolerated at sea level; however, the reduced partial pressure of oxygen at altitude could result in life-threatening hypoxia. This is particularly the case in unpressurized aircraft and is even a potential danger in pressurized airliners, where the usual cabin altitude is between 6000 and 8000 feet when flying at 40,000 feet. Minor diseases and injuries to the eyes may interfere with normal vision or depth perception and therefore compromise safety. Orthopedic injuries to either upper or lower extremities can interfere with normal operation of aircraft controls by the hands and feet. Such injuries could also endanger the pilot if emergency egress from the aircraft were required. Injuries that prevent the wearing of safety equipment such as shoulder and lap belts or oxygen masks must also be considered.

Medications

In general, the use of any medication by air crewmen while performing flying duties is contraindicated. The inflight use of medication by pilots requires knowledge of the drug's effect on the specific individual (not population generalizations), the drug's action in the flight environment, and the interval between the last dose of the drug and the resumption of flying duties (10,12,16,26,28).

Of even greater importance is the pathophysiology of the underlying illness. The discussion that follows examines different classes of drugs and their general compatability with flying. The side effects discussed are not all inclusive, but are the ones of most concern in the aviation environment.

The most commonly treated group of illnesses is upper respiratory infections. Generally, antihistamines, decongestants, or combinations of these are contraindicated in flying. The antihistamine's major side effect is drowsiness, and that of systemic decongestants can be central nervous system (CNS) stimulation. The simple nonnarcotic expectorants are safe as long as consideration is given to the severity of the underlying illness. The moderate use of locally acting nasal decongestants is allowed *as long as the crew member is still able to equalize pressure in his ears and sinuses.* Analgesics, such as aspirin and acetaminophen, are considered generally safe, although excessive aspirin use may cause acute gastrointestinal distress and possible bleeding. The use of narcotic analgesics precludes any flying duties, due to CNS depression and drowsiness. A 24-hour period from last use to control of an aircraft is recommended for these drugs. Topical agents, such as steroids or antibiotic creams and ointments, are also believed to be safe, but local allergic reactions must be considered. The primary concerns with antibiotic use are the early (anaphylactic) and late allergic reactions. To varying degrees, antibiotics can cause nausea, vomiting, and diarrhea. A specific adverse effect of sulfanilamide is a

marked decrease in tolerance to hypoxia (26,28). Except in cases of prophylactic use, the underlying illness will usually preclude flying.

With respect to gastrointestinal medications, antacids are generally considered safe. However, if straight sodium bicarbonate is used, the production of CO_2 in the intestines may cause severe difficulty with gaseous expansion at altitude (26). Antidiarrheics and antiemetics are both contraindicated in flying due to the CNS effects; however, the illness itself should prevent a pilot from flying. Sedatives, hypnotics, and tranquilizers are incompatible with the safe control of aircraft. Some of these medications have extremely long half-lives, due to active metabolites. With drugs such as diazepam and meprobamate, 2 weeks should elapse before resumption of flying duties. Sympathetic and parasympathetic stimulants or depressants are contraindicated due to their CNS and cardiovascular side effects, and generally require 24 hours after cessation of their use before resumption of flying. Cardiovascular illnesses, as well as the medications used to treat them, are generally not compatible with pilot duties. One exception to this rule is any thiazide diuretic used to treat essential hypertension. After an adequate symptom-free test period, a pilot taking such a medication will usually be allowed to return to flying duty. The β blocker propranolol, at a dose of 40 mg daily, has recently been approved by the FAA for use in flying in a few selected patients with hypertension. Hormonal agents must be considered individually in terms of their effect. Insulin, insulin substitutes, or stimulants are contraindicated due to the severity of symptoms from either over- or underdose. Thyroid replacement is acceptable for use while flying after adequate control has been demonstrated with no side effects. Estrogens and birth control pills also are acceptable after an initial side effect-free test period.

The use of a general or local anesthetic usually requires a minimum of 24 hours before resumption of duties, due to possible allergic reactions. The underlying reason for the anesthesia will usually preclude return to flying duties for a longer period. Immunizations generally require 24 hours of grounding to preclude possible allergic or severe systemic reactions. The reception of blood or blood products requires a minimum of 72 hours before the resumption of duties. Here again, the underlying illness itself will usually require a longer period of grounding. The donation of blood also requires 72 hours before flying duties are resumed in order to achieve plasma volume return. Table 8 summarizes the important information on medications.

To the treating physician, it may appear that the pilot should know when he should or should not fly. This is usually not the case, and the knowledgeable physician should always counsel the pilot-patient. The two considerations in determining fitness to fly are the underlying illness and the drug used to treat it. When there is any doubt in the mind of the physician, flying with a medication or an illness should be discouraged.

PASSENGERS

Physicians are often confronted with the evaluation of an individual's fitness to fly as a passenger. To answer such a question, one must understand the natural environment and the internal aircraft environment. With increased altitude, the total pressure and amount of available oxygen decrease. Flight in unpressurized aircraft exposes the passengers and crew to the ambient pressure at the flight altitude. Some pressurized aircraft are capable of maintaining a sea-level pressure, regardless of their flight altitude. Others, such as military high-performance jets, maintain a set differential with the ambient pressure. Most airline cabins maintain a 5:1 or 6:1 ratio with the ambient altitude pressure (a 6000- to 8000-foot pressure equivalent. Some aircraft cabins, however, might reach a cabin altitude of 10,000 feet. Therefore, most airline travel involves reduced total pressure and reduced partial pressure of oxygen. In addition, due to the altitude and the manner of replenishing the cabin environment, the humidity level is extremely low. Temperature is usually not a factor, because this is easily controlled. However, there have been numerous instances of undue exposure to heat and humidity in aircraft on the ground at terminals, and to cold in flight. Passengers should notify attendants of temperature difficulties.

In addition to purely environmental factors, there are passenger-related factors such as apprehension. This may be caused by exposure to a new mode of travel, changes in engine noise, or the story of a recent airline disaster. Turbulence may contribute to increased apprehension and possible motion or air sickness.

Minor illnesses influence the advisability of flying. A passenger with a head cold or sinus infection should be warned about the pressure changes and instructed how to equalize pressure in the middle ear with the Valsalva maneuver. The use of a local nasal decongestant prior to takeoff and landing may also help, but if possible, travel by air should be postponed. Passengers with upper respiratory infections should be warned of the lowered partial pressure of oxygen and the lower humidity, and should be advised to remain well hydrated if they must travel. The acute onset of unilateral ear pain, tinnitus, hearing loss, and vertigo may indicate oval window rupture. See Chapter 6 for a further discussion. Gastroenteritis with increased intestinal gas may be aggravated by the gaseous distention experienced at the lower pressure of 8000 feet (28). Passengers who have been scuba diving should receive proper warning. The exposure to reduced pressure within 24 hours after diving could easily induce evolved gas symptoms at cabin altitudes of 8000 feet, particularly if the cabin pressure cannot be maintained (17). The physician may be asked about the dangers of flying while pregnant. The decreased pressure or decreased oxygen has not been shown to have any detrimental effect upon the developing fetus. The only real danger is travel during the ninth month and the possibility of delivery in the air. If possible, the pregnant passenger should select a rear-facing seat (generally safer on impact) and should use the lap belt loosely across the legs only. She should also be warned of possible gas expansion in the gut and the possibility of dyspnea. False labor contractions following flying in the ninth month are not uncommon (7,21).

A physician who travels on an airliner should be aware that most airlines provide no medical equipment or supplies. There are current discussions among the FAA, the American Medical Association (AMA), and the airlines concerning this subject.

TABLE 8
Medications

Drug Type	Use While Flying		Undesirable Effects in Aviation	Time from Cessation to Flying
	Safe	Unsafe		
Antihistamines (alone or in combination)		X	Drowsiness, possible CNS stimulation; *note:* low-dose pseudoephedrine generally considered acceptable	24 hours
Analgesics				
Potent nonnarcotic		X	CNS depression, drowsiness	12–24 hours
Narcotic		X	CNS depression, drowsiness	12–24 hours
Aspirin/ acetaminophen	X		Possible GI effects should be considered	
Antibiotics	X		Reason for use often precludes flying; immediate allergic reaction or possible GI effects should be considered	—
Antacids	X		Generally safe except for possibility of masking severe GI distress	—
Barbiturates		X	CNS depression, drowsiness	24 hours
Cough mixtures				
Nonnarcotic	X		Underlying illness considered	—
Narcotic		X	CNS depression, drowsiness	24 hours
Antidiarrheics (Diphenoxylate, loperamide, paregoric)		X	Most common opiates and barbiturates which are contraindicated as above; *kaolin/pectin* alone is acceptable	24 hours
Antiemetic		X	CNS depression, drowsiness, allergic reaction	24 hours
Anesthetics				
General		X	Prolonged CNS depression	24 hours
Local or block		X	Possible allergic reaction	12 hours
Mood-changing drugs (Sedatives, hypnotics tranquilizers)		X	Mood alteration, CNS depression or stimulation, drowsiness; *note:* diazepam and meprobamate require 2 weeks before flying	24 hours–2 weeks
Topical decongestants	X		Generally safe, although some CNS stimulation may occur	—
Cardiovascular				
Antiarrythmics		X	Disease and use of drug prohibited with flying due to possible cardiac problems	
Antihypertensives				
Thiazides	X		After a 2–3 month symptom-free trial period	—
Propranolol	X		Recently approved by FAA in low doses of up to 40 mg/day; same guidelines as above	—

(continued)

TABLE 8 (*Continued*)

Drug Type	Use While Flying Safe	Use While Flying Unsafe	Undesirable Effects in Aviation	Time from Cessation to Flying
Other antihypertensives		X	Cardiac effects	—
Muscle relaxants		X	CNS depression	24 hours
Immunizations		X	Allergic reactions	24 hours
Blood donation		X	Due to depressed hematocrit	72 hours
Receiving blood or blood products		X	Allergic reaction; underlying illness usually precludes flying	72 hours
Steroids		X	Underlying illness usually procludes flying; CNS effects; topical steroids acceptable	24 hours

PATIENTS

Air transport of patients is commonplace. Acutely ill or injured patients are moved to emergency medical centers; stabilized patients are transported to definitive care centers; and recovering patients return to their homes by air. Military physicians have dealt with the aeromedical transportation of patients for more than 20 years; however, private physicians have only recently been offered this option. Air ambulance and emergency helicopter transport is now available in most major cities, and physicians who plan to utilize this means of transportation must understand its benefits and limitations. The sophistication of aircraft today allows the transport of many patients who were previously unacceptable. Basically, any patient believed to be transportable by any means may be transported by air as long as the proper support facilities are available (7). The physician should consider the decreased total pressure and consequent decreased partial pressure of oxygen. The low humidity and decreased cabin temperatures of many aircraft must be taken into account. The psychologic effects of noise and possible turbulence on the ill or injured patient, as well as the occurrence of motion sickness, must be considered. Aircraft with an alternating current (AC) power source for operation of medical equipment, humidified oxygen with a flow meter, litters anchored to the aircraft and stressed to the same G requirements as the aircraft, communication among pilot, attendant, and ground crew, and adequate lighting in the area of the litter are desirable.

Few regulations or even guidelines exist for air ambulance enterprises. The FAA has no regulations to cover the minimum support facilities required or the quality of medical care provided. All that is controlled is the air worthiness of the aircraft and its registration as an air ambulance. Consequently, the variation ranges from a pilot with an unpressurized aircraft, without a litter or room for an attendant, to the Air Force C-9A Nightingale, which is as well equipped as any modern hospital intensive care unit and can maintain a sea-level cabin pressure (28). It is the responsibility of the physician to know what support facilities are required and what is available on the transporting aircraft. Some air ambulance operations have physician consultants who are knowledgeable in aeromedical transportation of patients.

Helicopter transport is generally used intracity for its speed in getting a patient from an accident site to a medical treatment center. Fixed-wing transport is used intercity, interstate, or internationally to move patients for their convenience or to specialized care centers. Patient support considerations should be the same for either type of aircraft. However, there are some special considerations when helicopter transport is used. There is limited cockpit size and attendant access, depending on the type of helicopter, and the noise level is usually much greater than in fixed-wing aircraft. The helicopter is generally a fair weather aircraft. Instrument flying capability in clouds or fog is greatly limited.

Jetliners cruise at altitudes of 28,000–45,000 feet and are pressurized with atmospheric air to a differential of approximately 8.6 psi above ambient external pressure (1a). Thus, cabin pressure at 40,000 feet is equivalent to atmospheric pressure at 7500 feet. This factor is related to the partial pressure of oxygen (ppO$_2$), which corresponds to the equivalent at any given altitude. For example, at an aircraft altitude of 40,000 feet, the atmospheric pressure is 2.72 psi or 140 mmHg. With mechanical pressurization of 8.6 psi, the effective cabin pressure is 11.32 psi. This corresponds to an effective altitude of approximately 7500 feet, where the atmospheric ppO$_2$ would be 120 mmHg, the alveolar pressure of oxygen (pO$_2$) 65 mmHg, and the arterial pO$_2$ 60 mmHg.

Cardiovascular Diseases

Patients with reduced cardiac reserve or pulmonary dysfunction may not tolerate the relative hypoxia found at normal aircraft cabin altitudes. At altitudes above 22,500 feet, supplemental oxygen should be available. Once the need to move a patient has been established, there are few reasons that will preclude such transport. Humidified oxygen supplied by well-fitting masks and at flow rates that compensate for the reduced ambient oxygen must be supplied continuously. The nasal cannula supply is not adequate. Commercial airline standard masks do not exceed 4 liters/minute; therefore, an alternate must be supplied.

The American College of Chest Physicians has recommended guidelines on the transport of patients with cardiorespiratory disease. These limits apply to the actual flight altitude when considering unpressurized aircraft or the cabin altitude when considering pressurized aircraft.

1. *10,000 feet (3048 m)*: Any patient with symptomatic cardiorespiratory disease.
2. *8000 feet (2438 m)*: Patients with more than mildly symptomatic cardiorespiratory disease or marked ventilatory restriction.
3. *6000 feet (1829 m)*: Patients with recent myocardial infarction (8–24 weeks), angina pectoris, sickle cell disease, cyanosis, cor pulmonale, or respiratory acidosis. Oxygen should be available for all of these patients.
4. *4000 feet (1219 m)*: Patients with severe cardiac disease with cyanosis, or emphysema with cyanosis, unless continuous oxygen is available.
5. *2000 feet (610 m)*: Patients in cardiac failure or any myocardial infarction within 8 weeks of occurrence (8,9).

The restrictions, based on the acuteness of a myocardial infarct, should not be considered absolute. They are very conservative and do not take into consideration the variation in severity or speed of recovery. The major limitation to consider when transporting a patient with an infarct is the availability of adequate oxygen (25,28).

Hypertension in itself is not a contraindication, unless accompanied by other limiting cardiovascular disease. Long flights with immobilization may predispose some patients to the development of phlebitis.

Pulmonary Diseases

In addition to the previous guidelines, a decreased vital capacity to less than 50% of the predicted value should require continuous inflight oxygen. A better predictor is a sea-level arterial oxygen saturation of less than 90% (28).

Asthma that is controlled is not a contraindication to transport by air. Untreated pneumothorax, with free air in the chest, is a definite contraindication due to the gas expansion experienced at decreased barometric pressure. Any respiratory disease with increased secretions may be complicated by increased viscosity of these secretions, due to the low humidity found in aircraft atmospheres.

Hematologic Diseases

Patients with sickle cell disease are at risk of crisis due to the lowered oxygen partial pressure at altitude. Theoretically, a patient with sickle trait could also have a crisis, even at the low cabin altitudes of airliners. Reported cases, however, are few. In cases of anemia, it is recommended that patients with a hemoglobin of less than 8.5 g or a red blood cell count below 3 million cells per milliliter should have continuous oxygen while in flight (21,25,28). Hemophilia is a relative contraindication.

Ophthalmologic Disorders

Certain ophthalmologic conditions contraindicate the stress of hypoxia, or gas expansion. The injured or postsurgical eye may contain air in the anterior chamber. The gas expansion, even at a cabin altitude of 8000 feet, could be serious. Hypoxia at 10,000 feet produces measurable dilatation of the retinal and choroidal vessels, a rise in intraocular tension, and a decrease in pupil diameter. All of these can have adverse effects in the postsurgical or injured eye. The retina has the highest oxygen demand of any body tissue. Therefore, patients with eye conditions that affect the retina should be kept at cabin altitudes between sea level and 4000 feet (7, 22,28).

Gastrointestinal Disorders

Patients who have had gastrointestinal surgery are in potential danger from gas expansion. The intestine always harbors some gas and ordinarily handles its expansion by oral or rectal elimination. Occasionally, spasm or other functional obstruction renders this gas elimination difficult or impossible, and the intestine becomes distended. This is not desirable in acute abdominal or postsurgical cases. A 10-day delay between surgery and air transportation is suggested. Patients with perforated ulcers have continued peritoneal leakage, and this must be weighed against the potential benefit of transport. Patients who have had a colostomy should be warned of the gas expansion problem and advised to use larger colostomy bags during flight (22,25).

Orthopedic Disorders

Casted patients may require special consideration. A total body cast covering the abdomen may restrict abdominal gas expansion. Recently applied casts should be bivalved to allow for edema that might occur on a long flight. Patients in traction may be transported,

but changes in weight should be anticipated during possible turbulence and the accelerative forces of takeoff and landing. Spring-type traction apparatus is preferred in these cases. Air splints are easily transported but must be watched for expansion at altitude. Some of these splints have automatic relief valves.

Miscellaneous

Patients receiving intravenous fluids must be watched for sudden fluid surges with changes in cabin pressure. Pregnancy beyond 240 days is a relative contraindication (1a).

Any patient who has had a neurologic air study of the brain should not fly until all the air has been replaced with fluid, preferably not within 72 hours of the study. Patients with fractures of the mandible and wired jaws should not fly unless a rapid release mechanism exists in the wiring. If motion sickness and vomiting develop, aspiration could easily occur. Psychiatric patients may fly safely as long as the safety of other patients or passengers is considered. Epilepsy may worsen or become manifest at higher altitudes, probably due to a combination of apprehension, hyperventilation, and hypoxia.

Epidemiology

With the accessibility of air travel, once rare diseases in certain parts of the world have been seen in new settings. It is possible for the private physician to be confronted with a case of malaria, cholera, plague, typhus, or yellow fever. The rapid transit of servicemen between Vietnam and the United States, for instance, has introduced falciparum and lesser types of malaria and penicillin-resistant gonorrhea. The examining physician should always elicit a travel history, particularly in patients with confusing pictures of apparently infectious diseases. The physician who treats a patient with an infectious disease should also discourage any air travel while the patient is still infectious.

Accident Investigation and Prevention

Determination of the cause of aircraft accidents is of prime importance to the practice of aviation medicine. Specialists in aviation medicine emerged as a result of the unacceptable airplane accident rate of U.S. pilots in World War I. Accidents can be prevented only with knowledge of their causes, which requires medical participation in the investigation. In the military, this is a formalized process, and flight surgeons are trained to perform in this role. The FAA also has a formal investigative process that usually involves the aviation medical examiner. However, the AME may not be specifically trained for this role and is usually not the first physician at the scene of an accident. The first medical person at the scene of an accident will most likely be an emergency medical technician from an ambulance service, and the first notification of an accident may be when injured or dead persons arrive in the emergency room. The first order of business at the scene of an accident is the medical care and safety of the survivors. Second, consideration should be given to the medical aspects of the accident investigation, which are addressed in detail in the FAA Handbook *Aviation Medicine Participation in Aircraft Accident Investigations* (8025.1) (15). The following section summarizes the important considerations.

The major objective of the aeromedical portion of the accident investigation is the determination of possible pilot incapacitation as a primary or contributing cause of the accident. Several specific types of pilot incapacitation are spatial disorientation (vertigo), acute myocardial infarction, cerebrovascular accident, carbon monoxide or other toxic substance poisoning, hypoxia, alcohol intoxication, fatigue or hangover, and drug reaction. The time of death of the pilot is extremely important in the determination of possible incapacitation. A major safety consideration is the source of all incurred injuries. With fatalities, this is often best determined when the bodies are still in the aircraft. If they must be moved, photographs should be taken. This allows investigators to relate structure to injury. Recommendations may then be made for safety equipment and perhaps even aircraft design. Accurate identification and location of all bodies and parts are extremely important.

Autopsy of dead persons in general aviation accidents is important. Tissue, blood, and urine samples for toxicologic studies are ob-

tained before embalming. A general x-ray survey of the body is desirable to locate fractures missed on gross examination. The autopsy order is usually made by the coroner or medical examiner, but can also be ordered under the auspices of Public Law 87-810, which allows the procedure to be performed under federal statutes. Autopsy and toxicologic study expenses are covered by the FAA through the office of the Regional Flight Surgeon.

Certain material should be collected during the autopsy and forwarded for study to the Civil Aeromedical Institute (CAMI), FAA, in Oklahoma City:

1. Blood—20 ml or more (specify source of blood)
2. Urine—100 ml
3. Organs—50–100 g of liver, kidney, spleen, lung, muscle, brain
4. Gastric contents—100 ml
5. Drugs—on the person or in the wreckage

Even though the emergency physician will not usually investigate the accident, there are certain items he can carry to facilitate the investigation if he is first on the scene. Following is a list of FAA-recommended equipment for medical investigation of an aircraft accident:

1. Six sterile 10–20-ml screw-cap test tubes with 0.1 g sodium fluoride/10 ml
2. Three sterile syringes, 20 ml
3. Four no. 18 long needles and two no. 20 spinal needles
4. One surgical knife and blade
5. Two urinary catheters
6. Plastic bags (Baggies) and a supply of rubber bands
7. Camera, film, and flash equipment (35 mm color)
8. Paper and clipboard for taking notes
9. Appropriate clothing for the weather and site of the accident

Aviation Organizations

There are a number of agencies and organizations that are concerned with aviation, space, and their medical aspects.

FEDERAL AVIATION ADMINISTRATION (FAA)

The FAA, previously called the Federal Aviation Agency, is part of the Department of Transportation. It has the responsibility of regulating air commerce for the purpose of aviation safety. As part of this responsibility, the FAA regulates the national system of airports and maintains a common system of air traffic control and air navigation for both civilian and military aircraft. The FAA has the responsibility for medical certification of civilians to fly, which is accomplished through the aviation medical examiner (AME). The AME is a physician designated by the FAA Regional Flight Surgeon to perform FAA medical certification examinations.

NATIONAL TRANSPORTATION SAFETY BOARD (NTSB)

The NTSB is an independent agency of the federal government, and is composed of five members appointed by the president. Its primary job is to ensure the safety of all types of transportation in the United States. It investigates accidents and conducts safety studies, thereby making recommendations to other government agencies and the transportation industry. It is also responsible for promoting the safe transport of hazardous materials by both the government and private industry. The only medical relationships with the NTSB are in the area of aircraft accident investigation.

CIVIL AERONAUTICS BOARD (CAB)

The CAB is an independent regulatory agency which was established in 1938 by the Civil Aeronautics Act. The Airline Deregulation Act of 1978 altered the responsibility of the board, reduced its regulatory powers, and directed that it be abolished on January 1, 1985. At present, it is responsible for the promotion and regulation of the civil air transport industry within the United States and between the United States and foreign countries. The board grants authorization to U.S. air carriers to engage in interstate and foreign commerce. It also authorizes foreign air carriers to engage in air transportation between foreign countries and the United States. The board approves or disapproves proposed rates and fares, and proposed agreements or corporate relation-

ships between air carriers. The CAB has no direct or indirect medical responsibilities.

NATIONAL AERONAUTICS AND SPACE ADMINISTRATION (NASA)

NASA was established by the National Aeronautics and Space Act in 1958. The principal responsibility of NASA is to conduct research for the solution of problems of flight *within* and *outside* the earth's atmosphere, and to conduct all activities required for both manned and unmanned exploration of space. In addition, it is responsible for the effective utilization of U.S. resources in concert with other nations for the peaceful exploration of space. NASA has a headquarters in Washington, D.C., and 11 separate field installations. Two of the field installations, the Lyndon B. Johnson Space Center and Ames Research Center, have major life sciences and medical responsibilities.

INTERNATIONAL CIVIL AVIATION ORGANIZATION (ICAO)

The ICAO is often viewed as the international counterpart of the FAA. It is a specialized agency of the United Nations and was created in 1944. The purposes of the ICAO are to develop principles and techniques of international air navigation, to foster planning and development of international air transport, to encourage the design and operation of planes for peaceful purposes, and to meet the needs of the peoples of the world for safe, regular, efficient, and economical air transport. There is a medical section that coordinates the development of mutual medical standards, examination techniques, and aviation medical policies.

DEPARTMENT OF DEFENSE (DOD)

The DOD is mentioned here only as an agency concerned with aviation. All of the military services are involved with aviation to some degree. The promotion of safety, accident investigation, and medical support is a responsibility of each service. Aviation within the military services is internally regulated and fairly autonomous, except where involvement with civil aviation is concerned.

AEROSPACE MEDICAL ASSOCIATION (ASMA)

This is a professional society established in 1929 and originally called the Aero Medical Association. Most of its original 60 members were former military flight surgeons, some were pilots, and all were interested in the future of aviation. At that time, the primary medical concern was the physical qualification of new pilots. Members of this association have been instrumental in advancing aviation and aerospace medicine. The professional journal of the association, *Aviation, Space, and Environmental Medicine,* is the world's oldest continuously published periodical in aerospace medicine and the most influential in the field of aerospace medicine. In 1953, aviation (later aerospace) medicine became a recognized subspecialty of medicine under the control of the American Board of Preventive Medicine. The Aerospace Medical Association consists of the national experts in the field of aerospace medicine. The association's headquarters is located in Washington, D.C.

INTERNATIONAL ACADEMY OF AVIATION AND SPACE MEDICINE (IAASM)

The IAASM was founded in 1955 to promote and develop research in aviation and space medicine, and to facilitate international cooperation among physicians dedicated to this field. Membership is limited to an electorate of 250 based on their contributions to and eminence in the field. The secretariat currently is located in London.

OTHERS

The International Air Transport Association (IATA) is an organization of international air carriers with an active aviation medical section. The International Astronautical Federation (IAF) (headquartered in Paris) is active in space medicine through its Bioastronautics Committee. The American Institute of Aeronautics and Astronautics (AIAA) (headquartered in New York) has aerospace medical interests (although it is basically an engineering organization), and the Air Line Pilot's Association (ALPA) has been very active in affairs related to pilot medical qualification and length of flying service.

References

1. Benson, O. O., Jr., and Strughold, H. (eds.). *Physics and Medicine of the Atmosphere and Space* (New York: John Wiley & Sons, 1960).
1a. AMA Commission on Emergency Medical Services. *Medical Aspects of Transportation Aboard Commercial Aircraft. JAMA* **247:**7, 1007–1011, Feb 19, 1982.
2. Berry, C. A. Decompression sickness (caisson disease and Dysbarism). In *Traumatic Medicine and Surgery for the Attorney* (Butterworths, London, 1959), Vol. 9, pp. 424–40.
3. Berry, C. A. Medical legacy of Apollo. *Aerospace Medicine,* **45**(9):1045–52, 1974.
4. Berry, C. A. Medical legacy of Skylab as of May 9, 1974: The manned Skylab missions. *Aviation, Space and Environmental Medicine,* **47**(4): 418–24, 1976.
5. Berry, C. A. The current status of man's response to the space environment. In *The Eagle has Returned* (1976), Vol. 43, pp. 165–72.
6. Berry, C. A. The role of physical standards in jet and rocket aircraft flight. *The Journal of Aviation Medicine,* **29:**631–40, September 1958.
7. Berry, C. A. Transport of patients by air. *Texas State Journal of Medicine,* **54:**11–17, January 1958.
8. Committee on Medical Criteria of Aerospace Medical Association. Medical criteria for passenger flying. *Aerospace Medicine,* **32:**369–82, 1961.
9. Committee on Physiologic Therapy. American College of Chest Physicians: Air travel in cardio-respiratory disease. *Diseases of the Chest,* **37:**579–88, 1960.
10. Department of the Air Force. *Flight Surgeon's Guide.* AF Pamphlet No. 161–18 (Washington, D.C., 1962).
11. Department of the Air Force. *Physiology of Flight.* AF Pamphlet No. 160–10–4 (Washington, D.C., 1961).
12. Department of the Navy. *U.S. Naval Flight Surgeon's Manual* (Washington, D.C.: U.S. Government Printing Office, 1968).
13. Department of Transportation. *Guide for Aviation Medical Examiners.* (Federal Aviation Administration, Washington, D.C., June 1970).
14. Department of Transportation. *1980 Aeromedical Certification Statistical Handbook.* AC 8500–1 (Federal Aviation Administration, Civil Aeromedical Institute, Oklahoma).
15. Federal Aviation Administration. *Aviation Medicine Participation in Aircraft Accident Investigations* 8025.1 (Washington, D.C., 1970).
16. Federal Aviation Agency. *Guide to Drug Hazards in Aviation Medicine.* AC 91.11–1 (Washington, D.C.: Government Printing Office, 1962).
17. Fryer, D. I. *Subatmospheric Decompression Sickness in Man. AGARDograph 125* (Technivision Services, Slough, England, April 1969).
18. Gantry, K. F. (ed.). *Man in Space* (New York: Duell, Sloan and Pearce, 1959).
19. Gauer, O. H. and Zuidema, G. D. (eds.). *Gravita-*

tional Stress in Aerospace Medicine (Boston: Little, Brown, 1961).

20. Haber, H. *The Physical Environment of the Flyer* (USAF School of Aviation Medicine, 1954).

21. Johnson, A., Jr. Treatise on aeromedical evacuation I. Administration and some medical considerations. *Aviation, Space and Environmental Medicine,* **48**(6): 546–49, 1977.

22. Johnson, A., Jr. Treatise on aeromedical evacuation II. Some surgical considerations. *Aviation, Space and Environmental Medicine,* **48**(6):550–54, 1977.

23. Johnston, R. S., Dietlein, L. F., and Berry, C. A. (eds.). *Biomedical Results of Apollo* (National Aeronautics and Space Administration, Washington, D.C., 1975).

24. Johnston, R. S. and Dietlein, L. F. (eds.). *Biomedical Results from Skylab* (National Aeronautics and Space Administration, Washington, D.C., 1977).

25. Kimball, F. N. A guide for physicians regarding transportation of the incapacitated by aircraft. *International Record of Medicine,* **173**:20–30, 1960.

26. McFarland, R. A. *Human Factors in Air Transportation* (New York: McGraw-Hill, 1953).

27. National Aeronautics and Space Administration. *Bioastronautics Data Book,* 2d ed. (Washington, D.C., 1973).

28. Randel, H. W. (ed.). *Aerospace Medicine,* 2d ed. (Baltimore: Williams and Wilkins, 1971).

20 | DISASTER PLANNING

Joel Geiderman, M.D., and Paul M. Paris, M.D.

Other chapters of this book discuss emergency medical aspects of such areas as spaceflight, nuclear accidents, burns, smoke inhalation, and heat illness. For most of these conditions, *groups* of individuals, rather than single patients, may be involved: an orbiting Skylab crashes back to earth and lands on a school; 20 workers from a nuclear medicine laboratory are believed to be contaminated; 30 victims of a Las Vegas hotel fire suffer smoke inhalation, while scores more suffer major and minor burns; an Independence Day Parade is held in St. Louis, despite 100°F temperatures and 90% humidity that fell dozens of people. What is common to these scenarios is that they all involve large numbers of individuals and fall into the category of a disaster.

Many of the principles of disaster planning and management may be applied universally to seemingly diverse situations (76,79). The principles presented in this chapter, although often derived from industrial and mass transit incidents, can be applied equally well to natural disasters.

Defining a Disaster

"A disaster is a great sudden misfortune resulting in loss of life, serious injury and property loss. Strictly speaking, if such misfortune befalls even one person, it is a disaster. However, in current usage the term is used to refer to a sudden occurrence which kills and injures a relatively large number of persons" (24). A more functional definition is simply that a disaster is declared when the immediate patient load in the emergency medical services system is greater than that which can be handled by the normal number of personnel (68). Both of the above definitions of disaster are acceptable.

Generally, the sudden presentation of a large number of casualties is considered a disaster, no matter how well the emergency care system is prepared (3). However, a disaster may occur when a relatively small number of patients present to an emergency system that does not have the resources to deal with the situation effectively (13).

The number of victims most frequently used to quantify a disaster is 25 killed or seriously injured individuals. Using this definition, 1300 people have died in disasters every year of this century in the United States, with another 15,000 per year injured (24). Fortunately, the United States has been spared from tremendous disasters. The Bengal cyclone of November 1970 struck on a broad front in a densely populated and impoverished area; the most severely affected area (2000 square miles) had an estimated population of 1.7 million. Overall mortality was estimated at 14%, with a range of 4.7% in Antali to 46% in Tazummuddin; the absolute mortality was estimated at 224,000 (83). In 1962, an earthquake devastated a region in the central plateau of Iran. A total of 150 villages and 150,000 people were in the disaster area, with a resultant 12,000 dead, 1200 seriously injured, and 30,000 homeless (23). Hiroshima, with a population of 3 million, was devastated by a nuclear warhead, with 70,000 dead, 15,000 missing, and 80,000–100,000 injured (47).

Magnitude of Disaster

The magnitude of a disaster can be described as a multiple patient incident, multiple casualty incident, or mass casualty incident.

A *multiple patient incident* is one in which there are fewer than 10 casualties. This is frequently encountered in most facilities as multiple vehicle accidents. Usually, these incidents are well handled without implementing disaster plans. However, even a few seriously in-

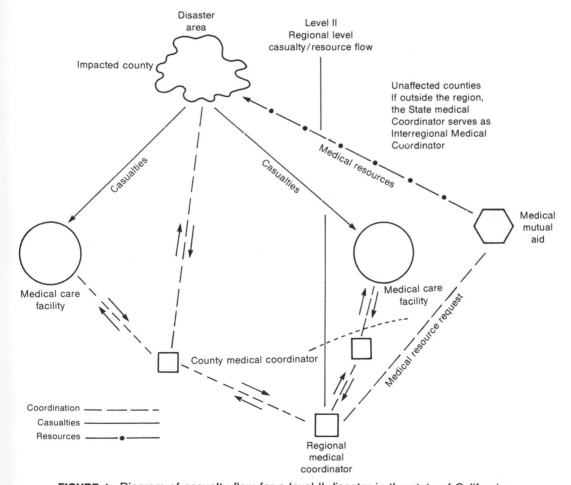

FIGURE 1   Diagram of casualty flow for a level II disaster in the state of California.

jured patients can stress the resources of a small facility, so that special plans must be put into effect. These plans may include calling in additional staff, transferring stabilized patients to other facilities, diverting further ambulance traffic, and the like. In any case, care must frequently be prioritized.

A *multiple casualty incident* is one in which there are 10–100 patients. Although only very minor injuries may be involved, the principles of disaster management (to be discussed later) must be used. These include triage and prioritization of patients, primary transportation of the most critical patients, first aid at the scene, effective use of communications, and control by a central authority.

A *mass casualty incident* involves more than 100 patients. These are the most likely to create panic and confusion, and must be

handled in a systematic fashion (17,18,26,34). Disasters of this magnitude frequently disrupt communications, power, water supply, and other vital services. Therefore, it is necessary for disaster plans to consider backup systems.

Three levels of mass casualty incidents have been described (67). In a level 1 disaster, the local community emergency medical system has adequate resources to provide on-scene triage, emergency first aid and stabilization, and transportation to local facilities capable of handling the patient load. Level 2 disasters are those in which a multicounty (or multicommunity) approach is necessary to deal adequately with the number of victims. A level 3 disaster requires state and/or federal assistance. Diagrams of casualty flow for level 2 and level 3 disasters for the California State Plan are depicted in Figures 1 and 2 (9,14).

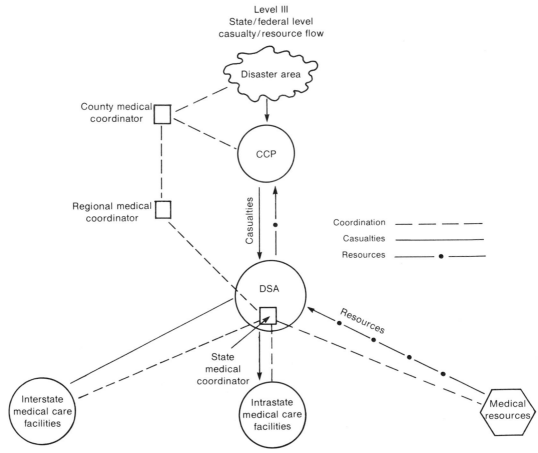

FIGURE 2 Diagram of casualty flow for a level III disaster in the state of California (CCP, casualty collection points; DSA, disaster support area).

TABLE 1
Potential Disasters

Hurricanes
Tornados
Cyclones
Volcanoes
Earthquakes
Floods
Fires
Explosions
Hazardous chemical and gas leaks
Falling aircraft or spacecraft
Exposure to radioactive materials
Riots
Civil disturbances
Wartime attack with conventional weapons
Wartime attack with thermonuclear weapons
Terrorist attacks
Transportation (road, rail, air, water)
Industrial accidents

Disasters are of many sizes and varieties. Table 1 lists some potential disasters (52).

Any community is susceptible to a disaster (62). With increasing numbers of nuclear-generating facilities, high-rise buildings, high-density housing, and terrorist threats, modern society faces increasing odds of experiencing a disaster (5,7). Because the principles of disaster planning apply equally to environmental and technological causes, the information contained herein will pertain to all types of disasters.

Disaster Planning

The purpose of disaster planning is to prevent and minimize mortality, disability, and suffering (41). This can be realized with a well-conceived, practiced, and inclusive disaster plan (67). Each hospital and community must have a plan that allows for the beneficial interplay of all aspects of the disaster team: hospital and paramedical personnel, policemen, firefighters, and the military (2). The plan must be flexible enough to cope with a wide variety of potential disasters.

In preparing a disaster plan, eight principles must be considered (24):

1. Whenever possible, prevent the occurrence of disaster.

2. If the disaster cannot be prevented, minimize the number of casualties.
3. Prevent further casualties after the initial impact of the disaster.
4. Rescue the victims.
5. Provide first aid to the victims.
6. Evacuate the injured to medical installations (59).
7. Administer definitive medical care.
8. Promptly reconstruct the lives of the victims.

"Disaster plans strive to set in motion a chain of events in response to an event that is unpredictable. Even with detailed rehearsals under the most realistically contrived circumstances, one can never be fully assured that a disaster plan will stand up" (42). This was demonstrated on May 6, 1975, when Omaha, Nebraska, was struck by the most devastating tornado to hit southeast Nebraska in a century. Although the twister killed only three persons in a city of 375,000, it involved more property destruction than any other in this nation's history. The need for flexibility in a disaster plan was highlighted by Archbishop Began Mercy Hospital, which suffered damage to the Emergency Room entrance, with power lines strewn across the emergency driveway. The disaster plan at this hospital included provisions for a second receiving area, which was the key to this hospital's success in handling this disaster (42).

For the successful operation of a hospital disaster plan, there are several essentials (63):

1. There must be provision for control of traffic at the entrances to the hospital grounds and buildings, the unloading area, and within the hospital, with the exclusion of vehicles and personnel not authorized to be in those areas immediately concerned with the unloading and triage of casualties.
2. There must be viable means of radio communication with central authorities and with other hospitals. Within the hospital, there must be dependable methods of communication between essential points: telephones, intercommunication speaker systems, and runners.
3. Competent, experienced personnel should be in charge at the triage point and available for immediate special assignment.
4. The supplies for emergency use to be kept ready in admitting or in the emergency area include the following:
   a. Hospital disaster maps showing the location of all emergency service areas.

b. Direction cards with arrows pointing to specific emergency services.
c. Prenumbered emergency medical tags in duplicate.
d. Emergency clinical records and hospital record jackets.
e. Clipboards for the admitting log or master casualty list (which is in triplicate).
f. Clipboard for the disposition or discharge log (which is in triplicate).
5. A tagging system should be established in order to attach important information to each casualty soon after his admission. This information includes the patient's name, address, time of arrival, tentative diagnosis, and time and nature of therapy.
6. The plan should be established around a few key positions necessary for the successful performance of the professional and administrative functions of the hospital when handling an unusual volume of casualties. It is important that available personnel be trained to fill key posts on short notice, and that performances of necessary functions not await the arrival of any one person. If positions are temporarily filled by junior personnel in an actual emergency, senior members of the staff can relieve the juniors as they arrive.
7. Assignment of personnel not involved directly in the central planning and operation of the hospital organization should be carried out through a central controlling point. As such persons are assigned to tasks, they are given limited, special responsibility and are expected to stay with the task until relieved or otherwise assigned.
8. General obedience to policy with regard to medical management as set down by key hospital personnel should be unquestioned under disaster conditions. To attain this level of obedience requires considerable indoctrination of most medical personnel. Under disaster conditions, the treatment of the injured will be based on the general principles that (a) adequate measures to combat shock will be instituted, (b) contaminated wounds should be handled by debridement and preparation for delayed closure, and (c) elective surgical procedures should be postponed.
9. There should be plans for the evacuation of patients already in the hospital so that space can be made available for casualties. Evacuation should be timed to minimize interference with the care of incoming casualties.
10. An adequate stock of supplies should always be on hand in the hospital, and sources of supplementary supplies should be readily available. Careful plans for replenishing supplies should be made, with coordination of these plans with other hospitals in the area.
11. Information should be made available to the public through official representatives of the hospital; an information center with its own means of outside communication is the best agency to carry this out. Such a center should not be located at the telephone switchboard and should be removed from the main channels of patient flow. Information gathering is aided by a system of duplicate tagging at the triage point, one record to be sent to the information center and the other to go with the patient.
12. Crowds of relatives, volunteers, the press, and blood donors must be prevented from interfering with the activities of the hospital. Bleeding of donors should be done at a site far from the areas in which patients are placed, and no blood should be drawn if this activity cannot be carried out effectively without hampering other functions of the hospital, or if facilities for handling and storing blood are inadequate.
13. Relatives seeking to view the unidentified dead and injured should be permitted access to the morgue in the company of a hospital representative. An available area for storage of the dead should be designated in advance; refrigeration is desirable.
14. The physical facilities of the hospital must be equipped and staffed for operation under disaster conditions. Auxiliary sources of power are essential. Elevator service must be reliable and should be controlled by operators.
15. The possibility of damage to the hospital itself must be anticipated; therefore, each institution must have both an external disaster plan for disasters occurring in the community and an internal disaster plan for those that occur within the hospital. Internal hospital plans require an in-depth study of normal hospital plant operations because many of these disasters will disrupt several of the hospital services.

The hospital plan should be developed by a committee who will be in charge of implementing the provisions if a disaster strikes. Functions of the committee include (24):

1. Preparation of the hospital plan
2. Coordination of the plan with existing community plans for disaster relief action
3. Assignment of responsibilities to each hospital department for programming emergency actions
4. Assignment of the functions, responsibilities, and tasks for each office for implementing the plan
5. Formulation of emergency care standards, with

FIGURE 3 "Anything that can go wrong will." Ambulances lie crushed under parking structure during Sylmar earthquake of 1971.

a view to avoiding errors, lost time, and duplicated effort

6. Development and supervision of training programs designed to ensure correct action in case of emergency
7. Organization and supervision of mock exercises to test various portions of the plan
8. Periodic review and updating of the plan
9. Forethought to the options available in the event of damage to the building's physical structure

Internal Disaster Planning

In planning for internal disasters, each hospital must keep in mind that anything that can go wrong, will (Figure 3). In July 1977, New York City was faced with a complete electricity disruption which forced local hospitals to use emergency generators for their power. The Jewish Hospital of Brooklyn and the Bellevue Hospital of Manhattan both had failures in their generating systems, leaving them without power (22). Neither hospital had ever considered the possibility of operating in total darkness or how to obtain power during generator failure. At Lee Hospital in Johnstown, Pennsylvania, a 1977 flood swept through the hospital basement, destroying many electrical systems and disrupting the telephone service. The damage rendered the emergency department entirely unusable (22). Not many disaster plans consider the internal disruption of power or communication, and are thus inadequate (56).

Action Cards

Despite disaster drills, there will be many hospital personnel who are unfamiliar with or who forget their duties because of the stress of the situation. To offset this reaction, each hospital disaster plan should include a set of action cards which describe the duties of each individual (66). These cards also allow previously untrained staff to assume roles without prior training. Each department within the hospital should have its own set of cards, and a master set should be included in the hospital disaster plan. Examples of cards used at the Cedars-Sinai Medical Center in Los Angeles are demonstrated in Figure 4. Multiple sets of action cards should be visible throughout the hospital in accessible locations.

Postdisaster Planning

An important feature of state and community disaster plans is the preparation for postdisaster cleanup and reinstitution of vital services. State and local plans must consider the management of disaster-related factors in the aftermath of the impact: vector-borne disease control, sanitation, relocation of survivors with their families, and establishment of shelters for the noninjured. Disasters have tremendous psychologic implications which will be discussed separately.

CRITICAL CARE TEAM PHYSICIAN

1. The objective of the team is to evaluate and stabilize one patient at a time, and to do so expeditiously.

2. You are responsible for assessing the patient and directing the team effort to stabilize and transport the patient.

3. You are responsible for determining the disposition of the patient from the E.D., whether it be to the O.R. or to an Intensive Care Unit.

4. The team must remain together at all times. Be aware of who is on your team, and do not allow the team to be separated during evaluation, treatment, and transport.

5. If you have to leave the team for an emergency elsewhere in the hospital or in the department, advise the Chief Disaster Medical Officer in the department.

6. You must be replaced by another physician before leaving the team.

7. After you complete one patient; return to the E.D., **as a team,** for another assignment to a serious or critical case.

DISASTER TRIAGE NURSE

1. Go to storeroom and obtain disaster triage station supplies:
   a) small table, disaster tags, disaster log sheet, pencils
   b) put on disaster identification bib
   c) small box of first-aid supplies: dressings, splints, tongue blades, airways

2. Set up **Triage Station** outside of Emergency Department Ambulance Entrance (between Ambulatory and Ambulance doors).

3. Be ready to tag all victims not tagged at the disaster scene and with the assistance of Triage Physician direct victims into the emergency care system.

4. Record visitor identification on tags and disaster triage log.

5. Keep pink copy of the triage tag—to be sent to Command Post, Room 1115 periodically via messenger.

6. Remain at Triage until all victims have been received.

DISCHARGE DISASTER NURSE

1. Put on disaster identification bib.

2. With the assistance of any other available staff, move all patients in the department that are able to be discharged at the time of the disaster notice to the E.D. Waiting Room.

3. Gather their medical records, have the physician assigned to the discharge task document follow-up instructions, and sign out the patient on the medical record face sheet.

4. Take the medical records to the waiting room, and discharge each patient with appropriate instructions for aftercare.

5. Discharged patients will be directed to the lobby of the North Tower to meet with relatives that may have been waiting, or to make necessary home calls to arrange for their transportation.

6. When all possible patients have been discharged, return to the coordinator in the treatment area for new assignment.

AMBULATORY CARE NURSE

1. Put on disaster identification bib.

2. During clinic hours, call extension 6311 and inform them of the need for space to be cleared in the surgical side waiting room and first two exam rooms because of disaster.

3. During nonclinic hours, **Stat** page Security to come and unlock Clinic doors.

4. Obtain supply cart from storeroom labeled "Ambulatory Disaster Supplies."

5. Set up work station with supply cart just outside the exam rooms in the surgery clinic waiting area just north of the clinic registration desk.

6. Complete E.D. treatment record on each disaster victim, write all orders, etc., on this sheet—not disaster tag.

7. Insurance information will be handwritten on a business office copy of the chart found on the disaster supply cart. This information can be obtained by the P.C.C. Secretary, Clerk, or any member of health care team.

8. Business office copy will go to registration desk in the clinic, where a plate will be made to be used to stamp all requisitions.

9. Call extension 6541 (Command Post) if more supplies or staff are needed.

10. Remain in Ambulatory Care until the last patient has been discharged.

11. Discharge patients through the Clinic registration desk.

O/R DISASTER COORDINATOR

1. Upon receiving notice from the Emergency Department via Beeper 689 that a disaster notification has been made, the O.R. Coordinator carrying that beeper will assess each O.R. as to availability of operating rooms and report to coordinator in the E.R., staff, surgeon, anesthesia availability.

2. The coordinator carrying beeper 689 will assign a coordinator to report directly to the Emergency Department Coordinator in person, obtaining disaster bib labeled "OR Coordinator" and requesting updated information from the E.D. Coordinator as to number of victims received, potential OR-type cases and information as to the total number of victims expected.

3. OR Coordinator is free to move about the Emergency Department to obtain whatever information they need to determine the need for OR support, and give updated information to beeper 689 stationed in Central Scheduling, command post for O.R. Services, to ensure direct updated status of disaster.

4. Informs E.D. Coordinator as to which OR the necessary disaster victims may be sent.

5. After clearance is given by either the E.D. Physician or the E.D. Coordinator that the disaster is over, will notify the OR of same.

FIGURE 4 Examples of disaster action cards used at Cedars-Sinai Medical Center in Los Angeles.

Triage

Triage is a military term for a process by which patients are classified according to the severity of their injuries at the time they are first seen (9). The cornerstone is categorization, so that immediate resuscitation is given to those in urgent need while the less severely injured are segregated for later treatment (33,35). Those who will require evacuation are identified, and those who are dead or hopelessly injured are isolated.

Perhaps the most difficult psychologic task of medical personnel is to resist the usual instinct to do as much as possible for a gravely ill patient. As has been noted in combat surgery and in massive casualty work, "the doctor must realize that there may be tens of hundreds of patients awaiting his services, and fruitless work on a hopeless case or too definitive a procedure on a patient who could wait without harm, may allow another patient to die for want of a hemostat applied to a bleeding vessel" (6).

Detailed guidelines on what constitutes a "hopeless case" cannot be given because this is a decision that must be made relative to the number of casualties and the resources available to care for them. For example, if a school bus were struck by an automobile, there could be 50 children with bruises, with the driver of the automobile near death. After very brief paramedic triage, if it was revealed that all the children had received only minor injuries, the rescuers would spend all their time with the driver of the automobile.

When many seriously ill casualties are present and resources are relatively stressed, then care should not be spent on persons who are unlikely to live, such as those who have suffered decapitation, total body burns with inhalation injuries, cardiac arrest following trauma, or massive open chest wounds.

A few years ago in Los Angeles, there was a fire that killed 25 people and injured 75. The front page of one of the newspapers displayed a photograph of paramedics performing advanced life support on a patient in cardiac arrest who had jumped from a window. Careful examination showed the patient to have a severe head injury, to be unconscious, apneic, and without pulse or blood pressure. The survival rate in such patients is zero. While paramedics were attending this victim, other victims were seen lying about without having been triaged. It is a natural reaction for many rescuers to seek out the most critical patient, but rescuers must be trained to realize that some patients are too critically injured to be saved.

There are several different triage systems used in the disaster literature (40,50,77). Figure 5 describes the two-, three-, four-, and five-tier systems. Many authorities presently favor the two-tier system because of its functional significance (31). In the two-tier system, the categories are "delayed" and "immediate." This system allows those patients in urgent need of hospital facilities to be transported first. Injuries assigned to each category are listed in Figure 6. Examples of disaster tags using the two- and four-tier systems are seen in Figure 7. If triage teams are able to identify those patients in whom early assignment of transportation may be lifesaving, then the goal of triage has been fulfilled.

The initial assessment of the patient should follow the guidelines suggested by the Committee on Trauma of the American College of Surgeons in their Advanced Trauma Life Support (ATLS) Course. The initial assessment starts with a primary survey based on the ABCs.

A—Airway maintenance with cervical spine control
B—Breathing (depth and presence of abnormal motion)
C—Circulation with hemorrhage control
D—Disability: neurologic status (Glasgow Coma Scale; see Figure 8)

Triage rating systems

Five-tier system (used in military triage)
 Dead or will die
 Life-threatening—readily correctable
 Urgent—must be treated within 1 to 2 hours
 Delayed—noncritical or ambulatory
 No injury—no treatment necessary

Four-tier system
 Immediate—seriously injured, reasonable chance of survival
 Delayed—can wait for care after simple first aid
 Expectant—extremely critical, moribund
 Minimal—no impairment of function, can either treat self or be treated by a
  nonprofessional

Three-tier system
 Life-threatening—readily correctable
 Urgent—must be treated within 1 to 2 hours
 Delayed—no injury, noncritical, or ambulatory

Two-tier system
 Immediate versus delayed
  Immediate—life-threatening injuries that are readily correctable on scene,
   and those that are urgent
  Delayed—no injury, noncritical injuries, ambulatory victims, moribund,
   and dead

FIGURE 5 Triage rating systems.

**Description of immediate and delayed cases
in simple triage during multiple casualty incidents,
and in military triage during mass casualty incidents***

Simple triage

Immediate (Priority I)

1. Asphyxia
2. Respiratory obstruction from mechanical causes
3. Sucking chest wounds
4. Tension pneumothorax
5. Maxillofacial wounds in which asphyxia exists or is likely to develop
6. Shock caused by major external hemorrhage
7. Major internal hemorrhage
8. Visceral injuries or evisceration
9. Cardiopericardial injuries
10. Massive muscle damage
11. Severe burns *over* 25% BSA
12. Dislocations
13. Major fractures
14. Major medical problems readily correctible
15. Closed cerebral injuries with increasing loss of consciousness

Delayed (Priority II)

1. Vascular injuries requiring repair
2. Wounds of the genitourinary tract
3. Thoracic wounds without asphyxia
4. Severe burns *under* 25% BSA
5. Spinal cord injuries requiring decompression
6. Suspected spinal cord injuries without neurological signs
7. Lesser fractures
8. Injuries of the eye
9. Maxillofacial injuries without asphyxia
10. Minor medical problems
11. Victims with little hope of survival under the best of circumstances of medical care

Mass casualty triage with an overwhelming number of injuries

Immediate (Priority I)

1. Asphyxia
2. Respiratory obstruction from mechanical causes
3. Sucking chest wounds
4. Tension pneumothorax
5. Maxillofacial wounds in which asphyxia exists or is likely to develop
6. Shock caused by major external hemorrhage
7. Dislocations
8. Severe burns *under* 25% BSA†
9. Lesser fractures†
10. Major medical problems that can be handled readily

Delayed (Priority II)

1. Major fractures (if able to stabilize)†
2. Visceral injuries or evisceration†
3. Cardiopericardial injuries†
4. Massive muscle damage†
5. Severe burns *over* 25% BSA†
6. Vascular injuries requiring repair
7. Wounds of the genitourinary tract
8. Thoracic wounds without asphyxia
9. Closed cerebral injuires with increasing loss of consciousness†
10. Spinal cord injuries requiring decompression†
11. Suspected spinal cord injuries without neurological signs
12. Injuries of the eye
13. Maxillofacial injuires without asphyxia
14. Complicated major medical problems†
15. Minor medical problems
16. Victims with little hope of survival under the best of circumstances of medical care

---

*Courtesy, Office of Emergency Services, State of California
†Conditions that have changed categories

FIGURE 6   Cases categorized by the simple triage rating system.

PRINT ALL INFORMATION

ATTACH TAG SECURELY TO PATIENT

DISASTER TAG

PINK COPY FOR: Administration
WHITE COPY FOR: Admitting
HARD COPY FOR: Patient Record

№ 317363

HOSPITAL

ADMITTING

NAME (Last) (First) (Initial)

LOCATION WHEN INJURED

ADDRESS | PHONE

DESCRIPTION (Height, Weight, Hair, Eyes, Complexion, Build, Race, Marks, Clothing, Articles)

DATE / / | TIME A.M. P.M. | AGE | SEX | RELIGION

NOTIFY IN CASE OF EMERGENCY | RELATIONSHIP

ADDRESS | PHONE

MEDICAL

ALLERGIC TO

TENTATIVE DIAGNOSIS

INITIAL TREATMENTS (See Details on Reverse Side)

☐ AIRWAY ☐ TOURNIQUET
☐ SPLINT ☐ INJECTION

INITIAL ROUTING DIRECTIONS

☐ MAJOR SURGERY ☐ MINOR SURGERY ☐ FIRST AID
☐ X-RAY ☐ ICU ☐ CCU ☐ OBSERVATION
☐ MORGUE ☐ OTHER ____________

TRIAGE

CARE CLASSIFICATION

☐ IMMEDIATE (Life Support)
☐ DELAYED
☐ DEAD

If Immediate Care Affix Red Label

If Delayed Care Affix Black Label

DO NOT DETACH TAG FROM PATIENT UNTIL INCORPORATED IN PATIENT'S RECORDS.

SEE REVERSE SIDE FOR TREATMENT RECORD, DISPOSITION AND INSTRUCTIONS

MEDICATIONS

Medications	Dose	Time	By
Tetanus Toxoid		AM PM	
Antitetanic Serum		AM PM	
T.A.T. With Gas Gangrene		AM PM	
		AM PM	
		AM PM	
		AM PM	

TOURNIQUETS

Limb	Time On	Time Off
	AM PM	AM PM
	AM PM	AM PM

CONDITION AND DISPOSITION

ADMITTED TO (Room, Surgery, ICU, CCU, Other)

TRANSFERRED TO | DATE / / | TIME A.M. P.M.

☐ DISCHARGED ☐ DIED | / / | A.M. P.M.

SIGNATURE OF DOCTORS

INSTRUCTIONS

1. Complete as many items as possible without delaying necessary care.
2. Be sure to attach label under "Care Classification" to indicate the level of care required.
   a. Immediate Care indicates a patient in need of life supporting medical service.
   b. Delayed Care indicates a patient where medical service needs are postponable without further endangering life.
3. Indicate time whenever tourniquet is released and reapplied.
4. Use the labels attached to identify patient's belongings or other records with this disaster tag.
5. Forward the top, pink copy to Administration, and the white copy to Admitting. Keep the hard copy with the Patient.

APPROVED BY HOSPITAL COUNCIL OF SOUTHERN CALIFORNIA 4/72

SECURLINE® DISASTER TAG
Reorder Number 2100
PRECISION GRAPHICS DIVISION
Precision Dynamics Corp. 3031 Thornton Ave., Burbank, Calif. 91504 · USA · (213) 849-6111

№ 317363
№ 317363
№ 317363
№ 317363

DELAYED

IMMEDIATE

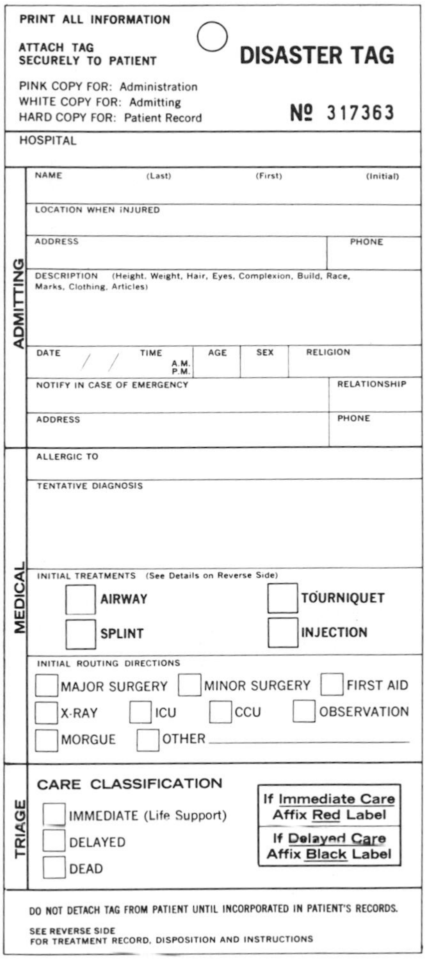

FIGURE 7 Examples of disaster tags. (Courtesy of Precision Graphics Division, Precision Dynamics Corp., Burbank, Calif.)

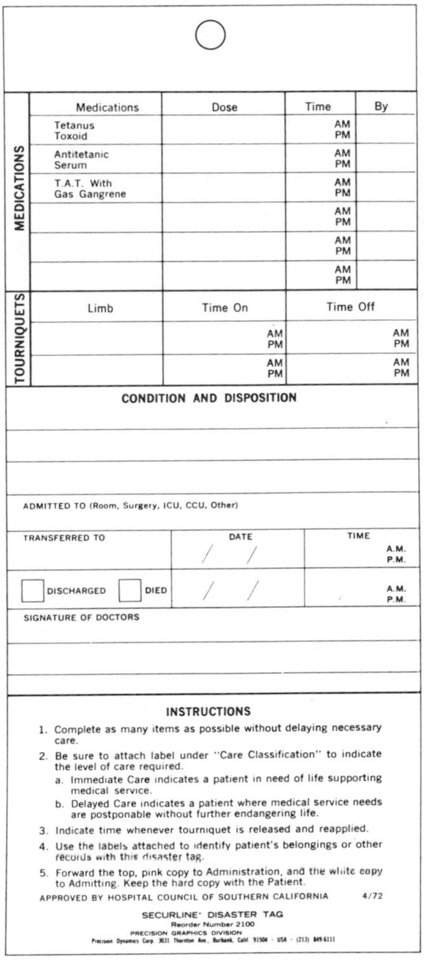

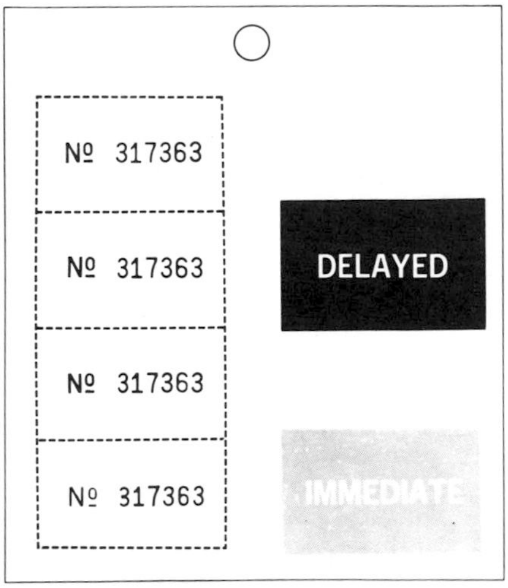

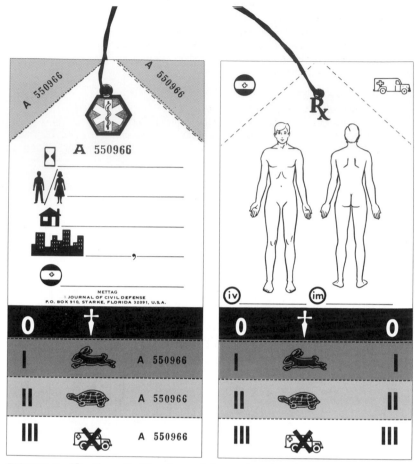

FIGURE 7   (Continued). (Courtesy of Journal of Civil Defense, Starke, Fla.)

E—Evaluate—List vital signs and delineate other injuries to the head, chest, abdomen, and extremities

As the primary survey is done, results should be listed on patient disaster tags. Emergency first aid should always be provided without delay, but procedures such as splinting of fractures or dressing of superficial wounds should be delayed until all patients have been triaged (80,81,83).

The triage team members must blend their individual skills to work together. One nicely described triage team is located in the San Fernando Valley (28). It is composed of seven physicians and a nurse, all on 24-hour emergency call. When summoned, the team is transported to the disaster site by surface vehicle and helicopter. The team carries medical

equipment in lightweight aluminum modules; members of the team are easily identified by white jumpsuits with appropriate insignias.

A few years ago, Sacramento, California, adopted a Mobile On-scene Triage Team (MOTT) composed of a senior emergency physician, a resident, a registered nurse, and a nurses' aide or emergency medical technician (20). The team is hospital based and capable of responding to a disaster within minutes of notification. The benefits demonstrated by the team have been immediate access, mobility, coordinated evacuation, treatment and disposition of mass casualty victims, control of facility overload, and appropriate initial disposition to definitive care facilities. All these benefits are major goals of efficient triage. Figure 9 demonstrates the standard operating procedure for the MOTT team.

1. Eye Opening Response
   (4) Spontaneous—already open with blinking (normal)
   (3) To speech—not necessary to request eye opening
   (2) To pain—stimulus should not be to the face
   (1) None—make note if eyes are swollen shut

2. Verbal Response
   (5) Oriented—knows name, age, etc.
   (4) Confused conversation—still answers questions
   (3) Inappropriate words—speech is either exclamatory or at random
   (2) Incomprehensible sounds—do not confuse with partial respiratory
       obstruction
   (1) None—make note if intubation prevents speech

3. Best Upper Limb Motor Response (pain applied to fingernail)
   (6) Obeys—moves limb to command and pain is not required
   (5) Localizes—changing the location of the painful stimulus causes the limb
       to follow
   (4) Withdraws—pulls away from painful stimulus
   (3) Abnormal flexion—decorticate posturing
   (2) Extensor response—decerebrate posturing
   (1) None—Indicate if limb is restrained

FIGURE 8   Glasgow coma scale (GCS).

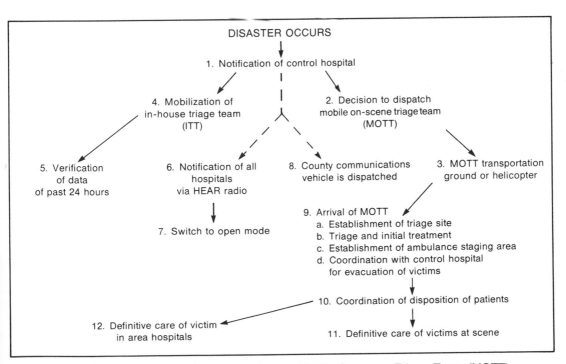

FIGURE 9   Standard operating procedure for Mobile On-scene Triage Team (MOTT).

Each community would do well to examine its own resources in an effort to design a triage team which is capable of demonstrating the same benefits that the Sacramento MOTT team has accomplished.

Telemetry Protocols

In most urban disasters occurring in the United States, much of the prehospital care will be provided by paramedics in radio communication with a specially trained nurse or physician at a base station or other command post. Frequently, due to the large number of patients, the orders to deliver care may not be given directly by a physician. Therefore,

it is necessary for protocols to be written in advance to ensure that the providers of emergency first aid have proper guidelines. Examples of protocols used by the Medical Intensive Care Nurses (MICNs) at Cedars-Sinai Medical Center in Los Angeles are seen in Figure 6.

Another option which allows early vital treatment without the direct intervention of a physician is the use of standing order protocols to be used by paramedics. This system is most useful when there is an overload or breakdown in the communication system. Examples of protocols developed by Dr. Ronald Stewart for the Pittsburgh Paramedic System are seen in Figures 10 and 11.

Traumatic Shock

Immediate transport is essential for optimal resuscitation (transfusions, emergency surgery, etc.)

1. Maintain airway and support ventilation.
2. Give 100% O_2 by mask; assist ventilations if necessary.
3. Protect C-spine.
4. Apply MAST Suit to:
   a. autotransfuse if patient is in shock—one should aim to maintain the systolic BP above 80 mmHg.
   b. tamponade all hemorrhaging injuries below the diaphragm
   c. splint lower extremity fractures
   d. increase peripheral resistance
5. Single attempt at largest bore IV at scene. If unable to establish, continue attempts enroute up to 2 times. Continue RL infusion wide open to maintain systolic BP 80-90 mmHg. Collect 1 purple and 2 red tops (if possible) prior to establishing the IV.
6. Control bleeding where possible with pressure dressing.
7. Splint all fractures and dress all open wounds.
8. Retrieve avulsed parts and transport in sterile saline solution.

Near drowning

Assess:
Level of consciousness
Respiration
Status of cervical spine in diving accidents

1. Clear airway
2. Ventilate
3. If unable to ventilate, consider dry drowning syndrome and use Heimlich maneuver
4. Protect C-spine if indicated
5. Nasal O_2 6-8 liters/minute, or support ventilations as needed
6. IV D5W TKO
7. CPR protocol supersedes drowning protocol
8. Transport code 3

FIGURE 10 Paramedic standing order protocols for major trauma and near drowning.

Neck injuries should be assumed on all patients who are unresponsive following trauma to the head, and as well in all severe facial injuries. Reports of cervical fractures being present in patients who have not complained of pain at the scene of the accident are contained in the literature. Basic care of spinal injuries by paramedical personnel in the field consists of airway control, an initial motor and sensory examination, careful extrication following immobilization, and treatment of any complications of the injury.

Such complications may include respiratory compromise in high cervical lesions, lack of temperature control, and hypotension due to loss of peripheral resistance. Treatment of airway problems includes oxygen administration and assisted ventilation. The patient requires protection from exposure to weather, etc., and as well must be handled with the thought of protection against bodily injury.

Shock resulting from loss of peripheral resistance should be managed with fluid infusions, usually a crystalloid. External pneumatic counterpressure can be used, but only the lower extremity chambers should be inflated because of the possibility of restriction of diaphragmatic movement which may result from the increase in intra-abdominal pressure obtained with the garment.

It should be noted that an initial brief motor and sensory examination should be done, if possible, before any movement; this brief examination should be repeated following extrication and in transport to hospital. This practice ensures both medical and legal data collection.

Goals
- Protection of the patient against further injury
- Maintenance of vital functions in the patient with actual or suspected spinal cord damage
- Data recording for both medical and medicolegal considerations

Indications

- Patients who have suffered a head injury sufficient to impair consciousness
- Patients who demonstrate any loss of motor or sensory findings following trauma
- Patients with facial lacerations, swelling, or deformity of the facial structure

Tools

- Extrication and immobilization devices, as appropriate
- Oxygen and airway control equipment
- MAST
- Intravenous lines and solutions

Technique

- Support patient psychologically; explain all procedures
- Control airway; run oxygen at 8-10 liters/minute
- Extricate with care, using immobilization procedures as necessary
- Application of *firm* cervical collar is mandatory
- Begin IV lines prior to extrication; Ringer's lactate
- If patient in shock, prepare MAST
- Open IV lines if patient in shock; otherwise, KVO
- Record all data by written and verbal means

FIGURE 11 Paramedic standing order protocol for spinal cord injury.

Emergency First Aid

Most current literature promotes the idea of field stabilization and triage when disaster occurs outside of the hospital. There are some proponents of simple, rapid transportation of victims to hospitals with a minimum of field intervention. Many of the deaths that have occurred, however, were potentially preventable with early basic first aid maneuvers. An excellent example was seen on February 28, 1975, when a subway train crashed into the blind end of a tunnel in the Moorgate Station in London (53). Autopsies showed that of the 39 deaths, 20 were attributed to *traumatic asphyxia,* a term suggesting the occurrence of airway compromise that was potentially treatable (45). The philosophy of field stabilization is nicely summarized by Nagan (54) in an article describing the disaster planning used in Israel (4):

The strategy of management and evacuation from the battle field is based upon the principle that evacuation is not urgent—only primary treatment and preparation for evacuation are urgent. Primary treatment includes first-aid and life saving procedures (keeping air passages free, hemostasis, antishock treatment, and the proper preparation of the wounded for evacuation. . . . These procedures performed as close as possible to the battle field greatly reduce the urgency of prompt evacuation.

A major principle that has emerged from examining previous disasters is that it is essential to prevent transferring a disaster from the field to the hospital. Simply transporting all the victims of a large disaster to the nearest hospital without field stabilization only accomplishes a change in the location of a disaster. The sudden arrival of a large number of unstable patients at a single hospital emergency room is a classic situation in which the resources available for patient care are overwhelmed. With field stabilization and sophisticated communication systems, patients can be distributed to facilities in a rational manner, allowing the most effective patient care.

Emergency first aid at a disaster site may be delivered by a stratified physician team or well-trained paramedics (64). Much of the British literature suggests sending a team of hospital-based physicians. One suggested combination consists of an anesthesiologist, chief surgical resident, and chief medical resident. With the evolution of paramedic programs and their expanding hospital-directed prehospital care, it is also possible to rely on paramedics to do much of the stabilization and field triage. Simple procedures such as clearing an airway, providing hemostasis with direct pressure, volume resuscitation through fluid replacement, and application of the military antishock trousers (MAST) suit will save lives regardless of which qualified individuals performs these tasks (51). As with other aspects of disaster planning, each community must examine its resources to determine the most effective means of providing emergency first aid.

Analgesia

Many disasters involve patients trapped for long periods of time before extrication is successful. A recent example of this was the Hyatt Regency Hotel disaster in Kansas City, where two aerial walkways collapsed into a crowded lobby, killing hundreds of people under twisted metal, glass, and concrete. In such cases, trapped casualties most often endure extreme pain without the use of analgesics. Other patients also may have painful injuries but may be low on the transportation priority list; they should be treated with analgesics in the field. Narcotics have frequently been used for this purpose in the past but have produced several undesirable effects, including respiratory depression, decreased left ventricular filling pressure, frequent emesis, and altering levels of consciousness, that make physical findings on future examinations unreliable.

An analgesic with many advantages is self-administered nitrous oxide. Utilizing a 50% nitrous oxide, 50% oxygen mixture, patients have some control over the level administered. Using a hand-held mask prevents patients from becoming overly obtunded. Nitrous oxide was extremely effective in the Moorgate disaster of London, in which several victims were trapped in mangled wreckage for long periods.

Environmental Factors

Increasing numbers of individuals are pursuing recreational and business ventures in rugged and rural areas each year. Consideration must be given to the unique approaches to disaster management in diverse environments, such as a desert, forest, cave, mine, mountain, or body of water (11,21,57).

At the scene of an accident or disaster, careful consideration must be given to the advisability of attempting a rescue operation. "Conditions may be so hazardous, and the chance of success so low, that rescue should be delayed until additional equipment and personnel have been obtained. Unduly jeopardizing men to retrieve or transport a dead body is never justified. Self-sacrifice is spiritually commendable, but under rare conditions it can have the effect of sacrificing everyone" (19).

In potentially dangerous environments, rescuers must always consider their own safety before attempting any rescue of victims. On June 14, 1981, three paramedics died in Lancaster, Pennsylvania, because of failure to obey this basic principle. These paramedics were called to rescue an 8 year old who had fallen into a septic tank. The first paramedic failed to use an air-pack in his attempted rescue and was quickly overcome and became unresponsive. The second paramedic used an air-pack but took it off in an attempt to save his partner; he also became unconscious. The third paramedic went to the aid of his two colleagues without an air-pack. All three died. This tragedy could have been prevented by adhering to the principle of protecting oneself before attempting any first aid or rescue.

The use of helicopters and fixed-wing aircraft has made a great improvement in wilderness rescue. The limitations of both types of aircraft must be appreciated. Both are ineffective at extremely high altitudes due to a lack of sufficient air density. Fixed-wing aircraft need a landing site and are greatly limited by terrain. Helicopters can pluck individuals from cliffs, glaciers, and inaccessible locations, but require a large horizontal sweep for their rotors.

Easy fatigue and exhaustion of rescuers should be anticipated when they must endure extremes of temperature, elevation, dampness, or otherwise hazardous environments. Frequent rests and changes in personnel are necessary to control stress and fatigue-induced errors (25,38).

Disaster Drills

Another major principle in disaster planning is the need for periodic, realistic disaster drills; the effectiveness of an emergency plan should not be determined for the first time during an actual disaster (37,70,71,73). The Joint Commission on the Accreditation of Hospitals (JCAH) requirements call for each hospital to have two disaster drills per year, but frequently these are done superficially, the only goal being to satisfy the JCAH. To make sure that the plan will be effective under actual conditions, it should be thoroughly tested under simulated emergency conditions and involve large numbers of moulaged casualties. These tests often show deficiencies in the plan, highlighting problem areas that require revision. Those responsible for the administration of the program will undergo valuable review of their own functions.

The types of problems discovered may be major. In Suffolk County, Massachusetts, new emergency vehicles purchased a few years ago did not fit through their roadway turnstiles. Usually, several small problems are discovered. At a recent drill at Evanston Hospital, problems included inability to hear the hospital page system's announcement of the disaster, mishandling of disaster tags, a runner reporting to the admitting office instead of the emergency department, and unavailability of elevator keys. The changes made after each disaster drill are necessary to keep a disaster plan a realistic and workable document, as opposed to a static plan unresponsive to the demands of a real disaster.

When disaster drills are held with moulaged victims, it is a good idea to have a tracking card attached to each victim (12). These cards should list the type of injury, time of triage, triage category, initial treatment, time and initial triage category upon arrival in the emergency room, and definitive management. An example of a tracking card is seen in Figure

1. Injuries and vital signs: _____
   _____

2. Initial triage category: _____
   _____

3. Time of initial triage: _____
4. Initial first aid measures: _____
   _____

5. Time and location of arrival at hospital: _____
   _____

6. Triage category upon arrival at hospital: _____
   _____

7. Definitive diagnostic and treatment measures at hospital: _____
   _____

8. Miscellaneous comments: _____
   _____

FIGURE 12   Patient tracking card.

12. Another aid in the evaluation of disaster drills is the use of videotape, which can be carefully reviewed and critiqued at a later date.

Because of the difficulties in performing realistic disaster drills where many key personnel may not be involved, an innovative approach is described to ensure greater participation in testing of disaster plans (43). In this approach, a scenario describing in general terms a credible disaster is presented individually to members of medical, administrative, and nursing staff by members of the disaster committee. After the disaster scenario is read and digested, questionnaires are distributed. Slightly different questions are given to each person depending on his job description. All questionnaires test the individual's ability to make decisions and set priorities. The completed questionnaires are then critiqued in terms of communication, assessment, triage, flexibility of function, use of personnel, resources, and planning. Scenarios, questionnaires, and critiques are used as a basis for a workshop for all personnel involved.

An example of such a plan is an explosion and fire in the hospital cafeteria spreading to the inpatient building and other areas of the hospital. Sample questions are:

1. Who would you notify of the disaster, and what would you tell them?
2. Where would triage be located?

3. What would you tell the general staff of the disaster?
4. The Fire Chief wants to know how many persons are in the disaster; how would you obtain this information?
5. What medical personnel would you need immediately, and how would you get in touch with them?
6. What medical implications would the disaster have immediately and for the succeeding 2 or 3 days?
7. What could be done to relieve general panic and facilitate staff evacuation?

The most important feature of the new approach to disaster planning is that it stimulates individual thought and concern. Each person is involved and cannot hide behind other members of the team. This novel approach has many advantages, including low cost, surprise drills, minimal disruption of routine hospital activities, ability to be done at frequent intervals, and the possibility of involving all key members of the hospital staff, leading to disaster awareness. Such a plan is not meant to replace realistic drills involving multiple casualties, but may be used as an excellent adjunct to periodic mock drills.

Central Authority

The larger the disaster, the more important the official organization of authority. The only way that the huge number of decisions and problems can be handled successfully in a major disaster is with a prearranged organizational chart. The purpose of the organizational chart is the delegation of authority, which is essential (24).

A central authority in charge of disaster management is a need frequently expressed in the available studies of civilian disasters. Such a central authority must be arranged in advance and should reside in several key persons or their designated replacements (27). Among those assigned to this central group are the regional head of civil defense (disaster control agency), the head of police function in the area, and the ranking official in public health or his representative. Cooperation among the heads of the involved agencies is of maximum importance to the success of the effort. If the authority of a central agency is not made clear, its directives may be ignored in the time of stress; if the organizational ability is poor, confusion will exist and no plan can be executed in orderly fashion. The authority of this group should clearly be superior to that of other local agencies. Further, the right of the central authority to issue orders utilizing hospital facilities and personnel must be unquestioned. It should be arranged in advance, by mutual agreement, and it requires considerable education, both of the public and of medical personnel. Practice drills are essential to demonstrate the role of the central authority and to accustom others to this role.

An agreement reached between the Federal Civil Defense Administration (disaster control agency) and the American National Red Cross in order to avoid disputes between agencies assigns to the former the responsibility for rescue, evacuation, and first aid and to the latter the responsibility for relief and welfare activities when disasters occur. This agreement should be clearly understood by local representatives of the two agencies. If a change in assignment of the major responsibility for direction and control in disaster management becomes necessary before the work is completed, some well-defined method of determining the point of shift of responsibility should be established. The exact interaction of these agencies varies in different communities and should be incorporated into local plans.

With regard to the physician component of this group, the growth of emergency medicine as a specialty, with greatly increasing numbers of residency-trained emergency physicians, provides individuals who are uniquely trained to assume a leadership role in disaster planning and disaster plan execution. The American College of Emergency Physicians summarizes their position (1):

. . . the emergency physician, through training, practice and day-to-day involvement with large numbers of undifferentiated patients, has developed a responsibility and unique role in mass casualty/disaster management involving the totality of the emergency care system. Emergency physicians should be involved in the planning, management and evacuation phases of the system at the local, state and federal levels. They should be involved at the site of the disaster and the emergency operations center in the hospital.

Radio communications should be provided for the central authority at a point convenient for the management of the entire area. Auxiliary communication centers should be designated and radio facilities provided so that the destruction of the main radio transmitter will not destroy the effectiveness of the system. The surviving representative of the central authority would move to a functioning auxiliary communication center if the main transmitters were silenced.

In an actual disaster, each hospital would keep the central authority informed of its current patient load relative to its resources. The central authority would then direct the evacuation personnel in the disaster zone and at traffic control points to guide the vehicles bearing the injured to the hospitals currently best able to care for them. Evacuation of casualties with minor injuries in areas remote from the disaster should be performed at the discretion of the central authority (24).

An ideal central authority during the initial phase of a disaster would be one that is already in existence. It should be accustomed to operating in emergency conditions and be operative on a 24-hour schedule. An excellent prototype of such a central authority is present in Los Angeles County, where the Medical Alert Center (MAC) assumes this role. Its daily functions include broadcasting special messages, such as the blood needs of various hospitals, alerts from local law enforcement agencies, and air quality alerts; maintaining a hyperbaric (recompression) chamber; and keeping records of all available burn unit beds and arranging transfers from community hospitals to county facilities. MAC operates in any situation with more than five casualties, assuming responsibility for prehospital care, communications, triage, and assignment of patients to facilities. Ideally, all large cities should create a similar centralized communications authority.

Communications

The major development of the last 20 years that has upgraded disaster procedures has been the implementation of sophisticated two-way radio communication networks. The major impetus behind the growth of emergency radio systems was provided by the Federal Communications Commission's ruling of December 1960 that granted hospitals the use of specific frequencies for both emergency and day-to-day activities (63). Without coordinated communications between hospitals and related agencies, any attempt to provide vital emergency services will become a tragic series of misdirected efforts (63).

One of the most efficient communication systems in the country is presently operated in southern California. The system is the Hospital Emergency Administrative Radio, otherwise known as the HEAR radio. Examining the accomplishments and capabilities of the system shows the value of radio communications. An excellent example of the value of the system was seen in the Los Angeles earthquake on February 9, 1971. The earthquake was the worst in 33 years, made more serious by the destruction of two hospitals (accounting for 47 of the 66 total deaths) and the near-destruction of two more, forcing evacuation. The remaining hospitals were severely taxed by the burden of 3000 injured victims and the necessity of receiving 1167 patients from facilities damaged in the earthquake. Contributing to the postquake disorganization were: (1) the need to evacuate 80,000 residents living below a seriously weakened reservoir, (2) loss of telephone communications in the heavily damaged disaster zone, (3) the blocking of streets and freeways by damage or debris that impaired the operation of emergency vehicles, (4) the rupture of gas and sewer lines that almost forced a fifth hospital to close, and (5) the disruption of power lines, causing widespread blackouts marked by the failure of auxiliary power units in several hospitals.

In this chaotic environment, effective disaster operations would have been seriously hampered without the coordinated system of communications provided by the emergency radio network. The system was utilized as follows (4):

1. To determine the nature, extent, and location of damages
2. To arrange for transfer of more than 1000 patients from damaged or destroyed hospitals by coordinating the dispatch of ambulances, buses, helicopters, and station wagons
3. To determine on a continuing basis the emergency capability and available beds of all hospitals still able to provide assistance
4. To locate specific blood types, drugs, supplies, and equipment and to arrange for their transportation by helicopter or police car
5. To coordinate and arrange for triage teams to be sent to the disaster scene by helicopter or emergency vehicle
6. To locate emergency sources of water for hospitals in need
7. To arrange for prepared meals to be sent to hospitals that lost the use of their kitchens
8. To advise hospitals on how and where to get physicians and key personnel through police lines located around the evacuation site
9. To locate physicians with specialty skills and direct them to requesting hospitals
10. To arrange emergency staff privileges to enable physicians to follow their transferred patients
11. To maintain continuous emergency operation for several days, issuing public health department reports and police bulletins, tracing transferred patients, and updating bed availability reports from community hospitals

A high-level task force from the White House Office of Emergency Preparedness, which investigated every facet of the disaster operations during the Los Angeles earthquake, reported that to their knowledge, this was the first major civil disaster in which a separate, self-sufficient medical and hospital radio communication network played a major role. The system worked effectively and undoubtedly made the difference between a chaotic and an orderly response to the hospital and medical needs of the affected areas (4). The HEAR radio system of southern California has also demonstrated other advantages, including quickly locating the amount or type of blood available at any hospital in the system (extremely useful for locating a rare blood type), notifying all area emergency rooms of potential criminals who may be seeking medical aid for crime-related injuries, notifying area emergency rooms of suspected drug abusers (such as narcotic addicts frequenting local emergency rooms), keeping a record of the number of monitored critical care beds available at any time in the various hospitals, and notifying paramedic units of closures of various hospitals to critical care patients due to lack of appropriate beds.

The system described is relatively inexpensive and can be easily combined with the radio system that is linked to paramedic units for the prehospital care of critically ill patients.

The necessary elements of an effective communication system have been summarized by Simoneau (67):

1. The principal coordination center must have direct communication links with medical facilities receiving victims, with law enforcement officials, with all rescue units (including ties to mutual aid agencies), and with fire units and other support agencies.
2. Rescue units must have the capability of communicating with one another, with law enforcement agencies, and with the receiving medical facilities. Any roving disaster coordinating vehicle must be similarly equipped.
3. Communication between disaster vehicles and the coordination center with the National Guard and state police is desirable.
4. Field triage operations require hand-held walkie-talkie radios capable of communicating with the communications center, all rescue units, and other hand-held field radios.
5. The coordination center must provide a means for recording all essential transmissions. A master tape of all transmissions is desirable.

One desirable feature that aids all aspects of emergency care is the availability of a 911 emergency telephone number. With such a system, the possibility exists for a central communications center to receive calls efficiently and quickly dispatch the necessary services. A 911 number also allows the public quickly to report a potential disaster that can possibly be averted or one that has already occurred.

In wilderness environments, effective communications is a major priority. Because of the specialized skills and equipment that may be necessary for search, rescue, and extrication, the first rescuers should assume a triage role, quickly evaluate the total needs at the scene, and then communicate them by two-way radio to local authorities. When two-way radio equipment is not available, one may have to use ordinary channels of a CB radio or revert to telephone communication. Word of mouth is notoriously poor for conveying the necessary information (82). This was well demonstrated in the Moorgate disaster in London, when a physician asked a paramedic for more Entonox (nitrous oxide); after this message was conveyed to another rescue worker, the physician received an "empty box." Modern technology can now bring sophisticated relief efforts to wilderness environments by use of radio technology and advances in transportation.

Medical Records

The maintenance of accurate medical records during a disaster serves many functions. Records are necessary for following patient treatment, collecting vital statistics, notifying relatives, preparing press releases, filling out insurance papers, fulfilling legal responsibilities, and performing a detailed study of the management of the disaster (10).

Prearranged, streamlined, brief medical record forms should be a part of each hospital's disaster plan. Prenumbered emergency disaster tags are a vital part of record keeping. During triage, a disaster tag, which contains the results of the initial 60-second assessment, is attached to the arm of each patient. The colored tag should correspond to the patient's general triage category. The card may read as follows:

1. Black—Dead/death imminent
2. Red—Critically ill but salvageable
3. Yellow—Salvageable (not immediately critical), but requires definitive medical care
4. Green—Walking wounded

The following information is essential for each tag:

1. Name or identifying features
2. Vital signs (timed)
3. List of injuries
4. Medicines or therapeutic measures received
5. Allergies

Three sample tags are shown in Figure 7.

If possible, no casualty should be treated before being tagged; however, lifesaving measures should not be withheld simply to prepare a tag. It is possible to process casualties more efficiently by having the triage team send patients with yellow tags, or those needing only minimal first aid, to a separate emergency department or outpatient area. A separate admitting log should be kept of those cases as soon as it is filed. A copy should be sent to the master casualty list.

When a casualty cannot answer questions, a search of the body should be made for some means of identification. Otherwise, a description of the person, indicating remarkable physical characteristics, including when and where found by the rescue squad, should be written on the emergency medical tag. A special person should be assigned to identify the dead. Valuables taken from all admitted casualties should be placed in paper bags, which are marked properly with the patient's name and tag number and the signature of the person taking the valuables. These bags are then sent by messengers to the business office for safekeeping. As soon as the emergency medical tag is filled out, the messenger should take the original of the tag to the admitting office (63).

For the patient to be admitted, a formal medical record should be kept with the patient's medical tag, which includes mention of diagnostic procedures performed and treatment received (39). A person experienced in medical record keeping and thoroughly familiar with the disaster record-keeping system must be available to oversee record keeping and to update the master list continually. An updated master casualty list will allow situation reports to be given to the disaster coordinator in order to allow a proper flow of patients into various areas. After the emergency, a file for future reference should be made by collecting the original or duplicate of the emergency medical tags, admitting and discharge logs, interim reports, newspaper clippings, and any written evaluation of the emergency service during the incident.

A printed disaster packet would greatly help organize disaster activities. Examples of the types of materials that can be used are as follows:

1. A multiple casualty incident form allows each base station to keep a record of the treatment given to all expected patients and allows the hospital to prepare for the types of victims that will be arriving and when to expect them.
2. The emergency department capacity inventory can be used to determine accurately the staffing needs of the emergency department based upon the estimated number of critical and noncritical patients that will be expected to arrive.
3. The disaster staff call-in list neatly records the response of staff called to participate in disaster relief activities. It documents the expected time of arrival of these staff and also which staff must be recalled.
4. The disaster assignment sheet lists the role of each staff member.
5. The master disaster log lists all patients seen during the disaster and their disposition.
6. The bed census sheet lists data regarding occupancy in all areas of the hospital so that admissions can be made to the most appropriate bed available. It also allows the central authority to be notified of data such as the number of neurosurgical beds, intensive care unit beds, coronary care unit beds, and other specialty beds.

Disaster Prevention

Disasters usually occur without any warning, but this may not always be the case. Two important aspects of disaster management are preparing for an expected disaster and being aware of situations in which adequate preparation may prevent a disaster from occurring.

When there is a warning that a disaster may occur, appropriate officials must decide how to notify the public without worsening the situation by generating panic. In environmental disasters such as floods, evacuation may decrease morbidity, but without a coordinated effort, injuries may be increased (67). Knowledge gained through several studies conducted on evacuation procedures indicates that at least four factors play a part in an individual's decision to participate in an evacuation process or to respond to a warning. These include (29):

The individual's assessment of personal threat
The reality of the disaster threat
The content of the warning message
The number of times the warning message was received

In order to evacuate an area effectively, residents must either have prior knowledge of an existing evacuation plan or be informed of the procedure when warned. Safe routes must be identified for exit from the area, and appropriate destinations must be defined for the public. In observations of flood warning response, it has been noted that families were warned through one of three distinct parties: authorities, peers, or mass media. Those warned by an authority such as a roving police car with a loudspeaker emitting the warning were less likely to be skeptical. It is reasonable to conclude from the foregoing information that a community plan for warning and evacuation should incorporate the following points:

1. The warning message should be as detailed as possible, including information regarding the location of expected impact, how severe the impact is expected to be, how and when evacuation will be conducted, and, if necessary, safe routes for exit and appropriate destinations.
2. The warning message must be repeated as urgently and often as possible.
3. The warning message must come from authorities in the community.

Public Gatherings

Many situations occur in which the impact of the disaster can be greatly diminished through proper planning. Detailed planning should occur any time several thousand people gather for athletic events, concerts, or similar occurrences (36). When 10,000–100,000 people gather in a relatively small area, plans should always be designed to minimize the risk of disaster and to provide routine first aid which may be necessary. The magnitude of the problem is appreciated by considering the work of Rooen (65) on rock concerts. He suggested that the health facility receiving patients from such an event could plan for one casualty per 500 paid attendance per 1 hour of concert. Based on these figures, a 6-hour concert in a stadium of 50,000 people would be expected to generate 600 casualties. The type of preparation that is necessary for such an event has been described detailing plans for an Arizona rock concert for 61,000 people. During the event, 299 patients presented minor problems and 10 patients needed to be seen at the university hospital. Preventive measures contributing to an orderly performance included:

1. Advance publicity by the news media regarding suggestions, traffic patterns, and available health facilities. Advance notice that alcohol would not be provided in the stadium was also given.
2. Support by the performers, who appealed to the audience to respect the stadium property and announced that help was available if any problem arose.
3. Adequate access obviating unnecessary crowding at the gates, with sufficient control of people flow to allow the enforcement of liquor prohibition at the gate.
4. Concessions with soft drinks and an adequate supply of ice during the hot late afternoon.
5. Maintenance of respectful attitudes by students for property and the performers, so that potential agitators in the crowd met unreceptive responses.
6. With random seating on the field, a light and sound mixer tower in front of the stage blocked vision for anyone sitting directly behind it. This then provided a badly needed aisle for the structure teams in such a situation.

Such simple factors cannot be overlooked in the planning of large events. Ignoring a seemingly small item such as the third occurred during a 1979 rock concert in Cincinatti, resulting in several deaths as youths were trampled when the gates opened and people scrambled to be admitted.

Medical planning for football games at Denver's Mile High Stadium, described by Pons et al., provides another excellent example of emergency preparation; the fact that two patients during the 1978 season survived cardiac arrest without neurologic sequelae is a tribute to their system (60). At each game there are 12 paramedics and seven physicians, all prepared to provide emergency care. Each of their first aid stations has radios for communication with a hospital base station in case of a disaster or other complicated medical problem.

Radiation Disasters

On March 31, 1979, a nuclear reactor at Three Mile Island in Harrisburg, Pennsylvania, came dangerously close to a meltdown, which would have resulted in a major radiation disaster (8). It is now frightfully clear that disaster plans must include the possibility of radiation disasters.

A brief discussion of the types of radiation is provided below. An extensive discussion of this topic may be found in the Appendix. There are three types of ionizing radiation to be considered.

Alpha particles are the same as the nucleus of a helium atom and therefore contain two protons and two neutrons. They have a high mass and electric charge and, as a consequence, have very poor powers of penetration. In air they penetrate only a few centimeters, and in tissue only several millimeters. Therefore, outside the body they are not dangerous, but they have potential for harm if ingested or inhaled. Specific instruments are necessary to measure α particles, but they can be predicted from the quantity of gamma radiation measured.

Beta particles are similar to electrons and can penetrate several meters in air and several centimeters in tissue, making them a significant biologic hazard.

Gamma rays are high-frequency electromagnetic rays similar to x-rays. They have a better penetrating power than α or β particles and are therefore the most significant biologic threat.

An emergency room must have a radiation counter to measure each of the above types of radiation. Personnel must be experienced in the proper use of the equipment for accurate monitoring to occur.

There are three types of radiation accidents that must be considered (48). The first is *contamination* in the form of particulate matter or liquid attached, or in close proximity to, a patient's body. The second situation is *incorporation,* which involves inhalation, ingestion, or contamination of an open wound with radioactive particles or liquid. The third situation is *radiation.* This occurs after exposure to x-rays or γ rays.

Patients with contamination must be carefully decontaminated. Once a patient has been irradiated, nothing can be done other than to watch the patient and treat any complications of the radiation syndrome.

It must be remembered that patients with skin and superficial contamination are a danger to hospital personnel until decontamination occurs. For adequate decontamination, a hospital must have a carefully detailed plan. All hospitals in close proximity to a nuclear power plant are best prepared if separate facilities exist for irradiation trauma and for treat-

ment. A prototype system is described by Galvin (23): "Basically the room is similar to an operating room, with the use of a deluge water system for decontamination purposes. The room possesses two water disposal systems: a portable tank system and an underground waste water tank for radioactive materials."

Each hospital disaster plan should include an individual who is in charge of all radiation accidents. His responsibility should include conducting radiation disaster drills, maintaining equipment, and supervising all radiation accidents. The essential elements of a radiation accident plan are well described by Leonard and Ricks (48).

The U.S. Department of Energy maintains regional offices which are willing to provide assistance for all radiation accidents. The Radiation Emergency Assistance Center/Training Site (REACTS) provides a 24-hour consultation service regarding all radiation accidents. REACTS, in addition to providing telephone advice, will send a team of experts to the accident site if necessary. REACTS can be contacted by calling (615) 576-3131, Monday through Friday, 8:00 A.M. to 4:40 P.M., or (615) 482-2441 (beeper 241) at any time. Written information can be obtained from REACTS, Box 117, Oak Ridge, Tennessee 37830.

Psychologic Aspects of Disaster

Any disaster can be expected to have large-scale psychologic impact on survivors, and on relatives of survivors and nonsurvivors, as well as on rescue personnel and hospital staff (16,72,75,76). Disaster planners should be aware of the expected reactions in an affected population and attempt to provide for their psychologic needs (44,55).

Disasters will produce at least transient psychologic effects in large numbers of individuals, regardless of their preexisting personalities; indeed, the notion that well-adjusted people can adapt successfully to any stressful situation is not supported by the evidence (15). When a disaster strikes, victims are suddenly exposed to a situation that is usually both unexpected and unfamiliar, rendering them emotionally and intellectually helpless. Additionally, there is little time and opportunity for effective action either to prevent or to escape the occurrence. Events are so overwhelming that the stimulus barrier becomes disrupted and sensory overload occurs beyond the integrative capacity of the nervous system. Unveiled, the organism responds in a characteristic psychologic manner (the *disaster syndrome*), briefly described below.

Several operational models have been prepared which attempt to define behavior patterns before, during, and after disaster impact. Such models permit an examination of the factors that may be involved in the prevention and treatment of behavioral problems at any particular stage of a disaster.

Various authors have used five to eight phases to describe the disaster period. The following five phases are modified from those of Tyhurst and Glass (30,75). One should appreciate that there is overlap between the phases, and that all phases may not exist for every disaster.

PREIMPACT PHASE

This period exists whenever there is a high probability that a disaster will occur. Characteristic behavior during this period consists of underactivity or ineffectiveness in preparing for the impact of the disaster. Denial is common and may be total, partial, or minimal. Denial may be manifested by joking, lack of interest, or total apathy. This occurs, in part, because acknowledgment of the danger would result in physical inconvenience and psychic stress.

Many persons adopt a fatalistic attitude which allows them to make no preparation, or adopt rationalizations which prove to them that the catastrophic event will never occur. The individual who feels helpless to affect his destiny therefore displaces responsibility to authorities "whose job it is" to worry about such things. Authorities should use this period to try to prepare and inform the population about what to expect and what protective measure to take. It has been shown that a population adequately forewarned is better able to cope with disaster.

WARNING PHASE

Danger is imminent, within minutes or hours. Denial may continue for a time, although many unprepared individuals will seek information as to how best to avoid the forthcoming impact. Once danger is admitted, ideas of faith, superstition, fantasy, and magical control flourish.

Ineffective behavior is revealed in overactivity. True panic is rare, but tends to occur during this period. *Panic* denotes irrational behavior in which judgment and perception of reality are so poor that self-destructive behavior may occur. True mass panic occurs when people perceive an immediate, severe danger and believe that there is only one or a limited number of escape routes. Under such circumstances, they lose all judgment and discretion and become impervious to communication or direction. Many situations have been noted in which large groups of people will rush toward one door, trampling one another, despite the fact that other nearby exits are completely open.

Leadership is of vital importance during the warning phase. Authorities must issue clear, specific advice via an adequate communication system in order to avoid panic and ensure compliance with appropriate defensive or evasive measures.

IMPACT PHASE

Little is known of behavior during the true brief impact phase, but it probably involves measures aimed mainly at staying alive, such as seeking shelter or protecting oneself from flying debris, or holding on to something to avoid being swept away. It is estimated that during the immediate postimpact period, 12–25% of all victims will remain effective, 12–25% will be in a state of panic or confusion, and 50–75% will be dazed, stunned, or bewildered. This last group of victims experience what has been termed the disaster syndrome, characterized by absence of emotion, inhibition of activity, docility, indecisiveness, withdrawal, denial, and automatic behavior, such as aimless walking or running. These can be viewed as maladaptive attempts at fight or flight, prompted by the inability to process in an orderly fashion the overwhelming stimuli being received in the wake of the disaster. Additionally, the individual displays physiologic manifestations of automatic arousal: tremors, sweating, the startle reaction, palpitations, hyperventilation, and crying. Keeping busy with a task, supplying leadership, or alleviating others' distress may help one to regain self-control.

RECOIL PHASE

This phase, also referred to as the *inventory phase,* begins when the initial stresses have ceased and physical escape has been managed. Individual self-awareness and recall begin to return, along with emotional expression; victims begin taking stock and assimilating impressions. They may become dependent, talkative, or childlike, form unstable groups, or seek safety. Recovery from the disaster syndrome will occur at various rates. In general, during recoil, there is an overinvolvement in rescue activities and an uncritical acceptance of and strong loyalty to leaders who emerge during the rescue activities.

Pathologic emotional recoil may also occur, resulting in psychopathic activities such as looting, rape, and heavy drinking. Alternatively, some individuals may exhibit the *counter-disaster syndrome* of overconscientiousness, hyperactivity, loss of efficiency, and irrational behavior. An example of such irrational behavior was seen recently, as rescue workers pulled tangled bodies from the rubble at the Hyatt Regency Hotel disaster in Kansas City; a hotel official was seen standing on top of the debris and telling firefighters not to break any windows (49).

Although one might expect panic to be a common occurrence following a disaster, it is in fact rare. The important thing to be aware of, from a management point of view, is that panic is contagious. One panic-stricken individual, if allowed to go free, may precipitate headlong mass flight. Consequently, early segregation and control are of urgent concern. Gentle firmness should be tried, but if this fails, it may be necessary for two or three individuals forcefully to restrain the panic victim and remove him to a treatment facility. If necessary, sedation is also acceptable.

General management during the recoil phase involves centralized treatment areas, which should be set up near the disaster scene as soon as possible. Victims should be provided with support, rest, and knowledge of what has happened and what can be expected, with frequent updating of news information. Most important is the opportunity and encouragement to communicate with other victims. Warm liquids, in the form of soup, coffee, tea, or the like, should be provided to create a safe, nurturing atmosphere.

POSTTRAUMATIC PHASE

This period may last from months to years. Initially, there is a rising tide of activity. People are called upon to perform heroic actions to save their property and that of others; altruism abounds. This early period has been termed by some (78) the *heroic phase,* followed by the *honeymoon, disillusionment,* and *reconstruction phases.* At the beginning, there is a strong sense of having shared and survived with other community members a dangerous and catastrophic experience. Victims are buoyed by an influx of official and governmental workers, and by promises. Later, anger, disappointment, resentment, and bitterness may surface when hopes and promises of aid fail to materialize and the full reason for and magnitude of the disaster have unfolded.

Anger may be individual or collective, and may be directed toward individuals or groups, including minority ethnic groups, the government, civic officials, large companies, or the financially successful. In many cases, this anger turns to scapegoating and may unleash latent hostility against certain groups. Examples are the Coconut Grove fire, after which Jews were blamed, or the sinking of the *Titanic,* for which Italians were held responsible.

As individuals become more aware of the disaster's impact, loss and bereavement are accompanied by the occurrence of psychiatric problems (32,58). These include guilt, depressive reactions, defensive neuroses, and phobias (46). Other changes which have been noted include increased smoking and drinking, and loss of interest in sex and socializing. Some of these long-term manifestations are discussed below.

Long-Term Psychiatric Manifestations

THE DEATH IMPRINT

The concept of a *death imprint* has been described following an extensive psychiatric investigation of survivors of the Buffalo Creek disaster (74). It consists of memories and images of the disaster, invariably associated with death, dying, and mass destruction. Such images are maintained years after a catastrophic event. That a disaster can produce such indelible images should not be surprising when one considers the horrific nature of such events. One especially vivid account described what happened on February 26, 1972, when a dam formed by the Buffalo Mining Company's "gob piles" gave way, setting loose 1 million gallons of water and black mud down the Buffalo Creek Valley. Everything was destroyed in the path of the flood, which killed 118 persons and left 4000 homeless. "This Appalachian tidal wave, carrying houses, human bodies, trailers, cars and all sorts of debris, completed its devastation of the 18 mile valley in no more than 15 minutes, and within 3 hours everything had washed into the Guyanelotte River" (74).

Indeed, with the mere printed word conjuring up such a horrible image, it is no surprise that a death imprint occurred. Associated symptoms are terrifying dreams, fears of crowds, and phobias. Phobias are especially strong in children, and are usually limited to the nature of the disaster. Victims of floods have been noted to hide in a stairwell at the start of a rain, while earthquake victims suffer inner terror as a truck rumbles down a street.

Guilt is another long-term neurosis among survivors. In some cases, this stems from a feeling that somehow they survived *because* someone else perished. Other victims are plagued by the irrational belief that they could have or should have done something to save those who died.

Special Risk Groups

CHILDREN

While reactions in children vary slightly with age, the predominant fear at all ages is separation from parents. Other problems include sleep disturbances, night terror, persistent fears about natural events, fears of future disasters, loss of interest in school, a loss of personal responsibility, and regressive symptoms. Adolescents may develop psychosomatic symptoms such as headaches and ab-

dominal pain and signs such as rashes, amenorrhea, and diarrhea.

THE ELDERLY

During the warning and impact phases, elderly persons may receive warnings later than the rest of the population, are less likely to leave their home, and can be expected to restrict their own rescue efforts to their immediate family and give less help to the community. A later psychologic reaction is characterized by a strong sense of deprivation with the loss of property and objects that symbolize ties with the past. The aged despair at the real improbability of ever restoring their former lives; the time is simply lacking.

RESCUE WORKERS AND HOSPITAL STAFF

Individuals involved in rescue and relief operations may show emotional reactions similar to those of victims, including hyperactivity, anger, denial, withdrawal, depression, irritability, nightmares, and insomnia. Because of their heavy professional responsibility, long hours, and daily exposure to victims of injury and acute stress, rescue and hospital personnel in the postdisaster period are at high risk of developing the *burnout syndrome*. Symptoms of burnout can be grouped into four categories, with examples listed for each:

1. *Thinking*—Mental confusion, slowness of thought, indecisiveness, lack of judgment
2. *Psychological*—Irritability, hyperexcitability, anxiety, depression
3. *Somatic*—Physical exhaustion, loss of energy, bowel disturbances, sleep disorders
4. *Behavioral*—Hyperactivity, social isolation, resentment

Burnout tends to creep up, unrecognized by the individual, and therefore must be recognized by co-workers or authorities. Workers suffering from burnout should be persuaded to take time off from work in order to recover.

Differential Diagnosis

The last word about psychologic sequelae of disasters is a reminder that physical disorders must not be mistaken for those that are psychologic. Various types of head injuries may occur during a disaster, including blast concussion, cerebral anoxia, toxic chemical reactions, or the effects of nuclear radiation. Other symptoms may arise as the result of contamination of food or water, or from the lack of usual medical care, especially among older or dependent individuals. Changes in physical surroundings may also result in water, food, or sleep deprivation. Examples of more insidious poisoning result from the disruption of a normal ventilation system.

Conclusion

Increasing technology, proliferating nuclear capabilities, increasing populations with high-density housing, increasing terrorism, and other such factors expose modern people to ever-increasing odds of experiencing a disaster. At the same time, as humans seek to escape civilization and return to the wilderness, individuals or groups of people are exposed to other dangers. Finally, there is a steady "background noise" of natural disasters that occur, and from which there is an ever-increasing expectation that people can be rescued. Communities in general, and medical facilities in particular, must therefore plan for the very real possibility of having to care for large numbers of individuals who have been injured or displaced in what is commonly called a disaster. While each community will have to plan according to its particular needs and resources, the principal elements of disaster planning and management, as detailed in this chapter, will remain the same.

Each of us can only hope that disaster does not touch our lives; however, if it does, it is satisfying and rewarding to know that we have minimized death and destruction through careful disaster planning and efficient implementation of the plan.

References

1. ACEP Position Paper: The role of the emergency physician in mass casualty disaster management. *JACEP,* **5:**901–2, 1976.

2. American Hospital Association: *Disaster Management—A Planning Guide for Hospital Administrators.* Chicago, 1966.
3. American Hospital Association: *Readings in Disaster Planning for Hospitals.* Chicago, 1966.
4. American Hospital Association: *Readings in Disaster Preparedness for Hospitals.* Chicago, 1973.
5. Barton, A.: *Communities in Disaster.* Doubleday and Co., New York, 1969.
6. Bowers, W., Hughes, C.: *Surgical Philosophies in Mass Casualty Management.* Charles C Thomas Publisher, Springfield, Ill., 1960.
7. Bowle, M., Parad, H., *et al.: Emergency and Disaster Management.* Charles Press Publishers, Inc., Bowie, Maryland, 1976.
8. Breo, D.: Nuclear scare tests hospital disaster plan. *Hospitals,* **53:**33–36, May, 1979.
9. Byrd, T.: Disaster medicine: Toward a more rational approach. *Milit Med,* **145:**270–73, April, 1980.
10. Camp, F.: Lessons learned applicable to civil disaster: Recipient identification and blood transfusion. *J Trauma,* **15:**743–44, August, 1975.
11. Christopher, P. J., Selig, M.: Medical Aspects of the Granville Rail Disaster. *Med J Aust,* **2:**383–85, September, 1970.
12. Demans, A., *et al.:* Victim tracking cards in a community disaster drill. *Ann Emerg Med,* **9:**207–9, 1980.
13. Disaster planning for mass casualties. In *Early Care of the Injured Patient:* 2nd ed., Kennedy, R. H. (ed.). W. B. Saunders Co., Philadelphia, 1976, pp. 433–37.
14. *Disaster Response Plan:* State of California, Department of Health Sciences. Approved March 13, 1980.
15. Drayer, C., *et al.:* Psychological first aid in community disasters. *JAMA,* **156:**36–41, 1954.
16. Edwards, J.: Psychiatric aspects of civilian disasters. *Br Med J,* **1:**944–47, 1976.
17. *Emergency Care in Natural Disasters: Views of an International Seminar, WHO Chron,* **34:**96–100, March, 1980.
18. Esqueda, K.: Is the nation prepared for an emergency? *Hospitals,* **53:**237–38, July, 1979.
19. Evren, L. W.: *Handbook of Emergency Care and Rescue.* Glencoe Press, London, 1976.
20. Fisher, C. J.: Mobile triage team in a community disaster plan. *JACEP,* **6:**10, 1971.
21. Fitzgerald, R.: Prehospital care of burned patients. *Crit Care Q,* **1**(3):13–23, 1978.
22. Friedman, E.: Updating disaster plans: A tale of three hospitals. *Hospitals,* **52:**95–101, 1978.
23. Galvin, J.: Hospital makes itself center for treatment of radiation victims. *Hospitals,* **53:**37–40, May, 1979.
24. Garb, S., Eng, E.: *Disaster Handbook.* Springer Publishing Co., New York.
25. General Services Administration: *Emergency War Surgery.* United States Government Printing Office, Washington, D.C., 1956.
26. Ghent, W.: Disaster. *CMA J,* **110:**917–18, 1974.
27. Gibson, W. H.: Disaster planning. *J Soc Occup Med,* **26:**136–38, 1976.
28. Gierson, E., Richman, L.: Valley triage: An approach to mass casualty care. *J Trauma,* **15:**193–96, 1975.
29. Glass, A. J.: Psychological aspects of disaster. *JAMA,* **171:**22–5, 1959.

30. Glass, A. The psychological aspects of emergency situations. In *Psychological Aspects of Stress,* Abram, H. A. (ed.), Charles C Thomas, Springfield, Ill., 1970, pp. 64–7.

31. Graham, N. K.: *Psychological Implications of Disasters.* St. Francis Conference on Disasters, Lynwood, Calif., 1981.

32. Grant, W. B., *et al.:* Psychiatric disturbance in Darwin evacuees following cyclone Tracy. *Med J Aust,* **1**:650–52, 1975.

33. Healy, R.: *Emergency and Disaster Planning.* John Wiley and Sons, Inc., New York, 1969.

34. Henry, S.: Mississauga Hospital: Largest evacuation in Canada's history. *CMA,* **121**:582–86, 1980.

35. Huckstep, R.: Simple Guidelines to Disasters. *Aust Fam Physician* **7**:36–48, 1978.

36. Hughes, J.: Disaster prevention—planning for a rock concert. *Ariz Med,* **35**:267–69, 1978.

37. Iacobell, F., Schodowski, L.: Fire reaction training that really works. *Hospitals,* **54**:64–6, February, 1980.

38. International Conference on Disaster Medicine: *S Afr Med J,* **11**:455–59, September, 1979.

39. Irving, M.: Major disasters: Hospital admission procedures. *Br J Surg,* **63**:731–34, 1976.

40. Jacobs, L., *et al.:* An emergency medical system approach to disaster planning. *J Trauma,* **19**:157–62, 1979.

41. Jimenez, L. S.: Planning health services for emergency situations. *PAHO Bull,* **11**:31–40, 1977.

42. Johnson, J.: Evaluating a disaster plan the hard way. *Cross Reference,* **6**:1–4, March–April, 1976.

43. Keller, E.: A realistic approach to disaster planning. *Hosp Medical Staff,* 18–23, May, 1977.

44. Kentsmith, D.: Minimizing the psychological effects of a wartime disaster on an individual. *Aviat Space Environ Med,* **51**:409–11, April, 1980.

45. King, E. G.: The Moorgate disaster: Lessons for the internist. *Ann Intern Med,* **83**:333–34, 1976.

46. Kingston, W., Rosser, R.: Disaster: Effects on mental and physical state. *J Psychosom Res,* **18**:437–65, 1974.

47. Lechat, M.: Disaster and public health. *Bull WHO,* **57**:11–17, 1979.

48. Leonard, R., Ricks, R.: Emergency department radiation accident protocol. *Ann Emerg Med,* **9**:462–70, 1980.

49. *Los Angeles Times,* July 18, 1931, p. 1, column 6.

50. Marian, J. P., Bougarte, W.: Disaster preparedness. In *Principles and Practice of Emergency Medicine,* Vol II, Schwartz, G. R., *et al.* (eds.). W. B. Saunders, Philadelphia, 1978, pp. 1422–27.

51. Mendelson, J.: The selection of plasma volume expanders for mass casualty planning. *J Trauma,* **14**:987–88, 1974.

52. Moles, T. M.: Planning for major disasters. *Br J Anaesth,* **49**:643, 1977.

53. Moorgate tube train disaster. *Br Med J,* **3**:927–31, September, 1975.

54. Naggan, L.: Medical planning for disaster in Israel. *Injury,* **7**:279–85, 1975.

55. National Institute of Mental Health: *Training Manual for Human Service Workers in Major Disasters.* Institute for the Studies of Destructive Behaviors and the Los Angeles Suicide Prevention Center, 1978.

56. O'Brien, P.: The hospital isn't closed—we've just relocated. A New Brunswick disaster plan. *CMA J,* **120**:1132–38, 1979.

57. Oliver, T.: A major rig disaster. *Prog Roy Soc Med,* **69**:20, 1969.

58. Parker, G.: Psychological disturbance in Darwin evacuees following cyclone Tracy. *Med J Aust,* **1**:650–52, 1975.

59. Perry, R. W.: Evacuation decision making in natural disasters. *Mass Emergencies,* **4**:25–37, 1979.

60. Pons, P., Holland, B., Alfrey, E., *et al.:* An advanced emergency medical care system at National Football League games. *Ann Emerg Med,* **9**:203–6, 1980.

61. Robinson, J. O.: Prepared for a disaster? *Br Med J,* **3**:727–31, September, 1975.

62. Queen, C. R.: Disaster. *Tex Med,* **73**:88–92, August, 1977.

63. Raker, J., *et al.: Emergency Medical Care in Disasters. A Summary of Recorded Experience.* Natural Academy of Sciences, Natural Research Committee, Washington, D.C., 1950.

64. Rerace, R.: Role of medical teams in a community disaster plan. *CMA J,* **120**:923–28, 1979.

65. Rooen, W.: Rock festival health services—hospitals should gear for rise in transient health problems. *Can Hosp,* **4**:8, 1971.

66. Savage, P. E.: Disaster planning: The use of action cards. *Br Med J,* **3**:942–43, 1972.

67. Simoneau, K., Barber, J., Budassi, S.: Disaster aspects of emergency nursing. In *Emergency Nursing Principles and Practice.* Barber, J., and Budassi, S. (eds.), C. V. Mosby Co., Saint Louis, 1981.

68. Stalcup, S. A., Oscherwitz, M., Cohen, M. S., *et al.:* Planning for a pediatric disaster: Experience gained from caring for 1600 Vietnamese orphans. *N Engl J Med,* **293**:691–95, 1976.

69. State of California, Office of Emergency Services: *Disaster Medical/Health Plan,* March, 1981.

70. Step-by-step emergency plan keeps hospital staff prepared. *Hospitals,* **52**(19):32, Oct. 1, 1978.

71. Stoll, M., Allen, E. W.: Ice storm tests disaster plan. *Dimens Health Serv,* **53**:32–3, 1976.

72. Winton, R. R.: The psychological management of disaster victims. *Med J Aust,* **1**:637–39, 1975.

73. Theoret, J.: Exercise London: A disaster exercise involving numerous casualties. *CMA J,* **114**:697–99, 1979.

74. Titchner, J. L., Kapp, F. T., Winget, C.: The Buffalo Creek syndrome. *Emergency and Disaster Management.* Parad, Resnik, Parad (eds.). Charles Press Publishers, Inc., Bowie, Maryland, 1976.

75. Tyhurst, J. S.: Psychological and social aspects of civilian disaster. *Can Med Assoc J,* **76**:385–93, 1957.

76. Tyhurst, J. S.: Individual reactions to community disaster. In *The Natural History of Psychiatric Phenomena.* 764–69.

77. United States Department of the Air Force: *Medical Planning for Disaster and Casualty Control.* United States Air Force Medical Service, 1967.

78. United States Department of Health, Education and Welfare. *Training Manual for Human Service Workers in Major Disasters,* 1978.

79. Whitton, J.: *Disasters.* University of Georgia Press, Athens, Ga., 1979.

80. Whyte, A.: Disaster wound treatment. *Br Med J,* **4:**43–4, October, 1975.
81. Wilkins, E., Jr.: The emergency ward and the community. In *M.G.H. Textbook of Emergency Medicine,* Wilkins, E. W., Dineen, J. J., Moncuré, A. C. (eds.). Williams & Wilkins Co., Baltimore, 1978, pp. 739–50.
82. Winch, R. D., *et al.:* Disaster procedures report: Report following the Moorgate train crash on February 28, 1975. *Injury,* **7:**288–91, 1976.
83. Zimmerman, J. M.: Casualty Management. In *The Management of Trauma,* 3rd ed., Ballinger, W. F., Rutherford, R. B., Zuidema, G. D. (eds.). W. B. Saunders Co., Philadelphia, 1979, pp. 780–94.

21 | INHALATION INJURIES

Brian D. Johnston, M.D.

Inhalation Injuries

In the discussion that follows, *inhalation injury* is defined as an injury to the respiratory system or to the body which results from inhalation of toxic or otherwise injurious material.

Inhalation injury causes a large and heterogeneous group of clinical entities ranging from slowly progressive and insidious pneumoconioses to rapidly fatal exposure to cyanide, hydrogen sulfide, and carbon monoxide. The cause of the injury may be obvious, as in smoke inhalation, which killed at least 5500 Americans and injured 18,000 more in 1979 (44,99). It may also be obscure, as in chronic carbon monoxide exposure (44,99). Patients may become ill and die hours after the exposure, as do some victims who breathe phosgene and hydrochloric acid. Patients who inhale metallic fumes typically present with fever, malaise, and myalgia 6 or more hours after exposure. Clearly, with exposure and onset of symptoms separated in time and mind,

making the proper diagnosis may present a real challenge to even the most astute physician. Thus, the physician who cares for such patients will need a great deal of information about the toxic properties of the material and the exposure and condition of the patient in order to determine the extent of injury and to move in orderly fashion to correct the physiologic derangements. Patients with inhalation injuries demand the highest level of knowledge and skill of their physicians.

TECHNOLOGY AND INHALATION INJURY

Inhalation injury is overwhelmingly a disease of civilization and technology; society becomes more vulnerable as the trend from one-story wood buildings to high-rise offices and apartments continues. The existing potential for inhalation injury is magnified by several factors:

1. Greater use of plastics and synthetic materials in buildings and conveyances

2. Increased dependence on controlled ventilation systems
3. Increased production and transportation of toxic chemicals

Thus, physicians will be increasingly forced to deal with people poisoned by smoke generated by structural and vehicular fires (11, 12,29). In particular, they will have to evaluate and treat those whose inability to escape forces them to breathe toxic gases, as well as to treat those who are exposed to noxious material at spills and transportation mishaps (8,9,47).

WILDERNESS SETTING

Inhalation injuries are not widely reported in wilderness settings. Nevertheless, the potential exists for such injuries to occur as a result of smoke inhalation from forest fires, exposure to carbon dioxide or methane collections in mines and caves, or exposure to hot gases and ash from volcanic eruptions (19,30). Campers and climbers are subject to carbon monoxide poisoning from fires built in shelters that are used for heat and preparation of food. High-altitude pulmonary edema does not fit the above definition of inhalation injury and thus is not included in this chapter.

SMOKE INHALATION, CLASSIC AND NEW

The previously single category of smoke inhalation can be divided into classic and new smoke inhalation. Although there are shared characteristics in these subgroups that create some overlap, the distinction calls attention to recent changes in the injury setting, the responsible agents, the character of the injury, and the potential clinical courses of the victims. *Classic* smoke inhalation refers to inhalation injuries seen in association with house fires, while *new* smoke inhalation refers to injuries caused by plastic-fueled fires that generate smoke and toxic thermal degradation products in closed or poorly ventilated spaces.

Classic Smoke Inhalation

There are numerous good summary articles on all aspects of this injury (22,48,93,103). In addition, because these injuries occur fre-

quently and are geographically well dispersed, there is considerable clinical experience with them in the medical community.

Residential fires are fueled by wood, natural fibers, and, to a lesser extent, paint and some plastics. Smoke generated by such fires contains carbon monoxide, carbon dioxide, acrolein or propanaldehyde, other aldehydes, and fine soot to which toxic material may adhere (85). There are indications that residential fires may generate significant levels of hydrogen cyanide, although the sources of the cyanide and its clinical important remain unclear (41,87,95).

RESIDENTIAL COMBUSTION PRODUCTS

The interactions of noxious substances which produce the clinical picture of classic smoke inhalation vary from fire to fire. However, some generalizations can be made about the toxic sources and their individual contributions to the clinical picture (Table 1) (88).

CARBON MONOXIDE

Although carbon monoxide (CO) is discussed in greater detail later in this chapter, a summary of its effects is included here. First, CO has an approximate 220-fold greater affinity for hemoglobin than does oxygen (71). Thus, in small concentrations, it displaces oxygen from hemoglobin and markedly diminishes the oxygen-carrying capacity of hemoglobin. In addition, it alters the tertiary configuration of the hemoglobin molecule, resulting in an unfavorable shift of the oxygen-hemoglobin dissociation constant (72). In the presence of carboxyhemoglobin (COHb), oxyhemoglobin unloads oxygen in the tissues less effectively (34). The resultant tissue hypoxia engages anaerobic metabolism, which produces progressive lactic acidosis if uncorrected (13).

To a lesser extent, carbon monoxide binds to myoglobin and intracellular cytochrome systems and can produce rhabdomyolysis and myoglobinuria (23). Further, carbon monoxide is cardiotoxic (2,91). Finally, cerebral hypoxia produces a continuum of neurologic symptoms that culminate in coma and death (74). Apparent recovery from severe carbon monoxide poisoning may be followed by delayed, severe central and peripheral nerve damage (35).

ACROLEIN

Acrolein, the three-carbon aldehyde, is the principal toxic product of wood combustion. Like common tissue fixatives, such as formaldehyde and glutaraldehyde, it denatures protein. Prolonged inhalation or exposure to concentrations of 150 parts per million (ppm) for as little as 10 minutes is lethal. Severe bronchorrhea and bronchospasm result from inhalation and contribute to the ventilation-perfusion mismatch frequently documented in smoke inhalation. This mismatch is thought to produce prolonged, severe hypoxia after the exposure to smoke is terminated (17,25,48, 59,67). Acrolein can also produce pulmonary edema with prolonged exposures to concentrations as low as 21 ppm (70).

CYANIDE

The presence of significant quantities of cyanide (HCN) in smoke from residential fires may previously have been underestimated (37). Its presence in the blood and tissues of fire victims in England and the United States has been documented (3,20,87,95). Hillenbrand and Wray reported 700 ppm HCN in the effluent gases of a typical American bedroom which was burned under experimental conditions (41).

The source of the HCN is not entirely clear. In Hillenbrand and Wray's report, the manifest of the contents of the room indicated that a chair with urethane foam padding was burned; no other significant source of urethane was detailed. In many American homes, urethane is found in mattresses, pillows, and carpet backing. Urethane, however, is not the only source of HCN. Paper generates nearly as much HCN as does urethane, and wool generates more than five times as much HCN as does urethane (90). Nylon, another source of HCN, can be found in carpets, clothing, and drapes.

Postmortem measurements of tissue cyanide in smoke inhalation victims is subject to considerable error. Further, it is seldom reported (20). Thus, it is difficult to know with any certainty the frequency and clinical significance of cyanide poisoning in victims of residential fires. The astute physician must include HCN poisoning in the differential diagnosis. The report of Clark *et al.* strongly suggested that the presence of a high percentage of carboxyhemoglobin was a valid indicator of concurrent cyanide poisoning (20). However, 26% of CO-poisoned victims in Wetherell's series had no concurrent cyanide poisoning (95). In view of the difficulty of obtaining cyanide levels rapidly, Clark *et al.* advocated treating suspected cyanide poisoning based upon the clinical presentation and significant carboxyhemoglobinemia. Wetherell's data do not support this conclusion.

CLINICAL FINDINGS

The clinical picture of classic smoke inhalation is a mosaic that reflects the different mechanisms of injury (33,101). It includes the contributions of carbon monoxide poisoning (tissue hypoxia), pulmonary irritants such as acrolein and other aldehydes (alveolar injury, bronchospasm, and bronchorrhea), and mismatched ventilation and perfusion. Hypoxia may also result from decreased ambient oxygen, but there is no consistent or convincing experimental data to demonstrate decreased ambient oxygen at fires (37,90). Thermal injuries of the airway and possibly HCN poisoning may contribute as well.

Underlying illnesses increase the vulnerability of certain patients to physiologic decompensation after smoke inhalation. Patients with preexisting heart disease have suffered myocardial infarctions, and patients with preexisting bronchospasm have had significant exacerbations of their underlying disease when exposed to heavy smoke concentrations (48). Thus, the physiologic insults of smoke inhalation must often be superimposed upon chronic obstructive lung disease, asthma, bronchitis, and atherosclerotic heart disease.

The clinical findings of classic smoke inhalation are chemical irritation or injury of the respiratory tree, response to inhaled soot and particulate matter, tissue hypoxia from either impaired ventilation exchange or cellular respiration, and thermal burns. Chemical irritation and injury result in conjunctivitis, lacrimation, rhinorrhea, bronchorrhea, bronchospasm, and perhaps pulmonary

TABLE 1
Noxious Gases

Source	Toxic Product	Toxicity/Clinical Syndrome	Remarks
A. Plastics	See below	See below	Increasing future use probable
1. Polyvinyl chloride	a. Hydrogen chloride	a. Dyspnea, burning mucous membranes, chest pain, lethal dysrhythmias, light-headedness, laryngeal and pulmonary edema	a. Toxic levels appear before significant amounts of smoke; persist for up to 1 hour after fire is extinguished
	b. Carbon monoxide	b. Light-headedness, nausea, dyspnea, chest pain, seizures, coma	b. Symptoms depend on carbon monoxide concentration, minute ventilation and reflect tissue hypoxia
2. Polyurethane	a. Carbon monoxide	a. See A.1.b. above	a. See A.1.b. above
	b. Toluene 2,4-diisocyanate	b. Light-headedness, nausea, dyspnea, chest pain, syncope	b. Potent pulmonary irritant; prolonged wheezing common
	c. Hydrocyanic acid	c. Weakness, vascular collapse, no cyanosis	c. Binds Fe^{3+} ions, interrupts cellular electron transport; R_x: sodium nitrite and sodium thiosulfate
3. Polystyrene	a. Carbon monoxide	a. See A.1.b. above	a. See A.1.b. above
	b. Styrene	b. Conjunctivitis, rhinorrhea, mucous membrane burning, central nervous system (CNS) depression	b. Less toxic than other noxious gases

4. Acrylics	Aircraft windows, textiles, wood finishes, wall coverings, furniture, piping	a. Carbon monoxide b. Acrolein	a. See A.1.b. above b. Burning mucous membranes, light-headedness, dyspnea	a. See A.1.b. above b. Toxicity results from denaturing proteins
5. Cellulosics	Film, fabrics, automobiles	a. Nitrogen dioxide b. Acetic acid c. Formic acid	a. Mucosal irritation and edema, pulmonary edema, bronchiolitis obliterans	a. Steroids may be indicated for bronchiolitis obliterans
B. Nylon	Carpeting, clothes, upholstery	a. Ammonia b. Hydrocyanic acid	a. Conjunctivitis, burning mucous membranes, laryngeal and pulmonary edema b. See A.2.c. above	a. Binds with cells and produces liquefaction necrosis; not neutralized by tissue fluids b. See A.2.c. above
C. Chlorine	Water purification, swimming pools, industrial and transportation mishaps	a. Chlorine gas	a. See A.1.a. above	a. Hydrolyzes in lung water to produce hydrochloric acid; not a lacrimator
D. Phosgene	Military weapons, synthesis of polypeptides	a. Carbonyl chloride Hydrogen chloride	a. See A.1.a. above	a. Prolonged latent period of up to 24 hours; may act as source of hydrochloric acid or denature protein by action of $C=0$ group on sulfhydrils
E. Anhydrous ammonia	Stored under pressure for use as fertilizer	a. Ammonia	a. See B.a. above	a. See B.a. above

edema. Chemical irritation can produce tracheolaryngeal mucosal edema, which can cause respiratory obstruction and even sloughing of entire tracheobronchial casts (68). Airway obstruction, altered mechanics of ventilation, ventilation-perfusion mismatch, and accumulated secretions may contribute to hypoxia and produce clinical cyanosis (22, 36,48,67,89,92,103). Smoke-injured patients typically complain of shortness of breath, difficulty in breathing (increased muscular work), and chest pain. They may have cough, wheezing, stridor, and dysphonia. On examination, tachypnea, wheezing, rhonchi, and, less commonly, rales may be present.

HYPOXIA

Tissue hypoxia, whether from poor ventilation, altered gas exchange, or disruption of cellular respiration, produces end organ failure in proportion to the oxygen requirement of the tissue. Tissue hypoxia from carbon monoxide intoxication, cyanide poisoning, or impaired oxygen delivery results in lactic acidemia and metabolic acidosis, which probably contribute to the tachypnea seen in smoke inhalation victims (13,38). Brain hypoxia results in a continuum of dysfunction that ranges from agitation to impaired judgment, stupor, coma, and death (26,74,78). Myocardial hypoxia may result in dysrhythmias, such as paroxysmal atrial fibrillation, angina, or myocardial infarction (2,6,48).

It has been proposed that decreased ambient oxygen contributes to hypoxia and the overall picture of smoke inhalation (Table 2). This mechanism is at least variably operant. In studies in which standing gasoline was ignited in a closed bunker, the fire self-extinguished, while the ambient oxygen remained at 14%, a survivable level (61). Subsequent work in which burning gasoline or napalm was injected into bunkers produced nearly complete and prolonged exhaustion of ambient oxygen. In light of the conflicting data, it is difficult to classify definitively situations in which decreased ambient oxygen and subsequent hypoxia of exposed individuals contribute to the clinical picture of smoke inhalation. Studies in which ambient oxygen was measured by firemen did not show significant depletion at the scene of the fire (37).

THERMAL INJURIES

Thermal injuries of the respiratory tract frequently contribute to the clinical picture of smoke inhalation. Persons trapped in a fire may have no choice but to breathe flame or very hot gases. This usually results in a thermal injury to the tissues of the upper airway and respiratory tract, which is most commonly confined to the nose, nasopharynx, mouth, oropharynx, hypopharynx, larynx, and upper trachea. These injuries may result in edema accumulation that may obstruct the airway and produce asphyxia. Thermal injury to the respiratory tract can also cause tracheitis and mediastinitis.

Thermal injury to the airway should be suspected when thermal injuries to the head, face, and neck are noted. Suspicion is heightened by the presence of singed facial or nasal hair, burns of the nasal, oral, or pharyngeal mucosa, and stridor and/or dysphonia (62,85,102). In association with a history of exposure to flame and hot gases in a closed space, these clinical findings strongly suggest the presence of a thermal injury to the airway. In view of the potential for acute airway obstruction, there is obvious urgency in establishing this diagnosis. Most experts who treat thermal injuries of the tracheobronchial tree advocate early visualization of the vocal cords by laryngos-

TABLE 2
Human Response to Decreased Ambient Oxygen at Sea Level

Ambient Oxygen	Human Response
20.9%	Normal function
16–18%	Decreased stamina and capacity for work
12–15%	Dyspnea with walking; impaired coordination; variably impaired judgment
10–12%	Dyspnea at rest; consciousness preserved; impaired judgment, coordination, concentration
6–8%	Loss of consciousness; death without prompt reversal
Less than 6%	Death in 6–10 minutes

copy and bronchoscopy (63). Bronchoscopy is proving to be a useful predictor of the clinical course and urgency of intensive care unit (ICU) intervention. In addition, there is one report of a significantly increased incidence of pneumonia and late mortality in persons with facial burns as compared to those without them (98).

Burns of the lower trachea are rarely reported. In fact, injuries to and beyond the carina are difficult to produce when the trachea is cannulated and hot gases are delivered in the anesthetized dog (61,100). Air has a very low specific heat and is therefore a poor conductor of thermal energy. In addition, the thermal exchange systems of the upper airway are quite efficient. The hot gases or flame are cooled sufficiently in the upper airway so that they do not burn the bronchi or more distal structures. It should be noted, however, that although water or steam in the hot gas mixture is probably rare, it is a far more efficient conductor of heat and permits significant thermal injury to the lower trachea and bronchi.

A delayed onset (2–24 hours after smoke inhalation) of pulmonary edema and the adult respiratory distress syndrome is widely reported and should be anticipated. Whether this results from direct injury to alveoli, prolonged hypotension, or cerebral hypoxia and cerebral edema is unclear.

New Smoke Inhalation

The advent and wide use of synthetic fabrics and building materials in the past 20 years have markedly increased the likelihood and subsequent complications of inhalation injury (12). The substrates that produce the gases are new, the noxious gases have only recently been characterized, and their effects both at the fire and in the hours afterward may be misconstrued or overlooked (Table 1) (28, 29,97).

Persons who suffer new smoke inhalation are frequently confined, as in an aircraft, bus, train, or high-rise building (26,56). They are typically exposed to toxic materials such as carbon monoxide, acrolein, HCN, hydrogen chloride (HCl), ammonia, toluene 2,4-diisocyanate, nitrogen dioxide (NO_2), styrene, or sulfur dioxide (SO_2).

PLASTIC COMBUSTION PRODUCTS

Polyvinyl Chloride

The most widely studied and documented plastic is polyvinyl chloride (PVC) (Figure 1) (54,80). According to the Society of Plastics Industry, 5.47 billion pounds of PVC were manufactured in the United States in 1980 (79). First introduced in 1927, this material has physical properties that allow its use in the manufacture of unbreakable bottles, electrical insulation, wall coverings, wall and furniture moldings, structural and decorative components of business machines, and the interiors of automobiles, buses, aircraft, and other conveyances.

The combustion products of PVC vary, depending upon the availability of oxygen, the manner in which the polymer is formulated, and the substrate to which it is applied (92). When PVC is heated, it may release up to 58% of its original weight as invisible HCl. PVC burns at 475°C, producing hydrogen chloride (HCl) and CO (Figure 3). Burning PVC also produces dense smoke, which may hamper efforts to exit the fire scene or to find trapped persons.

Polyurethane

Polyurethane (Figure 2), introduced in 1954, is another ubiquitous plastic (54). In 1980, 1.9 billion pounds were produced in the United States (Figures 3 and 4) (12,79). Polyurethane can be produced as a moldable solid, as well as in sheets, films, and both soft and hard foams. Addition of halogen atoms, such as fluorine (F−), chlorine (Cl−), and bromine (Br−), to the urethane structure confers considerable resistance to heat, allowing it to be used as a thermal insulation in buildings, refrigerators, freezers, and vehicles. The rigid foam can be cut into panels and used in non-weight-bearing portions of walls. The soft

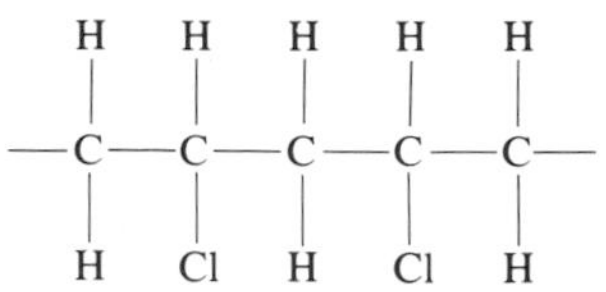

FIGURE 1 Polyvinyl chloride.

$$R - O - \underset{\underset{\displaystyle H}{|}}{\overset{\overset{\displaystyle O}{\|}}{C}} - N - R'$$

FIGURE 2 Polyurethane.

foam padding is commonly used for seat cushions and carpet backing. More than 1.8 million mattresses are made of polyurethane each year in this country. In 1979, the average American passenger car contained 45 pounds of polyurethane, compared to 19 pounds in 1970 (79). Total polyurethane use in transportation in 1980 was 288 million pounds (79).

Polyurethane can be explosively flammable once its heat of ignition is achieved (75). Upon combustion, it releases about 16,000 British thermal units (BTUs)/pound. This compares with 7100 BTUs/pound for cotton and 7700 BTUs/pound for polyvinyl chloride (79).

The products of polyurethane combustion and their characteristics are highly variable, depending upon the formulation, molecular modification during manufacture, availability of oxygen, and the substrate to which they are applied. The most abundant product is carbon monoxide, followed by toluene 2,4-di-isocyanate and hydrocyanic acid (Figure 4) (97). If halides (Cl^-, Br^-, F^-) have been incorporated in the urethane structure, their corresponding acids (HCl, HBr, HF) can be expected as well.

Styrene

Styrene (phenylethylene), introduced in 1938, is another commonly encountered plastic (Figure 5) (54). It is often found in buildings and vehicles as lightweight structural elements, packaging material, wall covering, telephones, appliances, luggage, and food containers. With the decline in the availability of hardwood and the increasing scarcity and cost of woodworking skills, styrene is rapidly replacing wood in the manufacture of furni-

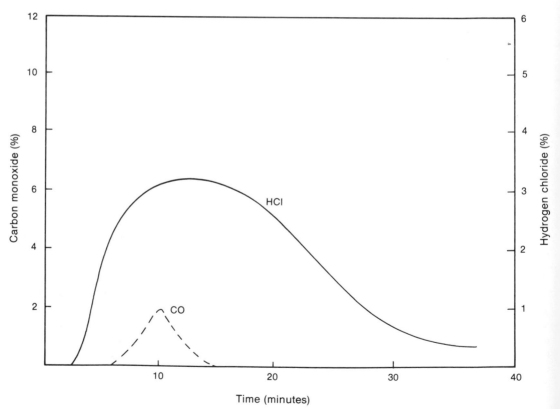

FIGURE 3 Toxic gas production from wood-PVC fire. (From Bowes, P. C.: Smoke and toxicity hazards of plastics in fire. *Ann Occup Hyg,* **17:** 143–57, 1974, with permission.)

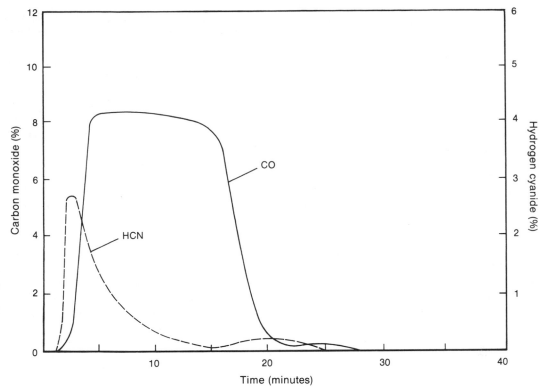

FIGURE 4 Toxic gas production from polyurethane fire. (From Bowes, P. C. Smoke and toxicity hazards of plastics in fire. *Ann Occup Hyg,* **17:** 143–57, 1974, with permission.)

ture. In 1980, 3.5 billion pounds were manufactured in the United States (79).

When burned, polystyrene produces styrene monomer and CO. The monomer is irritating but considerably less toxic than the chemical products mentioned previously. Under proper conditions, however, volatilized styrene can explode. This danger is principally encountered in its manufacture and has not been reported as a risk in structure fires.

Acrylics

Acrylics comprise a large and heterogeneous group of plastics. The basic core is acrylic acid and its corresponding aldehyde (Figures

6 and 7) (54). It can be polymerized as a polyester or as a polyamide (acrylamide) (see Figure 8) (54), with a wide variety of resultant compounds.

Acrylics are found in almost any structure or vehicle of recent manufacture and will be increasingly relied upon by engineers and designers. For instance, polymethylmethacrylate is frequently used as a substitute for glass. Its strength, weight, and wide temperature tolerance make it desirable for use in light diffusers, aircraft canopies, and windows. Further, acrylic textiles, mostly esters, are widely accepted and used. Acrylic paints, varnishes, wax, and other wood finishes are commonplace. Acrylonitrile-butadiene-styrene (ABS) is

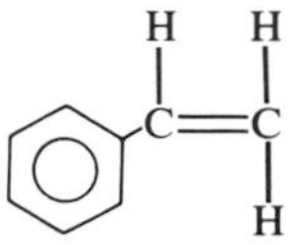

FIGURE 5 Styrene.

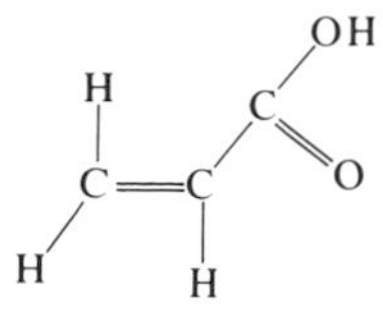

FIGURE 6 Acrylic acid.

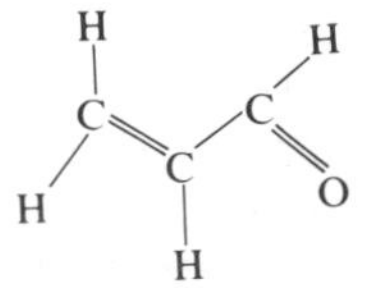

FIGURE 7   Aldehyde.

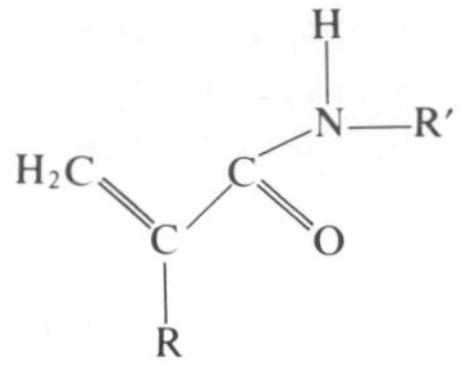

FIGURE 8   Acrylamide.

currently gaining wide acceptance as a piping material and in luggage. In 1980, 920 million pounds of ABS were manufactured in the United States (79).

Acrolein (Figure 9) (54), the aldehyde discussed previously, is the principal toxic product of the combustion of acrylics.

Nylon

Nylon is synthesized through the polycondensation of adipic acid and hexamethylene diamine (Figure 10) (54). In 1980, 248 billion pounds of nylon were manufactured; 77 billion pounds were used in automobiles and trucks, while 34 billion pounds found electrical and electronic application. Consumer products accounted for only 21 billion pounds, or less than 10% of production (79).

Ammonia and hydrocyanic acid are produced when nylon burns.

Cellulose-Based Polymers

Cellulose (Figure 11) (54) is a polymer of natural occurrence. It is modified by nitration, HNO_3, and H_2SO_4 to produce nitrocellulose. (Nitration is the substitution of NO_3 and other

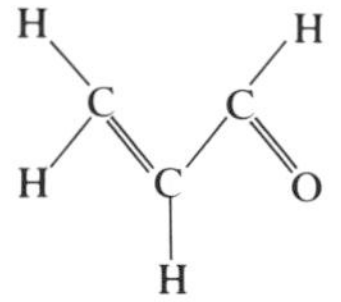

FIGURE 9   Acrolein.

$$HOOC(CH_2)\,4COOH + H_2N(CH_2)\,6NH_2$$

FIGURE 10   Nylon.

oxides of nitrogen in strong acids.) Nitrocellulose, the oldest plastic, was introduced in 1868. Some forms of this substance are called *celluloid*.

Nitrocellulose, which is quite flammable, produces nitrogen dioxide, carbon dioxide, and carbon monoxide on combustion (54).

Cellulose can be modified by a process similar to that noted above in which acetate residues are substituted, producing cellulose acetate. Probably the most widely known product manufactured by this process is the fabric Celanese.

TOXICITIES OF SPECIFIC PLASTIC COMBUSTION PRODUCTS

Hydrochloric Acid

Hydrogen chloride (HCl), the principal thermal degradation product of PVC, produces strong acid on hydrolysis. Hydrolysis is a reaction with water which results in an alteration in the dissociation equilibrium of water (H_2O), producing a relative increase in the OH− or H+ concentration of the resulting solution. When inhaled, HCl hydrolyzes on the moist surfaces of the mucosa of the tracheobronchial tree and the terminal respiratory units. Hydrochloric acid denatures protein and destroys the cells with which it has contact.

When heated, the ambient concentration of HCl may rise before the appearance of significant amounts of smoke; toxic levels may persist for up to 1 hour after the fire has been extinguished. This represents a significant risk to firefighters who remove their self-contained breathing apparatus based upon a visual estimate of the air quality and is particularly true of the cleanup or overhaul phase of a fire. Firefighters have taken off their masks and tanks and inhaled dangerous amounts of HCl during overhaul (28). Most persons exposed to smoke and fumes from burning PVC complain of shortness of breath, burning of the mucous membranes, and a squeezing tightness of the anterior chest, often associated with light-headedness.

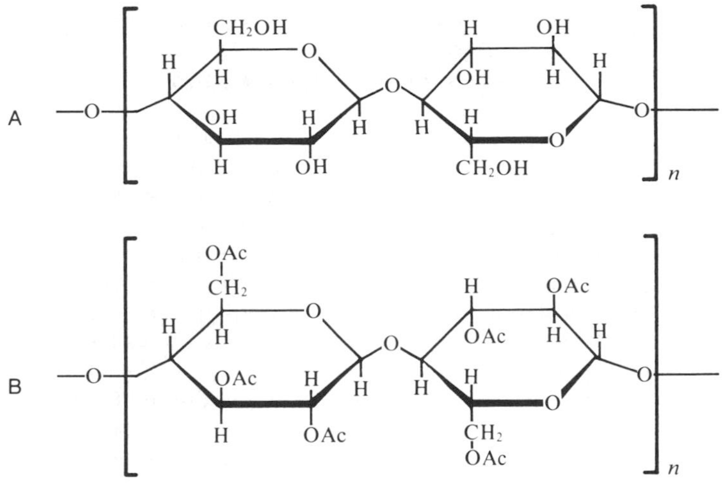

FIGURE 11 Cellulose (*A*) and cellulose triacetate (*B*). (From Mark H. F., Gaylord N. G. (eds.): *Encyclopedia of Polymer Science and Technology*, Vol. III. New York, John Wiley & Sons, 1969, with permission.)

Another form of toxicity from PVC smoke is cardiac dysrhythmia. Dyer and Esch reported the case of a firefighter who suffered a syncopal episode and transient respiratory tract irritation after a single 20-minute exposure to PVC smoke (28). He died 24 hours later in circumstances that suggested cardiac dysrhythmia. Subsequent studies of firefighters have indicated that about 20% have extrasystoles for several hours after PVC exposure; in approximately two-thirds of that group, the extrasystoles are premature ventricular contractions. Any person exposed to PVC fumes who complains of palpitations or who is found to have an irregular pulse should be monitored. If PVCs are demonstrated, hospitalization should be encouraged.

The maximum allowable concentration of HCl accepted by the American Conference of Governmental Industrial Hygienists for brief exposure is 5 ppm (70,83). Concentrations of up to 100 ppm have been tolerated for up to 1 hour (70). Laryngeal and pulmonary edema have been reported, but precise concentrations and exposure times required to produce these tissue reactions are not known (24). Although HCl is a powerful lacrimator, some firemen who work in a toxic environment have been observed to be unaffected by the noxious lacrimatory effect. This may result from a decreased sensitivity, due to the CNS effect of concurrent carbon monoxide toxicity. Acclimatization, or rise in the sensory threshold, may occur in the absence of concurrent carbon monoxide intoxication (70). Physicians who treat HCl inhalation should be aware that the lacrimatory effect may be blunted and that there may be a 2- to 12-hour latent period before the onset of pulmonary edema.

Chlorine Gas

Another source of pulmonary injury due to HCl is exposure to chlorine gas (Cl_2) (21,40,45). Chlorine gas hydrolyzes with body water to produce HCl (Figure 12) (70). Chlorine is detectable by odor at a concentration of 3.5 ppm. At a concentration of 15 ppm, it produces lacrimation. It is fatal at a concentration of 430 ppm breathed for only 30 minutes (40,70). The sequence, as with HCl, is lacrimation, mucosal burns and edema, variable laryngeal edema with respiratory obstruction, alveolitis, and pulmonary edema leading to death from hypoxia. Most serious poisonings result from transportation mishaps that involve cylinders of the gas or leakage of Cl_2 at water treatment facilities. Human exposure may result from an unwise or ignorant admixture of compounds that releases chlorine or HCl, but these exposures rarely result in clinically significant illness (32).

$$2Cl_2 + 2H_2O \longrightarrow 4HCl + O_2$$

FIGURE 12 Hydrolysis of chlorine gas into hydrochloric acid.

Phosgene

Another agent which may act in the same manner as HCl and chlorine is phosgene, or carbonyl chloride (Figure 13) (70), which has wide industrial and limited military applications.

Concentrations of 4.8 ppm phosgene produce coughing. Exposure to 50 ppm may be rapidly fatal (70). It is more dangerous than HCl, because it does not induce lacrimation and its odor is inoffensive. In addition to these treacherous properties, a latent period of 2–24 hours is required for the hydrolysis reaction to proceed (31). One theory of phosgene's mode of action is that it hydrolyzes to produce HCl in the respiratory tract. Another theory is that the carbonyl group reacts with tissue proteins in a manner similar to that of acrolein. Acting on this assumption, phosgene-poisoned patients have been treated with apparent success by infusing hexamethylenetetramine (methenamine) intravenously prior to the onset of symptoms (81). This therapy is based on the assumption that phosgene reacts preferentially with methenamine, thereby protecting tissue proteins.

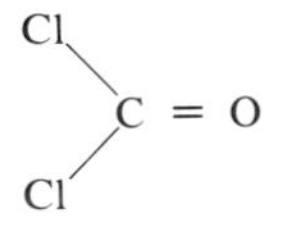

Fortunately, phosgene is not commonly encountered in fires. Nonetheless, health care personnel should be aware of the possibility of industrial or accident-related exposure which may threaten large numbers of people.

Carbon Monoxide

Carbon monoxide poisoning has been carefully studied and widely reviewed in the medical literature (10,49,57,71,76,90). Carbon monoxide acts principally by binding avidly to hemoglobin and preventing oxygen binding. The avidity with which CO binds is pH dependent, but ranges between 210 and 240 times that of oxygen. When CO binds to hemoglobin, forming carboxyhemoglobin (COHb), two factors immediately conspire to reduce tissue oxygenation. First, the oxygen available in the lungs cannot readily displace the CO from the carboxyhemoglobin, and is thus not exchanged and transported for oxidative metabolism in the tissues. Second, the presence of carboxyhemoglobin affects oxygen release by the remaining oxyhemoglobin, further reducing the oxygen-delivering capacity of the remaining oxyhemoglobin. This is called the *pheonectic effect,* and is readily demonstrated by comparing the normal oxygen-hemoglobin dissociation curve with the oxygen-hemoglo-

$$\begin{matrix} Cl \\ \diagdown \\ & C = O \\ \diagup \\ Cl \end{matrix}$$

FIGURE 13 Phosgene (carbonyl chloride).

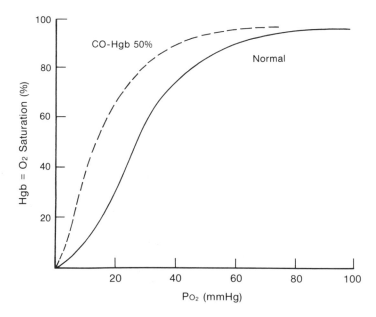

FIGURE 14 Normal oxygen-hemoglobin dissociation curve compared with oxyhemoglobin dissociation curve of 50% carboxyhemoglobinemia.

bin dissociation curve of 60% carboxyhemoglobinemia (Figure 14) (71).

Carbon monoxide binds to cytochrome a_3, thereby potentially crippling intracellular electron transport (16). This inhibition is not complete, and compensatory mechanisms exist to correct the defect partially. However, it demonstrates that CO is a molecular poison with properties similar to those of cyanide. In high concentrations, carbon monoxide also binds to myoglobin.

CO is produced endogenously as the result of porphyrin metabolism, resulting in normal levels of up to 1% carboxyhemoglobin (77). Persons with a hemolytic anemia, which produces accelerated porphyrin synthesis and degradation, will have higher levels, but this is not thought to have significant health consequences. Cigarette smokers typically have carboxyhemoglobin levels of 4–6%. Exposure to traffic or other engine exhaust gases can raise this level (5,50).

CO is almost totally excreted via the lungs; less than 0.1% is enzymatically converted intracellularly to CO_2. Pulmonary exchange in room air at 1 atmosphere is a slow process, with a half-life ($T_{1/2}$) of approximately 250 minutes. $T_{1/2}$ can be shortened to 40–50 minutes by breathing pure oxygen. Exposure to hyperbaric oxygen will further shorten $T_{1/2}$ to 15 minutes and simultaneously improve oxygen transport to tissues by markedly increasing the plasma O_2 carrying capacity.

PHYSIOLOGIC EFFECTS

The physiologic effects of acute CO poisoning are principally those of hypoxia at the cellular level (66). CO inhalation does not stimulate ventilation, although persons who become hypoxic and acidotic can be expected to demonstrate tachycardia, tachypnea, and increased cardiac output (71). Persons severely poisoned may subsequently suffer pulmonary edema, but this is more likely a result of hypoxia and decreased tissue perfusion or CNS insult than a direct toxic effect on the lung.

The effect of CO on the nervous system is dramatic (Table 3). Starting at levels of 5% carboxyhemoglobin, there is subtle impairment of vision, hearing, discrimination, and performance of complex tasks (7,39,58,60,

TABLE 3
Physiologic Effects of Carbon Monoxide

% COHb	Signs and Symptoms
0–5	None
5–10	Exacerbation of angina, decreased exercise tolerance, impaired concentration and fine discrimination, decreased visual acuity
10–20	Impaired performance of complex tasks; mild headache
20–30	Throbbing headache, decreased vision, nausea
30–40	Severe headache, confusion, decreased hearing, vision, and color perception, difficulty in walking, nausea and vomiting, tachypnea
40–50	Disorientation, syncope, acidemia, tachycardia, tachypnea
50–60	Collapse, coma, convulsions, cardiovascular collapse, cherry red mucosae
60–70	Coma, convulsions, cardiovascular collapse, death

74,96). From that level upward, coordination and motivation are progressively impaired. Nausea and vomiting occur at 25–35% COHb. Difficulty in walking is experienced at levels of 30% CoHb. Syncope and coma supervene above 40% COHb, with deep coma, convulsions, and death associated with levels of 60% COHb or more.

Carbon monoxide is cardiotoxic. Myocardial hypoxia results in dysrhythmia, myocardial ischemia, and infarction (2,90). Persons with preexistent coronary artery disease are far more susceptible. Aronow and Isbell have reported decreased exercise tolerance and onset of angina with COHb levels of 5% (5).

The pathologic findings in all major tissues of persons poisoned by carbon monoxide consist of cellular edema, petechiae, focal hemorrhages, and cellular necrosis. Persons with severe carbon monoxide poisoning may develop a delayed neurologic syndrome typified by encephalopathy, dementia, ataxia, apraxia, agnosia, peripheral sensory neuropathy, and motor paralysis. These findings are associated with central and peripheral demyelination, cerebral atrophy, and gliosis (35,69).

The physician who treats inhalation injuries should remember several key facts about carbon monoxide poisoning. First, CO intoxication should be suspected at the fire scene in much the same way that neck trauma is suspected with head injuries: it is present until proved otherwise. Second, the degree of poisoning parallels the victim's antecedent minute ventilation and cardiac output. Victims who have been more active will have higher blood CO levels. Third, CO toxicity may present as myocardial ischemia or infarction. Fourth, physicians should not expect patients to appear "cherry red"; those who do will probably have carboxyhemoglobin levels in excess of 50% (102,103). Fifth, CO poisoning should be identified quickly by measuring carboxyhemoglobin levels. Treatment with maximal inspired oxygen should be initiated if intoxication is *suspected*. Metabolic acidosis should be substantiated with arterial blood gas measurement. Finally, apparent recovery in a previously unconscious patient may be followed by cerebral edema or severe, delayed neurologic dysfunction. Thus, physicians should be cautious in the early discharge of patients or in premature prognostication (86).

Cyanide

The probable extent of cyanide poisoning in smoke inhalation has only recently been appreciated (20,26,52,76,87,95). Cyanide binds ferric iron in cellular cytochromes, blocking electron transport and thus oxidative metabolism (46). Because cyanide is quite soluble, high tissue levels are reached very rapidly, producing nearly instantaneous collapse in massive poisonings. Death results from exposure to 135 ppm for 30 minutes, 180 ppm for 10 minutes, or 270 ppm for 6–8 minutes (70). Persons with sublethal exposures complain of weakness, headache, confusion, nausea, and vomiting. Persons heavily exposed exhibit cardiovascular collapse, pulmonary edema, lactic acidosis, coma, and convulsions (38). Because oxidative metabolism is inhibited, venous blood may appear bright red. Cyanide in small amounts can be detoxified by an endogenous enzyme, rhodanase, but this mechanism is of minor significance in clinical cyanide poisoning.

Proper management begins with the suspicion of cyanide poisoning. The classic therapy is the oxidation of a significant fraction (approximately 30%) of ferrous hemoglobin iron to the ferric state by infusion of sodium nitrite solution. Ferric hemoglobin, or methemoglobin, then provides an alternative binding site for cyanide ions bound to ferric cytochrome oxidase iron. The resulting cyanomethemoglobin reacts with intravenous sodium thiosulfate to produce sodium thiocyanate, which is excreted by the kidneys.

The induction of methemoglobinemia in an individual who may be hypoxic or acidotic or has impaired cellular respiration and tissue perfusion is not without risk. Clark *et al.* advocate traditional treatment for HCN poisoning on clinical grounds in the presence of a high carboxyhemoglobin (20). They cite data that suggest that CO and HCN poisoning are predictably concurrent. Their findings have not been substantiated by other workers. Wetherell found significant carboxyhemoglobinemia without concurrent cyanide poisoning in 26% of his sample (95). An experimental alternative is treatment with hydroxocobalamin, which converts cyanide to cyanocobalamin (vitamin B_{12}), without the risk of inducing methemoglobinemia (38). No good comparative studies have yet been reported between hydroxocobalamin treatment and the classic sodium nitrite/sodium thiosulfate method. Therefore, symptomatic patients in the appropriate clinical setting should be treated by the induction of methemoglobinemia.

Hydrogen Sulfide

Hydrogen sulfide poisoning is comparable in many ways to cyanide poisoning (14). Hydrogen sulfide binds to ferric iron in the cytochrome oxidase enzyme, producing inhibition of electron transport and oxidative metabolism in a manner similar to that of cyanide. In addition to its effect on cytochrome oxidase, hydrogen sulfide is a powerful lacrimator, respiratory depressant, and a cardiotoxic agent. It can be displaced by sodium nitrite induction of methemoglobinemia, and has been successfully treated by this regimen (84).

Ammonia

Ammonia is produced by the combustion of nylon, but this source of exposure is thought to be clinically insignificant. Exposure to anhydrous ammonia, which is transported and stored throughout agricultural areas of the country, is potentially much more important. Anhydrous ammonia, which is used as a fertilizer throughout the United States, yields a pH of 11.6 when hydrolyzed. It destroys tissue by alkaline hydrolysis; liquefaction necrosis is demonstrated on histologic examination.

Severe eye injuries with opacification and loss of the cornea have resulted from contact with household ammonia solutions in the range of 5–10% NH_3. Concentrations of 50 ppm NH_3 in the atmosphere are readily detectable by odor. Concentrations of 1000 ppm will result in lacrimation and conjunctivitis. Blindness can result from prolonged exposure to ammonia at this level. At 1500 ppm, laryngeal edema results, and at 5000 ppm, pulmonary edema and death occur (15,73). Such exposure levels can be anticipated in the setting of a transport or other industrial mishap.

Unlike acid substances, alkaline materials are not neutralized by tissue fluids. They continue to react until they are removed or neutralized. Unfortunately, alkaline burns tend to be underrated initially. Consequently, much more extensive injury results from delayed or inadequate treatment than occurs with acid injuries. No attempt should be made to neutralize alkaline material, since the reaction is exothermic. Affected areas should be washed with copious amounts of normal saline or, if saline is unavailable, with water.

Acrolein

Acrolein is an aldehyde. Aldehydes, such as formaldehyde, are used to fix or denature proteins in such diverse situations as the tanning of leather and the embalming of bodies. Aldehydes in general, and acrolein or propanaldehyde in particular, bond readily to sulfhydryl groups and denature most proteins, especially sulfhydryl-dependent enzymes. Burning lumber is a good source of acrolein. While wood is not found in large amounts in highrise buildings or vehicles, polyethylene and acrylics are quite abundant and produce acrolein when burned.

Exposure to 0.25 ppm causes mucosal irritation; at 1.0 ppm, it becomes intolerable in minutes. Prolonged exposure to 21 ppm can cause pulmonary edema. Deaths have been reported following exposure to as little as 10 ppm, but

are not predictable until exposures of 150 ppm for 10 minutes are encountered (70). The maximum allowable concentration for industrial exposure is 0.5 ppm.

Toluene 2,4-Diisocyanate

Toluene 2,4-diisocyanate, a product of urethane combustion, is a pulmonary irritant which many authorities believe is responsible for much of the smog-induced bronchospasm experienced by asthmatics and persons with chronic obstructive lung disease. It can cause severe bronchospasm at a concentration of 0.02 ppm (70). Interestingly, this is below the olfactory threshold of 0.1–1.0 ppm. Marked bronchospasm and dyspnea can be expected following brief, high-level exposures, particularly in those with a prior history of asthma or chronic obstructive lung disease. There is also evidence to suggest that such exposure will sensitize some persons and predispose them subsequently to more severe and longlasting bronchospastic episodes.

Styrene

Styrene has an olfactory threshold of 0.1 ppm. People exposed to 376 ppm for 60 minutes experience mucosal irritation, headache, nausea, and incoordination (70). Those who are exposed to concentrations of 10,000 ppm for 30–60 minutes will become unconscious and probably die as a result of direct depression of the respiratory center of the central nervous system.

Nitrogen Dioxide

Nitrogen dioxide is the agent responsible for silo fillers' disease (53). Clinically significant human exposures have resulted from breathing smoke from burning nitrocellulose films and automobiles, exposure to fresh silage, and chemical mishaps (4,42,65). Studies with mice have shown increased capillary permeability following exposure to 10 ppm (76). Human exposure for 1 hour to 25 ppm produces lacrimation, cough, and chest pain. Exposure to 50 ppm can produce pulmonary edema and bronchiolitis obliterans. The latter is a pathologic entity characterized by inflammatory bronchiolar infiltrates and fibrosis, which may result from inhalation of several different poisons, including chlorine, HCl, and nitrogen dioxide. Brief exposures at 250 ppm produce cough, severe bronchorrhea, pulmonary edema, and bronchiolitis obliterans (70).

Prehospital Evaluation and Treatment

TRIAGE

Patients who are unconscious, manifest respiratory distress, or have a known heavy exposure or a history of syncope or transient respiratory distress should all be treated for inhalation injuries.

HISTORY

A history should be taken at the scene to answer the following questions:

What was the source of the noxious gas?
What was burning?
Was the fire in a closed space?
What type of ventilation was available?
How long was the victim exposed?
Was protective gear used?
Was it ever taken off?
Was the patient ever unconscious?
Is there any time that cannot be accounted for by the victim?

The victim's medical history will have a direct bearing on the risk of morbidity from inhalation of noxious gases. Patients with a history of asthma, bronchitis or chronic obstructive lung disease, smoking, ischemic heart disease, or dysrhythmia are at special risk.

Paramedics and ambulance personnel should specifically inquire about symptoms of skin or mucous membrane irritation; burning of the airway or chest; neck or back pain; cough; wheezing or shortness of breath; angina; and palpitations.

EXAMINATION

A careful physical examination should be performed with special attention to the following areas:

Singed facial or nasal hair and burns of the nasal or pharyngeal mucosa. (Such findings suggest the need for urgent hospitalization, laryngoscopy, and perhaps bronchoscopy, even if the patient appears to be stable.)
Inability to swallow, drooling.
Dysphonia, stridor, barking cough.
Conjunctivitis, rhinorrhea, and other signs of mucosal irritation that suggest exposure to acids, aldehydes, bases, or other irritants.
Rate and depth of respiration, noting any hyperventilation.
Rales or wheezes.
Blood pressure.
Rate and regularity of the pulse. (Monitoring, if feasible in the field, should be carried out if the pulse is irregular.)

Patients whose complaints suggest myocardial infarction should be treated for this condition until ischemic heart disease is definitively excluded as a diagnosis. Burns and trauma should be treated in the usual manner.

Hospital Evaluation and Treatment

HISTORY

The field history and physical examination are repeated in greater detail in the controlled environment of the emergency department (64).

EVALUATION

Tests should include the following:

A chest x-ray to demonstrate or exclude an infiltrate and to serve as a baseline.
An electrocardiogram (ECG) to demonstrate changes of ischemia or infarction and to serve as a baseline. (A normal tracing does not exclude these diagnoses. The patient should be monitored when dysrhythmia is suspected.)
Arterial blood gases to detect hypoxemia, document its severity, and assess the adequacy of ventilation as well as the patient's acid-base status.
A carboxyhemoglobin test (A lethal level of CO will not affect the oxygen pressure or the *calculated* oxygen saturation).
Xenon lung scans, spirometric tests, and nitrogen washout if there is some doubt as to the extent of pulmonary parenchymal involvement (1,67).
Laryngoscopy (indirect, direct, or fiberoptic) and occasionally bronchoscopy in all persons in

whom there is evidence of thermal injury to the respiratory tract and in cases in which the setting of the fire makes respiratory tract burns likely (63,89).

Patients who have been exposed to classic smoke inhalation may have a 2–48-hour interval during which their symptoms are unimpressive. This has been observed in HCl, chlorine, and phosgene poisoning as well. Persons who have had toxic exposure to CO or have suffered severe hypoxia may also have a quiescent interval followed by neurologic deterioration. These syndromes and the documented high cardiac risk of smoke inhalation, chemical inhalation injury, or CO poisoning argue for a low threshold for admission.

TREATMENT

Specific criteria have been enumerated for admission (22):

1. Presence of significant thermal or other injuries
2. Symptoms, signs, or laboratory evidence of cardiac or central nervous system dysfunction
3. Physical findings of tachypnea, hoarseness, stridor, wheezes, rales, or rhonchi
4. Carboxyhemoglobin saturation above 15–20% on arrival
5. Abnormal results of chest x-ray, arterial blood gas measurements, or pulmonary function tests
6. Deterioration in clinical status, arterial blood gases, or pulmonary function tests

The generally accepted treatment of inhalation injuries is bed rest, oxygen, humidification, hydration, and bronchodilators in the presence of bronchospasm. Patients at risk of CO poisoning should receive high-flow oxygen through a reservoir mask to approach 100% inspired oxygen. Intermittent positive-pressure breathing (IPPB) or continuous positive airway pressure (CPAP) can reduce the effort of breathing, prevent atelectasis, and deliver aerosolized medications. In the presence of laryngeal and/or tracheal edema, either from chemical or thermal injury, obstruction should be anticipated and treated prophylactically with endotracheal intubation.

The use of steroids is controversial in the absence of definitive research. Some authors report decreased mortality, while others report no benefit in humans treated in randomized studies with glucocorticoids (27,51, 62,63,94). Pending further information, there are no convincing data to support the use of glucocorticoids in the treatment of smoke inhalation. Although direct chemical injuries with nitrogen dioxide, chlorine, HCl, and phosgene have been treated successfully in the past with glucocorticoids, no double-blind controlled studies are available to form the basis for a recommendation (4,18,42,45). Review of the above authors' reports reasonably supports the use of glucocorticoids in pure chemical injury.

Phosgene poisoning has been treated with intravenous infusion of methenamine (81). This treatment is based on the assumption that phosgene toxicity results from the action of the carbonyl group (Figure 13) on tissue proteins, rather than from the hydrolysis which produces HCl. If further research supports the hypothesis that carbonyl groups are responsible for phosgene toxicity and controlled studies show methenamine to be effective, it should then be tried in the treatment of acrolein and other aldehyde poisonings.

In view of forensic research findings and the recent demonstration of lethal levels of HCN generated by the combustion of a standard American bedroom, cyanide toxicity should be considered in the evaluation and treatment of smoke inhalation victims (3, 20,41,95). With the risks inherent in converting a significant portion of hemoglobin to methemoglobin, embarking on therapy in the absence of strong indications is not advocated. However, in the presence of vascular collapse and lactic acidosis without cyanosis, or with the knowledge that the patient was exposed to smoke from burning urethane or another source of CN^-, treatment for cyanide poisoning should be instituted. COHb and cyanide levels (if available) should be obtained, and treatment for cyanide and carbon monoxide poisoning should be instituted. Oxygen should be delivered through a tight-fitting reservoir mask or by endotracheal tube so as to achieve as close to 100% inspired oxygen as possible (43). Sodium nitrite (0.3–0.5 g intravenously over 3–4 minutes) should be administered to induce methemoglobinemia if the patient does not improve clinically with oxygen therapy.

If sodium nitrate is not readily available, amyl nitrite inhalation (30 seconds every 2 minutes) may be effective. Following induction of methemoglobinemia, sodium thiosulfate (12.5 g in a 50-ml diluent over 10 minutes intravenously) should be administered. Recurrent symptoms are treated with the entire regimen, using a half-dosage. Hydroxocobalamin should be considered an experimental alternative therapy. It is administered in an intravenous dose of 200–500 mg/kg.

CLINICAL COURSE

The clinical course is variable and depends on the circumstances and duration of exposure, the concentration of noxious and asphyxiant gases, the composition of the smoke, and the preexisting diseases of the victim. Some authors have divided the time course of inhalation injury into four successive stages characterized by changes in cardiac output, blood gas analyses, minute ventilation, lung compliance, and dead space/tidal volume (Vd/Vt) ratios (17,82):

Stage I: during smoke inhalation
  Hypoxemia, hypercapnia, acidosis
  Low cardiac output
  Hyperpnea decreasing to apnea
  Bronchospasm
  Carbon monoxide poisoning
  Unconsciousness
Stage II: immediate period (*up to 2 hours*)
  Hypercapnia, mild hypoxemia
  Severely depressed cardiac output
  Severe vascular constriction
  Increased Vd/Vt
  Hyperventilation
  Carbon monoxidemia
Stage III: progression of injury (*2–24 hours*)
  Increased hypoxemia
  Decreased compliance
  Normal Vd/Vt
  Cardiovascular status tending toward normal
  Edema formation in lung
  Hyperventilation
  Absence of lung failure
Stage IV: pulmonary failure or recovery (*>24 hours*)
  Bacterial pneumonia progressing to lung failure
  Absence of bacterial pneumonia progressing to recovery

No general scenario such as that outlined above applies to all patients. However, numer-ous reports about the clinical course of residential smoke inhalation victims indicate that many victims appear deceptively well shortly after exposure. Between 2 and 24 hours later, these patients deteriorate from one or several mechanisms: (1) airway obstruction from thermal injury, (2) pulmonary edema from chemical insult, or (3) exacerbation of bronchospasm. Still later, pneumonia and respiratory failure or the neurologic sequelae of carbon monoxide poisoning or hypoxia may develop (55). Thus, the physician who evaluates smoke inhalation victims should seriously consider admitting these patients for observation.

Conclusion

Inhalation injury should demand the full attention of emergency physicians in particular and the medical community at large. Increasing reliance on synthetics will undoubtedly increase the prevalence of new smoke inhalation injuries. The use of plastics and synthetic materials in buildings and conveyances will also doubtless increase the frequency with which we are required to recognize and treat what now seem to be exotic chemical injuries. More studies are needed on the gases, vapors, and particulate matter that constitute smoke in various types of fires. When the physiologic derangements are understood, therapy can then be developed. The key is to recognize the seriousness and frequency of inhalation injury in our society.

References

1. Agee, R. N., Long, J. M., Hunt, J. L., *et al.:* Use of [133]Xenon in early diagnosis of inhalation injury. *J Trauma,* **16:**218–24, 1976.
2. Anderson, R. F., Allensworth, D. C., DeGroot, W. H.: Myocardial toxicity from carbon monoxide poisoning. *Ann Intern Med,* **67:**1172–82, 1967.
3. Ansell, M., Lewis, F. A. S.: A record of cyanide found in human organs. *J Forensic Sci,* **17:**148–55, 1970.
4. Arora, N. S., Aldrich, T. K.: Bronchiolitis obliterans from a burning automobile. *South Med J,* **73:**507–10, 1980.
5. Aronow, W. S., Isbell, M. W.: Carbon monoxide effect on exercise-induced angina pectoris. *Ann Intern Med,* **79:**392, 1973.
6. Bass, H. N., Hildreth, B. F.: Paroxysmal atrial fibril-

lation and exposure to smoke (letter). *Lancet,* **1:**1036, 1979.

7. Beard, R. R., Grandstaff, N.: Carbon monoxide exposure and cerebral function. *Ann NY Acad Sci,* **174:**385–95, 1970.

8. Best, R.: Rapid transit train fire. *Fire Command,* **46:**28–32, August 1979.

9. Best, R.: Analyzing BART and other rapid-transit system fires. *Fire J,* **74:**51–9, May 1980.

10. Boutros, A. R., Hoyt, J. L.: Management of carbon monoxide poisoning in the absence of hyperbaric oxygenation chamber. *Crit Care Med,* **4:**144–47, 1976.

11. Bowes, P. C.: Casualties attributed to toxic gas and smoke at fires: A survey of statistics. *Med Sci Law,* **16:**104–10, April 1976.

12. Bowes, P. C.: Smoke and toxicity hazards of plastics in fire. *Ann Occup Hyg,* **17:**143–57, 1974.

13. Buehler, J. H., Berns, A. S., Webster, J. R.: Lactic acidosis from carboxyhemoglobinemia after smoke inhalation. *Ann Intern Med,* **82:**803–5, 1975.

14. Burnett, W. W., King, E. G., *et al.:* Hydrogen sulfide poisoning: Review of five years' experience. *Can Med Assoc J,* **117:**1277–80, 1977.

15. Caplin, O.: Ammonia gas poisoning: 47 cases in a London shelter. *Lancet,* **2:**95–6, 1941.

16. Chance, B., Erecinska, M., Wagner, M.: Mitochondrial responses to carbon monoxide toxicity. *Ann NY Acad Sci,* **174:**193–204, 1970.

17. Charnock, E. L., Meehan, J. J.: Postburn respiratory injuries in children. *Pediatr Clin North Am,* **27:**661–76, 1980.

18. Chester, E. H., Kaimal, P. J., Payne, C. B., *et al.:* Pulmonary injury following exposure to chlorine gas. Possible beneficial effects of steroid treatment. *Chest,* **72:**247–50, 1977.

19. Cho, K. S., Lee, S. H.: Occupational health hazards of mine workers. *Bull WHO,* **56:**205–18, 1978.

20. Clark, C. J., Campbell, D., Reid, W. H.: Blood carboxyhemoglobin and cyanide levels in fire survivors. *Lancet,* **1:**1332–35, 1981.

21. Colardyn, F., Van Der Straeten, M., Lamont, H.: Acute inhalation-intoxication by combustion of polyvinylchloride. *Int Arch Occup Environ Health,* **38:**121–27, 1976.

22. Coleman, D. L.: Smoke inhalation. *West J Med,* **135:**300–9, 1981.

23. Cooper, D. Y., Schleyer, H., Rosenthal, O.: Some chemical properties of cytochrome P-450 and its carbon monoxide compound. *Ann NY Acad Sci,* **174:**205–17, 1970.

24. Cordasco, E. M., Stone, F. D.: Pulmonary edema of environmental origin. *Chest,* **64:**182–85, 1973.

25. Dodge, R. R.: Smoke inhalation. *Ariz Med,* **34:**749, 1977.

26. Dressler, D. P., Skornik, W. A., *et al.:* Smoke toxicity of common aircraft carpets. *Aviat Space Environ Med,* **46:**1141–43, 1975.

27. Dressler, D. P., Skornik, W. A., *et al.:* Corticosteroid treatment of experimental smoke inhalation. *Ann Surg,* **193:**46–52, 1976.

28. Dyer, R. F., Esch, V. H.: Polyvinyl chloride toxicity in fires. *JAMA,* **235:**393–97, 1976.

29. Einhorn, I. N.: Physiological and toxicological aspects of smoke produced during the combustion of polymeric materials. *Environ Health Perspect,* **2:**163–89, 1975.

30. Eisele, J. W., O'Halloran, R. L., Reay, D. T., *et al.:* Deaths during the May 18, 1980 eruption of Mount St. Helen's. *N Engl J Med,* **305:**931–36, 1981.

31. Everett, E. D., Overholt, E. L.: Phosgene poisoning. *JAMA,* **205:**103–6, 1968.

32. Faigel, H. C.: Mixtures of household cleaning agents. *N Engl J Med,* **271:**618, 1964.

33. Fein, A., Leff, A., Hopewell, P. C.: Pathophysiology and management of the complications resulting from fire and the inhaled products of combustion: Review of the literature. *Crit Care Med,* **8:**94–8, February 1980.

34. Forster, R. E.: Carbon monoxide and the partial pressure of oxygen in tissue. *Ann NY Acad Sci,* **174:**233–41, 1970.

35. Garland, H., Pearce, J.: Neurological complications of carbon monoxide poisoning. *Q J Med,* **144:**445–55, 1967.

36. Genovesi, M. G., *et al.:* Transient hypoxemia in firemen following inhalation of smoke. *Chest,* **71:**441–44, 1977.

37. Gold, A., Burgess, W. A., Clougherty, E. V.: Exposure of firefighters to toxic air contaminants. *Am Ind Hyg Assoc J,* **39:**534–39, 1978.

38. Graham, D. L., Laman, D., Theodore, J., *et al.:* Acute cyanide poisoning complicated by lactic acidosis and pulmonary edema. *Arch Intern Med,* **137:**1051–55, 1977.

39. Hanks, T. G.: Human performance of a psychomotor test as a function of exposure to carbon monoxide. *Ann NY Acad Sci,* **174:**421–24, 1970.

40. Hedges, J. R., Morrissey, W. L.: Acute chlorine gas exposure. *JACEP,* **8:**59–63, 1979.

41. Hillenbrand, L. J., Wray, J. A.: Space-age contribution to residential fire safety (full-scale fire tests of bedroom furnishings). *Fire J,* **68:**18–25, 1974.

42. Horvath, E. P., DoPico, G. A., Barbee, R.: Nitrogen dioxide-induced pulmonary disease. *J Occup Med,* **20:**103–10, 1978.

43. Isom, G. E., Way, J. L.: Effect of oxygen on cyanide intoxication. VI. Reactivation of cyanide-inhibited glucose metabolism. *J Pharmacol Exp Ther,* **189:**235–43, 1974.

44. Karter, M. J.: Fire loss in the United States during 1979. *Fire J,* **74:**52–65, 1980.

45. Kaufman, J., Burkons, D.: Clinical, roentgenologic and physiologic effects of acute chlorine exposure. *Arch Environ Health,* **23:**29–34, 1971.

46. Klaasen, C. D.: Non-metallic toxicants, air pollutants, solvents and vapors, and pesticides. In *The Pharmacological Basis of Therapeutics,* 6th ed. Gilman, A. G., Goodman, L. S., Gilman, A. (eds). New York, Macmillan, 1980, pp. 1638–59.

47. Kutsumi, A., Kuroiwa, Y., Takeda, R.: Medical report on casualties in the Hokuriku Tunnel train fire in Japan with special reference to smoke-gas poisoning. *Mt Sinai J Med,* **46:**469–74, 1979.

48. Landa, J., Avery, W. G., Sachner, M. A.: Some physiologic observations in smoke inhalation. *Chest,* **61:**62–4, 1972.

49. Larkin, J. M., *et al.:* Treatment of carbon monoxide poisoning: Prognostic factors. *J Trauma,* **16:**111–14, 1976.

50. Lawther, P. J., Commins, B. T.: Cigarette smoking and exposure to carbon monoxide. *Ann NY Acad Sci,* **174:**135–47, 1970.

51. Levine, B. A., Petroff, P. A., Szade, C. L., *et al.:* Prospective trials of dexamethasone and aerosolized gentamycin in the treatment of inhalation injury in the burned patient. *J Trauma,* **18:**188–93, 1978.

52. Levine, M. S., Radford, E. P.: Occupational exposure to cyanide in Baltimore firefighters. *J Occup Med,* **20:**53–6, 1978.

53. Lowry, T., Schuman, L. M.: Silo fillers' disease—A syndrome caused by nitrogen dioxide. *JAMA,* **162:**153–60, 1956.

54. Mark, H. F., Gaylord, N. G. (eds): *Encyclopedia of Polymer Science and Technology.* New York, John Wiley & Sons, 1969. Vol. I, p. 173; Vol. III, pp. 305–7, 329; Vol. XI, pp. 506–63; Vol. XIII, p. 400.

55. Markley, K.: Burn care: Infection and smoke inhalation (editorial). *Ann Intern Med,* **90:**269–70, 1979.

56. Mason, R. V.: Smoke and toxicity hazards in aircraft cabin furnishings. *Ann Occup Hyg,* **17:**159–65, 1974.

57. McBay, A. J.: Carbon monoxide poisoning. *N Engl J Med,* **272:**252, 1965.

58. McFarland, R. A.: The effects of exposure to small quantities of carbon monoxide on vision. *Ann NY Acad Sci,* **174:**301–12, 1970.

59. Mellins, R. B., Park, S.: Respiratory complications of smoke inhalation in victims of fires. *J Pediatr,* **87:**1–7, 1975.

60. Mikulka, P., O'Donnell, R., Heinig, P., *et al.:* The effect of carbon monoxide on human performance. *Ann NY Acad Sci,* **174:**409–20, 1970.

61. Moritz, A. A., Henriques, F. C., *et al.:* The effect of inhaled heat on the air passages and lungs. *Am J Pathol,* **21:**311–31, 1945.

62. Moylan, J. A.: Smoke inhalation and burn injury. *Surg Clin North Am,* **60:**1533–40, 1980.

63. Moylan, J. A., *et al.:* Early diagnosis of inhalation injury using [133]xenon lung scan. *Ann Surg,* **176:**477–83, 1973.

64. Myers, R. A.: Treatment protocol for smoke inhalation victims. *Occup Health Saf,* **49:**56–7, 59–60, 1980.

65. Nichols, B. H.: The clinical effects of the inhalation of nitrogen dioxide. *Am J Roentgenol,* **23:**516–20, 1930.

66. Otis, A. B.: The physiology of carbon monoxide poisoning and evidence for acclimatization. *Ann NY Acad Sci,* **174:**242–45, 1970.

67. Petroff, P. A., Hander, E. W., *et al.:* Pulmonary function studies after smoke inhalation. *Am J Surg,* **132:**346–51, 1976.

68. Pietak, S. P., Delahoye, D. J.: Airway obstruction following smoke inhalation. *CMA J,* **115:**329–31, 1976.

69. Plum, F., Posner, J. B., Hain, R. F.: Delayed neurological deterioration after anoxia. *Arch Intern Med,* **110:**56–63, 1962.

70. Proctor, N. H., Hughes, J. P.: *Chemical Hazards of the Workplace.* Philadelphia, JB Lippincott, 1978, pp. 87–88 (acrolein), 156–57 (Cl_2), 286–87 (HCl), 293–94 (H_2S), 382–83 (NO_2), 414–15 (phosgene), 449–50 (styrene), 483–84 (toluene 2,4-diisocyanate).

71. Root, W. S.: Carbon monoxide. In *Handbook of Physiology,* Field, J. (ed.). Sect. 3, Vol. II, Berne, R. M. (ed.), Chapt. 43. Bethesda, Maryland, American Physiological Society, 1965, pp. 1087–98.

72. Roughton, F. J. W.: Transport of oxygen and carbon dioxide. In *Handbook of Physiology,* Field, J. (ed.). Sect. 3, Vol. II, Berne, R. M. (ed.), Chapt. 31. Bethesda, Maryland, American Physiological Society, 1965, pp. 767–825.

73. Sax, N. I.: *Dangerous Properties of Industrial Materials,* 4th ed. New York, Van Nostrand Reinhold Co., 1975.

74. Schulte, J. E.: Effects of mild carbon monoxide intoxication. *Arch Environ Health,* **7:**524–30, 1963.

75. Shaw, G., Gillette, R.: Polyurethane: Hazardous to your health. *Los Angeles Times,* January 21, 1979.

76. Sherwin, R. P., Richters, V.: Lung capillary permeability: Nitrogen dioxide exposure and leakage of tritiated serum. *Arch Intern Med,* **128:**61, 1971.

77. Sjostrand, T.: Early studies of CO production. *Ann NY Acad Sci,* **174:**5–10, 1970.

78. Smith, P. W., Crane, C. R., Sanders, D. C., *et al.:* Effects of exposure to carbon monoxide and hydrogen cyanide. In *Physiological and Toxicological Aspects of Combustion Products.* Committee on Fire Research, National Research Council, National Academy of Sciences, 1976, pp. 75–88.

79. Society of Plastics Industry: *Facts and Figures of the Plastics Industry.* New York, 1981.

80. Sorenson, W. R.: Polyvinyl chloride in fires. *JAMA,* **236:**1449, 1976.

81. Stavrakis, P.: The use of hexamethylenetetramine (HMT) in treatment of acute phosgene poisoning. *Industr Med,* **40:**30–1, 1971.

82. Stephenson, S. F., Esrig, B. C., *et al.:* The pathophysiology of smoke inhalation injury. *Ann Surg,* **182:**652–60, 1975.

83. Gases, vapors, mists and dusts. *In Toxicology—Mechanisms and Analytical Methods,* Vol. II, Stewart, C. P., Stolman, A. (eds). New York, Academic Press, 1961, pp. 17–54.

84. Stine, R. J., Slosberg, B., Beacham, B. E.: Hydrogen sulfide intoxication. *Ann Intern Med,* **85:**756–58, 1976.

85. Stone, J. P., Hazlett, R. N., Johnson, J. E., *et al.:* The transport of hydrogen chloride by soot from burning polyvinyl chloride. *J Fire Flammability,* **4:**42–51, 1973.

86. Strohl, K. P., Feldman, N. T., Saunders, N. A., *et al.:* Carbon monoxide poisoning in fire victims: A reappraisal of prognosis. *J Trauma,* **20:**78–80, 1980.

87. Symington, I. S., *et al.:* Cyanide exposure in fires. *Lancet,* **2:**91–2, 1978.

88. Terrill, J. B., Montgomery, R. R., Reinhardt, C. F.: Toxic gases from fires. *Science,* **200**(4348):1343–47, 1978.

89. Trunkey, D. D.: Inhalation injury. *Surg Clin North Am,* **58:**1133–40, 1978.

90. Turino, G. M.: Effect of carbon monoxide on the cardiorespiratory system. Carbon monoxide toxicity: Physiology and biochemistry. *Circulation,* **63:**253A–59A, 1981.

91. Unger, K. M., Snow, R. M., Mestas, J. M., *et al.:* Smoke inhalation in firemen. *Thorax,* **35:**838–42, 1980.

92. Waksman, D., Ferguson, J. B.: Fire tests of building interior covering systems. *Fire Technology,* 211–20. August 1974.

93. Webster, J. R., McCabe, M. M., Karp, M.: Recognition and management of smoke inhalation. *JAMA,* **201:**71–4, 1976.

94. Welch, G. W., Lull, R. J., Petroff, P. A., *et al.:* The use of steroids in inhalation injury. *Surg Gynecol Obstet,* **145:**539–44, 1977.

95. Wetherell, H. R.: The occurrence of cyanide in the blood of fire victims. *J Forensic Sci,* **11:**167–73, 1966.

96. Winter, P. M., Miller, J. D.: Carbon monoxide poisoning. *JAMA,* **236:**1502–4, 1976.

97. Wooley, W. D.: Nitrogen-containing products from the thermal decomposition of flexible polyurethane foams. *Br Polymer J,* **4:**27–43, 1972.

98. Wroblewski, D. A., Bower, G. C.: The significance of facial burns in acute smoke inhalation. *Crit Care Med,* **7:**335–38, 1979.

99. Yuill, C. H.: Smoke—What's in it? *Fire J,* **66:**1–9, 1972.

100. Zapp, J. A.: Fires, toxicity and plastics. In *Physiological and Toxicological Products.* Committee on Fire Research, National Research Council, National Academy of Sciences, 1976, pp. 58–74.

101. Zawaki, B. E., Jung, R. C., Joyce, J., *et al.:* Smoke burns and the nature of inhalation injury in fire victims: A correlation of experimental data and clinical data. *Ann Surg,* **185:**100, 1977.

102. Zikria, B. A., Starner, W. Q., *et al.:* Respiratory tract damage in burns: Pathophysiology and treatment. *Ann NY Acad Sci,* **150:**618, 1968.

103. Zikria, B. A., Budd, D. C., *et al.:* What is clinical smoke poisoning? *Ann Surg,* **181:**151–56, 1973.

APPENDIX

THE EMERGENCY RESPONSE TO RADIATION ACCIDENTS

Frederick A. Mettler, Jr., M.D., M.P.H.
Sydney W. Porter, Jr., C.H.P.

Radiation accidents are characterized by their infrequency and complexity. This appendix provides a basic understanding of the principles involved in preparation of supplies, training of personnel, and management of the primary phase of a radiation accident. It is intended for use by physicians, hospital administrators, nurses, emergency medical technicians, nuclear plant personnel, and other persons interested in radiation accidents. Many of the procedures are presented in a stepwise fashion so that the material may be used during accident management.

The procedures contained in this text are based on training methods that are currently in practice at many nuclear facilities and that have been tested by drills or actual emergency situations. Emphasis has been placed on the medical effects of radiation and the preservation of human life.

A radiation incident or accident may complicate a mechanical accident, but if recovery personnel are adequately prepared, there should be minimal hazard in handling the initial radiation aspects. Although it is assumed for purposes of this appendix that most events will involve only one or two patients, the principles of care and handling can be expanded to involve larger numbers.

Primary consideration should always be given to first aid principles, which are not covered in this text. In addition, the complicated aspects of radiation and health physics, such as exact dosimetry, are left to experts responsible for the management of the secondary phase.

Two texts are highly recommended: NCRP Report No. 65, Management of Persons Accidentally Contaminated with Radionuclides, and the REACTS International Conference Proceedings, The Medical Basis for Radiation Accident Preparedness (1,2). The first is an essential text for preparation for the initial management of radiation accident patients.

The second is an excellent summary of significant exposure accidents, their clinical courses, and lessons learned in medical preparedness and planning.

Radiation in Perspective

Radiation is derived from either natural or man-made sources (Figure 1). Natural background radiation is derived from three sources: the sky (cosmic), the earth (terrestrial), and the human body (internal). This varies throughout the United States from about 80 to 200 millirems/year. (The *millirem,* or *mrem,* is a unit used to equate biologic effects of different types of radiation. *Millirad,* or *mrad,* describes the energy absorbed by tissue from radiation. In this text, the terms

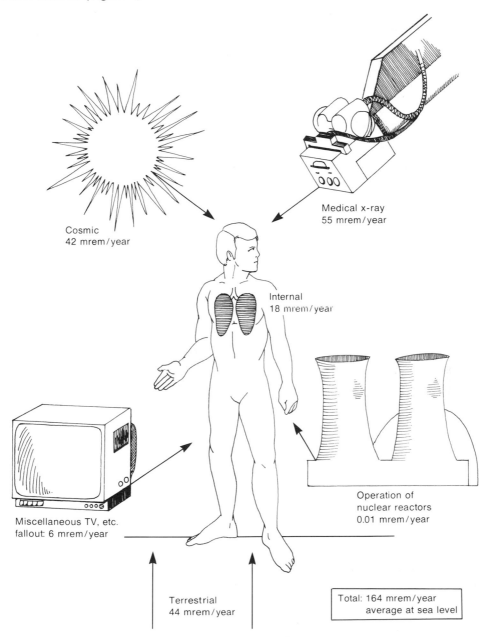

Cosmic
42 mrem/year

Medical x-ray
55 mrem/year

Internal
18 mrem/year

Miscellaneous TV, etc.
fallout: 6 mrem/year

Operation of
nuclear reactors
0.01 mrem/year

Terrestrial
44 mrem/year

Total: 164 mrem/year
average at sea level

FIGURE 1 Sources of radiation exposure.

TABLE 1
Environmental Radiation Exposure

Source	Average Annual Whole Body Dose Equivalent (mrem)
Natural sources	
Cosmic (sea level)	41
(10,000 feet)	120
(80,000 feet, supersonic transport flight level)	4000
Internal	18
Terrestrial	44
	Total 103 (at sea level)
Man-made sources	
Medical x-rays	55
Fallout	4
Miscellaneous, including television	2
Nuclear power plant operation	0.01
	Total 61

will be used interchangeably.) For example, on the eastern coast of the United States, this amounts to approximately 100 mrem/year; in Denver, Colorado, due to the higher elevation, the population is exposed to a dose of approximately 175 mrem/year. Background radiation varies considerably throughout the world. In some areas of France, the annual exposure is 350 mrem; India, 1500 mrem, Egypt, 400 mrem; and some areas of Brazil, 13,000 mrem. Some of this variation is due to differences in the natural radionuclide content of the soil.

Normally, humans are well shielded from cosmic radiation by the atmosphere. If they go to the top of a mountain or fly in a jetliner, they lose some of the benefit of atmospheric shielding and the radiation exposure increases. At an altitude of 10,000 feet, they receive more cosmic radiation (80 mrem/year) than they would at sea level (42 mrem/year). A cross-country trip in a jetliner exposes a person to about 4 mrem.

Another source of natural radiation is the earth itself, along with building materials which contain many radioactive elements. Granite and concrete, for example, give off more natural radiation than does wood. Consequently, a person living in a brick house receives more radiation than one who lives in a wooden dwelling. Measurements in New York City's Grand Central Station, which is constructed of Vermont granite, show dose rates as high as 300–500 mrem/year. However, only a person who stood in this building 24 hours a day, 365 days a year, would receive this total dose.

There are radioactive elements (mostly carbon-14, potassium-40, and radium-226) in food, which are incorporated into body tissues and emit radiation. These sources have been present for as long as humans have inhabited the earth. A list of average annual doses received is provided in Table 1.

Man-made sources applied to certain body organs almost double the radiation exposure from natural background sources. The primary man-made source is medical x-rays; 55 mrem/year is the average medical x-ray dose rate per person (Table 1) in the United States. Since many people do not receive x-rays, those who do are subjected to considerably higher doses. Approximate doses from medical x-rays are presented in Table 2. It is clear from these figures that several diagnostic studies will expose a patient to radiation far in excess of the natural background level and at least 1000 times greater than the radiation exposure to the population from the operation of nuclear reactors (0.01 mrem/year).

Thus far, no conclusive evidence of any biologic effect has been attributed to low natural background levels (102 mrem/year), and some authors even argue that some radiation may be beneficial, although this remains unproven.

TABLE 2
Average Dose from Medical X-Ray

X-Ray Procedure	Skin Dose (mrem)	Gonadal Dose	
		Males	Females
Chest	66	0.09	0.3
Abdomen (two films)	1,920	97	221
Lumbar spine (four films)	10,000	218	721
Upper gastrointestinal series	2,840	1	171
Barium enema	2,640	175	903
Teeth (full mouth)	900	8	0.6
Mammogram (two films)	5,000 (females)		

The evidence that radiation bears a cause-and-effect relationship to cancer is based on a minimum level of exposure of about 30,000 mrad. It is possible that repetitive low doses of medical x-rays may have some harmful effects. This possible risk is generally considered to be justified if the information obtained is useful in arriving at a diagnosis or monitoring the treatment of a patient.

The U.S. Code of Federal Regulations (Title 10, Part 20), contains the legal rediation exposure limits (Maximum Permissible Doses) for people engaged in radiation work. However, the maximum values shown in Table 3 are not to be used as average acceptable values. These permissible levels are considerably below those at which biologic effects have been observed in the human. The accepted principle is that these doses should be kept as low as practicable. Few radiation workers approach the 5000 mrem/year standard. Radiologists

TABLE 3
Radiation Dose Limits

Radiation worker (allowable limits)
Whole body, gonads,
eyes	5,000 mrem in any one year
Hands	75,000 mrem in any one year
Forearms	30,000 mrem in any one year
Skin	30,000 mrem in any one year

Lifesaving emer-
gency	100,000 mrem

Nonlifesaving
emergency	25,000 mrem

Nonoccupational Exposure (including minors)
Individuals	500 mrem in any one year
Population average	170 mrem in any one year

and x-ray technicians seldom exceed 300–400 mrem/year.

In the management of a patient, if lifesaving procedures are being performed, a one-time exposure of the attendant of up to 100 rem (100,000 mrem) may be justified on a voluntary basis (Table 3). Under nonlifesaving emergency conditions, a dose of 25 rem (25,000 mrem) could be received by an attendant voluntarily on a one-time basis. This dose will not cause any symptoms and carries only a small risk of late effects.

As will be discussed, although such exposures may be justified, they rarely need to be reached. Simple precautions can generally reduce the hazard to the attendants from radiation to a negligible level.

In summary, there are many sources of radiation, both natural and man-made. Levels near background have not been shown to be either beneficial or harmful. The greatest source of man-made radiation exposure to the public is the medical x-ray. On the whole, these levels are justified since the patient derives an overwhelming benefit.

In the management of a radiation accident, simple procedures can be used to ensure that paramedical and medical attendants are not exposed to levels of radiation even approaching those created by medical x-ray procedures.

Basic Atomic and Nuclear Physics

NUCLEUS

The nucleus is that part of the atom in which the total positive electric charge and most of the mass are concentrated. The nucleus contains protons, or positively charged

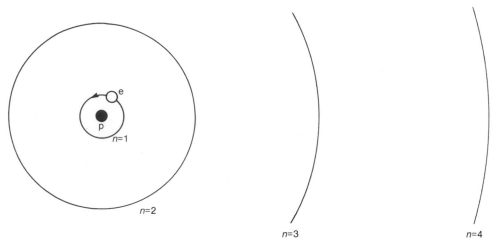

FIGURE 2 The Bohr model of the hydrogen atom. The electron is in its lowest stationary state. The relative orbital radii are as shown, but the proton and electron have been enlarged relatively about 10^3 times.

particles, and neutrons, or uncharged particles. The mass of the proton and the mass of the neutron are approximately equal. The number of protons found in the nucleus determines the atomic number of the substances of interest (Figure 2).

ELECTRON CLOUD

The electron cloud surrounds the nucleus and contains electrons, or stable elementary particles having a negative electrical charge. In a neutral atom, the number of electrons equals the number of protons in the nucleus. If an atom becomes ionized, there will be more or fewer electrons in the cloud than there are protons in the nucleus.

BINDING ENERGY

The binding energy is the amount of energy that is needed to separate the nucleus into its individual component parts.

NUCLEAR STABILITY

Nuclear stability is concerned with the probability that an element will undergo radioactive decay. In general, most elements have a nearly equal number of neutrons and protons in their nucleus. However, as the number of neutrons comes to exceed the number of protons, nuclear stability decreases. Elements in which the number of neutrons barely

exceeds the number of protons typically decay by β particle emission; elements with a great excess of neutrons (e.g., uranium) typically decay by α particle emission or possibly by spontaneous fission (see the section on radioactivity).

NOTES ON FIGURES

Figures 2, 3, and 4 help to demonstrate these principles. Figure 2 portrays a generalized atom. Figure 3 demonstrates the variation

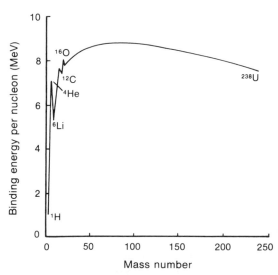

FIGURE 3 Variation of binding energy per nucleon with atomic mass number.

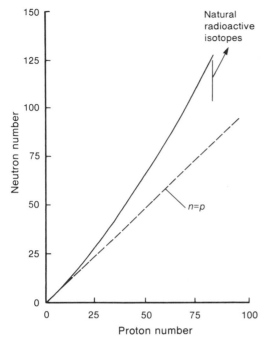

FIGURE 4 Nuclear stability curve. The line represents the best fit to the neutron-proton coordinates of stable isotopes.

of binding energy per nucleon with an atomic mass number, the mass number being the sum of the protons and neutrons. It is seen that the binding energy per nucleon, as measured in million electron volts (MeV), rapidly increases with increasing mass number, until a near-maximum is reached which has a binding energy slightly less than 8 MeV. Figure 4 shows a nuclear stability curve. The dashed line is a line of slope 1, in which the number of neutrons and protons are equal. The upper solid line represents a plot of the elements

$$\alpha = {}^{210}_{84}\text{Po} \rightarrow {}^{4}_{2}\text{He} + {}^{206}_{82}\text{Pb}$$

$$\beta = {}^{32}_{15}\text{P} \rightarrow {}^{32}_{16}\text{S} + {}^{0}_{-1}\text{e} + \gamma$$

$$\text{Positron} = {}^{22}_{11}\text{Na} \rightarrow {}^{22}_{10}\text{Ne} + {}^{0}_{1}\text{e} + \gamma$$

$$\text{Electron capture} = {}^{22}_{11}\text{Na} + {}^{0}_{-1}\text{e} \rightarrow {}^{22}_{10}\text{Ne} + \gamma$$

$$\text{Internal conversion} = {}^{137}_{55}\text{Cs} \rightarrow {}^{137}_{56}\text{Ba} + {}^{0}_{-1}\text{e} + \gamma$$

FIGURE 5 Various decay mechanisms. ${}^{210}_{84}\text{Po}$ is the symbol for polonium. The mass number is 210, which is the number of protons plus neutrons in the nucleus. The atomic number is 84, which is the number of protons in the nucleus. γ is a gamma photon; ${}_{-1}^{0}\text{e}$ is an electron; ${}_{+1}^{0}\text{e}$ is a positron.

as we know them, and a note is made of where the naturally radioactive isotopes begin.

Radioactivity

RADIOACTIVE DECAY

Radioactive decay is the means by which an atom disintegrates to form a different atom. There are many different means by which this may occur. These are diagrammed in Figure 5. The various decay mechanisms are as follows:

Alpha—In α decay, an α particle, which is a helium nucleus that has two protons and two neutrons, is ejected from the nucleus of the parent material. This results in a new compound which has an atomic number two less than the parent and an atomic weight four less than the parent.

Beta—In β decay, an electron which carries a negative charge is released from the nucleus of the parent material. This results in a compound which has an atomic number one greater than the parent and the same atomic weight.

Positron—In this case, a positively charged particle which has a mass similar to that of an electron is given off from the nucleus. In this particular instance, the atomic number drops by one and the atomic mass remains the same.

Electron capture—In this case, the compound pulls an electron from the electron cloud into the nucleus. The atomic number decreases by one and the atomic mass remains constant.

Internal conversion—In this instance, an electron is given off from the nucleus of the parent material. The atomic number increases by one and the mass remains the same.

RADIOACTIVE HALF-LIFE

The half-life of any radioactive material is the amount of time it takes for one-half of it to disappear. Each radioactive isotope has a specific half-life, which does not change. This average half-life relates to the amount of time, mathematically at least, for the decaying radionuclide to disappear completely. Figure 6 shows an example of a half-life curve.

CURIE

A Curie is a measure of the amount of radioactivity present. It is numerically equal to 3.7×10^{10} disintegrations per second (dps)

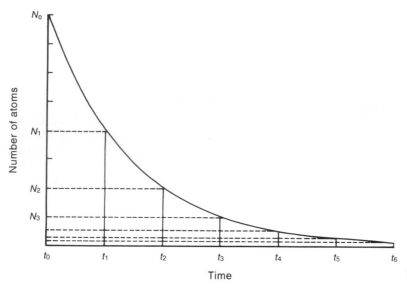

FIGURE 6   Half-life curve.

TABLE 4
Some Low Atomic Numbered Naturally Occurring Radioisotopes

Nuclide	Isotopic Abundance (%)	Half-life (Years)	Principal Radiations	
			Particles	Gamma
^{40}K	0.012	1.3×10^9	1.35 MeV[a]	1.46 MeV
^{87}Rb	27.85	5×10^{10}	0.275 MeV	None
^{138}La	0.09	1.1×10^{11}	1.0 MeV	0.80, 1.43 MeV
^{147}Sm	15.07	1.3×10^{11}	2.18 MeV	None
^{176}Lu	2.6	3×10^{10}	0.43 MeV	0.20, 0.31 MeV
^{137}Re	62.93	5×10^{10}	0.043 MeV	None

[a] MeV = million electron volts.

or 2.22×10^{12} dpm—disintegrations per minute (due to decay of radioactive materials).

SPECIFIC ACTIVITY

The specific acitivity of any element or compound is the amount of radioactivity found in a measured amount of that compound.

RADIOACTIVITY

There are essentially three forms of radioactivity: radionuclides found in a series (thonium, neptunium, uranium, actinium); naturally occurring, nonseries radioactive isotopes (Table 4); and radioactive materials created by bombarding a stable nucleus with atomic particles (Table 5).

TABLE 5
Induced Radioactivity

$^{14}_{7}N + ^{4}_{2}He \rightarrow ^{18}_{9}F$

$^{17}_{8}O + ^{1}_{1}H \rightarrow ^{18}_{9}F$

$^{2}_{1}H + \gamma \rightarrow ^{1}_{1}H + ^{1}_{1}n$

$^{79}_{35}Br + ^{1}_{0}n \rightarrow ^{80}_{35}Br + \gamma \ (n, \gamma)$

$^{14}_{7}N + ^{1}_{0}n \rightarrow ^{14}_{6}C + ^{1}_{1}H \ (n, p)$

$^{19}_{9}F + ^{1}_{0}n \rightarrow ^{16}_{7}N + ^{4}_{2}He \ (n, \alpha)$

$^{12}_{6}C + ^{1}_{0}n \rightarrow ^{11}_{5}C + ^{1}_{0}n + ^{1}_{0}n \ (n, 2n)$

$^{59}_{27}Co + ^{1}_{0}n \rightarrow ^{60}_{27}Co + ^{0}_{-1}\beta + \gamma + \gamma \ (n, \gamma)$

$^{58}_{28}Ni + ^{1}_{0}n \rightarrow ^{59}_{27}Co + ^{0}_{+1}\beta + \gamma \ (n, p)$

n = neutron; α = alpha; γ = gamma; ρ = proton; β = beta.

Interaction of Radiation with Matter

ALPHA PARTICLES

An α particle is a helium nucleus that contains two neutrons and two protons; as such, it has an atomic number of 2 and an atomic weight of 4. It is a relatively heavy particle and travels in a straight line, knocking everything else out of its way before it comes to rest. Refer to Figure 7 and note that even the most energetic α particles, i.e., those measuring 4 MeV, may travel only a few centimeters in air before losing all of their energy. Refer to Figure 8 (the number of ion pairs formed in air by a moving α particle), and

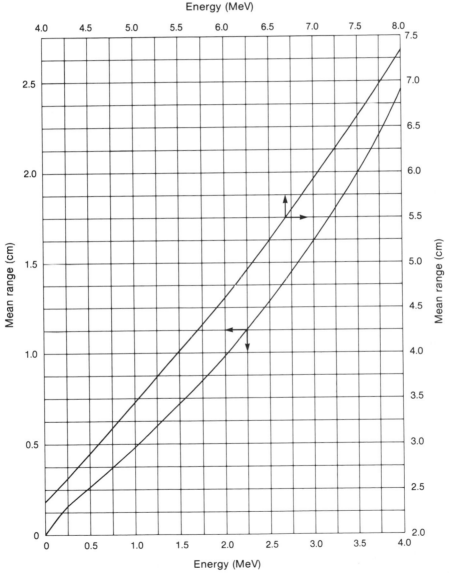

FIGURE 7 Range versus energy for α particles in air (STP). Adapted from Radiological Health Handbook, 1960. Department of Health, Education, and Welfare, Bureau of Radiologic Health (Superintendent of Documents, U.S. Government Printing Office, Washington, D.C.)

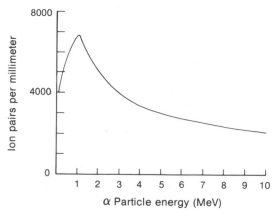

FIGURE 8 Bragg curve of specific ionization by α particles in air (STP).

note that α particles of 1 MeV will form the largest number of ion pairs per millimeter of air. Alpha particles have short penetration (through only the thickness of a sheet of paper) and are generally of low hazard. Because they dissipate energy quickly, they are dangerous upon inhalation or ingestion. Externally, they do not penetrate beyond the keratin layer of the epidermis.

BETA PARTICLES

Beta particles are electrons that have a charge of 1 and an exceedingly small mass (1/7000th that of an α particle). Because of this mass, as electrons travel through any medium, they are bounced from particle to particle traveling in a straight line. Typically, the distance that a β particle will travel in some medium is measured in milligrams per square centimeter. Figure 9 shows the actual range in inches that a β particle travels in many different media. Beta particles can penetrate more deeply into tissue than can α particles, but do not cause as much damage.

GAMMA RAYS

Gamma rays (photons which have no charge) are absorbed in a medium by three general processes. These processes, which are shown in Figures 10, 11, and 12, are the pho-

toelectric effect, the Compton effect, and pair production.

Photoelectric effect—An incoming γ ray causes an electron to be split away from the nucleus.
Compton effect—An incoming photon hits an electron in the electron cloud, splitting it away from the nucleus and the photon itself. Having hit the electron with a glancing blow, the photon moves away at another angle.
Pair production—An incoming photon is absorbed by the nucleus of an atom, which emits a positively charged and a negatively charged electron.

Figure 13 shows the energy requirements for the above three effects.

Gamma rays and x-rays differ only in that γ radiation originates in the nucleus, while x-irradiation is produced outside it. Both types of radiation have high penetration (meters) in air and can cause significant tissue damage when externally applied.

NEUTRONS

A neutron is an uncharged particle found in the nucleus with a mass approximately equal to that of a proton. Neutrons are produced in reactors, by the combination of certain radioactive elements such as polonium-beryllium, and in fission reactions. In general, they are classified as thermal, having very low energies; slow, having slightly higher energies; and fast, having relatively high energies. Neutrons interact with material in a variety of ways; they may be absorbed, or they may scatter in much the same way as γ rays. They have greater tissue penetration than the other particles and pose the greatest external hazard.

Radiation Dosimetry

ROENTGEN

The roentgen is a measure of the radioactivity in the air. It is that quantity of radiation which will cause the formation of 2.083×10^9 ion pairs per cubic centimeter of air at standard conditions.

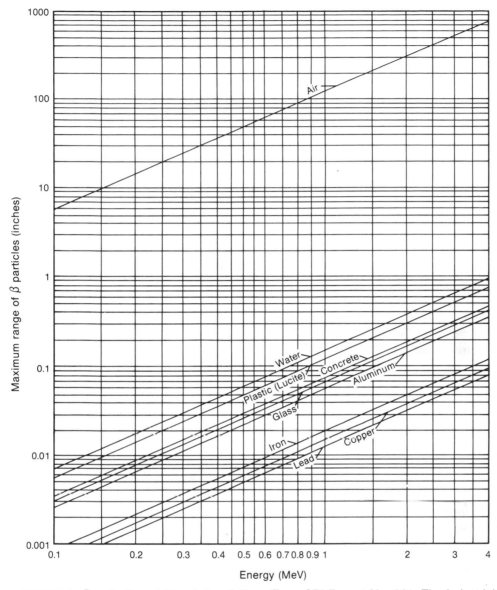

FIGURE 9 Penetration ability of β radiation. (From SRI Report No. 361, The industrial uses of radioactive fission products. With permission of the Stanford Research Institute and the U.S. Atomic Energy Commission.)

RAD

The rad is the unit of absorbed dose which is equal to 100 ergs of energy per gram of absorbing material.

RBE

The RBE, or relative biologic effectiveness, is a measure of the biologic damage caused by any particle. RBE values range from 1 to approximately 20; x-rays, γ rays, and most β particles have an RBE of 1, while neutrons, α particles, and others have higher RBEs.

REM

This special unit is equal to the number of rads multiplied by the RBE for the particles

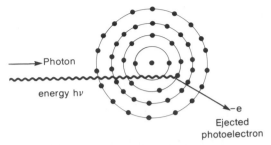

FIGURE 10 The photoelectric effect.

of interest. It is a method of measuring an absorbed dose.

QF

The QF, or quality factor, is related to the RBE (Table 6) but is mathematically derived. Table 7 gives the QFs for various types of radiation.

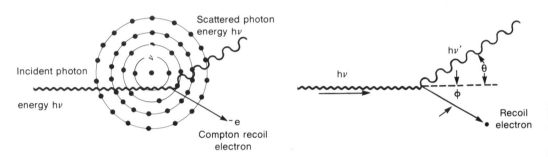

A

B

FIGURE 11 (*A*) The Compton effect. (*B*) Diagram of the Compton effect.

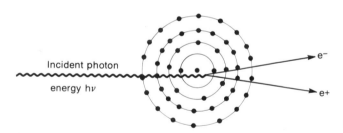

FIGURE 12 Pair production.

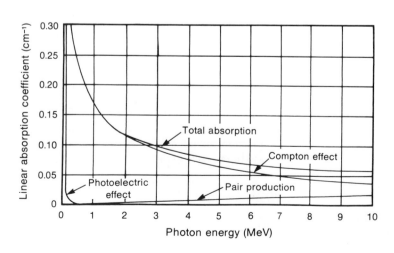

FIGURE 13 Linear absorption coefficients for γ rays in aluminum (0–10 MeV).

TABLE 6
Relationship Between Linear Energy Transfer (LET) and Quality Factor (QF)

LET (KeV/μm in water)[a]	QF
3.5 or less	1
3.5–7.0	1–2
7.0–23	2–5
23–53	5–10
53–175	10–20

[a] KeV = thousand electron volts.

TABLE 7
Quality Factor (QF) for Various Forms of Radiation

Radiation	QF
γ rays from radium in equilibrium with its decay products (filtered by 0.5 mm of platinum)	1
X-rays	1
β rays and electrons of energy >0.03 MeV	1
β rays and electrons of energy <0.03 MeV	1.7
Thermal neutrons	3
Fast neutrons	10
Protons	10
α rays	10
Heavy ions	20

EXTERNAL DOSIMETRY

Dosimetry is the process whereby the radiation dose absorbed by an individual can be measured. The series of equations in Figure 14 give many different methods for measuring the absorbed dose.

INTERNAL DOSIMETRY

This is the same as external dosimetry, but refers to doses from radionuclides which may be ingested or breathed into the body. The parameters of interest here are the biologic half-life (the amount of time it takes for the body to remove or detoxify one-half of the absorbed material) and the effective half-life (a combination of the biologic and physical half-lives). These relationships and the dose due to an internal β emitter are shown in

Figure 15. Other methods for performing internal dosimetry are found in International Committee on Radiation Protection (ICRP) publications, National Council on Radiation Protection (NCRP) publications, and the As Low as Practical Final Environmental Statement.

Basic Biology: Effects of Radiation

DOSE-RESPONSE CHARACTERISTICS

In general, the higher the absorbed dose for any form of ionizing or nonionizing radiation, the greater will be the biologic effect (10). Figure 16 shows two generalized dose-response curves. It should be noted that as the dose increases, the percentage response also increases. There are two ways in which these effects occur.

Direct action—Direct action (Figures 17 and 18) occurs when incoming energy causes a break in a chromosome or in a strand of nucleic acid. Depending on the type and severity of the break, there may be some effect or none, because the chromosome or the nucleic acid recombines incorrectly or is incapable of recombination.

Indirect action—Indirect action is caused by the action of radiation on molecules of water. This is shown in a series of equations in Figure 19. The net result is the formation of hydrogen peroxide and hydrogen dioxide, which are very reactive compounds. Their potent oxidizing action produces the results observed.

RADIATION EFFECTS

Radiation effects are manifested in either acute or delayed form. Figures 20 and 21 demonstrate a series of acute effects based on the absorbed dose. The delayed effects that may occur due to radiation are cancer, shortening of life, or the formation of cataracts. It is exceedingly difficult to relate the exposure to any of these delayed effects.

CHROMOSOME ABERRATION ANALYSIS

In this method, the dose of radiation received by an individual can be determined by examining defects that have occurred in the chromosomes of a cell.

1. *Exposure rate* (from a point source). (Equation assumes that one ion pair in air causes an average energy expenditure of 32.7 eV.)

$$I_\gamma = 0.156nE(10^5\mu_a)$$

where I_γ = milliroentgen per hour at 1 m/mCi
n = γ quanta per disintegration
E = energy of γ quanta in megaelectron volts
μ_a = energy absorption coefficient for γ in air (STP) per centimeter

2. *Exposure rate* (from point source of radium, 0.5 mm Pt cover)

$$\text{mR/hour} = \frac{\text{mg Ra}}{\text{yd}^2}$$

where yd = distance to source (yd)

$$\text{mR/hour} = \frac{8400 \text{ mg Ra}}{\text{cm}^2}$$

cm = distance (cm)

3. *Exposure rate, approximate* (from any γ-point source)

R/hr at 1 foot $\cong$ 6 C *En*
mR/hour per mCi at 1 m $\cong$ 0.5 nE

where C = number of curies
E = γ ray energy (MeV)
n = γ quanta/dis

4. *Exposure rate* (from any γ = point source)

$$\text{mR/hour} = nI_\gamma/s^2$$

where n = number of millicuries
I_γ = mR/hour at 1 m/mCi
s = distance (meters)

5. *Exposure rate* (from a linear γ = emitter source)

where S = source of activity in photons per second per unit length

ϕ = flux at point of interest in photons per square centimeter per second

r = distance from source to point of interest, P

θ = angle in degrees

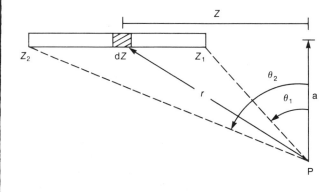

$$\phi = \int_{Z_1}^{Z_2} \frac{S(dZ)}{4\pi r^2}$$

$$\phi = \frac{S}{4\pi a} (\theta_2 - \theta_1)$$

FIGURE 14 γ Emitter dose in air.

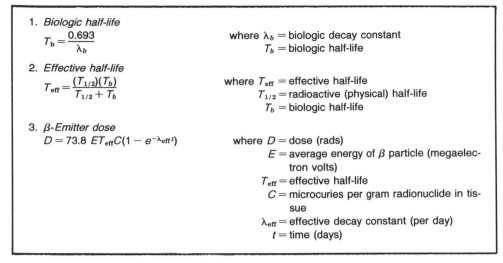

1. *Biologic half-life*
$$T_b = \frac{0.693}{\lambda_b}$$
    where λ_b = biologic decay constant
    T_b = biologic half-life

2. *Effective half-life*
$$T_{eff} = \frac{(T_{1/2})(T_b)}{T_{1/2} + T_b}$$
    where T_{eff} = effective half-life
    $T_{1/2}$ = radioactive (physical) half-life
    T_b = biologic half-life

3. *β-Emitter dose*
$$D = 73.8\ ET_{eff}C(1 - e^{-\lambda_{eff}t})$$
    where D = dose (rads)
    E = average energy of β particle (megaelectron volts)
    T_{eff} = effective half-life
    C = microcuries per gram radionuclide in tissue
    λ_{eff} = effective decay constant (per day)
    t = time (days)

FIGURE 15   Internal radiation dosage due to an internal β emitter.

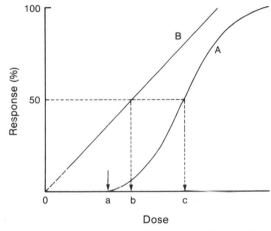

FIGURE 16   Dose-response curves. Curve *A* is the characteristic shape for a biological effect that exhibits a threshold dose (point *a*). The spread of the curve, from the threshold at *a* to the 100% response, is thought to be due to biologic variability around the mean dose, point *c*, which is called the 50% dose. Curve *B* represents a nonthreshold, or linear response; point *b* represents the 50% dose for the nonthreshold biologic effect.

SOME DEFINITIONS

Gene—a specific point on a chromosome
Chromosome—biologic structure which carries the hereditary (genetic) code

Biologic effect—any change in the normal function or structure of a biologic entity
Nucleic acid—the chemical which is responsible for the hereditary (genetic) code
Reactive compound—a chemical which reacts readily with other chemicals
Acute effect—any effect which occurs quickly (seconds to days)
LD_{100}, LD_{50}, LD_0—that level of effect which is lethal to 100%, 50%, or 0% of a population
Mutation—a change in the genetic material (usually deleterious)

Instrumentation

The instrumentation used in measuring radiation exposure at a nuclear facility is very complex and will not be considered here. Table 4.1 of Reference 1 provides an excellent summary of radiation measurement techniques and instruments.

Two types of instrumentation are employed in handling radiation accidents during the hospital phase. First, there are detectors to determine whether radioactive materials are present in the environment and, if so, their location and level. Such detectors are generally of the Geiger-Müller or ionization type. Second, there are devices known as *personnel dosimeters* or *ionization chambers* (5). They are concerned with measuring exposure to the attendants.

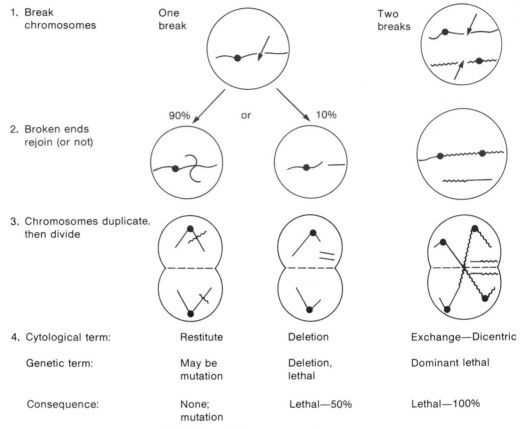

1. Break chromosomes

One break

Two breaks

90% or 10%

2. Broken ends rejoin (or not)

3. Chromosomes duplicate, then divide

4. Cytological term:	Restitute	Deletion	Exchange—Dicentric
Genetic term:	May be mutation	Deletion, lethal	Dominant lethal
Consequence:	None; mutation	Lethal—50%	Lethal—100%

FIGURE 17 Chromosome damage.

DETECTORS

The most common radiation detectors respond to ionizing particles by producing an electrical pulse. These pulses may be read on a meter or may be heard as a click or other audible signal. Such Geiger-Müller-type detectors are simple to use, inexpensive, reliable, and extremely sensitive to radiation.

Two such detectors are depicted in Figure 22. The first type of detector consists of an instrument box to which a probe is attached. When the probe is brought near a radioactive source, there is an increase in the number of audible clicks or the sound of an alarm. The audible response feature of such instruments is desirable, since it is impractical to watch the meter constantly. This type of detector does not indicate the amount or type of radiation. It merely confirms the presence and location of the radioactive material. Since these detectors are so sensitive, even a small amount of radioactive material produces a large audible signal. It is important not to become frightened by the magnitude of the response. Even the radium dial of a wrist watch will evoke an impressive number of clicks.

The second type of Geiger-Müller detector gives a reading on a meter of counts per minute and, if properly calibrated for fission products, in millirads (mrads) per hour. (As we have discussed previously, millirads are equal to millirems for our purposes.) The detector on this device is located on the end of a telescoping rod, permitting measurements to be made at some distance from the operator. The indicated reading refers to the dose that would be received by a person standing at a location at the probe end of the rod for 1 hour.

Both of these devices are battery operated and must be checked on a semiannual basis to ensure reliability. Care should be taken that

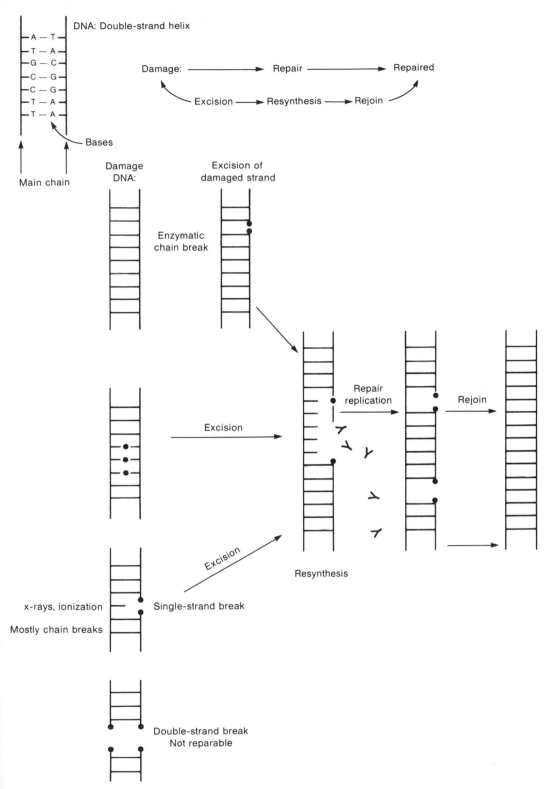

FIGURE 18 DNA radiation damage and repair.

$$H_2O \rightarrow H_2O^+ + e^-$$

$$H_2O^+ \rightarrow H^+ + OH$$

$$H_2O + e^- \rightarrow H_2O^-$$

$$H_2O^- \rightarrow H + OH^-$$

$$OH + OH \rightarrow H_2O_2$$

$$H + O_2 \rightarrow HO_2$$

FIGURE 19 The effect of radiation on water.

any Geiger-Müller device purchased is of the type that will function even at extremely high radiation levels and at low temperatures, and will provide a positive response to any malfunction.

Although there are many sources of uncertainty, Geiger-Müller counters, when used with care, enable the operator to assess the location and relative amount of radioactive material and to follow the efficacy of decontamination efforts. They are useful for civil radiation authorities in the examination of a suspected radiation accident. These devices may also be used to monitor persons and objects that leave an area of potential contamination, thus restricting the spread of radioactive material. Although there is some debate as to the hospital's need for monitoring equip-

ment of its own, this gives the hospital a capability independent of the nuclear facility and enables it to deal with minor radiation accidents, such as loss of radium needles or medical radiopharmaceutical spills.

Personnel Dosimeters

While Geiger-Müller detectors provide an estimate of the potential hazard in treating a patient, it is necessary to know more precisely the dose received by every attendant involved in treating the patient. A surgeon who removes a radioactive metallic fragment from a wound will generally receive a higher dose to his hand than to his body. Personnel dosimeters are used to determine what these doses are.

Two types of personnel dosimeters can be used. One type, thermoluminescent dosimeters (TLDs), are very small plasticlike buttons or rods. They store information about the dose received, but they must be processed in order to be read. Thus, TLDs reveal exposure after the fact. They are very accurate and reliable, have a large dose range, and are not subject to problems such as moisture effects or light leakage that occur with film badges. TLDs may be worn as a badge or ring. The badge TLD is worn under the outer layer of protective clothing on the chest. The ring TLD is

Time	Dose $\geq$ LD$_{100}$ >600 rad	LD$_{50}$ 450 rad	LD$_0$ $\leq$200 rad
Hour 2 through week 1 (days 2–6)	Severe nausea	Severe nausea	None
	Diarrhea, vomiting, sore throat, loss of appetite	Same, but less severe	No special symptoms
Week 2 (days 7–14)	Fever, weight loss, severe malaise	No special symptoms	No special symptoms
	Death, day 14		
Week 3 (days 15–21)	———	Loss of appetite, weight, hair; fever	Same symptoms, less severe
		50% die, days 15–21	None die
Week 4 and later	———	Recovery: Later detect mutations, cancer, premature aging	Same, but lower frequency

FIGURE 20 Radiation syndrome in the human.

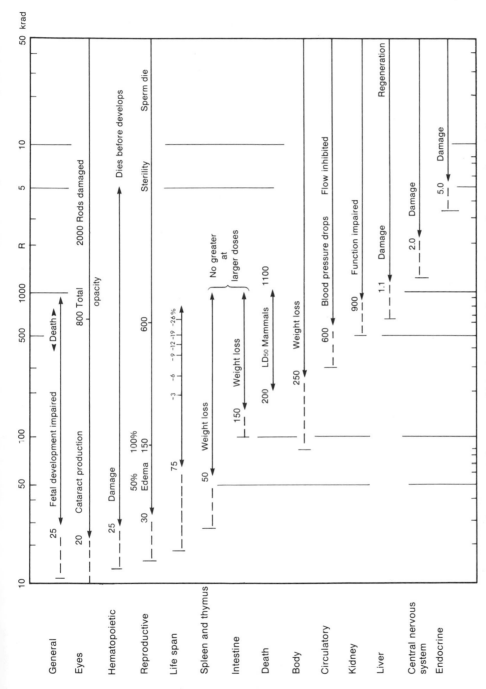

FIGURE 21 Organ and tissue sensitivity in mammals. The dose values are for whole-body, acute, x-ray, or γ-ray exposures. For low-intensity or fractionated exposure, the lines would be moved toward the right (higher doses). Note that radiosensitivity is roughly in order of proliferative rate or necessity of the organs.

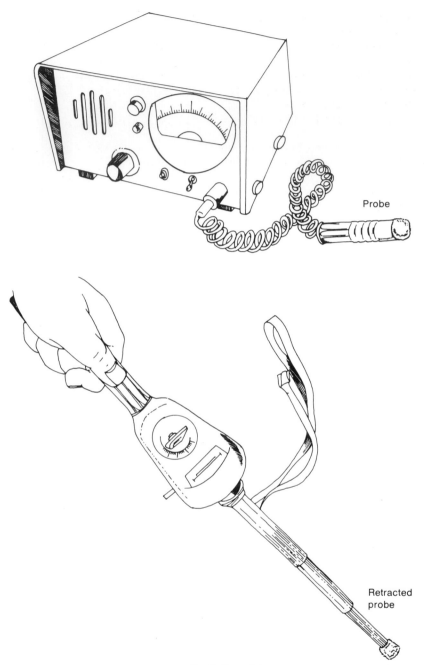

Probe

Retracted
probe

FIGURE 22 Radiation detectors.

worn on the ring finger of the right hand on a right-handed person and on the left hand of a left-handed person. It should be worn under latex gloves.

The second type of dosimeter is the self-reading pen type. This provides the user with an estimate of the dose he or she is currently receiving. When it is looked through like a small telescope, a scale and pointer can be seen. If the pointer reads 20 mrad before one enters a possibly contaminated area and 50 mrad 20 minutes later, then one has received the difference, or 30 mrad. With this device there is no need to wait for processing of the dosimeter. Pen-type dosimeters, however, are much less accurate than TLDs.

As a general rule, if personnel dosimeters are available, they should be worn by all persons handling the patient. If two different types of dosimeters are available, both should be worn.

Each dosimeter has an identifying number stamped on it. Accurate records of the identifying number of each dosimeter and the name of the person to whom it was issued are imperative. A dosimeter with a reading of 500 mrem is of no value unless the wearer can be identified.

A pocket alarm is the size of a package of cigarettes and is also battery operated. The alarm can be set at a desired level of 500–1000 mrem/hour. If such an alarm sounds, the wearer knows that the exposure is significant.

In summary, hospital personnel should have simple, reliable radiation detection devices. If radiation is detected, personnel dosimeters will provide information about the dose each attendant has received while treating the patient. Many other detection devices, often available at nuclear facilities, are too complicated for use without specific training and should remain in the hands of a competent health physicist.

Types of Accidents

Accidents that involve employees at nuclear facilities have been very rare. To date, fewer than 20 deaths have been attributed to overexposure to radiation, and none of these has occurred at a commercial nuclear power facility. The overall safety record at nuclear facilities for all types of accidents is better than for most industries.

There are six general types of accidents, that are reviewed below (6).

MECHANICAL ACCIDENTS

As with any industrial facility, the majority of accidents at nuclear facilities are caused by mechanical injury, such as a workman falling from a ladder. The first question the atten-

dant should consider is whether radiation is involved at all. Plant personnel have instrumentation available to determine the existence of radiation exposure. Mechanical accidents can be prevented by employing good industrial safety practices.

EXTERNAL EXPOSURE

An example of this type of injury is exposure of a patient to penetrating radiation similar to x-rays. The patient is *not* radioactive and presents no hazard to attendants. This injury is identical to that of a cancer patient who has received radiation therapy. Since the patient has not come in contact with radioactive material, he is not contaminated. Exposure is terminated by removing the patient from the radiation area. However, there may be some exposure to plant personnel if the patient needs help in leaving the radiation area.

WOUND WITH SHRAPNEL

An explosion or other violent destruction of a piece of equipment could result in a wound in which a fragment of radioactive metal is embedded. Care is required during removal of the metallic fragment to prevent exposure to the physician's hands. The radioactive fragment may be a hazard to other attendants and to the patient; shielding may be needed. Prompt removal and proper disposal of the fragment are required.

INTERNAL CONTAMINATION

The two most common forms of internal contamination are inhalation and ingestion. The former may be incurred by radiation workers who enter an area where radioactive products are present either in gaseous form or as airborne suspended particles. As an example of the latter, a worker may drink something he has accidentally contaminated, resulting in ingestion. Inhalation and ingestion often occur together, since some material deposited in the lungs and pharynx will normally be coughed up with mucus and then swallowed. Generally speaking, such internal deposition of radioactive material represents minimal, if any, hazard to the attendants. People contaminated in this fashion are very similar to patients who have received radioactive iodine for the diagnosis of thyroid abnormalities.

The patient's subsequent course is determined by the solubility of the material and the nature of the radionuclide. Insoluble material that enters the lungs is difficult to remove, whereas insoluble material that is ingested is excreted. Soluble materials may enter the tissues and be deposited in certain organs. Elimination of such radionuclides does occur to some extent.

Internal contamination can be avoided only by containment of radioactive material. Although accumulation of a radionuclide in a specific organ (such as radioactive iodine in the thyroid) can cause radiation damage locally, it practically never causes an acute radiation syndrome (described later).

PATIENT CONTAMINATION

A spill of radioactive material may cause workers to be contaminated externally with radioactive liquid or dust. The material is generally deposited on the clothing and skin. A break in the skin may allow some of the radioactive material to enter the body. Care must be exercised to restrict spread of the radioactive material while first aid is being administered. As a rule, such patients may be substantially decontaminated (95% or more) by removal of clothing and a wash procedure (7,9). If time does not permit decontamination at the site of the accident, the patient must be carefully transported to the hospital and decontaminated. This type of patient may be a hazard to attendants if contamination is not controlled.

COMBINED ACCIDENT

Combinations of the above types of accidents may occur. A thorough understanding of the basic types is essential to facilitate proper handling of the patient and to ensure the safety of the attendants. For example, a patient with a compound leg fracture and an inhalation exposure should be treated for the fracture without delay. The contaminated and injured patient presents the most difficult emergency problem. The severely overexposed patient poses the most difficult treatment problem, while the internally contaminated patient presents the most complex investigative problem.

Advance Planning

Effective management of any accident, radiation or otherwise, at an industrial facility necessitates previous planning, arrangements, and properly preplaced equipment. A list of general needs must consider the following:

Emergency organization
Action criteria
    For notification of off-site groups
    For initiation of protective measures
Updating provisions
First aid and decontamination facilities
    Personnel monitoring equipment
    Decontamination facilities and supplies
    First aid facilities and supplies
    On-site medical assistance arrangements
    Transportation arrangements
Treatment facilities off-site
Training provisions
Exercises and drills

PLANT PHASE

Each facility must have a specific person responsible for maintaining a first aid station and ensuring that adequate supplies (Tables 8–11) are kept on hand at all times. There must be a designated first aid area or room, located adjacent to but outside the high radiation area and en route to a prearranged ambulance pickup point (8). Equipment arrangements for a first aid room include a decontamination table, a shower hose, a collapsible stretcher, and a reasonable amount of cabinet space. Good lighting is required. A telephone should be available in the first aid room so that adequate communication may be maintained with outside agencies and assistants.

Additional requirements are a kit for taking samples, including urine samples, tissue samples, metallic fragment samples, and nose swabs. These kits should be used if one suspects that exposure to radioactive material has occurred. A second kit containing bandages, decontaminating materials, and antiseptic solutions should be available. These supplies should be accompanied by a simplified set of instructions placed on top of the outside of the packing to ensure that an individual unfa-

TABLE 8
Decontamination Kit

1. *Skin decontamination*
   a. *Utensils*
      Absorbent balls, extra large
      Sponge-holding forceps
      Solution bowl, plastic (to hold decontaminant)
      Plastic beaker, large (to discard used sponges)
      Preoperative sponges (for large area decontamination)
      Surgical hand brushes (for decontamination of hands or feet)
      Wash bottle (to hold water for decontamination)
   b. *Decontaminants*
      Mild liquid soap, bottles (for first decontamination effort, general)
      Aqueous solution of chlorine (Clorox), diluted before use (for second decontamination effort)
      Antiseptic cleansing agent (for decontamination of skin around wounds, abrasions, etc.)
2. *Wound cleansing*
   a. *Utensils*
      Sterile gauze pads, 4 × 4 inches, in box
      Surgical gloves, assorted sizes, sterile pair
      Solution bowl, sterile
      Irrigating syringes, 50 ml, sterile
      Aperture drapes, sterile
      Sponge-holding forceps, sterile
      Cotton-tipped applicators, sterile, in box
   b. *Cleansing agents*
      Normal saline solution, sterile, bottle
      Hydrogen peroxide, 3% solution, bottle
3. *Nose irrigation*
   a. *Utensils*
      Irrigator, plastic
      Tubing and applicator, set
      Paper container (to collect irrigation fluid)
   b. *Irrigation fluids*
      Water or normal saline solution, bottle
4. *Miscellaneous materials*
   Collodion, bottle (to seal residual skin contamination)
   Mild skin cream (Nivea) (to apply on dry skin after complete decontamination)
   Hair clippers, pair
   Preparation kit (for clipping and shaving)
   Nail clippers
   Bandage scissors, large pair
   Patient radiation and medical status record sheets (for recording essential data on patient's medical and radiation status)

Skin marker (permanent ink) (to mark contaminated areas on skin)
Plastic bags, assortment (to hold decontamination materials after use)
Tags, with wire (to indicate contents of containers and bags)
Tissue paper, box
Notebook
Pencils

TABLE 9
Medical Emergency Supplies, List 1

1. Suction, portable, with table and vacuum pump
2. Stretcher, complete
3. Head-foot board
4. Strap, restraint
5. Stool, revolving, conductive
6. Stand, Mayo
7. Stool, foot operating, conductive
8. Frame, basin, conductive casters
9. Tray, utility
10. Cart, on wheels
11. Spotlight, surgical
12. Stethoscope
13. Sphygmomanometer, portable
14. Clippers, hair, hand-operated
15. Forceps, tissue, Allis
16. Forceps, tissue (mouse tooth type)
17. Forceps, hemostatic, curved crile
18. Forceps, splinter
19. Forceps, instrument
20. Holder, needle
21. Probe, flexible
22. Scissors, suture
23. Scissors, dissecting, straight
24. Aprons, lead-lined, fluoroscopic
25. Clamps, mosquito, straight (for each surgical kit)
26. Procaine, 1%
27. Tray, tracheotomy, disposable
28. Tray, cut-down, disposable
29. Resuscitation bag, with large mask and O_2 tubing
30. Airway, plastic, large, oral
31. Airway, plastic, medium, nasal
32. Intravenous cannulas, no. 16-, 18-, 20-, and 22-gauge
33. Syringe, 50 ml
34. Tourniquet
35. Needle, cardiac
36. Armboard, large
37. Tube, tracheotomy, no. 32, cuffed Magill
38. Tube, tracheotomy, no. 36, cuffed Magill
39. Cardiac arrest drugs
40. Ethyl chloride

TABLE 10
Medical Emergency Supplies, List 2

1. Stethoscope
2. Blanket
3. Sphygmomanometer
4. Gown, patient
5. Sheet, cotton
6. Bed pan, plastic
7. Scissors, bandage
8. Tape, adhesive, 2-inch width
9. Razor, safety (with extra blades)
10. Brush, surgeon's, soft
11. Syringe, irrigation
12. Basin, irrigation
13. Large cotton ball container, glass, with stainless steel top
14. Ball, cotton
15. Swab, cotton (Q-tips)
16. Telfa, 3 × 4 inches, sterile
17. Sponge, gauze, 4 × 4 inches, sterile
18. Bandage, gauze, 2 × 3 inches, sterile
19. Bandage, Ace, 4 inches
20. Alcohol, 70%
21. Kits, intravenous, saline, isotonic (for intravenous use)
22. Saline, isotonic, sterile
23. Vials, 10 ml, oxalated
24. Zinc sulfate, 2 g each
25. Magnesium sulfate, 15 g each

TABLE 11
Health Physics Emergency Supplies

1. Coverall sets (yellow)—eight
   gloves (green plastic)
   gloves (white collon)
   hood
   shoe covers
2. Coverall sets (white)—seven
   gloves (rubber)
   gloves (white cotton)
   shoe covers
3. Gloves white cotton—four dozen
4. Gloves, green plastic—one dozen
5. Caps, surgeon's—four
6. Coverall, white cotton, sizes 42 and 46—seven each
7. Gloves, rubber, medium weight—15 pair
8. Respirators, half mask, with spare filters—two each

9. Bags, plastic, heavy, 55-gallon capacity—10
10. Pail, plastic, 14–20-quart capacity—three
11. Brush, scrubbing—three
12. Sanitary napkins—two boxes
13. Marker, black, felt tip—two
14. Paper, blotter or absorbent—one roll
15. Notebook, hard-cover—one
16. Pen, ball point (or pencil)—two each
17. Pins, safety, assorted sizes—2 dozen
18. Polyethylene sheeting, 100′ × 12′ × 4 mil—five rolls
19. Paper, heavy duty, brown, 26 inches wide (to cover floor)—two rolls
20. Sign, radiation warning—three, plus cords
21. Rope, radiation warning—50 feet
22. Sign, radiation, pressure sensitive—15 each
23. Detergent—6 pounds
24. Tape, gray, 2-inch width—six rolls
25. Towel, paper—10 packs
26. Bottles, sample, plastic, 32-ounce capacity—12
27. Preservative, 10% thymol in 2-propanol—1 pint
28. Formalin solution—1 quart
29. Container, pint or quart (for bioassay samples—three
30. Cans, 5-gallon—four
31. Scissors—one pair
32. Vials, blood sample—three
33. Mops, sponges—three each
34. Tags, radiation, prestrung—25
35. Paint, spray, magenta—one can
36. Cloth, wash—12
37. Towel, bath—12
38. Meter, survey, Geiger-Müller—one
39. Smears, paper disc—25
40. Tags, self-sticking—25
41. Envelopes, small—50
42. Mild liquid soap—1 gallon

For skin decontamination
43. Detergent—three boxes
44. Corn meal—1–2 pounds
45. Powder, titanium dioxide—1 pound
46. Lanolin, hydrous, USP[a]—1 pound
47. Crystals, potassium permanganate, USP—1 pound
48. Sodium bisulfite—1 pound
49. Sulfuric acid, 0.2 N—1 pound
50. Powder, sodium citrate, USP—1 pound
51. Radiation monitor, 0.1 mrad–100 rad/hour—one
52. Set, decontamination and sample taking, consisting of three containers—one each
53. Shield, movable, leaded glass and lead—one each
54. Decontamination table top with protective side shield, hose, and plastic container—one
55. High-activity sample container—one

---

[a] USP - United States Pharmacopeia

miliar with the contents and use of the kits can use them without previous instruction. The kits should be inventoried every 6 months to ensure that nothing has been removed and that outdated components have been replaced. Excellent prepared kits and lightweight decontamination tables are commercially available.

Planning to handle an accident involves the training of special groups, such as first aid and radiation teams. The specific functions of both of these teams are well known to plant personnel. There should be one central location where these teams can pick up appropriately calibrated monitoring devices and comprehensive first aid kits to take to the scene of an accident.

As soon as it is ascertained that there is a potentially serious injury, the accident control center should be notified. The control room should then notify an ambulance, the supporting hospital, and civil authorities, if necessary (see "Transportation Phase"). It is better to call an ambulance to the scene unnecessarily than to wait to discover the seriousness of the injury at the cost of the patient's health.

In summary, the objectives of planning for the plant phase are related to:

Evaluation
Emergency treatment
Decontamination
Preparation for transportation
Notification of other participating groups

TRANSPORTATION PHASE

Three transport mechanisms must be provided. Each has several options.

1. Transport in-plant
   a. Stretcher kit with case
   b. Basket stretcher
   c. Folding or solid wheel stretcher
2. Transport from plant to supporting hospital
   a. Plant emergency vehicle
   b. Local ambulance
   c. Local rescue squad
   d. Helicopter
3. Transport from supporting hospital to regional medical center
   a. Plant emergency vehicle
   b. Ambulance
   c. Helicopter
   d. Fixed-wing aircraft

The length of time it takes the ambulance to respond to a call from the accident control center should be known in advance. This will determine what should be done in terms of decontamination and first aid while awaiting the ambulance's arrival.

A system must be devised so that security of the plant is maintained when an ambulance arrives. A security escort must be waiting to direct the ambulance to the pickup point.

The plant health physicist will need to have personnel dosimetry available for the rescue squad if levels of contamination are high.

The rescue squad should have a plastic sheet to place under a stretcher in order to minimize contamination of the ambulance.

HOSPITAL PHASE

One of the most important steps in the successful management of a radiation accident is prior planning at the nearest hospital. A contaminated and injured patient who is brought to an emergency room without notice causes confusion and apprehension. This may delay necessary first aid.

Regular drills and training will greatly facilitate treatment of even the unannounced patient. It is strongly recommended that NCRP Report no. 65, Management of Persons Accidentally Contaminated with Radionuclides (1), be utilized for hospital preparation for radiation accident patients and as an overall reference for treatment of the patient.

THE RADIATION EMERGENCY AREA

This is a designated area within the hospital that can be used simultaneously for emergency treatment, stabilization, and decontamination. Preferably, it should:

1. Have a separate outside entrance
2. Have controlled access and egress
3. Be of sufficient size to allow stabilization and decontamination of at least one patient by three persons
4. Have adequate lighting
5. Have an ample water supply
6. Contain appropriate supplies for a radiation accident
7. Be in a portion of the hospital that is not essential for routine hospital use

The regular emergency department is unsuitable. If decontamination of the facility itself were needed, this could immobilize the use of the emergency department in a small community hospital for a long period of time.

Any combination of hallways and rooms may be used if the above criteria are met. Often, the autopsy room is a suitable place. It is usually on the ground level and has an outside entrance. A table with a water supply and drain is available for decontamination of patients. The floors are often impervious to liquid, making cleanup much easier. Because an autopsy room is optional (on an immediate basis), if it needs to be decontaminated, the hospital will not be inconvenienced. Wastes from such decontamination procedures can be disposed of by the nuclear facility.

All supplies should be kept locked to ensure that they are available when needed. The doors providing access to permanent supplies should be of a dispensable type in case the key cannot be found.

The use of monitoring equipment by hospital personnel is the subject of some debate. Often, if a patient is arriving from a nuclear facility, he will be accompanied by a health physicist with monitoring equipment. If, however, an unannounced accident victim arrives or the health physicist is unable to tolerate viewing the first aid procedures, simple monitoring devices should be available to hospital attendants to determine whether radioactivity is present and where it is located. Precise determination of the exact exposure is of secondary importance.

Prior thought needs to be devoted to the personnel traffic flow pattern within the radiation emergency area in order to restrict the spread of possible contamination (Figure 23). There are three distinct zones: a potentially contaminated area, a buffer zone, and a clean area, all separated by ropes. Hospital traffic passing into the contaminated area or buffer zone should be issued protective clothing and personnel dosimeters. *Nothing* should leave either the decontamination room or the buffer zone until it has been monitored for radioactive material.

A phone or other means of communication should exist so that the physician can obtain consultation if necessary. Washing facilities, preferably a shower, a change area, and a storage area for supplies should exist within the buffer zone for possible decontamination of the physician and attendants after the patient has been treated.

The ventilation system should be checked to see that a filter can be placed over the exhaust. (Although not essential, a 95% efficient dust-type filter may be used.) A lead container should be available for disposal of highly radioactive metallic fragments. A portable leaded glass shield is recommended for use during removal of radioactive shrapnel.

Some hospitals have devised separate plumbing systems and holding tanks for the runoff from the autopsy table in case a patient is contaminated. Holding tanks, although desirable, are not necessary. The runoff from the table may be collected in a suitable container from a valve under the table. The container should be placed 6–8 feet from the attendants. In the event of an accident, preparation of such an area before arrival of the patient involves (1) ensuring availability of supplies, (2) setting up control points, (3) covering the floors to facilitate cleanup later, and (4) issuing protective clothing and dosimeters to designated persons.

After the unannounced arrival of a patient, whose form of contamination is determined only after he is in the emergency room, the equipment may be taken to the emergency room and used there.

USE OF PROTECTIVE CLOTHING

All personnel should wear protective clothing within the radiation emergency area regardless of the degree of contamination of the patient. Standard protective clothing consists of the items used in operating rooms—i.e., a scrub suit, surgical gown, latex gloves, mask, and cap, augmented by shoe covers and a vinyl apron. Standard protective clothing may be assumed to be sufficient unless the plant health physicist states that full protective suits are necessary. Three such full suits should be available at a hospital near a nuclear facility.

USE OF DOSIMETERS (13)

Types of dosimeters have previously been discussed. The pen dosimeters, badge TLD dosimeters, and ring TLD dosimeters should

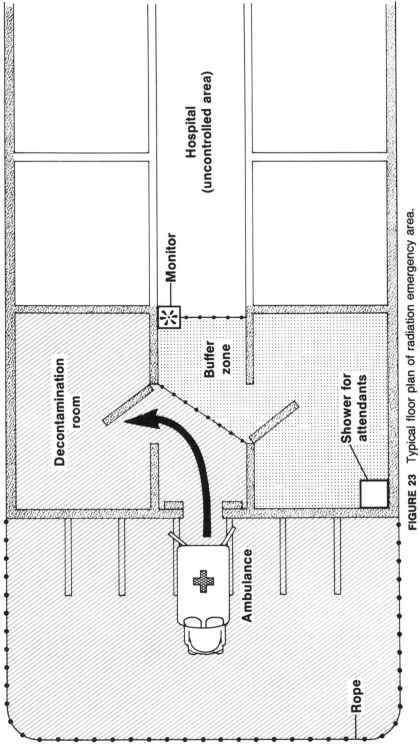

FIGURE 23 Typical floor plan of radiation emergency area.

631

be issued to all personnel who enter the radiation control area. The pen and badge dosimeters should be worn on the scrub suit at chest level, under the outer layer of protective clothing.

Dosimeters provide information about the dose received by attendants. They are not a substitute for careful procedures. If available, they should always be worn.

Protective clothing should be removed upon leaving the contaminated area, and dosimeters should be turned in at the control point. Care needs to be taken to record the name of the person using each dosimeter.

In summary, for adequate management of a radiation accident, a significant amount of advance planning must take place. Equipment requirements must be fulfilled and ready. Procedures and coordination mechanisms must be carefully thought out with regard to:

Evaluation of the patient's status
Treatment of urgent conditions
Further decontamination
Stabilization
Observation

MEDICAL BACKUP CAPABILITIES

With the exception of the removal of gross external contamination and the extraction of radioactive metallic fragments, there is little a primary care physician can do for an exposed patient once he has been stabilized. As has been noted, the radiation exposure problems of a patient who has received sublethal whole body exposure do not need to be treated for 24–48 hours.

Ingestion and inhalation may need to be treated promptly (1). The exact nature of the contaminant needs to be known, as well as the body burden (Table 12), with the exception of potassium iodide used for thyroid dose prophylaxis (4). Many of the drugs required for treatment are themselves toxic, and such therapy should not be undertaken without considerable thought. The specifics of therapy are outlined in Reference 1.

The planning phase must include development of the capability for consultation with an expert on a 24-hour basis.

If a patient has received a whole body dose of radiation in the near-lethal range, he will require very complex facilities that have the ability to do leukocyte transfusions, bone marrow transplants, and surgical removal of "hot" foreign bodies.

Complex laboratories are also required to evaluate the excreta and debrided tissue of such patients, perform chromosome analyses, and to do whole body and wound counting. All of these facilities are very expensive to maintain, particularly since there are very few accidents in such high dosage ranges. It is for this reason that the concept of regional centers for the treatment of such patients has been developed.

The Radiation Emergency Assistance Training Site (REACTS) provides 24-hour consultation for any person who requests advice in handling radiation accidents. REACTS can send a team of experts to assist or can accept a badly contaminated/irradiated patient at the Oak Ridge, Tennessee, Hospital. The telephone number is (615) 576-3131; on "off" hours, it is (615) 482-2441.

CIVIL

In the unlikely event of an expected or actual release of a significant amount of radioactive material from a nuclear facility, civil authorities should be notified. An effective civil response plan can play a major role in protecting the population.

Such response plans are the responsibility of the state and local authorities. Criteria should be included that cover airborne radioactive materials, exposure through food, and exposure from the materials deposited on the ground. Guidelines are currently being formulated by the Environmental Protection Agency. Generally, responses to be considered should include evacuation, medication (potassium iodide in the event of a radioiodine release), and food and water control and distribution. The value of evacuation is subject to much debate since it is not feasible at certain sites and often depends on weather conditions. Facts that need to be known in advance are the population at risk, density and distribution of the population, geographical facts, and possible exposure routes. Respiratory protective devices are not usually effective in reducing exposure to individuals. Remaining within a closed shelter, however, can contribute significantly to dose reduction.

Following the release of a large dose of radiation, the decisions of the civil authorities are based on estimates of the amount and duration of exposure, prevailing meteorologic conditions, and estimation of the risks and costs against the expected benefits of protective action.

Initial Management at the Accident Site

IN-PLANT ACCIDENTS

When an accident is reported in a plant (11), a radiation team is dispatched to the area to investigate it. Upon arriving at the accident scene with monitors, the radiation team's function will differ according to the type of accident, the trauma sustained by the patient, and the radiologic hazard involved.

It should be general policy that:

1. In case of critical injuries, attention will first be given to lifesaving measures; decontamination is of secondary concern.
2. All injuries that occur in a controlled area will be managed as if contaminated, until monitored and cleared by radiation safety personnel.
3. All classes of medical injuries will be reported to the supervisor. If contamination is involved, radiation safety personnel will be notified.

As has been previously discussed, NCRP guidelines provide that a dose of 100 rem (100,000 mrem) to the whole body may be incurred in a lifesaving procedure. (For the NCRP criteria, see Table 13). Twenty-five rem may be incurred in a nonlifesaving emergency. The radiation team must evaluate the exposure without neglecting first aid and lifesaving functions. These ABCs are:

1. A: establishing an *airway*
2. B: determining the status of *breathing*
3. C: *cardiopulmonary resuscitation* (circulation)

If the exposure is extremely high and the patient has obviously been in the contamination area for a long time, efforts may be adjusted accordingly. It should be borne in mind, however, that conditions in the reactor containment almost never exceed 3000 rem/hour (penetrating radiation). If the patient had not been in these conditions for more than 10 minutes, there is still a significant probability of saving his life from the radiologic standpoint. In incurring a dose of 100 rem, it is still possible under these circumstances to make a quick examination of the situation and either leave the room to get the necessary equipment in order to extract the patient from a trapped condition or to drag the patient to an area of lower exposure.

If the dose is significantly lower, one may have time to enter the area and perform first aid functions without moving the patient until stretchers and other first aid equipment have arrived.

The administration of first aid to a patient may involve several types of exposure to the attendants other than penetrating radiation. These include contamination of the attendants' skin by radioactive fission products. It is important to note that contamination of an area of skin of 100 cm² with an activity level of 2×10^{10} dpm for 1 hour results in a skin exposure of 1000 rem. It is extremely unlikely that surface contamination would reach such levels. It is also unlikely that any attendant would allow the contamination to remain on his skin for a period of 1 hour. If such levels were reached, a dose of 1000 rem would result in erythema within several days, and long-term effects would be unlikely.

A second possible type of exposure to the rescuing attendants is inhalation. This occurs with retrieval of a patient in a room in which radioactive iodine is suspended in the air. It has been calculated that if one spent 15 minutes inhaling an aerosol with a concentration of 10^{-2} μCi/ml of I-131, this would approach the level of irreparable damage to an adult thyroid if no therapy were given. Actually, several hours are available in which to block the uptake of the radioactive iodine by the thyroid, using potassium iodide (4). Immediate access to potassium iodide (although it is a prescription drug) has been suggested by some groups. It has been tentatively approved by the Food and Drug Administration in the event of a radioiodine release. It does have a limited shelf life. Again, such environmental concentrations are very unlikely in reactor accidents, and, if they were reached, it is unlikely

TABLE 12
Information on Selected Radionuclides[a]

(1) Nuclide	(2) Radiation	(3) Rhm/Curie	(4) Measurement Methods	
			External	Internal
Americium-241	α, γ	0.01	A, BG(SP), S	IVC, F, NS, U
Americium-243	α, γ, D	0.02	A, BG(SP), S	IVC, F, NS, U
Arsenic-74	β, γ	0.42	BG, S	BC, NS
Arsenic-77	β, γ, D	0.006	BG, S	BC, NS
Barium-140	β, γ, D	0.14	BG, S	BC, NS, U
Cadmium-109	γ, D	0	BG(S), S	F, U
Calcium-45	β	—	BG, S	U
Calcium-47	β, γ, D	0.54	BG, S	BC, NS, U
Californium-252	γ, α, neutron, D	—	A, BG, S	BC, U, NS
Carbon-14	β	—	S(LS), BG(SP)	U, F, B(CO_2)
Cerium-141	β, γ, D	0.033	BG, S	BC, F, NS, U
Cerium-141	β, γ, D	0.008	BG, S	BC, F, NS, U
Cesium-137	β, γ, D	0.32	BG, S	BC, F, NS, U
Chromium-51	γ	0.018	BG, S	BC, F, U
Cobalt-57	γ	0.093	BG, S	BC, F, U
Cobalt-58	β, γ	0.54	BG, S	BC, F, U
Cobalt-60	β, γ	1.3	BG, S	BC, F, U
Curium-242	α, neutron, γ	—	A, BG, S	BC, F, U
Curium-243	α, γ	0.041	A, BG, S	BC, F, U
Curium-244	α, neutron, γ	—	A, BG, S	BC, F, U
Europium-152	β, γ, D	0.53	BG, S	BC, F, U
Europium-154	β, γ	0.63	BG, S	BC, F, U
Europium-155	β, γ	0.021	BG, S	BC, F, U
Fission products	β, γ	—	BG, S	BC, F, NS, U
Fluorine-18	β, γ	0.56	BG, S	BC
Gallium-72	β, γ	1.16	BG, S	BC
Gold-198	β, γ	0.23	BG, S	BC, F, U
Hydrogen-3 (tritium)	β	—	BG(SP), S(LS)	U
Indium-114m	β, γ, D	0.042	BG, S	BC
Iodine-125	β, γ	0.07	BG, S	BC, IVC, U
Iodine-131	β, γ, D	0.21	BG, S	BC, IVC, U
Iron-55	γ	—	BG, S	F
Iron-59	β, γ	0.63	BG, S	BC, F
Lead-210	β, γ, D	0.002	BG, S	F, U, IVC
Mercury-197	γ	0.037	BG, S	BC, U
Mercury-203	β, γ	0.013	BG, S	BC, U
Molybdenum-99	β, γ, D	0.076	BG, S	BC, NS, F, U
Neptunium-237	β, γ, D	0.017	A, BG, S	BC, U
Neptunium-239	β, γ	0.05	A, BG, S	BC, U
Phosphorus-32	β	—	BG, S	BC, U
Plutonium-238	α, γ	0.001	A, BG(SP)	IVC, F, NS, U
Plutonium-239	α, γ	<0.001	A, BG(SP)	IVC, F, NS, U

| (5) Half-life | | (6) MPBB μCi | (7) Critical organ[a] | (8) Dose (rem/μCi in organ) | | | |
| Physical | Effective | | | Critical organ | | Lung (Inhalation) | |
				13 week	50 yr	13 week	50 yr
458 years	139 years	0.05	Bone	190	30,000	250	2100
7950 years	195 years	0.05	Bone	180	30,000	240	2000
18 days	17 days	—	Total body	0.009	0.01	0.36	0.36
39 hours	24 hours	—	Total body	0.0004	0.0004	0.028	0.028
13 days	11 days	—	Bone	0.49	0.49	1.3	1.3
453 days	140 days	20	Liver	0.19	0.53	0.36	1.5
165 days	162 days	30	Bone	0.24	0.74	0.20	0.24
4.5 days	4.5 days	—	Bone	0.12	0.12	0.25	0.25
2.6 years	2.2 years	0.01	Bone	710	11,000	890	5100
5730 years	12 days	—	Total body	0.0006	0.0006	0.14	0.20
32 days	30 days	—	Liver	0.29	0.23	0.36	0.41
284 days	280 days	5	Bone	3.7	16	5.1	17
30 years	70 days	—	Total body	0.03	0.04	1.1	1.5
28 days	27 days	—	Total body	0.0006	0.0007	0.025	0.027
270 days	9 days	—	Total body	0.0009	0.0009	0.13	0.16
71 days	8 days	—	Total body	0.005	0.005	0.55	0.62
5.3 years	10 days	—	Total body	0.015	0.015	1.9	2.6
163 days	155 days	0.05	Liver	180	540	230	580
32 years	27.5 days	0.09	Liver	160	15,000	260	2100
17.6 years	16.7 years	0.1	Liver	160	11,000	260	2100
13 years	3 years	20	Kidney	3.8	69	1.4	11
16 years	3 years	5	Bone	1.8	34	3.7	29
2 years	1.3 years	70	Kidney	1.2	9.3	0.4	1.9
—	—	—	—	—	—	—	—
2 hours	2 hours	—	Total body	0.00007	0.0007	0.003	0.003
14 hours	12 hours	—	Liver	0.024	0.024	0.047	0.047
2.7 days	2.6 days	—	Total body	0.001	0.001	0.087	0.087
12 years	12 days	—	Total body	0.0002	0.002		
49 days	27 days	—	Kidney, Spleen	5.6	6.2	1.6	1.7
60 days	42 days	—	Thyroid	4.2	5.4		
8 days	8 days	—	Thryoid	6.5	6.5		
2.6 years	1 year	1000	Spleen	0.19	1.2	0.016	0.023
46 days	42 days	—	Spleen	5.5	7.0	0.69	0.74
20 years	1.3 years	0.4	Kidney	150	1200	66	92
2.7 days	2.3 days	—	Kidney	0.022	0.022	0.009	0.009
46 days	11 days	—	Kidney	0.30	0.30	0.30	0.31
2.8 days	1.5 days	—	Kidney	0.17	0.17	0.094	0.094
2×10^6 years	200 years	0.06	Bone	170	28,000	220	1800
2.3 days	2.3 days	—	GI(LLI)	0.023	0.023	0.027	0.027
14 days	14 days	—	Bone	0.10	0.10	0.56	0.56
88 years	63 years	0.04	Bone	190	26,000	250	2100
2.4×10^4 years	197 years	0.04	Bone	180	30,000	230	2000

(Continued)

TABLE 12 (*Continued*)

(1) Nuclide	(2) Radiation	(3) Rhm/Curie	(4) Measurement methods	
			External	Internal
Polonium-210	α	<0.001	A	U, F
Potassium-42	β, γ	0.14	BG, S	BC, U
Promethium-147	β	—	BG, S	F, U, NS
Promethium-149	β, γ	0.004	BG, S	F, U, BC, NS
Radium-224	α, γ, D	—	A, BG	BC
Radium-226	α, γ, D	0.825	A, BG, S	BC, B
Rubidium-86	β, γ	0.05	BG	BC, F, U
Ruthenium-106	β, D	0.11	BG	BC, F, U
Scandium-46	β, γ	1.1	BG	BC, F, U
Silver-110m	β, γ, D	1.4	BG	BC, U
Sodium-22	β, γ	1.2	BG	BC, U
Sodium-24	β, γ	1.8	BG, S	BC, U
Strontium-85	γ	0.3	BG, S	BC, U, F
Strontium-90	β, D	—	BG, S	U, IVC, F
Sulfur-35	β	—	BG(SP), S(LS)	F, U
Technetium-99m	γ	0.059	BG, S	BC, NS, U
Technetium-99	β	—	BG, S	U
Thorium-230	α, γ	—	A, BG, S	BC, IVC, F, U
Thorium-232	α, γ, D	—	A, BG, S	BC, IVC, F, U
Thorium-natural	α, β, γ	—	A, BG, S	BC, IVC, F, U
Tritium (see hydrogen-3)				
Uranium-235[b]	α, γ, D	—	A, BG	BC, IVC, U
Uranium-238	α, γ, D	—	A, BG	BC, IVC, U
Uranium-natural	α, β, γ	—	A, BG	BC, IVC, U
Yttrium-90	β	—	BG, S	U
Zinc-65	β(+), γ	0.3	BG, S	BC, U
Zirconium-95	β, γ, D	0.4	BG, S	BC, U

Source: From Reference 1.   Column explanations:

Column (1) *Nuclide.* The name of the element and the atomic mass of the particular isotope are listed alphabetically by element.

Column (2) *Radiations.* The primary radiations are listed. For simplicity, some liberties have been taken in listing the radiations. β refers to both positron and electron emission. γ includes conversion x-ray emissions as well as gamma rays. The letter D refers to the possible presence of daughters with a half-life of less than 25 years. The radiations of the daughters are not included in the listing.

Column (3) *Rhm per Ci.* Roentgens per hour at 1 m from 1 Curie. These values are only approximate. A dash in the column indicates that the number was not evaluated because daughter radiations contribute appreciably to the γ dose rate; because of an uncertain or complex decay scheme; or because the isotope emits no appreciable gamma radiation, as in the case of pure β emitters.

Column (4) *Measurement Methods.* The following symbols are used to indicate principal techniques for measuring external contamination or indicating internal exposure. The order of the symbols has no significance in the listing.

External: A-α counting techniques.

BG-β-γ counting and detection techniques. Start all monitoring with detector unshielded.

BG(SP)-Special attention necessary to select appropriate low-energy monitoring techniques.

S-Smear or swipe sample counted in laboratory.

S(LS)-Liquid scintillation counting of samples.

Internal: BC-Whole body count (standard γ detection methods), including nuclear medicine counters.

F-Feces sample analyses.

IVC-Special *in vivo* counting techniques useful for low-energy counting, e.g., wound-monitoring, thyroid counting, or special low-energy x-ray or γ detectors for chest counts, e.g., plutonium or americium counting.

| (5) Half-life | | (6) MPBB μCi | (7) Critical organ[a] | (8) Dose (rem/μCi in organ) | | | |
| | | | | Critical organ | | Lung (Inhalation) | |
Physical	Effective			13 week	50 yr	13 week	50 yr
138 days	46 days	—	Spleen	880	1100	120	150
12 hours	12 hours	—	Total body	0.00	0.00	0.056	0.056
2.6 years	1.6 years	60	Bone	0.22	2.2	0.29	1.7
2.2 days	2.2 days	—	Bone	0.044	0.044	0.071	0.071
3.6 days	3.6 days	—	Bone	11	11	70	70
1600 years	44 years	0.1	Bone	73	10,000	290	410
19 days	13.2 days	—	Total body	0.009	0.009	0.66	0.66
368 days	2.5 days	—	Kidney	0.80	0.80	5.6	22
84 days	40 days	—	Liver	0.64	0.70	1.3	1.5
255 days	5 days	—	Total body	0.008	0.008	3.3	0
950 days	11 days	—	Total body	0.018	0.018	0.0012	0.0012
15 hours	14 hours	—	Total body	0.0017	0.0017	0.0023	0.0023
65 days	65 days	—	Total body	0.014	0.022	0.30	0.33
28 years	15 years	2	Bone	3.6	320	2.9	4.1
88 days	44 days	—	Testis	22	40	0.00008	0.00008
6 hours	5 hours	—	Total body	0.00001	0.000011	0.00064	0.00064
2×10^5 years	20 days	—	Kidney	0.12	0.13	0.09	0.13
8×10^4 years	200 years	0.05	Bone	160	29000	210	1800
1.4×10^{10} years	200 years	0.04	Bone	180	33000	210	1800
—	200 years	0.01	Bone	180	33000	200	1700
7.1×10^8 years	15 days	—	Kidney	170	170	200	1700
4.5×10^9 years	15 days	—	Kidney	160	160	190	1600
4.5×10^9 years	15 days	—	Kidney	170	170	200	1700
64 hours	64 hours	—	Bone	0.12	0.12	0.17	0.17
245 days	194 days	60	Total body	0.018	0.066	0.36	0.46
66 days	56 days	—	Total body	0.003	0.003	0.97	1.09

NS-Nose swipe counted in laboratory if inhalation suspected.

U-Urine sample analyses.   B-Breath analysis for gases.

Column (5) *Half-Life.* The radioactive and the effective half-lives are taken from ICRP (1960), except for the transuranic elements which were taken from ICRP (1972).

Column (6) *MPBB.* The maximum permissible body burden (MPBB) is listed for those radioisotopes with effective half-lives in excess of 120 days. For isotopes with shorter effective half-lives, the estimated dose to the critical organ is more meaningful for emergency decisions (see Column 8). The MPBB is based on a life-time continued exposure under conditions in which an equilibrium is established, or at least approached between intake and elimination. It should not be used in the sense implied in this table for a single exposure situation.

Column (7) *Critical Organ.* The organ that receives the highest dose or has the most significant biological effect. Only one organ has been listed for each radioisotope. This is an artificial representation since different chemical forms and modes of exposure will determine the critical organ; this table is intended to give only a limited presentation on one principal organ at risk until more complete information can be obtained.

Column (8) *Dose.* An approximate dose equivalent in rem is calculated for 1 microcurie of the radionuclide in the *critical organ* (Column 7) or lung, in the case of inhalation, after 13 weeks and 50 years residence time in that organ. These are approximate values to assist in rapid dose estimates if body (or organ) burden can be estimated. They are not definitive dose determinations particularly since they do not take into account the radionuclide distribution in the total body to the listed critical organ. Thus the physiologic chemistry and solubility of the material involved in an actual exposure is not taken into account in this table. The Curie for isotopes with radioactive daughters is defined as 3.7×10^{10} disintegrations per second of the parent only. Thus a curie of natural uranium includes only the activity of the [238]U parent and not activity of the daughter such as [234]U.

TABLE 13
NCRP Lifesaving Guidelines

GUIDANCE FOR PLANNED OCCUPATIONAL EXPOSURES UNDER EMERGENCY CONDITIONS

It is compatible with the concept of risk to accept exposure leading to radiation doses considerably in excess of those appropriate for lifetime use when recovery from an accident or major operational difficulty is necessary. Saving lives, circumventing substantial exposures to population groups, or even preserving valuable installations may all be sufficient cause for accepting above-normal exposures. Dose limits cannot be specified. They should be commensurate with the significance of the objective and held to the lowest practical level that the emergency permits. The following is offered as general guidance.

Lifesaving Actions
These guidelines apply to the search for and removal of injured persons, or entry to prevent conditions that would probably injure numbers of people.
1. Rescue personnel should be volunteers or professional rescue personnel (e.g., firemen who "volunteer" by their choice of employment).
2. Rescue personnel should be broadly familiar with the consequences of exposure.
3. Women capable of reproduction should not take part in these actions.
4. Other things being equal, volunteers above the age of 45 should be selected.
5. Planned whole body dose should not exceed 100 rem.
6. The hands and forearms may receive an additional dose of up to 200 rem (i.e., a total of 300 rem).
7. Internal exposure should be minimized by the use of the best available respiratory protection, and contamination should be controlled by the use of available protective clothing.
8. Normally, exposure under these conditions shall be limited to once in a lifetime.
9. Persons receiving exposures as indicated above should avoid procreation for a period of a few months.

Actions in Less Urgent Emergencies
These guidelines apply to less stressful circumstances in which it is still desirable to enter a hazardous area in order to protect facilities, eliminate further escape of effluents, or control fires.
1. Persons performing the planned actions should be volunteers broadly familiar with the consequences of exposure.
2. Women capable of reproduction should not take part in these actions.
3. The planned whole body dose should not exceed 25 rem.
4. The planned dose to the hands and forearms should not exceed 100 rem (including the whole body component).
5. Internal exposure should be minimized by respiratory protection and contamination controlled by the use of protective clothing.
6. Normally, if the retrospective dose from these actions is a substantial fraction of the prospective limits, the actions should be limited to once in a lifetime.

Source: From Basic Radiation Protection Criteria, NCRP: Report No. 39, 1971 (NCRP Publications, Washington, D.C.), with permission.

that the attendants would spend 15 minutes in such an area.

If a respirator is immediately available, it should be worn. If it is not available, one can hold one's breath for 30 seconds while removing the patient from the contaminated area.

In a reactor accident, the initial controlling factor in medical terms is the penetrating whole body radiation (γ dose) to the rescue team rather than contamination or inhalation

(11). At the scene of an accident, it is always difficult to assess such quantities as 10^{10} dpm/ minute of surface contamination over 100 cm^2 or a concentration in the air of 10^{-2} μCi/ml of radioiodine, but the whole body γ dose can be determined rather accurately and quickly with conventional monitoring equipment. Attendants should make every effort to decontaminate themselves as soon as possible following appropriate management of the patient. All unnecessary exposure should be avoided, time and the medical condition of the patient permitting.

Priority should be given to administering first aid to the patient and performing lifesaving procedures. The simple concepts of time, distance, and shielding may be used effectively to reduce the radiation exposure to both the patient and the attendants. It is only common sense to assume that a patient with a broken leg in a high-exposure area should be moved, even if no splint is available for his leg. If the exposure rate is for example, 10 rem/hour and a splint can be obtained within 5 minutes, it may be advisable to keep the patient immobile until a splint has arrived. The nature of the injury and the exposure field in which the patient is located will together dictate the first few actions.

Once the radiologic status of the area and the medical status of the patient have been assessed, the accident control center should be immediately notified of the patient's medical condition and the expected evacuation route. The hospital, in turn, should be notified by the accident control center, and the main gate should be alerted regarding the location of the patient for pickup by the ambulance.

A patient may be taken to the first aid station, where a telephone, adequate lighting for treatment, and medical supplies are available; these are invaluable if the patient's medical condition worsens. The first aid station is a convenient location to begin the patient's decontamination while stabilizing his condition until the ambulance arrives. This will greatly reduce the radiation hazard to the attendants and the staff at the supporting hospital.

TRANSPORTATION AND OFF-SITE MANAGEMENT

If a vehicle carrying radioactive material is encountered with injured occupants who require hospitalization, they should be given first aid, wrapped in blankets, and taken to the hospital. Wrapping the patient in a blanket will restrict the spread of radioactive material. Any contamination of the hands and clothing of attendants is of *no* medical urgency. Hand washing will generally remove 95% or more of any contamination present.

Federal regulations require stringent packing of radioactive materials before transportation. The containers are very strong and contain absorbent material if a liquid is stored inside. Consequently, it is very unlikely that any transportation accident will release medically significant amounts of radioactive material. If there is some doubt about a spill of such materials, first aid should be given promptly. The area should then be cordoned off until state radiation officials arrive with appropriate instruments. All individuals who do not need medical attention must be detained at the site until radiation experts arrive. The names and addresses of all individuals should be obtained.

Certainly, the most difficult accident for the emergency medicine technician (EMT) to handle is the transportation accident. Since the EMT does not carry radiation detection equipment, and is often the first person to arrive at the scene of an accident, he does not know whether radiation and/or contamination are present. If the accident involves a vehicle displaying a "radioactive material" sign, the EMT must assume that radiation is present in some form. Such an accident should be handled in the following manner:

1. Perform lifesaving functions, even if this involves mouth-to-mouth resuscitation. Manage trauma appropriately.
2. If a pair of gloves and coveralls are present, put them on. Remember, it may be difficult to feel a pulse or apply a bandage with gloves on, and they may have to be removed for this purpose.
3. Place the patient directly on a stretcher. Do not put a blanket between the patient and the stretcher. A blanket may be placed over the patient.
4. If the patient will not be transported to the hospital immediately, move him at least 20 yards from the accident vehicle.
5. Other people who were involved in the accident, and who were not seriously injured, should be instructed to stay 20 yards away from the vehicle but not to leave the scene of the accident until it can be ascertained whether they have been contaminated.
6. Place a blanket *under* the stretcher, and wrap both the stretcher and the patient in the blanket. This will prevent the spread of contamination in the ambulance and at the hospital. If the patient requires medical assistance while

being transported in the ambulance, the blanket may be unwrapped.

7. If radio communications exist between the hospital and the ambulance, notify the hospital that a *possibly* contaminated and injured patient is en route. Ask whether the hospital has a specific area for handling such patients. Many hospitals do have a special radiation emergency area, which is distinct and often completely separate from the routine emergency department.

8. Inform the hospital of the nature of the patient's injury, so that special equipment can be prepared and taken to the radiation emergency area.

9. If possible en route, notify the State Police of a suspected radiation accident. The State Police often have radiation detection equipment available or know where it can be obtained.

10. Upon arrival at the hospital, bring the patient (keeping the blanket wrapped, as previously described) to the area designated by the personnel on duty.

11. Place the stretcher on the floor and unwrap the blanket.

12. Cut off the patient's clothing, but leave the clothing on the blanket. If surface contamination is present, removal of the clothing will remove at least 90% of it.

13. Lift the patient onto a clean hospital stretcher. The hospital staff should be gowned in regular operating room garb (shoe covers, surgeon's cap, mask, gloves, and gown).

14. The EMT should next remove his outer clothing and place it either in a plastic bag or on the aforementioned blanket. The blanket should be wrapped up, enclosing the stretcher, the patient's clothes, and the EMT's outer clothing.

15. Although it has proved very difficult to suspend contamination in ambient air, care should be taken to avoid shaking the blanket or clothing.

16. When possible, the EMT should ask hospital personnel for soap, a washcloth, and a basin. He should wash the face and hands (in that order) (both the patient's and his own) and place the washcloths on the blanket. He should not leave the immediate area. If contamination is present, it may be on his shoes and could be spread to other parts of the hospital or emergency room.

17. The EMT should return to the ambulance the same way he entered the hospital and lock the back door. Other people should be kept away from it until someone with a radiation detector has confirmed that there is no contamination on the EMT or in the ambulance.

18. If there are multiple patients in the accident,

the EMT may return to the scene and proceed as before. He should be sure to borrow another clean blanket, surgeon's gloves, and gown for his use.

The role of the EMT in radiation accidents is exceptionally crucial. An understanding of radiation is important, yet the regular medical concerns, with which the EMT is already familiar, remain of primary importance.

To date, there has been little or no training of EMTs in handling radiation accidents. Perhaps the exceptions are rescue squads near operational nuclear plants. Transportation and industrial accidents will certainly become more frequent in the next few years. Training for radiation accidents should be part of the EMT course curriculum rather than solely part of the advanced paramedic training. Currently, there are only a few training courses; however, more are being developed.

Transportation to the Supporting Hospital

It is the responsibility of the personnel at the accident control center to mobilize the appropriate ambulance or transport mechanism.

At the pickup point, it is the duty of the health physicist involved to alert the ambulance personnel to the medical nature of the injury and the extent of radiologic contamination. He must also provide adequate personnel dosimetry for the ambulance personnel if necessary. The health physicist should travel to the hospital with the patient and take along appropriate monitoring devices.

At the time the patient is picked up by the ambulance, the accident control center personnel should notify the hospital of the expected time of arrival of the patient or patients, the number of patients involved, the extent of the injuries, the extent of expected contamination, and the names of the patients (if known). This is essential information so that the hospital can prepare adequately for the patients' arrival. At the hospital, procedures for handling a radiation accident should have been activated at the time of the initial call. The types of injuries may necessitate the use of certain special equipment, which may not have been foreseen by the hospital personnel unless appropriate advice was provided by the accident control center in advance.

Upon arrival at the hospital, the ambulance will find an area cordoned off outside the radiation entrance. This will be a restricted area. The radiation entrance generally is *not* the emergency department entrance, and the ambulance personnel will then bring the patient into the radiation emergency area and transfer him to the physician and nurses. The health physicist should provide the physician with as many facts as are known concerning the type and nature of the accident at the plant, the extent of injuries, the extent of radiologic contamination, the hazard to the physician, and the treatment that was carried out at the plant or en route to the hospital. The hospital staff will keep a record of this information.

The ambulance personnel should return to the ambulance and await clearance from the health physicist before leaving. If possible, a second health physicist will have come from the plant and will ascertain the possible contamination of the ambulance. As previously mentioned, this may have been minimized initially by placing a plastic sheet underneath the stretcher and wrapping the patient in a blanket. The plastic sheet should not be wrapped around the patient, since it prevents adequate ventilation. If a second health physicist is not available to clear the ambulance, the ambulance attendants should remain unless more patients have been collected at the plant for transportation by this particular group.

The health physicist who has traveled with the patient should remain with the physician and the patient until he is no longer needed. He may then return outside to determine the status of the ambulance and its attendants. If the ambulance is contaminated, it may be decontaminated on the spot. If the levels of contamination are too high within the ambulance, the staff should drive it back to the plant, where it will undergo more extensive decontamination procedures.

Mechanisms are available at most plants for transportation of patients by other methods, such as helicopter. General experience indicates that in the interest of time, the ambulance is the preferred mode of travel. Helicopters are subject to weather and delays, and involve time in preparing a pilot and making the appropriate conversions necessary for carrying a stretcher. Helicopters may be useful under certain conditions (e.g., snow) in which travel by ambulance is, at best, slow and dangerous.

Procedures for Patient Decontamination and Sample Taking

GENERAL

To standardize and simplify the measures to be taken for decontaminating patients and taking specimens, the supplies at both the plant and hospital should include:

1. A decontamination kit
2. A sample-taking kit (Figure 24). These kits provide all the necessary items for decontamination and sample-taking purposes, with the exception of items needed for protection of attendants.

As the collection of specimens is an essential prerequisite for a thorough evaluation of the medical and radiation status of the patient, and as it is performed in conjunction with decontamination activities, the combined and proper use of both kits is of the utmost importance.

DECONTAMINATION PROCEDURES

Principles

1. The objectives of decontamination are:
   a. To prevent ongoing injury to the contaminated patient caused by the presence of radioactive substances on his body
   b. To prevent the spread of contamination over and into the patient and his environment
   c. To protect attending personnel from becoming contaminated or (in extreme cases) from being exposed to a source of radiation
2. Although decontamination should be started as soon as possible, *primary attention should be given to the alleviation of life-threatening conditions* created by traumatic injury.
3. Decontamination is essentially the physical removal of radioactive dirt from the skin, wounds, or body orifices. Most decontaminants contain detergents or other chemical agents to facilitate this removal. As a consequence, some decontaminants are suitable for decontamination of the intact skin only—i.e., they are not appropriate for cleansing wounds or irrigating body orifices.

The general principle dictates that samples be obtained in all cases of *suspected* radiation accidents. The establishment of baseline data is exceptionally important. All samples need to be labeled with the patient's name, type of sample, time of accident, time of sample collection, and suspected radionuclides, if known.

1. *Blood sampling*
   Vacutainers, heparinized, 10 ml sterile
   Vacutainers, uncoated, 10 ml sterile
   Vacutainers, oxalated, 10 ml sterile
   Needle-holder combination, sterile
   Alcohol wipes, sterile, prepackaged
2. *Wound fluid, nose swabs*
   Cotton-tipped applicators, in test tube, sterile
   Q-tips, box
   Dropper bottles, ¼ oz.
   Envelopes, waterproof (for storage of nose swabs)
   Tissue paper, box (for nose blows)
3. *Small specimens* (hairs, nails, tissue samples, sputum)
   Vials, glass, 25 ml
   Bottles, widemouth, 100 ml

4. *Excreta, irrigation fluids, vomitus*
   Feces (and vomitus): jar, brown plastic, paper containers
   Urine (and irrigation fluid): specitainers, 2500 ml bottles, widemouth, 500 ml
5. *Skin smears:*
   Smear pads, with envelopes, in box
6. *Miscellaneous items*
   Plastic bags, assorted sizes
   Tags, with wire
   Labels, self-sticking
   Patient radiation and medical status record sheets (to record specimens collected)
   Notebook
   Pencils

FIGURE 24   Sample-taking kit.

4. Decontamination is performed:
   a. To reduce the level of contamination
   b. Starting with the simplest procedure (e.g., soap and water) and progressing to more complicated ones
   c. With due regard to contamination of wounds, body orifices, etc. (see below for specific guidelines)
5. Usually, the effect of decontamination is greatest in the earliest stages—i.e., most of the radioactive material is removed during the first decontamination effort. Continued decontamination may show diminishing effectiveness. At this point, one must decide either to accept some residual contamination or to proceed with the use of more potent decontaminants (more specific guidelines are given below).

Measures to be Taken by the Physician before Decontamination

1. Assuming that gross decontamination has been performed at the plant, it can be expected that general contamination is minor and/or that more serious contamination is localized—e.g., around and in a wound. Before continuing the decontamination, the following steps should be taken:
   a. Judge whether the patient's condition requires immediate intervention; if so, proceed,
   covering the contaminated area with a plastic drape or a towel.
   b. Obtain a briefing from the plant health physicist, who accompanies the patient, on the radiation and contamination status of the patient and the specific measures to be taken by attending personnel for their protection.
   c. Record all observations (Figures 25 and 26).
   d. Monitor the patient with the hospital survey instrument by scanning the entire body surface (holding the probe about 2 inches from the skin), and decide in which order skin decontamination shall be performed.
   e. Inspect wounds, inquire about their decontamination at the plant, and decide whether further wound decontamination or treatment can safely be postponed until skin decontamination has been completed.
   f. Decide whether certain samples should be taken.
2. If no decontamination has been performed at the plant (most likely because of an urgent need for emergency surgical treatment):
   a. Try to perform at least gross decontamination by removing all clothing and obvious dirt and debris. If immediate operative intervention is necessary, cover the contaminated area with a plastic drape and proceed.
3. After the emergency treatment, proceed with the applicable steps described under 1a–f above.

Name of patient: _____ Age: ____ yr ____
Location, date, and time of incident: _____
Summary description of incident: _____

TYPE OF EXPOSURE/INJURY

Wounds
yes/no
where? *indicate overleaf*
how serious? _____

general condition? _____

External Exposure
yes/no
where? • whole body _____
　　　　• local _____
how much? ~ _____ rems
　　　　　(likely/possible)
what? β | γ | neutron

Skin Contamination
yes/no
where? *indicate overleaf*
how much? *indicate meter*
　　　　　readings overleaf
what? mixed fission products? _____
other (describe): _____

Internal Contamination
yes/no
how? *wounds/ingestion/inhal*
how much? _____
what? mixed fission products? _____
other (describe): _____

MEASURES TAKEN

time: _____

first aid: _____

symptoms?　nausea　+/−
　　　　　　vomiting　+/−
　　　　　　skin erythema　+/−
other? _____
Symptomatic treatment? _____

medical: _____

blood samples taken? _____

badge taken? _____

wound decon:
how: _____

NEUTRON IRRADIATION ONLY:
ring taken? _____
buttons, hair, nail clippings
taken?

effect: _____

time: _____

decon:
technique: _____

effect: _____
*(indicate decontaminated
areas overleaf)*
residual contamination
at time of transfer? _____
(describe; mark on skin):

time: _____

nose blow:
sample kept? _____

decon of orifices:
where? _____
how? _____

decon fluids kept? _____

other samples taken:
urine? _____
feces? _____
other? _____

Course/follow-up: _____

FIGURE 25 Patient radiation and medical status record sheet (to accompany patient).

643

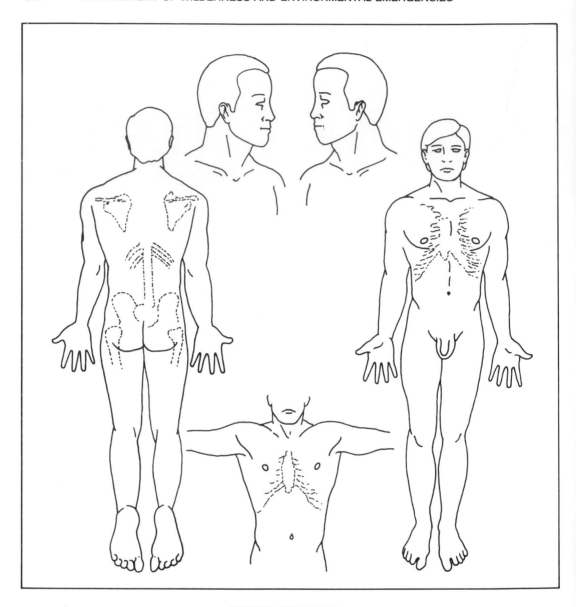

TYPE OF METER USED: _____
(Indicate model and number)

FIGURE 26 Form used to indicate contaminated areas as to location, degree of contamination, decon effort, and wounds. (Additional sheets may be used if necessary.)

Decontamination Techniques

1. Two general rules apply to the performance of decontamination:
   a. Continuously check the effectiveness of the technique applied by monitoring periodically and recording the results.

b. Avoid spreading radioactive materials from the area being decontaminated to areas of lesser contamination. Cover the adjacent area. Except when prohibitive degrees of contamination are present on or in any of the locations listed below, decontamination is performed in the following order:

a. Wounds and adjacent skin
b. Body orifices and adjacent skin
c. Other skin areas

2. Decontamination of wounds
   a. Use an aperture drape to isolate the contaminated area and take a sample (see "Sample-Taking Techniques and Indications," item 1.
   b. Decontaminate the skin adjacent to the wound, as described below.
   c. Depending on the size of the surface and depth of the wound, irrigate with sterile saline, dab with gauze pads and sterile saline, or use applicators to cleanse the wound. Collect all materials used and label the containers.
   d. Remove obviously necrotic and devitalized tissue surgically; keep all tissue specimens removed (see "Procedures for Sample Taking").
   e. Monitor the wound and record the results.
   f. If contamination persists, consult with the health physicist to determine any further course of action.
   g. If the wound is clean, treat it according to accepted technique.

3. Decontamination of body orifices
   a. Take samples for radiologic activity from the nares, ear canals, and other orifices, as indicated (see "Sample-Taking Techniques and Indications, item 1.
   b. Decontaminate the area surrounding the orifices, as described below.
   c. Gently clean the orifices using wet swabs.
   d. If a nose swab indicates significant radioactivity in the nasal cavity, irrigate it.
   e. Collect all materials used and label containers.

4. Decontamination of skin
   a. Take a smear sample of an area of skin (see "Sample-Taking Techniques and Indications," item 1.
   b. Protect the adjacent area by covering it with a plastic drape or towels.
   c. Cleanse the skin
      (1) Cleanse the skin around wounds and orifices with liquid soap and tepid water, using large, absorbent balls. Cover the entire contaminated surface with a good lather, repeatedly renewing the cotton balls. Remove the lather after 2–3 minutes by wiping the skin repeatedly with wet cotton balls. Monitor and record the result.
      (2) Other skin areas should be washed thoroughly with soap and tepid water, using either cotton balls, preoperative sponges, or hand brushes. Cover the area with a good lather; rinse off the lather after 2–

3 minutes with running water. Monitor and record the result.
   d. If contamination persists, repeat step (c) once.
   e. If contamination still persists, try gentle application of dilute bleach or hydrogen peroxide. (*Note:* Keep these substances out of the wound or body openings.) Repeat a few times, using new cotton balls. Remove decontaminants with water. Monitor and record the result.
   f. After complete decontamination, dry the skin and apply Nivea cream.
   g. If residual contamination is present, consult with the health physicist to decide whether further efforts are indicated. If it is decided to accept residual contamination, dry the skin and apply collodion. Mark the area involved. Record.
   h. Collect all materials used and label containers.

Notes:
In case of serious contamination around a wound, most of the radioactivity can be rapidly removed by shaving the skin.
If there is serious contamination of hair or under nails, clip.

PROCEDURE FOR SAMPLE TAKING

Principles

1. The objectives of collecting specimens from a radiation accident victim are:
   a. To evaluate the amount and composition of the radioactive contaminants on and in the body
   b. To obtain data on the patient's exposure to external radiation
   c. To supply information on the biologic injury inflicted by the radiation

2. To meet these objectives, the following types of specimens are collected routinely:
   a. Materials containing the external contaminant (swabs, smears, tissue samples, contaminated cleansing fluids, etc.)
   b. Specimens containing the internal contaminant (feces, stools, sputum, etc.)
   c. In case of neutron irradiation, materials in which neutron-induced radioactivity may be present (gold rings, buttons, hair, nail clippings)
   d. Hematologic specimens (whole blood in heparinized, oxalated, and uncoated tubes; blood smears, leukocyte counts)

3. As the analysis of radioactive samples with regard to their composition is possible only in sam-

ples with relatively high radioactivity, care should be taken to collect and store these samples separately from the usually bulky samples with rather low radioactivity (such as cleansing fluids, drapes, and towels).

4. A sample whose source (location, time taken) is not identifiable may be practically worthless. Therefore, take care to collect, store, and mark all samples properly.

Sample-Taking Techniques and Indications

1. External contamination: Before attempting any (further) decontamination, the following samples shall be obtained:
   a. Skin smears: use saturated solution potassium iodide (SSKI) smear pads, moisten them with a few drops of water, and smear a skin area of about 100 cm² (~4 × 4 inches), if possible, by allowing the sticky side of the smear to adhere to gloves, and rubbing the smear pad over the surface to be sampled. Place the smear on record paper and record the location, time, and area smeared if it is not 100 cm².
   b. Wound samples: use either of the following methods:
      (1) Large wounds with visible blood or wound fluid: obtain a few milliliters using a dropper, transfer this material to a bottle, and label it.
      (2) Superficial wounds: rub gently with a cotton swab, return the swab to the tube, and label it.
      (3) Wounds with visible dirt or debris: remove material with an applicator or use tweezers and transfer a sample to a small glass vial with a label.
2. Internal contamination
   a. Body orifices: wet a Q-tip with a few drops of water, swab, store in a waterproof envelope, and label it.
   b. In all cases in which internal contamination is suspected: collect all urine and feces in containers supplied; record the time of voiding.
3. External exposure: In all cases in which a whole body dose of more than 10 rads is suspected:
   a. Obtain a blood smear for differentiation.
   b. Obtain a leukocyte count.
   c. Obtain 30 ml of blood in vacutainers (heparinized, uncoated, and oxalated, 10 ml each). Record the time these samples were taken.

References

1. NCRP (1980). National Council on Radiation Protection and Measurements, Management of Persons Accidentally Contaminated with Radionuclides, NCRP Report No. 65 (NCRP Publications, Box 30175, Washington, D.C. 20014).
2. Hübner, K. E., and Fry, S. A. (1980). The Medical Basis for Radiation Accident Preparedness, Proceedings of REAC/TS International Conference, October 1979 (Elsevier North-Holland, Inc., New York).
3. NCRP (1971). Basic Radiation Protection Criteria, NCRP Report No. 39 (NCRP Publications, Box 30175, Washington, D.C. 20014).
4. NCRP (1977). Protection of the Thyroid Gland in the Event of Releases of Radioiodine, NCRP Report No. 55 (NCRP Publications, Box 30175, Washington, D.C. 20014).
5. NCRP (1978). Instrumentation and Monitoring Methods for Radiation Protection, NCRP Report No. 57 (NCRP Publications, Box 30175, Washington, D.C. 20014).
6. ICRP 1978. International Commission on Radiological Protection, The Principles and General Procedures for Handling Emergency and Accidental Exposures of Workers, ICRP Publication No. 28 (Pergamon Press, New York).
7. Saenger, E. L. (1968). Management of the early phase of radioactive contamination in human beings. In *Diagnosis and Treatment of Deposited Radionuclides*, Kornberg, H. A., and Norwood, W. D., editors (Excerpta Medica Foundation, Amsterdam).
8. Holland, R. W., Jr. (1969). Planning a medical unit for handling contaminated persons following a radiation accident, *Nuclear Safety*, **10:**72.
9. Lincoln, T. A. (1963). Decontamination of radioactive materials from the skin. In *Proceedings of the XIV International Congress on Occupational Health*, Vol. III, International Congress Series No. 62 (Excerpta Medica Foundation, New York).
10. BRH (1960). *Radiological Health Handbook*, Department of Health, Education, and Welfare, Bureau of Radiological Health (Superintendent of Documents, U.S. Government Printing Office, Washington, D.C.).
11. NRC (1980). Criteria for Preparation and Evaluation of Radiological Emergency Response Plans and Preparedness in Support of Nuclear Power Plants, NUREG-0654 Rev. 1, U.S. Nuclear Regulatory Commission. (GPO Sales, Division of Technological Information and Document Control, USNRC, Washington, D.C.).
12. Saenger, E. R. (1963). *Medical Aspects of Radiation Accidents*, U.S. Atomic Energy Commission (U.S. Government Printing Office, Washington, D.C.).
13. IAEA (1965). Personnel Dosimetry for Radiation Accidents, *IAEA/WHO Symposium*, Vienna, 1965 (IAEA, National Agency for International Publications, New York).

INDEX

Acclimatization:
  edema and, 69
  heat illness and, 71–72
  to high altitudes, 7, 9, 15, 20–21
Acetaldehyde, 419
Acetaminophen, 368
Acetazolamide (Diamox), 3, 7, 15,
  19, 20–23, 113
Achilles tendon, rupture of, 141
Acid burns, 492
Acidosis in hypothermia, 35–36, 38
Acrolein, 587, 594, 599
Acromioclavicular (AC) joint,
  sprains of, 152–153
Acrylics, burning of, 593–594
Acute mountain sickness (AMS),
  19–21
  causes of, 4, 19
  prevention of, 20–21
  symptoms of, 13, 19–20
  treatment of, 3, 15, 17, 20
Adult respiratory distress (ARDS)
  syndrome, 14, 198
Adenosine triphosphate (ATP), 67–
  68
Adrenal function in heat stroke, 75
Aerodontalgia, 532
Aerospace Medical Association
  (ASMA), 554
Aerospace medicine, 522–555
  aviation organizations and, 552–
  554
  crews and, 544–547, 552
  flight environment and, 523–529
  history of, 522–523
  passengers and, 547
  patients and, 549–551
  physiologic effects of flight and,
  529–544

Aerospace Rescue and Recovery
  Service (ARRS), 83–84
AGE (arterial gas embolism), 165,
  172–176
Age of patient:
  disaster impact and, 581
  drowning risk and, 190
  heat illness and, 72
  spider bites and, 290, 291
Air Force Rescue Coordination
  Center (AFRCC), 83–84, 86,
  88
Air searches, 87–88
Alcohol:
  heat illness and, 73
  submersion incidents and, 191
Alcohol (isopropyl):
  coma from topical, 78
  for stings by marine coelenterates,
  229
Algae:
  dermatitis from, 262
  infections caused by, 262–263
Alkali burns, 492
Alkaloids, 381–397
  amine, 397
  indole derivatives, 395
  isoquinoline and quinoline group,
  394–395
  purine, 396–397
  pyridine-piperidine group, 392–
  393
  pyrrolizidine, 395
  quinolizidine, 395–396
  steroid, 396
  tropane, 393–394
Alkalosis:
  heat stroke and, 76–77
  hypothermia and, 35, 38, 39

Allergies:
  cold urticaria, 57
  contact dermatitis and, 426–430
  from diving equipment, 268
  to the sun, 437–442, 447–448
Alpha particles, 611, 613–614
Altitude sickness, 1–26
  acute mountain sickness, 3, 4, 13,
  15, 17, 19–21
  altitude throat, 24
  chronic mountain polycythemia,
  24–25
  chronic or subacute mountain
  sickness, 21–22
  definitions of altitude and, 1–2
  high-altitude deterioration,
  (HAD), 22
  high-altitude encephalopathy
  (HAE), 17–19
  high-altitude flatus expulsion
  (HAFE), 23
  high-altitude pulmonary edema
  (HAPE), 7–17, 19, 22
  high-altitude retinal hemorrhages
  (HARH), 22–23
  high-altitude systemic edema
  (HASE), 22
  oxygen needs and, 113–114
  physiological consequences of
  high-altitude exposure and, 2–
  7
  pulmonary hypertension, 10, 13,
  25
  ultraviolet keratitis (snow blindness), 24, 57
  venous thrombosis and pulmonary embolism, 19
  See also Aerospace medicine
Altitude throat, 24

Amanita species (mushroom), 405–407, 416–417
AME (aviation medical examiners), 545, 552, 553
Amebic meningoencephalitis, 255
American hellebore, 396
American Rescue Dog Association (ARDA), 84
Ammonia, inhalation of, 598–599
Amnesia from lightning strikes, 512
Amphotericin-B, 255
AMS. *See* Acute mountain sickness
Amygdalin, 398
Ana-Kit, 281
Anaphylaxis, 279–280
Anemones, sea, 227–228
Ankle sprains and fractures, 138–141, 143, 160
Annelid worms, 234
Anoxia, 530–531
Anterior drawer test, 147–148
Antibacterial agents for burn wounds, 496
Antibiotics:
  for bite wounds, 320–321, 323–327, 344
  for burn wounds, 493, 497
  for lightning injury, 518
  for snake bites, 367
  use of, in aerospace activities, 546
  See also specific antibiotics
Antivenin
  snakes, 365–367
  Sea wasp, 229–230
  Stone fish, 244
  Black widow spider, 290–291
  Funnel-web spider, 295
  scorpion, 298
Ant stings, 276–281
Apnea, sleep, and high altitudes, 3
Appley test, 149
Arachnid bites, 287–302
  of centipedes, 301
  of millipedes, 301–302
  from scorpionlike arachnids, 298
  of scorpions, 295–298
  of spiders, 287–295
  of ticks, 287, 299–301
  See also Insect bites
Arthritis (Lyme disease), 301
Aspirin:
  for fever, 66
  for heat stroke, 77
Assassin bug, 283
Asthma, diving and, 186
Atarax (hydroxyzine), 429
Ataxia, high altitude and, 13, 18–20
Atropine (hyoscyamine), 44, 298, 393–394, 396, 420
Autopsy, in aviation accidents, 552
Avalanches, snow, 98–113
  causes of, 98–99
  control of, in skiing areas, 105

danger signs in, 105
rescue procedures for, 106–113
survival techniques for, 105–106
travel in avalanche country and, 103–105
types of, 99–103
Aviation. *See* Aerospace medicine
Aviation medical examiner (AME), 545, 552, 553

Back. *See* Spine injuries
Bacteria, dermatitis from marine, 267–268
  in animal bite wounds, 317, 323–331
Barbiturates, 208–210. *See also specific barbiturates*
Barosinusitis, 169–170
Barotitis, 169
Barotrauma. *See* Diving
Barracuda, 219–220
Bats, 346–347
Beaded lizard, 370
Bears, 256, 347
Bedbug, 283
Bee stings, 276–281
Beetle bites, 285–286
Belladonna alkaloids, 393–394
Benadryl (diphenhydramine hydrochloride), 129, 260, 366, 429
Bends, 180–181, 533
Bennett fracture, 156
Benzene hexachloride (Kwell, Gamene), 307–309
Beta particles, 611, 614
Biologic dressings for burn wounds, 497–498
Biotoxicity, 214
Bites:
  arachnid. *See* Arachnid bites
  crocodile, 348
  insect. *See* Insect bites
  mammalian. *See* Mammalian bites
  ostrich, 348
  snake. *See* Snake bites
  spider. *See* Spider bites
Black widow bites, 288–291
Blebs with frostbite, 51, 53, 56
Blister beetle, 285
Blood gas:
  arterial gas embolism (AGE), 165, 172–176
  changes in, with high altitude, 2–5
  diving and, 176–185
  submersion incidents and, 205
Bloodsucking fly, 286–287
Bluebottle, 226
Bone lesions, 534
Boyle's law, 166, 168, 169, 171, 524
Breath-hold diving, 171
Bretylium, 44
Bronchitis, diving and, 187

Brown recluse spider, 291–293
Brucellosis, 338
Buffalo bites, 345
Buflomedil hydrochloride, 56
Bumblebee, 276
Burnout syndrome, 581
Burn wounds, 481–499
  burn unit management and, 493–496
  care of, 496–498
  electrical, 489, 492, 493, 508–510
  emergency department treatment of, 489–493
  epidemiology of, 482
  extent of injury in, 482–483
  immediate treatment of, 483–489
  from lightning, 502, 510, 512–514, 516, 518
  mechanism of injury in, 482
  morbidity and mortality in, 499
  outpatient treatment of, 493
  septic thrombophlebitis and, 498–499
  smoke inhalation and, 590–591
  stress gastritis and, 498
Burow's solution, 429, 447

Caffeine, 396–397
Caisson disease. *See* Decompression sickness
Calcium, loss of, in space flight, 541, 544
Calcium chloride, 44, 129
Camel bites, 345–346
Candiru, 241
Carbon monoxide poisoning, 114, 178–179, 470–471
  burn wounds and, 485–487
  effects of, 586–587, 596–598
  treatment of, 601
Cardiac arrest:
  in hypothermia, 43–44
  in submersion incidents, 202–204, 206
Cardiopulmonary resuscitation (CPR):
  for avalanche victims, 108
  in burn injuries, 485
  for hypothermia, 43–44
  for lightning victims, 502–503, 516
  in submersion incidents, 202–204
Cardiovascular system:
  aerospace activity and, 540–541, 543, 550
  air transport and, 550
  changes in, with high altitude, 5–6
  frostbite and, 47–48
  hypothermia and, 33
  lightning strikes and, 511–512, 514, 517
  snake bite and, 359

submersion incidents and, 199, 207, 208
weightlessness and, 540–541, 543
Carolina jessamine, 395
Castor bean, 401–402
Cat bites, 311–312, 323, 341–343
Caterpillar bites, 281–283
Catfish, 240–242
Cat-scratch disease, 327, 335–336
Cattle bites, 313, 345
Cave rescues, 92–94
  problems of, 93
  procedures for, 93–94
  rescue organization for, 86
  unique character of, 93
Cellulose-based polymers, burning of, 594
Centipede bites, 301
Central nervous system:
  decompression sickness and, 181
  heat stroke impact on, 74, 78–79
  high altitude and, 6, 19
  hypothermia effects on, 32–33
  lightning strike impact on, 512, 518
  medication in aerospace activity and, 546–549
  oxygen poisoning and, 178–179
  submersion incidents and, 199
Cephalexin, 344
Charles' law, 524
Chemical burns, 485, 492
Cheyne-Stokes breathing, 3
Chilblains, 47
Chlorine gas, inhalation of, 595
Chlorpromazine (Thorazine), 78
Chokes in decompression sickness, 181, 533
Ciguatera fish poisoning, 249–251
Cimetidine, 79
Circulation. *See* Cardiovascular system
Civil Aeronautics Board (CAB), 553
Civil Air Patrol (CAP), 84, 88
Clams:
  giant, 222
  poisoning from ingestion of, 252–254
Clavicle, fracture of, 152
Clothing:
  for cold weather, 115–116, 118–119
  for fire safety, 476–477
  lightning impact on, 510, 514
  protective, for radiation, 630
  ultraviolet rays and, 436
Clupeotoxication, 251
Clysis, subeschar, for burn wounds, 497
Cocaine, 393
Coelenterates, 223–230
Colchicine, 397

Cold injuries:
  cold urticaria, 57
  frostbite. *See* Frostbite
  ophthalmic injuries, 57
  snow blindness, 24, 57
  trenchfoot (immersion foot), 29, 46–47
  See also Hypothermia
Cold weather survival, 113–127
  clothing for, 115–116, 118–119
  fire building in, 122–126
  food in, 126
  increasing heat production in, 118
  maintaining body temperature in, 115–117
  oxygen use in, 113–114
  warmth and shelter in, 114–115, 119–122
  water in, 127
Coma:
  in heat stroke treatment, 78
  in hypothermia, 32–33
  submersion incidents and, 206–207, 210
Compressed air illness. *See* Decompression sickness
Computed tomography (CT) scanning, 210, 517, 518
Cone shells, 230–232
Coniine, 393
Copperhead, 361
Coral, 230
  fire, 225–226
Coral snakes (Elapidae), 353, 360, 363, 367
Corneas, freezing of, 57
Coronary artery disease, diving and, 186
Counter-disaster syndrome, 580
CPR. *See* Cardiopulmonary resuscitation
Cramps:
  heat, 73
  from skiing, 160
Crinotoxin, 214
Crocodiles, 348
Crotalidae (pit vipers), 353, 357–360, 362–363, 365–366
Crown-of-thorns sea star, 235–236
CT (computed tomography) scanning, 210, 517, 518
Curie, 611–612
Cyanide poisoning, 398–400
  in smoke inhalation, 587, 598
  treatment of, 601

Dalton's law, 176, 524
DAN (United States National Diving Accident Network), 183
Dantrolene sodium, 68
Daphne, 400
Death camus, 396
Death imprint, 580–581

Debridement of bite wounds, 315, 319–320
Decompression sickness, 165, 179–185
  air embolism compared to, 172
  etiology of, 179–180
  from high altitudes, 532–535
  symptoms of, 180–182, 532–534
  treatment of, 183–185, 534–535
Decontamination, radioactive, 641–645
Deet, 305–306
Dehydration:
  fire and, 477–478
  high altitudes and, 7, 19
Department of Defense (DOD), 553
Dermatitis:
  allergic contact, 426–430
  creeping eruption, 266–267
  from diving equipment, 268
  Dogger Bank itch, 257, 261–262
  hot tub, 268
  irritant contact, 430
  from marine bacteria, 267–268
  from marine coelenterates, 229
  mechanical irritant, 430–431
  photoallergic, 437–442, 443
  phytophotodermatitis, 431, 442
  sea louse, 266
  seaweed, 257, 261–263
  sea worm, 265–266
  soapfish, 267
  from sponges, 260–261
Desensitization, insect stings, 280–281
Detectors of radiation:
  Geiger-Müller, 619–622
  personal dosimeters, 622–625, 630–632
Deterioration, high-altitude (HAD), 22
Dexamethasone, 78, 129, 185, 210, 293
Dextran, 54–56
Diabetes, diving and, 185–186
Diamox (acetazolamide), 3, 7, 15, 19, 20–23, 113
Diazepam (Valium), 20, 79, 298, 368, 419, 421, 518, 546
Dibenzyline (phenoxybenzamine hydrochloride), 54, 56
Dicloxacillin, 325
Dieffenbachia, 400
Digitalis, 397
Dilantin (phenytoin), 79
Dimethyl phthalate (DMP), 305–306
Diphenhydramine hydrochloride (Benadryl), 129, 260, 366, 429
Diphenoxylate (Lomotil), 17
Diphenylhydantoin, 518

Disaster planning, 556–584
  action cards for, 561
  analgesia in, 570
  central authority in, 572–574
  communications in, 568–569,
    574–575, 579
  defining a disaster in, 556–557
  described, 559–561
  disaster prevention in, 576–577
  drills in, 571–572
  emergency first aid in, 570
  environmental factors in, 571
  internal, 561
  magnitude of disaster in, 557–559
  medical records and, 575–576
  postdisaster, 561
  psychological aspects of disasters
    and, 578–582
  for public gatherings, 577
  for radiation disasters, 577–578
  special risk groups in, 581
  telemetry protocols in, 568–569
  triage in, 562–568
  See also Fire; Radiation accidents
Disaster syndrome, 579–580
Dislocation:
  hip, 151–152
  patella, 149–150
  peroneal tendon, 141
  shoulder, 154–155
Diuresis, in immersion, 33
Diving, 164–188
  alterations in gas partial pressures
    in, 176–185
  dermatitis from equipment used
    in, 268
  diver training and selection for,
    185–187
  effects of pressure changes in,
    169–176
  equipment and techniques in,
    166–169, 268
  history of, 165
  marine life and. *See* Marine life
  rescue organizations for, 84–85
  underwater pressure in, 165–166
  See also Submersion incidents
Diving reflex, 193, 197–198
Dobutamine, 207, 210
Dog bites, 311–313, 314, 323, 339–
    341
  fatal attacks in, 340–341
  septic complications of, 325–326,
    341
  suturing of, 321–322
Dogger Bank itch, 257, 261–262
Dopamine, 44, 207, 209, 218
Dosimetry, radiation, 614–625,
    630–632
Drowning, defined, 192–193. *See
    also* Submersion incidents
Drugs:
  aerospace activity and, 546–549

  with cardiopulmonary resuscita-
    tion, 204
  as cause of hypothermia, 67–69,
    72–73, 78
  stability of, 128–129
  use of, and submersion incidents,
    191–192
  See also specific drugs
Duck embryo vaccine, 335
Dysbarism, 532–535
  diagnosis of, 534
  evolved gas syndromes and, 533–
    534
  onset and frequency of, 534
  trapped gas syndromes and, 532–
    533
  treatment and prevention of, 534–
    535

Ears:
  lightning impact on, 515, 516,
    518–519
  pain in, with high altitude, 532–
    533
  trauma to, in diving, 169–171,
    186
Edema:
  cerebral, 17–19, 78–79, 208–209
  with frostbite, 51
  heat, 69, 75, 77–79
  high-altitude systemic (HASE),
    22
  laryngeal, in burn injuries, 488
  pulmonary. *See* Pulmonary
    edema
  in spinal injuries, 157
Eels, moray, 220, 251
Elapidae (coral snakes), 353, 360,
    363, 367
Electrical burns, 489, 492, 493
  lightning injuries compared to,
    508–510
Electric fish, 256
Electrolytes:
  aerospace activity and, 542
  aspiration of water and, 196
  hypothermia and, 36, 38
  loss of, in sweating, 477–478
  snake bite and, 368
  submersion incidents and, 199–
    200
  weightlessness and, 542
Elephants, 346
Embolism:
  arterial gas (AGE), 165, 172–176
  fat, 151
  venous thrombosis and, 19
Emergency medical technicians
    (EMTs), 639–640
Emphysema, diving and, 172
Encephalopathy, high-altitude
    (HAE), 17–19
Enzymes, heat stroke and, 74, 76

Epi-Pen, 281
Epinephrine, 44, 229, 366, 423
Ergot, 395
Erysipelothrix dermatitis, 218, 267–
    268
Erythema chronicum migrans, 300–
    301
Erythromycin, 218, 324–325
Escharotomies in burn treatment,
    493
Essential oils, 402
Exercise:
  heat illness and, 66–67, 71–72
  for physical conditioning, 115
Exhaustion:
  cold, 162
  heat, 70
Exotic snakes, 372–377
Explorer Search and Rescue (SAR),
    84
Eyes:
  aerospace activity and, 551
  cold injuries and, 24, 57
  high altitude and, 22–23
  lightning impact on, 515, 516, 518

Fasciotomy, 369
  lightning injuries and, 509, 517–
    518
Feathering burns (in lightning), 513
Federal Aviation Administration
    (FAA), 87, 544, 546, 552–553
  accident investigation by, 552
  crew classification by, 545
Feet. *See* Foot injuries
Femur fractures, 150–151
Fever, hyperthermia compared to,
    66–67
Fibula fractures, 142
Fire, 451–480
  building of, 122–126
  injuries and fatalities related to,
    465–471
  management of, 456–458
  principles of behavior of, 460–465
  problems of wilderness, 451–456
  survival techniques for, 471–478
  wildland/urban interface and,
    458–460
Fire ant, 278
Fire coral, 225–226
Fire sponge, 222–223
First aid:
  emergency, in disaster planning,
    570
  for lightning strike victims, 516
  in radiation accidents, 633–639
  sample kit for, 131
  for snake bite, 363–364
Fish tapeworm, 255
Flatus, high-altitude, 23
Fly bites, 286–287, 305–306

Food:
poisonous marine animals, 247–256
warming effect of, 114, 118
wilderness sources of, 126
Foot injuries, 136–146
Achilles tendon rupture, 141
ankle sprains and fractures, 138–141, 160
fibula fractures, 142
peroneal tendon dislocations, 141
from pressure of footwear, 136–138
tibia fractures, 142–146
Footwear:
for cold weather, 119
pressure injuries from, 136–138
tibial fractures from, 146
Forest fires. See Fire
Foxglove, 397
Fractures:
ankle, 138–141
clavicle, 152
femur, 150–151
proximal humerus, 155
thoracolumbar spine, 158–159
thumb, 156
tibia, 142–146
Frenzel maneuver, 169
Frostbite, 22, 47–57, 162
clinical presentation of, 49–50
cold-induced vasodilation and, 48
cutaneous circulation and, 47–48
evaluation of, 51–52
pathologic phases of, 48–49
symptoms of, 50–51
treatment of, 52–57
Funnel-web spider, 294–295
Furocoumarin, 431, 442
Furosemide (Lasix), 15, 18, 21, 22, 129, 208, 518

Gamma benzene hexachloride lotions, 129
Gamma rays, 614
Gangrene:
frostbite and, 49
in trench foot, 47
Gases:
behavior of, 524
blood. See Blood gas
in the earth's atmosphere, 524–527
evolved, syndromes of, 533–535
trapped, syndromes of, 532–533
Gastrointestinal system:
aerospace activity and, 551
in heat stroke, 75
plant poisoning and. See Plant poisoning
thermal injury and, 498
Geiger-Müller radiation detectors, 619–622

Gila monster, 370–372
Globiferous pedicellariae, 236
Glucagon injection, 129
Glycosides, 397–400
anthraquinone, 400
cardiac, 397–398
coumarin, 400
cyanogenic, 398–400
saponin, 400
Gnat bites, 286–287, 305–306
Gorilla bites, 345
Gravity in aerospace activity, 527
effects of forces of, 537
null, 538–540
protection against effects of, 537–540
terminology for forces of, 535–536
weightlessness effects and, 540–544
Groupers, 220–221

HAE (high-altitude encephalopathy), 17–19
Half-life, radioactive, 611
Hand, bites of, 321–322
Headache:
driving and, 186
high altitude and, 17–19, 20
HEAR (Hospital Emergency Administrative Radio), 574–575
Heat, body:
loss of, 29–30, 114–117. See also Cold injuries; Hypothermia
production of, 29, 115, 118–119
rewarming and, 37, 39–42
shivering and, 29, 35, 78, 201
thermoregulation and, 29, 64–66, 114–117
See also Heat illness; Hyperthermia
Heated humidified inhalation (HHI), 40–41
Heat escape lessening posture (HELP), 194
Heat illness, 64–81
edema in, 69, 75, 77–79
exhaustion, 70
fever versus hyperthermia in, 66–67
fire and, 470
heat stroke. See Heat stroke
hyperthermia, 66–69, 72–73, 78
predisposing factors in, 70–73
syncope, 69–70
thermoregulation and, 64–66
Heat stress, 470
Heat stroke, 70, 73–80
defined, 73–74
diagnosis of, 74
laboratory findings in, 76–77
predisposing factors to, 70, 73

symptoms of, 74–76
treatment of, 77–80
Heimlich maneuver, 203
Helicopters, 108–113
arterial gas embolism and use of, 173
boarding and exiting of, 111–113
decompression sickness and use of, 183
landing zones for, 108–111
limitations of, 571
in oversnow rescue, 97
patient transport by, 549–550, 641
safety rules for, 108
Hematologic system:
aerospace activity and, 541, 550–551
snake bite and, 359
weightlessness and, 541, 543
See also Blood gas; Sickle cell disorders
Hemolysis, 200
Hemorrhage, high-altitude retinal (HARH), 22–23
Henry's law, 180, 524
Heparin, 55, 56, 79
Hernia, diving and, 187
Hexachlorophene, 317
High-altitude illness. See Altitude sickness
Hip, dislocation of, 151–152
Hippopotamuses, 346
Holothurin, 238
Honeybee, 276
Hornet, 276
Horse bites, 313
Horse serum, 365–366
Hospitals:
disaster plans for, 559–561
radiation accidents and, 629–630, 640–646
Hot tub dermatitis, 268
Human bites, 311–312, 343–344
Human diploid cell vaccine, 335
Human rabies immune globulin (HRIG), 335
Humerus, fracture of proximal, 155
Hydrochloric acid (HCl), 594–595
Hydrofluoric acid, 492
Hydrogen sulfide, 598
Hydroxyzine (Atarax or Vistaril), 429
Hyenas, 347
Hymenoptera, 276–280
Hyoscine (Scopolamine), 393–394, 544
Hyoscyamine (Atropine), 44, 298, 393–394, 396, 420
Hyperbaric oxygen therapy, 56, 293
Hyperglycemia, hypothermia and, 36, 38
Hyperkalemia, 77
Hyperpnea, 3

Hypertension:
  diving and, 187
  high-altitude pulmonary, 10, 13, 25
  spider bites and, 290, 291
Hyperthermia:
  drugs as cause of, 67–69, 72–73, 78
  fever versus, 66–67
  malignant, 67–69
  syndromes of, 67–69
Hyperventilation:
  in hypothermia, 31
  submersion incidents and, 179, 197, 208
Hypocalcemia, 77
Hypocapnia, 20
Hypoglycemia:
  from Caribbean akee fruit, 403
  from hypothermia, 36
Hypophosphatemia:
  from heat stroke, 76–77
  after hypothermia, 38
Hypotension:
  in decompression sickness, 181
  in heat stroke, 74–75
  in rewarming process, 40
Hypothermia, 22, 27–46, 162
  aftercare in, 44–45
  arrhythmia treatment in, 42–44
  of avalanche victims, 108
  classification of, 28–29
  complications from, 45
  epidemiology of, 28
  frostbite treatment and, 53, 56
  historical aspects of, 27–28
  physiology of, 29–36
  rewarming techniques in, 39–42
  submersion incidents and, 193–196, 208
  treatment of, 36–39, 45–46
  See also Cold injuries
Hypoventilation, 3
Hypoxia:
  from aerospace activity, 529–532
  aspiration of water and, 196, 198
  high altitude and, 2–6, 20, 23
  smoke inhalation and, 590
Ichthyosarcotoxin, 247–249

Immersion foot (trench foot), 29, 46–47
Immersion syndrome, 197–198
Indalone, 305–306
Indomethacin, 55, 447
Inhalation injuries, 585–605
  defined and described, 585–586
  hospital evaluation and treatment of, 600–602
  prehospital evaluation and treatment of, 600
  smoke. *See* Smoke inhalation

Insect bites, 270–287
  Coleoptera (beetles), 285–286
  Diptera (bloodsucking flies, mosquitoes, gnats and midges), 286–287, 305–306
  Hemiptera (sucking bugs), 283–285
  Hymenoptera (bees, wasps and ants), 276–281
  Lepidoptera (caterpillars), 281–283
  repellants and, 304–306
  See also Arachnid bites
Insulin, 38–39, 46, 185–186, 546
International Academy of Aviation and Space Medicine (IAASM), 554
International Association of Dive Rescue Specialists (IADRS), 84–85
International Civil Aviation Organization (ICAO), 553
Intracranial pressure (ICP), 199, 209–210, 518
Intravenous therapy:
  for burn wounds, 488–491, 494–495, 499
  for lightning victims, 517
  in rewarming after hypothermia, 41
Ipecac, 395
Irrigation of bite wounds, 317–319, 333–334
Irritant oils, 402
Isoproterenol (Isuprel), 44, 77
Itch plant, 430

Jamaican vomiting sickness, 403
Jellyfish, 226–227, 230
Jerusalem cherry, 396
Jimson weed, 393–394, 403
Joule's law, 509

Kayexalate (sodium polystyrene sulfonate), 77
Keratitis, ultraviolet, 24, 57
Keraunographic marking, 513–514
Kidneys:
  changes in, with high altitude, 7
  failure of, in submersion incidents, 199, 208
  heat stroke and, 75–76, 79
  snake bite and, 359, 368
Killer bee, 276
Knee injuries, 146–152
  femur fractures in, 150–151
  ligament sprains, 146–148
  meniscal injuries, 148–149
  patellar dislocations in, 149–150
  posterior hip dislocation, 151–152

Labyrinthine window rupture, 171
Lachman test, 147–148
Larvae, dermatitis from parasite, 266–267
Lasix (furosemide), 15, 18, 21, 22, 129, 208, 518
Leeches, 265
Leopard bites, 342
Leptospirosis, 327, 337–338
Lice bites, 308–309
Lichens, 442
Licorice, 400
Lidocaine (Xylocaine), 43, 44, 46, 129, 240, 244, 301
Ligaments, sprains of, 146–148
Lightning, 500–521
  forms of, 506–507
  historical overview of, 500–501
  injuries from. *See* Lightning injuries
  lightning rod invention, 503–504
  myths and superstitions on, 502–503
  physics of stroke of, 504–507
Lightning injuries:
  diagnosis of, 515–516
  incidence of, 501–502
  mechanisms of, 507–510
  precautions for avoiding, 519–520
  treatment of, 516–519
  types of, 510–515
Limb-bends, 180–181, 533
Lion bites, 342
Liver:
  heat stroke and, 76
  polar bear, poisoning from, 256
Lomotil (diphenoxylate), 17
Low back strain, in skiing, 161–162
Lyme disease (arthritis), 301

McMurray test, 149
Maculotoxin, 233
Magnesium citrate, 381
Mammalian bites, 310–351
  of cat family, 311–312, 323, 341–343
  of cattle and other herbivores, 313, 345–346
  diseases transmitted in, 327–339
  of dogs. *See* Dog bites
  of elephants, rhinoceroses and hippopotamuses, 346
  of human beings, 311–312, 343–344
  incidence of, 310–313
  prehospital treatment of, 314–315
  prevention of, 313–314
  of primates, 344–345
  of rodents. *See* Rodent bites
  septic complications of, 325–327
  of skunks, 330, 331, 345
  of vampire bats, 346–347
  of venomous animals, 347–348

of wolves, hyenas and bears, 347
wound care in, 315–325
Mannitol, 78, 79, 129, 208, 492, 517, 518
Man-o-war, Atlantic Portuguese, 226
Marijuana, 403
Marine life, 213–259
biotoxicity of, 214–215
hazardous plants, 257
poisonous on ingestion, 247–256
shocking (electric), 256
skin disorders from, 229, 257, 260–269
stinging animals, 222–247
traumatogenic, 215–222
Mask burn, 268
MAST (military antishock trousers), 37–38, 218, 537, 570
MAST (Military Assistance to Safety and Transportation), 85, 88
Medical records, disaster planning and, 575–576
Medroxyprogesterone acetate (Provera), 21, 22
Melanin, 435
Meniscus, injury to, 148–149
Meperidine hydrochloride, 129, 298, 492
Meprobamate, 546
Mescaline, 404
Methemoglobin, 398–400, 598, 601–602
Methylprednisolone, 210
Miconazole, 255
Microwave irradiation, 42
Midge bites, 286–287, 305–306
Migraine headaches, diving and, 186
Military antishock trousers (MAST), 37–38, 218, 537, 570
Military Assistance to Safety and Transportation (MAST), 85, 88
Millipede bites, 301–302
Minimum erythema dose (MED), 442–445
Mite bites, 287, 307–308
Mojave rattlesnake, 367
Mollusks, 231–234
M-1 maneuver, 537
Monkey bites, 344–345
Monkshood, 396
Morels, 418
Morphine, 15, 298, 492
Mosquito bites, 286–287, 305–306
Motion sickness, weightlessness and, 541, 544
Mountain Rescue Association (MRA), 85, 94
Mountain sickness:
acute (AMS), 3, 4, 13, 15, 17, 19–21
subacute (chronic), 21–22

Musculoskeletal system:
aerospace activity and, 541
skiing and, 161
weightlessness and, 541, 543
Mushroom poisoning, 380, 405–423
coprine or disulfiramlike poisoning, 408, 413–414, 419–420
deadly cyclopeptides, 407–417
gastrointestinal irritants, 409–411, 416, 423
hallucinogenic (*Psilocybe, Paneolus*) mushrooms, 409, 415–416, 421–423
isoxazole (*A. muscaria*) derivatives, 409, 415, 420–421
monomethylhydrazine (*Gyromitra*) poisoning, 408, 413, 417–419
muscarine (*Inocybe, Clitocybe*) poisoning, 408–409, 414–415, 420
Myoglobinuria, 79, 517, 518

Naloxone (Narcan), 45, 129
Narcosis, nitrogen, 176–177
National Aeronautics and Space Administration (NASA), 539, 544, 553
National Antivenin Index, 372
National Association for Search and Rescue (NASAR), 83, 85–86
National Cave Rescue Commission (NCRC), 86
National Park Service, 86
National Ski Patrol System Inc., 96
National Speleological Society, 86, 92
National Transportation Safety Board (NTSB), 553
Neck trauma, 157–158
Needlefish, 222
Nematocyst, 224
Neomycin, 417, 430
Neostigmine, 253
Neutrons, 614
Newton's law, 527
Nicotine, 392–393
"Night Sun," 84
Nitrogen dioxide, 599–600
Nitrogen narcosis, 176–177
Nitrous oxide, 570
Noise, aerospace activity and, 535
Nutmeg, 403
Nutrition, burn injuries and, 495
Nylon, burning of, 594

Octopuses, 232–234
Ohm's law, 509
Oleander, 397–398
Ophthalmic injuries. *See* Eyes
Osborne wave, 33
Ostriches, 348

Otitis:
from diving, 169
from high altitude, 532–533
Oversnow rescue, 95–97
Oxacillin, 324
Oxalates, 400–401
Oxygen:
aerospace activity and, 529–532
for carbon monoxide poisoning, 487
in cold weather survival, 113–114
diving and, 167–168, 180, 183
for high-altitude pulmonary edema, 14
hyperbaric, for frostbite, 56
hyperbaric, for spider bites, 293
poisoning from, in diving, 177–179
to prevent evolved gas syndromes, 534–535
in submersion incident treatment, 200–208
Oxyhemoglobin dissociation curve, 31–32
Oxyphenbutazone, 55
Ozone, 432, 433, 527–528

PABA (para-aminobenzoic acid), 445–447
Pancreas, heat stroke and, 76
Pancuronium, 210
Panic reactions, 579, 580
Para-aminobenzoic acid (PABA), 445–447
Paralysis, tick, 299–300
Paralytic shellfish poisoning, 252–253
Pascal's law, 166, 167
Patella, dislocation of, 149–150
PEEP. *See* Positive end-respiratory pressure
Penicillin, 129, 170, 218, 240, 324–325, 336–338, 493
Peritoneal dialysis:
for heat stroke, 78
in hypothermia treatment, 41–42, 46
Permethrin, 306
Peroneal tendon, dislocation of, 141
Phenobarbital, 209, 298, 421, 518
Phenol burns, 492
Phenoxybenzamine hydrochloride (Dibenzyline), 54, 56
Phenylephrine, 170
Phenytoin (Dilantin), 79
Phlebitis, 19, 498–499
Phosgene poisoning, 596, 601
Phosphorus burns, 492
Photosensitive eruptions, 436–442
photoallergic, 437–442, 443
treatment for, 447–448
Phytophotodermatitis, 431, 442

Phytotoxicology. *See* Plant poisoning
Pit vipers (Crotalidae), 353, 357–360, 362–363, 365–366
Plague, 338–339
Plant poisoning, 379–425
 alkaloids, 381–397
 element and nitrate absorption and, 402–403
 general considerations in, 380–381
 glycosides in, 397–400
 by hazardous marine plants, 257
 hypoglycemic agents and, 403
 irritant and essential oils, 402
 by mushrooms. *See* Mushroom poisoning
 oxalates in, 400–401
 phytotoxins, 401–402
 psychoactive plants, 403–405
 resins in, 401
Platypuses, 348
Pneumonia, 16
Pneumothorax, 171–172, 186
Poison hemlock, 393
Poison ivy (sumac and oak) dermatitis, 426, 427–429
Poisons:
 from ingestion of marine animals, 247–256
 venoms compared with, 214–215
 See also Plant poisoning; Snake bites
Polar bears, poisoning from livers of, 256
Polycythemia, chronic mountain, 24–25
Polyurethane, burning of, 591–592
Polyvinyl chloride (PVC), burning of, 591
Positive-end-respiratory pressure (PEEP), 10, 14, 77
 for submersion incidents, 203–204, 207, 208
Posterior drawer test, 148
Potassium, in heat stroke, 76, 80
Povidone-iodine, 317–319
Prednisone, 260, 262, 293, 447
Pregnancy:
 diving and, 187
 flying and, 547, 551
 lightning strike during, 515, 519
Pressure:
 air. *See* Aerospace medicine; Altitude sickness
 from ski boots, 136–138
 water, in diving, 165–166
Preventive Search and Rescue (PSAR), 85
Primate bites, 344–345
Procainamide, 68
Propranolol, 419, 546
Provera (medroxyprogesterone acetate), 21, 22

Pseudoephedrine, 170
Psilocybin, 422–423
Psychoactive plants, 403–405
Psychological aspects of disaster, 578–581
Public gatherings, disaster planning for, 577
Pufferfish, 251
Pulegone, 402
Pulmonary atresia, 10
Pulmonary edema:
 with heat stroke, 75, 77
 high-altitude (HAPE), 7–17, 19, 22
 hypothermia and, 39
 with smoke inhalation, 591
Pulmonary system:
 aerospace activity and, 550
 edema of. *See* Pulmonary edema
 fire and, 470
 snake bite and, 359, 368
 submersion incidents and, 198–199, 207
 See also Inhalation injuries
Puncture wounds from animal bites, 322
Pyridoxine hydrochloride, 419

Rabies, 315, 319, 327–335, 340, 343
 bats and, 346
 local treatment of, 333–335
Rad, 615
Radiation, 606–646
 accidents involving. *See* Radiation accidents
 aerospace activity and, 527–528
 atomic and nuclear physics and, 609–611
 background on, 607–609
 biological effects of, 617–619
 dosimetry of, 614–625, 630–632
 instrumentation for measuring, 619–625
 interaction of, with matter, 613–614
 radioactivity and, 611–612
 solar. *See* Sun
Radiation accidents, 625–646
 advance planning for, 577–578, 626–633
 onsite management of, 633–639
 patient decontamination and sample taking in, 641–646
 transportation, 639–640
 transportation to hospitals and, 640–641
 types of, 625–626
Radiation Emergency Assistance Center/Training Site (REACTS), 578, 632
Radio, disaster planning and, 568–569, 574–575
Radioactive decay, 611

Rain, clothing for, 119
Rappelling, 94
RAST (Radio-allergoimmunoassay), 280
Rat-bite fever, 336–337
Rattlesnakes, 356–360, 362–363, 367
RBE (relative biologic effectiveness), 615–617
REACTS (Radiation Emergency Assistance Center/Training Site), 578, 632
Recluse spider bites, 288, 291–293
Reel splint, 144
Rescue. *See* Search and rescue organizations
Reserpine, 47, 54–56
Resins, 401
Resmethrin, 306
Respiratory disorders:
 high altitude and, 3–4, 20
 in hypothermia, 34–35
 See also Inhalation injuries; Pulmonary system
Resuscitation:
 cardiopulmonary. *See* Cardiopulmonary resuscitation
 of lightning victims, 502–503, 516
 for submersion incidents, 200–210
Retinas:
 high-altitude hemorrhage (HARH) of, 22–23
 oxygen requirements of, 551
Rewarming:
 in frostbite treatment, 53–54, 56
 in hypothermia treatment, 37, 39–42
Rhabdomyolysis, 77
Rhinoceroses, 346
Rhubarb, 401
Rhus dermatitis, 427–429
Ricin, 401
River rescues, 94–95
Rodent bites, 311–312, 323, 331, 343
 plague and, 338–339
 rat-bite fever and, 336–337
Roentgen, 614
Rope for rescue operations, 90–92
Rotator cuff injuries, 155
Rove beetle, 285

Safety, fire, 471–478
 building as refuge and, 474–475
 clothing for, 476–477
 entrapment procedures and, 475–476
 personal gear for, 478
 vehicles as refuge and, 473–474
 watchout situations and, 472–473
 water intake and, 477–478
Salt supplements, 73, 80, 127

SAMS (subacute mountain sickness), 21–22
SAR. *See* Search and rescue organizations
Scabies, 307
Scarring in burn wounds, 495–496
Schistosomiasis, 263–264
Scombroid poisoning, 254–255
Scopolamine (hyoscine), 393–394, 544
Scorpionfish, 243–244
Scorpion stings, 295–298
SCUBA (self-contained underwater breathing apparatus) diving, 84–86, 164–165
  aircraft flight and, 534, 547
  See also Diving
Sea bathers' eruption, 264–265
Sea cucumbers, 238
Sea lice, dermatitis from, 266
Sea lions, 221
Sea nettles, 227
Sea urchins, 236–238
Sea wasp (Box jellyfish), 227, 229–230
Search and rescue (SAR) organizations, 82–133
  cave rescues and, 92–94
  cold weather survival and, 113–127
  described, 83–86
  equipment used by, 90–92
  oversnow rescues and, 95–97
  responsibility, authority, and mobilization of, 86–90
  snow avalanches and. *See* Avalanches, snow
  survival preparation and, 127–131
  technical rock rescues and, 94
  whitewater river rescues and, 94–95
Seaweed dermatitis, 257, 261–263
Sea worms, dermatitis from, 263–266
Sepsis, in animal bites, 325–327
Serum sickness, snake bite and, 369–370
Shallow water blackout, 179, 197
Sharks, 215–219
  clinical aspects of, 217
  feeding and attack by, 216–217
  life and habits of, 216
  prevention of attacks by, 218–219
  treatment of injury by, 217–218
Shellfish poisoning, 252–254
Shelters, 114–115, 119–122
  artificial, 120–122
  natural, 119–120
Shin splints, 160
Shivering, 29, 35, 78
  in submersion incidents, 201
Shoulder dislocation, 154–155

Shrews, 347–348
Sickle cell disorders:
  air transport and, 550–551
  diving and, 186
  frostbite and, 47
  high altitude and, 5
Sidewinder, 361
Sinusitis:
  from diving, 169–170
  from high altitude, 533
Skiing, 134–163
  cross-country, injuries in, 160–162
  foot injuries in, 136–146, 160
  high-altitude pulmonary edema and, 8
  knee injuries in, 146–152
  miscellaneous injuries in, 159
  oversnow rescues and, 95–97
  snow avalanches and. *See* Avalanches, snow
  upper extremity injuries in, 152–160
Skunk bites, 345
  rabies and, 330, 331
Skylight, 433
Sleeping disorders:
  heat illness and, 73
  high altitude and, 3–4, 19–21
Smoke inhalation, 586–600
  acrolein and, 587, 594, 599
  carbon monoxide and. *See* Carbon monoxide poisoning
  clinical findings of, 587–590
  cyanide and, 587, 598, 601
  hypoxia and, 590
  plastic combustion products, described, 591–594
  plastic combustion products, toxicity of, 594–600
  residential combustion products and, 586, 591–600
  thermal injuries and, 590–591
  See also Inhalation injuries
Snake bites, 352–370, 372–377
  characteristics of poisonous snakes, 356
  epidemiology of, 353–356
  by exotic snakes, 372–377
  habits and habitats of snakes and, 356–360
  prevention of, 370
  prognosis for, 370
  signs of envenomation in, 360–363
  treatment of, 363–370
Snakes, sea, 245–247
Snow:
  avalanche rescues. *See* Avalanches, snow
  oversnow rescue and, 95–97
Snow blindness, 24, 57
Soapfish, 267

Sodium bicarbonate, 129, 204, 207, 546
Sodium polystyrene sulfonate (Kayexalate), 77
Space medicine. *See* Aerospace medicine
Specific dynamic action (SDA) of food, 114, 118
Spider bites, 287–295
  black widows and other *Lactrodectan*, 288–291
  of other venomous spiders, 295
  recluse spiders (*Loxosceles*), 288, 291–293
  tarantulas, 288, 293–295
Spine injuries, 156–159
  decompression sickness and, 181, 185
  neck trauma and, 157–158
  submersion incidents and, 192, 205
  thoracolumbar fractures, 158–159
Splints:
  for ankle injuries, 139, 141, 143
  for burn wounds, 495
  for knee injuries, 148
  for snake bites, 364
Sponge diver's disease, 222, 223, 228
Sponges, 222–223
  dermatitis from, 260–261
Sprains:
  of acromioclavicular (AC) joint, 152–153
  ankle, 140, 160
  in knee injuries, 146–148
  of sternoclavicular joint, 153–154
Starfish, 235–236
Sternoclavicular joint, sprains of, 153–154
Steroids:
  for burn wounds, 493
  after contact with sponges, 222–223
  for heat stroke, 78, 79
  for hypothermia, 39, 44
  snake bite and, 369–370
  in submersion incidents, 207, 208
  sunburn and, 447, 448
Stingrays, 238–240
Stonefish, 243–244
Streptomycin, 337, 338
Strychnine, 395
Styrene (phenylethylene), 592–593, 599
Subacute mountain sickness (SAMS), 21–22
Submersion incidents, 179, 189–212
  classification and types of, 197–198
  marine life and. *See* Marine life
  pathophysiology of, 198–200
  prevention of, 192
  risk factors in, 190–192

Submersion incidents [Cont.]
  special considerations in, 193–196
  terminology of, 192–193
  trauma in, 197
  treatment for, 200–210
  type of water and, 196
  See also Diving
Surfactant, 318
Sun, 432–450
  anti-inflammatory agents for injury from, 446–447
  chronic UVL exposure and, 435–436
  electromagnetic radiation from, 433–434, 527–529
  interaction of light and the skin, 434
  modification of light from, 436, 447
  photosensitive eruptions and, 436–442, 447–448
  pigmentation and, 435
  sunburn from. *See* Sunburn
  sunscreens and, 24, 442–446
Sunburn, 434–435
  anti-inflammatory agents for, 446–447
  sunscreens for, 442–447
  treatment for, 447–448
Sun protective factor (SPF), 442–445
Sunscreens, 24, 442–446
Survival Education Association (SEA), 86
Suturing of animal bite wounds, 321–322
Swan-Ganz pulmonary artery catheter, 77, 207
Sweating, heat illness and, 71, 74, 470, 477–478
Swimmers' itch, 263–264
Swimming, lightning and, 508, 519.
  See also Diving; Submersion incidents
"Swimming pool" granulomas, 267
Sympathectomy for frostbite, 48, 54–56
Syncope, heat, 69–70

Tachycardia:
  heat regulation and, 66
  high altitude and, 5–6, 10, 20
Tapeworm, fish, 255
Tarantula bites, 288, 293–295
Tar burns, 489
Technical rescue:
  defined, 90
  equipment for, 90–92, 130
  in rivers, 94–95
  rock rescues, 94
Teeth, pain in, 532
Tendinitis, 160–161

Tetanus prophylaxis, 129, 218
  for animal bites, 320
  for burn injuries, 491, 493
  for Gila monster bites, 372
  for lightning injury, 518
  for snake bite, 367
Tetracycline, 338
Tetrodotoxin, 251
Thiabendazole, 266–267
Thioctic acid, 417
Thompson test, 141
Thoracolumbar junction, fractures of, 158–159
Thorazine (chlorpromazine), 78
Thrombophlebitis:
  burn wounds and, 498–499
  high altitude and, 19
Thumb injuries, 156
Thunder, 507
Thyroid extracts for hypothermia, 39
Tibia fractures, 142–146
Tick bites, 287, 299–301
Tick paralysis, 299–300
Tiger bites, 341–342
TLDs (thermoluminescent dosimeters), 622–625, 630
Toboggans for oversnow rescues, 97
Toluene 2,4-Diisocyanate, 599
Tracheostomy for burn injuries, 489
Trench foot (immersion foot), 29, 46–47
Trendelenburg position, 172–173, 203
Triage:
  in disaster planning, 562–568
  for inhalation injuries, 600
  of lightning victims, 516
  medical records and, 575–576
Tularemia, 327, 337
Turtles, 256

Ulcers, thermal injury and, 498
Ultraviolet light (UVL). *See* Sun
Unconsciousness, underwater, 179
Underwater injuries. *See* Diving; Submersion incidents
United States National Diving Accident Network (DAN), 183
Urticaria, cold, 57

Vagus nerve, 31
Valium (diazepam), 20, 79, 298, 368, 419, 421, 518, 546
Valsalva maneuver, 169, 170, 533, 547
Vampire bat, 346–347
Van Allen belt, 528–529
Vasodilatation, cold-induced (CIVD), 48
Vehicles as shelters, 122

Venom:
  catfish, 241
  Gila monster, 370–371
  from marine coelenterates, 223–224, 228–230
  of mollusks, 231–234
  poisons compared with, 214–215
  scorpionfish, 244
  of sea snakes, 245–247
  of sea urchins, 236–238
  snake. *See* Snake bites
  spider. *See* Spider bites
  of stingrays, 239
  weeverfish, 243
Vibrio parahemolyticus, 255
Vibrio vulnificus, 255
Vinegaroon, 298
Vistaril (hydroxyzine), 429

Wasp stings, 276–281
Water:
  aspiration of, and hypoxia, 196, 198
  in chemical burn treatment, 485
  dehydration and, 7, 19, 477–478
  hemlock, 401
  purification of, 127
  wilderness use of, 127
  See also Diving; River rescues; Submersion incidents
Water bug, 283
Weather information, 128
Weeverfish, 242–243
Weightlessness:
  cardiovascular system and, 540–541, 543
  countermeasures for effects of, 544
Weil's disease, 338
Wet bulb globe temperature, 70–71
Whales, killer, 221–222
Whirlpool dermatitis, 268
Wilderness search and rescue. *See* Search and rescue organizations
Windburn, 435
Wind chill, 115
Wintergreen, 402
Wolves, 347
Worms, marine annelid, 234, 265–266

Xanthinol nicotinate, 55
X-rays:
  lightning strikes and, 517
  submersion incidents and, 205
Xylocaine (lidocaine), 43, 44, 46, 129, 240, 244, 301

Yellow jacket, 276